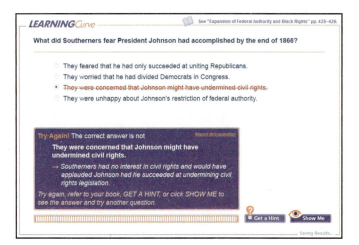

The American Promise

A History of the United States

The American Promise

A History of the United States

SIXTH EDITION
VOLUME 2: FROM 1865

James L. Roark
Emory University

Michael P. Johnson
Johns Hopkins University

Patricia Cline Cohen
University of California, Santa Barbara

Sarah Stage
Arizona State University

Susan M. Hartmann
The Ohio State University

BEDFORD/ST. MARTIN'S
BOSTON ◆ NEW YORK

FOR BEDFORD/ST. MARTIN'S

Vice President, Editorial, Macmillan Higher Education Humanities: Edwin Hill
Publisher for History: Mary V. Dougherty
Senior Executive Editor for History and Technology: William J. Lombardo
Director of Development for History: Jane Knetzger
Senior Developmental Editor: Heidi L. Hood
Production Editor: Kerri A. Cardone
Production Manager: Joe Ford
Executive Marketing Manager: Sandra McGuire
Editorial Assistant: Victoria Royal
Copy Editor: Lisa Wehrle
Indexer: Leoni Z. McVey
Cartography: Mapping Specialists Limited
Photo Researcher: Naomi Kornhauser
Senior Art Director: Anna Palchik
Text Design: Cenveo Publisher Services
Cover Design: William Boardman
Cover Photo: Grand opening of the Golden Gate Bridge.
© San Francisco Chronicle/Corbis
Composition: Cenveo Publisher Services
Printing and Binding: RR Donnelley and Sons

Manufactured in the United States of America.

9 8 7 6 5 4
f e d c b a

For information, write: Bedford/St. Martin's, 75 Arlington Street, Boston, MA 02116   (617-399-4000)

ISBN 978-1-4576–6838-8 (Combined Edition)   ISBN 978-1-4576-8887-4 (Loose-leaf Edition)
ISBN 978-1-4576-6841-8 (Volume 1)   ISBN 978-1-4576-8889-8 (Loose-leaf Edition,
ISBN 978-1-4576-6839-5 (Volume 2)   Volume 1)
                                                ISBN 978-1-4576-8888-1 (Loose-leaf Edition, Volume
                                                     2)

Preface: Why This Book This Way

What is the best way to engage and teach students in their history survey course? From the beginning, *The American Promise* has been shaped by our firsthand knowledge that the survey course is one of the most difficult to teach and, for many, also the most difficult to take. From the outset we have met this challenge by providing a story students enjoy for its readability, clear chronology, and lively voices of ordinary Americans, and by providing a full-featured text that instructors prize for its full narrative with political backbone, abundant documents and features for analysis and discussion, and the overall support for teaching. With this edition of *The American Promise* we have made meeting the challenges of the survey course a great deal easier through the introduction of **LaunchPad**, an intuitive new interactive e-book and course space with a wealth of primary sources and special critical thinking activities to help students learn key content and master essential skills. LaunchPad provides active learning assignments and dynamic course management tools that measure and analyze student progress, and can be used on its own or in conjunction with the printed text to give instructors and students the best of both worlds—the narrative text in an easy-to-read printed format as well as our highly acclaimed digital resources and tools designed for active learning and deep understanding. LaunchPad is loaded with the full-color e-book plus **LearningCurve,** an adaptive learning tool; the popular *Reading the American Past* documents collection; **additional primary sources**; special **skills-based assessment activities; videos; chapter summative quizzes;** and more.

New Tools for Teaching and Measuring Outcomes

With requests for clear and transparent learning outcomes coming from all quarters and with students who bring increasingly diverse levels of skills to class, even veteran teachers can find preparing for today's courses a trying matter. The introduction of **LaunchPad** to the sixth edition offers a breakthrough for instructors. With LaunchPad we have reconceived the textbook as a suite of tools in multiple formats that allows each format do what it does best to capture students' interest and help instructors create meaningful lessons. But one of the best benefits is that instructors using LaunchPad will find they have a number of assessment tools that allow them to see what it is their students do and don't know and measure student achievement all in one convenient space. For example, LaunchPad comes with **LearningCurve**—an adaptive learning tool that garners over a 90 percent student satisfaction rate and helps students master book content. When LearningCurve is assigned, the grade book results show instructors where the entire class or individual students may be struggling which in turn allows instructors to adjust lectures and course activities accordingly—a benefit not only for traditional classes but invaluable for hybrid, online, and newer "flipped" classes as well. In addition, not only can instructors assign all of the questions that appear in the print book and view the responses in the grade book, they have the option to assign automatically graded multiple choice questions for all of the book features. Plus many more pre-built **activities to foster critical reading and chronological reasoning skills** are available in LaunchPad along with a **test building tool,** as well as **additional primary sources** and **videos** that all can be used for customized assignments that will report into the grade book for simplified assessment. With LaunchPad for *The American Promise* we make the tough job of teaching simpler by providing everything an instructor needs in one convenient space so instructors can set and achieve the learning outcomes they desire. To learn more about the benefits of LearningCurve and LaunchPad, see the "Versions and Supplements" section on page xii.

What Makes *The American Promise* Special

Our experience as teachers and our frustrations with available textbooks inspired us to create a book that we could use effectively in our own classrooms. Our knowledge of classroom realities has informed every aspect of each edition and version of *The American Promise*. We began with a clear chronological, political framework. We have found that students need both the structure a political narrative provides *and* the insights gained from examining social and cultural experience. To write a comprehensive, balanced account of American history, we focus on the public arena—the place where politics intersects social and cultural developments—to show how Americans confronted the major issues of their day and created far-reaching historical change.

The unique approach of our narrative is reflected in our title, *The American Promise*. We emphasize human agency and demonstrate our conviction that the essence of America has been its promise. For millions, the nation has held out the promise of a better life, unfettered worship, equality before the law, representative government, democratic politics, and other freedoms seldom found elsewhere. But none of these promises has come with guarantees. Throughout the narrative we demonstrate how much of American history is a continuing struggle over the definition and realization of the nation's promise.

We also give special attention to the promise theme in our **Seeking the American Promise** biographical features. Each of the 19 essays explores a different promise of America—the promise of home ownership or the promise of higher education, for example—while recognizing that the promises fulfilled for some have meant promises denied to others. Popular essays profile people such as indentured servant Anne Orthwood and her struggle in colonial America, Stamp Act protestor Ebenezer Mackintosh, black Civil War soldiers, Russian Jews escaping the pogroms, progressive reformer Alice Hamilton, World War I servicewoman Nora Saltonstall, and Vietnamese immigrant-turned-politician Joseph Cao. All Seeking the American Promise features conclude with a set of short-answer questions that help students explore the subject further and understand its significance within the chapter and the book as a whole. In LaunchPad, these questions plus a multiple choice quiz for assessing comprehension can be assigned easily.

Our narrative also reflects our conviction that it is essential to situate American history in the global world in which students live. To underscore this emphasis in the narrative, we include 17 **Beyond America's Borders** features which consider the reciprocal relationships between the United States and the wider world and challenge students to think about the effects of transnational connections over time. In this edition we have added "Corn: An Ancient American Legacy" and brought back favorites such as "American Tobacco and European Consumers," "Transatlantic Abolition," "Imperialism, Colonialism, and the Treatment of the Sioux and the

Zulu," "Bolshevism," and "Transnational Feminism." With the goal of widening students' perspectives and helping students see that this country did not develop in isolation, these features are enhanced by short answer questions at the end of the essay, which can be easily assigned in LaunchPad, along with multiple choice quizzes that measure student comprehension.

We kept the needs and interests of the student reader foremost in our minds while writing and revising *The American Promise*. To engage students in this American story and to portray fully the diversity of the American experience, we stitch into our narrative **the voices of hundreds of contemporaries**. We further animate this story with a **vivid art and map program with captions and activities that prompt students to think critically** about what they see. To help students of all levels understand American history, we provide the best in **primary sources** and **pedagogical aids**. To help instructors teach important skills and evaluate student learning, we provide a **rich assortment of assignments and assessments** in both the print and LaunchPad formats. While this edition rests solidly on our original goals and premises, it has taken on a new role to address the specific needs of today's courses.

Better Prepared Students

Every instructor knows it can be a challenge to get students to complete assigned readings, and then to fully understand what is important once they do the reading. *The American Promise* addresses these problems head on with a suite of tools in LaunchPad that instructors can choose from.

To help students fully understand their reading and come to class prepared, instructors who adopt LaunchPad for *The American Promise* can assign the **LearningCurve** formative assessment activities. This online learning tool is popular with students because it helps them rehearse content at their own pace in a non-threatening, game-like environment. LearningCurve is also popular with instructors because the reporting features allow them to track overall class trends and spot topics that are giving their students trouble so they can adjust their lectures and class activities. When LearningCurve is assigned, students come to class better prepared and instructors can better evaluate and adjust their classes.

Encouraging active reading is another means for making content memorable and highlight what is truly important. To help students read actively and understand the central idea of the chapter, instructors who use LaunchPad can also assign our **new Guided Reading Exercises**. This new exercise, which appears at the start of each chapter, prompts students to collect information to be used to answer a broad analytic question central to the chapter as a whole.

To further encourage students to read and fully assimilate the text as well as measure how well they do this, instructors can assign the **new multiple-choice summative quizzes** in LaunchPad, where they are automatically graded. These secure tests not only encourage students to study the book, they can be assigned at specific intervals as high stakes testing and thus provide another means for analyzing class performance.

Extra Support

Another big challenge for survey instructors is meeting the needs of a range of students, particularly the students who need the most support. In addition to the formative assessment of LearningCurve, which adapts to the needs of students at any level, *The American Promise* offers a number of tools for the underprepared.

For those who need to know how to sort out what is important, each chapter opener includes **new Content Learning Objectives** to prepare students to read the chapter with purpose.

Once into the heart of the chapter, students are reminded to think about main ideas through **Review Questions** placed at the end of every major section. In print and LaunchPad these questions can be assigned as a chapter review activity.

Some students also have trouble connecting events and ideas, particularly with special boxed features. To address this, we have added a **new Connect to the Big Idea question** to each feature to help students understand the significance of the featured topic to the chapter as a whole. These questions are also available in the print and LaunchPad versions of the book.

Critical Thinking and Analysis

The American Promise also strives to turn students into critical thinkers who read actively and can analyze what they read. We have put this goal at the center of this revision through several activities that invite critical reading, evaluation of primary sources, and geographical literacy.

Critical Reading

To foster not only active reading but critical reading of the narrative, we introduce a **new Reflections assignment** at the end of each major section in LaunchPad, which uses a series of multiple choice and short answer questions to challenge students to think critically about the narrative as historical interpretation. To bring students' critical thinking skills to the next level, the **new Chronological Reasoning Activity** in LaunchPad encourages students to make connections among events and evaluate their importance, while the **new "What's Your Question"** activity, which builds naturally from the Reflections activities, presses students to formulate a solid historical question of their own based on their introspections about the chapter.

To demonstrate and engage students in various methods and perspectives of historical thinking, our 16 **Historical Questions** feature essays pose and interpret specific questions of continuing interest. Perennial favorites brought back in this edition range from "Was the New United States a Christian Country?" and "How Often Were Slaves Whipped?" to "Was There a Sexual Revolution in the 1920s?" and "Why Did the Allies Win World War II?" Short-answer questions at the end of the features prompt students to consider things such as evidence, beliefs and values, and cause and effect as they relate to the historical question at hand. Available both in print and online these features can be easily assigned in LaunchPad, along with multiple choice quizzes that measure student comprehension.

With this edition we also bring back two popular sets of end-of-chapter questions that help widen students' focus as they consider what they have read. **Making Connections** questions ask students to think about broad developments within the chapter, while **Linking to the Past** questions cross-reference developments in earlier chapters, encouraging students to make comparisons, see causality, and understand change over longer periods of time. Both sets of questions are assignable from the print and LaunchPad versions.

Evaluation of Primary Sources

Primary sources form the heart of the feature program in this edition as a means to engage students with history and to actively develop their critical thinking skills. We are pleased to offer **more Documenting the American**

Promise features than ever before—now 23 in all and 7 more than in the last edition. Each of these features juxtaposes two to four primary documents to reveal varying perspectives on a topic or an issue and to provide students with opportunities to build and practice their skills of historical interpretation. Feature introductions and document headnotes contextualize the sources, and short-answer questions at the end of the features promote critical thinking about primary sources. In addition to bringing back some favorites enjoyed in the past, new topics have been added that are rich with human drama and include "Reactions to the Boston Port Act Outside of Massachusetts," "The Gold Rush," "Ida B. Wells and Her Campaign to Stop Lynching," "The Songs of the Knights of Labor," "Americans Encounter the New Deal," and "Ending the War in Vietnam." These features are available both in print and online and they can be easily assigned in LaunchPad, along with multiple choice quizzes that measure student comprehension.

In addition, over 150 documents in the accompanying collection *Reading the American Past* are available free to users who package the documents collection with the main print text, and they are automatically included in the LaunchPad e-book. Not only can the short answers be easily assigned from within LaunchPad, but multiple choice questions are also available for assignment to measure comprehension and hold students accountable for their reading.

LaunchPad for The American Promise also comes with a collection of **over 135 additional primary sources** that instructors can choose to assign. These sources include letters, memoirs, court records, government documents, and more, and they include items by or about such people as John Smith, William Penn, Anne Hutchinson, Jonathan Edwards, Mary Jemison, Black Hawk, John C. Calhoun, Frederick Douglass, Abraham Lincoln, Mary Elizabeth Lease, William Jennings Bryan, Theodore Roosevelt, Nicolo Sacco and Bartolomeo Vanzetti, Huey P. Long, Franklin D. Roosevelt, Harry S. Truman, Paul Robeson, Richard Nixon, Ronald Reagan, and more.

This edition encourages students to think critically about visuals as primary source as well. Because students are so attuned to visuals and instructors deeply value their usefulness as primary sources, we have added 8 **more Visualizing History** features for a total of 20 across the book. A painting of colonial urban life, powder horns, early sketches of the great seal of the United States, a painting of a slave auction, Native American recreation, paintings

with differing viewpoints of Custer's last stand, Marshall Plan posters, and popular art about desegregation enrich this edition as sources for examination. By stressing the importance of historical context in the accompanying essay and, through new short-answer questions prompting critical analysis, each feature shows students how to mine visual documents for evidence about the past. Visualizing History features are available both in print and online and they can be easily assigned in LaunchPad, along with multiple choice quizzes that measure student comprehension.

To give students ample opportunity to practice thinking critically about primary source images, four pictures in each chapter—four times more than in the last edition—include a special **visual activity caption** that reinforces this essential skill. One set of questions in these activities prompts analysis of the image, while a second set of questions helps students connect the images to main points in the narrative. In LaunchPad, the answers to these questions can be submitted directly to the gradebook for convenient assessment.

Geographical Literacy

To help students think critically about the role of geography in American history, with two maps in each chapter we include a **map activity caption**. One set of questions in these activities prompts map analysis, while a second set of questions helps students connect the maps to main points in the narrative. In LaunchPad, the answers to these questions can be submitted directly to the gradebook for convenient assessment.

Acknowledgments

We gratefully acknowledge all of the helpful suggestions from those who have read and taught from previous editions of *The American Promise*, and we hope that our many classroom collaborators will be pleased to see their influence in the sixth edition. In particular, we wish to thank the talented scholars and teachers who gave generously of their time and knowledge to review this book: LeNie Adolphson, *Sauk Valley Community College;* Daniel Anderson, *Cincinnati State Technical and Community College;* Ian Baldwin, *University of Nevada, Las Vegas;* Dustin Black, *El Camino College;* Nawana Britenriker, *Pikes Peak Community College;* Elizabeth Broen, *South Florida State College;* Robert Bush, *Front*

Range Community College; Brian David Collins, *El Centro College;* Alexandra Cornelius, *Florida International University;* Sondra Cosgrove, *College of Southern Nevada;* Rodney E. Dillon, Jr., *Palm Beach State College;* Wayne Drews, *Georgia Institute of Technology;* Edward J. Dudlo, *Brookhaven College;* E. J. Fabyan, *Vincennes University;* Cecilia Gowdy-Wygant, *Front Range Community College;* William Grose, *Wytheville Community College;* Jeff Janowick, *Lansing Community College;* Juneann Klees, *Bay College;* Leonard V. Larsen, *Des Moines Area Community College;* Charles Levine, *Mesa Community College;* Mary Linehan, *University of Texas at Tyler;* Annie Liss, *South Texas College;* Patricia Loughlin, *University of Central Oklahoma;* Walter Miszczenko, *College of Western Idaho;* Rick Murray, *Los Angeles Valley College;* Richard Owens, *West Liberty University;* Stacey Pendleton, *University of Colorado Denver;* Michael J. Pfeifer, *John Jay College of Criminal Justice;* Chris Rasmussen, *Fairleigh Dickinson University;* Robert Sawvel, *University of Northern Colorado;* Benjamin G. Scharff, *West Virginia University;* Christopher Sleeper, *MiraCosta College;* Janet P. Smith, *East Tennessee State University;* John Howard Smith, *Texas A&M University–Commerce;* William Z. Tannenbaum, *Missouri Southern State University;* Ramon C. Veloso, *Palomar College;* and Kenneth A. Watras, *Paradise Valley Community College.*

A project as complex as this requires the talents of many individuals. First, we would like to acknowledge our families for their support, forbearance, and toleration of our textbook responsibilities. Naomi Kornhauser contributed her vast knowledge, tireless energy, and diligent research to make possible the useful and attractive illustration program.

We would also like to thank the many people at Bedford/St. Martin's and Macmillan Education who have been crucial to this project. No one has done more than our friend, senior editor Heidi Hood, who managed the entire revision and supplements program. Heidi, with help from senior editor Leah Strauss and associate editor Jennifer Jovin, guided us through every part of this complex revision, used unfailing good judgment, and saved us from many a misstep. Thanks also go to editorial assistant Victoria Royal for her assistance coordinating the pre-revision review, preparing the manuscript, and for working on the supplements, along with Jennifer Jovin. We are also grateful to Jane Knetzger, director of development for history; William J. Lombardo, senior executive editor for history; and Mary Dougherty, publisher for history, for their support and guidance. For their imaginative and tireless efforts to promote the book, we want to thank Sandi McGuire and Alex Kaufman. With great skill and professionalism, production editor Kerri Cardone pulled together the many pieces related to copyediting, design, and composition, with the guidance of managing editor Michael Granger. Production manager Joe Ford oversaw the manufacturing of the book. Designer Jerilyn Bockorick, copyeditor Lisa Wehrle, and proofreaders Jan Cocker and Nancy Benjamin attended to the myriad details that help make the book shine. Leoni McVey provided an outstanding index. The book's gorgeous cover was designed by William Boardman. Media producer Michelle Camisa managed the process that made sure that *The American Promise* remains at the forefront of technological support for students and instructors. Denise Wydra, vice president of editorial for the humanities, provided helpful advice throughout the course of the project. Finally, Charles H. Christensen, former president of Bedford/St. Martin's, took a personal interest in *The American Promise* from the start, and Joan E. Feinberg, former co-president of Macmillan Higher Education, encouraged us through each edition.

Versions and Supplements

Adopters of *The American Promise* and their students have access to abundant print and digital resources and tools, including documents, assessment and presentation materials, the acclaimed Bedford Series in History and Culture volumes, and much more. And for the first time, the full-featured LaunchPad course space provides access to the narrative with all assignment and assessment opportunities at the ready. See below for more information, visit the book's catalog site at **bedfordstmartins.com/roark/catalog**, or contact your local Bedford/St. Martin's sales representative.

Get the Right Version for Your Class

To accommodate different course lengths and course budgets, *The American Promise* is available in several different formats, including 3-hole punched loose-leaf Budget Books versions and low-priced PDF e-books, which include the *Bedford e-Book to Go for The American Promise* from our Web site and other PDF e-books from other commercial sources. And for the best value of all, package a new print book with LaunchPad at no additional charge to get the best each format offers—a print version for easy portability and reading with a LaunchPad interactive e-book and course space with loads of additional assignment and assessment options.

- **Combined Volume** (Chapters 1–31): available in paperback and e-book formats and in LaunchPad

- **Volume 1, To 1877** (Chapters 1–16): available in paperback, loose-leaf, and e-book formats and in LaunchPad

- **Volume 2, From 1865** (Chapters 16–31): available in paperback, loose-leaf, and e-book formats and in LaunchPad

As noted below, any of these volumes can be packaged with additional titles for a discount. To get ISBNs for discount packages, see the online catalog at **bedfordstmartins.com/roark** /catalog or contact your Bedford/St. Martin's representative.

NEW Assign LaunchPad—A Content-Rich and Assessment-Ready Interactive e-book and Course Space

Available for discount purchase on its own or for packaging with new books at no additional charge, LaunchPad is a breakthrough solution for today's courses. Intuitive and easy-to-use for students and instructors alike, LaunchPad is ready to use as is, and can be edited, customized with your own material, and assigned in seconds. *LaunchPad for The American Promise* includes Bedford/St. Martin's high-quality content all in one place, including the full interactive e-book and the *Reading the American Past* documents collection plus LearningCurve formative quizzing, guided reading activities designed to help students read actively for key concepts, additional primary sources, images, videos, chapter summative quizzes, and more.

Through a wealth of formative and summative assessments, including short answer, essay questions, multiple-choice quizzing, and the adaptive learning program of LearningCurve (see the full description ahead), students gain confidence and get into their reading *before* class. Map and visual activities engage students with visual analysis and critical thinking as they work through each unit, while special boxed features become more meaningful through automatically graded multiple choice exercises and short answer questions that prompt students to analyze their reading.

Best of all, each unit comes with a set of activities specially designed to make critical thinking a part of students' active reading experience. A set of "Reflections" questions at the end of every major section in the chapter exercises students' critical reading skills as they reflect on the narrative as historical interpretation, a "Chronological Reasoning" activity at the end of each chapter prompts students to consider the connections among events and why they are important, and the "What's Your Question?" activity at the end of the unit guides students to formulate their own historical questions.

LaunchPad easily integrates with course management systems and with fast ways to build assignments, rearrange chapters, and add new pages, sections, or links, it lets teachers build the courses they want to teach and hold students accountable. For more information, visit launchpadworks.com or to arrange a demo, contact us at history@bedfordstmartins.com.

✓ NEW Assign LearningCurve So Your Students Come to Class Prepared

Students using LaunchPad receive access to LearningCurve for *The American Promise*. Assigning LearningCurve in place of reading quizzes is easy for instructors, and the reporting features help instructors track overall class trends and spot topics that are giving students trouble so they can adjust their lectures and class activities. This online learning tool is popular with students because it was designed to help them rehearse content at their own pace in a nonthreatening, game-like environment. The feedback for wrong answers provides instructional coaching and sends students back to the book for review. Students answer as many questions as necessary to reach a target score, with repeated chances to revisit material they haven't mastered. When LearningCurve is assigned, students come to class better prepared.

Take Advantage of Instructor Resources

Bedford/St. Martin's has developed a rich array of teaching resources for this book and for this course. They range from lecture and presentation materials and assessment tools to course management options. Most can be found in LaunchPad or can be downloaded or ordered at bedfordstmartins.com/roark/catalog.

Instructor's Resource Manual. The instructor's manual offers both experienced and first-time instructors tools for preparing lectures and running discussions. It includes chapter content learning objectives, annotated chapter outlines, teaching strategies, and a guide to chapter-specific supplements available for the text, plus research paper topic ideas, suggestions on how to get the most out of LearningCurve, and a survival guide for first-time teaching assistants.

Guide to Changing Editions. Designed to facilitate an instructor's transition from the previous edition of *The American Promise* to the current edition, this guide presents an overview of major changes as well as other changes in each chapter.

Computerized Test Bank. The test bank includes a mix of fresh, carefully crafted multiple-choice, short-answer, and essay questions for each chapter. It also contains volume-wide essay questions. All questions appear in Microsoft Word format and in easy-to-use test bank software that allows instructors to add, edit, re-sequence, and print questions and answers. Instructors can also export questions into a variety of formats, including Blackboard, Desire2Learn, and Moodle.

The Bedford Lecture Kit: PowerPoint Maps and Images. Look good and save time with *The Bedford Lecture Kit*. These presentation materials are downloadable individually from the Instructor Resources tab at bedfordstmartins.com/roark/catalog. They include all maps, figures, and images from the textbook in JPEG and PowerPoint formats.

America in Motion: Video Clips for U.S. History. Set history in motion with *America in Motion*, an instructor DVD containing dozens of short digital movie files of events in twentieth-century American history. From the wreckage of the battleship *Maine* to FDR's fireside chats to Oliver North testifying before Congress, *America in Motion* engages students with dynamic scenes from key events and challenges them to think critically. All files are classroom-ready, edited for brevity, and easily integrated with PowerPoint or other presentation software for electronic lectures or assignments. An accompanying guide provides each clip's historical context, ideas for use, and suggested questions.

Package and Save Your Students Money

For information on free packages and discounts up to 50%, visit bedfordstmartins.com/roark/catalog, or contact your local Bedford/St. Martin's sales representative. The products that follow all qualify for discount packaging.

Reading The American Past, Fifth Edition. Edited by Michael P. Johnson, one of the authors of *The American Promise*, and designed to complement the textbook, *Reading the American Past* provides a broad selection of over 150 primary source documents, as well as editorial apparatus to help students understand the sources. Available free when packaged with the print text and included in the LaunchPad e-book. Also available on its own as a downloadable PDF e-book.

NEW **Bedford Digital Collections at macmillanhighered.com/launchpadsolo /BDC/USHistory/catalog.** This source collection provides a flexible and affordable online repository of discovery-oriented primary-source projects that you can easily customize and link to from your course management system or Web site.

The Bedford Series in History and Culture. More than 100 titles in this highly praised series combine first-rate scholarship, historical narrative, and important primary documents for undergraduate courses. Each book is brief, inexpensive, and focused on a specific topic or period. For a complete list of titles, visit **bedfordstmartins .com/history/series**.

Rand McNally Atlas of American History. This collection of over eighty full-color maps illustrates key events and eras from early exploration, settlement, expansion, and immigration to U.S. involvement in wars abroad and on U.S. soil. Introductory pages for each section include a brief overview, timelines, graphs, and photos to quickly establish a historical context.

Maps in Context: A Workbook for American History. Written by historical cartography expert Gerald A. Danzer (University of Illinois at Chicago), this skill-building workbook helps students comprehend essential connections between geographic literacy and historical understanding. Organized to correspond to the typical U.S. history survey course, *Maps in Context* presents a wealth of map-centered projects and convenient pop quizzes that give students hands-on experience working with maps.

The Bedford Glossary for U.S. History. This handy supplement for the survey course gives students historically contextualized definitions for hundreds of terms—from *abolitionism* to *zoot suit*—that they will encounter in lectures, reading, and exams.

U.S. History Matters: A Student Guide to U.S. History Online. This resource, written by Alan Gevinson, Kelly Shrum, and the late Roy Rosenzweig (all of George Mason University), provides an illustrated and annotated guide to 250 of the most useful Web sites for student research in U.S. history as well as advice on evaluating and using Internet sources. This essential guide is based on the acclaimed "History Matters" Web site developed by the American Social History Project and the Center for History and New Media.

Trade Books. Titles published by sister companies Hill and Wang; Farrar, Straus and Giroux; Henry Holt and Company; St. Martin's Press; Picador; and Palgrave Macmillan are available at a 50% discount when packaged with Bedford/ St. Martin's textbooks. For more information, visit **bedfordstmartins.com/tradeup**.

A Pocket Guide to Writing in History. This portable and affordable reference tool by Mary Lynn Rampolla provides reading, writing, and research advice useful to students in all history courses. Concise yet comprehensive advice on approaching typical history assignments, developing critical reading skills, writing effective history papers, conducting research, using and documenting sources, and avoiding plagiarism —enhanced with practical tips and examples throughout—have made this slim reference a best-seller.

A Student's Guide to History. This complete guide to success in any history course provides the practical help students need to be successful. In addition to introducin g students to the nature of the discipline, author Jules Benjamin teaches a wide range of skills from preparing for exams to approaching common writing assignments, and explains the research and documentation process with plentiful examples.

Going to the Source: The Bedford Reader in American History. Developed by Victoria Bissell Brown and Timothy J. Shannon, this reader's strong pedagogical framework helps students learn how to ask fruitful questions in order to evaluate documents effectively and develop critical reading skills. The reader's wide variety of chapter topics that complement the survey course and its rich diversity of sources—from personal letters to political cartoons—provoke students' interest as it teaches them the skills they need to successfully interrogate historical sources.

America Firsthand. With its distinctive focus on ordinary people, this primary documents reader, by Anthony Marcus, John M. Giggie, and David Burner, offers a remarkable range of perspectives on America's history from those who lived it. Popular Points of View sections expose students to different perspectives on a specific event or topic, and Visual Portfolios invite analysis of the visual record.

Brief Contents

 LearningCurve

PREFACE vii
VERSIONS AND SUPPLEMENTS xii
CONTENTS xvii
MAPS, FIGURES, AND TABLES xxvii
SPECIAL FEATURES xxix

16 Reconstruction, 1863–1877 433

17 The Contested West, 1865–1900 463

18 Railroads, Business, and Politics in the Gilded Age, 1865–1900 493

19 The City and Its Workers, 1870–1900 521

20 Dissent, Depression, and War, 1890–1900 553

21 Progressivism from the Grass Roots to the White House, 1890–1916 583

22 World War I: The Progressive Crusade at Home and Abroad, 1914–1920 613

23 From New Era to Great Depression, 1920–1932 645

24 The New Deal Experiment, 1932–1939 675

25 The United States and the Second World War, 1939–1945 707

26 Cold War Politics in the Truman Years, 1945–1953 741

27 The Politics and Culture of Abundance, 1952–1960 767

28 Reform, Rebellion, and Reaction, 1960–1974 795

29 Vietnam and the End of the Cold War Consensus, 1961–1975 827

30 America Moves to the Right, 1969–1989 857

31 The Promises and Challenges of Globalization: Since 1989 887

APPENDICES A-1
SELECTED BIBLIOGRAPHY B-1
GLOSSARY OF HISTORICAL VOCABULARY G-1
ACKNOWLEDGMENTS CR-1
INDEX I-1
U.S. POLITICAL/GEOGRAPHIC AND WORLD MAPS M-1
ABOUT THE AUTHORS LAST BOOK PAGE

Contents

PREFACE   vii

VERSIONS AND SUPPLEMENTS   xii

BRIEF CONTENTS   xvi

MAPS, FIGURES, AND TABLES   xxvii

SPECIAL FEATURES   xxix

CHAPTER 16
Reconstruction,
1863–1877   433

OPENING VIGNETTE: James T. Rapier emerges in the early 1870s as Alabama's most prominent black leader   433

Wartime Reconstruction   435
- "To Bind Up the Nation's Wounds"   435
- Land and Labor   437
- The African American Quest for Autonomy   438

   DOCUMENTING THE AMERICAN PROMISE: "The Meaning of Freedom"   438

Presidential Reconstruction   440
- Johnson's Program of Reconciliation   441
- White Southern Resistance and Black Codes   441
- Expansion of Federal Authority and Black Rights   443

Congressional Reconstruction   444
- The Fourteenth Amendment and Escalating Violence   444
- Radical Reconstruction and Military Rule   446
- Impeaching a President   446
- The Fifteenth Amendment and Women's Demands   447

The Struggle in the South   448
- Freedmen, Yankees, and Yeomen   448
- Republican Rule   448

   HISTORICAL QUESTION: "What Did the Ku Klux Klan Really Want?"   450
- White Landlords, Black Sharecroppers   452

   VISUALIZING HISTORY: "A Post-Slavery Encounter"   454

Reconstruction Collapses   455
- Grant's Troubled Presidency   455
- Northern Resolve Withers   457
- White Supremacy Triumphs   457
- An Election and a Compromise   459

Conclusion: "A Revolution But Half Accomplished"   460

CHAPTER REVIEW   462

LearningCurve

CHAPTER 17
The Contested West,
1865–1900   463

OPENING VIGNETTE: Frederick Jackson Turner delivers his "frontier thesis"   463

Conquest and Empire in the West   465
- Indian Removal and the Reservation System   465

   BEYOND AMERICA'S BORDERS: "Imperialism, Colonialism, and the Treatment of the Sioux and the Zulu"   466
- The Decimation of the Great Bison Herds   469
- Indian Wars and the Collapse of Comanchería   470
- The Fight for the Black Hills   470

   VISUALIZING HISTORY: "Custer's Last Stand"   472

Forced Assimilation and Indian Resistance   471
- Indian Schools and the War on Indian Culture   471
- The Dawes Act and Indian Land Allotment   474
- Indian Resistance and Survival   474

Mining the West   477
- Life on the Comstock Lode   478
- The Diverse Peoples of the West   480

Land Fever   482
- Moving West: Homesteaders and Speculators   483

   DOCUMENTING THE AMERICAN PROMISE: "Young Women Homesteaders and the Promise of the West"   484
- Ranchers and Cowboys   486
- Tenants, Sharecroppers, and Migrants   488
- Commercial Farming and Industrial Cowboys   488
- Territorial Government   490

Conclusion: The West in the Gilded Age   490

CHAPTER REVIEW   492

LearningCurve

CHAPTER 18
Railroads, Business, and Politics in the Gilded Age, 1865–1900 493

OPENING VIGNETTE: Mark Twain and the Gilded Age 493

Railroads and the Rise of New Industries 495
- Railroads: America's First Big Business 495
- **VISUALIZING HISTORY:** "Alva Vanderbilt and the Gilded Age" 498
- Andrew Carnegie, Steel, and Vertical Integration 500
- John D. Rockefeller, Standard Oil, and the Trust 501
- New Inventions: The Telephone and the Telegraph 503

From Competition to Consolidation 504
- J. P. Morgan and Finance Capitalism 505
- **HISTORICAL QUESTION:** "Social Darwinism: Did Wealthy Industrialists Practice What They Preached?" 506
- Social Darwinism, Laissez-Faire, and the Supreme Court 506

Politics and Culture 508
- Political Participation and Party Loyalty 508
- Sectionalism and the New South 508
- Gender, Race, and Politics 509
- **DOCUMENTING THE AMERICAN PROMISE:** "Ida B. Wells and Her Campaign to Stop Lynching" 510
- Women's Activism 512

Presidential Politics 513
- Corruption and Party Strife 513
- Garfield's Assassination and Civil Service Reform 514
- Reform and Scandal: The Campaign of 1884 514

Economic Issues and Party Realignment 516
- The Tariff and the Politics of Protection 516
- Railroads, Trusts, and the Federal Government 517
- The Fight for Free Silver 517
- Panic and Depression 518

Conclusion: Business Dominates an Era 519

CHAPTER REVIEW 520

✓ LearningCurve

CHAPTER 19
The City and Its Workers, 1870–1900 521

OPENING VIGNETTE: Workers build the Brooklyn Bridge 521

The Rise of the City 523
- The Urban Explosion: A Global Migration 523
- **SEEKING THE AMERICAN PROMISE:** "Seeking Refuge: Russian Jews Escape the Pogroms" 528
- Racism and the Cry for Immigration Restriction 528
- The Social Geography of the City 530

At Work in Industrial America 533
- America's Diverse Workers 533
- The Family Economy: Women and Children 534
- White-Collar Workers: Managers, "Typewriters," and Salesclerks 534

Workers Organize 537
- The Great Railroad Strike of 1877 537
- The Knights of Labor and the American Federation of Labor 539
- Haymarket and the Specter of Labor Radicalism 539
- **DOCUMENTING THE AMERICAN PROMISE:** "The Songs of the Knights of Labor" 540

At Home and at Play 543
- Domesticity and "Domestics" 543
- Cheap Amusements 543

City Growth and City Government 545
- Building Cities of Stone and Steel 545
- City Government and the "Bosses" 546
- White City or City of Sin? 547
- **BEYOND AMERICA'S BORDERS:** "The World's Columbian Exposition and Nineteenth-Century World's Fairs" 548

Conclusion: Who Built the Cities? 551

CHAPTER REVIEW 552

✓ LearningCurve

CHAPTER 20
Dissent, Depression, and War, 1890–1900   553

OPENING VIGNETTE: Frances Willard participates in the creation of the Populist Party in 1892   553

The Farmers Unite   555
- The Farmers' Alliance   555
- The Populist Movement   556

The Labor Wars   558
- The Homestead Lockout   558
- The Cripple Creek Miners' Strike of 1894   560
- Eugene V. Debs and the Pullman Strike   560

DOCUMENTING THE AMERICAN PROMISE: "The Press and the Pullman Strike: Framing Class Conflict"   562

Women's Activism   564
- Frances Willard and the Woman's Christian Temperance Union   564
- Elizabeth Cady Stanton, Susan B. Anthony, and the Movement for Woman Suffrage   565

Depression Politics   566
- Coxey's Army   566
- The People's Party and the Election of 1896   567

The United States and the World   570
- Markets and Missionaries   570
- The Monroe Doctrine and the Open Door Policy   571

BEYOND AMERICA'S BORDERS: "Regime Change in Hawai'i"   572
- "A Splendid Little War"   574

HISTORICAL QUESTION: "Did Terrorists Sink the *Maine*?"   576
- The Debate over American Imperialism   579

Conclusion: Rallying around the Flag   581

CHAPTER REVIEW   582

 LearningCurve

CHAPTER 21
Progressivism from the Grass Roots to the White House, 1890–1916   583

OPENING VIGNETTE: Jane Addams founds Hull House   583

Grassroots Progressivism   585
- Civilizing the City   585

SEEKING THE AMERICAN PROMISE: "Making the Workplace Safer: Alice Hamilton Explores the Dangerous Trades"   586
- Progressives and the Working Class   588

Progressivism: Theory and Practice   590
- Reform Darwinism and Social Engineering   590
- Progressive Government: City and State   590

Progressivism Finds a President: Theodore Roosevelt   592
- The Square Deal   592
- Roosevelt the Reformer   594

VISUALIZING HISTORY: "The Birth of Photojournalism"   596
- Roosevelt and Conservation   595

HISTORICAL QUESTION: "Progressives and Conservation: Should Hetch Hetchy Be Dammed or Saved?"   600
- The Big Stick   596
- The Troubled Presidency of William Howard Taft   600

Woodrow Wilson and Progressivism at High Tide   604
- Progressive Insurgency and the Election of 1912   604
- Wilson's Reforms: Tariff, Banking, and the Trusts   606
- Wilson, Reluctant Progressive   607

The Limits of Progressive Reform   607
- Radical Alternatives   607
- Progressivism for White Men Only   609

Conclusion: The Transformation of the Liberal State   611

CHAPTER REVIEW   612

LearningCurve

CHAPTER 22

World War I: The Progressive Crusade at Home and Abroad, 1914–1920 613

OPENING VIGNETTE: Doughboy George "Brownie" Browne sees combat on the front lines in France 613

Woodrow Wilson and the World 615
- Taming the Americas 615
- The European Crisis 617
- The Ordeal of American Neutrality 617
- The United States Enters the War 619

"Over There" 620
- The Call to Arms 620
- The War in France 621

The Crusade for Democracy at Home 624
- The Progressive Stake in the War 624
- Women, War, and the Battle for Suffrage 625
- **SEEKING THE AMERICAN PROMISE:** "Seeking to Serve: An American Woman in Wartime France" 626
- Rally around the Flag—or Else 628
- **DOCUMENTING THE AMERICAN PROMISE:** "The Final Push for Woman Suffrage" 630

A Compromised Peace 630
- Wilson's Fourteen Points 631
- The Paris Peace Conference 632
- The Fight for the Treaty 634

Democracy at Risk 635
- Economic Hardship and Labor Upheaval 636
- The Red Scare 637
- **BEYOND AMERICA'S BORDERS:** "Bolshevism" 638
- The Great Migrations of African Americans and Mexicans 640
- Postwar Politics and the Election of 1920 642

Conclusion: Troubled Crusade 642

CHAPTER REVIEW 644

 LearningCurve

CHAPTER 23

From New Era to Great Depression, 1920–1932 645

OPENING VIGNETTE: Henry Ford puts America on wheels 645

The New Era 647
- A Business Government 647
- Promoting Prosperity and Peace Abroad 649
- Automobiles, Mass Production, and Assembly-Line Progress 649
- Consumer Culture 650
- **VISUALIZING HISTORY:** "Advertising in a Consumer Age" 652

The Roaring Twenties 652
- Prohibition 653
- The New Woman 654
- **HISTORICAL QUESTION:** "Was There a Sexual Revolution in the 1920s?" 656
- The New Negro 658
- Entertainment for the Masses 658
- **SEEKING THE AMERICAN PROMISE:** "The Quest for Home Ownership in Segregated Detroit" 660
- The Lost Generation 660

Resistance to Change 662
- Rejecting the Undesirables 663
- The Rebirth of the Ku Klux Klan 663
- The Scopes Trial 664
- Al Smith and the Election of 1928 665

The Great Crash 665
- Herbert Hoover: The Great Engineer 666
- The Distorted Economy 667
- The Crash of 1929 667
- Hoover and the Limits of Individualism 667

Life in the Depression 669
- The Human Toll 669
- Denial and Escape 670
- Working-Class Militancy 671

Conclusion: Dazzle and Despair 672

CHAPTER REVIEW 674

LearningCurve

CHAPTER 24
The New Deal Experiment,
1932–1939   675

OPENING VIGNETTE: "Migrant Mother" Florence Owens struggles to survive in the Great Depression   675

Franklin D. Roosevelt: A Patrician in Government   677
- The Making of a Politician   677
- The Election of 1932   678

  BEYOND AMERICA'S BORDERS: "Fascism: Adolf Hitler and National Socialism"   680

Launching the New Deal   680
- The New Dealers   681
- Banking and Finance Reform   682
- Relief and Conservation Programs   684
- Agricultural Initiatives   685
- Industrial Recovery   686

  SEEKING THE AMERICAN PROMISE: "Textile Workers Strike for Better Wages and Working Conditions"   688

Challenges to the New Deal   687
- Resistance to Business Reform   687
- Casualties in the Countryside   690
- Politics on the Fringes   691

Toward a Welfare State   693
- Relief for the Unemployed   693

  DOCUMENTING THE AMERICAN PROMISE: "Americans Encounter the New Deal"   694
- Empowering Labor   696
- Social Security and Tax Reform   697
- Neglected Americans and the New Deal   698

The New Deal from Victory to Deadlock   700
- The Election of 1936   701
- Court Packing   701
- Reaction and Recession   701
- The Last of the New Deal Reforms   703

Conclusion: Achievements and Limitations of the New Deal   704

CHAPTER REVIEW   706

CHAPTER 25
The United States and the Second World War,
1939–1945   707

OPENING VIGNETTE: Colonel Paul Tibbets drops the atomic bomb on Hiroshima, Japan   707

Peacetime Dilemmas   709
- Roosevelt and Reluctant Isolation   709
- The Good Neighbor Policy   710
- The Price of Noninvolvement   710

The Onset of War   711
- Nazi Aggression and War in Europe   712
- From Neutrality to the Arsenal of Democracy   714
- Japan Attacks America   715

Mobilizing for War   716
- Home-Front Security   717
- Building a Citizen Army   718
- Conversion to a War Economy   719

  DOCUMENTING THE AMERICAN PROMISE: "Japanese Internment"   720

Fighting Back   720
- Turning the Tide in the Pacific   722
- The Campaign in Europe   723

The Wartime Home Front   725
- Women and Families, Guns and Butter   725
- The Double V Campaign   726
- Wartime Politics and the 1944 Election   727
- Reaction to the Holocaust   727

Toward Unconditional Surrender   728

  BEYOND AMERICA'S BORDERS: "Nazi Anti-Semitism and the Atomic Bomb"   730
- From Bombing Raids to Berlin   729

  HISTORICAL QUESTION: "Why Did the Allies Win World War II?"   734
- The Defeat of Japan   731
- Atomic Warfare   737

Conclusion: Allied Victory and America's Emergence as a Superpower   738

CHAPTER REVIEW   740

CHAPTER 26

Cold War Politics in the Truman Years, 1945–1953   741

OPENING VIGNETTE: Helen Gahagan Douglas, congresswoman and loyal Truman ally, supports the Marshall Plan, the creation of NATO, and the war in Korea   741

From the Grand Alliance to Containment   743
- The Cold War Begins   743

DOCUMENTING THE AMERICAN PROMISE: "The Emerging Cold War"   746
- The Truman Doctrine and the Marshall Plan   745

VISUALIZING HISTORY: "Selling the Marshall Plan"   750
- Building a National Security State   749
- Superpower Rivalry around the Globe   752

Truman and the Fair Deal at Home   753
- Reconverting to a Peacetime Economy   753
- Blacks and Mexican Americans Push for Their Civil Rights   755
- The Fair Deal Flounders   757
- The Domestic Chill: McCarthyism   759

SEEKING THE AMERICAN PROMISE: "An Immigrant Scientist Encounters the Anti-Communist Crusade"   760

The Cold War Becomes Hot: Korea   762
- Korea and the Military Implementation of Containment   762
- From Containment to Rollback to Containment   763
- Korea, Communism, and the 1952 Election   764
- An Armistice and the War's Costs   764

Conclusion: The Cold War's Costs and Consequences   765

CHAPTER REVIEW   766

✓ LearningCurve

CHAPTER 27

The Politics and Culture of Abundance, 1952–1960   767

OPENING VIGNETTE: Vice President Richard Nixon debates Russian premier Nikita Khrushchev   767

Eisenhower and the Politics of the "Middle Way"   769
- Modern Republicanism   769
- Termination and Relocation of Native Americans   770
- The 1956 Election and the Second Term   772

Liberation Rhetoric and the Practice of Containment   772
- The "New Look" in Foreign Policy   773
- Applying Containment to Vietnam   773
- Interventions in Latin America and the Middle East   774

SEEKING THE AMERICAN PROMISE: "Operation Pedro Pan: Young Political Refugees Take Flight"   776
- The Nuclear Arms Race   776

New Work and Living Patterns in an Economy of Abundance   779
- Technology Transforms Agriculture and Industry   779
- Burgeoning Suburbs and Declining Cities   780
- The Rise of the Sun Belt   782
- The Democratization of Higher Education   783

The Culture of Abundance   784
- Consumption Rules the Day   784
- The Revival of Domesticity and Religion   785
- Television Transforms Culture and Politics   785
- Countercurrents   786

The Emergence of a Civil Rights Movement   787
- African Americans Challenge the Supreme Court and the President   788

DOCUMENTING THE AMERICAN PROMISE: "The *Brown* Decision"   788

VISUALIZING HISTORY: "School Desegregation"   790
- Montgomery and Mass Protest   791

Conclusion: Peace and Prosperity Mask Unmet Challenges   793

CHAPTER REVIEW   794

✓ LearningCurve

CHAPTER 28
Reform, Rebellion, and Reaction, 1960–1974   795

OPENING VIGNETTE: Fannie Lou Hamer leads grassroots struggles of African Americans for voting rights and political empowerment   795

Liberalism at High Tide   797
- The Unrealized Promise of Kennedy's New Frontier   797
- Johnson Fulfills the Kennedy Promise   799
- Policymaking for a Great Society   800
- Assessing the Great Society   801
- The Judicial Revolution   803

The Second Reconstruction   804
- The Flowering of the Black Freedom Struggle   804
- The Response in Washington   805
- Black Power and Urban Rebellions   807

A Multitude of Movements   809
- Native American Protest   809
- Latino Struggles for Justice   810
- Student Rebellion, the New Left, and the Counterculture   811

DOCUMENTING THE AMERICAN PROMISE: "Student Protest"   812

VISUALIZING HISTORY: "Anti-Establishment Clothing"   814

- Gay Men and Lesbians Organize   816

The New Wave of Feminism   817
- A Multifaceted Movement Emerges   817

BEYOND AMERICA'S BORDERS: "Transnational Feminisms"   818

- Feminist Gains Spark a Countermovement   819

Liberal Reform in the Nixon Administration   821
- Extending the Welfare State and Regulating the Economy   821
- Responding to Environmental Concerns   822
- Expanding Social Justice   823

Conclusion: Achievements and Limitations of Liberalism   824

CHAPTER REVIEW   826

 LearningCurve

CHAPTER 29
Vietnam and the End of the Cold War Consensus, 1961–1975   827

OPENING VIGNETTE: Lieutenant Frederick Downs, Jr., is wounded in Vietnam and returns home to a country divided over the war   827

New Frontiers in Foreign Policy   829
- Meeting the "Hour of Maximum Danger"   829
- New Approaches to the Third World   831
- The Arms Race and the Nuclear Brink   832
- A Growing War in Vietnam   832

Lyndon Johnson's War against Communism   834
- An All-Out Commitment in Vietnam   834
- Preventing Another Castro in Latin America   835
- The Americanized War   837
- Those Who Served   838

A Nation Polarized   839
- The Widening War at Home   839
- The Tet Offensive and Johnson's Move toward Peace   840

BEYOND AMERICA'S BORDERS: "1968: A Year of Protest"   842

- The Tumultuous Election of 1968   843

Nixon, Détente, and the Search for Peace in Vietnam   845
- Moving toward Détente with the Soviet Union and China   845
- Shoring Up U.S. Interests around the World   846
- Vietnam Becomes Nixon's War   847

DOCUMENTING THE AMERICAN PROMISE: "Ending the War in Vietnam"   848

- The Peace Accords   850

SEEKING THE AMERICAN PROMISE: "From the Fall of Saigon to the House of Representatives"   852

- The Legacy of Defeat   852

Conclusion: An Unwinnable War   854

CHAPTER REVIEW   856

LearningCurve

CHAPTER 30
America Moves to the Right, 1969–1989 857

OPENING VIGNETTE: Phyllis Schlafly promotes conservatism 857

Nixon, Conservatism, and Constitutional Crisis 859
- Emergence of a Grassroots Movement 859
- Nixon Courts the Right 861

SEEKING THE AMERICAN PROMISE: "A Mother Campaigns for a Say in Her Children's Education" 862
- The Election of 1972 864
- Watergate 864
- The Ford Presidency and the 1976 Election 865

The "Outsider" Presidency of Jimmy Carter 866
- Retreat from Liberalism 867
- Energy and Environmental Reform 868
- Promoting Human Rights Abroad 869
- The Cold War Intensifies 870

Ronald Reagan and the Conservative Ascendancy 872
- Appealing to the New Right and Beyond 873
- Unleashing Free Enterprise 874
- Winners and Losers in a Flourishing Economy 875

Continuing Struggles over Rights 876
- Battles in the Courts and Congress 876
- Feminism on the Defensive 876

HISTORICAL QUESTION: "Why Did the ERA Fail?" 878
- The Gay and Lesbian Rights Movement 878

DOCUMENTING THE AMERICAN PROMISE: "Protecting Gay and Lesbian Rights" 880

Ronald Reagan Confronts an "Evil Empire" 882
- Militarization and Interventions Abroad 882
- The Iran-Contra Scandal 883
- A Thaw in Soviet-American Relations 884

Conclusion: Reversing the Course of Government 885

CHAPTER REVIEW 886

LearningCurve

CHAPTER 31
The Promises and Challenges of Globalization, Since 1989 887

OPENING VIGNETTE: Colin Powell adjusts to a post–Cold War world 887

Domestic Stalemate and Global Upheaval: The Presidency of George H. W. Bush 889
- Gridlock in Government 889

SEEKING THE AMERICAN PROMISE: "Suing for Access: Disability and the Courts" 890
- The Cold War Ends 891
- Going to War in Central America and the Persian Gulf 893
- The 1992 Election 896

The Clinton Administration's Search for the Middle Ground 896
- Clinton's Reforms 896
- Accommodating the Right 897
- Impeaching the President 898
- The Booming Economy of the 1990s 899

The United States in a Globalizing World 900
- Defining America's Place in a New World Order 900
- Debates over Globalization 902

BEYOND AMERICA'S BORDERS: "Jobs in a Globalizing Era" 904
- The Internationalization of the United States 903

President George W. Bush: Conservatism at Home and Radical Initiatives Abroad 905
- The Disputed Election of 2000 906
- The Domestic Policies of a "Compassionate Conservative" 906
- The Globalization of Terrorism 908
- Unilateralism, Preemption, and the Iraq War 909

The Obama Presidency: Reform and Backlash 911
- Governing during Economics Crisis and Political Polarization 911

VISUALIZING HISTORY: "Caricaturing the Candidates: Clinton and Obama in 2008" 914
- Redefining the War on Terror 912

Conclusion: Defining the Government's Role at Home and Abroad 913

CHAPTER REVIEW 916

LearningCurve

APPENDICES

I. Documents   A-1

The Declaration of Independence   A-1

The Constitution of the United States   A-3

Amendments to the Constitution with Annotations (including the six unratified amendments)   A-8

II. Government, and Demographics   A-23

- Presidential Elections   A-23
- Admission of States to the Union   A-26
- Population Growth, 1630–2010   A-27
- Major Trends in Immigration, 1820–2010   A-28

GLOSSARY   G-1

SELECTED BIBLIOGRAPHY   B-1

ACKNOWLEDGMENTS   CR-1

INDEX   I-1

U.S. POLITICAL/GEOGRAPHIC AND WORLD MAPS   M-1

ABOUT THE AUTHORS   LAST BOOK PAGE

Maps, Figures, and Tables

Maps

CHAPTER 16

SPOT MAP: Reconstruction Military Districts, 1867   446

MAP 16.1 A Southern Plantation in 1860 and 1881   455

MAP 16.2 The Election of 1868   456

MAP 16.3 The Reconstruction of the South   459

MAP 16.4 The Election of 1876   460

CHAPTER 17

SPOT MAP: Zululand and Cape Colony, 1878 (Beyond America's Borders)   466

MAP 17.1 The Loss of Indian Lands, 1850–1890   468

MAP 17.2 Western Mining, 1848–1890   478

SPOT MAP: Midwestern Settlement before 1862   486

MAP 17.3 Federal Land Grants to Railroads and the Development of the West, 1850–1900   487

CHAPTER 18

MAP 18.1 Railroad Expansion, 1870–1890   496

MAP 18.2 The Election of 1884   515

CHAPTER 19

MAP 19.1 Economic Regions of the World, 1890   524

MAP 19.2 The Impact of Immigration, to 1910   525

MAP 19.3 The Great Railroad Strike of 1877   537

CHAPTER 20

MAP 20.1 The Election of 1892   568

MAP 20.2 The Election of 1896   569

SPOT MAP: Samoan Islands, 1889   575

MAP 20.3 The Spanish-American War, 1898   578

MAP 20.4 U.S. Overseas Expansion through 1900   580

CHAPTER 21

MAP 21.1 National Parks and Forests   598

MAP 21.2 The Panama Canal, 1914   602

SPOT MAP: The Roosevelt Corollary in Action   598

SPOT MAP: Taft's "Dollar Diplomacy"   604

MAP 21.3 The Election of 1912   606

CHAPTER 22

MAP 22.1 U.S. Involvement in Latin America and the Caribbean, 1895–1941   616

SPOT MAP: U.S. Intervention in Mexico, 1916–1917   617

MAP 22.2 European Alliances after the Outbreak of World War I   618

SPOT MAP: Sinking of the *Lusitania*, 1915   619

MAP 22.3 The American Expeditionary Force, 1918   623

MAP 22.4 Women's Voting Rights before the Nineteenth Amendment   628

MAP 22.5 Europe after World War I   634

MAP 22.6 The Election of 1920   642

CHAPTER 23

MAP 23.1 Auto Manufacturing   646

SPOT MAP: Detroit and the Automobile Industry in the 1920s   649

MAP 23.2 The Shift from Rural to Urban Population, 1920–1930   662

MAP 23.3 The Election of 1928   665

SPOT MAP: Harlan County Coal Strike, 1931   671

CHAPTER 24

MAP 24.1 The Election of 1932   679

MAP 24.2 Electoral Shift, 1928–1932   679

MAP 24.3 The Tennessee Valley Authority   685

SPOT MAP: The Dust Bowl   691

CHAPTER 25

SPOT MAP: Spanish Civil War, 1936–1939   711

MAP 25.1 Axis Aggression through 1941   712

MAP 25.2 Japanese Aggression through 1941   715

SPOT MAP: Bombing of Pearl Harbor, December 7, 1941   716

MAP 25.3 Western Relocation Authority Centers   718

SPOT MAP: The Holocaust, 1933–1945   727

MAP 25.4 The European Theater of World War II, 1942–1945   733

MAP 25.5 The Pacific Theater of World War II, 1941–1945   736

CHAPTER 26

MAP 26.1 The Division of Europe after World War II   745

SPOT MAP: Berlin Divided, 1948   748

SPOT MAP: Israel, 1948   753

MAP 26.2 The Election of 1948   758

MAP 26.3 The Korean War, 1950–1953   762

CHAPTER 27

MAP 27.1 The Interstate Highway System, 1930 and 1970 771

SPOT MAP: Major Indian Relocations, 1950–1970 771

SPOT MAP: Geneva Accords, 1954 774

SPOT MAP: The Suez Crisis, 1956 775

MAP 27.2 The Rise of the Sun Belt, 1940–1980 782

CHAPTER 28

MAP 28.1 The Election of 1960 798

SPOT MAP: Civil Rights Freedom Rides, May 1961 805

MAP 28.2 The Rise of the African American Vote, 1940–1976 807

MAP 28.3 Urban Uprisings, 1965–1968 808

CHAPTER 29

MAP 29.1 U.S. Involvement in Latin America and the Caribbean, 1954–1994 830

SPOT MAP: Cuban Missile Crisis, 1962 832

MAP 29.2 The Vietnam War, 1964–1975 834

MAP 29.3 The Election of 1968 845

SPOT MAP: Chile 846

SPOT MAP: Israeli Territorial Gains in the Six-Day War, 1967 846

SPOT MAP: U.S. Invasion of Cambodia, 1970 847

CHAPTER 30

SPOT MAP: Integration of Public Schools, 1968 861

MAP 30.1 The Election of 1976 866

MAP 30.2 Worldwide Oil Reserves, 1980 870

MAP 30.3 The Middle East, 1948–1989 871

SPOT MAP: The Fight for the Equal Rights Amendment 876

SPOT MAP: El Salvador and Nicaragua 883

CHAPTER 31

MAP 31.1 Events in Eastern Europe, 1989–2002 892

MAP 31.2 Events in the Middle East, 1989–2011 894

SPOT MAP: Breakup of Yugoslavia 901

SPOT MAP: Events in Israel since 1989 902

MAP 31.3 The Election of 2000 906

SPOT MAP: Afghanistan 909

SPOT MAP: Iraq 909

MAP 31.4 The Election of 2012 913

Figures and Tables

FIGURE 16.1 Southern Congressional Delegations, 1865–1877 449

FIGURE 17.1 Changes in Rural and Urban Populations, 1870–1900 488

FIGURE 18.1 Iron and Steel Production, 1870–1900 501

THEMATIC CHRONOLOGY Notable American Inventions, 1865–1899 503

FIGURE 19.1 Global Comparison: European Emigration, 1870–1890 526

FIGURE 19.2 European Emigration, 1870–1910 526

FIGURE 19.3 Women and Work 1870–1890 535

FIGURE 20.1 Consumer Prices and Farm Income, 1865–1910 556

FIGURE 20.2 Expansion in U.S. Trade, 1870–1910 570

FIGURE 22.1 Global Comparison: Casualties of the First World War 624

FIGURE 22.2 Industrial Wages, 1912–1920 625

FIGURE 23.1 Production of Consumer Goods, 1921–1929 651

FIGURE 23.2 Manufacturing and Agricultural Income, 1920–1940 668

FIGURE 24.1 Bank Failures and Farm Foreclosures, 1932–1942 683

THEMATIC CHRONOLOGY Major Legislation of the New Deals' First Hundred Days 687

FIGURE 24.2 Global Comparison: National Populations and Economies, ca. 1938 703

THEMATIC CHRONOLOGY The Road to War: The United States and World War II 717

FIGURE 25.1 Global Comparison: Weapons Production by the Axis and Allied Powers during World War II 772

THEMATIC CHRONOLOGY Major Campaigns and Battles of World War II, 1939–1945 738

FIGURE 26.1 Women Workers in Selected Industries, 1940–1950 754

FIGURE 27.1 The Postwar Economic Boom: GNP and Per Capita Income, 1945–1970 784

THEMATIC CHRONOLOGY Reforms of the Great Society, 1964–1968 802

FIGURE 28.1 Poverty in the United States, 1960–1974 801

FIGURE 29.1 U.S. Troops in Vietnam, 1962–1972 836

TABLE 29.1 VIETNAM WAR CASUALTIES 854

THEMATIC CHRONOLOGY U.S. Involvement in Vietnam 850

FIGURE 30.1 Global Comparison: Energy Consumption per Capita, 1980 869

FIGURE 31.1 The Growth of Inequality: Changes in Family Income, 1969–1998 899

FIGURE 31.2 Global Comparison: Countries with the Highest Military Expenditures, 2005 900

Special Features

BEYOND AMERICA'S BORDERS

Imperialism, Colonialism, and the Treatment
  of the Sioux and the Zulu ... 466

The World's Columbian Exposition and
  Nineteenth-Century World's Fairs ... 548

Regime Change in Hawai'i ... 572

Bolshevism ... 638

Fascism: Adolf Hitler and National Socialism ... 680

Nazi Anti-Semitism and the Atomic Bomb ... 730

Transnational Feminisms ... 818

1968: A Year of Protest ... 842

Jobs in a Globalizing Era ... 904

DOCUMENTING THE AMERICAN PROMISE

The Meaning of Freedom ... 438

Young Women Homesteaders and the Promise
  of the West ... 484

Ida B. Wells and Her Campaign to Stop Lynching ... 510

The Songs of the Knights of Labor ... 540

The Press and the Pullman Strike: Framing Class
  Conflict ... 562

The Final Push for Woman Suffrage ... 630

Americans Encounter the New Deal ... 694

Japanese Internment ... 720

The Emerging Cold War ... 746

The *Brown* Decision ... 788

Student Protest ... 812

Ending the War in Vietnam ... 848

Protecting Gay and Lesbian Rights ... 880

HISTORICAL QUESTION

What Did the Ku Klux Klan Really Want? ... 450

Social Darwinism: Did Wealthy Industrialists
  Practice What They Preached? ... 506

Did Terrorists Sink the *Maine*? ... 576

Progressives and Conservation: Should Hetch
  Hetchy Be Dammed or Saved? ... 600

Was There a Sexual Revolution in the 1920s? ... 656

Why Did the Allies Win World War II? ... 734

Why Did the ERA Fail? ... 878

SEEKING THE AMERICAN PROMISE

Seeking Refuge: Russian Jews Escape the
  Pogroms ... 528

Making the Workplace Safer: Alice Hamilton
  Explores the Dangerous Trades ... 586

Seeking to Serve: An American Woman in
  Wartime France ... 626

The Quest for Home Ownership in Segregated
  Detroit ... 660

Textile Workers Strike for Better Wages and
  Working Conditions ... 688

An Immigrant Scientist Encounters the Anti-
  Communist Crusade ... 760

Operation Pedro Pan: Young Political Refugees
  Take Flight ... 776

From the Fall of Saigon to the House of
  Representatives ... 852

A Mother Campaigns for a Say in Her Children's
  Education ... 862

Suing for Access: Disability and the Courts ... 890

VISUALIZING HISTORY

A Post-Slavery Encounter ... 454

Custer's Last Stand ... 472

Alva Vanderbilt and the Gilded Age ... 498

The Birth of Photojournalism ... 596

Advertising in a Consumer Age ... 652

Selling the Marshall Plan ... 750

School Desegregation ... 790

Anti-Establishment Clothing ... 814

Caricaturing the Candidates: Clinton and
  Obama in 2008 ... 914

The American Promise

A History of
the United States

16 Reconstruction
1863–1877

CONTENT LEARNING OBJECTIVES

After reading and studying this chapter, you should be able to:

- Identify the challenges facing reconstruction efforts.

- Describe President Johnson's reconstruction plan and the ways in which it aligned and differed from Lincoln's.

- Recount the significance of the Fourteenth Amendment, and why President Johnson advised southern states to reject it. Explain the terms of radical reconstruction and how Johnson's interventions led some in Congress to seek his impeachment.

- Describe the provisions of the Fifteenth Amendment, and explain why some women's rights advocates were dissatisfied with it.

- Describe how congressional reconstruction altered life in the South. Explain why the North abandoned reconstruction, including the role of Grant's troubled presidency and the election of 1877 in this abandonment.

CARPETBAG

A carpetbag was a suitcase made from carpet. "Carpetbagger" was a derogatory name for rootless adventurers, which critics of Republican administrations in the South hurled at white Northerners who moved south during Reconstruction. © Elemental Studios/Alamy.

IN 1856, JOHN RAPIER, A FREE BLACK BARBER IN FLORENCE, ALABAMA, urged his four freeborn sons to flee the increasingly repressive and dangerous South. James T. Rapier chose Canada, where he went to live with his uncle in a largely black community and studied Greek and Latin in a log schoolhouse. In a letter to his father, he vowed, "I will endeavor to do my part in solving the problems [of African Americans] in my native land."

The Union victory in the Civil War gave James Rapier the opportunity to redeem his pledge. In 1865, after more than eight years of exile, the twenty-seven-year-old Rapier returned to Alabama, where he presided over the first political gathering of former slaves in the state. He soon discovered, however, that Alabama's whites found it agonizingly difficult to accept defeat and black freedom. They responded to the revolutionary changes under the banner "White Man—Right or Wrong—Still the White Man!"

During the elections of 1868, when Rapier and other Alabama blacks vigorously supported the Republican ticket, the recently organized Ku

Klux Klan went on a bloody rampage. A mob of 150 outraged whites scoured Rapier's neighborhood seeking four black politicians they claimed were trying to "Africanize Alabama." They caught and hanged three, but the "nigger carpetbagger from Canada" escaped. After briefly considering fleeing the state, Rapier decided to stay and fight.

In 1872, Rapier won election to the House of Representatives, where he joined six other black congressmen in Washington, D.C. Defeated for reelection in 1874 in a campaign marked by ballot-box stuffing, Rapier turned to cotton farming. But persistent black poverty and unrelenting racial violence convinced him that blacks could never achieve equality and prosperity in the South. He purchased land in Kansas and urged Alabama's blacks to escape with him. In 1883, however, before he could leave Alabama, Rapier died of tuberculosis at the age of forty-five.

Union general Carl Schurz had foreseen many of the troubles Rapier encountered in the postwar South. In 1865, Schurz concluded that the Civil War was "a revolution but half accomplished." Northern victory had freed the slaves, he observed, but it had not changed former slaveholders' minds about blacks' unfitness for freedom. Left to themselves, whites would "introduce some new system of forced labor, not perhaps exactly slavery in its old form but something similar to it." To defend their freedom, Schurz concluded, blacks would need federal protection, land of their own, and voting rights. Until whites "cut loose from the past, it will be a dangerous experiment to put Southern society upon its own legs."

As Schurz understood, the end of the war did not mean peace. Indeed, the nation entered one of its most turbulent eras—Reconstruction. Answers to the era's central questions—about the defeated South's status within the Union and the meaning of freedom for ex-slaves—came not only from Washington, D.C., where the federal government played an active role, but also from the state legislatures and county seats of the South, where blacks eagerly participated in politics. The Fourteenth and Fifteenth Amendments to the Constitution strengthened the claim of African Americans to equal rights. The struggle also took place on the South's farms and plantations, where former slaves sought to become free workers while former slaveholders clung to the Old South. A small band of white women joined in the struggle for racial equality, and soon their crusade broadened to include gender equality. Their attempts to secure voting rights for women were thwarted, however, just as were the effort of blacks and their allies to secure racial equality. In the contest to determine the consequences of Confederate defeat and emancipation, white Southerners prevailed.

James T. Rapier
In 1874, when Representative James T. Rapier spoke before Congress on behalf of a civil rights bill, he described the humiliation of being denied service at inns all along his route from Montgomery to Washington. Elsewhere in the world, he said, class and religion were invoked to defend discrimination. But in America, "our distinction is color." Alabama Department of Archives and History, Montgomery, Alabama.

▶ Wartime Reconstruction

Reconstruction did not wait for the end of war. As the odds of a northern victory increased, thinking about reunification quickened. Immediately, a question arose: Who had authority to devise a plan for reconstructing the Union? President Abraham Lincoln firmly believed that reconstruction was a matter of executive responsibility. Congress just as firmly asserted its jurisdiction. Fueling the argument were significant differences about the terms of reconstruction.

In their eagerness to formulate a plan for political reunification, neither Lincoln nor Congress gave much attention to the South's land and labor problems. But as the war rapidly eroded slavery and traditional plantation agriculture, Yankee military commanders in the Union-occupied areas of the Confederacy had no choice but to oversee the emergence of a new labor system. Freedmen's aspirations played little role in the plans that emerged.

"To Bind Up the Nation's Wounds"

As early as 1863, Lincoln began contemplating how "to bind up the nation's wounds" and achieve "a lasting peace." While deep compassion for the enemy guided his thinking about peace, his plan for reconstruction aimed primarily at shortening the war and ending slavery.

Lincoln's Proclamation of Amnesty and Reconstruction in December 1863 set out his terms. He offered a full pardon, restoring property (except slaves) and political rights, to most rebels willing to renounce secession and to accept emancipation. When 10 percent of a state's voting population had taken an oath of allegiance, the state could organize a new government and be readmitted into the Union. Lincoln's plan did not require ex-rebels to extend social or political rights to ex-slaves, nor did it anticipate a program of long-term federal assistance to freedmen. Clearly, the president looked forward to the rapid, forgiving restoration of the broken Union.

Lincoln's easy terms enraged abolitionists such as Wendell Phillips of Boston, who charged that the president "makes the negro's freedom a mere sham." He "is willing that the negro should be free but seeks nothing else for him."

CHRONOLOGY

1863	• Proclamation of Amnesty and Reconstruction.
1864	• Lincoln refuses to sign Wade-Davis bill.
1865	• Freedmen's Bureau established. • Lincoln assassinated; Andrew Johnson becomes president. • Black codes enacted. • Thirteenth Amendment becomes part of Constitution.
1866	• Congress approves Fourteenth Amendment. • Civil Rights Act. • American Equal Rights Association founded. • Ku Klux Klan founded.
1867	• Military Reconstruction Act. • Tenure of Office Act.
1868	• Impeachment trial of President Johnson. • Ulysses S. Grant elected president.
1869	• Congress approves Fifteenth Amendment.
1871	• Ku Klux Klan Act.
1872	• Liberal Party formed. • President Grant reelected.
1873	• Economic depression sets in. • *Slaughterhouse* cases. • Colfax massacre.
1874	• Democrats win majority in House of Representatives.
1875	• Civil Rights Act.
1876	• *United States v. Cruikshank*.
1877	• Rutherford B. Hayes becomes president; Reconstruction era ends.

Wartime Reconstruction

This cartoon from the presidential campaign of 1864 shows the "Rail Splitter" Abraham Lincoln leveraging the broken nation back together while his running mate, Andrew Johnson, who once was a tailor by trade, stitches the Confederate states securely back into the Union. Optimism that the task of reconstructing the nation after the war would be both quick and easy shines through the cartoon. The Granger Collection, New York.

Comparing Lincoln to the Union's most passive general, Phillips declared, "What McClellan was on the battlefield—'Do as little hurt as possible!'—Lincoln is in civil affairs—'Make as little change as possible!'" Phillips and other northern radicals called instead for a thorough overhaul of southern society. Their ideas proved to be too drastic for most Republicans during the war years, but Congress agreed that Lincoln's plan was inadequate.

In July 1864, Congress put forward a plan of its own. Congressman Henry Winter Davis of Maryland and Senator Benjamin Wade of Ohio jointly sponsored a bill that demanded that at least half of the voters in a conquered rebel state take the oath of allegiance before reconstruction could begin. The Wade-Davis bill also banned almost all ex-Confederates from participating in the drafting of new state constitutions. Finally, the bill guaranteed the equality of freedmen

before the law. Congress's reconstruction would be neither as quick nor as forgiving as Lincoln's. When Lincoln refused to sign the bill and let it die, Wade and Davis charged the president with usurpation of power.

Undeterred, Lincoln continued to nurture the formation of loyal state governments under his own plan. Four states—Arkansas, Louisiana, Tennessee, and Virginia—fulfilled the president's requirements, but Congress refused to seat representatives from the "Lincoln states." Lincoln admitted that a government based of only 10 percent was not ideal, but he argued, "We shall sooner have the fowl by hatching the egg than by smashing it." Massachusetts's senator Charles Sumner responded, "The eggs of crocodiles can produce only crocodiles." In his last public address in April 1865, Lincoln defended his plan but for the first time expressed publicly his endorsement of suffrage for southern blacks, at least "the very intelligent, and . . . those who serve our cause as soldiers." The announcement demonstrated that Lincoln's thinking about reconstruction was still evolving. Four days later, he was dead.

Land and Labor

Of all the problems raised by the North's victory in the war, none proved more critical than the South's transition from slavery to free labor. As federal armies invaded and occupied the Confederacy, hundreds of thousands of slaves became free workers. In addition, Union armies controlled vast territories in the South where legal title to land had become unclear. The Confiscation Acts passed during the war punished "traitors" by taking away their property. The question of what to do with federally occupied land and how to organize labor on it engaged ex-slaves, ex-slaveholders, Union military commanders, and federal government officials long before the war ended.

In the Mississippi valley, occupying federal troops announced a new labor code. It required landholders to give up whipping, sign contracts with ex-slaves, pay wages, and provide food, housing, and medical care. The code required black laborers to enter into contracts, work diligently, and remain subordinate and obedient. Military leaders clearly had no intention of promoting a social or economic revolution. Instead, they sought to restore traditional plantation agriculture with wage labor. The effort resulted in a hybrid system that one contemporary called "compulsory free labor," something that satisfied no one.

Planters complained because the new system fell short of slavery. Blacks could not be "transformed by proclamation," a Louisiana sugar planter declared. Without the right to whip, he argued, the new labor system did not have a chance. Either Union soldiers must "*compel* the negroes to work," or the planters themselves must "be authorized and sustained in using force."

African Americans found the new regime too reminiscent of slavery to be called free labor. Its chief deficiency, they believed, was the failure to provide them with land of their own. Freedmen believed they had a moral right to land because they and their ancestors had worked it without compensation for centuries. "What's the use of being free if you don't own land enough to be buried in?" one man asked. Several wartime developments led freedmen to believe that the

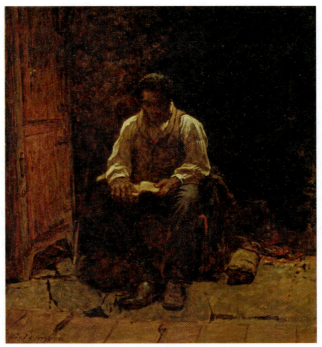

VISUAL ACTIVITY

The Lord Is My Shepherd, 1863

Maine-born Eastman Johnson (1824–1906) did this painting only months after the Emancipation Proclamation. Its title comes from Psalm 23, which begins "The Lord is my shepherd; I shall not want." The painting captures a humble black man quietly reading his Bible and reminds us of one of the reasons freedmen struggled so hard for literacy. Smithsonian American Art Museum, Washington, DC/Art Resource, NY.

READING THE IMAGE: What is the artist saying about ex-slaves' capacity to live as free people?

CONNECTIONS: Why did southern whites in the Reconstruction era consider literacy for former slaves less a religious impulse than a dangerous political act?

federal government planned to undergird black freedom with landownership.

In January 1865, General William Tecumseh Sherman set aside part of the coast south of Charleston for black settlement. By June 1865, some 40,000 freedmen sat on 400,000 acres of "Sherman land." In addition, in March 1865, Congress passed a bill establishing the Bureau of Refugees, Freedmen, and Abandoned Lands. The **Freedmen's Bureau**, as it was called, distributed food and clothing to destitute Southerners and eased the transition of blacks from slaves to free persons. Congress also authorized the agency to divide abandoned and confiscated land into 40-acre plots, to rent them to freedmen, and eventually to sell them "with such title as the

The Meaning of Freedom

Although the Emancipation Proclamation itself did not free any slaves, it transformed the character of the war. Black people resolutely focused on the possibilities of freedom.

DOCUMENT 1
Letter from John Q. A. Dennis to Edwin M. Stanton, July 26, 1864

John Q. A. Dennis, formerly a slave in Maryland, wrote to ask Secretary of War Edwin M. Stanton for help in reuniting his family.

Boston. Dear Sir I am Glad that I have the Honour to Write you a few line I have been in troble for about four yars my Dear wife was taken from me Nov 19th 1859 and left me with three Children and I being a Slave At the time Could Not do Anny thing for the poor little Children for my master it was took me Carry me some forty mile from them So I Could Not do for them and the man that they live with half feed them and half Cloth them & beat them like dogs & when I was admitted to go to see them it use to brake my heart & Now I say again I am Glad to have the honour to write to you to see if you Can Do Anny thing for me or for my poor little Children I was keap in Slavy untell last Novr 1863. then the Good lord sent the Cornel borne [federal colonel William Birney?] Down their in Marland in worsester Co So as I have been recently freed I have but letle to live on but I am Striveing Dear Sir but what I went too know of you Sir is it possible for me to go & take my Children from those men that keep them in Savery if it is possible will you pleas give me a permit from your hand then I think they would let them go. . . . I want get the little Children out of Slavery. . . .

Source: *Freedom: A Documentary History of Emancipation, 1861–1867*, ser. 1, vol. 1, *The Destruction of Slavery*, 386, edited by Ira Berlin, Joseph P. Reidy, and Leslie S. Rowland. Copyright © 1985. Reprinted with the permission of Cambridge University Press.

DOCUMENT 2
Report from Reverend A. B. Randall, February 28, 1865

A. B. Randall, the white chaplain of a black regiment stationed in Little Rock, Arkansas, affirmed the importance of legal marriage to freed slaves and emphasized their conviction that emancipation was only the first step toward full freedom.

Weddings, just now, are very popular, and abundant among the Colored People. They have just learned, of the Special Order No. 15. of Gen Thomas [Adjutant General Lorenzo Thomas] by which, they may not only be lawfully married, but have their Marriage Certificates, Recorded; in a book furnished by the Government. . . . I have married, during the month, at this Post; Twenty five couples; mostly, those, who have families; & have been living together for years. . . . The Colord People here, generally consider, this war not only; their exodus, from bondage; but the road, to Responsibility; Competency; and an honorable Citizenship—God grant that their hopes and expectations may be fully realized.

Source: *Freedom: A Documentary History of Emancipation, 1861–1867*, ser. 2, vol. 1, *The Black Military Experience*, 712, edited by Ira Berlin, Joseph P. Reidy, and Leslie S. Rowland. Copyright © 1982. Reprinted with the permission of Cambridge University Press.

United States can convey." By June 1865, the Bureau had situated nearly 10,000 black families on a half million acres abandoned by fleeing planters. Other ex-slaves eagerly anticipated farms of their own.

Despite the flurry of activity, wartime reconstruction failed to produce agreement about whether the president or Congress had the authority to devise policy or what proper policy should be.

The African American Quest for Autonomy

Ex-slaves never had any doubt about what they wanted from freedom. They had only to contemplate what they had been denied as slaves. (See "Documenting the American Promise," above.) Slaves had to remain on their plantations; freedom allowed blacks to see what was on the other side

DOCUMENT 3
Petition "to the Union Convention of Tennessee Assembled in the Capitol at Nashville," January 9, 1865

In January 1865, black Tennesseans petitioned a convention of white Unionists debating the reorganization of state government.

We the undersigned petitioners, American citizens of African descent, natives and residents of Tennessee, and devoted friends of the great National cause, do most respectfully ask a patient hearing of your honorable body in regard to matters deeply affecting the future condition of our unfortunate and long suffering race. . . .

In the contest between the nation and slavery, our unfortunate people have sided, by instinct, with the former. . . . We will work, pray, live, and, if need be, die for the Union, as cheerfully as ever a white patriot died for his country. The color of our skin does not lessen in the least degree, our love either for God or for the land of our birth. . . .

We know the burdens of citizenship, and are ready to bear them. We know the duties of the good citizen, and are ready to perform them cheerfully, and would ask to be put in a position in which we can discharge them more effectually. . . .

This is a democracy—a government of the people. It should aim to make every man, without regard to the color of his skin, the amount of his wealth, or the character of his religious faith, feel personally interested in its welfare. Every man who lives under the Government should feel that it is his property, his treasure, the bulwark and defence of himself and his family. . . .

This is not a Democratic Government if a numerous, law-abiding, industrious, and useful class of citizens, born and bred on the soil, are to be treated as aliens and enemies, as an inferior degraded class, who must have no voice in the Government which they support, protect and defend, with all their heart, soul, mind, and body, both in peace and war. . . .

The possibility that the negro suffrage proposition may shock popular prejudice at first sight, is not a conclusive argument against its wisdom and policy. No proposition ever met with more furious or general opposition than the one to enlist colored soldiers in the United States army. The opponents of the measure exclaimed on all hands that the negro was a coward; that he would not fight; that one white man, with a whip in his hand could put to flight a regiment of them. . . . Yet the colored man has fought so well . . . .

The Government has asked the colored man to fight for its preservation and gladly has he done it. It can afford to trust him with a vote as safely as it trusted him with a bayonet.

Source: *Freedom: A Documentary History of Emancipation, 1861–1867*, ser. 2, vol. 1, *The Black Military Experience*, 811–16, edited by Ira Berlin, Joseph P. Reidy, and Leslie S. Rowland. Copyright © 1982. Reprinted with the permission of Cambridge University Press.

Questions for Analysis and Debate

1. How does John Q. A. Dennis interpret his responsibility as a father?

2. Why do you think ex-slaves wanted their marriages legalized?

3. Why, according to petitioners to the Union Convention of Tennessee, did blacks deserve voting rights?

Connect to the Big Idea

C How did ex-slaves embrace freedom following the Civil War?

---

of the hill. Slaves had to be at work in the fields by dawn; freedom permitted blacks to sleep through a sunrise. Freedmen also tested the etiquette of racial subordination. "Lizzie's maid passed me today when I was coming from church *without speaking to me*," huffed one plantation mistress.

To whites, emancipation looked like pure anarchy. Blacks, they said, had reverted to their natural condition: lazy, irresponsible, and wild.

Actually, former slaves were experimenting with freedom, but they could not long afford to roam the countryside, neglect work, and casually provoke whites. Soon, most were back at work in whites' kitchens and fields.

But they continued to dream of land and independence. "The way we can best take care of ourselves is to have land," one former slave declared in 1865, "and turn it and till it by our

VISUAL ACTIVITY

Harry Stephens and Family, 1866
The seven members of the Stephens family sit proudly for a photograph just after the Civil War ended. Many black families were not as fortunate as these Virginians. Separated by slavery or war, former slaves desperately sought news of missing family members through newspaper advertisements.
G. Gable, Summer Scene, 1866. Gilman Collection, Purchase, The Horace W. Goldsmith Foundation Gift, through Joyce and Robert Menschel, 2005 (2005.100.277) Image copyright © The Metropolitan Museum of Art. Image source: Art Resource, NY.
READING THE IMAGE: How does the Stephens family signal that they are free people, not slaves?
CONNECTIONS: How would white Southerners likely respond to the message delivered by this photograph?

own labor." Slavery had deliberately kept blacks illiterate, and freedmen emerged from bondage eager to learn to read and write. "I wishes the Childern all in School," one black veteran asserted. "It is beter for them then to be their Surveing a mistes [mistress]."

The restoration of broken families was another persistent black aspiration. Thousands of freedmen took to the roads in 1865 to look for kin who had been sold away or to free those who were being held illegally as slaves. A black soldier from Missouri wrote his daughters that he was coming for them. "I will have you if it cost me my life," he declared. "Your Miss Kitty said that I tried to steal you," he told them. "But I'll let her know that god never intended for a man to steal his own flesh and blood." And he swore that "if she meets me with ten thousand soldiers, she [will] meet her enemy."

Independent worship was another continuing aspiration. African Americans greeted freedom with a mass exodus from white churches, where they had been required to worship when slaves. Some joined the newly established southern branches of all-black northern churches, such as the African Methodist Episcopal Church. Others formed black versions of the major southern denominations, Baptists and Methodists.

REVIEW To what extent did Lincoln's wartime plan for reconstruction reflect the concerns of newly freed slaves?

▶ Presidential Reconstruction

Abraham Lincoln died on April 15, 1865, just hours after John Wilkes Booth shot him at a Washington, D.C., theater. Chief Justice Salmon P. Chase immediately administered the oath of office to Vice President Andrew Johnson of Tennessee. Congress had adjourned in March and would not reconvene until December. Throughout the summer and fall, Johnson drew up and executed a plan of reconstruction without congressional advice.

Congress returned to the capital in December to find that, as far as the president and former Confederates were concerned, reconstruction was completed. Most Republicans, however, thought Johnson's plan made far too few demands of ex-rebels and made a mockery of the sacrifice of Union soldiers. They claimed that Johnson's leniency had acted as midwife to the rebirth of the Old South, that he had achieved political reunification at the cost of black freedom. Republicans in Congress then proceeded to dismantle Johnson's program and substitute a program of their own.

Johnson's Program of Reconciliation

Born in 1808 in Raleigh, North Carolina, Andrew Johnson was the son of illiterate parents. Self-educated and ambitious, Johnson moved to Tennessee, where he worked as a tailor, accumulated a fortune in land, acquired five slaves, and built a career in politics championing the South's common white people and assailing its "illegitimate, swaggering, bastard, scrub aristocracy." The only senator from a Confederate state to remain loyal to the Union, Johnson held the planter class responsible for secession. Less than two weeks before he became president, he announced what he would do to planters if he ever had the chance: "I would arrest them—I would try them—I would convict them and I would hang them."

A Democrat all his life, Johnson occupied the White House only because the Republican Party in 1864 had needed a vice presidential candidate who would appeal to loyal, Union-supporting Democrats. Johnson vigorously defended states' rights (but not secession) and opposed Republican efforts to expand the power of the federal government. A steadfast supporter of slavery, Johnson had owned slaves until 1862, when Tennessee rebels, angry at his Unionism, confiscated them. When he grudgingly accepted emancipation, it was more because he hated planters than sympathized with slaves. "Damn the negroes," he said. "I am fighting those traitorous aristocrats, their masters." The new president harbored unshakable racist convictions. Africans, Johnson said, were "inferior to the white man in

point of intellect—better calculated in physical structure to undergo drudgery and hardship."

Like Lincoln, Johnson stressed the rapid restoration of civil government in the South. Like Lincoln, he promised to pardon most, but not all, ex-rebels. Johnson recognized the state governments created by Lincoln but set out his own requirements for restoring the other rebel states to the Union. All that the citizens of a state had to do was to renounce the right of secession, deny that the debts of the Confederacy were legal and binding, and ratify the Thirteenth Amendment abolishing slavery, which became part of the Constitution in December 1865.

Johnson also returned all confiscated and abandoned land to pardoned ex-Confederates, even if it was in the hands of freedmen. Reformers were shocked. Instead of punishing planters as he had promised, Johnson canceled the promising beginnings made by General Sherman and the Freedmen's Bureau to settle blacks on land of their own. As one freedman observed, "Things was hurt by Mr. Lincoln getting killed."

White Southern Resistance and Black Codes

In the summer of 1865, delegates across the South gathered to draw up the new state constitutions required by Johnson's plan of reconstruction. They refused to accept even the president's mild requirements. Refusing to renounce secession, the South Carolina and Georgia conventions merely "repudiated" their secession ordinances, preserving in principle their right to secede. South Carolina and Mississippi refused to disown their Confederate war debts. Mississippi rejected the Thirteenth Amendment, and Alabama rejected it in part. Despite this defiance, Johnson did nothing. White Southerners began to think that by standing up for themselves they could shape the terms of reconstruction.

New state governments across the South adopted a series of laws known as **black codes**, which made a travesty of black freedom. The codes sought to keep ex-slaves subordinate to whites by subjecting them to every sort of discrimination. Several states made it illegal for blacks to own a gun. Mississippi made insulting gestures and language by blacks a criminal offense. The codes barred blacks from jury duty. Not a single southern state granted any black the right to vote.

At the core of the black codes, however, lay the matter of labor. Legislators sought to hustle

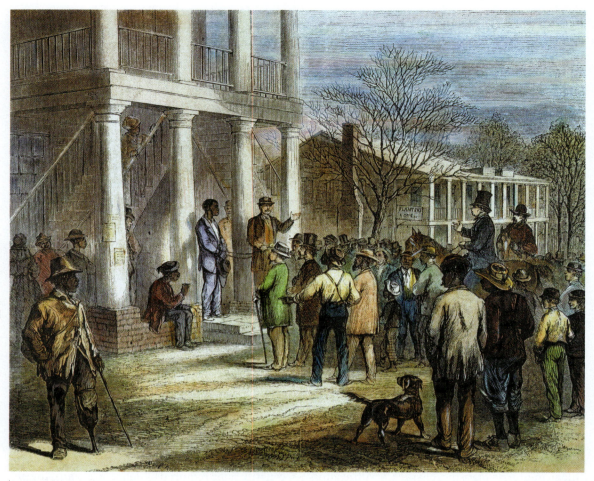

The Black Codes
Titled *Selling a Freeman to Pay His Fine at Monticello, Florida*, this 1867 drawing from a northern magazine equates black codes with the reinstitution of slavery. The laws stopped short of reenslavement but sharply restricted blacks' freedom. In southern states, certain acts, such as breaking a labor contract, were made criminal offenses, the penalty for which could be involuntary plantation labor for a year. The Granger Collection, New York

freedmen back to the plantations. Whites were almost universally opposed to black landowner-ship. Whitelaw Reid, a northern visitor to the South, found that the "man who should sell small tracts to them would be in actual personal danger." South Carolina attempted to limit blacks to either farmwork or domestic service by requiring them to pay annual taxes of $10 to $100 to work in any other occupation. Missis-sippi declared that blacks who did not possess written evidence of employment could be declared vagrants and be subject to involuntary planta-tion labor. Under so-called apprenticeship laws, courts bound thousands of black children—orphans and others whose parents they deemed

unable to support them—to work for planter "guardians."

Johnson refused to intervene. A staunch defender of states' rights, he believed that citizens of every state should be free to write their own constitutions and laws. Moreover, Johnson was as eager as other white Southern-ers to restore white supremacy. "White men alone must manage the South," he declared.

Johnson also recognized that his do-nothing response offered him political advantage. A conservative Tennessee Democrat at the head of a northern Republican Party, he had begun to look southward for political allies. Despite tough talk about punishing traitors, he personally pardoned fourteen thousand wealthy or high-ranking ex-Confederates. By pardoning powerful whites, by accepting governments even when they failed to satisfy his minimal demands, and by acquiescing in the black codes, he won useful southern friends.

In the fall elections of 1865, white Southerners dramatically expressed their mood. To represent them in Congress, they chose former Confederates. Of the eighty senators and representatives they sent to Washington, fifteen had served in the Confederate army, ten of them as generals. Another sixteen had served in civil and judicial posts in the Confederacy. Nine others had served in the Confederate Congress. One—Alexander Stephens—had been vice president of the Confederacy. As one Georgian remarked, "It looked as though Richmond had moved to Washington."

Expansion of Federal Authority and Black Rights

Southerners had blundered monumentally. They had assumed that what Andrew Johnson was willing to accept, Republicans would accept as well. But southern intransigence compelled even moderates to conclude that ex-rebels were a "generation of vipers," still untrustworthy and dangerous. The black codes became a symbol of southern intentions to "restore all of slavery but its name." "We tell the white men of Mississippi,"

the *Chicago Tribune* roared, "that the men of the North will convert the State of Mississippi into a frog pond before they will allow such laws to disgrace one foot of the soil in which the bones of our soldiers sleep and over which the flag of freedom waves."

The moderate majority of the Republican Party wanted only assurance that slavery and treason were dead. They did not champion black equality, the confiscation of plantations, or black voting, as did the radical minority within the party. But southern obstinacy had succeeded in forging unity (at least temporarily) among Republican factions. In December 1865, Republicans refused to seat the southern representatives elected in the fall elections. Rather than accept Johnson's claim that the "work of restoration" was done, Congress challenged his executive power.

Republican senator Lyman Trumbull declared that the president's policy meant that an ex-slave would "be tyrannized over, abused, and virtually reenslaved without some legislation by the nation for his protection." Early in 1866, the moderates produced two bills that strengthened the federal shield. The first, the Freedmen's Bureau bill, prolonged the life of the agency established by the previous Congress. Arguing that the Constitution never contemplated a "system for the support of indigent persons," President Andrew Johnson vetoed the bill. Congress failed by a narrow margin to override the president's veto.

The moderates designed their second measure, what would become the **Civil Rights Act of 1866**, to nullify the black codes by affirming African Americans' rights to "full and equal benefit of all laws and proceedings for the security of person and property as is enjoyed by white citizens." The act boldly required the end of racial discrimination in state laws and represented an extraordinary expansion of black rights and federal authority. The president argued that the civil rights bill amounted to "unconstitutional invasion of states' rights" and vetoed it. In essence, he denied that the federal government possessed the authority to protect the civil rights of African Americans.

In April 1866, an incensed Republican Party again pushed the civil rights bill through Congress and overrode the presidential veto. In July, it passed another Freedmen's Bureau bill and overrode Johnson's veto. For the first time in American history, Congress had overridden presidential vetoes of major legislation. As a worried South Carolinian observed, Johnson had succeeded in uniting the Republicans and probably touched off "a fight this fall such as has never been seen."

REVIEW When the southern states passed the black codes, how did the U.S. Congress respond?

Elizabeth Cady Stanton and Susan B. Anthony, 1870
Outspoken suffragists Elizabeth Cady Stanton (left) and Susan B. Anthony (right) were veteran reformers who advocated, among other things, better working conditions for labor, married women's property rights, liberalization of divorce laws, and women's admission into colleges and trade schools. Their passion for other causes led some conservatives to oppose women's political rights because they equated the suffragist cause with radicalism in general. ©Bettmann/Corbis.

▶ Congressional Reconstruction

By the summer of 1866, President Andrew Johnson and Congress had dropped their gloves and stood toe-to-toe in a bare-knuckle contest unprecedented in American history. Johnson made it clear that he would not budge on either constitutional issues or policy. Moderate Republicans responded by amending the Constitution. But the obstinacy of Johnson and white Southerners pushed Republican moderates ever closer to the radicals and to acceptance of additional federal intervention in the South. To end presidential interference, Congress voted to impeach the president for the first time since the nation was formed. Soon after, Congress also debated whether to make voting rights color-blind, while women sought to make voting sex-blind as well.

The Fourteenth Amendment and Escalating Violence

In June 1866, Congress passed the **Fourteenth Amendment** to the Constitution, and two years later the states ratified it. The most important provisions of this complex amendment made all native-born or naturalized persons American citizens and prohibited states from abridging the "privileges and immunities" of citizens, depriving them of "life, liberty, or property without due process of law," and denying them "equal protection of the laws." By making blacks national citizens, the amendment provided a national guarantee of equality before the law. In essence, it protected blacks against violation by southern state governments.

The Fourteenth Amendment also dealt with voting rights. It gave Congress the right to reduce the congressional representation of states that withheld suffrage from some of its adult male population. In other words, white Southerners could either allow black men to vote or see their representation in Washington slashed. Whatever happened, Republicans stood to benefit from the Fourteenth Amendment. If southern whites granted voting rights to freedmen, Republicans would gain valuable black votes. If whites refused, the representatives of southern Democrats would plunge.

The Fourteenth Amendment's suffrage provisions ignored the small band of women who had emerged from the war demanding "the ballot for the two disenfranchised classes, negroes and women." Founding the American Equal Rights Association in 1866, Susan B. Anthony and Elizabeth Cady Stanton lobbied for "a government by the people, and the whole people; for the people and the whole people." They felt betrayed when their old antislavery allies refused to work for their goals. "It was the Negro's hour," Frederick Douglass explained. Senator Charles Sumner suggested that woman suffrage could be "the great question of the future."

The Fourteenth Amendment provided for punishment of any state that excluded voters on the basis of race but not on the basis of sex. The amendment also introduced the word *male* into the Constitution when it referred to a citizen's right to vote. Stanton predicted that "if that word 'male' be inserted, it will take us a century at least to get it out."

Tennessee approved the Fourteenth Amendment in July, and Congress promptly welcomed the state's representatives and senators back. Had President Johnson counseled other southern states to ratify this relatively mild amendment, they might have listened. Instead, Johnson advised Southerners to reject the Fourteenth Amendment and to rely on him to trounce the Republicans in the fall congressional elections.

Johnson had decided to make the Fourteenth Amendment the overriding issue of the 1866 elections and to gather its white opponents into a new conservative party, the National Union Party. The president's strategy suffered a setback when whites in several southern cities went on rampages against blacks. Mobs killed thirty-four blacks in New Orleans and forty-six blacks in Memphis. The slaughter shocked Northerners and renewed skepticism about Johnson's claim that southern whites could be trusted. "Who doubts that the Freedmen's Bureau ought to be abolished forthwith," a New Yorker observed sarcastically, "and the

Memphis Riots, May 1866

South Memphis, pictured in this lithograph from *Harper's Weekly*, was a shantytown where the families of black soldiers stationed at nearby Fort Pickering lived. The army commander refused to send troops to protect soldiers' families and property in early May 1866 when white mobs ran wild. The Granger Collection, New York City.

blacks remitted to the paternal care of their old masters, who 'understand the nigger, you know, a great deal better than the Yankees can.'"

The 1866 elections resulted in an overwhelming Republican victory. Johnson had bet that Northerners would not support federal protection of black rights and that a racist backlash would blast the Republican Party. But the war was still fresh in northern minds, and as one Republican explained, southern whites "with all their intelligence were traitors, the blacks with all their ignorance were loyal."

Reconstruction Military Districts

Radical Reconstruction and Military Rule

When Johnson continued to urge Southerners to reject the Fourteenth Amendment, every southern state except Tennessee voted it down. "The last one of the sinful ten," thundered Representative James A. Garfield of Ohio, "has flung back into our teeth the magnanimous offer of a generous nation." After the South rejected the moderates' program, the radicals seized the initiative.

Each act of defiance by southern whites had boosted the standing of the radicals within the Republican Party. Except for freedmen themselves, no one did more to make freedom the "mighty moral question of the age." Radicals such as Massachusetts senator Charles Sumner and Pennsylvania representative Thaddeus Stevens united in demanding civil and political equality. Southern states were "like clay in the hands of the potter," Stevens declared in January 1867, and he called on Congress to begin reconstruction all over again.

In March 1867, Congress overturned the Johnson state governments and initiated military rule of the South. The **Military Reconstruction Act** (and three subsequent acts) divided the ten unreconstructed Confederate states into five military districts. Congress placed a Union general in charge of each district and instructed him to "suppress insurrection, disorder, and violence" and to begin political reform. After the military had completed voter registration, which would include black men, voters in each state would elect delegates to conventions that would draw up new state constitutions. Each constitution would guarantee black suffrage.

When the voters of each state had approved the constitution and the state legislature had ratified the Fourteenth Amendment, the state could submit its work to Congress. If Congress approved, the state's senators and representatives could be seated, and political reunification would be accomplished.

Radicals proclaimed the provision for black suffrage "a prodigious triumph," for it extended far beyond the limited suffrage provisions of the Fourteenth Amendment. When combined with the disfranchisement of thousands of ex-rebels, it promised to cripple any neo-Confederate resurgence and guarantee Republican state governments in the South.

Despite its bold suffrage provision, the Military Reconstruction Act of 1867 disappointed those who also advocated the confiscation of southern plantations and their redistribution to ex-slaves. Thaddeus Stevens agreed with the freedman who said, "Give us our own land and we take care of ourselves, but without land, the old masters can hire us or starve us, as they please." But most Republicans believed they had provided blacks with what they needed: equal legal rights and the ballot. Besides, confiscation was too radical, even for some Radicals. Confiscating private property, declared the *New York Times*, "strikes at the root of all property rights in both sections. It concerns Massachusetts quite as much as Mississippi." If blacks were to get land, they would have to gain it themselves.

Declaring that he would rather sever his right arm than sign such a formula for "anarchy and chaos," Andrew Johnson vetoed the Military Reconstruction Act, but Congress overrode his veto. With the passage of the Reconstruction Acts of 1867, congressional reconstruction was virtually completed. Congress left whites owning most of the South's land but, in a departure that justified the term "radical reconstruction," had given black men the ballot.

Impeaching a President

Despite his defeats, Andrew Johnson had no intention of yielding control of reconstruction. In a dozen ways, he sabotaged Congress's will and encouraged southern whites to resist. He issued a flood of pardons, waged war against the Freedmen's Bureau, and replaced Union generals eager to enforce Congress's Reconstruction Acts with conservative officers eager to defeat them. Johnson claimed that he was merely defending the "violated Constitution." At bottom, however, the president subverted congressional reconstruction to protect southern whites from what he considered the horrors of "Negro domination."

Radicals argued that Johnson's abuse of constitutional powers and his failure to fulfill constitutional obligations to enforce the law were impeachable offenses. According to the Constitution, the House of Representatives can impeach and the Senate can try any federal official for "treason, bribery, or other high crimes and misdemeanors." But moderates interpreted the Constitution to mean violation of criminal statutes. As long as Johnson refrained from breaking the law, impeachment (the process of formal charges of wrongdoing against the president or other federal official) remained stalled.

Then in August 1867, Johnson suspended Secretary of War Edwin M. Stanton from office. As required by the Tenure of Office Act, which demanded the approval of the Senate for the removal of any government official who had been appointed with Senate approval, the president requested the Senate to consent to Stanton's dismissal. When the Senate balked, Johnson removed Stanton anyway. "Is the President crazy, or only drunk?" asked a dumbfounded Republican moderate. "I'm afraid his doings will make us all favor impeachment."

News of Johnson's open defiance of the law convinced every Republican in the House to vote for a resolution impeaching the president. Supreme Court chief justice Salmon Chase presided over the Senate trial, which lasted from March until May 1868. When the vote came, thirty-five senators voted guilty and nineteen not guilty. The impeachment forces fell one vote short of the two-thirds needed to convict.

After his trial, Johnson called a truce, and for the remaining ten months of his term, congressional reconstruction proceeded unhindered by presidential interference. Without interference from Johnson, Congress revisited the suffrage issue.

The Fifteenth Amendment and Women's Demands

In February 1869, Republicans passed the **Fifteenth Amendment** to the Constitution, which prohibited states from depriving any citizen of the right to vote because of "race, color, or previous condition of servitude." The Reconstruction Acts of 1867 already required black suffrage in the South; the Fifteenth Amendment extended black voting nationwide.

Some Republicans, however, found the final wording of the Fifteenth Amendment "lame and halting." Rather than absolutely guaranteeing the right to vote, the amendment merely prohibited exclusion on grounds of race. The distinction would prove to be significant. In time, white Southerners would devise tests of literacy and property and other apparently nonracial measures that would effectively disfranchise blacks yet not violate the Fifteenth Amendment. But an amendment that fully guaranteed the right to vote courted defeat outside the South. Rising antiforeign sentiment—against the Chinese in California and European immigrants in the Northeast—caused states to resist giving up total control of suffrage requirements. In March 1870, after three-fourths of the states had ratified it, the Fifteenth Amendment became part of the Constitution.

Woman suffrage advocates, however, were sorely disappointed with the Fifteenth Amendment's failure to extend voting rights to women. Elizabeth Cady Stanton and Susan B. Anthony condemned the Republicans' "negro first" strategy and pointed out that women remained "the only class of citizens wholly unrepresented in the government." Increasingly, activist women concluded that woman "must not put her trust in man." The Fifteenth Amendment severed the early feminist movement from its abolitionist roots. Over the next several decades, feminists established an independent suffrage crusade that drew millions of women into political life.

Republicans took enough satisfaction in the Fifteenth Amendment to conclude that black suffrage was the "last great point that remained to be settled of the issues of the war" and promptly scratched the "Negro question" from the agenda of national politics. Even that steadfast crusader for equality Wendell Phillips concluded that the black man now held "sufficient shield in his own hands. . . . Whatever he suffers will be largely now, and in future, his own fault." Northerners had no idea of the violent struggles that lay ahead.

REVIEW Why did Congress impeach President Andrew Johnson?

▶ The Struggle in the South

Northerners believed they had discharged their responsibilities with the Reconstruction Acts and the amendments to the Constitution, but Southerners knew that the battle had just begun. Black suffrage had destroyed traditional southern politics and established the foundation for the rise of the Republican Party. Gathering outsiders and outcasts, southern Republicans won elections, wrote new state constitutions, and formed new state governments.

Challenging the established class for political control was dangerous business. Equally dangerous were the confrontations that took place on southern farms and plantations, where blacks sought to give fuller meaning to their newly won legal and political equality. Ex-masters had their own ideas about the labor system that should replace slavery, and freedom remained contested territory. Southerners fought pitched battles with one another to determine the contours of their new world.

Freedmen, Yankees, and Yeomen

African Americans made up the majority of southern Republicans. After gaining voting rights in 1867, nearly all eligible black men registered to vote as Republicans, grateful to the party that had freed them and granted them the franchise. "It is the hardest thing in the world to keep a negro away from the polls," observed an Alabama white man. Southern blacks did not all have identical political priorities, but they united in their desire for education and equal treatment before the law.

Northern whites who made the South their home after the war were a second element of the South's Republican Party. Conservative white Southerners called them **carpetbaggers**, opportunists who stuffed all their belongings in a single carpet-sided suitcase and headed south to "fatten on our misfortunes." But most Northerners who moved south were young men who looked upon the South as they did the West—as a promising place to make a living. Northerners in the southern Republican Party supported programs that encouraged vigorous economic development along the lines of the northern free-labor model.

Southern whites made up the third element of the South's Republican Party. Approximately one out of four white Southerners voted Republican. The other three condemned the one who did as a traitor to his region and his race and called him a **scalawag**, a term for runty horses and low-down, good-for-nothing rascals. Yeoman farmers accounted for the majority of southern white Republicans. Some were Unionists who emerged from the war with bitter memories of Confederate persecution. Others were small farmers who wanted to end state governments' favoritism toward plantation owners. Yeomen supported initiatives for public schools and for expanding economic opportunity in the South.

The South's Republican Party, then, was made up of freedmen, Yankees, and yeomen—an improbable coalition. The mix of races, regions, and classes inevitably meant friction as each group maneuvered to define the party. But Reconstruction represented an extraordinary moment in American politics: Blacks and whites joined together in the Republican Party to pursue political change. Formally, of course, only men participated in politics—casting ballots and holding offices—but white and black women also played a part in the political struggle by joining in parades and rallies, attending stump speeches, and even campaigning.

Most whites in the South condemned southern Republicans as illegitimate and felt justified in doing whatever they could to stamp them out. Violence against blacks—the "white terror"—took brutal institutional form in 1866 with the formation in Tennessee of the **Ku Klux Klan**, a social club of Confederate veterans that quickly developed into a paramilitary organization supporting Democrats. The Klan went on a rampage of whipping, hanging, shooting, burning, and throat-cutting to defeat Republicans and restore white supremacy. (See "Historical Question," page 450.) Rapid demobilization of the Union army after the war left only twenty thousand troops to patrol the entire South. Without effective military protection, southern Republicans had to take care of themselves.

Republican Rule

In the fall of 1867, southern states held elections for delegates to state constitutional conventions, as required by the Reconstruction Acts. About 40 percent of the white electorate stayed home because they had been disfranchised or because they had decided to boycott politics. Republicans won three-fourths of the seats. About 15 percent of the Republican delegates to the conventions were Northerners who had moved south, 25 percent were African Americans, and 60 percent were white Southerners. As a British visitor observed, the delegate elections reflected "the mighty revolution that had taken place in America."

The reconstruction constitutions introduced two broad categories of changes in the South: those that reduced aristocratic privilege and increased democratic equality and those that expanded the state's responsibility for the general welfare. In the first category, the constitutions adopted universal male suffrage, abolished property qualifications for holding office, and made more offices elective and fewer appointed. In the second category, they enacted prison reform; made the state responsible for caring for orphans, the insane, and the deaf and mute; and exempted debtors' homes from seizure.

To Democrats, however, these progressive constitutions looked like wild revolution. Democrats were blind to the fact that no constitution confiscated and redistributed land, as virtually every former slave wished, or disfranchised ex-rebels wholesale, as most southern Unionists advocated. And they were convinced that the new constitutions initiated "Negro domination." In fact, although 80 percent of Republican voters were black men, only 6 percent of Southerners in Congress during Reconstruction were black (Figure 16.1). The sixteen black men in Congress included exceptional men, such as Representative James T. Rapier of Alabama (see pages 433–34). No state legislature experienced "Negro rule," despite black majorities in the populations of some states.

Southern voters ratified the new constitutions and swept Republicans into power. When the former Confederate states ratified the Fourteenth Amendment, Congress readmitted them. Southern Republicans then turned to a staggering array of problems. Wartime destruction littered the landscape. Making matters worse, racial harassment and reactionary violence dogged Southerners who sought reform. Democrats mocked Republican officeholders as ignorant field hands who had only "agricultural degrees" and "brick yard diplomas," but Republicans began a serious effort to rebuild and reform the region.

Activity focused on three areas—education, civil rights, and economic development. Every

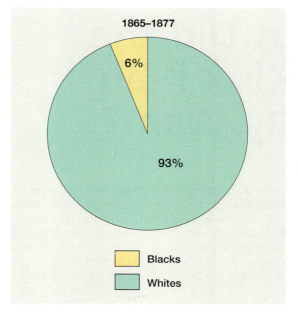

FIGURE 16.1 **Southern Congressional Delegations, 1865–1877**
The statistics contradict the myth of black domination of congressional representation during Reconstruction.

state inaugurated a system of public education. Before the Civil War, whites had deliberately kept slaves illiterate, and planter-dominated governments rarely spent tax money to educate the children of yeomen. By 1875, half of Mississippi's and South Carolina's eligible children were attending school. Although schools were underfunded, literacy rates rose sharply. Public schools were racially segregated, but education remained for many blacks a tangible, deeply satisfying benefit of freedom and Republican rule.

State legislatures also attacked racial discrimination and defended civil rights. Republicans especially resisted efforts to segregate blacks from whites in public transportation. Mississippi levied fines and jail terms for owners of railroads and steamboats that pushed blacks into "smoking cars" or to lower decks. But passing color-blind laws was one thing; enforcing them was another. A Mississippian complained: "Education amounts to nothing, good behavior counts for nothing, even money cannot buy for a colored man or woman decent treatment and the comforts that white people claim and can obtain." Despite the laws, segregation—later called Jim Crow—developed at white insistence. Determined to underscore the social inferiority

What Did the Ku Klux Klan Really Want?

In 1866, six Confederate veterans in Pulaski, Tennessee, founded the Ku Klux Klan for fun and fellowship. But by 1868, when congressional reconstruction went into effect, the Klan had spread across the South, and members had shifted to more serious matters.

According to former Confederate general and Georgia Democratic politician John B. Gordon, the Klan owed its popularity to the "instinct of self-preservation . . . the sense of insecurity and danger, particularly in those neighborhoods where the Negro population largely predominated." Everywhere whites looked, he said, they saw "great crime." Republican politicians marched ignorant freedmen to the polls, where they blighted honest government. Ex-slaves drove overseers from plantations and claimed the land for themselves. Black rapists made white women cower behind barred doors. It was necessary, Gordon declared, "in order to protect our families from outrage and preserve our own lives, to have something that we could regard as a brotherhood—a combination of the best men of the country, to act purely in self-defense."

Behind the Klan's high-minded and self-justifying rhetoric, however, lay another agenda. It was revealed in their actions, not their words.

Klansmen embarked on a campaign to reverse history. Garbed in robes and hoods, they engaged in guerrilla warfare against free labor, civil equality, and political democracy. They aimed to terrorize their enemies—ex-slaves and white Republicans—into submission. Changes in four particular areas of southern life proved flash points for Klan violence: racial etiquette, education, labor, and politics.

The Klan punished those blacks and whites who broke the Old South's racial code. The Klan considered "impudence" a punishable offense. Asked to define "impudence" before a congressional investigating committee, one white man responded: "Well, it is considered impudence for a negro not to be polite to a white man—not to pull off his hat and bow and scrape to a white man, as was done formerly." Klansmen whipped blacks for speaking disrespectfully, refusing to yield the sidewalk, and dressing well. Black women who "dress up and fix up like ladies" risked a midnight visit from the Klan. The Klan sought to restore racial subordination in every aspect of private and public life.

Klansmen also took aim at black education. White men found the sight of blacks in classrooms hard to stomach. Schools were easy targets,

and scores of them went up in flames. Teachers, male and female, were flogged, or worse. Klansmen drove northern-born teacher Alonzo B. Corliss from North Carolina for "teaching niggers and making them like white men." In Cross Plains, Alabama, the Klan hanged an Irish-born teacher along with four black men. Planters wanted ex-slaves back in the fields, not at desks. In 1869, an Alabama newspaper announced that the burning of a black school should be "a warning for them to stick here-after to 'de shovel and de hoe,' and let their dirty-backed primers go."

Planters turned to the Klan as part of their effort to preserve plantation agriculture. An Alabama white admitted that in his area the Klan was "intended principally for the negroes who failed to work." Hooded bands "punished Negroes whose landlords had complained of them." Sharecroppers who disputed their share at "settling up time" risked a visit from the night riders. It was dangerous for freedmen to consider changing employers. "If we got out looking for some other place to go," an ex-slave from Texas remembered, "them KKK they would tend to Mister negro good and plenty."

Above all, the Klan terrorized Republicans. Klansmen became the military arm of the Democratic Party. They drove blacks from the polls on election day and assaulted Republican officeholders. Klansmen gave Andrew Flowers, a black politician in Chattanooga, a brutal beating and told him that they "did not intend any nigger to hold office in the United States." Jack Dupree, president of the Republican Club in Monroe County, Mississippi, a man known to "speak

of blacks, whites saw to it that separation by race became a feature of southern life long before the end of the Reconstruction era.

Republican governments also launched ambitious programs of economic development. They envisioned a South of diversified agriculture, roaring factories, and booming towns. State legislatures chartered scores of banks and industrial companies, appropriated funds to fix ruined levees and drain swamps, and went on a railroad-building binge. These efforts fell far short of solving the South's economic troubles, however.

Klan murdered three scalawag members of the legislature and drove ten others from their homes. As one Georgia Republican commented after a Klan attack: "We don't call them [D]emocrats, we call them southern murderers."

It proved hard to arrest Klansmen and harder still to convict them. "If a white man kills a colored man in any of the counties of this State," observed a Florida sheriff, "you cannot convict him." Federal intervention—in the Ku Klux Klan Acts of 1870 and 1871—signaled an end to much of the Klan's power but not to counterrevolutionary violence in the South. Other groups continued the terror in the cause of white supremacy.

Ku Klux Klan Rider in Tennessee about 1868
During Reconstruction, Klansmen wore robes of various designs and colors. Hooded horses added another element to the Klan's terror. The Klansman holds a flag that probably contained a motto that supported white supremacy. Courtesy of the Tennessee State Museum.

Questions for Consideration

1. What changes during Reconstruction particularly provoked the Klan? Why do you think these issues were so important to Klansmen?

2. Why did Klansmen believe that their actions were justified? Why do you think they hid their identities?

3. What southern traditions did the Klan seek to perpetuate?

Connect to the Big Idea

C How did the Ku Klux Klan serve the counter-evolutionary goals of the South's Democratic Party?

his mind," had his throat cut and was disemboweled while his wife was forced to watch.

Political violence reached astounding levels. Arkansas experienced nearly three hundred political killings in the three months before the fall elections in 1868. Louisiana was even bloodier, suffering more than one thousand killings in the same year. In Georgia, the

Republican spending to stimulate economic growth also meant rising taxes and enormous debt that siphoned funds from schools and other programs.

The southern Republicans' record, then, was mixed. To their credit, the biracial party adopted an ambitious agenda to change the South. But money was scarce, the Democrats continued their harassment, and factionalism threatened the Republican Party from within. Moreover, corruption infected Republican governments. Nonetheless, the Republican Party

Students at a Freedmen's School in Virginia, ca. 1870s
"The people are hungry and thirsty after knowledge," a former slave observed immediately after the Civil War. African American leader Booker T. Washington remembered "a whole race trying to go to school." Students at this Virginia school stand in front of their log-cabin classroom reading books. For people long forbidden to learn to read and write, literacy symbolized freedom. Cook Collection, Valentine Richmond History Center, www.richmondhistorycenter.com.

made headway in its efforts to purge the South of aristocratic privilege and racist oppression. Republican governments had less success in overthrowing the long-established white oppression of black farm laborers in the rural South.

White Landlords, Black Sharecroppers

Ex-slaves who wished to escape slave labor and ex-masters who wanted to reinstitute old ways clashed repeatedly. Except for having to pay subsistence wages, planters had not been required to offer many concessions to emancipation. They continued to believe that African Americans would not work without coercion. A Tennessee man declared two years after the war ended that blacks were "a trifling set of lazy devils who will never make a living without Masters." Whites moved quickly to restore as much of slavery as they could get away with.

Ex-slaves resisted every effort to turn back the clock. They argued that if any class could be described as "lazy," it was the planters, who, as one former slave noted, "lived in idleness all their lives on stolen labor." They believed that land of their own would anchor their economic independence and end planters' interference in their personal lives. They could then, for example, make their own decisions about whether women and children would labor in the fields. Indeed, within months after the war, perhaps one-third of black women abandoned field labor to work on chores in their own cabins just as poor white women did. Black women also

Black Woman in Cotton Fields, Thomasville, Georgia
Few images of everyday black women during the Reconstruction era survive. This 1895 photograph poignantly depicts the post–Civil War labor struggle, when white landlords wanted emancipated slaves to continue working in the fields. Freedom allowed some women to escape field labor, but not this Georgian. Her headdress protected her from the fierce heat, and her bare feet reveal the hardships of her life. Courtesy, Georgia Archives, Vanishing Georgia Collection tho096.

negotiated about work ex-mistresses wanted done in the big house. (See "Visualizing History," page 454.) Hundreds of thousands of black children enrolled in school. But without their own land, ex-slaves had little choice but to work on plantations.

Although forced to return to the planters' fields, they resisted efforts to restore slavelike conditions. Instead of working for wages, a South Carolinian observed, "the negroes all seem disposed to rent land," which increased

their independence from whites. Out of this tug-of-war between white landlords and black laborers emerged a new system of southern agriculture.

Sharecropping was a compromise that offered something to both ex-masters and ex-slaves but satisfied neither. Under the new system, planters divided their cotton plantations into small farms that freedmen rented, paying with a share of each year's crop, usually half. Sharecropping gave blacks more freedom than the system of wages and labor gangs and released them from day-to-day supervision by whites. Black families abandoned the old slave quarters and built separate cabins for themselves on the patches of land they rented (Map 16.1). Still, most black families remained dependent on white landlords, who had the power to evict them at the end of each growing season. For planters, sharecropping offered a way to resume agricultural production, but it did not allow them to restore the old slave plantation.

Sharecropping introduced the country merchant into the agricultural equation. Land-lords supplied sharecroppers with land, mules, seeds, and tools, but blacks also needed credit to obtain essential food and clothing before they harvested their crops. Under an arrangement called a crop lien, a merchant would advance goods to a sharecropper in exchange for a *lien*, or legal claim, on the farmer's future crop. Some merchants charged exorbitant rates of interest, as much as 60 percent, on the goods they sold. At the end of the growing season, after the landlord had taken half of the farmer's crop for rent, the merchant took most of the rest. Sometimes, the farmer did not earn enough to repay the debt to the merchant, so he would have to borrow more from the merchant and begin the cycle again.

An experiment at first, sharecropping soon dominated the cotton South. Lien merchants forced tenants to plant cotton, which was easy to sell, instead of food crops. The result was excessive production of cotton and falling cotton prices, developments that cost thousands of small white farmers their land and pushed them into the great army of sharecroppers. The new sharecropping system of agriculture took shape just as the political power of Republicans in the South began to buckle under Democratic pressure.

REVIEW How did politics and economic concerns shape reconstruction in the South?

A Post-slavery Encounter

A Visit from the Old Mistress, 1876

Winslow Homer (1836–1910) is regarded by many as the nation's greatest nineteenth-century painter. He typically sketched and painted ordinary people in their everyday lives, and he was admired for his ability to convey drama and emotion on canvas. During the Civil War, Homer worked as an illustrator for *Harper's Weekly*, depicting scenes of the war for curious Northerners. In 1875, he traveled from his home in New York City to Virginia, where he observed firsthand the transformation of relationships between former slaves and their former owners. He composed *A Visit from the Old Mistress* from sketches he had made while traveling through Virginia.

In this painting, Homer captures the moment when a white woman arrives in the humble cabin of former slaves and encounters three black women, one of whom holds a toddler. Homer typically said little about his paintings, and there is much we don't know about the story being told in this work. Why has the old

mistress come? We can imagine that she has come to talk about work she wants done in the big house. If so, she would have come asking, not commanding, for the end of slavery meant that ex-slaves had control over their own labor and negotiated what they would be paid and the conditions under which they would work.

Notice the way Homer has arranged the subjects of his painting, with the former slaves on one side of the room and the former mistress on the other. What does the generous space between them suggest? How do the two sides compare? Look particularly at the women's clothing and their stance. What does the white woman's posture suggest? How are the three black women positioned, and what does this say about their attitude toward the old mistress? What do you detect in the facial expressions of the people in this image?

The end of slavery required wrenching readjustments in the lives of Southerners, black and white. Homer has captured a tense moment in that transition.

SOURCE: Smithsonian American Art Museum, Washington, DC/Art Resource, NY.

Questions for Analysis

1. How would you describe the conditions of these former slaves? Have they improved since emancipation?

2. White southerners often claimed that their slaves loved them. Do you see any signs of affection or loyalty in these black women for their former owner?

3. Do you think that this domestic scene reveals the artist's opinion about what he witnessed, or does *A Visit from the Old Mistress* try merely to capture truthfully a complex scene?

Connect to the Big Idea

C How might this painting have looked differently if it had been created before emancipation? (See chapters 13 and 15.)

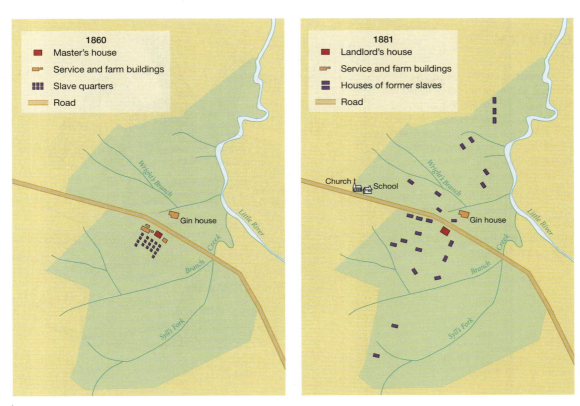

MAP ACTIVITY

Map 16.1 A Southern Plantation in 1860 and 1881
These maps of the Barrow plantation in Georgia illustrate some of the ways in which ex-slaves expressed their freedom. Freedmen and freedwomen deserted the clustered living quarters behind the master's house, scattered over the plantation, built family cabins, and farmed rented land. The former Barrow slaves also worked together to build a school and a church.

READING THE MAP: Compare the number and size of the slave quarters in 1860 with the homes of the former slaves in 1881. How do they differ? Which buildings were prominently located along the road in 1860, and which could be found along the road in 1881?

CONNECTIONS: How might the former master feel about the new configuration of buildings on the plantation in 1881? In what ways did the new system of sharecropping replicate the old system of plantation agriculture? In what ways was it different?

▶ Reconstruction Collapses

By 1870, after a decade of war and reconstruction, Northerners wanted to put "the southern problem" behind them. Practical business-minded men came to dominate the Republican Party, replacing the band of reformers and idealists who had been prominent in the 1860s. Civil war hero Ulysses S. Grant succeeded Andrew Johnson as president in 1869 and quickly be-came an issue himself, proving that brilliance on the battlefield does not necessarily translate into competence in the White House. As northern commitment to defend black freedom eroded, southern commitment to white supremacy intensified. Without northern protection, southern Republicans were no match for the Democrats' economic coercion, political fraud, and bloody violence. One by one, Republican state governments fell in the South. The election of 1876 both confirmed and completed the collapse of reconstruction.

Grant's Troubled Presidency

In 1868, the Republican Party's presidential nomination went to Ulysses S. Grant, the North's favorite general. His Democratic opponent, Horatio Seymour of New York, ran on a platform

VISUAL ACTIVITY

Grant and Scandal

This anti-Grant cartoon by Thomas Nast, the nation's most celebrated political cartoonist, shows the president falling headfirst into the barrel of fraud and corruption that tainted his administration. During Grant's eight years in the White House, many members of his administration failed him. Sometimes duped, sometimes merely loyal, Grant stubbornly defended wrongdoers, even to the point of perjuring himself to keep an aide out of jail. Picture Research Consultants & Archives.

READING THE IMAGE: How does Thomas Nast portray President Grant's role in corruption? According to this cartoon, what caused the problems?

CONNECTIONS: How responsible was President Grant for the corruption that plagued his administration?

that blasted reconstruction as "a flagrant usurpation of power . . . unconstitutional, revolutionary, and void." The Republicans answered by "waving the bloody shirt"—that is, they reminded voters that the Democrats were "the party of rebellion." Despite a reign of terror in the South, costing hundreds of Republicans their lives, Grant gained a narrow 309,000-vote margin in the popular vote and a substantial victory (214 votes to 80) in the electoral college (Map 16.2).

Grant was not as good a president as he was a general. The talents he had demonstrated on the battlefield—decisiveness, clarity, and resolution—were less obvious in the White House. Grant sought both justice for blacks and sectional reconciliation. But he surrounded himself with fumbling kinfolk and old friends from his army days and made a string of dubious appointments that led to a series of damaging scandals. Charges of corruption tainted his vice president, Schuyler Colfax, and brought down two of his cabinet officers. Though never personally implicated in any scandal, Grant was aggravatingly naive and blind to the rot that filled his administration. Republican congressman James A. Garfield declared: "His imperturbability is amazing. I am in doubt whether to call it greatness or stupidity."

In 1872, anti-Grant Republicans bolted and launched the Liberal Party. To clean up the graft and corruption, Liberals proposed ending the spoils system, by which victorious parties rewarded loyal workers with public office, and replacing it with a nonpartisan civil service commission that would oversee competitive examinations for appointment to office (as discussed in chapter 18). Liberals also demanded that the federal government remove its troops from the South and restore "home rule" (southern white control). Democrats liked the Liberals' southern policy and endorsed the Liberal presidential candidate, Horace Greeley,

MAP 16.2
The Election of 1868

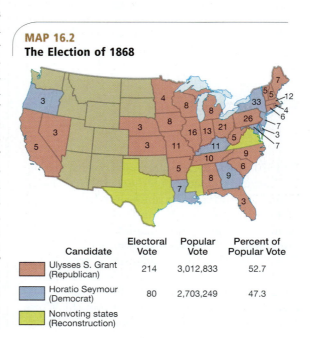

Candidate	Electoral Vote	Popular Vote	Percent of Popular Vote
Ulysses S. Grant (Republican)	214	3,012,833	52.7
Horatio Seymour (Democrat)	80	2,703,249	47.3
Nonvoting states (Reconstruction)			

the longtime editor of the *New York Tribune*. The nation, however, still felt enormous affection for the man who had saved the Union and reelected Grant with 56 percent of the popular vote.

Northern Resolve Withers

Although Grant genuinely wanted to see blacks' civil and political rights protected, he understood that most Northerners had grown weary of reconstruction and were increasingly willing to let southern whites manage their own affairs. Citizens wanted to shift their attention to other issues, especially after the nation slipped into a devastating economic depression in 1873. More than eighteen thousand businesses collapsed, leaving more than a million workers on the streets. Northern businessmen wanted to invest in the South but believed that recurrent federal intrusion was itself a major cause of instability in the region. Republican leaders began to question the wisdom of their party's alliance with the South's lower classes—its small farmers and sharecroppers. One member of Grant's administration proposed allying with the "thinking and influential native southerners ... the intelligent, well-to-do, and controlling class."

Congress, too, wanted to leave reconstruction behind, but southern Republicans made that difficult. When the South's Republicans begged for federal protection from increasing Klan violence, Congress enacted three laws in 1870 and 1871 that were intended to break the back of white terrorism. The severest of the three, the Ku Klux Klan Act (1871), made interference with voting rights a felony. Federal marshals arrested thousands of Klansmen and came close to destroying the Klan, but they did not end all terrorism against blacks. Congress also passed the Civil Rights Act of 1875, which boldly outlawed racial discrimination in transportation, public accommodations, and juries. But federal authorities never enforced the law aggressively, and segregation remained the rule throughout the South.

By the early 1870s, the Republican Party had lost its leading champions of African American rights to death or defeat at the polls. Other Republicans concluded that the quest for black equality was mistaken or hopelessly naive. In May 1872, Congress restored the right of office holding to all but three hundred ex-rebels. Many Republicans had come to believe that traditional white leaders offered the best hope for honesty, order, and prosperity in the South.

Underlying the North's abandonment of reconstruction was unyielding racial prejudice.

Northerners had learned to accept black freedom during the war, but deep-seated prejudice prevented many from accepting black equality. Even the actions they took on behalf of blacks often served partisan political advantage. Northerners generally supported Indiana senator Thomas A. Hendricks's harsh declaration that "this is a white man's Government, made by the white man for the white man."

The U.S. Supreme Court also did its part to undermine reconstruction. The Court issued a series of decisions that significantly weakened the federal government's ability to protect black Southerners. In the *Slaughterhouse* cases (1873), the Court distinguished between national and state citizenship and ruled that the Fourteenth Amendment protected only those rights that stemmed from the federal government, such as voting in federal elections and interstate travel. Since the Court decided that most rights derived from the states, it sharply curtailed the federal government's authority to defend black citizens. Even more devastating, the *United States v. Cruikshank* ruling (1876) said that the reconstruction amendments gave Congress the power to legislate against discrimination only by states, not by individuals. The "suppression of ordinary crime," such as assault, remained a state responsibility. The Supreme Court did not declare reconstruction unconstitutional but eroded its legal foundation.

The mood of the North found political expression in the election of 1874, when for the first time in eighteen years the Democrats gained control of the House of Representatives. As one Republican observed, the people had grown tired of the "negro question, with all its complications, and the reconstruction of Southern States, with all its interminable embroilments." Reconstruction had come apart. Rather than defend reconstruction from its southern enemies, Northerners steadily backed away from the challenge. By the early 1870s, southern Republicans faced the forces of reaction largely on their own.

White Supremacy Triumphs

Reconstruction was a massive humiliation to most white Southerners. Republican rule meant intolerable insults: Black militiamen patrolled town streets, black laborers negotiated contracts with former masters, black maids stood up to former mistresses, black voters cast ballots, and black legislators such as James T. Rapier enacted laws. Whites fought back by extolling the "great Confederate cause," or Lost Cause. They celebrated their soldiers, "the noblest band of men who ever

"White Man's Country"
This silk ribbon from the 1868 presidential campaign between Republican Ulysses S. Grant and his Democratic opponent, New York governor Horatio Seymour, openly declares the Democrats' goal of white supremacy. During the campaign, Democratic vice presidential nominee Francis P. Blair Jr. promised that a Seymour victory would restore "white people" to power by declaring the reconstruction governments in the South "null and void." © David J. & Janice L. Frent Collection/CORBIS.

Caucasian race, whose sovereignty on earth God has proclaimed." Local newspapers published the names of whites who kept company with blacks, and neighbors ostracized offenders.

Democrats also exploited the severe economic plight of small white farmers by blaming it on Republican financial policy. Government spending soared during reconstruction, and small farmers saw their tax burden skyrocket. "This is tax time," a South Carolinian reported. "We are nearly all on our head about them. They are so high & so little money to pay with" that farmers were "selling every egg and chicken they can get." In 1871, Mississippi reported that one-seventh of the state's land—3.3 million acres—had been forfeited for nonpayment of taxes. The small farmers' economic distress had a racial dimension. Because few freedmen succeeded in acquiring land, they rarely paid taxes. In Georgia in 1874, blacks made up 45 percent of the population but paid only 2 percent of the taxes. From the perspective of a small white farmer, Republican rule meant that he was paying more taxes and paying them to aid blacks.

If racial pride, social isolation, and financial hardship proved insufficient to drive yeomen from the Republican Party, Democrats turned to terrorism. "Night riders" targeted white Republicans as well as blacks for murder and assassination. Whether white or black, a "dead Radical is very harmless," South Carolina Democratic leader Martin Gary told his followers.

But the primary victims of white violence were black Republicans. Violence escalated to an unprecedented ferocity on Easter Sunday in 1873 in tiny Colfax, Louisiana. The black majority in the area had made Colfax a Republican stronghold until 1872, when Democrats turned to intimidation and fraud to win the local election. Republicans refused to accept the result and occupied the courthouse in the middle of the town. After three weeks, 165 white men attacked. They overran the Republicans' defenses and set the courthouse on fire. When the blacks tried to surrender, the whites murdered them. At least 81 black men were slaughtered that day. Although the federal government indicted the attackers, the Supreme Court ruled that it did not have the right to prosecute. And since local whites would not prosecute neighbors who killed blacks, the defendants in the Colfax massacre went free.

fought" and by making an idol of Robert E. Lee, the embodiment of the southern gentleman.

But the most important way white Southerners responded to reconstruction was their assault on Republican governments in the South. These Republican governments attracted more hatred than did any other political regimes in American history. The northern retreat from reconstruction permitted southern Democrats to set things right. Taking the name **Redeemers**, Democrats in the South promised to replace "bayonet rule" (a few federal troops continued to be stationed in the South) with "home rule." They promised that honest, thrifty Democrats would supplant corrupt tax-and-spend Republicans. Above all, Redeemers swore to save southern civilization from a descent into "African barbarism." As one man put it, "We must render this either a white man's government, or convert the land into a Negro man's cemetery."

Southern Democrats adopted a multipronged strategy to overthrow Republican governments. First, they sought to polarize the parties around race. They went about gathering all the South's white voters into the Democratic Party, leaving the Republicans to depend on blacks, who made up a minority of the population in almost every southern state. To dislodge whites from the Republican Party, Democrats fanned the flames of racism. A South Carolina Democrat crowed that his party appealed to the "proud

Even before adopting the all-out white supremacist tactics of the 1870s, Democrats had taken control of the governments of Virginia, Tennessee, and North Carolina. The new campaign brought fresh gains. The Redeemers

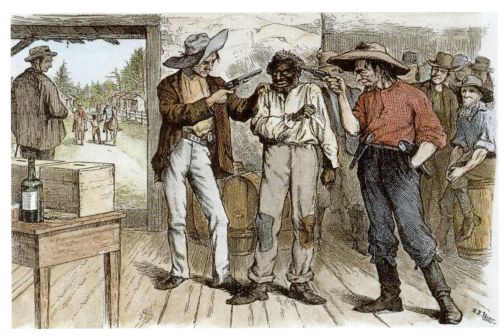

"Of Course He Wants to Vote the Democratic Ticket"
This Republican cartoon from the October 21, 1876, issue of *Harper's Weekly* comments sarcastically on the possibility of honest elections in the South. The caption reads: "You're free as air, ain't you? Say you are or I'll blow yer black head off." The cartoon demonstrates not only some Northerners' concern that violence would deliver the election to the Democrats but also the perception that white Southerners were crude, drunken, ignorant brutes. The Granger Collection, New York.

retook Georgia in 1871, Texas in 1873, and Arkansas and Alabama in 1874. As the state election approached in 1876, Governor Adelbert Ames appealed to Washington for federal troops to control the violence, only to hear from the attorney general that the "whole public are tired of these annual autumnal outbreaks in the South." Abandoned, Mississippi Republicans succumbed to the Democratic onslaught in the fall elections. By 1876, only three Republican state governments survived in the South (Map 16.3).

An Election and a Compromise

The year 1876 witnessed one of the most tumultuous elections in American history. The election took place in November, but not until March 2 of the following year did the nation know who would be inaugurated president on March 4. Sixteen years after Lincoln's election, Americans feared that a presidential election would again precipitate civil war.

The Democrats nominated New York's governor, Samuel J. Tilden, who immediately targeted the corruption of the Grant administration

and the "despotism" of Republican reconstruction. The Republicans put forward Rutherford B. Hayes, governor of Ohio. Privately, Hayes considered "bayonet rule" a mistake but concluded

MAP ACTIVITY

Map 16.3 The Reconstruction of the South

Myth has it that Republican rule of the former Confederacy was not only harsh but long. In most states, however, conservative southern whites stormed back into power in months or just a few years. By the election of 1876, Republican governments could be found in only three states, and they soon fell.

READING THE MAP: List in chronological order the readmission of the former Confederate states to the Union. Which states reestablished conservative governments most quickly?

CONNECTIONS: What did the former Confederate states need to do to be readmitted to the Union? How did reestablished conservative governments react to reconstruction?

Former Confederate states

1869 Date of readmission to the Union

1873 Date of reestablishment of conservative government

that waving the bloody shirt remained the Republicans' best political strategy.

On election day, Tilden tallied 4,288,590 votes to Hayes's 4,036,000. But in the all-important electoral college, Tilden fell one vote short of the majority required for victory. The electoral votes of three states—South Carolina, Louisiana, and Florida, the only remaining Republican governments in the South—remained in doubt because both Republicans and Democrats in those states claimed victory. To win, Tilden needed only one of the nineteen contested votes. Hayes had to have all of them.

Congress had to decide who had actually won the elections in the three southern states and thus who would be president. The Constitution provided no guidance for this situation. Moreover, Democrats controlled the House, and Republicans controlled the Senate. Congress created a special electoral commission to arbitrate the disputed returns. All of the commissioners voted their party affiliation, giving every state to the Republican Hayes and putting him over the top in electoral votes (Map 16.4).

Some outraged Democrats vowed to resist Hayes's victory. Rumors flew of an impending coup and renewed civil war. But the impasse was broken when negotiations behind the scenes resulted in an informal understanding known as the **Compromise of 1877**. In exchange for a Democratic promise not to block Hayes's inauguration and to deal fairly with the freedmen, Hayes vowed to refrain from using the army to uphold the remaining Republican regimes in the South and to provide the South with substantial federal subsidies for railroads.

Stubborn Tilden supporters bemoaned the "stolen election" and damned "His Fraudulency," Rutherford B. Hayes. Old-guard radicals such as William Lloyd Garrison denounced Hayes's bargain as a "policy of compromise, of credulity, of weakness, of subserviency, of surrender." But the nation as a whole celebrated, for the country had weathered a grave crisis. The last three Republican state governments in the South fell quickly once Hayes abandoned them and withdrew the U.S. Army. Reconstruction came to an end.

REVIEW   Why did northern support for reconstruction collapse?

▶ **Conclusion: "A Revolution but Half Accomplished"**

In 1865, when General Carl Schurz visited the South, he discovered "a revolution but half accomplished." White Southerners resisted the passage from slavery to free labor, from white racial despotism to equal justice, and from white political monopoly to biracial democracy. The old elite wanted to get "things back as near to slavery as possible," Schurz reported, while African Americans such as James T. Rapier and some whites were eager to exploit the revolutionary implications of defeat and emancipation.

Although the northern-dominated Republican Congress refused to provide for blacks' economic welfare, it employed constitutional amendments to require ex-Confederates to accept legal equality and share political power with black men. Congress was not willing to extend such power to women, however. Conservative southern whites fought ferociously to recover their power and privilege. When Democrats regained control of politics, whites used both state power and private violence to wipe out many of the gains of Reconstruction, leading one observer to conclude that the North had won the war but the South had won the peace.

The Redeemer counterrevolution, however, did not mean a return to slavery. Northern victory in the Civil War ensured that ex-slaves no longer faced the auction block and could send

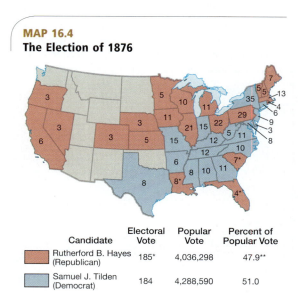

MAP 16.4
The Election of 1876

Candidate	Electoral Vote	Popular Vote	Percent of Popular Vote
Rutherford B. Hayes (Republican)	185*	4,036,298	47.9**
Samuel J. Tilden (Democrat)	184	4,288,590	51.0

*19 electoral votes were disputed.

**Percentages do not total 100 because some popular votes went to other parties.

their children to school, worship in their own churches, and work independently on their own rented farms. Sharecropping, with all its hardships, provided more autonomy and economic welfare than bondage had. It was limited freedom, to be sure, but it was not slavery.

The Civil War and emancipation set in motion the most profound upheaval in the nation's history. War destroyed the largest slave society in the New World and gave birth to a modern nation-state. The world of masters and slaves gave way to that of landlords and sharecroppers. Washington increased its role in national affairs, and the victorious North set the nation's compass toward the expansion of industrial capitalism and the final conquest of the West.

Despite massive changes, however, the Civil War remained only a "half accomplished" revolution. By not fulfilling the promises the nation seemed to hold out to black Americans at war's end, Reconstruction represents a tragedy of enormous proportions. The failure to protect blacks and guarantee their rights had enduring consequences. It was the failure of the first reconstruction that made the modern civil rights movement necessary.

See the Selected Bibliography for this chapter in the Appendix.

16 Chapter Review

MAKE IT STICK

LearningCurve

Go online and use LearningCurve to see what you know. Then review the key terms and answer the questions.

KEY TERMS

Freedmen's Bureau (p. 437)
black codes (p. 441)
Civil Rights Act of 1866 (p. 444)
Fourteenth Amendment (p. 444)
Military Reconstruction Act (p. 446)
Fifteenth Amendment (p. 447)
carpetbagger (p. 448)
scalawag (p. 448)
Ku Klux Klan (p. 448)
sharecropping (p. 451)
Redeemers (p. 458)
Compromise of 1877 (p. 460)

REVIEW QUESTIONS

1. To what extent did Lincoln's wartime plan for reconstruction reflect the concerns of newly freed slaves? (pp. 435–439)

2. When the southern states passed the black codes, how did the U.S. Congress respond? (pp. 441–444)

3. Why did Congress impeach President Andrew Johnson? (pp. 444–447)

4. How did politics and economic concerns shape reconstruction in the South? (pp. 448–455)

5. Why did northern support for reconstruction collapse? (pp. 456–461)

MAKING CONNECTIONS

1. Why and how did the federal government retreat from defending African Americans' civil rights in the 1870s?

2. Why was distributing plantation land to former slaves such a controversial policy? Why did Congress reject redistribution as a general policy?

3. After emancipation, how did ex-slaves exercise their new freedoms, and how did white Southerners attempt to limit them?

4. How did the identification of the Republican Party with Reconstruction policy affect the party's political fortunes in the 1870s?

LINKING TO THE PAST

1. In what ways did the attitudes and actions of President Johnson increase northern resolve to reconstruct the South and the South's resolve to resist reconstruction?

2. White women, abolitionists, and blacks all had hopes for a brighter future that were in some ways dashed during the turmoil of reconstruction. What specific goals of these groups slipped away? What political allies abandoned their causes, and why?

17

The Contested West
1865–1900

CONTENT LEARNING OBJECTIVES

After reading and studying this chapter, you should be able to:

- Explain federal policies toward Native Americans during the last decades of the nineteenth century. Describe how Native Americans resisted these policies and how the government quashed these acts of resistance.

- Recount how the late-nineteenth-century frenzy for gold and silver in the West transformed the region and explain how the development of the western mining industry mirrored the processes of industrialization in other parts of the country.

- Identify who worked and settled in the West and why they were drawn there.

- Describe the ways in which farming became increasingly commercialized and ranching became increasingly industrialized.

LAKOTA VEST
This late nineteenth-century Lakota vest displays the American flag, which was a common design in Indian bead art and testifies to the great changes that took place in the American West. Private Collection, photograph American Hurrah Archive, NYC.

TO CELEBRATE THE 400TH ANNIVERSARY OF COLUMBUS'S VOYAGE
to the New World, Chicago hosted the World's Columbian Exposition in 1893, creating a magical White City on the shores of Lake Michigan. Among the organizations vying to hold meetings at the fair was the American Historical Association, whose members gathered on a warm July evening to hear Frederick Jackson Turner deliver his landmark essay "The Significance of the Frontier in American History." Turner began by noting that the 1890 census no longer discerned a clear frontier line. His tone was elegiac: "The existence of an area of free land, its continuous recession, and the advance of settlement westward," he observed, "explained American development."

Of course, *west* has always been a comparative term in American history. Until the gold rush focused attention on California, the West for settlers lay beyond the Appalachians. But by the second half of the nineteenth century, the West stretched from Canada to Mexico, from the Mississippi River to the Pacific Ocean.

Turner, who originally studied the old frontier east of the Mississippi, viewed the West as a process as much as a place. The availability of land provided a "safety valve," releasing social tensions and providing opportunities for social mobility that worked to Americanize Americans. Turner's West demanded strength and nerve, fostered invention and adaptation, and produced self-confident, individualistic Americans. His frontier thesis underscored the exceptionalism of America's history, highlighting its difference from the rest of the world. His "frontier thesis" would earn him a professorship at Harvard and a permanent place in American history.

Yet the historians who applauded Turner in Chicago had short memories. That afternoon, many had crossed the midway to attend Buffalo Bill Cody's Wild West extravaganza—a cowboys-and-Indians shoot-um-up. The historians cheering in the stands that hot afternoon no doubt dismissed Buffalo Bill's history as amateur, but he made a point that Turner's thesis ignored: The West was neither free nor open. It was the story of a fierce and violent contest for land and resources.

In the decades following the Civil War, the United States pursued empire in the American West in Indian wars that lasted until 1890. Pushed off their land and onto reservations, Native Americans resisted as they faced waves of miners and settlers as well as the degradation of the environment by railroads, mines, barbed wire, and mechanized agriculture. The pastoral agrarianism Turner celebrated in his frontier thesis clashed with the urban, industrial West emerging on the Comstock Lode in Nevada and in the commercial farms of California.

Buffalo Bill's mythic West, with its heroic cowboys and noble savages, also obscured the complex reality of the West as a fiercely contested terrain. Competing groups of Anglos, Hispanics, former slaves, Chinese, and a host of others arrived seeking the promise of land and riches, while the Indians struggled to preserve their cultural identities. Turner's rugged white "frontierman" masked racial diversity and failed to acknowledge the role of women in community building.

Yet in the waning decade of the nineteenth century, as history blurred with nostalgia, Turner's evocation of the frontier as a crucible for American identity hit a nerve in a population facing rapid changes. A major depression started even before the Columbian Exposition opened its doors. Americans worried about the economy, immigration, and urban industrialism found in Turner's message a new cause for concern. Would America continue to be America now that the frontier was closed? Were the problems confronting the United States at the turn of the twentieth century—the exploitation of land and labor, the consolidation of capital, and vicious ethnic and racial rivalries—destined to play out under western skies?

VISUAL ACTIVITY

Buffalo Bill Poster

William (Buffalo Bill) Cody used colorful posters to publicize his Wild West show during the 1880s and 1890s. This poster from 1899 shows Indians attacking a wagon train and a village of tepees in the background. By the 1870s, the era of the wagon train had ended with the coming of the transcontinental railroads. The mythic West Cody (featured on the right) recreates, is already part of the past. Library of Congress.

READING THE IMAGE: How does Buffalo Bill contribute to the "myth of the old West" in this poster?

CONNECTIONS: What would Frederick Jackson Turner and the historians who gathered in Chicago have thought of the history of expansion depicted in Buffalo Bill's Wild West Show?

BUFFALO BILL'S WILD WEST
AND CONGRESS OF ROUGH RIDERS OF THE WORLD.

A CONGRESS OF AMERICAN INDIANS. REPRESENTING VARIOUS TRIBES, CHARACTERS AND PECULIARITIES OF THE WILY DUSKY WARRIORS IN SCENES FROM ACTUAL LIFE GIVING THEIR WEIRD WAR DANCES AND PICTURESQUE STYLE OF HORSEMANSHIP.

COL. W. F. CODY
BUFFALO BILL
WILL APPEAR
AT EVERY PERFORMANCE

▶ Conquest and Empire in the West

While the European powers expanded their authority and wealth through imperialism and colonialism in far-flung empires abroad, the United States focused its attention on its own western lands. From the U.S. Army attack on the remainder of the Comanche empire to the conquest of the Black Hills, whites pushed Indians aside as they moved West. As posited by Frederick Jackson Turner, American exceptionalism stressed how the history of the United States differed from that of European nations, citing America's western frontier as a cause. Yet expansion in the trans-Mississippi West involved the conquest, displacement, and rule over native peoples—a process best understood in the global context of imperialism and colonialism. (See "Beyond America's Borders," page 466.)

The U.S. government, through trickery and conquest, pushed tribes off their lands (Map 17.1) and onto designated Indian territories or reservations. The Indian wars depleted the Native American population and handed most Indian land to white settlers. The decimation of the bison herds pushed the Plains Indians onto reservations, where they lived as wards of the state. Thus did the United States, committed to an imperialist, expansionist ideology, colonize the West.

Indian Removal and the Reservation System

Manifest destiny—the belief that the United States had a "God-given" right to aggressively spread the values of white civilization and expand the nation from ocean to ocean—dictated U.S. policy toward Indians and other nations. In the name of manifest destiny, Americans forced the removal of the Five Civilized Tribes of the South (the Cherokee, Chocktaw, Chickasaw, Creek, and Seminole peoples) to Oklahoma in the 1830s; colonized Texas and won its independence from Mexico in 1836; conquered California, Arizona, New Mexico, and parts of Utah and Colorado in the Mexican-American War of 1846–1848; invaded Oregon in the mid-1840s; and paid Mexico for land in Arizona and New Mexico in the Gadsden purchase of 1854.

By midcentury, Western lands no longer seemed inexhaustible. Hoards of settlers crossed the Great Plains on their way to the goldfields of California or the rich farmland of Washington

CHRONOLOGY

1851	• First Treaty of Fort Laramie.
1862	• Homestead Act. • Great Sioux Uprising (Santee Uprising).
1864	• Sand Creek massacre.
1867	• Treaty of Medicine Lodge.
1868	• Washita massacre. • Second Treaty of Fort Laramie.
1869	• First transcontinental railroad completed.
1870s	• Hunters begin to decimate bison herds.
1873	• "Big Bonanza" discovered on Comstock Lode.
1874	• Discovery of gold in Black Hills.
1876	• Battle of the Little Big Horn.
1877	• Chief Joseph surrenders.
1879	• Carlisle Indian School opens. • Exodusters move to Kansas.
1881	• Sitting Bull surrenders.
1882	• Chinese Exclusion Act.
1886	• Geronimo surrenders.
1886–1887	• Severe blizzards decimate cattle.
1887	• Dawes Allotment Act.
1889	• Rise of Ghost Dance. • Two million acres in Oklahoma opened for settlement.
1890	• Sitting Bull killed. • Massacre at Wounded Knee, South Dakota.
1893	• Last land rush in Oklahoma Territory. • Frederick Jackson Turner presents "frontier thesis."

Imperialism, Colonialism, and the Treatment of the Sioux and the Zulu

Viewed through the lens of colonialism, the British war with the Zulu in South Africa offers a compelling contrast to the war of the United States against the Lakota Sioux. The Zulu, like the Sioux, came to power as a result of devastating intertribal warfare. In the area that is today the KwaZulu-Natal province of the Republic of South Africa, the Zulu king Shaka united his empire by 1826 with an army of more than twenty thousand. And like the Sioux, the Zulu earned a formidable reputation as brave warriors who fought to protect their land from white encroachment.

In 1806, the British seized the Cape of Good Hope to secure shipping interests, leading to conflicts with Dutch-speaking settlers known as the Boers, who had inhabited the southern tip of Africa since the seventeenth century. Clashes between Britons and Boers eventually resulted in the Great Trek, the migration of nearly twelve thousand Boers northeastward beginning in 1835. There they claimed land and established the South African Republic (the Transvaal) in 1853 and the Orange Free State in 1854, both independent of British rule. But the Great Trek brought the Boers into Zululand, where they met with bloody resistance.

The Zulu lived in a highly complex society, with regiments of warriors arranged by age and bound to local chiefs under the supreme command of the Zulu king. During his harsh reign, King Shaka inspected his regiments after each battle and put cowards to death on the spot. Young men could not start their own households without the local chief's permission, thus ensuring an ample stock of warriors and making the Zulu army, in the words of one English observer, "a celibate, man-slaying machine." The Boer settlers repeatedly faced the wrath of the Zulu, who slaughtered the first trekkers to arrive in Zululand and raided Boer settlements to steal cattle.

The British entered the fray in 1879, sparking the Anglo-Zulu War, which a recent historian has condemned as being "as unnecessary as it was unjust." Sir Theophilus Shepstone, British secretary for native affairs, hinted at Britain's motive when he wrote in 1878, "Had [its] 30,000 warriors been in time changed to labourers working for wages, Zululand would have been a prosperous peaceful country instead of what it is now, a source of perpetual danger to itself and its neighbors."

With aims of both placating the Boers and securing a source of labor for British economic expansion—made paramount by the discovery of diamonds in the region—British troops invaded Zululand. Leading soldiers armed with the latest rifles and artillery, Lt. Commander Lord Chelmsford—with a confidence reminiscent of that of George Armstrong Custer—expected to subdue the Zulu easily. But in January 1879, at the battle of Isandhlwana, the Zulu army of

Zululand and Cape Colony, 1878

British

Boer Republics

KALAHARI DESERT

TRANSVAAL

ORANGE FREE STATE

ZULULAND
• Isandlwana

CAPE COLONY

ATLANTIC OCEAN

INDIAN OCEAN

• Cape Town

and Oregon. In their path stood a solid wall of Indian land. To solve this "Indian problem," the U.S. government solution was to take Indian lands with the promise to pay annuities in return and put the Indians on lands reserved for their use—reservations. In 1851, some ten thousand Plains Indians came together at Fort Laramie in Wyoming to negotiate a treaty that ceded a wide swath of their land to allow passage to the West. In return, the government promised that the remaining Indian land would remain inviolate.

The Indians who "touched the pen" to the 1851 Treaty of Forth Laramie hoped to preserve their land and culture in the face of the white onslaught. Settlers and miners cut down trees, polluted streams, and killed off the bison. Whites brought alcohol, guns, and something even more deadly—disease. Between 1780 and 1870, the population of the Plains tribes declined by half. "If I could see this thing, if I knew where it came from, I would go there and fight it," a Cheyenne warrior anguished. Disease shifted the power

Zulu Warriors
Chief Ngoza (center) poses with Zulu men in full war dress. Their distinctive cowhide shields date to the reign of King Shaka. Each warrior also carried two or three throwing spears and an *ikwa*, or flat-bladed stabbing spear used in close combat. Zulu warriors marched at the double and could cover up to fifty miles a day. Campbell Collections of the University of KwaZulu-Natal.

may seem less exploitative if no less ruthless in its cultural imperialism.

Both the Little Big Horn and Isandhlwana became legends that spawned a romantic image of the "noble savage": fierce in battle, honored in defeat. Describing this myth, historian James Gump, who has chronicled the subjugation of the Sioux and the Zulu, observed, "Each western culture simultaneously dehumanized and glamorized the Sioux and Zulu," and noted that the noble savage mythology was "a product of the racist ideologies of the late nineteenth century as well as the guilt and compassion associated with the bloody costs of empire building." The imperial powers of Britain and the United States defeated indigenous rivals and came to dominate their lands (and, in the case of the Zulu, their labor) in the global expansion that marked the nineteenth century.

more than 25,000 surprised a British encampment. In less than two hours, more than 4,000 Zulu and British were killed. Only a handful of British soldiers managed to escape, and Chelmsford lost 1,300 officers and men.

When news of Isandhlwana reached London, commentators compared the massacre to Custer's defeat at the Little Big Horn and noted that native forces armed with spears had defeated a modern army.

The British immediately launched unconditional war against the Zulu. In the ensuing battles, neither side took prisoners. The Zulu beat the British twice more, but after seven months

the British finally routed the Zulu army and abandoned Zululand to its fate—partition, starvation, and civil war.

Historians would later compare the British victory to the U.S. Army's defeat of the Sioux in the American West, but the Zulu and Sioux met different economic fates. As Shepstone hinted in 1878, the British goal had been to subdue the Zulu and turn them into cheap labor. Compared to the naked economic exploitation of the Zulu, the U.S. policy toward the Sioux, with its forced assimilation on reservations and its misguided attempts to turn the nomadic tribes into sedentary, God-fearing farmers,

America in a Global Context

1. How was the British war with the Zulu similar to and different from the American war with the Sioux?

2. Compare the fate of the defeated Zulu with that of the Sioux.

Connect to the Big Idea

C Why did the American government put Native Americans on reservations during the late nineteenth century?

from Woodland agrarian tribes, whose proximity to whites meant they died at high rates, to the Lakota (Western) Sioux, who fled the contagion by pursuing an equestrian nomadic existence that displaced weaker tribes in the Western Plains.

In the Southwest, the Navajo people, in a removal similar to that of the Cherokee in the 1830s, endured a forced march called the "Long Walk" from their homeland to the desolate Bosque Redondo Reservation in New Mexico

in 1864. "This ground we were brought on, it is not productive," complained the Navajo leader Barboncito. "All the stock we brought here have nearly all died."

Poverty and starvation stalked the reservations. Confined by armed force, the Indians eked out an existence on stingy government rations. Styled as stepping-stones to "civilization," Indian reservations closely resembled colonial societies where native populations, ruled by outside bureaucrats, saw their culture assaulted,

MAP ACTIVITY

Map 17.1   The Loss of Indian Lands, 1850–1890

By 1890, western Indians were isolated on small, scattered reservations. Native Americans had struggled to retain their land in major battles, from the Santee Uprising in Minnesota in 1862 to the massacre at Wounded Knee, South Dakota, in 1890.

READING THE MAP: Where was the largest reservation located in 1890? Which states on this map show no reservations in 1890? Compare this map to Map 17.3.

CONNECTIONS: Why did the federal government force Native Americans onto reservations? What developments prompted these changes?

their religious practices outlawed, their children sent away to school, and their way of life attacked in the name of progress.

To Americans raised on theories of racial superiority, the Indians constituted, in the words of one Colorado militia major, constituted "an obstacle to civilization . . . [and] should be exterminated." This attitude pervaded the military. As a result, the massacre of Native American men, women, and children became commonplace in the West. In November 1864 at the Sand Creek in Colorado Territory, Colonel John M.

Chivington and his Colorado militia descended on a village of Cheyenne, mostly women and children. Their leader, Black Kettle, raised a white flag and an American flag to signal surrender, but the charging cavalry ignored his signal and butchered 270 Indians. Chivington watched as his men scalped and mutilated their victims and later justified the killing of Indian children with the terse remark, "Nits make lice." The city of Denver treated Chivington and his men as heroes, but a congressional inquiry eventually castigated the soldiers for their "fiendish malignity" and condemned the "savage cruelty" of the massacre. Four years later, Black Kettle, who had survived Sand Creek, died in another massacre when George Armstrong Custer slaughtered more than one hundred people on the banks of the Washita River in Oklahoma.

The Decimation of the Great Bison Herds

After the Civil War, the accelerating pace of industrial expansion brought about the near extinction of the American bison (buffalo). By 1850, the dynamic ecology of the Great Plains, with its droughts, fires, and blizzards, along with the demands of Indian buffalo-robe traders as well as whites and their cattle, had driven the bison herds onto the far western plains.

In the 1870s, industrial demand for heavy leather belting used in machinery and the development of larger, more accurate rifles combined to hasten the slaughter of the bison. The nations' transcontinental railroad systems cut the range in two and divided the dwindling herds. For the Sioux and other nomadic tribes of the plains, the buffalo constituted a way of life—a source of food, fuel, and shelter and a central part of religion and ritual. Railroad owners, however, considered bison a nuisance—at best a cheap source of meat for their workers and a target for sport.

Although the army took credit for the conquest of the Plains Indians, came about largely as a result of the decimation of the great bison herds was largely responsible for the Indians' fate. With their food supply gone, Indians had to choose between starvation and the reservation. "A cold wind blew across the prairie when the last buffalo fell," the great Sioux leader Sitting Bull lamented, "a death wind for my people."

On the southern plains in 1867, more than five thousand warring Comanches, Kiowas, and Southern Arapahos gathered at Medicine Lodge

VISUAL ACTIVITY

"Slaughtered for the Hide"
In 1874, *Harper's Weekly* featured this illustration of a buffalo-hide hunter skinning a carcass on the southwestern plains. City father Colonel Richard Dodge wrote of the carnage, "The air was foul with sickening stench, and the vast plain which only a short twelve months before teemed with animal life, was a dead, solitary putrid desert." Library of Congress.
READING THE IMAGE: What virtues and stereotypes of the West does this magazine cover extol?
CONNECTIONS: How did the slaughter of buffalo affect the lives of Plains Indians?

Creek in Kansas to negotiate the Treaty of Medicine Lodge, hoping to preserve limited land and hunting by moving the tribe to a reservation. Three years after the treaty became law, hide hunters poured into the region; within a decade, they had nearly exterminated the southern bison herds. Luther Standing Bear recounted the sight and stench: "I saw the bodies of hundreds of dead buffalo lying about, just wasting, and the odor was terrible. . . . They were letting our food lie on the plains to rot." Once an estimated 40 million bison roamed the West; by 1895, fewer than 1,000 remained. With the buffalo gone, the Indians faced starvation and reluctantly moved onto the reservations.

Indian Wars and the Collapse of Comanchería

The Indian wars in the West marked the last resistance of a Native American population devastated by disease and demoralized by the federal government's reservation policy. The Dakota Sioux in Minnesota went to war in 1862. For years, under the leadership of Chief Little Crow, the Dakota—also known as the Santee—had pursued a policy of accommodation, ceding land in return for the promise of annuities. But with his people on the verge of starvation (the local Indian agent told the hungry Dakota, "Go and eat grass"), Little Crow led his angry warriors in a desperate campaign against the intruders, killing more than 1,000 settlers. American troops quelled the Great Sioux Uprising (also called the Santee Uprising) and marched 1,700 Sioux to Fort Snelling, where 400 Indians were put on trial for murder and 38 died in the largest mass execution in American history.

Further west, the great Indian empire of **Comanchería** had once stretched from the Canadian plains to Mexico. By 1865, after two decades of what one historian has labeled "ethnic cleansing," fewer than 5,000 Comanche remained in west Texas and Oklahoma. Through decades of dealings with the Spanish and French, the Comanche had built a complex empire based on trade in horses, hides, guns, and captives. Expert riders, the Comanche waged war in the saddle, giving the U.S. Calvary reason to hate and fear them.

After the Civil War, President Ulysses S. Grant faced the prospect of protracted Indian war. Reluctant to spend more money and sacrifice more lives, Grant adopted a "peace policy" designed to segregate and control the Indians while opening up land to white settlers. This policy won the support of both friends of the Indians and those who coveted the Indians' land. The army herded the Indians onto reservations (see Map 17.1), where the U.S. Bureau of Indian Affairs hired agents who, in the words of Paiute Sarah Winnemucca, did "nothing but fill their pockets." In 1871, Congress determined to no longer deal with Indians as sovereign nations, but to eliminate treaties and treat Indians as wards of the state. Grant's peace policy in the West gave way to all-out warfare as the U.S. Army dispatched 3,000 soldiers to wipe out the remains of Comanchería. Raiding parties of Comanche virtually obliterated white settlements in west Texas. To defeat the Indians, the army adopted the practice of burning and destroying everything in its path, using the tactics that General William Tecumseh Sherman had perfected in his march through Georgia during the Civil War. At the decisive battle of Palo Duro Canyon in 1874, only three Comanche warriors died in battle, but U.S. soldiers took the Indians' camp; burned more than 200 tepees, hundreds of robes and blankets, and thousands of pounds of winter supplies; and shot more than 1,000 horses. Coupled with the decimation of the bison, the army's scorched-earth policy led to the final collapse of the Comanche people. The surviving Indians of Comanchería, now numbering fewer than 1,500, reluctantly retreated to the reservation at Fort Sill.

The Fight for the Black Hills

On the northern plains, the fever for gold fueled the conflict between Indians and Euro-Americans. In 1866, the Cheyenne united with the Sioux in Wyoming to protect their hunting grounds in the Powder River valley, which were threatened by the construction of the Bozeman Trail connecting Fort Laramie with the goldfields in Montana. Captain William Fetterman, who had boasted that with eighty men he could ride through the Sioux nation, died along with all of his troops at the hands of the Sioux. The Indians' impressive victories led to the second Treaty of Fort Laramie in 1868, in which the United States agreed to abandon the Bozeman Trail and guaranteed the Indians control of the **Black Hills**, land sacred to the Lakota Sioux.

The government's fork-tongued promises induced some of the tribes to accept the treaty. The great Sioux chief Red Cloud led many of his people onto the reservation. Red Cloud soon regretted his decision. "Think of it!" he told a visitor to the Pine Ridge Reservation. "I, who used to own . . . country so extensive that I could not ride through it in a week . . . must tell Washington when I am hungry. I must beg for that which I own." On a visit to Washington, D.C., in 1870, Red Cloud told the secretary of the interior, "We are melting like snow on the hillside, while you are grown like spring grass. . . . When the white man comes in my country he leaves a trail of blood behind him." As leadership of the Sioux passed to a new generation, younger chiefs, among them Crazy Horse and Sitting Bull, refused to sign the treaty and called for armed resistance. Crazy Horse later declared that he wanted no part of the "piecemeal penning" of his people.

In 1874, the discovery of gold in the Black Hills led the government to break its promise to Red Cloud. Miners began pouring into the Dakotas, and the Northern Pacific Railroad made plans to lay track. At first, the government offered to purchase the Black Hills. But the Lakota Sioux refused to sell. The army responded by issuing an ultimatum ordering all Lakota Sioux and Northern Cheyenne bands onto the Pine Ridge Reservation and threatening to hunt down those who refused.

In the summer of 1876, the army launched a three-pronged attack led by Lieutenant Colonel George Armstrong Custer, General George Crook, and Colonel John Gibbon. Crazy Horse stopped Crook at the Battle of the Rosebud. Custer, leading the second prong of the army's offensive, divided his troops and ordered an attack. On June 25, he spotted signs of the Indians' camp. Crying "Hurrah Boys, we've got them," he led 265 men of the Seventh Cavalry into the largest gathering of Indians ever assembled on the Great Plains (more than 8,000) camped along the banks of the Greasy Grass River. Indian warriors led by Sitting Bull and Crazy Horse set upon Custer and his men and quickly annihilated them. "It took us about as long as a hungry man to eat his dinner," the Cheyenne chief Two Moons recalled. (See "Visualizing History," page 472.)

"Custer's Last Stand," or the **Battle of the Little Big Horn,** soon became part of national mythology. But it proved to be the last stand for the Sioux. The nomadic bands that had massed at the Little Big Horn scattered, and the army hunted them down. "Wherever we went," wrote the Oglala holy man Black Elk, "the soldiers came to kill us." In 1877, Crazy Horse was captured and killed. Four years later, Sitting Bull surrendered. The government took the Black Hills and confined the Lakota to the reservation. The Sioux never accepted the loss of the Black Hills. In 1923, they filed suit, demanding the return of the land illegally taken from them. After a protracted court battle lasting nearly sixty years, the U.S. Supreme Court ruled in 1980 that the government had illegally violated the Treaty of Fort Laramie. Declaring "a more ripe and rank case of dishonorable dealings will never, in all probability, be found in our history," the Court awarded the tribes $122.5 million. The Sioux refused the settlement and continue to press for the return of the Black Hills.

> **REVIEW** How did the slaughter of the bison contribute to the Plains Indians' removal to reservations?

▶ Forced Assimilation and Indian Resistance

Imperialistic attitudes of whites toward Indians continued to evolve in the late nineteenth century. To "civilize" the Indians, the U.S. government sought to force assimilation on their children. Reservations became increasingly unpopular among whites who coveted Indian land and among friends of the Indians appalled by the conditions on the reservations. A new policy of allotment gained favor. It promised to put Indians on parcels of land, forcing them into farming, and then to redistribute the remaining land to settlers. In the face of this ongoing assault on their way of life, Indians actively resisted, contested, and adapted to colonial rule.

Indian Schools and the War on Indian Culture

Indian schools constituted the cultural battleground of the Indian wars in the West, their avowed purpose being, in the words of one of its fervent supporters, "To kill the Indian . . . and save the man." In 1877, Congress appropriated funds for Indian education, reasoning, in the words of one congressman, that it was less expensive to educate Indians than to kill them. That education effort focused on Native American boys and girls, from toddlers to teenagers. Virginia's Hampton Institute, created in 1868 to school newly freed slaves, accepted its first Indian students in 1878. Although many Indian schools operated on the reservations, authorities much preferred boarding facilities that isolated students from the "contamination" of tribal values.

Many Native American parents resisted sending their children away. When all else failed, the military kidnapped the children and sent them off to school. An agent at the Mescalero

"Custer's Last Stand"

Crazy Horse at the Little Big Horn, Amos Bad Heart Bull

No American soldier survived the Battle of the Little Big Horn. Yet many Indians remembered the battle and left pictures of it. In this pictograph, Amos Bad Heart Bull, an Oglala Sioux from the Pine Ridge Reservation, dramatized the battle at the river the Indians called the Greasy Grass. Although the artist was only seven years old in 1876 when the battle occurred, he based his pictures on the recollections of his uncle and other Oglala elders. Crazy Horse ritually prepared for battle by painting hailstones on his body, wearing a small stone tied behind one ear, and placing a single eagle feather in his hair. Featured at the center of the pictograph, he can be identified by his unique war paint. According to one Arapaho warrior who fought beside him, Crazy Horse "was the bravest man he ever saw."

Even at the time the Indian and white participants interpreted events differently. One of the soldiers cut off from Custer's group feared for his life as he heard "wild victory dances" coming from the Lakota camp. But what he heard, according to a Cheyenne warrior named Wooden Leg, were the songs of the Lakota and Cheyenne, mourning their sons, husbands, and fathers. The soldier, who huddled on Reno hill praying to live through the night, would not only survive, but live to 1950, making him the

Apache Agency in Arizona Territory reported in 1886 that "it became necessary to visit the camps unexpectedly with a detachment of police, and seize such children as were proper and take them away to school, willing or unwilling." The parents put up a struggle. "Some hurried their children off to the mountains or hid them away in camp, and the police had to chase and capture them like so many wild rabbits," the agent observed. "This unusual proceeding created quite an outcry. The men were sullen and muttering, the women loud in their lamentations and the children almost out of their wits with fright."

Once at school, the children were stripped and scrubbed, their clothing and belongings confiscated, and their hair hacked off and doused with kerosene to kill lice. Issued stiff new uniforms, shoes, and what Luther Standing Bear recalled as the "torture" of woolen long underwear, the children often lost not only their possessions but also their names. Children were asked to stand at the blackboard, take a pointer,

The Battle of Little Big Horn, 1889

last American to survive "Custer's Last Stand."

Many of the battle depictions by whites were little more than romantic idealism, with Custer on horseback leading a valiant charge. In this 1889 lithograph of the battle, Custer and his men are shown dismounted, firing at Indians on horseback. A much more accurate portrayal than many of the others in circulation at the time, the lithograph shows how badly Custer was outnumbered when he divided his forces and led one contingent into the largest gathering of Indians ever to meet on the Plains.

SOURCE: Crazy Horse: The Granger Collection, New York; battle: Private Collection/The Bridgeman Art Library.

Questions for Analysis

1. Compare the two portrayals. What strikes you about the Indian version in relationship to the Anglo lithograph?

2. Who is the center of the focus for the Indian? Who for the Anglos?

3. Would you know the outcome of the battle by looking at either picture? Why?

Connect to the Big Idea

C In what ways does the comparison of the two depictions of the Battle of the Little Big Horn point to conflicting interpretations of the American West?

and select a proper English name, recalled Standing Bear, who immediately became Luther.

The **Carlisle Indian School** in Pennsylvania, founded in 1879, became the model for later institutions. To encourage assimilation, Carlisle pioneered the "outing system"—sending students to live with white families during summer vacations. The policy reflected the school's slogan: "To civilize the Indian, get him into civilization. To keep him civilized, let him stay." The curriculum featured agricultural and manual arts for boys and domestic skills for girls, training designed to eliminate Indians' dependence on government support.

Merrill Gates, a member of the Board of Indian Commissioners, summed up the goal of Indian education: "To get the Indian out of the blanket and into trousers,—and trousers with a pocket in them, *and with a pocket that aches to be filled with dollars*!" Gates's faith in the "civilizing" power of the dollar reflected the unabashed

The Assimilation of Sioux Students at Carlisle Indian School
This pair of before and after photographs of Wounded Yellow Robe, Timber Yellow Robe, and Henry Standing Bear reveals the distinct turn away from tribal culture upon enrolling in Carlisle Indian School in 1883. The forced assimilation policy at such schools set out to divest the Indians of any remnant of their former lives. Archives and Special Collections, Dickinson College.

materialism of the age. But the cultural annihilation that Gates cheerfully predicted did not prove so easy.

Despite whites' efforts, Indians continued being Indians. Even in the "iron routine" of the "civilizing machine" at boarding school, Zitkala-Sa recounted how Indians retained their tribal loyalties and Indian identities. Luther Standing Bear, whose father enrolled him at Carlisle to learn white ways, confessed, "Though my hair had been cut and I wore civilian clothes, I never forsook the blanket." Students continued to speak tribal languages and attend tribal dances even though the punishment was whipping with a leather belt. The schools themselves ultimately subverted their goal by creating generations of Indians who shared a common language, English, and would later create a Pan Indian reform movement in the Progressive Era.

The Dawes Act and Indian Land Allotment

In the 1880s, the practice of rounding up and herding Indians onto reservations lost momentum in favor of allotment—a new policy designed to encourage assimilation through farming and the ownership of private property. Americans vowing to avenge Custer's defeat urged the government to get tough with the Indians. Reservations, they argued, took up too much good land that white settlers coveted and forced Americans to support

"lazy" reservation Indians. At the same time, people sympathetic to the Indians were appalled at the desperate poverty on the reservations and feared for the Indians' survival. Helen Hunt Jackson, in her classic work *A Century of Dishonor* (1881), convinced many readers that the Indians had been treated unfairly. "Our Indian policy," the *New York Times* concluded, "is usually spoliation behind the mask of benevolence."

The Indian Rights Association, a group of mainly white easterners formed in 1882, campaigned for the dismantling of the reservations, now viewed as obstacles to progress. To "cease to treat the Indian as a red man and treat him as a man" meant putting an end to tribal communalism and fostering individualism. "Selfishness," declared Senator Henry Dawes of Massachusetts, "is at the bottom of civilization." Dawes called for "allotment in severalty"—the institution of private property.

In 1887, Congress passed the **Dawes Allotment Act**, which divided up reservations and allotted parcels of land to individual Indians as private property. Each unmarried Indian man and woman as well as married men and children (married women were excluded) became eligible to receive 160 acres of land from reservation property. Indians who took allotments earned U.S. citizenship. This fostering of individualism through land distribution ultimately dealt a crippling blow to traditional tribal culture.

To protect Indians from land speculators, the government held most of the allotted land in trust—Indians could not sell it for twenty-five years. Since Indian land far surpassed the acreage needed for allotments, the government reserved the right to sell the "surplus" to white settlers. Many Indians sold their allotments and moved to urban areas where they lost touch with tribal ways.

The Dawes Act effectively reduced Indian land from 138 million acres to a scant 48 million. The legislation, in the words of one critic, worked "to despoil the Indians of their lands and to make them vagabonds on the face of the earth." By 1890, the United States controlled 97.5 percent of the territory formerly occupied by Native Americans.

Indian Resistance and Survival

Faced with the extinction of their entire way of life, different groups of Indians responded in different ways. In the 1870s, Comanche and Kiowa raiding parties frustrated the U.S. Army by brazenly using the reservations as a seasonal supply base during the winter months. When spring came they resumed their nomadic hunting as long as there were buffalo to hunt.

Some tribes, including the Crow and Shoshoni, chose to fight alongside the army against their old enemies, the Sioux. The Crow chief Plenty Coups explained why he allied with the United States: "Not because we loved the white man . . . or because we hated the Sioux . . . but because we plainly saw that this course was the only one which might save our beautiful country for us." The Crow and Shoshoni got to stay in their homelands and avoided the fate of other tribes shipped to reservations far away.

Indians who refused to stay on reservations risked being hunted down. The Nez Percé war is perhaps the most harrowing example of the army's policy. In 1863, the government dictated a treaty drastically reducing Nez Percé land. Most of the chiefs refused to sign the treaty and did not move to the reservation. When the army cracked down in 1877, some eight hundred Nez Percé people, many of them women and children, fled across the mountains of Idaho, Wyoming, and Montana, heading for the safety of Canada. After a 1,300-mile trek, 50 miles from freedom, they stopped in the Bear Paw Mountains to rest in the snow. The army caught up with them and attacked. Fewer than three hundred of the Indians eluded the army and made it to Canada. Yellow Wolf recalled the plight of those trapped:

"Children crying with cold. No fire. There could be no light. Everywhere the crying, the death wail." After a five-day siege, the Nez Percé leader, Chief Joseph, surrendered. His speech, reported by a white soldier, would become famous. "I am

Chief Joseph

Chief Joseph came to symbolize the heroic resistance of the Nez Percé. General Nelson Miles promised the Nez Percé that they could return to their homeland if they surrendered. But instead the Nez Percé were shipped off to Indian Territory (Oklahoma). In 1879, Chief Joseph traveled to Washington, D.C., to speak for his people. "Let me be a free man," he pleaded, "free to think and talk and act for myself—and I will obey every law." National Anthropological Archives, Smithsonian Institution (#01008900).

tired of fighting," he said as he surrendered his rifle. "Our chiefs are killed. It is cold and we have no blankets. The little children are freezing to death. . . . I am tired. My heart is sick and sad. From where the sun now stands, I will fight no more forever."

In the Southwest, the Apaches resorted to armed resistance. They roamed the Sonoran Desert of southern Arizona and northern Mexico, perfecting a hit-and-run guerrilla warfare that terrorized white settlers and bedeviled the army in the 1870s and 1880s. General George Crook combined a policy of dogged pursuit with judicious diplomacy. Crook relied on Indian scouts to track the raiding parties, recruiting nearly two hundred Apaches, Navajos, and Paiutes. By 1882, Crook had succeeded in persuading most of the Apaches to settle on the San Carlos Reservation in Arizona Territory. A desolate piece of desert inhabited by scorpions and rattlesnakes, San Carlos, in the words of one Apache, was "the worst place in all the great territory stolen from the Apaches."

Geronimo, a respected shaman (medicine man) of the Chiricahua Apache, refused to stay at San Carlos and repeatedly led raiding parties in the early 1880s. His warriors attacked ranches to obtain ammunition and horses. Among Geronimo's band was Lozen, a woman who rode with the warriors, armed with a rifle and a cartridge belt. Lozen's brother, a great chief, described her as being as "strong as a man, braver than most, and cunning in strategy." In the spring of 1885, Geronimo and his followers, including Lozen, went on a ten-month offensive, moving from the Apache sanctuary in the Sierra Madre to raid and burn ranches and towns on both sides of the Mexican border. General Crook caught up with Geronimo in the fall and persuaded him to return to San Carlos, only to have him slip away on the way back to the reservation. Chagrined, Crook resigned his post. General Nelson Miles, Crook's replacement, adopted a policy of hunt and destroy.

Geronimo's band of thirty-three Apaches, including women and children, eluded Miles's troops for more than five months. The pursuit left Miles's cavalry ragged. Over time, Lieutenant Leonard Wood had discarded his horse and was reduced to wearing nothing "but a pair of canton flannel drawers, and an old blouse, a pair of moccasins and a hat without a crown." Eventually, Miles's scouts cornered Geronimo in 1886 at Skeleton Canyon where he agreed to march north and negotiate a settlement. "We have not slept for six months," he admitted, "and we are worn out." Although fewer than three dozen Apaches had been considered "hostile," when General Miles induced them to surrender, the government rounded up nearly five hundred Apaches and sent them as prisoners to the South. By 1889, more than a quarter of them had died, some as a result of illnesses contracted in the damp lowland climate of Florida and Alabama and some by suicide. Their plight roused public opinion, and in 1892 they were moved to Fort Sill in Oklahoma and later to New Mexico.

Geronimo lived to become something of a celebrity. He appeared at the St. Louis Exposition in 1904 and rode in President Theodore Roosevelt's inaugural parade in 1905. In a newspaper interview, he confessed, "I want to go to my old home before I die. . . . Want to go back to the mountains again. I asked the Great White Father to allow me to go back, but he said no." None of the Apaches were permitted to return to Arizona; when Geronimo died in 1909, he was buried in Oklahoma.

On the plains, many tribes turned to a nonviolent form of resistance—a compelling new religion called the **Ghost Dance**. The Paiute shaman Wovoka, drawing on a cult that had developed in the 1870s, combined elements of Christianity and traditional Indian religion to found the Ghost Dance religion in 1889. Wovoka claimed that he had received a vision in which the Great Spirit spoke through him to all Indians, prophesying that if they would unite in the Ghost Dance ritual, whites would be destroyed in an apocalypse and the buffalo would return. His religion, born of despair and with a message of hope, spread like wildfire over the plains. The Ghost Dance was performed in Idaho, Montana, Utah, Wyoming, Colorado, Nebraska, Kansas, the Dakotas, and Indian Territory by tribes as diverse as the Sioux, Arapaho, Cheyenne, Pawnee, and Shoshoni. Dancers often went into hypnotic trances, dancing until they dropped from exhaustion.

The Ghost Dance was nonviolent, but it frightened whites, especially when the Sioux taught that wearing a white ghost shirt made Indians immune to soldiers' bullets. Soon whites began to fear an uprising. "Indians are dancing in the snow and are wild and crazy," wrote the Bureau of Indian Affairs agent at the Pine Ridge Reservation in South Dakota. Frantic, he pleaded for reinforcements. "We are at the mercy of these dancers. We need protection, and we need it now." President Benjamin Harrison dispatched several thousand federal troops to Sioux country to handle any outbreak.

Ghost Dancers
Arapaho women at the Darlington Agency in Indian Territory (Oklahoma) participate in the Ghost Dance. Different tribes performed variations of the dance, but generally dancers formed a circle and danced until they reached the trancelike state shown here. Whites feared the dancers and demanded that the army dispatch troops to subdue them. The result was the killing of Sitting Bull and the massacre at Wounded Knee. National Anthropological Archives, Smithsonian Institution (#81-9626).

In December 1890, when Sitting Bull attempted to join the Ghost Dance, he was killed by Indian police as they tried to arrest him at his cabin on the Standing Rock Reservation. His people, fleeing the scene, joined with a larger group of Miniconjou Sioux, who were apprehended by the Seventh Cavalry, Custer's old regiment, near Wounded Knee Creek, South Dakota. As the Indians laid down their arms, a soldier attempted to take a rifle from a deaf Miniconjou man and the gun went off. The soldiers opened fire. In the ensuing melee, more than two hundred Indian men, women, and children were mowed down in minutes by the army's brutally efficient Hotchkiss rapid-fire guns. Settler Jules Sandoz surveyed the scene the day after the massacre at **Wounded Knee**. "Here in ten minutes an entire community was as the buffalo that bleached on the plains," he wrote. "There was something loose in the world that hated joy and happiness as it hated brightness and color, reducing everything to drab agony and gray."

It had taken Euro-Americans 250 years to wrest control of the eastern half of the United States from the Indians. It took them only 40 years to take the western half. The subjugation of the American Indians marked the first chapter in a national mission of empire that would anticipate overseas imperialistic adventures in Asia, Latin America, the Caribbean, and the Pacific islands.

REVIEW   In what ways did different Indian groups defy and resist colonial rule?

▶ Mining the West

Mining stood at the center of the quest by the United States for empire in the West. The California gold rush of 1849 touched off the frenzy. The four decades following witnessed equally frenetic rushes for gold and other metals, most notably on the **Comstock Lode** in Nevada and later in New Mexico, Colorado, the Dakotas, Montana, Idaho, Arizona, and Utah (Map 17.2). At first glance, the mining West may seem much different from the East, but by the 1870s the term *urban industrialism* described

Virginia City, Nevada, as accurately as it did Pittsburgh or Cleveland. A close look at life on the Comstock Lode indicates some of the patterns and paradoxes of western mining. The diversity of peoples drawn to the West by the promise of mining riches and land made the region the most cosmopolitan in the nation, as well as the most contested. And although mining was often a tale of boom and bust, it was also a story of community building.

Life on the Comstock Lode

By 1859, refugees from California's played out goldfields flocked to the Washoe basin in Nevada. While searching for gold, Washoe miners stumbled on the richest vein of silver ore on the continent—the legendary Comstock Lode, named for prospector Henry Comstock.

To exploit even potentially valuable silver claims required capital and expensive technology well beyond the means of the prospector. An active San Francisco stock market sprang up to finance operations on the Comstock. Shrewd businessmen soon recognized that the easiest way to get rich was to sell their claims or to form mining companies and sell shares of stock. The most unscrupulous mined the wallets of gullible investors by selling shares in bogus mines. Speculation, misrepresentation, and outright thievery ran rampant. In twenty years, more than $300 million poured from the earth in Nevada alone, most of it going to speculators in San Francisco.

The promise of gold and silver drew thousands to the mines of the West. As Mark Twain observed in Virginia City's *Territorial Enterprise*, "All the peoples of the earth had representative adventures in the Silverland." Irish, Chinese, Germans, English, Scots, Welsh, Canadians, Mexicans, Italians, Scandinavians, French, Swiss, Chileans, and other South and Central Americans came to share in the bonanza. With them came a sprinkling of Russians, Poles, Greeks, Japanese, Spaniards, Hungarians, Portuguese, Turks, Pacific Islanders, and Moroccans, as well as other North Americans, African Americans, and American Indians. This polyglot population, typical of mining boomtowns, made Virginia City in the 1870s more cosmopolitan than New York or Boston. In the part of Utah Territory that eventually became Nevada, as many as 30 percent of the people came from outside

MAP 17.2

Western Mining, 1848–1890

Rich deposits of gold, silver, copper, lead, and iron larded the mountains of the West. Miners from all over the world flocked to the region. Few struck it rich, but many stayed on as paid workers in the increasingly mechanized corporate mines.

Mining on the Comstock
This photo of a miner at work shows the dangers faced on the Comstock Lode. Without a hardhat or miner's light, he is working with timbers to shore up the mineshaft. After the discovery of the "Big Bonanza" in 1875, six years after this picture was taken, silver mines honeycombed the hills of Nevada. National Archives.

the United States, compared to 25 percent in New York and 21 percent in Massachusetts.

Irish immigrants formed the largest ethnic group in the mining district. In Virginia City, fully one-third of the population claimed at least one parent from Ireland. Irish women constituted the largest group of women on the Comstock. As servants, boardinghouse owners, and washerwomen, they made up a significant part of the workforce. In contrast, the Chinese community, numbering 642 in 1870, remained overwhelmingly male. Virulent anti-Chinese sentiment barred the men from work in the mines, but despite this, the mining community came to depend on Chinese labor.

The discovery of precious metals on the Comstock spelled disaster for the Indians. No sooner had the miners struck pay dirt than they demanded that army troops "hunt Indians" and establish forts to protect transportation to and from the diggings. This sudden and dramatic intrusion left Nevada's native tribes—the Northern Paiute and Bannock Shoshoni—exiles in their own land. At first they resisted, but over time they adapted and preserved their culture and identity despite the havoc wreaked by western mining and settlement.

In 1873, Comstock miners uncovered a new vein of ore, a veritable cavern of gold and silver. This "Big Bonanza" speeded the transition from small-scale industry to corporate oligopoly, creating a radically new social and economic environment. The Comstock became a laboratory for new mining technology. Huge stamping mills pulverized rock with pistonlike hammers driven by steam engines. Enormous Cornish pumps sucked water from the mine shafts, and huge ventilators circulated air in the underground chambers. No backwoods mining camp, Virginia City was an industrial center with more than 1,200 stamping mills working on average a ton of ore every day. Almost 400 men worked in milling, nearly 300 labored in manufacturing industries, and roughly 3,000 toiled in the mines. The Gould and Curry mine covered sixty acres. Most of the miners who came to the Comstock ended up as laborers for the big companies.

New technology eliminated some of the dangers of mining but often created new ones. In the hard-rock mines of the West, accidents in the 1870s disabled one out of every thirty miners and killed one in eighty. Ross Moudy, who worked as a miner in Cripple Creek, Colorado, recalled how a stockholder visiting the mine nearly fell to his death. The terrified visitor told the miner next to him that "instead of being paid $3 a day, they ought to have all the gold they could take out." On the Comstock Lode, because of the difficulty of obtaining skilled labor, the richness of the ore, and the need for a stable workforce, labor unions formed early and held considerable bargaining power. Comstock miners commanded $4 a day, the highest wage in the mining West.

The mining towns of the "Wild West" are often portrayed as lawless outposts, filled with saloons and rough gambling dens and populated almost exclusively by men. The truth is more complex, as Virginia City's development attests. An established urban community built to serve an industrial giant, Virginia City in its first decade boasted churches, schools, theaters, an opera house, and hundreds of families. By 1870, women composed 30 percent of the population, and 75 percent of the women listed their occupation in the census as housekeeper. Mary McNair Mathews, a widow from Buffalo, New York, who lived on the Comstock in the 1870s, worked as a teacher, nurse, seamstress, laundress, and lodging-house operator. She later published a book on her adventures.

By 1875, Virginia City boasted a population of 25,000 people, making it one of the largest cities between St. Louis and San Francisco. The city, dubbed the "Queen of the Comstock," hosted American presidents as well as legions of lesser dignitaries. Virginia City represented, in the words of a recent chronicler, "the distilled essence of America's newly established course—urban, industrial, acquisitive, and materialistic, on the move, 'a living polyglot' of cultures that collided and converged."

The Diverse Peoples of the West

The West of the late nineteenth century was a polyglot place, as much so as the big cities of the East. The sheer number of peoples who mingled in the West produced a complex blend of racism and prejudice. One historian has noted, not entirely facetiously, that there were at least eight oppressed "races" in the West—Indians, Latinos, Chinese, Japanese, blacks, Mormons, strikers, and radicals.

African Americans who ventured out to the territories faced hostile settlers determined to keep the West "for whites only." In response, they formed all-black communities such as Nicodemas, Kansas. That settlement, founded by thirty black Kentuckians in 1877, grew to a community of seven hundred by 1880. Isolated and often separated by great distances, small black settlements grew up throughout the West, in Nevada, Utah, and the Pacific North-west, as well as in Kansas. Black soldiers who served in the West during the Indian wars often stayed on as settlers. Called buffalo soldiers because Native Americans thought their hair resembled that of the bison, these black troops numbered up to 25,000. In the face of discrimination, poor treatment, and harsh conditions, the buffalo soldiers served with distinction and boasted the lowest desertion rate in the army.

Hispanic peoples had lived in Texas and the Southwest since Juan de Oñate led pioneer settlers up the Rio Grande in 1598. Hispanics had occupied the Pacific coast since San Diego was founded in 1769. Overnight, they were reduced to a "minority" after the United States annexed Texas in 1845 and took land stretching to California after the Mexican-American War ended in 1848. At first, the Hispanic owners of large *ranchos* in California, New Mexico, and Texas greeted conquest as an economic opportunity. But racial prejudice soon ended their optimism.

Californios (Mexican residents of California), who had been granted American citizenship by the Treaty of Guadalupe Hidalgo (1848), faced discrimination by Anglos who sought to keep them out of California's mines and commerce. Whites illegally squatted on rancho land while protracted litigation over Spanish and Mexican land grants forced the Californios into court. Although the U.S. Supreme Court eventually validated most of their claims, it took so long— seventeen years on average—that many Californios sold their property to pay taxes and legal bills.

Swindles, trickery, and intimidation dispossessed scores of Californios. Many ended up segregated in urban barrios (neighborhoods) in their own homeland. Their percentage of California's population declined from 82 percent in 1850 to 19 percent in 1880 as Anglos migrated to the state. In New Mexico and Texas, Mexicans remained a majority of the population but became increasingly impoverished as Anglos dominated business and took the best jobs. Skirmishes between Hispanics and whites in northern New Mexico over the fencing of the open range lasted for decades. Groups of Hispanics with names such as *Las Manos Negras* (the Black Hands) cut fences and burned barns. In Texas, violence along the Rio Grande pitted Tejanos (Mexican residents of Texas) against the Texas Rangers, who saw their role as "keeping Mexicans in their place."

Mormons too, faced prejudice and hostility. The followers of Joseph Smith, the founder and prophet of the Church of Jesus Christ of Latter-Day Saints, fled west to Utah Territory in 1844 to avoid religious persecution. They believed they had a divine right to the land, and their messianic militancy made others distrust them. The Mormon practice of polygamy (church leader Brigham Young had twenty-seven wives) also came under attack. To counter the criticism of polygamy, the Utah territorial legislature gave women the right to vote in 1870, the first universal woman suffrage act in the nation. (Wyoming had granted suffrage to white women in 1869.) Although woman's rights advocates argued that the newly enfranchised women would "do away with the horrible institution of polygamy," it remained in force. Not until 1890 did the church hierarchy yield to pressure and renounce polygamy. The fierce controversy over polygamy postponed statehood for Utah until 1896.

The Chinese suffered the most brutal treatment of all the newcomers at the hands of employers and other laborers. Drawn by the promise of

VISUAL ACTIVITY

Mission Santa Clara

This 1880 painting of the Santa Clara Mission in California features a bucolic scene of farm labor that does not hint at the forced labor of Native Americans, who performed much of the manual labor at the missions. After the gold rush, when California became a state, the Jesuit order gained control of the mission and it became the University of Santa Clara, California's first college. The Granger Collection, New York.

READING THE IMAGE: What variety of peoples and occupations are portrayed in this image?
CONNECTIONS: How did American rule affect the life of Californios in the second half of the nineteenth century?

gold, more than 20,000 Chinese had joined the rush to California by 1852. Miners determined to keep "California for Americans" succeeded in passing prohibitive foreign license laws to keep the Chinese out of the mines. But Chinese immigration continued. In the 1860s, when white workers moved on to find riches in the bonanza mines of Nevada, Chinese laborers took jobs abandoned by the whites. Railroad magnate Charles Crocker hired Chinese gangs to work on the Central Pacific, reasoning that "the race that built the Great Wall" could lay tracks across the treacherous Sierra Nevada. Some 12,000 Chinese, representing 90 percent of Crocker's workforce, completed America's first transcontinental railroad in 1869.

By 1870, more than 63,000 Chinese immigrants lived in America, 77 percent of them in California. A 1790 federal statute that limited naturalization to "white persons" was modified after the Civil War to extend naturalization to blacks ("persons of African descent"). But the Chinese and other Asians continued to be denied access to citizenship. As perpetual aliens, they constituted a reserve army of transnational laborers that many saw as a threat to American labor.

In 1876, the Workingmen's Party formed to fight for Chinese exclusion. Racial and cultural animosities stood at the heart of anti-Chinese agitation. Denis Kearney, the fiery San Francisco leader of the movement, made clear this racist bent when he urged legislation to "expel every one of the moon-eyed lepers." Nor was California alone in its anti-immigrant nativism. As the country confronted growing ethnic and racial

Chinese Workers
Chinese section hands, wearing their distinctive conical hats, are shown here working on a railroad. Charles Crocker was the first to hire Chinese laborers to work on the Central Pacific railroad in the 1860s. Courtesy, California Historical Society, FN-25345.

diversity with the rising tide of global immigration in the decades following the Civil War, many questioned the principle of racial equality at the same time they argued against the assimilation of "nonwhite" groups. In this climate, Congress passed the **Chinese Exclusion Act** in 1882, effectively barring Chinese immigration and setting a precedent for further immigration restrictions.

The Chinese Exclusion Act led to a sharp drop in the Chinese population—from 105,465 in 1880 to 89,863 in 1900—because Chinese immigrants, overwhelmingly male, did not have families to sustain their population. Eventually, Japanese immigrants, including women as well as men, replaced the Chinese, particularly in agriculture. As "nonwhite" immigrants, they could not become naturalized citizens, but their children born in the United States claimed the rights of citizenship. Japanese parents, seeking to own land, purchased it in their children's names. Although anti-Asian prejudice remained strong in California and elsewhere in the West, Asian immigrants formed an important part of the economic fabric of the western United States.

> **REVIEW**   What role did mining play in shaping the society and economy of the American West?

► Land Fever

In the three decades following 1870, more land was settled than in all the previous history of the country. Americans by the hundreds of thousands packed up and moved west, goaded if not by the hope of striking gold, then by the promise of owning land to farm or ranch. The agrarian West shared with the mining West a persistent restlessness, an equally pervasive addiction to speculation, and a penchant for exploiting natural resources and labor.

Two factors stimulated the land rush in the trans-Mississippi West. The **Homestead Act of 1862** promised 160 acres free to any citizen or prospective citizen, male or female, who settled on the land for five years. Even more important, transcontinental railroads opened up new areas and actively recruited settlers. After the completion of the **first transcontinental railroad** in 1869, homesteaders abandoned the covered wagon, and by the 1880s, rampant railroad overbuilding meant that settlers could choose from four competing rail lines and make the trip west in a matter of days.

Although the country was rich in land and resources, not all who wanted to own land achieved their goal. During the transition from the family farm to large commercial farming,

small farms and ranches gave way to vast spreads worked by migrant labor or paid farmworkers and cowhands. Just as industry corporatized and consolidated in the East, the period from 1870 to 1900 witnessed corporate consolidation in mining, ranching, and agriculture.

Moving West: Homesteaders and Speculators

A Missouri homesteader remembered packing as her family pulled up stakes and headed west to Oklahoma in 1890. "We were going to God's Country," she wrote. "You had to work hard on that rocky country in Missouri. I was glad to be leaving it. . . . We were going to a new land and get rich."

Settlers who headed west in search of "God's Country" faced hardship, loneliness, and deprivation. To carve a farm from the raw prairie of Iowa, the plains of Nebraska, or the forests of the Pacific Northwest took more than fortitude and backbreaking toil. It took luck. Blizzards, tornadoes, grasshoppers, hailstorms, drought,

Young Women Homesteaders and the Promise of the West

The Homestead Act of 1862 allowed unmarried women and female heads of households to claim free land in the West, and many did. The number of women establishing homesteads in the West ranged from 5 percent of homesteaders in the early settlements to more than 20 percent after 1900.

Many women homesteaders were young. In the Dakotas, women between the ages of twenty-one and twenty-five constituted the largest percentage of women (53 percent) taking up claims.

Like Christine Sonnek, who took her mandolin along with her rifle, homesteading women prepared to enjoy their new environment despite its challenges. Their letters, diaries, and reminiscences reveal not only the hardships they faced but also the sense of promise that lured them west. Adventurous, resourceful, and exuberant, many of these young homesteading women seemed to relish their experiences.

DOCUMENT 1
The Varied Activities of a Woman Homesteader

Dakota homesteader Bess Cobb's letter to a friend reveals the optimism and high spirits that energized the young women who filed homesteading claims.

Suppose you girls are saying "poor Bess" and feeling dreadfully sorry for me out here in the wild and wooly uncivilized regions of America. But really time just seems to fly. You can see a team miles away—up one valley we can see ten miles, up to the Cannon Ball river—so when any one starts to our shack, if we see them in time we can comb our hair, change our gowns and get a good meal in running order before they arrive. You see Dakota has some redeeming qualities. Wish you could come out, but I suppose you think I am too far away. I have the neatest little shack I've ever seen and "my crops" are tip top. I know you would enjoy our camp life for a short time.

Source: "Excerpts from a letter written by Bess Cobb, Guide to Manuscripts 1364, State Historical Society, North Dakota Heritage Center, Bismarck," from pages 140–41 in *Land in Her Own Name:*

Women as Homesteaders in North Dakota by H. Elaine Lindgren. Copyright © 1996. Reprinted with permission of University of Oklahoma Press.

DOCUMENT 2
A Hard Winter

Lucy Goldthorpe, a young schoolteacher, came from Iowa to Dakota in 1905. Here she describes to a reporter her survival during the winter and contrasts her childhood fantasies with homestead reality.

There were many long, cold days and nights in my little homestead shack that winter!

Regardless of what I did the cold crept in through the thin walls. With no storm entry at the door and only single windows my little two-lid laundry stove with oven attached to the pipe had a real struggle to keep the place livable. . . .

A neighbor family returning to their claim "from the outside" brought me fresh vegetables. They were such a prized addition to my meals that I put the bag in bed with me at night to keep them from freezing. Night after night

prairie fires, accidental death, and disease were only a few of the catastrophes that could befall even the best farmer. Homesteaders on free land still needed as much as $1,000 for a house, a team of farm animals, a well, fencing, and seed. Poor farmers called "sodbusters" did without even these basics, living in houses made from sod (blocks of grass-covered earth) or dugouts carved into hillsides and using muscle instead of machinery.

"Father made a dugout and covered it with willows and grass," one Kansas girl recounted.

I stored food and my little alarm clock in the stove pipe oven; that was the only way I could keep the clock running and be sure of a non-frozen breakfast.

As a child I had enjoyed hearing my father tell of the hardships of the early days. They seemed so exciting to me as I listened in the warmth and security of our well built, fully winterized Iowa home. Like most youngsters I'd wished for the thrill of those other days. Little did I think that an opportunity for just that would come through homesteading alone, far out in the windswept, unsettled land. Believe me, it wasn't nearly as glamorous as the imagination would have it!

Source: Roberta M. Starry, "Petticoat Pioneer." Excerpt from page 48 in *The West* 7, no. 5, October 1967. Copyright © 1967. Reprinted with permission.

DOCUMENT 3
Socializing and Entertainment

Homesteading wasn't all hard times. Young, single homesteaders found time for fun. Here Effie Vivian Smith describes a "shack party" during the winter of 1906 on her Dakota claim.

I never enjoyed myself better in my life than I have this winter. We go some place or some one is here from 1 to 4 times a week. A week ago last Fri. a load of 7 drove out to my claim. Cliff, Clara, David, and I had gone out the Wed. before and such a time as we had. My shack is 10 feet 3 inches by 16 feet and I have only 2 chairs and a long bench for seats, a table large enough for 6, a single bed, and only 3 knives so 2 of them ate with paring knives & 1 with the butcher knife. We had two of them sit on the bed and moved the table up to them. . . . We played all the games we could think of both quiet and noisy and once all but Clara went out & snowballed. They brought a bu[shel] of apples, & a lot of nuts, candy, & gum & we ate all night. . . .

We have just started a literary society in our neighborhood. Had our first debate last Fri. The question was Resolved that city life is better than country life. All the judges decided in the negative. . . . Tomorrow our crowd is going to a literary [society] 6 or 7 miles from here, and the next night to a dance at the home of one of our bachelor boys. We always all go in our sleigh. I am learning to dance this winter but don't attend any except the ones we get up ourselves and they are just as nice & just as respectable as the parties we used to have at Ruthven [Iowa]. I just love to dance. . . .

Source: H. Elaine Lindgren, "Letter to her cousin, written on January 9, 1906." From pages 177–78 in *Land in Her Own Name: Women as Homesteaders in North Dakota*. Copyright © 1996 University of Oklahoma Press. Reprinted with permission.

DOCUMENT 4
Homesteading Pays Off

Homesteading proved rewarding for many women, not only economically but also because of the sense of accomplishment they experienced. Here Theona Carkin tells how the sale of her Dakota homestead helped finance her university degree.

Life in general was dotted with hardships but there were many good times also. I have always felt that my efforts on my homestead were very worthwhile and very rewarding, and I have always been proud of myself for doing it all.

By teaching off and on . . . and upon selling the homestead, I was able to pay all my own college expenses.

Source: "99-Year-Old U Graduate Recalls Early Childhood." From page 5 in *Alumni Review*, June 1985. Published by the University of North Dakota, Grand Forks.

Questions for Analysis and Debate

1. What sorts of hardships did the young women homesteaders encounter in the Dakotas?

2. How did their youth affect how they reacted to hardship?

3. What did the young women find particularly appealing about their experiences as homesteaders?

4. How did homesteading benefit women who chose not to remain on the land?

Connect to the Big Idea

Ⓒ What industrial developments encouraged settlement of the West?

When it rained, the dugout flooded, and "we carried the water out in buckets, then waded around in the mud until it dried." Rain wasn't the only problem. "Sometimes the bull snakes would get in the roof and now and then one would lose his hold and fall down on the bed. . . . Mother would grab the hoe . . . and after the fight was over Mr. Bull Snake was dragged outside."

For women on the frontier, obtaining simple daily necessities such as water and fuel meant backbreaking labor. Out on the plains, where water was scarce, women often had to trudge to the nearest creek or spring. "A yoke was made to place across [Mother's] shoulders, so as to carry at each end a bucket of water," one daughter recollected, "and then water was brought a half mile from spring to house." Gathering fuel was another heavy chore. Without ready sources of coal or firewood, the most prevalent fuel was "chips"—chunks of dried cattle and buffalo dung, found in abundance on the plains. (See "Documenting the American Promise," page 484.)

Despite the hardships, some homesteaders succeeded in building comfortable lives. The dugout made way for the sod hut—a more substantial dwelling; the log cabin yielded to a white clapboard home with a porch and a rocking chair. For others, the promise of the West failed to materialize. Already by the 1870s, much of the best land had been taken. Too often, homesteaders found that only the least desirable tracts were left—poor land, far from markets, transportation, and society. "There is plenty of land for sale in California," one migrant complained in 1870, but "the majority of the available lands are held by speculators, at prices far beyond the reach of a poor man." The railroads, flush from land grants provided by the state and federal governments, owned huge swaths of land in the West and actively recruited buyers. Altogether, the land grants totaled approximately 180 million acres—an area almost one-tenth the size of the United States (Map 17.3). Of the 2.5 million farms establish-ed between 1860 and 1900, homesteading accounted for only one in five; the vast majority of farmland sold for a profit.

As land grew scarce on the prairie in the 1870s, farmers began to push farther west, moving into western Kansas, Nebraska, and eastern Colorado—the region called the Great American Desert by settlers who had passed over it on their way to California and Oregon. Many agricultural experts warned that the semiarid land (where less than twenty inches of rain fell annually) would not support a farm

Midwestern Settlement Before 1862

on the 160 acres allotted to homesteaders. But their words of caution were drowned out by the extravagant claims of western promoters, many employed by the railroads to sell off land grants. "Rain follows the plow" became the slogan of western boosters, who insisted that cultivation would alter the climate of the region and bring more rainfall. Instead, drought followed the plow. Droughts were a cyclical fact of life on the Great Plains. Plowed up, the dry topsoil blew away in the wind. A period of relatively good rainfall in the early 1880s encouraged farming; then a protracted drought in the late 1880s and early 1890s forced thousands of starving farmers to leave, some in wagons carrying the slogan "In God we trusted, in Kansas we busted."

Fever for fertile land set off a series of spectacular land runs in Oklahoma. When two million acres of land in former Indian Territory opened for settlement in 1889, thousands of homesteaders massed on the border. At the opening pistol shot, "with a shout and a yell the swift riders shot out, then followed the light buggies or wagons," a reporter wrote. "Above all, a great cloud of dust hover[ed] like smoke over a battlefield." By nightfall, Oklahoma boasted two tent cities with more than ten thousand residents. In the last frenzied land rush on Oklahoma's Cherokee strip in 1893, several settlers were killed in the stampede, and nervous men guarded their claims with rifles. As public land grew scarce, the hunger for land grew fiercer for both farmers and ranchers.

Ranchers and Cowboys

Cattle ranchers followed the railroads onto the plains, establishing a cattle kingdom from Texas to Wyoming between 1865 and 1885. Cowboys drove huge herds, as many as three thousand head of cattle that grazed on public lands as they followed cattle tracks like the Chisholm Trail from Texas to railheads in Kansas.

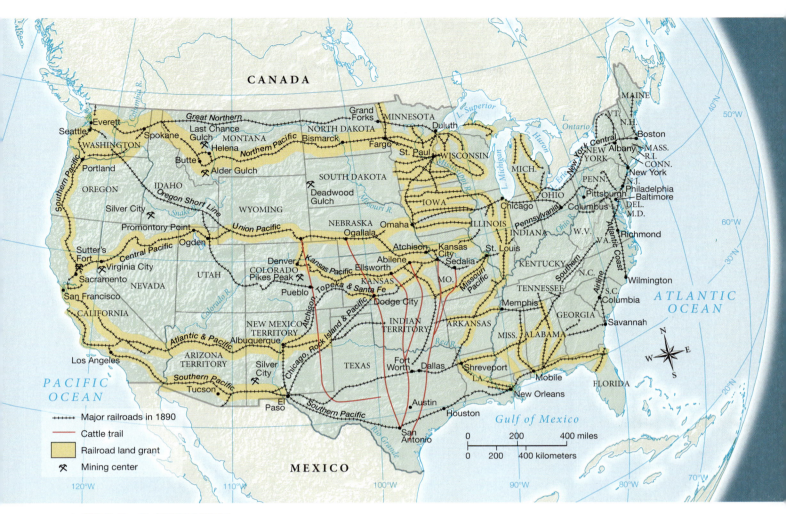

MAP ACTIVITY

Map 17.3 Federal Land Grants to Railroads and the Development of the West, 1850–1900
Railroads received more than 180 million acres, an area as large as Texas. Built well ahead of demand, the western railroads courted settlers, often onto land not fit for farming.

READING THE MAP: Which mining cities and towns were located directly on railroad lines? Which towns were located at the junction of more than one railroad line or branch?

CONNECTIONS: In what ways did the growth of the railroads affect the population of the West? What western goods and products did the railroads help bring east and to ports for shipping around the world?

Barbed wire, invented in 1874, revolutionized the cattle business and sounded the death knell for the open range. As the largest ranches in Texas began to fence, nasty fights broke out between big ranchers and "fence cutters," who resented the end of the open range. One old-timer observed, "Those persons, Mexicans and Americans, without land but who had cattle were put out of business by fencing." Fencing forced small-time ranchers who owned land but could not afford to buy barbed wire or sink wells to sell out for the best price they could get. The displaced ranchers, many of them Mexicans, ended up as wageworkers on the huge spreads owned by Anglos or by European syndicates.

On the range, the cowboy gave way to the cattle king and, like the miner, became a wage laborer. Many cowboys were African Americans (as many as five thousand in Texas alone). Writers of western literature chose to ignore the presence of black cowboys like Deadwood Dick (Nat Love), who was portrayed as a white man in the dime novels of the era.

By 1886, cattle overcrowded the range. Severe blizzards during the winter of 1886–87 decimated the herds. "A whole generation of cowmen," wrote one chronicler, "went dead broke." Fencing worsened the situation. During blizzards, cattle stayed alive by keeping on the move. But when they ran up against barbed wire fences, they froze to death. In the aftermath of the "Great Die Up," new labor-intensive forms of cattle ranching replaced the open-range model.

Tenants, Sharecroppers, and Migrants

In the post-Civil War period, as agriculture became a big business tied by the railroads to national and global markets, an increasing number of laborers worked land that they would never own. In the southern United States, farmers labored under particularly heavy burdens. The Civil War wiped out much of the region's capital, which had been invested in slaves, and crippled the plantation economy. "The colored folks stayed with the old boss man and farmed and worked on the plantations," a black Alabama sharecropper observed bitterly. "They were still slaves, but they were free slaves." Some freed people did manage to pull together enough resources to go west. In 1879, more than fifteen thousand black Exodusters, as the black settlers were known, moved from Mississippi and Louisiana to take up land in Kansas.

California's Mexican cowboys, or *vaqueros*, commanded decent wages throughout the Southwest. But by 1880, as the coming of the railroads ended the long cattle drives and as large feedlots began to replace the open range, the value of their skills declined. Many vaqueros ended up as migrant laborers, often on land their families had once owned. Similarly, in Texas, Tejanos found themselves displaced. After the heyday of cattle ranching ended in the late 1880s, cotton production rose in the southeastern regions of the state. Ranchers turned their pastures into sharecroppers' plots and hired displaced cowboys, most of them Mexicans, as seasonal laborers for as little as seventy-five cents a day, thereby creating a growing army of agricultural wageworkers.

Land monopoly and large-scale farming fostered tenancy and migratory labor on the West Coast. By the 1870s, less than 1 percent

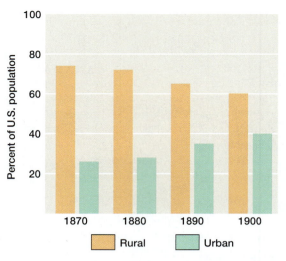

FIGURE 17.1   **Changes in Rural and Urban Populations, 1870–1900**
Between 1870 and 1900, both the number of urban dwellers and the number of farms increased, even as the number of rural inhabitants fell. Mechanization made it possible to farm with fewer hands, fueling the exodus from farm to city throughout the second half of the nineteenth century.

of California's population owned half the state's available agricultural land. The rigid economics of large-scale commercial agriculture and the seasonal nature of the crops spawned a ragged army of migratory agricultural laborers. Derisively labeled "blanket men" or "bindle stiffs," these transients worked the fields in the growing season and wintered in the flophouses of San Francisco. After passage of the Chinese Exclusion Act of 1882, Mexicans, Filipinos, and Japanese immigrants filled the demand for migratory workers.

Commercial Farming and Industrial Cowboys

In the late nineteenth century, the population of the United States remained overwhelmingly rural. The 1870 census showed that nearly 80 percent of the nation's people lived on farms and in villages of fewer than 8,000 inhabitants. By 1900, the figure had dropped to 66 percent (Figure 17.1). At the same time, the number of farms rose. Rapid growth in the West increased the number of farms from 2 million in 1860 to more than 5.7 million in 1900.

New technology and farming techniques revolutionized American farm life. Mechanized farm machinery halved the time and labor cost of production and made it possible to cultivate vast tracts of land. Meanwhile, urbanization provided farmers with expanding markets for their produce, and railroads carried crops to markets thousands of miles away. Even before the start of the twentieth century, American agriculture had entered the era of what would come to be called agribusiness—farming as a big business—with the advent of huge commercial farms.

As farming moved onto the prairies and plains, mechanization took command. Steel plows, reapers, mowers, harrows, seed drills, combines, and threshers replaced human muscle. Horse-drawn implements gave way to steam-powered machinery. By 1880, a single combine could do the work of twenty men, vastly increasing the acreage a farmer could cultivate. Mechanization spurred the growth of bonanza wheat farms, some more than 100,000 acres, in California and the Red River Valley of North Dakota and Minnesota. This agricultural revolution meant that Americans raised more than four times the corn, five times the hay, and seven times the wheat and oats they had before the Civil War.

Like cotton farmers in the South, western grain and livestock farmers increasingly depended on foreign markets for their livelihood. A fall in global market prices meant that a farmer's entire harvest went to pay off debts. In the depression that followed the panic of 1893, many heavily mortgaged farmers lost their land to creditors. As a Texas cotton farmer complained, "By the time the World Gets their Liveing out of the Farmer as we have to Feed the World, we the Farmer has nothing Left but a Bear Hard Liveing." Commercial farming, along with mining, represented another way in which the West developed its own brand of industrialism. The far West's industrial economy

Loggers in Washington, 1890
Loggers like these posed with a huge felled tree worked in all-male crews with a "faller" cutting down the tree, "buckers" cutting it into manageable pieces, and "whistle punks" relaying information. Logging brought massive deforestation, which continued and picked up speed as steam power replaced brawn and horsepower. Loggers lived hard, dirty lives in remote migratory camps, working long hours. ©CORBIS.

sprang initially from California gold and the vast territory that came under American control following the Mexican-American War. In the ensuing rush on land and resources, environmental factors interacted with economic and social forces to produce enterprises as vast in scale and scope as anything found in the East.

Two German immigrants, Henry Miller and Charles Lux, pioneered the West's mix of agriculture and industrialism. Beginning as meat wholesalers, Miller and Lux quickly expanded their business to encompass cattle, land, and land reclamation projects such as dams and irrigation systems. With a labor force of migrant workers, a highly coordinated corporate system, and large sums of investment capital, the firm of Miller & Lux became one of America's industrial behemoths. Eventually, these "industrial cowboys" grazed a herd of 100,000 cattle on 1.25 million acres of company land in California, Oregon, and Nevada and employed more than 1,200 migrant laborers on their corporate ranches. Miller & Lux dealt with the labor problem by offering free meals to migratory workers, thus keeping wages low while winning goodwill among an army of unemployed who competed for the work. When the company's Chinese cooks rebelled at washing all the dishes, the migrant laborers were forced to eat off dirty plates. By the 1890s, more than 800 migrants a year followed what came to be known as the "Dirty Plate Route" on Miller & Lux ranches throughout California.

Since the days of Thomas Jefferson, agrarian life had been linked with the highest ideals of a democratic society. Agrarianism had been transformed. The farmer was no longer a self-sufficient yeoman but often a businessman or a wage laborer tied to a global market. And even as farm production soared, industrialization outstripped it. More and more farmers left the fields for urban factories or found work in the "factories in the fields" of the new industrialized agribusinesses. Now that the future seemed to lie not with small farmers but with industrial enterprises, was democracy itself at risk? This question would ignite a farmers' revolt in the 1880s and dominate political debate in the 1890s.

Territorial Government

The federal government practiced a policy of benign neglect when it came to territorial government. A governor, a secretary, a few judges, an attorney, and a marshal held jurisdiction. In Nevada Territory, that meant a handful of officials governed an area the size of New England. Originally a part of the larger Utah Territory, Nevada, propelled by mining interests, moved on the fast tract to statehood, entering the Union in 1864.

More typical were the territories extant in 1870—New Mexico, Utah, Washington, Colorado, Dakota, Arizona, Idaho, Montana, and Wyoming. These areas remained territories for inordinately long periods ranging from twenty-three to sixty-two years. While awaiting statehood, they were subject to territorial governors, who won their posts due to party loyalty and who were largely underpaid, uninformed, often unqualified, and largely ignored by Washington. Wages rarely arrived on schedule, leading one cynic to observe, "Only the rich or those having 'no visible means of support,'" can afford to accept office." John C. Frémont, governor of Arizona Territory, complained he could not inspect the Grand Canyon because he was too poor to own a horse.

Western governors with fewer scruples accepted money from local interests—mine owners and big ranchers or lumber companies. Nearly all territorial appointees tried to maintain business connections in the East or take advantage of speculative opportunities in the West. Corruption ran rampant. Yet the distance from the nation's capital meant that few charges of corrupt dealings went investigated. Gun-toting Westerners served as another deterrent. One judge sent to New Mexico Territory in 1871 to investigate fraud "stayed three days, made up his mind that it would be dangerous to do any investigating, . . . and returned to his home without action."

Underfunded and overlooked victims of cronyism and prey to special interests, territorial governments mirrored the self-serving political and economic values of the era.

REVIEW   How did the fight for land and resources unfold in the West?

▶ Conclusion: The West in the Gilded Age

In 1871, author Mark Twain published *Roughing It*, a chronicle of his days spent in mining towns in California and Nevada. There he found the same corrupt politics, vulgar display, and mania for speculation that he later skewered in *The*

Gilded Age (1873), his biting satire of greed and corruption in the nation's capital. Far from being an antidote to the tawdry values of the East—an innocent idyll out of place and time—The American West, with its get-rich-quick ethos, addiction to gambling and speculation, and virulent racism, helped set the tone for the Gilded Age.

Twain's view countered that of Frederick Jackson Turner and perhaps better suited a West that witnessed the reckless overbuilding of railroads; the consolidation of business in mining and ranching; the rise of commercial farming; corruption and a penchant for government handouts; racial animosity; the exploitation of labor and natural resources, which led to the decimation of the great bison herds, the pollution of rivers with mining wastes, and the overgrazing of the plains; and the beginnings of an imperial policy that would provide a template for U.S. adventures abroad. Turner, intent on promoting what was unique about the frontier, failed to note that the same issues that came to dominate debate east of the Mississippi—the growing power of big business, the exploitation of land and labor, corruption in politics, and ethnic and racial tensions exacerbated by colonial expansion and unparalleled immigration—took center stage in the West at the end of the nineteenth century.

See the Selected Bibliography for this chapter in the Appendix.

17 Chapter Review

MAKE IT STICK

 **LearningCurve**

Go online and use LearningCurve to see what you know. Then review the key terms and answer the questions.

KEY TERMS

reservations (p. 464)
Comanchería (p. 470)
Black Hills (p. 470)
Battle of the Little Big Horn (p. 471)
Carlisle Indian School (p. 473)
Dawes Allotment Act (p. 474)
Ghost Dance (p. 476)
Wounded Knee (p. 477)
Comstock Lode (p. 477)
Chinese Exclusion Act (p. 482)
Homestead Act of 1862 (p. 482)
first transcontinental railroad (p. 482)

REVIEW QUESTIONS

1. How did the slaughter of the bison contribute to the Plains Indians' removal to reservations? (pp. 466–471)

2. In what ways did different Indian groups defy and resist colonial rule? (pp. 471–477)

3. What role did mining play in shaping the society and economy of the American West? (pp. 477–482)

4. How did the fight for land and resources unfold in the West? (pp. 482–490)

MAKING CONNECTIONS

1. Westward migration brought settlers into conflict with Native Americans. What was the U.S. government's policy toward Indians in the West, and how did it evolve over time?

2. How did innovations in business and technology transform mining and agriculture in the West?

3. In competition for work and land in the American West, why did Anglo-American settlers usually have the upper hand over settlers from other countries? How did legal developments contribute to this circumstance?

4. What role did railroads play in western settlement, industrialization, and agriculture? How did railroads affect Indian populations in the West?

LINKING TO THE PAST

1. In what ways were the goals of migrants to the West similar to those of the Northerners who moved to the South after the Civil War? How did they differ? (See chapter 16.)

2. How did the racism of the West compare with the racist attitudes against African Americans in the Reconstruction South? (See chapter 16.)

Railroads, Business, and Politics in the Gilded Age

1865–1900

ONE NIGHT OVER DINNER, MARK TWAIN AND CHARLES Dudley Warner teased their wives about the sentimental novels they read. When the two women challenged them to write something better, they set to work. Warner supplied the melodrama while Twain "hurled in the facts." The result, *The Gilded Age* (1873), was a runaway best seller, a savage satire of the "get-rich-quick" era that would forever carry the book's title.

Twain left no one unscathed in the novel—political hacks, Washington lobbyists, Wall Street financiers, small-town boosters, and the "great putty-hearted public." Underneath the glitter of the Gilded Age lurked vulgarity, crass materialism, and political corruption. In Twain's satire, Congress is for sale to the highest bidder:

Why the matter is simple enough. A Congressional appropriation costs money. . . . A majority of the House Committee, say $10,000 apiece—$40,000; a majority of the Senate Committee, the same each—say $40,000; a little extra to one or two chairmen of one or two such committees, say $10,000 each—$20,000; and there's $100,000 of the money gone, to begin with. Then, seven male lobbyists, at $3,000 each—$21,000; one female lobbyist, $3,000; a high moral Congressman or Senator here and there—the high moral ones cost more, because they give tone

CAMPAIGN PINS
Presidential campaign pins from 1884 depict James G. Blaine thumbing his nose at rival Grover Cleveland. The gilt pins symbolize the lavish wealth and corruption and political strife of the Gilded Age.
© David J. & Janice L. Frent Collection/CORBIS.

to a measure—say ten of these at $3,000 each, is $30,000; then a lot of small fry country members who won't vote for anything whatever without pay—say twenty at $500 apiece, is $10,000 altogether; lot of jimcracks for Congressmen's wives and children . . . well, those things cost in a lump, say $10,000 . . . and then comes your printed documents. . . . [W]ell, never mind the details, the total in clean numbers foots up $118,254.42 thus far!

The Gilded Age seemed to tarnished many who lived under its reign. No one knew that better than Twain, who, even as he attacked it as an "era of incredible rottenness," fell prey to its enticements. Born Samuel Langhorne Clemens, he grew up in a rough Mississippi River town, where he became a riverboat pilot. Taking the pen name Mark Twain, he wrote and played to packed houses as an itinerant humorist. But his work was judged too vulgar for the genteel tastes of the time. Boston banned his masterpiece, *The Adventures of Huckleberry Finn*, when it appeared in 1884. Huck Finn's creator eventually stormed the citadels of polite society and hobnobbed with the wealthy. Succumbing to the money fever of his age, he plunged into a scheme in the hope of making millions. By the 1890s, he faced bankruptcy. Twain's tale was common in an age when the promise of wealth led as many to ruin as to riches. Wall Street panics in 1873 and 1893 both plunged the country into depression.

The rush to build railroads and other industries and the corrupt interplay of business and politics strike the key themes in the Gilded Age. The runaway growth of the railroads and the surge in new inventions and technologies like electricity, the telephone, and the telegraph encouraged the rise of big business and led to an age of industrial capitalism.

Such rapid growth had alarming social and political implications. Economic issues increasingly shaped party politics. Social Darwinism, with its insistence on the "survival of the fittest," supported the power of the wealthy, while the poor and middle classes championed antimonopoly measures to restore competition, currency reform to ease debt, and civil service to end corruption. As always, race, class, and gender influenced politics and policy.

The hopes and fears of the Gilded Age were most evident in the public's attitude toward the business moguls of the day. Men like Jay Gould, Andrew Carnegie, and John D. Rockefeller sparked the popular imagination as the heroes and villains of industrialization. And as concern grew over the power of big business and the growing chasm between rich and poor, many Americans, women as well as men, looked to the government for solutions.

▶ Railroads and the Rise of New Industries

In the years following the Civil War, the American economy underwent a transformation. Where once wealth had been measured in tangible assets—property, livestock, buildings—the economy now ran on money and the new devices of business—paper currency, securities, and anonymous corporate entities. Wall Street, the heart of the country's financial system, increasingly affected Main Street. Driving the transition was the building of a transcontinental railroad system, which radically altered the scale and scope of American industry. Old industries like iron transformed into modern industries such as the behemoth U.S. Steel. Discovery and invention stimulated new industries, from oil refining to electric light and power. The overbuilding of the railroad in the decades after the Civil War played the key role in transforming the American economy as business came to rely on huge government subsidies, "friends" in Congress, and complicated financial transactions.

Jay Gould in railroads, Andrew Carnegie in steel, and John D. Rockefeller in oil pioneered new strategies to seize markets and consolidate power. Always with an eye to the main chance, these tycoons set the tone in the get-rich-quick era of freewheeling capitalism that came to be called the **Gilded Age**.

Railroads: America's First Big Business

The military conquest of America's inland empire and the dispossession of Native Americans (see chapter 17) was fed by an elaborate new railroad system in the West built on speculation and government giveaways. Between 1870 and 1880, the amount of track in the country doubled, and it nearly doubled again in the following decade. By 1900, the nation boasted more than 193,000 miles of railroad track—more than in all of Europe and Russia combined (Map 18.1). The railroads had become America's first big business. Credit fueled the railroad boom. Privately owned but publicly financed, and subsidized by enormous land grants from the federal government and the states, the railroads epitomized the insidious nexus of business and politics in the Gilded Age.

CHRONOLOGY

1869	• Completion of first transcontinental railroad. • National Woman Suffrage Association founded.
1870	• John D. Rockefeller incorporates Standard Oil Company.
1872	• Andrew Carnegie builds world's largest steel plant.
1873	• Wall Street panic leads to major economic depression.
1874	• Woman's Christian Temperance Union (WCTU) founded.
1876	• Alexander Graham Bell demonstrates telephone.
1877	• Rutherford B. Hayes sworn in as president. • *Munn v. Illinois.*
1880	• James A. Garfield elected president.
1881	• Garfield assassinated; Vice President Chester A. Arthur becomes president.
1882	• John D. Rockefeller develops the trust.
1883	• Pendleton Civil Service Act.
1884	• Grover Cleveland elected president.
1886	• *Wabash v. Illinois.*
1887	• Interstate Commerce Act.
1888	• Benjamin Harrison elected president.
1890	• McKinley tariff. • General Federation of Women's Clubs • Sherman Antitrust Act.
1892	• Ida B. Wells launches antilynching campaign.
1893	• Wall Street panic touches off national depression.
1895	• J. P. Morgan bails out U.S. Treasury.
1901	• U.S. Steel incorporated and capitalized at $1.4 billion.

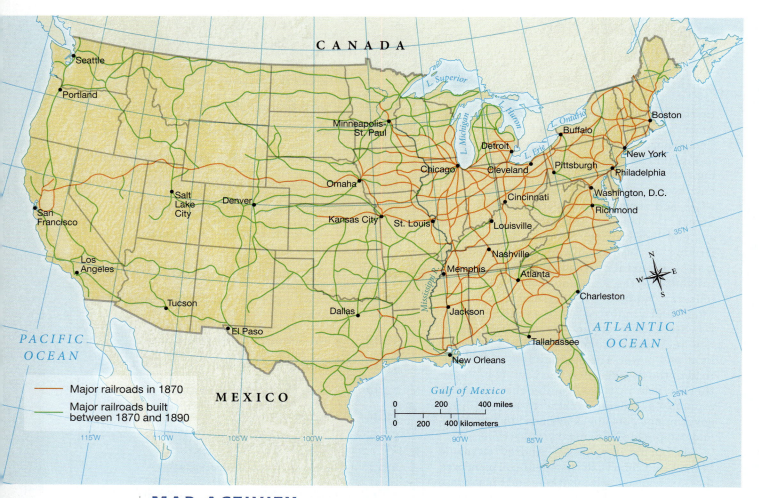

MAP ACTIVITY

Map 18.1   Railroad Expansion, 1870–1890
Railroad mileage nearly quadrupled between 1870 and 1890, with the greatest growth occurring in the trans-Mississippi West. The western lines were completed in the 1880s. Fueled by speculation and built ahead of demand, the western railroads made fortunes for individual speculators. But they rarely paid for themselves and speeded the demise of Native Americans.

READING THE MAP: Where were most of the railroad lines located in 1870? By 1890, how many railroads reached the west coast? What was the end point of the only western route?
CONNECTIONS: Why were so many rails laid between 1870 and 1890? How did the railroads affect the nation's economy?

To understand how the railroads came to dominate American life, there is no better place to start than with the career of Jay Gould, the era's most notorious speculator. Jason "Jay" Gould bought his first railroad before he turned twenty-five. It was only sixty-two miles long, in bad repair, and on the brink of failure, but within two years he sold it at a profit of $130,000.

The secretive Gould operated in the stock market like a shark, looking for vulnerable railroads, buying enough stock to take control, and threatening to undercut his competitors until they bought him out at a high profit. The railroads that fell into his hands often went bankrupt. Gould's genius lay not in providing transportation, but in cleverly buying and selling railroad stock on Wall Street. Gould soon realized that a corporate failure could still mean financial success. His strategy of expansion and consolidation encouraged overbuilding even as it stimulated a new national market.

The first transcontinental railway had been completed in 1869 at Promontory Point, Utah. In the 1880s, Gould moved to put together a

JUSTICE IN THE WEB.

VISUAL ACTIVITY

Jay Gould as a Spider

In this 1885 political cartoon titled "Justice in the Web," artist Frederick Burr Opper portrays Jay Gould as a hideous spider whose web, formed by Western Union telegraph lines, has entrapped "Justice" through its monopoly of the telegraph industry. Gould made his fortune through speculation on railroads, which often ran with telegraph lines alongside the tracks. Images like this one fueled the public's hatred of Gould. The Granger Collection, New York.

READING THE IMAGE: By portraying Gould as a spider, what is the cartoonist trying to say about him?

CONNECTIONS: In what ways did wealthy industrialists use manipulative techniques for personal gain?

second transcontinental railroad. To defend their interests, his competitors had little choice but to adopt his strategy of expansion. The railroads built ahead of demand, regardless of the social and environmental costs. Soon more railroads trailed into the West—by 1893, Kansas alone had at least six competing lines.

The railroad moguls put up little of their own money to build the roads and instead relied on the largesse of government and the sale of railroad bonds and stock. Bondholders were creditors who required repayment at a specific time. Stockholders bought a share in the company and received dividends if the company prospered. Thus, railroad moguls received money from these sales of financial interests but did not need to pay out until later. If the railroad failed, a receiver was appointed to determine how many pennies on the dollars shareholders would receive. The owners, astutely using the market, came out ahead. Novelist Charles Dudley Warner described how wrecking a railroad could yield profits:

> [They fasten upon] some railway that is prosperous, and has a surplus. They contrive to buy. . . . a controlling interest in it. . . . Then they absorb its surplus; they let it run down so that it pays no dividends, and by-and-by cannot even pay its interest; then they squeeze the bondholders, who may be glad to accept anything that is offered out of the wreck, and perhaps they throw the property into the hands of a receiver, or consolidate it with some other road at

a value far greater than it cost them in stealing it. Having one way or another sucked it dry, they look around for another road.

With help from railroad growth and speculation, the New York Stock Exchange expanded. The volume of stock increased sixfold between 1869 and 1901. The line between investment and speculation blurred, causing many Americans to question whether the manipulation of speculators fueled the boom and bust cycles that led to panic and depression in 1873 and again twenty years later. The dramatic growth of the railroads created the country's first big business. Before the Civil War, even the largest textile mill in New England employed no more than 800 workers. By contrast, the Pennsylvania Railroad by the 1870s boasted a payroll of more than 55,000 workers. Capitalized at more than $400 million, the Pennsylvania Railroad constituted the largest private enterprise in the world.

The big business of railroads bestowed enormous riches on a handful of tycoons. Both Gould and his competitor "Commodore" Cornelius Vanderbilt amassed fortunes estimated at $100 million. Such staggering wealth eclipsed the power and influence of upper-class Americans from previous generations and created an abyss between the nation's rich and poor. In its wake it left a legacy of lavish spending for an elite crop of ultra-rich heirs. (See "Visualizing History," page 498.)

Alva Vanderbilt and the Gilded Age

Nothing represented the Gilded Age better than the Gold Room of Marble House, the "cottage" Alva Vanderbilt opened in Newport, Rhode Island, in 1892. William K. Vanderbilt, Alva's husband, was the grandson of Cornelius Vanderbilt, the founder of the New York Central Railway and the richest man of his era. His sons doubled his wealth, and his grandsons spent it lavishly. Alva, who modeled Marble House after Marie Antoinette's retreat Petit Trianon at the palace of Versailles, liked to describe her architectural triumph as "Versailles improved."

The Gold Room, Alva's miniature version of Versailles's Hall of Mirrors, is a riot of neoclassical exuberance, with panels of Greek gods and goddesses adorning the walls and cavorting cupids and cherubs blowing trumpets on the walls and ceilings. The enormous chandeliers and wood panels painted in red, green, and gold are multiplied in their dazzling glory in the mirrors hung over each of the four doors, above the mantelpiece, and on the south wall. The Vanderbilt wealth and Alva's lavish spending made it hard for old-money New Yorkers, living in their staid brownstones, to compete. Alva and William's Fifth Avenue mansion in New York

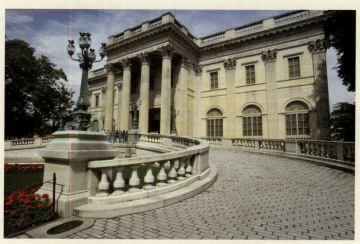

Marble House: The Vanderbilt Mansion in Newport, Rhode Island

The Gold Room in Marble House

The Republican Party, firmly entrenched in Washington after the Civil War, worked closely with business interests, subsidizing the transcontinental railroad system. Significant amounts of money changed hands to move bills through Congress. Along with "friends," often on the railroads' payrolls, lobbyists worked to craft legislation favorable to railroad interests. Friends of the railroads in state legislatures and Congress lavished the new Western roads with land grants of a staggering 100 million acres (mostly owned by the Indians) and $64 million in tax incentives and direct aid. States and local communities joined the railroad boom, betting that only those towns and villages along the tracks would grow and flourish. A revolution in communication accompanied and supported the growth of the railroads. The telegraph, developed by Samuel F. B. Morse, marched across the continent alongside the railroad.

City boasted a ballroom that accommodated 1,600 guests. At their legendary costume ball in 1883, Alva, pictured here dressed as a Venetian princess, releases live doves—perhaps representing her success in breaking down the social barriers designed to keep out the *nouveau* riche (vulgar newly rich). She had clearly arrived and taken her place in New York society. Defying convention, Alva divorced Vanderbilt, but kept Marble House, and later married Newport neighbor August Belmont. Her indomitable will, her quest for recognition, and her fearless defiance of convention led her to the women's rights cause. She would become a principal supporter of the National Woman's Party and serve as its president. On two occasions, she held fund-raisers at Marble House. In 1932, shortly before she died, Alva sold Marble House with the assurance that it would be kept as she had designed it. Today it is a National Historic Landmark open to the public. Alva Vanderbilt once described Marble House as "like a fourth child."

SOURCE: Marble House: © Dave G. Houser/Corbis; Gold Room: © Kelly-Mooney Photograph/Corbis; Alva Vanderbilt photo: Courtesy of The Preservation Society of Newport County.

Alva Vanderbilt Releasing the Doves

Questions for Analysis

1. Why might Alva have chosen to model her Newport home after a French queen's château?

2. Why do you think Alva chose classical figures for decoration?

3. Critics charged that Marble House, with its Gold Room, was "a symbol of the heartless, glittering emptiness of the Gilded Age." What did they mean by this criticism?

Connect to the Big Idea

C What economic changes took place in the Gilded Age that allowed for lavish personal wealth?

By transmitting coded messages along electrical wire, the telegraph formed the "nervous system" of the new industrial order. Telegraph service quickly replaced Pony Express mail carriers in the West and transformed business by providing instantaneous communication. Again Jay Gould took the lead. In 1879, through stock manipulation, he seized control of Western Union, the company that monopolized the telegraph industry.

The railroads soon fell on hard times. Already by the 1870s, lack of planning led to overbuilding. Across the nation, railroads competed fiercely for business. Manufacturers in areas served by competing railroads could get substantially reduced shipping rates in return for promises of steady business. Because railroad owners lost money through this kind of competition, they tried to set up agreements, or "pools," to divide up territory and set rates. But these informal gentlemen's agreements invariably failed because men like Gould, intent on undercutting all competitors, refused to play by the rules.

The public's alarm at the control wielded by the new railroad magnates and the tactics they employed came to light in the Credit Moblier scandal of 1872. Credit Moblier, a fiscal enterprise set up by partners including Thomas Durant, an executive of Union Pacific Railroad, would provide sole bids on construction work. Using money procured from investors and government bonds, the work was then subcontracted out, leaving profits in the hands of the financiers. With profits booming, senators clambered to profit as well. Charles Dana's *New York Sun* described the Credit Moblier money-making scheme as "The King of Frauds" and attempted to document the way the railroads controlled their friends in government with lavish gifts of stock. Although the press never got the financial dealings straight, the scandal and resulting investigation implicated the Union Pacific Railroad, the vice president, and numerous congressmen. The real revelation was how little the key players knew about how railroads were built or operated. The promoters knew little about building the roads; the investors had an even shakier grasp on what they were investing in; and the politicians who subsidized the roads, instead of overseeing them, remained vague on specifics and failed to provide governmental oversight. All that was clear was that the Union Pacific had sold stock below market prices to its friends. In the end, no one was punished and no money returned.

The Credit Moblier scandal increased public suspicion of the corrupt relationship between business and government, and led to a strong antipathy toward speculators and a movement to end monopoly.

Andrew Carnegie, Steel, and Vertical Integration

If Jay Gould was the man Americans loved to hate, Andrew Carnegie became one of America's heroes. Unlike Gould, Carnegie turned his back on speculation and worked to build something enduring—Carnegie Steel, the biggest steel business in the world during the Gilded Age.

The growth of the steel industry proceeded directly from railroad building. The first railroads ran on iron rails, which cracked and broke with alarming frequency. Steel, both stronger and more flexible than iron, remained too expensive for use in rails until Englishman Henry Bessemer developed a way to make steel more

Andrew Carnegie
A millionaire by his twenties, Carnegie, here in 1905 after he had retired, urged his fellow plutocrats to act as stewards of the people and to spend their money for the good of society. Before he died in 1919 he gave away an estimated $300 million to charitable causes. Library of Congress.

cheaply. Andrew Carnegie, among the first to champion the new "King Steel," came to dominate the emerging industry.

Carnegie, a Scottish immigrant, landed in New York in 1848 at the age of twelve. He rose from a job cleaning bobbins in a textile factory to become one of the richest men in America. Before he died, he gave away more than $300 million, most notably to public libraries. His generosity, combined with his own rise from poverty, burnished his public image.

While Carnegie was a teenager, his skill as a telegraph operator caught the attention of Tom Scott, superintendent of the Pennsylvania Railroad. Scott hired Carnegie, soon promoted him, and lent him the money for his first foray into Wall Street investment. As a result of this crony capitalism, Carnegie became a millionaire before his thirtieth birthday. At that point, Carnegie turned away from speculation. "My preference was always manufacturing," he wrote. "I wished to make something tangible." By applying the lessons of cost accounting and efficiency that he had learned with the Pennsylvania Railroad, Carnegie turned steel into the nation's first manufacturing big business.

In 1872, Andrew Carnegie built the world's largest, most up-to-date steel mill in Braddock, Pennsylvania. At that time, steelmakers produced about 70 tons a week. Within two decades, Carnegie's blast furnaces poured out an incredible 10,000 tons a week. His formula for success was simple: "Cut the prices, scoop the market, run the mills full; watch the costs and profits will take care of themselves." Carnegie pioneered a system of business organization called vertical integration in which all aspects of the business were under Carnegie's control—from the mining of iron ore, to its transport on the Great Lakes, to the production of steel. As one observer noted, "there was never a price, profit, or royalty paid to any outsider."

The great productivity Carnegie encouraged came at a high price. He deliberately pitted his managers against one another, firing the losers and rewarding the winners with a share in the company. Workers achieved the output Carnegie demanded by enduring low wages, dangerous working conditions, and twelve-hour days six days a week. One worker, observing the contradiction between Carnegie's generous endowment of public libraries and his labor policy, observed, "After working twelve hours, how can a man go to a library?"

By 1900, Andrew Carnegie had become the best-known manufacturer in the nation, and the age of iron had yielded to an age of steel. Steel from Carnegie's mills supported the elevated trains in New York and Chicago, formed the skeleton of the Washington Monument, supported the first steel bridge to span the Mississippi, and girded America's first skyscrapers. As a captain of industry, Carnegie's only rival was the titan of the oil industry, John D. Rockefeller.

John D. Rockefeller, Standard Oil, and the Trust

In the days before the automobile and gasoline, crude oil was refined into lubricating oil for machinery and kerosene for lamps, the major source of lighting in the nineteenth century. The amount of capital needed to buy or build an oil refinery in the 1860s and 1870s remained relatively low—roughly what it cost to lay one mile of railroad track. As a result, the new petroleum industry experienced riotous competition. Ultimately, John D. Rockefeller and his Standard Oil Company succeeded in controlling nine-tenths of the oil-refining business.

Rockefeller grew up the son of a shrewd Yankee who peddled quack cures for cancer. Under his father's rough tutelage, Rockefeller learned how to drive a hard bargain. In 1865, at the age of twenty-five, he controlled the largest oil refinery in Cleveland. Like a growing number of business owners, Rockefeller abandoned partnership or single proprietorship to embrace the corporation as the business structure best suited to maximize profit and minimize personal liability. In 1870, he incorporated his oil business, founding the Standard Oil Company.

As the largest refiner in Cleveland, Rockefeller demanded illegal rebates from the railroads in exchange for his steady business. The secret rebates enabled Rockefeller to drive out his competitors through predatory pricing. The railroads needed Rockefeller's business so badly that they gave him a share of the rates that his competitors paid. A Pennsylvania Railroad official later confessed that Rockefeller extracted such huge rebates that the railroad, which could not risk

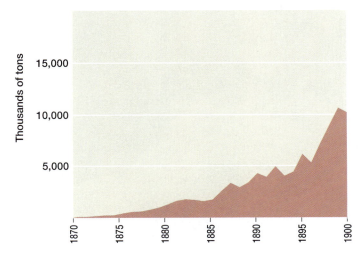

FIGURE 18.1 Iron and Steel Production, 1870–1900
Iron and steel production in the United States grew from nearly none in 1870 to 10 million tons a year by 1900. The secrets to such a great increase were the use of the Bessemer process and vertical integration, pioneered by Andrew Carnegie. By 1900, Carnegie's mills alone produced more steel than all of Great Britain. With corporate consolidation after 1900, the rate of growth in steel proved even more spectacular.

losing his business, sometimes ended up paying him to transport Standard's oil. Rebates enabled Rockefeller to undercut his competitors and pressure competing refiners to sell out or face ruin.

To gain legal standing for Standard Oil's secret deals, Rockefeller in 1882 pioneered a new form of corporate structure—the **trust**. The trust differed markedly from Carnegie's vertical approach in steel. Rockefeller used horizontal integration to control not the entire process, but only an aspect of oil production—refining. Several trustees held stock in various refinery companies "in trust" for Standard's stockholders. This elaborate stock swap allowed the trustees to coordinate policy among the refineries by gobbling up all the small, competing refineries. Often buyers did not know they were actually selling out to Standard. By the end of the century, Rockefeller enjoyed a virtual monopoly of the oil-refining business. The Standard Oil trust, valued at more than $70 million, paved the way for trusts in sugar, whiskey, matches, and many other products.

When the federal government responded to public pressure to outlaw the trust in 1890, Standard Oil changed tactics and reorganized as a holding company. Instead of stockholders in competing companies acting through trustees to set prices and determine territories, the holding company simply brought competing companies under one central administration. Now one business, not an assortment of individual refineries, Standard Oil controlled competition without violating antitrust laws that forbade competing companies from forming "combinations in restraint of trade." By the 1890s, Standard Oil ruled more than 90 percent of the oil business, employed 100,000 people, and was the biggest, richest, most feared, and most admired business organization in the world.

John D. Rockefeller enjoyed enormous success in business, but he was not well liked by the public. Editor and journalist Ida M. Tarbell's "History of the Standard Oil Company," which ran in serial form in *McClure's Magazine* (1902–1905), largely shaped the public's harsh view of

VISUAL ACTIVITY

"What a Funny Little Government"

The power wielded by John D. Rockefeller and his Standard Oil Company is satirized here by cartoonist Horace Taylor. Rockefeller is pictured holding the White House and the Treasury Department in the palm of his hand, while in the background the U.S. Capitol has been converted into an oil refinery. © Collection of the New-York Historical Society, USA/ The Bridgeman Art Library.

READING THE IMAGE: According to Horace Taylor, what kind of relationship did John D. Rockefeller have with the federal government? What did the public think of it?

CONNECTIONS: How much influence did industrialists such as Rockefeller exert over the national government in the late nineteenth century?

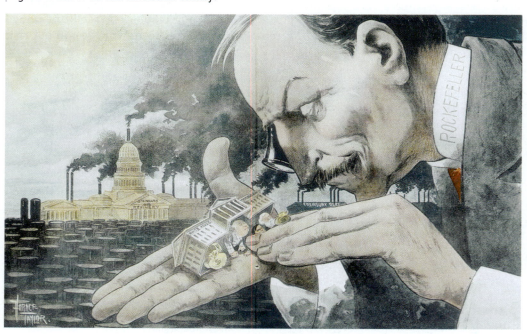

Ida M. Tarbell, Scourge of Standard Oil
Tarbell served as managing editor of the popular *McClure's Magazine*, where her "History of the Standard Oil Company" ran in serial form for three years. Her revelations of the ruthless railroad rebates John D. Rockefeller used to control the oil-refining business came from Tarbell's deep research but also from her experience growing up in the Pennsylvania oil fields where she witnessed how Standard Oil forced out its competitors. Tarbell: Library of Congress; magazine: The Ida Tarbell Collection, Special Collections, Pelletier Library, Allegheny College.

Rockefeller. Her history chronicled the illegal methods Rockefeller had used to take over the oil industry. By the time Tarbell finished her story, Rockefeller slept with a loaded revolver by his bed. Standard Oil and the man who created it had become the symbol of heartless monopoly.

New Inventions: The Telephone and the Telegraph

The second half of the nineteenth century was an age of invention. Men like Thomas Alva Edison and Alexander Graham Bell became folk heroes. But no matter how dramatic the inventors or the inventions, the new electric and telephone industries pioneered by Edison and Bell soon eclipsed their inventors and fell under the control of bankers and industrialists.

Alexander Graham Bell came to America from Scotland at the age of twenty-four with a passion to find a way to teach the deaf to speak (his wife and mother were deaf). Instead, he developed a way to transmit voice over wire—the telephone. Bell's invention astounded the world when he demonstrated it at the Philadelphia Centennial Exposition in 1876. In 1880, Bell's company, American Bell, pioneered "long lines" (long-distance telephone service), creating American Telephone and Telegraph (AT&T) as a subsidiary. In 1900, AT&T developed a

Notable American Inventions 1865–1899	
1865	Railroad sleeping car
1867	Typewriter
1868	Railroad refrigerator car
1870	Stock ticker
1874	Barbed wire
1876	Telephone
1877	Phonograph
1879	Incandescent lightbulb
1882	Electric fan
1885	Adding machine
1886	Coca-Cola
1888	Kodak camera
1890	Electric chair
1891	Zipper
1895	Safety razor
1896	Electric stove
1899	Tape recorder

complicated structure that enabled Americans to communicate not only locally but also across the country. And unlike a telegraph message, the telephone connected both parties immediately and privately. Bell's invention proved a boon to business, contributing to speed and efficiency. The number of telephones soared, reaching 310,000 in 1895 and more than 1.5 million in 1900.

Even more than Alexander Graham Bell, inventor Thomas Alva Edison embodied the old-fashioned virtues of Yankee ingenuity and rugged individualism that Americans most admired. A self-educated dynamo, he worked twenty hours a day in his laboratory in Menlo Park, New Jersey, vowing to turn out "a minor invention every ten days and a big thing every six months or so." He almost made good on his promise. At the height of his career, he averaged a patent every eleven days and invented such "big things" as the phonograph, the motion picture camera, and the filament for the incandescent lightbulb.

Edison, in competition with George W. Westinghouse, pioneered the use of electricity as an energy source. By the late nineteenth century, electricity had become a part of American urban life. It powered trolley cars and lighted factories, homes, and office buildings. Indeed, electricity became so prevalent in urban life that it symbolized the city, whose bright lights contrasted with rural America, left largely in the dark.

The day of the inventor quietly yielded to the heyday of the corporation. In 1892, the electric industry consolidated. Reflecting a nationwide trend in business, Edison General Electric dropped the name of its inventor, becoming simply General Electric (GE). For years, an embittered Edison refused to set foot inside a GE building. GE, a prime example of the trend toward business consolidation, soon dominated the market.

REVIEW   When, why, and how did the transcontinental railroad system develop, and what was its impact on American business?

▶ From Competition to Consolidation

Even as Rockefeller and Carnegie built their empires, the era of the "robber barons," as they were dubbed by their detractors, was drawing to a close. Increasingly, businesses replaced partnerships and sole proprietorships with the anonymous corporate structure that would come to dominate the twentieth century. At the same time, mergers led to the creation of huge new corporations.

Banks and financiers played key roles in this consolidation, so much so that the decades at the turn of the twentieth century can be characterized as a period of **finance capitalism**— investment sponsored by banks and bankers. When the depression that followed the panic of 1893 bankrupted many businesses, bankers stepped in to bring order and to reorganize major industries. During these years, a new social philosophy developed that helped to justify consolidation and to inhibit state or federal regulation of business. A conservative Supreme Court further frustrated attempts to control business by consistently declaring unconstitutional legislation designed to regulate railroads or to outlaw trusts and monopolies.

The Dangers of Electricity

This 1889 cartoon graphically portrays the dangers of electricity. Innocent pedestrians are electrocuted by the wires as a policeman runs for help. The skull in the wires attached to the electric lightbulb warns that this new technology can be deadly. And the carnage portrayed illustrates the point. The Granger Collection, New York City.

AN UNRESTRAINED DEMON.

J. P. Morgan and Finance Capitalism

John Pierpont Morgan, the preeminent finance capitalist of the late nineteenth century, loathed competition and sought whenever possible to eliminate it by substituting consolidation and central control. Morgan's passion for order made him the architect of business mergers. At the turn of the twentieth century, he dominated American banking, exerting an influence so powerful that his critics charged he controlled a vast "money trust" even more insidious than Rockefeller's Standard Oil.

Morgan acted as a power broker in the reorganization of the railroads and the creation of industrial giants such as General Electric. When the railroads collapsed, Morgan took over and eliminated competition by creating what he called "a community of interest." By the time he finished "Morganizing" the railroads, a handful of directors controlled two-thirds of the nation's track. Morgan's directors were bankers, not railroad men, and they saw the roads as little more than "a set of books." Their conservative approach aimed at short-term profit and discouraged the technological and organizational innovation necessary to running the railroads effectively.

In 1898, Morgan moved into the steel industry, directly challenging Andrew Carnegie. The pugnacious Carnegie cabled his partners in the summer of 1900: "Action essential: crisis has arrived . . . have no fear as to the result; victory certain." The press trumpeted news of the impending fight between the feisty Scot and the haughty Wall Street banker. But for all his belligerence, the sixty-six-year-old Carnegie yearned to retire to Scotland. Morgan, who disdained haggling, agreed to pay Carnegie's asking price, $480 million (the equivalent of about $10 billion in today's currency). According to legend, when Carnegie later teased Morgan, saying that he should have asked $100 million more, Morgan replied, "You would have got it if you had."

VISUAL ACTIVITY

Homestead Steelworks

The Homestead steelworks, outside Pittsburgh, is pictured shortly after J. P. Morgan created U.S. Steel, the precursor of today's USX. Try to count the smokestacks in the picture. Air pollution on this scale posed a threat to the health of citizens and made for a dismal landscape. Workers complained that trees would not grow in Homestead. The Granger Collection, New York.

READING THE IMAGE: What does the photo tell you about the purpose of Homestead? What does it say about the lives of the Homestead workers?

CONNECTIONS: How did the Homestead steelworks reflect Gilded Age values and interests?

Social Darwinism: Did Wealthy Industrialists Practice What They Preached?

Darwinism, with its emphasis on tooth-and-claw competition, seemed ideally suited to the get-rich-quick mentality of the Gilded Age. By placing the theory of evolution in an economic context, social Darwinism argued against government intervention in business while at the same time insisting that reforms to ameliorate the evils of urban industrialism would only slow evolutionary progress. Most of the wealthy industrialists of the day probably never read Charles Darwin or the exponents of social Darwinism. Nevertheless, the catchphrases of social Darwinism larded the rhetoric of business in the Gilded Age.

Andrew Carnegie, alone among the American business moguls, not only championed social Darwinism but also avidly read the works of its primary exponent, the British social philosopher Herbert Spencer. Significantly, Spencer, not Darwin, coined the catchphrase "survival of the fittest." Carnegie spoke of his indebtedness to Spencer in terms

Herbert Spencer

Herbert Spencer became a hero to industrialist Andrew Carnegie, who judged his steel business the apotheosis of survival of the fittest. But on a visit in 1882, the sage of social Darwinism proved a great disappointment to Carnegie. Hulton Archives/Getty Images.

usually reserved for religious conversion: "Before Spencer, all for me had been darkness, after him, all had become light—and right." In his autobiography, Carnegie wrote, "I had found the truth of evolution. 'All is well since all grows better' became my motto, my true source of comfort."

Not content to worship Spencer from afar, Carnegie assiduously worked to make his acquaintance and then would not rest until he had convinced the reluctant Spencer

Morgan's acquisition of Carnegie Steel signaled the passing of the old entrepreneurial order personified by Andrew Carnegie and the arrival of a new anonymous corporate world. Morgan quickly moved to pull together Carnegie's chief competitors to form a huge new corporation, United States Steel, known today as USX. Created in 1901 and capitalized at $1.4 billion, U.S. Steel was the largest corporation in the world.

Even more than Carnegie or Rockefeller, Morgan left his stamp on the twentieth century and formed the model for corporate consolidation that economists and social scientists justified with a new social theory later called social Darwinism.

Social Darwinism, Laissez-Faire, and the Supreme Court

John D. Rockefeller Jr., the son of the founder of Standard Oil, once remarked to his Baptist Bible class that the Standard Oil Company, like the American Beauty rose, resulted from "pruning the early buds that grew up around it." The elimination of competition, he declared, was "merely the working out of a law of nature and a law of God." The comparison of the business world to the natural world resembled the theory of evolution formulated by the British naturalist Charles Darwin. In his monumental work *On the Origin of Species* (1859), Darwin

to come to America. In Pittsburgh, Carnegie promised, Spencer could best view his evolutionary theories at work in the world of industry. Clearly, Carnegie viewed his steel-works as the apex of America's new industrial order, a testimony to the playing out of evolutionary theory in the economic world.

In 1882, Spencer undertook an American tour. Carnegie personally invited him to Pittsburgh, squiring him through the Braddock steel mills. But Spencer failed to appreciate Carnegie's achievement. The heat, noise, and pollution of Pittsburgh reduced Spencer to near collapse, and he could only choke out, "Six months' residence here would justify suicide." Carnegie must have been devastated.

How well Carnegie actually understood the principles of social Darwinism is debatable. In his 1900 essay "Popular Illusions about Trusts," Carnegie spoke of the "law of evolution that moves from the heterogeneous to the homogeneous," citing Spencer as his source. Spencer, however, had written of the movement "from an indefinite incoherent homogeneity to a definite coherent heterogeneity." Instead of acknowledging that the history of human evolution moved from the simple to the more complex, Carnegie seemed to insist that evolution moved from the complex to the simple. This confusion of the most basic evolutionary theory calls into question Carnegie's grasp of Spencer's ideas or indeed of Darwin's. Other business leaders too busy making money to read no doubt understood even less about the working of evolutionary theory and social Darwinism, which they so often claimed as their own.

The distance between preachment and practice is boldly evident in the example of William Graham Sumner, America's foremost social Darwinist. Ironically, Sumner, who often sounded like an apologist for the rich, aroused the wrath of the very group he championed. The problem was that strict social Darwinists like Sumner insisted absolutely that the government ought not to meddle in the economy. The purity of Sumner's commitment to laissez-faire led him to adamantly oppose the protective tariffs the pro-business Republicans enacted to inflate the prices of manufactured goods produced abroad so that U.S. businesses could compete against foreign rivals. Sumner outspokenly attacked the tariff and firmly advocated free trade from his chair in political economy at Yale University. In 1890, the same year Congress passed the McKinley tariff, Sumner's fulminations against this highest tariff in the nation's history so outraged Yale's wealthy alumni that they mounted a campaign (unsuccessful) to have him fired.

Inconsistency never seemed to trouble Carnegie, who did not acknowledge a contradiction between his worship of Spencer and his strong support for the tariff. The comparison of Carnegie's position and Sumner's underscores the reality that although in theory laissez-faire constrained the government from playing an active role in business affairs, in practice industrialists fought for government favors—whether tariffs, land grants, or subsidies—that worked to their benefit. Only when legislatures proposed taxes or regulation did business leaders cry foul and invoke the "natural laws" of social Darwinism and its corollary, laissez-faire.

Questions for Consideration

1. In what ways did American business moguls think that the notion of evolution applied to them?

2. Why were most industrialists inconsistent in invoking the principles of social Darwinism?

Connect to the Big Idea

C How had American industrialism transformed life for ordinary Americans?

---

theorized that in the struggle for survival, adaptation to the environment triggered among species a natural selection process that led to evolution. Herbert Spencer in Britain and William Graham Sumner in the United States developed the theory of **social Darwinism**. The social Darwinists insisted that societal progress came about as a result of relentless competition in which the strong survived and the weak died out.

In social terms, the idea of the "survival of the fittest," coined by Spencer, had profound significance, as Sumner, a professor of political economy at Yale University, made clear in his book *What Social Classes Owe to Each Other* (1883). "The drunkard in the gutter is just where he ought to be, according to the fitness and tendency of things," Sumner insisted. Conversely, "millionaires are the product of natural selection," and although "they get high wages and live in luxury," Sumner claimed, "the bargain is a good one for society."

Social Darwinists equated wealth and power with "fitness" and believed that any efforts by the rich to aid the poor would only tamper with the laws of nature and slow down evolution. Social Darwinism acted to curb social reform while glorifying great wealth. In an age when Rockefeller and Carnegie amassed hundreds of millions of dollars (billions in today's currency) and the average worker earned $500 a year, social Darwinism justified economic inequality. (See "Historical Question," page 506.)

Carnegie softened some of the harshness of social Darwinism in his essay "The Gospel of Wealth," published in 1889. The millionaire, Carnegie wrote, acted as a "mere trustee and agent for his poorer brethren, bringing to their service his superior wisdom, experience, and ability to administer, doing for them better than they could or would do for themselves." Carnegie preached philanthropy and urged the rich to "live unostentatious lives" and "administer surplus wealth for the good of the people." His **gospel of wealth** earned much praise but won few converts. Most millionaires followed the lead of Morgan, who contributed to charity but hoarded private treasures in his marble library.

With its emphasis on the free play of competition and the survival of the fittest, social Darwinism encouraged the economic theory of laissez-faire (French for "let it alone"). Business leaders argued that government should not meddle in economic affairs, except to protect private property (or support high tariffs and government subsidies). A conservative Supreme Court agreed. During the 1880s and 1890s, the Court increasingly reinterpreted the Constitution, judging corporations to be "persons" in order to protect business from taxation, regulation, labor organization, and antitrust legislation.

Only in the arena of politics did Americans tackle the social issues raised by corporate capitalism.

REVIEW   Why did the ideas of social Darwinism appeal to many Americans in the late nineteenth century?

▶ Politics and Culture

For many Americans, politics provided a source of identity, a means of livelihood, and a ready form of entertainment. No wonder voter turnout averaged a hefty 77 percent (compared to roughly 57.5 percent in the 2012 presidential election). A variety of factors contributed to the complicated interplay of politics and culture. Patronage provided an economic incentive for voter participation, but ethnicity, religion, sectional loyalty, race, and gender all influenced the political life of the period.

Political Participation and Party Loyalty

Political parties in power doled out federal, state, and local government jobs to their loyal supporters. With hundreds of thousands of jobs to be filled, the choice of party affiliation could mean the difference between a paycheck and an empty pocket. Money greased the wheels of this system of patronage, dubbed the **spoils system** from the adage "to the victor go the spoils." With their livelihoods tied to their party identity, government employees had a powerful incentive to vote in great numbers.

Political affiliation provided a sense of group identity for many voters proud of their loyalty to the Democrats or the Republicans. Democrats, who traced the party's roots back to Thomas Jefferson, called theirs "the party of the fathers." The Republican Party, founded in the 1850s, still claimed strong loyalties in the North as a result of its alignment with the Union during the Civil War. Republicans proved particularly adept at evoking Civil War loyalty, using a tactic called "waving the bloody shirt."

Religion and ethnicity also played a significant role in politics. In the North, Protestants from the old-line denominations, particularly Presbyterians and Methodists, flocked to the Republican Party, which championed a series of moral reforms, including local laws requiring business to close on Sunday in observance of the Sabbath. In the cities, the Democratic Party courted immigrants and working-class Catholic and Jewish voters and charged, rightly, that Republican moral crusades often masked attacks on immigrant culture.

Sectionalism and the New South

After the end of Reconstruction, most white voters in the former Confederate states remained loyal Democrats, creating the so-called solid South that lasted for the next seventy years. Labeling the Republican Party the agent of "Negro rule," Democrats urged white southerners to "vote the way you shot." Yet the South proved far from solid for the Democrats on the state and local levels, leading to shifting political alliances and to third-party movements that challenged Democratic attempts to define politics along race lines and maintain the Democrats as the white man's party.

The South's economy, devastated by the war, foundered at the same time the North experienced an unprecedented industrial boom. Soon an influential group of southerners called for a New South modeled on the industrial North. Henry Grady, the ebullient young editor of the *Atlanta Constitution*, used his paper's influence to exhort the South to use its natural advantages—cheap labor and abundant natural resources—to go head-to-head in competition with northern industry. And even as southern Democrats took back control of state governments, they embraced northern promoters who promised prosperity and profits.

The railroads came first, opening up the region for industrial development. Southern railroad mileage grew fourfold from 1865 to 1890. The number of cotton spindles also soared as textile mill owners abandoned New England in search of the cheap labor and proximity to raw materials promised in the South. By 1900, the South had become the nation's leading producer of cloth, and more than 100,000 southerners, many of them women and children, worked in the region's textile mills.

The New South prided itself most on its iron and steel industry, which grew up in the area surrounding Birmingham, Alabama. During this period, the smokestack replaced the white-pillared plantation as the symbol of the New South. Andrew Carnegie toured the region in 1889 and observed, "The South is Pennsylvania's most formidable industrial enemy." But southern industry remained controlled by northern investors, who had no intention of letting the South beat the North at its own game. Elaborate mechanisms rigged the price of southern steel, inflating it, as one northern insider confessed, "for the purpose of protecting the Pittsburgh mills and in turn the Pittsburgh steel users." Similarly, in the lumber and mining industries, investors in the North and abroad, not southerners, reaped the lion's share of the profits.

In only one industry did the South truly dominate—tobacco. Capitalizing on the invention of a machine for rolling cigarettes, the American Tobacco Company, founded by the Duke family of North Carolina, eventually dominated the industry. As cigarettes replaced chewing tobacco in popularity at the turn of the twentieth century, a booming market developed for Duke's "ready mades." Soon the company sold 400,000 cigarettes a day.

In practical terms, the industrialized New South proved an illusion. Much of the South remained agricultural, caught in the grip of the insidious crop lien system (see "White Landlords, Black Sharecroppers" in chapter 16). White southern farmers, desperate to get out of debt, some-times joined African Americans to pursue mutual political goals. Between 1865 and 1900, voters in every southern state experimented with political alliances that crossed the color line and threatened the status quo.

Gender, Race, and Politics

Gender—society's notion of what constitutes acceptable masculine or feminine behavior—influenced politics throughout the nineteenth century. From the early days of the Republic, citizenship had been defined in male terms. Citizenship and its prerogatives (voting and officeholding) served as a badge of manliness and rested on its corollary, patriarchy—the power and authority men exerted over their wives and families. With the advent of universal (white) male suffrage in the early nineteenth century, gender eclipsed class as the defining feature of citizenship; men's dominance over women provided the common thread that knit all white men together politically. The concept of separate spheres dictated political participation for men only. Once the public sphere of political participation became equated with manhood, women found themselves increasingly restricted to the private sphere of the home.

Women were not alone in their limited access to the public sphere. Blacks continued to face discrimination well after Reconstruction especially in the New South. Segregation, commonly practiced through **Jim Crow** laws (as discussed in "Progressivism for White Men Only" in chapter 21), prevented ex-slaves from riding in the same train cars as whites, from eating in the same restaurants, or from using the same toilet facilities.

Amid the turmoil of the post-Reconstruction South, some groups struck cross-racial alliances. In Virginia, the "Readjusters," a coalition of blacks and whites determined to "readjust" (lower) the state debt and spend more money on public education, captured state offices from 1879 to 1883. Groups like the Readjusters believed universal political rights could be extended to black males while maintaining racial segregation in the private sphere. Democrats fought back by arguing that black voting would lead to racial mixing, and many whites returned to the democratic fold to protect "white womanhood."

The notion that black men threatened white southern womanhood reached its most vicious form in the practice of lynching—the killing and mutilation of black men by white mobs. By 1892, the practice had become so prevalent that a courageous black editor, Ida B. Wells,

Ida B. Wells and Her Campaign to Stop Lynching

Ida B. Wells fearlessly crusaded to stop lynching in the South by researching and reporting lynchings in detail and by comparing coverage from black and white sources.

DOCUMENT 1
Ida B. Wells, Editorial Protesting the Lynching of Friends in Memphis, 1892

The lynching in 1892 of three friends who ran a grocery store outside of Memphis touched Wells deeply. She wrote an outraged editorial in the Free Press. *Later she would repeat the details in her first pamphlet,* Southern Horrors: Lynch Law in All Its Phases *(1892).*

On March 9, 1892, there were lynched in this same city three of the best specimens of young since-the-war Afro-American manhood. They were peaceful, law-abiding citizens and energetic business men. . . . They owned a flourishing grocery business in a thickly populated suburb of Memphis, and a white man named Barrett had one on the opposite corner. After a personal difficulty which Barrett sought by going into the "People's Grocery" drawing a pistol and was thrashed by Calvin McDowell, he (Barrett) threatened to "clean them out." These men were a mile beyond the city limits and the police protection; hearing that Barrett's crowd was coming to attack them Saturday night, they mustered forces and prepared to defend themselves against the attack.

When Barrett came he led a posse of officers, twelve in number, who afterward claimed to be hunting a man for whom they had a warrant. That twelve men in citizen's clothes should think it necessary to go in the night to hunt one man who had never before been arrested, or made any record as a criminal has never been explained. When they entered the back door the young men thought the threatened attack was on, and fired into them. Three of the officers were wounded, and when the defending party found it was officers of the law upon whom they had fired, they ceased and got away.

Thirty-one men were arrested and thrown in jail as "conspirators," although they all declared more than once they did not know they were firing on officers. Excitement was at fever heat until the morning papers, two days after, announced that the wounded deputy sheriffs were out of danger. This hindered rather than helped the plans of the whites. There was no law on the statute books which would execute an Afro-American for wounding a white man, but the "unwritten law" did. Three of these men, the president, the manager and the clerk of the grocery—"the leaders of the conspiracy"—were secretly taken from jail and lynched in a shockingly brutal manner. "The Negroes are getting too independent," they say "we must teach them a lesson."

What lesson? The lesson of subordination. "Kill the leaders and it will cow the Negro who dares to shoot a white man, even in self-defense."

Source: *Southern Horrors and Other Writings*, edited by Jacqueline Jones Royster (Boston: Bedford/St. Martins, 1997), 64–65.

launched an antilynching movement. That year, a white mob lynched a friend of Wells's whose grocery store competed too successfully with a white-owned store. Wells shrewdly concluded that lynching served "as an excuse to get rid of Negroes who were acquiring wealth and property and thus keep the race terrorized." (See "Documenting the American Promise.") She began to collect data on lynching and discovered that in the decade between 1882 and 1892, lynching rose in the South by an overwhelming 200 percent, with more than 241 black people killed. The vast increase in lynching testified to the retreat of the federal government following Reconstruction and to white southerners' determination to maintain supremacy through terrorism and intimidation.

Wells articulated lynching as a problem of gender as well as race. She insisted that the myth of black attacks on white southern women masked the reality that mob violence had more to do with economics and the shifting social structure of the South than with rape. She demonstrated in a sophisticated way how the southern patriarchal system, having lost its

DOCUMENT 2
Ida B. Wells, On Lack of Justice and Due Process for Accused Blacks, 1894

In her 1894 pamphlet The Red Record, *Wells insisted that lynching assumed all black men were guilty, thus denying them the constitutional right to defend themselves in front of a judge and jury.*

In lynching, opportunity is not given the Negro to defend himself against the unsupported accusations of white men and women. The word of the accuser is held to be true and the excited blood-thirsty mob demands that the rule of law be reserved and instead of proving the accused to be guilty, the victim of their hate and revenge must prove himself innocent. No evidence he can offer will satisfy the mob; he is bound hand and foot and swung into eternity. Then to excuse its infamy, the mob almost invariably reports the monstrous falsehood that its victim made a full confession before he was hanged."

Source: Royster, *Southern Horrors*, 153.

DOCUMENT 3
Ida B. Wells, On Mob Rule in New Orleans, 1900

In her last pamphlet, Mob Rule in New Orleans, *Wells describes the riot that occurred when a black man, Robert Charles, attacked by a police officer with a billy-club, retaliated. This led to a duel that then brought on further violence.*

During the entire time the mob held the city in its hands and went about holding up street cars and searching them, taking from them colored men to assault, shoot and kill, chasing colored men upon the public square, through alleys and into houses of anybody who would take them in, braking into the homes of defenseless colored men and women and beating aged and decrepit men and women to death, the police and the legally-constituted authorities showed plainly where their sympathies were, for in no case reported through the daily papers does there appear the arrest, trial and conviction of one of the mob for any of the brutalities which occurred. The ringleaders of the mob were at no time disguised. Men were chased, beaten and killed by white brutes, who boasted of their crimes, and the murderers still walk the streets of New Orleans, well known and absolutely exempt from prosecution. Not only were they exempt from prosecution by the police while the town was in the hands of the mob, but even now that law and order is supposed to resume control, these men, well known, are not now, nor ever will be, called to account for the unspeakable brutalities of that terrible week. On the other hand, the colored men who were beaten by the police and dragged into the station for purposes of intimidation were quickly called before the courts and fined or sent to jail upon the statement of the police.

Source: Royster, *Southern Horrors*, 181–182.

Questions for Analysis and Debate

1. Who is the audience for Wells's pamphlets, and what does she hope to achieve?

2. What do these documents tell you about the conditions in the post-Reconstruction South?

Connect to the Big Idea

C Why did the accusation of rape work as an excuse for mob violence? What other causes for lynching were masked by charges of rape?

control over blacks with the end of slavery, used its control over white women to circumscribe the liberty of black men.

Wells's outspoken stance immediately resulted in reprisal. While she was traveling in the North, vandals ransacked her office in Tennessee and destroyed her printing equipment. Yet the warning that she would be killed on sight if she ever returned to Memphis only stiffened her resolve. As she wrote in her autobiography, *Crusade for Justice* (1928), "Having lost my paper, had a price put on my life and been made an exile . . ., I felt that I owed it to myself and to my race to tell the whole truth now that I was where I could do so freely."

Lynching did not end during Wells's lifetime, but her forceful voice brought the issue to national and international prominence. At her funeral in 1931, black leader W. E. B. Du Bois eulogized Wells as the woman who "began the awakening of the conscience of the nation." Wells's determined campaign against lynching provided just one example of women's political activism during the Gilded Age. The suffrage and temperance movements, along with the growing popularity of women's clubs,

Ida B. Wells

Ida B. Wells began her antilynching campaign in 1892 after a friend's murder led her to examine lynching in the South. She spread her message in lectures and pamphlets like this one, distributed for fifteen cents. Wells brought the horror of lynching to national and international audiences and became a founding member of the National Association for the Advancement of Colored People (NAACP). Schomburg Center, NYPL/Art Resource, NY.

dramatized how women refused to be relegated to a separate sphere that kept them out of politics.

Women's Activism

In 1869, Elizabeth Cady Stanton and Susan B. Anthony formed the National Woman Suffrage Association (NWSA), the first independent woman's rights organization in the United States, to fight for the vote for women. But women found ways to act politically long before they voted and cleverly used their moral authority as wives and mothers to move from the domestic sphere into the realm of politics.

The extraordinary activity of women's clubs in the period following the Civil War provides just one example. Women's clubs proliferated beginning in the 1860s. Newspaper reporter Jane Cunningham Croly (pen name Jennie June) founded the Sorosis Club in New York City in 1868, after the New York Press Club denied entry to women journalists wishing to attend a banquet honoring the British author Charles Dickens. In 1890, Croly brought state and local clubs together under the umbrella of the General Federation of Women's Clubs (GFWC). Not wishing to alienate southern women, the GFWC barred black women's clubs from joining, despite vehement objections. Women's clubs soon abandoned literary pursuits to devote themselves to "civic usefulness," endorsing an end to child labor, supporting the eight-hour workday, and helping pass pure food and drug legislation.

The temperance movement (the movement to end drunkenness) attracted by far the largest number of organized women in the late nineteenth century. By the late 1860s and the 1870s, the liquor business was flourishing, with about one saloon for every fifty males over the age of fifteen. During the winter of 1873–74, temperance women adopted a radical new tactic. Armed with Bibles and singing hymns, they marched on taverns and saloons and refused to leave until the proprietors signed a pledge to quit selling liquor. Known as the Woman's Crusade, the movement spread like a prairie fire through small towns in Ohio, Indiana, Michigan, and Illinois and soon moved east into New York, New England, and Pennsylvania. Before it was over, more than 100,000 women had marched in more than 450 cities and towns.

The women's tactics may have been new, but the temperance movement dated back to the 1820s. Originally, the movement was led by Protestant men who organized clubs to pledge voluntary abstinence from liquor. By the 1850s, temperance advocates won significant victories when states, starting with Maine, passed laws to prohibit the sale of liquor. The Woman's Crusade dramatically brought the issue of temperance back into the national spotlight and led to the formation of a new organization, the **Woman's Christian Temperance Union (WCTU)** in 1874. Composed entirely of women, the WCTU advocated total abstinence from alcohol.

Temperance provided women with a respectable outlet for their increasing resentment of women's inferior status and their growing recognition of women's capabilities. In its first five years, the WCTU relied on education and moral suasion, but when Frances Willard became president in 1879, she politicized the organization

"Woman's Holy War"
This political cartoon styles the temperance campaign as "Woman's Holy War" and shows a woman knight in armor (demurely seated sidesaddle on her charger), wielding a battle-ax and trampling on barrels of liquor. The image of temperance women as ax-wielding Amazons proved a popular satiric image. The cartoon appeared in 1874, the year the Woman's Christian Temperance Union formed. Picture Research Consultants & Archives.

(as discussed in chapter 20). When the women of the WCTU joined with the Prohibition Party (formed in 1869 by a group of evangelical clergymen), one wag observed, "Politics is a man's game, an' women, childhern, and prohyibitionists do well to keep out iv it." By sharing power with women, the Prohibitionist men violated the old political rules and risked attacks on their honor and manhood.

Even though women found ways to affect the political process, especially in third parties, it remained true that politics, particularly presidential politics, remained an exclusively male prerogative.

REVIEW How did race and gender influence politics?

▶ Presidential Politics

The presidents of the Gilded Age, from Rutherford B. Hayes (1877–1881) to William McKinley (1897–1901), are largely forgotten men, primarily because so little was expected of them. The dominant creed of laissez-faire, coupled with

the dictates of social Darwinism, warned the presidents and the government to leave business alone (except when they were working in its interests). Still, presidents in the Gilded Age grappled with corruption and party strife, and they struggled toward the creation of new political ethics designed to replace patronage with a civil service system that promised to award jobs on the basis of merit, not party loyalty.

Corruption and Party Strife

The political corruption and party factionalism that characterized the administration of Ulysses S. Grant (1869–1877) (see "Grant's Troubled Presidency" in chapter 16) continued to trouble the nation in the 1880s. The spoils system remained the driving force in party politics at all levels of government. Pro-business Republicans generally held a firm grip on the White House, while Democrats had better luck in Congress. Both parties relied on patronage to cement party loyalty.

A small but determined group of reformers championed a new ethics that would preclude politicians from getting rich from public office. The selection of U.S. senators particularly concerned them. Under the Constitution, senators were selected by state legislatures, not directly elected by the voters. Powerful business interests often contrived to control state legislatures and through them U.S. senators. As journalist Henry Demarest Lloyd quipped, Standard Oil "had done everything to the Pennsylvania legislature except to refine it." In this climate, a constitutional amendment calling for the direct election of senators faced stiff opposition from entrenched interests.

Republican president Rutherford B. Hayes tried to steer a middle course between spoilsmen and reformers. Hayes proved a hardworking, well-informed executive who wanted peace, prosperity, and an end to party strife. Yet the Republican Party remained divided into factions led by strong party bosses who boasted that they could make or break any president.

Foremost among the Republican Senate bosses stood Roscoe Conkling of New York. He and his followers, who fiercely supported the patronage system, were known as "Stalwarts." Conkling's rival Senator James G. Blaine of Maine led the "Half Breeds," who were less openly corrupt yet still tainted by their involvement in the Credit Moblier scandal. A third group, called the "Mugwumps," consisted of reformers from Massachusetts and New York who deplored the spoils system and advocated civil service reform.

VISUAL ACTIVITY

Civil Service Exams

In this 1890 photograph, prospective police officers in Chicago take the written civil service exam. With the rise of a written exam, issues of class and status meant that many men, particularly immigrants and their sons, needed education and not simply connections to make the grade. © Chicago History Museum, USA/The Bridgeman Art Library

READING THE IMAGE: What types of people are sitting for the civil service exam? Would you expect to see women or people of color?

CONNECTIONS: Who pressed for civil service reform, and what were the repercussions for those who held government positions?

President Hayes's middle course pleased no one, and he soon managed to alienate all factions of his party. Few were surprised when he announced that he would not seek reelection in 1880. To avoid choosing among its factions, the Republican Party in 1880 nominated a dark-horse candidate, Representative James A. Garfield of Ohio. To foster party unity, they picked Stalwart Chester A. Arthur as the vice presidential candidate. The Democrats made an attempt to overcome sectionalism by selecting former Union general Winfield Scott Hancock. Hancock garnered only lukewarm support, receiving just 155 electoral votes to Garfield's 214, although the popular vote was less lopsided.

Garfield's Assassination and Civil Service Reform

"My God," Garfield swore after only a few months in office, "what is there in this place that a man should ever want to get into it? Garfield, like Hayes, faced the difficult task of remaining independent while pacifying the party bosses and placating the reformers. On July 2, 1881, less than four months after taking office, Garfield was shot and died two months later. His assailant, Charles Julius Guiteau, though clearly insane, turned out to be a disappointed office seeker, motivated by political partisanship. He told the police officer who arrested him, "I did it; I will go to jail for it: Arthur is president, and I am a Stalwart."

The press almost universally condemned Republican factionalism for creating the political climate that produced Guiteau. Attacks on the spoils system increased, and both parties claimed credit for passage of the Pendleton Civil Service Act of 1883, which established a permanent Civil Service Commission consisting of three members appointed by the president. Some fourteen thousand jobs came under a merit system that required examinations for office and made it impossible to remove jobholders for political reasons. The new law also prohibited federal jobholders from contributing to political campaigns, thus drying up the major source of the party bosses' revenue. Businesses soon stepped in as the nation's chief political contributors. Ironically, **civil service reform** gave business an even greater influence in political life.

Reform and Scandal: The Campaign of 1884

James G. Blaine assumed leadership of the Republican Party and at long last captured the presidential nomination in 1884. A magnetic Irish American, Blaine inspired such devotion

"Another Voice for Cleveland"
This political cartoon ran in the magazine *Judge* in the fall of 1884 during the presidential campaign. Grover Cleveland, the Democratic candidate, is pictured cringing from the cries of a babe in arms—an allusion to his admission that he had fathered an illegitimate child. Despite the lurid publicity, Cleveland won the election. Library of Congress.

that his supporters called themselves Blainiacs. But Mugwump reformers bolted the party and embraced the Democrats' presidential nominee, Governor Grover Cleveland of New York. The burly, beer-drinking Cleveland distinguished himself from a generation of politicians by the simple motto "A public office is a public trust." First as mayor of Buffalo and later as governor of New York, he built a reputation for honesty, economy, and administrative efficiency. The Democrats, who had not won the presidency since 1856, had high hopes for his candidacy, especially after the Mugwumps threw their support to Cleveland, announcing "The paramount issue this year is moral rather than political."

They soon regretted their words. In July, Cleveland's hometown paper, the *Buffalo Telegraph*, dropped the bombshell that the candidate had fathered an illegitimate child in an affair with a local widow. Cleveland, a bachelor, stoically accepted responsibility for the child. Crushed by the scandal, the Mugwumps lost much of their enthusiasm. At public rallies, Blaine's partisans taunted Cleveland, chanting, "Ma, Ma, where's my Pa?"

Blaine set a new campaign style by launching a whirlwind national tour. On a last-minute stop in New York City, the exhausted candidate committed a misstep that may have cost him the election. He overlooked a remark by a

supporter, a local clergyman who cast a slur on Catholic voters by styling the Democrats as the party of "Rum, Romanism, and Rebellion." Linking drinking (rum) and Catholicism (Romanism) offended Irish Catholic voters, whom Blaine had counted on to desert the Democratic Party and support him because of his Irish background.

With less than a week to go until the election, Blaine had no chance to recover from the negative publicity. He lost New York State by fewer than

MAP 18.2
The Election of 1884

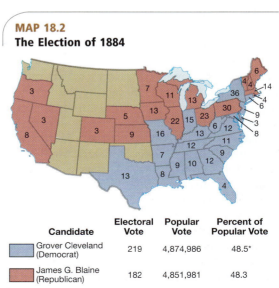

Candidate	Electoral Vote	Popular Vote	Percent of Popular Vote
Grover Cleveland (Democrat)	219	4,874,986	48.5*
James G. Blaine (Republican)	182	4,851,981	48.3

*Percentages do not total 100 because some popular votes went to other parties.

1,200 votes and with it the election. In the final tally, Cleveland defeated Blaine by a scant 23,005 votes nationwide but won with 219 electoral votes to Blaine's 182 (Map 18.2), ending twenty-four years of Republican control of the presidency. Cleveland's followers had the last word. To the chorus of "Ma, Ma, where's my Pa?" they retorted, "Going to the White House, ha, ha, ha."

> **REVIEW**   How did the question of civil service reform contribute to divisions within the Republican Party?

▶ Economic Issues and Party Realignment

Four years later, in the election of 1888, fickle voters turned Cleveland out, electing Republican Benjamin Harrison, the grandson of President William Henry Harrison. Then, in the only instance in American history when a president once defeated at the polls returned to office, the voters brought Cleveland back in the election of 1892. What factors account for such a surprising turnaround? The 1880s witnessed a remarkable political realignment as a set of economic concerns replaced appeals to Civil War sectional loyalties. The tariff, federal regulation of the railroads and trusts, and the campaign for free silver restructured American politics. Then a Wall Street panic in 1893 set off a major depression that further fed political unrest.

The Tariff and the Politics of Protection

The tariff became a potent political issue in the 1880s. The concept of a protective tariff to raise the price of imported goods and stimulate American industry dated back to the founding days of the Republic. Republicans turned the tariff to political ends in 1861 by enacting a measure that both raised revenues for the Civil War and rewarded their industrial supporters, who wanted protection from foreign competition. After the war, the pro-business Republicans continued to raise the tariff. Manufactured goods such as steel and textiles, and some agricultural products, including sugar and wool, benefited from protection. Most farm products, notably wheat and cotton, did not. By the 1880s, the tariff produced more than $2.1 billion in revenue. Not only did the high tariff pay off the nation's

Civil War debt and fund pensions for Union soldiers, but it also created a huge surplus that sat idly in the Treasury's vaults while the government argued about how (or even whether) to spend it.

To many Americans, particularly southern and midwestern farmers who sold their crops in a world market but had to buy goods priced artificially high because of the protective tariff, the answer was simple: Reduce the tariff. But the Republican Party seized on the tariff question to forge a new national coalition. "Fold up the bloody shirt and lay it away," Blaine advised a colleague in 1880. "It's of no use to us. You want to shift the main issue to protection." By encouraging an alliance among industrialists, labor, and western producers of raw materials—groups seen to benefit from the tariff—Blaine hoped to solidify the North, Midwest, and West against the solidly Democratic South. Although the tactic failed for Blaine in the presidential election of 1884, it worked for the Republicans four years later.

Cleveland, who had straddled the tariff issue in the election of 1884, startled the nation in 1887 by calling for tariff reform. The president attacked the tariff as a tax levied on American consumers by powerful industries. And he pointed out that high tariffs impeded the expansion of American markets abroad at a time when American industries needed to expand. The Republicans countered by arguing that "tariff tinkering" would only unsettle prosperous industries, drive down wages, and shrink the farmers' home market. Republican Benjamin Harrison, who supported the high tariff, ousted Cleveland from the White House in 1888, carrying all the western and northern states except Connecticut and New Jersey.

Back in power, the Republicans brazenly passed the highest tariff in the nation's history in 1890. The new tariff, sponsored by Republican representative William McKinley of Ohio, stirred up a hornet's nest of protest across the United States. The American people had elected Harrison to preserve protection but not to enact a higher tariff. Democrats condemned the McKinley tariff and labeled the Republican Congress that passed it the "Billion Dollar Congress" for its carnival of spending, which depleted the nation's surplus by enacting a series of pork barrel programs shamelessly designed to bring federal money to congressmen's constituencies. In the congressional election of 1890, angry voters swept the hapless Republicans, including tariff sponsor McKinley, out of office. Two years later, Harrison himself was defeated, and Grover Cleveland returned to the White House. Such were the changes in the political winds whipped up by the tariff issue.

Controversy over the tariff masked deeper divisions in American society. Conflict between workers and farmers on the one side and bankers and corporate giants on the other erupted throughout the 1880s and came to a head in the 1890s. Both sides in the tariff debate spoke to concerns over class conflict when they insisted that their respective plans, whether McKinley's high tariff or Cleveland's tariff reform, would bring prosperity and harmony. For their part, many working people shared the sentiment voiced by one labor leader that the tariff was "only a scheme devised by the old parties to throw dust in the eyes of laboring men."

Railroads, Trusts, and the Federal Government

American voters may have divided on the tariff, but increasingly they agreed on the need for federal regulation of the railroads and federal legislation to curb the power of the "trusts" (a term loosely applied to all large business combinations). As early as the 1870s, angry farmers in the Midwest who suffered from the unfair shipping practices of the railroads organized to fight for railroad regulation. The Patrons of Husbandry, or the Grange, founded in 1867 as a social and educational organization for farmers, soon became an independent political movement. By electing Grangers to state office, farmers made it possible for several midwestern states to pass laws in the 1870s and 1880s regulating the railroads. At first, the Supreme Court ruled in favor of state regulation (*Munn v. Illinois*, 1877). But in 1886, the Court reversed itself, ruling that because railroads crossed state boundaries, they fell outside state jurisdiction (*Wabash v. Illinois*). With more than three-fourths of railroads crossing state lines, the Supreme Court's decision effectively quashed the states' attempts at railroad regulation.

Anger at the *Wabash* decision finally led to the first federal law regulating the railroads, the Interstate Commerce Act, passed in 1887 during Cleveland's first administration. The act established the nation's first federal regulatory agency, the **Interstate Commerce Commission (ICC)**, to oversee the railroad industry. Railroad lobbyists worked furiously behind the scenes to make the new agency palatable to business leaders, many of whom felt a federal agency would be more lenient than state regulators. In its early years, the ICC was never strong enough to pose a serious threat to the railroads. For example, it could not end rebates to big shippers. In its early decades, the ICC proved more important as a precedent than effective as a watchdog.

Concern over the growing power of the trusts led Congress to pass the **Sherman Antitrust Act** in 1890. The act outlawed pools and trusts, ruling that businesses could no longer enter into agreements to restrict competition. It did nothing to restrict huge holding companies such as Standard Oil, however, and proved to be a weak sword against the trusts. In the following decade, the government successfully struck down only six trusts but used the law four times against labor by outlawing unions as a "conspiracy in restraint of trade." In 1895, the conservative Supreme Court dealt the antitrust law a crippling blow in *United States v. E. C. Knight Company*. In its decision, the Court ruled that "manufacture" did not constitute "trade." This semantic quibble drastically narrowed the law, in this case allowing the American Sugar Refining Company, which had bought out a number of other sugar companies (including E. C. Knight) and controlled 98 percent of the production of sugar, to continue its virtual monopoly. Yet the Court insisted the law could be used against labor unions.

Both the ICC and the Sherman Antitrust Act testified to the nation's concern about corporate abuses of power and to a growing willingness to use federal measures to intervene on behalf of the public interest. As corporate capitalism became more and more powerful, public pressure toward government intervention grew. Yet not until the twentieth century would more active presidents sharpen and use these weapons effectively against the large corporations.

The Fight for Free Silver

While the tariff and regulation of the trusts gained many backers, the silver issue stirred passions like no other issue of the day. On one side stood those who believed that gold constituted the only honest money. Many who supported the gold standard were eastern creditors who did not wish to be paid in devalued dollars. On the opposite side stood a coalition of western silver barons and poor farmers from the West and South who called for **free silver**. Farmers from the West and South hoped to increase the money supply with silver dollars and create inflation, which would give them some debt relief by enabling them to pay off their creditors with cheaper dollars. The mining interests, who had seen the silver bonanza in the West drive down the price of the precious metal, wanted the government to buy silver and mint silver dollars.

During the depression following the panic of 1873, critics of hard money organized the Greenback Labor Party, an alliance of farmers and urban wage laborers. The Greenbackers favored issuing paper currency not tied to the gold supply, citing the precedent of the greenbacks issued during the Civil War. The government had the right to define what constituted legal tender, the Greenbackers reasoned: "Paper is equally money, when . . . issued according to law." They proposed that the nation's currency be based on its wealth—land, labor, and capital—and not simply on its reserves of gold. The Greenback Labor Party captured more than a million votes and elected fourteen members to Congress in 1878. Although conservatives considered the Greenbackers dangerous cranks, their views eventually prevailed in the 1930s, when the country abandoned the gold standard.

After the Greenback Labor Party collapsed, proponents of free silver came to dominate the monetary debate in the 1890s. Advocates of free silver pointed out that until 1873 the country

had enjoyed a system of bimetallism—the minting of both silver and gold into coins. In that year, at the behest of those who favored gold, the Republican Congress had voted to stop buying and minting silver, an act silver supporters denounced as the "crime of '73." By sharply contracting the money supply at a time when the nation's economy was burgeoning, the Republicans had enriched bankers and investors at the expense of cotton and wheat farmers and industrial wageworkers. In 1878 and again in 1890, with the Sherman Silver Purchase Act, Congress took steps to ease the tight money policy and appease advocates of silver by passing legislation requiring the government to buy silver and issue silver certificates. Though good for the mining interests, the laws did little to promote the inflation desired by farmers. Soon monetary reformers began to call for "the free and unlimited coinage of silver," a plan whereby nearly all the silver mined in the West would be minted into coins circulated at the rate of sixteen ounces of silver—equal in value to one ounce of gold.

By the 1890s, the silver issue crossed party lines. The Democrats hoped to use it to achieve a union between western and southern voters. Unfortunately for them, Democratic president Grover Cleveland supported the gold standard as vehemently as any Republican. After a panic on Wall Street in the spring of 1893, Cleveland called a special session of Congress and bullied the legislature into repealing the Silver Purchase Act because he believed it threatened economic confidence. Repeal proved disastrous for Cleveland. It did nothing to bring prosperity and dangerously divided the country. Angry farmers warned Cleveland not to travel west of the Mississippi River if he valued his life.

Greenback Labor Party Seal
The Greenback Labor Party, active in the 1870s, pushed for an inflationary currency that would give farmers and workers more money in circulation to help pay off debts. Its party seal is progressive for the era, focusing on the family by picturing a girl child and not a man or boy—a sign of how important women were in the organization. The Granger Collection, New York.

Panic and Depression

President Cleveland had scarcely begun his second term in 1893 when the country plunged into the worst depression it had yet seen. In the face of economic disaster, Cleveland clung to the economic orthodoxy of the gold standard. In the winter of 1894–95, the president walked the floor of the White House, sleepless over the prospect that the United States might go bankrupt. Individuals and investors, rushing to trade in their banknotes for gold, strained the country's monetary system. The Treasury's gold reserves dipped so low that unless they could be buttressed, the unthinkable might happen: The U.S. Treasury might not be able to meet its obligations.

At this juncture, J. P. Morgan stepped in. A group of bankers pledged to purchase millions in U.S. government bonds, paying in gold. Cleveland knew that such a scheme would unleash a thunder of protest, yet to save the gold standard, the president had no choice. But if President Cleveland's action managed to salvage the gold standard, it did not save the country from hardship. In the winter of 1894–95, people faced unemployment, cold, and hunger. Cleveland, a firm believer in limited government, insisted that nothing could be done to help: "I do not believe that the power and duty of the General Government ought to be extended to the relief of individual suffering which is in no manner properly related to the public service or benefit." Nor did it occur to Cleveland that his great faith in the gold standard prolonged the depression, favored creditors over debtors, and caused immense hardship for millions of Americans.

REVIEW   What role did economic issues play in party realignment?

▶ Conclusion: Business Dominates an Era

The gold deal between J. P. Morgan and Grover Cleveland underscored a dangerous reality: the federal government was so weak that its solvency depended on a private banker. This lopsided power relationship signaled the dominance of business in the era Mark Twain satirically but accurately characterized as the Gilded Age. Birthed by the railroads, the new economy spawned greed, corruption, and vulgarity on a grand scale. Speculators like Jay Gould not only built but wrecked railroads to turn paper profits; the get-rich-quick ethic of the gold rush infused the whole continent; and business boasted openly of buying politicians, who in turn lined their pockets at the public's expense.

Nevertheless, the Gilded Age was not without its share of solid achievements. Where dusty roads and cattle trails once sprawled across the continent, steel rails now bound the country together, creating a national market that enabled America to make the leap into the industrial age. Factories and refineries poured out American steel and oil at unprecedented rates. Businessmen like Carnegie, Rockefeller, and Morgan developed new strategies to consolidate American industry. New inventions, including the telephone and electric light and power, transformed Americans' everyday lives.

By the end of the nineteenth century, the United States had achieved industrial maturity. It boasted the largest, most innovative, most productive economy in the world. The rise of Gilded Age industry came at a cost, however. The rampant railway building changed the nature of politics in the United States, entwining the state and the corporations and making a mockery of a free market economy. And as one historian speculated, had railroad magnates waited to build Western railroads to meet demand, their restraint might have resulted in less waste, less environmental degradation, less human suffering for Native Americans and whites alike.

The effects of American industry worried many Americans and gave rise to the era's political turmoil. Race and gender profoundly influenced American politics, leading to new political alliances. Fearless activist Ida B. Wells fought racism in its most brutal form—lynching. Women's organizations championed causes, notably suffrage and temperance, and challenged prevailing views of woman's proper sphere. Reformers fought corruption by instituting civil service. And new issues—the tariff, the regulation of the trusts, and currency reform—restructured the nation's politics.

The Gilded Age witnessed a nation transformed. Fueled by railroad building and expanding industry, cities grew exponentially, bulging at the seams with new inhabitants from around the globe and bristling with new bridges, subways, and skyscrapers. The frenzied growth of urban America brought wealth and opportunity, but also the exploitation of labor, racism toward newcomers, and social upheaval that lent a new urgency to calls for social reform.

See the Selected Bibliography for this chapter in the Appendix.

18 Chapter Review

MAKE IT STICK

 **LearningCurve**

Go online and use LearningCurve to see what you know. Then review the key terms and answer the questions.

KEY TERMS

Gilded Age (p. 495)
trust (p. 502)
finance capitalism (p. 504)
social Darwinism (p. 507)
gospel of wealth (p. 508)
spoils system (p. 508)
Jim Crow (p. 509)
Woman's Christian Temperance Union (WCTU) (p. 512)
civil service reform (p. 514)
Interstate Commerce Commission (ICC) (p. 517)
Sherman Antitrust Act (p. 517)
free silver (p. 517)

REVIEW QUESTIONS

1. When, why, and how did the transcontinental railroad system develop, and what was its impact on American business? (pp. 495–501)

2. Why did the ideas of social Darwinism appeal to many Americans in the late nineteenth century? (pp. 506–508)

3. How did race and gender influence politics? (pp. 508–513)

4. How did the question of civil service reform contribute to divisions within the Republican Party? (pp. 513–516)

5. What role did economic issues play in party realignment? (pp. 516–519)

MAKING CONNECTIONS

1. What were some of the key technology and business innovations in the late nineteenth century? How did they aid the maturation of American industry?

2. By the 1870s, what new issues displaced slavery as the defining question of American politics, and how did they shape new regional, economic, and racial alliances and rivalries?

3. How did the activism of women denied the vote contribute to Gilded Age electoral politics? Be sure to cite specific examples of political action.

4. Citing specific policies and court decisions, discuss how government helped augment the power of big business in the late nineteenth century.

LINKING TO THE PAST

1. In what ways did the military conquest of the trans-Mississippi West, with its dislocation of Native Americans, play a significant role in the industrial boom of the Gilded Age? (See chapter 17.)

2. In what ways did the rampant get-rich-quick mentality of western minters and land speculators help set the tone for the Gilded Age? Is the West the herald of the Gilded Age, or must we look to New York and Washington? (See chapter 17.)

19

The City and Its Workers

1870–1900

CONTENT LEARNING OBJECTIVES

After reading and studying this chapter, you should be able to:

- Identify the factors that led to rapid urbanization during the late nineteenth century. Describe how the social geography of the city changed and the reactions to those changes.

- Describe the diversity of American labor, including the role of women and children in the workforce.

- Understand why workers organized and how management responded to labor's demands. Analyze the impact of the Great Strike of 1877, the Knights of Labor, the American Federation of Labor, and the Haymarket bombing.

- Describe how notions of domesticity and everyday amusements reflected class divisions.

- Identify the nature of city government in the late nineteenth century and the growth of city amenities. Explain Americans' ambivalence toward cities.

"A TOWN THAT CRAWLED NOW STANDS ERECT, AND WE WHOSE backs were bent above the hearths know how it got its spine," boasted a steelworker surveying New York City. Where once wooden buildings stood rooted in the mire of unpaved streets, cities of stone and steel sprang up in the last decades of the nineteenth century. The labor of millions of workers, many of them immigrants, laid the foundations for urban America.

No symbol better represented the new urban landscape than the Brooklyn Bridge, opened in May 1883. The great bridge soared over the East River in a single mile-long span. Building the Brooklyn Bridge took fourteen years and cost the lives of twenty-seven men. To sink the foundation in the riverbed, laborers tunneled through the mud and worked in boxes that were open at the bottom and pressurized to keep the water out. Before long workers experienced the malady they called "bends" because it left them doubled over in pain when they rose to the surface. (Scientists later learned that nitrogen bubbles trapped in the bloodstream caused the bends, which could be prevented by allowing for decompression.) The first death occurred when the foundation reached a depth of seventy-one feet. A German immigrant complained that he did not feel well. He collapsed and died on his way home. Eight days later, another man dropped dead, and the entire workforce went out on strike. Terrified workers demanded a higher wage for fewer hours of work.

BROOKLYN BRIDGE FAN
This commemorative fan celebrates the opening of the bridge on May 24, 1883. It took fourteen years and cost the lives of twenty-seven men to complete the bridge.
© Museum of the City of New York, USA/The Bridgeman Art Library.

A scrawny sixteen-year-old from Ireland, Frank Harris, remembered the fearful experience of going to work on the bridge a few days after landing in America:

The six of us were working naked to the waist in the small iron chamber with the temperature of about 80 degrees Fahrenheit: In five minutes the sweat was pouring from us, and all the while we were standing in icy water that was only kept from rising by the terrific pressure. No wonder the headaches were blinding.

By his fifth day, Harris quit. Many immigrant workers walked off the job, often as many as a hundred a week. But a ready supply of immigrants meant that new workers took up the digging, where they could earn in a day more than they made in a week in Ireland or Italy.

Begun in 1869, the bridge was the dream of builder John Roebling, who died in a freak accident almost as soon as construction began. Washington Roebling took over as chief engineer after his father's death, routinely working twelve- to fourteen-hour days, six days a week. Soon he too fell victim to the bends. He directed the completion of the bridge through a telescope from his bedroom window in Brooklyn Heights. His wife, Emily Warren Roebling, acted as site superintendent and general engineer of the project.

At the end of the nineteenth century, the Brooklyn Bridge stood as a symbol of many things: the industrial might of the United States; the labor of the nation's immigrants; the ingenuity and genius of its engineers and inventors; the rise of iron and steel; and, most of all, the ascendancy of urban America. Poised on the brink of the twentieth century, the nation was shifting from a rural, agricultural society to an urban, industrial nation. The gap between rich and poor widened. In the burgeoning cities, tensions erupted into conflict as workers squared off to organize into labor unions and to demand safer working conditions, shorter hours, and better pay, sometimes with violent and bloody results. The explosive growth of the cities fostered political corruption as unscrupulous bosses and entrepreneurs cashed in on the building boom. Immigrants, political bosses, middle-class managers, poor laborers, and the very rich populated the nation's cities, crowding the streets, laboring in the stores and factories, and taking their leisure at the new ballparks, amusement parks, dance halls, and municipal parks. As the new century dawned, the city and its workers moved to center stage in American life.

VISUAL ACTIVITY

Workers on the Brooklyn Bridge

Illustrations show workers tunneling under the East River to lay the foundations for the Brooklyn Bridge. A cylindrical airlock took them down more than seventy feet. "What with the flaming lights, the deep shadows, the confusing noise of hammer, drills, and chains, the half-naked forms flitting about," wrote one reporter, the scene resembled hell. Library of Congress.

READING THE IMAGE: What would you guess about the age and the physical condition of the workers pictured?

CONNECTIONS: Who did the work of building America's new industrial infrastructure? How were they rewarded?

▶ The Rise of the City

"We cannot all live in cities, yet nearly all seem determined to do so," New York editor Horace Greeley complained. The last three decades of the nineteenth century witnessed an urban explosion. Cities and towns grew more than twice as rapidly as the total population. By 1900, the United States boasted three cities with more than a million inhabitants—New York, Chicago, and Philadelphia.

Patterns of **global migration** contributed to the rise of the city. In the port cities of the East Coast, more than fourteen million people arrived, many from southern and eastern Europe, and huddled together in dense urban ghettos. The word *slum* entered the American vocabulary along with a growing concern over the rising tide of newcomers. In the city, the widening gap between rich and poor became not just financial but physical. Changes in the city landscape brought about by advances in transportation and technology accentuated the great divide in wealth at the same time they put physical distance between rich and poor.

The Urban Explosion: A Global Migration

The United States grew up in the country and moved to the city, or so it seemed by the end of the nineteenth century. Between 1870 and 1900, eleven million people moved into cities. Burgeoning industrial centers such as Pittsburgh, Chicago, New York, and Cleveland acted as giant magnets, attracting workers from the countryside. But rural Americans were not the only ones migrating to cities. Millions of immigrants moved from their native countries to America. Worldwide in scope, the movement from rural areas to urban industrial centers attracted millions of immigrants to American shores.

By the 1870s, the world could be conceptualized as three interconnected geographic regions (Map 19.1). At the center stood an industrial core that encompassed the eastern United States and western Europe. Surrounding this industrial core lay a vast agricultural domain from the Canadian wheat fields to the hinterlands of northern China. Capitalist development in the late nineteenth century shattered traditional patterns of economic activity in this rural periphery. As old patterns broke down, these rural areas exported, along with other raw materials, new recruits for the industrial labor force.

CHRONOLOGY

1869	• Knights of Labor founded. • Cincinnati mounts first paid baseball team.
1871	• Boss Tweed's rule in New York ends. • Chicago's Great Fire.
1873	• Panic on Wall Street touches off depression.
1877	• Great Railroad Strike.
1880s	• Immigration from southern and eastern Europe rises.
1882	• Chinese Exclusion Act.
1883	• Brooklyn Bridge opens.
1886	• American Federation of Labor (AFL) founded. • Haymarket bombing.
1890s	• African American migration from the South begins.
1890	• Jacob Riis publishes *How the Other Half Lives*.
1892	• Ellis Island opens.
1893	• World's Columbian Exposition. • Panic on Wall Street touches off major economic depression.
1895	• Boston Public Library opens in Copley Square.
1896	• President Grover Cleveland vetoes immigrant literacy test.
1897	• Steeplechase Park opens on Coney Island. • Nation's first subway system opens in Boston.

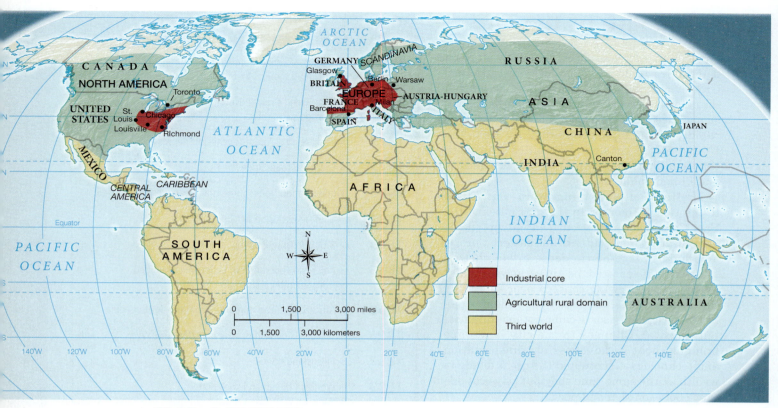

MAP ACTIVITY

Map 19.1 Economic Regions of the World, 1890
The global nature of the world economy at the turn of the twentieth century is indicated by three interconnected geographic regions. At the center stands the industrial core—western Europe and the northeastern United States. The second region—the agricultural periphery—supplied immigrant laborers to the industries in the core. Beyond these two regions lay a vast area tied economically to the industrial core by colonialism.

READING THE MAP: What types of economic regions were contained in the United States in this period? Which continents held most of the industrial core? Which held most of the agricultural rural domain? Which held the greatest portion of the third world?
CONNECTIONS: Which of these three regions provided the bulk of immigrant workers to the United States? What major changes prompted the global migration at the end of the nineteenth century?

Beyond this second circle lay an even larger third world. Colonial ties between this part of the world and the industrial core strengthened in the late nineteenth century, but most of the people living there stayed put. They worked on plantations and railroads, and in mines and ports, as part of a huge export network managed by foreign powers that staked out spheres of influence and colonies in this vast region.

In the 1870s, railroad expansion and low steamship fares gave the world's peoples a new-found mobility, enabling industrialists to draw on a global population for cheap labor. When Andrew Carnegie opened his first steel mill in 1872, his superintendent hired workers he called

"buckwheats"—young American boys just off the farm. By the 1890s, however, Carnegie's workforce was liberally sprinkled with other rural boys, Hungarians and Slavs who had migrated to the United States, willing to work for low wages.

Altogether, more than 25 million immigrants came to the United States between 1850 and 1920. They came from all directions: east from Asia, south from Canada, north from Latin America, and west from Europe (Map 19.2). Part of a worldwide migration, emigrants traveled to South America and Australia as well as to the United States. Yet more than 70 percent of all European emigrants chose North America as their destination.

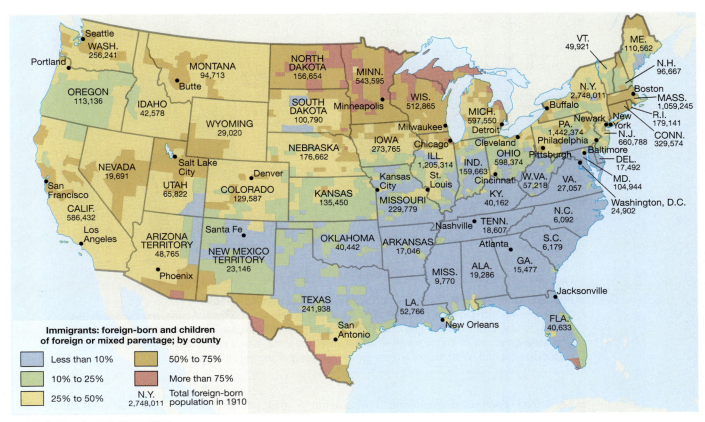

Immigrants: foreign-born and children of foreign or mixed parentage; by county

- Less than 10%
- 10% to 25%
- 25% to 50%
- 50% to 75%
- More than 75%

N.Y. 2,748,011 Total foreign-born population in 1910

MAP ACTIVITY

Map 19.2 The Impact of Immigration, to 1910

Immigration flowed in all directions—south from Canada, north from Mexico and Latin America, east from Asia, and west from Europe.

READING THE MAP: Which states had the high percentages of immigrants? Which cities attracted the most immigrants? Which cities attracted the fewest?

CONNECTIONS: Why did most immigrants gravitate toward the cities? Why do you think the South drew such a low percentage of immigrants?

Historically, the largest number of immigrants to the United States came from the British Isles and from German-speaking lands (Figure 19.1). The vast majority of immigrants were white; Asians accounted for fewer than one million immigrants, and other people of color numbered even fewer. Yet ingrained racial prejudices increasingly influenced the country's perception of immigration patterns. One of the classic formulations of the history of European immigration divided immigrants into two distinct waves that have been called the "old" and the "new" immigration. According to this theory, before 1880 the majority of immigrants came from northern and western Europe, with Germans, Irish, English, and Scandinavians making up approximately 85 percent of the newcomers. After 1880, the pattern shifted, with more and more ships

carrying passengers from southern and eastern Europe. Italians, Hungarians, eastern European Jews, Turks, Armenians, Poles, Russians, and other Slavic peoples accounted for more than 80 percent of all immigrants by 1896 (Figure 19.2). Implicit in the distinction was an invidious comparison between "old" pioneer settlers and "new" unskilled laborers. Yet this sweeping generalization spoke more to perception than to reality. In fact, many of the earlier immigrants from Ireland, Germany, and Scandinavia came not as settlers or farmers, but as wageworkers, and they were met with much the same disdain as the Italians and Slavs who followed them.

During good financial times, the need for cheap, unskilled labor for America's industries stimulated demand for immigrant workers. In 1873 and again in 1893, when the United States

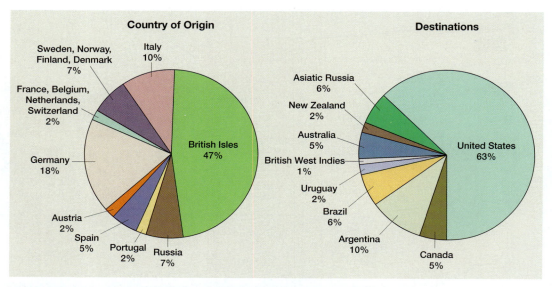

FIGURE 19.1   Global Comparison: European Emigration, 1870–1890
European emigration between 1870 and 1890 shows that people from Germany, Austria, and the British Isles formed the largest group of out-migrants. After 1890, the origin of European emigrants tilted south and east, with Italians and eastern Europeans growing in number. The United States took in nearly two-thirds of the Europeans emigrants. What factors account for the popularity of the United States?

experienced economic depressions, immigration slowed, only to pick up again when prosperity returned.

Steamship companies courted immigrants—a highly profitable, self-loading cargo. By the 1880s, the price of a ticket from Liverpool had dropped to less than $25. Would-be immigrants eager for information about the United States relied on letters from friends and relatives, advertisements, and word of mouth—sources that were not always dependable or truthful. As one Italian immigrant recalled, "News was colored, success

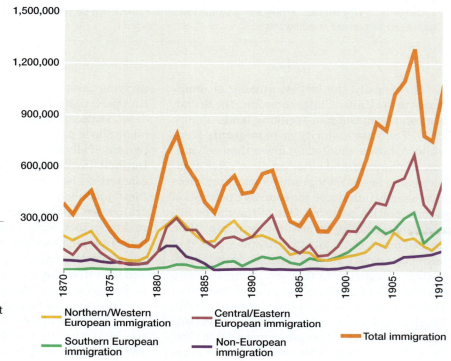

FIGURE 19.2   European Emigration, 1870–1910

Before 1880, more than 85 percent of U.S. immigrants came from northern and western Europe—Germany, Ireland, England, and the Scandinavian countries. After 1880, 80 percent of the "new" immigrants came from Italy, Turkey, Hungary, Armenia, Poland, Russia, and other Slavic countries.

magnified, comforts and advantages exaggerated beyond all proportions." Even photographs proved deceptive: Workers dressed in their Sunday best looked more prosperous than they actually were to relatives in the old country, where only the very wealthy wore white collars or silk dresses. No wonder people left for the United States believing, as one Italian immigrant observed, "that if they were ever fortunate enough to reach America, they would fall into a pile of manure and get up brushing the diamonds out of their hair."

Most of the newcomers stayed in the nation's cities. By 1900, almost two-thirds of the country's immigrant population resided in cities. Many of the immigrants were too poor to move on. (The average laborer immigrating to the United States carried only about $21.50.) Although the foreign-born rarely outnumbered the native-born population, taken together immigrants and their American-born children did constitute a majority in some areas, particularly in the nation's largest cities: Philadelphia, 55 percent; Boston, 66 percent; Chicago, 75 percent; and New York City, an amazing 80 percent in 1900.

Not all the newcomers came to stay. Perhaps eight million European immigrants—most of them young men—worked for a year or a season and then returned to their homelands. Immigration officers called these immigrants, many of them Italians, "birds of passage" because they followed a regular pattern of migration to and from the United States. By 1900, almost 75 percent of the new immigrants were young, single men. Willing to accept conditions other workers

regarded as intolerable, these young migrants showed little interest in labor unions. They organized only when the dream of returning home faded, as it did for millions who ultimately remained in the United States.

Women generally had less access to funds for travel and faced tighter family control. Because the traditional sexual division of labor relied on women's unpaid domestic labor and care of the very young and the very old, women most often came to the United States as wives, mothers, or daughters, not as single wage laborers. Only among the Irish, where the great potato famine presented the grim choice of starve or leave, did women immigrants outnumber men by a small margin from 1871 to 1891.

Jews from eastern Europe and Russia most often came with their families and came to stay. Fear of conscription into the Russian army motivated many young men to leave Russia. In addition, beginning in the 1880s, a wave of violent pogroms, or persecutions, in Russia and Poland prompted the departure of more than a million Jews in the next two decades. (See "Seeking the American Promise," page 528.) Mary Antin, a Jew leaving Poland for America, recalled her excitement: "So, at last I was going to America! Really going at last! The boundaries burst. The arch of heaven soared . . . America! America!" Most of the Jewish immigrants settled in the port cities of the East, creating distinct ethnic enclaves, like Hester Street in the heart of New York City's Lower East Side, which rang with the calls of pushcart peddlers and vendors hawking their wares, from pickles to feather beds.

Pushcart Peddlers in Little Italy
This photo shows banana sellers working from a pushcart in a street in New York's Little Italy. Italian immigrants constituted the majority of banana importers at the turn of the twentieth century. Library of Congress.

Seeking Refuge: Russian Jews Escape the Pogroms

Fifteen-year-old Abraham Bisno recalled running for his life. "I hid myself in a clay hole in an old brickyard on a hillside," he remembered. "I witnessed the mob coming down the hill to assault the Jewish settlement. I saw children and old people beaten—buildings burned—I heard women screaming."

Violent pogroms—deadly riots against Jews—erupted in Russia in 1881 in the wake of the assassination of Czar Alexander II. The city of Kiev, where Abraham Bisno lived with his parents, became the scene of a pogrom in late April. "For days on end," Bisno wrote, "entire neighborhoods were looted and largely destroyed by crowds estimated at over four thousand." Fanatical priests fed anti-Semitism (hatred of Jews) by denouncing the Jews as heartless "Christ-killers" who used the blood of Christian children in their rituals. The government failed to move quickly to put down the violence.

Bands of Russians swarmed through the Jewish quarters, breaking down doors and smashing windows, looting or destroying all the furnishings. They ripped to shreds feather beds and feather pillows, sending the white down into the breeze until it settled like snow over the scenes of violence and mayhem. No one knows precisely how many Jews died at the hands of the mob, but estimates range as high as five hundred. "The building we lived in and the place we worked in were assaulted at the same time," Bisno recalled. "Mother ran for her life while we struggled for ours; we were all separated by the mob— the shop was destroyed, the goods carried away."

These and subsequent pogroms and persecutions prompted a great wave of Jewish migration. Between 1880 and 1914, more than 2.7 million Jews sought refuge from religious persecution, the vast majority of them heading to the United States. Among the first to emigrate were Abraham Bisno and his family. When the Bisnos learned that Jewish groups in Europe and America had raised money to help Russian Jews emigrate, they scraped together forty rubles to get from Kiev to Brody in Galicia, where the refugees gathered. "Our family sold a sewing machine and whatever clothing could be spared—some from our very backs." In Brody, they had to wait six weeks, begging for bread on the streets, before they received aid to pay for their passage overland to Hamburg and from there to Liverpool and on to the United States.

The trip was long and arduous, particularly the ocean voyage. Crowded in steerage, immigrants suffered seasickness during the crossing, which took two to three weeks by steamer. Once in the United States, the Bisno family was sent on to Atlanta by an American committee formed to help the immigrants. The men quickly found work as tailors. Bisno struck out on his own, moving to Chattanooga, where he apprenticed to an English-speaking tailor and quickly picked up the language by reading signs and advertisements. But the Bisnos were unhappy in the South. Abraham's mother complained that she could not find a butcher who sold kosher meat, and his father fretted that there was no Orthodox synagogue in the neighborhood. So after nine months, the family moved to a larger Jewish community in Chicago.

The slums of the nation's big cities, where many of the Jewish immigrants ended up, were far from a "promised land." The Bisnos lived in a dilapidated shack above a stable with a yard "full of rags, junk, rats, and vermin." Other Jewish immigrants voiced their disappointment at the conditions they encountered in the United States. "The dirt, the noise, the confusion, the swarming hurrying crowds!" Goldie Stone exclaimed. "My heart sank. This was all so different from what I had expected or dreamed."

Racism and the Cry for Immigration Restriction

Ethnic diversity and racism played a role in dividing skilled workers (those with a craft or specialized ability) from the globe-hopping proletariat of unskilled workers (those who supplied muscle or tended machines). Skilled workers, frequently members of older immigrant groups, criticized the newcomers. One Irish worker complained, "There should be a law . . . to keep all the Italians from comin' in and takin' the bread out of the mouths of honest people."

The Irish worker's resentment brings into focus the impact racism had on America's immigrant laborers. Throughout the nineteenth century and into the twentieth, members of the educated elite as well as the uneducated viewed ethnic and even religious differences as racial characteristics, referring to the Polish or the Jewish "race." Americans judged immigrants of southern and eastern European "races" as

Bad as conditions were, the immigrant Jews appreciated the safe haven the United States afforded. And although the sweatshops where Bisno and other Jewish immigrants labored were dark and bleak, for most Jews the slums proved a temporary prison. The United States provided not only a refuge but also a chance to start over and prosper. Bisno watched as many of his friends and relatives, after saving or borrowing a little money, opened small businesses of their own. "All had to begin in a very small way," he recalled. "With a hundred or two hundred dollars they were able to start grocery stores, markets, cigar stores." Bisno quickly moved up in his trade, becoming a contractor in a sweatshop by the time he reached the age of sixteen. But then his life took a different course. Moved by the Haymarket martyrs, he converted to socialism in 1886, joined the Knights of Labor, and went on to become a labor organizer. The first president of the Chicago Cloak Makers' Union, he worked to improve the lot of garment workers until his death in 1929.

Jewish Refugees from the Pogroms
In this colorful depiction, Liberty, dressed in the Stars and Stripes, opens the gates of the country to a Jewish immigrant couple and their children fleeing the pogroms in Russia. Abraham Bisno and his family were among the first group of immigrants to flee Kiev after the pogroms of 1881 and to seek refuge in the United States. Yivo Institute for Jewish Research.

Questions for Consideration

1. Compare the Jewish immigrants from Russia with other immigrant groups discussed in this chapter. What attracted each group to America? What were their expectations? How did each group fare?

2. What aspects of Bisno's life in America led him to join the labor movement? How may his childhood in Russia have influenced him in this direction?

Connect to the Big Idea

C What developments in technology and industry encouraged global immigration during the Gilded Age?

inferior. Each wave of newcomers was deemed somehow inferior to the established residents. The Irish who criticized the Italians so harshly had themselves been stigmatized as a lesser "race" a generation earlier.

Immigrants not only brought their own religious and racial prejudices to the United States but also absorbed the popular prejudices of American culture. Social Darwinism, with its strongly racist overtones, decreed that whites stood at the top of the evolutionary ladder. But

who was "white"? Skin color supposedly served as a marker for the "new" immigrants—"swarthy" Italians; dark-haired, olive-skinned Jews. But even blond, blue-eyed Poles were not considered "white." The social construction of race is nowhere more apparent than in the testimony of an Irish dockworker, who boasted that he hired only "white men," a category that he insisted excluded "Poles and Italians." For the new immigrants, Americanization and assimilation would prove inextricably part of becoming "white."

For African Americans, the cities of the North promised not just economic opportunity but an escape from institutionalized segregation and persecution. Throughout the South, Jim Crow laws—restrictions that segregated blacks—became common in the decades following reconstruction. Intimidation and lynching terrorized blacks. "To die from the bite of frost is far more glorious than at the hands of a mob," proclaimed the *Defender*, Chicago's largest African American newspaper. In the 1890s, many blacks moved north, settling for the most part in the growing cities. Racism relegated them to poor jobs and substandard living conditions, but by 1900 New York, Philadelphia, and Chicago had the largest black communities in the nation. Although the most significant African American migration out of the South would occur during and after World War I, the great exodus was already under way.

On the West Coast, Asian immigrants became scapegoats of the changing economy. Hard times in the 1870s made them a target for disgruntled workers, who dismissed them as "coolie" labor. Contract laborers recruited by employers, or later by prosperous members of their own race or ethnicity, represented the antithesis of free labor to the workers who competed with them. In the West, the issue became racialized, and while the Chinese were by no means the only contract laborers, the Sinophobia that produced the scapegoat of the "coolie" permeated the labor movement. Prohibited from owning land, the Chinese migrated to the cities. In 1870, San Francisco housed a Chinese population estimated at 12,022, and it continued to grow until passage of the Chinese Exclusion Act in 1882 (see "The Diverse Peoples of the West" in chapter 17). For the first time in the nation's history, U.S. law excluded an immigrant group on the basis of race.

Some Chinese managed to come to America using a loophole in the exclusion law that allowed relatives to join their families. Meanwhile the number of Japanese immigrants rapidly grew until pressure to keep out all Asians led in 1910 to the creation of an immigration station at Angel Island in San Francisco Bay where immigrants were quarantined until judged fit to enter the United States.

On the East Coast, the volume of immigration from Europe in the last two decades of the century proved unprecedented. In 1888 alone, more than half a million Europeans landed in America, 75 percent of them in New York City. The Statue of Liberty, erected in 1886 as a gift from the people of France, stood sentinel in the harbor.

A young Jewish woman named Emma Lazarus penned the verse inscribed on Lady Liberty's base:

> Give me your tired, your poor,
> Your huddled masses yearning to breathe free,
> The wretched refuse of your teeming shore.
> Send these, the homeless tempest-tost to me,
> I lift my lamp beside the golden door!

Lazarus's poem stood both as a promise and a warning. With increasing immigration, some Americans soon would question whether the country really wanted the "huddled masses" or the "wretched refuse" of the world.

The tide of immigrants to New York City soon swamped the immigration office in lower Manhattan. After the federal government took over immigration in 1890, it built a facility on **Ellis Island**, in New York harbor, which opened in 1892. After fire gutted the wooden building, a new brick edifice replaced it in 1900. Able to process 5,000 immigrants a day, it was already inadequate by the time it opened. Its overcrowded halls became the gateway to the United States for millions.

To many Americans the new southern and eastern European immigrants appeared backward, uneducated, and outlandish in appearance—impossible to assimilate. "These people are not Americans," editorialized the popular journal *Public Opinion*, "they are the very scum and offal of Europe." Terence V. Powderly, head of the broadly inclusive Knights of Labor, complained that the newcomers "herded together like animals and lived like beasts." Blue-blooded Yankees led by Senator Henry Cabot Lodge of Massachusetts formed an unlikely alliance with leaders of organized labor—who feared that immigrants would drive down wages—to press for immigration restrictions. In 1896, Congress approved a literacy test for immigrants, but President Grover Cleveland promptly vetoed it. "It is said," the president reminded Congress, "that the quality of recent immigration is undesirable. The time is quite within recent memory when the same thing was said of immigrants, who, with their descendants, are now numbered among our best citizens."

The Social Geography of the City

During the Gilded Age, the social geography of the city changed enormously. Cleveland, Ohio, provides a good example. In the 1870s, Cleveland was a small city in both population and area. Oil magnate John D. Rockefeller could, and often did, walk from his large brick house on Euclid Avenue to his office downtown. On his way, he passed the small homes of his clerks and other middle-class families. Behind these homes ran miles of alleys crowded with the dwellings of Cleveland's working class. Farther out, on the shores of Lake Erie, close to the factories and foundries, clustered the shanties of the city's poorest laborers.

Within two decades, the Cleveland that Rockefeller knew no longer existed. The coming of mass transit transformed the walking city. In its place emerged a central business district surrounded by concentric rings of residences organized by ethnicity and income. First the horse car in the 1870s and then the electric streetcar in the 1880s made it possible for those who could afford the five-cent fare to work downtown and flee after work to the "cool green rim" of the city. Social segregation—the separation of rich and poor, and of ethnic and old-stock Americans—became one of the major social changes engendered by the rise of the industrial metropolis.

Race and ethnicity affected the way cities evolved. Newcomers to the nation's cities faced hostility and, not surprisingly, sought out their kin and country folk as they struggled to get ahead. Distinct ethnic neighborhoods often formed around a synagogue or church. African Americans typically experienced the greatest residential segregation, but every large city had its distinct ethnic neighborhoods—Little Italy, China-town, Bohemia Flats, Germantown—where English was rarely spoken.

Poverty, crowding, dirt, and disease constituted the daily reality of New York City's immigrant poor—a plight documented by photojournalist Jacob Riis in his best-selling book *How the Other Half Lives* (1890). By taking his camera into the hovels of the poor, Riis opened the nation's eyes to the filthy, overcrowded conditions in the city's slums (see chapter 21, "Visualizing History," page 594).

Pushcart for Sharpening Knives and Scissors

Joseph Antonucci, an Italian immigrant, used this cart to sharpen knives and scissors on Chicago's West Side in 1900. Sometimes he pushed his cart for miles to ply his trade outside the city in nearby towns. For poor immigrants who could not afford to rent a store, pushcarts provided a cheap means of livelihood. Street peddlers and vendors like Antonucci added to the bustle of urban streets. © Chicago History Museum, USA/The Bridgeman Art Library.

VISUAL ACTIVITY

The Arrival of the Electric Streetcar

The electric streetcar was part of the transformation of the cityscape in the late nineteenth century. This shiny new streetcar stands in front of Cincinnati's City Hall in 1890. © Bettmann/CORBIS.

READING THE IMAGE: What other type of transportation is pictured here, and what do you see that suggests the electric streetcar would be cleaner for the immediate environment?

CONNECTIONS: What did the coming of mass transit mean to the social geography of the city?

However, Riis's book, like his photographs, presented a world of black and white. There were many layers to the population Riis labeled "the other half"—distinctions deepened by ethnicity, religion, race, and gender. *How the Other Half Lives* must be read more as a reformer's call to action than as an entirely accurate portrayal of the varied and complex lives of "the other half." But it served its purpose. Tenement reform and city playgrounds grew out of Riis's exposé.

While Riis's audience shivered at his revelations about the "other half," many middle-class Americans worried equally about the excesses of the wealthy. They feared the class antagonism fueled by the growing chasm between rich and poor and shared Riis's view that "the real danger to society comes not only from the tenements, but from the ill-spent wealth which reared them."

The excesses of the Gilded Age's newly minted millionaires were nowhere more visible than in the lifestyle of the Vanderbilts. Cornelius "Commodore" Vanderbilt, the uncouth ferryman who built the New York Central Railroad, died in 1877. Today he still holds first place among the richest men in America (when adjusted for inflation). He left his son William $90 million. William doubled the sum, and his two sons proceeded to spend it on Fifth Avenue mansions and "cottages" in Newport, Rhode Island, that sought to rival the palaces of Europe (see chapter 18, "Visualizing History," page 498). Alva Vanderbilt, looked down on by the old-money matrons of New York, launched herself into New York society in 1883 with a costume party so opulent that her detractors had to cave in and accept her invitation. Alice Vanderbilt, her sister, topped all the guests by appearing as that miraculous new invention, the electric light, resplendent in a white satin evening dress studded with diamonds. The *New York World* speculated that Alva's party cost more than a quarter of a million dollars, more than $5 million in today's dollars.

Such ostentatious displays of wealth became especially alarming when they were coupled with disdain for the well-being of ordinary people. When a reporter in 1882 asked William Vanderbilt whether he considered the public good when running his railroads, he shot back, "The public be damned." The fear that America had become a plutocracy—a society ruled by the rich—gained credence from the fact that the wealthiest 1 percent of the population owned more than half the real and personal property in the country. As the new century dawned, reformers would form a progressive movement to address the problems of urban industrialism and the substandard living and working conditions it produced.

REVIEW   Why did American cities experience explosive growth in the late nineteenth century?

▶ At Work in Industrial America

The number of industrial wageworkers in the United States exploded in the second half of the nineteenth century, more than tripling from 5.3 million in 1860 to 17.4 million in 1900. These workers toiled in a variety of settings. Many skilled workers and artisans still earned a living in small workshops. But with the rise of corporate capitalism, large factories, mills, and mines increasingly dotted the landscape. Sweatshops and the contracting out of piecework, including finishing garments by hand, provided work experiences different from those of factory operatives and industrial workers. Pick-and-shovel labor constituted the lowest-paid labor, while managers, as well as women "typewriters" and salesclerks, formed a new white-collar segment of America's workforce. Children also worked in growing numbers in mills and mines across the country.

America's Diverse Workers

Common laborers formed the backbone of the American labor force. They built the railroads and subways, tunneled under New York's East River to anchor the Brooklyn Bridge, and helped lay the foundation of industrial America. These "human machines" generally came from the most recent immigrant groups. Initially, the Irish wielded the picks and shovels that built American cities, but by the turn of the century, as the Irish bettered their lot, Slavs and Italians took up their tools.

At the opposite end of labor's hierarchy stood skilled craftsmen like iron puddler James J. Davis, a Welsh immigrant who worked in the Pennsylvania mills. Using brains along with brawn, puddlers earned good wages—Davis drew up to $7 a day at a time when streetcar fare was 3 cents—when there was work. But most industry and manufacturing work in the nineteenth century remained seasonal; few workers could count on year-round pay. In addition, two major depressions twenty years apart, beginning in 1873 and 1893, brought unemployment and hardship. With no social safety net, even the best worker could not guarantee security for his family. "The fear of ending in the poor-house is one of the terrors that dog a man through life," Davis confessed.

Employers attempted to replace people with machines, breaking down skilled work into ever-smaller tasks that could be performed by unskilled factory operatives. New England's textile mills provide a classic example. Mary, a weaver at the mills in Fall River, Massachusetts, went to work in the 1880s at the age of twelve. Mechanization of the looms had reduced the job of the weaver to watching for breaks in the thread. "At first the noise is fierce, and you have to breathe the cotton all the time, but you get used to it," Mary told a reporter from *Independent* magazine. "When the bobbin flies out and a girl gets hurt, you can't hear her shout—not if she just screams, you can't. She's got to wait, 'till you see her. . . . Lots of us is deaf."

During the 1880s, the number of foreign-born mill workers almost doubled. At Fall River, Mary and her Scots-Irish family resented the new immigrants. "The Polaks learn weavin' quick," she remarked, using a common derogatory term to identify a rival group. "They just as soon live on nothin' and work like that. But it won't do 'em much good for all they'll make out of it." Employers encouraged racial and ethnic antagonism because it inhibited labor organization.

Mechanization transformed the garment industry as well. The introduction of the foot-pedaled sewing machine in the 1850s and the use of mechanical cloth-cutting knives drove out independent tailors who were replaced by pieceworkers. Sadie Frowne, a sixteen-year-old Polish Jew, worked in a Brooklyn **sweatshop** in the 1890s. Frowne sewed for eleven hours a day in a 20-by-14-foot room containing fourteen machines. "The machines go like mad all day, because the faster you work the more money you get," she recalled. She earned about $4.50 a week and, by rigid economy, tried to save $2. Young

Women at Work
Women workers labor under bright lights in this tenement hat shop in New York City. Often sweatshop workers labored in dim tenements belonging to the contractor who hired them. Garment workers frequently worked with highly combustible fabric in unsafe buildings. The Granger Collection, New York

and single, Frowne typified the woman wage earner in the late nineteenth century. In 1890, the average workingwoman was twenty-two and had been working since the age of fifteen, laboring twelve hours a day six days a week and earning less than $6 a week.

The Family Economy: Women and Children

In 1900, the typical male worker in manufacturing earned $500 a year, about $12,000 in today's dollars. Many working-class families, whether native-born or immigrant, lived in or near poverty, their economic survival dependent on the contributions of all family members, regardless of sex or age. "Father," asked one young immigrant girl, "does everybody in America live like this? Go to work early, come home late, eat and go to Sleep? And the next day again work, eat, and sleep?" Most workers did. The **family economy** meant that everyone contributed to maintain even the most meager household.

In the cities, boys as young as six years old plied their trades as bootblacks and newsboys. Often working under an adult contractor, these children earned as little as fifty cents a day. Many of them were homeless—orphaned or cast off by their families. "We wuz six, and we ain't

got no father," a child of twelve told reporter Jacob Riis. "Some of us had to go."

Child labor increased each decade after 1870. The percentage of children under fifteen engaged in paid labor did not drop until after World War I. The 1900 census estimated that 1,750,178 children ages ten to fifteen were employed, an increase of more than a million over thirty years. Children in this age range constituted more than 18 percent of the industrial labor force.

Women working for wages in nonagricultural occupations more than doubled in number between 1870 and 1900 (Figure 19.3). Yet white married women, even among the working class, rarely worked for wages outside the home. In 1890, only 3 percent were employed. Black women, married and unmarried, worked out of the home for wages in much greater numbers. The 1890 census showed that 25 percent of married African American women were employed, often as domestics in the houses of white families.

White-Collar Workers: Managers, "Typewriters," and Salesclerks

In the late nineteenth century, a managerial revolution created a new class of white-collar workers who worked in offices and stores. As

Bootblacks
The faces and hands of the two bootblacks shown here on a New York City street in 1896 testify to their grimy trade. Boys as young as six worked as bootblacks and newsboys, often for contractors who took a cut of their meager earnings. When families could no longer afford to feed their children, young boys often headed out on their own. Library of Congress.

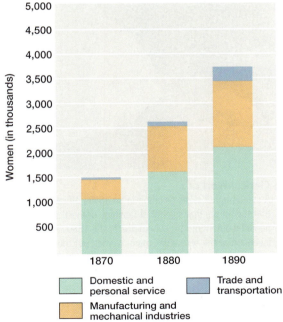

FIGURE 19.3 Women and Work, 1870–1890
In 1870, close to 1.5 million women worked in nonagricultural occupations. By 1890, that number had more than doubled to 3.7 million. More and more women sought work in manufacturing and mechanical industries, although domestic service still constituted the largest employment arena for women.

skilled workers saw their crafts replaced by mechanization, some moved into management positions. "The middle class is becoming a salaried class," a writer for the *Independent* magazine observed, "and is rapidly losing the economic and moral independence of former days." As large business organizations consolidated, corporate development separated management from ownership, and the job of directing the firm became the province of salaried executives and managers, the majority of whom were white men drawn from the 8 percent of Americans who held high school diplomas.

Until late in the century, when engineering schools began to supply recruits, many skilled workers moved from the shop floor to positions of considerable responsibility. Captain William "Billy" Jones, son of a Welsh immigrant, grew up in the heat of the blast furnaces, where he worked as an apprentice at the age of ten. Jones, by all accounts, the best steelman in the business, took as his motto "Good waged and good workmen." In 1872 Andrew Carnegie hired Jones as general superintendent of his new Pittsburgh steelworks. Although Carnegie constantly tried to force down workers' pay, Jones resisted, and he succeeded in shortening the shift from twelve to eight hours by convincing Carnegie that shorter hours reduced absenteeism and accidents. Jones demanded and received "a hell of a big salary"—$25,000, the same as the president of the United States.

The new white-collar workforce also included women **"typewriters"** and salesclerks. In the decades after the Civil War, as businesses became larger and more far-flung, the need for more elaborate and exact records, as well as the greater volume of correspondence, led to the hiring of more office workers. The adding machine, the cash register, and the typewriter came into general use in the 1880s. Employers seeking literate workers soon turned to nimble-fingered women. Educated men had many other career choices, but for middle-class white women, secretarial work constituted one of the very few areas where they could put their literacy to use for wages.

Sylvie Thygeson was typical of the young women who went to work as secretaries. Thygeson grew up in an Illinois prairie town and went to work as a country schoolteacher after graduating high school in 1884. Realizing that teaching school did not pay a living wage, she mastered typing and stenography and found work as a secretary to help support her family. According to her account, she made "a fabulous sum of money" (possibly $25 a month). Nevertheless, she gave up her job after a few years when she met and married her husband.

But by the 1890s, secretarial work was the overwhelming choice of native-born, single white women, who constituted more than 90 percent of the female clerical force. Not only considered more genteel than factory work or domestic labor, office work also meant more money for shorter hours. In 1883, Boston's clerical workers on average made more than $6 a week, compared with less than $5 for women working in manufacturing.

As a new consumer culture came to dominate American urban life in the late nineteenth century, department stores offered another employment opportunity for women in the cities. Boasting ornate facades, large plate-glass display windows, and marble and brass fixtures, stores such as Macy's in New York, Wanamaker's in Philadelphia, and Marshall Field in Chicago stood as monuments to the material promise of the era. Within these palaces of consumption, cash girls, stock clerks, and wrappers earned as little as $3 a week, while at the top of the scale, buyers like Belle Cushman of the fancy goods department at Macy's earned $25 a week, an unusually high salary for a woman in the 1870s. Salesclerks counted themselves a cut above factory workers.

Clerical Worker
A stenographer takes dictation in an 1890s office. Notice that the apron, that symbol of feminine domesticity, accompanied women into the workplace. In the 1880s, with the invention of the typewriter, many women put their literacy skills to use in the nation's offices. Brown Brothers.

Their work was neither dirty nor dangerous, and even when they earned less than factory workers, they felt a sense of superiority.

REVIEW   How did business expansion and consolidation change workers' occupations in the late nineteenth century?

Workers Organize

By the late nineteenth century, industrial workers were losing ground in the workplace. In the fierce competition to reduce prices and cut costs, industrialists invested heavily in new machinery that replaced skilled workers with unskilled labor. The erosion of skills and the redefinition of labor as mere "machine tending" left the worker with a growing sense of individual helplessness that spurred collective action. The 1870s and 1880s witnessed the emergence of two labor unions—the Knights of Labor and the American Federation of Labor. In 1877, in the midst of a depression, labor flexed its muscle in the Great Railroad Strike. But unionism would suffer a major setback after the mysterious Haymarket bombing in 1886.

The Great Railroad Strike of 1877

Economic depression following the panic of 1873 threw as many as three million people out of work. Those who were lucky enough to keep their jobs watched as pay cuts eroded wages until they could no longer feed their families. In the summer of 1877, the Baltimore and Ohio (B&O) Railroad announced a 10 percent wage cut at the same time it declared a 10 percent dividend to its stockholders. Angry brakemen in West Virginia, whose wages had already fallen from $70 to $30 a month, walked out on strike. One B&O worker described the hardship that drove him to take such desperate action: "We eat our hard bread and tainted meat two days old on the sooty cars up the road, and when we come home, find our wives complaining that they cannot even buy hominy and molasses for food."

The West Virginia brakemen's strike touched off the **Great Railroad Strike** of 1877, a nationwide uprising that spread rapidly to Pittsburgh and Chicago, St. Louis and San Francisco (Map 19.3). Within a few days, nearly 100,000 railroad workers had walked off the job. An estimated 500,000 sympathetic railway workers soon joined the strikers. In Reading, Pennsylvania, militiamen refused to fire on the strikers, saying, "We may be militiamen, but we are workmen first." Rail traffic ground to a halt; the nation lay paralyzed.

MAP 19.3
The Great Railroad Strike of 1877
Starting in West Virginia and Pennsylvania, the strike spread as far north as Albany, New York, and as far west as San Francisco, bringing rail traffic to a standstill. Called the Great Uprising, the strike heralded the beginning of a new era of working-class protest and trade union organization.

★ Strike activity

Destruction from the Great Railroad Strike of 1877
Pictures of the devastation caused in Pittsburgh during the strike shocked many Americans. When militiamen fired on striking workers, killing more than twenty strikers, the mob retaliated by destroying a two-mile area along the track, reducing it to a smoldering rubble. Property damage totaled $2 million. In the aftermath, the curious came out to view the destruction.
Carnegie Library of Pittsburgh.

Violence erupted as the strike spread. In Pittsburgh, militia brought in from Philadelphia fired on the crowds, killing twenty people. Angry workers retaliated by reducing an area two miles long beside the tracks to rubble. Before the day ended, the militia shot twenty workers and the railroad sustained more than $2 million in property damage.

Within eight days, the governors of nine states, acting at the prompting of the railroad owners and managers, defined the strike as an "insurrection" and called for federal troops. President Rutherford B. Hayes, after hesitating briefly, called out the army. By the time the troops arrived, the violence had run its course. Federal troops did not shoot a single striker in 1877. But they struck a blow against labor by acting as

strikebreakers—opening rail traffic, protecting nonstriking "scab" train crews, and maintaining peace along the line. In three weeks, the strike was over.

Middle-class Americans initially sympathized with the conditions that led to the strike. But they quickly condemned the strikers for the violence and property damage that occurred. The *New York Times* editorialized about the "dangerous classes," and the *Independent* magazine offered the following advice on how to deal with "rioters": "If the club of a policeman, knocking out the brains of the rioter, will answer then well and good; but if it does not promptly meet the exigency, then bullets and bayonets . . . constitutes [*sic*] the one remedy and one duty of the hour."

"The strikes have been put down by force," President Hayes noted in his diary on August 5. "But now for the real remedy. Can't something be done by education of the strikers, by judicious control of the capitalists, by wise general policy to end or diminish the evil? The railroad strikers, as a rule, are good men, sober, intelligent, and industrious." While Hayes acknowledged the workers' grievances, most businessmen condemned the idea of labor unions as agents of class warfare. For their part, workers quickly recognized that they held little power individually and flocked to join unions. As labor leader Samuel Gompers noted, the nation's first national strike dramatized the frustration and unity of the workers and served as an alarm bell to labor "that sounded a ringing message of hope to us all."

The Knights of Labor and the American Federation of Labor

The **Knights of Labor**, the first mass organization of America's working class, proved the chief beneficiary of labor's newfound consciousness. The Noble and Holy Order of the Knights of Labor had been founded in 1869 as a secret society of workers who envisioned a "universal brotherhood" of all workers, from common laborers to master craftsmen. Secrecy and ritual served to bind Knights together at the same time that they discouraged company spies and protected members from reprisals.

Although the Knights played no active role in the 1877 railroad strike, membership swelled as a result of the growing interest in labor organizing that followed the strike. In 1878, the Knights abandoned secrecy and launched an ambitious campaign to organize workers. (See "Documenting the American Promise," page 540.) The Knights attempted to bridge the boundaries of ethnicity, gender, ideology, race, and occupation. Leonora Barry served as general investigator for women's work from 1886 to 1890, helping the Knights recruit teachers, waitresses, housewives, and domestics along with factory and sweatshop workers. Women composed perhaps 20 percent of the membership. The Knights also recruited more than 95,000 black workers. That the Knights of Labor often fell short of its goals to unify the working class proved less surprising than the scope of its efforts.

Under the direction of Grand Master Workman Terence V. Powderly, the Knights became the dominant force in labor during the 1880s.

The organization advocated a kind of workers' democracy that embraced reforms including public ownership of the railroads, an income tax, equal pay for women workers, and the abolition of child labor. The Knights called for one big union to create a cooperative commonwealth that would supplant the wage system and remove class distinctions. Only the "parasitic" members of society—gamblers, stockbrokers, lawyers, bankers, and liquor dealers were denied membership.

The Knights of Labor was not without rivals. Many skilled workers belonged to craft unions organized by trade. Among the largest and richest of these unions stood the Amalgamated Association of Iron and Steel Workers, founded in 1876 and counting twenty thousand skilled workers as members. Trade unionists spurned the broad reform goals of the Knights and focused on workplace issues. Samuel Gompers founded the Organized Trades and Labor Unions in 1881 and reorganized it in 1886 into the **American Federation of Labor (AFL)**, which coordinated the activities of craft unions throughout the United States. His plan was simple: organize skilled workers such as machinists and locomotive engineers—those with the most bargaining power—and use strikes to gain immediate objectives such as higher pay and better working conditions. Gompers at first drew few converts. The AFL had only 138,000 members in 1886, compared with 730,000 for the Knights of Labor. But events soon brought down the Knights, and Gompers's brand of unionism came to prevail.

Haymarket and the Specter of Labor Radicalism

While the AFL and the Knights of Labor competed for members, more radical labor groups, including socialists and anarchists, believed that reform was futile and called instead for social revolution. Both the socialists and the anarchists, sensitive to criticism that they preferred revolution in theory to improvements here and now, rallied around the popular issue of the eight-hour day.

Since the 1840s, labor had sought to end the twelve-hour workday, which was standard in industry and manufacturing. By the mid-1880s, it seemed clear to many workers that labor shared too little in the new prosperity of the decade, and pressure mounted for the eight-hour day. Labor championed the popular issue and launched major rallies in cities across the nation.

The Songs of the Knights of Labor

From the 1870s, the Knights of Labor knew the power of song to knit together a movement. The Knights reported joyous singing scattered throughout their meetings. Glee clubs, bands, and quartets made up significant components of the local unions, uniting workers across the bounds of literacy. Songbooks, broadsides, and clippings testify to the role music played in union building and solidarity. The Knights' first songbook appeared in 1886. In the lyrics are found the values and virtues of fraternalism and the significance of the Order. Songs focused on corruption, greed, hypocrisy, tyranny, and workers' need to unite to bring things right. These early songs form a part of America's legacy of social protest.

DOCUMENT 1
"Storm the Fort"

This rousing anthem, written in 1882 by Thomas W. "Old Beeswax" Taylor and sung during the Homestead Lockout, became the trademark song of the Knights of Labor. It lays out the Knights' vision of a new economic landscape in which the producers have replaced the idle rich and created a new political and social order.

Chorus
Toiling millions now are waking,
See them marching on:
All the tyrants now are shaking,
Ere their power is gone

Chorus
Storm the fort ye Knights of Labor,
Battle for your cause;
Equal rights for every neighbor
Down with tyrant laws!

Lazy drones steal all the honey
From hard labor's hives;
Bankers control the nation's money
And destroy our lives.

Chorus
Do not load the workman's shoulder
With an unjust debt;
Do not let the rich bondholder
Live by blood and sweat.

Chorus
Why should those who fought for freedom
Wear old slavery's chains?
Working men will quickly break them
When they use their brains.

Source: Paul Krause, "The Forgotten Legacy of Labor Insurgency in Gilded Age America," in *The Human Tradition in American Labor History*, ed. Eric Arnesen. Wilmington, DE, Scholarly Resources, Inc. 2003, 59–60.

DOCUMENT 2
"The Noble Knights of Labor"

The Knights celebrated their history in song, going back to their founding in 1869 and celebrating Uriah Stephens, the Order's first leader. By using song as oral history, they kept their origins alive.

In the year of sixty-nine they commenced to fall
  in line,
The great Knights, the noble Knights of Labor.
Like the good old Knights of old, they cannot be bought
  or sold.
U.S. Stephens was the man this great order once began
The great Knights, the noble Knights of Labor.
And he started what they say is the strongest band today
The great Knights, the noble Knights of Labor.
Bless the mind that gave them birth, they're the finest
  men on Earth.

Source: Philip S. Foner, *American Labor Songs of the Nineteenth Century*. University of Illinois Press, 1975, 148.

DOCUMENT 3
"The Knights of Labor Song"

Kansas Knight Francis Goodwin penned this rousing song. Exhorting workers to organize, the Knights of Labor sang of vanquishing its foes and achieving justice. The song underlines the radical vision of the Knights, who wanted, in the words of a recent historian, "not just a larger piece of the pie, but a new recipe for a different kind of pie."

Ye valiant Knights of Labor, rise,
Unfurl your banners to the skies,
And go to work and organize.
   Until the world is won.
See the lordly nabobs* quake,
See the politicians shake,
Labor now is wide awake.
   Justice will be done.

*The rich.

Source: Robert Weir, *Beyond Labor's Veil: The Culture of the Knights of Labor*. The Pennsylvania University Press, University Park, PA.1996, 111–12.

DOCUMENT 4
"Organize the Hosts of Labor"

Will Minnick, a coal miner from Iowa, wrote in this song about the universality of the Knights' cause. Note that he includes industrial laborers, miners, and farmers as brother toilers who will organize and depose the nonproducing owners.

Organize the hosts of labor
  In one common brotherhood
He who drives the locomotive
  And the one who turns the sod.

Those who dig the dusky diamonds,
  And produce the shining gold.
Those in factory and in workshop,
  Bring them to the shepherd's fold . . .

Give them through united effort,
  Organize and drill with care
In the tactics of our Order
  Knighthood teaches everywhere.

Moving on in one direction,
  Labor's cause to guard and guide
By the wise and wholesome council
  Each assembly shall provide.

Source: Weir, *Beyond Labor's Veil*, 112–13.

DOCUMENT 5
"Only the Working Class"

The Knights of Labor employed Leonora Barry to organize women workers. At its peak, there were 50,000 female Knights. But male attitudes toward manliness and the fraternal ties that bound workers clashed with the women's belief in class over gender solidarity. An Ontario "sister" argued in the following lines that women made good Knights and had a key role to play in the struggle to liberate the working class.

It is not any woman's part
  We often hear folks say,
And it will mar our womanhood
  To mingle in the fray.
I fear I will never understand,
  Or realize it quite,
How a woman's fame can suffer
  In struggling for the right.

Source: Weir, *Beyond Labor's Veil*, 184.

Questions for Analysis and Debate

1. What common themes do the songs emphasize?

2. Who is the enemy the Knights seek to overthrow?

3. In what ways is the vision of the Knights of Labor political and social as well as economic? What role do women play in the Knights?

Connect to the Big Idea

C How did the Knights of Labor address the vast disparity of wealth in the Gilded Age?

Supporters of the movement set May 1, 1886, as the date for a nationwide general strike in support of the eight-hour workday.

All factions of the labor movement came together in Chicago on May Day. A group of labor radicals led by anarchist Albert Parsons, a *Mayflower* descendant, and August Spies, a German socialist, spearheaded the eight-hour movement in Chicago. Chicago's Knights of Labor rallied to the cause even though Powderly and the union's national leadership, worried about the increasing activism of the rank and file, refused to endorse the movement for shorter hours. Gompers was also on hand to lead the city's trade unionists, although he privately urged the AFL assemblies not to participate in the general strike.

The cautious labor leaders in their frock coats and starched shirts stood in sharp contrast to the dispossessed workers out on strike across town at Chicago's huge McCormick reaper works. There strikers watched helplessly as the company brought in strikebreakers to take their jobs and marched the "scabs" to work under the protection of the Chicago police and security guards supplied by the Pinkerton Detective Agency. Cyrus McCormick Jr., son of the inventor of the mechanical reaper, viewed labor organization as a threat to his power as well as to his profits; he was determined to smash the union.

During the May Day rally, 45,000 workers paraded peacefully down Michigan Avenue in support of the eight-hour day. Many sang what had become the movement's anthem:

> We want to feel the sunshine;
> We want to smell the flowers,
> We're sure that God has willed it,
> And we mean to have eight hours.
> Eight hours for work, eight hours for rest,
> Eight hours for what we will!

Trouble came two days later, when strikers attacked strikebreakers outside the McCormick works and police opened fire, killing or wounding six men. Angry radicals urged workers to "arm yourselves and appear in full force" at a rally in Haymarket Square.

On the evening of May 4, the turnout at Haymarket was disappointing. No more than two or three thousand gathered in the drizzle to hear Spies, Parsons, and the other speakers. Mayor Carter Harrison, known as a friend of labor, mingled conspicuously in the crowd,

VISUAL ACTIVITY

"The Chicago Riot"
Inflammatory pamphlets published in the wake of the Haymarket bombing aimed to scare the public. In this charged atmosphere, the anarchist speakers at the rally were tried and convicted for the bombing even though witnesses testified that none of them had thrown the bomb. Even today, the identity of the bomb thrower remains uncertain. © Chicago History Museum, USA /The Bridgeman Art Library.

READING THE IMAGE: What does the cover suggest about the views of the author of the pamphlet?
CONNECTIONS: In what ways does this pamphlet reflect the public climate following the Haymarket bombing?

pronounced the meeting peaceable, and went home to bed. Sometime later, police captain John "Blackjack" Bonfield marched his men into the crowd, by now fewer than three hundred people, and demanded that it disperse. Suddenly, someone threw a bomb into the police ranks. After a moment of stunned silence, the police drew their revolvers. "Fire and kill all you can," shouted a police lieutenant. When the melee ended, seven policemen and an unknown number of others lay dead. An additional sixty policemen and thirty or forty civilians suffered injuries.

News of the "Haymarket riot" provoked a nationwide convulsion of fear, followed by blind rage directed at anarchists, labor unions, strikers, immigrants, and the working class in general. Eight men, including Parsons and Spies, went on trial in Chicago, "Convict these men," thundered the state's attorney, Julius S. Grinnell, "make examples of them, hang them, and you save our institutions." Although the state could not link any of the defendants to the **Haymarket bombing**, the jury nevertheless found them all guilty. Four men hanged, one committed suicide, and three received prison sentences.

The bomb blast at Haymarket had lasting repercussions. To commemorate the death of the Haymarket martyrs, labor made May 1 an annual international celebration of the worker. But the Haymarket bomb, in the eyes of one observer, proved "a godsend to all enemies of the labor movement." It effectively scotched the eight-hour-day movement and dealt a blow to the Knights of Labor. With the labor movement everywhere under attack, many skilled workers turned to the AFL. Gompers's narrow economic strategy made sense at the time and enabled one segment of the workforce—the skilled—to organize effectively and achieve tangible gains.

REVIEW Why did membership in the Knights of Labor rise in the late 1870s and decline in the 1890s?

▶ At Home and at Play

The growth of urban industrialism not only dramatically altered the workplace but also transformed home and family life, and it gave rise to new forms of commercialized leisure. Industrialization redefined the very concepts of work and home. Increasingly, men went out to work for wages, while most white married women stayed home, either working in the home without pay—cleaning, cooking, and rearing children—or supervising paid domestic servants who did the housework.

Domesticity and "Domestics"

The separation of the workplace and the home that marked the shift to industrial society led to a new ideology, one that sentimentalized the home and women's role in it. The cultural idea that dictated a woman's place was in the home, where she would create a haven for her family, began to develop in the early 1800s. It has been called the **cult of domesticity**, a phrase used to prescribe an ideal of middle-class, white womanhood that dominated the period from 1820 to the end of the nineteenth century.

The cult of domesticity and the elaboration of the middle-class home led to a major change in patterns of hiring household help. The live-in servant, or domestic, became a fixture in the North, replacing the hired girl of the previous century. In American cities by 1870, 15 to 30 percent of all households included live-in domestic servants, more than 90 percent of them women. Earlier in the mid-nineteenth century, native-born women increasingly took up other work and left domestic service to immigrants. In the East, the maid was so often Irish that "Bridget" became a generic term for female domestics. The South continued to rely on poorly paid black female "help."

Servants by all accounts resented the long hours and lack of privacy. "She is liable to be rung up at all hours," one study of domestics reported. "Her very meals are not secure from interruption, and even her sleep is not sacred." Domestic service became the occupation of last resort, a "hard and lonely life" in the words of one female servant.

For women of the white middle class, domestics were a boon, freeing them from household drudgery and giving them more time to spend with their children, to pursue club work, or to work for reforms. Thus, while domestic service supported the cult of domesticity, it created for those women who could afford it opportunities that expanded their horizons outside the home. They became involved in women's clubs as well as the temperance and suffrage movements.

Cheap Amusements

Growing class divisions manifested themselves in patterns of leisure as well as in work and home life. The poor and working class took their leisure, when they had any, not in the crowded tenements that housed their families but increasingly in the cities' new dance halls, music houses, ballparks, and amusement arcades, which by the 1890s formed a familiar part of the urban landscape.

VISUAL ACTIVITY

Beach Scene at Coney Island

Coney Island became a symbol of commercialized leisure and mechanical excitement at the turn of the century. This fanciful rendering of Coney Island captures men and women frolicking in the waves. Notice the modest woolen bathing outfits. Men box and play ball, a woman flies on a parachute, a uniformed policeman wades into the fray, while the Ferris wheel dominates on shore. Sunday crowds reportedly reached 100,000. Library of Congress.

READING THE IMAGE: What does the scene present as the mood at Coney Island, and what does it tell us about who visited Coney Island and who didn't?

CONNECTIONS: Many reformers worried about the moral temptations mass leisure afforded city workers? Why?

Young workingwomen no longer met prospective husbands only through their families. Fleeing crowded tenements, the young sought each other's company in dance halls and other commercial retreats. Young workingwomen counted on being "treated" by men, a transaction that often implied sexual payback. Their behavior sometimes blurred the line between respectability and promiscuity. The dance halls became a favorite target of reformers who feared they lured teenaged girls into prostitution.

For men, baseball became a national pastime in the 1870s—then, as now, one force in urban life capable of uniting a city across class lines. Cincinnati mounted the first entirely paid team, the Red Stockings, in 1869. Soon professional teams proliferated in cities across the nation, and Mark Twain hailed baseball as "the very symbol, the outward and visible expression, of the drive and push and rush and struggle of the raging, tearing, booming nineteenth century."

The increasing commercialization of entertainment in the late-nineteenth-century city was best seen at Coney Island. A two-mile stretch of sand nine miles from Manhattan by trolley or steamship, Coney Island in the 1890s was transformed into the site of some of the largest and most elaborate amusement parks in the country. Promoter George Tilyou built Steeplechase Park in 1897, advertising "10 hours of fun for 10 cents." With its mechanical thrills and fun-house laughs, the amusement park encouraged behavior that one school-teacher aptly described as "everyone with the brakes off." By 1900, as many as a million New Yorkers flocked to Coney Island on any given weekend, making the amusement park the unofficial capital of a new mass culture.

REVIEW   How did urban industrialism shape home life and the world of leisure?

▶ City Growth and City Government

Private enterprise, not city planners, built the cities of the United States. With a few notable exceptions, cities simply mushroomed, formed by the dictates of profit and the exigencies of local politics. With the rise of the city came the need for public facilities, transportation, and services that would tax the imaginations of America's architects and engineers and set the scene for the rough-and-tumble of big-city government, politics, and bossism.

Building Cities of Stone and Steel

Skyscrapers and mighty bridges dominated the imagination and the urban landscape. Less imposing but no less significant were the paved streets, the parks and public libraries, and the subways and sewers. In the late nineteenth century, Americans rushed to embrace new technology of all kinds, making their cities the most modern in the world.

Structural steel made enormous advances in building possible. A decade after the completion of the Brooklyn Bridge, engineers used the new technology to construct the Williamsburg Bridge. More prosaic and utilitarian than its neighbor, the new bridge was never as acclaimed, but it was longer by four feet and completed in half the time. It became the model for future building as the age of steel supplanted the age of stone and iron.

Chicago, not New York, gave birth to the modern skyscraper. Rising from the ashes of the Great Fire of 1871, which destroyed three square miles and left eighteen thousand people homeless, Chicago offered a generation of skilled architects and engineers the chance to experiment. Commercial architecture became an art form at the hands of a skilled group of architects who together constituted the "Chicago school." Employing the dictum "Form follows function," they built startlingly modern structures.

Across the United States, municipal governments undertook public works on a scale never before seen. They paved streets, built sewers and water mains, replaced gas lamps with electric lights, ran trolley tracks on the old horsecar lines, and dug underground to build subways, tearing down the unsightly elevated tracks that had clogged city streets. Boston completed the nation's first subway system in 1897, and New York and Philadelphia soon followed.

Cities became more beautiful with the creation of urban public parks to complement the new buildings that quickly filled city lots. Much of the credit for America's greatest parks goes to one man—landscape architect Frederick Law Olmsted. New York City's Central Park, completed in 1873, became the first landscaped public park in the United States. Olmsted and his partner, Calvert Vaux, directed the planting of more than five million trees, shrubs, and vines to transform the eight hundred acres between 59th and 110th streets into an oasis for urban dwellers. "We want a place," he wrote, where people "may stroll for an hour, seeing, hearing, and feeling nothing of the bustle and jar of the streets."

American cities did not overlook the mind in their efforts at improvement. They created a comprehensive free public school system that educated everyone from the children of the middle class to the sons and daughters of immigrant workers. Yet the exploding urban population strained the system and led to crowded and inadequate facilities. In 1899, more than 544,000 pupils attended school in New York's five boroughs. Municipalities across the United States provided free secondary school education for all who wished to attend, even though only 8 percent of Americans completed high school.

To educate those who couldn't go to school, American cities created the most extensive free public library system in the world. In 1895, the Boston Public Library opened its bronze doors in its new Copley Square location under the inscription "Free to All." Designed in the style of a Renaissance palazzo, with more than 700,000 books on the shelves ready to be checked out, the library earned the description "a palace of the people."

Despite the Boston Public Library's legend "Free to All," the poor did not share equally in the advantages of city life. The parks, the libraries, and even the subways and sewers benefited some city dwellers more than others. Few library cards were held by Boston's laborers, who worked six days a week and found the library closed on Sunday. And in the 1890s, there was nothing central about New York's Central Park. It was a four-mile walk from the tenements of Hester Street to the park's entrance at 59th Street and Fifth Avenue. Then, as now, the

The Boston Public Library
When Boston moved the first public library in the country to Copley Square, the best artists and architects of the day lent their talents to create "a palace for the people." Architect Charles F. McKim designed the library; sculptor Augustus Saint-Gaudens modeled the marble lions on the grand stairway; and French muralist Puvis de Chavannes painted the allegorical mural representing literature and learning. Photo Copyright Richard Cheek for the Boston Public Library.

comfortable, not the indigent, reaped a disproportionate share of the benefits in the nation's big cities.

Any story of the American city, it seems, must be a tale of two cities—or, given the cities' great diversity, a tale of many cities within each metropolis. At the turn of the twentieth century, a central paradox emerged: The enduring monuments of America's cities—the bridges, skyscrapers, parks, and libraries—stood as the undeniable achievements of the same system of municipal government that reformers dismissed as boss-ridden, criminal, and corrupt.

City Government and the "Bosses"

The physical growth of the cities required the expansion of public services and the creation of entirely new facilities: streets, subways, elevated trains, bridges, docks, sewers, and public utilities. There was work to be done and money to be made. The professional politician—the colorful big-city boss—became a phenomenon of urban growth and **bossism** a national phenomenon. Though corrupt and often criminal, the boss saw to the building of the city and provided needed social services for the new residents in return for their political support. Yet not even the big-city boss could be said to rule the unruly city. The governing of America's cities resembled more a tug-of-war than boss rule.

The most notorious of all the city bosses was William Marcy "Boss" Tweed of New York. At midcentury, Boss Tweed's Democratic Party "machine" held sway. A machine was really no more than a political party organized at the grassroots level. Its purpose was to win elections and reward its followers, often with jobs on the city's payroll. New York's citywide Democratic machine, Tammany Hall, commanded an army of party functionaries. They formed a shadow government more powerful than the city's elected officials.

As chairman of the Tammany general committee, Tweed kept the Democratic Party together and ran the city through the use of bribery and graft. "As long as I count the votes," he shamelessly boasted, "what are you going to do about it?" The excesses of the Tweed ring soon led to a clamor for reform and cries of "Throw the rascals out." Tweed's rule ended in 1871. Eventually, he was tried and convicted, and later died in jail. New York was not the only city to experience bossism and corruption. The British visitor James Bryce concluded in 1888, "There is no denying that the government of cities is the one conspicuous failure of the United States." More than 80 percent of the nation's thirty largest cities experienced some form of boss rule in the decades around the turn of the twentieth century. However, infighting among powerful ward bosses often meant that no single boss enjoyed exclusive power in the big cities.

Urban reformers and proponents of good government (derisively called "goo goos" by their rivals) challenged machine rule and sometimes succeeded in electing reform mayors. But the reformers rarely managed to stay in office for long. Their detractors called them "mornin' glories," observing that they "looked lovely in the mornin' and withered up in a short time." The bosses enjoyed continued success largely because the urban political machine helped the cities' immigrants and poor, who remained the bosses' staunchest allies. "What tells in holding your district," a Tammany ward boss observed, "is to go right down among the poor and help them in the different ways they need help. It's philanthropy, but it's politics, too—mighty good politics."

The big-city boss, through the skillful orchestration of rewards, exerted powerful leverage and lined up support for his party from a broad range of constituents, from the urban poor to wealthy industrialists. In 1902, when journalist Lincoln Steffens began "The Shame of the Cities," a series of articles exposing city corruption, he found that business leaders who fastidiously refused to mingle socially with the bosses nevertheless struck deals with them. "He is a self-righteous fraud, this big businessman," Steffens concluded. "I found him buying boodlers [bribers] in St. Louis, defending grafters in Minneapolis, originating corruption in Pittsburgh, sharing with bosses in Philadelphia, deploring reform in Chicago, and beating good government with corruption funds in New York."

For all the color and flamboyance of the big-city boss, he was simply one of many actors in the drama of municipal government. Old-stock aristocrats, new professionals, saloon keepers, pushcart peddlers, and politicians all fought for their interests in the hurly-burly of city government. They didn't much like each other, and they sometimes fought savagely. But they learned to live with one another. Compromise and accommodation—not boss rule—best characterized big-city government by the turn of the twentieth century, although the cities' reputation for corruption left an indelible mark on the consciousness of the American public.

White City or City of Sin?

Americans have always been of two minds about the city. They like to boast of its skyscrapers and bridges, its culture and sophistication, and they pride themselves on its bigness and bustle. At the same time, they fear it as the city of sin, the home of immigrant slums, the center of vice and crime. Nowhere did the divided view of the American city take form more graphically than in Chicago in 1893. In that year, Chicago hosted the **World's Columbian Exposition**, the grandest world's fair in the nation's history. (See "Beyond America's Borders," page 548.) The fairground, only five miles down the shore of Lake Michigan from downtown Chicago, offered a lesson in what Americans on the eve of the twentieth century imagined a city might be. Christened the "White City," it seemed light-years away from Chicago, with its stockyards, slums, and bustling terminals. Frederick Law Olmsted and architect Daniel Burnham supervised the

The World's Columbian Exposition and Nineteenth-Century World's Fairs

The 1893 World's Columbian Exposition in Chicago, like the other great world's fairs of the nineteenth and twentieth centuries, represented a unique outgrowth of industrial capitalism and a testament to the expanding global market economy. The Chicago fair, named to celebrate the 400th anniversary of Columbus's arrival in the New World (the organizers missed the deadline by a year), offered a cornucopia of international exhibits, testifying to growing international influences ranging from cultural to technological exchange.

Great cities vied to host the fairs, as much to promote commercial growth as to demonstrate cultural refinement. Each successive fair sought to outdo its predecessor. Chicago's fair followed on the great success of the 1889 Universal Exposition in Paris, crowned by the 900-foot steel tower constructed by Alexander-Gustav Eiffel. How could Chicago, a prairie upstart, top that?

The answer was to create from scratch an ideal White City with monumental architecture, landscaped grounds, and the world's first Ferris wheel. The White City celebrated the classicism of the French Beaux Arts school, with massive geometric styling and elaborate detailing borrowed from Greek and Roman Renaissance architecture. Prairie architects Louis Sullivan and Frank Lloyd Wright later complained the fair was a "virus" that held back modern architecture for decades.

But beneath its Renaissance facade, the White City acted as an enormous emporium dedicated to the unabashed materialism of the Gilded Age. Fairgoers could view virtually every kind of manufactured product in the world inside the imposing Manufactures and Liberal Arts Building. As suited an industrial age, manufactured products and heavy machinery drew the largest crowds. Displays introduced visitors to the latest innovations, many the result of international influences. For five cents, fairgoers could put two hard rubber tubes into their ears and listen for the first time to a gramophone playing the popular tune "The Cat Came Back." The invention, the work of a German immigrant, Emile Berliner, signaled the beginning of the recorded music industry. Later Thomas Edison claimed credit for a similar invention, calling it the phonograph.

Such international influences were evident throughout the Columbian Exposition. At the Tiffany pavilion, Louis Comfort Tiffany displayed jewelry and objects influenced by Japanese art forms. The Colt firearms factory, known throughout the world for its revolver, was already international in scope, having opened a factory in England in 1851. At the fair Colt debuted its new automatic weapon, the machine gun—soon to play a major role on the world stage in both the Boxer uprising in China and the Spanish-American War.

All manner of foodstuffs tempted fairgoers—teas from India, whiskey from Ireland, and pastries and other confectioneries from Germany and France. American products such as Shredded Wheat, Aunt Jemima syrup, and Juicy Fruit gum debuted at the fair, where they competed for ribbons, like Pabst Blue Ribbon Beer. And the fair introduced two new foods—carbonated soda and the hamburger—destined to become America's best-known contributions to international cuisine.

By displaying technology in action, the White City tamed it and made it accessible to American and world consumers. The fair helped promote electric light and power, with its 90,000 electric lights, 5,100 arc lamps, electric fountains, an electric elevated railroad, and electric launches plying the lagoons. Fairgoers visited the Bell Telephone Company exhibit, marveled at General Electric's huge dynamo (electric generator), and gazed into the future at the all-electric home and model demonstration kitchen.

Consumer culture received its first major expression and celebration at the fair. Not only did this world's fair anticipate the mass marketing, packaging, and advertising of the twentieth century, but the vast array of products on display also cultivated the urge to consume. Thousands of concessionaires with

"All Nations Are Welcome"
Uncle Sam, flanked by the city of Chicago, welcomes representatives carrying the flags of many nations to the World's Columbian Exposition in 1893. In the background are the fairgrounds on the shores of Lake Michigan. More than one hundred nations participated in the fair by sending exhibits and mounting pavilions to showcase their cultures and products. © Chicago History Museum, USA /The Bridgeman Art Gallery.

products for sale sent a message that tied enjoyment inextricably to spending money and purchasing goods, both domestic and foreign. The Columbian Exposition encouraged the rise of a new middle-class consumer culture and made a powerful statement about the possibilities of urban life in an industrial age. As G. Brown Goode, head of the Smithsonian Institution observed, the Columbian Exposition was in many ways "an illustrated encyclopedia of civilization."

America in a Global Context

1. Would you describe the Columbian Exposition as a commercial venture, a cultural display, or an entertainment? Why?

2. What role did the fair play in popularizing new technologies?

3. What was meant by the observation that the fair was "an illustrated encyclopedia of civilization"?

4. How did the international flavor of the White City compare with the reality of global migration into America's fast-growing cities?

Connect to the Big Idea

⊙ How did the Columbian Fair, in general, and the White City, specifically, reflect changes in late-nineteenth-century America?

Chicago's White City

This painting by H. D. Nichols captures the monumental architecture of the White City built for the World's Columbian Exposition in 1893. In the foreground, the central Court of Honor features a Frederick MacMonnies fountain, with Christopher Columbus at the prow of his ship. In the distance is Daniel Chester French's sixty-foot gilded statue *Republic*. The awe-inspiring exposition drew millions of visitors from America and abroad. © Chicago History Museum, USA /The Bridgeman Art Gallery.

transformation of a swampy wasteland into a pristine paradise of lagoons, fountains, wooded islands, gardens, and imposing white buildings.

"Sell the cookstove if necessaray and come," novelist Hamlin Garland wrote to his parents on the farm. And come they did, in spite of the panic and depression that broke out only weeks after the fair opened in May 1893. In six months, fairgoers purchased more than 27 million tickets, turning a profit of nearly a half million dollars for promoters. Visitors from home and abroad strolled the elaborate grounds and visited the exhibits—everything from a model of the Brooklyn Bridge carved in soap to the latest goods and inventions. Half carnival, half culture, the great fair offered something for everyone. On the Midway Plaisance, crowds thrilled to the massive wheel built by Mr. Ferris and watched agog as Little Egypt danced the hootchy-kootchy.

In October, the fair closed its doors in the midst of the worst depression the country had yet seen. During the winter of 1894, Chicago's unemployed and homeless took over the grounds, vandalized the buildings, and frightened the city's comfortable citizens out of their wits. When reporters asked Daniel Burnham, its chief architect, what should be done with the moldering remains of the White City, he responded, "It should be torched." And it was. In July 1894, in a clash between federal troops and striking railway workers, incendiaries set fires that leveled the fairgrounds.

In the end, the White City remained what it had always been, a dreamscape. Buildings that looked like marble were actually constructed of staff, a plaster substance that began to crumble even before fire destroyed the fairgrounds. Perhaps it was not so strange, after all, that the legacy of the White City could be found on Coney Island, where two new amusement parks, Luna and Dreamland, sought to combine, albeit in a more tawdry form, the beauty of the White City and the thrill of the Midway Plaisance. More enduring than the White City itself was what it represented: the emergent industrial might of the United States, at home and abroad, with its inventions, manufactured goods, and growing consumer culture.

REVIEW How did municipal governments respond to the challenges of urban expansion?

▶ Conclusion: Who Built the Cities?

As great a role as industrialists, financiers, and engineers played in building the nation's cities common workers,—most of them immigrants,—provided the muscle that built the nation's cities. The unprecedented growth of urban, industrial America resulted from the labor of millions of men, women, and children who toiled in workshops and factories, in sweatshops and mines, on railroads and construction sites across America.

America's cities in the late nineteenth century teemed with life. Townhouses and tenements jostled for space with skyscrapers and great department stores, while parks, ball fields, amusement arcades, and public libraries provided the city masses with recreation and entertainment. Municipal governments, straining to build the new cities, experienced the rough-and-tumble of machine politics as bosses and their constituents looked to profit from city growth.

For America's workers, urban industrialism along with the rise of big business and corporate consolidation drastically changed the workplace. Industrialists replaced skilled workers with new machines that could be operated by cheaper unskilled labor. And during hard times, employers did not hesitate to cut workers' already meager wages. As the Great Railroad Strike of 1877 demonstrated, when labor united, it could bring the nation to attention. Organization held out the best hope for the workers; first the Knights of Labor and later the AFL won converts among the nation's working class.

The rise of urban industrialism challenged the American promise, which for decades had been dominated by Jeffersonian agrarian ideals. Could such a promise exist in the changing world of cities, tenements, immigrants, and huge corporations? In the great depression that came in the 1890s, mounting anger and frustration would lead farmers and workers to join forces and create a grassroots movement to fight for change under the banner of a new People's Party.

See the Selected Bibliography for this chapter in the Appendix.

19 Chapter Review

MAKE IT STICK

LearningCurve
Go online and use LearningCurve to see what you know. Then review the key terms and answer the questions.

KEY TERMS

global migration (p. 523)
Ellis Island (p. 530)
sweatshop (p. 533)
family economy (p. 534)
"typewriters" (p. 536)
Great Railroad Strike (p. 537)
Knights of Labor (p. 539)
American Federation of Labor (AFL) (p. 539)
Haymarket bombing (p. 543)
cult of domesticity (p. 543)
bossism (p. 546)
World's Columbian Exposition (p. 547)

REVIEW QUESTIONS

1. Why did American cities experience explosive growth in the late nineteenth century? (pp. 523–532)

2. How did business expansion and consolidation change workers' occupations in the late nineteenth century? (pp. 533–536)

3. Why did membership in the Knights of Labor rise in the late 1870s and decline in the 1890s? (pp. 537–543)

4. How did urban industrialism shape home life and the world of leisure? (pp. 543–544)

5. How did municipal governments respond to the challenges of urban expansion? (pp. 545–550)

MAKING CONNECTIONS

1. Americans expressed both wonder and concern at the nation's mushrooming cities. Why did cities provoke such divergent responses?

2. Why did patterns of immigration to the United States in the late nineteenth century change? How did Americans respond to the immigrants?

3. How did urban industrialization affect Americans' lives outside of work?

4. When workers began to embrace organization in the late 1870s, what did they hope to accomplish? Were they successful? Why or why not?

LINKING TO THE PAST

1. Compare the lives of migrant workers and industrial cowboys in the West to workers in the nation's cities. What are the major similarities? (See chapter 17.)

2. You have already looked at the development of America's industries in the nineteenth century from the vantage point of moguls such as Andrew Carnegie and John D. Rockefeller. How does your view of industrialism change when the focus is shifted to the nation's workers? (See chapter 18.)

20 Dissent, Depression, and War

1890–1900

After studying this chapter, you should be able to:

- Identify the economic and social ills American farmers and laborers faced at the turn of the century and how Farmers' Alliances and the Populist movement aimed to address some of these problems.

- Explain the factors that led to the labor wars of the 1890s.

- Characterize the political activism of American women during the last decades of the nineteenth century.

- Describe the political climate during the depression of 1893 and identify the defining issues of the election of 1896.

- Explain American expansionism in the late nineteenth century, how the United States emerged as a world power, and the resulting debate over American imperialism.

PEOPLE'S PARTY BANNER
This 1892 Populist convention banner promises to elect "Honest Men." The bison mascot was a poor choice for the new party, for just as the great herds were decimated, the People's Party was defeated in 1896. Nebraska State Historical Society.

FRANCES WILLARD TRAVELED TO ST. LOUIS IN FEBRUARY 1892 WITH high hopes. Political change was in the air, and Willard was there to help fashion a new reform party. As head of the Woman's Christian Temperance Union (WCTU), an organization with members in every state and territory in the nation, Willard wielded considerable clout. At her invitation, twenty-eight of the country's leading reformers met in Chicago to draft a set of principles to bring to St. Louis. No American woman before her had played such a central role in a political movement. At the height of her power, Willard took her place among the leaders on stage in St. Louis.

Exposition Music Hall presented a colorful spectacle. "The banners of the different states rose above the delegates throughout the hall, fluttering like the flags over an army encamped," wrote one reporter. The fiery orator Ignatius Donnelly attacked the money kings of Wall Street. Terence V. Powderly, head of the Knights of Labor, called on workers to join hands with farmers against the "nonproducing classes." And Frances Willard took the podium, urging the crowd to outlaw liquor and give women the vote.

Frances Willard

Frances Willard, the forward-thinking leader of the Woman's Christian Temperance Union, learned to ride a bicycle at age fifty-three. Willard brought her progressive ideas to the People's Party 1892 convention, where she shared a place on the platform with the new party's leaders. Courtesy of the Frances E. Willard Memorial Library and Archives (WCTU).

Delegates hammered out a series of demands, breathtaking in their scope. They tackled the tough questions of the day—the regulation of business, the need for banking and currency reform, the right of labor to organize and bargain collectively, and the role of the federal government in regulating business, curbing monopoly, and giving the people greater voice. But the new party was determined to stick to economic issues and resisted endorsing either temperance or woman suffrage. As a member of the platform committee, Willard fought for both and complained of the "crooked methods . . . employed to scuttle these planks."

The convention ended its work amid a chorus of cheers. According to one eyewitness, "Hats, paper, handkerchiefs, etc., were thrown into the air; . . . cheer after cheer thundered and reverberated through the vast hall reaching the outside of the building where thousands who had been waiting the outcome joined in the applause till for blocks in every direction the exultation made the din indescribable."

What was all the shouting about? The crowd, fed up with the Democrats and the Republicans, celebrated the birth of a new political party, officially named the People's Party. The St. Louis gathering marked an early milestone in one of the most turbulent decades in U.S. history. An agrarian revolt, labor strikes, a severe depression, and a war shook the 1890s. As the decade opened, Americans flocked to organizations including the Farmers' Alliance, the American Federation of Labor, the Woman's Christian Temperance Union, and the National Woman's Suffrage Association. Their political alliance gave birth to the People's (or Populist) Party. In a decade of unrest and uncertainty, the Populists countered laissez-faire economics by insisting that the federal government play a more active role to ensure economic fairness in industrial America.

This challenge to the status quo culminated in 1896 in one of the most hotly contested presidential elections in the nation's history. At the close of the tumultuous decade, the Spanish-American War brought the country together, with Americans rallying to support the troops. American imperialism and overseas expansion raised questions about the nation's role on the world stage as the United States stood poised to enter the twentieth century.

▶ The Farmers Unite

Hard times in the 1880s and 1890s created a groundswell of agrarian revolt. A bitter farmer wrote from Minnesota, "I settled on this Land in good Faith Built House and Barn. Broken up Part of the Land. Spent years of hard Labor in grubbing fencing and Improving." About to lose his farm to foreclosure, he lamented, "Are they going to drive us out like trespassers . . . and give us away to the Corporations?"

Farm prices fell decade after decade, even as American farmers' share of the world market grew. In parts of Kansas, corn sold for as little as ten cents a bushel, and angry farmers burned their crops for fuel rather than sell them on the market. At the same time, consumer prices soared (Figure 20.1). In Kansas alone, almost half the farms had fallen into the hands of the banks by 1894 through foreclosure. Farmers soon banded together into Farmers' Alliances that gave birth to a broad political movement.

The Farmers' Alliance

At the heart of the farmers' problems stood a banking system dominated by eastern commercial banks committed to the gold standard, a railroad rate system both capricious and unfair, and rampant speculation that drove up the price of land. In the West, farmers rankled under a system that allowed railroads to charge them exorbitant freight rates while granting rebates to large shippers (see "Railroads Trusts, and the Federal Government" in chapter 18). The practice of charging higher rates for short hauls than for long hauls meant that grainelevators could ship their wheat from Chicago to New York and across the Atlantic for less than a Dakota farmer paid to send his crop to mills in Minneapolis. In the South, lack of currency and credit drove farmers to the stopgap credit system of the crop lien. To pay for seed and supplies, farmers pledged their crops as collateral to local creditors (furnishing merchants). Determined to do something, farmers banded together to fight for change.

Farm protest was not new. In the 1870s, farmers had supported the Grange and the Greenback Labor Party. As the farmers' situation grew more desperate, they organized, forming regional alliances. The first **Farmers' Alliance** came together in Lampasas County, Texas, to fight "landsharks and horse thieves." In frontier farmhouses in Texas, in log cabins in the backwoods of Arkansas, and in the rural

CHRONOLOGY

1884	• Frances Willard calls for woman suffrage.
1890	• National American Woman Suffrage Association formed. • Wyoming only state allowing women to vote in national elections. • Southern Farmers' Alliance numbers three million members.
1892	• People's (Populist) Party founded. • Homestead lockout.
1893	• Stock market crash touches off economic depression. • President Grover Cleveland nixes attempt to annex Hawai'i.
1894	• Miners' strike in Cripple Creek, Colorado. • Coxey's army marches to Washington, D.C. • Pullman boycott crushed.
1895	• Cleveland enforces Monroe Doctrine in border dispute between British Guiana and Venezuela.
1896	• Democrats and Populists support William Jennings Bryan for president. • William McKinley elected president.
1898	• U.S. battleship Maine explodes in Havana harbor. • Congress declares war on Spain. • Admiral George Dewey destroys Spanish fleet in Manila Bay, the Philippines. • U.S. troops defeat Spanish forces in Cuba. • Treaty of Paris ends war with Spain. • United States annexes Hawai'i.
1899–1900	• Secretary of State John Hay enunciates Open Door policy in China. • Boxer uprising in China.
1901	• Boxer Protocol imposed on Chinese government.

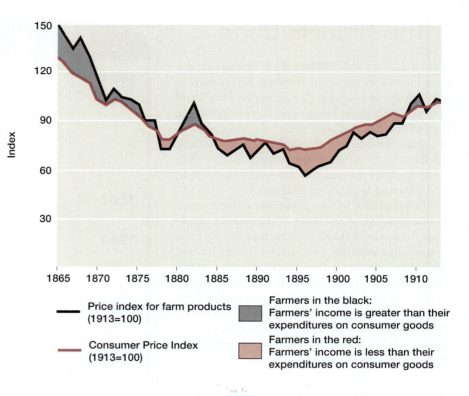

FIGURE 20.1 **Consumer Prices and Farm Income, 1865–1910**
Around 1870, consumer prices and farm income were about equal. During the 1880s and 1890s, however, farmers suffered great hardships as prices for their crops steadily declined and the cost of consumer goods continued to rise.

Price index for farm products (1913=100)

Consumer Price Index (1913=100)

Farmers in the black: Farmers' income is greater than their expenditures on consumer goods

Farmers in the red: Farmers' income is less than their expenditures on consumer goods

parishes of Louisiana, separate groups of farmers formed similar alliances for self-help.

As the movement grew in the 1880s, farmers' groups consolidated into two regional alliances: the Northwestern Farmers' Alliance, active in Kansas, Nebraska, and other midwestern Granger states; and the more radical Southern Farmers' Alliance. Traveling lecturers preached the Alliance message. Worn-out men and careworn women did not need to be convinced that something was wrong. By 1890, the Southern Farmers' Alliance alone counted more than three million members.

Radical in its inclusiveness, the Southern Alliance reached out to African Americans, women, and industrial workers. Through cooperation with the Colored Farmers' Alliance, an African American group founded in Texas in the 1880s, blacks and whites attempted to make common cause. As Georgia's Tom Watson, a Southern Alliance stalwart, pointed out, "The colored tenant is in the same boat as the white tenant, . . . and . . . the accident of color can make no difference in the interests of farmers, croppers, and laborers." The Alliance reached out to industrial workers as well as farmers. During a major strike against Jay Gould's Texas and Pacific Railroad in 1886, the Alliance vocally sided with the workers and rushed food and supplies to the strikers. Women as well as men rallied to the Alliance banner. "I am going to work for prohibition, the Alliance, and for Jesus as long as I live," swore one woman.

At the heart of the Alliance movement stood a series of farmers' cooperatives. By "bulking" their cotton—that is, selling it together—farmers could negotiate a better price. And by setting up trade stores and exchanges, they sought to escape the grasp of the merchant/creditor. Through the cooperatives, the Farmers' Alliance promised to change the way farmers lived. "We are going to get out of debt and be free and independent people once more," exulted one Georgia farmer. But the Alliance faced insurmountable difficulties in running successful cooperatives. Opposition by merchants, bankers, wholesalers, and manufacturers made it impossible for the cooperatives to get credit. As the cooperative movement died, the Farmers' Alliance moved into politics.

The Populist Movement

In the earliest days of the Alliance movement, a leader of the Southern Farmers' Alliance insisted, "The Alliance is a strictly white man's

The Farmer's Alliance and the Populist Party
Isaac Ware, from Southwest Custer County, Nebraska, proudly holds a copy of the *Alliance Independent*, a newspaper published in Lincoln, Nebraska. In 1892, before this picture was taken, Farmers' Alliance members came together in St. Louis to form the People's or Populist Party. Small local newspapers sprouted up all across the West and South to carry the message. Nebraska State Historical Society

nonpolitical, secret business association." But by 1892, it was none of those things. Advocates of a third party carried the day at the convention of laborers, farmers, and common folk in 1892 in St. Louis, where the Farmers' Alliance gave birth to the **People's Party** and launched the Populist movement. The same spirit of religious revival that animated the Farmers' Alliance infused the People's Party. Convinced that the money and banking systems worked to the advantage of the wealthy few, Populists demanded economic democracy. To help farmers get the credit they needed at reasonable rates, southern farmers hit on the ingenious idea of a subtreasury—a plan that would allow farmers to store their nonperishable crops until prices rose and to receive commodity credit from the federal government to obtain needed supplies. To the western farmer, the Populists promised land reform, championing a plan to claim excessive

Mary Elizabeth Lease
This photograph of Lease, taken in 1895 at the height of her activities as a Populist leader in Kansas, reflects her reputation as a hell raiser who supposedly exhorted Kansas farmers to "raise less corn and more hell." In the eyes of her detractors, she was "a lantern-jawed, google-eyed nightmare." Kansas State Historical Society.

land granted to railroads or sold to foreign investors. The Populists' boldest proposal called for government ownership of the railroads and the telegraph system to put an end to discriminatory rates.

The Populists solidly supported free silver, in the hope of increasing the nation's tight money supply. To empower the common people, the Populist platform called for the direct election of senators and for other electoral reforms, including the secret ballot and the right to initiate legislation, to recall elected officials, and to submit issues to the people by means of a referendum. In support of labor, the Populists supported the eight-hour workday.

The sweeping array of reforms enacted in the Populist platform changed the agenda of politics for decades to come. More than just a response to hard times, Populism presented an alternative vision of American economic democracy.

> **REVIEW** Why did American farmers organize alliances in the late nineteenth century?

▶ The Labor Wars

While farmers united to fight for change, industrial laborers fought their own battles in a series of bloody strikes historians have called the "labor wars." Industrial workers took a stand in the 1890s. At issue was the right of workers to organize and to speak through unions, to bargain collectively, and to fight for better working conditions, higher wages, shorter hours, and greater worker control in the face of increased mechanization. Three major conflicts—the lockout of steelworkers in Homestead, Pennsylvania, in 1892; the miners' strike in Cripple Creek, Colorado, in 1894; and the Pullman boycott that same year—raised fundamental questions about the rights of labor and the sanctity of private property.

The Homestead Lockout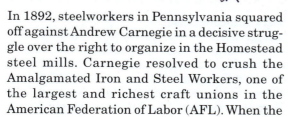

In 1892, steelworkers in Pennsylvania squared off against Andrew Carnegie in a decisive struggle over the right to organize in the Homestead steel mills. Carnegie resolved to crush the Amalgamated Iron and Steel Workers, one of the largest and richest craft unions in the American Federation of Labor (AFL). When the

Amalgamated attempted to renew its contract at Carnegie's Homestead mill, its leaders were told that since "the vast majority of our employees are Non union, the Firm has decided that the minority must give place to the majority." While it was true that only 800 skilled workers belonged to the elite Amalgamated, the union had long enjoyed the support of the plant's 3,000 non-union workers. Slavs, who did much of the unskilled work, made common cause with the Welsh, Scottish, and Irish skilled workers who belonged to the union.

Carnegie, who often praised labor unions, preferred not to be directly involved in the union busting, so that spring he sailed to Scotland and left Henry Clay Frick, the toughest antilabor man in the industry, in charge. By summer, a strike looked inevitable. Frick prepared by erecting a fifteen-foot fence around the Homestead plant and topping it with barbed wire. Workers aptly dubbed it "Fort Frick." Frick then hired 316 mercenaries from the Pinkerton National Detective Agency at the rate of $5 per day, more than double the wage of the average Homestead worker.

On June 28, the **Homestead lockout** began when Frick locked the doors of the mills and prepared to bring in strikebreakers. Hugh O'Donnell, the young Irishman who led the union, vowed to prevent "scabs" from entering the plant. On July 6 at 4 a.m., a lookout spotted two barges moving up the Monongahela River in the fog. Frick was attempting to smuggle his Pinkertons into Homestead.

Workers sounded the alarm, and within minutes a crowd of more than a thousand, hastily armed with rifles, hoes, and fence posts, rushed to the riverbank. When they attempted to come ashore, gunfire broke out, and more than a dozen Pinkertons and some thirty strikers fell, killed or wounded. The Pinkertons retreated to the barges. For twelve hours, the workers, joined by their family members, threw everything they had at the barges, from fireworks to dynamite. Finally, the Pinkertons hoisted a white flag and arranged with O'Donnell to surrender. With three workers dead and scores wounded, the crowd, numbering perhaps ten thousand, was in no mood for conciliation. As the hated "Pinks" came up the hill, they were forced to run a gantlet of screaming, cursing men, women, and children. When a young guard dropped to his knees, weeping for mercy, a woman used her umbrella to poke out his eye. One Pinkerton had been killed in the siege on the barges. In the grim rout that

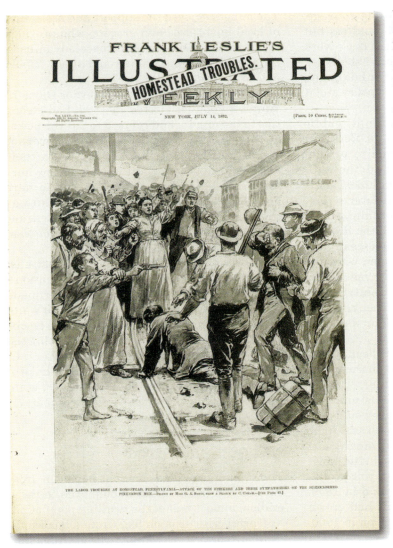

FRANK LESLIE'S
ILLUSTRATED
HOMESTEAD TROUBLES.
WEEKLY

NEW YORK, JULY 14, 1892.

THE LABOR TROUBLES AT HOMESTEAD, PENNSYLVANIA—ATTACK OF THE STRIKERS AND THEIR SYMPATHIZERS ON THE SURRENDERED PINKERTON MEN.

Homestead Workers Attack the Pinkertons

The nation's attention was riveted on labor strife at the Homestead steel mill in the summer of 1892. *Frank Leslie's Illustrated Weekly* ran a cover story on the violence that Pinkerton agents faced from an armed crowd of men, women, and children who were enraged that Frick had hired the Pinkertons to bring in strikebreakers. Beaten and overwhelmed by the strikers, the Pinkertons surrendered. The New York Society Library.

followed their surrender, not one avoided injury. The workers took control of the plant and elected a council to run the community. At first, public opinion favored their cause. A congressman castigated Carnegie for "skulking in his castle in Scotland." Populists, meeting in St. Louis, condemned the use of "hireling armies."

The action of the Homestead workers struck at the heart of the capitalist system, pitting the workers' right to their jobs against the rights of private property. The workers' insistence that "we are not destroying the property of the company—merely protecting our rights" did not prove as compelling to the courts and the state as the property rights of the owners. Four days after the confrontation, Pennsylvania's governor, who sympathized with the workers, nonetheless yielded to pressure from Frick and ordered eight

thousand National Guard troops into Homestead to protect Carnegie's property. The workers, thinking they had nothing to fear from the militia, welcomed the troops with a brass band. But the troops' occupation not only protected Carnegie's property but also enabled Frick to reopen the mills and bring in strikebreakers. "We have been deceived," one worker complained bitterly. "We have stood idly by and let the town be occupied by soldiers who come here, not as our protectors, but as the protectors of non-union men. . . . If we undertake to resist the seizure of our jobs, we will be shot down like dogs."

Then, in a misguided effort to ignite a general uprising, Alexander Berkman, a Russian immigrant and anarchist, attempted to assassinate Frick. Berkman bungled his attempt. Shot twice and stabbed with a dagger, Frick survived and showed considerable courage, allowing a doctor to remove the bullets but refusing to leave his desk until the day's work was completed. "I do not think that I shall die," Frick remarked coolly, "but whether I do or not, the Company will pursue the same policy and it will win."

After the assassination attempt, public opinion turned against the workers. Berkman was quickly tried and sentenced to prison. Although the Amalgamated and the AFL denounced his action, the incident linked anarchism and unionism. O'Donnell later wrote, "The bullet from Berkman's pistol, failing in its foul intent, went straight through the heart of the Homestead strike." The Homestead mill reopened in November, and the men returned to work, except for the union leaders, now blacklisted in every steel mill in the country. With the owners firmly in charge, the company slashed wages, reinstated the twelve-hour day, and eliminated five hundred jobs.

The workers at Homestead had been taught a lesson. They would never again, in the words of the National Guard commander, "believe the works are their's [sic] quite as much as Carnegie's." Another forty-five years would pass before steelworkers, unskilled as well as skilled, successfully unionized. In the meantime, Carnegie's production tripled, even in the midst of a depression. "Ashamed to tell you profits these days," Carnegie wrote a friend in 1899. And no wonder: Carnegie's profits had grown from $4 million in 1892 to $40 million in 1900.

The Cripple Creek Miners' Strike of 1894

Less than a year after the Homestead lockout, a panic on Wall Street in the spring of 1893 touched off a bitter economic depression. In the West, silver mines fell on hard times, leading to the **Cripple Creek miners' strike of 1894**. When mine owners moved to lengthen the workday from eight to ten hours, the newly formed Western Federation of Miners (WFM) vowed to hold the line in Cripple Creek, Colorado. In February 1894, the WFM threatened to strike all mines running more than eight-hour shifts. The mine owners divided: Some quickly settled with the WFM; others continued to demand ten hours, provoking a strike.

The striking miners received help from many quarters. Working miners paid $15 a month to a strike fund, and miners in neighboring districts sent substantial contributions.

The miners enjoyed the support and assistance of local businesses and grocers, who provided credit to the strikers. With these advantages, the Cripple Creek strikers could afford to hold out for their demands.

Even more significant, Governor Davis H. Waite, a Populist elected in 1892, had strong ties to the miners and refused to use the power of the state against the strikers. Governor Waite asked the strikers to lay down their arms and demanded that the mine owners disperse their hired deputies. The miners agreed to arbitration and selected Waite as their sole arbitrator. By May, the recalcitrant mine owners capitulated, and the union won an eight-hour day.

Governor Waite's intervention demonstrated the pivotal power of the state in the nation's labor wars. Having a Populist in power made a difference. A decade later, in 1904, with Waite out of office, mine owners relied on state troops to take back control of the mines, defeating the WFM and blacklisting all of its members. In retrospect, the Cripple Creek miners' strike of 1894 proved the exception to the rule of state intervention on the side of private property.

Eugene V. Debs and the Pullman Strike

The economic depression that began in 1893 swelled the ranks of the unemployed to three million, almost half of the working population. "A fearful crisis is upon us," wrote a labor publication. Nowhere were workers more demoralized than in the model town of Pullman, on the outskirts of Chicago.

In the wake of the Great Railroad Strike of 1877, George M. Pullman, the builder of Pullman railroad cars, moved his plant and workers nine miles south of Chicago and built a model town. The town of Pullman boasted parks, fountains, playgrounds, an auditorium, a library, a hotel, shops, and markets, along with 1,800 units of housing. Noticeably absent was a saloon.

The housing in Pullman was clearly superior to that in neighboring areas, but workers paid a high price to live there. Pullman's rents ran 10 to 20 percent higher than housing costs in nearby communities. In addition, George Pullman refused to "sell an acre under any circumstances." As long as he controlled the town absolutely, he held the powerful whip of eviction over his employees and could quickly get rid of "troublemakers." Although observers at first praised the beauty and orderliness of the town, critics by the 1890s compared Pullman's model town to a "gilded cage" for workers.

The depression brought hard times to Pullman. Workers saw their wages slashed five times between May and December 1893, with cuts totaling at least 28 percent. At the same time, Pullman refused to lower the rents in his model town, insisting that "the renting of the dwellings and the employment of workmen at Pullman are in no way tied together." When workers went to the bank to cash their paychecks, they found that the rent had been taken out. One worker discovered only forty-seven cents in his pay envelope for two weeks' work. When the bank teller asked him whether he wanted to apply it to his back rent, he retorted, "If Mr. Pullman needs that forty-seven cents worse than I do, let him have it." At the same time, Pullman continued to pay his stockholders an 8 percent dividend, and the company accumulated a $25 million surplus.

At the heart of the labor problems at Pullman lay not only economic inequity but also the company's attempt to control the work process, substituting piecework for day wages and undermining skilled crafts workers. During the spring of 1894, Pullman's desperate workers, seeking help, flocked to the ranks of the American Railway Union (ARU), led by the charismatic Eugene V. Debs. The ARU, unlike the skilled craft unions of the AFL, pledged to organize all railway workers—from engineers to engine wipers.

George Pullman responded to union organization at his plant by firing three of the union's leaders the day after they protested wage cuts. Angry men and women walked off the job in disgust. What began as a spontaneous protest in May 1894 quickly blossomed into a strike that involved more than 90 percent of Pullman's 3,300 workers. Pullman countered by shutting down the plant. In June, the Pullman strikers appealed to the ARU to come to their aid. Debs pleaded with the workers to find another solution. But when George Pullman refused arbitration, the ARU membership voted to boycott all Pullman cars. Beginning on June 29, switchmen across the United States refused to handle any train that carried Pullman cars.

The conflict escalated quickly. The General Managers Association (GMA), an organization of managers from twenty-four different railroads, acted in concert to quash the **Pullman boycott**. They recruited strikebreakers and fired all the protesting switchmen. Their tactics set off a chain reaction. Entire train crews walked off

A Pullman Crafts Worker
Pullman Palace cars were known for their luxurious details. Here, a painter working in the 1890s applies elaborate decoration to the exterior of a Pullman car. The Pullman workers' strike in 1894 stemmed in part from the company's efforts to undermine the status of crafts workers by reducing them to low-paid piecework. The fight to control the workplace contributed to the labor wars of the 1890s. © Chicago History Museum, USA / The Bridgeman Art Library.

the job in a show of solidarity with the Pullman workers. By July 2, rail lines from New York to California lay paralyzed. Even the GMA was forced to concede that the railroads had been "fought to a standstill."

The Press and the Pullman Strike: Framing Class Conflict

Newspaper coverage of the 1894 Pullman strike and the subsequent American Railway Union boycott provides a window into the way the press framed class conflict in the United States in the 1890s. The *Chicago Times*, for example, clearly supported the workers and the union. By contrast, the *Chicago Tribune* and most other Chicago newspapers sided with George M. Pullman and the General Managers Association. Nellie Bly, the era's most colorful investigative reporter, wrote a personal account of her experience with the striking workers for the *New York World*.

DOCUMENT 1
Chicago Tribune, May 12, 1894

PULLMAN MEN OUT
Discharges the Cause

Two thousand employees in the Pullman car works struck yesterday, leaving 800 others at their posts. This was not enough to keep the works going, so a notice was posted on the big gates at 6 o'clock . . . saying: "These shops closed until further notice."

Mr. Pullman said last night he could not tell when work would be resumed. The American Railway Union, which has been proselytizing for a week among the workmen, announces that it will support the strikers . . . [intimating] that the trainmen on the railways on which are organized branches of the union might refuse to handle any of the Pullman rolling stock.

DOCUMENT 2
Chicago Times, May 12, 1894

PULLMAN MEN OUT
Firing Three Men Starts It

Almost the entire force of men employed in the Pullman shops went on strike yesterday. Out of the 4,800 men and women employed in the various departments there were probably not over 800 at work at 6 o'clock last evening. The immediate cause of the strike was the discharge or laying off of three men in the iron machine shop. The real but remote cause is the question of wages over which the men have long been dissatisfied and on account of which they had practically resolved to strike a month ago. . . .

The position of the company is that no increase in wages is possible. . . . President George M. Pullman told the committee that the company was doing business at a loss even at the reduced wages paid the men and offered to show his books in support of his assertion.

DOCUMENT 3
Chicago Times, May 15, 1894

SKIMS OFF THE FAT
Pullman Company Declares a Dividend Today
Full Pockets Swallow $600,000 While Honest Labor Is Starving

Today the Pullman Company will declare a quarterly dividend of 2 per cent on its capital stock of $30,000,000 and President George M. Pullman is authority for the statement that his company owes no man a cent. This despite the assertion of Mr. Pullman that the works have been run at a loss for eight months. Six hundred thousand dollars to shareholders, while starvation threatens the workmen.

DOCUMENT 4
Chicago Tribune, July 1, 1894

MOBS BENT ON RUIN
Men Who Attempt to Work Are Terrorized and Beaten

Continued and menacing lawlessness marked the progress yesterday of Dictator Debs and those who obey his orders in their efforts at coercing the railroads of the country into obeying the mandates of the American Railway Union. . . . At Blue Island, anarchy reigned. The Mayor and police force of that town could do nothing to repress the riotous strikers and they did their own sweet will. . . .

DOCUMENT 5
Chicago Tribune, July 7, 1894

YARDS FIRE SWEPT
Rioters Prevent Firemen from Saving the Property

From Brighton Park to Sixty-First Street the yards of the Pan-Handle road were last night put to the torch by the rioters. Between 600 and 700 freight cars have been destroyed, many of them loaded. Miles and miles of costly track are in a snarled tangle of heat-twisted rails. Not less than $750,000—possibly a whole $1,000,000 of property—has been sacrificed to the caprice of a mob of drunken Anarchists and rebels.

DOCUMENT 6
Chicago Times, July 7, 1894

MEN NOT AWED BY SOLDIERS
Railway Union Is Confident of Winning against Armed Capital

Despite the presence of United States troops and the mobilization of five regiments of state militia, despite threats of martial law and total extermination of the strikers by bullet and bayonet, the great strike inaugurated by the American Railway Union holds three-fourths of the roads running out of Chicago in its strong fetters, and last night traffic was more fully paralyzed than at any time since the inception of the tie-up. . . .

If the soldiers are sent to this district, bloodshed and perhaps death will follow today, for this is the most lawless element in the city, as is shown by their riotous work yesterday. . . . But the perpetrators are not American Railway Union men. The people engaged in this outrageous work of destruction are not strikers, most of them are not even grown men. The persons who set the fires yesterday on the authority of the firemen and police are young hoodlums . . . and the police on the scene apparently didn't care to or would not make arrests.

DOCUMENT 7
New York World, July 14, 1894

CHEERS FOR NELLIE BLY
Nellie Bly Covers the Strike

I found in my mail this morning an earnest request from the Pullman A. R. U. for me to be present at a meeting which was to be held in the Turner Hall, Kensington. . . .

So I took my nerves in hand and my place before the table near where the speakers sat. I don't intend to repeat what I said, but I told them several truths. They were especially amused when I told them that I had come to Chicago very bitterly set against the strikers; that so far as I understood the question, I thought the inhabitants of the model town of Pullman hadn't a reason on earth to complain. With this belief I visited the town, intending in my articles to denounce the riotous and bloodthirsty strikers. Before I had been half a day in Pullman I was the most bitter striker in the town.

That is true. I've [flip]flopped, as they call it, and I am brave enough to confess it. If ever men and women had cause to strike, those men and women are in Pullman. I also said to these men, sitting so quietly and peaceably before me, hungry for a word of sympathy or a word of hope, that if any of them wished to make any statements to me I would be glad to have them do so. After the meeting I was besieged. If I attempted to tell half the tales of wrong I've listened to I could fill an entire copy of *The World*.

Questions for Analysis and Debate

1. How do the *Tribune* and *Times* articles differ in their portrayal of events and actors in the strike?

2. Which version of the strike do you think most middle-class readers, who tended to be sympathetic to the strikers but fearful of violence, would find most compelling?

3. Which version of the strike do you think was favored by business owners, who provided advertising revenue to the newspapers?

4. Do you think readers found Nellie Bly's article persuasive? Why or why not?

Connect to the Big Idea

C What economic and social conditions led workers to strike in the 1890s?

The boycott remained surprisingly peaceful. In contrast to the Great Railroad Strike of 1877, no major riots broke out, and no serious property damage occurred. Debs fired off telegrams to all parts of the country advising his followers to avoid violence and respect law and order. But the nation's newspapers, fed press releases by the GMA, distorted the issues and misrepresented the strike. Across the country, papers ran headlines like "Wild Riot in Chicago" and "Mob Is in Control." (See "Documenting the American Promise," page 562.)

In Washington, Attorney General Richard B. Olney, a lawyer with strong ties to the railroads, was determined to put down the strike. In his way stood the governor of Illinois, John Peter Altgeld, who, observing that the boycott remained peaceful, refused to call out troops. To get around Altgeld, Olney convinced President Grover Cleveland that federal troops had to intervene to protect the mails. To further cripple the boycott, two conservative Chicago judges issued an injunction so sweeping that it prohibited Debs from speaking in public. By issuing the injunction, the court made the boycott a crime punishable by a jail sentence for contempt of court, a civil process that did not require a jury trial. Even the conservative *Chicago Tribune* judged the injunction "a menace to liberty . . . a weapon ever ready for the capitalist." Furious, Debs risked jail by refusing to honor it.

Olney's strategy worked. President Grover Cleveland called out the army. On July 5, nearly 8,000 troops marched into Chicago. Violence immediately erupted. In one day, troops killed 25 workers and wounded more than 60. In the face of bullets and bayonets, the strikers held firm. "Troops cannot move trains," Debs reminded his followers, a fact that was borne out as the railroads remained paralyzed despite the military intervention. But if the army could not put down the boycott, the injunction did. Debs was arrested and imprisoned for contempt of court. With its leader in jail, its headquarters raided and ransacked, and its members demoralized, the ARU collapsed along with the boycott. Pullman reopened his factory, hiring new workers to replace many of the strikers and leaving 1,600 without jobs.

In the aftermath of the strike, a special commission investigated the events at Pullman, taking testimony from 107 witnesses, from the lowliest workers to George M. Pullman himself. Stubborn and self-righteous, Pullman spoke for the business orthodoxy of his era, steadfastly affirming the right of business to safeguard its interests through confederacies such as the GMA and at the same time denying labor's right to organize. "If we were to receive these men as representatives of the union," he stated, "they could probably force us to pay any wages which they saw fit."

From his jail cell, Eugene Debs reviewed the events of the Pullman strike. With the courts and the government ready to side with industrialists in defense of private property, strikes seemed futile, and unions remained helpless. Workers would have to take control of the state itself. Debs went into jail a trade unionist and came out six months later a socialist. At first, he turned to the Populist Party, but after its demise he formed the Socialist Party in 1900 and ran for president five times.

REVIEW What led to the labor wars of the 1890s?

▶ Women's Activism

"Do everything," Frances Willard urged her followers in 1881. The new president of the Woman's Christian Temperance Union (WCTU) meant what she said. The WCTU followed a trajectory that was common for women in the late nineteenth century. As women organized to deal with issues that touched their homes and families, they moved into politics, lending new urgency to the cause of woman suffrage. Urban industrialism dislocated women's lives no less than men's. Like men, women sought political change and organized to promote issues central to their lives, campaigning for temperance and woman suffrage.

Frances Willard and the Woman's Christian Temperance Union

A visionary leader, Frances Willard spoke for a group left almost entirely out of the U.S. electoral process. In 1890, only one state, Wyoming, allowed women to vote in national elections. But lack of the franchise did not mean that women were apolitical. The WCTU demonstrated the breadth of women's political activity in the late nineteenth century.

Women supported the temperance movement because they felt particularly vulnerable to the effects of drunkenness. Dependent on

men's wages, married women and their children suffered when money went for drink. The drunken, abusive husband epitomized the evils of a nation in which women remained second-class citizens. The WCTU, composed entirely of women, viewed all women's interests as essentially the same and therefore did not hesitate to use the singular *woman* to emphasize gender solidarity. Although mostly white and middle-class, WCTU members resolved to speak for their entire sex.

When Willard became president in 1879, she radically changed the direction of the organization. Social action replaced prayer as women's answer to the threat of drunkenness. Viewing alcoholism as a disease rather than a sin and poverty as a cause rather than a result of drink, the WCTU became involved in labor issues, joining with the Knights of Labor to press for better working conditions for women workers. Describing workers in a textile mill, a WCTU member wrote in the organization's *Union Signal* magazine, "It is dreadful to see these girls, stripped almost to the skin . . . and running like racehorses from the beginning to the end of the day." She concluded, "The hard slavish work is drawing the girls into the saloon."

Willard capitalized on the cult of domesticity as a shrewd political tactic. Using "home protection" as her watchword, she argued as early as 1884 that women needed the vote to protect home and family. By the 1890s, the WCTU's grassroots network of local unions included 200,000 dues paying members and had spread to all but the most isolated rural areas of the country.

Willard worked to create a broad reform coalition in the 1890s, embracing the Knights of Labor, the People's Party, and the Prohibition Party. Until her death in 1898, she led if not a woman's rights movement, then the first organized mass movement of women united around a woman's issue. By 1900, thanks largely to the WCTU, women could claim a generation of experience in political action—speaking, lobbying, organizing, drafting legislation, and running private charitable institutions. As Willard observed, "All this work has tended more toward the liberation of women than it has toward the extinction of the saloon."

Elizabeth Cady Stanton, Susan B. Anthony, and the Movement for Woman Suffrage

Unlike the WCTU, the organized movement for woman suffrage remained small and relatively weak in the late nineteenth century. In 1869, Elizabeth Cady Stanton and her ally, Susan B. Anthony, launched the National Woman Suffrage Association (NWSA) demanding the vote for women (see "Women's Activism" in chapter 18). A more conservative group, the American Woman Suffrage Association (AWSA), formed the same year. Composed of men as well as women,

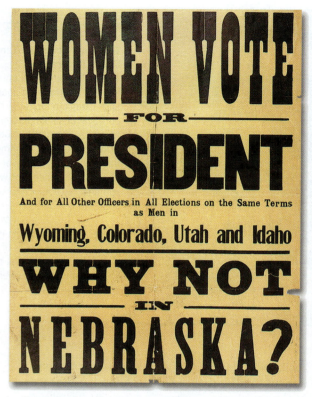

Campaigning for Woman Suffrage

In 1896, women voted in only four states—Wyoming, Colorado, Idaho, and Utah. The West led the way in the campaign for woman suffrage, with Wyoming Territory granting women the vote as early as 1869. The poster calls on Nebraska to join the suffrage column. Nebraska State Historical Society.

the AWSA believed that women should stick with the Republican Party and make suffrage the Sixteenth Amendment. Their optimism proved misplaced.

By 1890, the split had healed, and the newly united **National American Woman Suffrage Association (NAWSA)** launched campaigns on the state level to gain the vote for women. Twenty years had made a great change. Woman suffrage, though not yet generally supported, was no longer considered a crackpot idea, thanks in part to the WCTU's support of the "home protection" ballot. The NAWSA honored Elizabeth Cady Stanton by electing her its first president, but Susan B. Anthony, who took the helm in 1892, emerged as the leading figure in the new united organization.

Stanton and Anthony, both in their seventies, were coming to the end of their public careers. Since the days of the Seneca Falls woman's rights convention, they had worked for reforms for their sex, including property

rights, custody rights, and the right to education and gainful employment. But the prize of woman suffrage still eluded them. Suffragists won victories in Colorado in 1893 and Idaho in 1896. One more state joined the suffrage column in 1896 when Utah entered the Union. But women suffered a bitter defeat in a California referendum on woman suffrage that same year. Never losing faith, Anthony remarked in her last public appearance, in 1906, "Failure is impossible."

REVIEW   How did women's temperance activism contribute to the cause of woman suffrage?

▶ Depression Politics

The depression that began in the spring of 1893 and lasted for more than four years put nearly half of the labor force out of work, a higher percentage than during the Great Depression of the 1930s. The human cost of the depression was staggering. "I Take my pen in hand to let you know that we are Starving to death," a Kansas farm woman wrote to the governor in 1894. "Last cent gone," wrote a young widow in her diary. "Children went to work without their breakfasts." Following the harsh dictates of social Darwinism and laissez-faire, the majority of America's elected officials believed that it was inappropriate for the government to intervene. But the scope of the depression made it impossible for churches and local agencies to supply sufficient relief, and increasingly Americans called on the federal government to take action. Armies of the unemployed marched on Washington to demand relief, and the Populist Party experienced a surge of support as the election of 1896 approached.

Coxey's Army

Masses of unemployed Americans marched to Washington, D.C., in the spring of 1894 to call attention to their plight and to urge Congress to enact a public works program to end unemployment. Jacob S. Coxey of Massilon, Ohio, led the most publicized contingent. Convinced that men could be put to work building badly needed roads for the nation, Coxey proposed a scheme to finance public works through non-interest-bearing bonds. "What I am after," he maintained, "is to try to put this country in a

Coxey's Army
A contingent of Coxey's army stops to rest on its way to Washington, D.C. A "petition in boots," Coxey's followers were well dressed. Music was an important component of the march, including the anthem "Marching with Coxey." Band members are pictured on the right with their instruments. Despite their peaceful pose, the marchers stirred the fears of many Americans, who predicted an uprising of the unemployed. Courtesy of the Ohio Historical Society, OHS AL01139.

condition so that no man who wants work shall be obliged to remain idle." His plan won support from the AFL and the Populists.

Starting out from Ohio with one hundred men, **Coxey's army**, as it was dubbed, swelled as it marched east through the spring snows of the Alleghenies. In Pennsylvania, Coxey recruited several hundred from the ranks of those left unemployed by the Homestead lockout.

On May 1, Coxey's army arrived in Washington. When Coxey defiantly marched his men onto the Capitol grounds, police set upon the demonstrators with nightsticks, cracking skulls and arresting Coxey and his lieutenants. Coxey went to jail for twenty days and was fined $5 for "walking on the grass." But other armies of the unemployed, totaling possibly as many as five thousand people, were still on their way. The more daring contingents commandeered entire trains, stirring fears of revolution. Journalists who covered the march did little to quiet the nation's fears. They delighted in military terminology, describing themselves as "war correspondents." To boost newspaper sales, they gave to the episode a tone of urgency and heightened the sense of a nation imperiled.

By August, the leaderless, tattered armies dissolved. Although the "On to Washington" movement proved ineffective in forcing federal relief legislation, Coxey's army dramatized the plight of the unemployed and acted, in the words of one participant, as a "living, moving object lesson." Like the Populists, Coxey's army called into question the underlying values of the new industrial order and demonstrated how ordinary citizens turned to means outside the regular party system to influence politics in the 1890s.

The People's Party and the Election of 1896

Even before the depression of 1893, the Populists had railed against the status quo. "We meet in the midst of a nation brought to the verge of moral, political, and material ruin," Ignatius Donnelly had declared in his keynote address at the creation of the People's Party in St. Louis in 1892. "The fruits of the toil of millions are

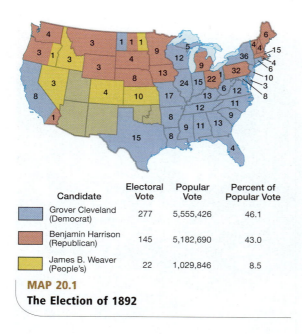

Candidate	Electoral Vote	Popular Vote	Percent of Popular Vote
Grover Cleveland (Democrat)	277	5,555,426	46.1
Benjamin Harrison (Republican)	145	5,182,690	43.0
James B. Weaver (People's)	22	1,029,846	8.5

MAP 20.1

The Election of 1892

boldly stolen to build up colossal fortunes for a few. . . . From the same prolific womb of governmental injustice we breed the two great classes—tramps and millionaires."

The fiery rhetoric frightened many who saw in the People's Party a call not to reform but to revolution. Throughout the country, the press denounced the Populists as "cranks, lunatics, and idiots." When one self-righteous editor dismissed them as "calamity howlers," Populist governor Lorenzo Lewelling of Kansas shot back, "If that is so I want to continue to howl until those conditions are improved."

The People's Party captured more than a million votes in the presidential election of 1892, a respectable showing for a new party (Map 20.1). But increasingly, sectional and racial animosities threatened its unity. Realizing that race prejudice obscured the common economic interests of black and white farmers, Populist Tom Watson of Georgia openly courted African Americans, appearing on platforms with black speakers and promising "to wipe out the color line." When angry Georgia whites threatened to lynch a black Populist preacher, Watson rallied two thousand gun-toting Populists to the man's defense. Although many Populists remained racist in their attitudes toward African Americans, the spectacle of white Georgians riding through the night to protect a black man from lynching was symbolic of the enormous changes the Populist Party promised in the South.

As the presidential election of 1896 approached, the depression intensified cries for reform not only from the Populists but also throughout the electorate. Depression worsened the tight money problem caused by the deflationary pressures of the gold standard. Once again, proponents of free silver stirred rebellion in the ranks of both the Democratic and the Republican parties. When the Republicans nominated Ohio governor William McKinley on a platform pledging the preservation of the gold standard, western advocates of free silver representing miners and farmers walked out of the convention. Open rebellion also split the Democratic Party as vast segments in the West and South repudiated President Grover Cleveland because of his support for gold. In South Carolina, Benjamin Tillman won his race for Congress by promising, "Send me to Washington and I'll stick my pitchfork into [Cleveland's] old ribs!"

The spirit of revolt animated the Democratic National Convention in Chicago in the summer of 1896. William Jennings Bryan of Nebraska, the thirty-six-year-old "boy orator from the Platte," whipped the convention into a frenzy with his passionate call for free silver with a ringing exhortation: "Do not crucify mankind upon a cross of gold." Pandemonium broke loose as delegates stampeded to nominate Bryan, the youngest candidate ever to run for the presidency.

The juggernaut of free silver rolled out of Chicago and on to St. Louis, where the People's Party met a week after the Democrats adjourned. Many western Populists urged the party to ally with the Democrats and endorse Bryan. A major obstacle in the path of fusion, however, was Bryan's running mate, Arthur M. Sewall. A Maine railway director and bank president, Sewall, who had been placed on the ticket to appease conservative Democrats, embodied everything the Populists detested. Moreover, die-hard southern Populists wanted no part of fusion. Southern Democrats had resorted to fraud and violence to steal elections from the Populists in southern states, and support for a Democratic ticket proved hard to swallow.

Populists struggled to work out a compromise. To show that they remained true to their principles, delegates first voted to support all the planks of the 1892 platform, added to it a call for public works projects for the unemployed, and only narrowly defeated a plank

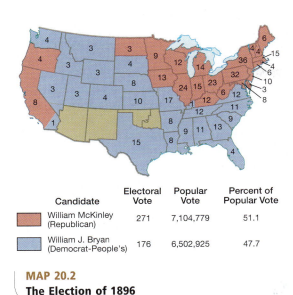

Candidate	Electoral Vote	Popular Vote	Percent of Popular Vote
William McKinley (Republican)	271	7,104,779	51.1
William J. Bryan (Democrat-People's)	176	6,502,925	47.7

MAP 20.2

The Election of 1896

visiting twenty-seven states and speaking to more than five million Americans.

On election day, four out of five voters went to the polls in an unprecedented turnout. The silver states of the Rocky Mountains lined up solidly for Bryan. The Northeast went for McKinley. The Midwest tipped the balance. In the end, the election hinged on between 100 and 1,000 votes in several key states, including Wisconsin, Iowa, and Minnesota. Although McKinley won twenty-three states to Bryan's twenty-two, the electoral vote showed a lopsided 271 to 176 in McKinley's favor (Map 20.2).

The biggest losers in 1896 turned out to be the Populists. On the national level, they polled fewer than 300,000 votes, a million less than in 1894. In the clamor to support Bryan, Populists in the South, determined to beat McKinley at any cost, swallowed their differences and drifted back to the Democratic Party.

REVIEW   Why was the People's Party unable to translate national support into victory in the 1896 election?

for woman suffrage. To deal with the problem of fusion, the convention selected the vice presidential candidate first. The nomination of Tom Watson undercut opposition to Bryan's candidacy. And although Bryan quickly sent a telegram to protest that he would not drop Sewall as his running mate, mysteriously his message never reached the convention floor. Fusion triumphed. Bryan won nomination by a lopsided vote. The Populists did not know it, but their cheers for Bryan signaled the death knell for the People's Party.

Few contests in the nation's history have been as fiercely fought as the presidential election of 1896. On one side stood Republican William McKinley, backed by the wealthy industrialist and party boss Mark Hanna. Hanna played on the business community's fears of Populism to raise a Republican war chest more than double the amount of any previous campaign. On the other side, William Jennings Bryan, with few assets beyond his silver tongue, struggled to make up in energy and eloquence what his party lacked in campaign funds. He crisscrossed the country in a whirlwind tour, by his own reckoning

VISUAL ACTIVITY

"Swallowed!"

This cartoon from 1900 shows William Jennings Bryan as a python swallowing the Democratic Party's donkey mascot. Bryan, who ran unsuccessfully in 1896, won the Democratic nomination again in 1900 and in 1908. Ironically, it was not the Democratic Party so much as the Populist Party that Bryan swallowed. By nominating the Democrat Bryan on their ticket in 1896, the Populist Party lost its identity. The Granger Collection, New York.

READING THE IMAGE: Does the image of a Populist Bryan swallowing the Democratic Party accurately reflect what happened in 1896? What happened to the Populists after 1896?

CONNECTIONS: What issues did the Populists support?

▶ The United States and the World

Throughout much of the second half of the nineteenth century, U.S. interest in foreign policy took a backseat to territorial expansion in the American West. The United States fought the Indian wars while European nations carved empires in Asia, Africa, Latin America, and the Pacific.

At the turn of the twentieth century, the United States pursued a foreign policy consisting of two currents—isolationism and expansionism. Although the determination to remain detached from European politics had been a hallmark of U.S. foreign policy since the nation's founding, Americans simultaneously believed in manifest destiny—the "obvious" right to expand the nation from ocean to ocean. With its own inland empire secured, the United States looked outward. Determined to protect its sphere of influence in the Western Hemisphere and to expand its trading in Asia, the nation turned away from isolationism and toward a more active role on the world stage that led to intervention in China's Boxer uprising and war with Spain.

Markets and Missionaries

The depression of the 1890s provided a powerful impetus to American commercial expansion. As markets weakened at home, American businesses looked abroad for profits. As the depression deepened, one diplomat warned that Americans "must turn [their] eyes abroad, or they will soon look inward upon discontent."

Exports constituted a small but significant percentage of the profits of American business in the 1890s (Figure 20.2). And where American interests led, businessmen expected the government's power and influence to follow to protect their investments. Companies like Standard Oil actively sought to use the U.S. government as their agent, often putting foreign service employees on the payroll. "Our ambassadors and ministers and consuls," wrote John D. Rockefeller appreciatively, "have aided to push our way into new markets and to the utmost corners of the world."

America's foreign policy often appeared little more than a sidelight to business development. In Hawai'i (first called the Sandwich Islands), American sugar interests fomented a rebellion in 1893, toppling the increasingly independent Queen Lili'uokalani. (See "Beyond America's Borders," page 572.) They pushed Congress to annex the islands to avoid the high McKinley tariff on sugar. When President Cleveland learned that Hawai'ians opposed annexation, he withdrew the proposal from Congress. But expansionists still coveted the islands and looked for an opportunity to push through annexation.

Business interests alone did not account for the new expansionism that seized the nation during the 1890s. As Alfred Thayer Mahan,

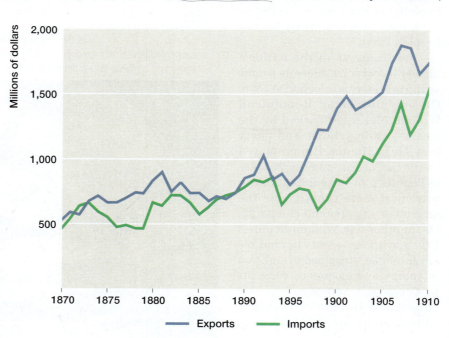

FIGURE 20.2 **Expansion in U.S. Trade, 1870–1910**
Between 1870 and 1910, American exports more than tripled. Imports generally rose, but they were held in check by the high protective tariffs championed by Republican presidents from Ulysses S. Grant to William Howard Taft. A decline in imports is particularly noticeable after the passage of the prohibitive McKinley tariff in 1890.

leader of a growing group of American expansionists, confessed, "Even when material interests are the original exciting cause, it is the sentiment to which they give rise, the moral tone which emotion takes that constitutes the greater force." Much of that moral tone was set by American missionaries intent on spreading the gospel of Christianity to the "heathen." No area on the globe constituted a greater challenge than China.

An 1858 agreement, the Tianjin (Tientsin) treaty, admitted foreign missionaries to China. Although Christians converted only 100,000 in a population of 400 million, the Chinese nevertheless resented the interference of missionaries in village life. Opposition to foreign missionaries took the form of antiforeign secret societies, most notably the Boxers, whose Chinese name translated to "Righteous Harmonious Fist." In 1899, the Boxers hunted down and killed Chinese Christians and missionaries in northwestern Shandong Province. With the tacit support of China's Dowager Empress, the Boxers, shouting "Uphold the Ch'ing Dynasty, Exterminate the Foreigners," marched on the cities. Their rampage eventually led to the massacre of some 30,000 Chinese converts and 250 foreign nuns, priests, and missionaries.

As the Boxer's spread terror throughout northern China, some 800 Americans and Europeans sought refuge in the foreign diplomatic buildings in Peking (today's Beijing). Along with missionaries from the countryside came thousands of their Chinese converts. Unable to escape and cut off from outside aid and communication, the Americans and Europeans in Beijing mounted a defense to face the Boxer onslaught. One American described the scene as 20,000 Boxers stormed the walls in June 1900:

> Their yells were deafening, while the roar of gongs, drums, and horns sounded like thunder. . . . They waved their swords and stamped on the ground with their feet. They wore red turbans, sashes, and garters over blue cloth. [When] they were now only twenty yards from our gate. Three or four volleys from the Lebel rifles of our marines left more than fifty dead on the ground.

For two months the little group held out under siege, eating mule and horse meat and losing 76 men in battle. Sarah Conger, wife of the U.S. ambassador, wrote wearily, "[The siege] was exciting at first, but night after night of this firing, horn-blowing, and yelling, and the whizzing of bullets has hardened us to it."

In August 1900, 2,500 U.S. troops joined an international force sent to rescue the foreigners and put down the uprising in the Chinese capital. The European powers imposed the humiliating Boxer Protocol in 1901, giving themselves the right to maintain military forces in Beijing and requiring the Chinese government to pay an exorbitant indemnity of $333 million.

In the aftermath of the **Boxer uprising**, missionaries voiced no concern at the paradox of bringing Christianity to China at gunpoint. "It is worth any cost in money, worth any cost in bloodshed," argued one bishop, "if we can make millions of Chinese true and intelligent Christians." Merchants and missionaries alike shared such moralistic reasoning. Indeed, they worked hand in hand; trade and Christianity marched into Asia together. "Missionaries," admitted the American clergyman Charles Denby, "are the pioneers of trade and commerce. . . . The missionary, inspired by holy zeal, goes everywhere and by degrees foreign commerce and trade follow."

The Monroe Doctrine and the Open Door Policy

The emergence of the United States as a world power pitted the nation against other colonial powers, particularly Germany and Japan, which posed a threat to the twin pillars of America's expansionist foreign policy. The first, the **Monroe Doctrine**, came to be interpreted as establishing the Western Hemisphere as an American "sphere of influence" and warned European powers to stay away or risk war. The second, the Open Door, dealt with maintaining market access to China.

American diplomacy actively worked to buttress the Monroe Doctrine, with its assertion of American hegemony (domination) in the Western Hemisphere. In the 1880s, Republican secretary of state James G. Blaine promoted hemispheric peace and trade through Pan-American cooperation but, at the same time, used American troops to intervene in Latin American border disputes. In 1895, President Cleveland risked war with Great Britain to enforce the Monroe Doctrine when a conflict developed between Venezuela and British Guiana. After American saber rattling, the British backed down and accepted U.S. mediation in the area despite their territorial claims in Guiana.

Regime Change in Hawai'i

Queen Lili'uokalani came to the throne in Hawai'i in 1891 determined to take back power for her monarchy and her people. As a member of Hawai'i's native royalty, or *ali'i*, she had received a first-rate education in missionary school. As a young woman, she converted to Christianity, adopted the English name Lydia, and married the white (*haole*) governor of Maui. Yet she maintained a reverence for traditional Hawai'ian ways and resented the treatment of her people by the white minority. Her brother, King Kalakaua, had proven a weak leader, coerced by the white elite into signing the "Bayonet Constitution," which put the government squarely in the hands of the whites. Determined to rule, not simply to reign, Lili'uokalani moved ahead with plans to wrest power from the minority she referred to as Hawai'i's "guests."

American missionaries first came to Hawai'i in 1820. Some intermarried with their Christian converts, creating a group of *hapa haole* (half whites), as well as a growing number of children born in Hawai'i to white parents. The temptations of wealth led many missionaries, like Amos Starr Cooke, to acquire land and take up sugar planting. In 1851, he founded Castle & Cooke, which became one of the world's largest sugar producers. By the end of the century, missionaries and planters had blended into one ruling class and gained control of extensive tracts of land. Thanks to the "Bayonet Constitution," they controlled the islands, even though native Hawai'ians and the Japanese and Chinese laborers imported to work on the sugar plantations outnumbered them ten to one.

Sugar became a booming business in Hawai'i as a result of favorable reciprocity treaties with the United States. But hard times came to the islands with the passage of the McKinley tariff in 1890. The tariff wiped out the advantage Hawai'ian sugar had enjoyed in the American market, with devastating results. Within two years, the value of Hawai'ian sugar exports plummeted from $13 million to $8 million.

One way to avoid the tariff was by incorporating Hawai'i into the United States through annexation. Foremost among those who championed this scheme was Lorrin Thurston, the thirty-five-year-old grandson of American missionaries. Thurston, born in Hawai'i and educated in the United States, was zealous in his belief that Hawai'i should be ruled by white Americans and their children. In 1892, he traveled to Washington, D.C., where he won the support of Republican secretary of state James G. Blaine. Thurston returned to Hawai'i knowing that annexation had friends in Washington.

Queen Lili'uokalani picked Saturday, January 14, 1893, as the day to promulgate her new constitution. Her aim was to return Hawai'i to Hawai'ians by allowing only those with native ancestry the right to vote. Learning of her intentions, Thurston quickly hatched a plot to overthrow the monarchy. Late that night, he called on John L. Stevens, the American minister to Hawai'i. Laying out his plan, he urged Stevens, a staunch annexationist, to support the overthrow of the queen and to pledge U.S. support for Thurston's actions. Without hesitating, Stevens promised to land Marines from the USS *Boston* "to protect American lives and property."

Two days later, 162 American Marines and sailors marched into Honolulu armed with carbines, howitzers (small cannons), and Gatling guns. The next day, Thurston and 17 of his confederates seized control of a government building and proclaimed themselves a "provisional government." Minister

In Central America, American business triumphed in a bloodless takeover that saw French and British interests routed. The United Fruit Company of Boston virtually dominated the Central American nations of Costa Rica and Guatemala, while an importer from New Orleans turned Honduras into a "banana republic" (a country run by U.S. business interests). Thus, by 1895, the United States, through business as well as diplomacy, had successfully achieved hegemony in Latin America and the Caribbean, forcing even the British to concur that "the infinite resources [of the United States] combined with its isolated position render it master of the situation and practically invulnerable as against any or all other powers."

At the same time that American foreign policy warned European powers to stay out of the Western Hemisphere, the United States competed for trade in the Eastern Hemisphere. As American interests in China grew, the United States became more aggressive in defending its

Stevens promptly recognized the revolutionaries as the legitimate government of Hawai'i.

To avoid bloodshed, Queen Lili'uokalani agreed to step aside. But in a masterstroke, she composed a letter addressed not to her enemies in the provisional government, but to the U.S. government. Protesting her overthrow, she yielded her authority "until such time as the Government of the United States, shall, upon the facts being presented to it, undo the action of its representatives and reinstate me in the authority which I claim as the constitutional sovereign of the Hawai'ian Islands." The action now shifted to Washington, where Grover Cleveland, a Democrat skeptical of America's adventures abroad, quickly squelched plans for annexation and supported the Hawai'ian queen. The provisional government, however, enjoyed the support of Republicans in Congress and refused to step down, biding its time, waiting for the Republicans to take back the White House.

In 1898, as the taste for empire swept the United States in the wake of the Spanish-American War, President William McKinley quietly signed a treaty annexing Hawai'i. His action pleased not only Hawai'i's sugar growers but also American expansionists, who judged Hawai'i strategically important in expanding U.S. trade with China.

"Hawai'i is ours," Grover Cleveland wrote sadly. "As I look back upon the first steps in this miserable business, and as I contemplate the means used to complete the outrage, I am ashamed of the whole affair."

Queen Lili'uokalani (1838–1917)
An accomplished woman who straddled two cultures, Lydia Kamakaeha Dominis, or Queen Lili'uokalani, spoke English as easily as her native Hawai'ian, was fluent in French and German as well, and traveled widely. Although Lili'uokalani never regained her throne. In 1993, Congress passed and President Bill Clinton signed a resolution offering an apology to native Hawai'ians for the overthrow of their queen. © Bettmann/Corbis

America in a Global Context

1. How did economic issues on the mainland affect the status of Hawai'i?

2. What role did party politics play in the annexation of Hawai'i?

Connect to the Big Idea

C What role did international markets play in American expansion in the 1890s?

presence in Asia and the Pacific. In 1889, it risked war with Germany to guarantee the U.S. navy access to Pago Pago in the Samoan Islands, a port for refueling on the way to Asia. Germany, seeking dominance over the islands, sent warships to the region. But before fighting broke out, a typhoon destroyed the German and American ships. The potential combatants later divided the islands amicably in the 1899 Treaty of Berlin.

In the 1890s, China, weakened by years of internal warfare, was partitioned into spheres of influence by Britain, Japan, Germany, France, and Russia. Concerned about the integrity of China and no less about American trade, Secretary of State John Hay in 1899–1900 wrote a series of notes calling for an "open door" policy that would ensure trade access to all and maintain Chinese sovereignty. The notes were greeted by the major powers with polite evasion. Nevertheless, Hay skillfully managed to maneuver them into doing his bidding, and in 1900 he boldly announced the Open Door as international policy.

VISUAL ACTIVITY

The Open Door
The trade advantage gained by the United States through the Open Door policy is portrayed in this political cartoon. Uncle Sam stands prominently in the "open door," while representatives of the other great powers seek admittance to the "Flowery Kingdom" of China. In fact, the Open Door policy promised equal access for all powers to the China trade, not U.S. preeminence as the cartoon implies. Culver Pictures.

READING THE IMAGE: How does the cartoon portray the role of the United States in international diplomacy?

CONNECTIONS: In what ways does this image misrepresent the reality of American and European involvement in China and of the Open Door policy?

The United States, by insisting on the **Open Door policy**, managed to secure access to Chinese markets, expanding its economic power while avoiding the problems of maintaining a far-flung colonial empire on the Asian mainland. But as the Spanish-American War soon demonstrated, Americans found it hard to resist the temptations of overseas empire.

"A Splendid Little War"

The **Spanish-American War** began as a humanitarian effort to free Cuba from Spain's colonial grasp and ended with the United States itself acquiring territory overseas and fighting a dirty guerrilla war with Filipino nationalists who, like the Cubans, sought independence. Behind the contradiction stood the twin pillars of American foreign policy: The Monroe Doctrine made Spain's presence in Cuba unacceptable; and U.S. determination to keep open the door to Asia made the Philippines attractive. Precedent for the nation's imperial adventures also came from the recent Indian wars in the American West, which provided a template for the subjugation of native peoples in the name of civilization.

Looking back on the Spanish-American War of 1898, Secretary of State John Hay judged it "a splendid little war; begun with the highest motives, carried on with magnificent intelligence and spirit, favored by that fortune which loves the brave." At the close of a decade marred by bitter depression, social unrest, and political upheaval, the war offered Americans a chance to wave the flag and march in unison. War fever proved as infectious as the tune of a John Philip Sousa march. Few argued the merits of the conflict until it was over and the time came to divide the spoils.

The war began with moral outrage over the treatment of Cuban revolutionaries, who had launched a fight for independence against the Spanish colonial regime in 1895. In an attempt to isolate the guerrillas, the Spanish general Valeriano Weyler herded Cubans into crowded and unsanitary concentration camps, where thousands died of hunger, disease, and ex-

The Samoan Islands, 1889

posure. Starvation soon spread to the cities. By 1898, fully a quarter of the island's population had perished in the Cuban revolution.

As the Cuban rebellion dragged on, pressure for American intervention mounted. American newspapers fueled public outrage at Spain. A fierce circulation war raged in New York City between William Randolph Hearst's *Journal* and Joseph Pulitzer's *World*. Their competition provoked what came to be called **yellow journalism**, named for the colored ink used in a popular comic strip. The Cuban war provided a wealth of dramatic copy. Newspapers fed the American people a daily diet of "Butcher" Weyler and Spanish atrocities. Hearst sent artist Frederic Remington to document the horror, and when Remington wired home, "There is no trouble here. There will be no

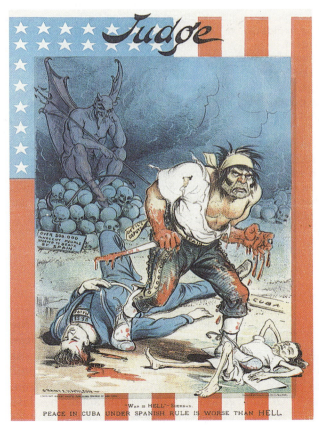

VISUAL ACTIVITY

Yellow Journalism

Most cartoonists promoted war with Spain. Cartoonist Grant Hamilton drew this cartoon for *Judge* magazine in March 1898. It shows a brutish Spain with bloody hands trampling on a sailor from the *Maine*. Cuba is prostrate, and a pile of skulls represents civilians "starved to death by Spain." © Collection of the New-York Historical Society, USA/The Bridgeman Art Library.

READING THE IMAGE: What case does the cartoon make for why the United States should go to war with Spain?

CONNECTIONS: How does the cartoon reflect American attitudes toward race in the late nineteenth century?

Did Terrorists Sink the *Maine*?

At 9:40 p.m. on the evening of February 15, 1898, the U.S. battleship *Maine* blew up in Havana harbor. "The shock threw us backward," reported one eyewitness. "From the deck forward of amidships shot a streak of fire as high as the tall buildings on Broadway. Then the glare of light widened out like a funnel at the top, and down through this bright circle fell showers of wreckage and mangled sailors." In all, 267 sailors drowned or burned to death in one of the worst naval catastrophes to occur during peacetime.

Captain Charles Dwight Sigsbee, the last man to leave the burning ship, filed a terse report saying that the *Maine* had blown up and "urging [that] public opinion should be suspended until further report." But the yellow press, led by William Randolph Hearst's *New York Journal*, ran banner headlines proclaiming, "The War Ship *Maine* Was Split in Two by an Enemy's Secret Infernal Machine!"

Public opinion quickly divided between those who suspected foul play and those who believed the explosion had been an accident. Foremost among the accident theorists was the Spanish government, along with U.S. business interests who hoped to avoid war. The "jingoes," as proponents of war were called, rushed to blame Spain. Even before the details were known, Assistant Secretary of the Navy Theodore Roosevelt wrote, "The *Maine* was sunk by an act of dirty treachery on the part of the Spaniards I believe; though we shall never find out definitely, and officially it will go down as an accident."

In less than a week, the navy formed a court of inquiry, and divers inspected the wreckage. The panel reported on March 25, 1898, that a mine had exploded under the bottom of the ship, igniting gunpowder in the forward magazine. The panel could not determine whether the mine had been planted by the Spanish government or by recalcitrant followers of Valeriano Weyler. The infamous Weyler had been ousted after the American press dubbed him "the Butcher" for his harsh treatment of the Cubans.

As time passed, however, more people came to view the explosion of the *Maine* as an accident. European experts concluded that the *Maine* had exploded accidentally, from a fire in the coal bunker adjacent to the reserve gunpowder. Perhaps poor design, not treachery, had sunk the *Maine*.

In 1910, New York congressman William Sultzer put it succinctly: "The day after the ship was sunk, you could hardly find an American who did not believe that she had been foully done to death by a treacherous enemy. Today you can hardly find an American who believes Spain had anything to do with it." The *Maine* still lay in the mud of Havana harbor, a sunken tomb containing the remains of many sailors. The Cuban government asked for the removal of the wreck, and veterans demanded a decent burial for the sailors. So in March 1910, Congress voted to raise the *Maine* and reinvestigate.

The "Final Report on Removing the Wreck of Battleship *Maine* from the Harbor of Habana, Cuba" appeared in April 1913. This report confirmed that the original naval inquiry was in error, but it ruled out the accident theory by concluding that the nature of the initial explosion indicated a homemade bomb—once again casting suspicion on Weyler's fanatic followers. Following the investigation and removal of human remains, the wreckage of the *Maine* was towed out to sea and, with full funeral honors, sunk in six hundred fathoms of water.

Controversy over the *Maine* proved harder to sink. In the Vietnam era, when faith in the "military establishment" plummeted, Admiral Hyman Rickover launched yet another investigation. Viewing the 1913 "Final Report" as a cover-up, he complained that the ship had been sunk so deep "that there will be no chance of the true facts being revealed." Rickover, a maverick who held the naval brass in low esteem, blamed "the warlike atmosphere in Congress and the press, and the natural tendency to look for reasons for the loss that did not reflect on the Navy." Judging

war," Hearst shot back, "You furnish the pictures and I'll furnish the war."

American interests in Cuba were, in the words of the U.S. minister to Spain, more than "merely theoretical or sentimental." American business had more than $50 million invested in Cuban sugar, and American trade with Cuba, a brisk $100 million a year before the rebellion, had dropped to near zero. Nevertheless, the business community balked, wary of a war with Spain. When industrialist Mark Hanna, the Republican kingmaker and senator from Ohio, urged restraint, a hotheaded Theodore Roosevelt exploded, "We will have this war for

the sinking an accident, Rickover warned, "We must make sure that those in 'high places' do not without more careful consideration of the consequences, exert our prestige and might."

Two decades later, the pendulum swung back. A 1995 study of the *Maine* published by the Smithsonian Institution concluded that zealot followers of General Weyler sank the battleship: "They had the opportunity, the means, and the motivation, and they blew up the *Maine* with a small low-strength mine they made themselves." According to this theory, the terrorists' homemade bomb burst the *Maine*'s hull, triggering a massive explosion. And in 1998 *National Geographic* employed computer models to show that an external explosion (bomb) was capable of sinking the *Maine*.

Questions for Consideration

1. How have explanations for the sinking of the *Maine* changed over time? Has the evidence changed, or have interpretations of the evidence shifted?

2. What does the word *terrorism* suggest about how our understanding of the event may have changed in the twenty-first century?

Connect to the Big Idea

C Why were the jingoists (war faction) so enthusiastic about a war with Spain? What were they trying to prove?

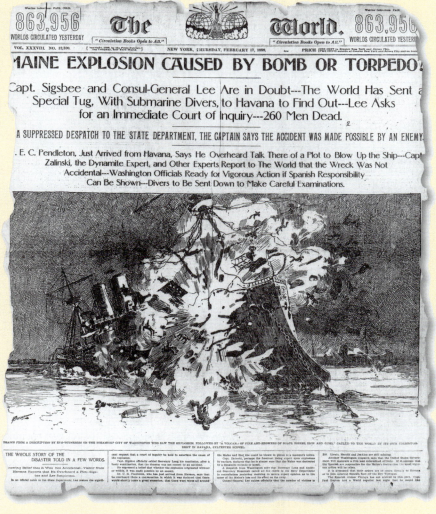

"Maine Explosion Caused by Bomb or Torpedo"
The front page of the *New York World* two days after the blast, trumpeted the news and graphically portrayed the destruction of the ship. The text insisted the explosion was not accidental, even though there was no evidence to back up the assertion. The extent of the destruction and the deaths of 267 sailors fueled war fever. © Collection of the New-York Historical Society, USA/The Bridgeman Art Library.

the freedom of Cuba, Senator Hanna, in spite of the timidity of commercial interests."

To expansionists like Roosevelt, more than Cuban independence was at stake. As assistant secretary of the navy, Roosevelt took the helm in the absence of his boss and, in the summer of 1897, audaciously ordered the U.S. fleet to be ready to steam to Manila in the Philippines. In the event of conflict with Spain, Roosevelt put the navy in a position to capture the islands and gain a stepping-stone to China.

President McKinley moved slowly toward intervention. In a show of American force, he dispatched the battleship *Maine* to Cuba. On

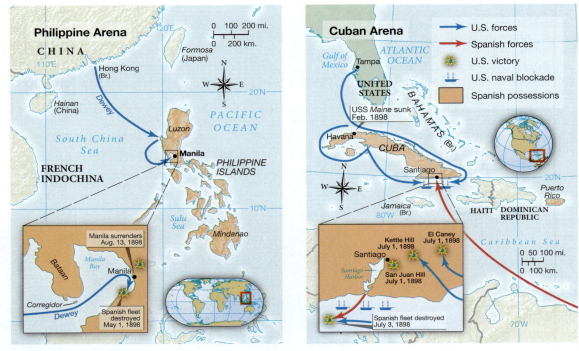

MAP ACTIVITY

Map 20.3   The Spanish-American War, 1898
The Spanish-American War was fought in two theaters, the Philippine Islands and Cuba. Five days after President William McKinley called for a declaration of war, Admiral George Dewey captured Manila. The war lasted only eight months. Troops landed in Cuba in mid-June and by mid-July had destroyed the Spanish fleet.

READING THE MAP: Which countries held imperial control over countries and territories immediately surrounding the Philippine Islands and Cuba?

CONNECTIONS: What role did American newspapers play in the start of the war? How did the results of the war serve American aims in both Asia and the Western Hemisphere?

the night of February 15, 1898, a mysterious explosion destroyed the *Maine*, killing 267 crew members. The source of the explosion remained unclear, but inflammatory stories in the press enraged Americans. (See Historical Question," page 576) Rallying to the cry "Remember the *Maine*," Congress declared war on Spain. In a surge of patriotism, more than a million men rushed to enlist. War brought with it a unity of purpose and national harmony that ended a decade of political dissent and strife. "In April, everywhere over this good fair land, flags were flying," wrote Kansas editor William Allen White. "At the stations, crowds gathered to hurrah for the soldiers, and to throw hats into the air, and to unfurl flags."

Five days after McKinley signed the war resolution, a U.S. Navy squadron destroyed the Spanish fleet in Manila Bay (Map 20.3). The stunning victory caught most Americans by surprise. Few had ever heard of the Philippines. Even McKinley confessed that he could not locate the archipelago on the map. Nevertheless he dispatched U.S. troops to secure the islands.

The war in Cuba ended almost as quickly as it began. The first troops landed on June 22, and after a handful of battles the Spanish forces surrendered on July 17. The war lasted just long enough to elevate Theodore Roosevelt to the status of bona fide war hero. Roosevelt resigned his navy post and formed the Rough Riders, a regiment composed of a sprinkling of Ivy League polo players and a number of western cowboys Roosevelt befriended during his stint as a cattle rancher in the Dakotas. The Rough Riders' charge up Kettle Hill and Roosevelt's role in the decisive battle of San Juan Hill made front-page news. Overnight, Roosevelt became the most famous man in America. By the time he sailed home from Cuba, a coalition of independent Republicans was already plotting his political future.

The Debate over American Imperialism

After a few brief campaigns in Cuba and Puerto Rico brought the Spanish-American War to an end, the American people woke up in possession of an empire that stretched halfway around the globe. As part of the spoils of war, the United States acquired Cuba, Puerto Rico, Guam, and the Philippines. And republicans quickly moved to annex Hawai'i in July 1898.

Contemptuous of the Cubans, whom General William Shafter declared "no more fit for self-government than gun-powder is for hell," the U.S. government directed a Cuban constitution and refused to give up military control of the island until the Cubans accepted the so-called Platt Amendment—a series of provisions that granted the United States the right to intervene to protect Cuba's "independence," as well as the power to oversee Cuban debt so that European creditors would not find an excuse for intervention. For good measure, the United States gave itself a ninety-nine-year lease on a naval base at Guantánamo. In return, McKinley promised to implement an extensive sanitation program to clean up the island, making it more attractive to American investors.

In the formal Treaty of Paris (1898), Spain ceded the Philippines to the United States along with the former Spanish colonies of Puerto Rico and Guam (Map 20.4). Empire did not come cheap. When Spain initially balked at these terms, the United States agreed to pay an indemnity of $20 million for the islands. Nor was the cost measured in money alone. Filipino revolutionaries under Emilio Aguinaldo, who had greeted U.S. troops as liberators, bitterly fought the new masters. It would take seven years and 4,000 American dead—almost ten times the number killed in Cuba—not to mention an estimated 20,000 Filipino casualties, to defeat Aguinaldo and secure American control of the Philippines.

At home, a vocal minority, mostly Democrats and former Populists, resisted the country's foray into overseas empire, judging it unwise, immoral, and unconstitutional. William Jennings Bryan, who enlisted in the army but never saw action, concluded that American expansionism only distracted the nation from problems

Columbia's Easter Bonnet
The United States, symbolized by the female figure of Columbia, tries on "World Power" in this cartoon from *Puck* that appeared in 1901 after the Spanish-American War left the United States in control of Spain's former colonies in Guam, the Philippines, and Puerto Rico. The bonnet, in the shape of an American battleship, indicates the key role the U.S. Navy played in the conflict. Library of Congress.

at home. Pointing to the central paradox of the war, Representative Bourke Cockran of New York admonished, "We who have been the destroyers of oppression are asked now to become its agents." But the expansionists won the day. As Senator Knute Nelson of Minnesota assured his colleagues, "We come as ministering angels, not as despots." Fresh from the conquest of Native Americans in the West, the nation largely embraced the heady mixture of racism and missionary zeal that fueled American adventurism abroad. The *Washington Post* trumpeted, "The taste of empire is in the mouth of the people," thrilled at the prospect of "an imperial policy, the Republic renascent, taking her place with the armed nations."

REVIEW Why did the United States largely abandon its isolationist foreign policy in the 1890s?

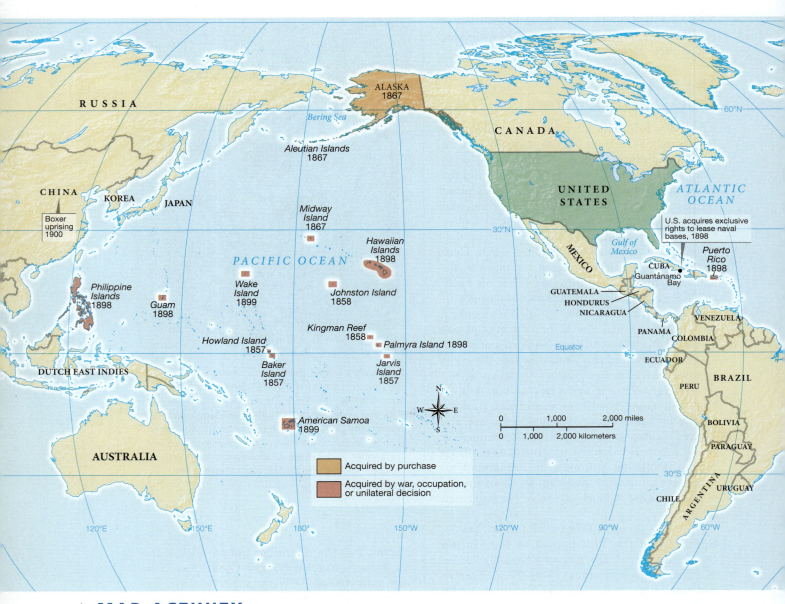

MAP ACTIVITY

Map 20.4   U.S. Overseas Expansion Through 1900

The United States extended its interests abroad with a series of territorial acquisitions. Although Cuba was granted independence, the Platt Amendment kept the new nation firmly under U.S. control. In the wake of the Spanish-American War, the United States woke up to find that it held an empire extending halfway around the globe.

READING THE MAP: Does the map indicate that more territory was acquired by purchase or by war, occupation, or unilateral decision? How many purchases of land outside the continental United States did the government make?

CONNECTIONS: What foreign policy developments occurred in the 1890s? How did American political leaders react to them? Where was U.S. expansion headed and why?

► Conclusion: Rallying around the Flag

A decade of domestic strife ended amid the blare of martial music and the waving of flags. The Spanish-American War drowned out the calls for social reform that had fueled the Populist politics of the 1890s. During that decade, angry farmers facing hard times looked to the Farmers' Alliances to fight for their vision of economic democracy, workers staged bloody battles across the country to assert their rights, and women like Frances Willard preached temperance and suffrage. Together they formed a new People's Party to fight for change.

The bitter depression that began in 1893 led to increased labor strife. The Pullman boycott brutally dramatized the power of property and the conservatism of the laissez-faire state. But workers' willingness to confront capitalism on the streets of Chicago, Homestead, Cripple Creek, and a host of other sites across America eloquently testified to labor's growing determination, unity, and strength.

As the depression deepened, the sight of Coxey's army of unemployed marching on Washington to demand federal intervention in the economy signaled a growing shift in the public mind against the stand-pat politics of laissez-faire. The call for the government to take action to better the lives of workers, farmers, and the dispossessed manifested itself in the fiercely fought presidential campaign of William Jennings Bryan in 1896. With the outbreak of the Spanish-American War in 1898, the decade ended on a harmonious note with patriotic Americans rallying around the flag. But even though Americans basked in patriotism and contemplated empire, old grievances had not been laid to rest. The People's Party had been beaten, but the Populist spirit lived on in the demands for greater government involvement in the economy, expanded opportunities for direct democracy, and a more equitable balance of profits and power between the people and the big corporations. A new generation of progressive reformers championed the unfinished reform agenda in the first decades of the twentieth century.

See the Selected Bibliography for this chapter in the Appendix.

20 Chapter Review

MAKE IT STICK

LearningCurve
Go online and use LearningCurve to see what you know. Then review the key terms and answer the questions.

KEY TERMS

Farmers' Alliance (p. 555)
People's Party (Populist Party) (p. 557)
Homestead lockout (p. 558)
Cripple Creek miners' strike of 1894 (p. 560)
Pullman boycott (p. 561)
National American Woman Suffrage Association (NAWSA) (p. 566)
Coxey's army (p. 567)
Boxer uprising (p. 571)
Monroe Doctrine (p. 571)
Open Door policy (p. 574)
Spanish-American War (p. 574)
yellow journalism (p. 575)

REVIEW QUESTIONS

1. Why did American farmers organize alliances in the late nineteenth century? (pp. 555–558)

2. What led to the labor wars of the 1890s? (pp. 558–564)

3. How did women's temperance activism contribute to the cause of woman suffrage? (pp. 564–566)

4. Why was the People's Party unable to translate national support into victory in the 1896 election? (pp. 566–569)

5. Why did the United States largely abandon its isolationist foreign policy in the 1890s? (pp. 570–579)

MAKING CONNECTIONS

1. Why did so many farmers and urban workers look to the government to help advance their visions of economic justice?

2. What circumstances gave rise to labor protests in the 1890s? How did they differ from those triggering earlier strikes?

3. How did women's activism in the late nineteenth century help advance the cause of woman suffrage?

LINKING TO THE PAST

1. How did the conquest of Native Americans in the West foreshadow U.S. expansion abroad? In what ways did the assumptions of racial superiority evident in U.S. Indian policy affect the treatment of Cubans and Filipinos? (See chapter 17.)

2. Why in the midst of burgeoning growth did the United States experience a major depression in the 1890s? Draw on your knowledge of the development of U.S. industries such as the railroads. (See chapter 18.)

21 Progressivism from the Grass Roots to the White House

1890–1916

CONTENT LEARNING OBJECTIVES

After reading and studying this chapter, you should be able to:

- Explain how and why grassroots progressivism arose near the start of the twentieth century and why proponents like Jane Addams and Hull House served as a spearhead for reform.

- Identify how President Theodore Roosevelt put his progressive activism to work toward big business, conservation, and international affairs and how successor Howard Taft stalled the progressive reforms Roosevelt had begun.

- Explain why progressives led an insurgent campaign during the election of 1912 and the factors that led to Woodrow Wilson's victory in 1912.

- Describe how Wilson sought to enact his "New Freedom" once in office and explain how he became a reluctant Progressive.

- Understand the limits of progressive reform, and identify the organizations that offered more radical visions of America's future.

IN THE SUMMER OF 1889, JANE ADDAMS LEASED TWO FLOORS OF A dilapidated mansion on Chicago's West Side. Her immigrant neighbors must have wondered why this well-dressed woman, who surely could afford better housing, chose to live on South Halsted Street. Yet the house, built by Charles Hull, precisely suited Addams's needs.

For Addams, personal action marked the first step in her search for solutions to the social problems created by urban industrialism. She wanted to help her immigrant neighbors, and she wanted to offer meaningful work to educated women like herself. Addams's emphasis on the reciprocal relationship between the social classes made Hull House different from other philanthropic enterprises. She wished to do things with, not just for, Chicago's poor.

In the next decade, Hull House expanded from two rented floors in the old brick mansion to some thirteen buildings housing a remarkable variety of activities. Addams provided public baths, opened a restaurant for working women too tired to cook after their long shifts, and sponsored a nursery and kindergarten. Hull House offered classes, lectures, art exhibits, musical instruction, and college extension courses.

PROGRESSIVE PARTY SOUVENIR BANDANA
This red bandana is a campaign souvenir from 1912, the year Theodore Roosevelt's followers broke with Republicans to form the Progressive Party. Roosevelt challenged laissez-faire liberalism and argued for government action for social justice.
© David J. & Janice L. Frent Collection / CORBIS.

It boasted a gymnasium, a theater, a manual training workshop, a labor museum, and the first public playground in Chicago.

From the first, Hull House attracted an extraordinary set of reformers who pioneered the scientific investigation of urban ills. Armed with statistics, they launched campaigns to improve housing, end child labor, fund playgrounds, and lobby for laws to protect workers.

Addams quickly learned that it was impossible to deal with urban problems without becoming involved in politics. Piles of decaying garbage overflowed Halsted Street's wooden trash bins, breeding flies and disease. To rectify the problem, Addams got herself appointed garbage inspector. Out on the streets at six in the morning, she rode atop the garbage wagon to make sure it made its rounds. Eventually, her struggle to aid the urban poor led her on to the state capitol and to Washington, D.C.

Under Addams's leadership, Hull House became a "spearhead for reform," part of a broader movement that contemporaries called progressivism. The transition from personal action to political activism that Addams personified became one of the hallmarks of this reform period, which lasted from the 1890s to World War I.

Classical liberalism, which opposed the tyranny of centralized government, did not address the enormous power of Gilded Age business giants. As the gap between rich and poor widened in the 1890s, progressive reformers demonstrated a willingness to use the government to counterbalance the power of private interests and, in doing so, redefined liberalism in the twentieth century.

Faith in activism united an otherwise diverse group of progressive reformers. A sense of Christian mission inspired some. Others, fearing social upheaval, sought to remove some of the worst evils of urban industrialism—tenements, child labor, and harsh working conditions. A belief in technical expertise and scientific management infused progressivism and made the cult of efficiency part of the movement.

Progressives shared a growing concern about the power of wealthy individuals and a distrust of the trusts, but they were not immune to the prejudices of their era. Although they called for greater democracy, many progressives sought to restrict the rights of African Americans, Asians, and even the women who formed the backbone of the movement.

Uplift and efficiency, social justice and social control, direct democracy and discrimination all came together in the Progressive Era at every level of politics and in the presidencies of Theodore Roosevelt and Woodrow Wilson. While in office, Roosevelt advocated conservation, pushed through antitrust reforms, and championed the nation as a world power. Roosevelt's successor, William Taft, failed to follow in Roosevelt's footsteps, and the resulting split in the Republican Party paved the way for Wilson's victory in 1912. A reluctant progressive, Wilson eventually presided over reforms in banking, business, and labor.

Jane Addams

Jane Addams was twenty-nine years old when she founded Hull House on South Halsted Street in Chicago. Her desire to live among the poor and her insistence that settlement house work benefited educated women such as her as well as her immigrant neighbors marked the distance from philanthropy to progressive reform. Her autobiographical *Twenty Years at Hull-House* was published in 1910. Photo: Jane Addams Memorial Collection (JAMC _8000_0005_0014), Special Collections, University of Illinois at Chicago, photographer: Max Platz; Book: Newberry Library, Chicago Illinois, USA/The Bridgeman Art Library.

▶ Grassroots Progressivism

Much of progressive reform began at the grassroots level and percolated upward into local, state, and eventually national politics as reformers attacked the social problems fostered by urban industrialism. Although **progressivism** flourished in many different settings across the country, urban problems inspired the progressives' greatest efforts. In their zeal to "civilize the city," reformers founded settlement houses, professed a new Christian social gospel, and campaigned against vice and crime in the name of "social purity." Allying with the working class, women progressives sought to better the lot of sweatshop garment workers and to end child labor. These local reform efforts often ended up being debated in state legislatures and in the U.S. Congress.

Civilizing the City

Progressives attacked the problems of the city on many fronts. **Settlement houses**, which began in England, spread in the United States. By 1893, the needs of poor urban neighborhoods that had motivated Jane Addams led Lillian Wald to recruit several other nurses to move to New York City's Lower East Side "to live in the neighborhood as nurses, identify ourselves with it socially, and . . . contribute to it our citizenship." Wald's Henry Street settlement pioneered public health nursing.

Women, particularly college-educated women like Addams and Wald, formed the backbone of the settlement house movement. Settlement houses gave college-educated women eager to use their knowledge a place to put their talents to work in the service of society and to champion progressive reform. (See "Seeking the American Promise," page 586.) Such reformers believed that only by living among the poor could they help bridge the growing class divide. Settlements like Hull House grew in number from six in 1891 to more than four hundred in 1911. In the process, settlement house women created a new profession—social work.

For their part, churches confronted urban social problems by enunciating a new **social gospel**, one that saw its mission as not simply to reform individuals but to reform society. The social gospel offered a powerful corrective to social Darwinism and the gospel of wealth, which fostered the belief that riches somehow

CHRONOLOGY

1889	• Jane Addams opens Hull House.
1896	• *Plessy v. Ferguson.*
1900	• Socialist Party founded.
1901	• William McKinley assassinated; Theodore Roosevelt becomes president.
1902	• Antitrust lawsuit filed against Northern Securities Company. • Roosevelt mediates anthracite coal strike.
1903	• Women's Trade Union League founded. • Panama Canal construction begins.
1904	• Roosevelt Corollary to Monroe Doctrine.
1905	• Industrial Workers of the World founded.
1906	• Pure Food and Drug Act and Meat Inspection Act. • Atlanta race riot. • Hepburn Act.
1907	• Panic on Wall Street. • "Gentlemen's Agreement" with Japan.
1908	• *Muller v. Oregon.* • William Howard Taft elected president.
1909	• Garment workers' strike. • National Association for the Advancement of Colored People formed.
1911	• Triangle Shirtwaist Company fire.
1912	• Roosevelt runs for president on Progressive Party ticket. • Woodrow Wilson elected president.
1913	• Suffragists march in Washington, D.C. • Federal Reserve Act.
1914	• Federal Trade Commission created. • Clayton Antitrust Act.
1916	• Margaret Sanger opens first U.S. birth control clinic.

Making the Workplace Safer: Alice Hamilton Explores the Dangerous Trades

Nothing in Alice Hamilton's middle-class, midwestern upbringing hinted at the leading role she would play in the progressive movement as a pioneer in the field of occupational health and safety. Yet at an early age, she resolved to become a doctor because, as she wrote, "as a doctor I could go anywhere I pleased—to the far-off lands or to city slums—and be quite sure that I could be of use anywhere."

This desire to be of use prompted Hamilton to earn a medical degree at the University of Michigan and to study bacteriology in Germany and at Johns Hopkins University. In September 1897, she fulfilled a long-time dream by moving into Hull House, where she, like most of the residents, worked a day job (at Northwestern University's Medical School) and participated in settlement activities in the evenings and on weekends. Hamilton soon focused on the area of public health, particularly the link between occupation and illness.

Through her work, Hamilton came to believe that the poor health of many immigrants resulted from unsafe conditions and noxious chemicals, especially lead dust, in the industrial workplace. Employers insisted that lead poisoning resulted from workers' failure to wash their hands before they ate, or they blamed workers' ill health on alcoholism, but Hamilton disagreed. As she noted, the United States was far behind Europe in the field of industrial toxicology and in the regulation of dangers in the workplace. "The employers [here] could, if they wished, shut their eyes to the dangers their workmen faced," Hamilton observed, "for nobody held them responsible, while the workers [largely immigrants] accepted the risks with fatalistic submissiveness as part of the price one must pay for being poor."

In 1910, at the age of thirty-two, Hamilton was appointed to the newly created Occupational Disease Commission of Illinois, the first investigative body of its kind in the United States. For the next decade, she relied primarily on "shoe leather epidemiology" to explore the dangerous trades. With her assistants, she visited factories, read hospital records, and interviewed workers in their homes to discover instances of lead poisoning. "No young doctor," she wrote, "can hope for work as exciting and rewarding." Lead poisoning builds up slowly in the body, leading to colic and convulsions. Lead harms the nervous system, causing paralysis and wrist drop, a condition in which the hands and fingers cannot be extended. In cases of chronic lead poisoning, victims suffer from weight loss, constipation, high blood pressure, anemia, abdominal pain, fatigue, and premature senility. One of Hamilton's case studies tells the grim story.

A Hungarian, thirty-six years old, worked for seven years grinding lead paint. During this time he had three attacks of colic, with vomiting and headache. I saw him in the hospital, a skeleton of a man, looking almost twice his age, his limbs soft and flabby, his muscles wasted. He was extremely emaciated, his color was a dirty grayish yellow, his eyes dull and expressionless. He lay in an apathetic condition, rousing when spoken to and answering rationally but slowly, with often an appreciable delay, then sinking back into apathy.

In 1911, Hamilton prepared a report making clear the connection between occupation and illness, leading to needed reforms in Illinois. In 1913, the U.S. commissioner of labor asked her to undertake a national study. "I had, as a Federal agent," she wrote, "no right to enter any establishment—that depended on the courtesy of the

signaled divine favor. Charles M. Sheldon's popular book *In His Steps* (1898) called on men and women to Christianize capitalism by asking the question "What would Jesus do?"

Ministers also played an active role in the social purity movement, the campaign to attack vice. To end the "social evil," as reformers delicately referred to prostitution, the social purity movement brought together ministers who wished to stamp out sin, doctors concerned about the spread of venereal disease, and women reformers. Advanced progressives linked prostitution to poverty and championed higher wages for women working in industrial or other jobs.

Attacks on alcohol went hand in hand with the push for social purity. The Anti-Saloon League, formed in 1895 under the leadership of

employer. I must discover for myself where the plants were, and the method of investigation to be followed. . . . Nobody would keep tabs on me, I should not even receive a salary." Using her intelligence and charm, she was rarely denied entry, and her experience at Hull House led her directly to the workers in their homes when she wanted the facts. Her powers of persuasion prompted several employers to institute reforms in their plants to cut down on lead dust.

By 1915, Hamilton had become the foremost American authority on lead poisoning and one of a handful of prominent specialists in industrial disease. When the Harvard Medical School began a program in industrial hygiene in 1916, Hamilton became the first woman invited to join the faculty. Until her retirement in 1935, she alternated a semester of teaching at Harvard with her field work "exploring the dangerous trades." In her long retirement (she lived to be 101), she continued to blend her commitment to social justice and civil rights, political activism, and concern for the poorest workers. Hamilton died on September 22, 1970, three months before Congress passed the Occupational Safety and Health Act, institutionalizing the reforms she had fought for her whole life.

Alice Hamilton
This picture of Alice Hamilton was taken the year she graduated from the University of Michigan medical school in 1893. A resident of Hull House, she pioneered the field of occupational health and safety. Schlesinger Library, Radcliffe Institute for Advanced Study, Harvard University.

Questions for Consideration

1. What was the importance of Hull House in Hamilton's career?

2. Hamilton observed that regulation of industry was much more advanced in Europe than in the United States, where, as she put it, the "subject was tainted with Socialism or with feminine sentimentality for the poor." In her own work, how did she overcome this attitude?

Connect to the Big Idea

C What kinds of social reforms did workers in other settlement houses address?

Protestant clergy, added to the efforts of the Woman's Christian Temperance Union in campaigning to end the sale of liquor. Reformers pointed to links between drinking, prostitution, wife and child abuse, unemployment, and industrial accidents. The powerful liquor lobby fought back, spending liberally in election campaigns, fueling the charge that liquor corrupted the political process.

An element of nativism (dislike of foreigners) ran through the movement for prohibition, as it did in a number of progressive reforms. The Irish, the Italians, and the Germans were among the groups stigmatized by temperance reformers for their drinking. Progressives campaigned to enforce the Sunday closing of taverns, stores, and other commercial establishments and pushed for state legislation to outlaw the sale of liquor. By 1912, seven states were "dry."

Progressives' efforts to civilize the city demonstrated their willingness to take action; their belief that environment, not heredity alone, determined human behavior; and their optimism that conditions could be corrected through government action without radically altering America's economy or institutions. All of these attitudes characterized the progressive movement.

Progressives and the Working Class

Day-to-day contact with their neighbors made settlement house workers particularly sympathetic to labor. When Mary Kenney O'Sullivan complained that her bookbinders' union met in a dirty, noisy saloon, Jane Addams invited them to meet at Hull House. And during the Pullman strike in 1894 (see chapter 20, "Documenting the American Promise," page 562), Hull House residents organized strike relief. "Hull-House has been so unionized," grumbled one Chicago businessman, "that it has lost its usefulness and become a detriment and harm to the community." But to the working class, the support of middle-class reformers marked a significant gain.

Attempts to forge a cross-class alliance became institutionalized in 1903 with the creation of the Women's Trade Union League (WTUL). The WTUL brought together women workers and middle-class "allies." Its goal was to organize working-women into unions under the auspices of the American Federation of Labor (AFL). Although the alliance between working-women, primarily immigrants and daughters of immigrants, and their middle-class allies was not without tension, the WTUL helped working-women achieve significant gains.

The WTUL's most notable success came in 1909 in the "uprising of the twenty thousand," when hundreds of women employees of the Triangle Shirtwaist Company in New York City went on strike to protest low wages, dangerous working conditions, and management's refusal to recognize their union, the International Ladies' Garment Workers Union. In support, an estimated twenty thousand garment workers, most of

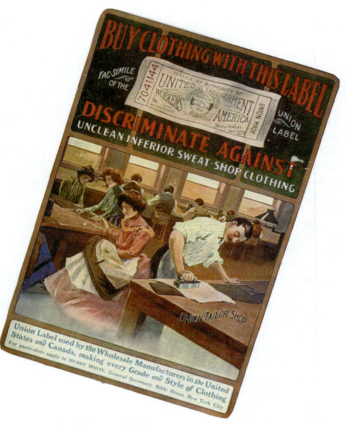

Garment Unions
This illustration urges consumers to fight sweatshops by buying only garments that carry the union label of the United Garment Workers of America. Unions provided important means for elevating working conditions and providing power to women workers. Picture Research Consultants & Archives.

them teenage girls and many of them Jewish and Italian immigrants, stayed out on strike through the winter, picketing in the bitter cold. Police and hired thugs harassed the picketing strikers, beating them up and arresting more than six hundred of them for "street walking" (prostitution). When WTUL allies, including J. P. Morgan's daughter Anne, joined the picket line, the harassment quickly stopped. By the time the strike ended in February 1910, the workers had won important demands in many shops. The solidarity shown by the women workers proved to be the strike's greatest achievement. As Clara Lemlich, one of the strike's leaders, exclaimed, "They used to say that you couldn't even organize women. They wouldn't come to union meetings. They were 'temporary' workers. Well we showed them!"

But for all its success, the uprising of the twenty thousand failed fundamentally to change conditions for women workers, as the tragic Triangle fire dramatized in 1911. A little over a year after the shirtwaist makers' strike ended, fire alarms sounded at the Triangle Shirtwaist factory. The ramshackle building, full of lint and combustible cloth, burned to rubble in half an hour. A WTUL member described the scene below on the street: "Two young girls whom I knew to be working in the vicinity came rushing toward me, tears were running from their eyes and they were white and shaking as they caught me by the arm. 'Oh,' shrieked one of them, 'they are jumping. Jumping from ten stories up! They are going through the air like bundles of clothes.'"

The terrified Triangle workers had little choice but to jump. Flames blocked one exit, and the other door had been locked to prevent workers from pilfering. The flimsy, rusted fire escape collapsed under the weight of fleeing workers, killing dozens. Trapped, 54 workers on the top floors jumped to their deaths. Of 500 workers, 146 died and scores of others were injured. The owners of the Triangle firm went to trial for negligence, but they avoided conviction when authorities determined that a careless smoker had started the fire. The Triangle Shirtwaist Company reopened in another firetrap within a matter of weeks.

Outrage and a sense of futility overwhelmed Rose Schneiderman, a leading WTUL organizer, who made a bitter speech at the memorial service for the dead Triangle workers. "I would be a traitor to those poor burned bodies if I came here to talk good fellowship," she told her audience. "We have tried you good people of the public and we have found you wanting. . . . I know from my experience it is up to the working people to save themselves . . . by a strong working class movement." The Triangle fire severely tested the bonds of the cross-class alliance. Schneiderman and other WTUL leaders determined that organizing and striking were no longer enough, particularly when the AFL paid so little attention to women workers. Increasingly, the WTUL turned its efforts to lobbying for protective legislation—laws that would limit hours and regulate women's working conditions.

The National Consumers League (NCL) also fostered cross-class alliance and advocated for protective legislation. When Florence Kelley took over the leadership of the NCL in 1899, she urged middle-class women to boycott stores and exert pressure for decent wages and working conditions for women employees. Frustrated by the reluctance of the private sector to reform, the NCL promoted protective legislation to better working conditions for women.

Advocates of protective legislation had won a major victory in 1908 when the U.S. Supreme Court, in *Muller v. Oregon*, reversed its previous rulings and upheld an Oregon law that limited

VISUAL ACTIVITY

Identifying the Dead

After the Triangle fire on March 26, 1911, New York City set up a makeshift morgue at the end of Manhattan's Charities Pier. There, the remains of more than a hundred young women and two dozen young men were laid out in coffins for their friends and relatives to identify. Often small personal items provided the only clues to the victim's identity. Hadwin Collection, Kheel Center, Cornell University, Ithaca, NY.

READING THE IMAGE: As you look at the picture, can you tell which Triangle victims would be easily identified and which would not?

CONNECTIONS: Why was the Triangle fire such an important turning point in U.S. labor history?

14. Viewing the unfortunates at the Morgue

to ten the number of hours women could work in a day. A mass of sociological evidence put together by Florence Kelley of the NCL and Josephine Goldmark of the WTUL convinced the Court that long hours endangered women and therefore the entire human race. The Court's ruling set a precedent, but one that separated the well-being of women workers from that of men by arguing that women's reproductive role justified special treatment. Later generations of women fighting for equality would question the effectiveness of this strategy and argue that it ultimately closed good jobs to women. The WTUL, however, greeted protective legislation as a first step in the attempt to ensure the safety of all workers.

Reform also fueled the fight for woman suffrage. For women like Jane Addams, involvement in social reform led inevitably to support for woman suffrage. These new suffragists emphasized the reforms that could be accomplished if women had the vote. Addams insisted that in an urban, industrial society, a good housekeeper could not be sure the food she fed her family, or the water and milk they drank, were pure unless she could vote.

REVIEW What types of people were drawn to the progressive movement, and why?

▶ Progressivism: Theory and Practice

Progressivism emphasized action and experimentation. Dismissing the view that humans should leave progress to the dictates of natural selection, a new group of reform Darwinists argued that evolution could be advanced more rapidly if men and women used their intellects to improve society. In their zeal for action, progressives often showed an unchecked admiration for speed and efficiency that promoted scientific management and a new cult to improve productivity. These varied strands of progressive theory found practical application in state and local politics, where reformers challenged traditional laissez-faire government.

Reform Darwinism and Social Engineering

The active, interventionist approach of the progressives directly challenged social Darwinism, with its insistence on survival of the fittest.

A new group of sociologists argued that progress could be advanced more rapidly if people used their intellects to alter their environment. The best statement of this **reform Darwinism** came from sociologist Lester Frank Ward in his book *Dynamic Sociology* (1883). Ward insisted the "blind natural forces in society must give way to human foresight." This theory condemned the laissez-faire approach, insisting that the liberal state should play a more active role in solving social problems.

Efficiency and *expertise* became progressives' watchwords. In *Drift and Mastery* (1914), journalist and critic Walter Lippmann called for skilled "technocrats" to use scientific techniques to control social change. Unlike the Populists, who advocated a greater voice for the masses, progressives, for all their interest in social justice, insisted that experts be put in charge. At its extreme, the application of expertise and social engineering took the form of scientific management.

Frederick Winslow Taylor pioneered "systematized shop management" in 1911. Obsessed with making humans and machines produce more and faster, he meticulously timed workers with a stop watch and attempted to break down their work into its simplest components, one repetitious action after another. He won many converts among corporate managers, but workers hated the monotony of systematized shop management and argued that it led to speedup—pushing workers to produce more in less time and for less pay. Nevertheless many progressives applauded the increased productivity and efficiency of Taylor's system.

Progressive Government: City and State

Progressivism burst forth at every level of government in 1900, but nowhere more forcefully than in Cleveland with the election of Democrat Thomas Loftin Johnson as mayor. A self-made millionaire by age forty, Johnson moved to Cleveland in 1899, where he began his career in politics. During his mayoral campaign, he pledged to reduce the streetcar fare from five cents to three cents. His election touched off a seven-year war between Johnson and the streetcar moguls. To get his three-cent fare, Johnson had Cleveland buy the streetcar system, a tactic of municipal ownership progressives called "gas and water socialism." Reelected four times, Johnson fought for fair taxation and championed greater democracy through the use of the initiative and, referendum to let voters introduce legislation, and

Tom Johnson Collage

Tom Johnson's greatest achievement as mayor of Cleveland is memorialized in this collage, which shows incidents from his successful fight to get a 3 cent streetcar for Cleveland. To get this low fare, Johnson finally instituted municipal ownership of the transit system. In the picture on the bottom right, he takes the controls of the city's first streetcar in 1906.
Library of Congress.

the recall to get rid of elected officials and judges. Under Johnson's administration, Cleveland became, in the words of journalist Lincoln Steffens, the "best governed city in America."

In Wisconsin, Republican Robert M. La Follette converted to the progressive cause early in the 1900s. La Follette capitalized on the grassroots movement for reform to launch his long political career as governor (1901–1905) and U.S. senator (1906–1925). La Follette brought scientists and professors into his administration and used the university, just down the street from the statehouse in Madison, as a resource. As governor, La Follette lowered railroad rates, raised railroad taxes, improved education, preached conservation, established factory regulation and workers' compensation, instituted the first direct primary in the country, and

inaugurated the first state income tax. Under his leadership, Wisconsin earned the title "laboratory of democracy." A fiery orator, "Fighting Bob" La Follette united his supporters around issues that transcended party loyalties. Democrats and Republicans like Tom Johnson and Robert La Follette crossed party lines to work for reform.

West of the Rockies, progressivism arrived somewhat later and found a champion in Republican Hiram Johnson of California, who served as governor from 1911 to 1917 and later as a U.S. senator. Since the 1870s, the Southern Pacific Railroad had dominated California the state. Johnson ran for governor in 1910 on the promise to "kick the Southern Pacific out of politics." With the support of the reform wing of the Republican Party and the promise "to return the government to the people," he handily won.

As governor, he introduced the direct primary; supported the initiative, referendum, and recall; strengthened the state's railroad commission; supported conservation; and signed an employer's liability law.

REVIEW How did progressives justify their demand for more activist government?

▶ Progressivism Finds a President: Theodore Roosevelt

On September 6, 1901, President William McKinley was shot by Leon Czolgosz, an anarchist, while attending the Pan-American Exposition in Buffalo, New York. Eight days later, McKinley died. When news of the assassination reached Republican boss Mark Hanna, he is said to have growled "Now that damned cowboy is president." He was speaking of Vice President

Theodore Roosevelt

Aptly described by a contemporary observer as "a steam engine in trousers," Theodore Roosevelt, at forty-two, was the youngest president ever to occupy the White House. He brought to the office energy, intellect, and activism in equal measure. Roosevelt boasted that he used the presidency as a "bully pulpit"—a forum from which he advocated reforms ranging from trust-busting to conservation. Library of Congress.

Theodore Roosevelt, the colorful hero of San Juan Hill, who had indeed cattle ranched in the Dakotas in the 1880s.

Roosevelt immediately reassured the shocked nation that he intended "to continue absolutely unbroken" the policies of McKinley. But Roosevelt was as different from McKinley as the nineteenth century from the twentieth. An activist and a moralist, imbued with the progressive spirit, Roosevelt would turn the Executive Mansion, which he insisted on calling the White House, into a "bully pulpit." Under his leadership, he achieved major reforms, advocating conservation and antitrust lawsuits, and championing the nation's emergence as a world power. In the process, Roosevelt would work to shift the nation's center of power from Wall Street to Washington.

After serving nearly two full terms as president, Roosevelt left office at the height of his powers. Any man would have found it difficult to follow in his footsteps, but his hand-picked successor, William Howard Taft, proved poorly suited to the task. Taft's presidency was marked by vigorous trust-busting but would end with a progressive stalemate and a bitter break with Roosevelt that ultimately caused a schism in the Republican Party.

The Square Deal

At age forty-two, Theodore Roosevelt became the youngest man ever to move into the White House. A patrician by birth and an activist by temperament, Roosevelt brought to the job enormous talent and energy. Early in his career, he had determined that the path to power did not lie in the good government leagues formed by his well-bred New York friends. "If it is the muckers that govern," he wrote, "then I want to see if I cannot hold my own with them." He served his political apprenticeship under a Republican ward boss in a grubby meeting hall above a saloon on Morton Street. Roosevelt's rise in politics was swift and sure. He went from the New York assembly at the age of twenty-three to the presidency with time out as a cowboy in the Dakotas, police commissioner of New York City, assistant secretary of the navy, and a colonel of the Rough Riders. Elected governor of New York in 1898, he alienated the Republican boss, who finagled to get him "kicked upstairs" as a candidate for the vice presidency in 1900. The party bosses reasoned Roosevelt could do little harm as vice president. But one bullet proved the error of their logic.

Once president, Roosevelt would harness his explosive energy to strengthen the power of the federal government, putting business on notice that it could no longer count on a laissez-faire government to give it free rein. In Roosevelt's eyes, self-interested capitalists like John D. Rockefeller, whose Standard Oil trust monopolized the refinery business, constituted "the most dangerous members of the criminal class—the criminals of great wealth." The "absolutely vital question" facing the country, Roosevelt wrote to a friend in 1901, was "whether or not the government has the power to control the trusts." The Sherman Antitrust Act of 1890 had been badly weakened by a conservative Supreme Court and by attorneys general more willing to use it against labor unions than against monopolies. To determine whether the law had any teeth left, Roosevelt, in one of his first acts as president, ordered his attorney general to begin a secret antitrust investigation of the Northern Securities Company, a behemoth that monopolized railroad traffic in the Northwest.

Just five months after Roosevelt took office, Wall Street rocked with the news that the government had filed an antitrust suit against Northern Securities. As one newspaper editor sarcastically observed, "Wall Street is paralyzed at the thought that a President of the United States would sink so low as to try to enforce the law." Roosevelt's thunderbolt put Wall Street on notice that the new president expected to be treated as an equal and was willing to use government as a weapon to curb business excesses. Roosevelt later recounted how Morgan had come to him, one Harvard man to another, to suggest that "if we have done anything wrong, send your man to my man and they can fix it up." Roosevelt's attorney general responded, "We don't want to fix it up, we want to stop it." Roosevelt chortled over the exchange, noting "this is a most illuminating illustration of the Wall Street point of view. Mr. Morgan could not help regarding me as a big rival operator." And indeed he was. Perhaps sensing the new mood, the Supreme Court, in a significant turnaround, upheld the Sherman Act and called for the dissolution of Northern Securities in 1904.

"Hurrah for Teddy the Trustbuster," cheered the papers. Roosevelt went on to use the Sherman Act against forty-three trusts, including such giants as American Tobacco, Du Pont, and Standard Oil. Always the moralist, he insisted on a "rule of reason." He would punish "bad" trusts (those that broke the law) and leave "good" ones alone. In practice, he preferred regulation to antitrust suits. In 1903, he pressured Congress to pass the Elkins Act, outlawing railroad rebates. And he created the new cabinet-level Department of Commerce and Labor with the subsidiary Bureau of Corporations to act as a corporate watchdog.

In his handling of the anthracite coal strike in 1902, Roosevelt again demonstrated his willingness to assert the authority of the presidency, this time to mediate between labor and management. In May, 147,000 coal miners in Pennsylvania went on strike. The United Mine Workers (UMW) demanded a reduction in the workday from twelve to ten hours, an equitable system of weighing each miner's output, and a 10 percent wage increase, along with recognition of the union. When asked about the appalling conditions in the mines that led to the strike, George Baer, the mine operators' spokesman, scoffed, "The miners don't suffer, why they can't even speak English."

Realist author Stephen Crane had already investigated life "In the Depths of a Coal Mine." There he found a vicious circle. Children worked as "breaker boys" separating out pieces of slate from streams of coal speeding by on conveyor belts. Paid 55 cents a day, the boys moved up to become miners where "having survived gas, the floods, the 'squeezes' of falling rocks, the cars shooting through little tunnels, the precarious elevators," they had little to look forward to: "when old and decrepit, he finally returns to the breaker where he started as a child."

The strike dragged on through the summer and into the fall. Hoarding and profiteering more than doubled the price of coal. As winter approached, coal shortages touched off near riots in the nation's big cities. At this juncture, Roosevelt stepped in. Instead of sending in troops, he determined to mediate. His unprecedented intervention served notice that government counted itself an independent force in business and labor disputes. At the same time, it gave unionism a boost by granting the UMW a place at the table.

At the meeting, Baer and the mine owners refused to talk with the union representative—a move that angered the attorney general and insulted the president. Beside himself with rage over the "woodenheaded obstinacy and stupidity" of management, Roosevelt threatened to seize the mines and run them with federal troops. This quickly brought management to the table. In the end, the miners won a reduction in hours and a wage increase, but the owners succeeded in preventing formal recognition of the UMW.

Breaker Boys

Child labor in America's mines and mills was common at the turn of the twentieth century, despite state laws that tried to restrict it. Here, "breaker boys," some as young as seven years old, pick over coal in a Pennsylvania mine. A committee investigating child labor found more than 10,000 children illegally employed in the Pennsylvania coalfields. Brown Brothers.

Taken together, Roosevelt's actions in the Northern Securities case and the anthracite coal strike marked a dramatic departure from the presidential passivity of the Gilded Age. Roosevelt's actions demonstrated conclusively that government intended to act as a countervailing force to the power of the big corporations. Pleased with his role in the anthracite strike, Roosevelt announced that all he had tried to do was give labor and capital a "square deal."

The phrase "Square Deal" became Roosevelt's campaign slogan in the 1904 election. Roosevelt easily defeated the Democrats, who abandoned their former candidate, William Jennings Bryan, to support Judge Alton B. Parker, a "safe" choice they hoped would lure business votes away from Roosevelt. In the months before the election, the president prudently toned down his criticism of big business. Roosevelt swept into office with the largest popular majority—57.9 percent—any candidate had polled up to that time.

Roosevelt the Reformer

"Tomorrow I shall come into my office in my own right," Roosevelt is said to have remarked on the eve of his election. "Then watch out for me!" Roosevelt's stunning victory gave him a mandate for reform. He would need all the popularity and political savvy he could muster, however, to guide his reform measures through Congress. The Senate remained controlled by a staunchly conservative Republican "Old Guard," with many senators on the payrolls of the corporations Roosevelt sought to curb. The *New York Times* suggested that "a millionaire could buy a Senate seat, just as he would buy an opera box, a yacht, or any other luxury."

Roosevelt's pet project remained railroad regulation. The Elkins Act prohibiting rebates had not worked. Roosevelt determined that the only solution lay in giving the Interstate Commerce Commission (ICC) real power to set rates and prevent discriminatory practices. But the right to determine the price of goods or services was an age-old prerogative of private enterprise, and one that business had no intention of yielding to government.

The Hepburn Act of 1906 marked the crowning legislative achievement of Roosevelt's presidency. It gave the ICC the power to set rates subject to court review. Committed progressives like La Follette judged the law a defeat for reform. Die-hard conservatives branded it a "piece of populism." Both sides exaggerated. The law left the courts too much power and failed to provide adequate means for the ICC to determine rates, but its passage proved a landmark in federal control of private industry. For the first time, a government commission had the power to investigate private business records and to set rates.

Always an apt reader of the public temper, Roosevelt witnessed a growing appetite for reform. Revelations of corporate and political wrongdoing as well as social injustice filled the papers and boosted the sales of popular magazines. Roosevelt counted many of the new investigative journalists among his friends. (See "Visualizing History," page 596.) But he warned them against going too far, citing the allegorical character in *Pilgrim's Progress* who was too busy raking muck to notice higher things. Roosevelt's criticism gave the American vocabulary a new word, *muckraker*, which journalists soon appropriated as a title of honor.

Muckraking, as Roosevelt well knew, provided enormous help in securing progressive legislation. In the spring of 1906, publicity generated by the muckrakers about poisons in patent medicines goaded the Senate, with Roosevelt's backing, into passing a pure food and drug bill. Opponents in the House of Representatives hoped to keep the legislation locked up in committee. There it would have died, were it not for the publication of Upton Sinclair's novel *The Jungle* (1906), with its sensational account of filthy conditions in meatpacking plants. Roosevelt, who read the book over breakfast, was sickened. He immediately invited Sinclair to the White House. Sinclair wanted socialism; Roosevelt wanted food inspection. But thanks to the publicity generated by *The Jungle*, a massive public outcry led to the passage of the Pure Food and Drug Act and the Meat Inspection Act in 1906.

In the waning years of his administration, Roosevelt allied with the more progressive elements of the Republican Party. In speech after speech, he attacked "malefactors of great wealth." Styling himself a "radical," he claimed credit for leading the "ultra conservative" party of McKinley to a position of "progressive conservatism and conservative radicalism."

When an economic panic developed in the fall of 1907, business interests quickly blamed the president. Once again, J. P. Morgan stepped in to avert disaster, this time switching funds from one bank to another to prop up weak institutions. For his services, Morgan dispatched his lieutenants to Washington, where they told Roosevelt that the sale of the Tennessee Coal and Iron company would aid the economy "but little benefit" U.S. Steel. Willing to take the word of a gentleman, Roosevelt tacitly agreed not to institute antitrust proceedings against U.S. Steel over the acquisition. Roosevelt's promise would give rise to the charge that he acted as a tool of the Morgan interests.

The charge of collusion between business and government underscored the extent to which corporate leaders like Morgan found federal regulation preferable to unbridled competition or harsher state measures. During the Progressive Era, enlightened business leaders cooperated with government in the hope of avoiding antitrust prosecution. Convinced that regulation and not trust-busting offered the best way to deal with big business, Roosevelt never acknowledged that his regulatory policies fostered an alliance between business and government that today is called corporate liberalism.

Roosevelt and Conservation

In the area of conservation, Roosevelt proved indisputably ahead of his time. When he took office, some 43 million acres of forestland remained as government reserves. He more than quadrupled that number to 194 million acres. To conserve natural resources, he fought western cattle barons, lumber kings, mining interests, and powerful leaders in Congress, including Speaker of the House Joseph Cannon, who vowed to spend "not one cent for scenery."

As the first president to have lived and worked in the West, Roosevelt came to the White House convinced of the need for better management of the nation's rivers and forests as well as the preservation of wildlife and wilderness. During his presidency, he placed the nation's conservation policy in the hands of scientifically trained experts like his chief forester, Gifford Pinchot. Pinchot preached conservation—the efficient use of natural resources. Willing to permit grazing, lumbering, and the development of hydroelectric power, conservationists fought private interests only when they felt business acted irresponsibly or threatened to monopolize water and electric power. Preservationists like John Muir, founder of the Sierra Club, believed that the wilderness needed to be protected. Roosevelt, a fervent Darwinian naturalist and an (overly) enthusiastic game hunter, a conservationist who built big

The Birth of Photojournalism

Photography changed the way Americans viewed their world. By the 1890s, any amateur could purchase the Kodak camera that George Eastman marketed with the slogan "You push the button, we do the rest." As the poet Oliver Wendell Holmes observed, the camera became not just "the mirror of reality" but "the mirror with a memory."

Yet for Jacob Riis, a progressive reformer wishing to document the grim horrors of tenement life, photography was useless because it required daylight or careful studio lighting. He could only crudely sketch the dim hovels, the criminal nightlife, and the windowless tenement rooms of New York. Then came the breakthrough: "One morning scanning my newspaper at my breakfast table, I put it down with an outcry. . . . There it was, the thing I had been looking for all these years. . . . A way had been discovered to take pictures by flashlight."

Riis set out to shine light in the dark corners of New York. "Our party carried terror wherever it went," Riis recalled. "The spectacle of strange men invading a house in the midnight hours armed with [flash] pistols which they shot off recklessly was hardly reassuring." But the results were a huge step forward for photojournalism.

Riis's book *How the Other Half Lives* (1890) made photographic

Five Cents a Spot

dams and a preservationist who saved the redwoods, aimed to have it both ways. (See "Historical Question," page 600.)

In 1907, Congress attempted to put the brakes on Roosevelt's conservation program by passing a law limiting his power to create forest reserves in six western states. In the days leading up to the law's enactment, Roosevelt feverishly created twenty-one new reserves and enlarged eleven more, saving 16 million acres from development. Once again, Roosevelt had outwitted his adversaries. "Opponents of the forest service turned handsprings in their wrath," he wrote, "but the threats . . . were really only a tribute to the efficiency of our action." Worried that private utilities were gobbling up water-power sites and creating a monopoly of hydroelectric power, he connived with Pinchot to withdraw 2,565 power sites from private use by designating them "ranger stations." Firm in his commitment to wild America, Roosevelt proved willing to stretch the law when it served his ends. His legacy is more than 234 million acres of American wilderness saved for posterity (Map 21.1).

The Big Stick

Roosevelt's activism extended to his foreign policy. A fierce proponent of America's interests abroad, he relied on executive power to pursue a vigorous foreign policy, sometimes stretching

history. Along with Riis's text and engravings of his drawings, it contained reproductions of seventeen photographs taken with his camera and flash. By looking at a line drawing side by side with the corresponding photograph, we can compare the impact of the two mediums.

Look at Riis's line drawing of a "Five Cents a Spot" lodgers' tenement that appeared in *How the Other Half Lives* and compare it with the photograph. On a police raid to evict tenement lodgers, Riis describes the room as "not thirteen feet either way," in which "slept twelve men and women, two or three in bunks in a sort of alcove, the rest on the floor." Note how the flash catches the sleepy faces and tired bodies, the crowding, dirt, and disorder.

Riis's pioneering photojournalism shocked the nation and led not only to tenement reform but also to the development of city playgrounds, neighborhood parks, and child labor laws.

SOURCE: *Five Cents a Spot*, drawing and photo: Library of Congress.

Five Cents a Spot

Questions for Analysis

1. How do you think photography affected American memory?

2. What details visible in the photograph are lost in the drawing? Which portrayal has a greater impact on the viewer?

3. Would you agree that Riis's photographs are "a mirror of reality," or did he interpret and frame the "reality" he photographed?

Connect to the Big Idea

C How was photojournalism part of the progressive movement?

the powers of the presidency beyond legal limits. In his relations with the European powers, he relied on military strength and diplomacy, a combination he aptly described with the aphorism "Speak softly but carry a big stick."

A strong supporter of the Monroe Doctrine, Roosevelt jealously guarded the U.S. sphere of influence in the Western Hemisphere. His proprietary attitude toward the Caribbean became evident in the case of the Panama Canal. Roosevelt had long been a supporter of a canal linking the Caribbean and the Pacific. By enabling ships to move quickly from the Atlantic to the Pacific, a canal would trim 8,000 miles from a coast-to-coast voyage and effectively double the U.S. Navy's power. Having decided on a route

across the Panamanian isthmus (a narrow strip of land connecting North and South America), then part of Colombia, Roosevelt in 1902 offered the Colombian government a one-time sum of $10 million and an annual rent of $250,000. When the government in Bogotá refused to accept the offer, Roosevelt became incensed at what he called the "homicidal corruptionists" in Colombia for trying to "blackmail" the United States. At the prompting of a group of New York investors, the Panamanians staged an uprising in 1903, and with unseemly haste the U.S. government recognized the new government within twenty-four hours. The Panamanians promptly accepted the $10 million, and the building got under way. The canal would take eleven years

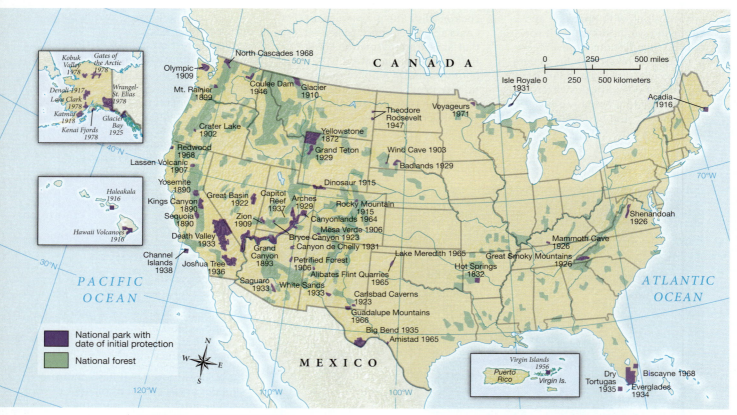

MAP ACTIVITY

Map 21.1   National Parks and Forests

The national park system in the West began with Yellowstone in 1872. Grand Canyon, Yosemite, Kings Canyon, and Sequoia followed in the 1890s. During his presidency, Theodore Roosevelt added six parks—Crater Lake, Wind Cave, Petrified Forest, Lassen Volcanic, Mesa Verde, and Zion.

READING THE MAP: Collectively, do national parks or national forests encompass more land? According to the map, how many national parks were created before 1910? How many were created after 1910?

CONNECTIONS: How do conservation and preservation differ? Why did Roosevelt believe that saving land in the West was important? What principles guided the national land use policy of the Roosevelt administration?

---

and $375 million to complete; it opened in 1914 (Map 21.2).

In the wake of the Panama affair, a confrontation with Germany over Venezuela, and yet another default on a European debt, this time in the Dominican Republic, Roosevelt grew concerned that financial instability in Latin America would lead European powers to interfere. In 1904, he announced the **Roosevelt Corollary** to the Monroe Doctrine in which he declared the United States had a right to act as "an international police power" in the Western

The Roosevelt Corollary in Action

Hemisphere. Roosevelt stated the United States would not intervene in Latin America as long as nations there conducted their affairs with "decency," but it would step in to stop "brutal wrongdoing." The Roosevelt Corollary served notice to the European powers to keep out.

In Asia, Roosevelt inherited the Open Door policy initiated by Secretary of State John Hay in 1899, designed to ensure U.S. commercial entry into China. As European powers raced to secure Chinese trade and territory, Roosevelt was tempted to use force to gain economic

THE WORLD'S CONSTABLE.

VISUAL ACTIVITY

"The World's Constable"

In this political cartoon from 1905, President Theodore Roosevelt, dressed as a constable, wields the club of "The New Diplomacy" in one hand with "Arbitration" tucked under his arm. The Roosevelt Corollary to the Monroe Doctrine made the United States the Western Hemisphere's policeman, a role Roosevelt relished. The Granger Collection, New York.

READING THE IMAGE: How does this political cartoon visually represent Roosevelt's foreign policy? Does it appear to be supportive or critical of his policies? How does it treat the other peoples of the world?

CONNECTIONS: What aspects of Roosevelt's foreign policy ideas and actions are depicted in the cartoon?

or possibly territorial concessions. Realizing that Americans would not support an aggressive Asian policy, the president sensibly held back.

In his relations with Europe, Roosevelt sought to establish the United States as a rising force in world affairs. When tensions flared between France and Germany in Morocco in 1905, Roosevelt mediated at a conference in Algeciras, Spain, where he worked to maintain a balance of power that helped neutralize German ambitions. His skillful mediation gained him a reputation as an astute player on the world stage and demonstrated the nation's new presence in world affairs.

Roosevelt earned the Nobel Peace Prize in 1906 for his role in negotiating an end to the Russo-Japanese War, which had broken out when the Japanese invaded Chinese Manchuria, threatening Russia's sphere of influence in the area. Once again, Roosevelt sought to maintain a balance of power, in this case working to curb Japanese expansionism. Roosevelt admired the Japanese, judging them "the most dashing fighters in the world," but he did not want Japan to become too strong in Asia.

When good relations with Japan were jeopardized by discriminatory legislation in California calling for segregated public schools for Asians, Roosevelt smoothed over the incident and negotiated the "Gentlemen's Agreement" in 1907, which allowed the Japanese to save face by voluntarily restricting immigration to the United States. To demonstrate America's naval power and to counter Japan's growing bellicosity, Roosevelt dispatched the Great White Fleet, sixteen of the navy's most up-to-date battleships, on a "goodwill mission" around the world. U.S. relations with Japan improved,

Progressives and Conservation: Should Hetch Hetchy Be Dammed or Saved?

In 1890, President Benjamin Harrison signed into law an act setting aside two million acres in California's Yosemite Valley and designating Yosemite a national park. For naturalist John Muir, the founder of the Sierra Club, the act marked a victory in his crusade to guarantee that "incomparable Yosemite" would be preserved for posterity. But Muir's fight was not yet over.

The growing city of San Francisco needed water and power, and Mayor James Phelan soon sought to obtain water rights in Hetch Hetchy, a spectacular mountain valley within Yosemite's borders. There, the Tuolumne River could easily be dammed and the valley flooded to create a reservoir large enough to ensure the city's water supply for one hundred years.

When Muir heard of the plan, he sprang into action to save Hetch Hetchy. "That any one would try to destroy such a place seems incredible," he wrote, describing the valley as "one of Nature's rarest and most precious mountain temples." All of Yosemite National Park, he argued, should remain sacrosanct. In 1903, the secretary of the interior concurred, denying San Francisco supervisors commercial use of Hetch Hetchy on the grounds that it lay within the national park.

But the San Francisco earthquake and resulting fire in 1906 created a groundswell of sympathy for the devastated city. In this climate, San Francisco renewed its efforts to obtain Hetch Hetchy and, in 1907, succeeded in gaining authorization to proceed with plans to dam the river and flood the valley.

Given President Theodore Roosevelt's commitment to conservation, how could his administration have agreed to the destruction of the Hetch Hetchy valley? Historians traditionally have styled the struggle as one that pitted conservationists against preservationists. Roosevelt's chief forester, Gifford Pinchot, represented the forces of conservation, or managed use. To him, the battle was not over preservation but over public versus private control of water and power. Roosevelt somewhat reluctantly agreed, although he softened the blow by designating a redwood sanctuary north of San Francisco a national monument in 1907 and naming it Muir Woods.

California progressives, who swept into office with the election of Hiram Johnson as governor in 1910, argued that if Congress did not grant the city of San Francisco the right to control Hetch Hetchy, the powerful Pacific Gas and Electric Company (PG&E) would monopolize the city's light and power industry. These progressives dismissed Muir and his followers as "nature fakers" and judged them little more than dupes in the machinations of PG&E.

For their part, Muir and the preservationists, although they fought for the integrity of the national parks, did not champion the preservation of wilderness for its own sake. The urban professional men and women who joined the Sierra Club saw nature as a retreat and restorative for city dwellers. The club hosted an annual camping trip to popularize Yosemite and spoke in glowing terms of plans to build new roads and hotels that would make the "healing power of Nature" accessible to "thousands of tired, nerve-shaken, over-civilized people." As historian Robert Righter has pointed out, the battle over Hetch Hetchy represented not so much conservation versus preservation, or managed use versus wilderness, as it did the victory of water and power over tourism and recreation.

Nevertheless, the engineers and irrigation men who dammed Hetch Hetchy demonstrated a breathtaking arrogance. Speaking for them, Franklin Lane, interior secretary under Woodrow Wilson, proclaimed, "The mountains are our enemy. We must pierce them and make them serve. The sinful rivers we must curb." Lane and the conservationists won the day. In 1913, Congress passed the Raker Act authorizing the building of the O'Shaughnessy Dam, completed a decade later. To build the dam, the Hetch Hetchy valley was first denuded of its trees and then

and in the 1908 Root-Takahira agreement the two nations pledged to maintain the Open Door and support the status quo in the Pacific. Roosevelt's show of American force constituted a classic example of his dictum "Speak softly but carry a big stick."

The Troubled Presidency of William Howard Taft

Roosevelt promised on the eve of his election in 1904 that he would not seek another term. So he retired from the presidency in 1909 at age

flooded under two hundred feet of water. Muir did not live to see the destruction of Hetch Hetchy. He died in 1914, cursing the "dark damn-dam-damnation." But his fight to save Hetch Hetchy galvanized the preservation movement and led to the passage of the National Park Service Act in 1916, creating a federal agency to protect the nation's parks.

The last chapter in the battle over Hetch Hetchy may yet be written. In 1987, President Ronald Reagan's secretary of the interior, Donald Hodel, shocked San Francisco by suggesting the removal of the O'Shaughnessy Dam and the restoration of the Hetch Hetchy valley. Although it is unlikely that the dam will be demolished (it supplies San Francisco not only with water but also with revenue from electric power), advocates for the restoration of the Hetch Hetchy valley continue to rally to the cause. As Ken Browner of the Sierra Club wrote, "Waiting in Yosemite National Park, under water, is a potential masterpiece of restoration" and a chance "to correct the biggest environmental mistake ever committed against the National Park System."

Questions for Consideration

1. What does the damming of Hetch Hetchy tell us about the Roosevelt administration's conservation policies in the West?

2. Given Roosevelt's conservation policies overall, are critics right in accusing him of failing to preserve the wilderness?

Connect to the Big Idea

ⓒ How did the goals of Progressive Era conservationists and preservationists differ?

Roosevelt and Muir in Yosemite
This 1903 photograph shows President Theodore Roosevelt on a camping trip in Yosemite National Park with John Muir. Muir later clashed with Chief Forester Gifford Pinchot over the flooding of the Hetch Hetchy valley in Yosemite to give San Francisco the right to dam the valley to supply water and power. Pinchot never bothered to visit the valley he condemned to a watery grave. Theodore Roosevelt Collection, Houghton Library, Harvard University.

fifty and removed himself from the political scene by going on safari in Africa. He turned the White House over to his handpicked successor, William Howard Taft, a lawyer who had served as governor-general of the Philippines. Affectionately known as "Big Bill," Taft had served as Roosevelt's right-hand man in the cabinet. In the presidential election of 1908, Taft soundly defeated the perennial Democratic candidate, William Jennings Bryan.

A genial man with a talent for law, Taft had no experience in elective office, no feel for

MAP ACTIVITY

Map 21.2 The Panama Canal, 1914
The Panama Canal, completed in 1914, bisects the isthmus in a series of massive locks and dams. As Theodore Roosevelt had planned, the canal greatly strengthened the U.S. Navy by allowing ships to move from the Atlantic to the Pacific in a matter of days.

READING THE MAP: How long was the trip from New York to San Francisco before the Panama Canal was built? After it was built?

CONNECTIONS: How did Roosevelt's desire for a canal lead to independence for Panama? How did the canal benefit the U.S. Navy?

politics, and no nerve for controversy. His ambitious wife coveted the office and urged him to seek it. He would have been better off listening to his mother, who warned, "Roosevelt is a good fighter and enjoys it, but the malice of politics would make you miserable." Sadly for Taft, his wife suffered a stroke in his first months in office, leaving him grieving and without his strongest ally.

Once in office, Taft proved a perfect tool in the hands of Republicans who yearned for a return to the days of a less active executive. A lawyer by training and instinct, Taft believed that it was up to the courts, not the president, to arbitrate social issues. Roosevelt had carried presidential power to a new level, often flouting the separation of powers and showing thinly veiled contempt for Congress and the courts. He believed that the president had the legal right to act as steward for the people, and to do anything necessary "unless the Constitution or the laws explicitly forbid him to do it." Taft found such presidential activism difficult to condone. Although he pursued the trusts vigorously, he acted more like a judge than a steward. Wary of the progressive insurgents in Congress, Taft relied increasingly on conservatives in the Republican Party. As a progressive senator lamented, "Taft is a ponderous and amiable

man completely surrounded by men who know exactly what they want."

Taft's troubles began on the eve of his inaugural, when he called a special session of Congress to deal with the tariff. Roosevelt had been too politically astute to tackle the troublesome tariff issue, even though he knew that rates needed to be lowered. Ida Tarbell, who lent her meticulous research skills to the tariff debate, concluded, "At a time when wealth is rolling up as never before, a vast number of hard-working people . . . are really having a more difficult time making ends meet than they have ever had before." Tarbell's articles proved a revelation to many, who had never understood the relationship between the tariff and the price of a pair of shoes.

Taft struggled to transform growing public sentiment against the tariff into legislation. But Taft blundered into the fray. The Payne-Aldrich bill that emerged was amended in the Senate so that it actually raised the tariff, benefiting big business and the trusts at the expense of consumers. As if paralyzed, Taft neither fought for changes nor vetoed the measure. On a tour of the Midwest in 1909, he was greeted with jeers when he claimed, "I think the Payne bill is the best bill that the Republican Party ever passed." In the eyes of a growing number of Americans,

THE LOST SKI.

William Howard Taft
In this 1911 *Puck* cartoon, the hapless William Howard Taft veers out of control, losing power in the House of Representatives as he skis down the nomination slide for 1912. Taft had little aptitude for politics and quickly lost the support of progressives in his party. Library of Congress.

Taft's praise of the tariff made him either a fool or a liar.

Taft's legalism soon got him into hot water in the area of conservation. He undid Roosevelt's work to preserve hydroelectric power sites when he learned that they had been improperly designated as ranger stations. And when Gifford Pinchot publicly denounced Taft's secretary of the interior as a tool of western land-grabbers, Taft fired Pinchot, touching off a storm of controversy that damaged Taft and alienated Roosevelt. When Roosevelt returned from Africa, Pinchot was among the first to greet him with a half dozen letters from progressives complaining of Taft's leadership.

Roosevelt returned to the United States in June 1910, where he received a hero's welcome and attracted a stream of visitors and reporters seeking his advice and opinions. Hurt, Taft kept his distance. By late summer, Roosevelt had taken sides with the progressive insurgents in his party. "Taft is utterly hopeless as a leader," Roosevelt confided to his son as he set out on a speaking tour of the West. Reading the mood of the country, Roosevelt began to sound more and more like a candidate.

With the Republican Party divided, the Democrats swept the congressional elections of 1910. Branding the Payne-Aldrich tariff "the mother of trusts," they captured a majority in the House of Representatives and won several key governorships. The revitalized Democratic Party could look to new leaders, among them the progressive governor of New Jersey, Woodrow Wilson.

The new Democratic majority in the House, working with progressive Republicans in the Senate, achieved a number of key reforms, including legislation to regulate railroad safety, to create the Children's Bureau in the

Department of Labor, and to establish an eight-hour day for federal workers and miners. Two significant constitutional amendments—the Sixteenth Amendment, which provided for a modest graduated income tax, and the Seventeenth Amendment, which called for the direct election of senators (formerly chosen by state legislatures)—went to the states, where they would win ratification in 1913. While Congress rode the high tide of progressive reform, Taft sat on the sidelines.

In foreign policy, Taft continued Roosevelt's policy of extending U.S. influence abroad, but here, too, Taft had a difficult time following Roosevelt. Taft's "dollar diplomacy" championed commercial goals rather than the strategic aims Roosevelt had pursued. Taft naively assumed he could substitute "dollars for bullets." In the Caribbean, he provoked anti-American feeling by dispatching U.S. Marines to Nicaragua and the Dominican Republic in 1912 pursuant to the Roosevelt Corollary. In Asia, he openly avowed his intent to promote "active intervention to secure for . . . our capitalists opportunity for profitable investment." Lacking Roosevelt's understanding of power politics, Taft failed to recognize that an aggressive commercial policy could not exist without the willingness to use military might to back it up.

Taft's "Dollar Diplomacy"

Taft faced the limits of dollar diplomacy when revolution broke out in Mexico in 1911. Under pressure to protect American investments, he mobilized troops along the border. In the end, however, with no popular support for a war with Mexico, he had to fall back on diplomatic pressure to salvage American interests.

Taft's greatest dream was to encourage world peace through the use of a world court and arbitration. He unsuccessfully sponsored a series of arbitration treaties that Roosevelt, who prized national honor more than international law, vehemently opposed as weak and cowardly. By 1910, Roosevelt had become a vocal critic of Taft's foreign policy.

The final breach between Taft and Roosevelt came in 1911, when Taft's attorney general filed an antitrust suit against U.S. Steel. In its brief against the corporation, the government cited Roosevelt's agreement with the Morgan interests in the 1907 acquisition of Tennessee Coal and Iron. The incident greatly embarrassed Roosevelt. Either he had been hoodwinked or he had colluded with Morgan. Neither idea pleased him. Thoroughly enraged, he lambasted Taft's "archaic" antitrust policy and hinted that he might be persuaded to run for president again.

REVIEW   How did Theodore Roosevelt advance the progressive agenda?

▶ Woodrow Wilson and Progressivism at High Tide

Disillusionment with Taft resulted in a split in the Republican Party and the creation of a new Progressive Party that rallied to Theodore Roosevelt. In the election of 1912, four candidates styled themselves "progressives," but it was Democrat Woodrow Wilson, with a minority of the popular vote, who won the presidency. He would continue Roosevelt's presidential power and help enact progressive legislation.

Progressive Insurgency and the Election of 1912

Convinced that Taft was inept, in February 1912, Roosevelt announced his candidacy for the Republican nomination announcing "My hat is in the ring." Taft, with uncharacteristic strength, refused to step aside. Roosevelt took advantage of newly passed primary election laws and ran in thirteen states, winning 278 delegates to Taft's 48. But at the Chicago convention, Taft's bosses refused to seat the Roosevelt delegates. Fistfights broke out on the convention floor as Taft won nomination on the first ballot. Crying robbery, Roosevelt's supporters bolted the party.

Seven weeks later, in the same Chicago auditorium, the hastily organized Progressive Party met to nominate Roosevelt. Full of reforming zeal, the delegates chose Roosevelt and Hiram Johnson to head the new party. Jane Addams seconded Roosevelt's nomination. "I have been fighting for progressive principles for thirty years," she told the enthusiastic crowd. "This is the first time there has been a chance to make them effective. This is the biggest day of my life." The new party lustily approved the most ambitious platform since that of the Populists. Planks called

1912 Election Cartoon
In this 1912 political cartoon, an elephant—the mascot of the Republican Party (the Grand Old Party, or GOP)—and a donkey—representing the Democratic Party—react in alarm as a bull moose charges into the fray. The bull moose, with its spectacles and gleaming teeth, caricatures Theodore Roosevelt, the new Progressive Party's presidential candidate. The Granger Collection, New York.

for woman suffrage, presidential primaries, conservation of natural resources, an end to child labor, workers' compensation, a living wage for both men and women workers, social security, health insurance, and a federal income tax.

Roosevelt arrived in Chicago to accept the nomination and announced that he felt "as fit as a bull moose," giving the new party a nickname and a mascot. With characteristic vigor, he launched his campaign with the exhortation, "We stand at Armageddon and do battle for the Lord!" But for all the excitement and the cheering, the new Progressive Party was doomed, and the candidate knew it. Privately he confessed to a friend, "I am under no illusion about it. It is a forlorn hope." The people may have supported the party, but the politicians, even progressives such as La Follette, refused to support the new party. The Democrats, delighted at the split in the Republican ranks, nominated Woodrow Wilson, the governor of New Jersey. After only eighteen months in office, the former professor of political science and president of Princeton University found himself running for president of the United States.

Voters in 1912 could choose among four candidates who claimed to be progressives. Taft, Roosevelt, and Wilson each embraced the label, and even the Socialist candidate, Eugene V. Debs, styled himself a progressive. That the term *progressive* could stretch to cover these diverse candidates underscored

major disagreements in progressive thinking about the relationship between business and government. Taft, in spite of his trust-busting, was generally viewed as the candidate of the Republican Old Guard. Debs urged voters to support the Socialist Party as the true spirit of the working class. The real contest for the presidency came down to a fight between Roosevelt and Wilson and the two political philosophies summed up in their respective campaign slogans: "**The New Nationalism**" and "**The New Freedom**."

The New Nationalism expressed Roosevelt's belief in federal planning and regulation. He accepted the inevitability of big business but demanded that government act as "a steward of the people" to regulate the giant corporations. Wilson, schooled in the Democratic principles of limited government and states' rights, set a markedly different course with his New Freedom. Wilson promised to use antitrust legislation to get rid of big corporations and to give small businesses and farmers better opportunities in the marketplace.

The energy and enthusiasm of the Bull Moosers made the race seem closer than it was. In the end, the Republican vote split, while the Democrats remained united. No candidate claimed a majority in the race. Wilson captured a bare 42 percent of the popular vote. Roosevelt and his Bull Moose Party won 27 percent, an unprecedented tally for a new party. Taft came

Candidate	Electoral Vote	Popular Vote	Percent of Popular Vote
Woodrow Wilson (Democrat)	435	6,293,454	41.9
Theodore Roosevelt (Progressive)	88	4,119,538	27.4
William H. Taft (Republican)	8	3,484,980	23.2
Eugene V. Debs (Socialist)	0	900,672	6.1

MAP 21.3
The Election of 1912

in third with 23 percent. The Socialist Party, led by Debs, captured a surprising 6 percent (Map 21.3). The Republican Party moved in a conservative direction, while the Progressive Party essentially collapsed after Roosevelt's defeat. It had always been, in the words of one astute observer, "a house divided against itself and already mortgaged."

Wilson's Reforms: Tariff, Banking, and the Trusts

Born in Virginia and raised in Georgia, Woodrow Wilson became the first southerner elected president since 1844 and only the second Democrat to occupy the White House since Reconstruction. A believer in states' rights, Wilson nevertheless promised legislation to break the hold of the trusts. This lean, ascetic scholar was, as one biographer conceded, a man whose "political convictions were never as fixed as his ambition." Building on the base built by Roosevelt in strengthening presidential power, Wilson exerted leadership to achieve banking reform and worked through his party in Congress to accomplish the Democratic agenda. Before he was finished, Wilson lent his support to many of the Progressive Party's social reforms.

With the Democrats thoroughly in control of Congress Wilson immediately called for tariff reform. "The object of the tariff," Wilson told Congress, "must be effective competition." The

Democratic House of Representatives hastily passed the Underwood tariff, which lowered rates by 15 percent. To compensate for lost revenue, the House approved a moderate federal income tax made possible by the ratification of the Sixteenth Amendment a month earlier. In the Senate, lobbyists for industries quietly went to work to get the tariff raised, but Wilson rallied public opinion by attacking the "industrious and insidious lobby." In the harsh glare of publicity, the Senate passed the Underwood tariff.

Wilson next turned his attention to banking. The panic of 1907 led the government to turn once again to J. P. Morgan to avoid economic catastrophe. But by the time Wilson came to office, Morgan's legendary power had come under close scrutiny. In 1913, a Senate committee investigated the "money trust," calling Morgan himself to testify. The committee uncovered an alarming concentration of banking power. J. P. Morgan and Company and its affiliates held 341 directorships in 112 corporations, controlling assets of more than $22 million (billions in today's dollars). The sensational findings led to reform.

The Federal Reserve Act of 1913 marked the most significant piece of domestic legislation of Wilson's presidency. It established a national banking system composed of twelve regional banks, privately controlled but regulated and supervised by the Federal Reserve Board, appointed by the president. It gave the United States its first efficient banking and currency system and, at the same time, provided for a greater degree of government control over banking. The new system made currency more elastic and credit adequate for the needs of business and agriculture.

Wilson, flush with success, tackled the trust issue next. When Congress reconvened in January 1914, he supported the introduction and passage of the Clayton Antitrust Act to outlaw "unfair competition"—practices such as price discrimination and interlocking directorates (directors from one corporation sitting on the board of another). In the midst of the successful fight for the Clayton Act, Wilson changed course and threw his support behind the creation of the Federal Trade Commission (FTC), precisely the kind of federal regulatory agency that Roosevelt had advocated in his New Nationalism. The FTC, created in 1914, had not only wide investigatory powers but also the authority to prosecute corporations for "unfair trade practices" and to enforce its judgments by issuing "cease and desist" orders. Despite his campaign promises, Wilson's antitrust program worked to regulate rather than to break up big business.

Wilson, Reluctant Progressive

By the fall of 1914, Wilson declared that the progressive movement had fulfilled its mission and that the country needed "a time of healing." Progressives watched in dismay as Wilson repeatedly obstructed or obstinately refused to endorse further reforms. He failed to support labor's demand for an end to court injunctions against labor unions. He twice threatened to veto legislation providing farm credits for nonperishable crops. He refused to support child labor legislation or woman suffrage. Wilson used the rhetoric of the New Freedom to justify his actions, claiming that his administration would condone "special privileges to none." But, in fact, his stance often reflected the interests of his small-business constituency.

In the face of Wilson's obstinacy, reform might have ended in 1913 had not politics intruded. In the congressional elections of 1914, the Republican Party, no longer split by Roosevelt's Bull Moose faction, won substantial gains. Democratic strategists recognized that Wilson needed to pick up support in the Midwest and the West by capturing votes from former Bull Moose progressives. Wilson responded belatedly by lending his support to reform in the months leading up to the election of 1916. In a sharp about-face, he cultivated union labor, farmers, and social reformers. To please labor, he appointed progressive Louis Brandeis to the Supreme Court. To woo farmers, he threw his support behind legislation to obtain rural credits. And he won praise from labor by supporting workers' compensation and the Keating-Owen child labor law (1916), which outlawed the regular employment of children younger than sixteen. When a railroad strike threatened in the months before the election, Wilson ordered Congress to establish an eight-hour day on the railroads. He had moved a long way from his New Freedom of 1912, and, as Wilson noted, the Democrats had "come very near to carrying out the platform of the Progressive Party." Wilson's shift toward reform, along with his claim that he had kept the United States out of the war in Europe (discussed in chapter 22), helped him win reelection in 1916.

REVIEW How and why did Wilson's reform program evolve during his first term?

▶ The Limits of Progressive Reform

While progressivism called for a more active role for the liberal state, at heart it was a movement that sought reforms designed to preserve American institutions and stem the tide of more radical change. Its basic conservatism can be seen by comparing it with the more radical movements of socialism, radical labor, and birth control—and by looking at the groups progressive reform left behind, including women, Asians, and African Americans.

Radical Alternatives

The year 1900 marked the birth of the Social Democratic Party in America, later called simply the **Socialist Party**. Like the progressives, the socialists were middle-class and native-born. They had broken with the older, more militant Socialist Labor Party precisely because of its dogmatic approach and immigrant constituency. The new group of socialists proved eager to appeal to a broad mass of disaffected Americans.

The Socialist Party chose as its presidential standard-bearer Eugene V. Debs, whose experience in the Pullman strike of 1894 (see "Eugene V. Debs and the Pullman Strike" in chapter 20) convinced him that "there is no hope for the toiling masses of my countrymen, except by the pathways mapped out by Socialism." Debs would run for president five times, in every election (except 1916) from 1900 to 1920. The socialism Debs advocated preached cooperation over competition and urged men and women to liberate themselves from "the barbarism of private ownership and wage slavery." In the 1912 election, Debs indicted both old parties as each dedicated to the preservation of capitalism and the continuation of the wage system. Styling the Socialist Party the "revolutionary party of the working class," he urged voters to rally to his standard. Debs's best showing came in 1912, when his 6 percent of the popular vote totaled more than 900,000 votes.

Further to the left and more radical than the socialists stood the **Industrial Workers of the World**, nicknamed the Wobblies. In 1905, Debs, along with Western Federation of Miners leader William Dudley "Big Bill" Haywood, created the IWW, "one big union" dedicated to organizing the most destitute segment of the workforce, the unskilled workers disdained by Samuel Gompers's AFL: western miners,

VISUAL ACTIVITY

Margaret Sanger's Brownsville Birth Control Clinic

Margaret Sanger opened the first birth control clinic in the United States in the Brownsville section of Brooklyn in 1916. Before police shut it down, more than 400 women visited the clinic. Sanger located her clinic in the heart of an immigrant neighborhood to prove that Italian Catholics and Russian Jews wanted birth control as much as their middle- and upper-class Protestant counterparts. Sophia Smith Collection, Smith College.

READING THE IMAGE: From this photo, what can you surmise about the women who sought birth control at Sanger's clinic in 1916? Why do so many of them have baby carriages?

CONNECTIONS: Why did Sanger consider birth control a radical cause?

migrant farmworkers, lumbermen, and immigrant textile workers. Haywood, a craggy-faced miner with one eye (he had lost the other in a childhood accident), was a charismatic leader and a proletarian intellectual. Seeing workers on the lowest rung of the social ladder as the victims of violent repression, the IWW advocated direct action, sabotage, and the general strike—tactics designed to trigger a workers' uprising and overthrow the capitalist state. The IWW never had more than 10,000 members at any one time, although possibly as many as 100,000 workers belonged to the union at one time or another in the early twentieth century. Nevertheless, the IWW's influence on the country extended far beyond its numbers (as discussed in chapter 22).

In contrast to political radicals like Debs and Haywood, Margaret Sanger promoted the **birth control movement** as a means of social change. Sanger, a nurse who had worked among the poor on New York's Lower East Side, coined the term *birth control* in 1915 and launched a movement with broad social implications. Sanger and her followers saw birth control not only as a sexual and medical reform but also as a means to alter social and political power relationships and to alleviate human misery. By having fewer babies, the working class could constrict the size of the workforce and make possible higher wages and at the same time refuse to provide "cannon fodder" for the world's armies.

The desire for family limitation was widespread, and in this sense birth control was noth-ing new. The birthrate in the United States had been falling consistently throughout the nineteenth century. The average number of children per family dropped from 7.0 in 1800 to 3.6 by 1900. But the open advocacy of contraception, the use of artificial means to prevent pregnancy, struck many people as both new and shocking. And it was illegal. Anthony Comstock, New York City's commissioner of vice, promoted laws in the 1870s making it a felony not only to sell contraceptive devices like condoms and cervical caps but also to publish information on how to prevent pregnancy.

When Sanger used her militant feminist paper, the *Woman Rebel*, to promote birth control, the Post Office confiscated Sanger's publication and brought charges of obscenity against her. Facing arrest, she fled to Europe, only to return in 1916 as something of a national celebrity. In her absence, birth control had become linked with free speech and had been taken up as a liberal cause. Under public pressure, the government dropped the charges against Sanger, who undertook a nationwide tour to publicize the birth control cause.

Sanger then took direct action, opening the nation's first birth control clinic in the Brownsville section of Brooklyn in October 1916. Located in the heart of a Jewish and Italian immigrant neighborhood, the clinic attracted 464 clients. On the tenth day, police shut down the clinic and threw Sanger in jail. By then, she had become a national figure, and the cause she championed had gained legitimacy, if not legality. Sanger soon reopened her clinic. After World War I, the birth control movement would become much less radical. Altering her tactics to suit the conservative temper of the times, Sanger sought support from medical doctors. She even jumped aboard the popular fad of eugenics, a racist genetic theory that warned against allowing the "unfit" to reproduce. But in its infancy, birth control was part of a radical vision for reforming the world that made common cause with the socialists and the IWW in challenging the limits of progressive reform.

Progressivism for White Men Only

The day before President Woodrow Wilson's inauguration in March 1913, the largest mass march to that date in the nation's history took place as more than five thousand demonstrators took to the streets in Washington to demand the vote for women. A rowdy crowd on hand to celebrate the Democrats' triumph attacked the marchers. Men spat at the suffragists and threw lighted cigarettes and matches at their clothing. "If my wife were where you are," a burly cop told one suffragist, "I'd break her head." But for all the marching, Wilson pointedly ignored woman suffrage in his inaugural address the next day.

The march served as a reminder that the political gains of progressivism were not spread equally throughout the population. As the twentieth century dawned, women still could not vote in most states, although they had won major victories in the West. Increasingly, however, woman suffrage had become an international movement.

Alice Paul, a Quaker social worker who had visited England and participated in suffrage activism there, returned to the United States in 1910 in time to plan the mass march on the eve of Wilson's inauguration and to lobby for a federal amendment to give women the vote. Paul's dramatic tactics alienated many in the National American Woman Suffrage Association. In 1916, Paul founded the militant National Woman's Party, which became the radical voice of the suffrage movement

Women weren't the only group left out in progressive reform. Progressivism, as it was practiced in the West and South, was tainted with racism by seeking to limit the rights of Asians and African Americans. Anti-Asian bigotry in the West led to a renewal of the Chinese Exclusion Act in 1902. At first, California governor Hiram Johnson stood against the strong anti-Asian prejudice of his state. But in 1913, he caved in to popular pressure and signed the Alien Land Law, which barred Japanese immigrants from purchasing land in California.

South of the Mason-Dixon line, the progressives' racism targeted African Americans. Progressives preached the disfranchisement of black voters as a "reform." During the bitter electoral fights that had pitted Populists against Democrats in the 1890s, the party of white supremacy held its power by votes purchased or

Woman Suffrage Parade
Women marched in a suffrage parade in Washington, D.C., in 1913. The women had to fend off angry crowds who attacked them and tried to break up the parade. Inez Milholland led the march on horseback, replicating the "white knight" on this program. When the crowd threatened the marchers, Milholland spurred her horse into the crowd shouting, "You men ought to be ashamed of yourselves." The Granger Collection, New York.

coerced from African Americans. Southern progressives proposed to reform the electoral system by eliminating black voters. Beginning in 1890 with Mississippi, southern states curtailed the African American vote through devices such as poll taxes (fees required for voting) and literacy tests.

The Progressive Era also witnessed the rise of Jim Crow laws to segregate public facilities. The new railroads precipitated segregation in the South where it had rarely existed before, at least on paper. Soon, separate railcars, separate waiting rooms, separate bathrooms, and separate dining facilities for blacks sprang up across the South. In courtrooms in Mississippi, blacks were required to swear on a separate Bible.

In the face of this growing repression, Booker T. Washington, the preeminent black leader of the day, urged caution and restraint. A former slave, Washington opened the Tuskegee Institute in Alabama in 1881 to teach vocational skills to African Americans. He emphasized education and economic progress for his race and urged African Americans to put aside issues of political and social equality. In an 1895 speech in Atlanta that came to be known as the Atlanta Compromise, he stated, "In all things that are purely social we can be as separate as the fingers, yet one as the hand in all things essential to mutual progress." Washington's accommodationist policy appealed to whites and elevated "the wizard of Tuskegee" to the role of national spokesman for African Americans.

The year after Washington proclaimed the Atlanta Compromise, the Supreme Court upheld the legality of racial segregation, affirming in *Plessy v. Ferguson* (1896) the constitutionality of the doctrine of "separate but equal." Blacks could be segregated in separate schools, restrooms, and other facilities as long as the facilities were "equal" to those provided for whites. Of course, facilities for blacks rarely proved equal.

VISUAL ACTIVITY

Booker T. Washington and Theodore Roosevelt Dine at the White House

Theodore Roosevelt invited Booker T. Washington to the White House in 1901, stirring up a hornet's nest of controversy that continued into the election of 1904. The Republican campaign piece pictured shows Roosevelt and a light-skinned Washington sitting under a portrait of Abraham Lincoln. Democrats' campaign buttons pictured Washington with darker skin and implied that Roosevelt had "painted the White House black" and favored "race mingling." © David J. & Janice L. Frent Collection / CORBIS.

READING THE IMAGE: In this Republican image of the famous meeting of Booker T. Washington and Theodore Roosevelt at the White House, what role does skin color play in the depiction?

CONNECTIONS: Why did African Americans in the South continue to ally with the Republican party?

DINNER GIVEN AT THE WHITE HOUSE BY PRESIDENT ROOSEVELT TO BOOKER T. WASHINGTON, OCTOBER 17th, 1901

Woodrow Wilson brought to the White House southern attitudes toward race and racial segregation. He instituted segregation in the federal workforce, especially the Post Office, and approved segregated drinking fountains and restrooms in the nation's capital. When critics attacked the policy, Wilson insisted that segregation was "in the interest of the Negro."

In 1906, a major race riot in Atlanta called into question Booker T. Washington's strategy of uplift and accommodation. For three days in September, the streets of Atlanta ran red with blood as angry white mobs chased and cornered any blacks they happened upon. An estimated 250 African Americans died in the riots—members of Atlanta's black middle class along with the poor and derelict. Professor William Crogman of Clark College noted the central irony of the riot: "Here we have worked and prayed and tried to make good men and women of our colored population," he observed, "and at our very doorstep the whites kill these good men." The riot caused many African Americans to question Washington's strategy of gradualism and accommodation.

Foremost among Washington's critics stood W. E. B. Du Bois, a Harvard graduate who urged African Americans to fight for civil rights and racial justice. In *The Souls of Black Folk* (1903), Du Bois attacked the "Tuskegee Machine," comparing Washington to a political boss who used his influence to silence his critics and reward his followers. Du Bois founded the Niagara movement in 1905, calling for universal male suffrage, civil rights, and leadership composed of a black intellectual elite. The Atlanta riot only bolstered his resolve. In 1909, the Niagara movement helped found the National Association for the Advancement of Colored People (NAACP), a coalition of blacks and whites that sought legal and political rights for African Americans through the courts. In the decades that followed, the NAACP came to represent the future for African Americans, while Booker T. Washington, who died in 1915, represented the past.

REVIEW How did race, class, and gender shape the limits of progressive reform?

▶ Conclusion: The Transformation of the Liberal State

Progressivism's goal was to reform the existing system—by government intervention if necessary—but without uprooting any of the traditional American political, economic, or social institutions. As Theodore Roosevelt, the bellwether of the movement, insisted, "The only true conservative is the man who resolutely sets his face toward the future." Roosevelt was such a man, and progressivism was such a movement. But although progressivism was never radical, progressives' willingness to use the power of government to regulate business and achieve a measure of social justice redefined liberalism in the twentieth century, tying it to the expanded power of the state.

Progressivism contained many paradoxes. A diverse coalition of individuals and interests, the progressive movement began at the grass roots but left as its legacy a stronger presidency and unprecedented federal involvement in the economy and social welfare. A movement that believed in social justice, progressivism often promoted social control. And while progressives called for greater democracy, they fostered elitism with their worship of experts and efficiency, and they often failed to champion equality for women and minorities.

Whatever its inconsistencies and limitations, progressivism took action to deal with the problems posed by urban industrialism. Progressivism saw grassroots activists address social problems on the local and state levels and search for national solutions. By increasing the power of the presidency and expanding the power of the state, progressives worked to bring about greater social justice and to achieve a better balance between government and business. Jane Addams and Theodore Roosevelt could lay equal claim to the movement that redefined liberalism and launched the liberal state of the twentieth century. War on a global scale would provide progressivism with yet another challenge even before it had completed its ambitious agenda.

See the Selected Bibliography for this chapter in the Appendix.

21 Chapter Review

MAKE IT STICK

 LearningCurve

Go online and use LearningCurve to see what you know. Then review the key terms and answer the questions.

KEY TERMS

progressivism (p. 585)
settlement houses (p. 585)
social gospel (p. 585)
reform Darwinism (p. 590)
muckraking (p. 595)
Roosevelt Corollary (p. 598)
The New Nationalism (p. 605)
The New Freedom (p. 605)
Socialist Party (p. 607)
Industrial Workers of the World (IWW) (p. 607)
birth control movement (p. 608)
Plessy v. Ferguson (p. 610)

REVIEW QUESTIONS

1. What types of people were drawn to the progressive movement, and why? (pp. 585–590)

2. How did progressives justify their demand for more activist government? (pp. 590–592)

3. How did Theodore Roosevelt advance the progressive agenda? (pp. 592–604)

4. How and why did Woodrow Wilson's reform program evolve during his first term? (pp. 604–607)

5. How did race, class, and gender shape the limits of progressive reform? (pp. 607–611)

MAKING CONNECTIONS

1. Roosevelt's foreign policy was summed up in the dictum "Speak softly but carry a big stick." Using two examples, describe how this policy worked.

2. Compare the legislative programs of Roosevelt and Wilson and the evolution of their policies over time.

3. What movements lay outside progressive reform? Why did progressivism coincide with the restriction of minority rights?

LINKING TO THE PAST

1. In what ways did Populism and progressivism differ? In what ways were they similar? (See chapter 20.)

2. During the Gilded Age, industrial capitalism concentrated power in the hands of corporations. How did Roosevelt respond to this problem? How did his approach differ from that of the Gilded Age presidents? Was his strategy effective? (See chapter 18.)

22

World War I: The Progressive Crusade at Home and Abroad

1914–1920

CONTENT LEARNING OBJECTIVES

After reading and studying this chapter, you should be able to:

- Explain the origins of World War I, and why Woodrow Wilson advocated U.S. neutrality. List the events that prompted the United States to enter the war.

- Describe how America geared up domestically and militarily to fight a foreign war.

- Recognize how the war transformed policy at home and understand how women's rights activists used U.S. involvement to secure woman suffrage.

- Explain Wilson's vision for a postwar world, and how that vision was compromised at Versailles. Chronicle the fate of the Paris peace treaty in the U.S. Senate, and explain why it faced so much opposition.

- Understand what threats democracy faced in the immediate postwar period.

GAS MASK
Both the Germans and Allies used poison gas during the First World War. Despite this gas mask's crude appearance, it proved highly effective. But many of those who were gassed and survived were left disabled. Collection of Colonel Stuart S. Corning Jr./ Picture Research Consultants & Archives.

GEORGE "BROWNIE" BROWNE WAS ONE OF TWO MILLION SOLDIERS who crossed the Atlantic during World War I to serve in the American Expeditionary Force in France. The twenty-three-year-old civil engineer from Waterbury, Connecticut, volunteered in July 1917, three months after the United States entered the war, serving with the 117th Engineers Regiment, 42nd Division. Two-thirds of the "doughboys" (American soldiers in Europe) saw action during the war, and few white troops saw more than Brownie did.

When the 42nd arrived at the front, veteran French troops taught Brownie's regiment of engineers how to build and maintain trenches, barbed-wire entanglements, and artillery and machine-gun positions. Although Brownie came under German fire each day, he wrote Martha Johnson, his girlfriend back home, "the longer I'm here the more spirit I have to 'stick it out' for the good of humanity and the U.S. which is the same thing."

Training ended in the spring of 1918 when the Germans launched a massive offensive in the Champagne region. The German bombardment made the night "as light as daytime, and the ground . . . was a mass of flames and whistling steel from the bursting shells." One doughboy from the 42nd remembered, "Dead bodies were all around me. Americans, French, Hun [Germans] in all phases and positions of death." Another declared that soon "the odor was something fierce. We had to put on our gas masks to keep from getting sick." Eight days of combat cost the 42nd nearly 6,500 dead, wounded, and missing, 20 percent of the division.

After only ten days' rest, Brownie and his unit joined in the first major American offensive, an attack against German defenses at Saint-Mihiel. On September 12, 3,000 American artillery launched more than a million rounds against German positions. This time the engineers preceded the advancing infantry, cutting through or blasting any barbed wire that remained. The battle cost the 42nd another 1,200 casualties, but Brownie was not among them.

At the end of September, the 42nd shifted to the Meuse-Argonne region, where it participated in the most brutal American fighting of the war. And it was there that Brownie's war ended. The Germans fired thousands of poison gas shells, and the gas, "so thick you could cut it with a knife," felled Brownie. When the war ended on November 11, 1918, he was recovering from his respiratory wounds at a camp behind the lines. Discharged from the army in February 1919, Brownie returned home, where he and Martha married. Like the rest of the country, they were eager to get on with their lives.

President Woodrow Wilson had never expected to lead the United States into the Great War, as the Europeans called it. When war erupted in 1914, he declared America's absolute neutrality. But trade and principle entangled the United States in Europe's troubles and gradually drew the nation into the conflict. Wilson claimed that America's participation would serve grand purposes and uplift both the United States and the entire world.

At home, the war helped progressives finally achieve their goals of national prohibition and woman suffrage, but it also promoted a vicious attack on Americans' civil liberties. Hyperpatriotism meant intolerance, repression, and vigilante violence. In 1919, Wilson sailed for Europe to secure a just peace. Unable to dictate terms to the victors, he accepted disappointing compromises. Upon his return to the United States, he met a crushing defeat that marked the end of Wilsonian internationalism abroad. Crackdowns on dissenters, immigrants, racial and ethnic minorities, and unions also signaled the end of the Progressive Era at home.

George "Brownie" Browne
Training at Fort Slocum, New York, Brownie complained about the army's red tape, bad food, shortage of equipment, inexperienced officers, lack of sleep, and physical exhaustion. Still, he enjoyed the camaraderie of the camp and was, as this photograph reveals, a happy soldier. When his unit arrived at Saint-Nazaire in October 1917, Brownie was proud to be one of the first doughboys in France. Courtesy of Janet W. Hansen.

▶ Woodrow Wilson and the World

Shortly after winning election to the presidency in 1912, Woodrow Wilson confided to a friend: "It would be an irony of fate if my administration had to deal with foreign affairs." Indeed, Wilson had focused his life and career on domestic concerns; in his campaign for the presidency, Wilson had hardly mentioned the world abroad.

Wilson, however, could not avoid the world and the rising tide of militarism, nationalism, and violence that beat against American shores. Economic interests compelled the nation outward. Moreover, Wilson was drawn abroad by his own progressive political principles. He believed that the United States had a moral duty to champion national self-determination, peaceful free trade, and political democracy. "We have no selfish ends to serve," he proclaimed. "We desire no conquest, no dominion. . . . We are but one of the champions of the rights of mankind." Yet as president, Wilson was as ready as any American president to apply military solutions to problems of foreign policy. This readiness led Wilson and the United States into military conflict in Mexico and then in Europe.

Taming the Americas

When he took office, Wilson sought to distinguish his foreign policy from that of his Republican predecessors. To Wilson, Theodore Roosevelt's "big stick" and William Howard Taft's "dollar diplomacy" appeared as crude flexing of military and economic muscle. To signal a new direction, Wilson appointed William Jennings Bryan, a pacifist, as secretary of state.

But Wilson and Bryan, like Roosevelt and Taft, also believed that the Monroe Doctrine gave the United States special rights and responsibilities in the Western Hemisphere. Issued in 1823 to warn Europeans not to attempt to colonize the Americas again, the doctrine had become a cloak for U.S. domination. Wilson thus authorized U.S. military intervention in Nicaragua, Haiti, and the Dominican Republic, paving the way for U.S. banks and corporations to take financial control. All the while, Wilson believed that U.S. actions were promoting order and democracy. "I am going to teach the South American Republics to elect good men!" he declared (Map 22.1).

Wilson's most serious involvement in Latin America came in Mexico. When General Victoriano

CHRONOLOGY

1914	• U.S. Marines occupy Veracruz, Mexico. • Archduke Franz Ferdinand assassinated. • Austria-Hungary declares war on Serbia. • Germany attacks Russia and France. • Great Britain declares war on Germany.
1915	• *Lusitania* sunk.
1916	• Pancho Villa attacks Americans in Mexico and New Mexico. • Wilson reelected.
1917	• Zimmermann telegram intercepted. • United States declares war on Germany. • Committee on Public Information created. • Selective Service Act. • Espionage Act and Trading with the Enemy Act.
1918	• Wilson gives Fourteen Points speech. • Russia arranges separate peace with Germany. • Sedition Act. • U.S. Marines see first major combat. • Armistice signed ending World War I.
1919	• Paris peace conference begins. • Treaty of Versailles signed. • Wave of labor strikes.
1920	• American Civil Liberties Union founded. • Prohibition begins. • Palmer raids. • Senate votes against ratification of Treaty of Versailles. • Women get the vote. • Warren G. Harding elected president.

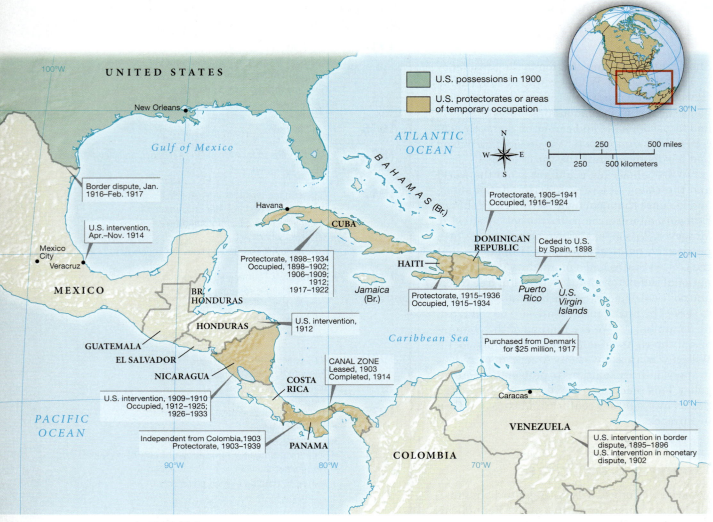

MAP 22.1

U.S. Involvement in Latin America and the Caribbean, 1895–1941

Victory against Spain in 1898 made Puerto Rico an American possession and Cuba a protectorate. The United States later gained control of the Panama Canal Zone. The nation protected its expanding economic interests with military force by propping up friendly, though not necessarily democratic, governments.

Huerta seized power by violent means in 1913, most European nations promptly recognized Mexico's new government, but Wilson refused, declaring that he would not support a "government of butchers." In April 1914, Wilson sent 800 Marines to seize the port of Veracruz to prevent the unloading of a large shipment of arms for Huerta. Huerta fled to Spain, and the United States welcomed a more compliant government.

But a rebellion erupted among desperately poor farmers who believed that the new government, aided by U.S. business interests, had betrayed the revolution's promise to help the common people. In January 1916, the rebel army, commanded by Francisco "Pancho" Villa, seized a train carrying gold to Texas from an American-owned mine in Mexico and killed the 17 American engineers aboard. In March, Villa's men crossed the border for a predawn raid on Columbus, New Mexico, where they killed 18 Americans. Wilson promptly dispatched 12,000 troops, led by Major General John J. Pershing. But Villa avoided capture, and in

January 1917, Wilson recalled Pershing so that he might prepare the army for the possibility of fighting in the Great War.

The European Crisis

Before 1914, Europe had enjoyed decades of peace, but just beneath the surface lay the potentially destructive forces of nationalism and imperialism. The consolidation of the German and Italian states into unified nations and the similar ambition of Russia to create a Pan-Slavic union initiated new rivalries throughout Europe. As the conviction spread that colonial possessions were a mark of national greatness, competition expanded onto the world stage. Most ominously, Germany's efforts under Kaiser Wilhelm II to challenge Great Britain's world supremacy by creating industrial muscle at home, an empire abroad, and a mighty navy threatened the balance of power and thus the peace.

European nations sought to avoid an explosion by developing a complex web of military and diplomatic alliances. By 1914, Germany, Austria-Hungary, and Italy (the **Triple Alliance**) stood opposed to Great Britain, France, and Russia (the **Triple Entente**, also known as "the Allies"). But in their effort to prevent war through a balance of power, Europeans had actually magnified the possibility of large-scale conflict (Map 22.2). Treaties, some of them secret, obligated members of the alliances to come to the aid of another member if attacked.

The fatal sequence began on June 28, 1914, in the city of Sarajevo, when a Bosnian Serb terrorist assassinated Archduke Franz Ferdinand, heir to the Austro-Hungarian throne. On July 18, Austria-Hungary declared war on Serbia. The elaborate alliance system meant that the war could not remain local. Russia announced that it would back the Serbs. Compelled by treaty to support Austria-Hungary, Germany on August 3 attacked Russia and France. In response, on August 4, Great Britain, upholding its pact with France, declared war on Germany. Within weeks, Europe was engulfed in war. The conflict became a world war when Japan, seeing an opportunity to rid itself of European competition in China, joined the cause against Germany.

U.S. Intervention in Mexico, 1916–1917

The evenly matched alliances would fight a disastrous war lasting more than four years, at a cost of 8.5 million soldiers' lives. A war that started with a solitary murder proved impossible to stop. Britain's foreign secretary, Edward Grey, lamented: "The lamps are going out all over Europe. We shall not see them lit again in our lifetime."

The Ordeal of American Neutrality

Woodrow Wilson promptly announced that because the war engaged no vital American interest and involved no significant principle, the United States would remain neutral. Neutrality entitled the United States to trade safely with all nations at war, he declared. Unfettered trade, Wilson believed, was not only a right under international law but also a necessity because in 1913 the U.S. economy had slipped into a recession that wartime disruption of European trade could drastically worsen.

Although Wilson proclaimed neutrality, his sympathies, like those of many Americans, lay with Great Britain and France. Americans gratefully remembered crucial French assistance in the American Revolution and shared with the British a language, a culture, and a commitment to liberty. Germany, by contrast, was a monarchy with strong militaristic traditions. Still, Wilson insisted on neutrality, in part because he feared the conflict's effects on the United States as a nation of immigrants. As he told the German ambassador, "We definitely have to be neutral, since otherwise our mixed populations would wage war on each other."

Britain's powerful fleet controlled the seas and quickly set up an economic blockade of Germany. The United States vigorously protested, but Britain refused to give up its naval advantage. The blockade actually had little economic impact on the United States. Between 1914 and the spring of 1917, while trade with Germany evaporated, war-related exports to Britain—food, clothing, steel, and munitions—escalated by some 400 percent, enough to pull the American economy out of its slump. Although the British blockade violated American neutrality, the Wilson administration gradually

MAP 22.2

European Alliances After the Outbreak of World War I
With Germany and Austria-Hungary wedged between their Entente rivals and all parties fully armed, Europe was poised for war when Archduke Franz Ferdinand of Austria-Hungary was assassinated in Sarajevo in June 1914.

acquiesced, thus beginning the fateful process of alienation from Germany.

Germany retaliated with a submarine blockade of British ports. German *Unterseebooten*, or U-boats, threatened notions of "civilized" warfare. Unlike surface warships that could harmlessly stop freighters and prevent them from entering a war zone, submarines relied on sinking their quarry. And once they sank a ship, the tiny U-boats could not pick up survivors. Nevertheless, in February 1915, Germany announced that it intended to sink on sight enemy ships en route to the British Isles. On May 7, 1915, a German U-boat torpedoed the British passenger liner *Lusitania*, killing 1,198 passengers, 128 of them U.S. citizens.

American newspapers featured drawings of drowning women and children, and some demanded war. Calmer voices pointed out that Germany had warned prospective passengers and that the *Lusitania* carried millions of rounds of ammunition and so was a legitimate target. Secretary of State Bryan resisted the hysteria and declared that a ship carrying war material "should not rely on passengers to protect her from attack—it would be like putting women and children in front of an army." He counseled Wilson to warn American citizens that they traveled on ships of belligerent countries at their own risk.

Wilson sought a middle course that would retain his commitment to peace and neutrality without condoning German attacks on passenger ships. On May 10, 1915, he announced that any further destruction of ships would be regarded as "deliberately unfriendly" and might lead the United States to break diplomatic relations with Germany. Wilson essentially demanded that Germany abandon unrestricted submarine warfare. Bryan resigned, predicting that the president had placed the United States on a collision course with Germany. Wilson replaced Bryan with Robert Lansing, who believed that Germany's antidemocratic character and goal of "world dominance" meant that it "must not be permitted to win this war."

Sinking of the *Lusitania*, 1915

After Germany apologized for the civilian deaths on the *Lusitania*, tensions subsided. And in 1916, Germany went further, promising no more submarine attacks without warning and without provisions for the safety of civilians. Wilson's supporters celebrated the success of his middle-of-the-road strategy.

Wilson's diplomacy proved helpful in his bid for reelection in 1916. In the contest against Republican Charles Evans Hughes, the Democratic Party ran Wilson under the slogan "He kept us out of war." Wilson felt uneasy with the claim, protesting that "they talk of me as though I were a god. Any little German lieutenant can push us into the war at any time by some calculated outrage." But the Democrats' case for Wilson's neutrality appealed to enough of those in favor of peace to eke out a majority. Wilson won, but only by the razor-thin margins of 600,000 popular and 23 electoral votes.

The United States Enters the War

Step by step, the United States backed away from "absolute neutrality." The consequence of protesting the German blockade of Great Britain but accepting the British blockade of Germany was that by 1916 the United States was supplying the Allies with 40 percent of their war material. When France and Britain ran short of money to pay for U.S. goods and asked for loans, Wilson argued that "loans by American bankers to any foreign government which is at war are inconsistent with the true spirit of neutrality." But rather than jeopardize America's wartime prosperity, Wilson allowed billions of dollars in loans that kept American goods flowing to Britain and France.

In January 1917, Germany decided that it could no longer afford to allow neutral shipping to reach Great Britain while Britain's blockage gradually starved Germany. It announced that its navy would resume unrestricted submarine warfare and sink without warning any ship, enemy or neutral, found in the waters off Great Britain. Germany understood that the decision would probably bring the United States into the war but gambled that its submarines would strangle the British economy and allow German armies to win a military victory in France before American troops arrived in Europe.

Resisting demands for war, Wilson continued to hope for a negotiated peace and only broke off diplomatic relations with Germany. Then, on February 25, 1917, British authorities informed Wilson of a secret telegram sent by the German foreign secretary, Arthur Zimmermann, to the German minister in Mexico. It promised that in the event of war between Germany and the United States, Germany would see that Mexico regained its "lost provinces" of Texas, New Mexico, and Arizona if Mexico would declare war against the United States. Wilson angrily responded to the Zimmermann telegram by asking Congress to approve a policy of "armed neutrality" that would allow merchant ships to fight back against attackers.

In March, German submarines sank five American vessels off Britain, killing 66 Americans. On April 2, the president asked Congress to issue a declaration of war. He accused Germany of "warfare against all mankind." Still, he called for a "war without hate" and declared that America fought only to "vindicate the principles of peace and justice." He promised a world made "safe for democracy." On April 6, 1917, by majorities of 373 to 50 in the House and 82 to 6 in the Senate, Congress voted to declare war.

Wilson feared what war would do at home. He said despairingly, "Once lead this people into war, and they'll forget there ever was such a thing as tolerance. To fight you must be brutal

"Chums"

This American war poster from 1918 depicts the devil seated with his arm around Germany's Kaiser Wilhelm, a devil-like figure himself who holds a bloody sword. The devil is congratulating Wilhelm for sinking the *Lusitania* three years earlier. The poster left no doubt that America was on the side of the angels and did the right thing by going to war. Library of Congress.

and ruthless, and the spirit of ruthless brutality will infect Congress, the courts, the policeman on the beat, the man in the street."

REVIEW Why did President Wilson fail to maintain U.S. neutrality during World War I?

▶ "Over There"

American soldiers sailed for France filled with a sense of democratic mission. Some doughboys, such as George Browne, maintained their idealism to the end. American soldiers, many of whom had been drafted, joined the fighting just after the Russians had withdrawn from the war, leaving France as the main battleground. Although black soldiers faced discrimination, many eventually won respect under the French command. The majority of American soldiers, however, found little that was gallant in rats, lice, and poison gas and—despite the progressives' hopes—little to elevate the human soul in a landscape of utter destruction and death.

The Call to Arms

When America entered the war, Britain and France were nearly exhausted after almost three years of conflict. Millions of soldiers had perished; food and morale were dangerously low. Another Allied power, Russia, was in turmoil. In March 1917, a revolution had forced Czar Nicholas II to abdicate, and eight months later, in a separate peace with Germany, the **Bolshevik** revolutionary government withdrew Russia from the war. Peace with Russia allowed Germany to withdraw hundreds of thousands of its soldiers from the eastern front and to deploy them against the Allies on the western front in France.

On May 18, 1917, Wilson signed a sweeping Selective Service Act, authorizing a draft of all young men into the armed forces. Conscription transformed a tiny volunteer armed force of 80,000 men into a vast army and navy. Draft boards eventually inducted 2.8 million men into the armed services, in addition to the 2 million, including George Browne, who volunteered.

Among the 4.8 million men under arms, 370,000 were black Americans. Although African Americans remained understandably skeptical about President Wilson's war for democracy, most followed W. E. B. Du Bois's advice to "close ranks" and to temporarily "forget our special grievances" until the nation had won the war. During training, black recruits suffered the same prejudices that they encountered in civilian life. Rigidly segregated, they faced abuse and miserable conditions, and they usually shouldered shovels rather than rifles.

"Men Wanted for the United States Army"
When America declared war on Germany in April 1917, its army numbered only 127,000, roughly the size of Chile's army. Wilson called for a draft, and within months 10 million men had registered. When the war ended, 2.8 million men had been drafted into military service. Another 2 million men volunteered. Brown Brothers.

Training camps sought to transform raw white recruits into fighting men. Progressives in the government were also determined that the camps turn out soldiers with the highest moral and civic values. To provide recruits with "invisible armor," YMCA workers and veterans of the settlement house and playground movements led them in games, singing, and college extension courses. The army asked soldiers to stop thinking about sex, explaining that a "man who is thinking below the belt is not efficient." Wilson's choice to command the army on the battlefields of France, Major General John "Black Jack" Pershing, was as morally upright as he was militarily uncompromising. Described by one observer as "lean, clean, keen," he gave progressives perfect confidence.

The War in France

At the front, the **American Expeditionary Force (AEF)** discovered a desperate situation. The war had degenerated into a stalemate of armies dug into hundreds of miles of trenches that stretched across France. Huddling in the mud among the corpses and rats, soldiers were separated from the enemy by only a few hundred yards of "no-man's-land." When ordered "over the top," troops raced desperately toward the enemy's trenches, only to be entangled in barbed wire, enveloped in poison gas, and mowed down by machine guns. The three-day battle of the Somme in 1916 cost the French and British forces 600,000 dead and wounded and the Germans 500,000. The deadliest battle of the war allowed the Allies to advance their trenches only a few meaningless miles.

Still, U.S. troops saw almost no combat in 1917. The major exception was the 92nd Division of black troops. When Pershing received an urgent call for troops from the French, he sent the 92nd to the front to be integrated with the French army because he did not want to lose command over the white troops he valued more. In the 191 days they spent in battle—longer

VISUAL ACTIVITY

Life in the Trenches

One U.S. soldier in a rat-infested trench watches for danger, while three others sit or lie in exhausted sleep. This trench is dry for the moment, but with the rains came mud so deep that wounded men drowned in it. Barbed wire, machine-gun nests, and mortars backed by heavy artillery protected the trenches. Trenches with millions of combatants stretched from French ports on the English Channel all the way to Switzerland. Such holes were miserable, but a decent shave with a Gillette safety razor and a friendly game of checkers offered doughboys temporary relief. Inevitably, however, the whistles would blow, sending the young men rushing toward enemy lines. Photo: © The Print Collector/Heritage/The Image Works; shaving kit and checkers set: Collection of Colonel Stuart S. Corning Jr./Picture Research Consultants & Archives.

READING THE IMAGE: What do these images suggest about the reality of life for American soldiers during World War I?

CONNECTIONS: How do you suppose the photograph of the trench compares with the doughboys' expectations of military service in France?

than any other American outfit—the 369th Regiment of the 92nd Division won more medals than any other American combat unit. Black soldiers recognized the irony of having to serve with the French to gain respect.

White troops continued to train and sightsee until March 1918 when a million German soldiers punched a hole in the Allied lines. Pershing finally committed the AEF to combat. In May and June, at Cantigny and then at Château-Thierry, the eager but green Americans checked the German advance with a series of assaults (Map 22.3). Then they headed toward the forest stronghold of Belleau Wood, moving against streams of retreating Allied soldiers who cried defeat: "La guerre est finie!" (The war is over!) A French

officer commanded the Americans to retreat with them, but the American commander replied sharply, "Retreat, hell. We just got here." After charging through a wheat field against withering machine-gun fire, the Marines plunged into hand-to-hand combat. Victory came hard, but a German report praised the enemy's spirit, noting that "the Americans' nerves are not yet worn out." Indeed, it was German morale that was on the verge of cracking.

In the summer of 1918, the Allies launched a massive counteroffensive that would end the war. A quarter of a million U.S. troops joined in the rout of German forces along the Marne River. In September, more than a million Americans took part in the assault that threw the Germans

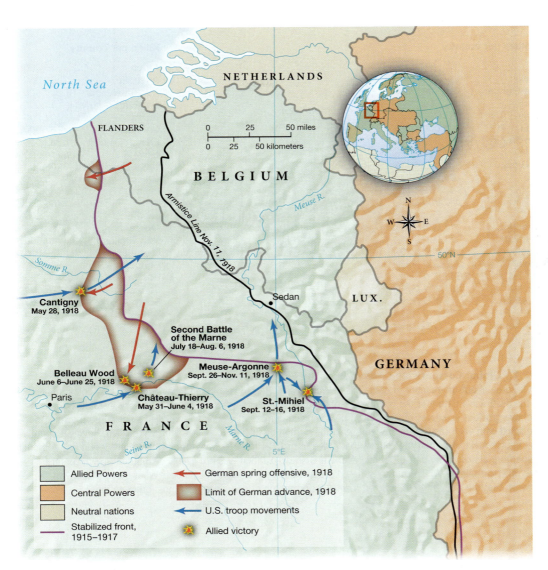

MAP ACTIVITY

Map 22.3   The American Expeditionary Force, 1918

In the last year of the war, the AEF joined the French army on the western front to respond to the final German offensive and pursue the retreating enemy until surrender.

READING THE MAP: Across which rivers did the Germans advance in 1918? Where did the armistice line of November 11, 1918, lie in relation to the stabilized front of 1915–1917? Through which countries did the armistice line run?

CONNECTIONS: What events paved the way for the AEF to join the combat effort in 1918? What characteristic(s) differentiated American troops from other Allied forces and helped them achieve victory?

back from positions along the Meuse River. In four brutal days, the AEF sustained 45,000 casualties. In November, a revolt against the German government sent Kaiser Wilhelm II fleeing to Holland. On November 11, 1918, a delegation from the newly established German republic met with the French high command to sign an armistice that brought the fighting to an end.

The adventure of the AEF was brief, bloody, and victorious. When Germany had resumed unrestricted U-boat warfare in 1917, it had been gambling that it could defeat Britain and France before the Americans could raise and train an army and ship it to France. The German military had miscalculated badly. By the end, 112,000 AEF soldiers perished from wounds and disease, while another 230,000 Americans, including George Browne, suffered casualties but survived. Only the Civil War, which lasted much longer, had cost more American lives. European nations,

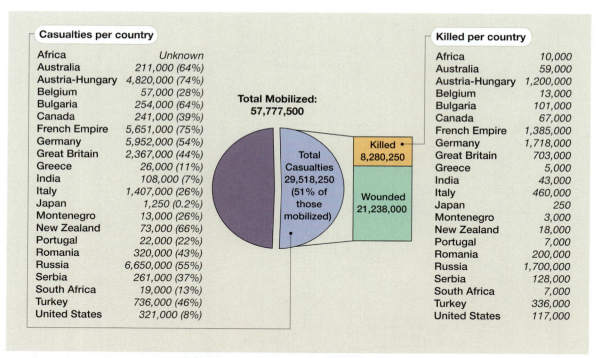

Casualties per country

Africa	*Unknown*
Australia	*211,000 (64%)*
Austria-Hungary	*4,820,000 (74%)*
Belgium	*57,000 (28%)*
Bulgaria	*254,000 (64%)*
Canada	*241,000 (39%)*
French Empire	*5,651,000 (75%)*
Germany	*5,952,000 (54%)*
Great Britain	*2,367,000 (44%)*
Greece	*26,000 (11%)*
India	*108,000 (7%)*
Italy	*1,407,000 (26%)*
Japan	*1,250 (0.2%)*
Montenegro	*13,000 (26%)*
New Zealand	*73,000 (66%)*
Portugal	*22,000 (22%)*
Romania	*320,000 (43%)*
Russia	*6,650,000 (55%)*
Serbia	*261,000 (37%)*
South Africa	*19,000 (13%)*
Turkey	*736,000 (46%)*
United States	*321,000 (8%)*

Total Mobilized:
57,777,500

Total Casualties
29,518,250
(51% of those mobilized)

Killed •
8,280,250

Wounded
21,238,000

Killed per country

Country	Killed
Africa	*10,000*
Australia	*59,000*
Austria-Hungary	*1,200,000*
Belgium	*13,000*
Bulgaria	*101,000*
Canada	*67,000*
French Empire	*1,385,000*
Germany	*1,718,000*
Great Britain	*703,000*
Greece	*5,000*
India	*43,000*
Italy	*460,000*
Japan	*250*
Montenegro	*3,000*
New Zealand	*18,000*
Portugal	*7,000*
Romania	*200,000*
Russia	*1,700,000*
Serbia	*128,000*
South Africa	*7,000*
Turkey	*336,000*
United States	*117,000*

FIGURE 22.1   Global Comparison: Casualties of the First World War
Historians disagree about the number of casualties in World War I. Record keeping in many countries was only rudimentary. Moreover, the destructive nature of the war meant that countless soldiers were wholly obliterated or instantly buried. The chart above provides estimates of casualties (the combined number of wounded and killed soldiers) per country. The percentage listed with each casualty figure represents the portion of soldiers mobilized who were killed. However approximate, these figures make clear that the conflict that raged from 1914 to 1918 was a truly catastrophic world war. Although soldiers came from almost every part of the globe, the human devastation was not evenly distributed. Which country suffered the most casualties? Which country suffered the greatest percentage of casualties? What do you think was the principal reason that the United States suffered a smaller percentage of casualties than most other nations?

however, suffered much greater losses: 2.2 million Germans, 1.9 million Russians, 1.4 million French, and 900,000 Britons (Figure 22.1). Where they had fought, the landscape was as blasted and barren as the moon.

REVIEW   How did the AEF contribute to the defeat of Germany?

▶ The Crusade for Democracy at Home

Many progressives hoped that the war would improve the quality of American life as well as free Europe from tyranny and militarism. Mobilization helped propel the crusades for woman suffrage and prohibition to success. Progressives enthusiastically channeled industrial and agricultural production into the vast war effort. Labor shortages caused by workers entering the military provided new opportunities for women in the booming wartime economy. With labor at a premium, unionized workers gained higher pay and shorter hours. To instill loyalty in Americans whose ancestry was rooted in the belligerent nations, Wilson launched a campaign to foster patriotism. But fanning patriotism led to suppressing dissent. When the government launched a harsh assault on civil liberties, mobs gained license to attack those whom they considered disloyal. As Wilson feared, democracy took a beating at home when the nation undertook its crusade for democracy abroad.

The Progressive Stake in the War

Progressives embraced the idea that the war could be an agent of national improvement. The

Wilson administration, realizing that the federal government would have to assert greater control to mobilize the nation's human and physical resources, created new agencies to manage the war effort. Bernard Baruch, a Wall Street stockbroker, headed the War Industries Board, charged with stimulating and directing industrial production. Baruch brought industrial management and labor together into a team that produced everything from boots to bullets and made U.S. troops the best-equipped soldiers in the world.

Herbert Hoover, a self-made millionaire engineer, headed the Food Administration. He led remarkably successful "Hooverizing" campaigns for "meatless" Mondays and "wheatless" Wednesdays and other ways of conserving resources. Guaranteed high prices, the American heartland not only supplied the needs of U.S. citizens and armed forces but also became the breadbasket of America's allies.

Wartime agencies multiplied: The Railroad Administration directed railroad traffic, the Fuel Administration coordinated the coal industry and other fuel suppliers, the Shipping Board organized the merchant marine, and the National War Labor Policies Board resolved labor disputes. Their successes gave most progressives reason to believe that, indeed, war and reform marched together.

Industrial leaders found that wartime agencies enforced efficiency, which helped corporate profits triple. Some working people also had cause to celebrate. Mobilization meant high prices for farmers and plentiful jobs at high wages in the new war industries (Figure 22.2). Because increased industrial production required peaceful labor relations, the National War Labor Policies Board enacted the eight-hour day, a living minimum wage, and collective bargaining rights in some industries. The American Federation of Labor (AFL) saw its membership soar from 2.7 million to more than 5 million.

The war also provided a huge boost to the crusade to ban alcohol. By 1917, prohibitionists had convinced nineteen states to go dry. Liquor's opponents now argued that banning alcohol would make the cause of democracy powerful and pure. At the same time, shutting down the distilleries would save millions of bushels of grain that could feed the United States and its allies. "Shall the many have food or the few drink?" the drys asked. Prohibition received an additional boost because many of the breweries had German names—Schlitz, Pabst, and Anheuser-Busch. In December 1917, Congress passed the **Eighteenth Amendment**, which banned the manufacture, transportation, and sale of alcohol. After swift ratification by the states, the prohibition amendment went into effect on January 1, 1920.

Women, War, and the Battle for Suffrage

Women had made real strides during the Progressive Era, and war presented new opportunities. More than 25,000 women served in France. About half were nurses. The others

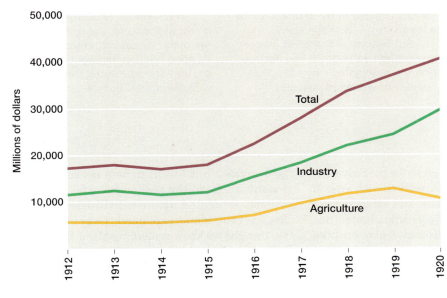

FIGURE 22.2 Industrial Wages, 1912–1920
With help from unions and progressive reformers, wageworkers gradually improved their economic condition. The entry of millions of young men into the armed forces during World War I caused labor shortages and led to a rapid surge in industrial wages.

Agriculture: cash receipts.
Industry: includes mining, electric power, manufacturing, construction, and communications.

Seeking to Serve: An American Woman in Wartime France

When World War I broke out in Europe in 1914, nineteen-year-old Nora Saltonstall was vacationing in Maine with other wellborn young people. A daughter of privilege, she belonged to one of Massachusetts's most distinguished families. But she was no silly, idle debutante. The Saltonstalls instilled in their children a strong sense of the obligation to serve. Within months, she was rolling bandages for the Red Cross in Boston and raising money for the relief of Belgian refugees. By the time the United States entered the war in April 1917, her two Harvard-educated brothers had already volunteered for military service. In October 1917, she volunteered for Red Cross work in France.

After an eleven-day voyage across the submarine-infested Atlantic, Saltonstall arrived in Bordeaux without any idea what she would be doing. She was assigned to long hours of dull work in Paris finding housing for refugees, and like many other American women in France, she contracted "frontline fever," an obsession with getting as far forward in the war zone as she could. She longed for what she called a "man's size job," something that would test her mettle and contribute to victory.

By January 1918, Saltonstall had found "real work," which would be "a direct help, even if it is the tiniest drop in the bucket." She joined a group of female Red Cross volunteers attached to a mobile surgical hospital that followed closely behind the French armies. Lacking training as a nurse, she became the unit's driver, responsible for chauffeuring personnel, transporting the wounded, and hauling supplies as the unit moved from place to place. Soon she was driving on muddy, shell-pocked roads in the dark without lights. She also became a mechanic, with the responsibility for maintaining and repairing the vehicles. "I usually cover myself with grease and oil every morning, tinker about a bit and do more harm than good," she wrote home shortly after arriving. But before long, she announced proudly, "I fixed the steering shaft on the Ford all by myself." Her life, she told her mother, consisted of "choked carburetors, broken springs, long hours on the road, food snatched when you can get it, and sleep." Her work brought changes. "I have developed a most enormous muscle in my right arm, and I am really rather ashamed of it because it literally stands out." She joked, "I'll have to try to direct it into a tennis stroke after the war."

But Saltonstall's sense of humor was tested by the death and destruction she confronted every day. The "stream of wounded men and refugees still makes me ache," she said. "I never hated the war so much before. I have seen enough wounds to hate them, and I don't see how people who have been in it for 3½ years can bear up at all, just one long unending hashing up of people." She lived, she said, in an "insane asylum."

At the same time, she never felt more alive. She believed that she was "learning more . . . than I could learn in years of regular living at home." Saltonstall loved being in the thick of things and "at last feeling as if I were doing something necessary here." She felt proud: "Because we are here, work is being done better and lives saved which might otherwise have been lost. . . . I love my job." She never expressed regrets about coming to France: "If I had not come over I would have felt not to have belonged to this generation and would have felt all my life as if there were something lacking to me on a level with all the up and coming crowd of my own age." Of this she was certain: "After the war there is going to be a difference between those who were in France and those not."

In November 1918, after nearly a year at the front, she scribbled in her diary: "Great excitement, guns stopped firing at midnight. Peace in the air." She celebrated the armistice with the others, but she also realized

drove ambulances; ran canteens for the Salvation Army, Red Cross, and YMCA; worked with French civilians in devastated areas; and acted as telephone operators and war correspondents. (See "Seeking the American Promise," above.) Like men who joined the war effort, they believed that they were taking part in a great national venture. "I am more than willing to live as a soldier and know of the hardships I would have to undergo," one canteen worker declared when applying to go overseas, "but I want to help my country. . . . I want . . . to do the *real* work." And like men, women struggled against disillusionment in France. One woman explained: "Over in America, we thought we knew something about the war . . . but when you get here the difference is [like the one between] studying the laws of electricity and being struck by lightning."

At home, long-standing barriers against hiring women fell when millions of workingmen

that her great adventure was almost over. She contemplated her return to the ordinariness of her civilian life: "I wonder when I get to Boston whether I will ever have the courage to motor 80 miles to a party, arrive at midnight, dance until 5 A.M. and then after a wonderful lunch and supper, motor back the next evening." Demobilization left her with a "very flat feeling." In December, the French government decorated Nora and her unit with the Croix de Guerre for their courageous service, and in March 1919 she sailed for home. Nora Saltonstall never got to confront her concerns about reentering American life, however. Just months after returning, on a camping trip in the West, she contracted typhoid fever and died.

Questions for Consideration

1. How did Nora Saltonstall's gender shape her wartime service? How was her experience different from or similar to that of George "Brownie" Browne?

2. Despite the blood and gore of the battlefield, Saltonstall found her service in France satisfying. Why?

Connect to the Big Idea

ⓒ Considering domestic developments during and just after the war (discussed later in this chapter), do you think that Saltonstall's worries about life in America after the war were justified? Why or why not?

Nora Saltonstall
Seen here at the wheel of the yawl *Comanche* off the coast of Maine, Nora Saltonstall grew into a self-assured, adventurous woman. Although no rebel (she wasn't a suffragist, for example), she was certain that she had something to offer to America's war effort. Unlike most Americans who arrived in Paris during the war, she had already spent a year studying art and history while touring Europe. © Massachusetts Historical Society, Boston, MA, USA/The Bridgeman Art Library.

became soldiers and few new immigrant workers crossed the Atlantic. Tens of thousands of women found work in defense plants as welders, metalworkers, and heavy machine operators and with the railroads. A black woman, a domestic before the war, celebrated her job as a laborer in a railroad yard: "We . . . do not have to work as hard as at housework which requires us to be on duty from six o'clock in the morning until nine or ten at night, with might[y] little time off and at very poor wages." Other women found white-collar work. Between 1910 and 1920, the number of women clerks doubled. Before the war ended, more than a million women had found work in war industries. One woman's rights advocate exaggerated when she declared: "At last . . . women are coming into the labor and festival of life on equal terms with men," but women had made real economic strides.

MAP ACTIVITY

Map 22.4 Women's Voting Rights Before the Nineteenth Amendment

The long campaign for women's voting rights reversed the pioneer epic that moved from east to west. From its first successes in the new democratic West, suffrage rolled eastward toward the entrenched, male-dominated public life of the Northeast and South.

READING THE MAP: What was the first state to grant woman suffrage? How many states extended full voting rights to women before 1914? How many extended these rights during World War I (1914–1918)?

CONNECTIONS: Suffragists redirected their focus during the war. What strategies did they use then?

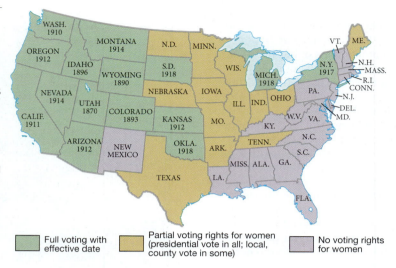

Full voting with effective date

Partial voting rights for women (presidential vote in all; local, county vote in some)

No voting rights for women

The most dramatic advance for women came in the political arena. Adopting a state-by-state approach before the war, suffragists had achieved some success (Map 22.4). More commonly, voting rights for women met strong hostility and defeat. After 1910, suffrage leaders added a federal campaign to amend the Constitution to the traditional state-by-state strategy for suffrage.

The radical wing of the suffragists, led by Alice Paul, picketed the White House, where the marchers unfurled banners that proclaimed "America Is Not a Democracy. Twenty Million Women Are Denied the Right to Vote." They chained themselves to fences and went to jail, where many engaged in hunger strikes. "They seem bent on making their cause as obnoxious as possible," Woodrow Wilson declared. His wife, Edith, detested the idea of "masculinized" voting women. But membership in the mainstream organization, the National American Woman Suffrage Association (NAWSA), led by Carrie Chapman Catt, soared to some two million. Seeing the handwriting on the wall, the Republican and Progressive Parties endorsed woman suffrage in 1916.

In 1918, Wilson finally gave his support to suffrage, calling the amendment "vital to the winning of the war." He conceded that it would be wrong not to reward the wartime "partnership of suffering and sacrifice" with a "partnership of privilege and right." By linking their cause to the wartime emphasis on national unity, the advocates of woman suffrage finally triumphed. In 1919, Congress passed the **Nineteenth Amendment**, granting women the vote, and by August 1920 the required two-thirds of the states had ratified it. (See "Documenting the American Promise," page 630.)

Rally Around the Flag—or Else

When Congress committed the nation to war, only a handful of peace advocates resisted the tide of patriotism. A group of professional women, led by settlement house leader Jane Addams and economics professor Emily Greene Balch, denounced what Addams described as "the pathetic belief in the regenerative results of war." After America entered the conflict, advocates for peace were labeled cowards and traitors.

To suppress criticism of the war, Wilson stirred up patriotic fervor. In 1917, the president created the Committee on Public Information under the direction of George Creel, a journalist who became the nation's cheerleader for war. Creel sent "Four-Minute Men," a squad of 75,000 volunteers, around the country to give brief pep talks that celebrated successes on the battlefields and in the factories. Posters, pamphlets, and cartoons depicted brave American soldiers and sailors defending freedom and democracy against the evil "Huns," the derogatory nickname applied to German soldiers.

America rallied around Creel's campaign. The film industry cranked out pro-war melodramas and taught audiences to hiss at the German kaiser. Colleges and universities generated war propaganda in the guise of scholarship. When Professor James McKeen Cattell of Columbia University urged that America seek peace with Germany short of victory, university president Nicholas Murray Butler fired him on the grounds that "what had been folly is now treason."

A firestorm of anti-German passion erupted. Across the nation, "100% American" campaigns enlisted ordinary people to sniff out disloyalty. German, the most widely taught foreign language in 1914, practically disappeared from the nation's schools. Targeting German-born Americans, the *Saturday Evening Post* declared that it was time to rid the country of "the scum of the melting pot." Anti-German action reached its extreme with the lynching of Robert Prager, a German-born baker with socialist leanings. Persuaded by the defense lawyer who praised what he called a "patriotic murder," the jury at the trial of the killers took only twenty-five minutes to acquit.

As hysteria increased, the campaign reached absurd levels. Menus across the nation changed German toast to French toast and sauerkraut to liberty cabbage. In Milwaukee, vigilantes mounted a machine gun outside the Pabst Theater to prevent the staging of Schiller's *Wilhelm Tell*, a powerful protest against tyranny. The fiancée of one of the war's leading critics, caught dancing on the dunes of Cape Cod, was held on suspicion of signaling to German submarines.

The Wilson administration's zeal in suppressing dissent contrasted sharply with its war aims of defending democracy. In the name of self-defense, the Espionage Act (June 1917), the Trading with the Enemy Act (October 1917), and the Sedition Act (May 1918) gave the government sweeping powers to punish any opinion or activity it considered "disloyal, profane, scurrilous, or abusive." When Postmaster General Albert Burleson blocked mailing privileges for dissenting publications, dozens of journals were forced to close down. Of the 1,500 individuals eventually charged with sedition, all but a dozen had merely spoken words the government found objectionable.

One of them was Eugene V. Debs, the leader of the Socialist Party, who was convicted under the Espionage Act and sentenced to ten years. In a speech on June 16, 1918, Debs declared that the United States was not fighting a noble war to make the world safe for democracy but had joined greedy European imperialists seeking to conquer the globe. The government claimed that Debs had crossed the line between legitimate dissent and criminal speech. From the Atlanta penitentiary, Debs argued that he was just telling the truth, like hundreds of his friends who were also in jail.

The president hoped that national commitment to the war would silence partisan politics, but his Republican rivals used the war as a weapon against the Democrats. The trick was to oppose Wilson's conduct of the war but not the war itself. Republicans outshouted Wilson on the nation's need to mobilize for war but then complained that Wilson's War Industries Board was a tyrannical agency that crushed free enterprise. As the war progressed, Republicans gathered power against the Democrats, who had narrowly reelected Wilson in 1916.

In 1918, Republicans gained a narrow majority in both the House and the Senate. The end of Democratic control of Congress not only halted further domestic reform but also meant that the United States would advance toward military victory in Europe with political power divided

D. W. Griffith's *Hearts of the World*
Hollywood joined in the government's efforts to stir up rage against the Germans. In a film made by D. W. Griffith, a hulking German is about to whip a defenseless farm woman (played by Lillian Gish). When the film premiered in 1918, First Lady Edith Wilson, who sought to moderate the hate campaign, wrote to Griffith, pleading with him to cut or soften the violent whipping scene. Library of Congress.

The Final Push for Woman Suffrage

By the early twentieth century, the women's movement had mobilized millions, who increasingly concentrated on the passage of an amendment to the U.S. Constitution to ensure women's voting rights. Nothing came easily to the suffragists, but in 1920 their passion and courage were rewarded by the ratification of the Nineteenth Amendment.

DOCUMENT 1
Politicking for Suffrage

While radical suffragists chained themselves to the White House fence and went on hunger strikes, other women followed more traditional political channels—methodically gathering petitions, lobbying legislators, building alliances, and rounding up votes. Mary Garrett Hay, vice president of the National American Woman Suffrage Association (NAWSA), reports her efforts with New York state legislators.

New York City, N.Y.
March 13th, 1919
Mrs. Maud Wood Park
1626 Rhode Island Avenue
Washington, D.C.

Dear Mrs. Park,

. . . I kept in very close touch on the telephone and telegraph wire with New York Congressmen and they reported to me, really twice a day what was going on, as far as Speaker, Floor Leader and Suffrage Committee was concerned. I can do more in the House than in the Senate, and I have asked Mr. Hays on the long distance telephone to try and see that things are perfectly straight for our Cause there.

Things will be all right, I believe, but I have made up my mind not to trust either Democrats or Republicans, until the Suffrage Amendment is passed; however, I do not say this to the men[,] only to you, and I shall keep my eyes and ears open and busy, and on the job all I can.

Source: *Women and Social Movements in the United States, 1600–2000*, "How Did Suffragists Lobby to Obtain Congressional Approval of a Woman Suffrage Amendment to the U.S. Constitution, 1917–1920?" Document #10. Courtesy of the Schlesinger Library, Radcliffe Institute, Harvard University (Cambridge, MA).

DOCUMENT 2
The President Intervenes

Although some people urged suffragists to muffle their demands during the war so that the nation could concentrate on victory, Carrie Chapman Catt, president of the NAWSA since 1915, pressed on, recognizing that the war offered a special opportunity. Catt prodded President Woodrow Wilson quietly but persistently, and on September 30, 1918, Wilson finally intervened directly, urging the Senate to pass the Nineteenth Amendment. His argument on behalf of democracy mirrored precisely that of radical suffragists who were protesting in front of the White House.

[The Senate's] adoption is, in my judgment, clearly necessary to the successful prosecution of the war and the successful realization of the objects for which the war is being fought.
. . . If we be indeed democrats and wish to lead the world to democracy, we can ask other peoples to accept in

between a Democratic president and a Republican Congress likely to challenge Wilson's plans for international cooperation.

REVIEW How did progressive ideals fare during wartime?

▶ A Compromised Peace

Wilson decided to reaffirm his noble war ideals by announcing his peace aims before the end of hostilities. He hoped the victorious Allies would

proof of our sincerity and our ability to lead them whither they wish to be led, nothing less persuasive and convincing than our actions.

. . . They are looking to the great, powerful, famous democracy of the West to lead them to a new day for which they have so long waited; and they think, in their logical simplicity, that democracy means that women shall play their part in affairs alongside men and upon an equal footing with them.

. . . We have made partners of the women in this war. Shall we admit them only to a partnership of suffering and sacrifice and toil and not to a partnership of privilege and right?

This war could not have been fought, either by the other nations engaged or by America, if it had not been for the services of the women—services rendered in every sphere. . . .

. . . I tell you plainly that this measure which I urge upon you is vital to the winning of the war and to the energies alike of preparation and of battle.

. . . And not to winning the war only. It is vital to the right solution of the great problems which we must settle, and settle immediately, when the war is over. We shall need in our vision of affairs, as we have never needed them before, the sympathy and insight and clear moral instinct of the women of the world. . . . We shall need their moral sense to preserve what is right and fine and worthy in our system of life as well as to discover just what it is that ought to be purified and reformed. Without their counsellings we shall be only half wise.

Source: "Appeal of President Wilson to the Senate of the United States to Submit the Federal Amendment for Woman Suffrage Delivered in Person Sept. 20, 1918," in *History of Woman Suffrage*, vol. 5, *1900–1920*, ed. Ida Husted Harper (New York: NAWSA, 1922), 760–63.

DOCUMENT 3
Reflections on Victory

Catt celebrates the passage of the Nineteenth Amendment in this letter to her staff at the NAWSA on Thanksgiving Day 1920. She reflects on the long road to victory and considers the satisfactions of the journey.

I have kept Thanksgiving sacred to reflections upon the long trail behind us, and the triumph which was its inevitable conclusion. John Adams said long after the Revolution that only about one third of the people were for it, a third being against it, and the remaining third utterly indifferent. Perhaps this proportion applies to all movements. At least a third of the women were for our cause at the end. . . . As I look back over the years . . . I realize that the greatest thing in the long campaign for us was not its crowning victory, but the discipline it gave us all. . . . It was a great crusade, the world has seen none more wonderful. . . . My admiration, love and reverence go out to that band which fought and won a revolution . . . with congratulations that we were permitted to establish a new and good thing in the world.

Source: Carrie Chapman Catt to NAWSA Office Staff, Thanksgiving Day 1920, in *Women's Suffrage in America: An Eyewitness History*, ed. Elizabeth Frost and Kathryn Cullen-DuPont (New York: Facts on File, 1992), 335–36.

Questions for Analysis and Debate

1. Why were some legislators in New York and elsewhere willing to work closely with suffragists such as Mary Garrett Hay?

2. What, according to Woodrow Wilson, would America's rejection of the Nineteenth Amendment have jeopardized?

3. What do you suppose Carrie Chapman Catt meant when she said that the greatest gain for women in the suffrage campaign was "discipline"?

Connect to the Big Idea

⊙ How was the final passage of the Nineteenth Amendment tied to World War I?

adopt his plan for international democracy, but he was sorely disappointed. America's allies understood that Wilson's principles jeopardized their own postwar plans for the acquisition of enemy territory, new colonial empires, and reparations. Wilson also faced strong opposition at home from those who feared that his enthusiasm for international cooperation would undermine American sovereignty.

Wilson's Fourteen Points

On January 8, 1918, ten months before the armistice in Europe, President Wilson revealed to Congress his **Fourteen Points**, his blueprint for a new democratic world order. The first five points affirmed basic liberal ideals: an end to secret treaties, freedom of the seas, removal of economic barriers to free trade, reduction of weapons of war, and recognition of the rights of colonized peoples. The next eight points supported the right to self-determination of European peoples who had been dominated by Germany or its allies. Wilson's fourteenth point called for a "general association of nations"— a **League of Nations**—to provide "mutual guarantees of political independence and territorial integrity to great and small states alike." A League of Nations reflected Wilson's lifelong dream of a "parliament of man." Only such an organization of "peace-loving nations," he believed, could justify the war and secure a lasting peace.

The Paris Peace Conference

From January 18 to June 28, 1919, the eyes of the world focused on Paris. Wilson, inspired by his mission, decided to head the U.S. delegation. He said he owed it to the American soldiers. "It is now my duty," he announced, "to play my full part in making good what they gave their life's blood to obtain." A dubious British diplomat retorted that Wilson was drawn to Paris "as a debutante is entranced by the prospect of her first ball." The decision to leave the country at a time when his political opponents challenged his leadership was risky enough, but his stubborn refusal to include prominent Republicans in the delegation proved foolhardy and eventually cost him his dream of a new world order.

After four terrible years of war, the common people of Europe almost worshipped Wilson, believing that he would create a safer, more decent world. When the peace conference convened at Louis XIV's magnificent palace at Versailles, however, Wilson encountered a different reception. To the Allied leaders, Wilson appeared a naive and impractical moralist. His desire to gather former enemies within a new international democratic order showed how little he understood hard European realities. Georges Clemenceau, premier of France, claimed that Wilson "believed you could do everything by formulas" and "empty theory." Disparaging the Fourteen Points, he added, "God himself was content with ten commandments."

The Allies wanted to fasten blame for the war on Germany, totally disarm it, and make it pay so dearly that it would never threaten its neighbors again. The French demanded retribution in the form of territory containing Germany's richest mineral resources. The British made it clear that they were not about to give up the powerful weapon of naval blockade for the vague principle of freedom of the seas.

The Allies forced Wilson to make drastic compromises. In return for France's moderating its territorial claims, he agreed to support Article 231 of the peace treaty, assigning war guilt to Germany. Though saved from permanently losing Rhineland territory to the French, Germany was outraged at being singled out as the instigator of the war and being saddled with more than $33 billion in damages. Many Germans felt that their nation had been betrayed. After agreeing to an armistice in the belief that peace terms would be based in Wilson's generous Fourteen Points, they faced hardship and humiliation instead.

Wilson had better success in establishing the principle of self-determination. But from the beginning, Secretary of State Robert Lansing knew that the president's concept of self-determination was "simply loaded with dynamite." Lansing wondered, "What unit has he in mind? Does he mean a race, a territorial area, or a community?" Even Wilson was vague about what self-determination actually meant. "When I gave utterance to those words," he admitted, "I said them without the knowledge that nationalities existed, which are coming to us day after day." Lansing suspected that the notion "will raise hopes which can never be realized. It will, I fear, cost thousands of lives. In the end it is bound to be discredited, to be called the dream of an idealist who failed to realize the danger until it was too late."

Yet partly on the basis of self-determination, the conference redrew the map of Europe and parts of the rest of the world. Portions of Austria-Hungary were ceded to Italy, Poland, and Romania, and the remainder was reassembled into Austria, Hungary, Czechoslovakia, and Yugoslavia—independent republics whose boundaries were drawn with attention to concentrations of major ethnic groups. More arbitrarily, the Ottoman empire was carved up into small mandates (including Palestine) run by local leaders but under the control of France and Great Britain. The conference reserved the mandate system for those regions it deemed insufficiently "civilized" to have full independence. Thus, the reconstructed nations—each beset with ethnic and nationalist rivalries—faced the challenge of making a new democratic

VISUAL ACTIVITY

"The Signing of Peace in the Hall of Mirrors, Versailles, 28th June 1919" by Sir William Orpen

Set in the dazzling Hall of Mirrors at Versailles, built for Louis XIV as a symbol of his power, this painting captures the moment when the treaty was signed in June 1919. The leaders in charge of putting the world back together after the Great War are gathered at the table. Wilson is seated fifth from the left, dignified but seemingly isolated, while the French premier Georges Clemenceau and the British Prime minister David Lloyd George are huddled together at Wilson's left. Imperial War Museum, London, UK/The Bridgeman Art Library.

READING THE IMAGE: What might have been the artist's message in depicting Wilson, Clemenceau, and George as he did?

CONNECTIONS: Diplomats and politicians hammered out the treaty. How did Americans back home respond to the work of Wilson and the other world leaders at Versailles?

government work (Map 22.5). Many of today's bitterest disputes—in the Balkans and Iraq, between Greece and Turkey, between Arabs and Jews—have roots in the decisions made in Paris in 1919.

Wilson hoped that self-determination would also dictate the fate of Germany's colonies in Asia and Africa. But the Allies, who had taken over the colonies during the war, went no further than allowing the League of Nations a mandate to administer them. Technically, the mandate system rejected imperialism, but in reality it allowed the Allies to maintain control. Thus, while denying Germany its colonies, the Allies retained and added to their own empires.

The cause of democratic equality suffered another setback when the peace conference rejected Japan's call for a statement of racial equality in the treaty. Wilson's belief in the superiority of whites, as well as his apprehension about how white Americans would respond to such a declaration, led him to oppose the clause. To soothe hurt feelings, Wilson agreed to grant Japan a mandate over the Shantung Peninsula in northern China, which had formerly been controlled by Germany. The gesture mollified Japan's moderate leaders, but the military faction preparing to take over the country used bitterness toward racist Western colonialism to build support for expanding Japanese power throughout Asia.

Closest to Wilson's heart was finding a new way to manage international relations. In Wilson's view, war had discredited the old strategy of balance of power. Instead, he proposed a League of Nations that would provide collective security. The league would establish rules of international conduct and resolve conflicts between nations through rational and peaceful means. When the Allies agreed to the

MAP 22.5

Europe After World War I
The post–World War I settlement redrew boundaries to create new nations based on ethnic groupings. Within defeated Germany and Russia, this outcome left bitter peoples who resolved to recover the territory taken from them.

league, Wilson was overjoyed. He believed that the league would rectify the errors his colleagues had forced on him in Paris.

To some Europeans and Americans, the **Versailles treaty** came as a bitter disappointment. Wilson's admirers were shocked that the president dealt in compromise like any other politician. But without Wilson's presence, the treaty that was signed on June 28, 1919, surely would have been more vindictive. Wilson returned home in July 1919 consoled that, despite his frustrations, he had gained what he most wanted—a League of Nations. In Wilson's judgment, "We have completed in the least time possible the greatest work that four men have ever done."

The Fight for the Treaty

The tumultuous reception Wilson received when he arrived home persuaded him, probably correctly, that the American people supported the treaty. When the president submitted the treaty to the Senate in July 1919, he warned that failure to ratify it would "break the heart of the world." By then, however, criticism of the treaty was mounting, especially from Americans convinced that their countries of ethnic origin—Ireland, Italy, and Germany—had not been given fair treatment. Others worried that the president's concessions at Versailles had jeopardized the treaty's capacity to provide a workable plan for rebuilding Europe and to guarantee world peace.

In the Senate, Republican "irreconcilables" condemned the treaty for entangling the United States in world affairs. A larger group of Republicans did not object to American participation in world politics but feared that membership in the League of Nations would jeopardize the nation's ability to act independently. No Republican, in any case, was eager to hand Wilson and the Democrats a foreign policy victory with the 1920 presidential election little more than a year away.

At the center of Republican opposition was Wilson's archenemy, Senator Henry Cabot Lodge of Massachusetts. Lodge was no isolationist, but he thought that much of the Fourteen Points was a "general bleat about virtue being better than vice." Lodge expected the United States' economic and military power to propel the nation into a major role in world affairs. But he insisted that membership in the League of Nations, which would require collective action to maintain peace, threatened the nation's independence in foreign relations.

With Lodge as its chairman, the Senate Foreign Relations Committee produced several amendments, or "reservations," that sought to limit the consequences of American membership in the league. For example, several reservations required approval of both the House and the Senate before the United States could participate in league-sponsored economic sanctions or military action.

It gradually became clear that ratification of the treaty depended on acceptance of the Lodge reservations. Democratic senators, who overwhelmingly supported the treaty, urged Wilson to accept Lodge's terms, arguing that they left the essentials of the treaty intact. Wilson, however, insisted that the reservations cut "the very heart out of the treaty."

Wilson decided to take his case directly to the people. On September 3, 1919, still exhausted from the peace conference, he set out by train on the most ambitious speaking tour ever undertaken by a president. On September 25 in Pueblo, Colorado, Wilson collapsed and had to return to Washington. There, he suffered a massive stroke that partially paralyzed him. From his bedroom, Wilson sent messages instructing Democrats in the Senate to hold firm against any and all reservations. Wilson commanded enough loyalty to ensure a vote against the Lodge reservations. But when the treaty without reservations came before the Senate in March 1920, the combined opposition of the Republican irreconcilables and reservationists

"Refusing to Give the Lady a Seat"
When stiff opposition to American membership in the League of Nations developed in the United States, friends of the league mounted a counterattack. This cartoon skewers the three leading Republican opponents of the league—Senators William Borah of Idaho, Henry Cabot Lodge of Massachusetts, and Hiram Johnson of California—who stubbornly refuse to budge an inch for the angel of peace. Picture Research Consultants & Archives.

left Wilson six votes short of the two-thirds majority needed for passage.

The nations of Europe organized the League of Nations at Geneva, Switzerland. Although Woodrow Wilson received the Nobel Peace Prize in 1920 for his central role in creating the league, the United States never became a member. Whether American membership could have prevented the world war that would begin in Europe in 1939 is highly unlikely, but the United States' failure to join certainly weakened the league from the start. In refusing to accept relatively minor compromises with Senate moderates, Wilson lost his treaty and American membership in the league.

REVIEW Why did the Senate fail to ratify the Versailles treaty?

► Democracy at Risk

The defeat of Wilson's plan for international democracy proved the crowning blow to progressives who had hoped that the war could boost reform at home. When the war ended, Americans wanted to demobilize swiftly. In the process, servicemen, defense workers, and farmers lost their war-related jobs. The volatile combination—of unemployed veterans returning home, a stalled economy, and leftover wartime patriotism looking for a new cause—threatened to explode. Wartime anti-German passion was quickly succeeded by the Red scare, an anti-radical campaign broad enough to ensnare unionists, socialists, dissenters, and African Americans and Mexicans who had committed no offense but to seek an escape from rural poverty as they moved north.

Economic Hardship and Labor Upheaval

Americans demanded that the nation return to a peacetime economy. The government abruptly abandoned its wartime economic controls and canceled war contracts. In a matter of months, 3 million soldiers mustered out of the military and flooded the job market just as war production ceased. Unemployment soared. At the same time, consumers went on a postwar spending spree that drove inflation skyward. In 1919 alone, prices rose 75 percent over prewar levels.

Most of the gains workers had made during the war evaporated. Freed from government controls, business turned against the eight-hour day and attacked labor unions. With inflation eating up their paychecks, workers fought back.

The year 1919 witnessed nearly 3,600 strikes involving 4 million workers. The most spectacular strike occurred in February 1919 in Seattle, where shipyard workers had been put out of work by demobilization. When a coalition of the radical Industrial Workers of the World (IWW, known as Wobblies) and the moderate American Federation of Labor (AFL) called a general strike, the largest work stoppage in American history shut down the city. Newspapers claimed that the walkout was "a Bolshevik effort to start a revolution." The suppression of the Seattle general strike by city officials cost the AFL many of its wartime gains and contributed to the destruction of the IWW soon afterward.

A strike by Boston policemen in the fall of 1919 underscored postwar hostility toward labor militancy. Although the police were paid less than pick-and-shovel laborers, they won little sympathy. Once the officers stopped walking their beats, looters sacked the city. Massachusetts governor Calvin Coolidge called in the National Guard to restore order and broke the Boston police strike. The public welcomed Coolidge's anti-union assurance that "there is no right to strike against the public safety by anybody, anywhere, any time."

Labor strife climaxed in the grim steel strike of 1919. Faced with the industry's plan to revert to seven-day weeks, twelve-hour days, and weekly wages of about $20, Samuel Gompers, head of the AFL, called for a strike. In September, 350,000 workers in fifteen states walked out.

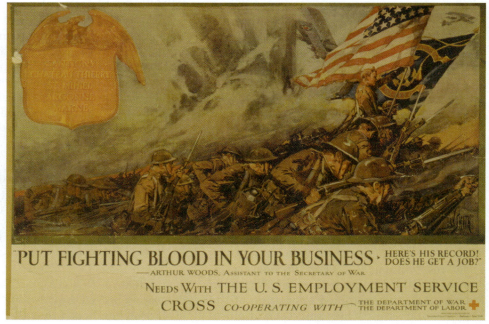

PUT FIGHTING BLOOD IN YOUR BUSINESS · HERE'S HIS RECORD! DOES HE GET A JOB?
—ARTHUR WOODS, ASSISTANT TO THE SECRETARY OF WAR.
NEEDS WITH THE U. S. EMPLOYMENT SERVICE
CROSS CO-OPERATING WITH THE DEPARTMENT OF WAR THE DEPARTMENT OF LABOR

The steel industry hired 30,000 strikebreakers and convinced the public that the strikers were radicals bent on subverting democracy and capitalism. In January 1920, after 18 striking workers were killed, the strike collapsed. That devastating defeat initiated a sharp decline in the fortunes of the labor movement, a trend that would continue for almost twenty years.

The Red Scare

Suppression of labor strikes was one response to the widespread fear of internal subversion that swept the nation in 1919. The **Red scare** ("Red" referred to the color of the Bolshevik flag) exceeded even the assault on civil liberties during the war. It had homegrown causes: the postwar recession, labor unrest, terrorist acts, and the difficulties of reintegrating millions of returning veterans. But unsettling events abroad also added to Americans' anxieties.

Two epidemics swept the globe in 1918. One was Spanish influenza, which brought on a lethal accumulation of fluid in the lungs. A nurse near the front lines in France observed that victims "run a high temperature, so high that we can't believe it's true. . . . It is accompanied by vomiting and dysentery. When they die, as about half of them do, they turn a ghastly dark gray and are taken out at once and cremated." Before the flu virus had run its course, 40 million people had died worldwide, including some 700,000 Americans.

The other epidemic was Russian bolshevism, which seemed to most Americans equally contagious and deadly. Bolshevism became even more menacing in March 1919, when the new Soviet leaders created the Comintern, a worldwide association of Communists sworn to revolution in capitalist countries. (See "Beyond America's Borders," page 638.) A Communist revolution in the United States was extremely unlikely, but edgy Americans, faced with a flurry of terrorist acts, believed otherwise. Dozens of prominent individuals had received bombs through the mail. On September 16, 1920, a wagon filled with dynamite and iron exploded on Wall Street, killing 38 and maiming 143 others. Authorities never caught the terrorists, and the successful attack on America's financial capital fed the nation's anger and fear.

Even before the Wall Street bombing, the government had initiated a hunt for domestic revolutionaries. Led by Attorney General A. Mitchell Palmer, who believed that "there could be no nice distinctions drawn between the theoretical ideals of the radicals and their actual violations of our national laws," the campaign targeted men and women for their ideas, not their illegal acts. In January 1920, Palmer ordered a series of raids that netted 6,000 alleged subversives. Finding no revolutionary conspiracies, Palmer nevertheless ordered 500 noncitizen suspects deported.

His action came in the wake of a campaign against the most notorious radical alien,

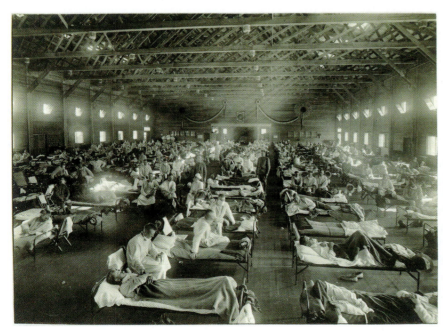

Emergency Hospital
Despite its name, the Spanish flu was first observed in 1918 in Kansas. Army camps, with their close troop quarters, proved perfect incubators. This emergency hospital at Camp Funston, Kansas, is filled with some of the flu's early victims. Crowded troopships quickly spread the virus to Europe. Civilians were not immune. In October 1918 in Philadelphia, more than 4,500 people died in a single week. National Museum of Health & Medicine Armed Forces Institute of Pathology.

Bolshevism

In March 1917, revolutionaries overthrew the Russian czar, whose conservative autocracy was the target of peasants and urban workers seeking a more democratic government. But Marxist radicals, who called themselves Bolsheviks, were not satisfied with the regime change. In November, the Bolsheviks seized control of Russia and made their leader, Vladimir Ilyich Lenin, ruler. Lenin scoffed at the idea that the Allies were fighting for democracy and insisted that greedy capitalists were waging war for international dominance. In March 1918, he shocked Woodrow Wilson and the Allies by signing a separate peace with Germany and withdrawing Russia from the war. Still locked in the desperate struggle with Germany, the Allies cried betrayal.

The Bolshevik regime dedicated itself to ending capitalism in Russia (known as the Soviet Union after 1922) and to instituting what it called a "dictatorship of the proletariat." In theory, workers—agricultural and industrial—would control the economy and exercise political power. But very quickly a gap opened between the workers and party leaders, who instituted a top-down apparatus that institutionalized the bloody repression of their opponents.

Prodded by British leader Winston Churchill, who declared that "the Bolshevik infant should be strangled in its cradle," Britain and France urged the United States to join them in sending troops to Russia in support of Russian democrats opposing the new revolutionary regime. Several prominent Americans spoke out against American intervention. Senator William Borah of Idaho declared: "The Russian people have the same right to establish a Socialist state as we have to establish a republic." But Wilson concluded that the Bolsheviks were a dictatorial party that had come to power through a violent coup that denied Russians political choice, and in September 1918 he ordered 14,000 U.S. troops to join British and French forces in Russia. U.S., British, and French troops fought to overthrow Lenin and annul the Bolshevik Revolution, but the Bolsheviks (by now calling themselves Communists) prevailed. U.S. troops withdrew from Russia in June 1919, after the loss of more than 200 American lives.

The Bolshevik regime also committed itself to overthrowing capitalist and imperialist regimes around the world. Clearly, Lenin's imagined future was at odds with Wilson's proposed liberal new world order. Wilson withheld U.S. diplomatic recognition of the Soviet Union (a policy that persisted until 1934) and joined the Allies in an economic boycott to bring down the Bolshevik government. Unbowed, Lenin promised that his party would "incite rebellion among all the peoples now oppressed," and revolutionary agitation became central to Soviet foreign policy. Just after the armistice, Communist revolutions erupted in Bavaria and Hungary. Though short-lived, the Communist regimes there sent shock waves throughout the West. In 1919, moreover, a Russian official bragged that monies being sent to Europe to foment Bolshevik rebellion were "nothing compared to the funds transmitted to New York for the purpose of spreading bolshevism in the United States." American attention shifted from revolutionaries in Europe to revolutionaries at home. The Red scare was on.

Attorney General A. Mitchell Palmer perceived a "blaze of Revolution sweeping over every American institution of law and order . . . licking the altars of churches . . . crawling into the sacred corners of American homes." In 1919, the U.S. government launched an all-out attack on the Communist ("Red") menace. In the same year, disgruntled socialists founded the American Communist Party, but it attracted only a handful of members, who spent most of their time arguing the fine points of doctrine, not manufacturing bombs. However,

Russian-born Emma Goldman. Before the war, Goldman's passionate support of labor strikes, women's rights, and birth control had made her a symbol of radicalism. In 1919, after she spent time in prison for denouncing military conscription, J. Edgar Hoover, the director of the Justice Department's Radical Division, ordered her deported.

The effort to rid the country of alien radicals was matched by efforts to crush troublesome citizens. Law enforcement officials and vigilante groups joined hands against so-called Reds. In November 1919 in the rugged lumber town of Centralia, Washington, a menacing crowd gathered in front of the IWW hall. Nervous Wobblies inside opened fire, killing three people. Three IWW members were arrested and later convicted of murder, but another, ex-soldier Wesley Everett, was carried off by the mob, which castrated him, hung him from a bridge, and then riddled his body with bullets. His death was officially ruled a suicide.

the few radicals who did resort to bombs prompted near panic in some quarters. Even mild dissenters faced bullying and threats. Workers seeking better wages and conditions, women and African Americans demanding equal rights, and anyone else pushing for change found the government hurling the epithet "Red" at them. Before the hysteria subsided, the nation witnessed beatings, jailings, and deportations.

The Bolshevik Revolution had endless consequences. In the Soviet Union, it initiated a brutal reign of terror that lasted for more than seven decades. In international politics, it set up a polarity that lasted nearly as long. In a very real sense, the Cold War, which set the United States and the Soviet Union at each other's throats after World War II, began in 1917. America's abortive military intervention against the Bolshevik regime and the Bolsheviks' call for worldwide revolution convulsed relations from the very beginning. In the United States, the rabid antiradicalism of the Red scare threatened traditional American values. Commitment to the protection of dissent succumbed to irrational anticommunism. Even mild reform became tarred with the brush of bolshevism. Although the Red scare quickly withered, the habit of crushing dissent in the name of security would live on. Years later, in the 1950s, when Americans' anxiety mounted and their confidence waned once again, witch-hunts against radicalism reemerged to undermine American democracy.

Vladimir Ilyich Lenin
After the Bolshevik success in Russia in 1917, Lenin became the face of the Communist revolution. His call for workers everywhere to rise against the ruling classes and end capitalism and imperialism sent chills down spines throughout much of Western Europe and the United States. Rather than viewing Lenin as a bloodthirsty monster, however, this dramatic portrait presents him as the courageous hero of the people's revolution.
AP Photo.

America in a Global Context

1. Why did U.S.-Bolshevik relations get off to such a rocky start? Were harsh relations the result of certain policy decisions or inherent in the clashing value systems?

2. In the United States, is there an inevitable tension between national security and free expression? Why or why not?

Connect to the Big Idea

C How did Lenin's and Wilson's aspirations for the post-WWI world differ?

Public institutions joined the attack on civil liberties. Local libraries removed dissenting books. Schools fired unorthodox teachers. Police shut down radical newspapers. State legislatures refused to seat elected representatives who professed socialist ideas. And in 1919, Congress removed its lone socialist representative, Victor Berger, on the pretext that he was a threat to national safety.

That same year, the Supreme Court provided a formula for restricting free speech. In upholding the conviction of socialist Charles Schenck for publishing a pamphlet urging resistance to the draft during wartime (*Schenck v. United States*), the Court established a "clear and present danger" test. Such utterances as Schenck's during a time of national peril, Justice Oliver Wendell Holmes wrote, were equivalent to shouting "Fire!" in a crowded theater.

In 1920, the assault on civil liberties provoked the creation of the American Civil Liberties Union (ACLU), which was dedicated to defending an individual's constitutional rights. One of the ACLU's founders, Roger Baldwin, declared, "So long as we have enough people in this country willing to fight for their rights, we'll be called a democracy." The ACLU championed the targets of Attorney General Palmer's campaign—politically radical immigrants, trade unionists, socialists and Communists, and antiwar activists who still languished in jail.

The Red scare eventually collapsed because of its excesses. In particular, the antiradical campaign lost credibility after Palmer warned that radicals were planning to celebrate the Bolshevik Revolution with a nationwide wave of violence on May 1, 1920. Officials called out state militias, mobilized bomb squads, and even placed machine-gun nests at major city intersections. When May 1 came and went without a single disturbance, the public mood turned from fear to scorn.

The Great Migrations of African Americans and Mexicans

Before the Red scare lost steam, the government raised alarms about the loyalty of African Americans. A Justice Department investigation concluded that Reds were fomenting racial unrest among blacks. Although the report was wrong about Bolshevik influence, it was correct in noticing a new stirring among African Americans.

In 1900, nine of every ten blacks still lived in the South, where poverty, disfranchisement, segregation, and violence dominated their lives. A majority of black men worked as dirt-poor tenants or sharecroppers, while many black women worked in the homes of whites as domestics. Whites remained committed to keeping blacks down. "If we own a good farm or horse, or cow, or bird-dog, or yoke of oxen," a black sharecropper in Mississippi observed in 1913, "we are harassed until we are bound to sell, give away, or run away, before we can have any peace in our lives."

The First World War provided African Americans with the opportunity to escape the South's cotton fields and kitchens. When war channeled almost 5 million American workers into military service and almost ended European immigration, northern industrialists turned to black labor. Black men found work in northern steel mills, shipyards, munitions plants, railroad yards, automobile factories, and mines. From 1915 to 1920, a half million blacks

(approximately 10 percent of the South's black population) boarded trains bound for Philadelphia, Detroit, Cleveland, Chicago, St. Louis, and other industrial cities.

Thousands of migrants wrote home to tell family and friends about their experiences in the North. One man announced proudly that he had recently been promoted to "first assistant to the head carpenter." He added, "I should have been here twenty years ago. I just begin to feel like a man. . . . My children are going to the same school with the whites and I don't have to [h]umble to no one. I have registered—will vote the next election and there ain't any 'yes sir'—it's all yes and no and Sam and Bill."

But the North was not the promised land. Black men stood on the lowest rungs of the labor ladder. Jobs of any kind proved scarce for black women, and most worked as domestic servants as they did in the South. The existing black middle class sometimes shunned the less educated, less sophisticated rural southerners crowding into northern cities. Many whites, fearful of losing jobs and status, lashed out against the new migrants. Savage race riots ripped through two dozen northern cities. The worst occurred in July 1917 when a mob of whites invaded a section of East St. Louis, Illinois, and murdered 39 people. In 1918, the nation witnessed 96 lynchings of blacks, some of them decorated war veterans still in uniform.

Still, most black migrants stayed in the North and encouraged friends and family to follow. By 1940, more than one million blacks had left the South, profoundly changing their own lives and the course of the nation's history. Black enclaves such as Harlem in New York and the South Side of Chicago, "cities within cities," emerged in the North. These assertive communities provided a foundation for black protest and political organization in the years ahead.

At nearly the same time, another migration was under way in the American Southwest. Between 1910 and 1920, the Mexican-born population in the United States soared from 222,000 to 478,000. Mexican immigration resulted from developments on both sides of the border. When Mexicans revolted against dictator Porfirio Díaz in 1910, initiating a ten-year civil war, migrants flooded northward. In the United States, the Chinese Exclusion Act of 1882 and later the disruption of World War I cut off the supply of cheap foreign labor and caused western employers in the expanding rail, mining, construction, and

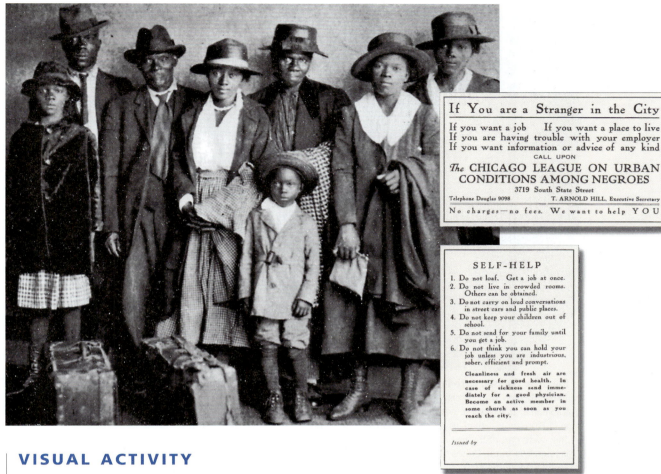

If You are a Stranger in the City

If you want a job   If you want a place to live
If you are having trouble with your employer
If you want information or advice of any kind
CALL UPON
The CHICAGO LEAGUE ON URBAN
CONDITIONS AMONG NEGROES
3719 South State Street
Telephone Douglas 9098   T. ARNOLD HILL, Executive Secretary
No charges—no fees. We want to help YOU

SELF-HELP

1. Do not loaf. Get a job at once.
2. Do not live in crowded rooms. Others can be obtained.
3. Do not carry on loud conversations in street cars and public places.
4. Do not keep your children out of school.
5. Do not send for your family until you get a job.
6. Do not think you can hold your job unless you are industrious, sober, efficient and prompt.

Cleanliness and fresh air are necessary for good health. In case of sickness send immediately for a good physician. Become an active member in some church as soon as you reach the city.

Issued by

VISUAL ACTIVITY

African Americans Migrate North

Wearing their Sunday best and carrying the rest of what they owned in two suitcases, this southern family waits to board a northern-bound train in 1912. In Chicago, the League on Urban Conditions among Negroes, which became the Urban League, sought to ease the transition of southern blacks to life in the North by distributing cards such as the one shown here (front and back). Photo: Schomburg Center, NYPL/Art Resource, NY; card: Arthur and Graham Aldis papers (APF_0001_0006a-01 a/b), Special Collections, The University Library, University of Illinois at Chicago.

READING THE IMAGE: This photograph captures the migration of a family. How many generations are represented?

CONNECTIONS: Why do you suppose the "Self-Help" card emphasizes hard work, cleanliness, and quiet?

agricultural industries to look south to Mexico for workers.

Like immigrants from Europe and black migrants from the South, Mexicans in the American Southwest dreamed of a better life. And like the others, they found both opportunity and disappointment. Wages were better than in Mexico, but life in the fields, mines, and factories was hard, and living conditions—in boxcars, labor camps, or urban barrios—were dismal. Signs warning "No Mexicans Allowed"

increased rather than declined. Mexicans were considered excellent prospects for manual labor but not for citizenship. By 1920, ethnic Mexicans made up about three-fourths of California's farm laborers.

Among Mexican Americans, some of whom had lived in the Southwest for more than a century, *los recién llegados* (the recent arrivals) encountered mixed reactions. One Mexican American expressed this ambivalence: "We are all Mexicans anyway because the gueros [Anglos]

Mexican Women Arriving in El Paso, 1911
These Mexican women, carrying bundles and wearing traditional shawls, try to get their bearings upon arriving in El Paso, Texas—the Ellis Island for Mexican immigrants. They were part of the first modern wave of Mexican immigration to the United States. Women like them found work in the fields, canneries, and restaurants of the Southwest, as well as at home taking in sewing, laundry, and boarders. New Mexico State University Library, Archives and Special Collections.

Candidate	Electoral Vote	Popular Vote	Percent of Popular Vote
Warren G. Harding (Republican)	404	16,143,407	60.5
James M. Cox (Democrat)	127	9,130,328	34.2
Eugene V. Debs (Socialist)	0	919,799	3.4

MAP 22.6
The Election of 1920

treat us all alike." But he also called for immigration quotas because the recent arrivals drove down wages and incited white prejudice that affected all ethnic Mexicans.

Despite friction, large-scale immigration into the Southwest meant a resurgence of the Mexican cultural presence, which became the basis for greater solidarity and political action for the ethnic Mexican population. In 1929 in Texas, Mexican Americans formed the League of United Latin American Citizens.

Postwar Politics and the Election of 1920

A thousand miles away in Washington, D.C., President Woodrow Wilson, bedridden and paralyzed, ignored the mountain of domestic troubles—labor strikes, the Red scare, race riots, immigration backlash—and insisted that the 1920 election would be a "solemn referendum"
on the League of Nations. Dutifully, the Democratic nominees for president, James M. Cox of Ohio, and for vice president, Franklin Delano Roosevelt of New York, campaigned on Wilson's international ideals. The Republican Party chose the handsome, gregarious Warren Gamaliel Harding, senator from Ohio.

Harding found the winning formula when he declared that "America's present need is not heroics, but healing; not nostrums [questionable remedies] but normalcy." But what was "normalcy"? Harding explained: "By 'normalcy' I don't mean the old order but a regular steady order of things. I mean normal procedure, the natural way, without excess." Eager to put wartime crusades and postwar strife behind them, voters responded by giving Harding the largest presidential victory ever: 60.5 percent of the popular vote and 404 out of 531 electoral votes (Map 22.6). Harding's election lifted the national pall, signaling a new, more easygoing era.

REVIEW   How did the Red scare contribute to the erosion of civil liberties after the war?

► Conclusion: Troubled Crusade

America's experience in World War I was exceptional. For much of the world, the Great War produced great destruction—blackened fields, ruined factories, and millions of casualties. But in the United States, war and prosperity marched hand in hand. America emerged from the war with the strongest economy in the world and a position of international preeminence.

Still, the nation paid a heavy price both at home and abroad. American soldiers and sailors encountered unprecedented horrors—submarines, poison gas, machine guns—and more than 100,000 died. But rather than redeeming the sacrifice of George Browne and others as Woodrow Wilson promised, the peace that followed the armistice tarnished it.

At home, rather than permanently improving working conditions, advancing public health, and spreading educational opportunity, as progressives had hoped, the war threatened to undermine the achievements of the previous two decades. Moreover, rather than promoting democracy, the war bred fear, intolerance, and repression that led to a crackdown on dissent and a demand for conformity. Reformers could count only woman suffrage as a permanent victory.

Woodrow Wilson had promised more than anyone could deliver. Progressive hopes of extending democracy and liberal reform nationally and internationally were dashed. In 1920, a bruised and disillusioned society stumbled into a new decade. The era coming to an end had called on Americans to crusade and sacrifice. The new era promised peace, prosperity, and a good time.

See the Selected Bibliography for this chapter in the Appendix.

22 Chapter Review

MAKE IT STICK

Go online and use LearningCurve to see what you know. Then review the key terms and answer the questions.

KEY TERMS

Triple Alliance (p. 617)
Triple Entente (p. 617)
Lusitania (p. 618)
Bolshevik (p. 620)
American Expeditionary Force (AEF) (p. 621)
Eighteenth Amendment (prohibition) (p. 625)
Nineteenth Amendment (woman suffrage) (p. 628)
Fourteen Points (p. 632)
League of Nations (p. 632)
Versailles treaty (p. 634)
Red scare (p. 637)
Schenck v. United States (p. 639)

REVIEW QUESTIONS

1. Why did President Wilson fail to maintain U.S. neutrality during World War I? (pp. 617–619)

2. How did the AEF contribute to the defeat of Germany? (pp. 620–623)

3. How did progressive ideals fare during wartime? (pp. 624–629)

4. Why did the Senate fail to ratify the Versailles treaty? (pp. 633–635)

5. How did the Red scare contribute to the erosion of civil liberties after the war? (pp. 637–640)

MAKING CONNECTIONS

1. Why did the United States at first resist intervening in World War I? Why did it later retreat from this policy and send troops?

2. How did World War I contribute to progressive-influenced domestic developments? Did they endure in peacetime?

3. After the war, what factors drove the conservative reaction in American politics, most vividly in the labor upheaval and Red scare that swept the nation? How did they shape the postwar political spectrum?

4. What drove African American and Mexican migration north? How did the war facilitate these changes? How was this migration significant?

LINKING TO THE PAST

1. How did America's experience in World War I compare with its experience during the Spanish-American War, its previous war abroad? Discuss the decision to go to war in each case, the military aspects, and the outcome. (See chapter 20.)

2. How did the experience of America's workers during World War I compare with their experience in the previous three decades? Consider the composition of the workforce, wages, conditions, and labor's efforts to organize. (See chapters 20 and 21.)

23
From New Era to Great Depression
1920–1932

CONTENT LEARNING OBJECTIVES

After reading and studying this chapter, you should be able to:

- Determine how business and industry contributed to a "new era" and the growth of mass consumer and popular culture in the 1920s.

- Describe the effectiveness of Prohibition in the 1920s.

- Explain how the "new woman" and the "new Negro" challenged social norms. Explain how some artists and intellectuals rejected America's mass culture.

- Evaluate ways in which social changes met with resistance, particularly in rural areas and how this affected the presidential election of 1928.

- Describe the various factors that contributed to the Great Crash of 1929. Explain President Hoover's response and why it proved to be inadequate.

- Describe how the Great Depression affected the lives of ordinary Americans.

MODEL T FORD
When Henry Ford introduced the Model T in 1908, Americans thought of automobiles as toys of the rich. But by the 1920s, millions of Americans owned Fords, and their lives were never the same. Division of Work & Industry, Archives Center, National Museum of American History, Smithsonian Institution.

AMERICANS IN THE 1920s CHEERED HENRY FORD AS AN AUTHENTIC American hero. When the decade began, he had already produced six million automobiles; by 1927, the figure reached fifteen million. In 1920, a Ford car cost $845; in 1928, the price was less than $300, within range of most of the country's skilled workingmen. Henry Ford put America on wheels, and in the eyes of most Americans he was an honest man who made an honest car: basic, inexpensive, and reliable.

Born in 1863 on a farm in Dearborn, Michigan, Ford at sixteen fled rural life for Detroit, where he became a journeyman machinist. In 1893, he put together one of the first successful gasoline-driven carriages in the United States. His ambition, he said, was to "make something in quantity." The product he chose reflected American restlessness. "Everybody wants to be someplace he ain't," Ford declared. "As soon as he gets there he wants to go right back." In 1903, Ford gathered twelve workers in a 250-by-50-foot shed and created the Ford Motor Company.

Ford's early cars were custom-made one at a time. By 1914, his cars were being built along a continuously moving assembly line. Workers bolted on parts brought to them by cranes and conveyor belts. In 1920, one car rolled off the Ford assembly line every minute; in 1925, one appeared every ten seconds. Ford made only one kind of car, the Model T, which became synonymous with mass production. Throughout the rapid expansion of the automotive industry, the Ford Motor Company remained the industry leader, peaking in 1925, when it outsold all its rivals combined (Map 23.1).

When Ford began his rise, progressive critics condemned the industrial giants of the nineteenth century as "robber barons" who lived in luxury while reducing their workers to wage slaves. Ford, however, identified with the common folk and saw himself as the benefactor of average Americans. But like the age in which he lived, Ford was more complex and more contradictory than this simple image suggests.

A man of genius whose compelling vision of modern mass production led the way in the 1920s, Ford was also cranky, tight fisted, and mean-spirited. He hated Jews and Catholics, bankers and doctors, and liquor and tobacco, and his money allowed him to act on his prejudices. His automobile plants made him a billionaire, but their regimented assembly lines reduced workers to near robots. On the cutting edge of modern technology, Ford nevertheless remained nostalgic about rural values. He sought to revive the past in Greenfield Village, where he relocated buildings from a bygone era, including his parents' farmhouse. His museum contrasted sharply with the roaring Ford assembly plant at River Rouge. Yet if Americans remained true to their agrarian past and managed to be modern and scientific at the same time, Ford insisted, all would be well.

Tension between traditional values and modern conditions lay at the heart of the conflicted 1920s. For the first time, more Americans lived in urban than in rural areas, and cities seemed to harbor everything rural people opposed. While millions admired urban America's sophisticated new style and consumer products, others condemned postwar society for its loose morals and vulgar materialism. The Ku Klux Klan and other champions of an older America resorted to violence as well as words when they chastised the era's "new woman," "New Negro," and surging immigrant populations. Those who sought to damn the tide of change proposed prohibition, Protestantism, and patriotism.

The public, disillusioned with the outcome of World War I, turned away from the Christian moralism and idealism of the Progressive Era. In the 1920s, Ford and businessmen like him replaced political reformers such as Theodore Roosevelt and Woodrow Wilson as the models of progress. The U.S. Chamber of Commerce crowed, "The American businessman is the most influential person in the nation." The fortunes of the era rose, then in 1929 crashed, according to the values and practices of the business community. When prosperity collapsed, the nation entered the most serious economic depression of all time.

MAP ACTIVITY

Map 23.1   Auto Manufacturing

By the mid-1920s, the massive coal and steel industries of the Midwest had made that region the center of the new automobile industry. A major road-building program by the federal government carried the thousands of new cars produced each day to every corner of the country.

READING THE MAP: How many states had factories involved with the manufacture of automobiles? In what regions was auto manufacturing concentrated?

CONNECTIONS: On what related industries did auto manufacturing depend? How did the integration of the automobile into everyday life affect American society?

Number of factories producing auto parts, materials, and vehicles

■ 8–20   ■ 21–50   ■ 51–100   ■ More than 100   — Major roads

▶ The New Era

Once Woodrow Wilson left the White House, energy flowed away from government activism and civic reform and toward private economic endeavor. The rise of a freewheeling economy and a heightened sense of individualism caused Secretary of Commerce Herbert Hoover to declare that America had entered a "New Era," one of many labels used to describe the complex 1920s. Some terms focus on the decade's high-spirited energy and cultural change: Roaring Twenties, Jazz Age, Flaming Youth. Others echo the rising importance of money—Dollar Decade, Golden Twenties—or reflect the sinister side of gangster profiteering—Lawless Decade. Still others emphasize the lonely confusion of the Lost Generation and the stress and anxiety of the Aspirin Age.

America in the twenties was many things, but President Calvin Coolidge got at an essential truth when he declared: "The business of America is business." Politicians and diplomats proclaimed business the heart of American civilization as they promoted its products at home and abroad. Average men and women bought into the idea that business and its wonderful goods were what made America great, as they snatched up the flood of new consumer items American factories sent forth. Nothing caught Americans' fancy more powerfully than the automobile.

A Business Government

Republicans controlled the White House from 1921 to 1933. The first of the three Republican presidents was Warren Gamaliel Harding, the Ohio senator who in his 1920 campaign called for a "return to normalcy," by which he meant the end of public crusades and a return to private pursuits. Harding appointed a few men of real stature to his cabinet. Herbert Hoover, the former head of the wartime Food Administration, became secretary of commerce. But wealth and friendship also counted: Andrew Mellon, one of the richest men in America, became secretary of the treasury, and Harding handed out jobs to his friends, members of his old "Ohio gang." This curious combination of merit and cronyism made for a disjointed administration.

When Harding was elected in 1920 (see chapter 22, Map 22.6), the unemployment rate hit 20 percent, the highest ever up to that point. The bankruptcy rate of farmers increased tenfold. Harding pushed measures to regain national prosperity—high tariffs to protect American businesses, price supports for agriculture, and

CHRONOLOGY

1920	• Prohibition begins. • Women get the vote. • Warren G. Harding elected president.
1921	• Sheppard-Towner Act. • Congress restricts immigration.
1922	• Five-Power Naval Treaty.
1923	• Equal Rights Amendment defeated in Congress. • Harding dies; Vice President Calvin Coolidge becomes president.
1924	• Dawes Plan. • Coolidge elected president. • Johnson-Reed Act. • Indian Citizenship Act.
1925	• Scopes trial.
1927	• Charles Lindbergh flies nonstop across the Atlantic. • Nicola Sacco and Bartolomeo Vanzetti executed.
1928	• Kellogg-Briand pact. • Herbert Hoover elected president.
1929	• St. Valentine's Day murders. • Agricultural Marketing Act. • Publication of *Middletown*. • Stock market collapses.
1930	• Congress authorizes $420 million for public works projects. • Hawley-Smoot tariff.
1931	• Scottsboro Boys arrested. • Harlan County, Kentucky, coal strike.
1932	• River Rouge factory demonstration. • Reconstruction Finance Corporation established. • National Farmers' Holiday Association formed.

the dismantling of wartime government control over industry in favor of unregulated private business. "Never before, here or anywhere else," the U.S. Chamber of Commerce said proudly, "has a government been so completely fused with business."

Harding's policies to boost American enterprise made him very popular, but ultimately his small-town congeniality and trusting ways did him in. Some of his friends in the Ohio gang were up to their necks in lawbreaking. Three of Harding's appointees would go to jail. Interior Secretary Albert Fall was convicted of accepting bribes of more than $400,000 for leasing oil reserves on public land in Teapot Dome, Wyoming, and "**Teapot Dome**" became a synonym for political corruption.

On August 2, 1923, when Harding died from a heart attack, Vice President Calvin Coolidge became president. Coolidge, who once said that "the man who builds a factory builds a temple, the man who works there worships there," continued and extended Harding's policies of promoting business and limiting government. Secretary of the Treasury Andrew Mellon reduced the government's control over the economy and cut taxes for corporations and wealthy individuals. New rules for the Federal Trade Commission severely restricted its power to regulate business. Secretary of Commerce Herbert Hoover hedged government authority by encouraging trade associations that ideally would keep business honest and efficient through voluntary cooperation.

Coolidge found an ally in the Supreme Court. For years, the Court had opposed federal regulation of hours, wages, and working conditions on the grounds that such legislation was the proper concern of the states. With Coolidge, the Court found ways to curtail a state's ability to regulate business. It ruled against closed shops—businesses where only union members could be employed—while confirming the right of owners to form exclusive trade associations. In 1923, the Court declared unconstitutional the District of Columbia's minimum-wage law for women, asserting that the law interfered with the freedom of employer and employee to make labor contracts. The Court and the president attacked government intrusion in the free market, even when the prohibition of government regulation threatened the welfare of workers.

The election of 1924 confirmed the defeat of the progressive principle that the state should take a leading role in ensuring the general welfare. To oppose Coolidge, the Democrats nominated John W. Davis, a corporate lawyer whose conservative views differed little from Republican principles. Only the Progressive Party and its presidential nominee, Senator Robert La Follette of Wisconsin, offered a genuine alternative. When La Follette championed labor unions, regulation of business, and protection of civil liberties, Republicans coined the slogan "Coolidge or Chaos." Voters chose Coolidge in a landslide. Coolidge was right when he declared, "This is a business country, and it wants a business government." What was true of the government's relationship to business at home was also true abroad.

VISUAL ACTIVITY

"Teapot Dome Scandal, 1924"
This cartoon shows Washington officials madly racing down the road to the White House in a desperate attempt to outrun the steamroller of scandal. Teapot Dome was only one example of the rampant corruption that tainted the Harding administration. The Granger Collection, New York.

READING THE IMAGE: How does the artist portray the fleeing politicians—as dignified public servants or something else?

CONNECTIONS: Why didn't Teapot Dome and the other scandals doom Republican chances in the elections of 1924?

Promoting Prosperity and Peace Abroad

After orchestrating the Senate's successful effort to block U.S. membership in the League of Nations, Henry Cabot Lodge boasted, "We have torn Wilsonism up by the roots." But repudiation of Wilsonian internationalism and rejection of collective security through the League of Nations did not mean that the United States retreated into isolationism. The United States emerged from World War I with its economy intact and enjoyed a decade of stunning growth. New York replaced London as the center of world finance, and the United States became the world's chief creditor. Economic involvement in the world and the continuing chaos in Europe made withdrawal impossible.

One of the Republicans' most ambitious foreign policy initiatives was the Washington Disarmament Conference, which convened in 1921 to establish a global balance of naval power. Secretary of State Charles Evans Hughes shaped the **Five-Power Naval Treaty of 1922** committing Britain, France, Japan, Italy, and the United States to a proportional reduction of naval forces. The treaty led to the scrapping of more than two million tons of warships, by far the world's greatest success in disarmament. By fostering international peace, Hughes also helped make the world a safer place for American trade.

A second major effort on behalf of world peace came in 1928, when Secretary of State Frank Kellogg joined French foreign minister Aristide Briand to produce the Kellogg-Briand pact. Nearly fifty nations signed the solemn pledge to renounce war and settle international disputes peacefully.

But Republican administrations preferred private-sector diplomacy to state action. With the blessing of the White House, a team of American financiers led by Charles Dawes swung into action when Germany suspended its war reparation payments in 1923. Impoverished, Germany was staggering under the massive bill of $33 billion presented by the victorious Allies in the Versailles treaty. When Germany failed to meet its annual payment, France occupied Germany's industrial Ruhr Valley, creating the worst international crisis since the war. In 1924, the Dawes Plan halved Germany's annual reparation payments, initiated fresh American loans to Germany, and caused the French to retreat from the Ruhr. Although the United States failed to join the League of Nations, it continued to exercise significant economic and diplomatic influence abroad. These Republican successes overseas helped fuel prosperity at home.

Automobiles, Mass Production, and Assembly-Line Progress

The automobile industry emerged as the largest single manufacturing industry in the nation. Henry Ford shrewdly located his company in Detroit, knowing that key materials for his automobiles were manufactured in nearby states (see Map 23.1). Keystone of the American economy, the automobile industry not only employed hundreds of thousands of workers directly but also brought whole industries into being—filling stations, garages, fast-food restaurants, and "guest cottages" (motels). The need for tires, glass, steel, highways, oil, and refined gasoline for automobiles provided millions of related jobs. By 1929, one American in four found employment directly or indirectly in the automobile industry. "Give us our daily bread" was no longer addressed to the Almighty, one commentator quipped, but to Detroit.

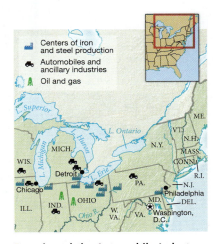

Detroit and the Automobile Industry in the 1920s

Automobiles changed where people lived, what work they did, how they spent their leisure, even how they thought. Hundreds of small towns decayed because the automobile enabled rural people to bypass them in favor of more distant cities and towns. In cities, streetcars began to disappear as workers moved to the suburbs and commuted to work along crowded highways. Nothing shaped modern America more than the automobile, and efficient mass production made the automobile revolution possible.

Mass production by the assembly-line technique became standard in almost every factory, from automobiles to meatpacking to cigarettes. To improve efficiency, corporations reduced assembly-line work to the simplest, most repetitive tasks. Changes on the assembly line and in management, along with technological advances, significantly boosted overall efficiency. Between 1922 and 1929, productivity in manufacturing increased 32 percent. Average wages, however, increased only 8 percent.

VISUAL ACTIVITY

Colorado Filling Station

By 1929, when Conoco (Continental Oil Company) produced this lavish map featuring Colorado's spectacular mountains, nearly every oil company was supplying road maps as part of its campaign to boost tourism. This appealing drive-through station is a far cry from the first retail outlets for gas—blacksmith shops and hardware stores, the same places individuals bought kerosene for their lamps. Because motorists did not trust what they could not see, companies in the 1910s introduced glass-cylinder, gravity-flow gas pumps. Courtesy, History Colorado.

READING THE IMAGE: What does this road map and accompanying image of a gravity-flow gasoline pump tell us about American consumer culture on the eve of the Great Depression?

CONNECTIONS: Does the road map accurately reflect the economic direction of the U.S. economy in 1929?

Industries also developed programs for workers that came to be called **welfare capitalism**. Some businesses improved safety and sanitation inside factories. They also instituted paid vacations and pension plans. Welfare capitalism encouraged loyalty to the company and discouraged traditional labor unions. One labor organizer in the steel industry bemoaned the success of welfare capitalism. "So many workmen here had been lulled to sleep by the company union, the welfare plans, the social organizations fostered by the employer," he declared, "that they had come to look upon the employer as their protector, and had believed vigorous trade union organization unnecessary for their welfare."

Consumer Culture

Mass production fueled corporate profits and national economic prosperity. During the 1920s, per capita income increased by a third, the cost of living stayed the same, and unemployment remained low. But the rewards of the economic boom were not evenly distributed. Americans who labored with their hands inched ahead, while white-collar workers enjoyed significantly more spending money and more leisure time to spend it. Mass production of a broad range of new products—automobiles, radios, refrigerators, electric irons, washing machines—produced a consumer goods revolution.

In this new era of abundance, more people than ever conceived of the American dream in terms of the things they could acquire. *Middletown* (1929), a study of the inhabitants of Muncie, Indiana, revealed that Muncie had become, above all, "a culture in which everything hinges on money." Moreover, faced with technological and organizational change beyond their comprehension, many citizens had lost confidence in their ability to play an effective role in civic affairs. More and more they became passive consumers, deferring to the supposed expertise of leaders in politics and economics.

The rapidly expanding business of advertising stimulated the desire for new products and attacked the traditional values of thrift and saving. Advertising linked material goods to the fulfillment of every spiritual and emotional need. Americans increasingly defined and measured their social status, and indeed their personal worth, on the yardstick of material possessions. Happiness itself rode on owning a car and choosing the right cigarettes and toothpaste. (See "Visualizing History," page 652.)

By the 1920s, the United States had achieved the physical capacity to satisfy Americans' material wants (Figure 23.1). The economic problem shifted from production to consumption: Who would buy the goods flying off American assembly lines? One solution was to expand America's markets in foreign countries, and government and business joined in that effort. Another solution to the problem of consumption was to expand the market at home.

Henry Ford realized early on that "mass production requires mass consumption." He understood that automobile workers not only produced cars but would also buy them if they made enough money. "One's own employees ought to be one's own best customers," Ford said. In 1914, he raised wages in his factories to $5 a day, more than twice the going rate. High wages made for workers who were more loyal and more exploitable, and high wages returned as profits when workers bought Fords.

Many people's incomes, however, were too puny to satisfy the growing desire for consumer goods. The solution was installment buying—a

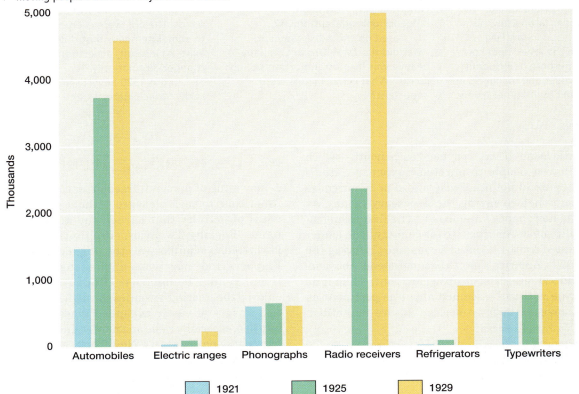

FIGURE 23.1   Production of Consumer Goods, 1921–1929
Transportation, communications, and entertainment changed the lives of consumers in the 1920s. Laborsaving devices for the home were popular, but the vastly greater sales of automobiles and radios showed that consumerism was powerful in moving people's attention beyond their homes.

Advertising in a Consumer Age

Just as American business changed dramatically from the 1880s to the 1920s, so, too, did advertising. Businesses in the New Era continued to promote their products, of course, but they sought to attract customers in very different ways. Here are two images that illustrate the changes.

Look at the Estey Organ Company advertisement from 1885. First and foremost, the ad features the company's huge industrial complex—two red brick kilns with smoke belching from their chimneys, surrounded by lumberyards and milling, woodworking, metalworking, and varnishing shops. Indeed, Estey was the world's largest organ manufacturer, selling 1,800 organs a year around the globe.

The men who presided over Estey's impressive manufacturing operation—founder Jason Estey, his son Julius, and his son-in-law Levi Fuller—appear in the lower right corner. What is the purpose of including the company founder and managers in the advertisement? In the other corner,

Estey Organ Company

the ad imagines an Estey organ in the parlor of a well-to-do family that gathers to hear one of its accomplished daughters play. How might this image influence potential customers?

Based on this advertisement, what did the Estey Organ Company believe was its most important selling factor? What other factors were important?

By the 1920s, companies employed advertising specialists who created ads that would appeal to the consumer's anxieties and personal needs. The ads were even designed to stimulate needs that didn't yet exist. As a result, advertisements changed dramatically.

In this 1929 advertisement for Lucky Strike cigarettes, the factory

little money down, a payment each month—which allowed people to purchase expensive items they could not otherwise afford or to purchase items before saving the necessary money. As one newspaper announced, "The first responsibility of an American to his country is no longer that of a citizen, but of a consumer." During the 1920s, America's motto became spend, not save. Old values—"Use it up, wear it out, make it do or do without"—seemed about as pertinent as a horse and buggy. American culture had shifted.

REVIEW How did the spread of the automobile transform the United States?

▶ The Roaring Twenties

A new ethic of personal freedom excited many Americans to seek pleasure without guilt in a whirl of activity that earned the decade the name "Roaring Twenties." Prohibition made lawbreakers of millions of otherwise decent folk. Flappers and "new women" challenged traditional gender boundaries. Other Americans enjoyed the Roaring Twenties through the words and images of vastly expanded mass communication, especially radio and movies. In America's big cities, particularly New York, a burst of creativity produced the "New Negro," who confounded and disturbed white Americans. The

Lucky Strike

the quoted slogans, the text, and the footnote. What health claims are made? Does the ad's small print undermine the main message?

Before the 1920s, advertising often focused on production. Even small businesses presented themselves as powerful and efficient producers of consumer goods such as organs, furniture, and stoves. In the consumer society of the 1920s, companies sought to teach Americans to judge themselves and others by what they bought, rather than by what they produced.

SOURCE: Organ ad: The Pease Collection of Historical Instruments; Lucky Strike ad: Picture Research Consultants & Archives.

Questions for Analysis

1. Why do you think the size of the factory was featured so prominently in the 1885 Estey Organ advertisement?

2. To whom is the 1929 Lucky Strike advertisement appealing?

3. How might an ad for Lucky Strike have looked if it had been done in 1885?

4. What might an Estey Organ Company ad have looked like in the 1920s?

Connect to the Big Idea

◉ How did the rise of mass production translate into the rise of mass consumption and mass culture?

and its owners are nowhere to be found. Instead, it offers a woman in a bathing suit. What does she have to do with cigarettes? Millions of Americans smoked billions of cigarettes in the 1920s. In countless tobacco advertisements, smoking promised instant maturity, sophistication, and worldliness. What is this ad's promise to smokers?

Look at the various elements of the ad—the headline, the pictures,

"Lost Generation" of writers, profoundly disillusioned with mainstream America's cultural direction, fled the country.

Prohibition

Republicans generally sought to curb the powers of government, but the twenties witnessed a great exception to this rule when the federal government implemented one of the last reforms of the Progressive Era: the Eighteenth Amendment, which banned the manufacture and sale of alcohol and took effect in January 1920 (see "The Progressive Stake in the War" in chapter 22). Drying up the rivers of liquor that Americans consumed, supporters of **prohibition** claimed, would eliminate crime, boost production, and lift the nation's morality. Prohibition would destroy the saloon, which according to a leading dry was the "most fiendish, corrupt and hell-soaked institution that ever crawled out of the slime of the eternal pit." Instead, prohibition initiated a fourteen-year orgy of lawbreaking unparalleled in the nation's history.

The Treasury Department agents charged with enforcing prohibition faced a staggering task. Although they smashed more than 172,000 illegal stills in 1925 alone, loopholes in the law almost guaranteed failure. Sacramental wine was permitted, allowing fake clergy to party with

Confiscated Liquor
Revenue agents, some holding rifles, proudly display the bootleg liquor they have confiscated during a raid in Washington, D.C., in 1922. The carefully staged scene and the photographer on the roof indicate that the agents were eager to publicize their success. Successes like this were common during prohibition, but the criminalization of liquor could not permanently defeat "Satan in a bottle." The Granger Collection, New York.

bogus congregations. Farmers were allowed to ferment their own "fruit juices." Doctors and dentists could prescribe liquor for medicinal purposes.

In 1929, a Treasury agent in Indiana reported intense local resistance to enforcement of prohibition. "Conditions in most important cities very bad," he declared. "Lax and corrupt public officials great handicap . . . prevalence of drinking among minor boys and the . . . middle or better classes of adults." The "speakeasy," an illegal nightclub, became a common feature of the urban landscape. Speakeasies' dance floors led to the sexual integration of the formerly all-male drinking culture, changing American social life forever. Detroit, probably America's wettest city, was home to more than 20,000 illegal drinking establishments, making the alcohol business the city's second-largest industry, behind automobile manufacturing.

Eventually, serious criminals took over the liquor trade. During the first four years of prohibition, Chicago witnessed more than two hundred gang-related killings as rival mobs struggled for control of the lucrative liquor trade. The most notorious event came on St. Valentine's Day 1929, when Alphonse "Big Al" Capone's Italian-dominated mob machine-gunned seven members of a rival Irish gang. Capone's bootlegging empire brought in $95 million a year, when a chicken dinner cost 5 cents. Federal authorities finally sent Capone to prison for income tax evasion. "I violate the

Prohibition law—sure," he told a reporter. "Who doesn't? The only difference is, I take more chances than the man who drinks a cocktail before dinner."

Americans overwhelmingly favored the repeal of the Eighteenth Amendment, the "noble experiment," as Herbert Hoover called prohibition. In 1931, a panel of distinguished experts reported that the experiment had failed. The social and political costs of prohibition outweighed the benefits. Prohibition fueled criminal activity, corrupted the police, demoralized the judiciary, and caused ordinary citizens to disrespect the law. In 1933, the nation ended prohibition, making the Eighteenth Amendment the only constitutional amendment to be repealed.

The New Woman

Of all the changes in American life in the 1920s, none sparked more heated debate than the alternatives offered to the traditional roles of women. Increasing numbers of women worked and went to college, defying older gender norms. Even mainstream magazines such as the *Saturday Evening Post* began publishing stories about young, college-educated women who drank gin cocktails, smoked cigarettes, and wore skimpy dresses and dangly necklaces. Before the Great War, the **new woman** dwelt in New York City's bohemian Greenwich Village, but afterward the mass media brought her into middle-class America's living rooms.

When the Nineteenth Amendment, ratified in 1920, granted women the vote, feminists felt liberated and expected women to reshape the political landscape. A Kansas woman declared, "I went to bed last night a *slave*[;] I awoke this morning a *free woman*." Women began pressuring Congress to pass laws that especially concerned women, including measures to protect women in factories and grant federal aid to schools. Black women lobbied particularly for federal courts to assume jurisdiction over the crime of lynching. But women's only significant national legislative success came in 1921 when Congress enacted the Sheppard-Towner Act, which extended federal assistance to states seeking to reduce high infant mortality rates.

A number of factors helped thwart women's political influence. Male domination of both political parties, the rarity of female candidates, and lack of experience in voting, especially among recent immigrants, kept many women away from the polls. In some places, male-run election machines actually disfranchised women, despite the Nineteenth Amendment. In the South, poll taxes, literacy tests, and outright terrorism continued to decimate the vote of African Americans, men and women alike.

Most important, rather than forming a solid voting bloc, feminists divided. Some argued for women's right to special protection; others demanded equal protection. The radical National Woman's Party fought for an Equal Rights Amendment that stated flatly: "Men and women shall have equal rights throughout the United States." The more moderate League of Women Voters feared that the amendment's wording threatened state laws that provided women special protection, such as preventing them from working on certain machines. Put before Congress in 1923, the Equal Rights Amendment went down to defeat, and radical women were forced to work for the causes of birth control, legal equality for minorities, and the end of child labor through other means.

Economically, more women worked for pay—approximately one in four by 1930—but they clustered in "women's jobs." The proportion of women working as secretaries, stenographers, and typists skyrocketed. Women almost monopolized the occupations of librarian, nurse, elementary school teacher, and telephone operator. Women also represented 40 percent of salesclerks by 1930. More female white-collar workers meant that fewer women were interested in protective legislation for women; new women wanted salaries and opportunities equal to men's.

Increased earnings gave working women more buying power in the new consumer culture. A stereotype soon emerged of the flapper, so called because of the short-lived fad of wearing unbuckled galoshes. The flapper had short "bobbed" hair, and she wore lipstick and rouge. She spent freely on the latest styles—dresses with short skirts, drop waists, bare arms, and no petticoats—and she danced all night to wild jazz. As F. Scott Fitzgerald described her in his novel *This Side of Paradise* (1920), she was "lovely and expensive and about nineteen."

The new woman both reflected and propelled the modern birth control movement. Margaret

VISUAL ACTIVITY

"The Girls' Rebellion"

The August 1924 cover of *Redbook*, a popular women's magazine, portrays the kind of postadolescent girl who was making respectable families frantic. Flappers scandalized their middle-class parents by flouting the old moral code. This young woman sports the "badges of flapperhood," including what one critic called an "intoxication of rouge." Fictionalized, emotion-packed stories such as this brought the new woman into every woman's home. Picture Research Consultants & Archives.

READING THE IMAGE: In addition to the rouge, what else identifies this young woman as a flapper?

CONNECTIONS: In addition to flappers, what other developments in the 1920s challenged America's traditional values?

25 Cents

August 1924

THE RED BOOK MAGAZINE

"The Girls' Rebellion"

A startling and revealing story of "the younger generation" that everyone should read

Was There a Sexual Revolution in the 1920s?

"Cigarette in hand, shimmying to the music of the masses, the New Woman and the New Morality have made their theatric debut upon the modern scene," lamented one commentator in 1926. A moral chasm, the *Atlantic* magazine declared, had opened between the generations. The old and young in America "were as far apart in point of view, codes, and standards as if they belonged to different races." Charlotte Perkins Gilman represented many older feminists who were disappointed with the outcome of recent advances for women: "It is sickening to see so many of the newly freed abusing that freedom in a mere imitation of masculine weakness and vice." Older Americans wholeheartedly agreed that the younger generation was in full-fledged revolt against traditional standards of morality and that

Heroes and Heroines

Two kinds of women look up adoringly at two kinds of 1920s heroes. A wholesome image is seen on the left in a 1927 cover of *People's Popular Monthly* magazine. The outdoor girl, smartly turned out in her raccoon coat and pennant, flatters a naive college football hero. On the right, Vilma Banky kneels imploringly before the hypnotic gaze of the movies' greatest heartthrob, Rudolph Valentino. Magazine: Picture Research Consultants & Archives; Poster: Mary Evans/FEATURE PICTURES INC/Ronald Grant/Everett Collection.

Sanger, the crusading pioneer for contraception during the Progressive Era (see "Radical Alternatives" in chapter 21), restated her principal conviction in 1920: "No woman can call herself free until she can choose consciously whether she will or will not be a mother." By shifting strategy in the twenties, Sanger courted the conservative American Medical Association; linked birth control with the eugenics movement, which advocated limiting reproduction among "undesirable" groups; and thus made contraception a respectable subject for discussion.

America was in danger of going to hell in a hand basket.

Critics had, it seemed, plenty of evidence. Between newspapers, movies, and magazines, even the small towns of America were "literally saturated with sex," one observer complained. Flappers and college coeds claimed the privileges of men, smoking cigarettes, drinking from hip flasks, and staying out all night. When eight hundred college women met to discuss life on campus and what "nice girls" should do, they concluded, "Learn temperance in petting, not abstinence." Anxious observers counseled intervention. The Ohio legislature debated whether to prohibit any "female over fourteen years of age" from wearing a "skirt which does not reach to that part of the foot known as the instep." The *Ladies' Home Journal* urged "legal prohibition" of jazz dancing.

But were the concerned observers correct? Was there really a sexual revolution in the 1920s? The principal movers of the new morality were youths, and without a doubt young, middle-class men and women felt freer than ever to express openly their feelings about sex. But we must separate the new candor from actual sexual behavior. Although solid evidence is difficult to come by, correspondence, diaries, and other personal documents; physicians' records; divorce proceedings; advice literature; and a few early sex surveys provide important clues.

A good place to begin the investigation is where youth congregated: college campuses. Campus life included a self-conscious ethos of experimentation and innovation, but as students demolished old rules, they also created new ones. One major innovation was "dating"—that is, going out unsupervised rather than receiving callers at home or meeting at church socials. Dating was encouraged by the automobile, that "house of prostitution on wheels," as one juvenile judge in Indiana labeled it. Dating led to a second innovation: "petting," or any sexual activity short of intercourse. One examination of coed behavior at the end of the 1920s found that 92 percent of women admitted engaging in petting.

Like dating, petting represented a significant change in female behavior. But it was not a total rejection of traditional morality because it took place within the search for the ideal marriage partner. There was also a modest increase in premarital sexual intercourse, made possible by the widespread acceptance of contraceptives. But sexual intercourse usually took place between partners who assumed they would marry. The new woman of the 1920s, though freer sexually, continued to focus on romance, marriage, and family.

Did the new sexual behavior mark a drastic change from the past? Evidence of sexual habits before World War I is even more difficult to come by than for the 1920s, but it appears that changes in attitudes and behaviors had been under way for decades. Nineteenth-century Victorian notions of sexless women who felt little or no passion had been eroding since at least the 1890s. A small survey of the sexual practices of middle-class women in the 1890s conducted by Dr. Clelia Duel Mosher, a physician at Stanford University, found that women were enthusiastic about sex and often found satisfaction. The primary ideologues of the sexual revolution, Havelock Ellis, who celebrated female passion, and Sigmund Freud, who stressed the centrality of sex in human endeavor, reached large American audiences before World War I.

Changes in sexual morality, therefore, were evolutionary rather than revolutionary. Still, liberal attitudes and behaviors had their greatest impact in the 1920s. American culture was being remade, and young people, especially women, were at the cutting edge. Now equal at the polling booth, women were also growing more economically independent. Changes in women's political and economic lives were reflected in their sexual attitudes and behaviors. In place of the idea that women were naturally pure, the new morality proclaimed the equality of desire. Only the boldest women rejected a "double standard" (the notion that the sexual behavior of women should be more circumscribed than that of men), but many jettisoned notions of female submission, obedience, and endless childbearing. Charges that the giddy flapper and her partner were bringing down American civilization were overblown, but young women certainly were changing the culture.

Questions for Consideration

1. What is the evidence for the contention that changes in sexual behavior in the 1920s were more evolutionary than revolutionary?

2. How did changes in women's political and economic lives affect their sexual behaviors?

Connect to the Big Idea

Ⓒ What was the relationship of the emergence of the "new woman" in the 1920s and the sexual habits of young women?

Flapper style and values spread from coast to coast through films, novels, magazines, and advertisements. New women challenged American convictions about separate spheres for women and men, the double standard of sexual conduct, and Victorian ideas of proper female appearance and behavior. (See "Historical Question," above.) Although only a minority of American women became flappers, all women, even those who remained at home, heard about girls gone wild and felt the great changes of the era.

The New Negro

The 1920s witnessed the emergence not only of the "new woman" but also of the "New Negro." African Americans who challenged the caste system that confined dark-skinned Americans to the lowest levels of society confronted whites who insisted that race relations would not change. As cheers for black soldiers faded after their return from World War I, African Americans faced grim days of economic hardship and race riots.

The prominent African American intellectual W. E. B. Du Bois and the National Association for the Advancement of Colored People (NAACP) aggressively pursued the passage of a federal antilynching law to counter mob violence against blacks in the South. At the same time, however, many disillusioned poor urban blacks turned to the new leadership of the Jamaican-born visionary Marcus Garvey, who urged African Americans to rediscover the heritage of Africa, take pride in their own achievements, and maintain racial purity by avoiding miscegenation. In 1917, Garvey launched the Universal Negro Improvement Association (UNIA) to help African Americans gain economic and political independence entirely outside white society. In 1919, the UNIA created its own shipping company, the Black Star Line, to support the "Back to Africa" movement among black Americans. In 1927, the federal government pinned charges of illegal practices on Garvey and deported him to Jamaica. Nevertheless, the issues Garvey raised about racial pride, black identity, and the search for equality persisted, and his legacy remains at the center of black nationalist thought.

Still, most African Americans maintained hope in the American promise. In New York City, hope and talent came together. The city's black population jumped 115 percent (from 152,000 to 327,000) in the 1920s, and in Harlem in uptown Manhattan an extraordinary mix of black artists, sculptors, novelists, musicians, and poets set out to create a distinctive African American culture that drew on their identities as Americans and Africans. As scholar Alain Locke put it in 1925, they introduced to the world the "**New Negro**," who rose from the ashes of slavery and segregation to proclaim African Americans' creative genius.

The emergence of the New Negro came to be known as the Harlem Renaissance. Building on the independence and pride displayed by black soldiers during the war, black artists sought to defeat the fresh onslaught of racial discrimination and violence with poems, paintings, and plays. "We younger Negro artists . . . intend to express our individual dark-skinned selves without fear or shame," poet Langston Hughes said of the Harlem Renaissance. "If white people are pleased, we are glad. If they are not, it doesn't matter. We know we are beautiful. And ugly, too."

The Harlem Renaissance produced dazzling talent. Black writer James Weldon Johnson, who in 1903 had written the Negro national anthem, "Lift Every Voice," wrote *God's Trombones* (1927), in which he expressed the wisdom and beauty of black folktales from the South. The poetry of Langston Hughes, Claude McKay, and Countee Cullen celebrated the vitality of life in Harlem. Zora Neale Hurston's novel *Their Eyes Were Watching God* (1937) explored the complex passions of black people in a southern community. Black painters, led by Aaron Douglas, linked African art, which had recently inspired European modernist artists, to the concept of the New Negro.

Despite such vibrancy, Harlem for most whites remained a separate black ghetto known only for its lively nightlife. Fashionable whites crowded into Harlem's segregated nightclubs, the most famous of which was the Cotton Club, where they believed they could hear "real" jazz, a relatively new musical form, in its "natural" surroundings. The vigor of the Harlem Renaissance left a powerful legacy for black Americans, but the creative burst did little in the short run to dissolve the prejudice of white society. (See "Seeking the American Promise," page 660.)

Entertainment for the Masses

In the 1920s, popular culture, like consumer goods, was mass-produced and mass-consumed. The proliferation of movies, radios, music, and sports meant that Americans found plenty to do, and in doing the same things, they helped create a national culture.

Nothing offered escapist delights like the movies. Hollywood, California, discovered the successful formula of combining opulence, sex, and adventure. Admission was cheap, and by 1929, the movies were drawing more than 80 million people in a single week, as many as lived in the entire country. Hollywood created "movie stars," glamorous beings whose every move was tracked by fan magazines. Rudolph Valentino, described as "catnip to women," and Clara Bow, the "It Girl" (everyone knew what *it* was), became household names. Most loved of all was the comic Charlie Chaplin, whose famous character, the wistful Little Tramp, showed an endearing

Duke Ellington Leads His Jazz Band
From 1927 to 1931, the Duke Ellington orchestra was the house band at the Cotton Club in Harlem, where black performers played for white audiences. The photograph captures something of the energy and exuberance that helped make Ellington America's greatest jazz composer and bandleader. ©Bettmann/CORBIS.

inability to cope with the rules and complexities of modern life.

Americans also found heroes in sports. Baseball solidified its place as the national pastime in the 1920s. It remained essentially a game played by and for the working class. In George Herman "Babe" Ruth, baseball had the most cherished free spirit of the time. The rowdy escapades of the "Sultan of Swat" demonstrated that sports offered a way to break out of the ordinariness of everyday life. By "his sheer exuberance," one sportswriter declared, Ruth "has lightened the cares of the world."

The public also fell in love with a young boxer from the grim mining districts of Colorado. As a teenager, Jack Dempsey had made his living hanging around saloons betting he could beat anyone in the house. When he took the heavyweight crown just after World War I, he was revered as the people's champ, a stand-in for the average American who felt increasingly confined by bureaucracy and machine-made culture. In Philadelphia in 1926, a crowd of 125,000 fans saw challenger Gene Tunney pummel and defeat the people's champ.

Football, essentially a college sport, held greater sway with the upper classes. The most famous coach, Knute Rockne of Notre Dame, celebrated football for its life lessons of hard work and teamwork. Let the professors make learning as exciting as football, Rockne advised, and the problem of getting young people to learn would disappear. But in keeping with the times, football moved toward a more commercial spectacle. Harold "Red" Grange, "the Galloping Ghost," led the way by going from stardom at the University of Illinois to the Chicago Bears in the new professional football league.

The decade's hero worship reached its zenith in the celebration of Charles Lindbergh, a young pilot who set out on May 20, 1927, to become the first person to fly nonstop across the Atlantic. Newspapers tagged Lindbergh "the Lone Eagle"— the perfect hero for an age that celebrated individual accomplishment. "Charles Lindbergh," one journalist proclaimed, "is the stuff out of which have been made the pioneers that opened up the wilderness. His are the qualities which we, as a people, must nourish." Lindbergh realized, however, that technical and organizational complexity was fast reducing chances for solitary achievement. Consequently, he titled his book about the flight *We* (1927) to include the machine that had made it all possible.

Another machine—the radio—became crucial to mass culture in the 1920s. The nation's first licensed radio station, KDKA in Pittsburgh, began broadcasting in 1920, and soon American airwaves buzzed with news, sermons, soap operas,

The Quest for Home Ownership in Segregated Detroit

Owning a place of one's own has always been important in America. In the nineteenth century, with the rise of industry and cities, the goal of a family farm gave way to the goal of a single-family house. Home ownership has been widely realized today, with roughly two-thirds of Americans (with the assistance of mortgage companies) owning their own homes.

In the 1920s, decent housing was in short supply in Detroit, America's great boomtown, as thousands poured in to work in Henry Ford's automobile factories. Arriving before World War I, blue-collar German, Irish, and Polish immigrants found homes in working-class neighborhoods scattered around the city center. The property owners resolved to keep their neighborhoods all-white by channeling the great migration of southern blacks into Black Bottom, the downtown ghetto. Although the U.S. Supreme Court had struck down a law mandating segregated housing in 1917, inventive white homeowners created other means to draw racial boundaries. Real estate agents refused to show blacks houses in white neighborhoods. Banks turned down blacks for mortgages. Whites signed restrictive covenants, promising not to sell their homes to blacks. If a black family managed to slip through their defenses, whites resorted to violence.

Dr. Ossian Sweet, a black physician, arrived in Detroit in 1921. He set up his medical practice in Black Bottom and prospered. He soon had the down payment for a home, but he refused to settle his wife and baby daughter in the congested, rat-infested ghetto. In 1925, Sweet bought a substantial bungalow at 2905 Garland Avenue, several blocks inside a working-class white neighborhood. His brother said later, "He wasn't looking for trouble. He just wanted to bring up his little girl in good surroundings." Sweet understood the danger; whites had recently run other black professionals out of their Detroit neighborhoods. "Well, we have decided we are not going to run," Sweet told a friend. "We're not going to look for any trouble, but we're going to be prepared to protect ourselves if trouble arises." When Gladys and Ossian Sweet moved into their home on September 8, 1925, nine friends and family members accompanied them. The moving van that brought their furniture also carried a shotgun, two rifles, six pistols, and four hundred rounds of ammunition.

Hundreds of white men quickly filled the streets, greatly outnumbering the few police who hoped to keep the peace. Shouting that they would send the "niggers" back where they belonged, the mob began throwing rocks, breaking windows, and advancing. Suddenly, gunfire erupted from the second story of the Sweet house, and two white men were shot; one was killed. The police kept the mob away long enough for a paddy wagon to haul the eleven blacks to the police station, where they were all indicted for murder.

Asked why he wanted to move to a white neighborhood, where there was likely to be trouble, Sweet said, "Because I bought the house, and it was my house, and I felt I had a right to live in it." The NAACP, which saw the case as an opportunity to strike a legal blow in favor of self-defense against racial violence, hired Clarence Darrow to defend the accused. Darrow was the most celebrated defense lawyer in the country and fresh from the Scopes trial in Tennessee (see page 664). Darrow told the jury that the facts were simple: "When they defended their home, they were arrested and charged with murder." He reminded the all-white jury that "every man's home is his castle, which even the king may not enter. Every man has a right to kill to defend himself or his family, or others, either in defense of the home, or in defense of themselves." A split jury caused the judge to declare a mistrial. A second trial ended in not guilty verdicts for all the defendants.

Over the next several decades, housing discrimination became entrenched throughout the nation. Blacks succeeded in breaking out of the inner cities and moving into the

sports, comedy, and music. Because they could now reach prospective customers in their own homes, advertisers bankrolled radio's rapid growth. Between 1922 and 1929, the number of radio stations in the United States increased from 30 to 606. In just seven years, homes with radios jumped from 60,000 to a staggering 10.25 million.

The Lost Generation

Some writers and artists felt alienated from America's mass-culture society, which they found shallow, anti-intellectual, and materialistic. Silly movie stars disgusted them. They believed that business culture blighted American life. In their minds, Henry Ford made a poor hero. Young,

Dr. Ossian Sweet and His House
Dr. Ossian Sweet's substantial two-story brick home is listed on the National Register of Historic Places. In September 1925, Sweet tried to move his family into the then all-white Detroit suburb where the house is located. Residents reacted violently, determined to uphold "the present high standards of the neighborhood." Dr. Sweet: Courtesy of the Burton Historical Collection, Detroit Public Library; house: Michigan State Historic Preservation Office.

suburbs, where today more than one-third of African Americans live, but breaching city boundaries did not mean leaving residential segregation behind. Of all the nation's segregated cities, none was more segregated than Detroit. As late as 1963, Martin Luther King Jr. declared: "I have a dream this afternoon that one day right here in Detroit Negroes will be able to buy a house or rent a house anywhere their money will carry them." As for Sweet,

he moved back into his home on Garland Avenue in 1928, but without his wife and daughter, both of whom had died. He stayed in the bungalow for more than twenty-five years, and when he left, the neighborhood around him was still largely white.

Questions for Consideration

1. Why did whites in Sweet's neighborhood oppose his living there?

2. Why didn't the Supreme Court's 1917 decision and Sweet's acquittal end residential segregation in Detroit and other American cities?

Connect to the Big Idea

C What does the case of Ossian Sweet say about the aspirations of middle-class black Americans during the 1920s?

white, and mostly college educated, these expatriates, as they came to be called, felt embittered by the war and renounced the progressives who had promoted it as a crusade. For them, Europe—not Hollywood or Harlem—seemed the place to seek their renaissance.

The American-born writer Gertrude Stein, long established in Paris, remarked famously as

the young exiles gathered around her, "They are the lost generation." Most of the expatriates, however, believed to the contrary that they had finally found themselves. The Lost Generation helped launch the most creative period in American art and literature in the twentieth century. The novelist whose spare, clean style best exemplified the expatriate efforts to make art mirror basic reality was Ernest Hemingway. Admirers found the terse language and hard lessons of his novel *The Sun Also Rises* (1926) to be perfect expressions of a world stripped of illusions.

Many writers who remained in America were exiles in spirit. Before the war, intellectuals had eagerly joined progressive reform movements. Afterward, they were more likely critics of American cultural vulgarity. Novelist Sinclair Lewis in *Main Street* (1920) and *Babbitt* (1922) satirized his native Midwest as a cultural wasteland. Humorists such as James Thurber created outlandish characters to poke fun at American stupidity and inhibitions. And southern writers, led by William Faulkner, explored the South's grim class and race heritage. Worries about

alienation surfaced as well. F. Scott Fitzgerald spoke sadly in *This Side of Paradise* (1920) of a disillusioned generation "grown up to find all Gods dead, all wars fought, all faiths in man shaken."

REVIEW   How did the new freedoms of the 1920s challenge older conceptions of gender and race?

▶ Resistance to Change

Large areas of the country did not share in the wealth of the 1920s. By the end of the decade, 40 percent of the nation's farmers were landless,

MAP ACTIVITY

Map 23.2   The Shift from Rural to Urban Population, 1920–1930

The movement of whites and Hispanics toward urban and agricultural opportunity made Florida, the West, and the Southwest the regions of fastest population growth. By contrast, large numbers of blacks left the rural South to find a better life in the North. Almost all migrating blacks went from the countryside to cities in distant parts of the nation, while white and Hispanic migrants tended to move shorter distances toward familiar places.

READING THE MAP: Which states had the strongest growth? To which cities did southern blacks predominantly migrate?

CONNECTIONS: What conditions in the countryside made the migration to urban areas appealing to many rural Americans? In what social and cultural ways did rural America view itself as different from urban America?

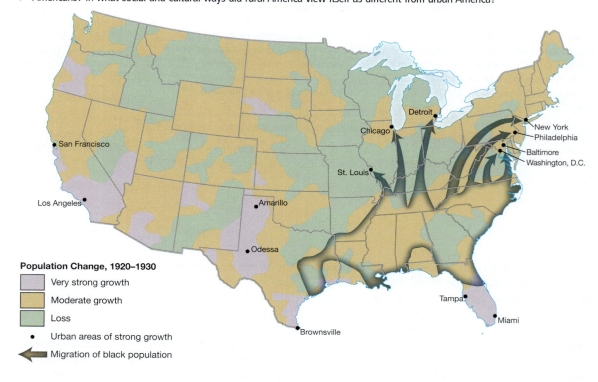

Population Change, 1920–1930

- Very strong growth
- Moderate growth
- Loss
- • Urban areas of strong growth
- ← Migration of black population

and 90 percent of rural homes lacked indoor plumbing, gas, or electricity. Rural America's traditional distrust of urban America turned to despair in the 1920s when the census reported that the majority of the population had shifted to the city (Map 23.2). Urban domination over the nation's political and cultural life and sharply rising economic disparity drove rural Americans in often ugly, reactionary directions.

Cities seemed to stand for everything rural areas stood against. Rural America imagined itself as solidly Anglo-Saxon (despite the presence of millions of African Americans in the South and Mexican Americans, Native Americans, and Asian Americans in the West), and the cities seemed to be filled with undesirable immigrants. Rural America was the home of old-time Protestant religion, and the cities teemed with Catholics, Jews, liberal Protestants, and atheists. Rural America championed old-fashioned moral standards—abstinence and self-denial—while the cities spawned every imaginable vice. In the 1920s, frustrated rural people sought to recapture their country by helping to push through prohibition, dam the flow of immigrants, revive the Ku Klux Klan, defend the Bible as literal truth, and defeat an urban Roman Catholic for president.

Rejecting the Undesirables

Before the war, when about a million immigrants arrived each year, some Americans warned that unassimilable foreigners were smothering the nation. War against Germany and its allies expanded nativist and antiradical sentiment. After the war, large-scale immigration resumed (another 800,000 immigrants arrived in 1921) at a moment when industrialists no longer needed new factory laborers. Returning veterans, as well as African American and Mexican migration, had relieved labor shortages. Moreover, union leaders feared that millions of poor immigrants would undercut their efforts to organize American workers. Rural America's God-fearing Protestants were particularly alarmed that most of the immigrants were Catholic or Jewish. In 1921, Congress responded by severely restricting immigration.

Three years later, Congress very nearly slammed the door shut. The **Johnson-Reed Act** of 1924 limited the number of immigrants to no more than 161,000 a year and established quotas for each European nation. The act revealed the fear and bigotry that fueled anti-immigration legislation. While it cut immigration by more

than 80 percent, it squeezed some nationalities far more than others. Backers of Johnson-Reed, who declared that America had become the "garbage can and the dumping ground of the world," manipulated quotas to ensure entry only to "good" immigrants from western Europe. The law, for example, allowed Great Britain 62,458 entries, but Russia could send only 1,992. Johnson-Reed effectively reversed the trend toward immigration from southern and eastern Europe, which by 1914 had amounted to 75 percent of the yearly total.

The 1924 law also reaffirmed the 1880s legislation barring Chinese immigrants and added Japanese and other Asians to the list of the excluded. But it left open immigration from the Western Hemisphere because farmers in the Southwest demanded continued access to cheap agricultural labor. During the 1920s some 500,000 Mexicans crossed the border. In addition, Congress in 1924 passed the Indian Citizenship Act, which extended suffrage and citizenship to all American Indians.

Rural Americans, who had most likely never laid eyes on a Polish packinghouse worker, a Slovak coal miner, an Armenian sewing machine operator, or a Chinese laundry worker, strongly supported immigration restriction, as did industrialists and labor leaders. The laws of the 1920s marked the end of the era symbolized by the Statue of Liberty's open-armed welcome to Europe's "huddled masses yearning to breathe free."

Antiforeign hysteria climaxed in the trial of two anarchist immigrants from Italy, Nicola Sacco and Bartolomeo Vanzetti. Arrested in 1920 for robbery and murder in South Braintree, Massachusetts, the men were sentenced to death by a judge who openly referred to them as "anarchist bastards." In response to doubts about the fairness of the verdict, a blue-ribbon review committee found the trial judge guilty of a "grave breach of official decorum" but refused to recommend a motion for retrial. When Massachusetts executed Sacco and Vanzetti on August 23, 1927, fifty thousand American mourners followed the caskets, convinced that the men had died because they were immigrants and radicals, not because they were murderers.

The Rebirth of the Ku Klux Klan

The nation's sour antiforeign mood struck a responsive chord in members of the secret society the **Ku Klux Klan**. The Klan first appeared

Sacco and Vanzetti
After the guilty verdicts were announced, American artist Ben Shahn produced a series of paintings to preserve the memory of Nicola Sacco and Bartolomeo Vanzetti, who many immigrants, liberals, and civil libertarians believed were falsely accused and unfairly convicted. Even today, the 1927 executions symbolize for some the shortcomings of American justice. Digital Image Ben Shahn, Bartolomeo Vanzetti and Nicola Sacco, 1931–32. Gouache on paper mounted on board, 10 7/8 x 14 5/8". Gift of Abby Aldrich Rockefeller. Digital Image © The Museum of Modern Art/Licensed by SCALA/Art Resource, NY. Art © Estate of Ben Shahn/Licensed by VAGA, New York, NY.

in the South during Reconstruction to thwart black freedom and expired with the reestablishment of white supremacy (see chapter 16). In 1915, the Klan was reborn at Stone Mountain, Georgia, but when the new Klan extended its targets beyond black Americans, it quickly spread beyond the South. Under a banner proclaiming "100 percent Americanism," the Klan promised to defend family, morality, and traditional American values against the threats posed by blacks, immigrants, radicals, feminists, Catholics, and Jews.

Building on the frustrations of rural America, the Klan in the 1920s spread throughout the nation, almost controlling Indiana and influencing politics in Illinois, California, Oregon, Texas, Louisiana, Oklahoma, and Kansas. In 1926, Klan imperial wizard Hiram Wesley Evans described the assault of modernity: "One by one all our traditional moral standards went by the boards or were so disregarded that they ceased to be binding," he explained. "The sacredness of our Sabbath, of our homes, of chastity, and finally even of our right to teach our own children in schools [represented] fundamental facts and truth torn away from us."

Eventually, social changes, along with lawless excess, crippled the Klan. Immigration restrictions eased the worry about invading foreigners, and sensational wrongdoing by Klan leaders cost it the support of traditional moralists. Grand Dragon David Stephenson of

Indiana, for example, went to jail for the kidnapping and rape of a woman who subsequently committed suicide. Yet the social grievances, economic problems, and religious anxieties of the countryside and small towns remained alive, ready to be ignited.

The Scopes Trial

In 1925 in a Tennessee courtroom, old-time religion and the new spirit of science went head-to-head. The confrontation occurred after several southern states passed legislation against the teaching of Charles Darwin's theory of evolution in the public schools. Scientists and civil liberties organizations clamored for a challenge to the law, and John Scopes, a young biology teacher in Dayton, Tennessee, offered to test his state's ban on teaching evolution. When Scopes came to trial, Clarence Darrow, a brilliant defense lawyer from Chicago, volunteered to defend him. Darrow, an avowed agnostic, took on the prosecution's William Jennings Bryan, three-time Democratic nominee for president, fervent fundamentalist, and symbol of rural America.

The **Scopes trial** quickly degenerated into a media circus. The first trial to be covered live on radio, it attracted a nationwide audience. When, under relentless questioning by Darrow, Bryan declared on the witness stand that he did indeed believe that the world had been created in six days and that Jonah had lived in the belly of a whale, his humiliation in the eyes of most urban observers was complete. Nevertheless, the Tennessee court upheld the law and punished Scopes with a $100 fine. Although fundamentalism won the battle, it lost the war. Baltimore journalist H. L. Mencken had the last word in a merciless obituary for Bryan, who died just a week after the trial ended. Portraying the "monkey trial" as a battle between the country and the city, Mencken flayed Bryan as a "charlatan, a mountebank, a zany without shame or dignity," motivated solely by "hatred of the city men who had laughed at him for so long."

As Mencken's acid prose indicated, Bryan's humiliation was not purely a victory of reason and science. It also revealed the disdain urban people felt for country people and the values they clung to. The Ku Klux Klan revival and the Scopes trial dramatized and inflamed divisions between city and country, intellectuals and the uneducated, the privileged and the poor, the scoffers and the faithful.

Al Smith and the Election of 1928

The presidential election of 1928 brought many of the developments of the 1920s—prohibition, immigration, religion, and the clash of rural and urban values—into sharp focus. Republicans emphasized the economic success of their party's pro-business government and turned to Herbert Hoover, the energetic secretary of commerce and leading public symbol of 1920s prosperity. But because both parties generally agreed that the American economy was basically sound, the campaign turned on social issues that divided Americans.

The Democrats nominated four-time governor of New York Alfred E. Smith. Smith adopted "The Sidewalk of New York" as a campaign theme song and seemed to represent all that rural Americans feared and resented. A child of immigrants, Smith got his start in politics with the help of New York City's Irish-dominated Tammany Hall political machine, to many the epitome of big-city corruption. He denounced immigration quotas, signed New York State's anti-Klan bill, and opposed prohibition, believing that it was a nativist attack on immigrant customs. Prohibition forces dubbed him "Alcohol Al," but Smith's greatest vulnerability in the heartland was his religion. He was the first Catholic to run for president. A Methodist bishop in Virginia denounced Roman Catholicism as "the Mother of ignorance, superstition, intolerance and sin" and begged Protestants not to vote for a candidate who represented "the kind of dirty people that you find today on the sidewalks of New York."

Hoover, who neatly combined the images of morality, efficiency, service, and prosperity, won the election by a landslide (Map 23.3). He received nearly 58 percent of the vote and gained 444 electoral votes to Smith's 87. The only bright spot for Democrats was the nation's cities, which voted Democratic, indicating the rising strength of ethnic minorities, including Smith's fellow Catholics.

REVIEW   How did some Americans resist cultural change?

MAP 23.3
The Election of 1928

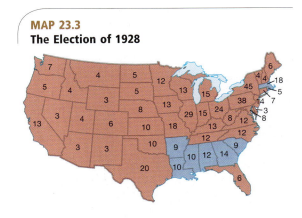

Candidate	Electoral Vote	Popular Vote	Percent of Popular Vote
Herbert Hoover (Republican)	444	21,391,381	57.4
Alfred E. Smith (Democrat)	87	15,016,443	40.3
Norman Thomas (Socialist)	0	881,951	2.3

▶ The Great Crash

At his inauguration in 1929, Hoover told the American people, "Given a chance to go forward with the policies of the last eight years, we shall soon with the help of God be in sight of the day when poverty will be banished from this nation." Those words came back to haunt Hoover when eight months later the prosperity he touted collapsed in the stock market crash of 1929. The nation ended nearly three decades of barely interrupted economic growth. Like much of the world, the United States fell into the most serious economic depression of all time. Hoover's reputation was among the first casualties, along with the reverence for business that had been the hallmark of the New Era.

Herbert Hoover: The Great Engineer

When Hoover became president in 1929, he seemed the perfect choice to lead a prosperous business nation. His rise from poor Iowa orphan to one of the world's most celebrated mining engineers by the time he was thirty personified America's rags-to-riches ideal. His success in managing efforts to feed civilian victims of the fighting during World War I won him acclaim as "the Great Humanitarian" and led Woodrow Wilson to name him head of the Food Administration once the United States entered the war. Hoover's reputation soared even higher as secretary of commerce in the Harding and Coolidge administrations.

Hoover belonged to the progressive wing of his party. "The time when the employer could ride roughshod over his labor[ers] is disappearing with the doctrine of 'laissez-faire' on which it is founded," he declared in 1909. He urged a limited business-government partnership that would manage the sweeping changes Americans were experiencing. Hoover brought a reform agenda to the White House: "We want to see a nation built of home owners and farm owners. We want to see their savings protected. We want to see them in steady jobs. We want to see more and more of them insured against death and accident, unemployment and old age. We want them all secure."

But Hoover also had ideological and political liabilities. Principles that appeared strengths in the prosperous 1920s—individual self-reliance, industrial self-management, and a limited federal government—became straitjackets when economic catastrophe struck. Moreover, Hoover had never held an elected public office, had a poor political touch, and was too thin-skinned to be an effective politician. Even so, most Americans considered him "a sort of superman" able to solve any problem. Prophetically, he confided to a friend his fear that "if some unprecedented calamity should come upon the nation . . . I would be sacrificed

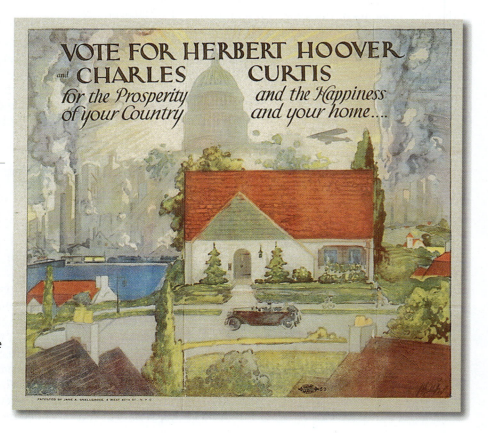

VISUAL ACTIVITY

Hoover Campaign Poster

This poster effectively illustrates Herbert Hoover's 1928 campaign message: Republican administrations in the 1920s had produced middle-class prosperity, complete with a house in the suburbs and the latest automobile. © David J. & Janice L. Frent Collection/CORBIS

READING THE IMAGE: What in the poster reminds voters that Hoover as secretary of commerce had helped create prosperity by promoting industry?

CONNECTIONS: How does the spirit of the poster compare with the actual campaign against the Democrat (and Catholic) Al Smith?

to the unreasoning disappointment of a people who expected too much." The distorted national economy set the stage for the calamity Hoover so feared.

The Distorted Economy

In the spring of 1929, the United States enjoyed a fragile prosperity. Although America had become the world's leading economy, it had done little to help rebuild Europe's shattered economy after World War I. Instead, the Republican administrations demanded that Allied nations repay their war loans, creating a tangled web of debts and reparations that sapped Europe's economic vitality. Moreover, to boost American business, the United States enacted tariffs that prevented other nations from selling their goods to Americans. Fewer sales meant that foreign nations had less money to buy American goods. American banks propped up the nation's export trade by extending credit to foreign customers, deepening their debt.

America's domestic economy was also in trouble. Wealth was badly distributed. Farmers continued to suffer from low prices and chronic indebtedness; the average income of farm families was only $240 per year. The wages of industrial workers, though rising during the decade, failed to keep up with productivity and corporate profits. Overall, nearly two-thirds of all American families lived on less than the $2,000 per year that economists estimated would "supply only basic necessities." In sharp contrast, the wealthiest 1 percent of the population received 15 percent of the nation's income—the amount received by the poorest 42 percent. The Coolidge administration worsened the deepening inequality by cutting taxes on the wealthy.

By 1929, the inequality of wealth produced a serious problem in consumption. The rich spent lavishly, but they could absorb only a tiny fraction of the nation's output. For a time, the new device of installment buying—buying on credit—kept consumer demand up. By the end of the decade, four out of five cars and two out of three radios were bought on credit.

Signs of economic trouble began to appear at mid-decade. New construction slowed down. Automobile sales faltered. Companies began cutting back production and laying off workers. Between 1921 and 1928, as investment and loan opportunities faded, five thousand banks failed, wiping out the life savings of hundreds of thousands.

The Crash of 1929

Even as the economy faltered, Americans remained upbeat. Hoping for even bigger slices of the economic pie, Americans speculated wildly in the stock market on Wall Street. Between 1924 and 1929, the values of stocks listed on the New York Stock Exchange increased by more than 400 percent. Buying stocks on margin—that is, putting up only part of the money at the time of purchase—accelerated. Many people got rich this way, but those who bought on credit could finance their loans only if their stocks increased in value. A Yale economist assured doubters that stock prices had reached "a permanently high plateau." Former president Calvin Coolidge declared that, at current prices, stocks were a bargain.

Finally, in the autumn of 1929, the market hesitated. Investors nervously began to sell their overvalued stocks. The dip quickly became a panic on October 24, the day that came to be known as Black Thursday. More panic selling came on Black Tuesday, October 29, the day the market suffered a greater fall than ever before. In the next six months, the stock market lost six-sevenths of its total value.

It was once thought that the crash alone caused the Great Depression. It did not. In 1929, the national and international economies were already riddled with severe problems. But the dramatic losses in the stock market crash and the fear of risking what was left acted as a great brake on economic activity. The collapse on Wall Street shattered the New Era's confidence that America would enjoy perpetually expanding prosperity.

Hoover and the Limits of Individualism

When the bubble broke, Americans expressed relief that Hoover resided in the White House. Not surprisingly for a man who had been such an active secretary of commerce, Hoover acted quickly to arrest the decline. In November 1929, to keep the stock market collapse from ravaging the entire economy, Hoover called a White House conference of business and labor leaders. He urged them to join in a voluntary plan for recovery: Businesses would maintain production and keep their workers on the job; labor would accept existing wages, hours, and conditions. Within a few months, however, the bargain fell apart. As demand for their products declined, industrialists cut production, sliced wages, and laid off workers. Poorly paid or unemployed workers could not buy much, and their decreased spending led to further cuts in production and further loss of jobs. Thus began the terrible spiral of economic decline.

To deal with the problems of rural America, Hoover got Congress to pass the Agricultural Marketing Act in 1929. The act created the Farm Board, which used its budget of $500 million to buy up agricultural surpluses and thus, it was hoped, raise prices. But prices continued to fall. To help end the decline, Hoover joined conservatives in urging protective tariffs on agricultural goods, and the Hawley-Smoot tariff of 1930 established the highest rates in history. The same year, Congress also authorized $420 million for public works projects to give the unemployed jobs and create more purchasing power. In three years, the Hoover administration nearly doubled federal public works expenditures.

But with each year of Hoover's term, the economy weakened. Tariffs did not end the suffering of farmers because foreign nations retaliated with increased tariffs of their own that crippled American farmers' ability to sell abroad. In 1932, Hoover hoped to help hard-pressed industry with the **Reconstruction Finance Corporation (RFC)**, a federal agency empowered to lend government funds to endangered banks and corporations. The theory was trickle-down economics: Pump money into the economy at the top, and in the long run the people at the bottom would benefit. Or, as one wag put it, "Feed the sparrows by feeding the horses." In the end, very little of what critics of the RFC called a "millionaires' dole" trickled down to the poor.

Meanwhile, hundreds of thousands of workers lost their jobs each month. By 1932, an astounding one-quarter of the American workforce—nearly thirteen million people—were unemployed. There was no direct federal assistance, and state services and private charities were swamped. The depression that began in 1929 devastated much of the world, but no other industrialized nation provided such feeble support to the jobless. Cries grew louder for the federal government to give hurting people relief.

Hoover was no do-nothing president, but there were limits to his conception of the government's proper role in fighting the economic disaster. He compared direct federal aid to the needy to the "dole" in Britain, which he thought destroyed the moral fiber of the chronically unemployed. "Prosperity cannot be restored by raids on the public Treasury,"

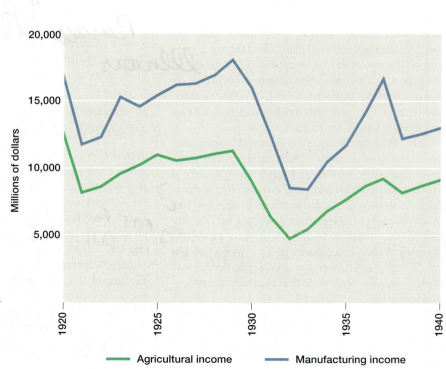

FIGURE 23.2 Manufacturing and Agricultural Income, 1920–1940
After economic collapse, recovery in the 1930s began under New Deal auspices.

Hoover declared. Besides, he said, the poor could rely on their neighbors to protect them "from hunger and cold." In 1931, he allowed the Red Cross to distribute government-owned agricultural surpluses to the hungry. In 1932, he relaxed his principles further to offer small federal loans, not gifts, to the states to help them in their relief efforts. But Hoover's restricted notions of legitimate government action proved vastly inadequate to address the problems of restarting the economy and ending human suffering.

REVIEW   Why did the American economy collapse in 1929?

▶ Life in the Depression

In 1930, suffering on a massive scale set in. Men and women hollow-eyed with hunger grew increasingly bewildered and angry in the face of cruel contradictions. They saw agricultural surpluses pile up in the countryside and knew that their children were going to bed hungry. They saw factories standing idle, yet they knew that they and millions of others were willing to work. The gap between the American people and leaders who failed to resolve these contradictions widened as the depression deepened. By 1932, America's economic problems had created a dangerous social and political crisis.

The Human Toll

Statistics only hint at the human tragedy of the Great Depression. When Hoover took office in 1929, the American economy stood at its peak. When he left in 1933, it had reached its twentieth-century low (Figure 23.2). In 1929, national income was $88 billion. By 1933, it had declined to $40 billion. In 1929, unemployment was 3.1 percent, or 1.5 million workers. By 1933, unemployment stood at 25 percent, almost 13 million workers. In Cleveland, Ohio, 50 percent of the workforce was jobless, and in Toledo, 80 percent. By 1932, more than 9,000 banks had shut their doors, wiping out millions of savings accounts.

Jobless, homeless victims wandered in search of work, and the tramp, or hobo, became one of the most visible figures of the decade.

Hoboes, 1920s
Out-of-work men gather around a fire in front of the train that may have brought them to this unnamed place in the Midwest. With no work at home, many decided to "ride the rails" for free in search of a job. Hoboing was dangerous because of accidents and the violence of the railroad security staffs, nicknamed "bulls." The Granger Collection, New York.

Riding the rails or hitchhiking, a million vagabonds moved southward and westward looking for seasonal agricultural work. Other unemployed men and women, sick or less hopeful, huddled in doorways, overcome, one man remembered, by "helpless despair and submission." Scavengers haunted alleys behind restaurants in search of food. One writer told of an elderly woman who always took off her glasses to avoid seeing the maggots crawling over the garbage she ate. In 1931, four New York City hospitals reported ninety-five deaths from starvation. "I don't want to steal," a Pennsylvania man wrote to the governor, "but I won't let my wife and boy cry for something to eat. . . . How long is this going to keep up? I cannot stand it any longer."

Rural poverty was most acute. Tenant farmers and sharecroppers, mainly in the South, came to symbolize how poverty crushed the human spirit. Eight and a half million people, three million of them black, crowded into cabins without plumbing, electricity, or running water. They subsisted—just barely—on salt pork, cornmeal, molasses, beans, peas, and whatever they could hunt or fish. When economist John Maynard Keynes was asked whether anything like this degradation had existed before, he replied, "Yes, it was called the Dark Ages and it lasted four hundred years."

There was no federal assistance to meet this human catastrophe, only a patchwork of strapped charities and destitute state and local agencies. For a family of four without any income, the best the city of Philadelphia could do was provide $5.50 per week. That was not enough to live on but better than Detroit, which allotted 60 cents a week before the city ran out of money altogether.

The deepening crisis roused old fears and caused some Americans to look for scapegoats. Among the most thoroughly scapegoated were Mexican Americans. During the 1920s, cheap agricultural labor from Mexico flowed legally across the U.S. border, welcomed by the large farmers. In the 1930s, however, the public denounced the newcomers as dangerous aliens who took jobs from Americans. Government officials, most prominently those in Los Angeles County, targeted Mexican residents for deportation regardless of citizenship status. As many as half a million Mexicans and Mexican Americans were deported or fled to Mexico.

The depression deeply affected the American family. Young people postponed marriage. When they did marry, they produced few children. White women, who generally worked in low-paying service areas, did not lose their jobs as often as men who worked in steel, automobile, and other heavy industries. Idle husbands suffered a loss of self-esteem. "Before the depression," one unemployed man reported, "I wore the pants in this family, and rightly so." Jobless, he lost "self-respect" and also "the respect of my children, and I am afraid that I am losing my wife." Employers discriminated against married women workers, but necessity continued to drive women into the marketplace. As a result, by 1940 some 25 percent more women were employed for wages than in 1930.

Denial and Escape

President Hoover assured the American nation that economic recovery was on its way, but the president's optimism was contradicted by makeshift shantytowns, called "Hoovervilles," that sprang up on the edges of America's cities. Newspapers used as cover by those sleeping on the streets were "Hoover blankets." An empty pocket turned inside out was a "Hoover flag," and jackrabbits caught for food were "Hoover hogs." Bitter jokes circulated about the increasingly unpopular president. One told of Hoover asking for a nickel to telephone a friend. Flipping him a dime, an aide said, "Here, call them both."

While Hoover practiced denial, other Americans sought refuge from reality at the movies. Throughout the depression, between 60 million and 75 million people (nearly two-thirds of the nation) scraped together enough change to fill the movie palaces every week. Box office hits such as *Forty-second Street* and *Gold Diggers of 1933* capitalized on the hope that prosperity lay just around the corner. But a few filmmakers grappled with realities rather than escape them. *The Public Enemy* (1931) taught hard lessons about gangsters' ill-gotten gains. Indeed, under the new production code of 1930, designed to protect public morals, all movies had to find some way to show that crime did not pay.

Despite Hollywood's efforts to keep Americans on the right side of the law, crime increased. In the countryside, the plight of people who had lost their farms to bank foreclosures led to the romantic idea that bank robbers were only getting back what banks had stolen from the poor. Woody Guthrie, the populist folksinger from

Oklahoma, captured the public's tolerance for outlaws in his tribute to a murderous bank robber with a choirboy face, "The Ballad of Pretty Boy Floyd":

> Yes, as through this world I've wandered
> I've seen lots of funny men;
> Some will rob you with a six-gun,
> And some with a fountain pen.
> And as through your life you'll travel,
> Yes, as through your life you roam,
> You won't never see an outlaw
> Drive a family from their home.

Working-Class Militancy

The nation's working class bore the brunt of the economic collapse. By 1931, William Green, head of the American Federation of Labor (AFL), had turned militant. "I warn the people who are exploiting the workers," he shouted, "that they can drive them only so far before they will turn on them and destroy them. They are taking no account of the history of nations in which governments have been overturned. Revolutions grow out of the depths of hunger."

The American people were slow to anger, but on March 7, 1932, several thousand unemployed autoworkers massed at the gates of Henry Ford's River Rouge factory in Dearborn, Michigan, to demand work. Pelted with rocks, Ford's private security forces responded with gunfire, killing four demonstrators. Forty thousand outraged citizens turned out for the unemployed men's funerals.

Farmers mounted uprisings of their own. When Congress refused to guarantee farm prices, several thousand farmers created the National Farmers' Holiday Association in 1932, so named because its members planned to take a "holiday" from shipping crops to market. Farm militants also resorted to what they called "penny sales." When banks foreclosed and put farms up for auction, neighbors warned others not to bid, bought the foreclosed property for a few pennies, and returned it to the bankrupt owners. Militancy won farmers little in the way of long-term solutions, but one individual observed that "the biggest and finest crop of revolutions you ever saw is sprouting all over the country right now."

Even those who had proved their patriotism by serving in World War I rose up in protest against the government. In 1932, tens of thousands of unemployed veterans traveled to Washington, D.C., to petition Congress for the immediate payment of the pension (known as a "bonus") that Congress had promised them in 1924. Hoover feared that the veterans would spark a riot and ordered the U.S. Army to evict the **Bonus Marchers** from their camp on the outskirts of the city. Tanks destroyed the squatters' encampments while five hundred soldiers wielding bayonets and tear gas sent the protesters fleeing. The spectacle of the army driving peaceful, petitioning veterans from the nation's capital further undermined public support for the beleaguered Hoover.

The Great Depression—the massive failure of capitalism—catapulted the Communist Party to its greatest size and influence in American history. Some 100,000 Americans—workers, intellectuals, college students—joined the Communist Party in the belief that only an overthrow of the capitalist system could save the victims of the depression. In 1931, the party, through its National Miners Union, moved into Harlan County, Kentucky, to support a strike by brutalized coal miners. Mine owners unleashed thugs against the strikers and eventually beat the miners down. But the Communist Party gained a reputation as the most dedicated and fearless champion of the union cause.

Harlan County Coal Strike, 1931

The left also led the fight against racism. While both major parties refused to challenge segregation in the South, the Socialist Party, led by Norman Thomas, attacked the system of sharecropping that left many African Americans in near servitude. The Communist Party also took action. When nine young black men in Scottsboro, Alabama (the **Scottsboro Boys**), were arrested on trumped-up rape charges in 1931, a team of lawyers sent by the party saved the defendants from the electric chair.

Radicals on the left often sparked action, but protests by moderate workers and farmers occurred on a far greater scale. Breadlines, soup kitchens, foreclosures, unemployment, government violence, and cold despair drove patriotic men and women to question American capitalism. "I am as conservative as any man could be," a Wisconsin farmer explained, "but

"Scottsboro Boys"
Nine black youths, ranging in age from thirteen to twenty-one, were convicted of the rape of two white women and sentenced to death by an all-white jury in March 1931. None was executed, and eventually the state dropped the charges against the youngest four and granted paroles to the others. The last "Scottsboro Boy" left jail in 1950. © Bettmann/Corbis.

any economic system that has in its power to set me and my wife in the streets, at my age—what can I see but red?"

REVIEW   How did the depression reshape American politics?

▶ Conclusion: Dazzle and Despair

In the aftermath of World War I, America turned its back on progressive crusades and embraced conservative Republican politics, the growing influence of corporate leaders, and business values. Changes in the nation's economy—Henry Ford's automobile revolution, mass production, advertising—propelled fundamental change throughout society. Living standards rose,

economic opportunity increased, and Americans threw themselves into private pleasures—gobbling up the latest household goods and fashions, attending baseball and football games and boxing matches, gathering around the radio, and going to the movies. As big cities came to dominate American life, the culture of youth and flappers became the leading edge of what one observer called a "revolution in manners and morals." At home in Harlem and abroad in Paris, American literature, art, and music flourished.

For many Americans, however, none of the glamour and vitality had much meaning. Instead of seeking thrills at the speakeasies, plunging into speculation on Wall Street, or escaping abroad, the vast majority struggled to earn a decent living. Blue-collar America did not participate fully in white-collar prosperity. Rural America was almost entirely left out of the Roaring Twenties. Country folk, deeply suspicious and profoundly discontented, championed prohibition, revived the Klan, attacked immigration, and defended old-time Protestant religion.

The crash of 1929 and the depression that followed starkly revealed the economy's crises of international trade and consumption. Hard times swept high living off the front pages of the nation's newspapers. Different images emerged: hoboes hopping freight trains, strikers confronting police, malnourished sharecroppers staring blankly into the distance, empty apartment buildings alongside cardboard shantytowns, and mountains of food rotting in the sun while guards with shotguns chased away the hungry.

The depression hurt everyone, but the poor were hurt most. As farmers and workers sank into aching hardship, businessmen rallied around Herbert Hoover to proclaim that private enterprise would get the country moving again. But things fell apart, and Hoover faced increasingly radical opposition. Membership in the Socialist and Communist Parties surged, and more and more Americans contemplated desperate measures. By 1932, the depression had nearly brought the nation to its knees. America faced its greatest crisis since the Civil War, and citizens demanded new leaders who would save them from the "Hoover Depression."

See the Selected Bibliography for this chapter in the Appendix.

23 Chapter Review

MAKE IT STICK

 **LearningCurve**

Go online and use LearningCurve to see what you know. Then review the key terms and answer the questions.

KEY TERMS

Teapot Dome (p. 648)
Five-Power Naval Treaty of 1922 (p. 649)
welfare capitalism (p. 650)
prohibition (p. 653)
new woman (p. 654)
New Negro (p. 658)
Johnson-Reed Act (p. 663)
Ku Klux Klan (p. 663)
Scopes trial (p. 664)
Reconstruction Finance Corporation (RFC) (p. 668)
Bonus Marchers (p. 671)
Scottsboro Boys (p. 671)

REVIEW QUESTIONS

1. How did the spread of the automobile transform the United States? (pp. 645–646, 649–651)

2. How did the new freedoms of the 1920s challenge older conceptions of gender and race? (pp. 652–662)

3. How did some Americans resist cultural change? (pp. 662–665)

4. Why did the American economy collapse in 1929? (pp. 665–669)

5. How did the depression reshape American politics? (pp. 669–671)

MAKING CONNECTIONS

1. What drove popular opinion in the 1920s to unrestrained confidence in American business? How did it influence Republicans' approach to governance and the development of the American economy in the 1920s?

2. Americans' encounters with the wealth and increased personal freedom characteristic of the 1920s varied greatly. Why did some embrace the era's changes, while others resisted them?

3. How did shifting government policy contribute to both the boom of the 1920s and the bust of 1929?

4. How did Americans attempt to lessen the impact of the Great Depression?

LINKING TO THE PAST

1. How did America's experience in World War I—both at home and abroad—help shape the 1920s? (See chapter 22.)

2. How did attitudes toward government in the Progressive Era differ from those in the 1920s? (See chapter 21.)

24 The New Deal Experiment

1932–1939

CONTENT LEARNING OBJECTIVES

After reading and studying this chapter, you should be able to:

- Explain which issues shaped the presidential campaign of 1932 and how the candidates' strategies differed. Determine the significance of Roosevelt's victory.

- Analyze which factors united New Deal reformers and what kinds of policies they endorsed. Describe the initial reforms enacted during Roosevelt's first one hundred days in office.

- Recount why critics resisted the New Deal.

- Explain how the Second New Deal moved the country toward a welfare state and describe the kinds of programs reformers proposed. Evaluate why some Americans were left out of the New Deal.

- Identify the final phase of the New Deal and why it ultimately reached a deadlock.

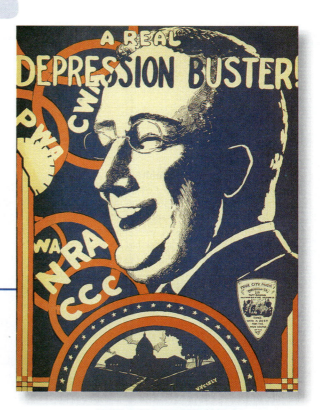

NEW DEAL PRESIDENTIAL CAMPAIGN POSTER

This 1936 poster proclaims President Franklin D. Roosevelt a "Real Depression Buster," without mentioning his name. The acronyms on the poster refer to the New Deal programs that exemplified Roosevelt's commitment to an activist government.
© David J. & Janice L. Frent Collection /CORBIS.

IN MARCH 1936, FLORENCE OWENS PILED HER SEVEN children into her old Hudson. They had been picking beets in southern California, near the Mexican border, but the harvest was over now. Owens headed north where she hoped to find work picking lettuce. About halfway there, her car broke down. She coasted into a labor camp of more than two thousand migrant workers who were hungry and out of work. They had been attracted by advertisements of work in the pea fields, only to find the crop ruined by a heavy frost. Owens set up a lean-to shelter and prepared food for her family while two of her sons worked on the car. They ate half-frozen peas from the field and small birds the children killed. Owens recalled later, "I started to cook dinner for my kids, and all the little kids around the camp came in. 'Can I have a bite? . . .' And they was hungry, them people was."

Florence Owens was born in 1903 in Oklahoma, then Indian Territory. Both of Florence's parents were Cherokee. When she was seventeen, Florence married Cleo Owens, a farmer who moved his growing family to California, where he worked in sawmills. Cleo died of tuberculosis in 1931, leaving Florence a widow with six young children.

Florence began to work as a farm laborer in California's Central Valley to support herself and her children. She picked cotton, earning about $2 a day. "I'd leave home before daylight and come in after dark," she explained. "We just existed!" To survive, she worked nights as a waitress, making "50-cents a day and the leftovers." Sometimes, she remembered, "I'd carry home two water buckets full" of leftovers to feed her children.

Like tens of thousands of other migrant laborers, Owens followed the crops, planting, cultivating, and harvesting as jobs opened up in the fields along the West Coast from California to Oregon and Washington. Joining Owens and other migrants—many of whom were Mexicans and Filipinos—were Okie refugees from the Dust Bowl, the large swath of Great Plains states that suffered drought, failed crops, and foreclosed mortgages during the 1930s.

Soon after Florence Owens fed her children at the pea pickers' camp, a car pulled up, and a woman with a camera got out and began to take photographs of Owens. The woman was Dorothea Lange, a photographer employed by a New Deal agency to document conditions among farmworkers in California. Lange snapped six photos of Owens, and climbed back in her car and headed to Berkeley. Owens and her family, their car now repaired, drove off to look for work in the lettuce fields.

Lange's last photograph of Owens, subsequently known as *Migrant Mother*, became an icon of the desperation among Americans that President Franklin Roosevelt's New Deal sought to alleviate. While *Migrant Mother* became Dorothea Lange's most famous photograph, Florence Owens continued to work in the fields, "ragged, hungry, and broke," as a San Francisco newspaper noted.

Unlike Owens, her children, and other migrant workers, many Americans received government help from Roosevelt's New Deal initiatives to provide relief for the needy, to speed economic recovery, and to reform basic economic and governmental institutions. Roosevelt's New Deal elicited bitter opposition from critics on the right and the left, and it failed to satisfy fully its own goals of relief, recovery, and reform. But within the Democratic Party, the New Deal energized a powerful political coalition that helped millions of Americans withstand the privations of the Great Depression. In the process, the federal government became a major presence in the daily lives of most American citizens.

Florence Owens and Children
This classic photograph of migrant farm laborer Florence Owens and her children was taken in 1936 in the labor camp of a pea field in California by New Deal photographer Dorothea Lange. The photo depicts the privations common among working people during the depression, but it also evokes a mother's leadership, dignity, and affection, qualities that helped shelter her family from poverty and joblessness. Library of Congress.

▶ Franklin D. Roosevelt: A Patrician in Government

Unlike the millions of impoverished Americans, Franklin Roosevelt came from a wealthy and privileged background that contributed to his optimism, self-confidence, and vitality. He drew on these personal qualities in his political career to bridge the economic, social, and cultural chasm that separated him from the struggles of ordinary people like Florence Owens. During the twelve years he served as president (1933–1945), many elites came to hate him as a traitor to his class, while millions more Americans in his New Deal coalition, especially the hardworking poor and dispossessed, revered him because he cared about them and their problems.

The Making of a Politician

Born in 1882, Franklin Delano Roosevelt grew up on his father's leafy estate at Hyde Park on the Hudson River, north of New York City. Roosevelt prepared for a career in politics, hoping to follow in the political footsteps of his fifth cousin, Theodore Roosevelt. In 1905 Franklin married his distant cousin, Eleanor Roosevelt, and Theodore Roosevelt—the current president of the United States and Eleanor's uncle—gave the bride away. Unlike cousin Teddy, Franklin Roosevelt sought his political fortune in the Democratic Party. In 1920, he catapulted to the second spot on the national Democratic ticket as the vice presidential candidate of presidential nominee James M. Cox. Although Cox lost the election (see "Postwar Politics and the Election of 1920" in chapter 22), Roosevelt's energetic campaigning convinced Democratic leaders that he had a bright future.

In the summer of 1921, at the age of thirty-nine, Roosevelt caught polio, which paralyzed both his legs. For the rest of his life, he wore heavy steel braces, and he could walk a few steps only by leaning on another person. Tireless physical therapy helped him regain his vitality and intense desire for high political office, although he carefully avoided being photographed in the wheelchair he used routinely.

After his polio attack, Roosevelt frequented a polio therapy facility at Warm Springs, Georgia. There, he got to know southern Democrats, which helped make him a rare political creature: a New Yorker from the Democratic Party's urban and

CHRONOLOGY

1933
- Franklin D. Roosevelt becomes president.
- Roosevelt's "the Hundred Days" launches the New Deal.
- Roosevelt's four-day "bank holiday."
- Federal Emergency Relief Administration created.

1934
- Securities and Exchange Commission created.
- Upton Sinclair loses California governorship bid.
- American Liberty League founded.
- Dr. Francis Townsend devises Old Age Revolving Pension scheme.
- Indian Reorganization Act.

1935
- Works Progress Administration created.
- Wagner Act.
- Committee for Industrial Organization founded.
- Social Security Act.
- Father Charles Coughlin begins National Union for Social Justice.

1936
- Franklin Roosevelt reelected by a landslide.

1937
- Sit-down strike at General Motors plant in Flint, Michigan.
- Roosevelt's court-packing legislation defeated.
- Economic recession.

1938
- Second Agricultural Adjustment Act.
- Fair Labor Standards Act.
- Congress rejects antilynching bill.

immigrant wing who got along with whites from the party's entrenched southern wing.

By 1928, Roosevelt had recovered sufficiently to campaign for governor of New York, and he squeaked out a victory. As governor of the nation's most populous state, Roosevelt showcased his activist policies, which became a dress rehearsal for his presidency.

As the Great Depression spread hard times throughout the nation, Governor Roosevelt believed that government should intervene to protect citizens from economic hardships rather than wait for the law of supply and demand to improve the economy. According to the laissez-faire views of many conservatives—especially Republicans, but also numerous Democrats—the depression simply represented market forces separating strong survivors from weak losers. Unlike Roosevelt, conservatives believed that government help for the needy sapped individual initiative and impeded the self-correcting forces of the market by rewarding people for losing the economic struggle to survive. Roosevelt lacked a full-fledged counterargument to these conservative claims, but he sympathized with the plight of poor people. "To these unfortunate citizens," he proclaimed, "aid must be extended by governments, not as a matter of charity but as a matter of social duty. . . . [No one should go] unfed, unclothed, or unsheltered."

To his supporters, Roosevelt seemed to be a leader determined to attack the economic crisis without deviating from democracy—unlike the fascist parties gaining strength in Europe—or from capitalism—unlike the Communists in power in the Soviet Union. (See "Beyond America's Borders," page 680.) Roosevelt's ideas about how to revive the economy were vague. A prominent journalist described Roosevelt in 1931 as "a kind of amiable boy scout . . . who, without any important qualifications for the office, would very much like to be president." Roosevelt's many supporters appreciated his energy and his conviction that government should do something to help Americans climb out of the economic abyss, and they propelled him into the front ranks of the national Democratic Party.

The Election of 1932

Democrats knew that Herbert Hoover's unpopularity gave them a historic opportunity to recapture the White House in 1932. Since Abraham Lincoln's election, Republicans had occupied the White House three-fourths of the time, a trend Democrats hoped to reverse. Democrats, however, had to overcome warring factions that divided the party by region, religion, culture, and commitment to the status quo. The southern, native-born, white, rural, Protestant,

VISUAL ACTIVITY

Roosevelt Campaigning
This photo of Franklin Roosevelt on the campaign trail in rural Georgia in October 1932 displays the candidate's support for ordinary Americans. The carefully posed photo illustrates Roosevelt's attempt to reach across the class divide that separated his patrician upbringing and lifestyle from the experience of the vast majority of Americans who lacked his privileges.
© Hulton-Deutsch Collection/CORBIS.

READING THE IMAGE: How does the photo contrast the lives of rural people with that of the presidential candidate? What is the significance of Roosevelt sitting atop the seat back in the car to shake hands?

CONNECTIONS: Why was it important in the 1932 election for the presidential candidates to seek the support of rural Americans?

conservative wing of the Democratic Party found little common ground with the northern, immigrant, urban, disproportionately Catholic, liberal wing. Eastern-establishment Democratic dignitaries shared few goals with angry farmers and factory workers. Still, this unruly coalition managed to agree on Franklin Roosevelt as its presidential candidate.

In his acceptance speech, Roosevelt vowed to help "the forgotten man at the bottom of the pyramid" with "bold, persistent experimentation." Highlighting his differences with Hoover and the Republicans, he pledged "a new deal for the American people." Few details about what Roosevelt meant by "a new deal" emerged in the presidential campaign. He declared that "the people of America want more than anything else . . . two things: work . . . and a reasonable measure of security . . . for themselves and for their wives and children." Voters decided that whatever Roosevelt's new deal might be, it was better than reelecting Hoover.

Roosevelt won the 1932 presidential election in a historic landslide. He received 57 percent of the nation's votes, the first time a Democrat had won a majority of the popular vote since 1852 (Map 24.1). He amassed 472 electoral votes to Hoover's 59, carrying state after state that had voted Republican for years (Map 24.2). Roosevelt's coattails swept Democrats into control of Congress by large margins. The popular mandate for change was loud and clear.

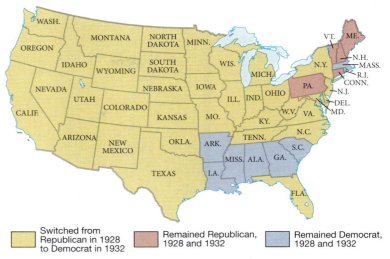

| Switched from Republican in 1928 to Democrat in 1932 | Remained Republican, 1928 and 1932 | Remained Democrat, 1928 and 1932 |

MAP ACTIVITY

Map 24.2 Electoral Shift, 1928–1932

The Democratic victory in 1932 signaled the rise of a New Deal coalition within which women and minorities, many of them new voters, made the Democrats the majority party for the first time in the twentieth century.

READING THE MAP: How many states voted Democratic in 1928? How many states voted Republican in 1932? How many states shifted from Republican to Democratic between 1928 and 1932?

CONNECTIONS: What factions within the Democratic Party opposed Franklin Roosevelt's candidacy in 1932, and why did they do so? To what do you attribute his landslide victory?

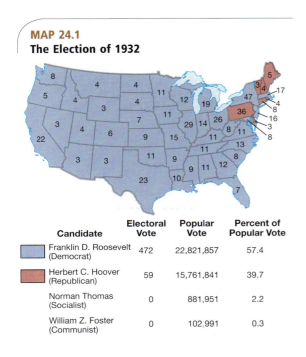

MAP 24.1
The Election of 1932

Candidate	Electoral Vote	Popular Vote	Percent of Popular Vote
Franklin D. Roosevelt (Democrat)	472	22,821,857	57.4
Herbert C. Hoover (Republican)	59	15,761,841	39.7
Norman Thomas (Socialist)	0	881,951	2.2
William Z. Foster (Communist)	0	102,991	0.3

Roosevelt's victory represented the emergence of what came to be known as the **New Deal coalition**. Attracting support from farmers, factory workers, immigrants, city folk, African Americans, women, and progressive intellectuals, Roosevelt launched a realignment of the nation's political loyalties. The New Deal coalition dominated American politics throughout Roosevelt's presidency and remained powerful long after his death in 1945. United less by their ideologies or support for specific policies, voters in the New Deal coalition instead expressed faith in Roosevelt's promise of a government that would somehow change things for the better. Nobody, including Roosevelt, knew exactly what the New Deal would change or whether the changes would revive the nation's ailing economy and improve Americans' lives. But Roosevelt and many others knew that the future of American capitalism and democracy was at stake.

REVIEW Why did Franklin D. Roosevelt win the 1932 presidential election by such a large margin?

Fascism: Adolf Hitler and National Socialism

The Great Depression paralyzed economies around the globe and seemed to demonstrate that capitalism had failed. Individual working people and even businesses could do little to restore prosperity. Only governments had the power to kick-start the economy. Many people believed that democracies such as the United States were too weak and divided to take the necessary steps.

President Franklin Roosevelt optimistically declared that the "democratic faith" of Americans in 1933 was "too sturdy" to turn to "alien ideologies like communism and fascism." But authoritarian, antidemocratic Communist and fascist parties battled to seize control of national governments across Europe. In Germany, Adolf Hitler and his fascist National Socialist Party, also known as the Nazis, came to power in 1933 and improved the economy while crushing democracy.

Hitler rose to power as the leader of a political coalition (composed of Nazis, other conservative parties, and the army) that sought to bring order to Germany in the years following World War I. Hitler stoked discontent by proclaiming his fantasy that an international conspiracy of Communists and financiers—mostly Jews—caused Germany's defeat and was responsible for its postwar woes. During the 1920s, economic distress and political turmoil increased support for Hitler's National Socialist Party among disgruntled veterans, farmers, residents of small towns, shopkeepers, artisans, and other members of the middle and lower-middle classes. The Nazis became the most popular political party by 1932, but they still commanded only one-third of the vote when Hitler became head of the German government in January 1933.

Within a few months, Hitler seized dictatorial power. The Nazis outlawed all political opposition, murdering hundreds and imprisoning more than 100,000 Communists, socialists, union members, and others in the summer of 1933, creating a one-party government. To stifle any lingering dissent, the Nazis seized control of every institution in German society, from local governments to choirs and hiking clubs. They created an elaborate system of spies who punished anyone suspected of questioning Nazi rule. Hitler boasted that "every person should know for all time that if he raises his hand to strike at the [Nazi] State, certain death will be his lot." The Nazi Gestapo (secret police) routinely carried out Hitler's threat, making lawless, life-threatening terror a reality throughout German society.

Hitler's obsessive anti-Semitism made Jews a special target of the Nazi police state. The Nazis organized boycotts of Jewish businesses, destroyed and confiscated Jews' property, purged Jews from civilian and military employment, and passed laws prohibiting marriages between Jews and non-Jews. In reality, Jews accounted for only about 1 percent of the German population, and most of them were fully acculturated members of German society. Hitler claimed, however, that Jews and other "enemies of the people"—such as Gypsies, homosexuals, the chronically ill, and the mentally or physically disabled—polluted the purity of the German race. Hitler and the Nazis relished the persecution of Jews, profited from robbing Jews of their property, and constantly warned about the grave threat Jews posed to Germany—a claim that was completely false.

Hitler's fascist dictatorship had one overriding goal: to rearm Germany and expand German territory until it encompassed all of Europe and much of the Soviet Union. Hitler grandiosely planned a campaign of conquest that would result in the Nazis' thousand-year dominion over the world. He announced in 1933 that "the re-armament of the German people . . . must always and

▶ Launching the New Deal

At noon on March 4, 1933, Americans gathered around their radios to hear the inaugural address of the newly elected president. Roosevelt began by asserting his "firm belief that the only thing we have to fear is fear itself—nameless, unreasoning, unjustified terror which paralyzes needed efforts to convert retreat into advance." He promised "direct, vigorous action," and the first months of his administration, termed "the Hundred Days," fulfilled that promise in a whirlwind of government initiatives that launched the New Deal.

Roosevelt and his advisers had three interrelated objectives: to provide relief to the destitute, especially the one out of four Americans who were unemployed; to foster the economic recovery of farms and businesses,

everywhere stand in the foreground." In consultation with military leaders, the Nazis mobilized German industries to build tanks, ships, aircraft, and weapons as rapidly as possible, all in violation of the terms of the Versailles treaty.

Unlike the Communists in the Soviet Union, fascists in Nazi Germany worked with privately owned industrial firms, which welcomed military production that brought them increased investment, productivity, and profits. The re-armament campaign reduced unemployment from more than 11 million in 1933 to less than 1 million by 1937. Likewise, although the peace treaty limited the size of the German military to 100,000 men, the Nazis had nearly 2.5 million men in uniform by 1939. They financed this massive militarization by forcing civilians to consume less and work more and by extortion and robbery of private wealth.

The Nazis barraged Germany with propaganda designed to promote a cult of Hitler worship. The führer (leader) was portrayed as having almost superhuman powers. The famous Nazi film director Leni Riefenstahl echoed this Hitler cult when she wrote to the führer, "You exceed anything human imagination has the power to conceive, achieving deeds without parallel in the history of mankind." Hitler welcomed such flattery, which masked the underlying terror, lawlessness, and corruption of his fascist dictatorship. The Nazis reduced unemployment and brought a measure of prosperity to many Germans during the 1930s by outlawing democracy, suppressing

Germans Salute a Nazi Parade
This photograph depicts the enthusiasm of German men, women, and children who raise their hands in the Nazi salute as fascist officials parade through the streets of Nuremberg in 1938. Most Germans welcomed the economic prosperity and political order imposed by Hitler and willingly cooperated with the Nazis' reign of terror, persecution, and rearmament. United States Holocaust Memorial Museum.

dissent, imprisoning and murdering tens of thousands of people, and preparing for a war that would leave Germany a smoldering ruin twelve years after Hitler seized power.

America in a Global Context

1. How did Hitler's Nazism compare with Roosevelt's New Deal?

2. To what degree was Roosevelt correct about the "democratic faith" of Americans compared, for example, with that of Germans?

Connect to the Big Idea

C Compared to Hitler, how did Roosevelt view democracy and react to political opposition?

thereby creating jobs and reducing the need for relief; and to reform the government and economy in ways that would reduce the risk of devastating consequences in future economic slumps and thereby strengthen capitalism. The New Deal never fully achieved these goals of relief, recovery, and reform. But by aiming for them, Roosevelt's experimental programs enormously expanded government's role in the nation's economy and society.

The New Dealers

To design and implement the New Deal, Roosevelt needed ideas and people. He convened a "Brains Trust" of economists and other leaders to offer suggestions and advice about the problems facing the nation. No New Dealers were more important than the president and his wife Eleanor. The gregarious president radiated charm and good cheer, giving the New Deal's bureaucratic regulations a benevolent

Fireside Chat
President Roosevelt explained New Deal programs to ordinary Americans in his frequent radio broadcasts. People throughout the nation, like the man shown here, listened to Roosevelt's fireside chats in the quiet of their homes. The chats reassured many Americans that Washington cared about their suffering and was trying to relieve it. Franklin D. Roosevelt Library.

human face. Eleanor Roosevelt became the New Deal's unofficial ambassador. She served, she said, as "the eyes and ears of the New Deal," traveling throughout the nation meeting Americans of all colors and creeds. A North Carolina woman's rights activist recalled, "One of my greatest pleasures was meeting Mrs. Roosevelt. . . . [S]he was so free of prejudice . . . and she was always willing to take a stand, and there were stands to take about blacks and women."

As Roosevelt's programs swung into action, the millions of beneficiaries of the New Deal became grassroots New Dealers who expressed their appreciation by voting Democratic on election day. In this way, the New Deal created a durable political coalition of Democrats that reelected Roosevelt in 1936, 1940, and 1944.

Four guiding ideas shaped New Deal policies. First, Roosevelt and his advisers sought capitalist solutions to the economic crisis. They had no desire to eliminate private property or impose socialist programs, such as public ownership of productive resources. Instead, they hoped to save the capitalist economy by remedying its flaws.

Second, Roosevelt's Brains Trust persuaded him that the greatest flaw of America's capitalist economy was **underconsumption**, the root cause of the current economic paralysis. Underconsumption, New Dealers argued, resulted from the gigantic productive success of capitalism. Factories and farms produced more than they could sell to consumers, causing factories to lay off workers and farmers to lose money on bumper crops. Workers without wages and farmers without profits shrank consumption and choked the economy. Somehow, the balance between consumption and production needed to be restored.

Third, New Dealers believed that the immense size and economic power of American corporations needed to be counterbalanced by government and by organization among workers and small producers. Unlike progressive trustbusters, New Dealers did not seek to splinter big businesses. Roosevelt and his advisers hoped to counterbalance big economic institutions with government programs focused on protecting individuals and the public interest.

Fourth, New Dealers believed that government must somehow moderate the imbalance of wealth created by American capitalism. Wealth concentrated in a few hands reduced consumption by most Americans and thereby contributed to the current economic gridlock. Government needed to find a way to permit ordinary working people to share more fully in the fruits of the economy. "Our task now," Roosevelt declared during the presidential campaign, "is . . . meeting the problem of underconsumption, . . . adjusting production to consumption, . . . [and] distributing wealth and products more equitably."

Banking and Finance Reform

Roosevelt wasted no time making good on his inaugural pledge for "action now." As he took the oath of office on March 4, the nation's banking system was on the brink of collapse. Roosevelt immediately devised a plan to shore up banks and restore depositors' confidence. Working round the clock, New Dealers drafted the Emergency Banking Act, propped up the private banking system with federal funds, and subjected banks to federal regulation and oversight. To secure the confidence of depositors, Congress passed the Glass-Steagall Banking Act, setting up the **Federal Deposit Insurance Corporation (FDIC)**, which guaranteed bank customers that the federal government would reimburse them for deposits if their banks failed. In addition, the act required the separation of commercial banks (which accept deposits and make loans to individuals and small businesses) and investment banks (which make speculative investments with their funds), in an effort to insulate the finances of Main Street America from the risky speculations of Wall Street wheeler-dealers.

On Sunday night, March 12, while the banks were still closed, Roosevelt broadcast the first of a series of **fireside chats**. Speaking in a friendly, informal manner, he explained the new banking legislation that, he said, made it "safer to keep your money in a reopened bank than under the mattress." With such plain talk, Roosevelt translated complex matters into common sense. This and subsequent fireside chats forged a direct connection—via radio—between Roosevelt and millions of Americans,

a connection felt by a man from Paris, Texas, who wrote to Roosevelt, "You are the one & only President that ever helped a Working Class of People. . . . Please help us some way I Pray to God for relief."

The banking legislation and fireside chat worked. Within a few days, most of the nation's major banks reopened, and they remained solvent as reassured depositors switched funds from their mattresses to their bank accounts (Figure 24.1). One New Dealer boasted, "Capitalism was saved in eight days." The rescue of the banking system took much longer to succeed, though.

In his inaugural address, Roosevelt criticized financiers for their greed and incompetence. To prevent the fraud, corruption, and insider trading that had tainted Wall Street and contributed to the crash of 1929, New Dealers created the Securities and Exchange Commission (SEC) in 1934 to oversee financial markets by licensing investment dealers, monitoring all stock transactions, and requiring corporate officers to make full disclosures about their companies. To head the SEC, Roosevelt appointed an ambitious Wall Street financier, Joseph P. Kennedy (father of the future president John F. Kennedy), who had a shady reputation for stock manipulation. Under Kennedy's leadership, the SEC helped clean up and regulate Wall Street, which slowly recovered.

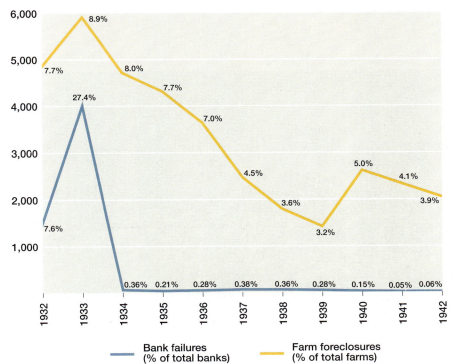

FIGURE 24.1 Bank Failures and Farm Foreclosures, 1932–1942
New Deal legislation to stabilize the economy had its most immediate and striking effect in preventing banks, along with their depositors, from going under and farmers from losing their land.

Bank failures (% of total banks)

Farm foreclosures (% of total farms)

Relief and Conservation Programs

Patching the nation's financial structure provided little relief for the hungry and unemployed. A poor man from Nebraska asked Eleanor Roosevelt "if the folk who was borned here in America . . . are this Forgotten Man, the President had in mind, [and] if we are this Forgotten Man then we are still Forgotten." Since its founding, the federal government had never assumed responsibility for needy people, except in moments of natural disaster or emergencies such as the Civil War. Instead, churches, private charities, county and municipal governments, and occasionally states assumed the burden of poor relief, usually with meager payments. The depression necessitated unprecedented federal relief efforts, according to New Dealers. As a New Yorker who still had a job wrote the government, "We work, ten hours a day for six days. In the grime and dirt of a nation [for] . . . low pay [making us] . . . slaves—slaves of the depression!"

The Federal Emergency Relief Administration (FERA), established in May 1933, supported four million to five million households with $20 or $30 a month. FERA also created jobs for the unemployed on thousands of public works projects, organized into the Civil Works Administration (CWA), which put paychecks worth more than $800 million into the hands of previously jobless workers. Earning wages between 40 and 60 cents an hour, laborers renovated schools, dug sewers, and rebuilt roads and bridges.

The most popular work relief program was the **Civilian Conservation Corps (CCC)**, established in March 1933. It offered unemployed young men a chance to earn wages while working to conserve natural resources, a long-standing interest of Roosevelt. Women were excluded from working in the CCC until Eleanor Roosevelt demanded that a token number of young women be hired. By the end of the program in 1942, three million CCC workers had left a legacy of vast new recreation areas, along with roads that made those areas accessible to millions of Americans. Just as important, the CCC, CWA, and other work relief efforts replaced the stigma of welfare with the dignity of jobs. As one woman said about her husband's work relief job, "We aren't on relief anymore. My husband is working for the Government."

The New Deal's most ambitious and controversial natural resources development project was the Tennessee Valley Authority (TVA), created in May 1933 to build dams along the Tennessee River to supply impoverished rural communities with cheap electricity (Map 24.3). The TVA set out to demonstrate that a partnership between the federal government and local residents could overcome the barriers of state governments and private enterprises to make efficient use of abundant natural resources and break the ancient cycle of poverty. The TVA improved the lives of millions in the region

Civil Conservation Corps (CCC)
During the New Deal, the CCC provided work and wages for about two-and-a-half million young men to improve parks, build roads, plant trees, and engage in other conservation projects. CCC workers earned wages of about $30 a month, all but $5 of which went to their parents. Everett Collection.

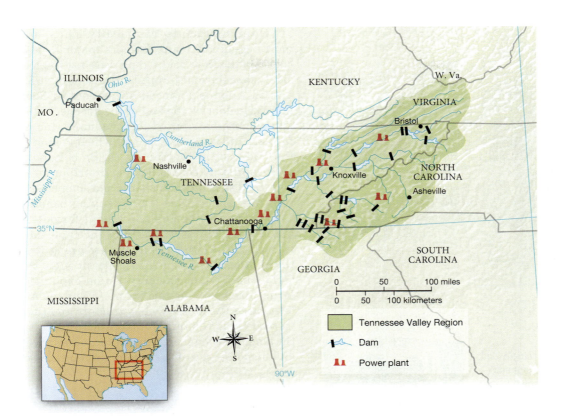

MAP ACTIVITY

Map 24.3 The Tennessee Valley Authority
The New Deal created the Tennessee Valley Authority to modernize a vast impoverished region with hydroelectric power dams and, at the same time, to reclaim eroded land and preserve old folkways.

READING THE MAP: How many states were affected by the TVA? How many miles of rivers (approximately) were affected?

CONNECTIONS: What kinds of benefits—economic as well as social and cultural—did TVA programs bring to the region? How might the lives of a poor farming family in Alabama or Tennessee have changed after the mid-1930s owing to these programs?

with electric power, flood protection, soil reclamation, and jobs.

New sources of hydroelectric power helped the New Deal bring the wonders of electricity to country folk, fulfilling an old progressive dream. When Roosevelt became president, 90 percent of rural Americans lacked electricity. Private electric companies refused to build transmission lines into the sparsely settled countryside when they had a profitable market in more accessible and densely populated urban areas. Beginning in 1935, the Rural Electrification Administration (REA) made low-cost loans available to local cooperatives for power plants and transmission lines to serve rural communities. Within ten years, the REA delivered electricity to nine out of ten farms, giving rural Americans access for the first time to modern conveniences that urban people had enjoyed for decades.

Agricultural Initiatives

Farmers had been mired in a depression since the end of World War I. New Dealers diagnosed the farmers' plight as a classic case of overproduction and underconsumption. Following age-old practices, farmers tried to compensate for low crop prices by growing more crops. Of course, producing more crops pushed prices lower still. Farm families' income sank to $167 a year, barely one-tenth of the national average in 1932.

New Dealers sought to cut agricultural production, thereby raising crop prices and farmers' income. With more money in their pockets, farm families—who made up one-third of all Americans—would then buy more goods and lift consumption in the entire economy. To reduce production, the **Agricultural Adjustment Act (AAA)** passed in May 1933 authorized the

Crop allotments, commodity loans, and mortgage credit made farmers major beneficiaries of the New Deal. Crop prices rose impressively, farm income jumped 50 percent by 1936, and FCA loans financed 40 percent of farm mortgage debt by the end of the decade. These gains were distributed fairly equally among farmers in the corn, hog, and wheat region of the Midwest. In the South's cotton belt, however, landlords controlled the distribution of New Deal agricultural benefits and shamelessly rewarded themselves while denying benefits to many sharecroppers and tenant farmers—blacks and whites—by taking the land they worked out of production and assigning it to the allotment program. As the president of the Oklahoma Tenant Farmers' Union explained, large farmers who got "Triple-A" payments often used the money to buy tractors and then "forced their tenants and[share]croppers off the land," causing these "Americans to be starved and dispossessed of their homes in our land of plenty."

Industrial Recovery

Unlike farmers, industrialists cut production with the onset of the depression. Between 1929 and 1933, industrial production fell more than 40 percent in an effort to balance low demand with low supply and thereby maintain prices. But falling industrial production meant that millions of working people lost their jobs. Unlike farmers, most working people needed jobs to eat. Mass unemployment also reduced consumer demand for industrial products, contributing to a downward spiral in both production and jobs, with no end in sight. Industries responded by reducing wages for employees who still had jobs, further reducing demand—a trend made worse by competition among industrial producers. New Dealers struggled to find a way to break this cycle of unemployment and underconsumption—a way consistent with corporate profits and capitalism.

The New Deal's National Industrial Recovery Act opted for a government-sponsored form of industrial self-government through the **National Recovery Administration (NRA)**, established in June 1933. The NRA encouraged industrialists to agree on rules, known as codes, to define fair working conditions, to set prices, and to minimize competition. The idea behind codes was to stabilize existing industries and maintain their workforces.

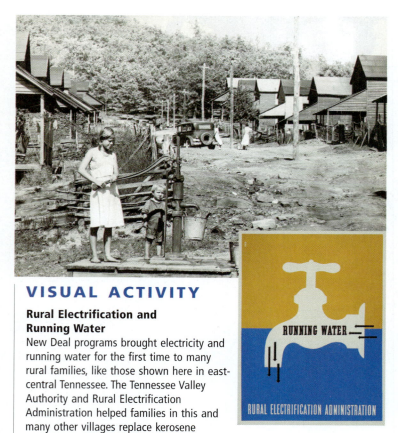

VISUAL ACTIVITY

Rural Electrification and Running Water

New Deal programs brought electricity and running water for the first time to many rural families, like those shown here in east-central Tennessee. The Tennessee Valley Authority and Rural Electrification Administration helped families in this and many other villages replace kerosene lamps with electric lights and to have access to clean, safe water.

Pump: FDR Library; poster: Lester Beall, Running Water-Rural Electrification Administration, 1937. Gift of the Artist. Digital Image © The Museum of Modern Art/Licensed by SCALA/Art Resource, NY. © VAGA, NY.

READING THE IMAGE: Where can you see evidence of New Deal benefits in this photo? What difference did electricity and running water make in the lives of people like the children depicted here at the pump?

CONNECTIONS: Why did New Deal programs devote so much attention to improving the lives of rural Americans?

"domestic allotment plan," which paid farmers not to grow crops. Individual farmers who agreed not to plant crops on a portion of their fields (their "allotment") would receive a government payment compensating them for the crops they did not plant. While millions of Americans like Florence Owens and her children went to bed hungry, farmers slaughtered livestock and destroyed crops to qualify for their allotment payments.

With the formation of the Commodity Credit Corporation, the federal government allowed farmers to hold their harvested crops off the market and wait for a higher price. New Dealers also sponsored the Farm Credit Act (FCA) to provide long-term credit on mortgaged farm property, allowing debt-ridden farmers to avoid foreclosures that were driving thousands off their land (see Figure 24.1).

Industry after industry wrote elaborate codes addressing detailed features of production, pricing, and competition. In exchange for the relaxation of federal antitrust regulations that prohibited such business agreements, the participating businesses promised to recognize the right of working people to organize and engage in collective bargaining. To encourage consumers to patronize businesses with NRA codes, posters with the NRA's Blue Eagle appeared in shop windows throughout the nation.

New Dealers hoped that NRA codes would yield businesses with a social conscience, ensuring fair treatment of workers and consumers as well as promotion of the general economic welfare. Instead, NRA codes tended to strengthen conventional business practices. Large corporations wrote codes that served primarily their own interests rather than the needs of workers or the welfare of the national economy. (See "Seeking the American Promise," page 688.) The failure of codes to cover domestic workers or agricultural laborers like Florence Owens led one woman to complain to Roosevelt that the NRA "never mentioned the robbery of the Housewives" by the privations caused by the depression.

Many business leaders criticized NRA codes as heavy-handed government regulation of private enterprise. In reality, compliance with NRA codes was voluntary, and government enforcement efforts were weak to nonexistent. The NRA did little to reduce unemployment, raise consumption, or relieve the depression. In effect, it represented a peace offering to business leaders by Roosevelt and his advisers, conveying the message that the New Deal did not intend to wage war against profits or private enterprise. The peace offering failed, however. Most corporate leaders became bitter opponents of Roosevelt and the New Deal.

REVIEW   How did the New Dealers try to steer the nation toward recovery from the Great Depression?

▶ Challenges to the New Deal

The first New Deal initiatives engendered fierce criticism and political opposition. From the right, Republicans and businesspeople charged that New Deal programs were too radical, undermining private property,

economic stability, and democracy. Critics on the left faulted the New Deal for its failure to allay the human suffering caused by the depression and for its timidity in attacking corporate power and greed.

Resistance to Business Reform

New Deal programs rescued capitalism, but business leaders lambasted Roosevelt, even though their economic prospects improved more than those of most other Americans during the depression. Republicans and business leaders denounced New Deal efforts to regulate or reform what they considered their private enterprises.

Major Legislation of the New Deal's First Hundred Days		
	Name of Act	**Basic Provisions**
March 9, 1933	Emergency Banking Act	Provides for reopening stable banks and authorizing the Reconstruction Finance Corporation to supply funds.
March 31, 1933	Civilian Conservation Corps Act	Provides jobs for unemployed young men.
May 12, 1933	Agricultural Adjustment Act	Provides funds to pay farmers for not growing crops.
May 12, 1933	Federal Emergency Relief Act	Provides relief funds for the destitute.
May 18, 1933	Tennessee Valley Authority Act	Creates the TVA to bring electric power and conservation to the area.
June 16, 1933	National Industrial Recovery Act	Specifies cooperation among business, government, and labor in setting fair prices and working conditions.
June 16, 1933	Glass-Steagall Banking Act	Creates the Federal Deposit Insurance Corporation (FDIC) to insure bank deposits.

Textile Workers Strike for Better Wages and Working Conditions

"The 'Stretch-out System' is the cause of the whole trouble," a textile worker declared in 1930, echoing the sentiments of thousands of other mill workers. The "stretch-out" was the term coined by mill workers for the cost-cutting efficiencies implemented by mill owners that led to layoffs and poor working conditions for textile workers during the 1920s and 1930s. Textile manufacturers drastically increased the workload of their employees to cut labor costs and raise productivity. A mill worker who tended thirty looms in 1920 was responsible for ninety or more looms by 1929—if she or he still had a job. Layoffs of mill hands in the midst of the Great Depression contributed to further deterioration in wages and working conditions. So many people were desperate for work, no matter what the wage, that manufacturers were able to cut wages in half. The result, as one textile worker wrote Roosevelt, was that "the ones who are Still at Work are Being Treated as Bad or Worse tha[n] the Slaves were in Slavery times."

Like so many other textile workers who faced the tough choice of working with the stretch-out or not working, Icy Norman was relieved to find work in 1929 at Burlington Mills in Piedmont Heights, North Carolina, where the supervisor happened to be a friend of her deceased father's. He hired Norman to wind thread onto bobbins for weaving. At first,

she earned only 15 cents a day, but as she became more skilled, her wages rose to $10 a week, a little over 15 cents an hour. "After I got used to being in there," Norman recalled, "I really loved my work. . . . I got pleasure out of it and it made me happy to do my job." Still, as one mill worker wrote to Roosevelt, "every textile worker in the South would walk out of the mill today if they were not afraid of starvation."

In September 1934, hundreds of thousands of textile workers throughout the nation overcame their fears and walked out of the mills in the largest strike in American history. Strikers shut down mills from Maine to Alabama. More than half of all textile workers nationwide and about two-thirds of mill hands in the southern heartland of the textile industry walked out, including Icy Norman. Loosely organized by the Textile Workers' Union, the strikers demanded better working conditions and wages through enforcement of the textile code established by the New Deal's National Recovery Administration (NRA).

Like other NRA codes, the textile code was written and administered by the leading textile manufacturers. It provided for a maximum forty-hour workweek, a minimum weekly wage of $12 for southern mill hands, and the right of workers to organize unions. Textile workers celebrated the

passage of the NRA in June 1933. "It seemed too good to be true," one textile worker observed. Mill hands told a New Dealer, "We trust in the Supreme Being and Franklin Roosevelt. . . . [We] know that the President will see that [we] have work and proper wages; and that the stretchout will be abandoned."

But their faith was misplaced, and the code was widely ignored. When workers complained that mill owners continued the stretch-out, cutting wages and firing any mill hands they suspected of union sympathies, their grievances were heard by the textile manufacturers who headed the NRA code authority. In the year before the strike, the textile code authority received nearly 4,000 complaints, investigated 96, and resolved just 1 in favor of a worker. Boiling with frustration over the failure of the textile code, more than 400,000 mill hands went on strike. Seeking to realize what they viewed as the unfulfilled promises of the New Deal's NRA, they aimed to organize a union to bargain with mill owners to improve wages and working conditions.

The strike lasted three weeks and led to numerous violent confrontations with police and the National Guard. It ended because of the combination of the mill owners' intransigence, the Textile Workers' Union's lack of resources, the mill workers' increasingly desperate financial situation, and Roosevelt's

By 1935, two major business organizations, the National Association of Manufacturers and the Chamber of Commerce, had become openly anti–New Deal. Their critiques were amplified by the American Liberty League, founded in 1934, which blamed the New Deal

for betraying basic constitutional guarantees of freedom and individualism. To them, the AAA was a "trend toward fascist control of agriculture," relief programs marked "the end of democracy," and the NRA was a plunge into the "quicksand of visionary experimentation."

Striking Mill Workers Jeer Strikebreakers
Textile workers on strike against the Cannon Textile Mills in North Carolina in September 1934 shouted taunts and curses at employees who refused to honor the strikers' picket line. Why do you think strikers and strikebreakers wore different styles of clothing? Although thousands of women joined the strike, there are no women among the strikers shown here. Why might that be? © Bettmann/Corbis.

focus on the need for industrial peace to achieve economic recovery.

The mill hands achieved virtually nothing as a result of the strike. Mill owners continued to flout the textile codes, the stretch-out continued without interruption, and working conditions did not improve. Angry mill owners fired and blacklisted strike leaders, succeeding in their efforts to crush workers' organizations.

Icy Norman went back to work after the strike ended, and since she was not a union activist, she managed to keep her job until she retired in 1976, after forty-seven years at Burlington Mills. For her efforts, the company rewarded her with a free visit to a local hairdresser, a tour of the Burlington executive suite, and a farewell handshake.

Questions for Consideration

1. How did the stretch-out contribute to unemployment for textile workers?

2. Why was textile workers' faith in Roosevelt and NRA codes misplaced?

3. Why do you think unions failed to organize textile workers when they succeeded in organizing autoworkers, for example?

Connect to the Big Idea

C In what ways did the New Deal affect industrial workers differently than farmers and other workers?

Economists who favored rational planning in the public interest and labor leaders who sought to influence wages and working conditions by organizing unions attacked the New Deal from the left. In their view, the NRA stifled enterprise by permitting monopolistic practices. They pointed out that industrial trade associations twisted NRA codes to suit their aims, thwarted competition, and engaged in price gouging. Labor leaders especially resented the NRA's willingness to allow businesses to form company-controlled unions while blocking workers from organizing genuine grassroots unions to bargain for themselves.

The Supreme Court stepped into this cross fire of criticisms in May 1935 and declared that the NRA unconstitutionally conferred powers reserved to Congress on an administrative agency. The NRA codes soon lost the little authority they had. The failure of the NRA demonstrated the depth of many Americans' resistance to economic planning and the stubborn refusal of business leaders to yield to government regulations or reforms.

Casualties in the Countryside

The AAA weathered critical battering by champions of the old order better than the NRA. Allotment checks for keeping land fallow and crop prices high created loyalty among farmers with enough acreage to participate. As a white farmer in North Carolina declared, "I stand for the New Deal and Roosevelt . . . , the AAA . . . and crop control."

Protests stirred, however, among those who did not qualify for allotments. The Southern Farm Tenants Union argued passionately that the AAA enriched large farmers while it impoverished small farmers who rented rather than owned their land. One black share-cropper explained why only $75 a year from New Deal agricultural subsidies trickled down to her: "De landlord is landlord, de politicians is landlord, de judge is landlord, de shurf [sheriff] is landlord, ever'body is landlord, en we [sharecroppers] ain' got nothin'!" Like the NRA, the AAA tended to help most those who least needed help. Roosevelt's political dependence on southern Democrats caused him to avoid confronting economic and racial inequities in the South.

Evicted Sharecroppers
The New Deal's Agricultural Adjustment Administration maintained farm prices by reducing acreage in production often resulted in the eviction of tenant farmers when the land they worked was left idle. These African American sharecroppers protested AAA policies that caused cotton farmers to evict them from their homes. They were among the many rural laborers whose lives were made worse by New Deal agricultural policies. © Bettmann/Corbis.

Displaced tenants often joined the army of migrant workers like Florence Owens who straggled across rural America during the 1930s, some to flee Great Plains dust storms. Many migrants came from Mexico to work Texas cotton, Michigan beans, Idaho sugar beets, and California crops of all kinds. But since the number of people willing to take agricultural jobs usually exceeded the number of jobs available, wages fell and native-born white migrants fought to reserve even these low-wage jobs for themselves. Hundreds of thousands of "Okies" streamed out of the Dust Bowl of Oklahoma, Kansas, Texas, and Colorado, where chronic drought and harmful agricultural practices blasted crops and hopes. Parched, poor, and windblown, Okies—like the Joad family immortalized in John Steinbeck's novel *The Grapes of Wrath* (1939)—migrated to the lush fields and orchards of California, congregating in labor camps and hoping to find work and a future. But migrant laborers seldom found steady or secure work. As one Okie said, "When they need us they call us migrants, and when we've picked their crop, we're bums and we got to get out."

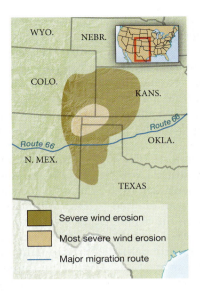

The Dust Bowl

Politics on the Fringes

Politically, the New Deal's staunchest opponents were in the Republican Party—organized, well-heeled, mainstream, and determined to challenge Roosevelt at every turn. But the New Deal also faced challenges from the political fringes, fueled by the hardship of the depression and the hope for a cure-all.

Socialists and Communists accused the New Deal of being the handmaiden of business elites and of rescuing capitalism from its self-inflicted crisis. Socialist author Upton Sinclair ran for governor of California in 1934 on a plan that the state take ownership of idle factories and unused land and then give them to cooperatives of working people, a first step toward putting the needs of people above profits. Sinclair lost the election, ending the most serious socialist electoral challenge to the New Deal.

Some intellectuals and artists sought to advance the cause of more radical change by joining left-wing organizations, including the American Communist Party. At its high point in the 1930s, the party had only about thirty thousand members, the large majority of them immigrants, especially Scandinavians in the upper Midwest and eastern European Jews in major cities. Individual Communists worked to organize labor unions, protect the civil rights of black people, and help the destitute, but the party preached the overthrow of "bourgeois democracy" and the destruction of capitalism in favor of Soviet-style communism. Such talk attracted few followers among the nation's millions of poor and unemployed. They wanted jobs and economic security within American capitalism and democracy, not violent revolution to establish a dictatorship of the Communist Party.

More powerful radical challenges to the New Deal sprouted from homegrown roots. Many Americans felt overlooked by New Deal programs that concentrated on finance, agriculture, and industry but did little to produce jobs or aid the poor. The merciless reality of the depression also continued to erode the security of people who still had jobs but worried constantly that they, too, might be pushed into the legions of the unemployed and penniless.

A Catholic priest in Detroit named Charles Coughlin spoke to and for many worried Americans in his weekly radio broadcasts, which reached a nationwide audience of 40 million. Father Coughlin expressed outrage at the suffering and inequities that he blamed on Communists, bankers, and "predatory capitalists" who, he claimed, appealing to widespread anti-Semitic sentiments, were mostly Jews. Coughlin became frustrated by Roosevelt's refusal to grant him influence, turned against the New Deal, and in 1935 founded the National Union for Social Justice, or Union Party, to challenge Roosevelt in the 1936 presidential election.

Dr. Francis Townsend, of Long Beach, California, also criticized the timidity of the New Deal. Angry that many of his retired patients lived in misery, Townsend proposed in 1934 the creation of the Old Age Revolving Pension, which would pay every American over age sixty a pension of $200 a month. To receive the pension, senior citizens had to agree to spend the entire amount within thirty days, thereby stimulating the economy.

Townsend organized pension clubs and petitioned the federal government to enact his scheme. When the major political parties ignored his impractical plan, Townsend merged his forces with Coughlin's Union Party in time for the 1936 election.

A more formidable challenge to the New Deal came from the powerful southern wing of the Democratic Party. Huey Long, son of a backcountry Louisiana farmer, was elected governor of the state in 1928 with his slogan "Every man a king, but no one wears a crown." Unlike nearly all other southern white politicians who harped on white supremacy, Long championed the poor over the rich, country people over city folk, and the humble over elites. As governor, "the Kingfish"—as he liked to call himself—delivered on his promises to provide jobs and build roads, schools, and hospitals, but he also behaved ruthlessly to achieve his goals. Long delighted his supporters, who elected him to the U.S. Senate in 1932, where he introduced a sweeping "soak the rich" tax bill that would outlaw personal incomes of more than $1 million and inheritances of more than $5 million. When the Senate rejected his proposal, Long decided to run for president, mobilizing more than five million Americans behind his "Share Our Wealth" plan. "Is that right," Long asked, "when . . . more [is] owned by 12 men than . . . by 120,000,000 people? . . . They own the banks, they own the steel mills, they own the railroads, they own the bonds, they own the mortgages, they own the stores, and they have chained the country from one end to the other." Like Townsend's scheme, Long's program promised far more than it could deliver. The Share Our Wealth campaign died when Long was assassinated in 1935, but his constituency and the wide appeal of a more equitable distribution of wealth persisted.

The challenges to the New Deal from both right and left stirred Democrats to solidify their winning coalition. In the midterm congressional elections of 1934—normally a time when a president loses support—voters gave New Dealers a landslide victory. Democrats increased their majority in the House of Representatives and gained a two-thirds majority in the Senate.

REVIEW   Why did groups at both ends of the political spectrum criticize the New Deal?

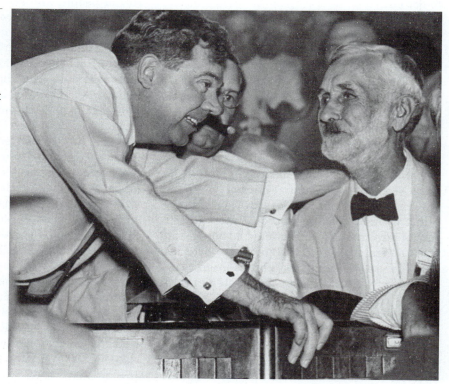

Huey Long
Huey Long, U.S. senator and former governor of Louisiana, pressured delegates at the 1932 Democratic convention into supporting Franklin Roosevelt, as depicted here. After Roosevelt's election, Long challenged the president from the left with his Share Our Wealth plan and, until he was assassinated in 1935, campaigned to replace Roosevelt on the Democratic ticket in the next presidential election. NY Daily News via Getty Images.

VISUAL ACTIVITY

City Activities Mural

During the 1930s, artists—many of them employed by New Deal agencies—painted thousands of murals depicting the variety of American life. These murals often appeared in public buildings. The mural shown here, by Missouri-born artist Thomas Hart Benton, illustrates the seductive pleasures and the spirit found in American cities. Thomas Hart Benton, *America Today*, City Activities with Subway, 1930–31. Image copyright © The Metropolitan Museum of Art. Gift of AXA Equitable, 2012 (2012.478a-j). Image Source: Art Resource, NY

READING THE IMAGE: What features of urban experience does Benton emphasize in this mural? What ideas and attitudes, if any, link the people shown here?

CONNECTIONS: To what extent does the mural highlight activities distinct to U.S. cities, compared with urban life in Europe, Africa, or Asia?

▶ Toward a Welfare State

The popular mandate for the New Deal revealed by the congressional elections persuaded Roosevelt to press ahead with bold new efforts to achieve relief, recovery, and reform. Despite the initiatives of the Hundred Days, the depression still strangled the economy. In 1935, Roosevelt capitalized on his congressional majorities to enact major new programs that signaled the emergence of an American welfare state.

Taken together, these New Deal efforts stretched a safety net under the lives of ordinary Americans, including such landmark initiatives as Social Security, which provided modest pensions for the elderly, and the Wagner Act, which encouraged the organization of labor unions. Although many citizens remained unprotected, New Deal programs helped millions with jobs, relief, and government support. Knitting together the safety net was the idea that, when individual Americans suffered because of forces beyond their control, the federal government had the responsibility to support and protect them. The safety net of welfare programs tied the political loyalty of working people to the New Deal and the Democratic Party. As a North Carolina mill worker said, "Mr. Roosevelt is the only man we ever had in the White House who would understand that my boss is a sonofabitch."

Relief for the Unemployed

First and foremost, Americans still needed jobs. Since the private economy left eight million people jobless by 1935, Roosevelt and

Americans Encounter the New Deal

Americans in all walks of life encountered New Deal measures in their daily lives. In 1938 and 1939, the Federal Writers Project, a part of the WPA, interviewed thousands of ordinary citizens throughout the nation, and many expressed their opinions about the New Deal. A sample of their views of the depression, Franklin Roosevelt, the WPA, the CIO, as well as political and economic power can be found in the following excerpts from three interviews.

DOCUMENT 1
Charles Fusco, On the Value of Relief Work during the Depression, December 6, 1938

An Italian American machinist in a munitions plant in Hampden, Connecticut, explained the value of the relief work provided by the WPA.

I can get a job today even if we got a depression. I don't mean that I wasn't on relief when things got tough because there was a time when everything was shut down and I had to get on relief for a job. It isn't so long ago I was working on WPA. Believe me it was a big help. But it wasn't the kind of a job I should have had because this town is Republican and I am a Republican and I was a good worker for the party—making voters and helping a lot of people out. . . . Getting jobs for them. When it came my turn that I needed help the politicians told me that I had to go on relief—well, when I did I was handed a shovel and pick. . . . Roosevelt is a damn good man. . . . You know there shouldn't be a depression in this country . . . the Democrats are in power and the Republicans won't let loose with the money. Well I say that the money men started this thing and I believe the government should

make laws to force these capitalists to bring back prosperity. They can do it if they wanted to.

Source: Interview with Charles Fusco, Manuscript. U.S. Work Projects Administration, Federal Writers Project. From Library of Congress, *Folklore Project, Life Histories, 1936–39,* GIF. http://www.loc.gov /resource/wpalh0.09030115/seq-1#seq-1 (accessed December 3, 2013).

DOCUMENT 2
Myron Buxton, The Benefits of WPA Projects, July 25, 1939

A native-born draftsman and assistant to an engineer working on WPA building projects in Newburyport, Massachusetts, illuminated the WPA's benefits to the community and to the individual workers.

One reason people here don't like WPA is because they don't understand it's not all bums and drunks and aliens! Nobody ever explains to them that they'd never have had the new High School they're so goddam proud of if it hadn't been for WPA. They don't stop to figure that new brick sidewalks wouldn't be there, the shade trees wouldn't be all dressed up to look at along High Street

his advisers launched a massive work relief program. Roosevelt believed that direct government handouts crippled recipients with "spiritual and moral disintegration . . . destructive to the human spirit." Jobs, by contrast, bolstered individuals' "self-respect . . . self-confidence, . . . courage, and determination." With a congressional appropriation of nearly

$5 billion—more than all government revenues in 1934—the New Deal created the **Works Progress Administration (WPA)** to give unemployed Americans government-funded jobs on public works projects. The WPA put millions of jobless citizens to work on roads, bridges, parks, public buildings, and more. In addition, Congress passed over Roosevelt's

and all around town, if it weren't for WPA projects. To most in this town, and I guess it's not much different in this, than any other New England place, WPA's just a racket, we set up to give a bunch of loafers and drunks steady pay to indulge in their vices! They don't stop to consider that on WPA are men and women who have traveled places and seen things, been educated and found their jobs folded up and nothing to replace them with. . . . The working guy in this country never had such a swell chance to get a toe-hold as he's had in the last four years! The louder the Republicans yell, the more of a toe-hold you can figure the ordinary guy's got!

Source: Seymour D. Buck. Interview with Myron Buxton. Manuscript. U.S. Work Projects Administration, Federal Writers Project. From Library of Congress, *Folklore Project, Life Histories, 1936–39*, GIF. http://www.loc.gov/resource/wpalh1.14030415/#seq-1 (accessed December 3, 2013).

DOCUMENT 3
Jim Cole, Overcoming Racism in the Unions, May 18, 1939

An African American packing house worker near Chicago, Illinois, explained how the CIO united workers from different racial and ethnic backgrounds when other unions turned them away.

I'm working in the Beef Kill section. Butcher on the chain. Been in the place twenty years, I believe. You got to have a certain amount of skill to do the job I'm doing. Long ago, I wanted to join the AFL union, the Amalgamated Butchers and Meat Cutters, they called it and wouldn't take me. Wouldn't let me in the union. Never said it to my face, but reason of it was plain. Negro. That's it. Just didn't want a Negro man to have what he should. That's wrong. You know that's wrong. Long about 1937 the CIO come. Well, I tell you, we Negroes was glad to see it come. Well, you know, sometimes the bosses, or either the company stooges try to keep the white boys from joining the union. They say,

"you don't want to belong to a black man's organization. That's all the CIO is." Don't fool nobody, but they got to lie, spread lyin' words around. There's a many different people, talkin' different speech, can't understand English very well, we have to have us union interpreters for lots of our members, but that don't make no mind, they all friends in the union, even if they can't say nothin' except 'Brother', an' shake hands. Well, my own local, we elected our officers and it's the same all over. We try to get every people represented. President of the local, he's Negro. First V. President, he's Polish. Second V[ice] President, he's Irish. Other officers, Scotchman, Lithuanian, Negro, German. . . . I don't care if the union don't do another lick of work raisin' our pay, or settling grievances about anything, I'll always believe they done the greatest thing in the world gettin' everybody who works in the yards together, and breakin' up the hate and bad feelings that used to be held against the Negro.

Source: Betty Burke. Interview with Jim Cole. Manuscript. U.S. Work Projects Administration, Federal Writers Project. From Library of Congress, *Folklore Project, Life Histories, 1936–39*, GIF. http://www.loc.gov/resource/wpalh0.07050602/seq-1#seq-1 (accessed December 3, 2013).

Questions for Analysis and Debate

1. What did Fusco, Buxton, and Cole see as successes and shortcomings of the New Deal?

2. Who did these men identify as opponents of New Deal measures and why?

3. What attitudes did these men believe other Americans had about the WPA, the CIO, and the New Deal in general?

Connect to the Big Idea

C How did the New Deal programs influence the lives of ordinary American citizens?

veto the bonus long sought by Bonus Marchers, giving veterans an average of $580 and further stimulating the economy.

By 1936, WPA funds provided jobs for 7 percent of the nation's labor force. In effect, the WPA made the federal government the employer of last resort, creating useful jobs when the capitalist economy failed to do so.

In hiring, WPA officials tended to discriminate in favor of white men and against women and racial minorities. Still, WPA made major contributions to both relief and recovery, putting thirteen million men and women to work earning paychecks worth $10 billion. (See "Documenting the American Promise," above.)

About three out of four WPA jobs involved construction and renovation of the nation's physical infrastructure. WPA workers built 572,000 miles of roads, 78,000 bridges, 67,000 miles of city streets, 40,000 public buildings, and much else. In addition, the WPA gave jobs to thousands of artists, musicians, actors, journalists, poets, and novelists. The WPA also organized sewing rooms for jobless women, giving them work and wages. These sewing rooms produced more than 100 million pieces of clothing that were donated to the needy. Throughout the nation, WPA projects displayed tangible evidence of the New Deal's commitment to public welfare.

Empowering Labor

During the Great Depression, factory workers who managed to keep their jobs worried constantly about being laid off while their wages and working hours were cut. When workers tried to organize labor unions to protect themselves, municipal and state governments usually sided with employers. Since the Gilded Age, state and federal governments had been far more effective at busting unions than at busting trusts. The New Deal dramatically reversed the federal government's stance toward unions. With legislation and political support, the New Deal encouraged an unprecedented wave of union organizing among the nation's working people. When the head of the United Mine Workers, John L. Lewis, told coal miners that "the President wants you to join a union," he exaggerated only a little. New Dealers believed that unions would counterbalance the organized might of big corporations by defending working people, maintaining wages, and replacing the bloody violence that often accompanied strikes with economic peace and commercial stability.

Violent battles on the nation's streets and docks showed the determination of militant labor leaders to organize unions that would protect jobs as well as wages. In 1934, striking workers in Toledo, Minneapolis, San Francisco, and elsewhere were beaten and shot by police and the National Guard. In Congress, labor leaders lobbied for the National Labor Relations Act, a bill sponsored by Senator Robert Wagner of New York that authorized the federal government to intervene in labor disputes and supervise the organization of labor unions. The **Wagner Act**, as it came to be called, guaranteed industrial workers the right to organize unions, putting the might of federal law behind the appeals of labor

leaders. If the majority of workers at a company voted for a union, the union became the sole bargaining agent for the entire workplace, and the employer was required to negotiate with the elected union leaders. Roosevelt signed the Wagner Act in July 1935, for the first time providing federal support for labor organization—the most important New Deal reform of the industrial order.

The achievements that flowed from the Wagner Act and renewed labor militancy were impressive. When Roosevelt became president in 1933, union membership—composed almost entirely of skilled workers in trade unions affiliated with the American Federation of Labor (AFL)—stood at three million. With the support of the Wagner Act, union membership expanded to fourteen million by 1945. By then, 30 percent of the workforce was unionized, the highest in American history.

Most of the new union members were factory workers and unskilled laborers, many of them immigrants, women, and African Americans. For decades, established AFL unions had no desire to organize factory and unskilled workers. In 1935, under the aggressive leadership of the mine workers' John L. Lewis and the head of the Amalgamated Clothing Workers, Sidney Hillman, a coalition of unskilled workers formed the **Committee for Industrial Organization** (CIO; later the Congress of Industrial Organizations). The CIO, helped by the Wagner Act, mobilized organizing drives in major industries, including the bitterly antiunion automobile and steel industries.

The bloody struggle by the CIO-affiliated United Auto Workers (UAW) to organize workers at General Motors climaxed in January 1937. Striking workers occupied the main assembly plant in Flint, Michigan, in a sit-down strike that slashed the plant's production of 15,000 cars a week to a mere 150. Stymied, General Motors eventually surrendered and agreed to make the UAW the sole bargaining agent for all the company's workers and to refrain from interfering with union activity. The UAW expanded its campaign until, after much violence, the entire industry was unionized by 1941.

The CIO hoped to ride organizing success in auto plants to victory in the steel mills. But after unionizing the giant U.S. Steel, the CIO ran up against determined opposition from smaller steel firms. Following a police attack that killed ten strikers at Republic Steel outside Chicago in May 1937, the battered steelworkers halted their organizing campaign. In steel and other major industries, such as the stridently antiunion southern textile mills, organizing efforts stalled until after 1941, when military mobilization created labor shortages that gave workers greater bargaining power.

Social Security and Tax Reform

The single most important feature of the New Deal's emerging welfare state was **Social Security**. An ambitious, far-reaching, and permanent reform, Social Security was designed to provide a modest income to relieve the poverty of elderly people. Only about 15 percent of older Americans had private pension plans, and during the depression corporations and banks often failed to pay the meager pensions they had promised. Corporations routinely fired or demoted employees to avoid or reduce pension payments. Prompted by the popular but impractical panaceas of Dr. Townsend, Father Coughlin, and Huey Long, Roosevelt told Congress that "it is our plain duty to provide for that security upon which welfare depends . . . and undertake the great task of furthering the security of the citizen and his family through social insurance."

The political struggle for Social Security highlighted class differences among Americans. Support for the measure came from a coalition of advocacy groups for the elderly and the poor, traditional progressives, leftists, social workers, and labor unions. Arrayed against them were economic conservatives, including the American Liberty League, the National Association of Manufacturers, the Chamber of Commerce, and the American Medical Association. Enact the Social Security system, these conservatives and other Republicans warned, and the government will ruin private property, destroy initiative, and reduce proud individuals to spineless loafers.

The large New Deal majority in Congress passed the Social Security Act in August 1935. The act provided that contributions from workers and their employers would fund pensions for the elderly, giving contributing workers a personal stake in the system and making it politically invulnerable. When

VISUAL ACTIVITY

Women's Emergency Brigade Supports Sit-Down Strikers
General Motors cut wages and employment in half during the depression, causing a wave of strikes by autoworkers. During the famous sit-down strike in Flint, Michigan, in 1937, the wives of striking workers organized the Emergency Brigade, shown here, to support the strikers. The photo does not show the thousands of armed police and National Guardsmen that surrounded the plant. © Bettmann/Corbis.
READING THE IMAGE: Why do you think the woman leading the Emergency Brigade carried an American flag? What kind of support did the Women's Emergency Brigade appear to provide to the striking autoworkers, according to the photo?
CONNECTIONS: In what ways did the New Deal support labor unions?

eligible workers reached retirement age, they were not subject to a means test to prove that they were needy. Instead, they had earned benefits based on their contributions and years of work. Social Security also created unemployment insurance that provided modest benefits for workers who lost their jobs.

Not all workers benefited from the Social Security Act. It excluded domestic and agricultural workers like Florence Owens, thereby making ineligible about half of all African Americans and more than half of all employed women—about five million people in all. The law also excluded employees of religious and nonprofit organizations, such as schools and hospitals, thereby rendering even more women and minorities ineligible.

Social Security provided states with multimillion dollar grants to help them support dependent children, blind people, and public health services.   After the Supreme Court upheld Social Security in 1937, the program was expand-ed to include benefits for dependent survivors of deceased recipients. Although the first Social Security check (for $41.30) was not issued until 1940, the system gave millions of working people the assurance that, when they became too old to work, they would receive a modest income from the federal government. This safety net protected many ordinary working people from fears of a penniless and insecure old age.

Fervent opposition to Social Security struck New Dealers as evidence that the rich had learned little from the depression. Roosevelt had long felt contempt for the moneyed elite who ignored the suffering of the poor. He looked for a way to redistribute wealth that would weaken conservative opposition, advance the cause of social equity, and defuse political challenges from Huey Long and Father Coughlin. Roosevelt charged in 1935 that large fortunes put "great and undesirable concentration of control in [the hands of] relatively few individuals," He urged a graduated tax on corporations, an inheritance tax, and an increase in maximum personal income taxes. Congress endorsed Roosevelt's basic principle by taxing those with higher incomes at a somewhat higher rate.

Neglected Americans and the New Deal

The patchwork of New Deal reforms erected a two-tier welfare state. In the top tier, orga-nized workers in major industries were the greatest beneficiaries of New Deal initiatives. In the bottom tier, millions of neglected Americans—women, children, and old folks, along with the unorganized, unskilled, uneducated, and unemployed—often fell through the New Deal safety net. Many working people remained more or less untouched by New Deal benefits. The average unemployment rate for the 1930s stayed high—17 percent. Workers in industries that resisted unions received little help from the Wagner Act or the WPA. Tens of thousands of women in southern textile mills, for example, commonly received wages of less than ten cents an hour and were fired if they protested. Domestic workers, almost all of them women, and agricultural work-ers—many of them African, Hispanic, or Asian Americans—were neither unionized nor eli-gible for Social Security.

The New Deal neglected few citizens more than African Americans. About half of black Americans in cities were jobless, more than double the unemployment rate among whites. In the rural South, where the vast majority of African Americans lived, conditions were worse, given the New Deal agricultural policies such as the AAA that favored landowners, who often pushed blacks off the land they farmed. Only 11 of more than 10,000 WPA supervisors in the South were black, even though African Americans accounted for a third of the region's population. Disfranchisement by in-timidation and legal subterfuge prevented southern blacks from protesting their plight at the ballot box. Protesters risked vicious retaliation from local whites. Bitter critics charged that the New Deal's NRA stood for "Negro Run Around" or "Negroes Ruined Again."

Roosevelt responded to such criticisms with great caution since New Deal reforms required the political support of powerful conservative, segregationist, southern white Democrats who would be alienated by pro-grams that aided blacks. A white Georgia relief worker expressed the common view that "any Nigger who gets over $8 a week is a spoiled Nigger, that's all." Stymied by the political clout of entrenched white racism, New Dealers still attracted support from black voters. Roosevelt's overtures to African Americans prompted northern black voters in the 1934 congress-ional elections to shift from the Republican to the Democratic Party, helping elect New Deal Democrats.

Eleanor Roosevelt sponsored the appointment of Mary McLeod Bethune—the energetic cofounder of the National Council of Negro Women—as head of the Division of Negro Affairs in the National Youth Administration. The highest-ranking black official in Roosevelt's administration, Bethune used her position to guide a small number of black professionals and civil rights activists to posts within New Deal agencies. Ultimately, about one in four African Americans got access to New Deal relief programs.

Mary McLeod Bethune

At the urging of Eleanor Roosevelt, Mary McLeod Bethune, a southern educational and civil rights leader, became director of the National Youth Administration's Division of Negro Affairs. The first black woman to head a federal agency, Bethune used her position to promote social change. Here, Bethune protests the discriminatory hiring practices of the Peoples Drug Store chain in the nation's capital. Moorland-Spingarn Research Center, Howard University.

Despite these gains, by 1940 African Americans still suffered severe handicaps. Most of the thirteen million black workers toiled at low-paying menial jobs, unprotected by the New Deal safety net. Segregated and unequal schools were the norm, and only 1 percent of black students earned college degrees. In southern states, vigilante violence against blacks went unpunished. For these problems of black Americans, the New Deal offered few remedies.

Hispanic Americans fared no better. About a million Mexican Americans lived in the United States in the 1930s, most of them first- or second-generation immigrants who worked crops throughout the West. During the depression, field workers saw their low wages plunge lower still to about a dime an hour. Ten thousand Mexican American pecan shellers in San Antonio, Texas, earned only a nickel an hour. To preserve scarce jobs for U.S. citizens, the federal government choked off immigration from Mexico, while state and local officials deported tens of thousands of Mexican Americans, many with their American-born children. New Deal programs throughout the West often discriminated against Hispanics and other people of color. A New Deal study concluded that "the Mexican is . . . segregated from the rest of the community as effectively as the Negro . . . [by] poverty and low wages."

Asian Americans had similar experiences. Asian immigrants were still excluded from U.S. citizenship and in many states were not permitted to own land. By 1930, more than half of Japanese Americans had been born in the United States, but they were still liable to discrimination. One young Asian American expressed the frustration felt by many others: "I am a fruit-stand worker. I would much rather it were doctor or lawyer . . . but my aspirations [were] frustrated long ago by circumstances. . . . I am only what I am, a professional carrot washer."

Native Americans also suffered neglect from New Deal agencies. As a group, they remained the poorest of the poor. Since the Dawes Act of 1887 (see "The Dawes Act and Indian Land Allotment" in chapter 17), the federal government had encouraged Native Americans to assimilate—to abandon their Indian identities and adopt the cultural norms of the majority society. Under the leadership of the New Deal's commissioner of Indian affairs, John Collier, the New Deal's Indian Reorganization Act (IRA) of 1934 largely reversed that policy. Collier claimed that "the most interesting and important fact about

Mexican Migrant Farmworkers
These Mexican immigrants are harvesting sugar beets in 1937 in northwestern Minnesota. Between 1910 and 1940, when refugees from the Mexican revolution poured across the American border, the Hispanic-American Alliance and other such organizations sought to protect Mexican Americans' rights against nativist fears and hostility. The alliance steadfastly emphasized Mexican Americans' desire to receive permanent legal status in the United States. Library of Congress.

Indians" was that they "do not expect much, often they expect nothing at all; yet they are able to be happy." Given such views, the IRA provided little economic aid to Native Americans, but it did restore their right to own land communally and to have greater control over their own affairs. The IRA brought little immediate benefit to Native Americans, but it provided an important foundation for Indians' economic, cultural, and political resurgence a generation later.

Voicing common experiences among Americans neglected by the New Deal, singer and songwriter Woody Guthrie traveled the nation for eight years during the 1930s and heard other rambling men tell him "the story of their life": "how the home went to pieces, how . . . the crops got to where they wouldn't bring nothing, work in factories would kill a dog . . . and—always, always [you] have to fight and argue and cuss and swear . . . to try to get a nickel more out of the rich bosses."

REVIEW   What features of a welfare state did the New Deal create and why?

▶ The New Deal from Victory to Deadlock

To accelerate the sputtering economic recovery, Roosevelt shifted the emphasis of the New Deal in the mid-1930s. Instead of seeking cooperation from conservative business leaders, he decided to rely on the growing New Deal coalition to enact reforms over the strident opposition of the Supreme Court, Republicans, and corporate interests. Roosevelt's conservative opponents reacted to the massing of New Deal forces by intensifying their opposition to the welfare state.

While he continued to lose conservatives' support, Roosevelt added new allies on the left in farm states and big cities. Throughout Roosevelt's first term, socialists and Communists denounced the slow pace of change and accused the New Deal of failing to serve the interests of the workers who produced the nation's wealth. But in 1935, the Soviet Union, worried about the threat of fascism in Europe, instructed Communists throughout the world to join hands with non-Communist progressives in a "Popular Front" to advance the fortunes of the working class. Many radicals soon switched from opposing the New Deal to supporting its relief programs and support for labor unions.

Roosevelt won reelection in 1936 in a landslide and soon concluded that the economy was improving. He reduced government spending in 1937, triggering a sharp recession that undermined economic recovery and prolonged the depression.

The Election of 1936

Roosevelt believed that the presidential election of 1936 would test his leadership and progressive ideals. The depression still had a stranglehold on the economy. Conservative leaders believed that the New Deal's failure to lift the nation out of the depression indicated that Americans were ready for a change. Left-wing critics insisted that the New Deal had missed the opportunity to displace capitalism with a socialist economy and that voters would embrace candidates who recommended more radical remedies.

Republicans turned to Kansas governor Alfred (Alf) Landon as their presidential nominee, a moderate who stressed mainstream Republican proposals to achieve a balanced federal budget and less government bureaucracy. Landon recommended that the perils of sickness and old age should be eased by old-fashioned neighborliness instead of a government program like Social Security.

Roosevelt put his faith in the growing New Deal coalition, whose members shared his conviction that the New Deal promised to liberate the nation from the long era of privilege and wealth for a few and "economic slavery" for the rest. He proclaimed that "the forces of selfishness and lust for power met their match" in his first term as president, and he hoped it would be said about his second term that "these forces met their master."

Roosevelt triumphed spectacularly. He won 60.8 percent of the popular vote, making it the widest margin of victory in a presidential election to date. Third parties—including the Socialist and Communist Parties—fell pitifully short of the support they expected and never again mounted a significant challenge to the New Deal. Congressional results were equally lopsided, with Democrats outnumbering Republicans more than three to one in both houses. In his inaugural address, Roosevelt announced, "I see one third of a nation ill-housed, ill-clad, [and] ill-nourished," and he promised to devote his second term to alleviating their hardship.

Court Packing

In the afterglow of his reelection triumph, Roosevelt pondered how to remove the remaining obstacles to New Deal reforms. He decided to target the Supreme Court. Conservative justices appointed by Republican presidents had invalidated eleven New Deal measures as unconstitutional interferences with free enterprise. Now, Social Security, the Wagner Act, the Securities and Exchange Commission, and other New Deal innovations were about to be considered by the justices.

To ensure that the Supreme Court did not dismantle the New Deal, Roosevelt proposed a **court-packing plan** that added one new justice for each existing judge who had served for ten years and was over the age of seventy. In effect, the proposed law would give Roosevelt the power to pack the Court with up to six New Dealers who could outvote the elderly, conservative, Republican justices.

But the president had not reckoned with Americans' deeply rooted deference to the independent authority of the Supreme Court. More than two-thirds of Americans believed that the Court should be free from political interference. Even New Deal supporters were disturbed by the court-packing scheme. The suggestion that individuals over age seventy had diminished mental capacity offended many elderly members of Congress, which defeated Roosevelt's plan in 1937.

Supreme Court justices still got the message. The four most conservative of the elderly justices—the "four horsemen of reaction," according to one New Dealer—retired. Roosevelt eventually named eight justices to the Court—more than any other president—ultimately giving New Deal laws safe passage through the Court.

Reaction and Recession

Emboldened by their defeat of the court-packing plan, Republicans and southern Democrats rallied around their common conservatism to obstruct additional reforms. Former president Herbert Hoover proclaimed that the New Deal was the "repudiation of Democracy" and that "the Republican Party alone [was] the guardian of . . . the charter of freedom." Democrats' arguments over whether the New Deal needed to be expanded—and if so, how—undermined the consensus among reformers and sparked antagonism between Congress and the White House. The ominous rise of belligerent regimes in Germany, Italy, and Japan also slowed reform as some Americans began to worry more about defending the nation than changing it.

Roosevelt himself favored slowing the pace of the New Deal. He believed that existing New Deal measures had steadily boosted the economy and largely eliminated the depression crisis. In fact, the gross national product in 1937 briefly equaled the 1929 level before dropping lower for the rest of the decade. Unemployment declined to 14 percent in 1937 but quickly spiked upward and stayed higher until 1940. Roosevelt's unwarranted optimism about the economic recovery persuaded him that additional deficit spending by the federal government was no longer necessary.

Roosevelt's optimism failed to consider the stubborn realities of unemployment and poverty, and the reduction in deficit spending reversed the improving economy. Even at the high-water mark of recovery in the summer of 1937, seven million people lacked jobs. In the next few months, national income and production slipped so steeply that almost two-thirds of the economic gains since 1933 were lost by June 1938.

This economic reversal hurt the New Deal politically. Conservatives argued that this recession proved that New Deal measures produced only an illusion of progress. The way to weather the recession was to tax and spend less as well as to wait for the natural laws of supply and demand to restore prosperity. Many New Dealers insisted instead that the continuing depression demanded that

Distributing Surplus Food to the Needy
When bountiful harvests produced surplus crops that would depress prices if they were sent to market, the New Deal arranged to distribute some of them to needy Americans. Here, farmworkers in east-central Arizona near the New Mexico border line up to receive a ration of potatoes authorized by the New Deal agent checking the box of index cards. Library of Congress.

Roosevelt revive federal spending and redouble efforts to stimulate the economy. In 1938, Congress heeded such pleas and enacted a massive new program of federal spending.

The recession scare of 1937–1938 taught the president the lesson that economic growth had to be carefully nurtured. The English economist John Maynard Keynes argued that only government intervention could pump enough money into the economy to restore prosperity, a concept that became known as Keynesian economics. Roosevelt never had the inclination or time to master Keynesian thought. But in a commonsense way, he understood that escape from the depression required a plan for large-scale spending to alleviate distress and stimulate economic growth (Figure 24.2).

The Last of the New Deal Reforms

From the moment he was sworn in, Roosevelt sought to expand the powers of the presidency. He believed that the president needed more authority to meet emergencies such as the depression and to administer the sprawling federal bureaucracy. Combined with a Democratic majority in Congress, a now-friendly Supreme Court, and the revival of deficit spending, the newly empowered White House seemed to be in a good position to move ahead with a revitalized New Deal.

Resistance to further reform was also on the rise, however. Conservatives argued that the New Deal had pressed government centralization

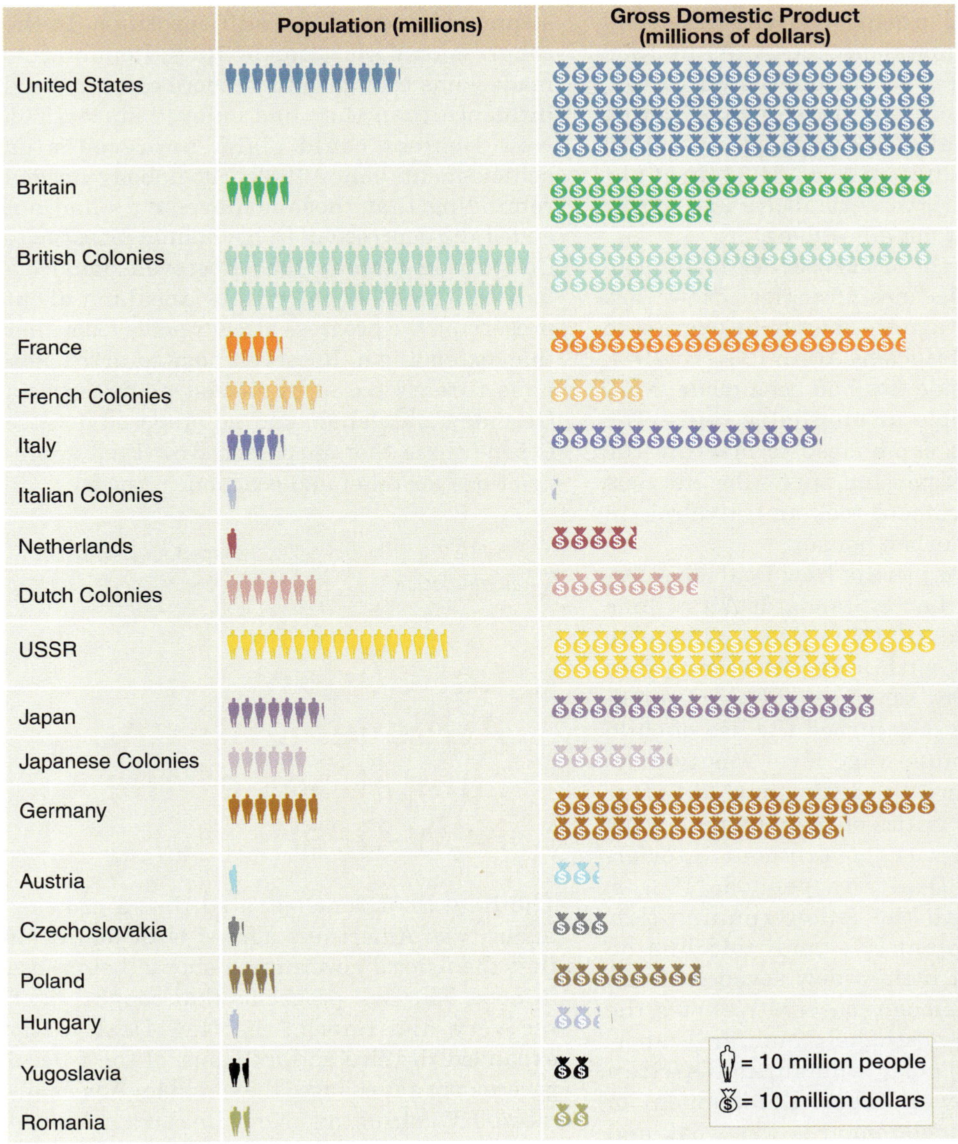

	Population (millions)	Gross Domestic Product (millions of dollars)
United States		
Britain		
British Colonies		
France		
French Colonies		
Italy		
Italian Colonies		
Netherlands		
Dutch Colonies		
USSR		
Japan		
Japanese Colonies		
Germany		
Austria		
Czechoslovakia		
Poland		
Hungary		
Yugoslavia		
Romania		

= 10 million people
= 10 million dollars

FIGURE 24.2   Global Comparison: National Populations and Economies, c. 1938
Throughout the Great Depression, the United States remained more productive than any other nation in the world. By 1938 the United States produced more than twice as much as its closest competitors, Germany and the USSR. If Germany had gained control of the other European nations listed here, it would have become the biggest economy in the world. What do these data suggest about the relationship between population and product?

too far. Even the New Deal's friends became weary of one emergency program after another while economic woes continued to shadow New Deal achievements. By the midpoint of Roosevelt's second term, restive members of Congress balked at new initiatives. But enough support remained for one last burst of reform.

Agriculture still had strong claims on New Deal attention in the face of drought, declining crop prices, and impoverished sharecroppers and tenants. In 1937, the Agriculture Department created the Farm Security Administration (FSA) to provide housing and loans to help tenant farmers become independent. A black tenant farmer in North Carolina who received an FSA loan told a New Deal interviewer, "I wake up in the night sometimes and think I must be half-dead and gone to heaven." For those who owned farms, the New Deal offered renewed prosperity with a second Agricultural Adjustment Act (AAA) in 1938 which placed production quotas on cotton, tobacco, wheat, corn, and rice while issuing food stamps to allow poor people to obtain surplus food. The AAA of 1938 brought stability to American agriculture and ample food to most—but not all—tables.

Advocates for the urban poor also made modest gains after decades of neglect. New York senator Robert Wagner convinced Congress to pass the National Housing Act in 1937. By 1941, some 160,000 residences had been made available to poor people at affordable rents. The program did not come close to meeting the need for affordable housing, but for the first time the federal government took an active role in providing decent urban housing.

The last major piece of New Deal labor legislation, the Fair Labor Standards Act of June 1938, reiterated the New Deal pledge to provide workers with a decent standard of living. The new law set wage and hours standards and at long last curbed the use of child labor. The minimum-wage level was twenty-five cents an hour for a maximum of forty-four hours a week. To critics of the minimum wage law who said it was "government interference," one New Dealer responded, "It was. It interfered with the fellow running that pecan shelling plant . . . [and] told him he couldn't pay that little widow seven cents an hour." To attract enough conservative votes, the act exempted domestic help and farm laborers—relegating most women and African Americans to lower wages. Enforcement of the minimum-wage standards was weak and

haphazard. Nevertheless, the Fair Labor Standards Act slowly advanced Roosevelt's inaugural promise to improve the living standards of the poorest Americans.

The final New Deal reform effort failed to make much headway against the hidebound system of racial injustice. Although Roosevelt denounced lynching as murder, he would not jeopardize his vital base of southern political support by demanding anti-lynching legislation, and Congress voted down attempts to make lynching a federal crime. Laws to eliminate the poll tax—used to deny blacks the opportunity to vote—encountered the same overwhelming resistance. The New Deal refused to confront racial injustice with the same vigor it brought to bear on economic hardship.

By the end of 1938, the New Deal had lost steam and encountered stiff opposition. In the congressional elections of 1938, Republicans made gains that gave them more congressional influence than they had enjoyed since 1932. New Dealers could claim unprecedented achievements since 1933, but nobody needed reminding that those achievements had not ended the depression. In his annual message to Congress in January 1939, Roosevelt signaled a halt to New Deal reforms by speaking about preserving the progress already achieved rather than extending it. Roosevelt pointed to the ominous threats posed by fascist aggressors in Germany and Japan, and he proposed defense expenditures that surpassed New Deal appropriations for relief and economic recovery.

REVIEW　Why did political support for New Deal reforms decline?

▶ Conclusion: Achievements and Limitations of the New Deal

The New Deal demonstrated that a growing majority of Americans agreed with Roosevelt that the federal government should help those in need. Through programs that sought relief, recovery, and reform, the New Deal vastly expanded the size and influence of the federal government and changed the way many Americans viewed Washington. New Dealers achieved significant victories, such as Social Security, labor's right to organize, and guarantees that farm prices would be maintained through controls on production and marketing. New Deal measures marked the emergence of a welfare state, but its limits left millions of needy Americans like Florence Owens and her children with little aid.

Full-scale relief, recovery, and reform eluded the New Deal. Even though millions of Americans benefited from New Deal initiatives, both relief and recovery were limited and temporary. In 1940, the depression still plagued the economy. Perhaps the most impressive achievement of the New Deal was what did not happen. Although authoritarian governments and anticapitalist policies were common outside the United States during the 1930s, they were shunned by the New Deal. The greatest economic crisis the nation had ever faced did not cause Americans to abandon democracy, as happened in Germany, where Adolf Hitler seized dictatorial power. Nor did the nation turn to radical alternatives such as socialism or communism.

Republicans and other conservatives claimed that the New Deal amounted to a form of socialism that threatened democracy and capitalism. But rather than attack capitalism, Franklin Roosevelt sought to save it. And he succeeded. That success also marked the limits of the New Deal's achievements. Franklin Roosevelt believed that a shift of authority toward the federal government would allow capitalist enterprises to be balanced by the nation's democratic tradition. The New Deal stopped far short of challenging capitalism either by undermining private property or by imposing strict national planning.

New Dealers repeatedly described their programs as a kind of warfare against the depression of the 1930s. In the next decade, the Roosevelt administration had to turn from the economic crisis at home to participate in a worldwide conflagration to defeat the enemies of democracy abroad.

Nonetheless, many New Deal reforms continued for decades to structure the basic institutions of banking, the stock market, union organizations, agricultural markets, Social Security, minimum-wage standards, and more. Opponents of these measures and of the basic New Deal notion of an activist government remained powerful, especially in the Republican Party. They claimed that government was the problem, not the solution—a slogan that Republicans championed during and after the 1980s and that led, with the cooperation of some Democrats, to the dismantling of a number of New Deal programs, including the regulation of banking. The deregulation of banking played a large role in the financial meltdown that began in 2008.

See the Selected Bibliography for this chapter in the Appendix.

24 Chapter Review

MAKE IT STICK

Go online and use LearningCurve to see what you know. Then review the key terms and answer the questions.

KEY TERMS

New Deal coalition (p. 679)
underconsumption (p. 682)
Federal Deposit Insurance Corporation (FDIC) (p. 683)
fireside chats (p. 683)
Civilian Conservation Corps (CCC) (p. 684)
Agricultural Adjustment Act (AAA) (p. 685)
National Recovery Administration (NRA) (p. 686)
Works Progress Administration (WPA) (p. 694)
Wagner Act (p. 696)
Committee for Industrial Organization (p. 696)
Social Security (p. 697)
court-packing plan (p. 701)

REVIEW QUESTIONS

1. Why did Franklin D. Roosevelt win the 1932 presidential election by such a large margin? (pp. 677–679)

2. How did the New Dealers try to steer the nation toward recovery from the Great Depression? (pp. 680–687)

3. Why did groups at both ends of the political spectrum criticize the New Deal? (pp. 687–692)

4. What features of a welfare state did the New Deal create and why? (pp. 693–700)

5. Why did political support for New Deal reforms decline? (pp. 700–704)

MAKING CONNECTIONS

1. How did Roosevelt build an effective interregional political coalition for the Democratic Party? How did the coalition shape the policies of the New Deal?

2. How effective were reform efforts targeting rural and industrial America?

3. Were any of Roosevelt's critics able to influence the New Deal? If so, how?

4. Who was in need of New Deal assistance but did not receive it? Why?

LINKING TO THE PAST

1. To what degree did the New Deal reflect a continuation of the progressive movement of the late nineteenth and early twentieth centuries? In what ways did the New Deal depart from progressive ideals? In general, how new was the New Deal? (See chapters 21 and 22.)

2. How did the New Deal coalition compare to the long-standing political coalition that had elected Republicans to the presidency since 1920? What accounted for the differences and similarities? (See chapter 23.)

25 The United States and the Second World War

1939–1945

CONTENT LEARNING OBJECTIVES

After reading and studying this chapter, you should be able to:

- Describe the foreign policy dilemmas that confronted the United States during the interwar years.

- Explain which events led to the onset of war and why the United States became involved. Describe the United States' war mobilization efforts.

- Outline the crucial military and diplomatic events of 1941 through 1943, demonstrating how the United States turned the tide in the Pacific and explaining its prime military objectives in the European theater.

- Analyze the impact of the war on American society including the effects it had on women and families, African Americans, and the 1944 presidential campaign.

- Assess which military and diplomatic events during 1943 to 1945 contributed to Allied victory in Europe and over Japan.

GI MAIL
Soldiers who engaged in deadly combat also stayed in touch with family and friends. The soldier who drew on this envelope emphasized that Uncle Sam was crushing the leaders of Germany and Japan. Stephen Douglas World War II Envelopes, Archives Center, National Museum of American History, Smithsonian Institution.

ON A SUN-DRENCHED FLORIDA AFTERNOON IN 1927, TWELVE-YEAR-OLD Paul Tibbets clambered into the front seat of the open cockpit of a biplane for his first airplane ride. While the pilot brought the plane in low over the Hialeah racetrack in Miami, Tibbets pitched Baby Ruth candy bars tethered to small paper parachutes to racing fans in the grandstands below. After repeating this stunt, sales of Baby Ruths soared, and Tibbets was hooked on flying.

In 1937, Tibbets joined the Army Air Corps and became a military pilot. Shortly after the Japanese attack on Pearl Harbor in December 1941 immediately overcame American isolationism and brought the United States into World War II, Tibbets flew on antisubmarine patrols against German U-boats lurking along the East Coast. When the heavily armored B-17 Flying Fortress bombers became available early in 1942, he took a squadron of the new planes to England. In August 1942, he led the first American daytime bombing raid on German-occupied Europe, releasing on railroad yards in northern France the first of some 700,000 tons of explosives dropped by American bombers during the air war in Europe.

After numerous raids over Europe, Tibbets was reassigned to the North African campaign. After eight months of combat missions, Tibbets returned to the United States and was ordered to test the new B-29 Super Fortress being built in Wichita, Kansas. The B-29 was much bigger than the B-17 and could fly higher and faster, making it ideal for the campaign against Japan. Tibbets's mastery of the B-29 caused him to be singled out in September 1944 to command a top-secret unit training for a special mission.

The mission was to be ready to drop on Japan a bomb so powerful that it might end the war. No such bomb yet existed, but American scientists and engineers were working around the clock to build one. In May 1945, Tibbets and his men went to Tinian Island in the Pacific, where they trained for their secret mission by flying raids over Japanese cities and dropping ordinary bombs. The atomic bomb arrived on Tinian on July 26, just ten days after a successful test explosion in the New Mexico desert. Nicknamed "Little Boy," the bomb packed the equivalent of 40 million pounds of TNT, or 200,000 of the 200-pound bombs Tibbets and other American airmen had dropped on Europe.

On August 6, 1945, Tibbets, his crew, and their atomic payload took off in the B-29 bomber *Enola Gay* and headed for Japan. Less than seven hours later, over the city of Hiroshima, Tibbets and his men released Little Boy from the *Enola Gay*'s bomb bay. Three days later, airmen from Tibbets's command dropped a second atomic bomb on Nagasaki, and within five days Japan surrendered.

Paul Tibbets's experiences traced an arc followed by millions of Americans during World War II. Like Tibbets, Americans joined their allies to fight the Axis powers in Europe and Asia. Like his *Enola Gay* crewmen—who hailed from New York, Texas, California, New Jersey, New Mexico, Maryland, North Carolina, Pennsylvania, Michigan, and Nevada—Americans from all regions united to help defeat the fascist aggressors in Asia and Europe. American industries mobilized to produce advanced bombers along with enough other military equipment to supply the American armed forces and their allies. At enormous cost in human life and suffering—including millions of civilians killed in military actions and millions more exterminated in the Holocaust of the Nazi's racist death camps—the war resulted in employment and prosperity to most Americans at home, ending the depression, providing new opportunities for women and African Americans, and ushering the nation into the postwar world as a triumphant economic and atomic superpower.

Colonel Paul Tibbets
Before taking off to drop the world's first atomic bomb on Hiroshima, Tibbets posed on the tarmac next to his customized B-29 Super Fortress bomber, named *Enola Gay* in honor of his mother. A crew of eleven handpicked airmen accompanied Tibbets on the top-secret mission. © Bettmann/Corbis.

▶ Peacetime Dilemmas

The First World War left a dangerous and ultimately deadly legacy. The victors—especially Britain, France, and the United States—sought to avoid future wars at almost any cost. The defeated nation, Germany, aspired to reassert its power and avenge its losses by means of renewed warfare. Italy and Japan felt humiliated by the Versailles peace settlement and saw war as a legitimate way to increase their global power. Japan invaded the northern Chinese province of Manchuria in 1931 with ambitions to expand throughout Asia. Italy, led by the fascist Benito Mussolini since 1922, hungered for an empire in Africa. In Germany, National Socialist Adolf Hitler rose to power in 1933 in a quest to dominate Europe and the world. (See chapter 24, "Beyond America's Borders," page 680.) These aggressive, militaristic, antidemocratic regimes seemed a smaller threat to most people in the United States during the 1930s than did the economic crisis at home. Shielded from external threats by the Atlantic and Pacific oceans, Americans hoped to avoid entanglement in foreign woes and to concentrate on climbing out of the nation's economic abyss.

Roosevelt and Reluctant Isolation

Like most Americans during the 1930s, Franklin Roosevelt believed that the nation's highest priority was to attack the domestic causes and consequences of the depression. But unlike most Americans, Roosevelt had long advocated an active role for the United States in international affairs.

The depression forced Roosevelt to retreat from his previous internationalism. He came to believe that energetic involvement in foreign affairs diverted resources and political support from domestic recovery. Once in office, Roosevelt sought to combine domestic economic recovery with a low-profile foreign policy that encouraged free trade and disarmament.

Roosevelt's pursuit of international amity was constrained by economic circumstances and American popular opinion. After an opinion poll demonstrated popular support for recognizing the Soviet Union—an international pariah since the Bolshevik Revolution in 1917—Roosevelt established formal diplomatic relations in 1933. But when the League of

CHRONOLOGY

1935–1937	• Neutrality acts.
1936	• Nazi Germany occupies Rhineland. • Italian armies conquer Ethiopia. • Spanish civil war begins.
1937	• Japanese troops capture Nanjing.
1938	• Hitler annexes Austria.
1939	• German troops occupy Czechoslovakia. • Nazi-Soviet nonaggression pact. • Germany's attack on Poland begins World War II.
1940	• Germany invades Denmark, Norway, France, Belgium, Luxembourg, and the Netherlands. • British and French evacuate from Dunkirk. • Battle of Britain. • Tripartite Pact.
1941	• Lend-Lease Act. • Germany invades Soviet Union. • Japanese attack Pearl Harbor.
1942	• Internment of Japanese Americans. • Japan captures Philippines. • Congress of Racial Equality founded. • Battles of Coral Sea and Midway. • Manhattan Project begins. • U.S. forces invade North Africa.
1943	• Allied leaders demand unconditional surrender of Axis powers. • U.S. and British forces invade Italy.
1944	• D Day.
1945	• Yalta Conference. • Roosevelt dies; Vice President Harry Truman becomes president. • Germany surrenders. • United States joins United Nations. • United States drops atomic bombs on Hiroshima and Nagasaki. • Japan surrenders, ending World War II.

Nations condemned Japanese and German aggression, Roosevelt did not support the league's attempts to keep the peace because he feared jeopardizing isolationists' support for New Deal measures in Congress. America watched from the sidelines when Japan withdrew from the league and ignored the limitations on its navy imposed after World War I. The United States also looked the other way when Hitler rearmed Germany and recalled its representative to the league in 1933. Roosevelt worried that German and Japanese actions threatened world peace, but he reassured Americans that the nation would not "use its armed forces for the settlement of any [international] dispute anywhere."

Americans All

The good neighbor policy emphasized the common interests of the United States and its Latin American neighbors. One consequence of the policy is illustrated by this World War II poster, which asserts the shared goal of Uncle Sam and sombrero-wearing Latin Americans to defeat the Axis powers. Above all, the United States sought to prevent Latin American nations from allying with German or Japan. United States Office of War Information.

The Good Neighbor Policy

In 1933, Roosevelt announced that the United States would pursue "the policy of the good neighbor" in international relations, which meant that no nation had the right to intervene in the internal or external affairs of another. He emphasized that this policy applied specifically to Latin America, where U.S. military forces had often intervened. The **good neighbor policy** did not indicate a U.S. retreat from empire in Latin America, though. Instead, it declared that, unlike in past decades, the United States would not depend on military force to exercise its influence in the region. Roosevelt refrained from sending troops to defend the interests of American corporations when Mexico nationalized American oil properties and revolution boiled over in Nicaragua, Guatemala, and Cuba during the 1930s. In 1934, Roosevelt withdrew American Marines from Haiti, which they had occupied since 1916. While Roosevelt's hands-off policy honored the principle of national self-determination, it also permitted the rise of dictators in Nicaragua, Cuba, and elsewhere, who exploited and terrorized their nations with private support from U.S. businesses.

Military nonintervention also did not prevent the United States from exerting its economic influence in Latin America. In 1934, Congress gave the president the power to reduce tariffs on goods imported into the United States from nations that agreed to lower their own tariffs on U.S. exports. By 1940, twenty-two nations had agreed to reciprocal tariff reductions, helping to double U.S. exports to Latin America, contributing to the New Deal's goal of boosting the domestic economy through free trade, and planting seeds of friendship and hemispheric solidarity.

The Price of Noninvolvement

In Europe, fascist governments in Italy and Germany threatened military aggression. Britain and France only made verbal protests. Emboldened, Hitler plotted to avenge defeat in World War I by recapturing territories with German inhabitants, all the while accusing Jews of polluting the purity of the Aryan master race. The virulent anti-Semitism of Hitler and his Nazi Party unified non-Jewish Germans and attracted sympathizers among many other Europeans, even in France and Britain.

In Japan, a stridently militaristic government planned to follow the invasion of Manchuria in 1931 with conquests extending throughout Southeast Asia. The Manchurian invasion bogged down in a long and vicious war when Chinese Nationalists rallied around their leader, Jiang Jieshi (Chiang Kai-shek), to fight against the Japanese. Preparations for new Japanese conquests continued, however. In 1936, Japan openly violated naval limitation treaties and began to build a battle-ready fleet to seek naval superiority in the Pacific.

In the United States, the hostilities in Asia and Europe reinforced isolationist sentiments. Popular disillusionment with the failure of Woodrow Wilson's idealistic goals caused many Americans to question the nation's participation in World War I. In 1933, Gerald Nye, a Republican from North Dakota, chaired a Senate committee that concluded that greedy "merchants of death"—American weapons makers, bankers, and financiers—dragged the nation into the war to line their own pockets. International tensions and the Nye committee report prompted Congress to pass a series of **neutrality acts** between 1935 and 1937 designed to avoid entanglement in foreign wars. The neutrality acts prohibited making loans and selling arms to nations at war.

By 1937, the growing conflicts overseas caused some Americans to call for a total embargo on all trade with warring countries. The Neutrality Act of 1937 attempted to reconcile the nation's desire for both peace and foreign trade with a "cash-and-carry" policy that required warring nations to pay cash for nonmilitary goods and to transport them in their own ships. This policy benefited the nation's economy, but it also helped foreign aggressors by supplying them with goods and thereby undermining peace.

The desire for peace in France, Britain, and the United States led Germany, Italy, and Japan to launch offensives on the assumption that the Western democracies lacked the will to oppose them. In March 1936, Nazi troops marched into the industry-rich Rhineland on Germany's western border, in blatant violation of the Treaty of Versailles. One month later, Italian armies completed their conquest of Ethiopia, projecting fascist power into Africa. In December 1937, Japanese invaders captured Nanjing (Nanking) and celebrated their triumph in the "Rape of Nanking," a deadly rampage that killed 200,000 Chinese civilians.

In Spain, a bitter civil war broke out in July 1936 when the Nationalists—fascist rebels led by General Francisco Franco—attacked the democratically elected Republican government. Both Germany and Italy reinforced Franco, while the Soviet Union provided much less aid to the Republican Loyalists. The Spanish civil war did not cause European democracies or the U.S. government to help the Loyalists, but more than 3,000 individual Americans enlisted in the Russian-sponsored Abraham Lincoln Brigade to fight alongside the Republicans. Abandoned by the Western nations, the Republican Loyalists were defeated in 1939, and Franco built a fascist bulwark in Spain.

Spanish Civil War, 1936–1939

Hostilities in Europe, Africa, and Asia alarmed Roosevelt and some Americans. The president sought to persuade most Americans to moderate their isolationism and find a way to support the victims of fascist aggression. He warned that an "epidemic of world lawlessness is spreading" and pointed out that "mere isolation or neutrality" offered no remedy. The popularity of isolationist sentiment caused Roosevelt to remark, "It's a terrible thing to look over your shoulder when you are trying to lead and find no one there." Roosevelt understood that he needed to maneuver carefully if the United States were to help prevent fascist aggressors from conquering Europe and Asia, leaving the United States an isolated island of democracy.

REVIEW Why did isolationism during the 1930s concern Roosevelt?

▶ The Onset of War

Between 1939 and 1941, fascist victories overseas eventually eroded American isolationism. At first, U.S. intervention was limited to providing material support to the enemies of Germany and Japan, principally Britain, China, and the Soviet Union. But Japan's surprise attack on

MAP 25.1
Axis Aggression through 1941
Through a series of surprise strikes before 1942 Mussolini sought to re-create the Roman empire in the Mediterranean while Hitler aimed to annex Austria and reclaim German territories occupied by France after World War I. World War II broke out when the German dictator attacked Poland.

Pearl Harbor eliminated that restraint, and the nation began to mobilize for an all-out assault on foreign foes.

Nazi Aggression and War in Europe

Under the spell of isolationism, Americans passively watched Hitler's relentless campaign to dominate Europe (Map 25.1). In 1938, Hitler incorporated Austria into Germany and turned his attention to Sudetenland, which had been granted to Czechoslovakia by the World War I peace settlement. Hoping to avoid war, British prime minister Neville Chamberlain offered Hitler terms of appeasement that would give the Sudetenland to Germany if Hitler agreed to leave the rest of Czechoslovakia alone. Hitler accepted the terms but didn't keep his promise. By 1939 Hitler had annexed Czechoslovakia and demanded that Poland return the German territory it gained after World War I. Recognizing that **appeasement** of Hitler had failed, Britain and France assured Poland that they would go to war with Germany if Hitler attacked. In turn, Hitler negotiated with his bitter enemy, Soviet premier Joseph Stalin, offering him concessions to prevent the Soviet Union from joining Britain and France in opposing a German attack on Poland. Despite the enduring hatred between fascist Germany and the Communist Soviet Union, the two powers signed the Nazi-Soviet treaty of nonaggression in August 1939, exposing Poland to an onslaught by both the German and Soviet armies.

At dawn on September 1, 1939, Hitler unleashed his *blitzkrieg* (literally, "lightning war") on Poland. "Act brutally!" Hitler exhorted his generals. "Send [every] man, woman, and child of Polish descent and language to their deaths, pitilessly and remorselessly." The attack triggered Soviet attacks on eastern Poland and declarations of war from France and Britain two days later, igniting a conflagration that raced around the globe. In September 1939, Germany seemed invincible, causing

many people to fear that all of Europe would soon share Poland's fate.

After the Nazis overran Poland, Hitler soon launched a westward blitzkrieg. In the first six months of 1940, German forces smashed through Denmark, Norway, the Netherlands, Belgium, and France. The speed of the German attack trapped more than 300,000 British and French soldiers, who retreated to the port of Dunkirk, where an improvised armada of British vessels ferried them to safety across the English Channel. By mid-June 1940, France had surrendered the largest army in the world, signed an armistice that gave Germany control of nearly two-thirds of the countryside, and installed a collaborationist government at Vichy. With an empire that stretched across Europe from Poland to France, Hitler seemed poised to attack Britain.

The new British prime minister, Winston Churchill, vowed that Britain, unlike France, would never surrender to Hitler. "We shall fight on the seas and oceans [and] . . . in the air," he proclaimed, "whatever the cost may be, we shall fight on the beaches, . . . and in the fields and in the streets." Churchill's defiance stiffened British resolve against Hitler's attack, which began in

Nazi Invasion of Poland

Adolf Hitler relished the early success of the German army's blitzkrieg against Poland in 1939. This photo shows Hitler reviewing a victory parade of his soldiers in Warsaw. After the conquest, Germans systematically murdered hundreds of thousands of Polish civilians and confined even more to slave labor camps. Hugo Jaeger/Time & Life Pictures/Getty Images.

mid-June 1940 when wave after wave of German bombers targeted British military installations and cities, killing tens of thousands of civilians. The outgunned Royal Air Force fought as doggedly as Churchill had predicted and finally won the Battle of Britain by November, clearing German bombers from British skies and handing Hitler his first defeat. Churchill praised the valiant British pilots, declaring that "never . . . was so much owed by so many to so few." Advance knowledge of German plans aided British pilots, who had access to the new technology of radar and to decoded top-secret German military communications. Battered and exhausted by German attacks, Britain needed American help to continue to fight, as Churchill repeatedly wrote Roosevelt in private.

From Neutrality to the Arsenal of Democracy

Most Americans condemned German aggression and favored Britain and France, but isolationism remained powerful. Roosevelt feared that if Congress did not repeal the arms embargo mandated by the Neutrality Act of 1937, France and Britain would soon succumb to the Nazi onslaught. "What worries me," Roosevelt wrote a friend, "is that public opinion . . . is patting itself on the back every morning and thanking God for the Atlantic Ocean (and the Pacific Ocean)" and underestimating "the serious implications" of the European war "for our own future." Congress agreed in November 1939 to allow belligerent nations to buy arms, as well as nonmilitary supplies, on a cash-and-carry basis.

In practice, the revised neutrality law permitted Britain and France to purchase American war materiel and carry it across the Atlantic in their own ships, thereby shielding American vessels from attack by German submarines lurking in the Atlantic. Roosevelt searched for a way to aid Britain short of entering a formal alliance or declaring war against Germany. Churchill pleaded for American destroyers, aircraft, and munitions, but he had no money to buy them under the prevailing cash-and-carry neutrality law. By late summer in 1940, as the Battle of Britain raged, Roosevelt concocted a scheme to deliver fifty old destroyers to Britain in exchange for American access to British bases in the Western Hemisphere, the first steps toward building a firm Anglo-American alliance against Hitler.

While German Luftwaffe (air force) pilots bombed Britain, Roosevelt decided to run for an unprecedented third term as president in 1940. But the presidential election, which Roosevelt won handily, provided no clear mandate for American involvement in the European war. The Republican candidate, Wendell Willkie, a former Democrat who generally favored New Deal measures and Roosevelt's foreign policy, attacked Roosevelt as a warmonger. Willkie's accusations caused the president to promise voters, "Your boys are not going to be sent into any foreign wars," a pledge counterbalanced by his repeated warnings about the threats to America posed by Nazi aggression.

Once reelected, Roosevelt maneuvered to support Britain in every way short of war. In a fireside chat shortly after Christmas 1940, he proclaimed that it was incumbent on the United States to become "the great arsenal of democracy" and send "every ounce and every ton of munitions and supplies that we can possibly spare to help the defenders who are in the front lines."

In January 1941, Roosevelt proposed the **Lend-Lease Act**, which allowed the British to obtain arms from the United States without paying cash but with the promise to reimburse the United States when the war ended. The purpose of Lend-Lease, Roosevelt proclaimed, was to defend democracy and human rights throughout the world, specifically the Four Freedoms: "freedom of speech and expression . . . freedom of every person to worship God in his own way . . . freedom from want . . . [and] freedom from fear." Lend-Lease started a flow of support to Britain that totaled more than $50 billion during the war, far more than all federal expenditures combined since Roosevelt had become president in 1933.

Stymied in his plans for an invasion of England, Hitler turned his massive army eastward and on June 22, 1941, sprang a surprise attack on the Soviet Union, his ally in the 1939 Nazi-Soviet nonaggression pact. Neither Roosevelt nor Churchill had any love for Joseph Stalin or communism, but they both welcomed the Soviet Union to the anti-Nazi cause. Both Western leaders understood that Hitler's attack on Russia would provide relief for the hard-pressed British. Roosevelt quickly persuaded Congress to extend Lend-Lease to the Soviet Union, beginning the shipment of millions of tons of trucks, jeeps, and other equipment that, in all, supplied about 10 percent of Russian war materiel.

As Hitler's Wehrmacht raced across the Russian plains and Nazi U-boats tried to choke off supplies to Britain and the Soviet Union, Roosevelt met with Churchill aboard a ship near

Newfoundland to cement the Anglo-American alliance. In August 1941, the two leaders issued the Atlantic Charter, pledging the two nations to freedom of the seas and free trade as well as the right of national self-determination.

Japan Attacks America

Although the likelihood of war with Germany preoccupied Roosevelt, Hitler exercised a measure of restraint in directly provoking America.

Japanese ambitions in Asia clashed more openly with American interests and commitments, especially in China and the Philippines. And unlike Hitler, the Japanese high command planned to attack the United States in order to pursue Japan's aspirations to rule an Asian empire it termed the Greater East Asia Co-Prosperity Sphere. Appealing to widespread Asian bitterness toward such white colonial powers as the British in India and Burma, the French in Indochina (now Vietnam), and the

MAP 25.2

Japanese Aggression Through 1941

Beginning with the invasion of Manchuria in 1931, Japan sought to extend its imperialist control over most of East Asia. Japanese aggression was driven by the need for raw materials for the country's expanding industries and by the military government's devotion to martial honor.

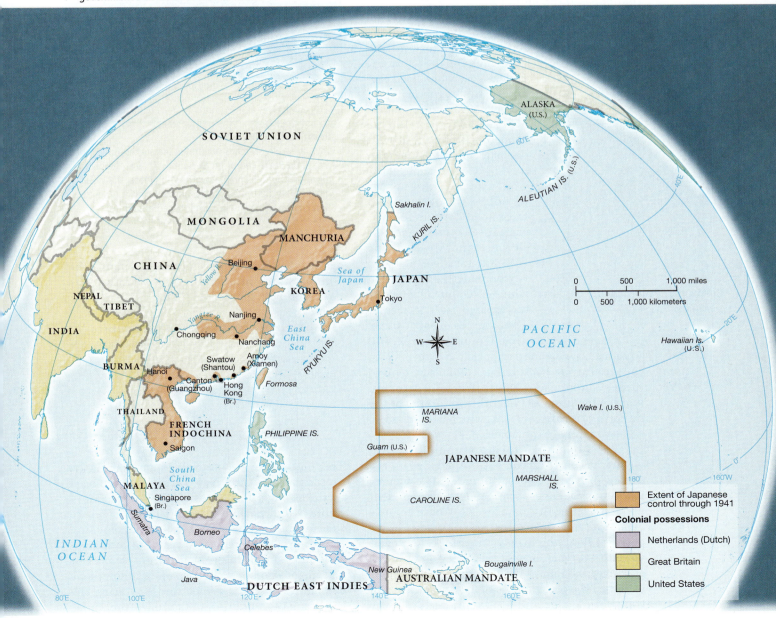

Dutch in the East Indies (now Indonesia), the Japanese campaigned to preserve "Asia for the Asians." Japan's invasion of China—which had lasted for ten years by 1941—proved that its true goal was Asia for the Japanese (Map 25.2). Japan coveted the raw materials available from China and Southeast Asia, and it ignored American demands to stop its campaign of aggression.

In 1940, Japan signaled a new phase of its imperial designs by entering a defensive alliance with Germany and Italy—the Tripartite Pact. To thwart Japanese plans to invade the Dutch East Indies, in July 1941 Roosevelt announced a trade embargo that denied Japan access to oil, scrap iron, and other goods essential for its war machines. Roosevelt hoped the embargo would strengthen factions within Japan that opposed the militarists.

Instead, the American embargo played into the hands of Japanese militarists headed by General Hideki Tojo, who seized control of the government in October 1941 and persuaded other leaders, including Emperor Hirohito, that swift destruction of American naval bases in the Pacific would leave Japan free to follow its destiny. On December 7, 1941, 183 aircraft lifted off six Japanese carriers and attacked the U.S. Pacific Fleet at Pearl Harbor on the Hawai'ian island of Oahu. The devastating surprise attack sank all of the fleet's battleships, killed more than 2,400 Americans, and almost crippled U.S. war-making capacity in the Pacific. Luckily for the United States, Japanese pilots failed to destroy oil storage facilities at Pearl Harbor or any of the nation's aircraft carriers, which happened to be at sea during the attack.

The Japanese scored a stunning tactical victory at Pearl Harbor, but in the long run the attack proved a colossal blunder. The victory made many Japanese commanders overconfident about their military prowess. Worse for the Japanese, Americans instantly united in their desire to fight and avenge the attack. Roosevelt vowed that "this form of treachery shall never endanger us again." On December 8, Congress endorsed the president's call for a declaration of war. Both Hitler and Mussolini declared war

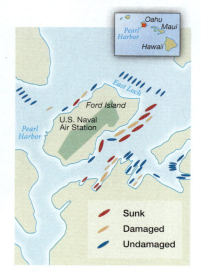

Bombing of Pearl Harbor, December 7, 1941

Sunk

Damaged

Undamaged

Pearl Harbor Attack
This Japanese postcard celebrates the successful surprise attack on Pearl Harbor on December 7, 1941, highlighting the airborne supremacy of the Japanese, the weak defenses of the United States, and the smoking destruction caused by Japanese carrier-based aircraft.
Museum of World War II, Natick, MA, www.museumofworldwarii.com.

against America on December 11, bringing the United States into all-out war with the Axis powers in both Europe and Asia.

REVIEW How did Roosevelt attempt to balance American isolationism with the military aggression of Germany and Japan in the late 1930s and early 1940s?

▶ Mobilizing for War

The time had come, Roosevelt announced, for the prescriptions of "Dr. New Deal" to be replaced by the stronger medicines of "Dr. Win-the-War." Military and civilian leaders rushed to secure the nation against possible attacks, causing Americans with Japanese ancestry to be stigmatized and sent to internment camps. Roosevelt and his advisers lost no time enlisting millions of Americans in the armed forces to bring the isolationist-era military to fighting strength for a two-front war. The war emergency also required economic mobilization unparalleled in the nation's history. As Dr. Win-the-War, Roosevelt set aside the New Deal goal of reform and plunged head-long into transforming the American economy into the world's greatest military machine, thereby achieving full employment and economic recovery, goals that had eluded the New Deal.

Home-Front Security

Shortly after declaring war against the United States, Hitler dispatched German submarines to hunt American ships along the Atlantic coast, where Paul Tibbets and other American pilots tried to destroy them. The U-boats had devastating success for about eight months, sinking hundreds of U.S. ships and threatening to disrupt the Lend-Lease lifeline to Britain and the Soviet Union. But by mid-1942, the U.S. Navy had chased German submarines into the mid-Atlantic.

Within the continental United States, Americans remained sheltered from the chaos and destruction the war was bringing to hundreds of millions in Europe and Asia. Nevertheless, the government worried constantly about espionage and internal subversion. Posters warned Americans that "Loose lips sink ships" and "Enemy agents are always near; if you don't talk, they won't hear." The campaign for patriotic vigilance focused on German and Japanese foes, but Americans of Japanese descent became targets of official and popular persecution because of Pearl Harbor and long-standing racial prejudice against people of Asian descent.

About 320,000 people of Japanese ancestry lived in U.S. territory in 1941, two-thirds of them in Hawai'i, where they largely escaped such wartime persecution because they were essential and valued members of society. On the mainland, however, Japanese Americans were a tiny minority—even along the West Coast, where most of them worked on farms and in small businesses. Although an official military survey concluded that Japanese Americans posed no danger, popular hostility fueled a campaign to round up all mainland Japanese Americans—two-thirds of them U.S. citizens. "A Jap's a Jap. . . . It makes no difference whether he is an American citizen or not," one official declared.

On February 19, 1942, Roosevelt issued Executive Order 9066, which authorized sending all Americans of Japanese descent to ten makeshift **internment camps** located in remote areas of the West (Map 25.3). Allowed little time to sell or secure their properties,

The Road to War: The United States and World War II

1931	Japan invades Manchuria.
1933	Franklin D. Roosevelt becomes U.S. president. Adolf Hitler becomes German chancellor.
1935–1937	Congress passes series of neutrality acts to protect United States from involvement in world conflicts.
1936	**March.** Nazi troops invade Rhineland, violating Treaty of Versailles.
	July. Civil war breaks out in Spain.
	Mussolini's fascist Italian regime conquers Ethiopia.
	November. Roosevelt reelected president.
1937	**December.** Japanese troops capture Nanjing, China.
1938	Hitler annexes Austria.
	September 29. Hitler accepts offer of "appeasement" in Munich from British prime minister Neville Chamberlain.
1939	**March.** Hitler invades Czechoslovakia.
	August. Hitler and Stalin sign Nazi-Soviet nonaggression pact.
	September 1. Germany invades Poland, beginning World War II. United States and Britain conclude cash-and-carry agreement for arms sales.
1940	**Spring.** German blitzkrieg smashes through Denmark, Norway, Belgium, Luxembourg, Netherlands, and northern France.
	Japan signs Tripartite Pact with Germany and Italy.
	May–June. German armies flank Maginot Line. British and French evacuated from Dunkirk. France surrenders to Germany.
	Summer/Fall. Germany conducts bombing campaign against England.
	November. Roosevelt wins third term as president. Royal Air Force wins Battle of Britain.
1941	**March.** Congress approves Lend-Lease Act, making arms available to Britain.
	June 22. Hitler invades Soviet Union.
	August. Roosevelt and Churchill issue Atlantic Charter.
	October. Militarists led by Hideki Tojo take over Japan.
	December 7. Japanese bomb Pearl Harbor. United States declares war on Japan.
	December 11. Germany and Italy declare war on United States.

VISUAL ACTIVITY

Japanese Internment
This photo shows Japanese Americans who were rounded up and confined to the horse barns and race track at Santa Anita, California, before being shipped out to internment camps throughout the western states. The imprisoned people on the left are saying goodbye to their friends seen waving from the windows of the train shown on the right, which was taking them to internment camps. ©CORBIS.

READING THE IMAGE: Why were these women, men, and children surrounded by high barbed-wire fences? What kinds of connections does the photo depict among the Japanese Americans at Santa Anita?

CONNECTIONS: How did World War II influence racial discrimination and civil rights in the United States?

into military service. In all, more than 16 million men and women served in uniform during the war, two-thirds of them draftees, mostly young men. Women were barred from combat duty, but they worked at nearly every noncombatant task, eroding traditional barriers to women's military service.

The Selective Service Act prohibited discrimination "on account of race or color," and almost a million African American men and women donned uniforms, as did half a million Mexican Americans, 25,000 Native Americans, and 13,000 Chinese Americans. The racial insults and discrimination suffered by all people of color made some soldiers ask, as a Mexican American GI did on his way to the European front, "Why fight for America when you have not been treated as an American?" Only black Americans were trained in segregated camps, confined in segregated barracks, and assigned to segregated units.

Most black Americans were consigned to manual labor, and relatively few served in combat until late in 1944, when the need for military manpower in Europe intensified. Then, as General George Patton told black soldiers in a tank unit in Normandy, "I don't care what color you are, so long as you go up there and kill those Kraut sonsabitches."

Japanese Americans lost homes and businesses worth about $400 million and lived out the war penned in by barbed wire and armed guards. (See "Documenting the American Promise," page 720.) Although several thousand Japanese Americans served with distinction in the U.S. armed forces and no case of subversion by a Japanese American was ever uncovered, the Supreme Court, in its 1944 Korematsu decision, upheld Executive Order 9066's blatant violation of constitutional rights as justified by "military necessity."

Building a Citizen Army

In 1940, Roosevelt encouraged Congress to pass the **Selective Service Act** to register men of military age who would be subject to a draft if the need arose. More than 6,000 local draft boards registered more than 30 million men and, when the war came, rapidly inducted them

MAP 25.3

Western Relocation Authority Centers
Responding to prejudice and fear of sabotage, President Roosevelt authorized the relocation of all Americans of Japanese descent in 1942. Taken from their homes in the cities and farmland of the far West, more than 120,000 Japanese Americans were confined in camps scattered as far east as the Mississippi River.

▲ WRA relocation camp

☐ States with more than 1,000 internees

African American Machine Gunners

Soldiers William Adam Leake and Adam Parham, shown here in May 1944, were among the first African American combat troops in the Pacific theater. They and thousands of other black soldiers fought in the Bougainville campaign to retake the Japanese-occupied portions of the Solomon Islands, just north of Australia, which continued until August 1945. The Granger Collection, New York.

Homosexuals also served in the armed forces, although in much smaller numbers than black Americans. Allowed to serve as long as their sexual preferences remained covert, gay Americans, like other minorities, sought to demonstrate their worth under fire. "I was superpatriotic," a gay combat veteran recalled. Another gay GI remarked, "Who in the hell is going to worry about [homosexuality]" in the midst of the life-or-death realities of war?

Conversion to a War Economy

In 1940, the American economy remained mired in the depression. Nearly one worker in seven was still unemployed, factories operated far below their productive capacity, and the total federal budget was less than $10 billion. Shortly after the attack on Pearl Harbor, Roosevelt announced the goal of converting the economy to produce "overwhelming . . . , crushing superiority of equipment in any theater of the world war." Factories were converted to assembling tanks and airplanes, and production soared to record levels. By the end of the war, jobs exceeded workers, plants operated at full capacity, and the federal budget topped $100 billion.

To organize and oversee this tidal wave of military production, Roosevelt called upon business leaders to come to Washington and, for the token payment of a dollar a year, head new government agencies such as the War Production Board, which set production priorities and pushed for maximum output. Contracts flowed to large corporations, often on a basis that guaranteed their profits. During the first half of 1942, the government issued contracts worth more than the entire gross national product in 1941.

Booming wartime employment swelled union membership. To speed production, the government asked unions to pledge not to strike. Despite the relentless pace of work, union members mostly kept their no-strike pledge, with the important exception of members of the United Mine Workers, who walked out of the coal mines in 1943, demanding a pay hike and earning the enmity of many Americans.

Overall, conversion to war production achieved Roosevelt's ambitious goal of "crushing superiority" in military goods. At a total cost of $304 billion during the war, the nation produced an avalanche of military equipment, more than double the combined production of

Japanese Internment

Determined that the bombing of Pearl Harbor would not be followed by more sneak attacks, military and political leaders on the West Coast targeted persons of Japanese descent—aliens and citizens alike—as potential saboteurs.

DOCUMENT 1
General John DeWitt, Final Recommendations of the Commanding General, Western Defense Command and Fourth Army, Submitted to the Secretary of War, 1942

Early in 1942, General John DeWitt, commander of the Western Defense Command, persuaded President Franklin Roosevelt to round up Japanese living in the United States and confine them to relocation camps for the duration of the war. DeWitt's recommendation expressed concern for military security and appealed to racist conceptions long used to curb Asian immigration. Japanese Americans and their supporters fought the internment order in the courts as a violation of fundamental constitutional rights, an argument rejected during the war by the U.S. Supreme Court.

February 14, 1942
Memorandum for the Secretary of War

Subject: Evacuation of Japanese and Other Subversive Persons from the Pacific Coast. . . .
Brief Estimate of the Situation.
1) . . . The following are possible and probable enemy activities: . . .
(a) Naval attack on shipping on coastal waters;
(b) Naval attack on coastal cities and vital installations;
(c) Air raids on vital installations, particularly within two hundred miles of the coast;
(d) Sabotage of vital installations throughout the Western Defense Command. . . .

Hostile Naval and air raids will be assisted by enemy agents signaling from the coastline and the vicinity thereof; and by supplying and otherwise assisting enemy vessels and by sabotage. . . .

In the war in which we are now engaged racial affinities are not severed by migration. The Japanese race is an enemy race and while many second and third generation Japanese born on United States soil, possessed of United States citizenship, have become "Americanized," the racial strains are undiluted. To conclude otherwise is to expect that children born of white parents on Japanese soil sever all racial affinity and become loyal Japanese subjects, ready to fight and, if necessary, to die for Japan in a war against the nation of their parents. . . .

It, therefore, follows that along the vital Pacific Coast over 112,000 potential enemies, of Japanese extraction, are at large today. There are indications that these are organized and ready for concerted action at a favorable opportunity. The very fact that no sabotage has taken place to date is a disturbing and confirming indication that such action will be taken.

Source: *Final Recommendations*, report by General John Lesesne DeWitt to the United States Secretary of War, February 14, 1942.

DOCUMENT 2
Charles Kikuchi, Prison Camp Diary, 1941–1942

Charles Kikuchi, a student at the University of California at Berkeley, sought in his prison camp diary to make sense of the internment and to judge where it would lead.

Germany, Japan, and Italy (Figure 25.1). This outpouring of military goods supplied not only U.S. forces but also America's allies, giving tangible meaning to Roosevelt's pledge to make America the "arsenal of democracy."

REVIEW How did the Roosevelt administration mobilize the human and industrial resources necessary to fight a two-front war?

▶ Fighting Back

The United States confronted a daunting military challenge in December 1941. The attack on Pearl Harbor destroyed much of its Pacific Fleet. In the Atlantic, Hitler's U-boats sank American ships, while German armies occupied most of western Europe and relentlessly advanced eastward into the Soviet

December 7, 1941

Berkeley, California

Pearl Harbor. We are at war! Jesus Christ, the Japs bombed Hawai'i and the entire fleet has been sunk. I just can't believe it. I don't know what in the hell is going to happen to us, but we will all be called into the Army right away.

. . . The next five years will determine the future of the Nisei [Japanese American citizens]. They are now at the crossroads. Will they be able to take it or will they go under? If we are ever going to prove our Americanism, this is the time. The Anti-Jap feeling is bound to rise to hysterical heights, and it is most likely that the Nisei will be included as Japs. I wanted to go to San Francisco tonight, but Pierre says I am crazy. He says it's best we stick on campus. In any event, we can't remain on the fence, and a positive approach must be taken if we are to have a place in fulfilling the Promise of America. I think the U.S. is in danger of going Fascist too, or maybe Socialist. . . .

I don't know what to think or do. Everybody is in a daze.

April 30, 1942, Berkeley

Today is the day that we are going to get kicked out of Berkeley. It certainly is degrading. . . .

I'm supposed to see my family at Tanforan as Jack told me to give the same family number. I wonder how it is going to be living with them as I haven't done this for years and years? I should have gone over to San Francisco and evacuated with them, but I had a last final to take. I understand that we are going to live in the horse stalls. I hope that the Army has the courtesy to remove the manure first. . . .

July 14, 1942

Marie, Ann, Mitch, Jimmy, Jack, and myself got into a long discussion about how much democracy meant to us as individuals. Mitch says that he would even go in the army and die for it, in spite of the fact that he knew he would be kept down. Marie said that although democracy was not perfect, it was the only system that offered any hope for a future, if we could fulfill its destinies. Jack was a little more skeptical. He even suggested that we [could] be in such grave danger that we would then realize that we were losing something. Where this point was he could not say. I said that this was what happened in France and they lost all. Jimmy suggested that the colored races of the world had reason to feel despair and mistrust the white man because of the past experiences. . . .

In reviewing the four months here, the chief value I got out of this forced evacuation was the strengthening of the family bonds. I never knew my family before this and this was the first chance that I have had to really get acquainted.

Source: Excerpts (pp. 43, 51, 183, 252) from *The Kikuchi Diary: Chronicle from an American Concentration Camp*, edited by John Modell. Copyright © 1973 by the Board of Trustees of the University of Illinois. Used with the permission of the University of Illinois Press and the author.

Questions for Analysis and Debate

1. What explains General DeWitt's insistence on evacuating the Japanese after he received the report of military investigators that no acts of sabotage had occurred?

2. How does the Kikuchi diary describe the meaning of internment for the detainees?

3. How did the internment camp experience influence the detainees' attitudes about their identity as Americans of Japanese descent?

Connect to the Big Idea

⊙ How did Americans and the American government treat minority citizens during World War II?

Union. Roosevelt and his military advisers believed that defeating Germany took top priority. To achieve that victory required preventing Hitler from defeating America's allies, Britain and the Soviet Union. If they fell, Hitler would command all the resources of Europe in a probable assault on the United States. To fight back effectively against Germany and Japan, the United States had to coordinate military and political strategy with its allies and muster all its human and economic assets. Victory over the Japanese fleet at the Battle of Midway, the successful elimination of Germany's menace to Allied shipping in the prolonged Battle of the Atlantic, and the Allied assault on North Africa and then Italy established Allied naval superiority in the Atlantic and Pacific and began to challenge German domination of southern Europe.

Turning the Tide in the Pacific

In the Pacific theater, Japan's leading military strategist, Admiral Isoroku Yamamoto, believed that if his forces did not quickly conquer and secure the territories they targeted, Japan would eventually lose the war because of America's far greater resources. Swiftly, the Japanese assaulted American airfields in the Philippines and captured U.S. outposts on Guam and Wake Island. After capturing Singapore and Burma, Japan sought to complete its domination of the southern Pacific with an attack in January 1942 on the American stronghold in the Philippines (see Map 25.5, page 734). American defenders surrendered to the Japanese in May. The Japanese victors sent captured American and Filipino soldiers on the infamous Bataan Death March to a concentration camp, causing thousands to die. By the summer of 1942, the Japanese had conquered the Dutch East Indies and were poised to strike Australia and New Zealand.

In the spring of 1942, U.S. forces launched a major two-pronged counteroffensive that military officials hoped would reverse Japanese advances. Forces led by General Douglas MacArthur, commander of the U.S. armed forces in the Pacific theater, moved north from Australia and eventually attacked the Japanese in the Philippines. Far more decisively, Admiral Chester W. Nimitz sailed his battle fleet west from Hawai'i to retake Japanese-held islands in the southern and mid-Pacific. On May 7–8, 1942, in the Coral Sea just north of Australia, the American fleet and carrier-based warplanes defeated a Japanese armada that was sailing around the coast of New Guinea.

Nimitz then learned from an intelligence intercept that the Japanese were massing an invasion force aimed at Midway Island, an outpost guarding the Hawai'ian Islands. Nimitz maneuvered his carriers and cruisers to surprise the Japanese at the Battle of Midway. In a furious battle that raged on June 3–6, American ships and planes delivered a devastating blow to the Japanese navy. The **Battle of Midway** reversed the balance of naval power in the Pacific and put the Japanese at a disadvantage for the rest of the war. Japan managed to build only six more large

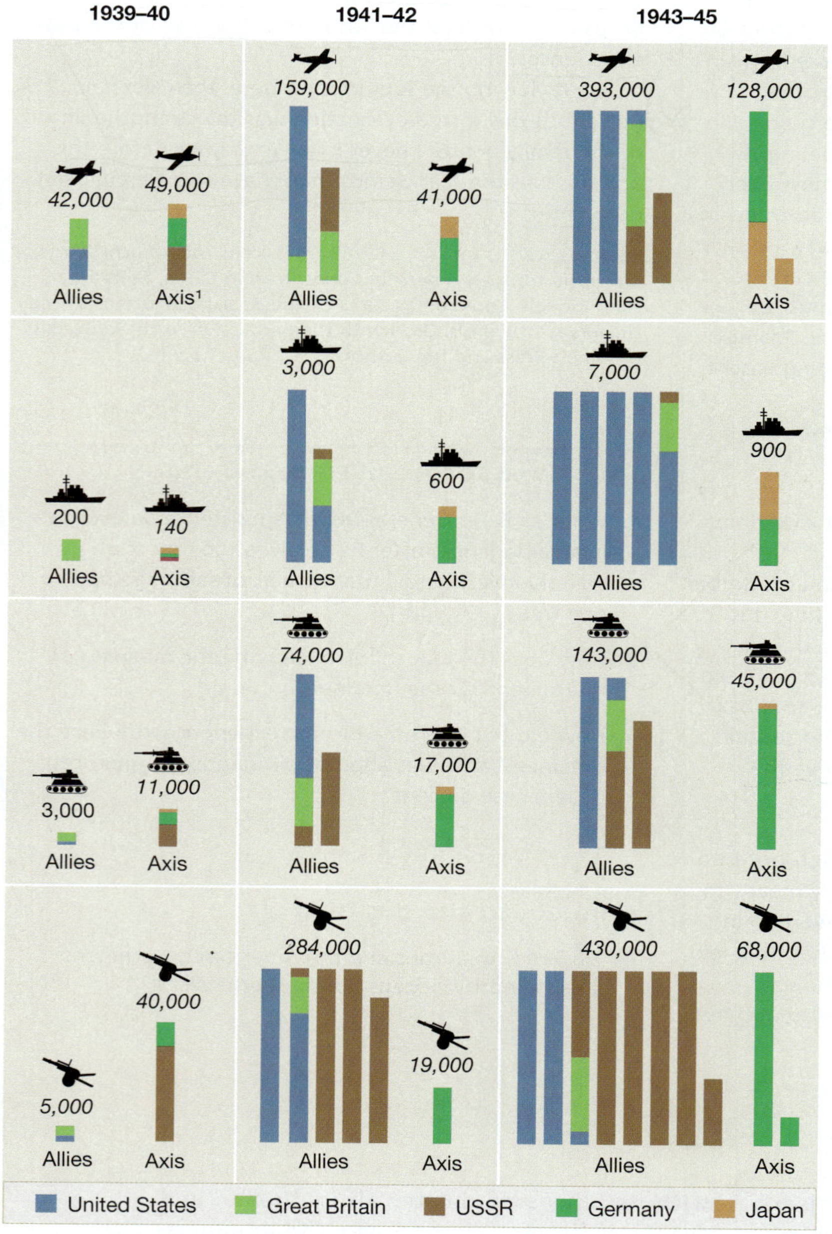

¹ The USSR was allied with Germany 1939–40.
² No reliable data exist for Japan.

FIGURE 25.1   Global Comparison: Weapons Production by the Axis and Allied Powers During World War II
U.S. weapons dominated the air and the sea during World War II. Together, the three Allied powers produced about three times as many aircraft and five to eight times as many warships as the two Axis powers. The Soviet Union led the other Allies in the production of tanks and artillery. What does the chronology of weapons production suggest about the kind of warfare emphasized by each belligerent nation and the course of the war?

Flamethrower in Combat in the Solomon Islands
American soldiers used flamethrowers in both the Pacific and European theaters. They were especially effective against enemy soldiers dug into bunkers that were difficult to penetrate by rifle or machine-gun fire. The Marine shown here, fighting in the Solomon Islands in 1943, carried on his back canisters of jellied gasoline and compressed air that were combined and projected through the gunlike machine. Soldiers: National Archives photo no. 111-SC-233458. Flamethrower: Armed Forces History Division, National Museum of American History, Smithsonian Institution.

aircraft carriers during the war, while the United States launched dozens, proving the wisdom of Yamamoto's prediction. But the Japanese still occupied and defended the many places they had conquered.

The Campaign in Europe

After Pearl Harbor, Hitler's eastern-front armies marched ever deeper into the Soviet Union while his western-front forces prepared to invade Britain. As in World War I, the Germans attempted to starve the British into submission by destroying their seaborne lifeline. In 1941 and 1942, they sank Allied ships faster than new ones could be built. Overall, the U-boat campaign sank 4,700 merchant vessels and almost 200 warships and killed 40,000 Allied seamen.

Until mid-1943, the outcome of the war in the Atlantic remained in doubt. Then, newly invented radar detectors and production of sufficient destroyer escorts for merchant vessels allowed the Allies to prey upon the lurking U-boats. After suffering a 75 percent casualty rate among U-boat crews, Hitler withdrew German submarines from the North Atlantic in late May 1943, allowing thousands

VISUAL ACTIVITY

Relief Column, Tunisia, North Africa

Peter Sanfilippo, a twenty-three year-old private from Brooklyn, New York, who fought in the Tunisian campaign in 1943, painted this column of American soldiers marching toward the front lines to relieve their wounded and exhausted comrades. Sanfilippo wrote that the arrival of a relief column "resurrected" among the "unnerved and wounded" soldiers "the spirit to thrive and . . . persevere into a new day." Peter Sanfilippo/Veterans History Project, Library of Congress, Institute on World War II and the Human Experience, Florida State University.

READING THE IMAGE: How do the soldiers in the relief column compare with the wounded soldiers they march past? How do the soldiers in the relief column appear to react to their wounded comrades?

CONNECTIONS: How did the physical and psychological challenges of combat affect ordinary soldiers and the war effort as a whole?

of American supply ships to cross the Atlantic unimpeded. Winning the battle of the Atlantic allowed the United States to continue to supply its British and Soviet allies for the duration of the war and to reduce the imminent threat of a German invasion of Britain.

The most important strategic questions confronting the United States and its allies were when and where to open a second front against the Nazis. Stalin demanded that America and Britain mount an immediate and massive assault across the English Channel into western France to force Hitler to divert his armies from the eastern front and relieve the pressure on the Soviet Union. Churchill and Roosevelt instead delayed opening a second front, allowing the Germans and the Soviets to slug it out. This drawn-out conflict weakened both the Nazis and the Communists and made an eventual Allied

attack on western France more likely to succeed. Churchill and Roosevelt decided to strike first in North Africa to help secure Allied control of the Mediterranean.

In October and November 1942, British forces at El-Alamein in Egypt halted German general Erwin Rommel's drive to capture the Suez Canal, Britain's lifeline to the oil of the Middle East and to British colonies in India and South Asia (see Map 25.4, page 732). In November, an American army under General Dwight D. Eisenhower landed far to the west, in French Morocco. Propelled by American tank units commanded by General George Patton, the Allied armies defeated the Germans in North Africa in May 1943. The North African campaign pushed the Germans out of Africa, made the Mediterranean safe for Allied shipping, and opened the door for an Allied invasion of Italy.

In January 1943, while the North African campaign was still under way, Roosevelt and Churchill met in Casablanca and announced that they would accept nothing less than the "unconditional surrender" of the Axis powers, ruling out peace negotiations. They concluded that they should capitalize on their success in North Africa and strike against Italy, consigning the Soviet Union to continue to bear the brunt of the Nazi war machine.

In July 1943, American and British forces landed in Sicily. Soon afterward, Mussolini was deposed in Italy, ending the reign of Italian fascism. Quickly, the Allies invaded the mainland, and the Italian government surrendered unconditionally. The Germans responded by rushing reinforcements to Italy, turning the Allies' Italian campaign into a series of battles to liberate Italy from German occupation.

German troops dug into strong fortifications and fought to defend every inch of Italy's rugged terrain. Allied forces continued to battle against stubborn German defenses for the remainder of the war, making the Italian campaign the war's deadliest for American infantrymen. One soldier wrote that his buddies "died like butchered swine."

REVIEW How did the United States seek to counter the Japanese in the Pacific and the Germans in Europe?

▶ The Wartime Home Front

The war effort mobilized Americans as never before. Factories churned out ever more bombs, bullets, tanks, ships, and airplanes, which workers rushed to assemble, leaving their farms and small towns and congregating in cities. Women took jobs with wrenches and welding torches, boosting the nation's workforce and fraying traditional notions that a woman's place was in the home rather than on the assembly line. Despite rationing and shortages, unprecedented government expenditures for war production brought prosperity to many Americans after years of depression-era poverty. Although Americans in uniform risked their lives on battlefields in Europe and Asia, Americans on the U.S. mainland enjoyed complete immunity from foreign attack—in sharp contrast to their Soviet and British allies. The wartime ideology that contrasted Allied support for human rights with Axis tyranny provided justification for the many sacrifices Americans were required to make in support of the military effort. It also established a standard of basic human equality that became a potent weapon in the campaign for equal rights at home and in condemning the atrocities of the Holocaust perpetrated by the Nazis.

Women and Families, Guns and Butter

Millions of American women gladly took their places on assembly lines in defense industries. At the start of the war, about a quarter of adult women worked outside the home, but few women worked in factories, except for textile mills and sewing industries. But wartime mobilization of the economy and the siphoning of millions of men into the armed forces left factories begging for women workers.

Government advertisements urged women to take industrial jobs by assuring them that their household chores had prepared them for work on the "Victory Line." One billboard proclaimed, "If you've sewed buttons, or made buttonholes, on a [sewing] machine, you can learn to do spot welding on airplane parts." Millions of women responded. Advertisers often referred to a woman who worked in a war industry as "Rosie the Riveter," a popular wartime term. By the end of the war, women working outside the home numbered 50 percent more than in 1939. Contributing to the war effort also paid off in wages. A Kentucky woman remembered her job at a munitions plant, where she earned "the fabulous sum of $32 a week. To us it was an absolute miracle. Before that we made nothing." Although men were paid an average of $54 for comparable wartime work, women accepted the pay differential and welcomed their chance to earn wages and help win the war at the same time.

The majority of married women remained at home, occupied with domestic chores and child care. But they, too, supported the war effort, planting Victory Gardens, saving tin cans and newspapers for recycling into war materiel, and buying war bonds. Many families scrimped to cope with the 30 percent inflation during the war, but men and women in manufacturing industries enjoyed wages that grew twice as fast as inflation.

The war influenced how all families spent their earnings. Buying a new washing machine

or car was out of the question since factories that formerly built them now made military goods. Many other consumer goods—such as tires, gasoline, shoes, and meat—were rationed at home to meet military needs overseas. But most Americans readily found things to buy, including movie tickets, cosmetics, and music recordings.

The wartime prosperity and abundance enjoyed by most Americans contrasted with the experiences of their hard-pressed allies. Personal consumption fell by 22 percent in Britain, and food output plummeted to just one-third of pre-war levels in the Soviet Union, creating widespread hunger and even starvation. Few went hungry in the United States as farm output grew 25 percent annually during the war, providing a cornucopia of food for export to the Allies.

The Double V Campaign

Fighting against Nazi Germany and its ideology of Aryan racial supremacy, Americans were confronted with the extensive racial prejudice in their own country. The *Pittsburgh Courier*, a leading black newspaper, asserted that the wartime emergency called for a **Double V campaign** seeking "victory over our enemies at home and victory over our enemies on the battlefields abroad." As a Mississippi-born African American combat veteran of the Pacific theater recalled, "We had two wars to fight: prejudice . . . and those Japs."

In 1941, black organizations demanded that the federal government require companies receiving defense contracts to integrate their workforces. A. Philip Randolph, head of the Brotherhood of Sleeping Car Porters, promised that 100,000 African American marchers would descend on Washington if the president did not eliminate discrimination in defense industries. Roosevelt decided to risk offending his white allies in the South and in unions, and he issued Executive Order 8802 in mid-1941. It authorized the Committee on Fair Employment Practices to investigate and prevent racial discrimination in employment.

Progress came slowly, however. In 1940, nine out of ten black Americans lived below the federal poverty line, and those who worked earned an average of just 39 percent of whites' wages. In search of better jobs and living conditions, 5.5 million black Americans migrated from the South to centers of industrial production in the North and West, making a majority of African Americans city dwellers for the first time in U.S. history. Severe labor shortages and government fair employment standards opened assembly-line jobs in defense plants to African Americans, causing black unemployment to drop by 80 percent during the war. But more jobs did not mean equal pay for blacks. The average income of black families rose during the war, but by the end of the conflict it still stood at only half of what white families earned.

Blacks' migration to defense jobs intensified racial antagonisms, which boiled over in the hot summer of 1943, when 242 race riots erupted in 47 cities. The worst mayhem occurred in Detroit, where a long-simmering conflict between whites and blacks over racially segregated housing ignited into a race war. In two days of violence, twenty-five blacks and nine whites were killed, and scores more were injured.

Racial violence created the impetus for the Double V campaign, officially supported by the National Association for the Advancement of Colored People (NAACP), which asserted black Americans' demands for the rights and privileges enjoyed by all other Americans—demands reinforced by the Allies' wartime ideology of freedom and democracy. While the NAACP focused on court challenges to segregation, a new organization founded in 1942, the Congress of Racial Equality, organized picketing and sit-ins against racially segregated restaurants and theaters. Still, the Double V campaign achieved only limited success against racial discrimination during the war.

Wartime Politics and the 1944 Election

Americans rallied around the war effort in unprecedented unity. In June 1944, Congress recognized the sacrifices made by millions of veterans, unanimously passing the landmark **GI Bill of Rights**, which gave military veterans government funds for education, housing, and health care, and it provided loans to help them start businesses and buy homes. The GI Bill put the financial resources of the federal government behind the abstract goals of freedom and democracy for which veterans were fighting, and it empowered millions of GIs to better themselves and their families after the war.

After twelve turbulent years in the White House, Roosevelt was exhausted and gravely ill with heart disease, but he was determined to remain president until the war ended. His poor health made the selection of a vice presidential candidate unusually important. Convinced that many Americans had soured on liberal reform, Roosevelt chose Senator Harry S. Truman of Missouri as his running mate. A reliable party man from a southern border state, Truman satisfied urban Democratic leaders while not worrying white southerners who were nervous about challenges to racial segregation.

The Republicans, confident of a strong conservative upsurge in the nation, nominated as their presidential candidate the governor of New York, Thomas E. Dewey, who had made his reputation as a tough crime fighter. In the 1944 presidential campaign, Roosevelt's failing health alarmed many observers, but his frailty was outweighed by Americans' unwillingness to change presidents in the midst of the war and by Dewey's failure to persuade most voters that the New Deal was a creeping socialist menace. Voters gave Roosevelt a 53.5 percent majority, his narrowest presidential victory, ensuring his continued leadership as Dr. Win-the-War.

Reaction to the Holocaust

Since the 1930s, the Nazis had persecuted Jews in Germany and every German-occupied territory, causing many Jews to seek asylum beyond Hitler's reach. (See "Beyond America's Borders," page 730.) Thousands of Jews sought to immigrate to the United States, but 82 percent of Americans opposed admitting them, and they were turned away. In 1942, numerous reports reached the United States that Hitler was sending Jews, Gypsies, religious and political dissenters, homosexuals, and others to

The Holocaust, 1933–1945

Principal German concentration and extermination camp

Mass Execution of Jewish Women and Children
On October 14, 1942, Jewish women and children from the village of Mizocz in present-day Ukraine were herded into a ravine, forced to undress and lie face down, and then shot at point-blank range by German officials. To centralize such executions, the Nazis built death camps, where they systematically slaughtered millions of Jews and other "undesirables." United States Holocaust Memorial Museum.

concentration camps, where old people, children, and others deemed too weak to work were systematically slaughtered and cremated, while the able-bodied were put to work at slave labor until they died of starvation and abuse. Other camps were devoted almost exclusively to murdering and cremating Jews. Despite reports of the brutal slave labor and killing camps, U.S. officials refused to grant asylum to Jewish refugees. Most Americans, including top officials, believed that reports were exaggerated. Only 152,000 of Europe's millions of Jews managed to gain refuge in the United States before America's entry into the war. Afterward, the number of Jewish refugees dropped to just 2,400 by 1944.

Desperate to stem the killing, the World Jewish Congress appealed to the Allies to bomb the death camps and the rail-road tracks leading to them in order to hamper the killing and block further shipments of victims. Intent on achieving military victory as soon as possible, the Allies repeatedly turned down such bombing requests, arguing that the air forces could not spare resources from their military missions.

The nightmare of the **Holocaust** was all too real. When Russian troops arrived at Auschwitz in Poland in January 1945, they found emaciated prisoners, skeletal corpses, gas chambers, pits filled with human ashes, and loot the Nazis had stripped from the dead, including hair, gold fillings, and false teeth. At last, the truth about

the Holocaust began to be known beyond the Germans who had perpetrated and tolerated these atrocities and the men, women, and children who had succumbed to the genocide. By then, it was too late for the 11 million civilian victims—mostly Jews—of the Nazis' crimes against humanity.

REVIEW   How did the war influence American society?

► Toward Unconditional Surrender

By February 1943, Soviet defenders had finally defeated the massive German offensive against Stalingrad, turning the tide of the war in Europe. After gargantuan sacrifices in fighting that had lasted for eighteen months, the Red Army forced Hitler's Wehrmacht to turn back toward the west. In the Pacific, the Allies had halted the expansion of the Japanese empire but now had the deadly task of dislodging Japanese defenders from the outposts they still occupied. Allied military planners devised a strategy to annihilate Axis resistance by taking advantage of America's industrial superiority. A secret plan to develop a super bomb harnessing atomic power came to fruition too late to use against Germany. But when the atomic bomb devastated the cities of Hiroshima and Nagasaki, Japan finally surrendered, cancelling the planned assault on the Japanese homeland by hundreds of thousands of American soldiers and sailors and their allies.

From Bombing Raids to Berlin

While the Allied campaigns in North Africa and Italy were under way, British and American pilots flew bombing missions from England to German-occupied territories and to Germany itself as an airborne substitute for the delayed second front on the ground. During night raids, British bombers targeted general areas, hoping to hit civilians, create terror, and undermine morale. Beginning with Paul Tibbets's flight in August 1942, American pilots flew heavily armored B-17s from English airfields in daytime raids on industrial targets vital for the German war machine.

German air defenses took a fearsome toll on Allied pilots and aircraft. In 1943, two-thirds of American airmen did not survive to complete their twenty-five-mission tours of duty. In all, 85,000 American airmen were killed in the skies over Europe. Many others were shot down and held as prisoners of war. In February 1944, the arrival of America's durable and deadly P-51 Mustang fighter gave Allied bombers superior protection. The Mustangs slowly began to sweep the Luftwaffe from the skies, allowing bombers to penetrate deep into Germany and pound civilian and military targets around the clock.

In November 1943, Churchill, Roosevelt, and Stalin met in Teheran to discuss wartime strategy and the second front. Roosevelt conceded to Stalin that the Soviet Union would exercise de facto control of the Eastern European countries that the Red Army occupied as it rolled back the still-potent German Wehrmacht. Stalin agreed to enter the war against Japan once Germany finally surrendered, in effect promising to open a second front in the Pacific theater. Roosevelt and Churchill promised that they would at last launch a massive second-front assault in northern France, code-named Overlord, scheduled for May 1944.

General Eisenhower was assigned overall command of Allied forces, and mountains of military supplies were stockpiled in England. The huge deployment of Hitler's armies in the east, which were trying to halt the Red Army's westward offensive, left too few German troops to stop the millions of Allied soldiers waiting to attack France. More decisive, years of Allied air raids had decimated the German Luftwaffe, which could send aloft only 300 fighter planes against 12,000 Allied aircraft.

After frustrating delays caused by stormy weather, Eisenhower launched the largest amphibious assault in world history on **D Day**, June 6, 1944 (Map 25.4). Allied soldiers finally succeeded in securing the beachhead. An officer told his men, "The only people on this beach are the dead and those that are going to die— now let's get the hell out of here." And they did, finally surmounting the cliffs that loomed over the beach and destroying the German defenses. One GI who made the landing recalled the soldiers "were exhausted and we were exultant. We had survived D Day!"

Within a week, a flood of soldiers, tanks, and other military equipment propelled Allied forces toward Germany. On August 25, the Allies liberated Paris from four years of Nazi occupation. As the giant pincers of the Allied and Soviet armies closed on Germany in December 1944, Hitler ordered a counterattack to capture the Allies' essential supply port at Antwerp, Belgium. In the Battle of the Bulge (December 16, 1944, to January 31, 1945), as the Allies termed it, German forces drove fifty-five miles into Allied lines before being stopped at Bastogne. More than 70,000 Allied soldiers were killed, including more Americans than in any other battle of the war. An American lieutenant recalled the macabre scene of "all the bodies . . . frozen stiff . . . many dead Americans and Germans . . . [many with] the ring finger . . . cut off in order to get the ring." The battle cost the Nazis hundreds of tanks and more than 100,000 men, fatally depleting Hitler's reserves.

In February 1945, while Allied armies relentlessly pushed German forces backward, Churchill, Stalin, and Roosevelt met secretly at the Yalta Conference (named for the Russian resort town where it was held) to discuss their plans for the postwar world. Roosevelt managed to secure Stalin's promise to permit votes of self-determination in the Eastern European countries occupied by the Red Army. The Allies pledged to support Jiang Jieshi (Chiang Kai-shek) as the leader of China. The Soviet Union obtained a role in the postwar governments of Korea and Manchuria in exchange for entering the war against Japan after the defeat of Germany.

The "Big Three" also agreed on the creation of a new international peacekeeping organization, the United Nations (UN). All nations

Nazi Anti-Semitism and the Atomic Bomb

During the 1930s, Jewish physicists fled Adolf Hitler's fanatical anti-Semitic persecutions and came to the United States, where they played a leading role in the research and development of the atomic bomb. In this way, Nazi anti-Semitism contributed to making the United States the first atomic power.

One of Germany's greatest scientists, Albert Einstein, won the Nobel Prize for physics in 1921. Among other things, Einstein's work demonstrated that the nuclei of atoms of physical matter stored almost inconceivable quantities of energy. A fellow scientist praised Einstein's discoveries as "the greatest achievements in the history of human thought." But Einstein was a Jew, and his ideas were ridiculed by German anti-Semites. A German physicist who had won the Nobel Prize in 1905 attacked Einstein for his "Jewish nonsense," which was "hostile to the German spirit." Einstein wrote to a friend, "Anti-Semitism is strong here [in Berlin] and political reaction is violent." Einstein's associates warned him that the anti-Semites had targeted him for assassination.

In his manifesto, *Mein Kampf*, Hitler proclaimed that Jews were "a foreign people," "inferior beings," the "personification of the devil,"

"a race of dialectical liars," "parasites," and "eternal bloodsuckers," who had the "clear aim of ruining the . . . white race." Hitler's rantings attracted a huge audience in Germany, and his personal Nazi army, which numbered 400,000 by 1933, terrorized and murdered anyone who got in the way.

In January 1933, just weeks before Franklin Roosevelt's inauguration as president of the United States, Hitler became chancellor of Germany on a tidal wave of popular support for his Nazi Party. Within months, he abolished freedom of speech and assembly, outlawed all political opposition, and exercised absolute dictatorial power. On April 7, Hitler announced the Law for the Restoration of the Professional Civil Service, which stipulated that "civil servants of non-Aryan descent must retire." A non-Aryan was defined as any person "descended from non-Aryan, especially Jewish, parents or grandparents." The law meant that scientists of Jewish descent who worked for state institutions, including universities, no longer had jobs. About 1,600 intellectuals in Germany immediately lost their livelihood and their future in Hitler's Reich. Among them were about a quarter of the physicists in Germany, including Einstein and ten other

Nobel Prize winners. The Nazis' anti-Semitism laws forced many leading scientists to leave Germany. Between 1933 and 1941, Einstein and about 100 other Jewish physicists joined hundreds of Jewish intellectuals in an exodus from Nazi Germany to the safety of the United States.

The refugee physicists scrambled to find positions at American universities and research institutes that would allow them to continue their studies. The accelerating pace of research in physics during the 1930s raised the possibility that a way might exist to release the phenomenal energy bottled up in atomic nuclei, perhaps even to create a superbomb. Einstein and other scientists considered that possibility remote. But many worried that if scientists loyal to Germany discovered a way to harness nuclear energy, Hitler would have the power to spread Nazi terror throughout the world. The refugee physicists asked Einstein to write a letter to President Roosevelt explaining the military and political threats posed by the latest research in nuclear physics.

In early October 1939, as Hitler's blitzkrieg swept through Poland, Roosevelt received Einstein's

would have a place in the UN General Assembly, but the Security Council would wield decisive power, and its permanent representatives from the Allied powers—China, France, Great Britain, the Soviet Union, and the United States—would possess a veto over UN actions. The Senate ratified the United Nations Charter in July 1945 by a vote of 89 to 2, reflecting the triumph of internationalism during the nation's mobilization for war.

While Allied armies sped toward Berlin, Allied warplanes dropped more bombs after D Day than in all the previous European bombing raids combined. By April 11, Allied armies reached the banks of the Elbe River and paused while the Soviets smashed into Berlin. The Red Army captured Berlin on May 2. Hitler had committed suicide on April 30, and the provisional German government surrendered unconditionally on May 7. The war in Europe was finally over, with the sacrifice of 135,576 American soldiers, nearly 250,000 British troops, and 9 million Russian combatants. (See "Historical Question," page 734.)

Roosevelt did not live to witness the end of the war. On April 12, he suffered a fatal stroke. Americans grieved for the man who had led them

letter and immediately grasped the central point, exclaiming, "What you are after is to see that the Nazis don't blow us up." Roosevelt quickly convened a small group of distinguished American scientists, who convinced the president to mount an all-out effort to learn whether an atomic bomb could be built and, if so, to build it. Only weeks before the Japanese attack on Pearl Harbor, Roosevelt decided to launch the Manhattan Project, the top-secret atomic bomb program.

Leading scientists from the United States and Britain responded to the government's appeal: "No matter what you do with the rest of your life, nothing will be as important to the future of the World as your work on this Project right now." Many of the most creative, productive, and irreplaceable scientists involved in the Manhattan Project were physicists who had fled Nazi Germany. Their efforts had brought the possibility of an atomic bomb to Roosevelt's attention. Having personally experienced Nazi anti-Semitism, they understood what was at stake—a world in which either Hitler had the atomic bomb or his enemies did.

In the end, Hitler's scientists failed to develop an atomic bomb, and Germany surrendered before the American bomb was ready to go. But the Manhattan Project succeeded, as Paul Tibbets proved over Hiroshima, Japan, on August 6, 1945. After the war, Leo Szilard, a leader among the refugee

Einstein Becomes a U.S. Citizen
Nazi anti-Semitism caused Albert Einstein to renounce his German citizenship, immigrate to the United States, and—in the 1940 naturalization ceremony recorded in this photo— officially become an American citizen. He is joined here by his secretary, Helen Dukas (right), and his stepdaughter, Margot Einstein (left).

physicists, remarked, "If Congress knew the true history of the atomic energy project . . . it would create a special medal to be given to meddling foreigners for distinguished services."

America in a Global Context

1. How did German anti-Semitism contribute to the United States' willingness to build and employ the atomic bomb?

2. In what ways were the United States' development and use of the atomic bomb "important to the future of the World"?

Connect to the Big Idea

C Why were German Jewish scientists accepted into American society at a time when Japanese Americans were isolated from the rest of the American population?

through years of depression and world war, and they worried about his untested successor, Vice President Harry Truman.

The Defeat of Japan

After the punishing defeats in the Coral Sea and at Midway, Japan had to fend off Allied naval and air attacks. In 1943, British and American forces, along with Indian and Chinese allies, launched an offensive against Japanese outposts in southern Asia, pushing through Burma and into China, where Jiang's armies continued to

resist conquest. In the Pacific, Americans and their allies attacked Japanese strongholds by sea, air, and land, moving island by island toward the Japanese homeland (Map 25.5).

The island-hopping campaign began in August 1942, when American Marines landed on Guadalcanal in the southern Pacific. For the next six months, a savage battle raged for control of the strategic area. Finally, during the night of February 8, 1943, Japanese forces withdrew. The terrible losses on both sides indicated to the Marines how costly it would be to defeat Japan. After the battle, Joseph Steinbacher, a twenty-

VISUAL ACTIVITY

The Allied War Effort

The Russian poster shown here illustrates the combined efforts of the Allies, declaring, "We won't let the evil enemy escape the noose. He will not evade it." Museum of World War II, Natick, MA, www.museumofworldwarii.com.

READING THE IMAGE: What does the depiction of Hitler on the Russian poster suggest about his leadership and character?

CONNECTIONS: What does the poster suggest about the importance of the alliance among the major Allied powers?

one-year-old from Alabama, sailed from San Francisco to New Guinea, where, he recalled, "all the cannon fodder waited to be assigned" to replace the killed and wounded.

In mid-1943, Allied forces launched offensives in New Guinea and the Solomon Islands that gradually secured the South Pacific. In the Central Pacific, amphibious forces conquered the Gilbert and Marshall islands, which served as forward bases for air assaults on the Japanese home islands. As the Allies attacked island after island, Japanese soldiers were ordered to refuse to surrender no matter how hopeless their plight.

While the island-hopping campaign kept pressure on Japanese forces, the Allies invaded the Philippines in the fall of 1944. In the four-

day Battle of Leyte Gulf, one of the greatest naval battles in world history, the American fleet crushed the Japanese armada, clearing the way for Allied victory in the Philippines. While the Philippine campaign was under way, American forces captured two crucial islands— Iwo Jima and Okinawa—from which they planned to launch an attack on the Japanese homeland. To defend Okinawa, Japanese leaders ordered thousands of suicide pilots, known as *kamikaze*, to crash their bomb-laden planes into Allied ships. But instead of destroying the American fleet, they demolished the last vestige of the Japanese air force. By June 1945, the Japanese were nearly defenseless on the sea and in the air. Still, their leaders prepared to fight to the death for their homeland.

Legend:
- Axis powers, including annexed territory
- Extent of Axis control, early Nov. 1942
- Allied powers
- Neutral nations
- Allied forces
- Major battle (Allied victory)

ICELAND

ATLANTIC OCEAN

NORWAY

SWEDEN

FINLAND

• Murmansk

• Archangel

Leningrad
Besieged
Sept. 1942–Jan. 1943

Sept. 1944

• Moscow

DENMARK

North Sea

Baltic Sea

GREAT BRITAIN

IRELAND

London •

NETH.

BELG.

Berlin
Captured
May 2, 1945

Danzig

Warsaw

SOVIET UNION

July 1944

Apr. 1945

GERMANY

POLAND

Mar. 1944

Aug. 1943

Normandy
D Day
June 6, 1944

LUX.

Battle of the Bulge
Dec. 16, 1944–Jan. 31, 1945

Stalingrad
Aug. 21, 1942–Jan. 31, 1943

Paris
Liberated
Aug. 25, 1944

FRANCE

SLOVAKIA

UKRAINE

Aug. 1944

SWITZ.

AUSTRIA

VICHY FRANCE

Aug. 1944

HUNGARY

ROMANIA

PORTUGAL

SPAIN

N
W   E
S

Corsica

CROATIA

SERBIA

Black Sea

BULGARIA

Adriatic Sea

ITALY

MONTENEGRO

TURKEY

Casablanca

SP. MOROCCO

Nov. 1942

Rome
Liberated
June 4, 1944

Sardinia

ALBANIA
(It.)

GREECE

MOROCCO

FRENCH NORTH AFRICA
(Vichy France)
Joined Allies Nov. 1942

Tunis
Occupied
May 12, 1943

Jul 1943

Sicily

TUNISIA

Rhodes
(It.)

Cyprus
(Br.)

LEBANON
(Fr.)

SYRIA

IRAQ

Crete (Gr.)

PALESTINE
(Br.)

TRANSJORDAN

Kasserine Pass
Feb. 14–26, 1943

Mediterranean Sea

Suez Canal

ALGERIA

El-Alamein
Oct. 23–Nov. 5, 1942

Alexandria

SAUDI ARABIA

0   200   400 miles
0   200   400 kilometers

LIBYA
(It.)

Nov. 1942

EGYPT

MAP ACTIVITY

Map 25.4   The European Theater of World War II, 1942–1945

The Russian reversal of the German offensive at Stalingrad and Leningrad, combined with Allied landings in North Africa and Normandy, trapped Germany in a closing vise of Allied armies on all sides.

READING THE MAP: By November 1942, which nations or parts of nations in the European theater were under Axis control? Which had been absorbed by the Axis powers before the war? Which nations remained neutral? Which ones were affiliated with the Allies?

CONNECTIONS: What were the three fronts in the European theater? When did the Allies initiate actions on each front, and why did Churchill, Stalin, and Roosevelt disagree on the timing of the opening of these fronts?

Why Did the Allies Win World War II?

An indispensable factor in Allied victory in World War II was the alliance among the major powers: the United States, Great Britain, and the Soviet Union. Fighting alone, none of the Allies could have prevailed against Nazi Germany. Together, they were able to defeat what had been the strongest military power in the world.

The major Axis nations—Germany and Japan—did almost nothing to help each other. In the Pacific, Japan fought alone against the United States and its other allies, especially Australia and China. Britain and the Soviet Union contributed relatively little to Allied efforts in the Pacific.

In Europe, Germany enjoyed the support of Hungary, Romania, Bulgaria, and Italy, but none of these nations had the resources and industrial might to field a fully modern army. The Germans conscripted tens of thousands of men from the territories they occupied as their armies swept east, but such coerced recruits made poorly motivated soldiers.

In contrast, the Allies had a single galvanizing purpose: to defeat Hitler. The United States devoted only about 15 percent of its war effort to defeat Japan; the remaining 85 percent was directed against Germany. Little else united the Allies. Political and ideological differences between the capitalist democracies and a Communist dictatorship produced suspicion and mistrust. Nonetheless, the Allies collaborated to force the unconditional surrender of Germany. Three militarily significant consequences of the wartime alliance stand out as decisive ingredients of Allied victory: American material support for Britain and the Soviet Union; American and British bombing campaigns and the D Day invasion of Europe; and the Red Army's success in stopping the eastward advance of the German army at Stalingrad, then driving it back to Berlin.

The flood of military supplies that poured out of American factories during the war made Allied victory possible. In total, the United States produced two-thirds of all Allied military equipment. In addition to shipping hundreds of millions of tons of supplies to Britain and stockpiling equipment for the D Day invasion, the United States sent more than half a million military vehicles to the Soviet Union, accounting for the bulk of the Red Army's motorized transportation. By 1944, American refineries supplied 90 percent of the Allies' high-octane gasoline, prompting Stalin to raise a toast at the Teheran conference "to the American auto industry and the American oil industry." American food shipments provided the equivalent of one meal a day for each Russian soldier. The American canned meat Spam was distributed so widely that Soviet troops called it "The Second Front," a sarcastic reference to the Americans' delay in opening a second front in western Europe.

The British and American bombing campaign against German targets in western Europe served as a crucial second-front surrogate until D Day, and it eventually allowed Allied pilots to rule the skies. The bombing campaign reduced the production of tanks, airplanes, and trucks by more than a third and diverted two-thirds of Germany's aircraft and three-quarters of its antiaircraft weapons from supporting the infantry on the eastern front to protecting German cities from Allied air attacks. Furthermore, improvements in Allied fighter planes allowed British and American pilots to decimate the Luftwaffe. Although the German civilian population and Allied air crews suffered huge casualties as a result of the air campaign, it decisively aided the Soviets' battle against the Germans on the eastern front.

But neither the bombing campaign nor the mountains of American supplies would have won the war if the Soviet Union had not stopped the seemingly unstoppable advance of the German Wehrmacht in the east. Within six months of Hitler's surprise attack on the Soviet Union in June 1941, Stalin's army had lost 4 million soldiers and nearly all its tanks and airplanes, and German armies threatened Moscow. U.S. military officials expected Stalin to capitulate within two or three months. Instead, the Red Army regrouped and managed to halt the Germans' eastward advance by early 1943.

Reversal of the German assault required colossal sacrifices by the people of the Soviet Union. As the German army swept east during

Soviet Counterattack on the Eastern Front
This photo depicts Russian soldiers, following a Red Army tank, participating in the massive Soviet counterattack in mid-1942 to push back the Nazi onslaught while snow is still on the ground. German soldiers firing from somewhere behind the smoke have killed two of the Russians as their comrades trudge doggedly ahead. The photo suggests the brutal, inch-by-inch, farmhouse-by-farmhouse fighting on the eastern front. © Bettmann/CORBIS.

1941, Russians frantically dismantled more than 1,500 industrial plants about to be captured by the Nazis, shipped them east of the Ural Mountains, and reassembled them there. They also built new plants and soon began producing thousands of new tanks, aircraft, and artillery to rearm the Soviet military. Through sheer hard work, the productivity of Soviet war industries more than doubled during the war. Meanwhile, food production plummeted, allowing the average Russian only one-fourth the amount of food available to the average German. Soviet casualties dwarfed the losses of the other Allies. For every American killed during the war, forty-five Soviets died. No contribution to Allied victory was more important than the monumental success of the Soviet Union on the eastern front.

Questions for Consideration

1. Specifically, how did the Allies help one another defeat the Axis powers?
2. Why was the eastern front so important to the Allied victory?

Connect to the Big Idea

C How did "Rosie the Riveter" help the Allies defeat Nazi Germany?

Legend:
- Extent of Japanese control, Aug. 1942
- Allies
- Neutral nations
- Allied forces
- Major battle
- Atomic bomb explosion

MAP ACTIVITY

Map 25.5 The Pacific Theater of World War II, 1941–1945

To drive the Japanese from their far-flung empire, the Allies launched two combined naval and military offensives—one to recapture the Philippines and then attack Japanese forces in China, the other to hop from island to island in the Central Pacific toward the Japanese mainland.

READING THE MAP: What was the extent of Japanese control up until August 1942? Which nations in the Pacific theater sided with the Allies? Which nations remained neutral?

CONNECTIONS: Describe the economic and military motivations behind Japanese domination of the region. How and when did they achieve this dominance? Judging from this map, what strategic and geographic concerns might have prompted Truman and his advisers to consider using the atomic bomb against Japan?

Hiroshima
This photo shows part of Hiroshima shortly after the atomic bomb dropped from the *Enola Gay*, leveling the densely populated city. Deadly radiation from the bomb maimed and killed Japanese civilians for years afterward. © Bettmann/CORBIS.

Joseph Steinbacher and other GIs who had suffered "horrendous" casualties in the Philippines were now told by their commanding officer, "Men, in a few short months we are going to invade [Japan]. . . . We will be going in on the first wave and are expecting ninety percent casualties the first day. . . . For the few of us left alive the war will be over." Steinbacher later recalled his mental attitude at that moment: "I know that I am now a walking dead man and will not have a snowball's chance in hell of making it through the last great battle to conquer the home islands of Japan."

Atomic Warfare

In mid-July 1945, as Allied forces prepared for the final assault on Japan, American scientists tested a secret weapon at an isolated desert site near Los Alamos, New Mexico. In 1942, Roosevelt had authorized the top-secret **Manhattan Project** to find a way to convert nuclear energy into a superbomb before the Germans added

such a weapon to their arsenal. More than 100,000 Americans, led by scientists, engineers, and military officers at Los Alamos, worked frantically to win the race for an atomic bomb. Germany surrendered two and a half months before the test on July 16, 1945, when scientists first witnessed an atomic explosion that sent a mushroom cloud of debris eight miles into the atmosphere. After watching the successful test of the bomb, J. Robert Oppenheimer, the head scientist at Los Alamos, remarked soberly, "Lots of boys not grown up yet will owe their life to it."

President Truman saw no reason not to use the atomic bomb against Japan if doing so would save American lives. Despite numerous defeats, Japan still had more than 6 million reserves at home for a last-ditch defense against the anticipated Allied assault, which U.S. military advisers estimated would kill at least 250,000 Americans. But first Truman issued an ultimatum: Japan must surrender unconditionally or face utter ruin. When the Japanese failed to respond by the deadline, Truman ordered that an atomic bomb be dropped on a Japanese city.

Major Campaigns and Battles of World War II, 1939–1945

September 1, 1939	Germany attacks Poland.
September 3, 1939	Britain and France declare war on Germany.
April 1940	Germany attacks Denmark and Norway.
May 1940	Germany invades Netherlands, Belgium, Luxembourg, and France.
June 1940	Italy joins Germany in war against Allies.
June–November 1940	Battle of Britain.
June 22, 1941	Germany invades Soviet Union.
December 7, 1941	Japan attacks Pearl Harbor.
December 8, 1941	U.S. Congress declares war on Japan.
December 11, 1941	Germany and Italy declare war on United States.
January 2–May 6, 1942	Battles of Bataan and Corregidor.
May 7–8, 1942	Battle of the Coral Sea.
June 3–6, 1942	Battle of Midway.
August 1942– February 1943	Battle of Guadalcanal.
August 21, 1942– January 31, 1943	Battle of Stalingrad.
October 23– November 5, 1942	British halt Germans at Battle of El-Alamein.
November 1942– May 1943	Allies mount North African campaign.
July 10, 1943	Allies begin Italian invasion through Sicily.
June 4, 1944	Allies liberate Rome from German occupation.
June 6, 1944	D Day—Allied forces invade Normandy.
August 25, 1944	Allies liberate Paris.
September 12, 1944	Allies enter Germany.
October 23–26, 1944	Battle of Leyte Gulf.
December 16, 1944– January 31, 1945	Battle of the Bulge.
February 19– March 16, 1945	Battle of Iwo Jima.
April 1–June 21, 1945	Battle of Okinawa.
May 2, 1945	Soviet forces capture Berlin.
August 6, 1945	United States drops atomic bomb on Hiroshima.
August 9, 1945	United States drops atomic bomb on Nagasaki.

The bomb that Colonel Paul Tibbets and his crew released over Hiroshima on August 6 leveled the city and incinerated about 100,000 people. Three days later, after the Japanese government still refused to surrender, the second atomic bomb killed nearly as many civilians at Nagasaki.

With American assurance that the emperor could retain his throne after the Allies took over, Japan surrendered on August 14. On a troop ship departing from Europe for what would have been the final assault on Japan, an American soldier spoke for millions of others when he heard the wonderful news that the killing was over: "We are going to grow to adulthood after all."

While all Americans welcomed peace, some worried about the consequences of unleashing atomic power. Almost every American believed that the atomic bomb had brought peace in 1945, but nobody knew what it would bring in the future.

REVIEW   Why did Truman elect to use the atomic bomb against Japan?

► Conclusion: Allied Victory and America's Emergence as a Superpower

At a cost of 405,399 American lives, the nation united with its allies to crush the Axis aggressors into unconditional surrender. Almost all Americans believed they had won a "good war" against totalitarian evil. The Allies saved Asia and Europe from enslavement and finally halted the Nazis' genocidal campaign against Jews and many others whom the Nazis considered inferior. To secure human rights and protect the world against future wars, the Roosevelt administration took the lead in creating the United Nations.

Wartime production lifted the nation out of the Great Depression. The gross national product soared to four times what it had been when Roosevelt became president in 1933. Jobs in defense industries eliminated chronic unemployment, provided wages for millions of women workers and African American migrants from southern farms, and boosted Americans' prosperity. Ahead stretched the challenge of maintaining that prosperity while reintegrating millions of uniformed men and women, with help from the benefits of the GI Bill.

By the end of the war, the United States had emerged as a global superpower. Wartime mobilization made the American economy the strongest in the world, buttressed by the military clout of the nation's nuclear monopoly. Although the war left much of the world a rubble-strewn wasteland, the American mainland had enjoyed immunity from attack. The Japanese occupation of China had left 50 million people without homes and millions more dead, maimed, and orphaned. The German offensive against the Soviet Union had killed more than 20 million Russian soldiers and civilians. Germany and Japan lay in ruins, their economies and societies as shattered as their military forces. But in the gruesome balance sheet of war, the Axis powers had inflicted far more grief, misery, and destruction on the global victims of their aggression than they had suffered in return.

As the dominant Western nation in the post-war world, the United States asserted its leadership in the reconstruction of Europe while occupying Japan and overseeing its economic and political recovery. America soon confronted new challenges in the tense aftermath of the war, as the Soviets seized political control of Eastern Europe, a Communist revolution swept China, and national liberation movements emerged in the colonial empires of Britain and France. The forces unleashed by World War II would shape the United States and the rest of the world for decades to come. Before the ashes of World War II had cooled, America's wartime alliance with the Soviet Union fractured, igniting a Cold War between the superpowers. To resist global communism, the United States became, in effect, the policeman of the free world, repudiating the pre–World War II legacy of isolationism.

See the Selected Bibliography for this chapter in the Appendix.

25 Chapter Review

MAKE IT STICK

 **LearningCurve**

Go online and use LearningCurve to see what you know. Then review the key terms and answer the questions.

KEY TERMS

good neighbor policy (p. 710)
neutrality acts (p. 711)
appeasement (p. 713)
Lend-Lease Act (p. 714)
internment camps (p. 717)
Selective Service Act (p. 718)
Battle of Midway (p. 722)
Double V campaign (p. 726)
GI Bill of Rights (p. 727)
Holocaust (p. 728)
D Day (p. 729)
Manhattan project (p. 737)

REVIEW QUESTIONS

1. Why did isolationism during the 1930s concern Roosevelt? (pp. 709–711)

2. How did Roosevelt attempt to balance American isolationism with the military aggression of Germany and Japan in the late 1930s and early 1940s? (pp. 711–716)

3. How did the Roosevelt administration mobilize the human and industrial resources necessary to fight a two-front war? (pp. 716–720)

4. How did the United States seek to counter the Japanese in the Pacific and the Germans in Europe? (pp. 720–725)

5. How did the war influence American society? (pp. 725–728)

6. Why did Truman elect to use the atomic bomb against Japan? (pp. 728–738)

MAKING CONNECTIONS

1. Did isolationism bolster or undermine national security and national economic interests? Discuss Roosevelt's evolving answer to this question.

2. Who benefited most from the wartime economy? What financial limitations did various members of society face, and why?

3. How did the United States play a decisive role in the Allies' victory?

4. How did minorities' contributions to the war effort draw attention to domestic racism? What were the political implications of these developments?

LINKING TO THE PAST

1. How did America's involvement in World War II differ from its participation in World War I? Consider diplomacy, allies and enemies, wartime military and economic policies, and social and cultural changes. (See chapter 22.)

2. Why did World War II succeed in creating the full economic recovery that remained elusive during the New Deal? Consider specifically the scope and limits of New Deal economic reforms and how they changed, if at all, during World War II. (See chapter 24.)

26 Cold War Politics in the Truman Years

1945–1953

CONTENT LEARNING OBJECTIVES

After reading and studying this chapter, you should be able to:

- Explain the origins of the Cold War, and describe where and how the containment policy was implemented.

- Describe President Truman's Fair Deal domestic agenda, and explain its successes and failures.

- Explain why the United States committed troops in Korea and how military objectives changed. Identify the war's costs and consequences.

HEADS TURNED WHEN CONGRESSWOMAN Helen Gahagan Douglas walked through the U.S. Capitol. Not only was she one of only ten female representatives in the 435-seat body, she also drew attention as an attractive former Broadway star and opera singer. Douglas served in Congress from 1945 to 1951 when the fate of the New Deal hung in the balance and the nation charted an unprecedented course in foreign policy.

Born in 1900, Helen Gahagan grew up in Brooklyn, New York, and left college early for the stage. She quickly won fame on Broadway, starring in show after show until she fell in love with one of her leading men, Melvyn Douglas. They married in 1931, and she followed him to Hollywood, where he hoped to advance his movie career and where she bore two children.

Helen Gahagan Douglas admired Franklin D. Roosevelt's leadership during the depression, and she and her husband joined Hollywood's liberal political circles. Douglas was drawn to the plight of poor migrant farmworkers when, visiting migrant camps, she saw "faces stamped with poverty and despair." Her work on their behalf led her to testify before Congress and become a friend of the Roosevelts. In 1944, she won election to Congress, representing not the posh Hollywood district where she lived but a multiracial district in downtown Los Angeles, which cemented her dedication to progressive politics.

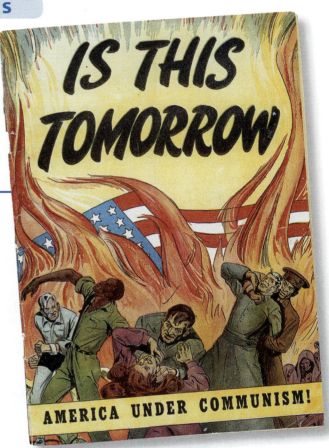

COLD WAR COMIC BOOK
After World War II, fear of communism pervaded American politics and popular culture. Four million copies of this 1947 comic book pictured the results of a Soviets takeover of the United States. Collection of Charles H. Christensen.

Like many liberals, Douglas was devastated by Roosevelt's death and unsure of his successor. "Who was Harry Truman anyway?" she asked. A compromise choice for the vice presidency, this "accidental president" lacked the charisma and political skills with which Roosevelt had transformed foreign and domestic policy, won four presidential elections, and forged a Democratic Party coalition that dominated national politics. Besides confronting domestic problems that the New Deal had not solved—how to avoid another depression without the war to fuel the economy—Truman faced new international challenges that threatened to undermine the nation's security.

By 1947, a new term described the hostility that had emerged between the United States and its wartime ally, the Soviet Union: Cold War. Truman and his advisers insisted that the Soviet Union posed a major threat to the United States, and they gradually shaped a policy to contain Soviet power wherever it threatened to spread. As a member of the House Foreign Affairs Committee, Douglas urged cooperation with the Soviet Union and initially opposed aid to Greece and Turkey, the first step in the new containment policy. Yet thereafter, Douglas was Truman's loyal ally, supporting the Marshall Plan, the creation of the North Atlantic Treaty Organization, and the war in Korea. The containment policy achieved its goals in Europe, but communism spread in Asia, and at home a wave of anti-Communist hysteria—a second Red scare—harmed many Americans and stifled dissent and debate.

Douglas's earlier links with leftist groups and her advocacy of civil rights and social welfare programs made her and other liberals easy targets for conservative politicians seeking to capitalize on the anti-Communist fervor that accompanied the Cold War. Running for the U.S. Senate in 1950, she faced Republican Richard M. Nixon, who had gained national attention for his efforts to expose Communists in government. Nixon's campaign labeled Douglas as "pink right down to her underwear" and sent thousands of voters the anonymous message, "I think you should know Helen Douglas is a Communist." Douglas's political career ended in defeat, just as much of Truman's domestic agenda fell victim to the Red scare.

Helen Gahagan Douglas at the Democratic National Convention

Long accustomed as an actress to appearing before an audience, the congresswoman from California was a popular campaigner and a featured speaker at Democratic National Conventions. Her appeal, shown in this photo from the 1948 convention, sparked interest in her for higher office. The *Washington Post* called it the "first genuine boom in history for a woman for vice-president." © Bettmann/Corbis.

▶ From the Grand Alliance to Containment

With Japan's surrender in August 1945, Americans besieged the government for the return of their loved ones. They were eager to dismantle the large military establishment and expected the United States and its allies, working with the United Nations, to cooperate in the management of international peace. Postwar realities quickly dashed these hopes. The wartime alliance forged by the United States, Great Britain, and the Soviet Union crumbled, giving birth to a Cold War. The United States began to develop the means for containing the spread of Soviet power around the globe, including a military buildup and an enormous aid program for Europe, known as the Marshall Plan.

The Cold War Begins

"The guys who came out of World War II were idealistic," reported Harold Russell, a young paratrooper who had lost both hands in a training accident. "We felt the day had come when the wars were all over." But such hopes were quickly dashed. Once the Allies had overcome a common enemy, the prewar mistrust and antagonism between the Soviet Union and the West resurfaced over their very different visions of the postwar world.

The Western Allies' delay in opening a second front in Western Europe aroused Soviet suspicions during the war. The Soviet Union made supreme wartime sacrifices, losing more than twenty million citizens and vast portions of its agricultural and industrial capacity. Soviet leader Joseph Stalin wanted to make Germany pay for Soviet economic reconstruction and to expand Soviet influence in the world. Above all, he wanted friendly governments on the Soviet Union's borders in Eastern Europe, through which his nation had been attacked twice in the past twenty-five years. A ruthless dictator, Stalin also wanted to maintain his own power.

In contrast to the Soviet devastation, American losses were relatively light, and the United States emerged from the war as the most powerful nation on the planet, with a vastly expanded economy and a monopoly on atomic weapons. That sheer power, along with U.S. economic interests and a belief in the superiority of American institutions and intentions,

CHRONOLOGY

1945	• Roosevelt dies; Truman becomes president.
1946	• Postwar labor unrest. • President's Committee on Civil Rights created. • George F. Kennan drafts containment policy. • United States grants independence to Philippines. • Employment Act. • Republicans gain control of Congress.
1947	• National Security Act. • Truman announces Truman Doctrine. • U.S. aid to Greece and Turkey. • Truman establishes loyalty program. • *Mendez v. Westminster*.
1948	• Marshall Plan approved. • Truman orders desegregation of military. • American GI Forum founded. • United States recognizes Israel. • Truman elected president.
1948–1949	• Berlin crisis and airlift.
1949	• Communists take over China • North Atlantic Treaty Organization formed. • Soviet Union explodes atomic bomb.
1950	• Senator Joseph McCarthy claims U.S. government harbors Communists. • Truman approves hydrogen bomb. • Korean War begins.
1951	• Truman fires General Douglas MacArthur. • U.S. occupation of Japan ends.
1952	• Dwight D. Eisenhower elected president.
1953	• Korean War ends.

all affected how American leaders approached the Soviet Union.

With the depression still fresh in their minds, American officials believed that a healthy economy depended on opportunities abroad. American companies needed access to raw materials, markets for their goods, and security for their investments overseas. These needs could be met best in countries with similar economic and political systems. As President Harry S. Truman put it in 1947, "The American system can survive in America only if it becomes a world system." Yet leaders and citizens alike regarded their foreign policy not as a self-interested campaign for economic advantage, but as the means to preserve national security and bring freedom, democracy, and capitalism to the rest of the world. Laura Briggs, a woman from Idaho, spoke for many Americans who believed "it was our destiny to prove that we were the children of God and that our way was right for the world."

Recent history also shaped postwar foreign policy. Americans believed that World War II might have been avoided had Britain and France resisted rather than appeased Hitler's initial aggression. Navy Secretary James V. Forrestal argued against trying to "buy [the Soviets'] understanding and sympathy. We tried that once with Hitler." The man with ultimate responsibility for U.S. policy was a keen student of history but came to the White House with little international experience beyond his service in World War I. Harry S. Truman anticipated Soviet-American cooperation, as long as the Soviet Union conformed to U.S. plans for the postwar world. Proud of his ability to make quick decisions, Truman determined to take a firm hand if the Soviets tried to expand, confident that America's nuclear monopoly gave him the upper hand.

The **Cold War** first emerged over clashing Soviet and American interests in Eastern Europe. Stalin insisted that wartime agreements gave him a free hand in the countries defeated or liberated by the Red Army, just as the United States was unilaterally reconstructing governments in Italy and Japan. The Soviet dictator used harsh methods to install Communist governments in neighboring Poland and Bulgaria. Elsewhere, Stalin initially tolerated non-Communist governments in Hungary and Czechoslovakia. In early 1946, he responded to pressure from the West and removed troops from Iran on the Soviet Union's southwest border, allowing U.S. access to the rich oil fields there.

Stalin saw hypocrisy when U.S. officials demanded democratic elections in Eastern Europe while supporting dictatorships friendly to U.S. interests in Latin America. The United States clung to its sphere of influence while opposing Soviet efforts to create its own. But the Western Allies were unwilling to match tough words with military force against the largest army in the world. They protested strongly but failed to prevent the Soviet Union from establishing satellite countries throughout Eastern Europe (Map 26.1).

In 1946, the wartime Allies contended over Germany's future. Both sides wanted to demilitarize Germany, but U.S. policymakers sought rapid industrial revival there to foster European economic recovery and thus America's own long-term prosperity. By contrast, the Soviet Union wanted Germany weak both militarily and economically, and Stalin demanded heavy reparations from Germany to help rebuild the devastated Soviet economy. Unable to settle their differences, the Allies divided Germany. The Soviet Union installed a puppet Communist government in the eastern section, and Britain, France, and the United States began to unify their occupation zones, eventually establishing the Federal Republic of Germany—West Germany—in 1949.

The war of words escalated early in 1946. Boasting of the superiority of the Soviet system, Stalin told a Moscow audience in February that capitalism inevitably produced war. One month later, Truman accompanied Winston Churchill to Westminster College in Fulton, Missouri, where the former prime minister denounced Soviet interference in Eastern Europe. "From Stettin in the Baltic to Trieste in the Adriatic, an **iron curtain** has descended across the Continent," Churchill said. (See "Documenting the American Promise," page 746.) Stalin saw Churchill's proposal for joint British-American action to combat Soviet aggression as "a call to war against the USSR."

In February 1946, George F. Kennan, a career diplomat and expert on Russia, wrote a comprehensive rationale for what came to be called the policy of **containment**. Downplaying the influence of Communist ideology in Soviet policy, he instead stressed Soviet insecurity and Stalin's need to maintain authority at home, which, he believed, prompted Stalin to exaggerate threats from abroad and expand Soviet power. Kennan believed that the Soviet Union would retreat from its expansionist efforts if the United States would respond with "unalterable counterforce." This approach, he predicted

MAP ACTIVITY

Map 26.1   The Division of Europe after World War II
The "iron curtain," a term coined by Winston Churchill to refer to the Soviet grip on Eastern Europe, divided the continent for nearly fifty years. Communist governments controlled the countries along the Soviet Union's western border, except for Finland, which remained neutral.

READING THE MAP: Is the division of Europe among NATO, Communist, and neutral countries about equal? Why would the location of Berlin pose a problem for the Western allies?
CONNECTIONS: When was NATO founded, and what was its purpose? How did the postwar division of Europe compare with the wartime alliances?

would eventually end in "either the breakup or the gradual mellowing of Soviet power."

Not all public figures agreed. In September 1946, Secretary of Commerce Henry A. Wallace urged greater understanding of the Soviets' national security concerns, insisting that "we have no more business in the political affairs of Eastern Europe than Russia has in the political affairs of Latin America." (See "Documenting the American Promise," page 746.) State Department officials were furious at Wallace for

challenging the administration's hard line against the Soviet Union, and Truman fired Wallace.

The Truman Doctrine and the Marshall Plan

In 1947, the United States began to implement the doctrine of containment that would guide foreign policy for the next four decades. It was not an easy transition; Americans approved of taking a hard line against the Soviet Union but

The Emerging Cold War

Early in 1946, Soviet and Western leaders began to express publicly distrust and attributed hostile motivations to each other. Within the United States, disagreement arose about how to deal with the Soviet Union.

DOCUMENT 1
Joseph Stalin, Address on the Strengths of the Soviet Social System, Moscow, February 9, 1946

In early 1946, Premier Joseph Stalin called on the Soviet people to support his program for economic development. Leaders in the West viewed his comments about communism and capitalism and his boasts about the strength of the Red Army as a threat to peace.

The [Second World War] arose as the inevitable result of the development of the world economic and political forces on the basis of monopoly capitalism. . . .

. . . The uneven development of the capitalist countries leads in time to sharp disturbances in their relations, and the group of countries which consider themselves inadequately provided with raw materials and export markets try usually to change this situation and to change the position in their favor by means of armed force. As a result of these factors, the capitalist world is split into two hostile camps and war follows. . . . The Soviet social system has proved to be more capable of life and more stable than a non-Soviet social system. . . .

. . . The Red Army heroically withstood all the adversities of the war, routed completely the armies of our enemies and emerged victoriously from the war. This is recognized by everybody—friend and foe.

[Stalin talks about his new Five-Year Plan.] Special attention will be focused on expanding the production of goods for mass consumption, on raising the standard of life of the working people by consistent and systematic reduction of the costs of all goods, and on wide-scale construction of all kinds of scientific research institutes to enable science to develop its forces. I have no doubt that if we render the necessary assistance to our scientists they will be able not only to overtake but also in the very near future to surpass the achievements of science outside the boundaries of our country.

Source: Excerpts from Joseph Stalin, "New Five-Year Plan for Russia," *Vital Speeches of the Day*, February 9, 1946, pp. 300–304.

DOCUMENT 2
Winston Churchill, "Iron Curtain" Speech, Westminster College, Fulton, Missouri, March 5, 1946

With Truman beside him, Winston Churchill, former prime minister of Great Britain, assessed Soviet actions in harsh terms. In response, Stalin equated Churchill with Hitler, a "firebrand of war."

. . . I have a strong admiration and regard for the valiant Russian people and for my war-time comrade, Marshal Stalin. . . . We understand the Russians need to be secure on her western frontiers from all renewal of German aggression. . . . It is my duty, however, to place before you certain facts. . . .

From Stettin in the Baltic to Trieste in the Adriatic, an iron curtain has descended across the Continent. Behind that line lie all the capitals of the ancient states of central and eastern Europe. Warsaw, Berlin, Prague, Vienna, Budapest, Belgrade, Bucharest and Sofia, all these famous cities and the populations around them lie in the Soviet sphere and all are subject in one form or another, not only to Soviet influence but to a very high and increasing measure of control from Moscow. . . . The Communist parties, which were very small in all these eastern states of Europe, have been raised to preeminence and power far beyond their numbers and are seeking everywhere to obtain totalitarian control. Police governments are prevailing in nearly every case. . . .

wanted to keep their soldiers and tax dollars at home. In addition to selling containment to the public, Truman had to gain the support of a Republican-controlled Congress, which included those who staunchly opposed to a strong U.S. presence in Europe.

Crises in two Mediterranean countries triggered the implementation of containment. In

. . . In a great number of countries, far from the Russian frontiers and throughout the world, Communist fifth columns are established and work in complete unity and absolute obedience to the directions they receive from the Communist center.

I do not believe that Soviet Russia desires war. What they desire is the fruits of war and the indefinite expansion of their power and doctrines. . . . Our difficulties and dangers will not be removed by . . . mere waiting to see what happens; nor will they be relieved by a policy of appeasement. . . . I am convinced that there is nothing [the Russians] admire so much as strength, and there is nothing for which they have less respect than for military weakness.

Source: Excerpts from Winston Churchill, "Alliance of English-Speaking People," *Vital Speeches of the Day*, March 5, 1946, 329–332.

DOCUMENT 3
Henry A. Wallace, Address on the Folly of the U.S. "Get Tough with Russia" Policy, Madison Square Garden, New York, September 12, 1946

Throughout 1946, Henry A. Wallace, Truman's secretary of commerce, urged the president to take a more conciliatory approach toward the Soviet Union, a position reflected in his speech to leftist and liberal groups.

We cannot rest in the assurance that we invented the atom bomb—and therefore that this agent of destruction will work best for us. He who trusts in the atom bomb will sooner or later perish by the atom bomb—or something worse. . . .

To achieve lasting peace, we must study in detail just how the Russian character was formed—by invasions of Tartars, Mongols, Germans, Poles, Swedes, and French; by the czarist rule based on ignorance, fear and force; by the intervention of the British, French and Americans in Russian affairs from 1919 to 1921; by the geography of the huge Russian land mass situated strategically between Europe and Asia; and by the vitality derived from the rich Russian soil and the strenuous Russian climate. Add to all this the tremendous emotional power which Marxism and Leninism gives to the Russian leaders—and then we can realize that we are reckoning with a force which cannot be handled successfully by a "Get tough

with Russia" policy. "Getting tough" never bought anything real and lasting—whether for schoolyard bullies or businessmen or world powers. The tougher we get, the tougher the Russians will get. . . .

We should recognize that we have no more business in the political affairs of Eastern Europe than Russia has in the political affairs of Latin America, Western Europe and the United States. . . . We have to recognize that the Balkans are closer to Russia than to us—and that Russia cannot permit either England or the United States to dominate the politics of that area. . . .

. . . Under friendly peaceful competition the Russian world and the American world will gradually become more alike. The Russians will be forced to grant more and more of the personal freedoms; and we shall become more and more absorbed with the problems of social-economic justice.

Source: Excerpts from Henry A. Wallace, "The Way to Peace," *Vital Speeches of the Day*, October 1, 1946, 738–741.

Questions for Analysis and Debate

1. What lessons did these three leaders draw from World War II? What did they see as the most critical steps to preventing another war?

2. What differences did these men see between the political and economic systems of the Soviet Union and those of the United States and Western Europe? How do their predictions about these systems differ?

3. What motives did these three men ascribe to Soviet actions? How do Churchill's and Wallace's proposals for the Western response to the Soviet Union differ?

4. Which leader do you think was most optimistic about the prospects for good relationships between Russia and the West? Which was most correct? Why?

Connect to the Big Idea

⬤ What motivations drove foreign policy in Great Britain, the United States, and the Soviet Union during the early years of the Cold War?

February 1947, Britain informed the United States that its crippled economy could no longer sustain military assistance to Greece, where the autocratic government faced economic disaster and a leftist uprising, and to Turkey, which was trying to resist Soviet pressures. Truman promptly sought congressional authority to send both countries military and economic aid. Meeting with congressional leaders, Undersecretary of State Dean Acheson predicted that if Greece and Turkey fell, communism would soon consume three-fourths of the world. After a stunned silence, Michigan senator Arthur Vandenberg, the Republican foreign policy leader, warned that to get approval, Truman would have to "scare hell out of the country."

Truman did just that. He warned that if Greece fell to the rebels, "confusion and disorder might well spread throughout the entire Middle East" and then create instability in Europe. According to what came to be called the **Truman Doctrine**, the United States must not only resist Soviet military power but also "support free peoples who are resisting attempted subjugation by armed minorities or by outside pressures." The president failed to convince Helen Gahagan Douglas and some of her congressional colleagues, who wanted the United States to work through the United Nations and opposed propping up the authoritarian Greek government. But the administration won the day, setting a precedent for forty years of Cold War interventions that would aid any kind of government if the only alternative appeared to be communism.

A much larger assistance program for Europe followed aid to Greece and Turkey. In May 1947, Acheson described a war-ravaged Western Europe, with "factories destroyed, fields impoverished, transportation systems wrecked, populations scattered and on the borderline of starvation." American citizens were sending generous amounts of private aid, but Europe needed large-scale assistance to keep desperate citizens from turning to socialism or communism.

In March 1948, Congress approved such assistance, which came to be called the **Marshall Plan**, after Secretary of State George C. Marshall, who proposed what a British official called "a lifeline to a sinking man." Over the next five years the United States spent $13 billion ($117 billion in 2010 dollars) to restore the economies of sixteen Western European nations. Marshall invited all European nations and the Soviet Union to cooperate in a request for aid, but the Soviets objected to the American insistence on free trade and financial disclosure. As U.S. officials had expected, the Soviets rejected the offer and ordered their Eastern European satellites to do the same.

Humanitarian impulses as well as the goal of keeping Western Europe free of communism drove the adoption of this enormous aid program. But the Marshall Plan also helped boost the U.S. economy because the participating European nations spent most of the dollars to buy American products and Europe's economic recovery created new markets and opportunities for American investment. And, by insisting that the recipient nations work together, the Marshall Plan marked the first step toward the European Union. (See "Visualizing History," p. 750.)

While Congress was debating the Marshall Plan, in February 1948 the Soviets staged a brutal coup and installed a Communist regime in Czechoslovakia, the last democracy left in Eastern Europe. Next, Stalin threatened Western access to Berlin. That former capital of Germany lay within Soviet-controlled East Germany, but all four Allies jointly occupied it. As the Western Allies moved to organize West Germany as a separate nation, the Soviets retaliated by blocking roads and rail lines between West Germany and the Western-held sections of Berlin, cutting off food, fuel, and other essentials to two million inhabitants.

"We stay in Berlin, period," Truman vowed. To avoid a confrontation with Soviet troops, for nearly a year U.S. and British pilots airlifted 2.3 million tons of goods to sustain the West Berliners. Stalin hesitated to shoot down these cargo planes, and in 1949 he lifted the blockade. The city was then divided into East Berlin, under Soviet control, and West Berlin, which became part of West Germany.

Building a National Security State

During the Truman years, advocates of the new containment policy fashioned a six-pronged defense strategy: (1) development of atomic weapons, (2) strengthening traditional military power, (3) military alliances with other nations, (4) military and economic aid to friendly nations, (5) an espionage network and secret means to subvert Communist expansion, and (6) a propaganda offensive to win friends around the world.

In September 1949, the Soviet Union detonated its own atomic bomb, ending the U.S. monopoly on atomic weapons.

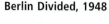

Berlin Divided, 1948

The Berlin Airlift
At the peak of the Berlin airlift in 1948, U.S. or British planes landed every three minutes twenty-four hours a day. These children, on top of a mountain of wartime rubble, may have been watching for Air Force pilot Gail S. Halvorsen, who, after meeting hungry schoolchildren, began to drop candy and gum as his plane approached the landing strip. Picture-alliance/dpa/AP Images.

Truman then approved the development of a hydrogen bomb—equivalent to five hundred atomic bombs—rejecting the counterarguments of several scientists who had worked on the atomic bomb and of George Kennan, who warned of an endless arms race. The "super bomb" was ready by 1954, but the U.S. advantage was brief. In November 1955, the Soviets exploded their own hydrogen bomb.

From the 1950s through the 1980s, deterrence formed the basis of American nuclear strategy. To deter a Soviet attack, the United States strove to maintain a nuclear force more powerful than that of the Soviets. Because the Russians pursued a similar policy, the superpowers became locked in an ever-escalating nuclear arms race amassing weapons that could destroy the earth many times over. Albert Einstein, whose mathematical discoveries had laid the foundations for nuclear weapons, commented grimly that the war that came after World War III would "be fought with sticks and stones."

Implementing the second component of containment, the United States beefed up its conventional military power to deter Soviet threats that might not warrant nuclear retaliation. The National Security Act of 1947 united the military branches under a single secretary of defense and created the National Security Council (NSC) to advise the president. During the Berlin crisis in 1948, Congress hiked military appropriations and enacted a peacetime draft. In addition, Congress granted permanent status to the women's military branches, though it limited their numbers, the jobs they could do, and the rank female servicemembers could attain. With 1.5 million men and women in uniform in 1950, the military strength of the United States had quadrupled since the 1930s, and defense expenditures claimed one-third of the federal budget.

Collective security, the third prong of containment strategy, marked a sharp reversal of the nation's traditional foreign policy. In 1949, the United States joined Canada and Western European nations in its first peacetime military alliance, the **North Atlantic Treaty Organization (NATO)**, designed to counter a Soviet threat to

Cold War Spying
"Intelligence," the gathering of information about the enemy, took on new importance with the Cold War and creation of the Central Intelligence Agency (CIA) in 1947. While much intelligence work took place in Washington, where analysts combed through Communist newspapers, official reports, and speeches, secret agents gathered information behind the iron curtain with bugs and devices such as these cameras hidden in cigarette packs. Jack Naylor Collection/Picture Research Consultants & Archives.

Selling the Marshall Plan

The United States launched the Marshall Plan in 1948 primarily to alleviate the devastation that might otherwise send Europeans into the arms of the Soviet Union. To promote and contain German reindustrialization by integrating its economy with those of other European countries, the United States required the European nations to coordinate their responses to Marshall's invitation to the European Recovery Program (ERP). With this requirement for cooperation, American policymakers allied with efforts of European leaders, such as French statesmen Jean Monnet and Robert Schuman and German Chancellor Konrad Audenauer, to knit together the European powers so that they could never again slaughter millions of each other's citizens as they had done twice in the past half century.

In 1950 the ERP launched a poster contest on the subject, "Intra-European Cooperation for a Better Standard of Living," and received more than 10,000 submissions from artists throughout Europe. Along with the themes of unity and prosperity suggested by the contest name, artists incorporated references to wartime devastation, peace, and the role of the United States.

Using the title of the competition itself for his work, German artist Alfred Lutz more pointedly appealed to individuals' material needs: The poster depicts a chef adorned with the flags of European nations stirring a pot that says ERP. The reference to food would have

"Intra-European Cooperation for Better Living Conditions"

resonated with Germans' memories of hunger and starvation in the early postwar years.

"We Build a New Europe," submitted by Austrian Kurt Krapeik, shows the wartime devastation in a burned tree and the promise of recovery in new shoots. The European nations are represented by flags in the nest, which is being supplied by doves, symbols of peace. How does the artist refer to American economic assistance?

First-prize winner, "All Our Colors to the Mast," by Dutch artist Reijn Dirksen more than any others here emphasizes intra-European cooperation. Why do you think he

Western Europe (see Map 26.1). For the first time in its history, the United States pledged to go to war if one of its allies was attacked.

The fourth element of defense strategy provided foreign assistance programs to strengthen friendly countries, such as aid to Greece and Turkey and the Marshall Plan. In addition, in 1949 Congress approved $1 billion of military aid to its NATO allies, and the government began economic assistance to nations in other parts of the world.

The fifth ingredient of containment improved the government's capacity to thwart communism through espionage and covert

"We Build a New Europe"

"All Our Colors to the Mast"

selected a ship as the main image? Note that it is a clipper ship, widely used for commerce in the nineteenth century, not a more modern vessel, which could be seen as a war ship. Dirksen has placed the flags of Belgium, Luxembourg, and the Netherlands at the front; those so called Benelux neighbors began efforts toward economic cooperation across national borders even before World War II had ended.

The vision portrayed by all the artists was most fully realized in 1993, when the European Union was born. It now has twenty-eight member countries.

SOURCES: "Intra-European Cooperation for Better Living Conditions": Deutsches Historisches Museum, Berlin, Germany / © DHM / The Bridgeman Art Library; "We Build a New Europe": Library of Congress; "All Our Colors to the Mast": Library of Congress.

Questions for Analysis

1. What attitudes about war and peace do you see reflected in the posters? How do the posters address these themes?

2. Which work do you find most compelling and why?

Connect to the Big Idea

⊙ How was the Marshall Plan similar to and different from other foreign assistance programs of the Truman administration?

activities. The National Security Act of 1947 created the **Central Intelligence Agency (CIA)** to gather information and to perform any activities "related to intelligence affecting the national security" that the NSC might authorize. Such functions included propaganda, sabotage, economic warfare, and support for "anti-communist elements in threatened countries of the free world." In 1948, secret CIA operations helped defeat Italy's Communist Party. Subsequently, CIA agents would intervene even more actively, helping to topple legitimate foreign governments and violating the rights of U.S. citizens.

Louis Armstrong in Düsseldorf
As one of its Cold War weapons, the United States sent representatives of American culture abroad. Jazz was especially popular around the world, and the State Department sponsored tours by black jazz artists in part to counter the image of the United States as a racist nation. Louis Armstrong, the great trumpet player, singer, and jazz innovator, is shown here captivating a German crowd in 1952. AP Photo.

Finally, the U.S. government created cultural exchanges and propaganda to win "hearts and minds" throughout the world. The Voice of America, established during World War II to broadcast U.S. propaganda abroad, expanded, and the State Department sent books, exhibits, jazz musicians, and other performers to foreign countries as "cultural ambassadors."

By 1950, the United States had abandoned age-old tenets of foreign policy. Isolationism and neutrality had given way to a peacetime military alliance and efforts to control events far beyond U.S. borders. Short of war, the United States could not stop the descent of the iron curtain, but it aggressively and successfully promoted economic recovery and a military shield for the rest of Europe.

Superpower Rivalry around the Globe

Efforts to implement containment moved beyond Europe. In Africa, Asia, and the Middle East, World War II accelerated a tide of national liberation movements against war-weakened imperial powers. By 1960, forty countries had won their independence. These nations, along with Latin America, came to be referred to collectively as the third world.

Like Woodrow Wilson during World War I, Roosevelt and Truman promoted the ideal of self-determination. The United States granted independence to the Philippines in 1946 and applauded the British withdrawal from India. As the Cold War intensified, however, the ideal of self-determination gave way to concern when new governments supplanting the old empires failed to emulate the American model. U.S. policymakers encouraged democracy and capitalism in emerging nations and sought to preserve opportunities for American trade, while U.S. corporations coveted the vast oil reserves in the Middle East. Yet leaders of many liberation movements, impressed with Russia's rapid economic growth, adopted socialist or Communist ideas. Although few of these movements had formal ties with the Soviet Union, American leaders saw them as a threatening extension of Soviet power. Seeking to hold communism at bay by fostering economic development and political stability, in 1949 the Truman administration began a small program of aid to developing nations.

Meanwhile civil war raged in China, where the Communists, led by Mao Zedong (Mao Tsetung), fought the official Nationalist government under Jiang Jieshi (Chiang Kaishek). While the Communists gained popular support for their land reforms, Jiang's corrupt, incompetent government alienated much of the population and his military forces had been devastated by the Japanese. Failing to promote a settlement between Jiang and Mao, the United States provided $3 billion in aid to the Nationalists. Yet, recognizing the ineptness of Jiang's government, Truman refused to divert further resources from Europe to China.

In October 1949, Mao established the People's Republic of China (PRC), and the Nationalists fled to the island of Taiwan. Fearing a U.S.-supported invasion to recapture China for the Nationalists, Mao signed a mutual defense treaty with the Soviet Union. The United States refused to recognize the PRC, blocked its admission to the United Nations, and supported the

Nationalist government in Taiwan. Only a massive U.S. military commitment could have stopped the Chinese Communists, yet some Republicans charged that Truman and "pro-Communists in the State Department" had "lost" China. China became a political albatross for the Democrats, who resolved never again to be vulnerable to charges of being soft on communism.

With China in turmoil, U.S. policy shifted to helping Japan rapidly reindustrialize. In a short time, the Japanese economy was flourishing, and the official military occupation ended when the two nations signed a peace treaty and a mutual security pact in September 1951. Like West Germany, Japan now sat squarely within the American orbit, ready to serve as an economic hub in a vital area.

The one place where Cold War considerations did not control American policy was Palestine. In 1943, then-senator Harry Truman spoke passionately about Nazi Germany's annihilation of the Jews, asserting, "This is not a Jewish problem, it is an American problem—and we must . . . face it squarely and honorably." As president, he made good on his words. Jews had been migrating to Palestine, their biblical homeland, since the nineteenth century, resulting in tension and hostilities with the Palestinian Arabs. After World War II, as hundreds of thousands of European Jews sought refuge and a national homeland in Palestine, fighting and terrorism escalated on both sides.

Truman's foreign policy experts sought American-Arab friendship to contain Soviet influence in the Middle East and to secure access to Arabian oil. Uncharacteristically defying his advisers, the president responded instead to pleas from Jewish organizations, his moral commitment to Holocaust survivors, and his interest in the American Jewish vote. When Jews in Palestine declared the state of Israel in May 1948, Truman quickly recognized the new country and made its defense the cornerstone of U.S. policy in the Middle East.

Israel, 1948

UN partition of Palestine, 1947

- Jewish state
- Arab state
- Boundary of Israel, 1949

REVIEW: What factors contributed to the emergence of the Cold War?

▶ Truman and the Fair Deal at Home

Referring to the Civil War general who coined the phrase "War is hell," Truman said in December 1945, "Sherman was wrong. I'm telling you I find peace is hell." Challenged by crises abroad, Truman also faced shortages, strikes, inflation, and other problems as the economy shifted to peacetime production. At the same time, he tried to expand New Deal reform with his own Fair Deal agenda of initiatives in civil rights, housing, education, and health care—efforts hindered by the wave of anti-Communist hysteria sweeping the country. In sharp contrast to the bipartisan support Truman won for his foreign policy, he won little support from Congress for his domestic agenda.

Reconverting to a Peacetime Economy

Despite scarcities and deprivations, World War II had brought most Americans a higher standard of living than ever before. Economic experts as well as ordinary citizens worried about sustaining that standard and providing jobs for millions of returning soldiers. To that end Truman asked Congress to enact a twenty-one-point program of social and economic re-forms. He wanted the government to continue regulating the economy while it adjusted to peacetime production, and he sought government programs to provide basic essentials such as housing and health care to those in need. "Not even President Roosevelt ever asked for as much at one sitting," exploded Republican leader Joseph W. Martin Jr.

Congress approved just one of Truman's key proposals—full-employment legislation—and then only after watering it down. The Employment Act of 1946 called on the federal government "to promote maximum employment, production, and purchasing power," thereby formalizing government's responsibility for maintaining a healthy economy. It created the Council of Economic Advisors to assist the president, but it authorized no new powers to translate the government's economic obligations into effective action.

Inflation, not unemployment, turned out to be the biggest problem. Consumers had $30 billion in wartime savings to spend, but shortages of meat, automobiles, housing, and other items persisted. Until industry could make more goods available, consumer demand would continue to drive up prices. With a basket of groceries on her arm to dramatize rising costs, Helen Gahagan Douglas urged Congress to maintain price and rent controls. Those efforts, however, fell to pressures from business groups and others determined to trim government powers.

Labor relations were another thorn in Truman's side. Organized labor emerged from the war with its 14.5 million members making up 35 percent of the civilian workforce. Yet union members feared the erosion of wartime gains and turned to the weapon they had surrendered during the war. Five million workers went out on strike in 1946, affecting nearly every major industry. Shortly before voting to strike, a former Marine and his coworkers calculated that an executive had spent more on a party than they would earn in a whole year at the steel mill. "That sort of stuff made us realize, hell we had to bite the bullet. . . . The bosses sure didn't give a damn for us." Although most Americans

approved of unions in principle, they became fed up with strikes, blamed unions for shortages and rising prices, and called for government restrictions on organized labor. When the strikes subsided, workers had won wage increases of about 20 percent, but the loss of overtime pay along with rising prices left their purchasing power only slightly higher than in 1942.

Women workers fared even worse. Polls indicated that 68 to 85 percent wanted to keep their wartime jobs, but most who remained in the workforce had to settle for relatively low-paying jobs in light industry or the service sector (Figure 26.1). Displaced from her shipyard work, Marie Schreiber took a cashier's job, lamenting, "You were back to women's wages, you know . . . practically in half." With the backing of women's organizations and union women, Congresswoman Douglas sponsored bills to require equal pay for equal work, to provide child care for employed mothers, and to create a government commission to study women's status. But at a time when women were viewed primarily as wives and mothers and opposition to further expansion of federal powers was strong, these initiatives got nowhere.

By 1947, the economy had stabilized, avoiding the postwar depression that so many had feared. Wartime profits enabled businesses to expand. Consumers could now spend their wartime savings on houses, cars, and appliances that had lain beyond their reach during the depression and war. Defense spending and foreign aid that enabled war-stricken countries to purchase American products also stimulated the economy. A soaring birthrate further sustained consumer demand. Although prosperity was far from universal, the United States entered into a remarkable economic boom that lasted through the 1960s (see "New Work and Living Patterns in an Economy of Abundance" in chapter 27).

Another economic boost came from the only large welfare measure passed after the New Deal. The Servicemen's Readjustment Act (GI Bill), enacted in 1944, offered 16 million veterans job training and education; unemployment compensation until they found jobs; and low-interest loans to purchase homes, farms, and small businesses. By 1948, some 1.3 million veterans had bought houses with government loans. Helping 2.2 million ex-soldiers attend college, the subsidies sparked a boom in higher education. A drugstore clerk before his military service, Don Condren was able to get an engineering degree and buy his first house. "I think the GI Bill gave the whole country an upward boost economically," he said.

FIGURE 26.1   Women Workers in Selected Industries, 1940–1950
Women demolished the idea that some jobs were "men's work" during World War II, but they failed to maintain their gains in the manufacturing sector after the war.

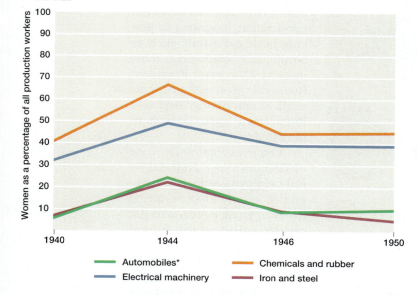

*During World War II, this industry did not produce cars, but rather military transportation such as jeeps, tanks, aircraft, etc.

Trying to catch up with your demands...THOUSANDS OF NEW PROCTOR IRONS AND TOASTERS

Here they come!

PROCTOR
AUTOMATIC ELECTRIC APPLIANCES

VISUAL ACTIVITY

Women's Role in Peacetime

Like many manufacturers during World War II, Proctor Electric Company, which had shifted its focus from making appliances to producing bomb fuses, cartridges, and airplane wing flaps, hoped to profit after the war from pent-up consumer demand. Even before the company had fully reconverted its plants, ads tempted consumers with products soon to come, as in this 1946 ad. Picture Research Consultants & Archives.

READING THE IMAGE: Why do you think a woman was featured in this ad? Considering the scene in the background, what message is conveyed about women's employment during and after the war?

CONNECTIONS: How did the shortage of consumer goods affect the postwar economy? What role did consumer goods play in the economic revival?

Yet the impact of the GI Bill was uneven. As wives and daughters of veterans, women benefited indirectly from the GI subsidies, but few women qualified for the employment and educational preferences available to some 15 million men. Moreover, GI programs were administered at the state and local levels, which resulted in routine discrimination especially in the South. Southern universities remained segregated, and historically black colleges could not accommodate all who wanted to attend. Black veterans were shuttled into menial labor. One decorated veteran reported that "my color bars

me from most decent jobs, and if, instead of accepting menial work, I collect my $20 a week readjustment allowance, I am classified as a 'lazy nigger.'" Thousands of black veterans did benefit, but the GI Bill did not help all ex-soldiers equally.

Blacks and Mexican Americans Push for Their Civil Rights

"I spent four years in the army to free a bunch of Frenchmen and Dutchmen," an African American corporal declared, "and I'm hanged if I'm going to let the Alabama version of the Germans kick me around when I get home." Black veterans along with civilians resolved not to return to the racial injustices of prewar America. The migration of two million African Americans to northern and western cities meant that they could now vote and participate in ongoing struggles to end discrimination in housing and education. Pursuing civil rights through the courts and Congress, the National Association for the Advancement of Colored People (NAACP) counted half a million members.

In the postwar years, individual African Americans broke through the color barrier, achieving several "firsts." Jackie Robinson integrated major league baseball, playing for the Brooklyn Dodgers and braving abuse from fans and players to win the Rookie of the Year Award in 1947. In 1950, Ralph J. Bunche received the Nobel Peace Prize for his United Nations work, and Gwendolyn Brooks won the Pulitzer Prize for poetry. Some organizations, such as the American Association of University Women and the American Medical Association in 1949, opened their doors to black members. Still, little had changed for most African Americans, especially in the South, where violence greeted their attempts to assert their rights. Armed white men prevented Medgar Evers (who would become a key civil rights leader in the 1960s) and four other veterans from voting in Mississippi. A mob lynched Isaac Nixon for voting in Georgia, and an all-white jury acquitted the men accused of his murder. Segregation and economic discrimination were widespread in the North as well.

The Cold War heightened U.S. leaders' sensitivity to racial issues, as the superpowers vied for the allegiance of newly independent nations with nonwhite populations, and Soviet propaganda repeatedly highlighted racial injustice in the United States. Secretary of State Dean Acheson noted that systematic segregation

Segregation
The segregation visible on this bus was a feature of life in the South from the late nineteenth century until the 1960s. African Americans could not use white hospitals, cemeteries, schools, libraries, swimming pools, restrooms, or drinking fountains. They were relegated to balconies in movie theaters and kept apart from whites in all public meetings. Stan Wayman/Time Life Pictures/Getty Images.

and discrimination endangered "our moral leadership of the free and democratic nations of the world."

"My very stomach turned over when I learned that Negro soldiers just back from overseas were being dumped out of army trucks in Mississippi and beaten," wrote Truman. Risking support from southern white voters, Truman spoke more boldly on civil rights than any previous president had. In 1946, he created the President's Committee on Civil Rights, and in February 1948 he asked Congress to enact the committee's comprehensive recommendations. The first president to address the NAACP, Truman asserted that all Americans should have equal rights to housing, education, employment, and the ballot.

As with much of his domestic program, Truman failed to act aggressively on his bold words. Congress rejected his proposals for national civil rights legislation, although some northern and western states did pass laws against discrimination in employment and public accommodations. Running for reelection in 1948 and hoping to appeal to northern black and liberal voters, Truman issued an executive order to desegregate the armed services, but it lay unimplemented until the Korean War, when the cost of segregation to military efficiency became apparent. Officers gradually integrated their ranks, and by 1953 nearly all African Americans served in mixed units. Although actual accomplishments fell far short of Truman's proposals, desegregation of the military and the administration's support of civil rights cases in the Supreme Court contributed to far-reaching changes.

Discussion of race and civil rights usually focused on African Americans, but Mexican Americans fought similar injustices. In 1929, they had formed the League of United Latin-American Citizens (LULAC) to combat discrimination and segregation in the Southwest. Like black soldiers, Mexican American veterans believed, as one insisted, that "we had earned our credentials as American citizens."

Problems with getting their veterans' benefits spurred the formation of a new organization in 1948 in Corpus Christi, Texas—the American GI Forum. Dr. Héctor Peréz García, president of the local LULAC and a Bronze Star combat surgeon, led the GI Forum, which became a national force for battling discrimination and electing sympathetic officials.

"Education is our freedom," read the GI Forum's motto, yet Mexican American children were routinely segregated in public schools. In 1945, with the help of LULAC, parents filed a class action suit in southern California, challenging school districts that barred their children from white schools. In the resulting decision, Mendez v. Westminster (1947), a federal *court* for the first time struck down school segregation. NAACP lawyer Thurgood Marshall filed a supporting brief in the case, which foreshadowed the landmark *Brown* decision of 1954 (see "African Americans Challenge the Supreme Court and the President" in chapter 27). Efforts to gain equal education, challenges to job discrimination in employment, and campaigns for political representation all demonstrated a growing mobilization of Mexican Americans in the Southwest.

The Fair Deal Flounders

Republicans capitalized on public frustrations with strikes and shortages in the 1946 congressional election, accusing the administration of "confusion, corruption, and communism." Helen Gahagan Douglas kept her seat, but the Republicans captured control of Congress for the first time in fourteen years. Many had campaigned against the New Deal in 1946, and in the Eightieth Congress they weakened some reform programs and enacted tax cuts favoring higher-income groups.

Organized labor took the most severe blow when Congress passed the **Taft-Hartley Act** over Truman's veto in 1947. Called a "slave labor" law by unions, the measure amended the Wagner Act (see "Empowering Labor" in chapter 24), putting restraints on unions that reduced their power to bargain with employers and made it more difficult to organize workers. States could now pass "right-to-work" laws, which banned the practice of requiring all workers to join a union once a majority had voted for it. Many states, especially in the South and West, rushed to enact such laws, encouraging industries to relocate there. Taft-Hartley main-

VISUAL ACTIVITY

Dr. Héctor P. García

Héctor García, shown here with patients, came from Mexico as a boy and became a doctor. While leading the GI Forum, García treated all who needed medical care regardless of whether they could pay for it. An associate referred to García, who was active in politics, as "a man who in the space of one week delivers 20 babies, 20 speeches, and 20 thousand votes." Héctor P. García Papers, Special Collections & Archives, Texas A&M University, Corpus Christi, Bell Library.

READING THE IMAGE: This photograph was taken in Dr. García's office in the early 1950s. Why might he have dressed in his military uniform? What do the other people in the photograph suggest about his medical practice? What in the photo suggests that his practice was successful?

CONNECTIONS: What were the goals of Dr. García's movement? What was the biggest gain for Mexican Americans in the postwar period?

tained the New Deal principle of government protection for collective bargaining, but it tipped the balance of power more in favor of management.

In the 1948 elections, Truman faced not only a resurgent Republican Party headed by New York governor Thomas E. Dewey but also two revolts within his own party. On the left, Henry A. Wallace, whose foreign policy views had cost him his cabinet seat, led the new Progressive Party. On the right, South Carolina governor J. Strom Thurmond headed the States' Rights Party—the Dixiecrats—formed by southern Democrats who walked out of the 1948 Democratic Party convention when it passed a liberal civil rights plank.

Truman launched a vigorous campaign, yet his prospects were so bleak that on election night the *Chicago Daily Tribune* printed its next day's issue with the headline "Dewey Defeats Truman." But even though the Dixiecrats won four southern states, Truman took 303 electoral

VISUAL ACTIVITY

Truman's Whistle-Stop Campaign

Harry Truman rallies a crowd from his campaign train in Bridgeport, Pennsylvania, in October 1948 as he campaigned across the country to shouts of "Give 'em hell, Harry!" Truman's support for civil rights cost him four southern states but helped him win votes from liberals and blacks. Norristown Times Herald

READING THE IMAGE: This photo was taken one month before the election. Why might his opponent's campaign have dismissed the importance of these large crowds in support of Truman?

CONNECTIONS: President Truman was under attack by the Republicans and could not enact his Fair Deal. Almost everyone thought he would lose the election. Why do you think the American people responded so well to his campaign? In what ways have presidential campaigns changed since Harry Truman's time?

Candidate	Electoral Vote	Popular Vote	Percent of Popular Vote
Harry S. Truman (Democrat)	303	24,105,695	49.5
Thomas E. Dewey (Republican)	189	21,969,170	45.1
J. Strom Thurmond (States' Rights)	39	1,169,021	2.4
Henry A. Wallace (Progressive)	0	1,156,103	2.4

MAP 26.2

The Election of 1948

votes to Dewey's 189, and his party regained control of Congress (Map 26.2). His unexpected victory attested to the broad support for his foreign policy and the enduring popularity of New Deal reform.

While most New Deal programs survived Republican attacks, Truman failed to enact his Fair Deal agenda. Congress made modest improvements in Social Security and raised the minimum wage, but it passed only one significant reform measure. The **Housing Act of 1949** authorized 810,000 units of government-constructed housing over the next six years and represented a landmark commitment by the government to address the housing needs of the poor. Yet it fell far short of actual need, and slum clearance frequently displaced the poor without providing alternatives.

With southern Democrats posing a primary obstacle, Congress rejected Truman's proposals for civil rights, a powerful medical lobby blocked plans for a universal health care program, and conflicts over race and religion thwarted federal aid to education. Truman's efforts to revise immigration policy were mixed. The McCarran-Walter Act of 1952 ended the outright ban on immigration and citizenship for Japanese and other Asians, but it authorized the government to bar suspected Communists and homosexuals and maintained the discriminatory quota system established in the 1920s.

Truman's concentration on foreign policy rather than domestic proposals contributed to the failure of his Fair Deal. By late 1950, the Korean War embroiled the president in controversy and depleted his power as a legislative leader (see pages 762–765). Truman's failure to make good on his domestic proposals set the United States apart from most European nations, which by the 1950s had in place comprehensive health, housing, and employment security programs to underwrite the material well-being of their populations.

The Domestic Chill: McCarthyism

Truman's domestic agenda also suffered from a wave of anticommunism that weakened liberals. "Red-baiting" (attempting to link individuals or ideas with communism) and official retaliation against leftist critics of the government had flourished during the Red scare at the end of World War I (see "The Red Scare" in chapter 22), and Republicans had attacked the New Deal as a plot of radicals. A second Red scare followed World War II, born of partisan politics, the collapse of the Soviet-American alliance, foreign policy setbacks, and disclosures of Soviet espionage.

Republicans jumped on events such as the Soviet takeover of Eastern Europe and the Communist triumph in China to accuse Democrats of fostering internal subversion. Wisconsin senator Joseph R. McCarthy avowed that "the Communists within our borders have been more responsible for the success of Communism abroad than Soviet Russia." McCarthy's charges—such as the allegation that retired general George C. Marshall belonged to a Communist conspiracy—were reckless and often ludicrous, but the press covered him avidly, and McCarthyism became a term synonymous with the anti-Communist crusade.

Revelations of Soviet espionage lent credibility to fears of internal communism. A number of ex-Communists, including Whittaker Chambers and Elizabeth Bentley, testified that they and others had provided secret documents to the Soviets. Most alarming of all, in 1950 a British physicist working on the atomic bomb project confessed that he was a spy and implicated several Americans, including Ethel and Julius Rosenberg. The Rosenbergs pleaded not guilty but were convicted of conspiracy to commit espionage and electrocuted in 1953.

VISUAL ACTIVITY

The Red Scare
The celebrated editorial cartoonist for the *Washington Post*, Herbert Lawrence Block, was a frequent critic of McCarthyism. In this 1949 cartoon, he addressed the intimidation of teachers, which occurred across the country in public schools and universities. Public officials demanded that teachers take loyalty oaths, grilled them about their past and present political associations, and fired those who refused to cooperate. A 1949 Herblock Cartoon, © The Herb Block Foundation.

READING THE IMAGE: What is the effect of portraying a female teacher and nine hefty male investigators? What does the man with scissors appear to be doing, and how does this ridicule the Red Scare? Do you think it was coincidental that the artist included a portrait of Thomas Jefferson, author of the Bill of Rights?

CONNECTIONS: How did the Red scare affect the prospects of Truman's domestic agenda?

An Immigrant Scientist Encounters the Anti-Communist Crusade

Qian Xuesen (Tsien Hsue-shen), whose name means "study to be wise," was born to a privileged family in Hangzhou, China, in 1911. Qian graduated at the top of his class from Jiaotong University in Shanghai, China's best engineering school. Deciding that aviation was the wave of the future and aware of how far behind his country lagged in this area, Qian looked abroad to further his education. In 1935, with his country torn by Japanese aggression and internal opposition to the Nationalist government, he accepted an American-sponsored scholarship and quickly earned a master's degree in aeronautical engineering from the Massachusetts Institute of Technology (MIT). One year later, he began doctoral work at the California Institute of Technology (Caltech) in Pasadena.

At Caltech, Qian joined a group of scientists working on questions about flight and contributed to the development of theoretical aerodynamics and jet propulsion, which eventually provided a foundation for America's space program. School officials were so impressed with Qian's work that they helped him get a visa extension, and in 1942 the government gave him security clearance so that he could work on secret military projects. Qian served on the air force's Scientific Advisory Board, and after World War II he went on a U.S. mission to interview Nazi scientists in Germany. He spent a year on the faculty at MIT and then traveled home to China amid the turmoil of a civil war between the Communists, led by Mao Zedong (Mao Tse-tung), and the Nationalist government of Jiang Jieshi (Chiang Kai-shek). There Qian spent time with his father, gave motivational speeches to large audiences of students, and married a woman he had known in childhood, an opera singer and the daughter of one of Jiang Jieshi's generals.

In 1949, when he returned to Caltech to direct the Jet Propulsion Center, teach, continue his research, and entertain a close circle of colleagues with classical music and elaborate dinners, Qian seemed to have everything necessary to lead a rich life and pursue his lifelong passion for science. He applied for U.S. citizenship. One year later, after the Communists had taken control of China, the U.S. government revoked Qian's security clearance. The FBI interrogated him about a group he had socialized with in the 1930s, which the FBI said was a cell of the Communist Party. Qian denied any participation in Communist activities, but the proud, angry, and humiliated scientist concluded that, given the "cloud of suspicion . . . the only gentlemanly thing left to do is to depart." The promise of a brilliant career shattered, he resisted Caltech officials who begged him to remain; instead, he readied a shipment of his belongings to send on to China. The government seized the shipment and accused Qian of taking secret documents. Although the claim was later refuted, the Immigration and Naturalization Service arrested him. He was released after two weeks, but for the next five years the government refused to let him go and kept him and his family under constant surveillance. Although Caltech administrators worked furiously to clear his name, some of his associates began to avoid him, fearing that they, too, would be caught up in the hunt for Communists. Finally, in 1955, he was deported as part of a prisoner of war exchange following the Korean War.

Qian disembarked in China with his wife and two children to a hero's reception and a career that would eventually earn him the title of "father of Chinese rocketry." Denied the full use of his talents by the United States, he organized and led China's rocketry program, developing its ballistic missiles and satellites.

Records opened in the 1990s showed that the Soviet Union did receive secret documents from Americans that probably hastened its development of nuclear weapons by a year or two. Yet the vast majority of individuals hunted down in the Red scare had done nothing more than at one time joining the Communist Party, associating with Communists, or supporting radical causes. And nearly all the accusations related to activities that had taken place long before the Cold War had made the Soviet Union an enemy.

The hunt for subversives was conducted by both Congress and the executive branch. Stung by charges of communism in the 1946 mid-term elections, Truman issued Executive Order 9835 in March 1947, establishing loyalty review boards to investigate every federal employee. "A nightmare from which there [was] no awakening" was how State Department employee Esther Brunauer described it when she and her husband, a chemist in the navy, both lost their jobs because he had joined a Communist youth organization in the 1920s and associated with suspected radicals. Government investigators allowed anonymous informers to make charges and placed the burden of proof on the accused. More than two thousand civil service employees lost their jobs, and an-

Like anyone who hoped to have a successful career in China, he became a trusted Communist Party official. Though the extremely private scientist said little about his experiences in the United States, he refused to return in 1979 to accept Caltech's Distinguished Alumni Award. Qian had lost faith in the U.S. government but maintained affection for the American people and sent both his children to study at American universities. Qian died in China in 2009 at the age of ninety-eight.

Questions linger about Qian's associations and intentions in the United States. A 1999 congressional report maintained that he had been a spy, but his supporters claimed that the report lacked evidence. Every one of his Caltech colleagues vouched for his integrity, and some went to great lengths to defend him against government charges. Dan A. Kimball, who was secretary of the navy in the early 1950s, later said that Qian's deportation "was the stupidest thing this country ever did. He was no more a Communist than I was—and we forced him to go." The Red scare dashed Qian's belief that America promised an opportunity for any talented individual to live a free and prosperous life. It also delivered a brilliant scientist to the nation's enemy.

Qian Xuesen

Qian Xuesen, the Chinese rocket scientist, teaches a class at the California Institute of Technology in 1955, shortly before his deportation back to China. Students who worked with him were "awe-struck" by his brilliance. They recalled that he generously mentored those whose mental powers matched his, but was impatient and harsh toward those he deemed intellectually incapable. © Bettmann/Corbis.

Questions for Consideration

1. What particular aspects of American life and institutions attracted Qian to the United States in the first place, and what made him want to stay in the country?

2. How did the timing of events in Qian's case correlate with domestic and international developments related to the Cold War and McCarthyism?

Connect to the Big Idea

C How were other people and ideas silenced during the Red scare?

---

other ten thousand resigned as Truman's loyalty program continued into the mid-1950s. Hundreds of homosexuals resigned or were fired over charges of "sexual perversion," which anti-Communist crusaders said could subject them to blackmail. Years later, Truman said privately that the loyalty program had been a mistake.

Congressional committees, such as the **House Un-American Activities Committee (HUAC)**, also investigated individuals' political associations. When those under scrutiny refused to name names, investigators charged that silence was tantamount to confession, and these "unfriendly witnesses" lost their jobs and suffered public ostracism. In 1947, HUAC investigated radical activity in Hollywood. Some actors and directors cooperated, but ten refused, citing their First Amendment rights. The "Hollywood Ten" served jail sentences for contempt of Congress—a punishment that Helen Gahagan Douglas fought—and then found themselves blacklisted in the movie industry.

The Truman administration went after the Communist Party directly, prosecuting its leaders under a 1940 law that made it a crime to "advocate the overthrow and destruction of the [government] by force and violence." Although civil libertarians argued that the guilty

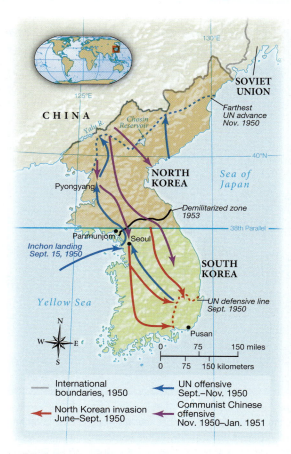

MAP ACTIVITY

Map 26.3   The Korean War, 1950–1953
Although each side had plunged deep into enemy territory, the war ended in 1953 with the dividing line between North and South Korea nearly where it had been before the fighting began.

READING THE MAP: How far south did the North Korean forces progress at the height of their invasion? How far north did the UN forces get? What countries border Korea, and what was the significance of these particular countries' presence so close to the territory in dispute?

CONNECTIONS: What dangers did the forays of MacArthur's forces to within forty miles of the Korean-Chinese border pose? Why did Truman forbid MacArthur to approach that border? What political considerations on the home front influenced Truman's policy and military strategy regarding Korea?

verdicts violated First Amendment freedoms of speech, press, and association, the Supreme Court ruled in 1951 that the Communist threat overrode constitutional guarantees.

The domestic Cold War spread beyond the nation's capital. State and local governments investigated citizens, demanded loyalty oaths, fired employees suspected of disloyalty, banned books from public libraries, and more. College

professors and public school teachers lost their jobs in New York, California, and elsewhere. (See "Seeking the American Promise," page 760.) Because the Communist Party had helped organize unions and championed racial justice, labor and civil rights activists fell prey to McCarthyism as well. African American activist Jack O'Dell remembered that segregationists pinned the tag of Communist on "anybody who supported the right of blacks to have civil rights."

McCarthyism caused untold harm to thousands of innocent individuals. Anti-Communist crusaders humiliated and discredited law-abiding citizens, hounded them from their jobs, and in some cases even sent them to prison. The anti-Communist crusade violated fundamental constitutional rights of freedom of speech and association and stifled the expression of dissenting ideas or unpopular causes.

REVIEW: Why did Truman have limited success in implementing his domestic agenda?

▶ The Cold War Becomes Hot: Korea

The Cold War erupted into a shooting war in June 1950 when troops from Communist North Korea invaded South Korea. For the first time, Americans went into battle to implement containment. Confirming the global reach of the Truman Doctrine, U.S. involvement in Korea also marked the militarization of American foreign policy. The United States, in concert with the United Nations, ultimately held the line in Korea, but at a great cost in lives, dollars, and domestic unity.

Korea and the Military Implementation of Containment

The **Korean War** grew out of the artificial division of Korea after World War II. Having expelled the Japanese, the United States and the Soviet Union created two occupation zones separated by the thirty-eighth parallel (Map 26.3). With Moscow and Washington unable to agree on unification, the United Nations sponsored elections in South Korea in July 1948. The American-favored candidate, Syngman Rhee, was elected president, and the United States withdrew most of its troops. In fall 1948, the Soviets established the People's Republic of North Korea under Kim Il-sung and also

On the Defensive in Korea
After UN troops approached the Yalu River, the Chinese entered the Korean War, throwing UN forces on the defensive and pushing deep into the South. In this photo, taken in April 1951, infantrymen are protecting a pontoon bridge so that UN trucks and tanks on the other side can escape the advancing Chinese army. Eventually, UN forces recaptured this territory. AP Photo/James Martenhoff.

withdrew. Although unsure whether Rhee's repressive government could sustain popular support, U.S. officials appreciated his anticommunism and provided economic and military aid to South Korea.

Skirmishes between North and South Korean troops at the thirty-eighth parallel began in 1948. Then, in June 1950, 90,000 North Koreans swept into South Korea. Truman's advisers assumed that the Soviet Union or China had instigated the attack (an assumption later proved incorrect), and the president quickly decided to intervene, viewing Korea as "the Greece of the Far East." With the Soviet Union absent from the Security Council, the United States obtained UN sponsorship of a collective effort to repel the attack. Authorized to appoint a commander for the UN force, Truman named World War II hero General Douglas MacArthur.

Sixteen nations sent troops to Korea, but the United States furnished most of the personnel and weapons, deploying almost 1.8 million troops and dictating strategy. By dispatching troops without asking Congress for a declaration of war, Truman violated the spirit if not the letter of the Constitution and contributed to the expansion of executive power that would characterize the Cold War.

The first American soldiers rushed to Korea unprepared and ill equipped: "I didn't even know how to dig a foxhole," recalled a nineteen-year-old Army reservist. As a result, U.S. forces suffered severe defeats early in the war. The North Koreans took the capital of Seoul and drove deep into South Korea, forcing UN troops to retreat to Pusan. Then, in September 1950, General MacArthur launched a bold counteroffensive at Inchon, 180 miles behind North Korean lines. By October UN and South Korean forces had retaken Seoul and pushed the North Koreans back to the thirty-eighth parallel. Now Truman had to decide whether to invade North Korea and seek to unify the country.

From Containment to Rollback to Containment

"Troops could not be expected . . . to march up to a surveyor's line and stop," remarked Secretary of State Dean Acheson, reflecting support for transforming the military objective from containment to elimination of the enemy and unification of Korea. Thus, for the only time during the Cold War, the United States tried to roll back communism by force. With UN approval, on September 27, 1950, Truman authorized MacArthur to cross the thirty-eighth parallel. Concerned about possible intervention by China, the president directed him to keep UN troops away from the Korean-Chinese border. Disregarding the order, MacArthur sent them to within forty miles of China, whereupon 300,000 Chinese soldiers crossed into Korea. With Chinese help, the North Koreans recaptured Seoul.

After three months of grueling battle, UN forces fought their way back to the thirty-eighth parallel. At that point, Truman decided to seek a negotiated settlement. MacArthur was furious

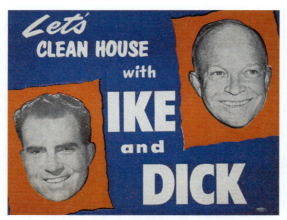

The 1952 Republican Ticket
This 1952 campaign poster shows Republican presidential nominee Dwight D. Eisenhower with his running mate Richard Nixon. The slogan refers to scandals involving Truman associates, but not Truman himself, and his failure to end the Korean War. © David J. & Janice L. Frent Collection/CORBIS

when the goal of the war reverted to containment, which to him represented defeat. Taking his case to the public, he challenged both the president's authority to conduct foreign policy and the principle of civilian control of the military. Fed up with MacArthur's insubordination, Truman fired him in April 1951. Many Americans sided with MacArthur, reflecting their frustration with containment. Why should Americans die simply to preserve the status quo? Why not destroy the enemy once and for all? Those siding with MacArthur assumed that the United States was all-powerful and blamed the stalemate in Korea on the government's ineptitude or willingness to shelter subversives.

When Congress investigated MacArthur's dismissal, all of the top military leaders supported the president. According to the chairman of the Joint Chiefs of Staff, MacArthur wanted to wage "the wrong war, at the wrong place, at the wrong time, with the wrong enemy." Yet Truman never recovered from the political fallout. Nor was he able to end the war. Negotiations began in July 1951, but peace talks dragged on for two more years while 12,000 more U.S. soldiers died.

Korea, Communism, and the 1952 Election

Popular discontent with Truman's war boosted Republicans in the 1952 election. Their presidential nominee, General Dwight D. Eisenhower, was a popular hero. As supreme commander in Europe, he won widespread acclaim for leading the Allied armies to victory over Germany in World War II,

and in 1950 Truman appointed Eisenhower the first supreme commander of NATO forces.

Although Eisenhower believed that professional soldiers should stay out of politics, he found compelling reasons to run in 1952. He largely agreed with Truman's foreign policy, but he deplored the Democrats' propensity to solve domestic problems with costly new federal programs. He also disliked the foreign policy views of leading Republican presidential contender, Senator Robert A. Taft, who attacked containment and sought to cut defense spending. Eisenhower defeated Taft for the nomination, but the old guard prevailed on the party platform. It excoriated containment as "negative, futile, and immoral" and charged the Truman administration with shielding "traitors to the Nation in high places." By choosing thirty-nine-year-old Senator Richard M. Nixon for his running mate, Eisenhower helped to appease the right wing of the party.

Richard Milhous Nixon grew up in southern California, worked his way through college and law school, served in the navy, and briefly practiced law, before winning election to Congress in 1946. Nixon quickly made a name for himself as a member of HUAC (see page 761) and a key anti-Communist, moving to the Senate with his victory over Helen Gahagan Douglas in 1950.

With his public approval ratings plummeting, Truman decided not to run for reelection. The Democrats nominated Adlai E. Stevenson, the popular governor of Illinois, but he could not escape the domestic fallout from the Korean War, nor match Eisenhower's widespread appeal. Shortly before the election, Eisenhower announced dramatically, "I shall go to Korea," and voters registered their confidence in his ability to end the war. Cutting sharply into traditional Democratic territory, Eisenhower won several southern states and garnered 55 percent of the popular vote overall. His coattails carried a narrow Republican majority to Congress.

An Armistice and the War's Costs

Eisenhower made good on his pledge to end the Korean War. In July 1953, the two sides reached an armistice that left Korea divided, again roughly at the thirty-eighth parallel, with North and South separated by a two-and-a-half-mile-wide demilitarized zone (see Map 26.3). The war fulfilled the objective of containment, since the United States had backed up its promise to help nations that were resisting communism. Both Truman and Eisenhower managed to contain what amounted to a world war—involving twenty nations altogether—within a single country and to avoid the use of nuclear weapons.

Yet the war took the lives of 36,000 Americans and wounded more than 100,000. Thousands of U.S. soldiers suffered as prisoners of war. South Korea lost more than a million people to war-related causes, and 1.8 million North Koreans and Chinese were killed or wounded.

Korea had an enormous effect on defense policy and spending. In April 1950, just before the war began, the National Security Council completed a top-secret report, known as **NSC 68**, on the United States' military strength, warning that national survival required a massive military buildup. The Korean War brought about nearly all of the military expansion called for in NSC 68, vastly increasing U.S. capacity to act as a global power. Military spending shot up from $14 billion in 1950 to $50 billion in 1953 and remained above $40 billion thereafter. By 1952, defense spending claimed nearly 70 percent of the federal budget, and the size of the armed forces had tripled.

To General Matthew Ridgway, MacArthur's successor as commander of the UN forces, Korea taught the lesson that U.S. forces should never again fight a land war in Asia. Eisenhower concurred. Nevertheless, during the Korean War the Truman administration had expanded its role in Asia by increasing aid to the French, who were fighting to hang on to their colonial empire in Indochina. As U.S. Marines retreated from a battle against Chinese soldiers in 1950, they sang, prophetically, "We're Harry's police force on call, / So put back your pack on, / The next step is Saigon."

> **REVIEW:** How did U.S. Cold War policy lead to the Korean War?

▶ Conclusion: The Cold War's Costs and Consequences

Hoping for continued U.S.-Soviet cooperation rather than unilateral American intervention to resolve foreign crises, Helen Gahagan Douglas initially opposed the implementation of containment. By 1948, however, she was squarely behind Truman's decision to fight communism throughout the world, a decision that marked the most momentous foreign policy initiative in the nation's history.

More than any development in the postwar world, the Cold War defined American politics and society for decades to come. It transformed the federal government, shifting its priorities from domestic to external affairs, greatly expanding its budget, and substantially increasing the power of the president. Military spending helped transform the nation itself, as defense contracts promoted economic and population booms in the West and Southwest. The nuclear arms race put the people of the world at risk, consumed resources that might have been used to improve living standards, and skewed the economy toward dependence on military projects.

In sharp contrast to foreign policy, the domestic policies of the postwar years reflected continuity with the 1930s. Douglas had come to Congress hoping to expand the New Deal, to help find "a way by which all people can live out their lives in dignity and decency." She avidly supported Truman's proposals for new programs in education, health, and civil rights, but a majority of her colleagues did not. Consequently, the poor and minorities suffered even while a majority of Americans enjoyed a higher standard of living in an economy boosted by Cold War spending and the reconstruction of Western Europe and Japan.

Another cost of the early Cold War years was the anti-Communist hysteria that swept the nation, denying Douglas a Senate seat, intimidating radicals and liberals, and narrowing the range of ideas acceptable for political discussion. Partisan politics and Truman's warnings about the Communist menace fueled McCarthyism, along with popular frustrations over the failure of containment to produce clear-cut victories. The Korean War, which ended in stalemate rather than the defeat of communism, exacerbated feelings of frustration. It would be a major challenge of the Eisenhower administration to restore national unity and confidence.

See the Selected Bibliography for this chapter in the Appendix.

26 Chapter Review

MAKE IT STICK

 **LearningCurve**

Go online and use LearningCurve to see what you know. Then review the key terms and answer the questions.

KEY TERMS

Cold War (p. 744)
iron curtain (p. 744)
containment (p. 744)
Truman Doctrine (p. 748)
Marshall Plan (p. 748)
North Atlantic Treaty Organization (NATO) (p. 749)
Central Intelligence Agency (CIA) (p. 751)
Taft-Hartley Act (p. 757)
Housing Act of 1949 (p. 758)
House Un-American Activities Committee (HUAC) (p. 761)
Korean War (p. 762)
NSC 68 (p. 765)

REVIEW QUESTIONS

1. What factors contributed to the emergence of the Cold War? (pp. 743–753)

2. Why did Truman have limited success in implementing his domestic agenda? (pp. 753–762)

3. How did U.S. Cold War policy lead to the Korean War? (pp. 762–765)

MAKING CONNECTIONS

1. What was the containment policy, and how successful was it up to 1953? Discuss both the supporters and the critics of the policy.

2. How did returning American soldiers change postwar domestic life in the areas of education and civil rights? Discuss how wartime experiences influenced their demands.

3. Why did anti-Communist hysteria sweep the country in the early 1950s? How did it shape domestic politics? Be sure to consider the influence of developments abroad and at home.

LINKING TO THE PAST

1. What events and decisions during World War II contributed to the rise of the Cold War in the late 1940s? (See chapter 25.)

2. What did the anti-Communist hysteria of the late 1940s and the 1950s have in common with the Red scare that followed World War I, and how did these two phenomena differ? (See chapter 22.)

27

The Politics and Culture of Abundance

1952–1960

After reading and studying this chapter, you should be able to:

- Explain the dominant issues of the Eisenhower administration and how Eisenhower's policies represented the politics of the "Middle Way."

- Describe how the Eisenhower administration practiced containment and explain how the "New Look" in foreign policy influenced its handling of world events.

- Explain the factors that led to an economy of abundance and how that abundance influenced Americans' lives.

- Analyze how the economy of abundance influenced consumption, religion, gender roles, and the media.

- Explain the origins of the modern civil rights movement and the strategies activists used to end racial segregation.

1959 CADILLAC
The automobile reflected 1950s prosperity and generated one of every six jobs. This Cadillac was manufactured by General Motors, the biggest and richest corporation in the world. Bill Philpot /Alamy.

TRAILED BY REPORTERS, VICE PRESIDENT RICHARD M. NIXON LED Soviet premier Nikita Khrushchev through the American National Exhibition in Moscow in July 1959. The display of American consumer goods was part of a cultural exchange that reflected a slight thaw in the Cold War after Khrushchev replaced Stalin. In Moscow, both Khrushchev and Nixon seized on the propaganda potential of the moment. As they examined the display, they exchanged a slugfest of words and gestures that reporters dubbed the kitchen debate.

Showing off a new color television set, Nixon said the Soviet Union "may be ahead of us . . . in the thrust of your rockets," but he insisted to Khrushchev that the United States outstripped the Soviets in consumer goods. Nixon linked capitalism with democracy, asserting that the array of products represented "what freedom means to us . . . our right to choose." Moreover, Nixon boasted that "any steelworker could buy this house," as they walked through a model of a six-room ranch-style home. Khrushchev retorted that in the Soviet Union "you are entitled to housing," whereas in the United States the homeless slept on pavements.

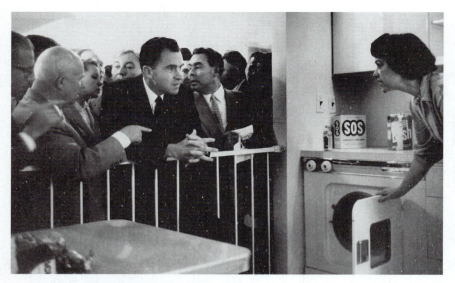

The Kitchen Debate
Soviet premier Nikita Khrushchev (left) and Vice President Richard M. Nixon (center) debate the relative merits of their nations' economies at the American National Exhibition held in Moscow in 1959. "You are a lawyer for capitalism and I am a lawyer for communism," Khrushchev told Nixon as each tried to outdo the other. Howard Sochurek/Time & Life Pictures/Getty.

Nixon declared that the household appliances were "designed to make things easier for our women." Khrushchev disparaged "the capitalist attitude toward women," maintaining that the Soviets appreciated women's contributions to the economy, not their domesticity. Nixon got Khrushchev to agree that it was "far better to be talking about washing machines than machines of war," yet Cold War tensions surfaced when Khrushchev later blustered, "We too are giants. You want to threaten—we will answer threats with threats."

In fact, the Eisenhower administration (1953–1961) had begun with threats, and the two nations engaged in an intense arms race throughout the decade and beyond. During the 1952 campaign, Republicans had vowed to roll back communism and liberate "enslaved" peoples under Soviet rule. In practice, President Dwight D. Eisenhower pursued a containment policy much like that of his predecessor, Harry S. Truman, though Eisenhower relied more on nuclear weapons and on Central Intelligence Agency (CIA) secret operations against left-leaning governments. Yet as Nixon's visit to Moscow demonstrated, Eisenhower seized on political changes in the Soviet Union to reduce tensions in Soviet-American relations.

Continuity with the Truman administration also characterized domestic policy. Although Eisenhower favored corporations with tax cuts and resisted strong federal efforts in health care, education, and race relations, he did not try to demolish the New Deal. He even extended the reach of the federal government with a massive highway program.

Although poverty clung stubbornly to one of every five Americans, the Moscow display testified to the unheard-of material gains savored by many in the postwar era. Cold War weapons production spurred the economy, whose vitality stimulated suburban development, contributed to the growth of the South and Southwest (the Sun Belt), and enabled millions of Americans to buy a host of new products. As new homes, television sets, and household appliances transformed living patterns, Americans took part in a consumer culture that celebrated the family and traditional gender roles, even as more and more married women took jobs outside the home. Challenging the dominant norms were dissenting writers known as the Beats and an emerging youth culture.

The Cold War and the economic boom helped African Americans mount the most dramatic challenge of the 1950s, a struggle against the system of segregation and disfranchisement that had replaced slavery. Large numbers of African Americans took direct action against the institutions of injustice, developing the organizations, leadership, and strategies to mount a civil rights movement of unprecedented size and influence.

▶ Eisenhower and the Politics of the "Middle Way"

Moderation was the guiding principle of Eisenhower's domestic agenda and leadership style. In 1953, he pledged a "middle way between untrammeled freedom of the individual and the demands for the welfare of the whole Nation," promising that his administration would "avoid government by bureaucracy as carefully as it avoids neglect of the helpless." Eisenhower generally resisted expanding the federal government's power, he acted reluctantly when the Supreme Court ordered schools to desegregate, and his administration terminated the federal trusteeship of dozens of Indian tribes. As a moderate Republican, however, Eisenhower supported the continuation of New Deal programs and in some cases, such as in the creation of a national highway system, he expanded federal action. Nicknamed "Ike," the confident war hero remained popular, but he was not able to lift the Republican Party to national dominance.

Modern Republicanism

In contrast to the old guard conservatives in his party who criticized containment and wanted to repeal much of the New Deal, Dwight D. Eisenhower preached "modern Republicanism." This meant resisting additional federal intervention in economic and social life, but not turning the clock back to the 1920s. "Should any political party attempt to abolish social security and eliminate labor laws and farm programs," he wrote privately in 1954, "you would not hear of that party again in our political history." Democratic control of Congress after the elections of 1954 further contributed to Eisenhower's moderate approach.

The new president attempted to distance himself from the anti-Communist fervor that had plagued the Truman administration, even as he intensified Truman's loyalty program, allowing federal executives to dismiss thousands of employees on grounds of loyalty, security, or "suitability." Reflecting his inclination to avoid controversial issues, Eisenhower refused to denounce Senator Joseph McCarthy publicly. But, in 1954, McCarthy began to destroy himself when he hurled reckless charges of communism against military personnel during televised hearings. When the army's lawyer demanded of McCarthy, "Have you left no sense of decency?"

CHRONOLOGY

1952	• Dwight D. Eisenhower elected president.
1953	• CIA-organized coup against Iranian government.
1954	• CIA coup against Guatemalan government. • Geneva accords. • United States begins aid to South Vietnam. • Operation Wetback. • *Hernandez v. Texas*. • *Brown v. Board of Education*. • Senate condemns Senator Joseph McCarthy.
1955	• Eisenhower and Khrushchev meet in Geneva.
1955–1956	• Montgomery, Alabama, bus boycott.
1956	• Interstate Highway and Defense System Act. • Eisenhower reelected.
1957	• Southern Christian Leadership Conference (SCLC) founded. • Soviets launch *Sputnik*. • Civil Rights Act of 1957.
1958	• National Aeronautics and Space Administration (NASA) established. • National Defense Education Act.
1959	• Kitchen debate between Nixon and Khrushchev.
1960	• Soviets shoot down U.S. U-2 spy plane. • One-quarter of Americans live in suburbs. • Thirty-five percent of women work outside the home.

those in the hearing room applauded. A Senate vote in 1954 to condemn him marked the end of his influence but not the end of searching out dissenters on the left.

Eisenhower sometimes echoed conservative Republicans' conviction that government was best left to the states and economic decisions to private business. Yet he signed laws bringing ten million more workers under Social Security, increasing the minimum wage, and creating a new Department of Health, Education, and Welfare. And when the spread of polio neared epidemic proportions, Eisenhower obtained funds from Congress to distribute a vaccine, even though conservatives wanted to leave that responsibility to the states.

Eisenhower's greatest domestic initiative was the **Interstate Highway and Defense System Act of 1956** (Map 27.1). Promoted as essential to national defense and an impetus to

economic growth, the act authorized construction of a national highway system, with the federal government paying most of the costs through increased fuel and vehicle taxes. The new highways accelerated the mobility of people and goods, spurred suburban expansion, and benefited the trucking, construction, and automobile industries that had lobbied hard for the law. Eventually, the monumental highway project exacted unforeseen costs in the form of air pollution, energy consumption, declining railroads and mass transportation, and decay of central cities.

In other areas, Eisenhower restrained federal activity in favor of state governments and private enterprise. His large tax cuts directed most benefits to business and the wealthy, and he resisted federal aid to primary and secondary education as well as strong White House leadership on behalf of civil rights. Eisenhower opposed national health insurance, preferring the growing practice of private insurance provided by employers. Although Democrats sought to keep nuclear power in government hands, Eisenhower signed legislation authorizing the private manufacture and sale of nuclear energy. The first commercial nuclear power plant opened in 1958 in northwest Pennsylvania.

Termination and Relocation of Native Americans

Eisenhower's efforts to limit the federal government were consistent with a new direction in Indian policy, which reversed the New Deal emphasis on strengthening tribal governments and preserving Indian culture (see "Neglected Americans and the New Deal" in chapter 24). After World War II, when some 25,000 Indians had left their homes for military service and another 40,000 for work in defense industries, policymakers began to favor assimilating Native Americans and ending their special relationships with the government.

To some officials, who reflected Cold War emphasis on conformity to dominant American values, the communal practices of Indians resembled socialism and stifled individual initiative. Eisenhower's commissioner of Indian affairs, Glenn Emmons, did not believe that tribal lands could produce income sufficient to eliminate poverty, but he also revealed the ethnocentrism of policymakers when he insisted that Indians wanted to "work and live like Americans." Moreover, Indians still held rights to water, land, minerals, and other resources that were increasingly attractive to state governments and private entrepreneurs.

The Polio Vaccine
Building on the work of other scientists, Dr. Jonas Salk, a researcher at the University of Michigan and the University of Pittsburgh, was the first to develop a successful polio vaccine. In this 1954 photo, he injects a boy during the trials that established the drug's success. Salk became a national hero when the vaccine became available to millions of children in 1955. AP Photo/National Foundation March of Dimes.

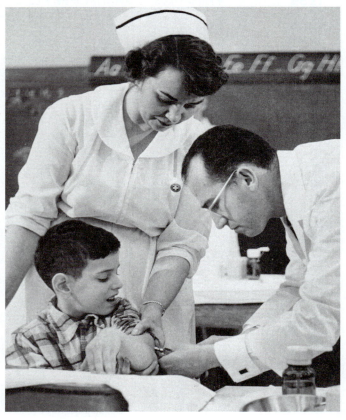

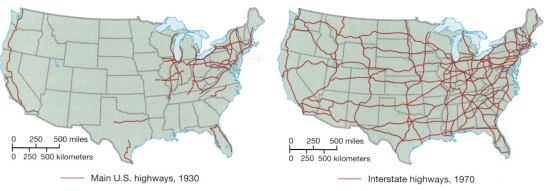

—— Main U.S. highways, 1930

—— Interstate highways, 1970

MAP ACTIVITY

Map 27.1   The Interstate Highway System, 1930 and 1970

Built with federal funds authorized in the Interstate Highway and Defense System Act of 1956, superhighways soon crisscrossed the nation. Trucking, construction, gasoline, and travel were among the industries that prospered, but railroads suffered from the subsidized competition.

READING THE MAP: What regions of the United States had main highways in 1930? What regions did not? How had the situation changed by 1970?

CONNECTIONS: What impact did the growth of the interstate highway system have on migration patterns in the United States? What benefits did the new interstate highways bring to Americans and at what costs?

By 1960, the government had implemented a three-part program of compensation, termination, and relocation. In 1946, Congress established the Indian Claims Commission to hear outstanding claims by Native Americans for land taken by the government. When it closed in 1978, the commission had settled 285 cases, with compensation exceeding $800 million. Yet the awards were based on land values at the time the land was taken and did not include interest.

The second policy, termination, also originated in the Truman administration when Commissioner Dillon S. Myer asserted that his Bureau of Indian Affairs should do "nothing for Indians which Indians can do for themselves." Beginning in 1953, Eisenhower signed bills transferring jurisdiction over tribal land to state and local governments and ending the trusteeship relationship between Indians and the federal government. The loss of federal hospitals, schools, and other special arrangements devastated Indian tribes. As had happened after passage of the Dawes Act in 1887 (see "The Dawes Act and Indian Land Allotment" in chapter 17), some corporate interests and individuals took advantage of the opportunity to purchase Indian land cheaply. The government abandoned termination in the 1960s after some 13,000 Indians and more than one million acres of their land had been affected.

The Indian Relocation Program, the third piece of Native American policy, began in 1948 and involved more than 100,000 Native Americans by 1973. The government encouraged Indians to move to cities, where relocation centers were supposed to help with housing, job training, and medical care. Even though Indians were moved far from their reservations, about one-third returned.

Most who stayed in cities faced racism, unemployment, poor housing, and the loss of their traditional culture. "I wish we had never left home," said one woman whose husband was out of work and drinking heavily. "It's dirty and noisy, and people all around, crowded. . . . It seems like I never see the sky or trees." Reflecting long-standing disagreements among Indians themselves, some who overcame these obstacles applauded the program. But most urban Indians remained poor, and even many who had welcomed relocation worried that "we would lose our identity as Indian people, lose our culture and our

Indian reservation, 1970

Relocation

Major Indian Relocations, 1950–1970

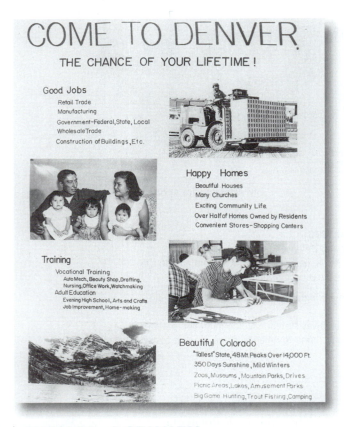

VISUAL ACTIVITY

Indian Relocation

As part of its new emphasis on assimilation in the late 1940s and the 1950s, the Bureau of Indian Affairs distributed this leaflet to entice Native Americans to move from their reservations to cities. Thousands of Indians relocated in the years after World War II. The percentage of Indians living in urban areas grew from 13.4 in 1950 to 44 in 1970. National Archives.

READING THE IMAGE: Which of the features shown in this leaflet do you think would have been the most appealing to Native Americans living on reservations? Which might have evoked little interest?

CONNECTIONS: In what ways did the government's plan to assimilate Native Americans succeed? In what ways did it fail?

[way] of living." Within two decades, a national pan-Indian movement—a by-product of this urbanization—emerged to resist assimilation and to demand much more for Indians (as discussed in "Native American Protest" in chapter 28).

The 1956 Election and the Second Term

Eisenhower easily defeated Adlai Stevenson in 1956, doubling his victory margin of 1952. Yet Democrats kept control of Congress, and in the midterm elections two years later, they all but wiped out the Republican Party, gaining a 64–34 majority in the Senate and a 282–135 advantage in the House. Although Ike captured voters' hearts, a majority of Americans remained wedded to the programs and policies of the Democrats.

Eisenhower faced more serious leadership challenges in his second term. When the economy plunged into a recession in late 1957, he fought with Congress over the budget and vetoed bills to expand housing, urban development, and public works projects. The president and Congress did agree on the first, though largely symbolic, civil rights law in a century and on a larger federal role in education, largely in the interest of national security (as discussed on pages 777 and 791).

In the end, the first Republican administration after the New Deal left the functions of the federal government intact, though it tipped policy benefits somewhat toward corporate interests. Even with two recessions, unparalleled prosperity graced the Eisenhower years, and inflation was kept low. Eisenhower celebrated what he called the "wide diffusion of wealth and incomes" across the United States, yet amid the remarkable abundance were some forty million impoverished Americans. Rural deprivation was particularly pronounced, as was poverty among the elderly, African Americans, and other minorities.

REVIEW: How did Eisenhower's domestic policies reflect his moderate political vision?

► Liberation Rhetoric and the Practice of Containment

At his first inauguration, Eisenhower warned that "forces of good and evil are massed and armed and opposed as rarely before in history." Like Truman, he saw communism as a threat to the nation's security and economic interests, and he wanted to keep the United States the most powerful country in the world. Eisenhower's foreign policy differed, however, in three areas: its rhetoric, its means, and—after Stalin's death in 1953—its movement toward accommodation with the Soviet Union.

Although some Republicans, such as Secretary of State John Foster Dulles, deplored containment as "negative, futile, and immoral," the Eisenhower administration did not attempt to roll back communism with force. Nuclear weapons and CIA secret operations took on a more prominent role in defense strategy, and the United States intervened at the margins of Communist power in Asia, Latin America, and the Middle East. Toward the end of his presidency, Eisenhower sought to ease tensions between the superpowers.

The "New Look" in Foreign Policy

To meet his goals of balancing the budget and cutting taxes, Eisenhower was determined to control military expenditures. Moreover, he feared that massive defense spending would threaten the nation's economic strength. Reflecting American confidence in technology and opposition to a large peacetime army, Eisenhower's "New Look" in defense strategy concentrated U.S. military strength in nuclear weapons and missiles to deliver them. Instead of maintaining large ground forces of its own, the United States would arm friendly nations and back them up with an ominous nuclear arsenal, providing, according to one defense official, "more bang for the buck." Dulles believed that America's willingness to "go to the brink" of war with its intimidating nuclear weapons—a strategy called brinksmanship—would block any Soviet efforts to expand.

Nuclear weapons could not stop a Soviet nuclear attack, but in response to one, they could inflict enormous destruction. This certainty of "massive retaliation" was meant to deter the Soviets from launching an attack. Because the Soviet Union could respond similarly to an American first strike, this nuclear stand-off became known as **mutually assured destruction,** or **MAD**. As leaders of both nations pursued an ever-escalating arms race, the United States stayed on top of the Soviet Union in nuclear warheads and delivery missiles.

Nuclear weapons could not roll back the iron curtain. When a revolt against the Soviet-controlled government began in Hungary in 1956, Dulles's liberation rhetoric proved to be empty. A radio plea from Hungarian freedom fighters cried, "SOS! They just brought us a rumor that the American troops will be here within one or two hours." But help did not come. Eisenhower was unwilling to risk U.S. soldiers and possible nuclear war, and Soviet troops soon suppressed the insurrection, killing or wounding thousands of Hungarians.

Applying Containment to Vietnam

A major challenge to the containment policy came in Southeast Asia. During World War II, Ho Chi Minh, a Vietnamese nationalist, had founded a coalition called the Vietminh to

Missiles in the Nuclear Age
By the 1950s, both the United States and the Soviet Union were arming missiles with nuclear weapons, and the U.S. Air Force had begun to deploy those missiles in Europe before it had achieved the capability to strike Moscow from a launching site in the United States. This photograph shows the first Thor Ballistic Missile arriving at an RAF Base in Norfolk, England, in 1958. © Mary Evans/The Image Works.

fight both the occupying Japanese forces and the French colonial rulers. In 1945, the Vietminh declared Vietnam's independence from France, and when France fought back, the area plunged into war. Because Ho declared himself a Communist, the Truman administration quietly began to provide aid to the French (see chapter 29, Map 29.2). American principles of national self-determination took a backseat to the battle against communism.

Eisenhower viewed communism in Vietnam much as Truman had regarded it in Greece and Turkey. In what became known as the **domino theory**, Eisenhower explained, "You have a row of dominoes, you knock over the first one, and what will happen to the last one is the certainty that it will go over very quickly." A Communist victory in Southeast Asia, he warned, could trigger the fall of Japan, Taiwan, and the Philippines. By 1954, the United States was paying 75 percent of the cost of France's war, but Eisenhower resisted a larger role. When the French asked for American troops and planes to avert almost certain defeat in the battle for Dien Bien Phu, Eisenhower, remembering the Korean War (see "The Cold War Becomes Hot: Korea" in chapter 26).

Dien Bien Phu fell to the Vietminh in May 1954, and two months later in Geneva a truce was signed. The Geneva accords recognized Vietnam's independence and temporarily partitioned it at the seventeenth parallel, separating the Vietminh in the north from the puppet government established by the French in the south. Within two years, the Vietnamese people were to vote in elections for a unified government. Some officials warned against U.S. involvement in Vietnam, envisioning "nothing but grief in store for us if we remained in that area." Eisenhower and Dulles nonetheless moved to prop up the dominoes with a new alliance and put the CIA to work infiltrating and destabilizing North Vietnam. Fearing a Communist victory in the elections mandated by the Geneva accords, they supported South Vietnamese prime minister Ngo Dinh Diem's refusal to hold the vote.

Geneva Accords, 1954

Between 1955 and 1961, the United States provided $800 million to the South Vietnamese army (ARVN). Yet the ARVN proved grossly unprepared for the guerrilla warfare that began in the late 1950s. With help from Ho Chi Minh's government in Hanoi, Vietminh rebels in the south stepped up their guerrilla attacks on the Diem government. The insurgents gained support from the largely Buddhist peasants, who were outraged by the repressive regime of the Catholic, Westernized Diem. Unwilling to abandon containment, Eisenhower left his successor with a deteriorating situation and a firm commitment to defend South Vietnam against communism.

Interventions in Latin America and the Middle East

While supporting friendly governments in Asia, the Eisenhower administration sought to topple unfriendly ones in Latin America and the Middle East. Officials saw internal civil wars in terms of the Cold War conflict between the superpowers and often viewed nationalist uprisings as Communist threats to democracy. They also acted against governments that threatened U.S. economic interests. The Eisenhower administration took this course of action out of sight of Congress and the public, making the CIA an important arm of foreign policy.

Guatemala's government, under the popularly elected reformist president Jacobo Arbenz, was not Soviet controlled, but it accepted support from the small local Communist Party (see "Meeting the 'Hour of Maximum Danger'" in chapter 29, Map 29.1). In 1953, Arbenz moved to help landless, poverty-stricken peasants by nationalizing land owned, but not cultivated, by the United Fruit Company, a U.S. corporation whose annual profits were twice the size of Guatemala's budget. United Fruit refused Arbenz's offer to compensate the company at the value of the land it had declared for tax purposes. Then, equating Arbenz's reformist government with the spread of communism, the CIA provided pilots and other support to an opposition army that overthrew the elected government and installed a military dictatorship in 1954. United Fruit kept its land, and Guatemala succumbed to destructive civil wars that lasted through the 1990s.

In 1959, when Cubans' desire for political and economic autonomy erupted into a revolution led by Fidel Castro, a CIA agent promised "to take care of Castro just like we took care of Arbenz." American companies controlled major Cuban resources, and decisions made in Washington directly influenced the lives of the Cuban people. The 1959 **Cuban revolution** drove out the U.S.-supported dictator Fulgencio Batista and led the CIA to warn Eisenhower that "Communists and other extreme radicals appear to have penetrated the Castro movement." When the United States denied Castro's requests for loans, he turned to the Soviet Union. And when U.S. companies refused Castro's offer to purchase their Cuban holdings at their assessed value, he began to nationalize their property. Many anti-Castro Cubans fled to the United States and reported his atrocities. (See "Seeking the American Promise," page 776.) Before leaving office, Eisenhower broke off diplomatic relations with Cuba and authorized the CIA to train Cuban exiles for an invasion to overthrow the Castro government.

In the Middle East, the CIA intervened in Iran to oust an elected government, support an unpopular dictatorship, and maintain Western access to Iranian oil (see "The Cold War Intensifies" in chapter 30, Map 30.3). In 1951, the Iranian parliament, led by Prime Minister Mohammed Mossadegh, nationalized the country's oil fields and refineries, which had been held primarily by a British company and from which Iran received less than 20 percent of profits. Britain strongly objected to the takeover and eventually sought help from the United States.

Advisers convinced Eisenhower that Mossadegh, whom *Time* magazine had called "the Iranian George Washington," left Iran vulnerable to communism, and the president wanted to keep oil-rich areas "under the control of people who are friendly." With Eisenhower's authorization, CIA agents instigated a coup, bribing army officers and financing demonstrations in the streets. In August 1953, Iranian army officers captured Mossadegh and reestablished the authority of the shah, Mohammad Reza Pahlavi, known for favoring Western interests and the Iranian wealthy classes. U.S. companies received a 40 percent share of Iran's oil concessions. But resentment over the intervention would poison U.S.-Iranian relations into the twenty-first century.

Elsewhere in the Middle East, Eisenhower continued Truman's support of Israel but also pursued friendships with Arab nations to secure access to oil and build a bulwark against communism. U.S. officials demanded that smaller nations take the American side in the Cold War,

The CIA Helps Restore the Shah of Iran

In 1952, *Time* magazine called Iranian premier Mohammed Mossadegh "the Iranian George Washington" for his commitment to nationalism and democracy. But Secretary of State John Foster Dulles believed that restoring Shah Reza Pahlavi to power would produce a more stable U.S. ally and persuaded President Eisenhower to approve a CIA-supported coup. Here supporters of the shah rally outside the home of Mossadegh, who was eventually forced out. AP Images.

even when those nations preferred neutrality. In 1955, as part of this effort to win Arab allies, Secretary of State Dulles began talks with Egypt about American support to build the Aswan Dam on the Nile River. The following year, Egypt's leader, Gamal Abdel Nasser, sought arms from Communist Czechoslovakia, formed a military alliance with other Arab nations, and recognized the People's Republic of China. In retaliation, Dulles called off the deal for the dam.

In July 1956, Nasser responded by seizing the Suez Canal, then owned by Britain and France but scheduled to revert to Egypt within seven years. In response to the seizure, Israel, whose forces had been skirmishing with Egyptian troops along their common border since 1948, attacked Egypt, with help from Britain and France. Eisenhower opposed

The Suez Crisis, 1956

Operation Pedro Pan: Young Political Refugees Take Flight

Six-year-old María was awakened before dawn one summer day in Cuba in 1962. Her parents drove her to the Havana airport, with one suitcase and her favorite doll. A paper pinned to her gingham dress gave her name and the phone number of family friends in Miami who were to meet her. She traveled with a six-year-old boy whose father in Miami had obtained the visa waivers the children would need to enter the United States. María, excited but anxious, had never been away from her parents before; she would not see them for four months.

On a different flight that summer, ten-year-old Carlos flew to Miami with his older brother, leaving behind a father they would never see again. Because of their age difference, the boys were separated on arrival and sent to different refugee camps in rural Florida. A family acquaintance—a Cuban lawyer working as a janitor in Miami—helped them gain temporary placement with foster families just ten blocks apart. A few months later, they were transferred to a juvenile delinquent facility that provided only one meal a day. Finally, a Cuban uncle arrived and took them with

him to a small midwestern town where no one spoke Spanish. After three years of traumatic separation, their mother fled Cuba and joined them.

María and Carlos were just two of more than fourteen thousand unaccompanied children, ages six to eighteen, who left Cuba as part of a special U.S. government–facilitated program called Operation Pedro Pan, which functioned from December 1960 to October 1962. With little money, no knowledge of English, and often no friends or relatives to receive them, the children faced daunting loneliness and possibly neglect. What drove the parents of these children to take such an extraordinary step?

The U.S. government had already made unusual accommodation for the large exodus of adults fleeing Cuba after Fidel Castro came to power in 1959. Assuming that the refugees would return as soon as Castro's government fell, the United States relaxed immigration restrictions for Cubans, allowed refugees to work, and authorized millions of dollars in relief and resettlement funds for people "subjected to the captivity of Communist despotism."

The U.S. government felt an obligation to shelter Cubans who had worked in the government or military of deposed dictator Fulgencio Batista, who had been a close U.S. ally. Many other Cubans who fled after the revolution had worked for U.S.-owned businesses. Still others were wealthy landowners, business owners, and professionals. By the fall of 1962, 248,000 Cubans had chosen to flee communism, furnishing the United States with a powerful symbolic statement of Cold War politics.

An even more potent symbol was Operation Pedro Pan, with its implication that Castro's Cuba had to be truly terrible for parents to part with their children, even though they expected to see their children soon. Cuban parents who opposed Castro feared not for their children's lives, but for their minds. Public schools in Cuba reportedly taught an escalating rhetoric of revolution, while private schools were shut down. Compulsory military service for boys and summer programs relocating teenagers to jobs teaching literacy in the rural countryside threatened parental rights to determine their children's activities.

---

the intervention, recognizing that the Egyptians had claimed their own territory and that Nasser "embodie[d] the emotional demands of the people . . . for independence." Calling on the United Nations to arrange a truce, he pressured Britain and France to pull back, forcing Israel to retreat.

Despite staying out of the Suez crisis, Eisenhower made it clear in a January 1957 speech that the United States would actively combat communism in the Middle East. In March, Congress approved aid to any Middle Eastern nation "requesting assistance against armed aggression from any country controlled by international communism." The president invoked this **Eisenhower Doctrine** to send aid to Jordan in 1957 and troops to Lebanon in 1958 to counter anti-Western pressures on those governments.

The Nuclear Arms Race

While Eisenhower moved against perceived Communist inroads abroad, he also sought to reduce superpower tensions. After Stalin's death in 1953, Nikita Khrushchev emerged as a more moderate leader. Like Eisenhower, who remarked privately that the arms race would

Relatively prosperous Cuban families did not benefit from Castro's reforms, which focused on improving health and education for the impoverished masses. Their fears of socialized child rearing were reinforced by a program of disinformation allegedly broadcast from a CIA radio station, which warned parents that "the Revolutionary Government will take [your children] away from you when they turn five and will keep them until they are eighteen." Rumors of Communist indoctrination ran rampant.

Fear of communism gripped the United States in the 1950s, and the Pedro Pan exodus both demonstrated and heightened that fear. The belief that Communists brainwashed children and turned them against their parents led some Cuban parents to try to save their children by sending them to a country that celebrated freedom. As with the adult refugees who had fled Cuba for the United States, parents of the Pedro Pan children believed that the trip would be temporary, until the fall of Castro's regime. Most children reunited with their parents in the United States, and some had prominent careers, such as Mel Martinez, who represented Florida in the U.S. Senate. María de los Angeles Torres and Carlos Eire, two among the thousands, grew up to become university professors in the United States. But some of the children, now grown, have ques-

Leaving Havana
A family camera captures María de los Angeles Torres (far left) at the airport in Havana, before her flight to Miami in July 1961. AP Photo.

tioned whether coming to America was worth the trauma they endured and have speculated that Cold War politics might have shaped the operation more than humanitarian concerns.

Questions for Consideration

1. What were the parents of the boys and girls in Operation Pedro Pan trying to save their children from?

2. What did the United States stand to gain from harboring Cuban exiles, especially children?

Connect to the Big Idea

C In what other ways did anticommunism shape relationships between the United States and Latin American countries?

---

lead "at worst to atomic warfare, at best to robbing every people and nation on earth of the fruits of their own toil," Khrushchev wanted to reduce defense spending and the threat of nuclear devastation. Eisenhower and Khrushchev met in Geneva in 1955 at the first summit conference since the end of World War II. Although the meeting produced no new agreements, it symbolized what Eisenhower called "a new spirit of conciliation and cooperation."

In August 1957, the Soviets test-fired their first intercontinental ballistic missile (ICBM) and, two months later, beat the United States into space by launching *Sputnik*, the first man-made satellite to circle the earth. The United States launched a successful satellite of its own in January 1958, but *Sputnik* raised fears that the Soviets led not only in missile development and space exploration but also in science and education. In response, Eisenhower established the National Aeronautics and Space Administration (NASA) with a huge budget increase for space exploration. He also signed the National Defense Education Act, providing support for students in math, foreign languages, and science and technology.

Eisenhower assured the public that the United States possessed nuclear superiority.

VISUAL ACTIVITY

The Age of Nuclear Anxiety

As schools routinely held drills to prepare for possible Soviet attacks, children directly experienced the anxiety and insecurity of the 1950s nuclear arms race. The federal government distributed this pamphlet about how to protect oneself from an atomic attack. Photo: Archive Photos/Getty Images; Pamphlet: Lynn Museum and Historical Society.

READING THE IMAGE: How effective do you think the strategy pictured here would be in a nuclear attack? Why would the government suggest that civilians could protect themselves?

CONNECTIONS: In what other ways did the Cold War shape the everyday lives of Americans?

In fact, during his presidency, the stockpile of nuclear weapons more than quadrupled. With ICBMs at home and in Britain, the United States was prepared to deploy more in Italy and Turkey. In 1960, the United States launched the first Polaris submarine carrying nuclear missiles, yet nuclear weapons could not guarantee security for either superpower because they both possessed sufficient nuclear capacity to devastate each other. Most Americans did not follow Civil Defense Administration recommendations to construct home bomb shelters, but they did realize how precarious nuclear weapons had made their lives.

In the midst of the arms race, the superpowers continued to talk, and by 1960, the two sides were close to a ban on nuclear testing. But just before a planned summit in Paris, a Soviet missile shot down an American U-2 spy plane over Soviet territory. The State Department first denied that U.S. planes had been violating Soviet airspace, but the Soviets produced the pilot and the photos taken on his flight. Eisenhower and Khrushchev met briefly in Paris, but the U-2 incident dashed all prospects for a nuclear arms agreement.

As Eisenhower left office, he warned about the growing influence of the **military-industrial complex.** Eisenhower had struggled against persistent pressures from defense contractors who, in tandem with the military, sought more dollars for newer, more powerful weapons systems. In his farewell address, he warned that the "conjunction of an immense military establishment and a large arms industry . . . exercised a total influence . . . in every city, every state house, every office of the federal government," but his administration had done little to curtail the defense industry's power. The Cold War had created a warfare state.

REVIEW: Where and how did Eisenhower practice containment?

▶ New Work and Living Patterns in an Economy of Abundance

Stimulated by Cold War spending and technological advances, economic productivity increased enormously in the 1950s. A multitude of new items came on the market, and consumption became the order of the day. Millions of Americans enjoyed new homes in the suburbs, and higher education enrollments skyrocketed. Although every section of the nation enjoyed the new abundance, the Southwest and South—the Sun Belt—especially boomed in production, commerce, and population.

Work itself was changing. Fewer people labored on farms, service sector employment overtook manufacturing jobs, women's employment grew, and union membership soared. Not all Americans benefited from these changes; forty million lived in poverty. Most Americans, however, enjoyed a higher standard of living, prompting economist John Kenneth Galbraith to call the United States "the affluent society."

Technology Transforms Agriculture and Industry

Between 1940 and 1960, agricultural output mushroomed even while the number of farmworkers declined by almost one-third. Farmers achieved unprecedented productivity through greater crop specialization, intensive use of fertilizers, and, above all, mechanization. A single mechanical cotton picker replaced fifty people and cut the cost of harvesting a bale of cotton from $40 to $5.

The decline of family farms and the growth of large commercial farming, or agribusiness, were both causes and consequences of mechanization. Benefiting handsomely from federal price supports begun in the New Deal, larger farmers could afford technological improvements, while smaller producers lacked capital to purchase the machinery necessary to compete. Consequently, average farm size more than doubled between 1940 and 1964, and the number of farms fell by more than 40 percent.

Many small farmers who hung on constituted a core of rural poverty. Southern landowners replaced sharecroppers and tenants with machines. Hundreds of thousands of African Americans moved to cities, where racial discrimination and a lack of jobs mired many in urban poverty. A

Technology Transforms Agriculture
The years from 1945 to 1970 saw a second agricultural revolution in the United States. In 1954, tractors outnumbered mules and horses on farms for the first time. In 1940, one farmer could feed 10.7 people. By 1970 that ratio was 1 to 75.8. This advertisement shows how one person could plant several rows of corn by barely lifting a finger. Picture Research Consultants & Archives. Used with permission by Navistar, Inc.

Mississippi mother reported that most of her relatives headed for Chicago when they realized that "it was going to be machines now that harvest the crops." Worrying that "it might be worse up there" for her children, she agonized, "I'm afraid to leave and I'm afraid to stay."

New technologies also transformed industrial production. Between 1945 and 1960 the number of labor-hours needed to manufacture a car fell by 50 percent. Technology revolutionized industries such as electronics, chemicals, and air transportation. It also promoted the growth of television, plastics, computers, and other newer industries. American businesses enjoyed access to cheap oil, ample markets abroad, and little foreign competition. Even with Eisenhower's conservative fiscal policies, government spending reached $80 billion annually and created new jobs.

The strength of labor unions contributed to prosperity by putting money into the hands of people who would spend it. Real earnings for production workers shot up 40 percent. One child of a steelworker remembered, "In 1946, we did not have a car, a television set, or a refrigerator. By 1952 we had all those things." In most industrial nations, government programs underwrote their citizens' security, but the United States developed a mixed system in which company-funded programs won by unions provided for retirement, health care, paid vacations, supplementary unemployment benefits, and more. This system, often called a private welfare state, resulted in wide disparities among workers, disadvantaging those who did not belong to strong unions and those with irregular employment.

While the number of organized workers continued to grow, union membership peaked at 27.1 percent of the labor force in 1957. Technological advances eliminated jobs in heavy industry. "You are going to have trouble collecting union dues from all of these machines," commented a Ford manager to union leader Walter Reuther. Moreover, the economy as a whole was shifting from production to service. Beginning in 1957, white-collar jobs outnumbered blue-collar jobs, as more workers distributed goods, performed services, provided education, and carried out government work. Unions made some headway in these fields, especially among government employees, but most service industries resisted unionization.

The growing clerical and service occupations swelled the demand for female workers. By the end of the 1950s, women held nearly one-third of all jobs. The vast majority of them worked in offices, light manufacturing, domestic service, teaching, and nursing; because these occupations were occupied primarily by women, wages were relatively low. In 1960, the average female full-time worker earned just 60 percent of the average male worker's wages. At the bottom of the employment ladder, black women took home only 42 percent of what white men earned.

Burgeoning Suburbs and Declining Cities

Although suburbs had existed since the nineteenth century, nothing symbolized the affluent society more than their tremendous expansion in the 1950s. Eleven million new homes went up in the suburbs, and by 1960 one in four Americans lived there. As Nixon boasted to Khrushchev during the kitchen debate, the suburban homes were accessible to families with modest incomes. Builder William J. Levitt adapted the factory assembly to home construction, building nearly identical units so that workers moved from house to house performing one specific job. In 1949, families could purchase mass-produced houses in his

The New Suburbs
William J. Levitt adapted the factory assembly-line process to home building, planning nearly identical units so that individual workers could move from house to house performing the same single operation. This photograph reflects a typical Levittown street in 1954. © Bettmann/Corbis.

17,000-home development, called Levittown, on Long Island, New York, for just under $8,000 each ($75,000 in 2012 dollars). Similar developments, as well as more luxurious ones, quickly went up throughout the country. The government subsidized home ownership by guaranteeing low-interest mortgages and by making interest on mortgages tax deductible. Government-funded interstate highways running through metropolitan areas also encouraged suburban development.

By the 1960s, suburbs came under attack for bulldozing the natural environment, creating groundwater contamination, and disrupting wildlife patterns. Social critic Lewis Mumford disparaged suburbia as "a multitude of uniform, unidentifiable houses in a treeless communal wasteland, inhabited by people of the same class, the same income, the same age group." Yet most families were thrilled to be able to own new homes. "It was a miracle to them," one man said of his working-class parents who moved to Levittown.

The suburbs did help polarize society, especially along racial lines. Each Levittown homeowner signed a contract pledging not to rent or sell to a non-Caucasian. The Supreme Court declared such covenants unenforceable in 1948, but suburban America remained dramatically segregated. Although some African Americans joined the suburban migration, most moved to cities in search of economic opportunity, doubling their numbers in major cities during the 1950s. These migrants, however, came to cities that were already in decline, losing not only population but also commerce, industry, and jobs to the suburbs or to southern and western states.

The Rise of the Sun Belt

No regions experienced the postwar economic and population booms more intensely than the South and Southwest (Map 27.2). California overtook New York as the most populous state. Sports franchises followed fans: In 1958, the Brooklyn Dodgers moved to Los Angeles, joined by the Minneapolis Lakers three years later.

A pleasant natural environment attracted new residents to the **Sun Belt**, but no magnet proved stronger than economic opportunity. As railroads had fueled western growth in the nineteenth century, so the automobile and airplane spurred the post–World War II surge. Air-conditioning cooled nearly eight million homes by 1960, and it facilitated industrial development and tourism. "Can you conceive a Walt Disney World in central Florida without its air-conditioned hotels?" asked a journalist.

So important was the defense industry to the South and Southwest that the area was later referred to as the "Gun Belt." The aerospace industry boomed in such cities as Los Angeles and Dallas–Fort Worth, and military bases helped underwrite prosperity in cities such as San Diego and San Antonio. Although defense dollars benefited other regions—military bases and aerospace plants were numerous in the Northwest—the Sun Belt captured the lion's share of Cold War spending. By the 1960s, nearly

VISUAL ACTIVITY

Air-Conditioning

The first air-conditioning system was installed in factories, but room air-conditioning began to appear in homes in the 1930s and spread rapidly in the 1950s. Fewer than one million homes had room air conditioners in 1950, but nearly eight million did in 1960, and more than half of all homes had some form of air-conditioning by 1975, as its status changed from a luxury to a necessity. Picture Research Consultants & Archives, courtesy of General Electric.

READING THE IMAGE: What does this ad promise consumers? What negative effects of air-conditioning does it leave out?

CONNECTIONS: How was air-conditioning related to the rise of the Sun Belt? What other factors contributed to its growth?

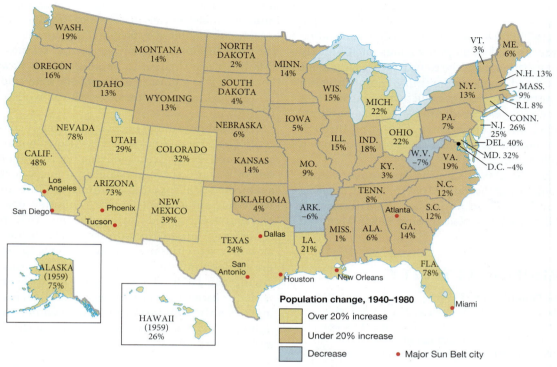

MAP ACTIVITY

Map 27.2   The Rise of the Sun Belt, 1940–1980

The growth of defense industries, a non-unionized labor force, and the spread of air-conditioning all helped spur economic development and population growth in the Southwest and the South. This made the Sun Belt the fastest-growing region of the country between 1940 and 1980.

READING THE MAP: Which states experienced population growth of more than 20 percent? Which states experienced the largest population growth?

CONNECTIONS: What stimulated the population boom in the Southwest? What role did the Cold War play in this expansion? What developments made the Southwest diverse in the composition of its population?

one of every three California workers held a defense-related job.

The surging populations and industries soon threatened the environment. Providing sufficient water and power to cities and to agribusiness meant building dams and reservoirs on free-flowing rivers. Native Americans lost fishing sites on the Columbia River, and dams on the Upper Missouri displaced nine hundred Indian families. Sprawling suburban settlement without efficient public transportation contributed to blankets of smog over Los Angeles and other cities.

The high-technology basis of economic development drew well-educated, highly skilled workers to the West, but economic promise also attracted the poor. "We see opportunity all around us here. . . . We smell freedom here, and maybe soon we can taste it," commented a black mother in California. Between 1945 and 1960, more than

one-third of the African Americans who left the South moved west.

The Mexican American population also grew, especially in California and Texas. To supply California's vast agribusiness industry, the government continued the bracero program begun in 1942, under which Mexicans were permitted to enter the United States to work for a limited period. Until the program ended in 1964, more than 100,000 Mexicans entered the United States each year to labor in the fields—and many of them stayed, legally or illegally. But perm-anent Mexican immigration was not as welcome as Mexicans' low-wage labor. In 1954, the government launched a series of raids called "Operation Wetback," sending more than a million Mexicans back across the border.

At the same time, Mexican American citizens gained a victory in their ongoing struggle

Rounding up Undocumented Migrants
Not all Mexican Americans who wanted to work in the United States were accommodated by the *bracero* program. In 1953, Los Angeles police arrested these men who did not have legal documents and were hiding in a freight train. © Bettmann/Corbis.

for civil rights in **Hernandez v. Texas**. In this 1954 case, the Supreme Court ruled unanimously that Mexican Americans constituted a distinct group and that their systematic exclusion from juries violated the Fourteenth Amendment guarantee of equal protection. Legal scholar Ian Haney-Lopez called *Hernandez* "huge for the Mexican American community. They now had the highest court in the land saying it's unconstitutional to treat Mexicans as if they're an inferior race."

Free of the discrimination faced by minorities, white Americans enjoyed the fullest prosperity in the West. In April 1950, when California developers opened Lakewood, a 17,500-home development in Los Angeles County, thirty thousand people lined up to buy houses at prices averaging $86,000 in 2013 dollars. Many of the new homeowners were veterans, blue-collar, and lower-level white-collar workers whose defense-based jobs at aerospace corporations enabled them to fulfill the American dream of the 1950s. A huge shopping mall, Lakewood Center, offered myriad products of the consumer culture, and the workers' children lived at commuting distance from community colleges and six state universities.

The Democratization of Higher Education

California's university system exemplified a spectacular transformation of higher education. Between 1940 and 1960, college enrollments in the United States more than doubled, and more than 40 percent of young Americans attended college by the mid-1960s. The federal government subsidized the education of more than two million veterans, and the Cold War sent millions of federal dollars to universities for defense-related research. State governments vastly expanded the number of public colleges and universities, while municipalities began to build two-year community colleges.

All Americans did not benefit equally from the democratization of higher education. Although their college enrollments surged from 37,000 in 1941 to 90,000 in 1961, African Americans constituted only about 5 percent of all college students. For a time the educational gap between white men and women grew, even though women's enrollments increased. In 1940, women had earned 40 percent of undergraduate degrees, but as veterans flocked to college campuses, women's proportion fell to 25 percent, rising to just 33 percent by 1960. Women were more likely than men to drop out of college after marriage, taking jobs to keep their husbands in school. Reflecting gender norms of the 1950s, most college women agreed that "it is natural for a woman to be satisfied with her husband's success and not crave personal achievement."

REVIEW: What fueled the prosperity of the 1950s?

► The Culture of Abundance

Prosperity in the 1950s intensified the transformation of the nation into a consumer society, changing the way Americans lived and converting the traditional work ethic into an ethic of consumption. The new medium of television both reflected and stimulated a consumer culture. People married at earlier ages, the birthrate soared, and dominant values celebrated family life and traditional gender roles. Undercurrents of rebellion, especially among young people, and women's increasing employment defied some of the dominant norms but did not greatly disrupt the complacency of the 1950s.

Consumption Rules the Day

Scorned by Khrushchev during the kitchen debate as unnecessary gadgets, consumer items flooded American society in the 1950s. Although the purchase and display of consumer goods was not new (See "Consumer Culture" in chapter 23), at midcentury consumption had become a reigning value, vital for economic prosperity and essential to individuals' identity and status. In place of the traditional emphasis on work and savings, the consumer culture encouraged satisfaction and happiness through the acquisition of new products.

The consumer culture rested on a firm material base. Between 1950 and 1960, both the gross national product (the value of all goods and services produced) and median family income grew by 25 percent in constant dollars (Figure 27.1). Economists claimed that 60 percent of Americans enjoyed middle-class incomes in 1960. By then, four-fifths of all families owned a television set, nearly all had a refrigerator, and most owned at least one car. The number of shopping centers quadrupled between 1957 and 1963.

Several forces spurred this unparalleled abundance. A population surge—from 152 million to 180 million during the 1950s—expanded demand for products and boosted industries ranging from housing to baby goods. Consumer borrowing also fueled the economic boom, as people made purchases on installment plans and began to use credit cards. Increasingly Americans enjoyed their possessions while they paid for them instead of saving their money for future purchases.

Although the sheer need to support themselves and their families explained most women's employment, a desire to secure some of the new abundance sent growing numbers of women to work. As one woman remarked, "My Joe can't put five kids through college . . . and the washer had to be replaced, and Ann was ashamed to bring friends home because the living room furniture was such a mess, so I went to work." The standards for family happiness imposed

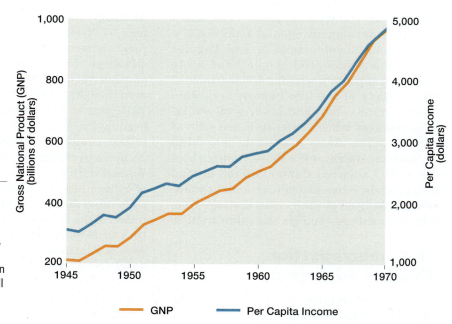

FIGURE 27.1 **The Postwar Economic Boom: GNP and Per Capita Income, 1945–1970**
American dominance of the worldwide market, innovative technologies that led to new industries such as computers and plastics, population growth, and increases in worker productivity all contributed to the enormous economic growth of the United States after World War II.

by the consumer culture increasingly required a second income.

The Revival of Domesticity and Religion

Despite married women's growing employment, a dominant ideology celebrated traditional family life and conventional gender roles. Both popular culture and public figures defined the ideal family as a male breadwinner, a full-time homemaker, and three or four children. Writer and feminist Betty Friedan gave a name to the idealization of women's domestic roles in her 1963 book *The Feminine Mystique*. Friedan criticized health professionals, scholars, advertisers, and public officials for assuming that biological differences dictated different roles for men and women. According to this feminine mystique that they promulgated, women should find fulfillment in devotion to their homes, families, and serving others. Not many women directly challenged these ideas, but writer Edith Stern maintained that "many arguments about the joys of housewifery have been advanced, largely by those who have never had to work at it."

Although the glorification of domesticity clashed with women's increasing employment, many Americans' lives did embody the family ideal. Postwar prosperity enabled people to marry earlier and to have more children. In the midst of a general downward trend over the century, the American birthrate soared between 1945 and 1960, peaking in 1957 with 4.3 million births and producing the **baby boom** generation. Experts encouraged mothers to devote even more attention to child rearing, while they also urged fathers to cultivate family "togetherness" by spending more time with their children.

Interest in religion also surged in the 1950s. From 1940 to 1960, membership in churches and synagogues rose from 50 to 63 percent of all Americans. Polls reported that 95 percent of the population believed in God. Evangelism took on new life, most notably in the nationwide crusades of Baptist minister Billy Graham. Congress linked religion more closely to the state by adding "under God" to the pledge of allegiance and by requiring that "In God We Trust" be printed on all currency.

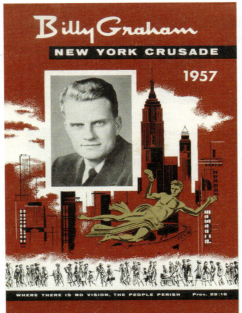

Evangelist Billy Graham Preaches in New York City

Billy Graham, a young Baptist minister from North Carolina, electrified mass audiences, exhorting them to find salvation in Jesus Christ and to uphold Christian moral standards. Americans flocked to his crusades, even as he implicitly condemned their avid participation in consumerism as "materialistic, worldly, secular, greedy, and covetous." Hundreds of thousands flocked to his New York Crusade in 1957, and millions watched on TV.

Religion helped to calm anxieties in the nuclear age, while ministers such as Graham made the Cold War a holy war, labeling communism "a great sinister anti-Christian movement masterminded by Satan." Some critics questioned the depth of the religious revival, attributing the growth in church membership to a desire for conformity and a need for social outlets. One commentator noted that 53 percent of Americans could not name a single book of the Christian New Testament.

Television Transforms Culture and Politics

Just as family life and religion offered a respite from Cold War anxieties, so too did the new medium of television. By 1960, nearly 90 percent of American homes boasted a television set, and the average viewer spent more than five hours each day in front of the screen. Audiences were especially attracted to situation comedies, which projected the family ideal and the feminine mystique into millions of homes. On TV, married women did not have paying jobs and they deferred to their husbands, though they often got the upper hand through subtle manipulation.

Television also began to affect politics. Eisenhower's 1952 presidential campaign used TV ads for the first time, although he was not happy that "an old soldier should come to this." By 1960, television played a key role in election campaigns. Reflecting on his narrow victory, president-elect John F. Kennedy remarked, "We wouldn't have had a prayer without that gadget." In addition, money played a much larger role in elections because candidates needed to pay for expensive TV spots. The ability to appeal directly to voters in their living rooms put a premium on personal attractiveness and encouraged candidates to build their own campaign organizations, relying less on political parties. The declining strength of parties and the growing power of money in elections were not new trends, but TV helped accelerate them.

Unlike government-financed television in Europe, private enterprise paid for American TV. What NBC called a "selling machine in every living room" became the major vehicle for fostering consumption, and advertisers did not hesitate to interfere with shows that might jeopardize the sale of their products. In 1961, Newton Minow, chairman of the Federal Communications Commission, called television a "vast wasteland." While acknowledging some of

TV's achievements, particularly documentaries and drama, Minow depicted it as "a procession of game shows, . . . formula comedies about totally unbelievable families, blood and thunder, mayhem, violence, sadism, murder . . . and cartoons." But viewers kept tuning in. In little more than a decade, television came to dominate Americans' leisure time, influence their consumption patterns, and shape their perceptions of the nation's leadership.

Countercurrents

Pockets of dissent underlay the complacency of the 1950s. Some intellectuals took exception to the materialism and conformity of the era. In *The Lonely Crowd* (1950), sociologist David Riesman lamented a shift from the "inner-directed" to the "other-directed" individual, as Americans replaced independent thinking with an eagerness to adapt to external standards of behavior and belief. Sharing that distaste for the importance

Jackson Pollock
One of the leading artists of the post–World War II revolution in painting, Jackson Pollock often worked with the canvas on the floor, dripping paint onto it with sticks, turkey basters, and hard brushes, prompting *Time* magazine to dub him "Jack the Dripper." He struggled with alcohol and died in 1956, at the age of forty-four, crashing his car while drunk and speeding near his Long Island home. Time & Life Pictures/Getty Images.

of "belonging," William H. Whyte Jr., in his popular book *The Organization Man* (1956), blamed the modern corporation for making employees tailor themselves to the group. Vance Packard's 1959 best seller, *The Status Seekers*, decried "the vigorous merchandising of goods as status-symbols."

Implicit in much of the critique of consumer culture was concern about the loss of traditional masculinity. Consumption was associated with women and their presumed greater susceptibility to manipulation. Men, required to conform to get ahead, moved further away from the masculine ideals of individualism and aggressiveness. Moreover, the increase in married women's employment compromised the male ideal of breadwinner. Into this gender confusion came *Playboy*, which began publication in 1953 and quickly gained a circulation of one million. The new magazine idealized masculine independence in the form of bachelorhood and assaulted the middle-class norms of domesticity and respectability. By associating the sophisticated bachelor with good wine, music, furnishings, and the like, the magazine made consumption more masculine while promoting sexual freedom, at least for men.

In fact, two books published by Alfred Kinsey and other researchers at Indiana University—*Sexual Behavior in the Human Male* (1948) and *Sexual Behavior in the Human Female* (1953)—disclosed that Americans' sexual behavior often departed from the postwar family ideal. Large numbers of men and women reported that they had engaged in premarital sex and adultery; one-third of the men and one-seventh of the women reported homosexual experiences. Although Kinsey's sampling procedures later cast doubt on his ability to generalize across the population, the books became best sellers.

Less direct challenges to mainstream standards appeared in the everyday behavior of young Americans. "Roll over Beethoven and tell Tchaikovsky the news!" belted out Chuck Berry in his 1956 hit record celebrating **rock and roll**, a new form of music that combined country with black rhythm and blues. White teenagers lionized Elvis Presley, who shocked their parents with his tight pants, hip-rolling gestures, and sensuous rock-and-roll music. "Before there was Elvis . . . I started going crazy for 'race music,'" recalled a white man of his teenage years. His recollection underscored African Americans' contributions to rock and roll, as well as the rebellion expressed by white youths' attraction to black music.

The most blatant revolt against conventionality came from the self-proclaimed Beat generation, a small group of primarily male literary figures based in New York City and San Francisco. Rejecting nearly everything in mainstream culture—patriotism, consumerism, technology, conventional family life, discipline—writers such as Allen Ginsberg and Jack Kerouac celebrated spontaneity and absolute personal freedom, including drug consumption and freewheeling sex. The Beats' lifestyles shocked "square" Americans, but both they and their lifestyles would provide a model for a new movement of youthful dissidents in the 1960s.

Bold new styles in the visual arts also showed the 1950s to be more than a decade of bland conventionality. In New York City, "action painting" or "abstract expressionism" flowered, rejecting the idea that painting should represent recognizable forms. Jackson Pollock and other abstract expressionists poured, dripped, and threw paint on canvases or substituted sticks and other implements for brushes. The new form of painting so captivated and redirected the Western art world that New York replaced Paris as its center.

REVIEW: Why did American consumption expand so dramatically in the 1950s, and what aspects of society and culture did it influence?

▶ The Emergence of a Civil Rights Movement

Building on the civil rights initiatives begun during World War II, African Americans posed the most dramatic challenge to the status quo of the 1950s as they sought to overcome discrimination and segregation. Every southern state mandated rigid segregation in public settings ranging from schools to cemeteries. Voting laws and practices in the South disfranchised the vast majority of African Americans. Employment discrimination kept blacks at the bottom throughout the country. Schools, restaurants, and other public spaces were often as segregated, though usually not by law, in the North as in the South.

Although black protest was as old as American racism, in the 1950s grassroots movements arose that attracted national attention

The *Brown* Decision

Responding to lawsuits argued by NAACP lawyers, *Brown v. Board of Education* was the culmination of a series of Supreme Court rulings that chipped away at an earlier Court's decision in *Plessy v. Ferguson* (1896) permitting "separate but equal" public facilities.

DOCUMENT 1
Brown v. Board of Education, May 1954

In 1954, Chief Justice Earl Warren delivered the unanimous opinion of the Supreme Court, declaring racial segregation in public education unconstitutional and explaining why.

It is doubtful that any child may reasonably be expected to succeed in life if he is denied the opportunity of an education. Such an opportunity, if the state has undertaken to provide it, is a right that must be made available to all on equal terms. . . .

We come then to the question presented: Does segregation of children in public schools solely on the basis of race, even though the physical facilities and other "tangible" factors may be equal, deprive the children of the minority group of equal educational opportunities?

We believe that it does. . . . In *McLaurin* [a 1950 case], the Court, in requiring that a Negro admitted to a white graduate school be treated like all other students, again resorted to intangible considerations: ". . . his ability to study, to engage in discussions and exchange views with other students, and, in general, to learn his profession." Such considerations apply with added force to children in grade and high schools. To separate them from others of similar age and qualifications solely because of their race generates a feeling of inferiority as to their status in the community that may affect their hearts and minds in a way unlikely ever to be undone.

We conclude that in the field of public education the doctrine of "separate but equal" has no place. Separate educational facilities are inherently unequal

Source: *Brown v. Board of Education*, 347 U.S. 483 (1954).

DOCUMENT 2
Southern Manifesto on Integration, March 1956

The Brown *decision outraged many southern whites. In 1956, more than one hundred members of Congress signed a manifesto pledging resistance to the ruling.*

We regard the decision of the Supreme Court in the school cases as a clear abuse of judicial power. It climaxes a trend in the Federal judiciary undertaking to legislate . . . and to encroach upon the reserved rights of the states and the people.

The original Constitution does not mention education. Neither does the Fourteenth Amendment nor any amendment. . . . The Supreme Court of the United States, with no legal basis for such action, undertook to exercise their naked judicial power and substituted their personal political and social ideas for the established law of the land.

This unwarranted exercise of power by the court, contrary to the Constitution, is creating chaos and confusion in the states principally affected. It is destroying the amicable relations between the white and negro races that have been created through ninety years of patient effort by the good people of both races. . . .

We pledge ourselves to use all lawful means to bring about a reversal of this decision which is contrary to the Constitution and to prevent the use of force in its implementation.

Source: "Southern Manifesto on Integration," *Congressional Record*, 84th Congress, 2nd Session, vol. 102, pt. 4 (Washington, DC: Governmental Printing Office, 1956), 4459–60.

and the support of white liberals. Pressed by civil rights groups, the Supreme Court delivered significant institutional reforms, but the most important changes occurred among blacks themselves. Ordinary African Americans in substantial numbers sought their own liberation, building a movement that would transform race relations in the United States.

African Americans Challenge the Supreme Court and the President

Several factors spurred black protest in the 1950s. Between 1940 and 1960, more than three million African Americans moved from the South into areas where they had a political voice. Black

DOCUMENT 3
A High School Boy in Oak Ridge, Tennessee, 1957

In the face of white hostility, black children carried the burden of implementing the Brown decision as these accounts testify.

I like it a whole lot better than the colored school. You have a chance to learn more and you have more sports. I play forward or guard on the basketball team, only I don't get to participate in all games. Some teams don't mind my playing. Some teams object not because of the fellows on the team, but because of the people in their community. Mostly it's the fans or the board of education that decides against me. . . . The same situation occurs in baseball. I'm catcher, but the first game I didn't get to participate in. A farm club of the major league wrote the coach that they were interested in seeing me play so maybe I'll get to play the next time.

Source: Dorothy Sterling, *Tender Warriors* (New York: Hill and Wang, 1958), 83. Copyright © 1958 by Hill and Wang. Reprinted with permission.

DOCUMENT 4
A High School Girl in the Deep South, May 1966

The first day a news reporter rode the bus with us. All around us were state troopers. In front of them were federal marshals. When we got to town there were lines of people and cars all along the road. A man without a badge or anything got on the bus and started beating up the newspaper reporter. . . . When we got to the school the students were all around looking through the windows. The mayor said we couldn't come there because the school was already filled to capacity. We turned around and the students started yelling and clapping. When we went back [after obtaining a court order] there were no students there at all. [The white students did not return, so the six black students finished the year by themselves.] The shocking thing was during the graduation ceremonies. All six of the students got together to make a speech. After we finished, I looked around and saw three teachers crying. The principal had tears in his eyes and he got up to make a little speech about us. He said at first he didn't think he would enjoy being around us. You could see in his face that he was really touched.

Source: *In Their Own Words: A Student Appraisal of What Happened after School Desegregation* (Washington, DC: Department of Health, Education, and Welfare, Office of Education, 1966), 17–18.

DOCUMENT 5
A High School Girl in the Deep South, May 1966

I chose to go because I felt that I could get a better education here. I knew that the [black] school that I was then attending wasn't giving me exactly what I should have had. As far as the Science Department was concerned, it just didn't have the chemicals we needed and I just decided to change. When I went over the students there weren't very friendly and when I graduated they still weren't. They didn't want us there and they made that plain, but we went there anyway and we stuck it out.

Source: *In Their Own Words: A Student Appraisal of What Happened after School Desegregation* (Washington, DC: Department of Health, Education, and Welfare, Office of Education, 1966), 44.

Questions for Analysis and Debate

1. What reasons did the Supreme Court give in favor of desegregation? What reasons did black students give for wanting to attend integrated schools? How do these reasons differ?

2. What arguments did the southern legislators make against the Supreme Court decision?

3. What obstacles remained for African American students to confront once they had been admitted to integrated schools?

4. What conditions do you feel would be worth enduring to obtain a better education?

Connect to the Big Idea

C Why did President Eisenhower initially resist desegregation, and what steps did he eventually take in support of integration?

---

leaders emphasized how racist practices at home tarnished the U.S. image abroad and handicapped the United States in its competition with the Soviet Union. The very system of segregation meant that African Americans controlled certain organizational resources, such as churches, colleges, and newspapers, where leadership skills could be honed and networks developed.

The legal strategy of the major civil rights organization, the National Association for the Advancement of Colored People (NAACP), reached its crowning achievement with the Supreme Court decision in *Brown v. Board of Education* in 1954, which consolidated five separate suits. Oliver Brown, a World War II veteran in Topeka, Kansas, filed suit because

School Desegregation

One of the best-known American painters of the twentieth century, Norman Rockwell produced more than 300 covers for the *Saturday Evening Post*, a popular bimonthly magazine, between 1916 and 1963. Unlike the abstract expressionists who enthralled the art establishment in the 1940s and 1950s, Rockwell believed that paintings should tell stories: His patriotic, sentimental, and often humorous works examined the everyday lives of ordinary Americans.

In 1963, Rockwell parted company with the *Post*, which had begun to favor pictures of celebrities over Rockwell's common-man covers and resisted Rockwell's growing desire to comment on social problems through his art. *Look* magazine proved more receptive and, in January 1964, published *The Problem We All Live With*, one of a number of Rockwell's paintings exploring civil rights, poverty, and other social issues.

The oil painting captured one moment in the tortured process of school desegregation. After six years of resistance to *Brown*, the New Orleans school board reluctantly began integration of its schools in 1960, starting with the first grade, with just two schools, and with only a handful of black children. Encouraged by the local NAACP, three African American girls enrolled in one school, and Ruby Bridges, the subject of Rockwell's painting, was sent to another all-white school. Federal marshals escorted her through hostile crowds, and white mothers, who were part of those mobs, rushed to take their own children out of school. Bridges, whose family faced economic retaliation, spent her first-grade year as the only student in her class.

Rockwell's painting compels the viewer to focus on young Ruby, who is placed near the center of the piece, a small, solitary figure. She appears dressed in her Sunday best, carrying her school supplies and a posture of determination. While a news photograph showed her dressed in a plaid dress and black shoes, Rockwell painted her clothed in all white. Why might he have taken liberties with reality, and what does his use of the color white for her clothes convey to the viewer?

With the marshals headless and dressed in neutral colors, viewers' eyes are drawn to Ruby, to the tomatoes splattered on the wall and ground, and to the word written on the wall. Why do you think Rockwell used inanimate objects to depict the screaming mob? Notice that something is sticking out of the first marshal's pocket, most likely the federal court order that ordered New Orleans to comply with the *Brown* decision. What is the effect of depicting the scene without the federal marshals' heads?

Rockwell's work became an iconic representation of the civil rights movement and hung in the White House in 2011.

SOURCE: Printed by permission of the Norman Rockwell Family Agency. Copyright © 2014 the Norman Rockwell Family Entities.

his daughter had to pass by a white school near their home to attend a black school more than a mile away. In Virginia, sixteen-year-old Barbara Johns initiated a student strike over wretched conditions in her black high school, leading to another of the suits joined in Brown. The NAACP's lead lawyer, future Supreme Court justice Thurgood Marshall, urged the Court to overturn the "separate but equal" precedent established in *Plessy v. Ferguson* in 1896 (see "Progressivism for White Men Only" in chapter 21). A unanimous Court, headed by Chief Justice Earl Warren, declared, "Separate educational facilities are inherently unequal" and thus violated the Fourteenth Amendment.

Ultimate responsibility for enforcement of the decision lay with President Eisenhower, but he refused to endorse *Brown*. He also kept silent in 1955 when whites murdered Emmett Till, a fourteen-year-old black boy who had alleg-edly whistled at a white woman in Mississippi. Reflecting his own prejudice, his preference for limited federal intervention in the states, and a leadership style that favored consensus and gradual progress, Eisenhower kept his distance from civil rights issues. Such inaction fortified southern resistance.

In September 1957, Governor Orval Faubus sent Arkansas National Guard troops to block the enrollment of nine black students in Little Rock's Central High School. Later, he allowed them to enter but withdrew the National Guard, leaving the students to face an angry white mob. "During those years when we desperately needed approval from our peers," Melba Patillo Beals remembered, "we were victims of the most harsh rejection imaginable." As television cameras transmitted the ugly scene, Eisenhower was forced to send regular army troops to Little Rock, the first federal military intervention in

The Problem We all Live With

Questions for Consideration

1. What elements in the painting suggest the dangers posed to African Americans who challenged racism?

2. Why do you think Rockwell titled his work *The Problem We All Live With*?

Connect to the Big Idea

C What areas of public life, in addition to education, did civil rights activists target in the 1950s?

the South since Reconstruction. Paratroopers escorted the "Little Rock Nine" into the school, but integration and resistance to it continued across the South. (See "Documenting the American Promise," page 788.)

School segregation outside the South was not usually sanctioned by law, but northern school districts separated black and white students by manipulating neighborhood boundaries and with other devices. Even before *Brown*, black parents in dozens of northern cities challenged the assignment of their children to inferior "colored" schools. While these protests reaped some successes, the structure of residential segregation, often supported by official action, made school segregation a reality for African Americans in both the North and South. (See "Visualizing History," above.)

Eisenhower ordered the integration of public facilities in Washington, D.C., and on military bases, and he supported the first federal civil

rights legislation since Reconstruction. Yet the Civil Rights Acts of 1957 and 1960 were little more than symbolic. Baseball star Jackie Robinson spoke for many African Americans when he wired Eisenhower in 1957, "We disagree that half a loaf is better than none. Have waited this long for a bill with meaning—can wait a little longer." Eisenhower appointed the first black professional to his White House staff, but E. Frederick Morrow confided in his diary, "I feel ridiculous . . . trying to defend the administration's record on civil rights."

Montgomery and Mass Protest

What set the civil rights movement of the 1950s and 1960s apart from earlier acts of black protest was its widespread presence in the South, the large number of people involved, their willingness to confront white institutions directly, and

VISUAL ACTIVITY

Civil Rights Activism in the North
While southern civil rights activism gained national attention in the 1950s, black protest had a long history in the North. African Americans and their allies battled job discrimination and segregation in schools, housing, and public accommodations. Here demonstrators march outside the Stork Club in New York City in 1951, protesting its refusal to serve the world famous dancer, singer, and actress Josephine Baker. Photo by Archive Photos/Getty Images.

READING THE IMAGE: Who sponsored this demonstration? What do the people in the photo tell you about the racial makeup of protest? How does one of the signs capitalize on Cold War rhetoric?

CONNECTIONS: How did this kind of protest in the North differ from that in the South?

the use of nonviolent protest and civil disobedience to bring about change. The Congress of Racial Equality and other groups had experimented with these tactics in the 1940s, organizing to integrate movie theaters, restaurants, and swimming pools in northern cities. In the South, the first sustained protest to claim national attention began in Montgomery, Alabama, on December 1, 1955.

That day, police arrested Rosa Parks for violating a local segregation ordinance. Riding a crowded bus home from work, she refused to give up her seat in the white section so that a man could sit down. She resisted not because she was physically tired, she recalled; rather she was "tired of giving in." The bus driver called the police, who promptly arrested her. Parks had long been active in the local NAACP,

headed by E. D. Nixon. They had already talked about challenging bus segregation. So had the Women's Political Council (WPC), led by Jo Ann Robinson, an English professor at Alabama State, who had once been humiliated by a bus driver when she accidentally sat in the white section.

When word came that Parks would fight her arrest, WPC leaders mobilized teachers and students to distribute fliers urging blacks to boycott the buses. E. D. Nixon called a mass meeting at a black church, where those assembled founded the Montgomery Improvement Association (MIA). The MIA arranged volunteer car pools and marshaled more than 90 percent of the black community to sustain the yearlong **Montgomery bus boycott**.

Elected to head the MIA was twenty-six-year-old Martin Luther King Jr., a young Baptist pastor with a doctorate in theology from Boston University. A captivating speaker, King addressed mass meetings at churches throughout the bus boycott, inspiring blacks' courage and commitment by linking racial justice to Christianity. He promised, "If you will protest courageously and yet with dignity and Christian love . . . historians will have to pause and say, 'There lived a great people—a black people— who injected a new meaning and dignity into the veins of civilization.'"

Montgomery blacks summoned their courage and determination in abundance. An older woman insisted, "I'm not walking for myself, I'm walking for my children and my grandchildren." Boycotters walked miles or carpooled to get to work, contributed their meager financial resources, and stood up to intimidation and police harassment. Authorities arrested several leaders, and whites firebombed King's house. Yet the movement persisted until November 1956, when the Supreme Court declared unconstitutional Alabama's laws requiring bus segregation.

King's face on the cover of *Time* magazine in February 1957 marked his rapid rise to national and international fame. In January, black clergy from across the South had chosen King to head the Southern Christian Leadership Conference (SCLC), newly established to coordinate local protests against segregation and disfranchisement. The prominence of King and other ministers obscured the substantial numbers and critical importance of black women in the movement. King's fame and the media's focus on the South also hid the national scope of racial injustice and the struggles for racial equality in the North that both encouraged and benefited from the black freedom struggle in the South.

REVIEW: What were the goals and strategies of civil rights activists in the 1950s?

▶ Conclusion: Peace and Prosperity Mask Unmet Challenges

At the American exhibit in Moscow in 1959, the consumer goods that Nixon proudly displayed to Khrushchev and the Cold War competition that crackled through their dialogue reflected two dominant themes of the 1950s: American prosperity and the superpowers' success in keeping their antagonism within the bounds of peace. The tremendous economic growth of the 1950s, which raised the standard of living for most Americans, resulted in part from Cold War defense spending.

Prosperity changed the very landscape of the United States. Suburban housing developments sprang up, interstate highways cut up cities and connected the country, farms declined in number but grew in size, and population and industry moved south and west. Daily habits and even values shifted as the economy became more service oriented and the appearance of television and a host of new products intensified the growth of a consumer culture.

The prosperity, however, masked a number of developments and problems that Americans would soon face head-on: rising resistance to racial injustice, a 20 percent poverty rate, married women's movement into the labor force, and the emergence of a youth rebellion. Although defense spending and housing, highway, and education subsidies helped to sustain the economic boom, in general Eisenhower tried to curb domestic programs and let private enterprise have its way. His administration maintained the welfare state inherited from the New Deal but resisted the expansion of federal programs.

In global affairs, Eisenhower exercised restraint on large issues, recognizing the limits of U.S. power. In the name of deterrence, he promoted the development of more destructive atomic weapons, but he withstood pressures for even larger defense budgets. Still, Eisenhower shared Truman's assumption that the United States must fight communism everywhere, and when movements in Iran, Guatemala, Cuba, and Vietnam seemed too radical, too friendly to communism, or too inimical to American economic interests, he tried to undermine them, often with secret operations. Eisenhower presided over eight years of peace and prosperity, but his foreign policy inspired anti-Americanism and forged commitments and interventions that plagued future generations. As Eisenhower's successors took on the struggle against communism and grappled with the domestic challenges of race, poverty, and urban decay that he had avoided, the tranquility and consensus of the 1950s would give way to turbulence and conflict in the 1960s.

See the Selected Bibliography for this chapter in the Appendix.

27 Chapter Review

MAKE IT STICK

 **LearningCurve**

Go online and use LearningCurve to see what you know. Then review the key terms and answer the questions.

KEY TERMS

Interstate Highway and Defense System Act of 1956 (p. 770)
mutually assured destruction (MAD) (p. 773)
domino theory (p. 774)
Cuban revolution (p. 775)
Eisenhower Doctrine (p. 776)
military-industrial complex (p. 778)
Sun Belt (p. 781)
Hernandez v. Texas (p. 783)
baby boom (p. 785)
rock and roll (p. 787)
Brown v. Board of Education (p. 789)
Montgomery bus boycott (p. 792)

REVIEW QUESTIONS

1. How did Eisenhower's domestic policies reflect his moderate political vision? (pp. 769–772)

2. Where and how did Eisenhower practice containment? (pp. 772–778)

3. What fueled the prosperity of the 1950s? (pp. 779–783)

4. Why did American consumption expand so dramatically in the 1950s, and what aspects of society and culture did it influence? (pp. 784–787)

5. What were the goals and strategies of civil rights activists in the 1950s? (pp. 787–793)

MAKING CONNECTIONS

1. How did Eisenhower's "modern Republicanism" address the New Deal legacy?

2. What economic and demographic changes contributed to the growth of suburbs and the Sun Belt? Consider both Americans who participated in these trends and those who did not.

3. What developments in American society in the 1950s were at odds with prevailing norms and values?

4. Explain how new policies and court decisions regarding minorities came about and their impact for better and for worse.

LINKING TO THE PAST

1. How did the policies of termination and relocation differ from the New Deal's policy toward Indians? (See chapter 24.)

2. What developments stemming from World War II influenced U.S. foreign policy in such areas as Vietnam and Latin America? (See chapter 25.)

28 Reform, Rebellion, and Reaction

1960–1974

CONTENT LEARNING OBJECTIVES

After reading and studying this chapter, you should be able to:

- Identify the ways in which liberalism was manifested in President Johnson's Great Society.

- Identify the strategies civil rights activists used during the 1960s and describe Washington's response. Explain the rise of the black power movement and its influence on American society.

- Explain how the civil rights movement inspired protest movements among other groups, including Native Americans, Chicanos, students, and gays and lesbians.

- Define the origins of the feminist movement and identify its various strategies and criticisms of society. Explain feminism's achievements and the backlash it provoked.

- Describe the ways in which liberalism persisted during the Nixon administration.

PROTEST BANNER
In the 1960s Americans carried banners to broadcast a variety of political positions. This pennant represents the black freedom struggle, which inspired a host of other movements. Collection of Mark Hooper.

ON AUGUST 31, 1962, FORTY-FIVE-YEAR-OLD FANNIE LOU HAMER boarded a bus carrying eighteen African Americans to the county seat in Indianola, Mississippi, where they intended to register to vote. Blacks constituted a majority of Sunflower County's population but only 1.2 percent of registered voters. Before civil rights activists arrived in Ruleville to start a voter registration drive, Hamer recalled, "I didn't know that a Negro could register and vote." The poverty, exploitation, and political disfranchisement she experienced typified the lives of most blacks in the rural South. The daughter of sharecroppers, Hamer began work in the cotton fields at age six, attending school in a one-room shack from December to March and only until she was twelve. After marrying Perry Hamer, she moved onto a plantation, where she worked in the fields, did domestic work for the owner, and recorded the cotton that sharecroppers harvested.

At the Indianola County courthouse, Hamer had to pass through a hostile, white, gun-carrying crowd. Refusing to be intimidated, she registered to vote on her third attempt, attended a civil rights leadership training conference, and began to mobilize others to vote. In 1963, she and other activists were arrested in Winona, Mississippi, and beaten so brutally that Hamer went from jail to the hospital.

Fannie Lou Hamer's courage and determination made her a prominent figure in the black freedom struggle, which shook the nation's conscience, provided a protest model for other groups, and pressured the government. After John F. Kennedy was assassinated in November 1963, Lyndon B. Johnson launched the Great Society—a multitude of efforts to promote racial justice, education, medical care, urban development, environmental and economic health, and more. Those who struggled for racial justice made great sacrifices, but by the end of the decade American law had caught up with the American ideal of equality.

Yet strong civil rights legislation and pathbreaking Supreme Court decisions could not alone mitigate the deplorable economic conditions of African Americans nationwide, on which Hamer and others increasingly focused after 1965. Nor were liberal politicians reliable supporters, as Hamer found out in 1964 when President Johnson and his allies rebuffed black Mississippi Democrats' efforts to be represented at the Democratic National Convention. By 1966, a minority of African American activists were demanding black power; the movement soon splintered, while white support sharply declined. The war in Vietnam stifled liberal reform, while a growing conservative movement condemned the challenge to American traditions and institutions mounted by blacks, students, and others.

Though disillusioned and often frustrated, Fannie Lou Hamer remained an activist until her death in 1977, participating in new social movements stimulated by the black freedom struggle. In 1969, she supported students at Mississippi Valley State College who demanded black studies courses and a voice in campus decisions. In 1972, she attended the first conference of the National Women's Political Caucus, established to challenge sex discrimination in politics and government.

Feminists and other groups, including ethnic minorities, environmentalists, and gays and lesbians, carried the tide of reform into the 1970s. They pushed Richard M. Nixon's Republican administration to sustain the liberalism of the 1960s, with its emphasis on a strong government role in regulating the economy, guaranteeing the welfare and rights of all individuals, and improving the quality of life. Despite its conservative rhetoric, the Nixon administration implemented affirmative action and adopted pathbreaking measures in environmental regulation, equality for women, and justice for Native Americans. The years between 1960 and 1974 witnessed the greatest efforts to reconcile America's promise with reality since the New Deal.

Mississippi Freedom Democratic Party Rally
Fannie Lou Hamer (left) and other activists rally at the 1964 Democratic National Convention, supporting the Mississippi Freedom Democratic Party (MFDP) in its challenge to the all-white delegation sent by the state party. Next to Hamer is civil rights lawyer Eleanor Holmes Norton, and Ella Baker (far right), who helped organize the Southern Christian Leadership Conference. In the straw hat is SNCC leader, Stokely Carmichael. © George Ballis/Take Stock/The Image Works.

► Liberalism at High Tide

At the Democratic National Convention in 1960, John F. Kennedy proclaimed "a New Frontier" that would confront "unsolved problems of peace and war, unconquered pockets of ignorance and prejudice, unanswered questions of poverty and surplus." Four years later, Lyndon B. Johnson invoked the ideal of a "Great Society, [which] rests on abundance and liberty for all [and] demands an end to poverty and racial injustice." Acting under the liberal faith that government should use its power to solve social and economic problems, end injustice, and promote the welfare of all citizens, the Democratic administrations of the 1960s won legislation on civil rights, poverty, education, medical care, housing, consumer safeguards, and environmental protection. These measures, along with pathbreaking Supreme Court decisions, responded to demands for rights from African Americans and other groups and addressed problems arising from rapid economic growth.

The Unrealized Promise of Kennedy's New Frontier

John F. Kennedy grew up in privilege, the child of an Irish Catholic businessman who became a New Deal official and nourished political ambitions for his sons. Helped by a distinguished World War II navy record, Kennedy won election to the House of Representatives in 1946 and the Senate in 1952. With a powerful political machine, his family's fortune, and a dynamic personal appeal, Kennedy won the Democratic presidential nomination in 1960. He stunned many Democrats by choosing as his running mate Lyndon B. Johnson of Texas, whom liberals disparaged as a typical southern conservative.

In the general election, Kennedy narrowly defeated his Republican opponent, Vice President Richard M. Nixon, by a 118,550-vote margin (Map 28.1). African American voters contributed to his victory, Johnson helped carry the South, and Kennedy also benefited from the nation's first televised presidential debates, at which he appeared cool and confident beside a nervous and pale Nixon.

At forty-three, Kennedy was the youngest man to be elected president. His administration projected energy, idealism, and glamour, while the press kept from the public his serious health

CHRONOLOGY

1960	• John F. Kennedy elected president. • Student Nonviolent Coordinating Committee founded. • Students for a Democratic Society established.
1961	• Freedom Rides.
1962	• United Farm Workers founded.
1963	• President's Commission on the Status of Women issues report. • Equal Pay Act. • *Baker v. Carr.* • *Abington School District v. Schempp.* • March on Washington. • President Kennedy assassinated; Lyndon B. Johnson becomes president.
1964	• Civil Rights Act. • Mississippi Freedom Summer Project.
1964–1966	• Congress passes most of Johnson's Great Society domestic programs.
1965	• Voting Rights Act.
1965–1968	• Riots in major cities.
1966	• Black Panther Party for Self-Defense founded. • *Miranda v. Arizona.* • National Organization for Women founded.
1968	• Martin Luther King Jr. assassinated. • American Indian Movement founded. • Richard M. Nixon elected president.
1969	• Stonewall riots.
1970	• Environmental Protection Agency established. • Clean Air Act.
1972	• Title IX. • "Trail of Broken Treaties" caravan to Washington, D.C.
1973	• *Roe v. Wade.*

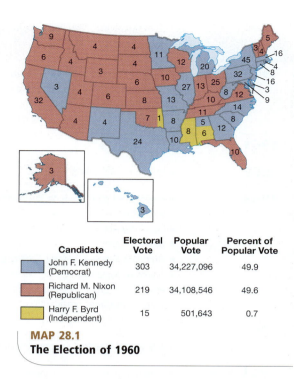

Candidate	Electoral Vote	Popular Vote	Percent of Popular Vote
John F. Kennedy (Democrat)	303	34,227,096	49.9
Richard M. Nixon (Republican)	219	34,108,546	49.6
Harry F. Byrd (Independent)	15	501,643	0.7

MAP 28.1
The Election of 1960

but Kennedy failed to persuade Congress to expand the welfare state with federal education and health care programs. Moreover, he resisted leadership on behalf of racial justice until civil rights activists gave him no choice.

Moved by the desperate conditions he observed while campaigning in Appalachia, Kennedy pushed poverty onto the national agenda. In 1962, he read Michael Harrington's *The Other America*, which described poverty that left more than one in five Americans "maimed in body and spirit, existing at levels beneath those necessary for human decency." By 1962, Kennedy had won support for a $2 billion urban renewal program, providing incentives to businesses to locate in economically depressed areas and job training for the unemployed. In the summer of 1963, he asked aides to plan a full-scale attack on poverty.

With economic growth a key objective, Kennedy called for an enormous tax cut in 1963, which he promised would increase demand and create jobs. Passed in February 1964, the law contributed to an economic boom, as unemployment fell to 4.1 percent and the gross national product shot up. Some liberal critics of the tax cut, however, noted that it favored the well-off and argued instead for increased spending on social programs.

problems and extramarital affairs. At his inauguration, Kennedy called on Americans to serve the common good. "Ask not what your country can do for you," he implored, "ask what you can do for your country." That idealism inspired many,

The Kennedy Appeal
The freshness and glamor of the Kennedy administration are apparent in this photo of the candidate and his wife riding through New York City a few weeks before his election in 1960. The couple's second child was born between his election and inauguration, further contributing to his youthful image. NY Daily News via Getty Images.

Kennedy's domestic efforts were in their infancy when an assassin's bullets struck him down on November 22, 1963. Within minutes of the shooting—which occurred as Kennedy's motorcade passed through Dallas, Texas—radio and television broadcast the unfolding horror to the nation. Stunned Americans struggled to understand what had happened. Soon after the assassination, police arrested Lee Harvey Oswald and concluded that he had fired the shots from a nearby building. Two days later, while officers were transferring Oswald from one jail to another, a local nightclub operator killed him. Suspicions arose that Oswald was murdered to cover up a conspiracy by ultraconservatives who hated Kennedy or by Communists who supported Castro's Cuba (see "Meeting the 'Hour of Maximum Danger'" in chapter 29). To get at the truth, President Johnson appointed a commission headed by Chief Justice Earl Warren, which concluded that both Oswald and his assassin had acted alone.

Kennedy's domestic record had been unremarkable in his first two years, but his attention to taxes, civil rights, and poverty in 1963 suggested an important shift. Whether Kennedy could have persuaded Congress to enact his proposals remained in question. Journalist James Reston commented, "What was killed was not only the president but the promise. . . . We saw him only as a rising sun."

Johnson Fulfills the Kennedy Promise

Lyndon B. Johnson assumed the presidency with a wealth of political experience. A self-made man from the Texas Hill Country, he had won election in 1937 to the House of Representatives and in 1948 to the Senate, where he served skillfully as Senate majority leader. His modest upbringing, his admiration for Franklin Roosevelt, and his ambition to outdo the New Deal president all spurred his commitment to reform. Equally compelling were external pressures generated by the black freedom struggle and the host of movements it helped inspire.

Lacking Kennedy's sophistication, Johnson excelled behind the scenes, where he could entice, maneuver, or threaten legislators to support his objectives. His persuasive power, the famous "Johnson treatment," became legendary. In his ability to achieve his legislative goals, Johnson had few peers in American history.

Johnson entreated Congress to act so that "John Fitzgerald Kennedy did not live or die in vain." He pushed through Kennedy's tax cut bill by February 1964. More remarkable was passage of the **Civil Rights Act of 1964,** which made discrimination in employment, education, and public accommodations illegal. The strongest such measure since Reconstruction required every ounce of Johnson's political skill to pry sufficient votes from Republicans to balance the "nays" of southern Democrats. Senate Republican leader Everett Dirksen's aide reported that Johnson "never left him alone for thirty minutes." In proportion to their numbers in Congress, more Republicans voted for the measure than Democrats.

Antipoverty legislation followed fast on the heels of the Civil Rights Act. Johnson announced "an unconditional war on poverty" in his January 1964 State of the Union message, and in August Congress passed the Economic Opportunity Act. The law authorized ten new programs, allocating $800 million—about 1 percent of the federal budget—for the first year. Many provisions targeted children and youths, including Head Start for preschoolers, work-study grants for college students, and the Job Corps for unemployed young people. The Volunteers in Service to America (VISTA) program paid modest wages to volunteers working with the disadvantaged, and a legal services program provided lawyers for the poor.

The "Johnson Treatment"

Abe Fortas, a distinguished lawyer who had argued a major criminal rights case, *Gideon v. Wainwright* (1963), before the Supreme Court, was a close friend of and adviser to President Johnson. This photograph of the president and Fortas taken in July 1965 illustrates how Johnson used his body as well as his voice to bend people to his will. Yoichi R. Okamoto/LBJ Library Collection.

The most novel and controversial part of the law, the Community Action Program (CAP), required "maximum feasible participation" of the poor themselves in antipoverty projects. Poor people began to organize to make welfare agencies, school boards, police departments, and housing authorities more accountable to the people they served. When the local Democratic officials complained, Johnson backed off from pushing genuine representation for the poor. Still, CAP gave people usually excluded from government an opportunity to act on their own behalf and develop leadership skills.

Policymaking for a Great Society

As the 1964 election approached, Johnson projected stability and security in the midst of a booming economy. Few voters wanted to risk the dramatic change promised by his Republican opponent, Arizona senator Barry M. Goldwater, who attacked the welfare state and entertained the use of nuclear weapons in Vietnam. Johnson achieved a record-breaking 61 percent of the popular vote, and Democrats won resounding majorities in the House (295–140) and Senate (68–32). Still, Goldwater's considerable grassroots support marked a growing movement on the right (see "Emergence of a Grassroots Movement" in chapter 30) and a threat to Democratic control of the South.

"I want to see a whole bunch of coonskins on the wall," Johnson told his aides, using a hunting analogy to stress his ambitious legislative goals for what he called the "Great Society." The large Democratic majorities in Congress, his own political skills, and pressure from the black freedom struggle and other movements enabled Johnson to obtain legislation on discrimination, poverty, education, medical care, housing, consumer and environmental protection, and more. Reporters called the legislation of the Eighty-ninth Congress (1965–1966) "a political miracle."

The Economic Opportunity Act of 1964 was the opening shot in the **War on Poverty**. Congress doubled the program's funding in 1965, enacted new economic development measures for depressed regions, and authorized more than $1 billion to improve the nation's slums. Direct aid included a new food stamp program, giving poor people

greater choice in obtaining food, and rent supplements that provided alternatives to public housing. Moreover, a movement of welfare mothers, the National Welfare Rights Organization, assisted by antipoverty lawyers, pushed administrators of Aid to Families with Dependent Children (AFDC) to ease restrictions on welfare recipients. The number of families receiving assistance jumped from less than one million in 1960 to three million by 1972, benefiting 90 percent of those eligible.

Central to Johnson's War on Poverty were efforts to equip the poor with the skills necessary to find jobs. His Elementary and Secondary Education Act of 1965 marked a turning point by involving the federal government in K–12 education. The measure sent federal dollars to local school districts and provided equipment and supplies to private and parochial schools serving the poor. That same year, Congress passed the Higher Education Act, vastly expanding federal assistance to colleges and universities for buildings, programs, scholarships, and loans.

The federal government's responsibility for health care marked an even greater watershed. Faced with a powerful medical lobby that opposed national health insurance as "socialized medicine," Johnson focused on the elderly, who constituted a large portion of the nation's poor. Congress responded with the **Medicare** program, providing the elderly with universal medical insurance financed largely through Social Security taxes. A separate program, **Medicaid**, authorized federal grants to supplement state-paid medical care for poor people. By the twenty-first century, these two programs covered 87 million Americans, nearly 30 percent of the population.

Whereas programs such as Medicare fulfilled New Deal and Fair Deal promises, the Great Society's civil rights legislation represented a break with tradition. Racial minorities were neglected or discriminated

A Tribute to Johnson for Medicare

George Niedermeyer, who lived in Hollywood, Florida, and received a Social Security pension, painted pieces of wood and glued them together to create this thank-you to President Johnson for establishing Medicare. Niedermeyer entrusted his congressional representative, Claude Pepper, known for his support of the interests of the elderly, to deliver the four-foot-tall tribute to Johnson in 1967. LBJ Library, photo by Henry Groskinsky.

against in many New Deal programs, and Truman's civil rights proposals bore few results. By contrast, the Civil Rights Act of 1964 made discrimination in employment, education, and public accommodations illegal. The **Voting Rights Act of 1965** banned literacy tests, which were often impossibly complicated in order to disqualify black voters, and authorized federal intervention to ensure access to the voting booth.

Another form of bias fell with the **Immigration and Nationality Act of 1965**, which abolished quotas based on national origins that discriminated against non-western European immigrants. The law maintained caps on the total number of immigrants and, for the first time, included the Western Hemisphere in those limits; preference was now given to immediate relatives of U.S. citizens and to those with desirable skills. The measure's unanticipated consequences triggered a surge of immigration in the 1980s and thereafter (see "The Internationalization of the United States" in chapter 31).

Great Society benefits reached well beyond victims of discrimination and the poor. Medicare covered the elderly, regardless of income. A groundswell of consumer activism won legislation making cars safer and raising standards for the food, drug, and cosmetics industries. Johnson insisted that the Great Society meet "not just the needs of the body but the desire for beauty and hunger for community." In 1965, he sent Congress the first presidential message on the environment, obtaining measures to control water and air pollution and to preserve the natural beauty of the American landscape. In addition, the National Arts and Humanities Act of 1965 funded artists, musicians, writers, and scholars and brought their work to public audiences.

The flood of reform legislation dwindled after 1966, when Democratic majorities in Congress diminished and a backlash against government programs arose. The Vietnam War dealt the largest blow to Johnson's ambitions, diverting his attention, spawning an antiwar movement that crippled his leadership, and devouring tax dollars that might have been used for reform (see "The Widening War at Home" in chapter 29).

In 1968, Johnson pried out of Congress one more civil rights law,

which banned discrimination in housing and jury service. He also signed the National Housing Act of 1968, which authorized an enormous increase in low-income housing—1.7 million units over three years—and put construction and ownership in private hands.

Assessing the Great Society

The reduction in poverty in the 1960s was considerable. The number of poor Americans fell from more than 20 percent of the population in 1959 to around 13 percent in 1968. Those who in Johnson's words "live on the outskirts of hope" saw new opportunities. To Rosemary Bray, what turned her family of longtime welfare recipients into taxpaying workers "was the promise of the civil rights movement and the war on poverty." A Mexican American who learned to be a sheet metal worker through a jobs program reported, "[My children] will finish high school and maybe go to college. . . . I see my family and I know the chains are broken."

Certain groups, especially the aged, fared better than others. Many male-headed families rose out of poverty, but impoverishment among

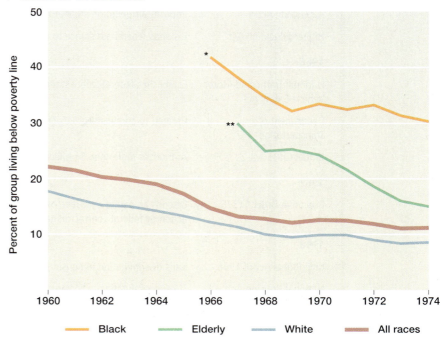

FIGURE 28.1   **Poverty in the United States, 1960–1974**

The short-term effects of economic growth and the Great Society's attack on poverty are seen here. Which groups experienced the sharpest decline in poverty, and what might account for the differences?

*Statistics on blacks for years 1960–1965 not available.
**Statistics on the elderly for years 1960–1966 not available.

Reforms of the Great Society, 1964–1968

1964

Twenty-fourth Amendment	Abolishes poll tax as prerequisite for voting.
Tax Reduction Act	Provides $10 billion in tax cuts in 1964 and 1965.
Civil Rights Act	Bans discrimination in public accommodations, public education, and employment and extends protections to American Indians on reservations.
Economic Opportunity Act	Creates programs for the disadvantaged, including Head Start, VISTA, the Job Corps, and CAP.

1965

Elementary and Secondary Education Act	Provides $1.3 billion in aid to elementary and secondary schools.
Medical Care Act	Provides health insurance (Medicare) for all citizens age sixty-five and over and extends federal health benefits to welfare recipients (Medicaid).
Voting Rights Act	Bans literacy tests and other voting restrictions and authorizes the federal government to act directly to enable African Americans to both register and vote.
Executive Order 11246	Bans discrimination on the basis of race, religion, and national origin by employers awarded government contracts and requires them to "take affirmative action to ensure equal opportunity."
Department of Housing and Urban Development	Created to provide programs to improve housing and neighborhoods in urban areas.
National Arts and Humanities Act	Creates National Endowment for the Arts (NEA) and Humanities (NEH) to support the work of artists, musicians, writers, and scholars.
Water Quality Act	Requires states to set and enforce water quality standards.
Immigration and Nationality Act	Abolishes fifty-year-old discriminatory quotas based on national origins and sets equal limits for all countries.
Air Quality Act	Imposes air pollution standards for motor vehicles.
Higher Education Act	Expands federal assistance to colleges and universities.

1966

National Traffic and Motor Vehicle Safety Act	Establishes federal safety standards.
Department of Transportation	Created to administer transportation programs and policies.
Model Cities Act	Authorizes more than $1 billion to ameliorate the nation's slums.

1967

Executive Order 11375	Extends an earlier executive order banning discrimination and requiring affirmative action by federal contractors to cover women.

1968

Civil Rights Act of 1968	Bans discrimination in housing and jury service.
National Housing Act	Subsidizes the private construction of 1.7 million units of low-income housing.

female-headed families actually increased. Whites escaped poverty faster than racial and ethnic minorities. Great Society programs contributed to a burgeoning black middle class, yet one in three African Americans remained poverty-stricken (Figure 28.1).

Conservative critics charged that Great Society programs discouraged initiative by giving the poor "handouts." Liberal critics claimed that focusing on training and education wrongly blamed the poor themselves rather than an economic system that could not provide enough adequately paying jobs. In contrast to the New Deal, the Great Society avoided structural reform of the economy and spurned public works projects as a means of providing jobs for the disadvantaged.

Some critics insisted that ending poverty required raising taxes in order to create jobs, overhaul welfare systems, and rebuild slums. Great Society programs did invest more heavily in the public sector, but the Great Society was funded from economic growth rather than from new taxes on the rich or middle-class. There was no significant redistribution of income, despite large increases in subsidies for food stamps, housing, medical care, and AFDC. Economic prosperity allowed spending for the poor to rise and improved the lives of millions, but that spending never approached the amounts necessary to claim victory in the War on Poverty.

The Judicial Revolution

A key element of liberalism's ascendancy emerged in the Supreme Court under Chief Justice Earl Warren (1953–1969). In contrast to the federal courts of the Progressive Era and New Deal, which blocked reform, the **Warren Court** often moved ahead of Congress and public opinion. Expanding the Constitution's promise of equality and individual rights, the Court's decisions supported an activist government to prevent injustice and provided new protections to disadvantaged groups and accused criminals.

Following the pathbreaking *Brown v. Board of Education* school desegregation decision of 1954 (see "African Americans Challenge the Supreme Court and the President" in chapter 27), the Court struck down southern states' maneuvers to avoid integration and defended civil rights activists' rights to freedom of assembly and speech. In addition, a unanimous Court in *Loving v. Virginia* (1967) invalidated state laws banning interracial marriage, calling marriage one of the "basic civil rights of man."

Chief Justice Warren considered *Baker v. Carr* (1963) his most important decision. The case grew out of a complaint that inequitably drawn Tennessee electoral districts gave sparsely populated rural districts far more representatives than densely populated urban areas. Using the Fourteenth Amendment guarantee of "equal protection of the laws," the Court established the principle of "one person, one vote" for state legislatures and for the House of Representatives. As states redrew electoral districts, legislatures became more responsive to metropolitan interests.

The Warren Court also reformed the criminal justice system, overturning a series of convictions on the grounds that the accused had been deprived of "life, liberty, or property, without due process of law," guaranteed in the Fourteenth Amendment. In decisions that dramatically altered law enforcement practices, the Court declared that states, as well as the federal government, were subject to the Bill of Rights. *Gideon v. Wainwright* (1963) ruled that when an accused criminal could not afford to hire a lawyer, the state had to provide one. *Miranda v. Arizona* (1966) required police officers to inform suspects of their rights upon arrest. The Court also overturned convictions based on evidence obtained by unlawful arrest, by electronic surveillance, or without a search warrant. Critics accused the justices of "handcuffing the police" and letting criminals go free; liberals argued that these rulings promoted equal treatment in the criminal justice system.

The Court's decisions on religion provoked even greater outrage. *Abington School District v. Schempp* (1963) ruled that requiring Bible reading and prayer in public schools violated the First Amendment principle of separation of church and state. Later judgments banned official prayer in public schools even if students were not required to participate. The Court's supporters declared that the religion cases protected the rights of non-Christians and atheists. They noted that the Court left students free to pray on their own, but the decisions infuriated many Christians. Billboards demanding "Impeach Earl Warren" spoke for critics of the Court, who joined a larger backlash mounting against Great Society liberalism.

REVIEW: How did the Kennedy and Johnson administrations exemplify a liberal vision of the federal government?

▶ The Second Reconstruction

As much as Supreme Court decisions, the black freedom struggle distinguished the liberalism of the 1960s from that of the New Deal. Before the Great Society reforms—and, in fact, contributing to them—African Americans had mobilized a movement that struck down legal separation and discrimination in the South and secured their voting rights. Whereas the first Reconstruction reflected the power of northern Republicans in the aftermath of the Civil War, the second Reconstruction depended heavily on the courage and determination of black people themselves to stand up to racist violence.

Civil rights activism that focused on the South and on legal rights won widespread acceptance in most of the country. But when African Americans stepped up protests against racial injustice outside the South and challenged the economic deprivation that equal rights left untouched, a strong backlash developed as the movement itself lost cohesion.

The Flowering of the Black Freedom Struggle

The Montgomery bus boycott of 1955–1956 gave racial issues national visibility and produced a leader in Martin Luther King Jr. In the 1960s, protest expanded dramatically, as blacks directly confronted the people and institutions that segregated and discriminated against them: retail establishments, public parks and libraries, buses and depots, voting registrars, and police forces.

Massive direct action in the South began in February 1960, when four African American college students in Greensboro, North Carolina, requested service at the whites-only Woolworth's lunch counter. Within days, hundreds of young people joined them, and others launched sit-ins in thirty-one southern cities. From Southern Christian Leadership Conference headquarters, Ella Baker telephoned her young contacts at black colleges: "What are you going to do? It's time to move."

In April, Baker helped student activists form a new organization, the Student Nonviolent Coordinating Committee (SNCC). Embracing King's civil disobedience and nonviolence principles, activists would confront their oppressors and stand up for their rights, but they would not respond if attacked. In the words of SNCC leader James Lawson, "Nonviolence nurtures the atmosphere in which reconciliation and justice become actual possibilities." SNCC, however, rejected the top-down leadership of King and the established civil rights organizations, adopting a structure that fostered decision making and leadership development at the grassroots level.

The activists' optimism and commitment to nonviolence soon underwent severe tests. Although some cities quietly met student demands,

---

VISUAL ACTIVITY

Lunch Counter Sit-in

Tougaloo College Professor John Salter Jr. and students Joan Trumpauer and Anne Moody take part in a 1963 sit-in at the Woolworth's lunch counter in Jackson, Mississippi. Shortly before this photograph was taken, whites had thrown two students to the floor, and police had arrested one student. In 1968, Moody published *Coming of Age in Mississippi*, a book about her experiences in the black freedom struggle. The Granger Collection, New York.

READING THE IMAGE: What does the photograph tell you about how civil rights protests were staged and how others responded to them the early 1960s?

CONNECTIONS: How would you describe the changes in race relations between African Americans and whites in the United States in the first half of the 1960s?

more typically activists encountered violence. Hostile whites poured food over demonstrators, burned them with cigarettes, called them "niggers," and pelted them with rocks. Local police attacked protesters with dogs, clubs, fire hoses, and tear gas, and they arrested thousands of demonstrators.

Another wave of protest occurred in May 1961, when the Congress of Racial Equality (CORE) organized Freedom Rides to implement Court orders for integrated transportation. When a group of six whites and seven blacks reached Alabama, whites bombed their bus and beat them with baseball bats so fiercely that an observer "couldn't see their faces through the blood." CORE rebuffed President Kennedy's pleas to call off the rides. But after a huge mob attacked the riders in Montgomery, Alabama, Attorney General Robert Kennedy dispatched federal marshals to restore order. Nonetheless, Freedom Riders arriving in Jackson, Mississippi, were promptly arrested, and several hundred spent weeks in jail. All told, more than four hundred blacks and whites participated in the Freedom Rides.

In the summer of 1962, SNCC and other groups began the Voter Education Project to register black voters in southern states. They, too, met violence. Whites bombed black churches, threw tenant farmers out of their homes, and beat and jailed activists such as Fannie Lou Hamer. In June 1963, a white man gunned down Mississippi NAACP leader Medgar Evers in front of his house. Similar violence met King's 1963 campaign in Birmingham, Alabama, to integrate public facilities and open jobs to blacks. The police attacked demonstrators, including children, with dogs, cattle prods, and fire hoses—brutalities that television broadcast around the world.

The largest demonstration drew 250,000 blacks and whites to the nation's capital in August 1963 in the March on Washington for Jobs and Freedom, inspired by the strategy of A. Philip Randolph in 1941 (see "The Double V Campaign" in chapter 25). Speaking from the Lincoln Memorial, King put his indelible stamp on the day. "I have a dream," he repeated again and again, imagining the day "when all of God's children . . . will be able to join hands and sing . . .

Civil Rights Freedom Rides, May 1961

'Free at last, free at last; thank God Almighty, we are free at last.'"

The euphoria of the March on Washington faded as activists returned to face continued violence in the South. In 1964, the Mississippi Freedom Summer Project mobilized more than a thousand northern black and white college students to conduct voter registration drives. Resistance was fierce, and by the end of the summer, only twelve hundred new voters had been allowed to register. Southern whites had killed several activists, beaten eighty, arrested more than a thousand, and burned thirty-five black churches. Hidden resistance came from the federal government itself, as the Federal Bureau of Investigation (FBI) spied on King and other leaders and expanded its activities to "expose, disrupt, misdirect, discredit, or otherwise neutralize" black protest.

Still, the movement persisted. In March 1965, Alabama state troopers used such violent force to turn back a voting rights march from Selma to the state capitol in Montgomery that the incident earned the name "Bloody Sunday" and compelled President Johnson to call up the Alabama National Guard to protect the marchers. Battered and hospitalized on Bloody Sunday, John Lewis, chairman of SNCC (and later a congressman from Georgia), called the Voting Rights Act, which passed that October, "every bit as momentous as the Emancipation Proclamation." Referring to the Selma march, he said, "we all felt we'd had a part in it."

The Response in Washington

Civil rights leaders would have to wear sneakers, Lyndon Johnson said, if they were going to keep up with him. But both Kennedy and Johnson, reluctant to alienate southern voters and their congressional representatives, tended to move only when events gave them little choice. In June 1963, Kennedy finally made good on his promise to seek strong antidiscrimination legislation. Pointing to the injustice suffered by blacks, Kennedy asked white Americans, "Who among us would then be content with the counsels of patience and delay?" Johnson took up Kennedy's commitment with passion, as scenes of violence

VISUAL ACTIVITY

Selma March

The fifty-four-mile voting rights march from Selma, Alabama, to the state capital, Montgomery, gained national attention because of the violent reaction to the marchers from onlookers and state officials. The protest helped get the 1965 Voting Rights Act through Congress, a measure that eventually rewrote politics in the South. © Bruce Davidson/Magnum Photos.

READING THE IMAGE: Why do you think the young boy lowered the flag to cover his body? What do the presence of the priest in the background and the signs behind him reflect about the breadth of the black freedom struggle?

CONNECTIONS: How was this protest like and different from other civil rights protests during the 1960s?

banning discrimination in employment, not only attacked racial discrimination but also outlawed discrimination against women. Because Title VII applied to every aspect of employment, including wages, hiring, and promotion, it represented a giant step toward equal employment opportunity for white women as well as for racial minorities.

Responding to black voter registration drives in the South, Johnson demanded legislation to remove "every remaining obstacle to the right and the opportunity to vote." In August 1965, he signed the Voting Rights Act, empowering the federal government to intervene directly to enable African Americans to register and vote, thereby launching a major transformation in southern politics. Black voting rates shot up dramatically (Map 28.2). In turn, the number of African Americans holding political office in the South increased from a handful in 1964 to more than a thousand by 1972. Such gains translated into tangible benefits as black officials upgraded public facilities, police protection, and other basic services for their constituents.

Johnson also declared the need to realize "not just equality as a right and theory, but equality as fact and result." To this end, he issued an executive order in 1965 to require employers holding government contracts (affecting about one-third of the labor force) to take affirmative action to ensure equal opportunity. Extended to cover women in 1967, the affirmative action program required employers to counter the effects of centuries of discrimination by acting forcefully to align their labor force with the available pool of qualified candidates. Most corporations came to see affirmative action as a good employment practice that could make them more successful in "today's increasingly global marketplace".

In 1968, Johnson maneuvered one final bill through Congress. While those in other regions often applauded the gains made by the black freedom struggle in the South, whites were just as likely to resist claims for racial justice in their own locations. In 1963, California voters rejected a law passed by the legislature banning discrimination in housing. And when Martin Luther King Jr. launched a campaign against de facto segregation in Chicago in 1966, thousands of whites jeered and threw stones at demonstrators. Johnson's efforts to get a federal open-housing law succeeded only in the wake of King's assassination in 1968. The Civil Rights Act of 1968 banned racial discrimination in housing and jury selection, and it authorized federal intervention when states failed to protect civil rights workers from violence.

against peaceful demonstrators appalled television viewers across the world. The resulting public support, the "Johnson treatment," and the president's appeal to memories of the martyred Kennedy all produced the most important civil rights law since Reconstruction.

The Civil Rights Act of 1964 guaranteed access for all Americans to public accommodations, public education, employment, and voting, and it extended constitutional protections to Indians on reservations. Title VII of the measure,

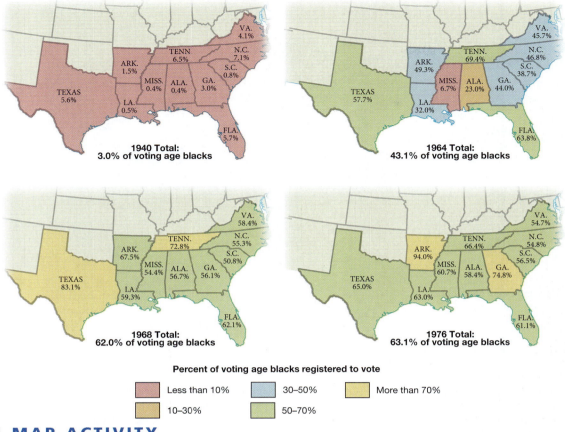

1940 Total:
3.0% of voting age blacks

1964 Total:
43.1% of voting age blacks

1968 Total:
62.0% of voting age blacks

1976 Total:
63.1% of voting age blacks

Percent of voting age blacks registered to vote

Less than 10%	30–50%	More than 70%
10–30%	50–70%	

MAP ACTIVITY

Map 28.2   The Rise of the African American Vote, 1940–1976
Voting rates of southern blacks increased gradually in the 1940s and 1950s but shot up dramatically in the deep South after the Voting Rights Act of 1965 provided for federal agents to enforce African Americans' right to vote.

READING THE MAP: When did the biggest change in African American voter registration occur in the South? In 1968, which states had the highest and which had the lowest voter registration rates?
CONNECTIONS: What role did African American voters play in the 1960 election? What were the targets of two major voting drives in the 1960s?

Black Power and Urban Rebellions

By 1966, black protest engulfed the entire nation, demanding not just legal equality but also economic justice and abandoning passive resistance as a basic principle. These developments were not completely new. African Americans had waged campaigns for decent jobs, housing, and education outside the South since the 1930s. Some African Americans had always armed themselves in self-defense, and many protesters doubted that their passive absorption of violent attacks would change the hearts of racists. Still, the black freedom struggle began to appear more threatening to the white majority.

The new emphases resulted from a combination of heightened activism and unrealized promise. Legal equality could not quickly ameliorate African American poverty, and black rage at oppressive conditions erupted in waves of urban uprisings from 1965 to 1968 (Map 28.3). In a situation where virtually all-white police forces patrolled black neighborhoods, incidents between police and local blacks typically sparked the riots and resulted in looting, destruction of property, injuries, and deaths. The worst riots occurred in Watts (Los Angeles) in August 1965, Newark and Detroit in July 1967, and the nation's capital in April 1968, but violence visited hundreds of cities, and African Americans suffered most of the casualties.

MAP ACTIVITY

Map 28.3   Urban Uprisings, 1965–1968

When a white police officer in the Watts district of Los Angeles struck a twenty-one-year-old African American, whom he had just pulled over for driving drunk, one onlooker shouted, "We've got no rights at all—it's just like Selma." The altercation sparked a five-day uprising, during which young blacks set fires, looted, and attacked police and firefighters. When the riot ended, 34 people were dead, more than 3,000 were arrested, and scores of businesses had been wiped out. Similar but smaller-scale violence erupted in dozens of cities across the nation during the next three summers.

READING THE MAP: In what regions and cities of the United States were the 1960s uprisings concentrated? What years saw the greatest unrest?

CONNECTIONS: What were some of the causes of racial unrest in America's cities during this period? Whom did whites generally hold responsible for the violence and why?

In the North, Malcolm X posed a powerful challenge to the ethos of nonviolence. Calling for black pride and autonomy, separation from the "corrupt [white] society," and self-defense against white violence, Malcolm X attracted a large following, especially in urban ghettos. At a June 1966 rally in Greenwood, Mississippi, SNCC chairman Stokely Carmichael gave the ideas espoused by Malcolm X a new name when he shouted, "We want black power." Carmichael rejected integration and assimilation because they implied white superiority. African Americans were encouraged to develop independent businesses and control their own schools, communities, and political organizations. The phrase "Black is beautiful" emphasized pride in African American culture and connections to dark-skinned people around the world who were claiming their independence from colonial domination. Black power quickly became the rallying cry in SNCC and CORE as well as other organizations such as the Black Panther Party for Self-Defense, organized to combat police brutality.

The press paid inordinate attention to the **black power movement,** and civil rights activism met with a severe backlash from whites. Although the urban riots of the mid-1960s erupted spontaneously, triggered by specific incidents of alleged police mistreatment, horrified whites blamed black power militants. By 1966, 85 percent of the white population—up from 34 percent two years earlier—thought that African Americans were pressing for too much too quickly.

Martin Luther King Jr. agreed with black power advocates about the need for economic justice and "a radical reconstruction of society,"

Black Power
Black Panthers in San Francisco organized a number of community centers where they provided free breakfasts to poor children, distributed party literature, organized protests, and operated "liberation schools." Here adults and children give the black power salute outside the Panther school in the Fillmore district in 1969. Such shows of militancy struck fear into many whites. © Bettmann/Corbis.

yet he clung to nonviolence and integration as the means to this end. In 1968, the thirty-nine-year-old leader went to Memphis to support striking municipal sanitation workers. There, on April 4, he was murdered by an escaped white convict.

Although black power organizations captured the headlines, they failed to gain the massive support from African Americans that King and other leaders had attracted. Nor could they alleviate the poverty and racism entrenched in the entire country. Black radicals were harassed by the FBI and jailed; some encounters left both black militants and police dead. Yet black power's emphasis on racial pride and its critique of American institutions resonated loudly and helped shape the protest activities of other groups.

REVIEW: How and why did the civil rights movement change in the mid-1960s?

▶ A Multitude of Movements

The civil rights movement's undeniable moral claims helped make protest more respectable, while its successes encouraged other groups with grievances. Native Americans, Latinos, college

students, women, gay men and lesbians, and others drew on the black freedom struggle for inspiration and models of activism. Many of these groups engaged in direct-action protests, expressed their own cultural nationalism, and challenged dominant institutions and values. Their grievances gained attention in the political arena, and they expanded justice and opportunity for many of their constituents.

Native American Protest

The cry "red power" reflected the influence of black radicalism on young Native Americans, whose activism took on fresh militancy and goals in the 1960s. The termination and relocation programs of the 1950s, contrary to their intent, stirred a sense of Indian identity across tribal lines and a determination to preserve traditional culture. Native Americans demonstrated and occupied land and public buildings, claiming rights to natural resources and territory they had owned collectively before European settlement.

In 1969, Native American militants captured world attention when several dozen seized Alcatraz Island, an abandoned federal prison in San Francisco Bay, claiming their right of "first discovery" of this land. For nineteen months, they used the occupation to publicize injustices against Indians, promote pan-Indian cooperation, and celebrate traditional cultures. One of the organizers, Dr. LaNada Boyer, the first Native American to attend the University of California, Berkeley, said of Alcatraz, "We were able to reestablish our identity as Indian people, as a culture, as political entities."

In Minneapolis in 1968, two Chippewa Indians, Dennis Banks and George Mitchell, founded the **American Indian Movement (AIM)** to attack problems in cities, where about 300,000 Indians lived. AIM sought to protect Indians from police

Native Americans Occupy Alcatraz Island

Beginning in November 1969, some one hundred Native Americans occupied Alcatraz Island in San Francisco Bay. Calling themselves "Indians of All Tribes" to reflect their diversity, they demanded the deed to the island and the creation of an Indian university, museum, and cultural center. Although failing to achieve their goals, they brought attention to the Native American cause and spurred further activism. © Dennis Stock/Magnum Photos

harassment, secure anti-poverty funds, and establish "survival schools" to teach Indian history and values. The movement's appeal quickly spread and filled many Indians with a new sense of purpose. Lakota activist and author Mary Crow Dog wrote that AIM's visit to her South Dakota reservation "loosened a sort of earthquake inside me." AIM leaders helped organize the "Trail of Broken Treaties" caravan to the nation's capital in 1972, when activists occupied the Bureau of Indian Affairs to express their outrage at the bureau's policies and interference in Indians' lives. In 1973, a much longer siege occurred on the Lakota Sioux reservation in South Dakota. Conflicts there between AIM militants and older tribal leaders led AIM to take over for seventy-two days the village of Wounded Knee, where U.S. troops had massacred more than one hundred Sioux Indians in 1890 (see "Indian Resistance and Survival" in chapter 17).

Although these dramatic occupations failed to achieve their specific goals, Indians won the end of relocation and termination policies, greater tribal sovereignty and control over community services, protection of Indian religious practices, and a measure of respect and pride. A number of laws and court decisions restored rights to ancestral lands and compensated tribes for land seized in violation of treaties.

Latino Struggles for Justice

The fastest-growing minority group in the 1960s was Latino, or Hispanic American, an extraordinarily varied population encompassing people of Mexican, Puerto Rican, Caribbean, and other Latin American origins. (The term *Latino* stresses their common bonds as a minority group in the United States. The older, less political term *Hispanic* also includes people with origins in Spain.) People of Puerto Rican and Caribbean descent populated East Coast cities, but more than half of the nation's Latino population—including some six million Mexican Americans—lived in the Southwest. In addition, thousands illegally crossed the border between Mexico and the United States yearly in search of economic opportunity.

Political organization of Mexican Americans dated back to the League of United Latin-American Citizens (LULAC), founded in 1929, which fought segregation and discrimination through litigation (see "Blacks and Mexicans Push for Their Civil Rights" in chapter 26). In the 1960s, however, young Mexican Americans increasingly rejected traditional politics in favor of direct action. One symbol of this generational challenge was young activists' adoption of the term *Chicano* (from *mejicano*, the Spanish word for "Mexican").

The **Chicano movement** drew national attention to California, where Cesar Chavez and Dolores Huerta organized a movement to overcome the exploitation of migrant agricultural workers. As the child of migrant farmworkers, Chavez lived in soggy tents, saw his parents cheated by labor contractors, changed schools frequently, and encountered indifference and discrimination. One teacher, he recalled, "hung a sign on me that said, 'I am a clown, I speak Spanish.'" After serving in World War II, Chavez began to organize voter registration drives among Mexican Americans.

In contrast to Chavez, Dolores Huerta grew up in an integrated urban neighborhood and avoided the farmworkers' grinding poverty but witnessed subtle forms of discrimination. Once, a high school teacher challenged her authorship of an essay because it was so well written. Believing that collective action was the key to progress, she and Chavez founded the United Farm Workers (UFW) union in 1962. To gain leverage for striking workers, the UFW mounted a nationwide boycott of California grapes, winning support from millions of Americans and gaining a wage increase for the workers in 1970. Although the UFW struggled and lost membership during the 1970s, it helped politicize Mexican Americans and improve farmworkers' lives.

Other Chicanos pressed the Equal Employment Opportunity Commission (EEOC) to act against job discrimination against Mexican Americans. After LULAC, the American GI Forum (see "Blacks and Mexicans Push for Their Civil Rights" in chapter 26), and other groups picketed government offices, President Johnson responded in 1967 by appointing Vicente T. Ximenes as the first Mexican American EEOC commissioner and creating a special committee on Mexican American issues.

Claiming "brown power," Chicanos organized to end discrimination in education, gain political power, and combat police brutality. In Denver, Rodolfo "Corky" Gonzales set up "freedom schools" where Chicano children learned Spanish and Mexican American history. The nationalist strains of Chicano protest were evident in La Raza Unida (the United Race), a political party founded in 1970 based on cultural pride and brotherhood. Along with blacks and Native Americans, Chicanos continued to be disproportionately impoverished, but they gradually won more political offices, more effective enforcement of antidiscrimination legislation, and greater respect for their culture.

Student Rebellion, the New Left, and the Counterculture

Although materially and legally more secure than their African American, Indian, and Latino counterparts, white youths also expressed dissent, participating in the black freedom struggle, student protests, the antiwar movement, and the new feminist movement. Challenging establishment institutions, young activists were part of a larger international phenomenon of student movements around the globe.

The central organization of white student protest was Students for a Democratic Society

Cesar Chavez and Dolores Huerta
Under posters showing Senator Robert Kennedy and Mahatma Gandhi, Chavez and Huerta confer in 1968 during the United Farm Workers' struggle with grape growers for better wages and working conditions. Chavez, like Martin Luther King, had studied the ideas of Gandhi, who used civil disobedience and nonviolence to gain independence for India. People across the country, including Robert Kennedy, supported the UFW's grape boycott. Arthur Schatz/Time & Life Pictures/Getty Images.

Student Protest

Although only a minority of college students participated in the rebellions of the 1960s, a sizable number at all kinds of colleges challenged traditional authority, criticized established institutions, and demanded a voice in decision making.

DOCUMENT 1
Edward Schwartz, Student Power, October 1967

Student activist Edward Schwartz wrote this statement to represent the views of the National Student Association, the largest college student organization in the 1960s.

Let this principle apply—he who must obey the rule should make it.

Students should make the rules governing dormitory hours, boy-girl visitation, student unions, student fees, clubs, newspapers, and the like. Faculty and administrators should advise—attempt to persuade, even. Yet the student should bear the burden of choice.

Students and faculty should co-decide curricular policy.

Students, faculty, and administration should co-decide admissions policy, overall college policy affecting the community, even areas like university investment. . . . Student power should not be argued on legal grounds. It is not a legal principle. It is an educational principle.

Student power is threatening to those who wield power now, but this is understandable. A student should threaten his administrators outside of class, just as bright students threaten professors inside of class.

Student power ultimately challenges everyone in the university—the students who must decide; the faculty and administrators who must rethink their own view of community relations in order to persuade.

People who say that student power means anarchy imply really that students are rabble who have no ability to form community and to adhere to decisions made by community. Student power is not the negation of rules—it is the creation of a new process for the enactment of rules. Student power is not the elimination of authority,

it is the development of a democratic standard of authority.

Source: Excerpt from "He Who Must Obey the Rule Should Make It," from *The University Crisis Reader*, vol. 1, *The Liberal University under Attack* by Immanuel Wallerstein and Paul Starr, eds., pp. 482–84. Copyright © 1971 by Random House, Inc.

DOCUMENT 2
SDS Explanation of the Columbia Strike, September 1968

One of the longest, most violent student protests occurred in New York City at Columbia University in spring 1968. A key issue was the university's expansion through buying up land in neighboring Harlem and evicting black tenants. Members of the Columbia chapter of SDS rationalized their actions below.

When we seized five buildings at Columbia University, we engaged the force of wealth, privilege, property—and the force of state violence that always accompanies them—with little more than our own ideals, our fears, and a vague sense of outrage at the injustices of our society. Martin Luther King had just been shot, his name demeaned by Columbia officials who refused to grant a decent wage to Puerto Rican workers, and who had recently grabbed part of Harlem for a student gym. . . .

For years Columbia Trustees had evicted tenants from their homes, taken land through city deals, and fired workers for trying to form a union. For years they had trained officers for Vietnam who, as ROTC literature indicates, killed Vietnamese peasants in their own country. In secret work for the IDA [Institute for Defense Analysis] and the CIA, in chemical-biological war research

(SDS), formed in 1960. In 1962, the organizers wrote in their statement of purpose, "We are people of this generation, bred in at least modest comfort, housed now in universities, looking uncomfortably at the world we inherit." The idealistic students criticized the complacency of their elders, the remoteness of decision makers, and the powerlessness and alienation generated

for the Department of War, the Trustees implicated their own University in genocide. They had consistently . . . lied to their own constituents and published CIA books under the guise of independent scholarship. . . . Columbia, standing at the top of a hill, looked down on Harlem. . . . People who survived in Harlem had been evicted by the Trustees from Morningside or still paid rent to Columbia. . . . We walked to our classrooms across land that had been privatized; we studied in buildings that had once been homes in a city that is underhoused; and we listened to the apologies for Cold War and capital in our classes.

Columbia professors often claim that the University is a neutral institution. . . . A University could not, even if it wanted, choose to be really value-free. It can choose good values; it can choose bad values; or it can remain ignorant of the values on which it acts. . . . A social institution should at least articulate its own perspective, so that its own values may be consciously applied or modified. It is a typical fallacy of American teaching, that to remain silent on crucial issues is to be objective with your own constituents. Actually a "neutral" institution is far more manipulative than a University committed to avowed goals and tasks.

Source: Excerpt from "The Columbia Statement," Columbia SDS, from *The University Crisis Reader*, vol. 1, *The Liberal University under Attack* by Immanuel Wallerstein and Paul Starr, eds., pp. 23–47. Copyright © 1971 by Random House, Inc.

DOCUMENT 3
Counterthrust on Student Power, Spring 1967

While the majority of students simply avoided involvement in campus rebellions, some students actively criticized the protesters. A leaflet titled "Student Power Is a Farce" reflected the views of Counterthrust, a conservative group at Wayne State University in Michigan.

Our University is being treated to the insanity of Left-Wing students demanding the run of the University. . . . Wayne students are told by the Left that "student power" merely means more democracy on campus. This is an outright lie! Student power is a Left-Wing catchword symbolizing campus militancy and radicalism. In actuality, the Left-Wing, spearheaded by the SDS, want to radically alter the university community. . . .

The Leftists charge a sinister plot by private enterprise to train students for jobs at taxpayers' expense. Evidently it never occurred to the SDS that private enterprise is also the biggest single taxpayer for schools. But, of course, that would require a little thought on the part of the SDS which they have already demonstrated they are incapable of. . . .

The byword of student power-union advocates is Radicalism. . . . Fraternities and student Governments will have no place in student power-unions since both are considered allies of the status quo and thus useless. . . . As responsible Wayne students, we cannot allow our University to be used by Leftists for their narrow purposes. We were invited to this campus by the Michigan Taxpayer to receive an education. Let us honor that invitation.

Source: "Student Power Is a Farce," Counterthrust, from *The University Crisis Reader*, vol. 1, *The Liberal University under Attack* by Immanuel Wallerstein and Paul Starr, eds., pp. 487–88. Copyright © 1971 by Random House, Inc.

Questions for Analysis and Debate

1. How do the statements by Edward Schwartz and the Columbia SDS chapter differ in terms of the issues they address?

2. What did Counterthrust see as the biggest problem with student protesters?

3. Do you agree or disagree with the Columbia SDS chapter's assertion that it is impossible for a university to be neutral or value-free? Explain your position.

4. To what extent do your own campus policies and practices suggest that student protest during the 1960s and 1970s made a difference?

Connect to the Big Idea

C In what ways did student protests differ from other protest movements of the 1960s?

by a bureaucratic society. SDS aimed to mobilize a "New Left" around the goals of civil rights, peace, and universal economic security. Other forms of student activism soon followed.

The first large-scale white student protest arose at the University of California, Berkeley, in 1964, when university officials banned students from setting up tables to recruit support for

Anti-Establishment Clothing

In the new counterculture emerging in the 1960s, youthful hippies embraced distinctive and colorful clothing to reflect their identities as rebels. The well-worn artifacts shown here typify the self-expression of young people who scorned the older generation's button-down shirts, business suits, teased bouffant hair, sheath dresses, and all that they stood for.

Hippie first emerged as a new word in 1965, derived from hip and hipster, slang words from the realm of jazz and beatniks. But the teenagers and young adults who became hippies came disproportionately from the middle-class suburbs that symbolized the success of the American dream. Hippies rejected the classic aspirations of steady work, home ownership, and consumer goods. In the summer of 1967, some 100,000 of them converged on the Haight-Ashbury district of San Francisco, lured by the call of the "Summer of Love." Those who stayed beyond the summer lived in voluntary poverty, relying on panhandling, crash pads, soup kitchens, and free clinics to support their freedom from middle-class values. Hippie enclaves sprouted in low-rent districts of cities and in rural communes.

Blue jeans became almost a uniform for the student movement of the 1960s, but hippies took things one step further in expressing their disdain for the Establishment, as reflected in this pair of patched bell-bottom jeans. Why would someone take the time to sew on all those patches? Think about the typical stress points in pants. Are the patches functional or decorative? What attitudes about consumption and conservation are displayed in these jeans?

Bell-Bottom Jeans

The jacket illustrates two common themes: the Native American/cowboy-style fringe and the red-white-blue motif. How might mainstream patriots have regarded this jacket? Was it intentionally inflammatory, or might the wearer be expressing an alternative form of patriotism? Most states had decades-old laws forbidding the desecration of the U.S. flag. Would this jacket have put its wearer at risk for arrest? What was rebellious about the denim shorts and halter top? Can you think of any time or place when such immodest dress would have been acceptable? Can you guess how high school dress codes responded to these innovations? How the fashion industry responded?

Authentic hippie clothing remains rare; most of it probably fell apart and was junked by the mid-1970s, with occasional garments showing up in thrift stores or vintage clothing shops. By the 1980s, patterned bell-bottoms and daring short shorts looked as old-fashioned as a flapper dress from the 1920s. Nevertheless, mainstream designers copied many of the hippie styles, and the impact of counterculture clothing on conventional dress was profound, leading within a few years to a much greater informality in everyday attire, even among the Establishment.

various causes. Led by whites returning from civil rights work in the South, the "free speech" movement occupied the administration building, and more than seven hundred students were arrested before the California Board of Regents overturned the new restrictions.

Hundreds of student rallies and building occupations followed on campuses across the country, especially after 1965, when opposition to the Vietnam War mounted and students protested against universities' ties with the military (see "The Widening War at Home" in chapter 29). Students also challenged the collegiate environment. Women at the University of Chicago, for example, charged in 1969 that all universities "discriminate against women, impede their full intellectual development, deny them places on the faculty, exploit talented women and mistreat women students." At Howard University, African American students called for a "Black

SOURCE: Jacket: Collection of Mark Hooper; jeans: Michael G. Stewart / Vintage-Haberdashers; halter and shorts: Picture Research Consultants & Archives.

Questions for Analysis

1. How might establishment types and high school officials have responded to these kinds of clothing?

2. Do the clothes of today's youth resemble any elements of resistance to conventional norms expressed in these garments?

Connect to the Big Idea

C In what ways did the clothing of young protesters reflect their political agenda in the 1960s?

Halter and Shorts

Fringed Jacket

Awareness Research Institute," demanding that academic departments "place more emphasis on how these disciplines may be used to effect the liberation of black people." Across the country, students won curricular reforms such as black studies and women's studies programs, more financial aid for minority and poor students, independence from paternalistic rules, and a larger voice in campus decision making. (See "Documenting the American Promise," page 812.)

Student protest sometimes blended into a cultural revolution against nearly every conventional standard of behavior. Drawing on the ideas of the Beats of the 1950s (see "Countercurrents" in chapter 27), the "hippies," as they were called, rejected mainstream values such as consumerism, order, and sexual discipline. Seeking personal rather than political change, they advocated "Do your own thing" and drew attention with their long hair, wildly colorful clothing, and drug use.

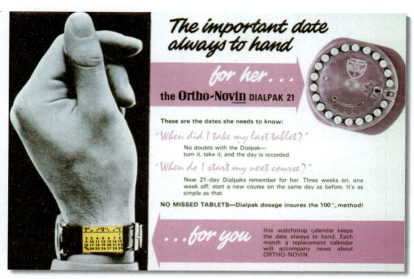

The Pill
Urged on by longtime birth control advocate Margaret Sanger and funded by Katharine Dexter McCormick, scientists discovered how to prevent ovulation. In 1960, the Food and Drug Administration approved the first birth control pill, which soon became the leading form of contraception for American women. This 1965 ad shows doctors how the Ortho-Novin Dialpak will help women remember to take the daily tablet. Division of Medicine & Science, Archives Center, National Museum of American History, Smithsonian Institution.

Across the country, thousands of radicals established communes in cities or on farms, where they renounced private property and shared everything. (See "Visualizing History," page 814.)

Rock and folk music defined both the counterculture and the political left. Music during the 1960s often carried insurgent political and social messages that reflected radical youth culture. "Eve of Destruction," a top hit of 1965, reminded young men at a time when the voting age was twenty-one, "You're old enough to kill but not for votin'." The 1969 Woodstock Music Festival, attended by 400,000 young people, epitomized the centrality of music to the youth rebellion. Hippies faded away in the 1970s, but many elements of the counterculture—rock music, jeans, and long hair, as well as new social attitudes—filtered into the mainstream. More tolerant approaches to sexual behaviors spawned what came to be called the "sexual revolution," with help from the birth control pill, which became available in the 1960s. Self-fulfillment became a dominant concern of many Americans, and questioning of authority became more widespread.

Gay Men and Lesbians Organize

More permissive sexual norms did not stretch easily to include tolerance of homosexuality. Gay men and lesbians escaped discrimination and ridicule only by concealing their very identities. Those who couldn't or wouldn't found themselves fired from jobs, arrested for their sexual activities, deprived of their children, or accused of being "perverted." Despite this, some gays and lesbians began to organize.

Some of the first gay activism challenged the government's aggressive efforts to keep homosexuals out of the civil service. In October 1965, picketers outside the White House held signs calling discrimination against homosexuals "as immoral as discrimination against Negroes and Jews." Not until ten years later, however, did the Civil Service Commission formally end its anti-gay policy.

A turning point in gay activism came in 1969 when police raided a gay bar, the Stonewall Inn, in New York City's Greenwich Village, and gay men and lesbians fought back. "Suddenly, they were not submissive anymore," a police officer remarked. Energized by the defiance shown at the Stonewall riots, gay men and lesbians organized a host of new groups, such as the Gay Liberation Front and the National Gay and Lesbian Task Force.

In 1972, Ann Arbor, Michigan, passed the first antidiscrimination ordinance, and two years later Elaine Noble's election to the Massachusetts legislature marked the first time an openly gay candidate won state office. In 1973, gay activists persuaded the American Psychiatric Association to withdraw its designation of homosexuality as a mental disease. It would take decades for these initial gains to improve conditions for most homosexuals, but by the mid-1970s gay men and lesbians had a movement through which they could claim equal rights and express pride in their identities.

REVIEW: What other movements emerged in the 1960s, and how were they influenced by the black freedom struggle?

▶ The New Wave of Feminism

On August 26, 1970, on the fiftieth anniversary of women's suffrage, tens of thousands of women across the country—from radical women in jeans to conservatively dressed suburbanites, peace activists, and politicians—took to the streets. They carried signs reading "Sisterhood Is Powerful" and "Don't Cook Dinner—Starve a Rat Today." Some of the banners opposed the war in Vietnam, others demanded racial justice, but women's own liberation stood at the forefront.

Becoming visible by the late 1960s, a multifaceted women's movement reached its high tide in the 1970s and persisted into the twenty-first century. By that time, despite a powerful countermovement, women had experienced tremendous transformations in their legal status, public opportunities, and personal and sexual relationships, while popular expectations about appropriate gender roles had shifted dramatically.

A Multifaceted Movement Emerges

Beginning in the 1940s, large demographic changes laid the preconditions for a resurgence of feminism. As more and more women took jobs, the importance of their paid work to the economy and their families challenged traditional views of women and awakened many women workers, especially labor union women, to the inferior conditions of their employment. The democratization of higher education brought more women to college campuses, where their aspirations exceeded the confines of domesticity and of routine, subordinate jobs.

Policy initiatives in the early 1960s reflected both these larger transformations and the efforts of women's rights activists. In 1961, Assistant Secretary of Labor Esther Peterson persuaded President Kennedy to create the President's Commission on the Status of Women (PCSW). Its 1963 report documented widespread discrimination against women and recommended remedies, although it did not challenge women's domestic roles. One of the commission's concerns was addressed even before it issued its report, when Congress passed the Equal Pay Act of 1963, making it illegal to pay women less than men for the same work.

Like other movements, the rise of feminism owed much to the black freedom struggle. Women gained protection from employment discrimination through Title VII of the Civil Rights Act of 1964 and the extension of affirmative action to women by piggybacking onto civil rights measures. They soon grew impatient when the government failed to take these new policies seriously. Determining the need for "an NAACP for women," to put pressure on the government and other institutions, Betty Friedan, civil rights activist Pauli Murray, several union women, and others founded the **National Organization for Women (NOW)** in 1966.

Simultaneously, a more radical feminism grew among mostly white young women active in the black freedom struggle and the New Left. Frustrated when male leaders dismissed and ridiculed their claims of sex discrimination, many women walked out of New Left organizations and created independent women's liberation groups throughout the nation.

Women's liberation began to gain public attention, especially when dozens of women picketed the Miss America beauty pageant in 1968, protesting against being forced "to compete for male approval [and] enslaved by ludicrous 'beauty' standards." Women began to speak publicly about personal experiences that had always been shrouded in secrecy, such as rape and abortion. Throughout the country, women joined consciousness-raising groups, where they discovered that what they had considered "personal" problems reflected an entrenched system of discrimination against and devaluation of women.

Radical feminists, who called their movement "women's liberation," differed from feminists in NOW and other more mainstream groups in several ways. NOW focused on equal treatment for women in the public sphere; women's liberation emphasized ending women's subordination in family and other personal relationships. Groups such as NOW wanted to integrate women into existing institutions; radical groups insisted that women's liberation required a total transformation of economic, political, and social institutions. Differences between these two strands of feminism blurred in the 1970s, as NOW and other mainstream groups embraced many of the issues raised by radicals.

Although NOW elected a black president, Aileen Hernandez, in 1970, the new feminism's leadership and constituency were predominantly white and middle-class. Women of color criticized white feminists for their inadequate attention

Transnational Feminisms

Organizations of women across national borders originated in the nineteenth century, but global connections among women increased dramatically in 1945 with the creation of the United Nations, whose charter affirmed "the equal rights of men and women." In 1947, the UN established a Commission on the Status of Women, creating a forum for women from around the globe to meet and be heard; in 1948 it adopted a Universal Declaration of Human Rights, which explicitly rejected sex discrimination. These commitments to justice for women went far beyond any rights guaranteed to women in the United States or most other nations, thereby setting standards and raising expectations.

The UN helped launch a global feminist movement of unparalleled size and diversity when it declared 1975 International Women's Year and sponsored a conference in Mexico City. In addition to official delegates from 125 nations, six thousand women came to Mexico City on their own. The assembly approved the World Plan of Action for Women and prompted the UN to declare 1976 to 1985 the UN Decade for Women.

In response to the call for action in individual countries, the U.S. government funded the National Women's Conference in Houston, Texas, in 1977. More than two thousand state delegates attended, representing a cross section of American womanhood. They adopted the National Plan of Action, not only supporting ratification of the ERA and reproductive freedom but also addressing the needs of specific groups of women, including the elderly, lesbians, racial minorities, women with disabilities, rural women, and homemakers. For the first time, the U.S. women's movement had a comprehensive national agenda setting goals for decades to come.

The three themes of the UN Decade for Women—equality, development, and peace—reflected an effort to address the enormously diverse needs of women throughout the world. Feminists from Western nations who focused on equal rights met criticism from women who represented colonized, impoverished third world countries and insisted that "to talk feminism to a woman who has no water, no food, and no home is to talk nonsense." Ever larger UN-sponsored meetings followed Mexico City—Copenhagen in 1980, Nairobi in 1985, and Beijing in 1995, where twenty thousand women gathered. These global exchanges taught American feminists that to participate in a truly international movement, they would have to revise their Western-centered perspective on women's needs and understand that women's issues must include economic development and anticolonialism.

American feminists also learned that theirs was not always the most advanced nation when it came to women's welfare and status. Employed women in most industrialized countries had access to paid maternity leave and public child care. By 2013, women had headed governments in more than thirty countries, including India, Israel, Britain, and Germany. Many nations, such as Argentina, Egypt, and members of the European Union, had some form of affirmative action to increase the numbers of women in government. And whereas American women held just 20 percent of the seats in Congress, women constituted more than 35 percent of national legislatures in such countries as Sweden, South Africa, Costa Rica, and Belgium.

Despite enormous differences among women around the world, internationally minded feminists continued to seek common ground. As Gertrude Mongella, secretary general of the Beijing conference, insisted in 1995, "A revolution has begun and there is no going back. . . . This revolution is too just, too important, and too long overdue."

to the disproportionate poverty experienced by minority women and to the particular forms of oppression women of color experienced when gender combined with race or ethnicity. To black women, who were much more frequently compelled to work in the lowest-paying jobs for their families' survival, employment did not necessarily look like liberation.

In addition to struggling with vast differences among women, feminism also contended with the media's refusal to take women's grievances seriously. For instance, when the House of Representatives passed an equal rights amendment to the U.S. Constitution in 1970, the *New York Times* criticized it in an editorial titled "The Henpecked House." After Gloria Steinem founded *Ms: The New Magazine for Women* in 1972, feminists had their own mass-circulation periodical controlled by women and featuring articles on a broad range of feminist issues.

Ms. reported on a multifaceted movement that reflected the tremendously diverse experiences, backgrounds, and goals of American women. New women's organizations represented ethnic and racial minorities, labor union women, religious women, welfare mothers,

International Women's Year Tribune
Along with the official UN conference in Mexico City in 1975, nongovernmental organizations associated with the UN sponsored a tribune, where six thousand women gathered. Participants expressed the conflicting priorities of Western women and women from developing countries, arguing over whether issues such as apartheid in South Africa and self-government for Palestinians were women's issues. Despite their disagreements, most women left Mexico City enlightened and energized. ©Bettye Lane. From the Sallie Bingham Center for Women's History and Culture, Duke University.

America in a Global Context

1. What were the three themes of the UN Decade for Women? How were these three themes related to women's status and well-being?

2. In what ways were women in the United States ahead of women in other countries? In what ways were they behind? What might account for the differences?

Connect to the Big Idea

⊙ What goals did the feminist movements in the United States and abroad have in common with other protest movements of the 1960s?

---

lesbians, and more. Other new groups focused on single issues such as health, education, abortion rights, and violence against women. In addition, U.S. women connected with women abroad, joining a movement that crossed national boundaries. (See "Beyond America's Borders," above.)

Common threads underlay the great diversity of organizations, issues, and activities. Feminism represented the belief that women were barred from, unequally treated in, or poorly served by the entire male-dominated public arena, including politics, medicine, law, education, culture, and religion. Many feminists also sought equality in the private sphere, challenging traditional norms that identified women primarily as wives and mothers or sex objects who accommodated themselves to men's needs and interests.

Feminist Gains Spark a Countermovement

Although more an effect than a cause of women's rising employment, feminism lifted female aspirations and helped lower barriers to posts

VISUAL ACTIVITY

Ms. Magazine

In 1972, Gloria Steinem and other journalists and writers published the premier issue of the first mass-circulation magazine for and controlled by women. *Ms.: The New Magazine for Women* shunned the recipes and fashion tips typical of women's magazines and instead featured literature by women writers and articles on a broad range of women's issues. Reprinted by permission of *Ms.* magazine, © 1972.

READING THE IMAGE: What concerns are suggested by this cover of the first issue? What is the significance of the woman's multiple arms?

CONNECTIONS: In addition to male-controlled media, what other institutions did feminists try to change?

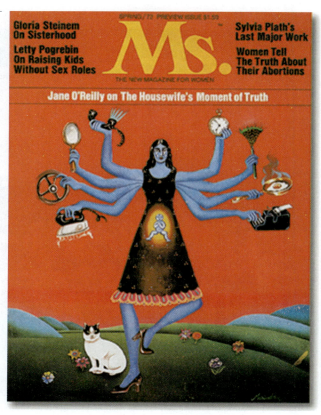

monopolized by men. Between 1970 and 2000, women's share of law degrees shot up from 5 percent to nearly 50 percent, and their proportion of medical degrees from less than 10 percent to more than 35 percent. Women gained political offices very slowly; yet by 2014, they constituted about 20 percent of Congress and nearly 25 percent of all state legislators.

Despite outnumbering men in college enrollments and making some inroads into male-dominated occupations, women still concentrated in low-paying, traditionally female jobs, and an earnings gap between men and women persisted into the twenty-first century. Employed women continued to bear primary responsibility for taking care of their homes and families, thereby working a "double day." Unlike in other advanced countries, women in the United States were not entitled to paid maternity leave, and government provisions for child care lagged far behind.

By the mid-1970s feminism faced a powerful countermovement, organized around opposition to an Equal Rights Amendment (ERA) to the Constitution that would outlaw differential treatment of men and women under all state and federal laws. After Congress passed the ERA in 1972, Phyllis Schlafly, a conservative activist in the Republican Party, mobilized thousands of antifeminist women who feared that the ERA would devalue what they believed were their God-given roles as wives and mothers. These women, marching on state capitols, persuaded enough male legislators to block ratification so that when the time limit ran out in 1982, only thirty-five states had done so, three short of the necessary three-fourths majority. (See Chapter 30, "Historical Question," page 878.)

Powerful opposition likewise arose to feminists' quest for abortion rights. "Without the full capacity to limit her own reproduction," abortion rights activist Lucinda Cisler insisted, "a woman's other 'freedoms' are tantalizing mockeries that cannot be exercised." In 1973, the Supreme Court ruled in the landmark *Roe v. Wade* decision that the Constitution protects the right to abortion, which states cannot prohibit in the early stages of pregnancy. This decision galvanized many Americans who believed that abortion constituted murder. Like ERA opponents, with whom they often overlapped, right-to-life activists believed that abortion disparaged motherhood and that feminism threatened their traditional roles. Beginning in 1977, abortion foes pressured Congress to restrict the right to abortion by prohibiting coverage under Medicaid and other government-financed health programs, and the Supreme Court allowed states to impose additional obstacles.

Despite resistance, feminists won other lasting gains. Title IX of the Education Amendments Act of 1972 banned sex discrimination in all aspects of education, such as admissions, athletics, and hiring. Congress also outlawed sex discrimination in credit in 1974, opened U.S. military academies to women in 1976, and prohibited discrimination against pregnant workers in 1978. Moreover, the Supreme Court struck down laws that treated men and women differently in Social Security, welfare and military benefits, and workers' compensation.

At the state and local levels, women saw reforms in areas that radical feminists had first introduced. They won laws forcing police departments and the legal system to treat rape victims more justly and humanely. Activists also pushed domestic violence onto the public agenda, obtaining government financing for shelters for battered women as well as laws ensuring both greater protection for victims of domestic violence and more effective prosecution of abusers.

REVIEW: What were the key goals of feminist reformers, and why did a countermovement arise to resist them?

▶ Liberal Reform in the Nixon Administration

Opposition to civil rights measures, Great Society reforms, and protest groups—along with frustrations over the war in Vietnam (see "A Nation Polarized" in chapter 29)—delivered the White House to Republican Richard M. Nixon in 1968. Nixon attacked the Great Society for "pouring billions of dollars into programs that have failed" and promised to represent the "forgotten Americans, the non-shouters, the non-demonstrators." Yet, his administration either promoted or accepted important elements of the liberal reform agenda, including greater federal assistance to the poor, new protections for women and minorities, and environmental reforms.

Extending the Welfare State and Regulating the Economy

A number of factors shaped the liberal policies of the Nixon administration. Democrats continued to control Congress, the Republican Party contained significant numbers of liberals and moderates, and Nixon saw political advantages in accepting some liberal programs, especially those promoted by grassroots movements that persisted into the 1970s. Serious economic problems also compelled new approaches, and although Nixon's real passion lay in foreign policy, he was eager to establish a domestic legacy.

Under Nixon, government assistance programs such as Social Security, housing, and food stamps grew, and Congress enacted a new billion-dollar program that provided Pell grants for low-income students to attend college. Noting the disparity between what Nixon said and what he did, his speechwriter, the archconservative Pat Buchanan, grumbled, "Vigorously did we inveigh against the Great Society, enthusiastically did we fund it."

Nixon also acted contrary to his anti-government rhetoric when economic crises and energy shortages induced him to increase the federal government's power in the marketplace. By 1970, both inflation and unemployment had surpassed 6 percent, an unprecedented combination dubbed "stagflation." Domestic troubles were compounded by the decline of American dominance in the international economy. With Japan and Western Europe fully recovered from the devastation of World War II, foreign cars, electronic equipment, and other products now competed favorably with American goods. In 1971, for the first time in decades, the United States imported more than it exported. Because the amount of dollars in foreign hands exceeded U.S. gold reserves, the nation could no longer back up its currency with gold.

In 1971, Nixon abandoned the convertibility of dollars into gold and devalued the dollar to increase exports by making them cheaper. To protect domestic manufacturers,

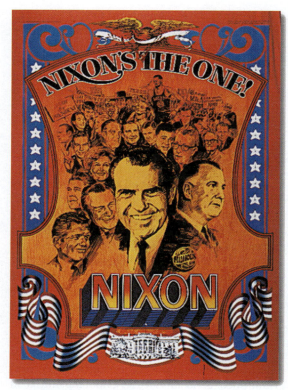

Nixon's 1968 Campaign

Attempting to appeal to a broad spectrum of voters, this poster includes the liberal Republican Nelson Rockefeller and the conservative Barry Goldwater. While Nixon's slogan "Champion of Forgotten America" spoke to whites alienated by Great Society programs for minorities and the poor, the poster's inclusion of black Republican senator Edward Brooke and basketball player Wilt Chamberlain gave a nod to African Americans. © David J. & Janice L. Frent Collection/CORBIS

he imposed a 10 percent surcharge on most imports, and he froze wages and prices, thus enabling the government to stimulate the economy without fueling inflation. In the short run, these policies worked, and Nixon was resoundingly reelected in 1972. Yet by 1974, unemployment had crept back up and inflation soared.

Skyrocketing energy prices intensified stagflation. Throughout the post–World War II economic boom, abundant domestic oil deposits and access to cheap Middle Eastern oil had encouraged the building of large cars and skyscrapers with no concern for fuel efficiency. By the 1970s, the United States was consuming one-third of the world's fuel resources.

In the fall of 1973, the United States faced its first energy crisis. Arab nations, furious at the administration's support of Israel during the Yom Kippur War (see "Shoring Up U.S. Interests around the World" in chapter 29), cut off oil shipments to the United States. Long lines formed at gas stations, where prices had nearly doubled, and many homes were cold. In response, Nixon authorized temporary emergency measures allocating petroleum and establishing a national 55-mile-per-hour speed limit to save gasoline. The energy crisis eased, but the nation had yet to come to grips with its seemingly unquenchable demand for fuel and dependence on foreign oil.

Responding to Environmental Concerns

The oil crisis dovetailed with a rising environmental movement, which was pushing the government to conserve energy and protect nature and human beings from the hazards of rapid economic growth. Like the conservation movement born in the Progressive Era (see "Roosevelt and Conservation" in chapter 21), the new environmentalists sought to preserve natural areas for recreational and aesthetic purposes and to conserve natural resources for future use. Especially in the West, the post–World War II explosion of economic growth and mushrooming population, with the resulting demands for electricity and water, made such efforts seem even more critical. Already in the 1950s, environmental groups mobilized to stop construction of dams that would disrupt national parks and wilderness.

The new environmentalists, however, went beyond conservationism to attack the ravaging effects of industrial development and technological advances on human life and health. The polluted air and water and spread of deadly chemicals attending economic growth threatened wildlife, plants, and the ecological balance that sustained human life. Biologist Rachel Carson drew national attention in 1962 with her best seller *Silent Spring*, which described the harmful effects of toxic chemicals such as the pesticide DDT. The Sierra Club and other older conservation organizations expanded their agendas, and a host of new groups arose. Millions of Americans expressed environmental concerns on the first observation of Earth Day in April 1970. The locally organized, grassroots events addressed a host of topics, including oil spills, water pollution, recycling, industrial waste, automobile emissions, and many more.

Responding to these concerns, Nixon built on efforts begun under Johnson. He called "clean

VISUAL ACTIVITY

Earth Day 1970

Building on the success of teach-ins about the Vietnam War, Democratic senator Gaylord Nelson of Wisconsin came up with the idea of Earth Day "to shake up the political establishment and force this issue [environmentalism] onto the national agenda." As a result, on April 22, 1970, some twenty million people participated in grassroots demonstrations throughout the country. Above are demonstrators in New York City. © Dennis Stock/Magnum Photos.

READING THE IMAGE: What aspects of environmentalism are reflected in the colored faces in the forefront and in the banner behind? Why might young people have been especially drawn to the environmental movement?

CONNECTIONS: What new environmental policies were enacted in the early 1970s?

air, clean water, open spaces . . . the birthright of every American" and urged Congress to "end the plunder of America's natural heritage." In 1970, he created the **Environmental Protection Agency (EPA)** to enforce environmental laws, conduct research, and reduce human health and environmental risks from pollutants. He also signed the landmark Occupational Safety and Health Act (OSHA), protecting workers against job-related accidents and disease, the Clean Air Act of 1970, restricting factory and automobile emissions of carbon dioxide and other pollutants, and the Endangered Species Act of 1973. Although environmentalists claimed that Nixon failed to do enough, pointing particularly to his veto of the Clean Water Act of 1972, which Congress overrode, his environmental initiatives far surpassed those of previous administrations.

Expanding Social Justice

Nixon's 1968 campaign had appealed to southern Democrats and white workers by exploiting hostility to black protest and new civil rights policies, but his administration had to answer to the courts and to Congress. In 1968, fourteen years after the *Brown* decision, school desegregation had barely touched the South. Like Eisenhower, Nixon was reluctant to use federal power to compel integration, but the Supreme Court overruled the administration's efforts to delay court-ordered desegregation. By the time Nixon left office, fewer than one in ten southern black children attended totally segregated schools.

Nixon also began to implement affirmative action among federal contractors and unions, and his administration awarded more government contracts and loans to minority businesses. Congress took the initiative in other areas. In 1970, it extended the Voting Rights Act of 1965, and in 1972 it strengthened the Civil Rights Act of 1964 by enlarging the powers of the Equal Employment Opportunity Commission. In 1971, Congress also responded to the massive youth movement with the Twenty-sixth Amendment to the Constitution, reducing the voting age to eighteen. And in 1973, Nixon signed legislation outlawing discrimination against people with disabilities in all programs receiving federal funds.

Several measures of the Nixon administration also specifically attacked sex discrimination, as the president confronted a growing feminist movement that included Republican women. Nixon vetoed a comprehensive child care bill and publicly opposed abortion, but he signed the pathbreaking Title IX, guaranteeing equality in all aspects of education, and allowed his Labor Department to push affirmative action.

President Nixon gave more public support for justice to Native Americans than to any other protest group. He told Congress that Indians were "the most deprived and most isolated minority group . . . the heritage of centuries of injustice." While not bowing to radical demands, his administration dealt cautiously with extreme protests such as the occupations of Alcatraz and the Bureau of Indian Affairs. Nixon signed measures recognizing claims of Alaskan and New Mexican Indians, restored tribal status to groups that undergone termination, and set in motion legislation restoring tribal lands and granting Indians more control over their schools and other service institutions.

REVIEW: How did liberal reform fare under President Nixon?

▶ Conclusion: Achievements and Limitations of Liberalism

Senate majority leader Mike Mansfield was not alone in concluding that Lyndon Johnson "has done more than FDR ever did, or ever thought of doing." Building on initiatives from John F. Kennedy's New Frontier, the Great Society expanded the New Deal's focus on economic security, refashioning liberalism to embrace individual rights and to extend material well-being to groups left out of or discriminated against in New Deal programs. Yet opposition to Johnson's leadership grew so strong that by 1968 his liberal vision lay in ruins. "How," he asked, "was it possible that all these people could be so ungrateful to me after I have given them so much?"

Fannie Lou Hamer could have responded by pointing out how slowly the government acted when efforts to win African Americans' rights met with violence. In addition, Hamer's failed attempts to use Johnson's antipoverty programs to help poor blacks in Mississippi reflected, in part, some of the more general shortcomings of the War on Poverty. Hastily planned and inadequately funded, antipoverty programs focused more on remediating individual shortcomings than on structural reforms that would ensure adequately paying jobs for all. Because Johnson launched an all-out war in Vietnam and refused to ask for sacrifices from prosperous Americans, the Great Society never commanded the resources necessary for victory over poverty.

Furthermore, black aspirations exceeded white Americans' commitment to genuine equality. Most whites supported overturning the crude and blatant forms of racism in the South, but when the civil rights movement attacked racial barriers long entrenched throughout the nation and sought equality in fact as well as in law, it faced a powerful backlash. By the end of the 1960s, the revolution in the legal status of African Americans was complete, but the black freedom struggle had lost momentum, and African Americans remained, with Native Americans and Chicanos, at the bottom of the economic ladder.

Johnson's critics overlooked the Great Society's more successful and lasting elements. Medicare and Medicaid continue to provide access to health care for the elderly and the poor. Federal aid for education and housing became permanent elements of national policy. Moreover, Richard Nixon's otherwise conservative administration implemented school desegregation in the South and affirmative action, initiated environmental reforms, and secured new rights for Native Americans and women. Women benefited from the decline of discrimination, and significant numbers of African Americans and other minority groups began to enter the middle class.

Yet the perceived shortcomings of government programs contributed to social turmoil and fueled the resurgence of conservative politics. Young radicals launched direct confrontations with the government and universities that together with racial conflict, escalated into political discord and social disorder. The Vietnam War polarized American society as much as did domestic change; it devoured resources that might have been used for social reform and undermined faith in government.

See the Selected Bibliography for this chapter in the Appendix.

MAKE IT STICK

LearningCurve

Go online and use LearningCurve to see what you know. Then review the key terms and answer the questions.

KEY TERMS

Civil Rights Act of 1964 (p. 799)
War on Poverty (p. 800)
Medicare and Medicaid (p. 800)
Voting Rights Act of 1965 (p. 801)
Immigration and Nationality Act of 1965 (p. 801)
Warren Court (p. 803)
black power movement (p. 808)
American Indian Movement (AIM) (p. 810)
Chicano movement (p. 811)
National Organization for Women (NOW) (p. 817)
Roe v. Wade **(p. 820)**
Environmental Protection Agency (EPA) (p. 823)

REVIEW QUESTIONS

1. How did the Kennedy and Johnson administrations exemplify a liberal vision of the federal government? (pp. 797–803)

2. How and why did the civil rights movement change in the mid-1960s? (pp. 804–809)

3. What other movements emerged in the 1960s, and how were they influenced by the black freedom struggle? (pp. 809–816)

4. What were the key goals of feminist reformers, and why did a countermovement arise to resist them? (pp. 817–819)

5. How did liberal reform fare under President Nixon? (pp. 819–824)

MAKING CONNECTIONS

1. Why were Johnson's reforms so much more far-reaching than Kennedy's?

2. What specific gains did the civil rights movement achieve in the 1960s and how were those gains limited?

3. What common characteristics did all reform movements of the 1960s share?

LINKING TO THE PAST

1. How was Lyndon Johnson's approach to poverty different from Franklin Roosevelt's? Which was more successful? (See chapter 24.)

2. What changes that had been taking place in the United States since 1940 laid a foundation for the rise of a feminist movement in the 1960s? (See chapters 25 and 26.)

29

Vietnam and the End of the Cold War Consensus

1961–1975

CONTENT LEARNING OBJECTIVES

After reading and studying this chapter, you should be able to:

- Describe President Kennedy's more aggressive implementation of the containment policy. Identify his approach toward the third world, and explain U.S. involvement in Cuba and Vietnam.

- Explain why Johnson escalated involvement in Vietnam and evaluate the effectiveness of this strategy.

- Explain how the war polarized the nation, and contributed to a year of upheaval in 1968.

- Describe Nixon's approach to communism, including his pursuit of détente with the Soviet Union and China, and anticommunism efforts in the third world. Explain how Nixon ended the war in Vietnam and the legacies of the war.

CAMOUFLAGE HELMET
The anti-war buttons on this military helmet reflect the bitter divisions that the Vietnam War produced in the United States, even among some of the soldiers themselves. Doug Steley B / Alamy.

LIEUTENANT FREDERICK DOWNS GREW UP ON AN INDIANA farm and enlisted in the army after three years of college. Leaving a ten-month-old daughter behind, he completed officer training and arrived in Vietnam in September 1967. The infantry platoon leader and his men went to Vietnam, "cocky and sure of our destiny, gung ho, invincible."

That confidence was tempered by the conditions they found in Vietnam. Unlike most of America's previous wars, there was no fixed battle front; helicopters ferried fighting units all over South Vietnam, as U.S. and South Vietnamese troops attempted to defeat the South Vietnamese insurgents and their North Vietnamese allies. In a civil war characterized by guerrilla tactics, Downs and his men struggled to distinguish civilians from combatants and destroyed villages just because they might be used by the enemy. He had faith that his country could win the war, but he found its ally, the South Vietnamese army, to be lazy and ineffective. "Maybe the people in Nam are worth saving, but their army isn't worth shit," he wrote in his memoir. Downs won several medals for bravery, but his one-year stint in Vietnam ended when a land mine blew off his left arm and wedged shrapnel into his legs and back.

Downs served in Vietnam at the height of a U.S. engagement that began with the Cold War commitments made by Presidents Harry S. Truman and Dwight D. Eisenhower. John F. Kennedy wholeheartedly took on those commitments, promising more flexible and vigorous efforts to thwart communism, declaring that the United States would "pay any price, bear any burden, meet any hardship, support any friend, oppose any foe to assure the survival and the success of liberty."

Kennedy sent increasing amounts of American arms and personnel to sustain the South Vietnamese government, and Lyndon B. Johnson dramatically escalated that commitment in 1965, turning a civil war among the Vietnamese into America's war. At peak strength in 1968, 543,000 U.S. military personnel served in Vietnam; all told, some 2.6 million saw duty there. Yet this massive intervention failed to defeat North Vietnam and created intense discord at home, "poisoning the soul of America," in Downs's words. Some Americans supported the government's goal in Vietnam and decried only the failure to pursue it effectively. Others believed that preserving a non-Communist South Vietnam was neither a vital interest of the United States nor within its capacity or moral right to achieve. Back home in college after months of surgery, Downs encountered a man who asked about the hook descending from his sleeve. When he said that he had lost his arm in Vietnam, the man shot back, "Serves you right."

This internal conflict was just one of the war's great costs. Like Downs, more than 150,000 soldiers suffered severe wounds, and more than 58,000 lost their lives. The war derailed domestic reform, depleted the federal budget, disrupted the economy, kindled domestic discord, and led to the violation of protesters' rights, leaving a lasting mark on the nation.

Even while fighting communism in Vietnam and in other third world countries, American leaders moved to ease Cold War tensions. After a tense standoff with the Soviet Union during the Cuban missile crisis, the United States began to cooperate with its Cold War enemy to limit the spread of nuclear weapons. In addition, Richard M. Nixon made a historic visit to China in 1972, abandoning the policy of isolating China and paving the way for normal diplomatic relations by the end of the 1970s.

► New Frontiers in Foreign Policy

John F. Kennedy moved quickly to pursue containment more aggressively and with more flexible means. In contrast to the Eisenhower administration's emphasis on nuclear weapons, Kennedy expanded both the nation's nuclear capacity and its ability to fight conventional battles and engage in guerrilla warfare. Kennedy also accelerated the nation's space exploration program and increased engagement with the third world. When the Soviets tried to establish a nuclear outpost in Cuba in 1962, Kennedy took the United States to the brink of war. Less dramatically, Kennedy sent increasing amounts of American arms and personnel to save the South Vietnamese government from Communist insurgents.

Meeting the "Hour of Maximum Danger"

Underlying Kennedy's foreign policy was an assumption that the United States had "gone soft—physically, mentally, spiritually soft," as he put it in 1960. Calling the Eisenhower era "years of drift and impotency," Kennedy warned in his inaugural address that the nation faced a grave peril: "Each day the crises multiply. . . . Each day we draw nearer the hour of maximum danger."

Although the president exaggerated the threat to national security, several developments in 1961 heightened the sense of crisis and provided a rationalization for his military buildup. Shortly before Kennedy's inauguration, Soviet premier Nikita Khrushchev publicly encouraged "wars of national liberation," thereby aligning the Soviet Union with independence movements in the third world that were often anti-Western. His statement reflected in part the Soviet competition with China for the allegiance of emerging nations, but U.S. officials saw it as a threat to the status quo of containment.

Cuba, just ninety miles off the Florida coast, posed the first crisis for Kennedy. The revolution led by Fidel Castro had moved Cuba into the Soviet orbit, and Eisenhower's Central Intelligence Agency (CIA) had been planning an invasion of the island by Cuban exiles living in Florida. Kennedy ordered the invasion to proceed even though his military advisers gave it only a fair chance of success.

On April 17, 1961, about 1,400 anti-Castro exiles trained and armed by the CIA landed at

CHRONOLOGY

1961	• Bay of Pigs invasion.
	• Berlin Wall erected.
	• Kennedy increases military aid to South Vietnam.
	• Peace Corps created.
1962	• Cuban missile crisis.
1963	• President Kennedy assassinated; Lyndon B. Johnson becomes president.
1964	• Gulf of Tonkin Resolution.
1965	• Operation Rolling Thunder begins.
	• First combat troops to Vietnam.
	• U.S. troops invade Dominican Republic.
1967	• Arab-Israeli Six-Day War.
1968	• Demonstrations against Vietnam War increase.
	• Tet Offensive.
	• Johnson decides not to seek second term.
	• Violence near Democratic convention in Chicago.
	• Richard M. Nixon elected president.
1969	• American astronauts land on moon.
1970	• Nixon orders invasion of Cambodia.
	• Students killed at Kent State and Jackson State.
1971	• *Pentagon Papers* published.
1972	• Nixon becomes first U.S. president to visit China.
	• Nixon signs arms limitation treaties with Soviets.
1973	• Paris Peace Accords.
	• CIA-backed military coup in Chile.
	• Arab oil embargo following Yom Kippur War.
1975	• North Vietnam takes over South Vietnam, ending the war.
	• Helsinki accords.

MAP ACTIVITY

Map 29.1   U.S. Involvement in Latin America and the Caribbean, 1954–1994
During the Cold War, the United States frequently intervened in Central American and Caribbean countries to suppress Communist or leftist movements.

READING THE MAP: How many and which Latin American countries did the United States invade directly? What was the extent of indirect U.S. involvement in other upheavals in the region?
CONNECTIONS: What role, if any, did geographic proximity play in U.S. policy toward the region? What was the significance of the Cuban missile crisis for U.S. foreign policy?

the **Bay of Pigs** on the south shore of Cuba (Map 29.1). Contrary to U.S. expectations, no popular uprising materialized to support the anti-Castro brigade. Kennedy refused to provide direct military support, and the invaders quickly fell to Castro's forces. The disaster humiliated Kennedy and the United States, posing a stark contrast to the president's inaugural promise of a new, more effective foreign policy. And it alienated Latin Americans who saw it as another example of Yankee imperialism.

Days before the Bay of Pigs invasion, the Soviet Union delivered a psychological blow when a Soviet astronaut became the first human to orbit the earth. Kennedy then called for a huge new commitment to the space program, with the goal of sending a man to the moon by 1970. Congress authorized the **Apollo program** and boosted appropriations for space exploration. John H. Glenn orbited the earth in 1962, and the United States beat the Soviets to the moon, landing two astronauts there in 1969.

Kennedy was determined to show American toughness to Khrushchev, but when the two met in June 1961 in Vienna, Austria, Khrushchev took the offensive. The stunned Kennedy reported privately, "He just beat [the] hell out of me. . . . If he thinks I'm inexperienced and have no guts . . . we won't get anywhere with him." Khrushchev demanded an agreement recognizing the existence of two Germanys, and he threatened U.S. occupation rights in and access to West Berlin.

The Soviet premier was concerned about the massive exodus of East Germans into West Berlin, a major embarrassment for the Communists. To stop this flow, in August 1961 East Germany erected a wall between East and West Berlin. With the **Berlin Wall** stemming the tide of escapees and Kennedy declaring West Berlin "the great testing place of Western courage and will," Khrushchev backed off from his threats. A decade later the superpowers recognized East and West Germany as separate nations and guaranteed Western access to West Berlin.

Kennedy used the Berlin crisis to add $3.2 billion to the defense budget. He increased draft calls and mobilized the reserves and National Guard, adding 300,000 troops to the military. This buildup of conventional forces provided for a "flexible response," offering "a wider choice than humiliation or all-out nuclear action," yet Kennedy also more than doubled the nation's nuclear force within three years.

New Approaches to the Third World

Complementing Kennedy's hard-line policy toward the Soviet Union were fresh approaches to the nationalist movements that had multiplied since the end of World War II. In 1960 alone, seventeen African nations gained their independence. Much more than his predecessors, Kennedy publicly supported third world aspirations, believing that the United States could win the hearts and minds of people in developing nations by helping to fulfill hopes for autonomy and material well-being.

Kennedy launched his most dramatic third world initiative in 1961 with an idea borrowed from Senator Hubert H. Humphrey: the **Peace Corps**. The program recruited young people to work in developing countries, attracting many who had been moved by Kennedy's appeal for idealism and sacrifice in his inaugural address. One volunteer spoke of having been "born between clean sheets when others were issued into the dust with a birthright of hunger." Peace Corps volunteers worked directly with local people, opening schools, providing basic health care, and assisting with agriculture and small economic enterprises. By the mid-1970s, more than 60,000 volunteers had served in Latin America, Africa,

Peace Corps Volunteers Build a School in Gabon
Young Americans who joined the Peace Corps helped increase food production, build public works, and curb diseases in developing countries, but the majority worked on educational projects. In 1964, these volunteers worked side-by-side with a local resident to build a school in the west central African nation of Gabon, which had won its independence from France in 1960. James P. Blair/National Geographic/Getty Images.

and Asia. Peace Corps projects were generally welcomed, but they did not address the receiving countries' larger economic and political structures.

Kennedy also used direct military means to bring political stability to the third world. He rapidly expanded the elite special forces corps established under Eisenhower to aid groups fighting against Communist-leaning movements. These counterinsurgency forces, including the army's Green Berets and the navy's SEALs, were trained to wage guerrilla warfare and equipped with the latest technology. They would get their first test in Vietnam.

The Arms Race and the Nuclear Brink

The final piece of Kennedy's foreign policy was to strengthen American nuclear dominance. He upped the number of nuclear weapons based in Europe from 2,500 to 7,200 and multiplied fivefold the supply of intercontinental ballistic missiles (ICBMs). Concerned that this buildup would enable the United States to launch a first strike and wipe out Soviet missile sites before they could respond, the Soviet Union stepped up its own ICBM program. Thus began the most intense arms race in history.

U.S. blockade zone
Range of Soviet missiles
Soviet missile and jet bomber base

Cuban Missile Crisis, 1962

The superpowers came perilously close to using their weapons during the **Cuban missile crisis** in 1962. Khrushchev decided to install nuclear missiles in Cuba to protect Castro's regime from further U.S. attempts at intervention and to balance the U.S. missiles aimed at the Soviet Union from Europe. On October 22, after the CIA showed Kennedy aerial photographs of missile launching sites under construction in Cuba, Kennedy announced that the military was on full alert and that the navy would turn back any Soviet vessel suspected of carrying offensive missiles to Cuba. He warned that any attack launched from Cuba would trigger a full nuclear assault against the Soviet Union.

With the superpowers on the brink of nuclear war, both Kennedy and Khrushchev also exercised caution. Kennedy refused advice from the military to bomb the missile sites. On October 24, Russian ships carrying nuclear warheads toward Cuba suddenly turned back. When one ship crossed the blockade line, Kennedy ordered the navy to follow the ship rather than attempt to stop it.

While Americans experienced the Cold War's most dangerous days, Kennedy and Khrushchev negotiated an agreement. The Soviets removed the missiles and pledged not to introduce new offensive weapons into Cuba. The United States promised not to invade the island. Secretly, Kennedy also agreed to remove U.S. missiles from Turkey. The Cuban crisis contributed to Khrushchev's fall from power two years later, while Kennedy emerged triumphant. The image of an inexperienced president fumbling the Bay of Pigs invasion gave way to that of a strong leader.

Having proved his toughness, Kennedy worked to ease superpower hostilities. In a major speech in June 1963, Kennedy called for a reexamination of Cold War assumptions, asking Americans "not to see conflict as inevitable." Acknowledging the superpowers' differences, Kennedy stressed what they had in common: "We all breathe the same air. We all cherish our children's future and we are all mortal." In August 1963, the United States, the Soviet Union, and Great Britain signed a limited nuclear test ban treaty, reducing the threat of radioactive fallout from nuclear testing and raising hopes for further superpower accord.

A Growing War in Vietnam

In 1963, Kennedy criticized the idea of "a Pax Americana enforced on the world by American weapons of war," but he had already increased the flow of those weapons into South Vietnam. Kennedy's strong anticommunism and attachment to a vigorous foreign policy prepared him to expand the commitment that he had inherited from Eisenhower.

By the time Kennedy took office, more than $1 billion in aid and seven hundred U.S. military advisers had failed to stabilize South Vietnam. Two major obstacles stood in the way. First, the South Vietnamese insurgents—whom Americans derisively called Vietcong—were an indigenous force whose initiative came from within. Because the Saigon government refused to hold elections, the rebels saw no choice but to take up arms. Increasingly, Ho Chi Minh's Communist government in North Vietnam supplied them with weapons and soldiers, aiming eventually to unify all of Vietnam.

Cuban Missile Crisis
During the Cuban missile crisis, while many Americans prepared for the worst possible outcome, U.S. Navy pilots dodged anti-aircraft fire to conduct low-altitude reconnaissance. This photo, taken on October 23, 1962, shows details of the missile site in Cuba. © Bettmann/Corbis.

Second, the South Vietnamese government refused to satisfy insurgents' demands, but the Army of the Republic of Vietnam (ARVN) could not defeat them militarily. Ngo Dinh Diem, South Vietnam's premier from 1954 to 1963, chose self-serving military leaders for their personal loyalty rather than for their effectiveness. Many South Vietnamese, the majority of whom were Buddhists, saw the Catholic Diem as a corrupt and brutal tool of the West. In contrast, Ho Chi Minh and his associates consolidated their power through land reform and their anticolonialist credentials on the one hand and imprisonment and mass executions on the other.

Stability and popular support enabled the Hanoi government in the North to wage war in the South. In 1960, it established the National Liberation Front (NLF), composed of South Vietnamese rebels but directed by the northern army. In addition, Hanoi constructed a network of infiltration routes, called the Ho Chi Minh Trail, in neighboring Laos and Cambodia, through which it sent people and supplies to help liberate the South (Map 29.2). Violence escalated between 1960 and 1963, bringing the Saigon government close to collapse.

In response, Kennedy gradually escalated the U.S. commitment. By spring 1963, military aid had doubled, and 9,000 Americans served in Vietnam as military advisers, occasionally participating in actual combat. The South Vietnamese government promised reform but never made good on its promises.

American officials assumed that technology and sheer power could win in Vietnam. Yet advanced weapons were ill suited to the guerrilla warfare practiced by the enemy, whose surprise attacks were designed to weaken support for the South Vietnamese government. Moreover, U.S. weapons and strategy harmed

MAP ACTIVITY

Map 29.2 The Vietnam War, 1964–1975
The United States sent 2.6 million soldiers to Vietnam and spent more than $150 billion on the longest war in American history, but it was unable to prevent the unification of Vietnam under a Communist government.

READING THE MAP: What accords divided Vietnam into two nations? When were these accords signed, and where was the line of division drawn? Through what countries did the Ho Chi Minh Trail go?
CONNECTIONS: What was the Gulf of Tonkin incident, and how did the United States respond? What was the Tet Offensive, and how did it affect the war?

the very people they were intended to save. Thousands of peasants were uprooted or fell victim to bombs—containing the highly flammable substance napalm—dropped by the South Vietnamese air force to quell the Vietcong. In 1962, U.S. planes began to spray herbicides such as **Agent Orange** to destroy the Vietcong's jungle hideouts and food supply.

With tacit permission from Washington, South Vietnamese military leaders executed a coup against Diem and his brother, who headed the secret police, in November 1963. Kennedy expressed shock at the murders but indicated no change in policy. In a speech to be given on the day he was assassinated, Kennedy referred specifically to Southeast Asia and warned, "We dare not weary of the task." At his death, 16,700 Americans were stationed in Vietnam, and 100 had died there.

REVIEW: Why did Kennedy believe that engagement in Vietnam was crucial to his foreign policy?

► Lyndon Johnson's War against Communism

Lyndon B. Johnson shared the Cold War assumptions that had shaped Kennedy's foreign policy. Retaining Kennedy's key advisers—Secretary of State Dean Rusk, Secretary of Defense Robert McNamara, and National Security Adviser McGeorge Bundy—Johnson continued the massive buildup of nuclear weapons as well as conventional and counterinsurgency forces. In 1965, he made the fateful decisions to order U.S. troops into combat in Vietnam and to initiate sustained bombing of the North. That same year, Johnson sent U.S. Marines to the Dominican Republic to crush a leftist rebellion.

An All-Out Commitment in Vietnam

The president who wanted to make his mark on domestic policy was compelled to deal with the commitments his predecessors had made in Vietnam. Some advisers, politicians, and international leaders questioned the wisdom of greater intervention there, recognizing the situation as a civil war rather than Communist aggression.

Agent Orange
For more than a decade, U.S. planes like these sprayed herbicides in Vietnam, Cambodia, and Laos, destroying 5.5 million acres of forest and farmland to eliminate sources of food and enemy hiding places. The most common chemical used, Agent Orange, contained dioxin, which left land contaminated for decades and ruined the health of Vietnamese and American soldiers.
Time & Life Pictures/Getty Images.

Most U.S. allies did not consider Vietnam crucial to containing communism and were not prepared to share the military burden. Senate majority leader Mike Mansfield wondered, "What national interests in Asia would steel the American people for the massive costs of an ever-deepening involvement?" Disregarding the opportunity for disengagement that these critics saw in 1964, Johnson expressed his own doubt privately: "I don't think it's worth fighting for and I don't think we can get out."

Like Kennedy, Johnson remembered how Truman had suffered politically when the Communists took over China, and he determined not "to be the president who saw Southeast Asia go the way China did." Along with most of his advisers, he believed that American credibility as a bulwark against communism was on the line, and he believed that conceding defeat in Vietnam would undermine his ability to achieve his Great Society.

Johnson understood the ineffectiveness of his South Vietnamese allies and agonized over sending young men into combat. Yet he continued to dispatch more military advisers, weapons, and economic aid and, in August 1964, seized an opportunity to increase the pressure on North Vietnam. While spying in the Gulf of Tonkin, off the coast of North Vietnam, two U.S. destroyers reported that North Vietnamese gunboats had fired on them (see Map 29.2). Johnson quickly ordered air strikes on North Vietnamese torpedo bases and oil storage facilities. Concealing the uncertainty about whether the second attack had even occurred, he won from Congress the **Gulf of Tonkin Resolution**, authorizing him to take "all necessary measures to repel any armed attacks against the forces of the United States and to prevent further aggression."

Soon after winning the election of 1964, Johnson widened the war. He dismissed reservations expressed by prominent Democrats and he rejected peace overtures from North Vietnam, which insisted on American withdrawal and a coalition government in South Vietnam as steps toward unification of the country. In February 1965, Johnson authorized Operation Rolling Thunder, a strategy of gradually intensified bombing of North Vietnam. Less than a month later, Johnson ordered the first U.S. combat troops to South Vietnam, and in July he shifted U.S. troops from defensive to offensive operations, dispatching 50,000 more soldiers (Figure 29.1). Although the administration downplayed the import of these decisions, they marked a critical turning point. Now it was genuinely America's war.

Preventing Another Castro in Latin America

Closer to home, Johnson faced persistent problems in Latin America. Thirteen times during the 1960s, military coups toppled Latin American

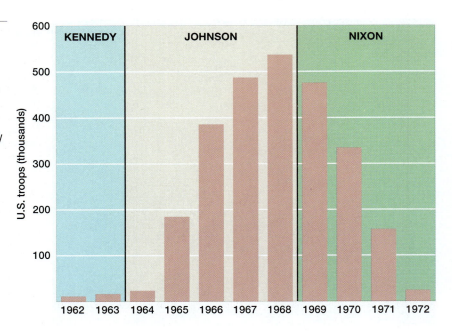

FIGURE 29.1 U.S. Troops in Vietnam, 1962–1972
The steepest increases in the American military presence in Vietnam came with Johnson's escalation of the war in 1965 and 1966. Although Nixon reduced troop levels significantly in 1971 and 1972, the United States continued massive bombing attacks.

governments, and local insurgencies grew apace. The administration's response varied from case to case but centered on the determination to prevent any more Castro-type revolutions.

In 1964, riots erupted in the Panama Canal Zone, instigated by Panamanians who viewed the United States as a colonial power because it had held the territory since early in the century (see "The Big Stick" in chapter 21). Johnson sent troops to quell the disturbance, but he also initiated negotiations that eventually returned the canal to Panamanian authority in 2000.

Elsewhere, Johnson's Latin American policy generated new cries of "Yankee imperialism." In 1961, voters in the Dominican Republic ousted a longtime dictator and elected a constitutional government headed by reformist Juan Bosch, who was overthrown by a military coup two years later. In 1965, when Bosch supporters launched an uprising against the military government, Johnson sent more than 20,000 soldiers to suppress what he perceived to be a leftist revolt and to take control of the island.

U.S. Troops in the Dominican Republic
These U.S. paratroopers were among the 20,000 troops sent to the Dominican Republic in April and May 1965. The invasion restored peace but kept the popularly elected government of Juan Bosch from regaining office. Dominicans greeted the U.S. troops with anti-American slogans throughout the capital, Santo Domingo. Bosch himself said, "This was a democratic revolution smashed by the leading democracy in the world." © Bettmann/Corbis.

This first outright show of Yankee force in Latin America in four decades damaged the administration. Although Johnson had justified intervention as necessary to prevent "another Cuba," no Communists were found among the rebels, and U.S. intervention kept the reform-oriented Boschists from returning to power. Moreover, the president had not consulted the Dominicans or the Organization of American States (OAS), to which the United States had promised it would respect national sovereignty in Latin America.

The Americanized War

Military success in the Dominican Republic no doubt encouraged the president to press on in Vietnam. From 1965 to early 1968, the U.S. military presence grew to more than 500,000 troops as it escalated attacks on North Vietnam and on its ally, the National Liberation Front, in South Vietnam. To minimize protest at home and avoid provoking Chinese or Soviet involvement, Johnson expanded the war slowly. "I'm going up old Ho Chi Minh's leg an inch at a time," he crowed.

Eventually, U.S. pilots dropped 643,000 tons of bombs on North Vietnam and more than twice that amount in the South, a total surpassing all the explosives the United States dropped in World War II. The North Vietnamese withstood monthly death tolls of more than 2,000 from the bombing. "They turned their hatred into activity," said one North Vietnamese about his comrades, who applied ingenuity and sheer effort to compensate for the destruction of transportation lines, industry sites, and power plants. In South Vietnam, the massive U.S. bombing campaign destroyed villages and fields, alienating the very population that the Americans had come to save and turning the former leading rice producer into a rice importer.

On the ground, General William Westmoreland's strategy of attrition was designed to seek out and kill the Vietcong and North Vietnamese regular army. With no fixed battle front, helicopters carried troops to conduct offensives all over South Vietnam, and officials calculated progress not in territory seized but in "body counts" and "kill ratios"—the number of enemies killed relative to the cost in American and ARVN lives. "To win a battle, we had to kill them," explained Lieutenant Frederick Downs. "For them to win, all they had to do was survive." After U.S. troops fought and bled to take ground, the enemy would withdraw, only to come back whenever they liked. The Americans "never owned anything except the ground they stood on." And even though U.S.-ARVN forces achieved high kill ratios, North Vietnam sent in or recruited new communist forces faster than they could be eliminated.

The Military Helicopter
In Vietnam, for the first time, helicopters played a central role in warfare. Choppers carried infantry units all over South Vietnam, transported artillery and ammunition, performed reconnaissance, picked up downed pilots, and evacuated the dead and wounded. Mounted with machine guns and grenade launchers, helicopters also served as attack vehicles. Here soldiers leap from a helicopter as they begin a reconnaissance mission. © Bettmann/Corbis.

Those Who Served

Teenagers fought the Vietnam War, in contrast to World War II, in which the average soldier was twenty-six years old. All the men in Frederick Downs's platoon were between the ages of eighteen and twenty-one, and the average age for all soldiers was nineteen. Until the Twenty-sixth Amendment to the Constitution dropped the voting age from twenty-one to eighteen in 1971, most soldiers could not even vote for the officials who sent them to war. Men of all classes had fought in World War II, but in Vietnam the poor and working class constituted about 80 percent of the troops. More privileged youths avoided the draft by using college deferments or family connections to get into the National Guard. Sent from Plainville, Kansas, to Vietnam in 1965, Mike Clodfelter could not recall "a single

middle-class son of the town's businessmen, lawyers, doctors, or ranchers from my high school graduating class who experienced the Armageddon of our generation."

Much more than World War II, Vietnam was a men's war. Because the United States did not undergo full mobilization for Vietnam, officials did not seek women's sacrifices for the war effort. Still, between 7,500 and 11,000 women served in Vietnam, the vast majority of them nurses. Some women were exposed to enemy fire, and eight died. Many more struggled with their helplessness to repair the maimed and dead bodies they attended.

Early in the war, African Americans constituted 31 percent of combat troops, often choosing the military over the meager opportunities in the civilian economy. Special forces ranger Arthur E. Woodley Jr. recalled, "The only way

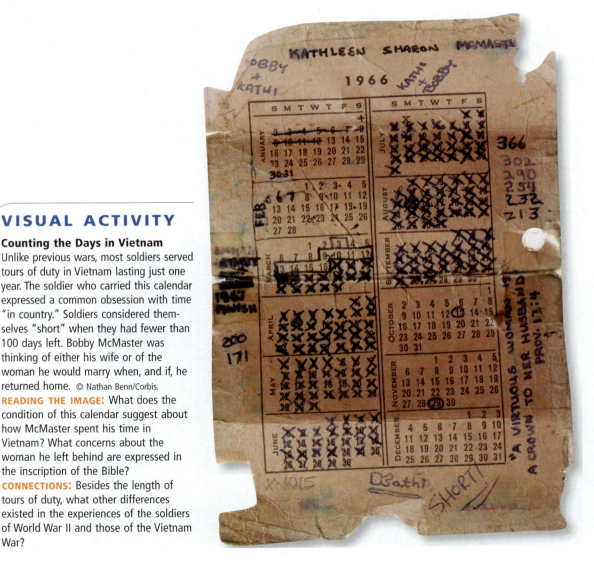

VISUAL ACTIVITY

Counting the Days in Vietnam
Unlike previous wars, most soldiers served tours of duty in Vietnam lasting just one year. The soldier who carried this calendar expressed a common obsession with time "in country." Soldiers considered themselves "short" when they had fewer than 100 days left. Bobby McMaster was thinking of either his wife or of the woman he would marry when, and if, he returned home. © Nathan Benn/Corbis.
READING THE IMAGE: What does the condition of this calendar suggest about how McMaster spent his time in Vietnam? What concerns about the woman he left behind are expressed in the inscription of the Bible?
CONNECTIONS: Besides the length of tours of duty, what other differences existed in the experiences of the soldiers of World War II and those of the Vietnam War?

I could possibly make it out of the ghetto was to be the best soldier I possibly could." Death rates among black soldiers were disproportionately high until 1966, when the military adjusted personnel assignments to achieve a better racial balance.

The young troops faced extremely difficult conditions. Frederick Downs's platoon fought in thick leech-ridden jungles, in rain and oppressive heat, always vulnerable to sniper bullets and land mines. Soldiers in previous wars had served "for the duration," but in Vietnam a soldier served a one-year tour of duty. A commander called it "the worst personnel policy in history," because men had less incentive to fight near the end of their tours, wanting merely to stay alive and whole. American soldiers inflicted great losses on the enemy, yet the war remained a stalemate. Many Vietnamese saw the South Vietnamese government as a tool of Western imperialism, full of graft and corruption. Moreover, in the intensified fighting and with the inability to distinguish friend from foe, ARVN and American troops killed and wounded thousands of South Vietnamese civilians and destroyed their villages. By 1968, nearly 30 percent of the population had become refugees. According to Downs, "all Vietnamese had a common desire—to see us go home." The failure to stabilize South Vietnam even as the U.S. military presence expanded enormously created grave challenges for the administration at home.

REVIEW: Why did massive amounts of airpower and ground troops fail to bring U.S. victory in Vietnam?

► A Nation Polarized

Soon President Johnson was fighting a war on two fronts, as domestic opposition to the war swelled after 1965. In March 1968, torn between his domestic critics and the military's clamor for more troops, Johnson announced a halt to the bombing, a new effort at negotiations, and his decision not to pursue reelection. Throughout 1968, demonstrations, violence, and assassinations convulsed the increasingly polarized nation. Vietnam took center stage in the election, and voters narrowly favored the Republican candidate, former vice president Richard Nixon, who promised to achieve "peace with honor."

The Widening War at Home

Johnson's authorization of Operation Rolling Thunder expanded the previously quiet doubts and criticism into a mass movement against the war. In April 1965, Students for a Democratic Society (SDS) recruited 20,000 people for the first major antiwar protest in Washington, D.C. Thousands of students protested against Reserve Officers Training Corps (ROTC) programs, CIA and defense industry recruiters, and military research projects on their campuses. Environmentalists attacked the use of chemical weapons, such as the deadly Agent Orange.

Antiwar sentiment entered society's mainstream. By 1968, media critics included the *New York Times*, the *Wall Street Journal*, *Life* magazine, and popular TV anchorman Walter Cronkite. Clergy, businesspeople, scientists, and physicians formed their own groups to pressure Johnson to stop the bombing and start negotiations. Prominent Democratic senators urged Johnson to substitute negotiation for force.

Opposition to the war took diverse forms, including letter-writing to officials, public demonstrations, draft card burnings, and attempts to stop troop trains. Although the peace movement never claimed a majority of the population, it focused media attention on the war and severely limited the administration's options. The twenty-year-old consensus around Cold War foreign policy had shattered.

Many refused to serve. The World Boxing Association stripped Muhammad Ali of his heavyweight title when he refused to "drop bombs and bullets on brown people in Vietnam while so-called negro people in Louisville are treated like dogs." More than 170,000 men gained conscientious objector status and performed nonmilitary duties at home or in Vietnam. About 60,000 fled the country to escape the draft, and more than 200,000 were accused of failing to register or of committing other draft offenses.

Opponents of the war held diverse views. Those who saw the conflict in moral terms wanted total withdrawal, claiming that their country had no right to interfere in a civil war and stressing the suffering of the Vietnamese people. A larger segment of antiwar sentiment reflected practical considerations—the belief that the war could not be won at a bearable cost. Those activists wanted Johnson to stop bombing North Vietnam and seek negotiations. Working-class people were no more antiwar than other groups, but they recognized the class dimensions of the war and the antiwar movement. A firefighter

VISUAL ACTIVITY

Mothers Against the War
Founded in 1961 to work for nuclear disarmament, Women Strike for Peace (WSP) began to protest the Vietnam War in 1963. As "concerned housewives" and mothers, members mobilized around the slogan "Not Our Sons, Not Your Sons, Not Their Sons." In February 1967, more than 2,000 women, some shown here, protested at the Pentagon, banging on doors, which were locked as they approached.

READING THE IMAGE: Notice how these women look. Do they appear threatening to you? Why do you think Pentagon officials locked them out? How do their banners draw on their roles as mothers?
CONNECTIONS: How are the antiwar arguments made by WSP similar to and different from other opponents of the Vietnam War?

optimistic statements and concealing officials' doubts about the possibility of success in Vietnam. Johnson ordered the CIA to spy on peace advocates, and without the president's specific authorization, the FBI infiltrated the peace movement, disrupted its work, and spread false information about activists. Even the resort to illegal measures failed to subdue the opposition.

The Tet Offensive and Johnson's Move toward Peace

The year 1968 was marked by violent confrontations around the world. Protests against governments erupted from Mexico City to Paris to Tokyo, usually led by students in collaboration with workers. (See "Beyond America's Borders," page 842.) American society became increasingly polarized. On one side, the so-called hawks charged that the United States was fighting with one hand tied behind its back and called for intensification of the war. The doves wanted de-escalation or withdrawal. As U.S. troop strength neared half a million and military deaths approached 20,000 by the end of 1967, most people were torn between weariness with the war and a desire to fulfill the U.S. commitment. As one woman said, "I want to get out but I don't want to give up."

whose son had died in Vietnam said bitterly, "It's people like us who give up our sons for the country."

The antiwar movement outraged millions of Americans who supported the war. Some members of the generation who had fought against Hitler could not understand younger men's refusal to support their government. They expressed their anger at war protesters with bumper stickers that read "America: Love It or Leave It."

By 1967, the administration realized that "discontent with the war is now wide and deep." President Johnson used various means to silence critics. He equated opposition to the war with communism and assistance to the enemy. His administration deceived the public by making

Grave doubts penetrated the administration itself. Secretary of Defense Robert McNamara, a principal architect of U.S. involvement, now believed that the North Vietnamese "won't quit no matter how much bombing we do." He feared for the image of the United States, "the world's greatest superpower, killing or seriously injuring 1,000 noncombatants a week, while trying to pound a tiny, backward nation into submission on an issue whose merits are hotly disputed." McNamara left the administration in early 1968 but did not publicly oppose the war.

A critical turning point came with the **Tet Offensive**. On January 30, 1968, the North Vietnamese and Vietcong launched a campaign of attacks on key cities, every major American base, and the U.S. Embassy in Saigon during Tet, the Vietnamese New Year holiday. Although the enemy lost ten times as many soldiers as ARVN and U.S. forces, Tet was psychologically devastating to the United States because it exposed the credibility gap between official statements and the war's reality. Newsman

Walter Cronkite wondered, "What the hell is going on? I thought we were winning the war." The attacks created a million more South Vietnamese refugees as well as widespread destruction. Public approval of Johnson's handling of the war dropped to 26 percent.

In the aftermath of Tet, Johnson conferred with advisers in the Defense Department and an unofficial group of foreign policy experts who had been key architects of Cold War since the 1940s. Dean Acheson, who had been Truman's secretary of state, summarized their conclusion: "We can no longer do the job we set out to do in the time we have left and we must begin to take steps to disengage."

On March 31, 1968, Johnson announced that the United States would sharply curtail its bombing of North Vietnam and that he was prepared to begin peace talks. He added the stunning declaration that he would not run for reelection. The gradual escalation of the war was over, and military strategy shifted from "Americanization" to "Vietnamization" of the war. But this was not

The Battle for Hue

During the Tet Offensive in early 1968, North Vietnamese troops captured the city of Hue, the ancient capital of Vietnam, rich with the country's history and culture. It took nearly a month of brutal house-to-house fighting for U.S. and ARVN troops to retake the city, 80 percent of which had by then been destroyed. Here U.S. Marines are pinned down near the center of Hue. © Bettmann/Corbis.

1968: A Year of Protest

To many people living through it, 1968 looked like the start of a worldwide political revolution. A surge of protests against the U.S. war in Vietnam and demands for greater democracy and economic justice jumped over borders and challenged authorities in many countries around the world. Although local grievances ignited many of the protests, a common feature of them all was the central role played by university students. The protests of 1968 unfolded rapidly, giving rise to excitement and apprehension. From February to December, demonstrations erupted in North and South America, Europe, and Asia. Many demonstrators expressed transnational solidarity by carrying the flag of Vietnam's National Liberation Front or placards bearing the image of Ernesto "Che" Guevara, a Latin American radical killed by the Bolivian military in 1967. And yet there was little international coordination of events or any shared plan for remaking the world.

One of the first large-scale protests occurred in February at West Berlin's Free University, where some 10,000 participants from ten countries at the "Vietnam Congress" called for "an international manifestation of solidarity" with the people of Vietnam. Protests continued throughout the spring, prompting the West German government to pass emergency laws to stifle disorder. In February and March, demonstrations flared up in Madrid, Warsaw, Rome, São Paulo, and London, met by police with clubs. As with the protesters,

police also took their cues from worldwide events, reacting more forcefully to demonstrations in light of commotions in other countries. Charges of police brutality, disseminated in television and newspaper reports, fed the cycle of protest further.

In April and May, violence erupted in the United States. Martin Luther King Jr.'s assassination on April 4 ignited riots in many U.S. cities. Less than a month later, students at Columbia University in New York City seized buildings and shut down the campus, leading to a bloody showdown between police and protesters.

In May, rebellion paralyzed France. It began with students' complaints about services at a university north of Paris and spread to the Sorbonne in the capital city. Police teargassed a small rally, only to face tens of thousands of students streaming into Paris over the next few days. Violence escalated as protesters barricaded streets. Independent radio stations broadcast live interviews with demonstrators, and soon a million people were in the streets. Workers joined the rebellion, shutting down factories across France. Students proclaimed that "exceptional domestic and international conditions" had brought powerless students and workers together around the world. By late May, France was in deep crisis.

Prague, the capital of Communist Czechoslovakia, also stirred in May. A liberal president, Alexander Dubček, pushed for

reforms against heavy-handed Soviet control, giving rise to hopes for greater freedom. Students demonstrated, and thousands signed manifestos. But this "Prague Spring" was cut short in August when Soviet tanks rumbled into the country and Dubček was arrested. Throughout Europe, students marched on Soviet embassies to protest the crackdown. At the same moment in the United States, Chicago police battled young protesters near the Democratic National Convention.

In July, Mexican police attacked marchers carrying posters of Fidel Castro and Che Guevara. When thousands rallied against the violence, police fired into the crowd, killing several students. Violent clashes continued into August and September, as activists protested the Olympic Games, scheduled to open in Mexico City in October. Insisting that the money spent on the Olympics should have been used to alleviate the country's widespread poverty, protesters chanted, "We don't want Olympic Games; we want revolution." The upcoming Olympics created pressure for the authorities to clear the city of dissidents. When some 10,000 students assembled for a rally on October 2, jeeps with machine guns arrived. At least 100 to 200 protesters were killed, and another several hundred were wounded. The Olympic Games went on as scheduled ten days later.

In the wake of the massacre, protesters staged demonstrations and

a shift in policy. The goal remained a non-Communist South Vietnam; the United States would simply rely more heavily on the South Vietnamese to achieve it.

Negotiations began in Paris in May 1968. The United States would not agree to recognize the Hanoi government's National Liberation Front, to allow a coalition government, or to withdraw. The North Vietnamese would agree to nothing less. Although the talks continued, so did the fighting.

Meanwhile, violence escalated at home. Protests struck two hundred college campuses in spring 1968. In the bloodiest action, students occupied buildings at Columbia University in New York City, condemning the university's war-related research and its treatment of African Americans. (See Chapter 28, "Documenting the American Promise," page 812.) When negotiations failed, university officials called in the city police, who cleared the buildings, injuring scores of demonstrators and arresting

Prague Spring
Czech students march in the capital of Czechoslovakia in support of proposals introduced in the spring of 1968 that would loosen Soviet control of the Communist satellite and promote freedom of speech and economic reform. Their banner reads, "Never Again with the Soviet Union," mocking an earlier Czecho-Stalinist slogan, "Forever with the Soviet Union."
© Bettmann/Corbis.

attacks on Mexican embassies in Latin America and Europe. By December, more episodes of violence against protesters occurred in Spain, Pakistan, and Northern Ireland. In the United States, violence diminished generally, but not in urban ghettos.

By year's end, a kind of stunned exhaustion set in. The Soviets had shut down the Prague Spring, the student-led protests in France and Germany had reached a stalemate, and Republican Richard Nixon had won the U.S. presidential election with promises to maintain law and order at home and to end the war in Vietnam. The year of global protest ended with despair and fear on all sides. Student protest did not disappear, but the excitement of worldwide revolutionary solidarity was blunted by the very real threat of fatal consequences faced by protesters.

America in a Global Context

1. What did the global protests of 1968 have in common?

2. How did protest in the United States differ from that in other countries, both in the composition of the protesters and in the reaction from authorities?

Connect to the Big Idea

C How did protest in the United States influence the Johnson administration and national politics?

hundreds. An ensuing student strike prematurely ended the academic year.

The Tumultuous Election of 1968

Disorder and violence also entered the election process. In June, two months after the murder of Martin Luther King Jr. and the riots that followed, antiwar candidate Senator Robert F. Kennedy, campaigning for the Democratic Party's presidential nomination, was killed by a Palestinian Arab refugee because of his support for Israel.

In August, protesters battled the police in Chicago, site of the Democratic Party national convention. Several thousand demonstrators came to the city, some to support peace candidate Senator Eugene McCarthy, others to cause disruption. On August 25, when demonstrators jeered at orders to disperse, police attacked them with tear gas and clubs. Street battles continued for three days, culminating in a police riot on the night of August 28. Taunted by the crowd, the police sprayed Mace and clubbed not only those who had come to provoke violence but also reporters, peaceful demonstrators, and convention delegates.

The bloodshed in Chicago had little effect on the convention's outcome. Vice President Hubert H. Humphrey believed that the nation was "throwing lives and money down a corrupt rat hole" in Vietnam, but he kept his views to himself and trounced the remaining antiwar candidate, McCarthy, by nearly three to one for the Democratic nomination.

In contrast to the turmoil in Chicago, the Republican convention met peacefully and nominated former vice president Richard Nixon. In a bid for southern support, Nixon chose Maryland governor Spiro T. Agnew for his running mate. A strong third candidate entered the race when the American Independent Party nominated staunch segregationist George C. Wallace. The former Alabama governor appealed to Americans' dissatisfaction with the reforms and rebellions of the 1960s and their outrage at the assaults on traditional values. Nixon guardedly played on resentments that fueled the Wallace campaign, calling for "law and order" and attacking liberal Supreme Court decisions, busing for school desegregation, and protesters.

The two major party candidates differed little on the central issue of Vietnam. Nixon promised "an honorable end" to the war but did not indicate how to achieve it. Humphrey had reservations about U.S. policy in Vietnam, yet as vice president he was tied to Johnson's policies. Winning nearly 13 percent of the total popular vote, Wallace produced the strongest third-party finish since 1924. Nixon edged out Humphrey by just half a million popular votes but won 301 electoral college votes to Humphrey's 191 and Wallace's 46 (Map 29.3). The Democrats maintained control of Congress.

The 1968 election revealed deep cracks in the coalition that had maintained Democratic dominance in Washington for the previous thirty years. Johnson's liberal policies on race shattered a century of Democratic Party rule in the South, which delivered all its electoral votes to Wallace and Nixon. Elsewhere, large numbers of blue-collar workers broke with labor's traditional alliance with the Democrats to vote for Wallace or Nixon, as did other groups that associated the Democrats with racial turmoil, poverty programs, changing sexual mores, and failure to turn the tide in Vietnam. These resentments would soon be mobilized into a resurging right in American politics (see chapter 30).

REVIEW: How did the war in Vietnam polarize the nation?

Protest in Chicago
The worst violence surrounding the 1968 Democratic National Convention in Chicago came near the Hilton Hotel, where most of the delegates stayed. When some 3,000 protesters marching toward the convention site came up against a line of police, the police attacked not only the demonstrators but also reporters, hotel guests, and bystanders, driving a crowd through the plate-glass window of the hotel and injuring hundreds. AP Photo/Michael Boyer.

Candidate	Electoral Vote	Popular Vote	Percent of Popular Vote
Richard M. Nixon (Republican)	301	31,770,237	43.4
Hubert H. Humphrey (Democrat)	191	31,270,533	42.7
George C. Wallace (American Independent)	46	9,906,141	13.5

Note: North Carolina split its vote, with one elector voting for Wallace.

MAP 29.3
The Election of 1968

these two nations might be used to help the United States extricate itself from Vietnam.

Following two years of secret negotiations, in February 1972 Nixon became the nation's first president to set foot on Chinese soil, an astonishing move by one who had built his career on anticommunism. Although his visit was largely symbolic, cultural and scientific exchanges followed, and American manufacturers began to find markets in China—small steps in the process of globalization that would take giant strides in the 1990s (see "The United States in a Globalizing World" in chapter 31). In 1979, the United States and China establish-ed formal diplomatic relations.

As Nixon and Kissinger had hoped, the warming of U.S.-Chinese relations furthered their strategy of **détente**, their term for easing conflict with the Soviet Union. Détente did not mean abandoning containment; instead it

▶ Nixon, Détente, and the Search for Peace in Vietnam

Richard M. Nixon hoped to make his mark on history by applying his broad understanding of international relations to a changing world. Diverging from Republican orthodoxy, he made dramatic overtures to the Soviet Union and China. Yet anticommunism remained central to U.S. policy. Nixon backed repressive regimes around the world and aggressively pursued the war in Vietnam, despite mounting opposition to his policies. He expanded the conflict into Cambodia and Laos and ferociously bombed North Vietnam. In the end, however, he was forced to settle for peace without victory.

Moving toward Détente with the Soviet Union and China

Nixon perceived that the "rigid and bipolar world of the 1940s and 1950s" was changing, and America's European allies were seeking to ease East-West tensions. Moreover, Nixon and his national security adviser Henry A. Kissinger believed they could exploit the increasing discord between the Soviet Union and China. In addition,

Nixon in China
"This was the week that changed the world," proclaimed President Nixon in February 1972, emphasizing the stunning turnaround in relations with America's former enemy, the People's Republic of China. Nixon's trip was planned to dramatize the event on television and, aside from criticism from some conservatives, won overwhelming support from Americans. Here, Nixon and his wife Pat visit the Great Wall of China. Nixon Presidential Materials Project, National Archives and Record Administration.

focused on issues of common concern, such as arms control and trade. Containment now would be achieved not just by military threat but also by ensuring that the Soviets and Chinese had stakes in a stable international order. Nixon's goal was "a stronger healthy United States, Europe, Soviet Union, China, Japan, each balancing the other."

Arms control, trade, and stability in Europe were three areas where the United States and the Soviet Union had common interests. In May 1972, Nixon visited Moscow, signing agreements on trade and cooperation in science and space. Most significantly, Soviet and U.S. leaders concluded arms limitation treaties that had grown out of the **Strategic Arms Limitation Talks (SALT)** begun in 1969, agreeing to limit antiballistic missiles (ABMs) to two each. Giving up pursuit of a defense against nuclear weapons was a crucial move because it denied both nations an ABM defense so secure against a nuclear attack that they would risk a first strike.

Although détente made little progress after 1974, U.S., Canadian, Soviet, and European leaders signed a historic agreement in 1975 in Helsinki, Finland, that formally recognized the post–World War II boundaries in Europe. Conservatives excoriated the **Helsinki accords** because they acknowledged the status quo: Soviet domination over Eastern Europe. Yet the agreement also committed the signing countries to recognize "the universal significance of human rights and fundamental freedoms." Dissidents in the Soviet Union and its Eastern European satellites used this official promise of rights to challenge the Soviet dictatorship and help force its overthrow fifteen years later.

Chile

Israeli Territorial Gains in the Six-Day War, 1967

Israel before 1967

Land gained by Israel in Six-Day War

Land returned to Egypt, 1973–1981

Shoring Up U.S. Interests around the World

Despite the thaw in U.S. relations with the Soviet Union and China, in other parts of the world Nixon and Kissinger continued to view left-wing movements as threats to U.S. interests and actively resisted social revolutions that might lead to communism. For example, the Nixon administration helped overthrow Salvador Allende, a self-proclaimed Marxist who was elected president of Chile in 1970. Since 1964, the CIA and U.S. corporations concerned about nationalization of their Chilean properties had assisted Allende's opponents. After Allende's election, Nixon ordered the CIA director to destabilize Allende's government and the economy, and in 1973, the CIA helped the Chilean military engineer a coup, killing Allende and establishing a brutal dictatorship under General Augusto Pinochet.

In other parts of the world, too, the Nixon administration backed repressive regimes. In southern Africa, it eased pressures on white minority governments that tyrannized blacks. In the Middle East, the United States sent massive arms shipments to support the shah of Iran's harsh regime because Iran had enormous petroleum reserves and seemed a stable anti-Communist ally.

Like his predecessors, Nixon pursued a delicate balance between defending Israel's security and seeking the goodwill of Arab nations strategically and economically important to the United States. Conflict between Israel and the Arab nations had escalated into the **Six-Day War** in 1967, when Israel attacked Egypt after Egypt had massed troops on the Israeli border and cut off sea passage to

Israel's southern port. Although Syria and Jordan joined the war on Egypt's side, Israel won a stunning victory, seizing the Sinai Peninsula and Gaza Strip from Egypt, the Golan Heights from Syria, and the West Bank, where hundreds of thousands of Palestinians lived, from Jordan.

That decisive victory did not quell Middle Eastern turmoil. In October 1973, on the Jewish holiday Yom Kippur, Egypt and Syria surprised Israel with a full-scale attack. When the Nixon administration sided with Israel, Arab nations retaliated with an oil embargo that created severe shortages in the United States. After Israel repulsed the attack, tensions remained high. The Arab countries refused to recognize Israel's right to exist, Israel began to settle its citizens in the West Bank and other territories it had seized during the Six-Day War, and no solution could be found for the Palestinian refugees who had been displaced by the creation of Israel in 1948. The simmering conflict contributed to anti-American sentiment among Arabs who viewed the United States as Israel's supporter.

Vietnam Becomes Nixon's War

"I'm going to stop that war. Fast," Nixon asserted. He gradually withdrew ground troops, but he was no more willing than his predecessors to be the president who let South Vietnam fall to the Communists. (See "Documenting the American Promise," page 848.) That goal was tied to the larger objective of maintaining American credibility. Regardless of the wisdom of the initial intervention, Kissinger asserted, "the commitment of 500,000 Americans has settled the importance of Vietnam. For what is involved now is confidence in American promises."

From 1969 to 1972, Nixon and Kissinger pursued a three-pronged approach. First, they tried to strengthen the South Vietnamese military and government. ARVN forces grew to more than a million, and the South Vietnamese air force became the fourth largest in the world. The United States also promoted land reform, village elections, and the building of schools, hospitals, and transportation facilities.

Second, Nixon gradually reduced the U.S. presence in Vietnam, a move that somewhat disarmed the antiwar movement at home. American forces decreased from 543,000 in 1968 to 140,000 by the end of 1971, although casualties remained high. Third, the United States replaced U.S. forces with intensive bombing. In spring 1969, Nixon began a ferocious air war in Cambodia, hiding it from Congress and the public for more than a year. Seeking to knock out North Vietnamese sanctuaries in Cambodia, Americans dropped more than 100,000 tons of bombs but succeeded only in sending the enemy to other hiding places. Echoing Johnson, Kissinger believed that a "fourth-rate power like North Vietnam" had to have a "breaking point," but the massive bombing failed to find it.

To support a new, pro-Western Cambodian government installed through a military coup and "to show the enemy that we were still serious about our commitment in Vietnam," Nixon ordered a joint U.S.-ARVN invasion of Cambodia in April 1970. He accompanied that action with a belligerent speech emphasizing the importance of U.S. credibility: "If when the chips are down, the world's most powerful nation

U.S. Invasion of Cambodia, 1970

VISUAL ACTIVITY

Pro-War Demonstrators
Supporters as well as opponents of the war in Vietnam took to the streets, as these New Yorkers did in support of the U.S. invasion of Cambodia in May 1970. Construction workers—called "hard hats"—and other union members marched with American flags and posters championing President Nixon's policies and blasting New York mayor John Lindsay for his antiwar position. Paul Fusco/Magnum Photos, Inc.
READING THE IMAGE: What do the hard hats in the photograph symbolize in terms of identity and politics?
CONNECTIONS: How were these union members related to the unraveling of the Democratic Party coalition?

Ending the War in Vietnam

By 1969, a clear majority of Americans wanted their country out of Vietnam. As these documents suggest, disagreement abounded over how to get out and what would be the consequences of U.S. withdrawal.

DOCUMENT 1
Richard Nixon Explains His Policy of Vietnamization, November 3, 1969

Elected on the promise of ending the war, Nixon adopted a plan of Vietnamization, strengthening South Vietnam so that it could take over its own defense and U.S. forces could come home. Here Nixon explains why he chose Vietnamization over immediate withdrawal.

But the question facing us today is: Now that we are in the war, what is the best way to end it?

In January I could only conclude that the precipitate withdrawal of American forces from Vietnam would be a disaster not only for South Vietnam but for the United States and for the cause of peace.

For the South Vietnamese, our precipitate withdrawal would inevitably allow the Communists to repeat the massacres which followed their takeover in the North 15 years before. . . .

For the United States, this first defeat in our Nation's history would result in a collapse of confidence in American leadership, not only in Asia but through-out the world. Three American Presidents have recognized the great stakes involved in Vietnam and understood what had to be done. . . .

For the future of peace, precipitate withdrawal would thus be a disaster of immense magnitude.

—A nation cannot remain great if it betrays its allies and lets down its friends.

—Our defeat and humiliation in South Vietnam without question would promote recklessness in the councils of those great powers who have not yet abandoned their goals of world conquest.

—This would spark violence wherever our commitments help maintain the peace in the Middle East, in Berlin, eventually even in the Western Hemisphere. . . .

I pledged in my campaign for the Presidency to end the war in a way that we could win the peace. I have initiated a plan of action which will enable me to keep that pledge.

The more support I can have from the American people, the sooner that pledge can be redeemed; for the more divided we are at home, the less likely the enemy is to negotiate at Paris.

Let us be united for peace. Let us also be united against defeat. Because let us understand: North Vietnam cannot defeat or humiliate the United States. Only Americans can do that.

Source: Excerpt from *Public Papers of the Presidents of the United States: Richard Nixon, 1969* (Washington, DC: U.S. Government Printing Office, 1971), 901–09.

DOCUMENT 2
A Vietnam Veteran Urges Congress to End the War, April 22, 1971

John Kerry was a decorated Navy lieutenant who served in Vietnam in 1968 and 1969 and later became a U.S. senator and secretary of state. He provided this testimony as a leader of Vietnam Veterans against the War.

acts like a pitiful helpless giant, the forces of totalitarianism and anarchy will threaten free nations" everywhere.

In response, more than 100,000 people protested in Washington, D.C., and students boycotted classes on hundreds of campuses. At a rally on May 4 at Kent State University in Ohio, National Guard troops opened fire, killing four and wounding ten others. "They're starting to treat their own children like they treat us," commented a black woman in Harlem. In a confrontation at Jackson State College in Mississippi on May 14, police shot into a dormitory, killing two black students.

Congressional reaction to the invasion of Cambodia revealed increasing concern about abuses of presidential power. In the name of national security, presidents since Franklin

. . . In our opinion, and from our experience, there is nothing in South Vietnam, nothing which could happen that realistically threatens the United States of America. And to attempt to justify the loss of one American life in Vietnam, Cambodia, or Laos by linking such loss to the preservation of freedom . . . is to us the height of criminal hypocrisy, and it is that kind of hypocrisy which we feel has torn this country apart. . . .

We found that not only was it a civil war, an effort by a people who had for years been seeking their liberation from any colonial influence whatsoever, but also we found that the Vietnamese . . . were hard put to take up the fight against the threat we were supposedly saving them from.

We found most people didn't even know the difference between communism and democracy. They only wanted to work in rice paddies without helicopters strafing them and bombs with napalm burning their villages and tearing their country apart. They wanted everything to do with the war, particularly with this foreign presence of the United States of America, to leave them alone in peace, and they practiced the art of survival by siding with whichever military force was present at a particular time, be it Vietcong, North Vietnamese, or American.

We found also that all too often American men were dying in those rice paddies for want of support from their allies. We saw firsthand how money from American taxes was used for a corrupt dictatorial regime. We saw that many people in this country had a one-sided idea of who was kept free by our flag, as blacks provided the highest percentage of casualties. We saw Vietnam ravaged equally by American bombs as well as by search and destroy missions, as well as by Vietcong terrorism, and yet we listened while this country tried to blame all of the havoc on the Viet Cong. . . .

We watched the U.S. falsification of body counts, in fact the glorification of body counts. We listened while month after month we were told the back of the enemy was about to break. We fought using weapons against "oriental human beings," with quotation marks around that. We fought using weapons against those people

which I do not believe this country would dream of using were we fighting in the European theater . . . .

Now we are told that the men who fought there must watch quietly while American lives are lost so that we can exercise the incredible arrogance of Vietnamizing the Vietnamese. . . .

Each day to facilitate the process by which the United States washes her hands of Vietnam someone has to give up his life so that the United States doesn't have to admit something that the entire world already knows, so that we can't say that we have made a mistake. Someone has to die so that President Nixon won't be, and these are his words, "the first President to lose a war."

We are asking Americans to think about that because how do you ask a man to be the last man to die in Vietnam? How do you ask a man to be the last man to die for a mistake?

Source: Excerpt from *Legislative Proposals Relating to the War in Southeast Asia, Hearings before the U.S. Senate Committee on Foreign Relations*, 92nd Cong. 180–210 (April–May 1971).

Questions for Analysis and Debate

1. Why did President Nixon consider it crucial to remain engaged until South Vietnam's freedom from Communist control was assured?

2. What reasons did Kerry give for placing U.S. withdrawal from Vietnam above all other considerations?

3. What did each man have to say about the disunity that racked the nation?

Connect to the Big Idea

C In which ways were Nixon and Kerry both correct about what happened when the United States left Vietnam?

Roosevelt had conducted foreign policy without the consent or sometimes even the knowledge of Congress—for example, Eisenhower in Iran and Johnson in the Dominican Republic. But in their determination to win the war in Vietnam, Johnson and Nixon had taken extreme measures to deceive the public and silence their critics. The aggression into Cambodia infuriated enough legislators that the Senate voted to terminate

the Gulf of Tonkin Resolution and to cut off funds for the Cambodian operation. The House refused to go along, but by the end of June 1970 Nixon had pulled all U.S. troops out of Cambodia.

In 1971, Vietnam veterans became a visible part of the peace movement, the first men in U.S. history to protest a war in which they had fought. They held a public investigation of "war crimes" in Vietnam, rallied in front of the Capitol,

U.S. Involvement in Vietnam

1954
French colonial presence ends with Vietnamese victory at Dien Bien Phu.

Geneva accords establish temporary division of North and South Vietnam at seventeenth parallel and provide for free elections.

United States joins with European, East Asian, and other nations to form Southeast Asia Treaty Organization.

Eisenhower administration begins to send weapons and military advisers to South Vietnam to bolster Diem government.

1955–1961
United States sends $800 million in aid to South Vietnamese army (ARVN) to support its struggle with South Vietnamese rebels and their North Vietnamese allies.

1961–1963
Under Kennedy administration, military aid to South Vietnam doubles, and number of military advisers reaches 9,000.

1963
South Vietnamese military overthrows Diem's government.

1964
President Johnson uses Gulf of Tonkin incident to escalate war.

1965
Johnson administration initiates Operation Rolling Thunder, intensifying bombing of North Vietnam.

1965–1967
Number of U.S. troops in Vietnam increases, reaching 543,000 in 1968, but U.S. and ARVN forces make only limited progress against the guerrilla forces, resulting in a stalemate.

1968
Tet Offensive causes widespread destruction and heavy casualties.

Johnson announces reduction in bombing of North Vietnam, plans for peace talks, and his decision not to run for another presidential term.

1969
Nixon administration initiates secret bombing of Cambodia, increases bombing of North Vietnam while reducing U.S. troops in the South, and pursues peace talks.

1970
Nixon orders joint U.S.-ARVN invasion of Cambodia.

1970–1971
U.S. troops in Vietnam decrease from 334,600 to 140,000.

1972
With peace talks stalled in December, Nixon administration orders the war's most devastating bombing of North Vietnam.

1973
On January 27, United States, North Vietnam, and South Vietnam sign formal accord in Paris marking end of U.S. involvement.

1975
North Vietnam launches new offensive in South Vietnam, defeating ARVN. Vietcong troops occupy Saigon, renaming it Ho Chi Minh City.

---

and cast away their war medals. In May 1971, veterans numbered among the 40,000 protesters who engaged in civil disobedience in an effort to shut down Washington. Officials made more than 12,000 arrests, which courts later ruled violations of protesters' rights.

After the spring of 1971, there were fewer massive antiwar demonstrations, but opposition to the war continued. Public attention focused on the court-martial of Lieutenant William Calley, which began in November 1970. During the trial, Americans learned that in March 1968 Calley's company had killed every inhabitant of the hamlet of My Lai, even though it had encountered no enemy forces and the four hundred villagers were nearly all old men, women, and children. The military covered up the massacre for more than a year before a journalist exposed it. Eventually, twelve officers and enlisted men were charged with murder or assault, but only Calley was convicted.

Administration policy suffered another blow in June 1971 when the New York Times published portions of the **Pentagon Papers**, a secret internal study of the war begun in 1967. Nixon sent government lawyers to court to stop further publication, in part out of fear that other information would be leaked. The Supreme Court, however, ruled that suppression of the publication violated the First Amendment. Subsequent circulation of the *Pentagon Papers*, which revealed pessimism among officials even as they made rosy promises, heightened disillusionment with the war by casting doubts on the government's credibility. More than 60 percent of Americans polled in 1971 considered it a mistake to have sent American troops to Vietnam; 58 percent believed the war to be immoral.

Military morale sank in the last years of the war. Having been exposed to the antiwar movement at home, many soldiers had less faith in the war than their predecessors had had. Racial tensions among the troops mounted, many soldiers sought escape in illegal drugs, and enlisted men committed hundreds of "fraggings," attacks on officers. In a 1971 report, *The Collapse of the Armed Forces*, a retired Marine Corps colonel described the lack of discipline: "Our army that now remains in Vietnam [is] near mutinous."

The Peace Accords

Nixon and Kissinger continued to believe that intensive firepower could bring the North Vietnamese to their knees. In March 1972, responding to a North Vietnamese offensive, the United States resumed sustained bombing of the North, mined Haiphong and other harbors for the first time, and announced a naval blockade. With peace talks stalled, in December Nixon ordered the most devastating bombing yet. Though costly to both sides, it brought renewed negotiations. On January 27, 1973, representatives of the United States, North Vietnam, South Vietnam, and the Vietcong (now called the Provisional Revolutionary Government) signed a formal peace accord in Paris. The agreement required removal of all U.S. troops and military advisers from South Vietnam but allowed North Vietnamese forces to remain. Both sides agreed to return prisoners of war. Nixon called the agreement "peace with honor," but in fact it allowed only a face-saving withdrawal.

Fighting resumed immediately among the Vietnamese. Nixon's efforts to support the South Vietnamese government, and indeed his ability to govern at all, were increasingly eroded by what came to be known as the Watergate scandal, which forced him to resign in 1974 (see "Watergate" in chapter 30). In 1975, North Vietnam launched a new offensive, seizing Saigon on April 30. The Americans remaining in the U.S. Embassy and their Marine guard hastily evacuated, along with 150,000 of their South Vietnamese allies. Confusion, humiliation, and tragedy marked the rushed departure. The United States lacked sufficient transportation capacity and time to evacuate all those who had supported the South Vietnamese government and were desperate to leave. A U.S. diplomat who escaped Saigon commented, "The rest of our lives we will be haunted by how we betrayed those people." Eventually more than 600,000 Vietnamese fled to the United States, but others lost their lives trying to escape, and many who could not get out suffered from political repression or poverty. (See "Seeking the American Promise," page 852.)

During the four years it took Nixon to end the war, he had expanded the conflict into Cambodia and Laos and launched massive bombing campaigns. Although increasing numbers of legislators criticized the war, Congress never denied the funds to fight it. Only after the peace accords did the legislative branch try to reassert its constitutional authority in the making of war. The War Powers Act of 1973 required the president to secure congressional approval for any substantial, long-term deployment of troops abroad. The new law, however, did little to dispel the distrust of government that resulted from Americans' realization that their leaders had not told the truth about Vietnam.

VISUAL ACTIVITY

Evacuating South Vietnam

As Communist troops approached Saigon in the spring of 1975, desperate South Vietnamese attempted to flee along with the departing Americans. Here they attempt to scale the wall of the U.S. Embassy to reach evacuation helicopters. Thousands were left behind, while South Vietnamese president Nguyen Van Thieu fled with fifteen tons of baggage on a U.S. plane. AP Images/Neal Ulevich.

READING THE IMAGE: What in the photo suggests the desperation of the South Vietnamese? How might this kind of photo have been viewed in the United States by supporters of the war and opponents?

CONNECTIONS: What besides the hasty departure from Saigon left a bitter taste in the mouths of Americans about the Vietnam War?

The war produced widespread criticism of the draft from both the left and right. As the United States withdrew from Vietnam, Nixon and Congress agreed to abandon conscription, which had been part of the Cold War since its beginning. Replacing the principle of obligation with the offer of opportunity, military leaders predicted that an all-volunteer army would make a more disciplined and professional fighting force. At the same time, ending service as a common

From the Fall of Saigon to the House of Representatives

Near the end of April 1975, eight-year-old Anh Quang Cao was rushed to the crowded airfield near Saigon, South Vietnam, along with his brother and sister and their aunt. Anh's father had been an officer in the South Vietnamese army, which put the entire family at extreme risk as North Vietnamese forces approached from the north for the final assault on Saigon. Anh's mother could send only three of her children; five more remained with their parents.

South Vietnam's capital was in an uproar, with tens of thousands of people who had worked for or cooperated with the Americans seeking escape. Two days after Anh's plane departed, rockets and artillery fire heavily damaged the airport. Thereafter helicopters shuttled thousands out of Saigon, as thousands more made for the docks to get passage on any seaworthy vessel, seeking safety in the U.S. Seventh Fleet, anchored just beyond Vietnamese territorial waters.

The ships and planes headed for a U.S. military base on Guam, where large camps had been rapidly constructed. Anh found himself among some 64,000 other refugees in a huge tent city where he located an uncle. Three times a day, the refugees lined up for eggs and bacon, hamburgers, mashed potatoes, fruit cocktail, and other classics of the American diet. The new food was part of a U.S. program dubbed "Operation New Life," to deal with the refugees, who by summer's end numbered 130,000.

After three weeks on Guam, Anh and his uncle joined an airlift of five hundred flights taking refugees to four military bases in the United States. The two landed at Fort Chaffee, an army reserve base in northwest Arkansas. There they received a limited program of English-language instruction and awaited resettlement.

The U.S. plan for the initial wave of refugees was to disperse them in small numbers to communities in all fifty states. Charitable groups were encouraged to sponsor refugees with minimal government assistance—just $500 per person. Anh and his uncle were sponsored by a Lutheran church in Goshen, Indiana, where the boy entered first grade and his uncle worked in a fast-food restaurant. Anh learned to love snow, and he took an Americanized name: Joseph Cao. After four years in Goshen, Cao and his uncle moved to Texas.

By 1978, a second and larger exodus began leaving Vietnam by water. Some 20,000 "boat people" per month paid extortionate fees and endured great hardship in crossing the South China Sea. As many as 100,000 people perished, but some half a million came to the United States, aided by the Refugee Act of 1980, which accepted the international definition of a refugee as a person unable to return to his or her country because of a "well-founded fear of persecution." Among late arrivals in this migration stream were Cao's family, his father severely traumatized by nearly seven years of imprisonment and torture in a Communist "reeducation" camp.

An able student, Cao completed high school and earned degrees in physics at Baylor University, in philosophy at Fordham University, and in law at Loyola University. Along the way, he continued to practice Catholicism, the religion of his childhood in Saigon, and he spent six

sacrifice distanced most Americans from the horrors of warfare and from the military, whose ranks would be disproportionately filled by poorer Americans and people of color.

The Legacy of Defeat

Four presidents had declared that the survival of South Vietnam was essential for U.S. containment policy, but their predictions that a Communist victory in South Vietnam would set the dominoes cascading did not materialize. Although Vietnam, Laos, and Cambodia all fell within the Communist camp in the spring of 1975, the rest of Southeast Asia did not. When China and Vietnam reverted to their historically hostile relationship, the myth of a monolithic Communist power overrunning Asia evaporated.

Antigovernment sentiment was just one of the war's legacies. It also left bitter divisions among Americans and diverted money from domestic programs. The war created federal budget deficits and triggered inflation that contributed to ongoing economic crises throughout the 1970s (as discussed in chapter 30).

The long pursuit of victory in Vietnam complicated the United States' relations with other nations, as even its staunchest ally, Britain,

Congressman Cao
Vietnamese American Ahn "Joseph" Cao speaks to constituents at a town hall meeting in Westwego, Louisiana, in August 2009. AP Photo/Bill Haber.

American to be elected to the House of Representatives.

In office, Cao proved to be an unconventional Republican, one who called out Wall Street bankers in hearings and cast the lone Republican vote in 2009 for the first version of what became Obamacare. His 2010 campaign for reelection was an uphill battle, and he lost decisively to a Democrat. Cao has returned to his law practice and his young family in New Orleans. In a *New York Times* interview before the election, he credited his philosophical studies for teaching him that "life is absurd but one cannot succumb to the absurdity of it," a fitting adage for his remarkable life story.

Questions for Consideration

1. Why did Cao have to leave Vietnam?

2. What made it possible for Cao to get to and succeed in the United States?

Connect to the Big Idea

○ In addition to the hundreds of thousands of Vietnamese immigrants who arrived in the United States, what were other unforeseen consequences of the Vietnam War?

years in a Jesuit seminary, doing missionary work among the poor. He became an immigration lawyer, serving the Vietnamese community in New Orleans. After Hurricane Katrina destroyed his house, he developed political ambitions and ran as an independent for the Louisiana state legislature.

Cao failed in that bid, but Republican Party leaders in Louisiana tapped him to run for Congress in 2008 in a heavily Democratic district. Cao agreed to run as a Republican, citing the debt he felt to John McCain, that year's Republican presidential candidate, who had spent five and a half years in a Hanoi POW camp. In a close election, Cao defeated the incumbent (who was embroiled in corruption charges) and thus became the first Vietnamese

---

doubted the wisdom of the war. The use of terrifying American power against a small Asian country alienated many in the third world and compromised efforts to win the hearts and minds of people in developing nations.

The cruelest legacy of Vietnam fell on those who had served. "The general public just wanted to ignore us," remembered Frederick Downs, while opponents of the war "wanted to argue with us until we felt guilty about what we had done over there." Many veterans believed in the war's purposes and felt betrayed by the government for not letting them win it. Others blamed the government for sacrificing the nation's youth in an immoral, unnecessary war, expressing their sense of the war's futility by referring to their dead comrades as having been "wasted." Veterans of color had more reason to doubt the nobility of their purpose. A Native American soldier assigned to resettle Vietnamese civilians found it to be "just like when they moved us to the rez [reservation]. We shouldn't have done that."

Because the Vietnam War was a civil war involving guerrilla tactics, combat was especially brutal (Table 29.1). The terrors of conventional warfare were multiplied, and so were the motivations to commit atrocities. The

TABLE 29.1	VIETNAM WAR CASUALTIES
United States	
Battle deaths	47,434
Other deaths	10,786
Wounded	153,303
South Vietnam	
Killed in action	110,357
Military wounded	499,026
Civilians killed	415,000
Civilians wounded	913,000
Communist Regulars and Guerrillas	
Killed in action	66,000

Source: U.S. Department of Defense.

1968 massacre at My Lai was only the most widely publicized war crime. To demonstrate the immorality of the war, peace advocates stressed the atrocities, contributing to a distorted image of the Vietnam veteran as dehumanized and violent.

Most veterans came home to public neglect. Government benefits were less generous to Vietnam veterans than they had been to those of the previous two wars. While two-thirds of Vietnam veterans said that they would serve again, and while most veterans readjusted well to civilian life, some suffered long after the war ended. The Veterans Administration estimated that nearly one-sixth of the veterans suffered from post-traumatic stress disorder, experiencing recurring nightmares, feelings of guilt and shame, violence, substance abuse, and suicidal tendencies. Thirty years after performing army intelligence work in Saigon, Doris Allen "still hit the floor sometimes when [she heard] loud bangs." Some who had served in Vietnam began to report birth defects, cancer, severe skin disorders, and other ailments. Veterans claimed a link between those illnesses and Agent Orange, which had exposed many to the deadly poison dioxin in Vietnam. In 1991, Congress began to provide assistance to veterans with diseases linked to the poison.

By then, the climate had changed. The war began to enter the realm of popular culture, with novels, TV shows, and hit movies depicting a broad range of military experience—from soldiers reduced to brutality, to men and women serving with courage and integrity. The incorporation of the Vietnam War into the collective experience was symbolized most dramatically in the Vietnam Veterans Memorial unveiled in Washington, D.C., in November 1982. Designed by Yale architecture student Maya Lin, the black, V-shaped wall inscribed with the names of 58,200 men and women lost in the war became one of the most popular sites in the nation's capital. In an article describing the memorial's dedication, a Vietnam combat veteran spoke to and for his former comrades: "Welcome home. The war is over."

REVIEW: What strategies did Nixon implement to bring American involvement in Vietnam to a close?

▶ Conclusion: An Unwinnable War

Lieutenant Frederick Downs fought in America's longest war. The United States spent $111 billion (more than $600 billion in 2014 dollars) and sent 2.6 million men and women to Vietnam. Of those, 58,200 never returned, and 150,000, like Downs, suffered serious injury. The war shattered consensus at home, increased presidential power at the expense of congressional authority and public accountability, weakened the economy, diminished trust in government, and contributed to the downfall of two presidents.

Even as Nixon and Kissinger took steps to ease Cold War tensions with the major Communist powers—the Soviet Union and China—they also acted vigorously throughout the third world to install or prop up anti-Communist governments. They embraced their predecessors' commitment to South Vietnam as a necessary Cold War engagement: To do otherwise would threaten American credibility and make the United States appear weak. Defeat in Vietnam did not make the United States the "pitiful helpless giant" predicted by Nixon, but it did mark a relative decline of U.S. power and the impossibility of containment on a global scale.

One of the constraints on U.S. power was the tenacity of revolutionary movements determined to achieve national independence. Overestimating the effectiveness of American technological superiority, U.S. officials badly underestimated the sacrifices that the enemy was willing to make and failed to realize how easily the United States could be perceived as a colonial intruder. A second constraint on Eisenhower, Kennedy, Johnson, and Nixon was their resolve to avoid a major confrontation with the Soviet Union or China. For Johnson, who conducted the largest escalation of the war, caution was critical so as not to provoke direct intervention by the Communist superpowers. After China exploded its first atomic bomb in 1964, the potential heightened for the Vietnam conflict to escalate into worldwide disaster.

Third, in Vietnam the United States sought to prop up an extremely weak ally engaged in a civil war. The South Vietnamese government failed to win the support of its people, and the intense devastation the war brought to civilians only made things worse. Short of taking over the South Vietnamese government and military, the United States could do little to strengthen South Vietnam's ability to resist communism.

Finally, domestic opposition to the war, which by 1968 had spread to mainstream America, constrained the options of Johnson and Nixon. As the war dragged on, with increasing American casualties and growing evidence of the damage being inflicted on innocent Vietnamese, more and more civilians wearied of the conflict. Even some who had fought in the war joined the peace movement, sending their military ribbons and bitter letters of protest to the White House. In 1973, Nixon and Kissinger bowed to the resoluteness of the enemy and the limitations of U.S. power. As the war wound down, passions surrounding it contributed to a rising conservative movement that would substantially alter the post–World War II political order.

See the Selected Bibliography for this chapter in the Appendix.

MAKE IT STICK

 **LearningCurve**

Go online and use LearningCurve to see what you know. Then review the key terms and answer the questions.

KEY TERMS

Bay of Pigs (p. 830)
Apollo program (p. 830)
Berlin Wall (p. 831)
Peace Corps (p. 831)
Cuban missile crisis (p. 832)
Agent Orange (p. 834)
Gulf of Tonkin Resolution (p. 835)
Tet Offensive (p. 841)
détente (p. 845)
Strategic Arms Limitation Talks (SALT) (p. 846)
Helsinki accords (p. 846)
Six-Day War (p. 846)
Pentagon Papers (p. 850)

REVIEW QUESTIONS

1. Why did Kennedy believe that engagement in Vietnam was crucial to his foreign policy? (pp. 829–834)

2. Why did massive amounts of airpower and ground troops fail to bring U.S. victory in Vietnam? (pp. 834–839)

3. How did the war in Vietnam polarize the nation? (pp. 839–844)

4. What strategies did Nixon implement to bring American involvement in Vietnam to a close? (pp. 845–854)

MAKING CONNECTIONS

1. How did Cuba figure into President Kennedy's Cold War policies?

2. Explain the Gulf of Tonkin incident and its significance to American foreign policy. How did President Johnson respond to the incident and why?

3. Discuss the range of American responses to the war in Vietnam. How did they change over time?

LINKING TO THE PAST

1. What commitments were made in the Truman and Eisenhower administrations that resulted in the United States' full-scale involvement in Vietnam? (See chapters 26 and 27.)

2. Compare American public sentiment during World War II to that during the Vietnam War. What policies, events, attitudes, and technological advancements contributed to the differences? (See chapter 25.)

30

America Moves to the Right

1969–1989

CONTENT LEARNING OBJECTIVES

After reading and studying this chapter, you should be able to:

- Explain the emergence of a grassroots conservative movement and how Nixon courted the right. Identify the events that led to Nixon's resignation.

- Describe the "outsider" presidency of Jimmy Carter and explain his approach to energy and environmental regulation, human rights, and the Cold War.

- Explain how Ronald Reagan's presidency represented ascendant conservatism and the factors behind Reagan's broad appeal.

- Explain how minority groups, feminists, gays and lesbians, and lower-income Americans struggled during the 1980s.

- Describe Reagan's foreign policies including increased militarization and interventions in the Middle East, Latin America, and Asia. Explain what led to a thaw in Soviet-American relations.

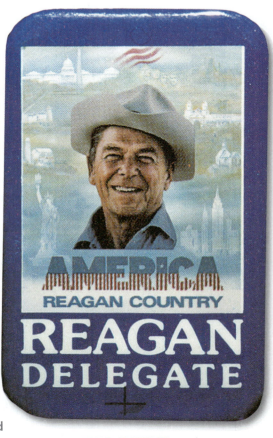

MAKING AMERICA "REAGAN COUNTRY"
This delegate badge from the 1980 Republican National Convention displayed key themes of Ronald Reagan's presidency and politics in the 1980s—patriotism and the rugged individualism of the West.
Division of Political History, National Museum of American History, Smithsonian Institution.

HEARING REPUBLICAN BARRY GOLDWATER ADDRESS THE Federation of Republican Women in 1963 was for Phyllis Schlafly "one of the most exciting days of my life." Schlafly wanted the United States to do more than just contain communism; she, like Goldwater, wanted to eliminate that threat entirely. She also wanted to cut back the federal government, especially its role in providing social welfare and enforcing civil rights. Goldwater's loss to Lyndon Johnson in 1964 did not diminish Schlafly's conservative commitment. She added new issues to the conservative agenda, cultivating a grassroots movement that would redefine the Republican Party and American politics into the twenty-first century.

Phyllis Stewart was born in St. Louis in 1924, attended Catholic schools, and worked her way through Washington University testing ammunition at a World War II defense plant. After earning a master's degree in government from Radcliffe College, she worked at the American Enterprise Institute, where she imbibed the think tank's conservatism. Returning to the Midwest, she married Fred Schlafly, an Alton, Illinois, attorney, and bore six children. "I don't think there's anything as much fun as taking care of a baby," Schlafly claimed.

Yet while insisting that caring for home and family was women's most important career, Schlafly spent much of her time writing or on the road, speaking, leading Republican women's organizations, and testifying before legislative committees. She ran twice for Congress but lost in her heavily Democratic district in Illinois. Her 1964 book, *A Choice Not an Echo*, pushed Barry Goldwater for president and sold more than three million copies. In 1967, she began publishing *The Phyllis Schlafly Report*, a monthly newsletter about current political issues. Throughout the 1950s and 1960s, Schlafly advocated stronger efforts to combat communism, a more powerful military, and a government less active in domestic affairs.

In the 1970s, Schlafly expanded the agenda of conservatism, addressing new issues such as feminism, abortion, gay rights, busing for racial integration, and religion in the schools. Her ideas resonated with Americans who were fed up with the expansion of government, liberal Supreme Court decisions, protest movements, and the loosening of moral standards that seemed to define the 1960s. Although Richard Nixon did not embrace the entire conservative agenda, he won the presidency in 1968 on a platform that sought to make the Republicans the dominant party by appealing to disaffected blue-collar and southern white Democrats. The Watergate revelations forced Nixon to resign the presidency in 1974, and his Republican successor, Gerald Ford, served only two years, but the political spectrum continued to shift right even when Democrat Jimmy Carter captured the White House in 1976. Carter advanced environmental and energy legislation, but an economy beset by both inflation and unemployment and a crisis in U.S.-Iranian relations burdened his campaign for reelection.

Consequently, Phyllis Schlafly's call for "a choice not an echo" was realized when Ronald Reagan won the presidency in 1980. Cutting taxes, government regulations, and social programs, expanding the nation's military capacity, and pressuring the Soviet Union and communism in the third world, Reagan addressed the hopes of the traditional right. Like Schlafly, he also championed the concerns of Christian conservatives, opposing abortion and sexual permissiveness as well as supporting a larger role for religion in public life.

Reagan's goals encountered resistance from feminists, civil rights groups, environmentalists, and others, and he failed to enact the entire conservative agenda. Although he enormously increased the national debt, and his aides engaged in illegal activities to thwart communism in Latin America, his popularity boosted the Republican Party. And Reagan's optimism and spirited leadership contributed to a revival in national pride and confidence.

The Phyllis Schlafly Report

Phyllis Schlafly began her newsletter in 1967. When Congress passed the ERA in 1972, the *Report* added antifeminism and other concerns of the New Right to its agenda. Schlafly had more than 35,000 newsletter subscribers in the mid-1970s; she also had many adversaries, including feminist leader Betty Friedan, who called her "a traitor to your sex." Courtesy of Phyllis Schlafly.

▶ Nixon, Conservatism, and Constitutional Crisis

Richard Nixon acquiesced in continuing most Great Society programs and even approved pathbreaking environmental, minority, and women's rights measures, prompting Phyllis Schlafly to call him "too liberal." Yet his public rhetoric and some of his actions signaled the country's rightward move. Whereas John F. Kennedy had summoned Americans to contribute to the common good, Nixon invited Americans to "ask—not just what will government do for me, but what can I do for myself?," invoking individualism and reliance on private enterprise rather than on government. These preferences would grow stronger in the nation during the 1970s and beyond, as a new strand of conservatism joined the older movement that focused on anticommunism, a strong national defense, and limited government in domestic affairs. New conservatives wanted to restore what they considered traditional moral values.

Just two years after Nixon won reelection by a huge margin, his abuse of power and efforts to cover up crimes committed by subordinates, revealed in the so-called Watergate scandal, forced the first presidential resignation in history. His successor, Gerald Ford, faced the aftermath of Watergate and severe economic problems, which returned the White House to the Democrats in 1976.

Emergence of a Grassroots Movement

Hidden beneath Lyndon B. Johnson's landslide victory over Arizona senator Barry Goldwater in 1964 lay a rising conservative movement. Defining his purpose as "enlarging freedom at home and safeguarding it from the forces of tyranny abroad," Goldwater argued that government intrusions into economic life hindered prosperity, stifled personal responsibility, and interfered with individuals' rights to determine their own values. Conservatives assailed big government in domestic affairs but demanded a strong military to eradicate "Godless communism."

The grassroots movement supporting Goldwater's nomination was especially vigorous in the South and West, and it included middle-class suburban women and men, members of the

CHRONOLOGY

1968	• Richard Nixon elected president.
1969	• Warren E. Burger appointed chief justice of Supreme Court.
1971	• Nixon vetoes child care bill.
1972	• Watergate arrests. • Nixon reelected president.
1974	• Nixon resigns; Gerald Ford becomes president. • Ford pardons Nixon.
1976	• Jimmy Carter elected president.
1977	• Panama Canal treaty.
1978	• *Regents of University of California v. Bakke*. • Congress deregulates airlines.
1979	• Camp David accords. • Carter establishes formal diplomatic relations with China. • Soviet Union invades Afghanistan. • Iranian hostage crisis begins. • Moral Majority founded.
1980	• Congress deregulates banking, trucking, and railroad industries. • Congress passes Superfund legislation. • Ronald Reagan elected president.
1981	• AIDS virus discovered. • Economic Recovery Tax Act.
1983	• Terrorist bomb kills 241 U.S. Marines in Beirut, Lebanon. • Reagan announces Strategic Defense Initiative ("Star Wars"). • Family Research Council founded.
1984	• Reagan reelected president.
1986	• Iran-Contra scandal.
1987	• INF agreement.
1988	• Civil Rights Restoration Act.

rabidly anti-Communist John Birch Society, and college students in the new Young Americans for Freedom (YAF). In 1966, California conservatives helped Ronald Reagan defeat the liberal incumbent governor, whom Reagan linked to the Watts riot, student disruptions at California universities, and rising taxes.

A number of Sun Belt characteristics made conservatism strong in places such as Orange County, California; Dallas, Texas; and Scottsdale, Arizona. Such predominantly white areas contained relatively homogeneous, skilled, and economically comfortable populations, as well as military bases and defense plants. The West harbored a long-standing tradition of Protestant morality, individualism, and opposition to interference by a remote federal government. That tradition continued with the emergence of the New Right, even though it was hardly

consistent with the Sun Belt's economic dependence on defense spending and on huge federal projects providing water and power for the burgeoning region. The South, which also benefited from military bases and the space program, shared the West's antipathy toward the federal government, but hostility to racial change was much more central to the South's conservatism. After signing the Civil Rights Act of 1964, President Johnson remarked privately, "I think we just delivered the South to the Republican Party." Indeed, Goldwater carried five southern states in 1964.

Grassroots movements proliferated around what conservatives believed marked the "moral decline" of their nation. For example, in 1962 Mel and Norma Gabler got the Texas board of education to drop books that they believed undermined "the Christian-Judeo morals, values, and standards as given to us by God through . . . the Bible." Sex education roused the ire of Eleanor Howe in Anaheim, California, who felt that "nothing [in the sex education curriculum] depicted my values." (See "Seeking the American Promise, page 862.) The U.S. Supreme Court's liberal decisions on school prayer, obscenity, and abortion also galvanized conservatives to restore "traditional values."

In the 1970s, grassroots protests against taxes grew alongside concerns about morality. As Americans struggled with inflation and unemployment, many found themselves paying higher taxes, especially higher property taxes as the value of their homes increased. Some were incensed to see their taxes fund government programs for people they considered undeserving. In 1978, Californians revolted in a popular referendum, reducing property taxes by more than one-half and limiting the state legislature's ability to raise taxes. What a newspaper called a "primal scream by the People against Big Government" spread to other states.

Law and order was yet another rallying cry of the right, who were concerned about skyrocketing rates of crime, which were due in part to baby boomers maturing into the age group most prone to crime. Conservatives lumped together common crime with civil disobedience and antiwar protest into a cry for law and order, and blamed liberals for Great Society programs that had failed to reduce crime, permissive attitudes toward protesters, and Supreme Court decisions that coddled criminals. A Pennsylvania man called "crime, the streets being unsafe, strikes, the trouble with the colored, all this dope-taking . . . a breakdown of the American way of life."

VISUAL ACTIVITY

The Tax Revolt

Neighbors gather in Los Angeles to rally for Proposition 13, an initiative launched by conservative Howard Jarvis in 1978. Many homeowners rallied to Jarvis's antitax movement because rising land values had increased their property taxes sharply. After Californians passed Proposition 13, some thirty-seven states cut property taxes, and twenty-eight reduced income taxes. The tax issue helped the Republican Party end decades of Democratic dominance. Tony Korody/Time & Life Pictures/Getty Images.

READING THE IMAGE: Considering the signs, what is the main concern of the people pictured here? What kinds of people are pictured here, and what are their stakes in the property tax issue?

CONNECTIONS: What other issues did Republicans capitalize on in the 1970s and 1980s?

Nixon Courts the Right

Highlighting law and order in his 1968 presidential campaign, Nixon appealed to "forgotten Americans, those who did not indulge in violence, those who did not break the law." He also exploited hostility to black protest and new civil rights policies to woo white southerners and a considerable number of northern voters away from the Democratic Party. As president, he used this "southern strategy" to make further inroads into traditional Democratic strongholds in the 1972 election.

Nixon reluctantly enforced court orders to achieve high degrees of integration in southern schools, but he resisted efforts to deal with segregation outside the South. In northern and western cities, where segregation resulted from discrimination in housing and in the drawing of school district boundaries, half of all African American children attended nearly all-black schools. After courts began to order the transfer of students between schools in white and black neighborhoods to achieve desegregation, busing became a hot-button issue. "We've had all we can

Percent of black students statewide attending schools more than 50% white

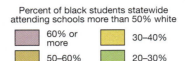

60% or more	30–40%
50–60%	20–30%
40–50%	20% or less

Integration of Public Schools, 1968

take of judicial interference with local schools," Phyllis Schlafly railed in 1972.

Children had been riding buses to school for decades, but busing for racial integration provoked fury. Violence erupted in Boston in 1974 when a district judge found that school officials had maintained what amounted to a dual system based on race and ordered busing "if necessary to achieve a unitary school system." The whites most affected by busing came from working-class families who were left in cities abandoned by the more affluent and whose children often rode buses to predominantly black, overcrowded schools with deficient facilities. Clarence McDonough denounced the liberal officials who bused his "kid half way around Boston so that a bunch of politicians can end up their careers with a clear conscience." African Americans themselves were conflicted about sending their children on long rides to schools where white teachers might not welcome or respect them.

Whites eventually became more accepting of integration, especially after the creation of schools with specialized programs and other

School Busing
Controversy over busing as a means to integrate public schools erupted in Boston during the 1974–1975 school year. Residents in white neighborhoods particularly opposed busing; they resented liberal, suburban judges assigning them the burden of integration. Clashes between blacks and whites in South Boston, and nearby communities, such as this one in February 1975 outside Boston's Hyde Park High School, prompted authorities to dispatch police to protect black students. AP Photo/DPG.

A Mother Campaigns for a Say in Her Children's Education

Although historians usually trace the rise of conservatism through national politics, the most intense political battles of the 1970s and 1980s were often fought at the local level. None were more impassioned than those mounted by parents over what their children should be taught in public schools. The introduction of sex education and new textbooks in the Kanawha County, West Virginia, school district prompted Alice Moore to challenge instruction she deemed harmful to her children and to organize a parents movement to gain control over their children's education.

The diverse school district of Kanawha County encompassed the state capital of Charleston as well as surrounding towns and rural areas containing chemical plants, coal mines, and small hamlets. Alice Moore, a native of Mississippi, and her husband, a fundamentalist minister, lived in a small town on the outskirts of Charleston, where their four children attended local schools. When she heard that sex education was coming to Kanawha County, she rallied like-minded citizens and won a seat on the five-person school board in 1970. She failed to terminate the sex education program, which she found a "humanistic, atheistic attack on God," but managed to dilute the curriculum.

The district's adoption of a new English language arts curriculum in 1974 provoked even greater controversy. The program, similar to those sweeping school districts across the country, sought to teach children about the larger world, incorporated writings by African Americans and other minority groups, and encouraged students to think critically and independently.

Objecting to both the philosophy and the content of the new curriculum, Moore began to mobilize opposition, calling on fundamentalist ministers and holding meetings in churches. In June 1974, at a meeting before an impassioned crowd of more than a thousand, she persuaded the school board to eliminate 8 of the curriculum's 325 books but failed to prevent adoption of the curriculum by a vote of three to two. Opponents then redoubled their efforts, echoing concerns that were energizing the Christian Right across the country.

Protesters condemned the new materials for containing what they considered disrespect for authority, American patriotism, and the free enterprise system. One of Moore's allies, a conservative chemical company owner, vilified the curriculum as "liberal, socialist, even communist-inspired." Textbook opponents also challenged the authority of distant "experts" to decide what was best for their children.

Furthermore, Moore and her supporters objected to the curriculum's multicultural materials, designed to illustrate the diversity of American society. They disliked the nonstandard English that appeared in some of the literature, as well as what they considered the "trashy" aspects of urban ghetto life. "Why the hell do we have to indoctrinate our children out here in semi-rural communities with the problems of the inner city?" a protester asked.

The new sexual permissiveness of the 1960s also aroused anti-textbook forces. The sexual realism in some of the materials inflamed fundamentalist protesters above all because it defied their belief in the system of right and wrong laid out in the Bible, which they interpreted literally. To Moore, morality was not a relative issue: "God's law is absolute."

Such deeply held beliefs inspired opponents to keep their children home when school opened in September, achieving a 20 percent absentee rate. Defying their union leadership, thousands of miners went out on a sympathy strike while protesters set up picket lines and staged demonstrations. Three schools were bombed, district headquarters were dynamited, and guns were fired on both sides. Anti-textbook supporters streamed into Charleston, including representatives from the Heritage Foundation, the John Birch Society, and the Ku Klux Klan. The violence gradually subsided, but protests went on through April 1975.

new mechanisms for desegregation offered greater choice. Nonetheless, integration propelled white flight to the suburbs. Nixon failed to persuade Congress to end court-ordered busing, but after he had appointed four new justices, the Supreme Court imposed strict limits on the use of that tool to achieve racial balance.

Nixon's judicial appointments also reflected the southern strategy. He criticized the Supreme Court under Chief Justice Earl Warren for being "unprecedentedly politically active . . . using their interpretation of the law to remake American society according to their own social, political, and ideological precepts." When

RE-ELECT
ALICE MOORE
FOR
BOARD of EDUCATION

Dear Friends,

The schools belong to the people who pay for them, not Washington Bureaucrats, not School Administrators, not National Education Organizations.

Nationally, education is costing us more than 61 billion dollars a year, more than is spent on education by all the rest of the world combined. This is a 1000 percent increase in 20 years while enrollment has barely doubled. Yet, almost one third of our high school graduates cannot pass college placement exams and this number increases annually.

Are your children getting the education you want for them? I am convinced most parents expect the schools, for which we pay and for which we provide the children, to:

- Offer the best academic education possible with emphasis on basic skills.

- Respect family privacy and our right as parents to rear our children according to our own moral, ethical and religious beliefs without interference.

- Provide a disciplined and morally up-lifting educational climate for the safety and peace of mind for both students and teachers. Stop coddling the class trouble-makers at the expense of serious minded students.

- Operate the schools as efficiently as private enterprise.

As a board member, I have tried to represent the public interest, not an Educational Bureaucracy. This is the kind of education I want for my five children. If this is what you want, please give me your vote and contact your friends on my behalf.

Sincerely yours,

(Mrs.) Alice Moore

The final board vote is at the May 11 primary. Democrats, Republicans and Independents can vote for me, for this non-partisan position.

Alice Moore Campaigns for the School Board
Alice Moore's 1976 campaign for reelection to the Kanawha County Board of Education emphasized moral issues and attacked government bureaucrats and expenditures. Her first campaign's slogan had been "We need a mother on the board of education." She bore her fifth child while on the board, but one of the policies she championed prohibited pregnant girls from attending high school because she considered them "disruptive." West Virginia State Archives.

looked favorably on different forms of government, or that "intrude[d] into the privacy of students' homes by asking personal questions about the inner feelings or behavior of themselves or their parents."

Conflicts over public school curricula, involving such topics as evolution, continued to strike communities throughout the nation, although none equaled the war in Kanawha County. Some conservative parents retreated from the public schools entirely. By 2007, parents were homeschooling 1.5 million children, and the number of private Christian schools soared, accommodating parents who, in Moore's words, "can't put their children in public schools and allow them to have their beliefs torn away." Those who believed that students should be exposed to a diversity of ideas in order to form their own beliefs were in the majority, but Christian conservatives such as Moore continued to fight for control over what their children were taught.

Questions for Consideration

1. What specific features of the new English arts curriculum did Alice Moore and her supporters object to?

2. What values of the New Right were reflected in the anti-textbook campaign?

Connect to the Big Idea

C How successful were conservatives in getting their objectives into federal policy?

The school board ended up keeping most of the new curriculum, but parents were allowed to designate those books they did not want their children to read. Many teachers avoided hassles by not using any of the new books. The board also set new guidelines for choosing textbooks, which included banning materials that contained profanity, that

Warren resigned in 1969, Nixon replaced him with Warren E. Burger, a federal appeals court judge who was a strict constructionist, inclined to interpret the Constitution narrowly and to limit government intervention on behalf of individual rights. The Burger Court restricted somewhat the protections of individual rights established by its predecessor, but it upheld many of the liberal programs of the 1960s. For example, *Regents of the University of California v. Bakke* (1978) limited the range of affirmative action but allowed universities to attack the results of past discrimination if they avoided strict quotas and racial classifications.

Nixon's southern strategy and other repercussions of the civil rights revolution of the 1960s ended the Democratic hold on the "solid South." Beginning in 1964, a number of conservative southern Democrats changed their party affiliation; by 2005, Republicans held the majority of southern seats in Congress and governorships in seven southern states.

In addition to exploiting racial fears, Nixon appealed to anxieties about women's changing roles and new demands. In 1971, he vetoed a bill providing federal funds for day care centers with a message that combined the old and new conservatism. Parents should purchase child care services "in the private, open market," he insisted, not rely on government. He appealed to social conservatives by warning about the measure's "family-weakening implications." In response to the movement to liberalize abortion laws, Nixon sided with "defenders of the right to life of the unborn," anticipating the Republican Party's eventual embrace of the issue.

The Election of 1972

Nixon's ability to attract Democrats and appeal to concerns about Vietnam, race, law and order, and traditional morality heightened his prospects for reelection in 1972. Although the war in Vietnam continued, antiwar protests diminished with the decrease in American ground forces and casualties. Nixon's economic initiatives had temporarily checked inflation and unemployment (see "Extending the Welfare State and Regulating the Economy" in chapter 28), and his attacks on busing and antiwar protesters had won increasing support from the right.

A large field of contenders vied for the Democratic nomination, including New York congresswoman Shirley Chisholm, the first African American to make a serious bid for the presidency. South Dakota senator George S. McGovern came to the Democratic convention as the clear leader and was easily nominated by the delegates, who included unprecedented numbers of women, minorities, and youth. But McGovern struggled as Republicans portrayed him as a left-wing extremist, while his support for busing, a generous welfare program, and immediate withdrawal from Vietnam alienated some Democrats.

Nixon achieved a landslide victory, winning 60.7 percent of the popular vote and every state except Massachusetts. Although the Democrats maintained control of Congress, Nixon won majorities among traditional Democrats—southerners, Catholics, urbanites, and blue-collar workers. The president, however, had little time to savor his triumph, as revelations began to emerge about crimes committed to ensure the victory.

Watergate

During the early-morning hours of June 17, 1972, five men working for Nixon's reelection crept into Democratic Party headquarters in the Watergate complex in Washington, D.C. Intending to repair a bugging device installed in an earlier break-in, they were discovered and arrested. Nixon and his aides then tried to cover up the intruders' connection to administration officials, setting in motion the scandal reporters dubbed **Watergate**.

Nixon was not the first president to lie to the public or to misuse power. Every president since Franklin D. Roosevelt had enlarged the powers of his office in the name of national security. This expansion of executive powers, often called the "imperial presidency," weakened the traditional checks and balances on the executive branch and opened the door to abuses. No president, however, had dared go as far as Nixon, who saw opposition to his policies as a personal attack and was willing to violate the Constitution to stop it.

Upon learning of the Watergate arrests, Nixon plotted to manipulate the Central Intelligence Agency (CIA) and Federal Bureau of Investigation (FBI) to conceal links between the burglars and the White House, while publicly denying any connection. In April 1973, after investigations by a grand jury and the Senate suggested that White House aides had been involved in the cover-up effort, Nixon accepted official responsibility for Watergate but denied any knowledge of the break-in or cover-up. He also announced the resignations of three White House aides and the attorney general. In May, he authorized the appointment of an independent special prosecutor, Archibald Cox, to conduct an investigation.

Meanwhile, speaking before a Senate investigating committee headed by Democrat Samuel J. Ervin of North Carolina, White House counsel John Dean described projects to harass "enemies" through tax audits and other illegal means and implicated the president in efforts to cover up the Watergate break-in. Another White House aide struck the decisive blow when he disclosed that all conversations in the Oval Office were taped. Both Cox and Ervin immediately asked for the tapes related to

Watergate. When Nixon refused, citing executive privilege and separation of powers, they won a unanimous decision from the Supreme Court ordering him to release the tapes.

Additional disclosures exposed Nixon's misuse of federal funds and tax evasion. In August 1973, Vice President Spiro Agnew resigned after an investigation revealed that he had taken bribes while governor of Maryland. Nixon's choice of House minority leader Gerald Ford of Michigan to succeed Agnew won widespread approval, but Agnew's resignation further tarnished the administration, and Nixon's popular support plummeted.

In February 1974, the House of Representatives voted to begin an impeachment investigation. In April, Nixon began to release edited transcripts of the tapes. The transcripts revealed Nixon's orders to aides in March 1973: "I don't give a shit what happens. I want you all to stonewall it, let them plead the Fifth Amendment, cover up or anything else, if it'll save it—save the plan." House Republican leader Hugh Scott of Pennsylvania called the documents a "deplorable, shabby, disgusting, and immoral performance by all."

In July 1974, the House Judiciary Committee voted to impeach the president on three counts: obstruction of justice, abuse of power, and contempt of Congress. Seven or eight Republicans on the committee sided with the majority, and it seemed certain that the House would follow suit. Georgia state legislator and civil rights activist Julian Bond commented, "The prisons of Georgia are full of people who stole $5 or $10, and this man tried to steal the Constitution."

To avoid impeachment, Nixon announced his resignation to a national television audience on August 8, 1974. Acknowledging some incorrect judgments, he insisted that he had always tried to do what was best for the nation. The next morning, Nixon ended a rambling, emotional farewell to his staff with some advice: "Always give your best, never get discouraged, never get petty; always remember, others may hate you, but those who hate you don't win unless you hate them, and then you destroy yourself." Had he followed his own advice, he might have saved his presidency.

The Ford Presidency and the 1976 Election

Upon taking office, Gerald R. Ford announced, "Our long national nightmare is over." But he shocked many Americans one month later by granting Nixon a pardon "for all offenses against the United States which he . . . has committed or may have committed or taken part in" during his presidency. Prompted by Ford's concern for Nixon's health and by his hope to get the country beyond Watergate, this sweeping pardon saved Nixon from nearly certain indictment and trial, and it provoked a tremendous outcry from Congress and the public. Democrats made impressive gains in the November congressional elections, while Ford's action gave Nixon a new political life. Without having to admit that he had violated the law, Nixon rebuilt his image over the next two decades into that of an elder statesman. Thirty of his associates ultimately pleaded guilty to or were convicted of crimes related to Watergate.

Nixon Resigns
The first U.S. president to resign, Nixon refused to admit guilt, even though tapes of his conversations indicated that he had obstructed justice, abused his power, and lied. In the decades after his resignation, he gradually rehabilitated his reputation and became an elder statesman. Here, he and his wife Pat are escorted by his successor Gerald Ford, and his wife Betty, as they leave the White House. © CORBIS

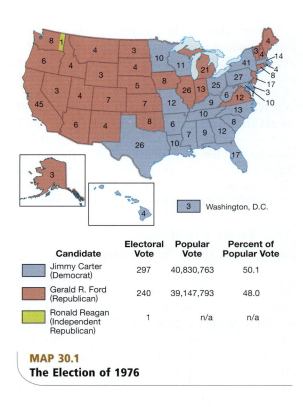

Candidate	Electoral Vote	Popular Vote	Percent of Popular Vote
Jimmy Carter (Democrat)	297	40,830,763	50.1
Gerald R. Ford (Republican)	240	39,147,793	48.0
Ronald Reagan (Independent Republican)	1	n/a	n/a

MAP 30.1
The Election of 1976

Congress's efforts to guard against the types of abuses revealed in the Watergate investigations had only limited effects. The Federal Election Campaign Act of 1974 established public financing of presidential campaigns and imposed some restrictions on contributions to curtail the selling of political favors. Yet politicians found other ways of raising money—for example, through political action committees (PACs), to which individuals could contribute more than they could to candidates. Moreover, the Supreme Court struck down limitations on campaign spending as violations of freedom of speech. Ever-larger campaign donations flowed to candidates from interest groups, corporations, labor unions, and wealthy individuals.

Congressional investigating committees discovered a host of illegal FBI and CIA activities stretching back to the 1950s, including surveillance of American citizens like Martin Luther King. Jr., harassment of political dissenters, and plots to assassinate Fidel Castro and other foreign leaders. In response to these revelations, President Ford established new controls on covert operations, and Congress created permanent committees to oversee the intelligence agencies. Yet these measures did little to diminish the public's cynicism about their government or to curtail massive government surveillance of

private communications that accompanied terrorist threats to the United States in the twenty-first century. Disillusionment grew as the Ford administration struggled with serious economic problems: a low growth rate, high unemployment, a foreign trade deficit, and soaring energy prices. Ford carried these burdens into the election campaign of 1976, while contending with a major challenge from the Republican right. Blasting Nixon's and Ford's foreign policy of détente for causing the "loss of U.S. military supremacy," California governor Reagan came close to capturing the nomination.

The Democrats nominated James Earl "Jimmy" Carter Jr., former governor of Georgia. A graduate of the U.S. Naval Academy, Carter spent seven years as a nuclear engineer in the navy before returning to Plains, Georgia, to run the family peanut farming business. Carter stressed his faith as a "born-again Christian" and his distance from the government in Washington. Although he selected liberal senator Walter F. Mondale of Minnesota as his running mate, Carter's nomination nonetheless marked a rightward turn in the party.

Carter had considerable appeal as a candidate who carried his own bags, lived modestly, and taught a Bible class at his Baptist church. He also benefited from Ford's failure to solve the country's economic problems, which helped him win the traditional Democratic coalition of blacks, organized labor, and ethnic groups and even recapture some of the white southerners who had voted for Nixon in 1972. Still, Carter received just 50 percent of the popular vote to Ford's 48 percent, while Democrats retained substantial margins in Congress (Map 30.1).

REVIEW: How did Nixon's policies reflect the increasing influence of conservatives on the Republican Party?

▶ The "Outsider" Presidency of Jimmy Carter

Carter promised a government that was "competent" as well as "decent, open, fair, and compassionate." He also warned Americans "that even our great Nation has its recognized limits, and that we can neither answer all questions nor solve all problems." Carter's humility and personal integrity helped revive trust in the presidency, but he faltered in the face of domestic and foreign crises.

Energy shortages and stagflation worsened, exposing Carter's deficiencies in working with Congress and rallying public opinion. He achieved notable advances in environmental and energy policies, and he oversaw foreign policy successes concerning the Panama Canal, China, and the Middle East. Yet near the end of his term, Soviet-American relations deteriorated, new crises emerged in the Middle East, and the economy plummeted.

Retreat from Liberalism

Jimmy Carter vowed "to help the poor and aged, to improve education, and to provide jobs," but at the same time "not to waste money." When these goals conflicted, reform took second place to budget balancing. Carter's approach pleased Americans unhappy about their tax dollars being used to benefit the disadvantaged while stagflation eroded their own standard of living. But his fiscal stringency frustrated liberal Democrats pushing for major welfare reform and a national health insurance program. Carter himself said, "In many cases I feel more at home with the conservative Democratic and Republican members of Congress than I do with the others."

Although Carter did fulfill liberals' desire to make government more inclusive by appointing unprecedented numbers of women and minorities to cabinet, judicial, and diplomatic posts, a number of factors thwarted Carter's policy goals. His outsider status helped him win the election but left him without strong ties to party leaders in Congress. Democrats complained that Carter flooded them with comprehensive proposals without consultation or a strategy to get them enacted. Even if he had possessed Lyndon Johnson's political skills, Carter might not have done much better. The economic problems he inherited—unemployment, inflation, and sluggish economic growth—confounded economic doctrine. Usually, rising prices accompanied a humming economy with a strong demand for labor. Now, however, stagflation burdened the economy with both steep inflation and high unemployment and contributed to a federal budget deficit.

Carter first targeted unemployment, signing bills that pumped $14 billion into the economy through public works and public service jobs programs and cutting taxes by $34 billion. Unemployment receded, but then inflation surged. Working people, wrote one journalist, "winced and ached" as their paychecks bought less and less, "hollowing their hopes and dreams, their plans for a house or their children's college education." To curb inflation, Carter curtailed federal spending, and the Federal Reserve Board tightened the money supply. Not only did these measures fail to halt inflation, which surpassed 13 percent in 1980, but they also contributed to rising unemployment, reversing the gains made in Carter's first two years.

Carter's commitment to holding down the federal budget frustrated Democrats pushing for comprehensive welfare reform, national health insurance, and a substantial jobs program that

Jimmy Carter Honors Martin Luther King Jr.
In 1979, President Carter and his wife Rosalyn observed King's birthday at Ebenezer Baptist Church in Atlanta, Georgia, where King had been pastor. Carter pushed to establish King's birthday as a national holiday, but Congress did not enact such a law until 1983. With the Carters are Martin Luther King Sr.; Andrey Young, Carter's ambassador to the United Nations; and King's widow Coretta Scott King. Jimmy Carter Presidential Library.

VISUAL ACTIVITY

The Fuel Shortage

This billboard appeared in 1980 while Iran held Americans hostage in Tehran (see page 872). The Iranian revolution brought to power Ayatollah Ruholla Khomeini, pictured on the billboard, and created gasoline shortages and rising gas prices, vexing motorists all over the United States. The ad urges drivers to observe the fuel-saving 55-mile-per-hour speed limit imposed in 1974 during the first oil crisis. Outdoor Advertising Association of America (OAAA) Archives, David M. Rubenstine Rare Books & Manuscript Library, Duke University

READING THE IMAGE: What assumptions does the billboard make about Americans' reactions to the Iran hostage crisis? What reasons does the ad give for drivers to respect the speed limit? What reasons are not mentioned?

CONNECTIONS: What impact did the hostage and oil crises have on American politics?

would make government the employer of the last resort. His refusal to propose a comprehensive national health insurance plan, long a key Democratic Party objective, led to a bitter split with Massachusetts senator Ted Kennedy, who fought Carter for the 1980 presidential nomination. Carter's agreement to legislation to ensure solvency in the Social Security system resulted in higher payroll taxes on lower- and middle-income Americans.

By contrast, corporations and wealthy individuals gained from new legislation, such as a sharp cut in the capital gains tax. When the Chrysler Corporation approached bankruptcy, Congress provided $1.5 billion in loan guarantees to bail out the auto giant. Congress also acted on Carter's proposals to deregulate airlines in 1978 and the banking, trucking, and railroad industries in 1980, beginning a policy turn toward implementing conservatives' attachment to a free market and unfettered private enterprise.

Energy and Environmental Reform

Complicating the government's battle with stagflation was the nation's enormous energy consumption and dependence on foreign nations to fill one-third of its energy demands. Consequently, Carter proposed a comprehensive program to conserve energy, and he elevated its importance by establishing the Department of Energy. Beset with competing demands among energy producers and consumers, Congress picked Carter's program apart. The **National Energy Act of 1978** penalized manufacturers of gas-guzzling automobiles and provided other incentives for conservation and development of alternative fuels, such as wind and solar power, but the act fell far short of a long-term, comprehensive program.

In 1979, a new upheaval in the Middle East, the Iranian revolution, created the most severe energy crisis yet. In midsummer, shortages caused 60 percent of gasoline stations to close down, resulting in long lines and high prices. In response, Congress reduced controls on the oil and gas industry to stimulate American production and imposed a windfall profits tax on producers to redistribute some of the profits they would reap from deregulation.

European nations were just as dependent on foreign oil as was the United States, but they more successfully controlled consumption. They levied high taxes on gasoline, causing people to rely more on public transportation and manufacturers to produce more energy-efficient cars. In the automobile-dependent United States, however, with inadequate public transit, a sprawling population, and an aversion to taxes, politicians dismissed that approach. By the end of the century, the United States, with 6 percent of the world's population, would consume more than 25 percent of global oil production (Figure 30.1 and Map 30.2).

A vigorous environmental movement opposed nuclear energy as an alternative fuel, warning of radiation leakage, potential accidents, and the hazards of radioactive wastes. In 1976, hundreds of members of the Clamshell Alliance went to jail for attempting to block construction of a nuclear power plant in Seabrook, New Hampshire; other groups sprang up across the country to demand an environment safe from nuclear radiation and waste. The perils of nuclear energy claimed international attention in March 1979, when a meltdown of the reactor core was narrowly averted at the nuclear facility near Harrisburg, Pennsylvania. Popular opposition and the great expense of building nuclear power plants stalled further development

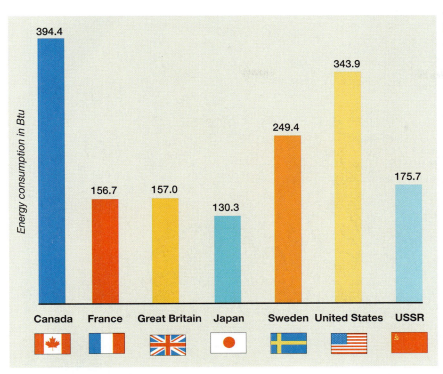

FIGURE 30.1 **Global Comparison: Energy Consumption Per Capita, 1980**
By 1980, the United States consumed more energy than most other industrialized nations, with a per capita rate of consumption that was more than double that of Britain, France, and Japan and nearly twice as high as that of the Soviet Union. A number of factors influence a nation's energy consumption, including standard of living, climate, size of landmass, population distribution, availability and price of energy, and government policies.

of the industry, which provided 10 percent of the nation's electricity in the 1970s.

A disaster at Love Canal in Niagara Falls, New York, advanced other environmental goals by underscoring the human costs of unregulated development. Residents suffering high rates of serious illness discovered that their homes sat amid highly toxic waste products from a nearby chemical company. Finally responding to the residents' claims in 1978, the state of New York agreed to help families relocate, and the Carter administration sponsored legislation in 1980 that created the so-called Superfund, $1.6 billion for cleanup of hazardous wastes left by the chemical industry around the country.

Carter also signed bills to improve clean air and water programs; to expand the Arctic National Wildlife Refuge (ANWR) preserve in Alaska; and to control strip-mining, which left destructive scars on the land. During the 1979 gasoline crisis, Carter attempted to balance the development of domestic fuel sources with environmental concerns, winning legislation to conserve energy and to provide incentives for the development of solar energy and environmentally friendly alternative fuels.

Promoting Human Rights Abroad

"We're ashamed of what our government is as we deal with other nations around the world," Jimmy Carter charged, promising to reverse

U.S. support of dictators, secret diplomacy, interference in the internal affairs of other countries, and excessive reliance on military solutions. Human rights formed the cornerstone of his approach. The Carter administration applied economic pressure on governments that denied their citizens basic rights, refusing aid or trading privileges to nations such as Chile and El Salvador, as well as to the white minority governments of Rhodesia and South Africa. Yet in other instances, Carter sacrificed human rights ideals to strategic and security considerations, invoking no sanctions against repressive governments in Iran, South Korea, and the Philippines.

Carter's human rights principles faced another test when a popular movement overthrew an oppressive dictatorship in Nicaragua. U.S. officials were uneasy about the leftist Sandinistas who led the rebellion and had ties to Cuba. Once they assumed power in 1979, however, Carter recognized the new government and sent economic aid, signaling that the way a government treated its citizens was as important as how anti-Communist and friendly to American interests it was.

Applying moral principles to relations with Panama, Carter sped up negotiations over control of the Panama Canal and in 1977 signed a treaty providing for Panama's takeover of the canal in 2000. Supporters viewed the treaty as restitution for the use of U.S. power to gain control of the territory in 1903. Opponents insisted

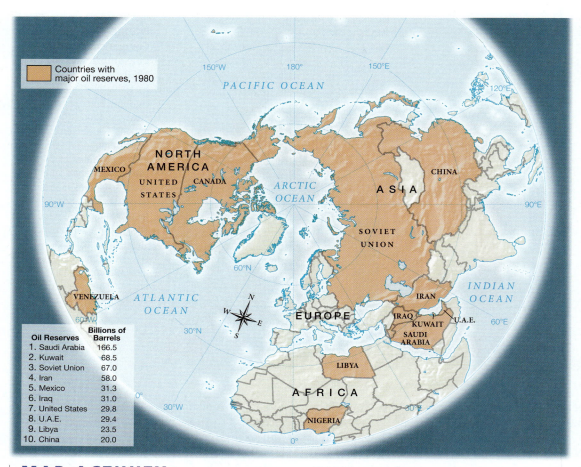

Oil Reserves	Billions of Barrels
1. Saudi Arabia	166.5
2. Kuwait	68.5
3. Soviet Union	67.0
4. Iran	58.0
5. Mexico	31.3
6. Iraq	31.0
7. United States	29.8
8. U.A.E.	29.4
9. Libya	23.5
10. China	20.0

MAP ACTIVITY

Map 30.2   Worldwide Oil Reserves, 1980
Geologists and engineers can estimate the size of "proved oil reserves," quantities recoverable with existing technology and prices. In 1980, worldwide reserves were estimated at 645 billion barrels. Recovery of reserves depends on many factors, including the location of the oil. Large portions of U.S. reserves, for example, lie under the Gulf of Mexico, where it is expensive to drill and where hurricanes can disrupt operations.

READING THE MAP: Where did the United States rank in 1980 in the possession of oil reserves? About what portion of the total oil reserves were located in the Middle East?
CONNECTIONS: When during the 1970s did the United States experience oil shortages? What caused these shortages?

on retaining the vital waterway. "We bought it, we paid for it, it's ours," claimed Ronald Reagan during the presidential primaries of 1976. It took a massive effort by the administration to get Senate ratification of the **Panama Canal treaty**.

Seeking to promote peace in the Middle East, Carter seized on the courage of Egyptian president Anwar Sadat, the first Arab leader to risk his political career by talking directly with Israeli officials. In 1979, Carter invited Sadat and Israeli prime minister Menachem Begin to Camp David, Maryland, where he applied his tenacious diplomacy for thirteen days. These talks led to the **Camp David accords**, whereby Egypt became

the first Arab state to recognize Israel, and Israel agreed to gradual withdrawal from the Sinai Peninsula, which it had seized in the 1967 Six-Day War (Map 30.3). Although Israel maintained control of other Palestinian land (the West Bank and Gaza) and continued to settle Israelis there, Carter had nurtured the first meaningful steps toward peace in the Middle East.

The Cold War Intensifies

Consistent with his human rights approach, Carter preferred to pursue national security through nonmilitary means and initially sought accommodation with the nation's Cold War enemies. Following up on Nixon's initiatives, in 1979 he opened formal diplomatic relations with the People's Republic of China and signed a second strategic arms reduction treaty with Soviet premier Leonid Brezhnev.

Yet that same year, Carter decided to pursue a military buildup when the Soviet Union invaded neighboring Afghanistan, whose recently installed Communist government was threatened by Muslim opposition (see Map 30.3). Carter imposed economic sanctions on the Soviet Union, barred U.S. participation in the 1980 Summer Olympic Games in Moscow, and obtained legislation requiring all nineteen-year-old men to register for the draft.

Claiming that Soviet actions jeopardized oil supplies from the Middle East, the president announced the "Carter Doctrine," threatening the use of any means necessary to prevent an outside force from gaining control of the Persian Gulf. His human rights policy fell by the wayside as the United States stepped up aid to the military dictatorship in Afghanistan's neighbor, Pakistan, and the CIA funneled secret aid through Pakistan to the Afghan rebels. Finally, Carter called for hefty increases in defense spending.

Events in Iran also encouraged this hard-line approach. Generous U.S. arms and aid had not enabled the shah to crush Iranian dissidents who still resented the CIA's role in the overthrow of the Mossadegh government in 1953 (see "Interventions in Latin America and the Middle East" in chapter 27), condemned the shah's brutal attempts to silence opposition, and detested his adoption of Western culture and values.

MAP ACTIVITY

Map 30.3   The Middle East, 1948–1989

Determination to preserve access to the rich oil reserves of the Middle East and commitment to the security of Israel were fundamental—and often conflicting—principles of U.S. foreign policy in that region.

READING THE MAP: Where did the United States become involved diplomatically or militarily in the Middle East between 1948 and 1989?

CONNECTIONS: What role did U.S. foreign policy regarding the Middle East and events in Israel play in provoking the 1973 Arab oil embargo against the United States? What precipitated the taking of U.S. hostages in Iran in 1979?

American Hostages in Iran
Less than a month after Iranian militants seized the U.S. Embassy in Tehran and took Americans hostage, the Iranian leader Ayatollah Khomeini ordered the release of thirteen hostages, all women or African Americans, because he believed they were not spies and had already endured "the oppression of American society." Here, in front of propaganda, they are presented to the press shortly before their release. © Bettmann/Corbis.

These grievances erupted into a revolution in 1979 that forced the shah out of Iran and brought to power Shiite Islamic fundamentalists led by Ayatollah Ruholla Khomeini, whom the shah had exiled in 1964.

Carter's decision to allow the shah into the United States for medical treatment enraged Iranians, who believed that the United States would restore the shah to power as it had done in 1953. On November 4, 1979, a crowd broke into the U.S. Embassy in Iran's capital, Teheran, and seized sixty-six U.S. diplomats, CIA officers, citizens, and military attachés. Refusing the captors' demands that the shah be returned to Iran for trial, Carter froze Iranian assets in U.S. banks and placed an embargo on Iranian oil. In April 1980, he sent a small military operation into Iran, but the rescue mission failed.

The disastrous rescue attempt and scenes of blindfolded U.S. citizens paraded before TV cameras fed Americans' feelings of impotence, simmering since the defeat in Vietnam. These frustrations in turn increased support for a more militaristic foreign policy. Opposition to Soviet-American détente, combined with the Soviet invasion of Afghanistan, nullified the thaw in superpower relations that had begun in the 1960s. Iran released a handful of the captives (primarily women and African Americans), but the **Iran hostage crisis** dominated the news during the 1980 presidential campaign and contributed to Carter's defeat. Iran freed the remaining 52 hostages the day he left office, but relations with the United States remained tense.

REVIEW: How did Carter implement his commitment to human rights, and why did human rights give way to other priorities?

▶ Ronald Reagan and the Conservative Ascendancy

The election of Ronald Reagan in 1980 marked the most important turning point in politics since Franklin D. Roosevelt's election in 1932.

Reagan's victory established conservatism's dominance in the Republican Party, while Democrats searched for votes by moving toward the right. The United States was not alone in this political shift. Conservatives rose to power in Britain with the election of Prime Minister Margaret Thatcher, and they led governments in Germany, Canada, and Sweden, while socialist and social democratic governments elsewhere trimmed their welfare states.

The Reagan administration embraced the conservative Christian values of the New Right, but it left its most important mark on the economy: victory over inflation, deregulation of industry, enormous tax cuts, and a staggering federal budget deficit. Popular culture celebrated financial success, but poverty increased and economic inequality grew. Although the Reagan era did not see a policy revolution comparable to that of the New Deal, it dealt a sharp blow to the liberalism that had informed American politics since the 1930s.

Appealing to the New Right and Beyond

Sixty-nine-year-old Ronald Reagan was the oldest candidate ever nominated for the presidency. Coming first to national attention as a movie actor, he initially shared the politics of his staunchly Democratic father but moved to the right in the 1940s and 1950s and campaigned for Barry Goldwater in 1964.

Reagan's political career took off when he was elected governor of California in 1966. He ran as a conservative, but in office he display-ed flexibility, approving a major tax increase, a strong water pollution bill, and a liberal abortion law. Displaying similar agility in the 1980 presidential campaign, he softened earlier attacks on programs such as Social Security and chose the moderate George H. W. Bush as his running mate.

Some Republicans balked at his nomination and the party platform, which reflected the concerns of the party's right wing. For example, after Phyllis Schlafly persuaded the party to reverse its forty-year support for the Equal Rights Amendment, moderate and liberal Republicans protested outside the convention hall. Moderate John B. Anderson, congressman from Illinois, deserted his party to run as an independent.

Reagan's campaign capitalized on the economic recession and the international challenges symbolized by the Americans held hostage in Iran. Repeatedly, Reagan asked voters, "Are you better off now than you were four years ago?"

He promised to "take government off the backs of the people" and to restore Americans' morale and other nations' respect. Reagan won the election, while Republicans took control of the Senate for the first time since the 1950s.

While the economy and the Iran hostage crisis sealed Reagan's victory, he also benefited from the burgeoning grassroots conservative movements. His support from religious conservatives, predominantly Protestants who had traditionally refrained from partisan politics, constituted a relatively new phenomenon known as the **New Right** or **New Christian Right**. During the 1970s, evangelical and fundamentalist Christianity claimed thousands of new adherents. Evangelical ministers such as Pat Robertson preached to huge television audiences, attacking feminism, abortion, and homosexuality. They called for the restoration of old-fashioned "family values." A considerable number of Catholics, such as Phyllis Schlafly, shared the fundamentalists' goal of a return to "Christian values."

Conservatives created political organizations such as the Moral Majority, founded by the Reverend Jerry Falwell in 1979, to fight "left-wing, social welfare bills, . . . pornography, homosexuality, [and] the advocacy of immorality in school textbooks." Dr. James Dobson, a clinical psychologist with a popular Christian talk show, founded the Family Research Council in 1983 to lobby Congress for measures to curb abortion, divorce, homosexuality, and single motherhood. The instruments of more traditional conservatives, who stressed limited government at home and militant anticommunism abroad, likewise flourished, while Phyllis Schlafly's monthly newsletter merged the sentiments of the old and new right.

Reagan spoke for the New Right on such issues as abortion and school prayer, but he did not push hard for so-called moral or social policies. Instead, his major achievements fulfilled goals of the older right—strengthening the nation's anti-Communist posture as well as reducing taxes and government restraints on free enterprise. "In the present crisis," Reagan declared, "government is not the solution to our problem, government is the problem."

Reagan was extraordinarily popular, appealing even to Americans who opposed his policies but warmed to his optimism, confidence, and easygoing humor. Ignoring the darker moments of the American past, he presented a version of history that Americans could feel good about. Declaring that it was "morning in America," he promised an even more glorious future.

Ronald Reagan Addresses Religious Conservatives
Reagan's victory in 1980 helped to reshape the Republican Party by attracting millions of evangelical Christians. In his 1983 address to the National Association of Evangelicals, Reagan called the Soviet Union an "evil empire" and appealed to religious conservatives with strong words about abortion and prayer in the schools, rejoicing that "America is in the midst of a spiritual awakening and a moral renewal." Ronald Reagan Presidential Library.

Unleashing Free Enterprise

Reagan's first domestic objective was a massive tax cut. To justify tax cuts in the face of a large budget deficit, Reagan relied on a new theory called **supply-side economics**, which held that cutting taxes would actually increase revenue by enabling businesses to expand, encouraging individuals to work harder because they could keep more of their earnings (especially the wealthy who enjoyed the greatest tax savings), and increase the production of goods and services—the supply—which in turn would boost demand. Reagan promised that the economy would grow so much that the government would recoup the lost taxes, but instead it incurred a galloping deficit.

In the summer of 1981, Congress passed the **Economic Recovery Tax Act**, the largest tax reduction in U.S. history. Rates were cut from 14 percent to 11 percent for the lowest-income individuals and from 70 percent to 50 percent for the wealthiest, who also benefited from reduced levies on corporations, capital gains, gifts, and inheritances. A second measure, the Tax Reform Act of 1986, cut taxes still further. Although the 1986 law narrowed loopholes used primarily by the wealthy, affluent Americans saved far more on their tax bills than did average taxpayers, and the distribution of wealth tipped further in favor of the rich.

Carter had confined deregulation to particular industries, such as air transportation and banking, while increasing health, safety, and environmental regulations. The Reagan administration, by contrast, pursued across-the-board deregulation. It declined to enforce the Sherman Antitrust Act (see "Railroads, Trusts, and the Federal Government" in chapter 18), which limited monopolies, against an unprecedented number of business mergers and takeovers. Reagan also loosened regulations protecting employee health and safety, and he weakened labor unions. When members of the Professional Air Traffic Controllers Organization—one of the few unions to support Reagan in 1980—struck in 1981, the president fired them, destroying the union and intimidating organized labor.

Reagan blamed environmental laws for the nation's sluggish economic growth and targeted them for deregulation. His first secretary of the interior, James Watt, declared, "We will mine more, drill more, cut more timber," and released federal lands to private exploitation. Meanwhile, the head of the Environmental Protection Agency relaxed enforcement of air and water pollution standards. Of environmentalists, Reagan wisecracked, "I don't think they'll be happy until the White House looks like a bird's nest," but their numbers grew in opposition to his policies. Popular support for environmental protection forced several officials to resign and blocked full realization of Reagan's deregulatory goals.

Deregulation of the banking industry, begun under Carter with bipartisan support, created a crisis in the savings and loan industry. Some of the newly deregulated savings and loan institutions (S&Ls) extended enormous loans to real estate developers and invested in other high-yield but risky ventures. S&L owners reaped lavish profits, and their depositors enjoyed high interest rates, but when real estate values began to plunge, hundreds of S&Ls went bankrupt creating the largest financial scandal in U.S. history thus far. The government bail out of the industry in 1989 cost American taxpayers more than $100 billion.

The S&L crisis deepened the federal deficit. Reagan cut funds for food stamps, job training, student aid, and other social welfare programs, and hundreds of thousands of people lost benefits. Yet increases in defense spending far exceeded the budget cuts and along with the tax cuts caused the deficit to soar. The nation's debt tripled to $2.3 trillion, consuming one-seventh of all federal expenditures. Despite Reagan's antigovernment rhetoric, the number of federal employees increased from 2.9 million to 3.1 million during his presidency.

It took the severest recession since the 1930s to squeeze inflation out of the U.S. economy. Unemployment approached 11 percent late in 1982, and record numbers of banks and businesses closed. The threat of unemployment further undermined organized labor, forcing unions to make concessions that management insisted were necessary for industry's survival. In 1983, the economy recovered and entered a period of unprecedented growth.

That economic upswing and Reagan's own popularity posed a formidable challenge to the Democrats in the 1984 election. They nominated Carter's vice president, Walter F. Mondale, to head the ticket, but even his precedent-breaking move in choosing a woman as his running mate—New York representative Geraldine A. Ferraro—did not save the Democrats from a humiliating defeat. Reagan charged his opponents with concentrating on America's failures, while he emphasized success and possibility. Democrats, he claimed, "see an America where every day is April 15th [the deadline for income tax returns] . . . we see an America where every day is the Fourth of July." Reagan was reelected in a landslide victory, winning 59 percent of the popular vote and every state but Mondale's Minnesota.

Winners and Losers in a Flourishing Economy

After the economy took off in 1983, some Americans won great fortunes. Popular culture celebrated making money and displaying wealth. Books by business wizards topped best seller lists, the press described lavish million-dollar parties, and a new television show, *Lifestyles of the Rich and Famous*, drew large audiences. College students listed making money as their primary ambition.

Many of the newly wealthy got rich from moving assets around rather than from producing goods, making money by manipulating debt and restructuring corporations through mergers and takeovers. Notable exceptions included Steven Jobs, who invented the Apple computer in his garage; Bill Gates, who transformed the software industry; and Liz Claiborne, who created a billion-dollar fashion enterprise. Most financial wizards operated within the law, but greed sometimes led to criminal convictions.

Older industries faced increasing international pressures, as German and Japanese corporations overtook U.S. manufacturing in steel, automobiles, and electronics. International competition forced the collapse of some companies, while others moved factories and jobs abroad to be closer to foreign markets or to benefit from the low wages in countries such as Mexico and Korea. Service industries expanded and created new jobs at home, but at substantially lower wages. The number of full-time workers earning wages below the poverty level ($12,195 for a family of four in 1990) rose from 12 percent to 18 percent of all workers in the 1980s.

The weakening of organized labor combined with the decline in manufacturing to erode the position of blue-collar workers. Chicago steelworker Ike Mazo, who contemplated the $6-an-hour jobs available to him, fumed, "It's an attack on the living standards of workers." Increasingly, a second income was needed to stave off economic decline. By 1990, nearly 60 percent of married women with young children worked outside the home. Yet even with two incomes, families struggled. Speaking of her children, Mazo's wife confessed, "I worry about their future every day. Will we be able to put them through college?" The average $10,000 gap between men's and women's annual earnings made things even harder for the nearly 20 percent of families headed by women.

In keeping with conservative philosophy, Reagan adhered to trickle-down economics, insisting that the benefits of a booming economy would trickle down to everyone. Average personal income did rise during his tenure, but the trend toward greater economic inequality that had begun in the 1970s intensified in the 1980s, encouraged in part by his tax policies. During Reagan's presidency, the percentage of Americans living in poverty increased from 11.7 to 13.5, the highest poverty rate in the industrialized world. Social Security and Medicare helped to stave off destitution among the elderly. Less fortunate were other groups that the economic boom had bypassed: racial minorities, female-headed families, and children. One child in five lived in poverty.

REVIEW: What conservative goals were realized in the Reagan administration?

▶ Continuing Struggles over Rights

The rise of conservatism put liberal social movements on the defensive, as the government moved away from the commitment to equal opportunity undertaken in the 1960s and the president's federal court appointments reflected that shift. Feminists and minority groups fought to keep protections they had recently won, and the newer gay and lesbian rights movement made some gains.

Battles in the Courts and Congress

Ronald Reagan agreed with conservatives that the nation had moved too far in guaranteeing rights to minority groups. Crying "reverse discrimination," conservatives maintained that affirmative action unfairly hurt whites. Instead they called for "color-blind" policies, ignoring statistics showing that minorities and

white women still lagged far behind white men in opportunities and income.

Intense mobilization by civil rights groups, educational leaders, labor, and even corporate America prevented the administration from abandoning affirmative action, and the Supreme Court upheld important antidiscrimination policies. Moreover, against Reagan's wishes, Congress extended the Voting Rights Act with veto-proof majorities. The administration did, however, limit civil rights enforcement by appointing conservatives to the Justice Department, the Civil Rights Commission, and other agencies as well as by slashing their budgets.

Congress stepped in to defend antidiscrimination programs after the Justice Department, in the case of *Grove City v. Bell* (1984), persuaded the Supreme Court to severely weaken Title IX of the Education Amendments Act of 1972, a key law promoting equal opportunity in education. In 1988, Congress passed the Civil Rights Restoration Act over Reagan's veto, reversing the administration's victory in *Grove City* and banning government funding of any organization that practiced discrimination on the basis of race, color, national origin, sex, disability, or age.

The *Grove City* decision reflected a rightward movement in the federal judiciary, upon which liberals had become accustomed to count as a powerful ally. With the opportunity to appoint half of the 761 federal court judges and three new Supreme Court justices, President Reagan encouraged this trend by carefully selecting conservative candidates. The full impact of these appointments became clear after Reagan left office, as the Court allowed states to impose restrictions that weakened access to abortion for poor and rural women, reduced protections against employment discrimination, and whittled down legal safeguards against the death penalty.

Feminism on the Defensive

A signal achievement of the New Right was capturing the Republican Party's position on women's rights. For the first time in its history, the party took an explicitly antifeminist tone, opposing both the **Equal Rights Amendment (ERA)** and abortion rights, key goals of women's rights activists. When the time limit for ratification of the ERA

Ratified the ERA
Did not ratify the ERA
Ratified and then voted to rescind ratification

The Fight for the Equal Rights Amendment

ran out in 1982, Phyllis Schlafly and her followers celebrated the defeat of a central feminist objective. (See "Historical Question," page 878.)

Cast on the defensive, feminists focused more on women's economic and family problems, where they found some common ground with the Reagan administration. The Child Support Enforcement Amendments Act helped single and divorced mothers collect court-ordered child support payments from absent fathers. The Retirement Equity Act of 1984 benefited divorced and older women by strengthening their claims to their husbands' pensions and enabling women to qualify more easily for private retirement pensions.

The Reagan administration had its own concerns about women, specifically about the gender gap in voting—women's tendency to support liberal and Democratic candidates in larger numbers than men did. Reagan appointed three women to cabinet posts and, in 1981, selected the first woman, Sandra Day O'Connor, a moderate conservative, for the Supreme Court, despite the Christian Right's objection to her support of abortion. But these actions accompanied a general decline in the number of women and minorities in high-level government positions. And with higher poverty rates than men, women suffered most from Reagan's cuts in social programs.

Although Supreme Court decisions allowed increasing restrictions on women's ability to obtain abortions, feminists fought successfully to retain the basic principles of Roe v. Wade. Moreover, they won a key decision from the

VISUAL ACTIVITY

The Abortion Debate

After the *Roe v. Wade* decision in 1973, several states enacted restrictions on abortion. In 1989, the Supreme Court upheld a Missouri law prohibiting public employees from performing abortions except to save a woman's life. It also banned abortions in public buildings and required physicians to perform viability tests on the fetus after twenty weeks. Here, activists on both sides rally before the Supreme Court. AP Photo/Ron Edmonds.

READING THE IMAGE: What arguments do the signs of the abortion opponents make?

CONNECTIONS: How did other elements of the feminist agenda fare in the 1980s?

Supreme Court ruling that sexual harassment in the workplace constituted sex discrimination. Feminists also made some gains at the state level on such issues as pay equity, rape, and domestic violence.

VISUAL ACTIVITY

Gay Rights Parade

Annual gay rights parades in the United States began in June 1970, the first anniversary of Stonewall (see chapter 28). More than 150,000 people marched in this parade in New York City in 1989, including many friends and relatives of homosexuals. Here, E. G. Smith wears the "rainbow" colors of the movement, while his grandmother, Norma Isaacs, demonstrates her support. AP Photo/Sergio Florez.

READING THE IMAGE: Notice the building on the parade route. Why would the organizers have chosen this street? How might bystanders have responded to the presence of Norma Isaacs?

CONNECTIONS: What gains did the gay and lesbian rights movement make during the 1980s?

Why Did the ERA Fail?

The proposed Equal Rights Amendment to the U.S. Constitution guaranteed that "equality of rights under the law shall not be denied or abridged by the United States or by any State on account of sex." Two more short sections gave Congress enforcement powers and provided that the ERA would take effect two years after ratification. By the 1970s, it had become the symbol of the women's movement, and the controversy it sparked revealed profound differences in beliefs and values among Americans.

The National Woman's Party, a militant suffrage organization that had helped win the vote for women in 1920, first proposed an equal rights amendment to the Constitution in 1923. It won little support, however, before the resurgence of feminism in the late 1960s, when the National Organization for Women and other women's groups made the ERA a key objective.

Both houses of Congress passed the ERA in March 1972 by overwhelming margins, 354–23 in the House and 84–8 in the Senate. Within three hours, Hawaii rushed to become the first state to ratify, and twenty-three states quickly followed. Public opinion heavily favored ratification, peaking at 74 percent in favor in 1974 and never falling below 52 percent, while opposition never topped 31 percent. Yet even after Congress extended the ratification period until 1982, the ERA fell three short of the three-fourths of the states required by the Constitution (see The Fight for the Equal Rights Amendment map on page 000). (see The Fight for the Equal Rights Amendment map on page 000). Why did a measure with so much congressional and popular support fail?

The ERA encountered well-organized and passionate opposition linked to the growing conservative forces in the 1970s. Conservatives' opposition to the ERA reflected in part their distaste for big government, but even more it signaled the New Right's determination to preserve traditional gender roles and "family values." What feminists saw as a simple measure to ensure equal rights for all citizens, ERA opponents saw as a threat to women's God-given and natural right to be protected and supported by men. They raised fears by suggesting extravagant ways in which courts might interpret the amendment. Senator Samuel J. Ervin Jr. claimed that the ERA would eliminate laws against rape, require coed housing for prisoners, and deprive women of alimony and child support. Others claimed it would legalize homosexual marriage and send women into combat.

Anti-ERA arguments drew on conservative Christian beliefs. Evangelical minister and politician Jerry Falwell declared the ERA "a definite violation of holy Scripture [and its] mandate that 'the husband is the head of the wife.'" Anti-ERA rhetoric also appealed to some women's understandings of their own self-interest. Many ERA opponents were full-time housewives who had no stake in equal treatment in the marketplace and who feared that the amendment would eliminate the duty of men to support their families.

Phyllis Schlafly and other conservatives skillfully mobilized women who saw their traditional roles threatened. In October 1972, she established a national movement called STOP (Stop Taking Our Privileges) ERA, whose members deluged legislators with letters and lobbied them personally in state capitols. In Illinois, they gave lawmakers apple pies with notes that read, "My heart and my hand went into this dough / For the sake of the family please vote 'no.'" Opponents also brought baby girls to the legislature wearing signs that pleaded, "Please don't draft me."

ERA opponents had an easier task than supporters because the framers of the Constitution had stacked the odds against revision. All opponents had to do was to convince a minority of legislators in a minority of states to preserve the status quo. In addition, unlike their suffragist predecessors, ERA forces had concentrated on winning Congress and were not prepared for the state campaigns.

The very gains feminists made in the 1960s and 1970s also worked against ratification. Congress had banned sex discrimination in employment, education, and other areas, and the Supreme Court had struck down several discriminatory laws, thus making it harder for ERA advocates to demonstrate the urgency of constitutional revision.

The ERA failed because a handful of men in a handful of state legislatures voted against it. The shift of only a few votes in states such as Illinois and North Carolina would have meant ratification. Schlafly's forces played a key role in the defeat because men could vote "no" and take cover behind the many women who

The Gay and Lesbian Rights Movement

In contrast to feminism and other social movements, gay and lesbian rights activism grew during the 1980s, galvanized in part by the discovery in 1981 of a devastating disease, acquired immune deficiency syndrome (AIDS). Because initially the disease disproportionately affected male homosexuals in the United States, activists mobilized to promote public funding for AIDS education, prevention, and treatment.

The gay and lesbian rights movement encouraged closeted homosexuals to "come out," and their visibility increased awareness, if not

opposed it. And those women proved willing to commit time, energy, and money to block ratification because they were convinced that the ERA threatened their very way of life.

Feminists did not leave the ERA battle empty-handed, however. Thousands of women were mobilized across the political spectrum, participating in the public arena for the first time. Fourteen states passed their own equal rights amendments after 1970. And feminists continued to fight legislative and judicial battles for the expansion of women's rights into the twenty-first century.

Questions for Consideration

1. In what ways did the New Right see the ERA as a threat to traditional values?

2. How did attitudes about the ERA differ from those about woman suffrage in the period leading up to ratification of the Nineteenth Amendment? (See chapter 22.)

Connect to the Big Idea

◉ What other issues on the New Right agenda were related to the concern about women and the family?

Phyllis Schlafly Derails the ERA in Illinois
Illinois was one of the most hotly contested states in the battle over ratification of the ERA. Here Schlafly rallies ERA opponents in the state capitol in 1975. Schlafly's STOP ERA movement succeeded in Illinois, her home state and the only northern state that failed to ratify. Despite political activities that required extensive traveling and speaking, Schlafly insisted on calling herself a housewife. © Bettmann/Corbis.

always acceptance, of homosexuality among the larger population. Beginning with the election of Elaine Noble to the Massachusetts legislature in 1974, several openly gay politicians won offices ranging from mayor to member of Congress, and the Democrats began to include gay rights in their party platforms. Activists organized gay rights marches throughout the country, turning out half a million people in New York City in 1987.

Popular attitudes about homosexuality moved toward greater tolerance but remained complex, leading to uneven changes in policies. (See "Documenting the American Promise," page 880.) Dozens of cities banned job discrimination against homosexuals, and beginning

Protecting Gay and Lesbian Rights

Since the 1970s, the gay and lesbian rights movement has sought measures to protect homosexuals from discrimination. In 1982, Wisconsin became the first state to ban discrimination on the basis of sexual orientation, following several cities that passed gay rights ordinances in the 1970s. By 2013, twenty-one states and the District of Columbia outlawed employment discrimination against gays, and dozens of cities did so.

DOCUMENT 1
Ordinance of the City of Minneapolis, 1974

In 1974, the city council of Minneapolis amended its civil rights ordinance to include discrimination based on sexual orientation. The law provided a rationale for banning discrimination and covered a broad range of activities.

It is determined that discriminatory practices based on race, color, creed, religion, national origin, sex, or affectional or sexual preference, with respect to employment, labor union membership, housing accommodations, property rights, education, public accommodations, and public services, or any of them, tend to create and intensify conditions of poverty, ill health, unrest, civil disobedience, lawlessness, and vice and adversely affect the public health, safety, order, convenience, and general welfare; such discriminatory practices threaten the rights, privileges, and opportunities of all inhabitants of the city and such rights, privileges, and opportunities are hereby to be declared civil rights.

Source: From *The Rights of Gay People: The Basic ACLU Guide to a Gay Person's Rights*, ed. E. Carrington Boggan, et al (New York: Avon Books, 1975), 251.

DOCUMENT 2
Paul Moore, Letter to the Editor of the *New York Times*, November 23, 1981

Paul Moore, Episcopal bishop of New York, made a religious argument for gay rights.

I quote our diocesan resolution: "Whereas this Convention, without making any judgment on the morality of homosexuality, agrees that homosexuals are entitled to full civil rights. Now therefore be it resolved this Convention supports laws guaranteeing homosexuals all civil rights guaranteed to other citizens." The Bible stands for justice and compassion for all of God's children. To deny civil rights to anyone for something he or she cannot help is against the clear commandment of justice and love, which is the message of the word of God. As a New Yorker I find it incredible that this great city, populated by more gay persons than any other city in the world, still denies them basic human rights. They make an enormous contribution to the commercial, artistic, and religious life of our city.

Source: Paul Moore, reprinted with permission.

DOCUMENT 3
Vatican Congregation for the Doctrine of the Faith, August 6, 1992

The following statement from the Roman Catholic Church reflects the views of many religious groups that deem homosexuality immoral.

"Sexual orientation" does not constitute a quality comparable to race, ethnic background, etc., in respect to nondiscrimination. Unlike these, homosexual orientation is an objective disorder and evokes moral concern.

There are areas in which it is not unjust discrimination to take sexual orientation into account, for example, in the placement of children for adoption or foster care, in employment of teachers or athletic coaches, and in military recruitment.

Source: From Vatican Doctrine of the Faith, *Origins*, August 6, 1992. Used by permission of the United States Conference of Catholic Bishops.

DOCUMENT 4
Charles Cochrane Jr., Testimony before the House Subcommittee on Employment Opportunities of the Committee on Education and Labor, January 27, 1982

Congress has considered, but never enacted, legislation banning discrimination on the basis of sexual orientation. Charles Cochrane Jr., an army veteran and police sergeant, testified on behalf of such a bill.

I am very proud of being a New York City policeman. And I am equally proud of being gay. I have always been gay.

I have been out of the closet for 4 years. November 6 was my anniversary. It took me 34 years to muster enough courage to declare myself openly.

We gays are loathed by some, pitied by others, and misunderstood by most. We are not cruel, wicked, cursed, sick, or possessed by demons. We are artists, business people, police officers, and clergymen. We are scientists, truck drivers, politicians; we work in every field. We are loving human beings who are in some ways different. . . .

During the early years of my association with the New York City Police Department a great deal of energy did go into guarding and concealing my innermost feelings. I believed that I would be subjected to ridicule and harassment were my colleagues to learn of my sexual orientation. Happily, when I actually began to integrate the various aspects of my total self, those who knew me did not reject me.

Then what need is there for such legislation as H.R. 1454? The crying need of others, still trapped in their closets, who must be protected, who must be reassured that honesty about themselves and their lives will not cost them their homes or their jobs. . . .

The bill before you will not act as a proselytizing agent in matters of sexual orientation or preference. It will not include affirmative action provisions. Passage of this bill will protect the inherent human rights of all people of the United States, while in no way diminishing the rights of those who do not see the need for such legislation.

Source: *Hearing on H.R. 1454 Before the U.S. House Subcommittee on Employment Opportunities of the Committee on Education and Labor*, 97th Cong. 54–56 (1982).

DOCUMENT 5
Carl F. Horowitz, "Homosexuality's Legal Revolution," May 1991

Carl Horowitz, a policy analyst at the Heritage Foundation, a conservative think tank, argues against gay rights.

Homosexual activists have all but completed their campaign to persuade the nation's educational establishment that homosexuality is normal "alternative" behavior, and thus any adverse reaction to it is akin to a phobia, such as fear of heights, or an ethnic prejudice, such as anti-Semitism.

The movement now stands on the verge of fully realizing its use of law to . . . intimidate heterosexuals uncomfortable about coming into contact with it. . . . The movement seeks to win sinecures through the state, and over any objections by "homophobic" opposition. With a cloud of a heavy fine or even a jail sentence hanging over a mortgage lender, a rental agent, or a job interviewer who might be discomforted by them, homosexuals under these laws can win employment, credit, housing, and other economic entitlements. Heterosexuals would have no right to discriminate against homosexuals, but apparently, not vice versa. . . .

Heterosexuals and even "closeted" homosexuals will be at a competitive disadvantage for jobs and housing. . . .

The new legalism will increase heterosexual anger—and even violence—toward homosexuals.

Source: Carl F. Horowitz, "Homosexuality's Legal Revolution," *Freeman*, May 1991.

Questions for Analysis and Debate

1. Which of these documents discuss how heterosexuals would be affected by laws protecting gay and lesbian rights? What effects do they anticipate?

2. Which of these documents suggest that the civil rights movement influenced the authors' views on homosexual rights?

3. What do you think is the strongest argument for government protection of homosexual rights? What do you think is the strongest argument against government protection?

Connect to the Big Idea

C What advances did gay rights activists make in the 1980s, and what helped them secure those gains?

with Wisconsin in 1982, eleven states made sexual orientation a protected category under civil rights laws. Local governments and large corporations began to offer health insurance and other benefits to same-sex domestic partners.

Yet a strong countermovement challenged the drive for gay rights. The Christian Right targeted gays and lesbians as symbols of national immorality, and they succeeded in overturning some homosexual rights measures, which already lagged far behind protections for women and minorities. Many states removed antisodomy laws from the books, but in 1986 the Supreme Court upheld the constitutionality of such laws. Until the Court reversed that opinion in 2003, more than a dozen states retained statutes that left homosexuals vulnerable to criminal charges for private consensual behavior.

REVIEW: What gains and setbacks did minorities, feminists, and gays and lesbians experience during the Reagan years?

▶ Ronald Reagan Confronts an "Evil Empire"

Reagan accelerated Carter's arms buildup and harshly censured the Soviet Union, calling it "an evil empire." Yet despite the new aggressiveness—or, as some argued, because of it—Reagan presided over the most impressive thaw in superpower conflict since the Cold War had begun. On the periphery of the Cold War, however, Reagan practiced militant anti-communism, assisting anti-leftist movements in Asia, Africa, and Central America and dispatching troops to the Middle East and the Caribbean.

Militarization and Interventions Abroad

Reagan expanded the military with new bombers and missiles, an enhanced nuclear force in

Nuclear Freeze Campaign
In the early 1980s, millions of Europeans and Americans worked to end the nuclear arms race. People marched even in the Soviet Union, where they passed the U.S. Embassy to make sure that news of their demonstration could not be censored. Here 750,000 march in New York City in 1982. The movement pushed Reagan and Gorbachev toward the nuclear arms limitation treaty signed in 1987. Getty Images.

Europe, a larger navy, and a rapid-deployment force. Throughout Reagan's presidency, defense spending averaged $216 billion a year, up from $158 billion in the Carter years and higher even than in the Vietnam era.

Reagan startled many of his own advisers in March 1983 by announcing plans for research on the **Strategic Defense Initiative (SDI)**. Immediately dubbed "Star Wars" by critics who doubted its feasibility, the project would deploy lasers in space to destroy enemy missiles before they could reach their targets. Such a defense would allow the United States to strike first and not fear retaliation. The Soviets reacted angrily because SDI violated the 1972 Antiballistic Missile Treaty and because they would have to make huge investments to develop their own Star Wars technology to maintain the nuclear balance. Subsequent administrations continued to spend billions on SDI research without producing a working system.

Reagan justified the military buildup and SDI as a means to negotiate with the Soviets from a position of strength, but he provoked an outburst of pleas to halt the arms race. In 1982, a rally demanding a freeze on additional nuclear weapons drew 700,000 people in New York City. That same year the National Conference of Catholic Bishops issued a strong call for nuclear disarmament. Hundreds of thousands demonstrated across Europe, stimulated by fears of new U.S. missiles scheduled for deployment there in 1983.

The U.S. military buildup was powerless before the growing threat of terrorism by non-state organizations seeking to gain political objectives by attacking civilian populations. Terrorism had a long history throughout the world, but in the 1970s and 1980s Americans saw it escalate among groups hostile to Israel and Western policies. In 1972, for example, after the Israeli occupation of the West Bank, Palestinian terrorists murdered eleven Israeli athletes at the Munich Olympics. The terrorist organization Hezbollah, composed of Shiite Muslims and backed by Iran and Syria, arose in Lebanon in 1982 after Israeli forces invaded that country to stop the Palestine Liberation Organization from using sanctuaries in Lebanon to launch attacks on Israel.

Reagan's effort to stabilize Lebanon by sending 2,000 Marines to join an international peace-keeping mission failed. In April 1983, a suicide attack on the U.S. Embassy in Beirut killed 63 people, and in October a Hezbollah fighter drove a bomb-filled truck into a U.S. barracks there, killing 241 Marines. The attack prompted the withdrawal of U.S. troops, signaling that political violence could affect U.S. policy. Lebanon remained in chaos, while incidents of murder, kidnapping, and hijacking by various Middle Eastern extremist groups continued.

Following a Cold War pattern begun under Eisenhower, the Reagan administration sought to contain leftist movements across the globe. In October 1983, 5,000 U.S. troops invaded Grenada, a small Caribbean nation where Marxists had staged a successful coup. In Asia, the United States quietly aided the Afghan rebels' war against Afghanistan's Soviet-backed government. In the African nation of Angola, the United States armed rebel forces against the government supported by the Soviet Union and Cuba. Reagan also sided with the South African government, which was brutally suppressing black protest against apartheid, forcing Congress to override his veto in order to impose economic sanctions against South Africa.

Administration officials were most fearful of left-wing movements in Central America, which Reagan claimed could "destabilize the entire region from the Panama Canal to Mexico." When a leftist uprising occurred in El Salvador in 1981, the United States sent money and military advisers to prop up the authoritarian government. In neighboring Nicaragua, the administration secretly aided the Contras, an armed coalition seeking to unseat the left-wing Sandinistas, who had toppled a long-standing dictatorship.

El Salvador and Nicaragua

The Iran-Contra Scandal

Fearing being drawn into another Vietnam, many Americans opposed aligning the United States with reactionary forces not supported by the majority of Nicaraguans. Congress repeatedly instructed the president to stop aiding the Contras, but the administration continued to secretly provide them with weapons and training. It also helped wreck the Nicaraguan economy. With support for his government under-mined, Nicaragua's president, Daniel Ortega, agreed to a political settlement, and when he was defeated by a coalition of all the opposition groups, he stepped aside.

The Fireside Summit
This photograph captures the warmth that developed between President Ronald Reagan and Soviet leader Mikhail Gorbachev, shown here at their first meeting at Geneva in November 1985. Although the meeting did not produce any key agreements, the two men began to appreciate each other's concerns and to build trust, launching a relationship that would lead to nuclear arms reductions and the end of the Cold War. Ronald Reagan Presidential Library.

Secret aid to the Contras was part of a larger project that came to be known as the **Iran-Contra scandal**. It began in 1985 when officials of the National Security Council and CIA covertly arranged to sell arms to Iran, then in the midst of an eight-year war with neighboring Iraq, even while the United States openly supplied Iraq with funds and weapons. The purpose was to get Iran to pressure Hezbollah to release American hostages being held in Lebanon. Funds from the arms sales were then channeled through Swiss bank accounts to aid the Nicaraguan Contras. Over the objections of his secretary of state and secretary of defense, Reagan approved the arms sales to Iran, but the three subsequently denied knowing that the proceeds were diverted to the Contras.

When news of the affair surfaced in November 1986, the Reagan administration faced serious charges. The president's aides had defied Congress's express ban on military aid to the Contras. Investigations by an independent prosecutor appointed by Reagan led to a trial in which seven individuals pleaded guilty or were convicted of lying to Congress and destroying evidence. One felony conviction was later overturned on a technicality, and President George H. W. Bush pardoned the other six officials in December 1992. The independent prosecutor's final report found no evidence that Reagan had broken the law, but it concluded that he had

known about the diversion of funds to the Contras and had "knowingly participated or at least acquiesced" in covering up the scandal.

A Thaw in Soviet-American Relations

A momentous reduction in Cold War tensions soon overshadowed the Iran-Contra scandal. The new Soviet-American accord depended both on Reagan's flexibility and profound desire to end the possibility of nuclear war and on an innovative Soviet head of state who recognized that his country's domestic problems demanded an easing of Cold War antagonism. Mikhail Gorbachev assumed power in 1985 determined to revitalize an economy incapable of satisfying basic consumer needs. Hoping to stimulate production and streamline distribution of consumer goods, Gorbachev introduced some elements of free enterprise and proclaimed a new era of *glasnost* (greater freedom of expression), eventually allowing contested elections and challenges to Communist rule.

Concerns about immense defense budgets moved both Reagan and Gorbachev to the negotiating table. Enormous military expenditures stood between the Soviet premier and his goal of economic revival. With growing popular support for arms reductions, Reagan made disarmament a major goal in his last years in office and readily responded when Gorbachev took the initiative. A positive personal chemistry developed between them, and the two leaders met four times between 1985 and 1988. Reagan had to fend off criticism from the hard anti-Communist right, and his insistence on proceeding with SDI nearly killed the talks. But by December 1987, the superpowers had completed an **intermediate-range nuclear forces (INF) agreement,** marking a major turning point in U.S.-Soviet relations. The treaty eliminated all short- and medium-range missiles from Europe and provided for on-site inspection for the first time. This was also the first time that either nation had agreed to eliminate weapons already in place.

In 1988, Gorbachev further reduced tensions by announcing a gradual withdrawal from Afghanistan, which had become the Soviet equivalent of America's Vietnam. In addition, the Soviet Union, the United States, and Cuba agreed on a political settlement of the civil war in Angola. In the Middle East, both superpowers supported a cease-fire and peace talks in the eight-year war between Iran and Iraq. Within three years, the Cold War that had defined the world for nearly half a century would be history.

REVIEW: How did anticommunism shape Reagan's foreign policy?

▶ Conclusion: Reversing the Course of Government

"Ours was the first revolution in the history of mankind that truly reversed the course of government," boasted Ronald Reagan in his farewell address in 1989. The word revolution exaggerated the change, but his administration did mark the slowdown or reversal of expanding federal budgets for domestic programs and regulations that had taken off in the 1930s. Although he did not deliver on the social or moral issues dear to the heart of the New Right, Reagan represented the "choice not an echo" that Phyllis Schlafly had called for in 1964, using his skills as "the Great Communicator" to cultivate antigovernment sentiment and undermine the liberal assumptions of the New Deal.

Antigovernment sentiment grew along with the backlash against the reforms and cultural changes of the 1960s and the conduct of the Vietnam War. Watergate and other lawbreaking by Nixon administration officials further disillusioned Americans. Presidents Ford and Carter restored morality to the White House, but neither could solve the gravest economic problems since the Great Depression—slow economic growth, stagflation, and an increasing trade deficit. Even the Democrat Carter gave higher priority to fiscal austerity than to social reform, stressed the limitations of what government could or should do, and began the government's retreat from regulation of key industries.

A new conservative movement helped Reagan win the presidency and flourished during his administration. Reagan's tax cuts, combined with hefty increases in defense spending, created a federal deficit crisis that justified cuts in social welfare spending, made new federal initiatives unthinkable, and burdened the country for years to come. These policies also contributed to a widening income gap between the rich and poor, weighing especially heavily on minorities, female-headed families, and children. Many Americans continued to support specific federal programs—especially those, such as Social Security and Medicare, that reached beyond the poor—but public sentiment about the government in general had taken a U-turn from the Roosevelt era. Instead of seeing the government as a helpful and problem-solving institution, many believed that not only was it ineffective at solving national problems but it also often made things worse. As Reagan appointed new justices, the Supreme Court retreated from liberalism, curbing the government's authority to protect individual rights and regulate the economy.

With the economic recovery that set in after 1982 and his optimistic rhetoric, Reagan lifted the confidence of Americans about their nation and its promise—confidence that had eroded with the economic and foreign policy blows of the 1970s. Beginning his presidency with harsh rhetoric against the Soviet Union and a huge military buildup, he left office having helped move the two superpowers to the highest level of cooperation since the Cold War began. Although that accord was not welcomed by strong anti-Communist conservatives like Phyllis Schlafly, it signaled developments that would transform American-Soviet relations—and the world—in the next decade.

See the Selected Bibliography for this chapter in the Appendix.

30 Chapter Review

MAKE IT STICK

LearningCurve

Go online and use LearningCurve to see what you know. Then review the key terms and answer the questions.

KEY TERMS

Watergate (p. 864)
National Energy Act of 1978 (p. 869)
Panama Canal treaty (p. 870)
Camp David accords (p. 870)
Iran hostage crisis (p. 872)
New (Christian) Right (p. 873)
supply-side economics (p. 874)
Economic Recovery Tax Act (p. 874)
Equal Rights Amendment (ERA) (p. 876)
Strategic Defense Initiative (SDI) (p. 883)
Iran-Contra scandal (p. 884)
intermediate-range nuclear forces (INF) agreement (p. 885)

REVIEW QUESTIONS

1. How did Nixon's policies reflect the increasing influence of conservatives on the Republican Party? (pp. 859–866)

2. How did Carter implement his commitment to human rights, and why did human rights give way to other priorities? (pp. 866–872)

3. What conservative goals were realized in the Reagan administration? (pp. 872–876)

4. What gains and setbacks did minorities, feminists, and gays and lesbians experience during the Reagan years? (pp. 876–882)

5. How did anticommunism shape Reagan's foreign policy? (pp. 882–885)

MAKING CONNECTIONS

1. What was Watergate's legacy for American politics in the following decade? In your answer, explain what led to Nixon's resignation.

2. How did the Republican and Democratic parties change in the 1970s and 1980s? Discuss how those changes shaped American politics.

3. How did Americans' memory of the Vietnam War affect foreign policy in the 1970s and 1980s?

4. Why was grassroots conservatism particularly strong in the Sun Belt in the 1970s and 1980s?

LINKING TO THE PAST

1. How were the conservatives of the 1980s similar to and different from the conservatives who opposed the New Deal in the 1930s? (See chapter 24.)

2. Presidents Jimmy Carter and Woodrow Wilson both claimed human rights as a central principle of their foreign policy. Which one was more successful in spreading human rights? Explain your answer. (See chapter 22.)

31 The Promises and Challenges of Globalization,

Since 1989

CONTENT LEARNING OBJECTIVES

After reading and studying this chapter, you should be able to:

- Explain the limited domestic initiatives of George H. W. Bush's presidency, and explain U.S. interventions in Central America and the Persian Gulf.

- Explain the Clinton administration's search for a middle ground in domestic policy, and outline the factors that guided the administration's military interventions around the world.

- Describe the debates over globalization and its effects on the United States.

- Explain George W. Bush's key domestic initiatives and his foreign policy of preemption and unilateralism, including the invasion of Iraq in 2003.

- Describe the historic 2008 presidential election, how President Obama's domestic agenda fared, and the challenges he faced around the world.

CONTAINER BOX
Using truck-size boxes to move goods without loading and unloading individual items became the norm by the 1980s. The container box's efficiency stimulated global industrial development and gave Americans greater access to cheap goods. Shutterstock Images LLC.

IN HIS MOSCOW HOTEL ROOM IN APRIL 1988, RONALD REAGAN'S national security adviser, Colin L. Powell, contemplated Premier Mikhail Gorbachev's reforms that would dramatically alter the Soviet Union's government and economy. Powell recalled, "I realized that one phase of my life had ended, and another was about to begin. Up until now, as a soldier, my mission had been to confront, contain, and, if necessary, combat communism. Now I had to think about a world without a Cold War."

Colin Powell was born in Harlem in 1937, the son of Jamaican immigrants who worked in a garment factory. At the City College of New York, he joined the army's Reserve Officers Training Corps (ROTC) program and, on graduation in 1958, began a lifelong career in military and public service, rising to the highest rank of four-star general. He stayed in the army because "I loved what I was doing," but he also knew that "for a black, no other avenue in American society offered so much opportunity." Powell's service in Vietnam taught him that "you do not squander courage and lives without clear purpose, without the country's backing, and without full commitment." In his subsequent positions as national security adviser to Ronald Reagan, chairman of the Joint Chiefs of Staff under George H. W. Bush and Bill Clinton, and secretary of state under George W. Bush, Powell endeavored to keep his country out of "halfhearted warfare for half-baked reasons that the American people could not understand or support."

Powell's sense that Gorbachev's reforms would transform the Cold War became a reality more quickly than anyone anticipated. Eastern Europe threw off communism in 1989, and the Soviet Union disintegrated in 1991. Throughout the 1990s, as the lone superpower, the United States deployed military and diplomatic power during episodes of instability in Latin America, the Middle East, Eastern Europe, and Asia, almost always in concert with the other major nations. In 1991, the United States led a United Nations–authorized force of twenty-eight nations to repel Iraq's invasion of Kuwait.

In the 1990s, Powell remarked that "neither of the two major parties fits me comfortably." Many Americans seemed to agree: From 1988 to 2012 they elected two Republicans—George H. W. Bush and George W. Bush—and two Democrats—Bill Clinton and Barack Obama—as president, and each faced Congresses where the opposing party controlled at least one house. Bipartisan cooperation produced a few initiatives, including disability rights legislation, welfare reform, drug benefits under Medicare, and expanded federal involvement in public education. But the most far-reaching law—expansion and reform of health care—passed without one Republican vote.

All four presidents supported globalization. As capital, products, information, and people crossed national boundaries in greater numbers and at greater speed, a surge of immigration rivaled the stream that had brought Powell's parents to the United States. Powell shared the world-wide shock when in September 2001 terrorist attacks in New York City and Washington, D.C., exposed American vulnerability to horrifying threats and sent U.S. soldiers into Afghanistan to overthrow the government that harbored the attackers. The administration's response to terrorism overwhelmed Secretary of State Powell's commitments to internationalism, multilateralism, and military restraint when, in 2003, George W. Bush began a second war against Iraq. The unpopularity of that war and a severe financial crisis helped the Democrats regain power and elect Barack Obama as the first African American president in 2008. After ending the war in Iraq and achieving legislation to fight the economic crisis, reform the financial industry, and substantially expand health insurance coverage, Obama won election to a second term in 2012.

▶ Domestic Stalemate and Global Upheaval: The Presidency of George H. W. Bush

Vice President George H. W. Bush announced his bid for the presidency in 1988, declaring, "We don't need radical new directions." As president, Bush proposed few domestic initiatives, but he signed key environmental and disability rights legislation. More dramatic changes swept through the world, shattering the free-world-versus-communism framework of the Cold War years. Most Americans approved of Bush's handling of the disintegration of the Soviet Union and its hold over Eastern Europe, and his response to Iraq's invasion of neighboring Kuwait. But voters' concern over a sluggish economy limited him to one term as president.

Gridlock in Government

The son of a wealthy U.S. senator from New England, George Herbert Walker Bush fought in World War II, served in Congress, and headed the Central Intelligence Agency under Richard Nixon and Gerald Ford. When Ronald Reagan tapped him for second place on the Republican ticket in 1980, Bush tailored his more moderate positions to Reagan's conservative agenda. At the end of Reagan's second term, Republicans rewarded him with the presidential nomination.

Several candidates competed for the Democratic nomination in 1988. The civil rights leader Reverend Jesse Jackson—whose Rainbow Coalition campaign centered on the needs of minorities, women, the working class, and the poor—won several primaries and seven million votes. But the centrist candidate, Massachusetts governor Michael Dukakis, won the nomination. On election day, Bush won 54 percent of the vote but the Democrats gained seats in Congress.

Promising "a kinder, gentler nation," President Bush was more inclined than Reagan to approve government activity in the private sphere. For example, Bush approved the **Clean Air Act of 1990**, the strongest, most comprehensive environmental law in history. Some forty million Americans benefited when Bush signed another regulatory measure in 1990, the **Americans with Disabilities Act (ADA),** banning discrimination against and requiring that private businesses

CHRONOLOGY

1988	• George H. W. Bush elected president.
1989	• Communism collapses in Eastern Europe.
1990	• Americans with Disabilities Act.
1991	• Persian Gulf War.
1992	• Bill Clinton elected president.
1993	• Israel and PLO peace accords. • North American Free Trade Agreement.
1994	• World Trade Organization established.
1995	• Bombing of federal building in Oklahoma City.
1996	• Personal Responsibility and Work Opportunity Reconciliation Act.
1998–2000	• United States bombs Iraq.
1999	• Senate trial rejects impeachment of Clinton.
2000	• George W. Bush elected president.
2001	• Terrorists attack World Trade Center and Pentagon. • U.S.-led coalition drives Taliban government out of Afghanistan. • USA Patriot Act. • $1.35 trillion tax cut.
2002	• No Child Left Behind Act.
2003	• United States attacks Iraq.
2005	• Hurricane Katrina.
2008	• Financial crisis. • Barack Obama elected president.
2009	• American Recovery and Reinvestment Act.
2010	• Patient Protection and Affordable Care Act. • Wall Street Reform and Consumer Protection Act. • United States ends combat operations in Iraq, increases troops in Afghanistan.
2011	• Osama bin Laden killed.
2013	• U.S. Supreme Court overturns Defense of Marriage Act.

Suing for Access: Disability and the Courts

When the ADA passed in 1990, Beverly Jones expressed her elation: "For me, the passage of the ADA was like opening a door that had been closed to me for so long." The measure promised to protect people with disabilities from discrimination by private employers, public agencies, and state and local governments. This civil rights act providing equal access and opportunity followed in a long tradition of Americans fighting for their rights, struggles not only to enact laws but also to see them enforced.

Jones, a single mother with two children, joined the ranks of the 2.2 million Americans who use a wheelchair after she was in an automobile accident in 1984 that resulted in paraplegia. Determined not to "allow what I wanted in life to be denied because of . . . physical limitations," she trained as a court reporter and went to work to support her family. But Jones discovered that despite the requirements of the ADA, in Tennessee seven out of ten courthouses were not wheelchair accessible. "I was often forced to ask complete strangers to carry me up the stairs," Jones recalled, and she found the experiences "humiliating and frightening."

Jones pleaded in vain with local, state, and federal officials to obtain compliance with the law. "The door that I thought had been opened was still closed and my freedom to live my dream was turning into a nightmare," she said. Finally, in 1998, after having to ask a judge to carry her to a restroom, she decided to appeal to the courts.

Jones filed a lawsuit against the state of Tennessee, joining five other plaintiffs who alleged that the state was in violation of Title II of the ADA, which prohibits governmental entities from denying public services, programs, and activities to individuals because of a disability. Another plaintiff, George Lane, had injured his hip and pelvis in a car accident. Cited for reckless driving, he went to the courthouse in a wheelchair but had to crawl up the stairs. When the court adjourned for lunch, he crawled back down. That afternoon, he refused to crawl upstairs again and was jailed for failing to appear in court. Lane said that he would never forget the humiliation of having to drag his body up the thirty tile steps of the Polk County Courthouse. Lane, Jones, and the four other plaintiffs sought legal redress and damages of $250,000 each.

Tennessee immediately countersued, challenging the constitutionality of the ADA's requirement that states make public facilities accessible to people with disabilities. Finally, in 2004, the case of *Tennessee v. Lane* reached the Supreme Court, where conservative justices espoused a "new federalism" that challenged the right of Congress to tell the states what to do. Citing sovereign immunity (protection from lawsuits), granted to states by the Eleventh Amendment to the Constitution, courts began to question the right of Congress to make federal laws binding on the states. In 2001, in a dramatic example of the trend to limit Congress's power, the Supreme Court held that Congress lacked a constitutional basis for permitting states to be sued under Title I of the ADA, which applies to state employment.

In *Tennessee v. Lane,* the state cited this decision, claiming sovereign

and public facilities be accessible to people with disabilities. As a breeze rippled over the White House lawn at the signing ceremony, disability advocate Cynthia Jones said, "It was kind of like a new breath of air was sweeping across America. . . . People knew they had rights. That was wonderful." (See "Seeking the American Promise," above.)

Yet Bush also needed to satisfy party conservatives to whom he had pledged "Read my lips: No new taxes." Bush vetoed thirty-six bills, including those extending unemployment benefits, raising taxes, and mandating family and medical leave for workers. Press reports increasingly used the words *stalemate* and *divided government*.

Continuing a trend begun during the Reagan years, some states compensated for this paralysis with their own innovations. State legislatures enacted laws to establish parental leave policies, improve food labeling, and protect the environment. Dozens of cities passed ordinances requiring businesses receiving tax abatements or other benefits to pay wages well above the federal minimum wage. And in 1999, California passed a much tougher gun control bill than reformers had been able to get through Congress.

The huge federal budget deficit inherited from Reagan impelled Bush in 1990 to abandon his "no new taxes" pledge, outraging conservatives. The new law modestly raised taxes on high-income Americans and increased levies on

immunity and challenging the constitutionality of the ADA. Carol Westlake, executive director of the Tennessee Disability Coalition, pointed out that Tennessee's claim of states' rights was the same argument used to deny civil rights to African Americans in the 1950s and 1960s. In January 2004, as the Supreme Court heard arguments in the case, activists demonstrated outside the Court, chanting, "Justice for all; we won't crawl."

At stake was not only the right of people with disabilities to sue a state when denied access to public facilities but also the right of Congress to make federal laws binding on the states. In May 2004, in a five-to-four decision, the Supreme Court ruled that states failing to make their courthouses accessible to people with disabilities could be sued for damages under federal disability law. But it confined its ruling to the specific context presented in the case: access to courts. By the narrowest possible margin, with the crucial fifth vote cast by Justice Sandra Day O'Connor, the Court focused on one narrow application of the ADA and upheld it in the face of Tennessee's claim of constitutional immunity.

"My case is over," Jones acknowledged. "We have accomplished what we wanted to be achieved." Nonetheless, the narrow

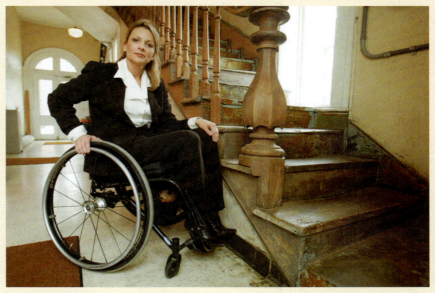

Beverly Jones

Beverly Jones is shown here next to one of the courthouse stairways that made her job as a court reporter so difficult. Jones filed suit under the ADA in 1998. In 2004, the Supreme Court upheld her right to enforce the protections the ADA granted to those with disabilities. AP Photo/John Russell.

grounds on which the Court decided her case meant that people with disabilities would continue to seek judicial acknowledgment of their rights to opportunity and access.

Questions for Consideration

1. What arguments did Tennessee use in its effort to defeat Jones's lawsuit?

2. In what ways was the struggle for disability rights similar to and different from minority rights movements?

Connect to the Big Idea

G Why was disability rights legislation one of the few pieces of reform legislation that passed in the 1990s?

---

gasoline, cigarettes, alcohol, and luxury items, while leaving intact most of Reagan's massive tax cuts. Neither the new revenues nor controls on spending curbed the deficit, which was boosted by rising costs for Social Security, Medicare, Medicaid, and natural disasters relief.

Like Reagan, Bush created a more conservative Supreme Court. His first nominee was a moderate, but in 1991, when the only African American on the Court, Justice Thurgood Marshall, retired, Bush nominated Clarence Thomas, a conservative black appeals court judge who had opposed affirmative action when he headed the Equal Employment Opportunity Commission (EEOC) under Reagan. Charging that Thomas would not protect minority rights,

civil rights groups and other liberal organizations fought the nomination. Then Anita Hill, a black law professor and former EEOC employee, accused Thomas of sexual harassment. Thomas angrily denied the charges, and the Senate voted narrowly to confirm him. The hearings angered many women, who noted that only two women sat in the Senate and denounced the male senators for not taking sexual harassment seriously.

The Cold War Ends

Although domestic policy remained fairly constant during Bush's presidency, the world experienced enormous changes. The progressive forces that Gorbachev had encouraged in the

MAP ACTIVITY

Map 31.1   Events in Eastern Europe, 1989–2002

The overthrow of Communist governments throughout Eastern Europe and the splintering of the Soviet Union into more than a dozen separate nations were among the most momentous changes in world history since World War II.

READING THE MAP: Which country was the first to overthrow its Communist government? Which was the last? In which nations did elections usher in a change in government?

CONNECTIONS: What problems did Mikhail Gorbachev try to solve, and how did he try to solve them? What policy launched by Ronald Reagan contributed to Soviet dilemmas? (See "Ronald Reagan Confronts an 'Evil Empire'" in chapter 30.) Did it create any problems in the United States?

Communist world (see "A Thaw in Soviet-American Relations" in chapter 30) swept through Eastern Europe in 1989, where popular uprisings demanded an end to state repression and inefficient economic bureaucracies. Communist governments toppled like dominoes (Map 31.1), virtually without bloodshed, because Gorbachev refused to prop them up with Soviet armies. East Germany opened its border with West Germany, and in November 1989 ecstatic Germans danced on the Berlin Wall.

Unification of East and West Germany sped to completion in 1990. Soon Poland, Hungary,

and other former iron curtain countries lined up to join the North Atlantic Treaty Organization (NATO). Although U.S. military forces remained in Europe as part of NATO, Europe no longer depended on the United States for its security. Its economic clout also grew as Western Europe formed a common economic market in 1992. Inspired by the liberation of Eastern Europe, republics within the Soviet Union soon sought their own independence. In December 1991, Boris Yeltsin, president of the Russian Republic, announced that Russia and eleven other

VISUAL ACTIVITY

Fall of the Berlin Wall

After 1961, the Berlin Wall stood as the prime symbol of the Cold War and the iron grip of communism over Eastern Europe and the Soviet Union. More than four hundred Eastern Europeans were killed trying to flee to the West. After Communist authorities opened the wall on November 9, 1989, permitting free travel between East and West Germany, Berliners from both sides gathered at the wall to celebrate. Gamma-Rapho via Getty Images.

READING THE IMAGE: What does the image tell you about the revolutions in Eastern Europe in 1989?

CONNECTIONS: What were the major factors that made possible the dismantling of the Berlin Wall?

republics had formed a new entity, the Commonwealth of Independent States, and other former Soviet states declared their independence. With nothing left to govern, Gorbachev resigned. The Soviet Union had dissolved, and with it the Cold War conflict that had defined U.S. foreign policy for decades.

Democracy also prevailed in South Africa, which began to dismantle apartheid, a process that led to the election of its first black president, Nelson Mandela, in 1994. Colin Powell joked that he was "running out of villains. I'm down to Castro and Kim Il Sung," the North Korean dictator who, along with China's leaders, resisted the liberalizing tides sweeping the world. In 1989, Chinese soldiers killed hundreds of pro-democracy demonstrators in Beijing, and the Communist government arrested some ten thousand reformers. North Korea remained a Communist dictatorship, committed to developing nuclear weapons.

"The post–Cold War world is decidedly not post-nuclear," declared one U.S. official. In 1990, the United States and the Soviet Union signed the Strategic Arms Reduction Talks (START) treaty, which cut about 30 percent of each superpower's nuclear arsenal. And in 1996, the United Nations General Assembly overwhelmingly approved a total nuclear test ban treaty. Yet India and Pakistan, hostile neighbors, refused to sign the treaty, and both exploded atomic devices in 1998. Moreover, the Republican-controlled U.S. Senate defeated ratification of the treaty. The potential for rogue nations and terrorist groups to develop nuclear weapons posed an ongoing threat.

Going to War in Central America and the Persian Gulf

Near its borders, the United States continued to exercise its military power. In Central

America, U.S. officials had developed close ties to Panamanian dictator Manuel Noriega whom they valued for his anticommunism. But in 1989, after an American grand jury indicted Noriega for drug trafficking and after his troops killed an American Marine, Bush ordered 25,000 military personnel into Panama. U.S. forces quickly overcame Noriega's troops, sustaining 23 deaths, while hundreds of Panamanians, including many civilians, died. Colin Powell noted that "our euphoria over our victory was not universal." Both the United Nations and the Organization of American States censured the unilateral action by the United States.

By contrast, Bush's second military engagement rested solidly on international approval. Viewing Iran as America's major enemy in the Middle East, U.S. officials had quietly assisted the Iraqi dictator Saddam Hussein in the Iran-Iraq war, which began in 1980 and ended inconclusively in 1988. In August 1990, Hussein invaded the small country of Kuwait (Map 31.2), and his troops soon neared the Saudi Arabian border, threatening the world's largest oil

MAP ACTIVITY

Map 31.2   Events in the Middle East, 1989–2011

The Arab League supported the war to liberate Kuwait in 1991, and after September 11, 2001, it also approved of U.S. military operations in Afghanistan. Yet only the countries where the United States had military bases supported the American invasion of Iraq in 2003. Arab hostility toward the United States also reflected the deterioration of Israeli-Palestinian relations after 1999.

READING THE MAP: In what countries are the sources of oil located? In what countries does the United States have military bases?

CONNECTIONS: What conditions prompted the U.S. military interventions in Iraq and Afghanistan in 1991, 2001, and 2003? What were the U.S. goals in each of these interventions? To what extent were those goals realized?

reserves. President Bush quickly ordered a massive military mobilization and assembled an international coalition to stand up to Iraq. He invoked principles of national self-determination and international law, but access to Middle Eastern oil was also a key concern.

Reflecting the easing of Cold War tensions, the Soviet Union supported a UN embargo on Iraqi oil and authorization for using force if Iraq did not withdraw from Kuwait by January 15, 1991. By then, the United States had deployed more than 400,000 soldiers to Saudi Arabia, joined by 265,000 troops from two dozen other nations, including several Arab states. "The community of nations has resolutely gathered to condemn and repel lawless aggression," Bush announced. "With few exceptions, the world now stands as one."

When the UN-imposed deadline for Iraqi withdrawal expired, Bush asked Congress to approve war. Many legislators favored waiting to see whether the embargo would force Hussein to back down, a position quietly urged within the administration by Colin Powell. Congress debated for three days and then authorized war by a margin of five votes in the Senate and sixty-seven in the House, with most Democrats opposed. On January 17, 1991, U.S. forces led a forty-day bombing campaign against Iraqi military targets, power plants, oil refineries, and transportation networks. Having severely crippled Iraq by air, the coalition then stormed into Kuwait, forcing Iraqi troops to withdraw (see Map 31.2).

"By God, we've kicked the Vietnam syndrome once and for all," President Bush exulted on March 1. Most Americans found no moral ambiguity in the **Persian Gulf War** and took pride in the display of military prowess. The United States stood at the apex of global leadership, steering a coalition in which Arab nations fought beside their former colonial rulers.

Some Americans wondered why the Bush administration ended the war without deposing Hussein. Bush pointed to the limited UN mandate and to Middle Eastern leaders' concerns that invading Iraq would destabilize the region. His secretary of defense, Richard Cheney, doubted that a stable government could be created to replace Hussein and considered the price of a long occupation too high. Instead, administration officials counted on Hussein's pledge not to rearm or develop weapons of mass destruction, secured by a system of UN inspections, to contain him.

Yet Middle Eastern stability remained elusive. Israel, which had endured Iraqi missile attacks, was more secure, but the Israeli-Palestinian conflict seethed. Despite military losses, Hussein remained in power and turned his war machine on Iraqi Kurds and Shiite Muslims whom the United States had encouraged to rebel. Hussein also found ways to conceal arms from UN weapons inspectors before he threw the inspectors out in 1998. Finally, the

The Gulf War
On Thanksgiving 1990, during the buildup to the Gulf War, President George H. W. Bush visited U.S. troops deployed to Saudi Arabia. Here he talks with a woman, one of 33,000 stationed throughout the area. For the first time, women served in combat support positions, piloting planes and helicopters, directing artillery, and fighting fires. Time & Life Pictures/ Getty Images.

decision to keep U.S. troops based in Saudi Arabia, the holy land of Islam, fueled the hatred and determination of Muslim extremists like Osama bin Laden.

The 1992 Election

Bush's popularity after the Gulf War caused the most prominent Democrats to opt out of the presidential race of 1992. But that did not deter William Jefferson "Bill" Clinton, who at age forty-five had served as governor of Arkansas for twelve years. Like Carter in 1976, Clinton and his running mate, Tennessee senator Albert Gore Jr., presented themselves as "New Democrats" and sought to rid the party of its liberal image.

Clinton identified his campaign with the "forgotten middle class," who "do the work, pay the taxes, raise the kids, and play by the rules." He promised a tax cut for the middle class, pledged to reinvigorate government and the economy, and vowed "to put an end to welfare as we know it." Bush was vulnerable to an unemployment rate of 7 percent and to a challenge from self-made Texas billionaire H. Ross Perot, whose third-party organization revealed Americans' frustrations with government and the major parties. Clinton won 43 percent of the popular vote, Bush 38 percent, and Perot 19 percent—the strongest third-party finish in eighty years.

> **REVIEW:**   How did George H. W. Bush respond to threats to U.S. interests as the Cold War came to an end?

▶ The Clinton Administration's Search for the Middle Ground

Bill Clinton's assertion that "the era of big government is over" reflected the Democratic Party's move to the right that had begun with Jimmy Carter, but Clinton did not completely abandon liberal principles. He extended benefits for the working poor; delivered incremental reforms to feminists, environmentalists, and other groups; and spoke out for affirmative action and gay rights. Yet his administration restricted welfare benefits and attended more to the concerns of middle-class Americans than to the needs of the disadvantaged.

Clinton's eight-year presidency witnessed the longest economic boom in history and ended with a budget surplus. Although various factors generated the prosperity, many Americans identified Clinton with the buoyant economy, elected him to a second term, and supported him even when his reckless sexual behavior led to impeachment, which crippled his leadership in his last years in office.

Clinton's Reforms

Clinton wanted to restore confidence in government as a force for good while not alienating antigovernment voters. Yet he inherited a huge budget deficit—$4.4 trillion in 1993—that precluded substantial federal initiatives. Moreover, Clinton failed to win a majority of the popular vote in both 1992 and 1996, and the Republicans controlled Congress after 1994. Throughout his presidency, Clinton was burdened by investigations into past financial activities and private indiscretions.

Despite these obstacles, Clinton achieved a number of reforms. He issued executive orders easing restrictions on abortion and signed several bills that Republicans had previously blocked. In 1993, Congress enacted gun control legislation and the Family and Medical Leave Act, which mandated unpaid leave for childbirth, adoption, and family medical emergencies for workers in larger companies. The Violence against Women Act of 1994 authorized $1.6 billion and new remedies for combating sexual assault and domestic violence. Clinton won stricter air pollution controls and greater protection for national forests and parks. Other liberal measures included a minimum-wage increase and a large expansion of aid for college students.

Most significantly, Clinton pushed through a substantial increase in the **Earned Income Tax Credit (EITC).** Begun in 1975, EITC gave tax breaks to people who worked full-time at meager wages or, if they owed no taxes, a subsidy to lift their family income above the poverty line. By 2003, some fifteen million low-income families were benefiting from the EITC, almost half of them minorities. One expert called it "the largest antipoverty program since the Great Society." The program implicitly recognized the inability of the free market to secure a living wage for all workers.

Shortly before Clinton took office, the economy had begun to rebound. Economic expansion, along with spending cuts, tax increases, and declining unemployment, produced in 1998 the first budget surplus since 1969. Clinton failed, however, in his major domestic initiative to provide universal health insurance and to curb skyrocketing medical costs. Congress enacted important smaller reforms, such as underwriting health care for five million uninsured children, yet forty million Americans remained uninsured.

Pledging to make the face of government "look like America," Clinton built on the gradual progress women and minorities had made since the 1960s. For example, African Americans and women had become mayors in major cities from New York to San Francisco. Virginia had elected the first black governor since Reconstruction, and Florida the first Latino. Clinton's cabinet appointments included six women, three African Americans, two Latinos, and an Asian American. His judicial appointments had a similar cast, and in 1993 he named the second woman to the Supreme Court, Ruth Bader Ginsburg, whose arguments as an attorney had won key women's rights rulings from that Court.

Accommodating the Right

The 1994 midterm elections swept away the Democratic majorities in Congress and helped push Clinton to the right. Led by Representative Newt Gingrich of Georgia, Republicans claimed the 1994 election as a mandate for their "contract with America," a conservative platform to end "government that is too big, too intrusive, and too easy with the public's money" and to elect "a Congress that respects the values and shares the faith of the American family."

The most extreme antigovernment sentiment developed far from Washington in the form of grassroots armed militias that stockpiled weapons, celebrated white Christian supremacy, and reflected conservatives' hostility to such diverse institutions as taxes and the United Nations. The militia movement grew after passage of new gun control legislation and after government agents stormed the headquarters of an armed religious cult in Waco, Texas, in April 1993, killing more than 80. On the second anniversary of that event, militia sympathizers bombed a federal building in Oklahoma City, taking 169 lives in the worst terrorist attack in the nation's history up to that point.

Clinton bowed to conservative views on gay and lesbian rights, and, following the advice of military leaders, backed away from his promise to lift the ban on gays in the military. Homosexual soldiers would be safe from discharge

Domestic Terrorism
The most devastating product of antigovernment extremism was the explosion of the Alfred P. Murrah Federal Building in Oklahoma City in April 1995. The building housed a day care center, and nineteen infants and toddlers were among the 169 killed. Timothy McVeigh, who drove the bomb-rigged truck, was executed in 2001, and his co-conspirator, Terry Nichols, was sentenced to life imprisonment without parole. © Charles Porter IV/ZUMAPRESS.com

only if they kept their sexual orientations secret. Cathleen Glover, an army specialist in Arabic who lost her position along with thousands of other soldiers, lamented, "The army preaches integrity, but asks you to lie to everyone around you." In addition, in 1996, Clinton signed the Defense of Marriage Act (DOMA), prohibiting the federal government from recognizing state-licensed marriages between same-sex couples.

Nonetheless, attitudes and practices relating to homosexuality were changing rapidly. By 2006, a majority of the largest companies provided health benefits to same-sex domestic partners and included sexual orientation in their nondiscrimination policies. A majority of states banned discrimination in public employment, and many of those laws extended to private employment, housing, and education. By 2014, gay marriage was legal in seventeen states and the District of Columbia, while thirty-three states banned it. And in 2013, the

Supreme Court overturned DOMA as a violation of the Constitution's equal protection guarantee. Gay spouses were now entitled to equal treatment in such areas as federal insurance benefits, immigration, and tax filing.

Clinton's efforts to dissociate his party from liberalism were apparent in his handling of the New Deal program Aid to Families with Dependent Children (AFDC), popularly called welfare. He responded to changing public sentiment that tended to blame poverty on the poor themselves and on welfare programs that trapped the poor in cycles of dependency, rather than on external circumstances, such as lack of adequate jobs and childcare. Many questioned why they should subsidize poor mothers when so many women worked outside the home. Defenders of AFDC doubted that the economy could provide sufficient jobs at decent wages and pointed to the substantial subsidies the government provided to other groups, such as large farmers, corporations, and homeowners.

After vetoing two welfare bills, Clinton signed a less punitive measure as the 1996 election approached. The **Personal Responsibility and Work Opportunity Reconciliation Act** replaced AFDC with Temporary Assistance for Needy Families, which provided grants to the states to assist the poor. It limited welfare payments to two consecutive years, with a lifetime maximum of five years.

Clinton's signature on the new law denied Republicans a partisan issue in the 1996 presidential campaign. The Republican Party also moved to the center, nominating Kansan Robert Dole, a World War II hero and former Senate majority leader. Clinton won 49 percent of the votes; 41 percent went to Dole and 9 percent to third-party candidate Ross Perot. Voters sent a Republican majority back to Congress.

In 1999, Clinton and Congress further deregulated the financial industry by repealing key aspects of the Glass-Steagall Act, passed during the New Deal to avoid another Great Depression. The Financial Services Modernization Act ended the separation between banking, securities, and insurance services, allowing financial institutions to engage in all three areas, practices that contributed to the severe financial meltdown of 2008.

Impeaching the President

Clinton's magnetism, his ability to capture the middle ground, and the nation's economic

VISUAL ACTIVITY

The end of Welfare
After signing the bill that sharply curtailed government support for poor mothers and their children, Bill Clinton made it a part of his 1996 campaign for reelection. He highlighted the issue especially when campaigning in more conservative regions, as this photo from a campaign stop in Daytona, Florida, shows. AFP/Getty Images.

READING THE IMAGE: What does the poster behind Clinton say about the importance of welfare as an issue in 1996? What "American values" do you think it refers to?

CONNECTIONS: What other programs that addressed the issue of poverty did Clinton advance?

resurgence enabled him to survive scandals and impeachment. Early in his presidency, charges related to firings of White House staff, political use of Federal Bureau of Investigation records, and real estate investments that the Clintons had made in Arkansas led to an official investigation by an independent prosecutor.

In January 1998, the independent prosecutor, Kenneth Starr, began to investigate a charge that Clinton had had sexual relations with a twenty-one-year-old White House intern and then lied about it to a federal grand jury. Starr prepared a case for the House of Representatives, which in December 1998 voted to impeach the president for perjury and obstruction of justice. Clinton became the second president (after Andrew Johnson, in 1868) to be impeached by the House and tried by the Senate.

Most Americans condemned the president's behavior but approved of the job he was doing and opposed his removal from office. Some saw Starr as a fanatic invading individuals' privacy. Those favoring removal insisted that the president must set a high moral standard and that lying to a grand jury, even over a private matter, was a serious offense. With a two-thirds majority needed for conviction, the Senate voted 45 to 55 on the perjury count and 50 to 50 on the obstruction of justice count. A majority, including some Republicans, seemed to agree with a Clinton supporter that the president's behavior, though "indefensible, outrageous, unforgivable, shameless," did not warrant his removal from office. The investigation that led up to impeachment ended in 2000 when the independent prosecutor reported insufficient evidence of illegalities.

The Booming Economy of the 1990s

Clinton's ability to weather impeachment owed much to the prosperous economy, which in 1991 began a period of tremendous expansion. During the 1990s, the gross domestic product grew by more than one-third, thirteen million new jobs were created, inflation remained in check, unemployment reached 4 percent—its lowest point in twenty-five years—and the stock market soared.

Clinton's policies contributed to the boom. He made deficit reduction a priority, and in exchange the Federal Reserve Board and bond market traders encouraged economic expansion by lowering interest rates. Businesses also prospered because they had lowered their costs

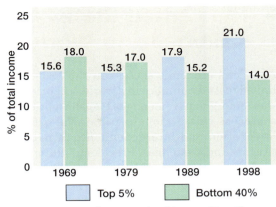

FIGURE 31.1   The Growth of Inequality: Changes in Family income, 1969–1998
For most of the post–World War II period, income increased for all groups on the economic ladder. But after 1979, the income of the poorest families actually declined, while the income of the richest 20 percent of the population grew substantially. Adapted from the *New York Times*, 1989.

through corporate restructuring and employee layoffs. Economic problems in Europe and Asia helped American firms become more competitive in the international market. And the computer revolution and the application of information technology boosted productivity.

People at all income levels benefited from the economic boom, but income inequality, rising since the 1970s, endured (Figure 31.1). The growing use of computer technology increased demand for highly skilled workers, while the movement of manufacturing jobs abroad diminished opportunities and wages for the less skilled. Moreover, deregulation and the continuing decline of unions hurt lower-skilled workers, tax cuts favored the better-off, and the minimum wage failed to keep up with inflation.

Although more minorities than ever attained middle-class status, people of color overall remained lowest on the economic ladder. For instance, in 1999 the median income for white households surpassed $45,000, but it stood at only $29,423 and $33,676 for African American and Latino households, respectively. In 2000, poverty afflicted more than 20 percent of African Americans and Latinos, in contrast to 7.5 percent of whites.

REVIEW: How did President Clinton seek a middle ground in American politics?

▶ The United States in a Globalizing World

America's economic success in the 1990s was linked to its dominance in a world economy that was undergoing tremendous transformations in a process called globalization—the growing integration and interdependence of national citizens and economies. President Clinton lowered a number of trade barriers, despite critics who emphasized the economic deprivation and environmental devastation that often resulted. Debates likewise arose over the large numbers of immigrants entering the United States.

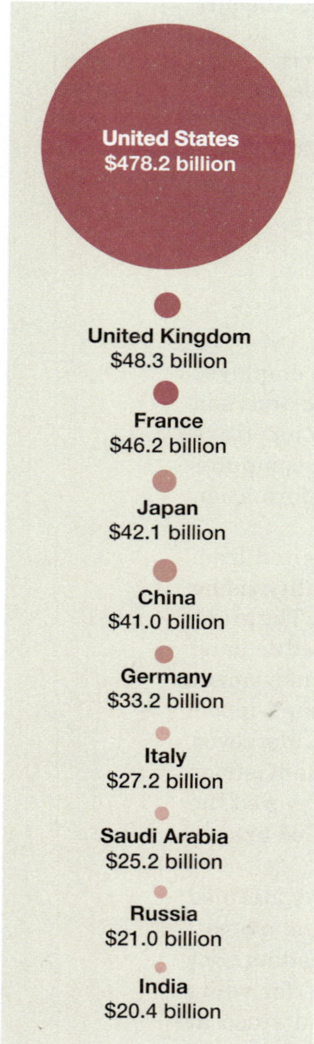

Clinton agreed with Bush that the United States must retain its supreme position in the world. He took military action in Somalia, Haiti, the Middle East, and Eastern Europe, and he pushed hard to ease the conflict between Israelis and Palestinians. Clinton also strove to safeguard American interests from terrorist attacks around the world, a challenge in some ways more difficult than combating communism.

Defining America's Place in a New World Order

In 1991, President George H. W. Bush declared a "new world order" emerging from the ashes of the Cold War. As the sole superpower, the United States was determined to let no nation challenge its military superiority or global leadership: it spent ten times more on defense than its nearest competitor, China (Figure 31.2). Defining principles for the use of that power in a post–Cold War world remained a challenge.

Africa, where civil wars and extreme human suffering rarely evoked a strong U.S. response, was a case in point. In 1992, President Bush had attached U.S. forces to a UN operation in the northern African country of Somalia, where famine and civil war raged. In 1993, President Clinton allowed that humanitarian mission to turn into "nation building"—an effort to establish a stable government—and eighteen U.S. soldiers were killed. The outcry after Americans saw film of a soldier's corpse dragged through the streets suggested that most citizens were unwilling to sacrifice lives when no vital interest was threatened. Indeed, both the United States and the UN stood by in 1994 when more than half a million people were massacred in a brutal civil war in Rwanda.

As always, the United States was more inclined to use force nearer its borders. In 1994, after a military coup overthrew Jean-Bertrand Aristide, Haiti's democratically elected president, Clinton persuaded the United Nations to impose economic sanctions on Haiti and to authorize military intervention. Hours before U.S. forces were to invade, Haitian military leaders promised to step down. U.S. forces peacefully landed, and Aristide was restored to power, but Haiti continued to face grave economic challenges and political instability.

In Eastern Europe, the collapse of communism ignited a severe crisis. During the Cold War, the Communist government of Yugoslavia had held together a federation of six republics. After the Communists were swept out in 1989, ruthless leaders exploited ethnic differences to bolster their power. Yugoslavia splintered into separate states and fell into civil war.

The Serbian aggression under President Slobodan Milosevic against Bosnian Muslims, which included rape, torture, and mass killings, horrified much of the world, but European and U.S. leaders hesitated to use military force. Finally, in 1995, Clinton ordered U.S. fliers to join NATO forces in intensive bombing of Serbian military concentrations. That effort and successful offensives by the Croatian and Bosnian armies forced Milosevic to the bargaining table, where representatives from Serbia, Croatia, and Bosnia hammered out a peace treaty.

In 1998, new fighting broke out in the southern Serbian province of Kosovo, where ethnic Albanians, who constituted 90 percent of the population, demanded independence. When the

United States
$478.2 billion

United Kingdom
$48.3 billion

France
$46.2 billion

Japan
$42.1 billion

China
$41.0 billion

Germany
$33.2 billion

Italy
$27.2 billion

Saudi Arabia
$25.2 billion

Russia
$21.0 billion

India
$20.4 billion

FIGURE 31.2 Global Comparison: Countries with the Highest Military Expenditures, 2005
During the Cold War, the military budgets of the United States and the Soviet Union were relatively even. Even before the Iraq War began in 2003, the U.S. military budget constituted 47 percent of total world military expenditures. Massive defense budgets reflected the determination of Democratic and Republican administrations alike to maintain dominance in the world, even while the capacities of traditional enemies shrunk.

Serbian army retaliated, in 1999, NATO launched a U.S.-led bombing attack on Serbian military and government targets that, after three months, forced Milosevic to agree to a settlement. Serbians voted Milosevic out of office in October 2000, and he died in 2006 while on trial for genocide by a UN war crimes tribunal.

Elsewhere, Clinton deployed U.S. power when he could send missiles rather than soldiers, and he was prepared to act without international support or UN sanction. In August 1998, bombings at the U.S. embassies in Kenya and Tanzania killed 12 Americans and more than 250 Africans.

Breakup of Yugoslavia

Clinton retaliated with missile attacks on terrorist training camps in Afghanistan and facilities in Sudan controlled by Osama bin Laden, a Saudi-born millionaire who financed Al Qaeda, the Islamic-extremist terrorist network linked to the embassy attacks. Clinton also launched air strikes against Iraq in 1993 when a plot to assassinate former president Bush was uncovered, in 1996 after Saddam Hussein attacked the Kurds in northern Iraq, and repeatedly between 1998 and 2000 after Hussein expelled UN weapons inspectors. Whereas Bush had acted in the Gulf War

VISUAL ACTIVITY

Ethnic Strife in Kosovo
In 1999, American troops joined a NATO peacekeeping force in the former Yugoslav province of Kosovo. Here, an ethnic Albanian boy walks beside Specialist Brent Baldwin as the soldier patrols the town of Gnjilane in southeast Kosovo in May 2000. AP Photo.

READING THE IMAGE: What attitude about the U.S. soldiers does this boy display? What did the presence of American troops mean to people like him?

CONNECTIONS: Where else did President Clinton deploy military force in the 1990s?

Israel and PLO sign accords, 1993
Israel and Jordan sign peace treaty, 1994
Progress of Israeli-Palestinian negotiations halts and violence escalates, 2000
Israel withdraws from Gaza, 2005
Israel at war with Hezbollah in Lebanon, 2006
Israel invades Gaza, 2008

Events in Israel since 1989

with the support of an international force that included Arab states, Clinton acted unilaterally and in the face of Arab opposition.

To defuse the Israeli-Palestinian conflict, Clinton applied diplomatic rather than military power. In 1993, Norwegian diplomats had brokered an agreement between Yasir Arafat, head of the Palestine Liberation Organization (PLO), and Yitzhak Rabin, Israeli prime minister, to recognize the existence of each other's states. Israel agreed to withdraw from the Gaza Strip and Jericho, allowing for Palestinian self-government there. In July 1994, Clinton presided over another turning point as Rabin and King Hussein of Jordan signed a declaration of peace. Yet difficult issues remained, especially control of Jerusalem and the presence of more than 200,000 Israeli settlers in the West Bank, the land seized by Israel in 1967, where three million Palestinians were determined to establish their own state.

Debates over Globalization

Building on efforts by Reagan and Bush, Clinton sought to speed up the growth of a "global marketplace" with new measures to ease restrictions on international commerce. Although the process of globalization was centuries old, new communications technologies such as the Internet and cell phones connected nations, corporations, and individuals at much faster speeds and much lower costs than ever before. To advance globalization and the U.S. economy, in 1993, Clinton won congressional approval of the **North American Free Trade Agreement (NAFTA)**, which eliminated all tariffs and trade barriers among the United States, Canada, and Mexico. Fearing loss of jobs and industries to Mexico, a majority of Democrats opposed NAFTA, but Republican support ensured approval. In 1994, the Senate ratified the General Agreement on Tariffs and Trade, establishing the **World Trade Organization (WTO)** to enforce substantial tariff and import quota reductions among some 135 member nations. And in 2005, Clinton's successor, George W. Bush, lowered more trade barriers with the passage of the Central American–Dominican Republic Free Trade Agreement.

The free trade issue was intensely contested. Much of corporate America welcomed the elimination of trade barriers. "Ideally, you'd have every plant you own on a barge," remarked Jack Welch, CEO of General Electric. Critics linked globalization to the loss of good jobs, the weakening of unions, and the growing gap between rich and poor. (See "Beyond America's Borders," page 904.) Demanding "fair trade" rather than simply free trade, critics wanted treaties to require decent wage and labor standards. Environmentalists wanted countries seeking increased commerce with the United States to reduce pollution and prevent the destruction of endangered species.

Globalization controversies often centered on relationships between the United States, which dominated the world's industrial core, and developing nations on the periphery, whose cheap labor and lax environmental standards

VISUAL ACTIVITY

The Internet

In 1958, in response to the Soviet launch of *Sputnik,* President Eisenhower created the Advanced Research Projects Agency (ARPA), which produced a system that routed digitized messages between computers to facilitate military communications. The technology spread beyond the military; by 2000, even the poorest countries had some access to what became the Internet. By 2011, Internet-enabled "smart phones" were abundant. Activists used digital networks to organize protests and broadcast their stories and images during the Arab Spring of 2011. © Ron Haviv/VII/Corbis

READING THE IMAGE: What forms of technology do you see among these Egyptian protesters? What are some pros and cons of using these technologies for political activism?

CONNECTIONS: How did the Obama administration respond to the Arab Spring revolutions?

caught investors' eyes. United Students against Sweatshops, for example, attacked the international conglomerate Nike, which paid Chinese workers $1.50 to produce a pair of shoes selling for more than $100 in the United States. Yet leaders of developing nations actively sought foreign investment because wages deemed pitiful by Americans often provided their impoverished people a much better living than they could otherwise obtain. At the same time, developing countries often pointed to American hypocrisy in advocating free trade in industry while heavily subsidizing the U.S. agricultural sector. "When countries like America, Britain and France subsidize their farmers," complained a grower in Uganda, "we get hurt."

Whereas globalization's cheerleaders pointed to the cheap consumer goods available to Americans and argued that everyone would benefit in the long run, critics focused on the short-term victims. American businessman George Soros conceded that international trade and investments generated wealth, "but they cannot take care of other social needs, such as the preservation of peace, alleviation of poverty, protection of the environment, labor conditions, or human rights." In 2000, President Clinton responded to such criticism by ordering an environmental impact review before the signing of any trade agreement. Beyond the United States, officials from the World Bank and the International Monetary Fund, along with representatives from wealthy economies, promised to provide poor nations more debt relief and a greater voice in decisions about loans and grants. According to World Bank president James D. Wolfensohn, "Our challenge is to make globalization an instrument of opportunity and inclusion—not fear."

The Internationalization of the United States

The United States experienced the dynamic forces of globalization in many ways. Already in the 1980s, Japanese, European, and Middle Eastern investors had purchased U.S. stocks and bonds, real estate, and corporations. Local communities welcomed foreign capital, and states competed to recruit foreign automobile plants. By 2002, the paychecks of nearly four million American workers came from foreign-owned companies, such as Honda and BMW.

Globalization was also transforming American society, as the United States experienced a tremendous surge of immigration, part of a worldwide trend that counted some 214 million immigrants across the globe in 2010. By 2006, the United States' 35.7 million immigrants constituted 12.4 percent of the population. In contrast to earlier immigrants, who had come largely from Europe, by the 1980s the vast majority came from Asia, Latin America, and the Caribbean. Consequently, immigration changed the racial and ethnic composition of the nation. By 2012, 53 million Latinos constituted—at 17 percent—the largest minority group in the nation. The promise of economic opportunity, as always, lured immigrants to America, and the Immigration and Nationality Act of 1965 enabled them to come. The law allowed close relatives of U.S. citizens to enter above the annual ceiling of 270,000 immigrants, thus creating family migration chains. Moreover, during the Cold War, U.S. immigration policy was generous to refugees from communism, welcoming more than 800,000 Cubans and more than 600,000 Vietnamese, Laotians, and Cambodians.

The racial composition of the new immigration heightened the long-standing wariness of native-born Americans toward newcomers. Pressure for more restrictive policies stemmed from beliefs that immigrants took jobs from the native-born, suppressed wages by accepting low pay, strained social services, or eroded the dominant culture and language. Americans expressed particular hostility toward immigrants who were in the country illegally, estimated at 11.7 million

Immigrant Labor
Large commercial farms depended on Latino workers, who constituted more than 45 percent of crop workers in 2002. The dependence of agriculture and service industries on immigrant labor helped block movements for greater immigration restrictions. The workers here are harvesting strawberries near Carlsbad, California. In 2002, the median weekly pay for migrant farmworkers was $300. Sandy Huffaker/Getty Images.

Jobs in a Globalizing Era

In 2001, Paul Sufronko, a supervisor at Rocky Shoes and Boots in Nelsonville, Ohio, handed out final paychecks to the company's last sixty-seven employees in the United States, ending a process of outsourcing that had begun in the 1980s. Before his own job ended, Sufronko traveled to Rocky plants in Puerto Rico and the Dominican Republic to train local workers to replace him. Asked about his job loss, the thirty-six-year-old said, "I had other plans. Things just didn't work out."

Other Americans did not take the loss of their jobs to foreign workers so philosophically. An autoworker believed that "corporations are looking for a disposable workforce. . . . No commitment to community; no commitment to country."

In 1960, American workers made 96 percent of all shoes bought in the United States; by 2000, nearly all shoes came from abroad. The globalizing process was not a new experience for Julio Lopez, a temporary beneficiary of Rocky's outsourcing of labor. After Lopez lost his job of twenty-three years when his employer moved production overseas, he found work at Rocky's Puerto Rico plant at a rate of $5.15 an hour, less than half of what Nelsonville workers had earned. Lopez hoped that the factory would

stay in Puerto Rico for eight more years. "Then I will be sixty-two, and I can retire." Lillian Chaparro, the plant manager, spoke about the perpetual motion of jobs: "It's like a chain, you know? The jobs leave the U.S. They come here. Then they go to the Dominican, to China. That's why I push people—we have to be able to compete."

The athletic shoe manufacturer Nike was one of the first to exploit the advantages of production abroad, turning to Japan in the 1960s. When labor costs there began to rise, Nike shifted production to South Korea. When Korean workers demanded better wages and working conditions, Nike turned to China and other Asian countries. Local contractors in Indonesia paid workers as little as fifteen cents an hour as they produced seventy million pairs of shoes in 1996.

Charles Seitz, who lost his job at Eastman Kodak when the company moved some operations to China and Mexico, was not entirely wrong when he said, "There's nothing made here anymore." The proportion of American workers in manufacturing jobs fell from one-third in the 1950s to 10 percent by the twenty-first century. Of course, not all the job losses resulted from outsourcing. At Kodak, for example, a

machine replaced fourteen workers who previously had mixed filmmaking ingredients. In the 1980s and 1990s, American corporations sought increased productivity so that they could downsize their workforces and reduce costs. Moreover, some companies built plants abroad to be close to burgeoning markets there. Because so many companies, like Nike, contracted out production to foreign companies rather than employing foreign workers directly, the number of U.S. jobs lost to foreign workers is difficult to calculate.

The outsourcing of work did not end with manufacturing jobs. Corporations began to employ workers abroad, especially in India, for a wide range of service and professional work. For example, 1,700 engineers and scientists conducted research for General Electric in Bangalore, India. Technology experts in Bangalore provided telephone help for Dell computer users, and American schoolchildren received online tutoring from teachers in Cochin, India. A research firm executive pointed to the power of technology to overcome distance and noted, "You can get crackerjack Java programmers in India right out of college for $5,000 a year versus $60,000."

in 2013, even though the economy depended on their cheap labor.

The new immigration was once again making America an international, interracial society. The largest numbers of immigrants flocked to California, New York, Texas, Florida, New Jersey, and Illinois, but new immigrants dispersed throughout the country. Taquerias, sushi bars, and Vietnamese restaurants appeared in southeastern and midwestern towns; cable TV companies added Spanish-language stations; and the international sport of soccer soared in popularity. Mixed marriages displayed the growing fusion of cultures, recognized in 2000 on Census Bureau forms, where Americans could check

more than one racial category. Like their predecessors, the majority of post-1965 immigrants were unskilled and poor. They took the lowest-paying jobs, constituting nearly half of all farmworkers and housekeepers. Yet a significant number of immigrants were highly skilled workers, sought after by burgeoning high-tech industries. By 2006, nearly one-third of all software developers were foreign-born, as were 28 percent of all physicians.

REVIEW: What were the costs and benefits to the United States of globalization in the 1990s and early 2000s?

The flight of jobs has not been entirely one-way. Seeking to move production closer to its market, in 1983 Japan's second-largest auto-maker, Nissan, opened a plant in Smyrna, Tennessee, which would become the largest auto plant in the United States. The plant was non-union, and wages were lower than those of Michigan autoworkers. Yet Daren Shanks, who came from a Tennessee farming town, felt that his job on the engine line gave him "the opportunity to do stuff for my kids that I'd never have had the opportunity to do." By 2007, nearly 5 percent of all American workers, and more than 10 percent of those in manufacturing, received their paychecks from foreign companies operating in the United States.

The majority of manufacturing jobs, however, moved in the opposite direction. In 2003, Levi Strauss and Company closed its last plants in the United States, contracting out its work in fifty other countries from Latin America to Asia. Marivel Gutierez, a side-seam operator in the San Antonio plant, acknowledged that workers in Mexico and elsewhere would benefit, suggesting the globalization of the American dream. "But what happens to our American dream?" Workers like Gutierez stood as stark reminders that as many reaped the benefits of free enterprise across national borders, globalization left multitudes of victims in its wake.

Making Nikes in Vietnam

In 1995, Nike began to contract with Vietnamese factories to produce footwear. In the United States, Nike faced protests and boycotts over working conditions in Vietnamese plants, but their wages surpassed those available to most Vietnamese. These workers in a plant just outside of Ho Chi Minh City were among some 130,000 Vietnamese producing Nike products in 2005. AP Photo/Richard Vogel.

America in a Global Context

1. Why did manufacturing jobs move from the United States to other countries in the 1980s and beyond?

2. What impact did the outsourcing of jobs have on workers in the United States and elsewhere?

Connect to the Big Idea

🅒 In what other ways did globalization directly affect the lives of millions of Americans?

▶ President George W. Bush: Conservatism at Home and Radical Initiatives Abroad

Although failing to capture a plurality of the popular vote in 2000, George W. Bush made his mark in domestic policy with key legislation to improve public school education, subsidize prescription drugs for elderly citizens, and greatly reduce taxes for the wealthy. The tax cuts, along with spending on new crises, created the largest budget deficit in the nation's history, and a financial crisis near the end of his presidency sent the economy into a recession.

As Islamist terrorism replaced communism as the primary threat to U.S. security, the Bush administration launched a war in Afghanistan in 2001 and invaded Iraq in 2003. Bush won reelection in 2004, but stability in Iraq and Afghanistan remained elusive, and he confronted serious foreign and domestic crises in his second term. Democrats capitalized on widespread dissatisfaction with his administration to gain control of Congress in 2006 and the White House in 2008.

The Disputed Election of 2000

The oldest son of former president George H. W. Bush, George W. Bush was the governor of Texas when he won the Republican presidential nomination. Inexperienced in national and international affairs, Bush chose for his running mate a seasoned official, Richard B. Cheney, who had served in three previous Republican administrations. Many observers predicted that the thriving economy would give the Democratic contender, Vice President Al Gore, the edge, and he did surpass Bush by more than half a million votes. But Florida's 25 electoral college votes would decide the presidency. Bush's tiny margin in Florida prompted an automatic recount of the votes, which eventually gave him an edge of 537 popular votes in that state.

The Democrats asked for hand-counting of Florida ballots in several heavily Democratic counties where machine errors and confusing ballots may have left thousands of Gore votes unrecorded. The Republicans, in turn, went to court to try to stop the hand-counts. The outcome of the 2000 election hung in the balance for weeks as cases went all the way to the Supreme Court. Finally, a sharply divided Court ruled five to four against allowing the state to conduct further recounts. While critics charged partisanship, noting that the conservative justices had abandoned their principle of favoring

state over federal authority, Gore conceded the presidency to Bush. For the first time since 1888, a president who failed to win the popular vote took office (Map 31.3). Despite the lack of a popular mandate, the Bush administration set out to make dramatic policy changes.

The Domestic Policies of a "Compassionate Conservative"

Bush had promised to govern as a "compassionate conservative." Embracing the nation's diversity and following in Clinton's footsteps, he appointed African Americans, Latinos, and Asian Americans to his cabinet. A devout born-again Christian, he immediately established the White House Office of Faith-Based and Community Initiatives, funding religious groups to run programs for prison inmates, the unemployed, and others. Conservatives praised the initiatives, which encouraged private institutions to replace government as the provider of welfare, but others charged that they violated the constitutional separation of church and state. Federal courts ruled in several dozen cases that faith ministries were using government funds to indoctrinate the people they served. More substantial was Bush's achievement of legislation authorizing a $15 billion anti-AIDS program in Africa that eventually saved millions of lives.

By contrast, Bush's fiscal policies were more compassionate toward the rich than toward average Americans. In 2001, he signed a bill reducing taxes over the next ten years by $1.35 trillion. A 2003 tax law slashed another $320 billion. The laws heavily favored the rich by reducing income taxes, phasing out estate taxes, and cutting tax rates on capital gains and dividends. They also provided benefits for married couples and families with children and offered tax deductions for college expenses.

The tax cuts helped turn the budget surplus that Bush had inherited into a mushrooming federal deficit—the highest in U.S. history. In 2009, the deficit surpassed $1 trillion as the government struggled to combat a recession. By then, the national debt had risen to $9.6 trillion, making the United States increasingly dependent on China and other foreign investors, who held more than half of the debt.

Bush used executive powers to weaken environmental protection as part of his larger goals of reducing government regulation, promoting economic growth, and increasing energy production. The administration opened millions of wilderness acres to mining, oil, and

MAP 31.3
The Election of 2000

Candidate	Electoral Vote	Popular Vote	Percent of Popular Vote
George W. Bush (Republican)	271	50,456,062	47.8
Al Gore (Democrat)	267	50,996,862	48.4
Ralph Nader (Green Party)	0	2,858,843	2.7
Patrick J. Buchanan (Reform Party)	0	438,760	0.4

timber industries and relaxed standards under the Clean Air and Clean Water Acts. To worldwide dismay, the administration withdrew from the Kyoto Protocol on global warming, signed in 1997 by 178 nations to reduce greenhouse gas emissions that cause global warming.

Conservatives hailed Bush's two appointments to the Supreme Court. In 2005, John Roberts, who had served in the Reagan and George H. W. Bush administrations, was named chief justice. When the moderate Sandra Day O'Connor resigned, Bush nominated Samuel A. Alito, a staunch conservative who won confirmation by a narrow margin. While the Court upheld the rights of homosexuals and stood up to the administration in rulings on the rights of accused terrorists, it also upheld increasing restrictions on abortion and struck down regulations in the areas of gun control, sex discrimination in employment, campaign financing, and business practices.

In contrast to the partisan conflict over judicial appointments and tax and environmental policy, Bush won bipartisan support for the **No Child Left Behind Act** of 2002, marking the first substantial expansion of the federal government in public education since the 1960s. Promising to end, in Bush's words, "the story of children being just shuffled through the system," the law required every school to meet annual testing standards, penalized failing schools, and allowed parents to transfer their children out of such schools. But the law was never adequately funded, and as states struggled to finance the new standards and administer new tests, school officials began to criticize the one-size-fits-all approach. They pointed to family and community impoverishment as sources of student deficiencies, which schools alone could not overcome.

The Bush administration's second effort to co-opt Democratic Party issues constituted what the president hailed as "the greatest advance in health care coverage for America's seniors" since Medicare became law in 1965. In 2003, Bush signed a bill authorizing prescription drug benefits for the elderly and also expanding the role of private insurers in the Medicare system. Most Democrats opposed the legislation because it subsidized private insurers with federal funds, banned imports of low-priced drugs, and prohibited the government from negotiating with drug companies to reduce prices. The law was a boon to the elderly, but medical costs overall continued to soar, and the number of uninsured Americans surpassed forty million in 2008.

One domestic undertaking of the Bush administration found little approval anywhere: its handling of Hurricane Katrina, which in August 2005 devastated the coasts of Alabama, Louisiana, and Mississippi and ultimately resulted in some fifteen hundred deaths. The catastrophe that ensued when the levees in New Orleans broke, flooding 80 percent of the city, shook a deeply rooted assumption of Americans that government owed its citizens protection from natural disasters. New Orleans residents who were too old, too poor, or too sick to flee the flooding spent anguished days waiting on rooftops for help; wading in filthy, toxic water; and enduring the heat, disorder, and lack of basic necessities at the centers where they had been told to go for safety and protection. "How can we save the world if we can't save our own people?" wondered one Louisianan. Since so many of Katrina's hardest-hit victims were poor

Hurricane Katrina
Residents of the poverty-stricken Lower Ninth Ward of New Orleans pleaded for help in the flooding that followed Hurricane Katrina in August 2005. The boat was useless because it had lost its motor. Some residents waited as long as five days to be rescued. A historian of the disaster wrote, "Americans were not used to seeing their country in ruins, their people in want." AP Photo/David J. Phillip.

9/11

The magnitude of the destruction and loss of lives in the 9/11 attacks made Americans feel more vulnerable than they had since the Cold War ended. The attacks also affected people around the world, who streamed to U.S. embassies or expressed their shock and sympathy in other ways. Steve Ludlum/The New York Times/Redux.

and black, the disaster also highlighted the injustices and deprivations remaining in American society.

The Globalization of Terrorism

The response to Hurricane Katrina contrasted sharply with the government's decisive reaction to the horror that had unfolded four years earlier on the morning of September 11, 2001. Nineteen terrorists hijacked four planes and flew two of them into the twin towers of New York City's World Trade Center and one into the Pentagon in Washington, D.C.; the fourth crashed in a field in Pennsylvania. The attacks took nearly 2,800 lives, including U.S. citizens and people from ninety countries.

The hijackers belonged to Osama bin Laden's Al Qaeda international terrorist network. Organized from Afghanistan, ruled by the radical Muslim Taliban government, the attacks reflected Islamic extremists' rage at the spread of Western culture and values into the Muslim world. The attacks also demonstrated their opposition to the 1991 Persian Gulf War against Iraq and the stationing of American troops in Saudi Arabia. Bin Laden sought to rid the Middle East of Western influence and install puritanical Muslim control.

The 9/11 terrorists and others who came after them ranged from poor to well-off; some lived in Middle Eastern homelands governed by undemocratic and corrupt governments, others in Western cities where they felt alienated and despised. All saw the West, especially the United States, as the evil source of their humiliation and the supporter of Israel's oppression of Palestinian Muslims.

In the wake of the September 11 attacks, President Bush sought a global alliance against terrorism and won at least verbal support from most governments. On October 11, with NATO support, the United States and Britain began bombing Afghanistan, and American special forces aided the Northern Alliance, the Taliban government's main opposition. By December, the Taliban government was destroyed, but bin Laden eluded capture, continuing to direct Al Qaeda forces throughout the world, until U.S. special forces killed him in Pakistan in 2011. Afghans elected a new national government, but the Taliban remained strong in large parts of the country, continued to challenge U.S. and NATO troops, and contributed to economic stability and insecurity.

After the September 11 attacks, anti-immigrant sentiment revived throughout the United States, and residents appearing to be Middle Eastern or practicing Islam often aroused suspicion. Authorities arrested more than a thousand Arabs and Muslims, and a Justice Department study later reported that many people with no connection to terrorism spent months in jail, denied their rights. "I think America overreacted . . . by singling out Arab-named men like myself," said Shanaz Mohammed, who was jailed for eight months for an immigration violation.

In October 2001, Congress passed the **USA Patriot Act,** which gave the government new powers to monitor suspected terrorists and their associates, including the ability to access personal information. It soon provoked calls for revision from both conservatives and liberals. Kathleen MacKenzie, a councilwoman in Ann Arbor, Michigan, explained why the council opposed the Patriot Act: "As concerned as we were about national safety, we felt that giving up [rights] was too high a price to pay." A security official countered, "If you don't violate someone's human rights some of the time, you probably aren't doing your job." A decade past 9/11, the government continued to gather personal information on individual citizens, seeming to some to have sacrificed too much liberty for security.

Insisting that presidential powers were virtually limitless in times of national crisis, Bush stretched his authority as commander in chief until he met resistance from the courts and Congress. The U.S. detained more than 700 prisoners captured in Afghanistan and taken to the U.S. military base at Guantánamo, Cuba, where, until the courts acted, they had no rights and some were tortured. Although President Barack Obama promised to close the detention camp, he met resistance from Congress, and more than one hundred prisoners remained there in 2014.

The government also sought to protect Americans from future terrorist attacks through the greatest reorganization of the executive branch since 1948. In November 2002, Congress authorized the new Department of Homeland Security, combining 170,000 federal employees from twenty-two agencies responsible for various aspects of domestic security. Chief among the department's duties were intelligence analysis; immigration and border security; chemical, biological, and nuclear countermeasures; and emergency preparedness and response.

Unilateralism, Preemption, and the Iraq War

The Bush administration sought collective action against the Taliban, but on most international issues it adopted a go-it-alone approach. In addition to withdrawing from the Kyoto Protocol on global warming and violating international rules about the treatment of military prisoners, it scrapped the 1972 Antiballistic Missile Treaty to develop the space-based Strategic Defense Initiative first proposed by

Ronald Reagan. Bush also withdrew the nation from the UN's International Criminal Court, and he rejected an agreement to enforce bans on biological weapons that all of America's European allies had signed.

Afghanistan

Nowhere was the policy of unilateralism more striking than in a new war against Iraq, a war pushed by Vice President Dick Cheney and Secretary of Defense Donald H. Rumsfeld, but not by Secretary of State Colin Powell. Addressing West Point graduates in June 2002, President Bush proclaimed a new security strategy based not on containment but on preemption: "Traditional concepts of deterrence will not work against a terrorist enemy whose avowed tactics are wanton destruction and the targeting of innocents; whose so-called soldiers seek martyrdom in death and whose most potent protection is statelessness." Because even weak countries and small groups could strike devastating blows at the United States, as Al Qaeda had done on 9/11, the nation had to "be ready for preemptive action." The president's claim that the United States had the right to start a war was at odds with international law and with many Americans' understanding of their nation's ideals. It distressed most of America's great-power allies.

Nonetheless, the Bush administration soon applied the doctrine of preemption to Iraq, whose dictator, Saddam Hussein, appeared to be violating UN resolutions from the 1991 Gulf War restricting Iraqi development of nuclear, chemical, and biological weapons. In November 2002, the United States persuaded the UN Security Council to pass a resolution demanding that Iraq disarm or face "serious consequences." When Iraq failed to comply fully with new UN inspections, the Bush administration decided on war. Making claims that were subsequently refuted that Hussein had links to Al Qaeda and harbored terrorists and that Iraq possessed weapons of mass destruction, the president insisted that the threat was immediate and great enough

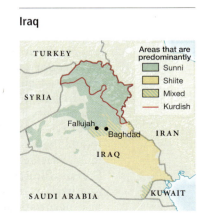

Iraq

Areas that are predominantly		
Sunni		
Shiite		
Mixed		
Kurdish		

to justify pre-emptive action. Despite the absence of UN approval and opposition from the Arab world and most major nations—including France, Germany, China, and Russia—the United States and Britain invaded Iraq on March 19, 2003, supported by some thirty nations (see Map 31.2). Coalition forces won an easy victory, and Bush declared the end of the **Iraq War** on May 1. Saddam Hussein remained at large until December 2003.

Chaos followed the quick victory. Damage from U.S. bombing and widespread looting resulting from the failure of U.S. troops to secure order and provide basic necessities left Iraqis wondering how much they had gained. "With Saddam there was tyranny, but at least you had a salary to put food on your family's table," said a young father. A Baghdad hospital worker complained, "They can take our oil, but at least they should let us have electricity and water." Five years after the invasion, continuing violence had caused 2 million to flee their country and displaced 1.9 million within Iraq.

The administration had not planned adequately for the occupation and failed to send sufficient troops to Iraq. The 140,000 American forces there came under attack almost daily from remnants of the former Hussein regime, religious extremists, and hundreds of foreign terrorists now entering the chaotic country. Seeking to divide Iraqis and undermine the occupation, terrorists launched assaults that killed tens of thousands of Iraqis. By the end of the Iraq war, nearly 4,500 U.S. soldiers had lost their lives, and many returned home grievously wounded.

The war became an issue in the presidential campaign of 2004. U.S. senator John Kerry, the Democratic nominee, criticized Bush's unilateralist foreign policy and the administration's conduct of the war. A slim majority of voters, however, indicated their belief that Bush would better protect American security than Kerry. The president eked out a 286 to 252 victory in the electoral college, winning 50.7 percent of the popular vote and carrying Republican majorities into Congress.

In June 2004, the United States transferred sovereignty to an interim Iraqi government, and in January 2005 Iraqis elected a national assembly, which then had to organize a government satisfactory to Iraq's three major groups— Sunnis, Shiites, and Kurds. Violence escalated against government officials, Iraqi civilians, and occupation forces. A nineteen-year-old Iraqi confined to his house by his parents, who feared he could be killed or lured into terrorist activities, said, "If I'm killed, it doesn't even matter because I'm dead right now." By 2006, a majority of Americans told pollsters that the Iraq War was a mistake.

Bush's conduct of the war faced criticism that crossed party lines and included military leaders. Critics acknowledged that the United States had felled a brutal dictator, but coalition forces were not large enough or adequately prepared for the turmoil that followed. Nor did they find the weapons of mass destruction or links to Osama bin Laden that administration officials had insisted made the war necessary. Rather, in the chaos induced by the invasion, more than a thousand terrorists entered Iraq—the place, according to one expert, "for fundamentalists to go . . . to stick it to the West."

The war and occupation exacted a steep price in American and Iraqi lives, dollars (more than $750 billion), U.S. relations with other great powers, and the nation's reputation in the world, especially among Arab nations. Revelations of prisoner abuse in the Abu Ghraib prison in Iraq and in the Guantánamo detention camp housing captives from the Afghan war further tarnished the image of the United States, as Anti-Americanism rose around the world. The budget deficit swelled, and resources were diverted to Iraq from other national security challenges, including the stabilization of Afghanistan, the elimination of bin Laden and Al Qaeda, and the threats posed by North Korea's and Iran's pursuit of nuclear weapons.

Voters registered their dissatisfaction in 2006, when Democrats captured both houses of Congress for the first time since 1994. The Bush administration displayed more willingness to work with other nations in dealing with Iraq, Iran, and North Korea. In 2007, it began a troop surge in Iraq, increasing U.S. forces there to 160,000. The surge, along with actions by Iraqi leaders, contributed to a significant reduction in violence, and the administration began planning for the withdrawal of U.S. forces, which was completed at the end of 2011. Peace eluded the Iraqis, however, who continued to live amidst sectarian violence that killed hundreds of people each month in 2013.

REVIEW: What impact did the terrorist attacks on September 11, 2001, have on U.S. foreign and domestic policies?

▶ The Obama Presidency: Reform and Backlash

Bush's successor, Barack Hussein Obama, aimed to turn the page in both domestic and foreign policy. He achieved major health care reform and some antirecession measures, but a determined grassroots movement on the Republican right pushed the party to oppose the president at every turn. In foreign policy, Obama oversaw the withdrawal of troops from Iraq and generally sought a less aggressive, more multilateral approach to challenges around the world.

Governing during Economic Crisis and Political Polarization

Obama won an election that represented momentous changes in American politics. The Republican nominee, Senator John McCain of Arizona, a Vietnam War hero, chose as his running mate Alaska governor Sarah Palin, the first Republican woman to run for vice president. Even more historic changes occurred in the Democratic Party when, for the first time, an African American and a woman were the top two contenders. (See "Visualizing History," page 914.) In hard-fought primary battles, Barack Obama edged out New York senator and former First Lady Hillary Clinton for the nomination.

Born to a white mother and a Kenyan father and raised in Hawai'i and Indonesia, Obama was the first African American to head the *Harvard Law Review*. He settled in Chicago, served in the Illinois Senate, and won election to the U.S. Senate in 2004. At the age of forty-seven, he won the Democratic presidential nomination with brilliant grassroots and Internet organizing and by appealing to deep-seated longings for a new kind of politics and racial reconciliation. Obama won 53 percent of the popular vote and defeated McCain 365 to 173 in the electoral college to become the first African American president, while Democrats increased their majorities in the House and Senate.

Defining "individual responsibility and mutual responsibility" as "the essence of the American promise," Obama hoped to work across party lines as he pursued reforms in health care, education, the environment, and immigration policy, but he confronted a severe economic crisis. A recession had struck in late 2007, fueled by a breakdown in financial institutions that had accumulated trillions of dollars of bad debt, much of it from risky home mortgages. As the recession spread to other parts of the economy and the world, home mortgage foreclosures skyrocketed, major companies went bankrupt, and unemployment rose to 9.8 percent in late 2010, the highest rate in more than twenty-five years.

The crisis was so severe that Congress passed the Bush administration's $700 billion Troubled Asset Relief Program in 2008 to inject credit into the economy and shore up banks as well as other businesses. Obama followed with the American Recovery and Reinvestment Act of 2009, $787 billion worth of spending and tax cuts to stimulate the economy and relieve unemployment. He also arranged a federal bailout of General Motors and Chrysler, saving an estimated one million jobs related to the automobile industry. Finally, to address the conditions that triggered the financial crisis, Congress expanded governmental regulation with the Wall Street Reform and Consumer Protection Act in 2010.

Backed by a Democrat-controlled Congress for only the first two years of his presidency, Obama's domestic achievements fell short of his promises. His judicial appointments increased the number of women on the Supreme Court to three and included the first ever Latina justice, and he signed legislation that strengthened women's right to equal pay. In addition, Congress ended discrimination against gays in the military and rolled back some of the Bush tax cuts that favored the wealthy.

Obama's paramount domestic achievement was passage of health care reform, putting the United States in step with all the other advanced nations, which subsidized some kind of health care for all citizens. The **Patient Protection and Affordable Care Act** of 2010 required that nearly everyone carry health insurance, and to that end, it provided subsidies and compelled larger businesses to offer coverage to employees. The law also imposed new regulations on insurance companies to protect health care consumers and contained provisions to limit medical costs. Although liberals failed to get a public option to allow government-managed programs to compete with private insurance plans, the law represented the largest expansion of government since the Great Society. Even though Republicans had previously endorsed key elements of the measure, and it resembled the health care reform that Republican governor Mitt Romney had achieved in Massachusetts, not a single Republican voted for it.

"Obamacare" (a derisive label that was later embraced by its supporters), along with the government bailouts of big corporations, helped

Health Care Reform Repeated breakdowns of the federal government's Web site when it opened for health insurance enrollment in October 2013 added fuel to the critics of the Patient Protection and Affordable Care Act. President Obama chose Faneuil Hall in Boston, where former governor Mitt Romney had signed a similar health reform measure for Massachusetts, to defend the law and promise that the Web site would be fixed. Boston Globe via Getty Images.

fuel a grassroots movement of mostly white, middle-class, and older voters funded by billionaire conservatives and encouraged by conservative media. These Americans, who identified themselves as members of the Tea Party movement, raged at what they considered an overreaching government and the sense that they and their values were being displaced. As one Tea Party supporter put it, "The government is taking over everything—I want my freedom back." Most Tea Party activists defended Social Security and Medicare as programs they had "earned" but resisted any new federal entitlement programs. Even after the Supreme Court upheld the constitutionality of Obamacare by a five-to-four vote, House Republicans, urged on by Tea Party groups, held dozens of votes in futile efforts to repeal it. Many Republican governors impeded its implementation in their states.

The Tea Party movement helped Republicans issue a sharp rebuke to Obama in the 2010 midterm elections, turning over the House to the Republicans and cutting into the Democratic majority in the Senate. Although the stock market had rebounded, nearly 10 percent of American workers remained unemployed, and the federal deficit that Obama had inherited from the Bush administration soared to $1.4 trillion.

The intensely polarized political environment posed a roadblock to reducing unemployment and lowering the federal debt. It also thwarted Obama's efforts to reform environmental and immigration policy. With Republicans in Congress blocking him at every turn, Obama used his executive authority to stiffen requirements on motor vehicle emissions, encourage alternative energy, and protect from deportation undocumented immigrants brought to the United States as children.

Obama carried the burden of a nearly 8 percent unemployment rate into the 2012 election, where he faced Republican Mitt Romney. With the electorate deeply divided over the role of the federal government, Obama won easily in the electoral college, with 332 votes to Romney's 206, and he captured 51 percent of the popular vote to Romney's 47 percent (Map 31.4). The Democrats made small gains in Congress, but Republicans still controlled the House, and, within that majority, Tea Party allies determined to block any legislation that did not cut federal spending.

This stalemate, much more severe than the one during the first Bush administration, prevented the government from getting employment back to prerecession levels and from dealing with a staggering (though shrinking) national deficit and debt. Only the wealthiest 5 percent of Americans had completely recovered from the recession. The richest Americans continued to increase their share of national income, and, in 2013, the United States had the greatest degree of income inequality since the 1920s.

Redefining the War on Terror

Obama criticized much of his predecessor's foreign policy, embodied in Bush's term "global war on

Candidate	Electoral Vote	Popular Vote	Percent of Popular Vote
Barack Obama (Democrat)	332	65,899,660	51.1
Mitt Romney (Republican)	206	60,932,152	47.2

3 Washington, D.C.

MAP 31.4
The Election of 2012

terror." Obama believed that that concept exaggerated the threat, rationalized disastrous decisions like the invasion of Iraq, sacrificed American ideals in the pursuit of security, and distracted attention from the need to solve serious problems at home. In office, however, Obama left many Bush initiatives in place. The use of torture had been ended in the Bush administration, but more than a hundred prisoners remained, without rights, at Guantánamo. Obama greatly increased the use of unmanned drone strikes in other countries, killing hundreds of people, both terrorists and innocent citizens. Continuing Bush's surveillance programs, the Obama administration secretly collected data about millions of citizens' telephone calls and e-mail correspondence.

Obama followed the Bush administration's plan to withdraw from Iraq, and the last troops departed in 2011, leaving a country that continued to endure terrorist violence. Even though corruption permeated Afghanistan's government and a majority of Americans now opposed the war there, which had taken more than 2,000 American lives, Obama dispatched 50,000 more military personnel. He promised that the United States could fully withdraw by 2014, but it seemed unlikely that Afghanistan would prove a stable ally in the region. In May 2011, U.S. Special Forces killed Osama bin Laden, who was hiding in Pakistan, weakening, but not destroying, Al Qaeda and its offshoots.

Obama reached out to regain the trust of Muslim nations, but he sometimes floundered in the face of difficult decisions about what role the United States should take when popular uprisings, called the "Arab Spring," sought reforms from long-standing dictators. The calamity of the Iraq War and the desire to improve the nation's international reputation made policymakers wary of intervention. In 2011, when rebellions arose in Tunisia, Egypt, Libya, and Syria, the United States participated in military action only in Libya, only with UN approval, and only in concert with NATO and the Arab League. Each country had experienced long-standing internal divisions, decades of official corruption, and neglect of the basic needs of the populations, such as water and food; moreover, terrorists operated in each country, hoping to exploit the situation to install a radical fundamentalist Islamic state. Although the rebellions toppled corrupt dictators, such as Libya's Muammar al-Gaddafi and Egypt's Hosni Mubarak, little progress was made toward stability, constitutional government, equal rights, and economic security.

Congress and the American people rebuffed Obama in 2013 when he sought approval for a missile strike against government military resources in Syria. Protests in that country had turned into a civil war in which more than 100,000 people were killed, many by their government's use of poison gas against rebels and children. Obama insisted that the United States must remain engaged in the Middle East and pledged to concentrate on two daunting undertakings: resolving the Israeli-Palestinian conflict and working with a new, more moderate government in Iran to keep it from developing nuclear weapons. Obama's conversation with the Iranian president in September 2013 marked the first contact between the leaders of the two nations since 1979. Hope rose that progress in the Middle East might enable the administration to pursue its initial goal of turning attention to Asia, where China grew more powerful economically and militarily.

REVIEW: What obstacles stood in the way of Obama's reform agenda?

▶ Conclusion: Defining the Government's Role at Home and Abroad

More than two hundred years after the birth of the United States, Colin Powell referred to the unfinished nature of the American promise when he declared that the question of America's role in

Caricaturing the Candidates: Clinton and Obama in 2008

In the Democratic presidential primaries of 2008, political cartoonists faced an unusual challenge. For the first time, a woman and an African American squared off as major rivals. How could they portray a woman and a black man without raising charges of sexism or racism?

Hillary Clinton had a history in political cartoons as First Lady and then as senator from New York. Her supporters had already criticized the press for caricatures they felt were as personal as they were political.

Political cartoonists drawing Barack Obama faced the challenge of avoiding obvious racial stereotypes. In his 2004 Democratic convention keynote address, Obama had already described himself as "a skinny kid with big ears and a funny name," and cartoonists capitalized on that image.

In the first cartoon, from February 2008, Hillary Clinton is in the driver's seat of "The Clinton

"The Clinton Machine"

Machine," which is about to crush Barack Obama. Who is providing the power for the steamroller? How does the portrayal of Obama compare with that of Clinton in this cartoon? What does this cartoon imply

the world "isn't answered yet." In fact, the end of the Cold War, the rise of international terrorism, and the George W. Bush administration's doctrines of preemption and unilateralism sparked new debates over the long-standing question of how the United States should act beyond its borders.

Nor had Americans set to rest questions about the role of government at home. In a population greatly derived from people fleeing oppressive governments, Americans had always debated what responsibilities the government should shoulder and what was best left to private enterprise, families, churches, and other voluntary institutions. Far more than most industrialized democracies, the United States had relied on private rather than public obligation, individual rather than collective solutions. In the twentieth century, Americans had significantly enlarged the federal government's powers and responsibilities, but the years since the 1960s had seen a decline of trust in government's ability to improve people's lives, even as a poverty rate of 20 percent among children continued and a growing gap between rich and poor intensified in the twenty-first century.

The shifting of control of the government back and forth between Republicans and Democrats from 1989 to 2012 revealed a dynamic debate over government's role in domestic affairs. Both the first Bush administration's civil rights measure for people with disabilities and Clinton's incremental reforms built on a deep-rooted tradition that sought to realize the American promise of justice and human well-being. Those who mobilized against the ravages of globalization worked internationally for what populists, progressives, New Deal reformers, and activists of the 1960s

about Bill Clinton's role in his wife's campaign and her chances for capturing the Democratic nomination?

In the second cartoon, Clinton appears as "The Incredible Sulk," a monster threatening a nervous Obama as he contemplates choosing a running mate. The cartoon ran in June 2008, in the lead-up to the Democratic National Convention in Denver. Why do you think the artist styled Clinton as a cartoon character who morphs into a monster when provoked? Why do you think the artist portrayed Obama as cowering before his former rival?

These cartoons reproduced here are a tiny sample of the larger world of political commentary. Yet they convey many of the beliefs and attitudes held by the American public as the 2008 primary elections played out.

Although cartoonists tended to portray Clinton and Obama as bitter enemies throughout the primaries, the two politicians began an effective partnership when president-elect Obama selected Clinton for the position of secretary of state in November 2008.

"The Incredible Sulk"

Questions for Analysis

1. Do you think these cartoonists were successful in avoiding sexist or racist portrayals of the candidates? Do you see any sexual or racial stereotypes in the cartoons?

2. What message does the second cartoon send in having Clinton tower over Obama, even though he had just defeated her for the nomination?

Connect to the Big Idea

C In what ways was the election of 2008 groundbreaking?

---

had sought for the domestic population: protection of individual rights, curbs on capitalism, assistance for victims of rapid economic change, and fiscal policies that placed greater responsibility on those best able to pay for the collective good. Even the second Bush administration, which sought to limit government's reach, supported the No Child Left Behind Act and the Medicare prescription drug program; it departed from traditional conservative policy in a gigantic program to bail out failing businesses when the financial crisis hit the economy in 2008. The controversy surrounding Obama's efforts to stimulate the economy and reform health care and the financial industry replayed America's long-standing debate about the government's appropriate role.

The United States became more embedded in the global economy as products, information, and people crossed borders with amazing speed and frequency. New waves of immigration altered the face of the American population and the makeup of its culture. Although the end of the Cold War brought about unanticipated cooperation between the United States and its former enemies, globalization also contributed to the threat of deadly terrorism within America's own borders. In response to those dangers, the second Bush administration launched wars in Afghanistan and Iraq. Both Democratic and Republican presidents sought to maintain the preeminence in the world that the United States had held since World War II, but debate continued about where and how best to use America's power.

See the Selected Bibliography for this chapter in the Appendix.

MAKE IT STICK

LearningCurve
Go online and use LearningCurve to see what you know.
Then review the key terms and answer the questions.

KEY TERMS

Clean Air Act of 1990 (p. 889)
Americans with Disabilities Act (ADA) (p. 889)
Persian Gulf War (p. 895)
Earned Income Tax Credit (EITC) (p. 896)
Personal Responsibility and Work Opportunity
  Reconciliation Act (p. 898)
North American Free Trade Agreement (NAFTA)
  (p. 902)
World Trade Organization (WTO) (p. 902)
No Child Left Behind Act (p. 907)
USA Patriot Act (p. 909)
Iraq War (p. 910)
Patient Protection and Affordable Care Act (p. 911)

REVIEW QUESTIONS

1. How did George H. W. Bush respond to threats to U.S. interests as the Cold War came to an end? (pp. 889–896)

2. How did President Clinton seek a middle ground in American politics? (pp. 896–899)

3. What were the costs and benefits to the United States of globalization in the 1990s and early 2000s? (pp. 900–904)

4. What impact did the terrorist attacks on September 11, 2001, have on U.S. foreign and domestic policies? (pp. 905–910)

5. What obstacles stood in the way of Obama's reform agenda? (pp. 911–913)

MAKING CONNECTIONS

1. How did George H. W. Bush continue the policies of his predecessor, Ronald Reagan? How did he depart from them?

2. How did Clinton's policies differ from those of Democrats in the past?

3. Explain what economic globalization is, and describe how it affected the U.S. economy and population in the 1990s.

4. What gave rise to the 9/11 attacks? How did the United States respond?

LINKING TO THE PAST

1. How did George W. Bush's doctrine of preemption differ from the doctrine of containment? (See chapter 26.)

2. What features did immigration after 1980 have in common with immigration between 1880 and 1920? What was different? (See chapter 19.)

Appendix Directory

APPENDIX I.
Documents

The Declaration of Independence   A-1

The Constitution of the United States   A-3

Amendments to the Constitution with Annotations
(including the six unratified amendments)   A-8

APPENDIX II.
Government and Demographics

Presidential Elections   A-23

Admission of States to the Union   A-26

Major Trends in Immigration   A-28

THE DECLARATION OF INDEPENDENCE

In Congress, July 4, 1776,

THE UNANIMOUS DECLARATION OF THE THIRTEEN UNITED STATES OF AMERICA

When in the course of human events, it becomes necessary for one people to dissolve the political bands which have connected them with another, and to assume, among the powers of the earth, the separate and equal station to which the laws of nature and of nature's God entitle them, a decent respect to the opinions of mankind requires that they should declare the causes which impel them to the separation.

We hold these truths to be self-evident, that all men are created equal; that they are endowed by their Creator with certain unalienable rights; that among these, are life, liberty, and the pursuit of happiness. That, to secure these rights, governments are instituted among men, deriving their just powers from the consent of the governed; that, whenever any form of government becomes destructive of these ends, it is the right of the people to alter or to abolish it, and to institute a new government, laying its foundation on such principles, and organizing its powers in such form, as to them shall seem most likely to effect their safety and happiness. Prudence, indeed, will dictate that governments long established, should not be changed for light and transient causes; and, accordingly, all experience hath shown, that mankind are more disposed to suffer, while evils are sufferable, than to right themselves by abolishing the forms to which they are accustomed. But, when a long train of abuses and usurpations, pursuing invariably the same object, evinces a design to reduce them under absolute despotism, it is their right, it is their duty, to throw off such government and to provide new guards for their future security. Such has been the patient sufferance of these colonies, and such is now the necessity which constrains them to alter their former systems of government. The history of the present King of Great Britain is a history of repeated injuries and usurpations, all having, in direct object, the establishment of an absolute tyranny over these States. To prove this, let facts be submitted to a candid world: He has refused his assent to laws the most wholesome and necessary for the public good.

He has forbidden his governors to pass laws of immediate and pressing importance, unless suspended in their operation till his assent should be obtained; and, when so suspended, he has utterly neglected to attend to them.

He has refused to pass other laws for the accommodation of large districts of people, unless those people would relinquish the right of representation in the legislature; a right inestimable to them, and formidable to tyrants only.

He has called together legislative bodies at places unusual, uncomfortable, and distant from the depository of their public records, for the sole purpose of fatiguing them into compliance with his measures.

He has dissolved representative houses repeatedly for opposing, with manly firmness, his invasions on the rights of the people.

He has refused, for a long time after such dissolutions, to cause others to be elected; whereby the legislative powers, incapable of annihilation, have returned to the people at large for their exercise; the state remaining in the mean-time exposed to all the danger of invasion from without, and convulsions within.

He has endeavoured to prevent the population of these States; for that purpose, obstructing the laws for naturalization of foreigners, refusing to pass others to encourage their migration hither, and raising the conditions of new appropriations of lands.

He has obstructed the administration of justice, by refusing his assent to laws for establishing judiciary powers.

He has made judges dependent on his will alone, for the tenure of their offices, and the amount and payment of their salaries.

He has erected a multitude of new offices, and sent hither swarms of officers to harass our people, and eat out their substance.

He has kept among us, in times of peace, standing armies, without the consent of our legislature.

He has affected to render the military independent of, and superior to, the civil power.

He has combined, with others, to subject us to a jurisdiction foreign to our Constitution, and unacknowledged by our laws; giving his assent to their acts of pretended legislation:

For quartering large bodies of armed troops among us:

For protecting them by a mock trial, from punishment, for any murders which they should commit on the inhabitants of these States:

For cutting off our trade with all parts of the world:

For imposing taxes on us without our consent:

For depriving us, in many cases, of the benefit of trial by jury:

For transporting us beyond seas to be tried for pretended offences:

For abolishing the free system of English laws in a neighboring province, establishing therein an arbitrary government, and enlarging its boundaries, so as to render it at once an example and fit instrument for introducing the same absolute rule into these colonies:

For taking away our charters, abolishing our most valuable laws, and altering, fundamentally, the powers of our governments:

For suspending our own legislatures, and declaring themselves invested with power to legislate for us in all cases whatsoever.

He has abdicated government here, by declaring us out of his protection, and waging war against us.

He has plundered our seas, ravaged our coasts, burnt our towns, and destroyed the lives of our people.

He is, at this time, transporting large armies of foreign mercenaries to complete the works of death, desolation, and tyranny, already begun, with circumstances of cruelty and perfidy scarcely paralleled in the most barbarous ages, and totally unworthy the head of a civilized nation.

He has constrained our fellow citizens, taken captive on the high seas, to bear arms against their country, to become the executioners of their friends, and brethren, or to fall themselves by their hands.

He has excited domestic insurrections amongst us, and has endeavored to bring on the inhabitants of our frontiers, the merciless Indian savages, whose known rule of warfare is an undistinguished destruction of all ages, sexes, and conditions.

In every stage of these oppressions, we have petitioned for redress; in the most humble terms; our repeated petitions have been answered only by repeated injury. A prince, whose character is thus marked by every act which may define a tyrant, is unfit to be the ruler of a free people.

Nor have we been wanting in attention to our British brethren. We have warned them, from time to time, of attempts made by their legislature to extend an unwarrantable jurisdiction over us. We have reminded them of the circumstances of our emigration and settlement here. We have appealed to their native justice and magnanimity, and we have conjured them, by the ties of our common kindred, to disavow these usurpations, which would inevitably interrupt our connections and correspondence. They, too, have been deaf to the voice of justice and consanguinity. We must, therefore, acquiesce in the necessity which denounces our separation, and hold them as we hold the rest of mankind, enemies in war, in peace, friends.

We, therefore, the representatives of the United States of America, in general Congress assembled, appealing to the Supreme Judge of the world for the rectitude of our intentions, do, in the name, and by authority of the good people of these colonies, solemnly publish and declare, that these united colonies are, and of right ought to be, free and independent states: that they are absolved from all allegiance to the British Crown, and that all political connection between them and the state of Great Britain is, and ought to be, totally dissolved; and that, as free and independent states, they have full power to levy war, conclude peace, contract alliances, establish commerce, and to do all other acts and things which independent states may of right do. And, for the support of this declaration, with a firm reliance on the protection of Divine Providence, we mutually pledge to each other our lives, our fortunes, and our sacred honor.

The foregoing Declaration was, by order of Congress, engrossed, and signed by the following members:

JOHN HANCOCK

New Hampshire
Josiah Bartlett
William Whipple
Matthew Thornton

Massachusetts Bay
Samuel Adams
John Adams
Robert Treat Paine
Elbridge Gerry

Rhode Island
Stephen Hopkins
William Ellery

Connecticut
Roger Sherman
Samuel Huntington
William Williams
Oliver Wolcott

New York
William Floyd
Phillip Livingston
Francis Lewis
Lewis Morris

New Jersey
Richard Stockton
John Witherspoon
Francis Hopkinson
John Hart
Abraham Clark

Pennsylvania
Robert Morris
Benjamin Rush
Benjamin Franklin
John Morton
George Clymer
James Smith

George Taylor
James Wilson
George Ross

Delaware
Caesar Rodney
George Read
Thomas M'Kean

Maryland
Samuel Chase
William Paca
Thomas Stone
Charles Carroll,
    of Carrollton

North Carolina
William Hooper
Joseph Hewes
John Penn

South Carolina
Edward Rutledge
Thomas Heyward, Jr.
Thomas Lynch, Jr.
Arthur Middleton

Virginia
George Wythe
Richard Henry Lee
Thomas Jefferson
Benjamin Harrison
Thomas Nelson, Jr.
Francis Lightfoot Lee
Carter Braxton

Georgia
Button Gwinnett
Lyman Hall
George Walton

Resolved, That copies of the Declaration be sent to the several assemblies, conventions, and committees, or councils of safety, and to the several commanding officers of the continental troops; that it be proclaimed in each of the United States, at the head of the army.

THE CONSTITUTION OF THE UNITED STATES*

Agreed to by Philadelphia Convention, September 17, 1787. Implemented March 4, 1789.

Preamble

We the people of the United States, in order to form a more perfect union, establish justice, insure domestic tranquility, provide for the common defense, promote the general welfare, and secure the blessings of liberty to ourselves and our posterity, do ordain and establish this Constitution for the United States of America.

Article I

Section 1 All legislative powers herein granted shall be vested in a Congress of the United States, which shall consist of a Senate and a House of Representatives.

Section 2 The House of Representatives shall be composed of members chosen every second year by the people of the several States, and the electors in each State shall have the qualifications requisite for electors of the most numerous branch of the State Legislature.

No person shall be a Representative who shall not have attained to the age of twenty-five years, and been seven years a citizen of the United States, and who shall not, when elected, be an inhabitant of that State in which he shall be chosen.

Representatives and direct taxes shall be apportioned among the several States which may be included within this Union, according to their respective numbers, *which shall be determined by adding to the whole number of free persons, including those bound to service for a term of years and excluding Indians not taxed, three-fifths of all other persons.* The actual enumeration shall be made within three years after the first meeting of the Congress of the United States, and within every subsequent term of ten years, in such manner as they shall by law direct. The number of Representatives shall not exceed one for every thirty thousand, but each State shall have at least one Representative; *and until such enumeration shall be made, the State of New Hampshire shall be entitled to choose three, Massachusetts eight, Rhode Island and Providence Plantations one, Connecticut five, New York six, New Jersey four, Pennsylvania eight, Delaware one, Maryland six, Virginia ten, North Carolina five, South Carolina five, and Georgia three.*

When vacancies happen in the representation from any State, the Executive authority thereof shall issue writs of election to fill such vacancies.

The House of Representatives shall choose their Speaker and other officers; and shall have the sole power of impeachment.

Section 3 The Senate of the United States shall be composed of two Senators from each State, *chosen by the legislature thereof,* for six years; and each Senator shall have one vote.

Immediately after they shall be assembled in consequence of the first election, they shall be divided as equally as may be into three classes. The seats of the Senators of the first class shall be vacated at the expiration of the second year, of the second class at the expiration of the fourth year, and of the third class at the expiration of the sixth year, so that one-third may be chosen every second year; *and if vacancies happen by resignation or otherwise, during the recess of the legislature of any State, the Executive thereof may make temporary appointments until the next meeting of the legislature, which shall then fill such vacancies.*

No person shall be a Senator who shall not have attained to the age of thirty years, and been nine years a citizen of the United States, and who shall not, when elected, be an inhabitant of that State for which he shall be chosen.

The Vice-President of the United States shall be President of the Senate, but shall have no vote, unless they be equally divided.

The Senate shall choose their other officers, and also a President pro tempore, in the absence of the Vice-President, or when he shall exercise the office of President of the United States.

The Senate shall have the sole power to try all impeachments. When sitting for that purpose, they shall be on oath or affirmation. When the President of the United States is tried, the Chief Justice shall preside: and no person shall be convicted without the concurrence of two-thirds of the members present.

Judgment in cases of impeachment shall not extend further than to removal from the office, and disqualification to hold and enjoy any office of honor, trust or profit under the United States: but the party convicted shall nevertheless be liable and subject to indictment, trial, judgment and punishment, according to law.

*Passages no longer in effect are in italic type.

Section 4 The times, places and manner of holding elections for Senators and Representatives shall be prescribed in each State by the legislature thereof; but the Congress may at any time by law make or alter such regulations, except as to the places of choosing Senators.

The Congress shall assemble at least once in every year, and such meeting *shall be on the first Monday in December, unless they shall by law appoint a different day.*

Section 5 Each house shall be the judge of the elections, returns and qualifications of its own members, and a majority of each shall constitute a quorum to do business; but a smaller number may adjourn from day to day, and may be authorized to compel the attendance of absent members, in such manner, and under such penalties, as each house may provide.

Each house may determine the rules of its proceedings, punish its members for disorderly behavior, and with the concurrence of two-thirds, expel a member.

Each house shall keep a journal of its proceedings, and from time to time publish the same, excepting such parts as may in their judgment require secrecy; and the yeas and nays of the members of either house on any question shall, at the desire of one-fifth of those present, be entered on the journal.

Neither house, during the session of Congress, shall, without the consent of the other, adjourn for more than three days, nor to any other place than that in which the two houses shall be sitting.

Section 6 The Senators and Representatives shall receive a compensation for their services, to be ascertained by law and paid out of the treasury of the United States. They shall in all cases except treason, felony and breach of the peace, be privileged from arrest during their attendance at the session of their respective houses, and in going to and returning from the same; and for any speech or debate in either house, they shall not be questioned in any other place.

No Senator or Representative shall, during the time for which he was elected, be appointed to any civil office under the authority of the United States, which shall have been created, or the emoluments whereof shall have been increased, during such time; and no person holding any office under the United States shall be a member of either house during his continuance in office.

Section 7 All bills for raising revenue shall originate in the House of Representatives; but the Senate may propose or concur with amendments as on other bills.

Every bill which shall have passed the House of Representatives and the Senate, shall, before it become a law, be presented to the President of the United States; if he approve he shall sign it, but if not he shall return it with objections to that house in which it shall have originated, who shall enter the objections at large on their journal, and proceed to reconsider it. If after such reconsideration two-thirds of that house shall agree to pass the bill, it shall be sent, together with the objections, to the other house, by which it shall likewise be reconsidered, and, if approved by two-thirds of that house, it shall become a law. But in all such cases the votes of both houses shall be determined by yeas and nays, and the names of the persons voting for and against the bill shall be entered on the journal of each house respectively. If any bill shall not be returned by the President within ten days (Sundays excepted) after it shall have been presented to him, the same shall be a law, in like manner as if he had signed it, unless the Congress by their adjournment prevent its return, in which case it shall not be a law.

Every order, resolution, or vote to which the concurrence of the Senate and House of Representatives may be necessary (except on a question of adjournment) shall be presented to the President of the United States; and before the same shall take effect, shall be approved by him, or being disapproved by him, shall be repassed by two-thirds of the Senate and House of Representatives, according to the rules and limitations prescribed in the case of a bill.

Section 8 The Congress shall have power

To lay and collect taxes, duties, imposts, and excises, to pay the debts and provide for the common defense and general welfare of the United States; but all duties, imposts and excises shall be uniform throughout the United States;

To borrow money on the credit of the United States;

To regulate commerce with foreign nations, and among the several States, and with the Indian tribes;

To establish an uniform rule of naturalization, and uniform laws on the subject of bankruptcies throughout the United States;

To coin money, regulate the value thereof, and of foreign coin, and fix the standard of weights and measures;

To provide for the punishment of counterfeiting the securities and current coin of the United States;

To establish post offices and post roads;

To promote the progress of science and useful arts by securing for limited times to authors and inventors the exclusive right to their respective writings and discoveries;

To constitute tribunals inferior to the Supreme Court;

To define and punish piracies and felonies committed on the high seas and offences against the law of nations;

To declare war, grant letters of marque and reprisal, and make rules concerning captures on land and water;

To raise and support armies, but no appropriation of money to that use shall be for a longer term than two years;

To provide and maintain a navy;

To make rules for the government and regulation of the land and naval forces;

To provide for calling forth the militia to execute the laws of the Union, suppress insurrections and repel invasions;

To provide for organizing, arming, and disciplining the militia, and for governing such part of them as may be employed in the service of the United States, reserving to the States respectively the appointment of the officers, and the authority of training the militia according to the discipline prescribed by Congress;

To exercise exclusive legislation in all cases whatsoever, over such district (not exceeding ten miles square) as may, by cession of particular States, and the acceptance of Congress, become the seat of the government of the United States, and to exercise like authority over all places purchased by the consent of the legislature of the State, in which the same shall be, for erection of forts, magazines, arsenals, dock-yards, and other needful buildings;—and

To make all laws which shall be necessary and proper for carrying into execution the foregoing powers, and all other powers vested by this Constitution in the government of the United States, or in any department or officer thereof.

Section 9 *The migration or importation of such persons as any of the States now existing shall think proper to admit shall not be prohibited by the Congress prior to the year one thousand eight hundred and eight; but a tax or duty may be imposed on such importation, not exceeding ten dollars for each person.*

The privilege of the writ of habeas corpus shall not be suspended, unless when in cases of rebellion or invasion the public safety may require it.

No bill of attainder or ex post facto law shall be passed.

No capitation, or other direct, tax shall be laid, unless in proportion to the census or enumeration herein before directed to be taken.

No tax or duty shall be laid on articles exported from any State.

No preference shall be given by any regulation of commerce or revenue to the ports of one State over those of another; nor shall vessels bound to, or from, one State be obliged to enter, clear, or pay duties in another.

No money shall be drawn from the treasury, but in consequence of appropriations made by law; and a regular statement and account of the receipts and expenditures of all public money shall be published from time to time.

No title of nobility shall be granted by the United States: and no person holding any office of profit or trust under them, shall, without the consent of the Congress, accept of any present, emolument, office, or title, of any kind whatever, from any king, prince, or foreign state.

Section 10 No State shall enter into any treaty, alliance, or confederation; grant letters of marque and reprisal; coin money; emit bills of credit; make anything but gold and silver coin a tender in payment of debts; pass any bill of attainder, ex post facto law, or law impairing the obligation of contracts, or grant any title of nobility.

No State shall, without the consent of Congress, lay any imposts or duties on imports or exports, except what may be absolutely necessary for executing its inspection laws: and the net produce of all duties and imposts, laid by any State on imports or exports, shall be for the use of the treasury of the United States; and all such laws shall be subject to the revision and control of the Congress.

No State shall, without the consent of Congress, lay any duty of tonnage, keep troops, or ships of war in time of peace, enter into any agreement or compact with another State, or with a foreign power, or engage in war, unless actually invaded, or in such imminent danger as will not admit of delay.

Article II

Section 1 The executive power shall be vested in a President of the United States of America. He shall hold his office during the term of four years, and, together with the Vice-President, chosen for the same term, be elected as follows:

Each State shall appoint, in such manner as the legislature thereof may direct, a number of electors, equal to the whole number of Senators and Representatives to which the State may be entitled in the Congress; but no Senator or Representative, or person holding an office of trust or profit under the United States, shall be appointed an elector.

The electors shall meet in their respective States, and vote by ballot for two persons, of whom one at least shall not be an inhabitant of the same State with themselves. And they shall make a list of all the persons voted for, and of the number of votes for each; which list they shall sign and certify, and transmit sealed to the seat of government of the United States, directed to the President of the Senate. The President of the Senate shall, in the presence of the Senate and House of Representatives, open all the certificates, and the votes shall then be counted. The person having the greatest number of votes shall be the President, if such number be a majority of the whole number of electors appointed; and if there be more than one who have such majority, and have an equal number of votes, then the House of Representatives shall immediately choose by ballot one of them for President; and if no person have a majority, then from the five highest on the list said house shall in like manner choose the President. But in choosing the President the votes shall be taken by States, the representation from each State having one vote; a quorum for this purpose shall consist of a member or members from two-thirds of the States, and a majority of all the States shall be necessary to a choice. In every case, after the choice of the President, the person having the greatest number of votes of the electors shall be the Vice-President. But if there should remain two or more who have equal votes, the Senate shall choose from them by ballot the Vice-President.

The Congress may determine the time of choosing the electors, and the day on which they shall give their votes; which day shall be the same throughout the United States.

No person except a natural-born citizen, *or a citizen of the United States at the time of the adoption of this Constitution*, shall be eligible to the office of President; neither shall any person be eligible to that office who shall not have attained to the age of thirty-five years, and been fourteen years a resident within the United States.

In cases of the removal of the President from office or of his death, resignation, or inability to discharge the powers and duties of the said office, the same shall devolve on the Vice-President, and the Congress may by law provide for the case of removal, death, resignation, or inability, both of the President and Vice-President, declaring what officer shall then act as President, and such officer shall act accordingly, until the disability be removed, or a President shall be elected.

The President shall, at stated times, receive for his services a compensation, which shall neither be increased nor diminished during the period for which he shall have been elected, and he shall not receive within that period any other emolument from the United States, or any of them.

Before he enter on the execution of his office, he shall take the following oath or affirmation:—"I do solemnly swear (or affirm) that I will faithfully execute the office of the President of the United States, and will to the best of my ability preserve, protect and defend the Constitution of the United States."

Section 2 The President shall be commander in chief of the army and navy of the United States, and of the militia of the several States, when called into the actual service of the United States; he may require the opinion, in writing, of the principal officer in each of the executive departments, upon any subject relating to the duties of their respective offices, and he shall have power to grant reprieves and pardons for offenses against the United States, except in cases of impeachment.

He shall have power, by and with the advice and consent of the Senate, to make treaties, provided two-thirds of the Senators present concur; and he shall nominate, and by and with the advice and consent of the Senate, shall appoint ambassadors, other public ministers and consuls, judges of the Supreme Court, and all other officers of the United States, whose appointments are not herein otherwise provided for, and which shall be established by law: but Congress may by law vest the appointment of such inferior officers, as they think proper, in the President alone, in the courts of law, or in the heads of departments.

The President shall have power to fill up all vacancies that may happen during the recess of the Senate, by granting commissions which shall expire at the end of their next session.

Section 3 He shall from time to time give to the Congress information of the state of the Union, and recommend to their consideration such measures as he shall judge necessary and expedient; he may, on extraordinary occasions, convene both houses, or either of them, and in case of disagreement between them, with respect to the time of adjournment, he may adjourn them to such time as he shall think proper; he shall receive ambassadors and other public ministers; he shall take care that the laws be faithfully executed, and shall commission all the officers of the United States.

Section 4 The President, Vice-President and all civil officers of the United States shall be removed from office on impeachment for, and on conviction of, treason, bribery, or other high crimes and misdemeanors.

Article III

Section 1 The judicial power of the United States shall be vested in one Supreme Court, and in such inferior courts as the Congress may from time to time ordain and establish. The judges, both of the Supreme and inferior courts, shall hold their offices during good behavior, and shall, at stated times, receive for their services a compensation which shall not be diminished during their continuance in office.

Section 2 The judicial power shall extend to all cases, in law and equity, arising under this Constitution, the laws of the United States, and treaties made, or which shall be made, under their authority;—to all cases affecting ambassadors, other public ministers and consuls;—to all cases of admiralty and maritime jurisdiction;—to controversies to which the United States shall be a party;—to controversies between two or more States;—*between a State and citizens of another State*;—between citizens of different States;— between citizens of the same State claiming lands under grants of different States, and between a State, or the citizens thereof, and foreign states, citizens or subjects.

In all cases affecting ambassadors, other public ministers and consuls, and those in which a State shall be party, the Supreme Court shall have original jurisdiction. In all the other cases before mentioned, the Supreme Court shall have appellate jurisdiction, both as to law and fact, with such exceptions, and under such regulations, as the Congress shall make.

The trial of all crimes, except in cases of impeachment, shall be by jury; and such trial shall be held in the State where said crimes shall have been committed; but when not committed within any State, the trial shall be at such place or places as the Congress may by Law have directed.

Section 3 Treason against the United States shall consist only in levying war against them, or in adhering to their enemies, giving them aid and comfort. No person shall be convicted of treason unless on the testimony of two witnesses to the same overt act, or on confession in open court.

The Congress shall have power to declare the punishment of treason, but no attainder of treason shall work corruption of blood, or forfeiture except during the life of the person attainted.

Article IV

Section 1 Full faith and credit shall be given in each State to the public acts, records, and judicial proceedings of every other State. And the Congress may by general laws prescribe the manner in which such acts, records, and proceedings shall be proved, and the effect thereof.

Section 2 The citizens of each State shall be entitled to all privileges and immunities of citizens in the several States.

A person charged in any State with treason, felony, or other crime, who shall flee from justice, and be found in another State, shall on demand of the executive authority of the State from which he fled, be delivered up, to be removed to the State having jurisdiction of the crime.

No Person held to service or labor in one State, under the laws thereof, escaping into another, shall, in consequence of any law or regulation therein, be discharged from such service or labor, but shall be delivered up on claim of the party to whom such service or labor may be due.

Section 3 New States may be admitted by the Congress into this Union; but no new State shall be formed or erected within the jurisdiction of any other State; nor any State be formed by the junction of two or more States, or parts of States, without the consent of the legislatures of the States concerned as well as of the Congress.

The Congress shall have power to dispose of and make all needful rules and regulations respecting the territory or other property belonging to the United States; and nothing in this Constitution shall be so construed as to prejudice any claims of the United States, or of any particular State.

Section 4 The United States shall guarantee to every State in this Union a republican form of government, and shall protect each of them against invasion; and on application of the legislature, or of the executive (when the legislature cannot be convened), against domestic violence.

Article V

The Congress, whenever two-thirds of both houses shall deem it necessary, shall propose amendments to this Constitution, or, on the application of the legislatures of two-thirds of the several States, shall call a convention for proposing amendments, which, in either case, shall be valid to all intents and purposes, as part of this Constitution, when ratified by the legislatures of three-fourths of the several States, or by conventions in three-fourths thereof, as the one or the other mode of ratification may be proposed by the Congress; provided *that no amendments which may be made prior to the year one thousand eight hundred and eight shall in any manner affect the first and fourth clauses in the ninth section of the first article*; and that no State, without its consent, shall be deprived of its equal suffrage in the Senate.

Article VI

All debts contracted and engagements entered into, before the adoption of this Constitution, shall be as valid against the United States under this Constitution, as under the Confederation.

This Constitution, and the laws of the United States which shall be made in pursuance thereof; and all treaties made, or which shall be made, under the authority of the United States, shall be the supreme law of the land; and the judges in every State shall be bound thereby, anything in the Constitution or laws of any State to the contrary notwithstanding.

The Senators and Representatives before mentioned, and the members of the several State legislatures, and all executive and judicial officers, both of the United States and of the several States, shall be bound by oath or affirmation to support this Constitution; but no religious test shall ever be required as a qualification to any office or public trust under the United States.

Article VII

The ratification of the conventions of nine States shall be sufficient for the establishment of this Constitution between the States so ratifying the same.

Done in convention by the unanimous consent of the States present, the seventeenth day of September in the year of our Lord one thousand seven hundred and eighty-seven and of the Independence of the United States of America the twelfth. In witness whereof we have hereunto subscribed our names.

GEORGE WASHINGTON
PRESIDENT AND DEPUTY FROM VIRGINIA

New Hampshire
John Langdon
Nicholas Gilman

Massachusetts
Nathaniel Gorham
Rufus King

Connecticut
William Samuel
  Johnson
Roger Sherman

New York
Alexander Hamilton

New Jersey
William Livingston
David Brearley
William Paterson
Jonathan Dayton

Pennsylvania
Benjamin Franklin
Thomas Mifflin
Robert Morris
George Clymer
Thomas FitzSimons
Jared Ingersoll
James Wilson
Gouverneur Morris

Delaware
George Read
Gunning Bedford, Jr.
John Dickinson
Richard Bassett
Jacob Broom

Maryland
James McHenry
Daniel of St. Thomas
  Jenifer
Daniel Carroll

Virginia
John Blair
James Madison, Jr.

North Carolina
William Blount
Richard Dobbs Spaight
Hugh Williamson

South Carolina
John Rutledge
Charles Cotesworth
  Pinckney
Charles Pinckney
Pierce Butler

Georgia
William Few
Abraham Baldwin

AMENDMENTS TO THE CONSTITUTION WITH ANNOTATIONS (including the six unratified amendments)

IN THEIR EFFORT TO GAIN Antifederalists' support for the Constitution, Federalists frequently pointed to the inclusion of Article 5, which provides an orderly method of amending the Constitution. In contrast, the Articles of Confederation, which were universally recognized as seriously flawed, offered no means of amendment. For their part, Antifederalists argued that the amendment process was so "intricate" that one might as easily roll "sixes an hundred times in succession" as change the Constitution.

The system for amendment laid out in the Constitution requires that two-thirds of both houses of Congress agree to a proposed amendment, which must then be ratified by three-quarters of the legislatures of the states. Alternatively, an amendment may be proposed by a convention called by the legislatures of two-thirds of the states. Since 1789, members of Congress have proposed thousands of amendments. Besides the seventeen amendments added since 1789, only the six "unratified" ones included here were approved by two-thirds of both houses and sent to the states for ratification.

Among the many amendments that never made it out of Congress have been proposals to declare dueling, divorce, and interracial marriage unconstitutional as well as proposals to establish a national university, to acknowledge the sovereignty of Jesus Christ, and to prohibit any person from possessing wealth in excess of $10 million.*

Among the issues facing Americans today that might lead to constitutional amendment are efforts to balance the federal budget, to limit the number of terms elected officials may serve, to limit access to or prohibit abortion, to establish English as the official language of the United States, and to prohibit flag burning. None of these proposed amendments has yet garnered enough support in Congress to be sent to the states for ratification.

Although the first ten amendments to the Constitution are commonly known as the Bill of Rights, only Amendments 1–8 actually provide guarantees of individual rights. Amendments 9 and 10 deal with the structure of power within the constitutional system. The Bill of Rights was promised to appease Antifederalists who refused to ratify the Constitution without guarantees of individual liberties and limitations to federal power. After studying more than two hundred amendments recommended by the ratifying conventions of the states, Federalist James Madison presented a list of seventeen to Congress, which used Madison's list as the foundation for the twelve amendments that were sent

---

*Richard B. Bernstein, *Amending America* (New York: Times Books, 1993), 177–81.

to the states for ratification. Ten of the twelve were adopted in 1791. The first on the list of twelve, known as the Reapportionment Amendment, was never adopted (see page A-15). The second proposed amendment was adopted in 1992 as Amendment 27 (see page A-24).

Amendment I

Congress shall make no law respecting an establishment of religion, or prohibiting the free exercise thereof; or abridging the freedom of speech, or of the press; or the right of the people peaceably to assemble, and to petition the government for a redress of grievances.

◆ ◆ ◆

▶ *The First Amendment is a potent symbol for many Americans. Most are well aware of their rights to free speech, freedom of the press, and freedom of religion and their rights to assemble and to petition, even if they cannot cite the exact words of this amendment.*

The First Amendment guarantee of freedom of religion has two clauses: the "free exercise clause," which allows individuals to practice or not practice any religion, and the "establishment clause," which prevents the federal government from discriminating against or favoring any particular religion. This clause was designed to create what Thomas Jefferson referred to as "a wall of separation between church and state." In the 1960s, the Supreme Court ruled that the First Amendment prohibits prayer (see Engel v. Vitale, *online) and Bible reading in public schools.*

Although the rights to free speech and freedom of the press are established in the First Amendment, it was not until the twentieth century that the Supreme Court began to explore the full meaning of these guarantees. In 1919, the Court ruled in Schenck v. United States *(online) that the government could suppress free expression only where it could cite a "clear and present danger." In a decision that continues to raise controversies, the Court ruled in 1990, in* Texas v. Johnson, *that flag burning is a form of symbolic speech protected by the First Amendment.*

Amendment II

A well-regulated militia being necessary to the security of a free State, the right of the people to keep and bear arms shall not be infringed.

◆ ◆ ◆

▶ *Fear of a standing army under the control of a hostile government made the Second Amendment an important part of the Bill of Rights. Advocates of gun ownership claim that the amendment prevents the government from regulating firearms. Proponents of gun control argue that the amendment is designed only to protect the right of the states to maintain militia units.*

In 1939, the Supreme Court ruled in United States v. Miller *that the Second Amendment did not protect the right of an individual to own a sawed-off shotgun, which it argued was not ordinary militia equipment. Since then, the Supreme Court has refused to hear Second Amendment cases, while lower courts have upheld firearms regulations. Several justices currently on the bench seem to favor a narrow interpretation of the Second Amendment, which would allow gun control legislation. The controversy over the impact of the Second Amendment on gun owners and gun control legislation will certainly continue.*

Amendment III

No soldier shall, in time of peace, be quartered in any house without the consent of the owner, nor in time of war, but in a manner to be prescribed by law.

◆ ◆ ◆

▶ *The Third Amendment was extremely important to the framers of the Constitution, but today it is nearly forgotten. American colonists were especially outraged that they were forced to quarter British troops in the years before and during the American Revolution. The philosophy of the Third Amendment has been viewed by some justices and scholars as the foundation of the modern constitutional right to privacy. One example of this can be found in Justice William O. Douglas's opinion in* Griswold v. Connecticut *(online).*

Amendment IV

The right of the people to be secure in their persons, houses, papers, and effects, against unreasonable searches and seizures, shall not be violated, and no warrants shall issue but upon probable cause, supported by oath or affirmation, and particularly describing the place to be searched, and the persons or things to be seized.

◆ ◆ ◆

▶ *In the years before the Revolution, the houses, barns, stores, and warehouses of American colonists were ransacked by British authorities under "writs of assistance" or general warrants. The British, thus empowered, searched for seditious material or smuggled goods that could then be used as evidence against colonists who were charged with a crime only after the items were found. The first part of the Fourth Amendment protects citizens from "unreasonable" searches and seizures.*

The Supreme Court has interpreted this protection as well as the words search *and* seizure *in different ways at different times. At one time, the Court did not recognize electronic eavesdropping as a form of search and seizure, though it does today. At times, an "unreasonable" search has been almost any search carried out without a warrant, but in the two decades before 1969, the Court sometimes sanctioned warrantless searches that it considered reasonable based on "the total atmosphere of the case."*

The second part of the Fourth Amendment defines the procedure for issuing a search warrant and states the requirement of "probable cause," which is generally viewed as evidence indicating that a suspect has committed an offense.

The Fourth Amendment has been controversial because the Court has sometimes excluded evidence that has been seized in violation of constitutional standards. The justification is that excluding such evidence deters violations of the amendment, but doing so may allow a guilty person to escape punishment.

Amendment V

No person shall be held to answer for a capital, or otherwise infamous crime, unless on a presentment or indictment of a grand jury, except in cases arising in the land or naval forces, or in the militia, when in actual service in time of war or public danger; nor shall any person be subject for the same offence to be twice put in jeopardy of life or limb; nor shall be compelled in any criminal case to be a witness against himself, nor be deprived of life, liberty, or property, without due process of law; nor shall private property be taken for public use without just compensation.

◆ ◆ ◆

▶ *The Fifth Amendment protects people against government authority in the prosecution of criminal offenses. It prohibits the state, first, from charging a person with a serious crime without a grand jury hearing to decide whether there is sufficient evidence to support the charge and, second, from charging a person with the same crime twice. The best-known aspect of the Fifth Amendment is that it prevents a person from being "compelled . . . to be a witness against himself." The last clause, the "takings clause," limits the power of the government to seize property.*

Although invoking the Fifth Amendment is popularly viewed as a confession of guilt, a person may be innocent yet still fear prosecution. For example, during the Red-baiting era of the late 1940s and 1950s, many people who had participated in legal activities that were associated with the Communist Party claimed the Fifth Amendment privilege rather than testify before the House Un-American Activities Committee because the mood of the times cast those activities in a negative light. Since "taking the Fifth" was viewed as an admission of guilt, those people often lost their jobs or became unemployable. (See chapter 26.) Nonetheless, the right to protect oneself against self-incrimination plays an important role in guarding against the collective power of the state.

Amendment VI

In all criminal prosecutions, the accused shall enjoy the right to a speedy and public trial, by an impartial jury of the State and district wherein the crime shall have been committed, which district shall have been previously ascertained by law, and to be informed of the nature and cause of the accusation; to be confronted with the witnesses against him; to have compulsory process for obtaining witnesses in his favor, and to have the assistance of counsel for his defence.

◆ ◆ ◆

▶ *The original Constitution put few limits on the government's power to investigate, prosecute, and punish crime. This process was of great concern to the early Americans, however, and of the twenty-eight rights specified in the first eight amendments, fifteen have to do with it. Seven rights are specified in the Sixth Amendment. These include the right to a speedy trial, a public trial, a jury trial, a notice of accusation, confrontation by opposing witnesses, testimony by favorable witnesses, and the assistance of counsel.*

Although this amendment originally guaranteed these rights only in cases involving the federal government, the adoption of the Fourteenth Amendment began a process of applying the protections of the Bill of Rights to the states through court cases such as Gideon v. Wainwright (online).

Amendment VII

In suits at common law, where the value in controversy shall exceed twenty dollars, the right of trial by jury shall be preserved, and no fact tried by a jury shall be otherwise reexamined in any court of the United States, than according to the rules of the common law.

◆ ◆ ◆

▶ *This amendment guarantees people the same right to a trial by jury as was guaranteed by English common law in 1791. Under common law, in civil trials (those involving money damages) the role of the judge was to settle questions of law and that of the jury was to settle questions of fact. The amendment does not specify the size of the jury or its role in a trial, however. The Supreme Court has generally held that those issues are determined by English common law of 1791, which stated that a jury consists of twelve people, that a trial must be conducted before a judge who instructs the jury on the law and advises it on facts, and that a verdict must be unanimous.*

Amendment VIII

Excessive bail shall not be required, nor excessive fines imposed, nor cruel and unusual punishments inflicted.

◆ ◆ ◆

The language used to guarantee the three rights in this amendment was inspired by the English Bill of Rights of 1689. The Supreme Court has not had a lot to say about "excessive fines." In recent years it has agreed that, despite the provision against "excessive bail," persons who are believed to be dangerous to others can be held without bail even before they have been convicted.

Although opponents of the death penalty have not succeeded in using the Eighth Amendment to achieve the end of capital punishment, the clause regarding "cruel and unusual punishments" has been used to prohibit capital punishment in certain cases (see Furman v. Georgia, *online) and to require improved conditions in prisons.*

Amendment IX

The enumeration in the Constitution, of certain rights, shall not be construed to deny or disparage others retained by the people.

◆ ◆ ◆

▶ *Some Federalists feared that inclusion of the Bill of Rights in the Constitution would allow later generations of interpreters to claim that the people had surrendered any rights not specifically enumerated there. To guard against this, Madison added language that became the Ninth Amendment. Interest in this heretofore largely ignored amendment revived in 1965 when it was used in a concurring opinion in* Griswold v. Connecticut *(online). While Justice William O. Douglas called on the Third Amendment to support the right to privacy in deciding that case, Justice Arthur Goldberg, in the concurring opinion, argued that the right to privacy regarding contraception was an unenumerated right that was protected by the Ninth Amendment.*

In 1980, the Court ruled that the right of the press to attend a public trial was protected by the Ninth Amendment. While some scholars argue that modern judges cannot identify the unenumerated rights that the framers were trying to protect, others argue that the Ninth Amendment should be read as providing a constitutional "presumption of liberty" that allows people to act in any way that does not violate the rights of others.

Amendment X

The powers not delegated to the United States by the Constitution, nor prohibited by it to the States, are reserved to the States respectively, or to the people.

◆ ◆ ◆

▶ *The Antifederalists were especially eager to see a "reserved powers clause" explicitly guaranteeing the states control over their internal affairs. Not*

surprisingly, the Tenth Amendment has been a frequent battleground in the struggle over states' rights and federal supremacy. Prior to the Civil War, the Democratic Republican Party and Jacksonian Democrats invoked the Tenth Amendment to prohibit the federal government from making decisions about whether people in individual states could own slaves. The Tenth Amendment was virtually suspended during Reconstruction following the Civil War. In 1883, however, the Supreme Court declared the Civil Rights Act of 1875 unconstitutional on the grounds that it violated the Tenth Amendment. Business interests also called on the amendment to block efforts at federal regulation.

The Court was inconsistent over the next several decades as it attempted to resolve the tension between the restrictions of the Tenth Amendment and the powers the Constitution granted to Congress to regulate interstate commerce and levy taxes. The Court upheld the Pure Food and Drug Act (1906), the Meat Inspection Acts (1906 and 1907), and the White Slave Traffic Act (1910), all of which affected the states, but struck down an act prohibiting interstate shipment of goods produced through child labor. Between 1934 and 1935, a number of New Deal programs created by Franklin D. Roosevelt were declared unconstitutional on the grounds that they violated the Tenth Amendment. (See chapter 24.) As Roosevelt appointees changed the composition of the Court, the Tenth Amendment was declared to have no substantive meaning. Generally, the amendment is held to protect the rights of states to regulate internal matters such as local government, education, commerce, labor, and business, as well as matters involving families such as marriage, divorce, and inheritance within the state.

Unratified Amendment

Reapportionment Amendment (proposed by Congress September 25, 1789, along with the Bill of Rights)

After the first enumeration required by the first article of the Constitution, there shall be one Representative for every thirty thousand, until the number shall amount to one hundred, after which the proportion shall be so regulated by Congress, that there shall be not less than one hundred Representatives, nor less than one Representative for every forty thousand persons, until the number of Representatives shall amount to two hundred; after which the proportion shall be so regulated by Congress, that there shall not be less than two hundred Representatives, nor more than one Representative for every fifty thousand persons.

◆ ◆ ◆

▶ *If the Reapportionment Amendment had passed and remained in effect, the House of Representatives today would have more than 5,000 members rather than 435.*

Amendment XI

[Adopted 1798]

The judicial power of the United States shall not be construed to extend to any suit in law or equity, commenced or prosecuted against one of the United States by citizens of another State, or by citizens or subjects of any foreign state.

◆ ◆ ◆

▶ *In 1793, the Supreme Court ruled in favor of Alexander Chisholm, executor of the estate of a deceased South Carolina merchant. Chisholm was suing the state of Georgia because the merchant had never been paid for provisions he had supplied during the Revolution. Many regarded this Court decision as an error that violated the intent of the Constitution.*

Antifederalists had long feared a federal court system with the power to overrule a state court.

When the Constitution was being drafted, Federalists had assured worried Antifederalists that section 2 of Article 3, which allows federal courts to hear cases "between a State and citizens of another State," did not mean that the federal courts were authorized to hear suits against a state by citizens of another state or a foreign country. Antifederalists and many other Americans feared a powerful federal court system because they worried that it would become like the British courts of this period, which were accountable only to the monarch. Furthermore, Chisholm v. Georgia prompted a series of suits against state governments by creditors and suppliers who had made loans during the war.

In addition, state legislators and Congress feared that the shaky economies of the new states, as well as the country as a whole, would be destroyed, especially if loyalists who had fled to other countries sought reimbursement for land and property that had been seized. The day after the Supreme Court announced its decision, a resolution proposing the Eleventh Amendment, which overturned the decision in Chisholm v. Georgia, was introduced in the U.S. Senate.

Amendment XII

[Adopted 1804]

The electors shall meet in their respective States, and vote by ballot for President and Vice-President, one of whom, at least, shall not be an inhabitant of the same State with themselves; they shall name in their ballots the person voted for as President, and in distinct ballots the person voted for as Vice-President, and they shall make distinct lists of all persons voted for as President, and of all persons voted for as Vice-President, and of the number of votes for each, which lists they shall sign and certify, and transmit sealed to the seat of government of the United States, directed to the President of the Senate;—the President of the Senate shall, in the presence of the Senate and House of Representatives, open all the certificates and the votes shall then be counted;—the person having the greatest number of votes for President shall be the President, if such number be a majority of the whole number of electors appointed; and if no person have such majority, then from the persons having the highest numbers not exceeding three on the list of those voted for as President, the House of Representatives shall choose immediately, by ballot, the President. But in choosing the President, the votes shall be taken by States, the representation from each State having one vote; a quorum for this purpose shall consist of a member or members from two-thirds of the States, and a majority of all the States shall be necessary to a choice. And if the House of Representatives shall not choose a President whenever the right of choice shall devolve upon them, before the fourth day of March next following, then the Vice-President shall act as President, as in the case of the death or other constitutional disability of the President.

The person having the greatest number of votes as Vice-President shall be the Vice-President, if such number be a majority of the whole number of electors appointed; and if no person have a majority, then from the two highest numbers on the list the Senate shall choose the Vice-President; a quorum for the purpose shall consist of two-thirds of the whole number of Senators, and a majority of the whole number shall be necessary to a choice. But no person constitutionally ineligible to the office of President shall be eligible to that of Vice-President of the United States.

◆ ◆ ◆

▶ *The framers of the Constitution disliked political parties and assumed that none would ever form. Under the original system, electors chosen by the states would each vote for two candidates. The candidate who won the most votes would become president, while the person who won the second-highest number of votes would become vice president. Rivalries between Federalists and Antifederalists led to the formation of political parties, however, even before George Washington had left office. Though Washington was elected unanimously in 1789 and 1792, the elections of 1796 and 1800 were procedural disasters because of party maneuvering (see chapters 9 and 10). In 1796, Federalist John Adams was chosen as president, and his great rival, the Antifederalist Thomas Jefferson (whose party was called the Republican Party), became his vice president. In 1800, all the electors cast their two votes as one of two party blocs. Jefferson and his fellow Republican nominee, Aaron Burr, were tied with 73 votes each. The contest went to the House of Representatives, which finally elected Jefferson after 36 ballots. The Twelfth Amendment prevents these problems by requiring electors to vote separately for the president and vice president.*

Unratified Amendment

Titles of Nobility Amendment (proposed by Congress May 1, 1810)

If any citizen of the United States shall accept, claim, receive or retain any title of nobility or honor or shall, without the consent of Congress, accept and retain any present, pension, office or emolument of any kind whatever, from any emperor, king, prince or foreign power, such person shall cease to be a citizen of the United States, and shall be incapable of holding any office of trust or profit under them or either of them.

◆ ◆ ◆

▶ *This amendment would have extended Article 1, section 9, clause 8 of the Constitution, which prevents the awarding of titles by the United States and the acceptance of such awards from foreign powers without congressional consent. Historians speculate that general nervousness about the power of the emperor Napoleon, who was at that time extending France's empire throughout Europe, may have prompted the proposal. Though it fell one vote short of ratification, Congress and the American people thought the proposal had been ratified, and it was included in many nineteenth-century editions of the Constitution.*

The Civil War and Reconstruction Amendments (Thirteenth, Fourteenth, and Fifteenth Amendments)

▶ *In the four months between the election of Abraham Lincoln and his inauguration, more than 200 proposed constitutional amendments were presented to Congress as part of a desperate attempt to hold the rapidly dissolving Union together. Most of these were efforts to appease the southern states by protecting the right to own slaves or by disfranchising African Americans through constitutional amendment. None were able to win the votes required from Congress to send them to the states. The relatively innocuous Corwin Amendment seemed to be the only hope for preserving the Union by amending the Constitution.*

    The northern victors in the Civil War tried to restructure the Constitution just as the war had restructured the nation. Yet they were often divided in their goals. Some wanted to end slavery; others hoped for social and economic equality regardless of race; others hoped that extending the power of the ballot box to former slaves would help create a new political order. The debates over the Thirteenth, Fourteenth, and Fifteenth Amendments were bitter. Few of those who fought for these changes were satisfied with the amendments themselves; fewer still were satisfied with their interpretation. Although the

amendments put an end to the legal status of slavery, it took nearly a hundred years after the amendments' passage before most of the descendants of former slaves could begin to experience the economic, social, and political equality the amendments had been intended to provide.

Unratified Amendment

Corwin Amendment (proposed by Congress March 2, 1861)

No amendment shall be made to the Constitution which will authorize or give to Congress the power to abolish or interfere, within any State, with the domestic institutions thereof, including that of persons held to labor or service by the laws of said State.

◆ ◆ ◆

▶ *Following the election of Abraham Lincoln, Congress scrambled to try to prevent the secession of the slaveholding states. House member Thomas Corwin of Ohio proposed the "unamendable" amendment in the hope that by protecting slavery where it existed, Congress would keep the southern states in the Union. Lincoln indicated his support for the proposed amendment in his first inaugural address. Only Ohio and Maryland ratified the Corwin Amendment before it was forgotten.*

Amendment XIII

[Adopted 1865]

Section 1 Neither slavery nor involuntary servitude, except as a punishment for crime whereof the party shall have been duly convicted, shall exist within the United States, or any place subject to their jurisdiction.

Section 2 Congress shall have power to enforce this article by appropriate legislation.

◆ ◆ ◆

▶ *Although President Lincoln had abolished slavery in the Confederacy with the Emancipation Proclamation of 1863, abolitionists wanted to rid the entire country of slavery. The Thirteenth Amendment did this in a clear and straightforward manner. In February 1865, when the proposal was approved by the House, the gallery of the House was newly opened to black Americans who had a chance at last to see their government at work. Passage of the proposal was greeted by wild cheers from the gallery as well as tears on the House floor, where congressional representatives openly embraced one another.*

    The problem of ratification remained, however. The Union position was that the Confederate states were part of the country of thirty-six states. Therefore, twenty-seven states were needed to ratify the amendment. When Kentucky and Delaware rejected it, backers realized that without approval from at least four former Confederate states, the amendment would fail. Lincoln's successor, President Andrew Johnson, made ratification of the

Thirteenth Amendment a condition for southern states to rejoin the Union. Under those terms, all the former Confederate states except Mississippi accepted the Thirteenth Amendment, and by the end of 1865 the amendment had become part of the Constitution and slavery had been prohibited in the United States.

Amendment XIV
[Adopted 1868]

Section 1 All persons born or naturalized in the United States, and subject to the jurisdiction thereof, are citizens of the United States and of the State wherein they reside. No State shall make or enforce any law which shall abridge the privileges or immunities of citizens of the United States; nor shall any State deprive any person of life, liberty, or property, without due process of law; nor deny to any person within its jurisdiction the equal protection of the laws.

Section 2 Representatives shall be appointed among the several States according to their respective numbers, counting the whole number of persons in each State, excluding Indians not taxed. But when the right to vote at any election for the choice of Electors for President and Vice-President of the United States, Representatives in Congress, the executive and judicial officers of a State, or the members of the legislature thereof, is denied to any of the male inhabitants of such State, being twenty-one years of age and citizens of the United States, or in any way abridged, except for participation in rebellion, or other crime, the basis of representation therein shall be reduced in the proportion which the number of such male citizens shall bear to the whole number of male citizens twenty-one years of age in such State.

Section 3 No person shall be a Senator or Representative in Congress, or Elector of President and Vice-President, or hold any office, civil or military, under the United States, or under any State, who, having previously taken an oath, as a member of Congress, or as an officer of the United States, or as a member of any State legislature, or as an executive or judicial officer of any State, to support the Constitution of the United States, shall have engaged in insurrection or rebellion against the same, or given aid or comfort to the enemies thereof. Congress may, by a vote of two-thirds of each house, remove such disability.

Section 4 The validity of the public debt of the United States, authorized by law, including debts incurred for payment of pensions and bounties for services in suppressing insurrection or rebellion, shall not be questioned. But neither the United States nor any State shall assume or pay any debt or obligation incurred in aid of insurrection or rebellion against the United States, or any claim for the loss or emancipation of any slave; but all such debts, obligations, and claims shall be held illegal and void.

Section 5 The Congress shall have power to enforce, by appropriate legislation, the provisions of this article.

◆ ◆ ◆

▶ *Without Lincoln's leadership in the reconstruction of the nation following the Civil War, it soon became clear that the Thirteenth Amendment needed additional constitutional support. Less than a year after Lincoln's assassination, Andrew Johnson was ready to bring the former Confederate states back into the Union with few changes in their governments or politics. Anxious Republicans drafted the Fourteenth Amendment to prevent that from happening. The most important provisions of this complex amendment made all native-born or naturalized persons American citizens and prohibited states from abridging the "privileges or immunities" of citizens; depriving them of "life, liberty, or property, without due process of law"; and denying them "equal protection of the laws." In essence, it made all ex-slaves citizens and protected the rights of all citizens against violation by their own state governments.*

As occurred in the case of the Thirteenth Amendment, former Confederate states were forced to ratify the amendment as a condition of representation in the House and the Senate. The intentions of the Fourteenth Amendment, and how those intentions should be enforced, have been the most debated point of constitutional history. The terms due process and equal protection have been especially troublesome. Was the amendment designed to outlaw racial segregation? Or was the goal simply to prevent the leaders of the rebellious South from gaining political power?

The framers of the Fourteenth Amendment hoped Article 2 would produce black voters who would increase the power of the Republican Party. The federal government, however, never used its power to punish states for denying blacks their right to vote. Although the Fourteenth Amendment had an immediate impact in giving black Americans citizenship, it did nothing to protect blacks from the vengeance of whites once Reconstruction ended. In the late nineteenth and early twentieth centuries, section 1 of the Fourteenth Amendment was often used to protect business interests and strike down laws protecting workers on the grounds that the rights of "persons," that is, corporations, were protected by "due process." More recently, the Fourteenth Amendment has been used to justify school desegregation and affirmative action programs, as well as to dismantle such programs.

Amendment XV
[Adopted 1870]

Section 1 The right of citizens of the United States to vote shall not be denied or abridged by the United States or by any State on account of race, color, or previous condition of servitude.

Section 2 The Congress shall have power to enforce this article by appropriate legislation.

♦ ♦ ♦

▶ *The Fifteenth Amendment was the last major piece of Reconstruction legislation. While earlier Reconstruction acts had already required black suffrage in the South, the Fifteenth Amendment extended black voting rights to the entire nation. Some Republicans felt morally obligated to do away with the double standard between North and South since many northern states had stubbornly refused to enfranchise blacks. Others believed that the freedman's ballot required the extra protection of a constitutional amendment to shield it from white counterattack. But partisan advantage also played an important role in the amendment's passage, since Republicans hoped that by giving the ballot to northern blacks, they could lessen their political vulnerability.*

Many women's rights advocates had fought for the amendment. They had felt betrayed by the inclusion of the word "male" in section 2 of the Fourteenth Amendment and were further angered when the proposed Fifteenth Amendment failed to prohibit denial of the right to vote on the grounds of sex as well as "race, color, or previous condition of servitude." In this amendment, for the first time, the federal government claimed the power to regulate the franchise, or vote. It was also the first time the Constitution placed limits on the power of the states to regulate access to the franchise. Although ratified in 1870, the amendment was not enforced until the twentieth century.

The Progressive Amendments (Sixteenth–Nineteenth Amendments)

▶ *No amendments were added to the Constitution between the Civil War and the Progressive Era. America was changing, however, in fundamental ways. The rapid industrialization of the United States after the Civil War led to many social and economic problems. Hundreds of amendments were proposed, but none received enough support in Congress to be sent to the states. Some scholars believe that regional differences and rivalries were so strong during this period that it was almost impossible to gain a consensus on a constitutional amendment. During the Progressive Era, however, the Constitution was amended four times in seven years.*

Amendment XVI
[Adopted 1913]

The Congress shall have power to lay and collect taxes on incomes, from whatever source derived, without apportionment among the several States, and without regard to any census or enumeration.

♦ ♦ ♦

▶ *Until passage of the Sixteenth Amendment, most of the money used to run the federal government came from customs duties and taxes on specific items, such as liquor. During the Civil War, the federal government taxed incomes as an emergency measure. Pressure to enact an income tax came from those who were concerned about the growing gap between rich and poor in the United States. The Populist Party began campaigning for a graduated income tax in 1892, and support continued to grow. By 1909, thirty-three proposed income tax amendments had been presented in Congress, but lobbying by corporate and other special interests had defeated them all. In June 1909, the growing pressure for an income tax, which had been endorsed by Presidents Roosevelt and Taft, finally pushed an amendment through the Senate. The required thirty-six states had ratified the amendment by February 1913.*

Amendment XVII
[Adopted 1913]

Section 1 The Senate of the United States shall be composed of two Senators from each State, elected by the people thereof, for six years; and each Senator shall have one vote. The electors in each State shall have the qualifications requisite for electors of [voters for] the most numerous branch of the State legislatures.

Section 2 When vacancies happen in the representation of any State in the Senate, the executive authority of such State shall issue writs of election to fill such vacancies: Provided, that the Legislature of any State may empower the executive thereof to make temporary appointments until the people fill the vacancies by election as the Legislature may direct.

Section 3 This amendment shall not be so construed as to affect the election or term of any Senator chosen before it becomes valid as part of the Constitution.

♦ ♦ ♦

▶ *The framers of the Constitution saw the members of the House as the representatives of the people and the members of the Senate as the representatives of the states. Originally senators were to be chosen by the state legislators. According to reform advocates, however, the growth of private industry and transportation conglomerates during the Gilded Age had created a network of corruption in which wealth and power were exchanged for influence and votes in the Senate. Senator Nelson Aldrich, who represented Rhode Island in the late nineteenth and early twentieth centuries, for example, was known as "the senator from Standard Oil" because of his open support of special business interests.*

Efforts to amend the Constitution to allow direct election of senators had begun in 1826, but since any proposal had to be approved by the Senate, reform seemed impossible. Progressives tried to gain influence in the Senate by instituting party caucuses and primary elections, which gave citizens the chance to express their choice of a senator who could then be officially elected by the state legislature. By 1910, fourteen of the country's thirty senators received popular votes through a state primary before the state legislature made its selection. Despairing of getting a proposal through the Senate, supporters of a direct election amendment had begun in 1893 to seek a convention of representatives from two-thirds of the states to propose an amendment that could then be ratified. By 1905, thirty-one of forty-five states had endorsed such an amendment. Finally, in 1911, despite extraordinary opposition, a proposed amendment passed the Senate; by 1913, it had been ratified.

Amendment XVIII
[Adopted 1919; repealed 1933 by Amendment XXI]

Section 1 After one year from the ratification of this article the manufacture, sale, or transportation of intoxicating liquors within, the importation thereof into, or the exportation thereof from the United States and all territory subject to the jurisdiction thereof, for beverage purposes, is hereby prohibited.

Section 2 The Congress and the several States shall have concurrent power to enforce this article by appropriate legislation.

Section 3 This article shall be inoperative unless it shall have been ratified as an amendment to the Constitution by the legislatures of the several States, as provided by the Constitution, within seven years from the date of the submission thereof to the States by the Congress.

◆ ◆ ◆

▶ *The Prohibition Party, formed in 1869, began calling for a constitutional amendment to outlaw alcoholic beverages in 1872. A prohibition amendment was first proposed in the Senate in 1876 and was revived eighteen times before 1913. Between 1913 and 1919, another thirty-nine attempts were made to prohibit liquor in the United States through a constitutional amendment. Prohibition became a key element of the progressive agenda as reformers linked alcohol and drunkenness to numerous*

social problems, including the corruption of immigrant voters. While opponents of such an amendment argued that it was undemocratic, supporters claimed that their efforts had widespread public support. The admission of twelve "dry" western states to the Union in the early twentieth century and the spirit of sacrifice during World War I laid the groundwork for passage and ratification of the Eighteenth Amendment in 1919. Opponents added a time limit to the amendment in the hope that they could thus block ratification, but this effort failed. (See also Amendment XXI.)

Amendment XIX
[Adopted 1920]

Section 1 The right of citizens of the United States to vote shall not be denied or abridged by the United States or by any State on account of sex.

Section 2 Congress shall have the power to enforce this article by appropriate legislation.

◆ ◆ ◆

▶ *Advocates of women's rights tried and failed to link woman suffrage to the Fourteenth and Fifteenth Amendments. Nonetheless, the effort for woman suffrage continued. Between 1878 and 1912, at least one and sometimes as many as four proposed amendments were introduced in Congress each year to grant women the right to vote. While over time women won very limited voting rights in some states, at both the state and federal levels opposition to an amendment for woman suffrage remained very strong. President Woodrow Wilson and other officials felt that the federal government should not interfere with the power of the states in this matter. Others worried that granting suffrage to women would encourage ethnic minorities to exercise their own right to vote. And many were concerned that giving women the vote would result in their abandoning traditional gender roles. In 1919, following a protracted and often bitter campaign of protest in which women went on hunger strikes and chained themselves to fences, an amendment was introduced with the backing of President Wilson. It narrowly passed the Senate (after efforts to limit the suffrage to white women failed) and was adopted in 1920 after Tennessee became the thirty-sixth state to ratify it.*

Unratified Amendment
Child Labor Amendment (proposed by Congress June 2, 1924)

Section 1 The Congress shall have power to limit, regulate, and prohibit the labor of persons under eighteen years of age.

Section 2 The power of the several States is unimpaired by this article except that the operation of State laws shall be suspended to the extent necessary to give effect to legislation enacted by Congress.

◆ ◆ ◆

► *Throughout the late nineteenth and early twentieth centuries, alarm over the condition of child workers grew. Opponents of child labor argued that children worked in dangerous and unhealthy conditions, that they took jobs from adult workers, that they depressed wages in certain industries, and that states that allowed child labor had an economic advantage over those that did not. Defenders of child labor claimed that children provided needed income in many families, that working at a young age developed character, and that the effort to prohibit the practice constituted an invasion of family privacy.*

In 1916, Congress passed a law that made it illegal to sell goods made by children through interstate commerce. The Supreme Court, however, ruled that the law violated the limits on the power of Congress to regulate interstate commerce. Congress then tried to penalize industries that used child labor by taxing such goods. This measure was also thrown out by the courts. In response, reformers set out to amend the Constitution. The proposed amendment was ratified by twenty-eight states, but by 1925, thirteen states had rejected it. Passage of the Fair Labor Standards Act in 1938, which was upheld by the Supreme Court in 1941, made the amendment irrelevant.

Amendment XX

[Adopted 1933]

Section 1 The terms of the President and Vice-President shall end at noon on the 20th day of January, and the terms of Senators and Representatives at noon on the 3rd day of January, of the years in which such terms would have ended if this article had not been ratified; and the terms of their successors shall then begin.

Section 2 The Congress shall assemble at least once in every year, and such meeting shall begin at noon on the 3rd day of January, unless they shall by law appoint a different day.

Section 3 If, at the time fixed for the beginning of the term of the President, the President-elect shall have died, the Vice-President-elect shall become President. If a President shall not have been chosen before the time fixed for the beginning of his term, or if the President-elect shall have failed to qualify, then the Vice-President-elect shall act as President until a President shall have qualified; and the Congress may by law provide for the case wherein neither a President-elect nor a Vice-President-elect shall have qualified, declaring who shall then act as President, or the manner in which one who is to act shall be selected, and

such person shall act accordingly until a President or Vice-President shall have qualified.

Section 4 The Congress may by law provide for the case of the death of any of the persons from whom the House of Representatives may choose a President whenever the right of choice shall have devolved upon them, and for the case of the death of any of the persons from whom the Senate may choose a Vice-President whenever the right of choice shall have devolved upon them.

Section 5 Sections 1 and 2 shall take effect on the 15th day of October following the ratification of this article.

Section 6 This article shall be inoperative unless it shall have been ratified as an amendment to the Constitution by the Legislatures of three-fourths of the several States within seven years from the date of its submission.

◆ ◆ ◆

► *Until 1933, presidents took office on March 4. Since elections are held in early November and electoral votes are counted in mid-December, this meant that more than three months passed between the time a new president was elected and when he took office. Moving the inauguration to January shortened the transition period and allowed Congress to begin its term closer to the time of the president's inauguration. Although this seems like a minor change, an amendment was required because the Constitution specifies terms of office. This amendment also deals with questions of succession in the event that a president- or vice president-elect dies before assuming office. Section 3 also clarifies a method for resolving a deadlock in the electoral college.*

Amendment XXI

[Adopted 1933]

Section 1 The eighteenth article of amendment to the Constitution of the United States is hereby repealed.

Section 2 The transportation or importation into any State, Territory, or Possession of the United States for delivery or use therein of intoxicating liquors, in violation of the laws thereof, is hereby prohibited.

Section 3 This article shall be inoperative unless it shall have been ratified as an amendment to the Constitution by conventions in the several States, as provided in the Constitution, within seven years from the date of the submission thereof to the States by the Congress.

◆ ◆ ◆

► *Widespread violation of the Volstead Act, the law enacted to enforce prohibition, made the United*

States a nation of lawbreakers. Prohibition caused more problems than it solved by encouraging crime, bribery, and corruption. Further, a coalition of liquor and beer manufacturers, personal liberty advocates, and constitutional scholars joined forces to challenge the amendment. By 1929, thirty proposed repeal amendments had been introduced in Congress, and the Democratic Party made repeal part of its platform in the 1932 presidential campaign. The Twenty-first Amendment was proposed in February 1933 and ratified less than a year later. The failure of the effort to enforce prohibition through a constitutional amendment has often been cited by opponents to subsequent efforts to shape public virtue and private morality.

Amendment XXII
[Adopted 1951]

Section 1 No person shall be elected to the office of the President more than twice, and no person who has held the office of President, or acted as President, for more than two years of a term to which some other person was elected President shall be elected to the office of President more than once. But this article shall not apply to any person holding the office of President when this Article was proposed by the Congress, and shall not prevent any person who may be holding the office of President, or acting as President, during the term within which this Article becomes operative from holding the office of President or acting as President during the remainder of such term.

Section 2 This article shall be inoperative unless it shall have been ratified as an amendment to the Constitution by the legislatures of three-fourths of the several States within seven years from the date of its submission to the States by the Congress.

♦ ♦ ♦

▶ *George Washington's refusal to seek a third term of office set a precedent that stood until 1912, when former president Theodore Roosevelt sought, without success, another term as an independent candidate. Democrat Franklin Roosevelt was the only president to seek and win a fourth term, though he did so amid great controversy. Roosevelt died in April 1945, a few months after the beginning of his fourth term. In 1946, Republicans won control of the House and the Senate, and early in 1947 a proposal for an amendment to limit future presidents to two four-year terms was offered to the states for ratification. Democratic critics of the Twenty-second Amendment charged that it was a partisan posthumous jab at Roosevelt.*

Since the Twenty-second Amendment was adopted, however, the only presidents who might have been able to seek a third term, had it not existed, were Republicans Dwight Eisenhower, Ronald Reagan, and George W. Bush, and Democrat Bill

Clinton. Since 1826, Congress has entertained 160 proposed amendments to limit the president to one six-year term. Such amendments have been backed by fifteen presidents, including Gerald Ford and Jimmy Carter.

Amendment XXIII
[Adopted 1961]

Section 1 The District constituting the seat of Government of the United States shall appoint in such manner as the Congress may direct: A number of electors of President and Vice-President equal to the whole number of Senators and Representatives in Congress to which the District would be entitled if it were a State, but in no event more than the least populous State; they shall be in addition to those appointed by the States, but they shall be considered for the purposes of the election of President and Vice-President, to be electors appointed by a State; and they shall meet in the District and perform such duties as provided by the twelfth article of amendment.

Section 2 The Congress shall have the power to enforce this article by appropriate legislation.

♦ ♦ ♦

▶ *When Washington, D.C., was established as a federal district, no one expected that a significant number of people would make it their permanent and primary residence. A proposal to allow citizens of the district to vote in presidential elections was approved by Congress in June 1960 and was ratified on March 29, 1961.*

Amendment XXIV
[Adopted 1964]

Section 1 The right of citizens of the United States to vote in any primary or other election for President or Vice-President, for electors for President or Vice-President, or for Senator or Representative in Congress, shall not be denied or abridged by the United States or any State by reason of failure to pay any poll tax or other tax.

Section 2 The Congress shall have the power to enforce this article by appropriate legislation.

♦ ♦ ♦

▶ *In the colonial and Revolutionary eras, financial independence was seen as necessary to political independence, and the poll tax was used as a requirement for voting. By the twentieth century, however, the poll tax was used mostly to bar poor people, especially southern blacks, from voting. While conservatives complained that the amendment interfered with states' rights, liberals thought that the amendment did not go far enough because it barred the poll tax only in national elections and not in state or local elections. The amendment was ratified in 1964, however, and two years later, the Supreme Court ruled that poll taxes in state and local elections also violated the equal protection clause of the Fourteenth Amendment.*

Amendment XXV

[Adopted 1967]

Section 1 In case of the removal of the President from office or of his death or resignation, the Vice-President shall become President.

Section 2 Whenever there is a vacancy in the office of the Vice-President, the President shall nominate a Vice-President who shall take office upon confirmation by a majority vote of both Houses of Congress.

Section 3 Whenever the President transmits to the President pro tempore of the Senate and the Speaker of the House of Representatives his written declaration that he is unable to discharge the powers and duties of his office, and until he transmits to them a written declaration to the contrary, such powers and duties shall be discharged by the Vice-President as Acting President.

Section 4 Whenever the Vice-President and a majority of either the principal officers of the executive departments or of such other body as Congress may by law provide, transmit to the President pro tempore of the Senate and the Speaker of the House of Representatives their written declaration that the President is unable to discharge the powers and duties of his office, the Vice-President shall immediately assume the powers and duties of the office as Acting President.

Thereafter, when the President transmits to the President pro tempore of the Senate and the Speaker of the House of Representatives his written declaration that no inability exists, he shall resume the powers and duties of his office unless the Vice-President and a majority of either the principal officers of the executive department[s] or of such other body as Congress may by law provide, transmit within four days to the President pro tempore of the Senate and the Speaker of the House of Representatives their written declaration that the President is unable to discharge the powers and duties of his office. Thereupon Congress shall decide the issue, assembling within forty-eight hours for that purpose if not in session. If the Congress, within twenty-one days after receipt of the latter written declaration, or, if Congress is not in session, within twenty-one days after Congress is required to assemble, determines by two-thirds vote of both Houses that the President is unable to discharge the powers and duties of his office, the Vice-President shall continue to discharge the same as Acting President; otherwise, the President shall resume the powers and duties of his office.

♦ ♦ ♦

▶ *The framers of the Constitution established the office of vice president because someone was needed to preside over the Senate. The first president to die in office was William Henry Harrison, in 1841. Vice President John Tyler had himself sworn in as president, setting a precedent that was followed when seven later presidents died in office. The assassination of President James A. Garfield in 1881 posed a new problem, however. After he was shot, the president was incapacitated for two months before he died; he was unable to lead the country, while his vice president, Chester A. Arthur, was unable to assume leadership. Efforts to resolve questions of succession in the event of a presidential disability thus began with the death of Garfield.*

In 1963, the assassination of President John F. Kennedy galvanized Congress to action. Vice President Lyndon Johnson was a chain smoker with a history of heart trouble. According to the 1947 Presidential Succession Act, the two men who stood in line to succeed him were the seventy-two-year-old Speaker of the House and the eighty-six-year-old president of the Senate. There were serious concerns that any of these men might become incapacitated while serving as chief executive. The first time the Twenty-fifth Amendment was used, however, was not in the case of presidential death or illness, but during the Watergate crisis. When Vice President Spiro T. Agnew was forced to resign following allegations of bribery and tax violations, President Richard M. Nixon appointed House Minority Leader Gerald R. Ford vice president. Ford became president following Nixon's resignation eight months later and named Nelson A. Rockefeller as his vice president. Thus, for more than two years, the two highest offices in the country were held by people who had not been elected to them.

Amendment XXVI

[Adopted 1971]

Section 1 The right of citizens of the United States, who are eighteen years of age or older, to vote shall not be denied or abridged by the United States or by any State on account of age.

Section 2 The Congress shall have power to enforce this article by appropriate legislation.

♦ ♦ ♦

▶ *Efforts to lower the voting age from twenty-one to eighteen began during World War II. Recognizing that those who were old enough to fight a war should have some say in the government policies that involved them in the war, Presidents Eisenhower, Johnson, and Nixon endorsed* the idea. In 1970, the combined pressure of the antiwar movement and the demographic pressure of the baby boom generation led to a Voting Rights Act lowering the voting age in federal, state, and local elections.

In Oregon v. Mitchell (1970), the state of Oregon challenged the right of Congress to determine the age at which people could vote in state or local elections. The Supreme Court agreed with Oregon. Since the Voting Rights Act was ruled unconstitutional, the Constitution had to be amended to allow passage of a law that would lower the voting age. The amendment was ratified in a little more than three months, making it the most rapidly ratified amendment in U.S. history.

Unratified Amendment

Equal Rights Amendment (proposed by Congress March 22, 1972; seven-year deadline for ratification extended to June 30, 1982)

Section 1 Equality of rights under the law shall not be denied or abridged by the United States or by any State on account of sex.

Section 2 The Congress shall have the power to enforce, by appropriate legislation, the provisions of this article.

Section 3 This amendment shall take effect two years after the date of ratification.

◆ ◆ ◆

▶ In 1923, soon after women had won the right to vote, Alice Paul, a leading activist in the woman suffrage movement, proposed an amendment requiring equal treatment of men and women. Opponents of the proposal argued that such an amendment would invalidate laws that protected women and would make women subject to the military draft. After the 1964 Civil Rights Act was adopted, protective workplace legislation was removed anyway.

The renewal of the women's movement, as a byproduct of the civil rights and antiwar movements, led to a revival of the Equal Rights Amendment (ERA) in Congress. Disagreements over language held up congressional passage of the proposed amendment, but on March 22, 1972, the Senate approved the ERA by a vote of 84 to 8, and it was sent to the states. Six states ratified the amendment within two days, and by the middle of 1973 the amendment seemed well on its way to adoption, with thirty of the needed thirty-eight states having ratified it. In the mid-1970s, however, a powerful "Stop ERA" campaign developed. The campaign portrayed the ERA as a threat to "family values" and traditional relationships between men and women. Although thirty-five states ultimately ratified the ERA, five of those state legislatures voted to rescind ratification, and the amendment was never adopted.

Unratified Amendment

D.C. Statehood Amendment (proposed by Congress August 22, 1978)

Section 1 For purposes of representation in the Congress, election of the President and Vice-President, and article V of this Constitution, the District constituting the seat of government of the United States shall be treated as though it were a State.

Section 2 The exercise of the rights and powers conferred under this article shall be by the people of the District constituting the seat of government, and as shall be provided by Congress.

Section 3 The twenty-third article of amendment to the Constitution of the United States is hereby repealed.

Section 4 This article shall be inoperative, unless it shall have been ratified as an amendment to the Constitution by the legislatures of three-fourths of the several states within seven years from the date of its submission.

◆ ◆ ◆

▶ The 1961 ratification of the Twenty-third Amendment, giving residents of the District of Columbia the right to vote for a president and vice president, inspired an effort to give residents of the district full voting rights. In 1966, President Lyndon Johnson appointed a mayor and city council; in 1971, D.C. residents were allowed to name a nonvoting delegate to the House; and in 1981, residents were allowed to elect the mayor and city council. Congress retained the right to overrule laws that might affect commuters, the height of federal buildings, and selection of judges and prosecutors. The district's nonvoting delegate to Congress, Walter Fauntroy, lobbied fiercely for a congressional amendment granting statehood to the district. In 1978, a proposed amendment was approved and sent to the states. A number of states quickly ratified the amendment, but, like the ERA, the D.C. Statehood Amendment ran into trouble.

Opponents argued that section 2 created a separate category of "nominal" statehood. They argued that the federal district should be eliminated and that the territory should be reabsorbed into the state of Maryland. Although these theoretical arguments were strong, some scholars believe that racist attitudes toward the predominantly black population of the city were also a factor leading to the defeat of the amendment.

Amendment XXVII

[Adopted 1992]

No law, varying the compensation for the services of the Senators and Representatives, shall take effect, until an election of Representatives shall have intervened.

◆ ◆ ◆

▶ *While the Twenty-sixth Amendment was the most rapidly ratified amendment in U.S. history, the Twenty-seventh Amendment had the longest journey to ratification. First proposed by James Madison in 1789 as part of the package that included the Bill of Rights, this amendment had been ratified by only six states by 1791. In 1873, however, it was ratified by Ohio to protest a massive retroactive salary increase by the federal government. Unlike later proposed amendments, this one came with no time limit on ratification.*

In the early 1980s, Gregory D. Watson, a University of Texas economics major, discovered the "lost" amendment and began a single-handed campaign to get state legislators to introduce it for ratification. In 1983, it was accepted by Maine. In 1984, it passed the Colorado legislature. Ratifications trickled in slowly until May 1992, when Michigan and New Jersey became the thirty-eighth and thirty-ninth states, respectively, to ratify. This amendment prevents members of Congress from raising their own salaries without giving voters a chance to vote them out of office before they can benefit from the raises.

PRESIDENTIAL ELECTIONS

Year	Candidates	Parties	Popular Vote	Percentage of Popular Vote	Electoral Vote	Percentage of Voter Participation
1789	**GEORGE WASHINGTON (Va.)***				69	
	John Adams				34	
	Others				35	
1792	**GEORGE WASHINGTON (Va.)**				132	
	John Adams				77	
	George Clinton				50	
	Others				5	
1796	**JOHN ADAMS (Mass.)**	Federalist			71	
	Thomas Jefferson	Democratic-Republican			68	
	Thomas Pinckney	Federalist			59	
	Aaron Burr	Dem.-Rep.			30	
	Others				48	
1800	**THOMAS JEFFERSON (Va.)**	Dem.-Rep.			73	
	Aaron Burr	Dem.-Rep.			73	
	John Adams	Federalist			65	
	C. C. Pinckney	Federalist			64	
	John Jay	Federalist			1	
1804	**THOMAS JEFFERSON (Va.)**	Dem.-Rep.			162	
	C. C. Pinckney	Federalist			14	
1808	**JAMES MADISON (Va.)**	Dem.-Rep.			122	
	C. C. Pinckney	Federalist			47	
	George Clinton	Dem.-Rep.			6	
1812	**JAMES MADISON (Va.)**	Dem.-Rep.			128	
	De Witt Clinton	Federalist			89	
1816	**JAMES MONROE (Va.)**	Dem.-Rep.			183	
	Rufus King	Federalist			34	
1820	**JAMES MONROE (Va.)**	Dem.-Rep.			231	
	John Quincy Adams	Dem.-Rep.			1	
1824	**JOHN Q. ADAMS (Mass.)**	Dem.-Rep.	108,740	30.5	84	26.9
	Andrew Jackson	Dem.-Rep.	153,544	43.1	99	
	William H. Crawford	Dem.-Rep.	46,618	13.1	41	
	Henry Clay	Dem.-Rep.	47,136	13.2	37	
1828	**ANDREW JACKSON (Tenn.)**	Democratic	647,286	56.0	178	57.6
	John Quincy Adams	National Republican	508,064	44.0	83	
1832	**ANDREW JACKSON (Tenn.)**	Democratic	687,502	55.0	219	55.4
	Henry Clay	National Republican	530,189	42.4	49	
	John Floyd	Independent			11	
	William Wirt	Anti-Mason	33,108	2.6	7	

*State of residence when elected president.

Year	Candidates	Parties	Popular Vote	Percentage of Popular Vote	Electoral Vote	Percentage of Voter Participation
1836	**MARTIN VAN BUREN (N.Y.)**	Democratic	765,483	50.9	170	57.8
	W. H. Harrison	Whig			73	
	Hugh L. White	Whig	739,795	49.1	26	
	Daniel Webster	Whig			14	
	W. P. Mangum	Independent			11	
1840	**WILLIAM H. HARRISON (Ohio)**	Whig	1,274,624	53.1	234	78.0
	Martin Van Buren	Democratic	1,127,781	46.9	60	
	J. G. Birney	Liberty	7,069		—	
1844	**JAMES K. POLK (Tenn.)**	Democratic	1,338,464	49.6	170	78.9
	Henry Clay	Whig	1,300,097	48.1	105	
	J. G. Birney	Liberty	62,300	2.3	—	
1848	**ZACHARY TAYLOR (La.)**	Whig	1,360,099	47.4	163	72.7
	Lewis Cass	Democratic	1,220,544	42.5	127	
	Martin Van Buren	Free-Soil	291,263	10.1	—	
1852	**FRANKLIN PIERCE (N.H.)**	Democratic	1,601,117	50.9	254	69.6
	Winfield Scott	Whig	1,385,453	44.1	42	
	John P. Hale	Free-Soil	155,825	5.0	—	
1856	**JAMES BUCHANAN (Pa.)**	Democratic	1,832,995	45.3	174	78.9
	John C. Frémont	Republican	1,339,932	33.1	114	
	Millard Fillmore	American	871,731	21.6	8	
1860	**ABRAHAM LINCOLN (Ill.)**	Republican	1,866,452	39.8	180	81.2
	Stephen A. Douglas	Democratic	1,375,157	29.4	12	
	John C. Breckinridge	Democratic	847,953	18.1	72	
	John Bell	Union	590,631	12.6	39	
1864	**ABRAHAM LINCOLN (Ill.)**	Republican	2,213,665	55.1	212	73.8
	George B. McClellan	Democratic	1,805,237	44.9	21	
1868	**ULYSSES S. GRANT (Ill.)**	Republican	3,012,833	52.7	214	78.1
	Horatio Seymour	Democratic	2,703,249	47.3	80	
1872	**ULYSSES S. GRANT (Ill.)**	Republican	3,597,132	55.6	286	71.3
	Horace Greeley	Democratic; Liberal Republican	2,834,125	43.9	66	
1876	**RUTHERFORD B. HAYES (Ohio)**	Republican	4,036,298	48.0	185	81.8
	Samuel J. Tilden	Democratic	4,288,590	51.0	184	
1880	**JAMES A. GARFIELD (Ohio)**	Republican	4,454,416	48.5	214	79.4
	Winfield S. Hancock	Democratic	4,444,952	48.1	155	
1884	**GROVER CLEVELAND (N.Y.)**	Democratic	4,874,986	48.5	219	77.5
	James G. Blaine	Republican	4,851,981	48.3	182	
1888	**BENJAMIN HARRISON (Ind.)**	Republican	5,439,853	47.9	233	79.3
	Grover Cleveland	Democratic	5,540,309	48.6	168	
1892	**GROVER CLEVELAND (N.Y.)**	Democratic	5,555,426	46.1	277	74.7
	Benjamin Harrison	Republican	5,182,690	43.0	145	
	James B. Weaver	People's	1,029,846	8.5	22	
1896	**WILLIAM McKINLEY (Ohio)**	Republican	7,104,779	51.1	271	79.3
	William J. Bryan	Democratic-People's	6,502,925	47.7	176	
1900	**WILLIAM McKINLEY (Ohio)**	Republican	7,207,923	51.7	292	73.2
	William J. Bryan	Dem.-Populist	6,358,133	45.5	155	
1904	**THEODORE ROOSEVELT (N.Y.)**	Republican	7,623,486	57.9	336	65.2
	Alton B. Parker	Democratic	5,077,911	37.6	140	
	Eugene V. Debs	Socialist	402,283	3.0	—	
1908	**WILLIAM H. TAFT (Ohio)**	Republican	7,678,908	51.6	321	65.4
	William J. Bryan	Democratic	6,409,104	43.1	162	
	Eugene V. Debs	Socialist	420,793	2.8	—	

Year	Candidates	Parties	Popular Vote	Percentage of Popular Vote	Electoral Vote	Percentage of Voter Participation
1912	**WOODROW WILSON (N.J.)**	Democratic	6,293,454	41.9	435	58.8
	Theodore Roosevelt	Progressive	4,119,538	27.4	88	
	William H. Taft	Republican	3,484,980	23.2	8	
	Eugene V. Debs	Socialist	900,672	6.1	—	
1916	**WOODROW WILSON (N.J.)**	Democratic	9,129,606	49.4	277	61.6
	Charles E. Hughes	Republican	8,538,221	46.2	254	
	A. L. Benson	Socialist	585,113	3.2	—	
1920	**WARREN G. HARDING (Ohio)**	Republican	16,143,407	60.5	404	49.2
	James M. Cox	Democratic	9,130,328	34.2	127	
	Eugene V. Debs	Socialist	919,799	3.4	—	
1924	**CALVIN COOLIDGE (Mass.)**	Republican	15,725,016	54.0	382	48.9
	John W. Davis	Democratic	8,386,503	28.8	136	
	Robert M. La Follette	Progressive	4,822,856	16.6	13	
1928	**HERBERT HOOVER (Calif.)**	Republican	21,391,381	57.4	444	56.9
	Alfred E. Smith	Democratic	15,016,443	40.3	87	
	Norman Thomas	Socialist	881,951	2.3	—	
	William Z. Foster	Communist	102,991	0.3	—	
1932	**FRANKLIN D. ROOSEVELT (N.Y.)**	Democratic	22,821,857	57.4	472	56.9
	Herbert Hoover	Republican	15,761,841	39.7	59	
	Norman Thomas	Socialist	881,951	2.2	—	
1936	**FRANKLIN D. ROOSEVELT (N.Y.)**	Democratic	27,751,597	60.8	523	61.0
	Alfred M. Landon	Republican	16,679,583	36.5	8	
	William Lemke	Union	882,479	1.9	—	
1940	**FRANKLIN D. ROOSEVELT (N.Y.)**	Democratic	27,244,160	54.8	449	62.5
	Wendell Willkie	Republican	22,305,198	44.8	82	
1944	**FRANKLIN D. ROOSEVELT (N.Y.)**	Democratic	25,602,504	53.5	432	55.9
	Thomas E. Dewey	Republican	22,006,285	46.0	99	
1948	**HARRY S. TRUMAN (Mo.)**	Democratic	24,105,695	49.5	303	53.0
	Thomas E. Dewey	Republican	21,969,170	45.1	189	
	J. Strom Thurmond	States'-Rights Democratic	1,169,021	2.4	38	
	Henry A. Wallace	Progressive	1,156,103	2.4	—	
1952	**DWIGHT D. EISENHOWER (N.Y.)**	Republican	33,936,252	55.1	442	63.3
	Adlai Stevenson	Democratic	27,314,992	44.4	89	
1956	**DWIGHT D. EISENHOWER (N.Y.)**	Republican	35,575,420	57.6	457	60.6
	Adlai Stevenson	Democratic	26,033,066	42.1	73	
	Other	—	—		1	
1960	**JOHN F. KENNEDY (Mass.)**	Democratic	34,227,096	49.9	303	62.8
	Richard M. Nixon	Republican	34,108,546	49.6	219	
	Other	—	—		15	
1964	**LYNDON B. JOHNSON (Texas)**	Democratic	43,126,506	61.1	486	61.7
	Barry M. Goldwater	Republican	27,176,799	38.5	52	
1968	**RICHARD M. NIXON (N.Y.)**	Republican	31,770,237	43.4	301	60.9
	Hubert H. Humphrey	Democratic	31,270,533	42.7	191	
	George Wallace	American Indep.	9,906,141	13.5	46	
1972	**RICHARD M. NIXON (N.Y.)**	Republican	47,169,911	60.7	520	55.2
	George S. McGovern	Democratic	29,170,383	37.5	17	
	Other	—	—		1	
1976	**JIMMY CARTER (Ga.)**	Democratic	40,830,763	50.0	297	53.5
	Gerald R. Ford	Republican	39,147,793	48.0	240	
	Other	—	1,575,459	2.1	—	
1980	**RONALD REAGAN (Calif.)**	Republican	43,901,812	51.0	489	54.0
	Jimmy Carter	Democratic	35,483,820	41.0	49	
	John B. Anderson	Independent	5,719,722	7.0	—	
	Ed Clark	Libertarian	921,188	1.1	—	

Year	Candidates	Parties	Popular Vote	Percentage of Popular Vote	Electoral Vote	Percentage of Voter Participation
1984	**RONALD REAGAN (Calif.)**	Republican	54,455,075	59.0	525	53.1
	Walter Mondale	Democratic	37,577,185	41.0	13	
1988	**GEORGE H. W. BUSH (Texas)**	Republican	47,946,422	54.0	426	50.2
	Michael S. Dukakis	Democratic	41,016,429	46.0	112	
1992	**WILLIAM J. CLINTON (Ark.)**	Democratic	44,908,254	43.0	370	55.9
	George H. W. Bush	Republican	39,102,282	38.0	168	
	H. Ross Perot	Independent	19,721,433	19.0	—	
1996	**WILLIAM J. CLINTON (Ark.)**	Democratic	47,401,185	49.2	379	49.0
	Robert Dole	Republican	39,197,469	40.7	159	
	H. Ross Perot	Independent	8,085,294	8.4	—	
2000	**GEORGE W. BUSH (Texas)**	Republican	50,456,062	47.8	271	51.2
	Al Gore	Democratic	50,996,862	48.4	267	
	Ralph Nader	Green Party	2,858,843	2.7	—	
	Patrick J. Buchanan	—	438,760	0.4	—	
2004	**GEORGE W. BUSH (Texas)**	Republican	61,872,711	50.7	286	60.3
	John F. Kerry	Democratic	58,894,584	48.3	252	
	Other	—	1,582,185	1.3	—	
2008	**BARACK OBAMA (Illinois)**	Democratic	69,456,897	52.9	365	56.8
	John McCain	Republican	59,934,314	45.7	173	
2012	**BARACK OBAMA (Illinois)**	Democratic	65,899,660	51.1	332	—
	Willard Mitt Romney	Republican	60,932,152	47.2	152	

ADMISSION OF STATES TO THE UNION

State	Date of Admission	State	Date of Admission
Delaware	December 7, 1787	Florida	March 3, 1845
Pennsylvania	December 12, 1787	Texas	December 29, 1845
New Jersey	December 18, 1787	Iowa	December 28, 1846
Georgia	January 2, 1788	Wisconsin	May 29, 1848
Connecticut	January 9, 1788	California	September 9, 1850
Massachusetts	February 6, 1788	Minnesota	May 11, 1858
Maryland	April 28, 1788	Oregon	February 14, 1859
South Carolina	May 23, 1788	Kansas	January 29, 1861
New Hampshire	June 21, 1788	West Virginia	June 19, 1863
Virginia	June 25, 1788	Nevada	October 31, 1864
New York	July 26, 1788	Nebraska	March 1, 1867
North Carolina	November 21, 1789	Colorado	August 1, 1876
Rhode Island	May 29, 1790	North Dakota	November 2, 1889
Vermont	March 4, 1791	South Dakota	November 2, 1889
Kentucky	June 1, 1792	Montana	November 8, 1889
Tennessee	June 1, 1796	Washington	November 11, 1889
Ohio	March 1, 1803	Idaho	July 3, 1890
Louisiana	April 30, 1812	Wyoming	July 10, 1890
Indiana	December 11, 1816	Utah	January 4, 1896
Mississippi	December 10, 1817	Oklahoma	November 16, 1907
Illinois	December 3, 1818	New Mexico	January 6, 1912
Alabama	December 14, 1819	Arizona	February 14, 1912
Maine	March 15, 1820	Alaska	January 3, 1959
Missouri	August 10, 1821	Hawaii	August 21, 1959
Arkansas	June 15, 1836		
Michigan	January 16, 1837		

Population

FROM AN ESTIMATED 4,600 white inhabitants in 1630, the country's population grew to a total of more than 308 million in 2010. It is important to note that the U.S. census, first conducted in 1790 and the source of these figures, counted blacks, both free and slave, but did not include American Indians until 1860. The years 1790 to 1900 saw the most rapid population growth, with an average increase of 25 to 35 percent per decade. In addition to "natural" growth—birthrate exceeding death rate—immigration was also a factor in that rise, especially between 1840 and 1860, 1880 and 1890, and 1900 and 1910. The twentieth century witnessed slower growth, partly a result of 1920s immigration restrictions and a decline in the birthrate, especially during the depression era and the 1960s and 1970s. The U.S. population is expected to pass 340 million by the year 2020.

POPULATION GROWTH, 1630–2010

Year	Population	Percent Increase	Year	Population	Percent Increase
1630	4,600	—	1830	12,866,020	33.5
1640	26,600	473.3	1840	17,069,453	32.7
1650	50,400	89.1	1850	23,191,876	35.9
1660	75,100	49.0	1860	31,443,321	35.6
1670	111,900	49.1	1870	39,818,449	26.6
1680	151,500	35.4	1880	50,155,783	26.0
1690	210,400	38.9	1890	62,947,714	25.5
1700	250,900	19.3	1900	75,994,575	20.7
1710	331,700	32.2	1910	91,972,266	21.0
1720	466,200	40.5	1920	105,710,620	14.9
1730	629,400	35.0	1930	122,775,046	16.1
1740	905,600	43.9	1940	131,669,275	7.2
1750	1,170,800	30.0	1950	150,697,361	14.5
1760	1,593,600	36.1	1960	179,323,175	19.0
1770	2,148,100	34.8	1970	203,302,031	13.4
1780	2,780,400	29.4	1980	226,542,199	11.4
1790	3,929,214	41.3	1990	248,718,302	9.8
1800	5,308,483	35.1	2000	281,422,509	13.1
1810	7,239,881	36.4	2010	308,745,538	9.7
1820	9,638,453	33.1			

SOURCE: *Historical Statistics of the U.S.* (1960), *Historical Statistics of the U.S., Colonial Times to 1970* (1975), *Statistical Abstract of the U.S., 1996* (1996), *Statistical Abstract of the U.S., 2003* (2003), and United States Census (2010).

Major Trends in Immigration

THE QUANTITY AND CHARACTER OF IMMIGRATION to the United States has varied greatly over time. During the first major influx, between 1840 and 1860, newcomers hailed primarily from northern and western Europe. From 1880 to 1915, when rates soared even more dramatically, the profile changed, with 80 percent of the "new immigration" coming from central, eastern, and southern Europe. Following World War I, strict quotas reduced the flow considerably. Note also the significant falloff during the years of the Great Depression and World War II. The sources of immigration during the last half century have changed significantly, with the majority of people coming from Latin America, the Caribbean, and Asia. The latest surge during the 1980s and 1990s brought more immigrants to the United States than in any decade except 1901–1910.

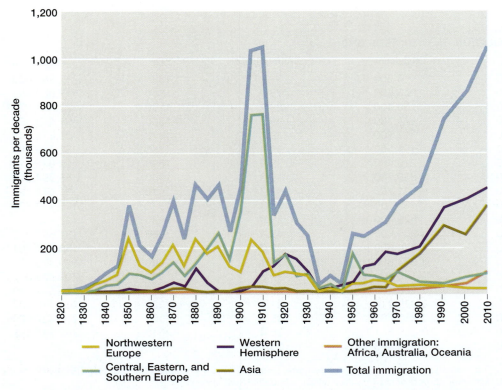

SOURCE: Data from *Historical Statistics of the U.S., Colonial Times to 1970* (1975), *Statistical Abstract of the U.S., 1999* (1999), and *Statistical Abstract of the U.S., 2011* (2011).

Selected Bibliography

Chapter 16

GENERAL WORKS

Thomas J. Brown, ed., *Reconstructions: New Perspectives on the Postbellum United States* (2006).

Michael W. Fitzgerald, *Splendid Failure: Postwar Reconstruction in the American South* (2007).

Eric Foner, *Reconstruction: America's Unfinished Revolution* (1988).

James M. McPherson, *Ordeal by Fire: The Civil War and Reconstruction* (3rd ed., 2000).

THE MEANING OF FREEDOM

Ira Berlin et al., eds., *Freedom: A Documentary History of Emancipation, 1861–1867*, 5 vols. (1982–2008).

Ronald E. Butchart, *Schooling the Freed People: Teaching, Learning, and the Struggle for Black Freedom, 1861–1876* (2010).

Jim Downs, *Sick for Freedom: African-American Illness and Suffering during the Civil War and Reconstruction* (2012).

John Hope Franklin and Loren Schweninger, *In Search of the Promised Land: A Slave Family in the Old South* (2006).

Thavolia Glymph, *Out of the House of Bondage: The Transformation of the Plantation Household* (2008).

Steven Hahn, *A Nation under Our Feet: Black Political Struggles in the Rural South, from Slavery to the Great Migration* (2003).

Leon F. Litwack, *Been in the Storm So Long: The Aftermath of Slavery* (1979).

Susan Eva O'Donovan, *Becoming Free in the Cotton South* (2007).

Joshua Paddison, *American Heathens: Religion, Race, and Reconstruction in California* (2012).

Howard N. Rabinowitz, *Race Relations in the Urban South, 1865–1890* (1978).

Roger L. Ransom and Richard Sutch, *One Kind of Freedom: The Economic Consequences of Emancipation* (1977).

Leslie Schwalm, *A Hard Fight for We: Women's Transition from Slavery to Freedom in South Carolina* (1997).

Loren Schweninger, *James T. Rapier and Reconstruction* (1978).

Rebecca J. Scott, *Degrees of Freedom: Louisiana and Cuba after Slavery* (2005).

Clarence E. Walker, *A Rock in a Weary Land: The African Methodist Episcopal Church during the Civil War and Reconstruction* (1982).

THE POLITICS OF RECONSTRUCTION

Richard F. Bensel, *Yankee Leviathan: The Origins of Central State Authority in America, 1859–1877* (1990).

Philip Dray, *Capitol Men: The Epic Story of Reconstruction Through the Lives of the First Black Congressmen* (2008).

Ellen Carol DuBois, *Feminism and Suffrage: The Emergence of an Independent Women's Movement in America, 1848–1869* (1978).

Laura Edwards, *Gendered Strife and Confusion: The Political Culture of Reconstruction* (1997).

James K. Hogue, *Uncivil War: Five New Orleans Street Battles and the Rise and Fall of Radical Reconstruction* (2006).

Richard L. Hume and Jerry B. Gough, *Blacks, Carpetbaggers, and Scalawags: The Constitutional Conventions of Radical Reconstruction* (2008).

Heather Cox Richardson, *The Death of Reconstruction: Race, Labor, and Politics in the Post–Civil War North, 1865–1901* (2001).

Leslie A. Schwalm, *Emancipation's Diaspora: Race and Reconstruction in the Upper Midwest* (2009).

Brooks D. Simpson, *The Reconstruction Presidents* (1998).

Mark Wahlgren Summers, *A Dangerous Stir: Fear, Paranoia, and the Making of Reconstruction* (2009).

Michael Vorenberg, *Final Freedom: The Civil War, the Abolition of Slavery, and the Thirteenth Amendment* (2001).

C. Vann Woodward, *Reunion and Reaction: The Compromise of 1877 and the End of Reconstruction* (1951).

THE STRUGGLE IN THE SOUTH

James Alex Baggett, *The Scalawags: Southern Dissenters in the Civil War and Reconstruction* (2003).

Nancy D. Bercaw, *Gendered Freedoms: Race, Rights, and the Politics of Household in the Delta, 1861–1875* (2003).

Stephen Budiansky, *The Bloody Shirt: Terror After the Civil War* (2008).

Jane Turner Censer, *The Reconstruction of White Southern Womanhood, 1865–1895* (2003).

Paul A. Cimbala, *Under the Guardianship of the Nation: The Freedmen's Bureau and the Reconstruction of Georgia, 1865–1870* (1997).

Jane E. Dailey, *Before Jim Crow: The Politics of Race in Post-emancipation Virginia* (2000).

Sarah E. Gardner, *Blood and Irony: Southern White Women's Narratives of the Civil War, 1861–1937* (2004).

Carole Faulkner, *Women's Radical Reconstruction: The Freedmen's Aid Movement* (2004).

Moon-Ho Jung, *Coolies and Cane: Race, Labor, and Sugar in the Age of Emancipation* (2006).

Stephen Kantrowitz, *Ben Tillman and the Reconstruction of White Supremacy* (2000).

Charles Lane, *The Day Freedom Died: The Colfax Massacre, the Supreme Court, and the Betrayal of Reconstruction* (2008).

Amy Feely Morsman, *The Big House After Slavery: Virginian Plantation Families and Their Postbellum Domestic Experiences* (2010).

George C. Rable, *But There Was No Peace: The Role of Violence in the Politics of Reconstruction* (1984).

James L. Roark, *Masters without Slaves: Southern Planters in the Civil War and Reconstruction* (1977).

Hannah Rosen, *Terror in the Heart of Freedom: Citizenship, Sexual Violence, and the Meaning of Race in the Postemancipation South* (2009).

Hyman Rubin III, *South Carolina Scalawags* (2006).

Christopher M. Span, *From Cotton Field to Schoolhouse: African American Education in Mississippi, 1862–1875* (2009).

Peter Wallenstein, *From Slave South to New South: Public Policy in Nineteenth-Century Georgia* (1987).

Chapter 17

GENERAL

Najia Aarin-Heriot, *Chinese Immigrants, African Americans, and Racial Anxiety in the United States, 1848–1882* (2003).

Robert V. Hine and John Mack Faragher, *The American West: A New Interpretive History* (2000).

Patricia Nelson Limerick, *Something in the Soil: Legacies and Reckonings in the New West* (2000).

Valerie Matsumoto and Blake Allmendinger, eds., *Over the Edge: Remapping the American West* (1999).

Louis S. Warren, *Buffalo Bill's America: William Cody and the Wild West Show* (2005).

Richard White, *"It's Your Misfortune and None of My Own": A New History of the American West* (1991).

Richard White, *Railroaded: The Transcontinentals and the Making of Modern America* (2011).

David M. Wrobel, *Promised Lands: Promotion, Memory, and the Creation of the American West* (2002).

INDIANS

David Wallace Adams, *Education for Extinction: American Indians and the Boarding School Experience, 1875–1928* (1995).

Gary Clayton Anderson, *The Conquest of Texas: Ethnic Cleansing in the Promised Land, 1820–1875* (2005).

Stuart Banner, *How the Indians Lost Their Land: Law and Power on the Frontier* (2005).

Ned Blackhawk, *Violence over the Land: Indian Empires in the Early American West* (2006).

Colin Calloway, *First Peoples: A Documentary Survey of American Indian History* (3rd ed., 2008).

James O. Gump, *The Dust Rose like Smoke: The Subjugation of the Zulu and the Sioux* (1994).

Pekka Hamalainen, *The Comanche Empire* (2008).

Andrew C. Isenberg, *The Destruction of the Bison: An Environmental History, 1730–1920* (2000).

Ari Kelman, *A Misplaced Massacre: Struggling over the Memory of Sand Creek* (2013).

Edward Lazarus, *Black Hills, White Justice: The Sioux Nation versus the United States, 1775 to the Present* (1991).

Jeffrey Ostler, *The Plains Sioux and U.S. Colonialism from Lewis and Clark to Wounded Knee* (2004).

Nathaniel Philbrick, *The Last Stand: Custer, Sitting Bull, and the Battle of the Little Bighorn* (2010).

Francis Paul Prucha, *The Great Father: The United States Government and the American Indian* (1986).

Charles M. Robinson III, *A Good Year to Die: The Story of the Great Sioux War* (1995).

Alan Trachtenberg, *Shades of Hiawatha: Staging Indians, Making Americans, 1880–1930* (2004).

MINING, RANCHING, AND FARMING

Suchen Chan, *This Bittersweet Soil: The Chinese in American Agriculture, 1860–1919* (1986).

Suchen Chan, Douglas Henry Daniels, Mario T. Garcia, and Terry P. Wilson, *Peoples of Color in the American West* (1994).

Roger Daniels, *Asian American: Chinese and Japanese in the United States since 1850* (1997).

Deborah Fitzgerald, *Every Farm a Factory: The Industrial Ideal in American Agriculture* (2003).

Manuel G. Gonzales, *Mexicanos: A History of Mexicans in the United States* (1999).

J. S. Holliday, *Rush for Riches: Gold Fever and the Making of California* (1999).

David Igler, *Industrial Cowboys: Miller & Lux and the Transformation of the Far West, 1850–1920* (2001).

Andrew C. Isenberg, *Mining California: An Ecological History* (2005).

Ronald M. James, *The Roar and the Silence: The History of Virginia City and the Comstock Lode* (1998).

William Loren Katz, *Black West: A Documentary and Pictorial History of the African American Role in the Westward Expansion of the United States* (2005).

Karen R. Merrill, *Public Lands and Political Meaning: Ranchers, the Government, and the Property between Them* (2002).

Rodman Wilson Paul, *Mining Frontiers of the Far West, 1848–1880* (rev. ed., 2001).

William G. Robbins, *Colony and Empire: The Capitalist Transformation of the American West* (1994).

Steven Stoll, *Larding the Lean Earth: Soil and Society in Nineteenth-Century America* (2002).

Chapter 18

GENERAL WORKS

Charles W. Calhoun, ed., *The Gilded Age: Essays on the Origins of Modern America* (1996).

Sean Dennis Cashman, *America in the Gilded Age: From the Death of Lincoln to the Rise of Theodore Roosevelt* (1993).

Rebecca Edwards, *New Spirits: Americans in the Gilded Age, 1865–1905* (2006).

Jackson Lears, *Rebirth of a Nation: The Making of Modern America, 1877–1920* (2009).

Richard While, *Railroaded: The Transcontinentals and the Making of Modern America* (2011).

BUSINESS

Kathleen Brady, *Ida Tarbell: Portrait of a Muckraker* (1984).

Edward Chancellor, *Devil Take the Hindmost: A History of Financial Speculation* (1999).

Ron Chernow, *Titan: The Life of John D. Rockefeller, Sr.* (1998).

Steve Fraser, *Every Man a Speculator: A Cultural History of Wall Street in America* (2005).

Morton J. Horowitz, *The Transformation of American Law, 1870–1960* (1992).

Walter Licht, *Industrializing America* (1995).

Carol Marvin, *When Technologies Were New* (1988).

David Nasaw, *Andrew Carnegie* (2006).

T. J. Stiles, *The First Tycoon: The Epic Life of Cornelius Vanderbilt* (2009).

Jean Strouse, *Morgan: American Financier* (1999).

Viviana A. Zelizer, *The Social Meaning of Money* (1994).

POLITICS

Paula Baker, *The Moral Framework of Public Life* (1991).

Richard F. Bensel, *The Political Economy of American Industrialization, 1877–1900* (2000).

Ruth Bordin, *Women and Temperance: The Quest for Power and Liberty, 1873–1900* (1990).

Alyn Brodsky, *Grover Cleveland: A Study in Character* (2000).

Robert W. Cherny, *American Politics in the Gilded Age, 1868–1900* (1997).

Jane Dailey, Glenda Elizabeth Gilmore, and Bryant Simon, eds., *Jumpin' Jim Crow: Southern Politics from the Civil War to Civil Rights* (2000).

Rebecca Edwards, *Angels in the Machinery: Gender in American Party Politics from the Civil War to the Progressive Era* (1997).

Dana Frank, *Buy American: The Untold Story of Economic Nationalism* (1999).

Paula Giddings, *Ida, a Sword among Lions: Ida B. Wells and the Campaign against Lynching* (2008).

Steven Hahn, *A Nation under Our Feet: Black Political Struggles in the Rural South from Slavery to the Great Migration* (2003).

Darlene Clark Hine and Kathleen Thompson, *A Shining Thread of Hope: The History of Black Women in America* (1998).

Ari Hoogenboom, *Rutherford B. Hayes: Warrior and President* (1995).

H. Paul Jeffers, *An Honest President: The Life and Presidencies of Grover Cleveland* (2000).

Ross Evans Paulson, *Liberty, Equality, and Justice: Civil Rights, Women's Rights, and the Regulation of Business, 1865–1932* (1997).

Dorothy Salem, *To Better Our World: Black Women in Organized Reform, 1890–1920* (1990).

Ian Tyrell, *Woman's World, Woman's Empire: The Woman's Christian Temperance Union in International Perspective, 1880–1930* (1991).

LeeAnn Whites, *Gender Matters: Civil War, Reconstruction, and the Making of the New South* (2005).

CULTURE

Ellen Gruber Garvey, *The Adman in the Parlor: Magazines and the Gendering of Consumer Culture, 1880s to 1910s* (1996).

Judy Arlene Hilkey, *Character Is Capital: Success Manuals and Manhood in Gilded Age America* (1997).

Jane H. Hunter, *How Young Ladies Became Girls: The Victorian Origins of American Girlhood* (2002).

Paulette D. Kilmer, *The Fear of Sinking: The American Success Formula in the Gilded Age* (1996).

Alan Trachtenberg, *The Incorporation of America: Culture and Society in the Gilded Age* (anniversary edition, 2009).

Chapter 19

IMMIGRATION

John Bodnar, *The Transplanted: A History of Immigration in Urban America* (1985).

Vincent J. Cannato, *American Passage: The History of Ellis Island* (2010).

Roger Daniels, *Guarding the Golden Door: American Immigration Policy and Immigrants since 1882* (2004).

Allan Dawley, *Struggles for Justice: Social Responsibility and the Liberal State* (1991).

Martha Gardner, *The Qualities of a Citizen: Women, Immigration, and Citizenship, 1870–1965* (2005).

Dirk Hoerder, *Cultures in Contact: World Migrations in the Second Millennium* (2002).

Matthew Frye Jacobson, *Whiteness of a Different Color: European Immigrants and the Alchemy of Race* (1998).

David M. Reimers, *Unwelcome Strangers* (1998).

David R. Roediger, *Working toward Whiteness: How America's Immigrants Became White* (2005).

Ronald Takaki, *Strangers from a Different Shore: A History of Asian Americans* (1998).

WORKERS AND UNIONS

Susan Porter Benson, *Counter Cultures: Saleswomen, Managers, and Customers in American Department Stores, 1890–1940* (1986).

Ileen A. DeVault, *United Apart: Gender and the Rise of Craft Unionism* (2004).

Hasia Diner, *Lower East Side Memories: A Jewish Place in America* (2000).

Leon Fink, *Workingman's Democracy: The Knights of Labor and American Politics* (1983).

James Green, *Death in the Haymarket: A Story of Chicago, the First Labor Movement, and the Bombing That Divided Gilded Age America* (2006).

Hamilton Hold, ed., *The Life Stories of Undistinguished Americans as Told by Themselves* (2000).

Jacqueline Jones, *American Work: Four Centuries of Black and White Labor* (1998).

Jackson Lears, *Rebirth of a Nation: The Making of Modern America, 1877–1920* (2009).

Susan Levine, *Labor's True Women: Carpet Weavers, Industrialization, and Labor Reform in the Gilded Age* (1984).

David Montgomery, *The Fall of the House of Labor: The Workplace, the State, and American Labor Activism, 1865–1925* (1987).

Roy Rosenzweig, *Eight Hours for What We Will: Workers and Leisure in an Industrial City, 1870–1920* (1983).

Timothy Spears, *Chicago Dreaming: Midwesterners and the City, 1871–1919* (2005).

Carole Srole, *Transcribing Class and Gender: Masculinity and Femininity in Nineteenth Century Courts and Offices* (2009).

Sharon Hartman Strom, *Beyond the Typewriter: Gender, Class, and the Origins of Modern American Office Work, 1900–1930* (1992).

Robert E. Weir, *Knights Unhorsed: Internal Conflict in a Gilded Age Social Movement* (2000).

THE CITY AND ITS AMUSEMENTS

LeRoy Ashby, *With Amusement for All: A History of American Popular Culture since 1830* (2006).

Sven Beckert, *The Monied Metropolis: New York City and the Consolidation of the American Bourgeoisie, 1850–1896* (2001).

Gary S. Cross and John K. Walton, *The Playful Crowd: Pleasure Places in the Twentieth Century* (2005).

Sarah Deutsch, *Women and the City: Gender, Space, and Power in Boston, 1870–1940* (2000).

Nan Enstad, *Ladies of Labor, Girls of Adventure: Working Women, Popular Culture, and Labor Politics at the Turn of the Twentieth Century* (1999).

Margaret Garb, *City of American Dreams: A History of Home Ownership and Housing Reform in Chicago, 1871–1919* (2005).

Richard Haw, *The Brooklyn Bridge: A Cultural History* (2005).

Elizabeth Hawes, *New York, New York: How the Apartment House Transformed Life in the City, 1869–1930* (1993).

Kathy Peiss, *Cheap Amusements: Working Women and Leisure in Turn-of-the-Century New York* (1986).

Roy Rosenzweig and Elizabeth Blackmar, *The Park and the People: A History of Central Park* (1992).

Witold Rybczynski, *A Clearing in the Distance: Frederick Law Olmsted and America in the Nineteenth Century* (1999).

Jules Tygiel, *Past Time: Baseball as History* (2000).

Chapter 20

WAR AND FOREIGN POLICY

THE FARMERS ALLIANCE, THE LABOR WARS, AND WOMEN'S ACTIVISM

Peter H. Argersinger, *The Limits of Agrarian Radicalism: Western Populism and American Politics* (1995).

Jean H. Baker, *Sisters: The Lives of America's Suffragists* (2005).

Donna A. Barnes, *The Louisiana Populist Movement, 1881–1900* (2011).

Ruth Bordin *Frances Willard: A Biography* (1986).

Alan Dawley, *Struggles for Justice: Social Responsibility and the Liberal State* (1991).

Ellen Carol DuBois, *Woman Suffrage and Women's Rights* (1998).

Gaither, *Blacks and the Populist Movement* (2013).

Michael Lewis Goldberg, *An Army of Women: Gender and Politics in Gilded Age Kansas* (1997).

Steven Hahn, *A Nation under Our Feet: Black Political Struggles in the Rural South from Slavery to the Great Migration* (2003).

Elizabeth Jameson, *All That Glitters: Class, Conflict, and Community in Cripple Creek* (1998).

Michael Kazin, *The Populist Persuasion: An American History* (rev. ed., 1998).

Paul Krause, *The Battle for Homestead, 1880–1892* (1992).

Connie L. Lester, *Up From the Mudsills of Hell: The Farmers' Alliance, Populism, and Progressive Agriculture in Tennessee, 1870–1915* (2006).

Theodore R. Mitchell, *Political Education in the Southern Farmers' Alliance, 1887–1900* (1987).

David Nasaw, *Andrew Carnegie* (2006).

Nick Salvatore, *Eugene V. Debs: Citizen and Socialist* (1982).

DEPRESSION AND THE ELECTION OF 1896

Louis L, Gould, *The Presidency of Willliam McKinley* (1981).

Stephen Kantrowitz, *Ben Tillman and the Reconstruction of White Supremacy* (2000).

Michael Kazin, *A Godly Hero: The Life of William Jennings Bryan* (2006).

Kenneth L. Kusmer, *Down and Out, on the Road: The Homeless in American History* (2002).

Gretchen Ritter, *Goldbugs and Greenbacks: The Antimonopoly Tradition in the Politics of Finance in America* (1997).

Carol A. Schwantes, *Coxey's Army: An American Odyssey* (1985).

Douglas Steeples and David O Whitten, *Democracy in Desperation: The Depression of 1892* (1998).

U.S. FOREIGN POLICY AND THE SPANISH-AMERICAN WAR

Fred Anderson and Andrew Cayton, *The Domination of War: Empire and Liberty in North America, 1500–2000* (2005).

Edward P. Crapol, *James G. Blaine: Architect of Empire* (1999).

Kristin Hoganson, *Fighting for American Manhood: How Gender Politics Provoked the Spanish-American and Philippine-American Wars* (1998).

Matthew Frye Jacobson, *Barbarian Virtues: The United States Encounters Foreign Peoples at Home and Abroad, 1876–1917* (2000).

Amy Kaplan, *The Anarchy of Empire in the Making of U.S. Culture* (2002).

Stephen Kinzer, *Overthrow: America's Century of Regime Change from Hawaii to Iraq* (2006).

Walter LaFeber, *The Cambridge History of American Foreign Relations*, vol. 2 *The American Search for Opportunity, 1865–1913* (1993).

Brian Linn, *The Philippine War, 1899–1902* (2000).

Paul T. McCartney, *Power and Progress: American National Identity, the War of 1898, and the Rise of American Imperialism* (2006).

Ivan Musicant, *Empire by Default: The Spanish American War and the Dawn of the American Century* (1998).

Thomas J. Osborne, *Annexation Hawaii* (1998).

Louis A. Perez Jr., *The War of 1898: The United States and Cuba in History and Historiography* (1998).

Diana Preston, *Besieged in Peking: The Story of the 1900 Boxer Uprising* (1999).

Lars Shoultz, *Beneath the United States* (1998).

Margaret Strobel, *Gender, Sex, and Empire* (1993).

Evan Thomas, *The War Lovers: Roosevelt, Lodge, Hearst, and the Rush to Empire, 1898* (2010).

David Traxel, *1898: The Birth of the American Century* (1999).

Walter Zimmerman, *First Great Triumph: How Five Americans Made Their Country a World Power* (2002).

Chapter 21

GENERAL

Maureen A. Flanagan, *America Reformed: Progressives and Progressivisms, 1890s–1920s* (2007).

Jackson Lears, *Rebirth of a Nation: The Making of Modern America, 1877–1920* (2009).

Michael McGerr, *A Fierce Discontent: The Rise and Fall of the Progressive Movement in America* (2005).

Eric Ruchway, *Blessed among Nations: How the World Made America* (2006).

GRASSROOTS PROGRESSIVISM

Victoria Bissell Brown, *The Education of Jane Addams* (2004).

Robert Kanigel, *The One Best Way: Frederick Winslow Taylor* (1997).

Louise W. Knight, *Citizen: Jane Addams and the Struggle for Democracy* (2005).

————*Jane Addams: Spirit in Action* (2010).

Seth Koven and Sonya Michel, eds., *Mothers of a New World: Maternalist Politics and the Origins of the Welfare State* (1993).

Robyn Muncy, *Creating a Female Dominion in American Reform* (1991).

Kathryn Kish Sklar, *Florence Kelley and the Nation's Work: The Rise of Women's Political Culture, 1830–1900* (1995).

Landon R. Y. Storre, *Civilizing Capitalism: The National Consumers' League, Women's Activism, and Labor Standards in the New Deal Era* (2000).

Nancy C. Unger, *Fighting Bob La Follette: The Righteous Reformer* (2000).

David Von Drehle, *Triangle: The Fire That Changed America* (2003).

PROGRESSIVE POLITICS AND DIPLOMACY

Douglas Brinkley, *The Wilderness Warrior: Theodore Roosevelt and the Crusade for America* (2009).

John Milton Cooper, *Woodrow Wilson: A Biography* (2009).

Alan Dawley, *Changing the World: American Progressives in War and Revolution* (2003).

Doris Kearns Goodwin, *The Bully Pulpit: Theodore Roosevelt, William Howard Taft, and ther Golden Age of Journalism* (2013).

Lewis L. Gould, *Four Hats in the Ring: The 1912 Election and the Birth of Modern American Politics* (2008); *William Howard Taft: Presidency* (2009).

————*William Howard Taft: Presidency* (2009).

Kristin Hoganson, *Consumers' Imperium: The Global Production of American Domesticity, 1865–1920* (2007).

Matthew Frye Jacobson, *Barbarian Virtues: The United States Encounters Foreign Peoples at Home and Abroad, 1876–1917* (2000).

Robert Johnston, *The Radical Middle Class: Populist Democracy and the Question of Capitalism in Progressive Era Portland, Oregon* (2003).

Walter LaFeber, *The Cambridge History of American Foreign Relations*, vol. 2 *The American Search for Opportunity, 1865–1913* (1993).

Kevin Matson, *Creating a Democratic Public: The Struggle for Urban Participatory Democracy during the Progressive Era* (1998).

Robert W. Righter, *The Battle over Hetch Hetchy: America's Most Controversial Dam and the Birth of Modern Environmentalism* (2005).

Daniel T. Rodgers, *Atlantic Crossings: Social Politics in a Progressive Age* (1998).

RADICALS, RACE RELATIONS, AND WOMAN SUFFRAGE

Mary Jo Buhle, *Women and American Socialism, 1870–1920* (1981).

Ellen Chesler, *Woman of Valor: Margaret Sanger and the Birth Control Movement in America* (1993).

Melvyn Dubofsky, *"Big Bill" Haywood* (1987).

Gary Gerstle, *American Crucible: Race and Nation in the Twentieth Century* (2002).

Glenda Elizabeth Gilmore, *Gender and Jim Crow: Women and the Politics of White Supremacy in North Carolina, 1896–1920* (1996).

David Fort Godshalk, *Veiled Visions: The 1906 Atlanta Race Riot and the Reshaping of American Race Relations* (2005).

Evelyn Higginbotham, *Righteous Discontent: The Women's Movement in the Black Baptist Church, 1880–1920* (1993).

David Levering Lewis, *W. E. B. Du Bois: Biography of a Race, 1868–1919* (1993).

Rebecca J. Mead, *How the Vote Was Won: Woman Suffrage in the Western United States, 1868–1914* (2004).

Nick Salvatore, *Eugene V. Debs: Citizen and Socialist* (1982).

Chapter 22

GENERAL WORKS

John Milton Cooper, *Woodrow Wilson: A Biography* (2009).

Thomas Fleming, *The Illusion of Victory: America in World War I* (2003).

Robert H. Zieger, *America's Great War: World War I and the American Experience* (2000).

"OVER THERE"

Gerald Astor, *The Right to Fight: A History of African Americans in the Military* (1998).

Peter Boyle, *American-Soviet Relations: From the Russian Revolution to the Fall of Communism* (1993).

Edward M. Coffman, *The War to End All Wars: The American Military Experience in World War I* (1968).

Byron Farwell, *Over There: The United States in the Great War, 1917–1918* (1999).

Lloyd C. Gardner, *Safe for Democracy: The Anglo-American Response to Revolution, 1913–1923* (1987).

Judith S. Graham, ed., *"Out Here at the Front": The World War I Letters of Nora Saltonstall* (2004).

Jennifer D. Keene, *Doughboys, the Great War, and the Remaking of America* (2001).

Thomas Knock, *To End All Wars: Woodrow Wilson and the Quest for a New World Order* (1992).

Edward G. Lengel, *To Conquer Hell: The Meuse-Argonne, 1918* (2008).

Margaret Olwen Macmillan, *Paris 1919: Six Months That Changed the World* (2002).

Gary Mead, *The Doughboys: America and the First World War* (2000).

Emily S. Rosenberg, *Financial Missionaries to the World: The Politics and Culture of Dollar Diplomacy, 1890–1930* (1999).

Gene Smith, *Until the Last Trumpet Sounds: The Life of General of the Armies John J. Pershing* (1998).

David L. Snead, ed., *An American Soldier in World War I: George Browne* (2006).

David F. Trask, *The AEF and Coalition Warmaking, 1917–1918* (1993).

Susan Zeiger, *In Uncle Sam's Service: Women with the AEF, 1917–1919* (1999).

THE HOME FRONT

Jean Baker, *Sisters: The Lives of America's Suffragists* (2005).

Nancy Cott, *The Grounding of American Feminism* (1987).

Leslie Midkiff DeBauche, *Reel Patriotism: The Movies and World War I* (1997).

Marc A. Eisner, *From Warfare State to Welfare State: World War I, Compensatory State Building, and the Limits of the Modern Order* (2000).

Ernest Freeberg, *Democracy's Prisoner: Eugene V. Debs, the Great War, and the Right to Dissent* (2008).

Elizabeth Frost and Kathryn Cullen-DuPont, eds., *Women's Suffrage in America: An Eyewitness History* (1992).

Maurine Weiner Greenwald, *Women, War, and Work: The Impact of World War I on Women Workers in the United States* (1980).

James N. Gregory, *Southern Diaspora: How the Great Migrations of Black and White Southerners Transformed America* (2005).

James R. Grossman, *Land of Hope: Chicago, Black Southerners, and the Great Migration* (1989).

David Kennedy, *Over Here: The First World War and American Society* (1980).

David Levering Lewis, *W. E. B. Du Bois: Biography of a Race, 1868–1919* (1993).

Robert K. Murray, *Red Scare: A Study in National Hysteria, 1919–1920* (1955).

Tammy M. Proctor, *Civilians in a World at War, 1914–1918* (2010).

George J. Sanchez, *Becoming Mexican American: Ethnicity, Culture, and Identity in Chicano Los Angeles, 1900–1945* (1993).

William H. Thomas Jr., *Unsafe for Democracy: World War I and the U.S. Justice Department's Covert Campaign to Suppress Dissent* (2008).

Joe William Trotter Jr., ed., *The Great Migration in Historical Perspective* (1991).

Chapter 23

GENERAL WORKS

David M. Kennedy, *Freedom from Fear: The American People in Depression and War, 1929–1945* (1999).

William E. Leuchtenburg, *The Perils of Prosperity, 1914–1932* (1958).

Michael Parrish, *Anxious Decades: America in Prosperity and Depression, 1920–1941* (1992).

POLITICS AND ECONOMY

Kristi Anderson, *After Suffrage: Women in Partisan and Electoral Politics before the New Deal* (1996).

Douglas Brinkley, *Wheels for the World: Henry Ford, His Company, and a Century of Progress, 1903–2003* (2003).

Kendrick A. Clements, *Hoover, Conservation, and Consumerism: Engineering the Good Life* (2000).

Warren I. Cohen, *Empire without Tears: America's Foreign Relations, 1921–1933* (1987).

Steve Fraser, *Every Man a Speculator: A History of Wall Street* (2005).

Colin Gordon, *New Deals: Business, Labor, and Politics in America, 1920–1935* (1994).

David Greenberg, *Calvin Coolidge* (2006).

Owen Gutfreund, *Twentieth-Century Sprawl: Highways and the Reshaping of the American Landscape* (2004).

Jill Jonnes, *Empires of Light: Edison, Tesla, and Westinghouse, and the Race to Electrify the World* (2003).

William E. Leuchtenburg, *Herbert Hoover: 31st President, 1929–1933* (2009).

Martha L. Olney, *Buy Now, Pay Later: Advertising, Credit, and Consumer Durables in the 1920s* (1991).

Lorrai Schuyler, *Weight of Their Votes: Southern Women and Political Leverage in the 1920s* (2006).

Steven Watts, *People's Tycoon: Henry Ford and the American Century* (2005).

SOCIETY AND CULTURE

Douglas Carl Abrams, *Selling the Old-Time Religion: American Fundamentalists and Mass Culture, 1920–1940* (2001).

Francisco E. Balderrama and Raymond Rodriguez, *Decade of Betrayal: Mexican Repatriation in the 1930s* (1995).

Kevin Boyle, *Arc of Justice: A Saga of Race, Civil Rights, and Murder in the Jazz Age* (2004).

Liz Conor, *Spectacular Modern Woman: Feminine Visibility in the 1920s* (2004).

Ruth Schwartz Cowan, *More Work for Mother: The Ironies of Household Technology from the Open Hearth to the Microwave* (1983).

Roger Daniels, *Guarding the Golden Door: American Immigration Policy and Immigrants since 1882* (2004).

Paula S. Fass, *The Damned and the Beautiful: American Youth in the 1920s* (1977).

David J. Goldberg, *Discontented America: The United States in the 1920s* (1999).

David M. Kennedy, *Birth Control in America: The Career of Margaret Sanger* (1970).

David E. Kyvig, *Daily Life in the United States, 1920–1940* (2002).

Edward J. Larson, *Summer of the Gods: The Scopes Trial and America's Continuing Debate over Science and Religion* (1997).

David Levering Lewis, *W. E. B. Du Bois: The Fight for Equality and the American Century, 1919–1963* (2000).

Nancy MacLean, *Behind the Mask of Chivalry: The Making of the Second Ku Klux Klan* (1994).

David E. Nye, *Electrifying America: Social Meanings of a New Technology, 1880–1940* (1990).

Daniel Okrent, *Last Call: The Rise and Fall of Prohibition* (2010).

David M. Reimers, *Unwelcome Strangers: American Identity and the Turn against Immigration* (1998).

Susan Smulyan, *Selling Radio: The Commercialization of American Broadcasting, 1920–1934* (1994).

Judith Stein, *The World of Marcus Garvey* (1986).

Andrew Wiese, *Places of Their Own: African American Suburbanization in the Twentieth Century* (2004).

Chapter 24
GENERAL WORKS

Gary Dean Best, *The Retreat from Liberalism: Collectivists versus Progressives in the New Deal Years* (2002).

William H. Chafe, ed., *The Achievement of American Liberalism: The New Deal and Its Legacies* (2003).

Morris Dickstein, *Dancing in the Dark: A Cultural History of the Great Depression* (2010).

Ronald Edsforth, *The New Deal: America's Response to the Great Depression* (2000).

Ira Katznelson, *Fear Itself: The New Deal and the Origins of Our Time* (2013)

David M. Kennedy, *Freedom from Fear: The American People in Depression and War, 1929–1945* (1999).

Alan Lawson, *A Commonwealth of Hope: The New Deal Response to Crisis* (2006).

William Edward Leuchtenburg, *Franklin D. Roosevelt and the New Deal, 1932–1940* (2009).

Amity Shlaes, *The Forgotten Man: A New History of the Great Depression* (2008).

NEW DEAL POLITICS

Roger Biles, *The South and the New Deal* (2006).

Kirstin Downey, *The Woman behind the New Deal: The Life and Legacy of Frances Perkins* (2010).

Alonzo L. Hamby, *For the Survival of Democracy: Franklin Roosevelt and the World Crisis of the 1930s* (2004).

Joseph E. Lowndes, *From the New Deal to the New Right: Race and the Southern Origins of Modern Conservatism* (2009).

Marian C. McKenna, *Franklin Roosevelt and the Great Constitutional War: The Court-Packing Crisis of 1937* (2002).

Kim Phillips-Fein, *Invisible Hands: The Businessmen's Crusade against the New Deal* (2010).

Theodore Rosenof, *Economics in the Long Run: New Deal Theorists and Their Legacies, 1933–1993* (1997).

Robert Shogan, *Backlash: The Killing of the New Deal* (2006).

Mary Triece, *On the Picket Line: Strategies of Working-Class Women during the Depression* (2007).

Clyde P. Weed, *The Nemesis of Reform: The Republican Party during the New Deal* (1994).

NEW DEAL POLICIES

Lizbeth Cohen, *Making a New Deal: Industrial Workers in Chicago, 1919–1939* (1990).

Kathleen G. Donohue, *Freedom from Want: American Liberalism and the Idea of the Consumer* (2004).

Timothy Eagan, *The Worst Hard Time: The Untold Story of Those Who Survived the Great American Dust Bowl* (2006).

Jan Goggans, *California on the Breadlines: Dorothea Lange, Paul Taylor, and the Making of a New Deal Narrative* (2010).

Linda Gordon, *Dorothea Lange: A Life beyond Limits* (2009).

Michael R. Grey, *New Deal Medicine: The Rural Health Programs of the Farm Security Administration* (1999).

Janet Irons, *Testing the New Deal: The General Textile Strike of 1934 in the American South* (2000).

Jennifer Klein, *For All These Rights: Business, Labor, and the Shaping of America's Public-Private Welfare State* (2003).

Lawrence Levine et al., *The Fireside Conversations: America Responds to FDR during the Great Depression* (2010).

Julie Novkov, *Constituting Workers, Protecting Women: Gender, Law, and Labor in the Progressive Era and New Deal Years* (2001).

Sarah Phillips, *This Land, This Nation: Conservation, Rural America, and the New Deal* (2007).

Patrick D. Reagan, *Designing a New America: The Origins of New Deal Planning, 1890–1936* (1999).

John A. Salmond, *The General Textile Strike of 1934: From Maine to Alabama* (2002).

Jason Scott Smith, *Building New Deal Liberalism: The Political Economy of Public Works, 1933–1956* (2005).

Landon R. Y. Stors, *Civilizing Capitalism: The National Consumers' League, Women's Activism, and Labor Standards in the New Deal Era* (2000).

David A. Taylor, *Soul of a People: The WPA Writers' Project Uncovers Depression America* (2010).

Chapter 25

GENERAL WORKS

Max Arthur, ed., *Forgotten Voices of the Second World War: A New History of World War Two in the Words of the Men and Women Who Were There* (2004).

Anthony Beevor, *The Second World War* (2013)

Richard Evans, *The Third Reich at War* (2010).

Thomas Fleming, *The New Dealers' War: Franklin D. Roosevelt and the War within World War II* (2001).

Max Hastings, *Inferno: The World at War, 1939–1945* (2011)

Peter Fritzsche, *Life and Death in the Third Reich* (2009).

David M. Kennedy, *Freedom from Fear: The American People in Depression and War, 1929–1945* (1999).

Mark Mazower, *Hitler's Empire: How the Nazis Ruled Europe* (2008).

Andrew Roberts, *The Storm of War: A New History of the Second World War* (2011)

Paul W. Tibbets Jr., *The Tibbets Story* (1978).

John Toland, *The Rising Sun: The Decline and Fall of the Japanese Empire, 1936–1945* (2001).

Adam Tooze, *The Wages of Destruction: The Making and Breaking of the Nazi Economy* (2006).

FOREIGN POLICY

Tokomo Akami, *Internationalizing the Pacific: The U.S., Japan, and the Institute of Pacific Relations in War and Peace, 1919–1945* (2002).

Elizabeth Borgwardt, *A New Deal for the World: America's Vision for Human Rights* (2005).

Tsuyoshi Hasegawa, *Racing the Enemy: Stalin, Truman, and the Surrender of Japan* (2005).

J. Robert Moskin, *Mr. Truman's War: The Final Victories of World War II and the Birth of the Postwar World* (2002).

David Reynolds, *From Munich to Pearl Harbor: Roosevelt's America and the Origins of the Second World War* (2001).

Gaddis Smith, *American Diplomacy during the Second World War, 1941–1945* (1985).

MOBILIZATION AND THE HOME FRONT

Gerald Astor, *The Right to Fight: A History of African Americans in the Military* (1998).

Jeffrey F. Burton et al., *Confinement and Ethnicity: An Overview of World War II Japanese American Relocation Sites* (2002).

Stephanie A. Carpenter, *On the Farm Front: The Women's Land Army in World War II* (2003).

Susan Hartmann, *The Home Front and Beyond: American Women in the 1940s* (1982).

Arthur Herman, *Freedom's Forge: How American Business Produced Victory in World War II* (2012)

John W. Jeffries, *Wartime America: The World War II Home Front* (1996).

Christopher Moore, *Fighting for America: Black Soldiers—The Unsung Heroes of World War II* (2005).

Wendy Ng, *Japanese American Internment during World War II* (2002).

MILITARY EVENTS

Rick Atkinson, *The Guns at Last Light: The War in Western Europe, 1944–1945* (2013).

Antony Beevor, *D-Day: The Battle for Normandy* (2009).

John Dower, *War without Mercy: Race and Power in the Pacific War* (1986).

Max Hastings, *Overlord: D-Day and the Battle for Normandy* (2006).

Peter Novick, *The Holocaust in American Life* (1999).

Richard Overy, *Why the Allies Won* (1996).

———*The Bombing War: Europe, 1939–1945* (2013)

Mary Louise Roberts, *What Soldiers Do: Sex and the American GI in World War II France* (2013).

Peter Schrijvers, *The GI War against Japan: American Soldiers in Asia and the Pacific during World War II* (2002).

Thomas W. Zeiler, *Unconditional Defeat: Japan, America, and the End of World War II* (2004).

Chapter 26

GENERAL WORKS

Rodolfo Acuña, *Occupied America: A History of Chicanos* (5th ed., 2004).

Carol Anderson, *Eyes off the Prize: The United Nations and the African American Struggle for Human Rights, 1944–1955* (2003).

Margot Canaday, *The Straight State: Sexuality and Citizenship in Twentieth-Century America* (2009).

Peter L. Hahn, *Caught in the Middle East: U.S. Policy toward the Arab-Israeli Conflict, 1945–1961* (2004).

Alonzo L. Hamby, *Man of the People: A Life of Harry S. Truman* (1995).

Ira Katznelson, *When Affirmative Action Was White: An Untold History of Racial Inequality in Twentieth- Century America* (2005).

James T. Patterson, *Grand Expectations: The United States, 1945–1974* (1996).

Brenda Gayle Plummer, *Rising Wind: Black Americans and U.S. Foreign Affairs, 1935–1960* (1996).

Julian E. Zelizer, *Arsenal of Democracy: The Politics of National Security—from World War II to the War on Terrorism* (2010).

DOMESTIC POLITICS AND POLICIES

Glenn C. Altschuler and Stuart M. Blumin, *The GI Bill: A New Deal for Veterans* (2009).

Jonathan Bell, *The Liberal State on Trial: The Cold War and American Politics in the Truman Years* (2004).

Kevin Boyle, *The UAW and the Heyday of American Liberalism, 1945–1968* (1995).

Mark Brilliant, *The Color of America Has Changed: How Racial Diversity Shaped Civil Rights Reform in California, 1941–1978* (2010).

Griffin Fariello, *Red Scare: Memories of the American Inquisition* (1995).

Kari Frederickson, *The Dixiecrat Revolt and the End of the Solid South, 1932–1968* (2001).

Michael D. Gambone, *The Greatest Generation Comes Home: The Veteran in American Society* (2005).

Ignacio M. García, *Hector P. García: In Relentless Pursuit of Justice* (2002).

Meg Jacobs, *Pocketbook Politics: Economic Citizenship in Twentieth-Century America* (2004).

David K. Johnson, *The Lavender Scare: The Cold War Persecution of Gays and Lesbians in the Federal Government* (2004).

Suzanne Mettler, *Soldiers to Citizens: The G.I. Bill and the Making of the Greatest Generation* (2005).

Henry A. J. Ramos, *The American GI Forum: In Pursuit of the Dream, 1948–1983* (1998).

Ellen W. Schrecker, *Many Are the Crimes: McCarthyism in America* (1998).

Ingrid Winther Scobie, *Center Stage: Helen Gahagan Douglas: A Life* (1992).

Robert Shogan, *Harry Truman and the Struggle for Racial Justice* (2013).

Philippa Strum, *Mendez v. Westminster: School Desegregation and Mexican-American Rights* (2010).

THE COLD WAR

Robert L. Beisner, *Dean Acheson: A Life in the Cold War* (2006).

Greg Behrman, *The Most Noble Adventure: The Marshall Plan and the Time When America Helped Save Europe* (2007).

Iris Chang, *Thread of the Silkworm* (1996).

Campbell Craig and Fredric Logevall, *America's Cold War: The Politics of Insecurity* (2009).

Robert Dallek, *The Lost Peace: Leadership in a Time of Horror and Hope, 1945–1953* (2010).

Carolyn Eisenberg, *Drawing the Line: The American Decision to Divide Germany, 1944–1949* (1996).

John L. Gaddis, *The Cold War: A New History* (2005).

Michael D. Gordin, *Red Cloud at Dawn: Truman, Stalin, and the End of the Atomic Monopoly.* (2010).

Daniel F. Harrington, *Berlin on the Brink: The Blockade, the Airlift, and the Early Cold War* (2012).

Lawrence S. Kaplan, 1948: *The Birth of the Transatlantic Alliance* (2007).

Melvyn Leffler, *For the Soul of Mankind: The United States, the Soviet Union, and the Cold War* (2007).

Richard Rhodes, *Dark Sun: The Making of the Hydrogen Bomb* (1995).

Katherine A. S. Sibley, *Red Spies in America: Stolen Secrets and the Dawn of the Cold War* (2004).

Odd Arne Westad, *The Global Cold War* (2005).

ASIA AND THE KOREAN WAR

Gordon H. Chang, *Friends and Enemies: The United States, China, and the Soviet Union, 1948–1972* (1990).

Bruce Cumings, *The Korean War* (2010).

Chae-Jin Lee, *A Troubled Peace: U.S. Policy and the Two Koreas* (2006).

Allen R. Millett, *The War for Korea, 1945–1950: A House Burning* (2005).

———*The War for Korea, 1950–1951: They Came from the North* (2010).

Michael Schaller, *Altered States: The United States and Japan since the Occupation* (1997).

Stanley Weintraub, *MacArthur's War: Korea and the Undoing of an American Hero* (2000).

Chapter 27

EISENHOWER'S ADMINISTRATION

Jeff Broadwater, *Eisenhower and the Anti-Communist Crusade* (2010).

Dino A. Brugioni, *Eyes in the Sky: Eisenhower, the CIA and Cold War Aerial Espionage* (2010).

Steven Z. Freiberger, *Dawn over Suez: The Rise of American Power in the Middle East, 1953–1957* (1992).

David Halberstam, *The Fifties* (1993).

Stephen Kinzer, *All the Shah's Men: An American Coup and the Roots of Middle East Terror* (2003).

William M. McClenaham, Jr., and William H. Becker, *Eisenhower and the Cold War Economy* (2011).

David A. Nichols, *A Matter of Justice: Eisenhower and the Beginning of the Civil Rights Revolution* (2007)

David A. Nichols, *Eisenhower 1956: The President's Year of Crisis—Suez and the Brink of War* (2011).

Chester J. Pach Jr. and Elmo Richardson, *The Presidency of Dwight D. Eisenhower* (rev. ed., 1991).

Kathryn C. Statler and Andrew L. Johns, eds., *The Eisenhower Administration, the Third World, and the Globalization of the Cold War* (2006).

Philip Taubman, *Secret Empire: Eisenhower, the CIA, and the Hidden Story of America's Space Espionage* (2003).

Salim Yaqub, *Containing Arab Nationalism: The Eisenhower Doctrine and the Middle East* (2004).

ECONOMIC AND SOCIAL DEVELOPMENTS

Lizabeth Cohen, *A Consumers' Republic: The Politics of Mass Consumption in Postwar America* (2003).

Gail Cooper, *Air-Conditioning America: Engineers and the Controlled Environment, 1900–1960* (1998).

Carlos Eire, *Waiting for Snow in Havana: Confessions of a Cuban Boy* (2004).

Kenneth T. Jackson, *Crabgrass Frontier: The Suburbanization of the United States* (1985).

Michael Johns, *Moment of Grace: The American City in the 1950s* (2002).

Fred Kaplan, *1959: The Year Everything Changed* (2009).

Jennifer Klein, *For All These Rights: Business, Labor, and the Shaping of America's Public-Private Welfare State* (2003).

Tom Lewis, *Divided Highways: Building the Interstate Highways, Transforming American Life* (1999).

David Oshinsky, *Polio: An American Story* (2005).

Adam Rome, *The Bulldozer in the Countryside: Suburban Sprawl and the Rise of American Environmentalism* (2001).

Bruce J. Schulman, *From Cotton Belt to Sunbelt: Federal Policy, Economic Development, and the Transformation of the South, 1938–1980* (1994).

GENDER, THE FAMILY, AND CULTURE

Glenn C. Altschuler, *All Shook Up: How Rock 'n' Roll Changed America* (2004).

Erik Barnouw, *Tube of Plenty: The Evolution of American Television* (rev. ed., 1990).

Stephanie Coontz, *The Way We Never Were: American Families and the Nostalgia Trip* (1992).

Robert Ellwood, *The Fifties Spiritual Marketplace: American Religion in a Decade of Conflict* (1997).

Elizabeth Fraterrigo, *Playboy and the Making of the Good Life in Modern America* (Oxford, 2009).

James Gilbert, *Men in the Middle: Searching for Masculinity in the 1950s* (2005).

James Howard Jones, *Alfred C. Kinsey: A Public/Private Life* (1998).

Elaine Tyler May, *Homeward Bound: American Families in the Cold War Era* (1988).

Anna McCarthy, *The Citizen Machine: Governing by Television in 1950s America* (2010).

Joanne Meyerowitz, ed., *Not June Cleaver: Women and Gender in Postwar America, 1945–1960* (1994).

Alan Petigny, *The Permissive Society: America, 1941-1965* (2009)

Lynn Spigel, *Make Room for TV: Television and the Family Ideal in Postwar America* (1992).

Steven Watson, *The Birth of the Beat Generation: Visionaries, Rebels, and Hipsters, 1944–1960* (1995).

MINORITIES AND CIVIL RIGHTS

Melba Patillo Beals, *Warriors Don't Cry: A Searing Memoir of the Battle to Integrate Little Rock's Central High* (1994).

Taylor Branch, *Parting the Waters: America in the King Years, 1954–1963* (1988).

Mary L. Dudziak, *Cold War Civil Rights: Race and the Image of American Democracy* (2000).

Donald L. Fixico, *Termination and Relocation: Federal Indian Policy, 1945–1960* (1986).

David J. Garrow, ed., *The Montgomery Boycott and the Women Who Started It: The Memoir of Jo Ann Gibson Robinson* (1987).

Michael J. Klarman, *From Jim Crow to Civil Rights: The Supreme Court and the Struggle for Racial Equality* (2004).

Richard Kluger, *Simple Justice: The History of Brown v. Board of Education and Black America's Struggle for Racial Equality* (rev. ed. 2004).

James T. Patterson, *Brown v. Board of Education: A Civil Rights Milestone and Its Troubled Legacy* (2001).

Barbara Ransby, *Ella Baker and the Black Freedom Movement* (2003).

Thomas J. Sugrue, *Sweet Land of Liberty: The Forgotten Struggle for Civil Rights in the North* (2008).

Patricia Sullivan, *Lift Every Voice: The NAACP and the Making of the Civil Rights Movement* (2009).

Juan Williams, *Thurgood Marshall: American Revolutionary* (1998).

Chapter 28

THE BLACK FREEDOM STRUGGLE

Raymond Arsenault, *Freedom Riders: 1961 and the Struggle for Racial Justice* (2006).

Martha Biondi, *To Stand and Fight: The Struggle for Civil Rights in Postwar New York City* (2003).

Taylor Branch, *America in the King Years*, 3 vols. (1988, 1998, 2006).

John D'Emilio, *Lost Prophet: the Life and Times of Bayard Rustin* (2003).

Wesley C. Hogan, *Many Minds, One Heart: SNCC's Dream for a New America* (2009).

William P. Jones, *The March on Washington: Jobs, Freedom, and the Forgotten History of Civil Rights* (2013).

Peniel E. Joseph, *Dark Days, Bright Nights: From Black Power to Barack Obama* (2010).

Chana Kai Lee, *For Freedom's Sake: The Life of Fannie Lou Hamer* (1999).

Manning Marable, *Malcolm X: A Life of Reinvention* (2011).

Gary May, *Bending toward Justice: The Voting Rights Act and the Transformation of American Democracy* (2013).

Jeffrey O. G. Ogbar, *Black Power: Radical Politics and African American Identity* (2005).

Charles Payne, *I've Got the Light of Freedom: The Organizing Tradition and the Mississippi Freedom Struggle* (1995).

Barbara Ransby, *Ella Baker and the Black Freedom Movement: A Radical Democratic Vision* (2003).

Timothy Tyson, *Radio Free Dixie: Robert F. Williams and the Roots of Black Power* (1999).

Bruce Watson, *Freedom Summer: The Savage Season That Made Mississippi Burn and Made America a Democracy* (2010).

POLITICS, POLICIES, AND COURT DECISIONS

David C. Carter, *The Music Has Gone Out of the Movement: Civil Rights and the Johnson Administration, 1965–1968* (2009).

Robert Dallek, *An Unfinished Life: John F. Kennedy, 1917–1963* (2003).

Maurice Isserman and Michael Kazin, *America Divided: The Civil War of the 1960s* (2000).

Michael B. Katz, *The Undeserving Poor: From the War on Poverty to the War on Welfare* (1989).

Nancy MacLean, *Freedom Is Not Enough: The Opening of the American Workplace* (2006).

Gerald Posner, *Case Closed: Lee Harvey Oswald and the Assassination of JFK* (1993).

Lucas A. Powe Jr., *The Warren Court and American Politics* (2000).

John D. Skrentny, *The Minority Rights Revolution* (2002).

Melvin Small, *The Presidency of Richard Nixon* (2003).

Irwin Unger, *The Best of Intentions: The Triumph and Failure of the Great Society* (1996).

Tom Wicker, *One of Us: Richard Nixon and the American Dream* (1991).

Randall B. Woods, *LBJ: Architect of American Ambition* (2006).

PROTEST MOVEMENTS

Adam Rome, *The Genius of Earth Day: How a 1970 Teach-in Unexpectedly Made the First Green Generation* (2013).

Terry H. Anderson, *The Movement and the Sixties* (1995).

David Barber, *A Hard Rain Fell: SDS and Why It Failed* (2010).

Stefan M. Bradley, *Harlem vs. Columbia University: Black Student Power in the Late 1960s* (2009).

Daniel M. Cobb, *Native Activism in Cold War America: The Struggle for Sovereignty* (2008).

John D'Emilio, William B. Turner, and Urvashi Vaid, *Creating Change: Sexuality, Public Policy, and Civil Rights* (2000).

Matt Garcia, *From the Jaws of Victory: The Triumph and Tragedy of Cesar Chavez and the Farm Worker Movement* (2012)

Troy R. Johnson, *The American Indian Occupation of Alcatraz Island: Red Power and Self-Determination* (2008).

Ian F. Haney López, *Racism on Trial: The Chicano Fight for Justice* (2003).

Daryl J. Maeda, *Chains of Babylon: The Rise of Asian America.* (2009).

F. Arturo Rosales, *Chicano! The History of the Mexican American Civil Rights Movement* (1997).

Randy Shaw, *Beyond the Fields: Cesar Chavez, the UFW, and the Struggle for Justice in the 21st Century* (2008).

Chapter 29

FOREIGN POLICY UNDER KENNEDY, JOHNSON, AND NIXON

Beth Bailey, *America's Army: Making the All-Volunteer Force* (2009).

Warren Bass, *Support Any Friend: Kennedy's Middle East and the Making of the U.S.-Israel Alliance* (2003).

H. W. Brands, *The Wages of Globalism: Lyndon Johnson and the Limits of American Power* (1995).

Robert Dallek, *Nixon and Kissinger: Partners in Power* (2007).

Michael Dobbs, *One Minute to Midnight: Kennedy, Khrushchev, and Castro on the Brink of Nuclear War* (2008).

Lawrence Freedman, *Kennedy's Wars: Berlin, Cuba, Laos, and Vietnam* (2000).

Michael Grow, *U.S. Presidents and Latin American Interventions: Pursuing Regime Change in the Cold War* (2008).

Elizabeth Cobbs Hoffman, *All You Need Is Love: The Peace Corps and the Spirit of the 1960s* (1998).

Howard Jones, *The Bay of Pigs* (2008).

Frederick Kempe, *Berlin 1961: Kennedy, Khrushchev, and the Most Dangerous Place on Earth* (2011).

Margaret Macmillan, *Nixon and Mao: The Week That Changed the World* (2007).

Walter A. McDougall, *The Heavens and the Earth: A Political History of the Space Age* (1985).

Keith L. Nelson, *The Making of Détente: Soviet-American Relations in the Shadow of Vietnam* (1995).

Robert B. Rakove, *Kennedy, Johndon, and the Nonaligned World* (2013).

Thomas Alan Schwartz, *Lyndon Johnson and Europe: In the Shadow of Vietnam* (2003).

Jeremi Suri, *Power and Protest: Global Revolution and the Rise of Détente* (2003).

THE WAR IN VIETNAM

Mark Philip Bradley, *Vietnam at War* (2009).

Arnold R. Isaacs, *Vietnam Shadows: The War, Its Ghosts, and Its Legacy* (1997).

David Kaiser, *American Tragedy: Kennedy, Johnson, and the Origins of the Vietnam War* (2000).

Jeffrey P. Kimball, *Nixon's Vietnam War* (1998).

A. J. Langguth, *Our Vietnam / Nuoc Viet Ta: A History of the War, 1954–1975* (2000).

Mark Atwood Lawrence, *The Vietnam War: A Concise International History* (2008).

Fredrik Logevall, *Choosing War: The Lost Chance for Peace and the Escalation of the War in Vietnam* (1999); *Embers of War: The Fall of an Empire and the Making of America's Vietnam* (2013).

They Marched into Sunlight: War, Peace, Vietnam, and America, October 1967 (2004).

James Willbanks, *The Tet Offensive: A Concise History* (2008). Those Who Served

Christian G. Appy, *Working-Class War: American Combat Soldiers in Vietnam* (1993).

Philip Caputo, *A Rumor of War* (1977).

David Donovan, *Once a Warrior King: Memories of an Officer in Vietnam* (1985).

Frederick Downs, *The Killing Zone: My Life in the Vietnam War* (1978); *Aftermath: A Soldier's Return from Vietnam* (1984); *No Longer Enemies, Not Yet Friends: An American Soldier Returns to Vietnam* (1991).

Harry Maurer, *Strange Ground: Americans in Vietnam, 1945–1975, an Oral History* (1998).

Tim O'Brien, *If I Die in a Combat Zone, Box me Up and Ship Me Home* (1992).

Al Santoli, *Everything We Had: An Oral History of the Vietnam War* (1981).

William J. Shkurti, *Soldiering On in a Dying War: The True Story of the Firebase Pace Incidents and the Vietnam Drawdown* (2011).

James E. Westheider, *Fighting on Two Fronts: African Americans and the Vietnam War* (1997).

Kara Dixon Vuic, *Officer, Nurse, Woman: The Army Nurse Corps in the Vietnam War* (2010).

POLITICS AND THE ANTIWAR MOVEMENT

Dan T. Carter, *The Politics of Race: George Wallace, the Origins of the New Conservatism, and the Transformation of American Politics* (1995).

Michael S. Foley, *Confronting the War Machine: Draft Resistance during the Vietnam War* (2007).

Adam Garfinkle, *Telltale Hearts: The Origins and Impact of the Vietnam Anti-War Movement* (1997).

Lewis L. Gould, *1968: The Election That Changed America* (rev. ed., 2010).

Simon Hall, *Rethinking the American Anti-War Movement* (2011).

Andrew E. Hunt, *The Turning: A History of Vietnam Veterans against the War* (1999).

Rhodri Jeffreys-Jones, *Peace Now! American Society and the Ending of the Vietnam War* (1999).

Martin Klimke, *The Other Alliance: Student Protest in West Germany and the United States in the Global Sixties* (2009).

Lorena Orpesa, *Raza Sí!, Guerra No!: Chicano Protest and Patriotism During the Viet Nam War Era* (2005).

David Rudenstine, *The Day the Presses Stopped: A History of the Pentagon Papers Case* (1996).

Scanlon, Sandra, *The Pro-War Movement: Domestic Support for the Vietnam War and the Making of Modern American Conservatism.* (2013).

Amy Swerdlow, *Women Strike for Peace: Traditional Motherhood and Radical Politics in the 1960s* (1993).

Chapter 30

GENERAL WORKS

Edward D. Berkowitz, *Something Happened: A Political and Cultural Overview of the Seventies* (2006).

Thomas Borstelman, *The 1970s: A New Global History from Civil Rights to Economic Inequality* (2011).

Robert Collins, *Transforming Americas: Politics and Culture in the Reagan Years* (2007).

Laura Kalman, *Right Star Rising: A New Politics, 1974–1980* (2010).

Burton I. Kaufman and Scott Kaufman, *The Presidency of James Earl Carter, Jr.* (2006).

Robert Mason, *Richard Nixon and the Quest for a New Majority* (2004).

Keith W. Olson, *Watergate: The Presidential Scandal That Shook America* (2003).

James T. Patterson, *Restless Giant: The United States from Watergate to* Bush v. Gore (2005).

Gil Troy, *Morning in America: How Ronald Reagan Invented the 1980s* (2005).

Sean Wilentz, *The Age of Reagan: A History, 1974–2008* (2008).

FOREIGN POLICY

David Farber, *Taken Hostage: The Iran Hostage Crisis and America's First Encounter with Radical Islam* (2004).

David Crist, *The Twilight War: The Secret History of America's Thirty-Year Conflict with Iran* (2012).

Marc Ensalaco, *Middle Eastern Terrorism: From Black September to September 11* (2008).

Frances FitzGerald, *Way Out There in the Blue: Reagan, Star Wars, and the End of the Cold War* (2000).

Scott Kaufman, *Plans Unraveled: The Foreign Policy of the Carter Administration* (2008).

William M. LeoGrande, *Our Own Backyard: The United States in Central America, 1977–1992* (1998).

Douglas Little, *American Orientalism: The United States and the Middle East since 1945* (2002).

James Mann, *The Rebellion of Ronald Reagan: A History of the End of the Cold War* (2009).

THE ECONOMY, ENERGY, AND THE ENVIRONMENT

W. Carl Biven, *Jimmy Carter's Economy: Policy in an Age of Limits* (2003).

Elizabeth D. Blum, *Love Canal Revisited: Race, Class, and Gender in Environmental Activism* (2008).

Phillip J. Cooper, *The War against Regulation: From Jimmy Carter to George W. Bush.* (2009).

Jefferson Cowie, *Stayin' Alive: The 1970s and the Last Days of the Working Class* (2010).

Samuel P. Hays, *A History of Environmental Politics since 1945* (2000).

Robert J. Samuelson, *The American Dream in the Age of Entitlement, 1945–1995* (1996).

John W. Sloan, *The Reagan Effect: Economics and Presidential Leadership* (1999).

Judith Stein, *Pivotal Decade: How the United States Traded Factories for Finance in the Seventies* (2010).

SOCIAL MOVEMENTS AND CONTESTS OVER RIGHTS

Terry H. Anderson, *The Pursuit of Fairness: A History of Affirmative Action* (2004).

John A. Andrew, *The Other Side of the Sixties: Young Americans for Freedom and the Rise of Conservative Politics* (1997).

Donald T. Critchlow, *Phyllis Schlafly and Grassroots Conservatism: A Woman's Crusade* (2005).

J. Brooks Flippen. *Jimmy Carter, the Politics of Family, and the Rise of the Religious Right.* (2011).

Linda Hirshman, *Victory: The Triumphant Gay Revolution—How a Despised Minority Pushed Back, Beat Death, Found Love, and Changed America for Everyone* (2012).

J. Anthony Lukas, *Common Ground: A Turbulent Decade in the Lives of Three American Families* (1986).

Bradford Martin, *The Other Eighties: A Secret History of America in the Age of Reagan* (2011).

William Martin, *With God on Our Side: The Rise of the Religious Right in America* (1996).

Donald G. Mathews and Jane Sherron De Hart, *Sex, Gender, and the Politics of the ERA* (1990).

Lisa McGirr, *Suburban Warriors: The Origins of the New American Right* (2001).

Kim Phillips-Fein, *Invisible Hands: The Making of the Conservative Movement from the New Deal to Reagan* (2009).

Robert O. Self, *All in the Family: The Realignment of American Democracy since the 1960s* (2012).

James F. Simon, *The Center Holds: The Power Struggle inside the Rehnquist Court* (1995).

Daniel K. Williams, *God's Own Party: The Making of the Christian Right* (2010).

Chapter 31

DOMESTIC POLITICS, POLICIES, AND ECONOMIC CHANGE

Jonathan Alter, *The Center Holds: Obama and His Enemies* (2013).

Alan S. Blinder, *After the Music Stopped: The Financial Crisis, the Response, and the Work Ahead* (2013).

Douglas Brinkley, *The Great Deluge: Hurricane Katrina, New Orleans, and the Mississippi Gulf Coast* (2006).

Alfred D. Chandler Jr., *Inventing the Electronic Century: The Epic Story of the Consumer Electronics and Computer Science Industries* (2001).

Robert Draper, *"Dead Certain": The Presidency of George W. Bush* (2007).

John F. Harris, *The Survivor: Bill Clinton in the White House* (2005).

Bruce D. Meyer and Douglas Holtz-Eakin, *Making Work Pay: The Earned Income Tax Credit and Its Impact on America's Families* (2002).

Jack N. Rakove, ed., *The Unfinished Election of 2000* (2001).

Theda Skocpol and Vanessa Williamson, *The Tea Party and the Remaking of Republican Conservatism* (2012).

Richard K. Scotch, *From Good Will to Civil Rights: Transforming Federal Disability Policy* (rev. ed., 2001).

David K. Shipler, *The Working Poor: Invisible in America* (2004).

Paul Starr, *Remedy and Reaction: The Peculiar American Struggle over Health Care Reform* (2011).

Julian E. Zelizer, ed., *The Presidency of George W. Bush: A First Historical Assessment* (2010).

GLOBALIZATION AND IMMIGRATION

Frank D. Bean and Gillian Stevens, *America's Newcomers and the Dynamics of Diversity* (2003).

Jeremy Brecher, Tim Costello, and Brendan Smith, *Globalization from Below* (2000).

Otis L. Graham, *Unguarded Gates: A History of America's Immigration Crisis* (2004).

John R. MacArthur, *The Selling of "Free Trade": NAFTA, Washington, and the Subversion of American Democracy* (2000).

David M. Reimers, *Other Immigrants: The Global Origins of the American People* (2005).

Joseph E. Stiglitz, *Globalization and Its Discontents* (2002).

FOREIGN POLICY AFTER THE COLD WAR

Andrew J. Bacevich, *American Empire: The Realities and Consequences of U.S. Diplomacy* (2002).

David Crist, *The Twilight War: The Secret History of America's Thirty-Year Conflict with Iran* (2012).

Ivo H. Daalder and James M. Lindsay, *America Unbound: The Bush Revolution in Foreign Policy* (2003).

Karen DeYoung, *Soldier: The Life of Colin Powell* (2006).

David Halberstam, *War in a Time of Peace: Bush, Clinton, and the Generals* (2001).

James Mann, *Rise of the Vulcans: The History of Bush's War Cabinet* (2004).

Christopher Maynard, *Out of the Shadow: George H.W. Bush and the End of the Cold War* (2008).

Richard Sale, *Clinton's Secret Wars: The Evolution of a Commander in Chief* (2009).

TERRORISM AND THE AFGHAN AND IRAQ WARS

Peter L. Bergen, *The Longest War: The Enduring Conflict Between America and Al Quaeda* (2011).

Seth G. Jones, *In the Graveyard of Empires: America's War in Afghanistan* (2009).

Daniel Levitas, *The Terrorist Next Door: The Militia Movement and the Radical Right* (2002).

Jane Mayer, *The Dark Side: The Inside Story of How the War on Terror Turned into a War on American Ideals* (2008).

National Commission on Terrorist Attacks, *The 9/11 Commission Report: Final Report of the National Commission on Terrorist Attacks upon the United States* (2004).

George Packer, *The Assassins' Gate: America in Iraq* (2005).

Gary Rosen, ed., *The Right War? The Conservative Debate on Iraq* (2005).

Anthony Shadid, *Night Draws Near: Iraq's People in the Shadow of America's War* (2005)

Glossary

A NOTE TO STUDENTS: For definitions and discussions of words not included here, consult a dictionary and the book's index, which will point you to topics covered at greater length in the book.

Acoma pueblo revolt Revolt against the Spaniards by Indians living at the Acoma pueblo in 1599. Juan de Oñate violently suppressed the uprising, but the Indians revolted again later that year, after which many Spanish settlers returned to Mexico.

Agent Orange Herbicide used extensively during the Vietnam War to destroy the Vietcong's jungle hideouts and food supply. Its use was later linked to a wide range of illnesses that veterans and the Vietnamese suffered after the war, including birth defects, cancer, and skin disorders.

Agricultural Adjustment Act (AAA) New Deal legislation passed in May 1933 aimed at cutting agricultural production and raising crop prices and, consequently, farmers' income. Through the "domestic allotment plan," the AAA paid farmers to not grow crops.

Algonquian Indians People who inhabited the coastal plain of present-day Virginia, near the Chesapeake Bay, when English colonists first settled the region.

Alien and Sedition Acts 1798 laws passed to suppress political dissent. The Sedition Act criminalized conspiracy and criticism of government leaders. The two Alien Acts extended the waiting period for citizenship and empowered the president to deport or imprison without trial any foreigner deemed a danger.

American Colonization Society An organization dedicated to sending freed slaves and other black Americans to Liberia in West Africa. Although some African Americans cooperated with the movement, others campaigned against segregation and discrimination.

American Expeditionary Force (AEF) American armed forces under the command of General John Pershing who fought under a separate American command in Europe during World War I. They helped defeat Germany when they entered the conflict in full force in 1918.

American Federation of Labor (AFL) Organization created by Samuel Gompers in 1886 that coordinated the activities of craft unions throughout the United States. The AFL worked to achieve immediate benefits for skilled workers. Its narrow goals for unionism became popular after the Haymarket bombing.

American Indian Movement (AIM) Organization established in 1968 to address the problems Indians faced in American cities, including poverty and police harassment. AIM organized Indians to end relocation and termination policies and to win greater control over their cultures and communities.

American system The practice of manufacturing and then assembling interchangeable parts. A system that spread quickly across American industries, the use of standardized parts allowed American manufacturers to employ cheap unskilled workers.

American Temperance Society Organization founded in 1826 by Lyman Beecher that linked drinking with poverty, idleness, ill-health, and violence. Temperance lecturers traveled the country gaining converts to the cause. The temperance movement had considerable success, contributing to a sharp drop in American alcohol consumption.

Americans with Disabilities Act (ADA) Legislation signed by President George H. W. Bush in 1990 that banned discrimination against the disabled. The law also required handicapped accessibility in public facilities and private businesses.

Antifederalists Opponents of ratification of the Constitution. Antifederalists feared that a powerful and distant central government would be out of touch with the needs of citizens. They also complained that the Constitution failed to guarantee individual liberties in a bill of rights.

antinomians Individuals who believed that Christians could be saved by faith alone and did not need to act in accordance with God's law as set forth in the Bible. Puritan leaders considered this belief to be a heresy.

Apollo program Project initiated by John F. Kennedy in 1961 to surpass the Soviet Union in space exploration and send a man to the moon.

appeasement British strategy aimed at avoiding a war with Germany in the late 1930s by not objecting to Hitler's policy of territorial expansion.

Archaic Indians Hunting and gathering peoples that descended from Paleo-Indians and dominated the Americas from 10,000 BP to between 4000 and 3000 BP, approximately.

Articles of Confederation The written document defining the structure of the government from 1781 to 1788 under which the union was a confederation of equal states, with no executive and limited powers, existing mainly to foster a common defense.

baby boom The surge in the American birthrate between 1945 and 1965, which peaked in 1957 with 4.3 million births. The baby boom both reflected and promoted Americans' postwar prosperity.

Bacon's Rebellion An unsuccessful rebellion against the colonial government in 1676, led by frontier settler Nathaniel Bacon, that arose when increased violence between Indians and colonists pushing westward was met with government refusal to protect settlers or allow them to settle Indian lands.

Barbados Colonized in the 1630s, this island in the British West Indies became an enormous sugar producer and a source of wealth for England. The island's African slaves quickly became a majority of the island's population despite the deadliness of their work.

battle of Antietam Battle fought in Maryland on September 17, 1862, between the Union forces of George McClellan and Confederate troops of Robert E. Lee. The battle, a Union victory that left 6,000 dead and 17,000 wounded, was the bloodiest day of the war.

battle of Bull Run (Manassas) First major battle of the Civil War, fought at a railroad junction in northern Virginia on July 21, 1861. The Union suffered a sobering defeat, while the Confederates felt affirmed in their superiority and the inevitability of Confederate nationhood.

battle of Bunker Hill Second battle of the Revolutionary War, on June 16, 1775, involving a massive British attack on New England militia units on a hill facing Boston. The militiamen finally yielded the hill, but not before inflicting heavy casualties on the British.

battle of Gettysburg Battle fought at Gettysburg, Pennsylvania (July 1–3, 1863), between Union forces under General Meade and Confederate forces under General Lee. The Union emerged victorious, and Lee lost more than one-third of his men. Together with Vicksburg, Gettysburg marked a major turning point in the Civil War.

Battle of the Little Big Horn 1876 battle begun when American cavalry under George Armstrong Custer attacked an encampment of Indians who refused to remove to a reservation. Indian warriors led by Crazy Horse and Sitting Bull annihilated the American soldiers, but their victory was short-lived.

battle of Long Island First major engagement of the new Continental army, defending against 45,000 British troops newly arrived on western Long Island (today Brooklyn). The Continentals retreated, with high casualties and many taken prisoner.

Battle of Midway June 3–6, 1942, naval battle in the Central Pacific in which American forces surprised and defeated the Japanese who had been massing an invasion force aimed at Midway Island. The battle put the Japanese at a disadvantage for the rest of the war.

battle of New Orleans The final battle in the War of 1812, fought and won by General Andrew Jackson and his militiamen against the much larger British army in New Orleans. The celebrated battle made no difference since the peace had already been negotiated.

battle of Oriskany A punishing defeat for Americans in a ravine named Oriskany near Fort Stanwix in New York in August 1777. German American militiamen aided by allied Oneida warriors were ambushed by Mohawk and Seneca Indians, and 500 on the revolutionary side were killed.

battle of Saratoga A multistage battle in New York ending with the decisive defeat and surrender of British general John Burgoyne on October 17, 1777. France was convinced by this victory to throw its official support to the American side in the war.

battle of Shiloh Battle at Shiloh Church, Tennessee, on April 6–7, 1862, between Albert Sidney Johnston's Confederate forces and Ulysses S. Grant's Union army. The Union army ultimately prevailed, though at great cost to both sides. Shiloh ruined the Confederacy's bid to control the war in the West.

battle of Tippecanoe An attack on Shawnee Indians at Prophetstown on the Tippecanoe River in 1811 by American forces headed by William Henry Harrison, Indiana's territorial governor. The Prophet Tenskwatawa fled with his followers. Tecumseh, his brother, deepened his resolve to make war on the United States.

battle of Yorktown October 1781 battle that sealed American victory in the Revolutionary War. American troops and a French fleet trapped the British army under the command of General Charles Cornwallis at Yorktown, Virginia.

Bay of Pigs Failed U.S.-sponsored invasion of Cuba by anti-Castro forces in 1961 who planned to overthrow Fidel Castro's government. The disaster humiliated Kennedy and the United States. It alienated Latin Americans who saw the invasion as another example of Yankee imperialism.

Beringia The land bridge between Siberia and Alaska that was exposed by the Wisconsin glaciation, allowing people to migrate into the Western Hemisphere.

Berlin Wall Structure erected by East Germany in 1961 to stop the massive exodus of East Germans into West Berlin, which was an embarrassment to the Communists.

Bill of Rights The first ten amendments to the Constitution, officially ratified by 1791. The First through Eighth Amendments dealt with individual liberties, and the Ninth and Tenth concerned the boundary between federal and state authority.

birth control movement Movement launched in 1915 by Margaret Sanger in New York's Lower East Side. Birth control advocates hoped contraception would alter social and political power relationships by reducing the numbers of the working class to induce higher wages and by limiting the supply of soldiers to end wars.

black codes Laws passed by state governments in the South in 1865 that sought to keep ex-slaves subordinate to whites. At the core of the black codes lay the desire to force freedmen back to the plantations.

Black Death A disease that in the mid-fourteenth century killed about a third of the European population and left a legacy of increased food and resources for the survivors as well as a sense of a world in precarious balance.

Black Hills Mountains in western South Dakota and northeast Wyoming that are sacred to the Lakota Sioux. In the 1868 Treaty of Fort Laramie, the United States guaranteed Indians control of the Black Hills but broke its promise after gold was discovered there in 1874.

black power movement Movement of the 1960s and 1970s that emphasized black racial pride and autonomy. Black power advocates encouraged African Americans to assert community control, and some within the movement also rejected the ethos of nonviolence.

"Bleeding Kansas" Term for the bloody struggle between proslavery and antislavery factions in Kansas following its organization in the fall of 1854. Corrupt election tactics led to a proslavery victory, but free-soil Kansans established a rival territorial government, and violence quickly ensued.

Bolshevik Russian revolutionary. Bolsheviks forced Czar Nicholas II to abdicate and seized power in Russia in 1917. In a separate peace with Germany, the Bolshevik government withdrew Russia from World War I.

Bonus Marchers World War I veterans who marched on Washington, D.C., in 1932 to lobby for immediate payment of the pension ("bonus") promised them in 1924. President Herbert Hoover believed the bonuses would bankrupt the government and sent the U.S. Army to evict the veterans from the city.

bossism Pattern of urban political organization that arose in the late nineteenth century in which an often corrupt "boss" maintains an inordinate level of power through command of a political machine that distributes services to its constituents.

Boston Massacre March 1770 incident in Boston in which British soldiers fired on an American crowd, killing five. The Boston Massacre became a rallying point for colonists who increasingly saw the British government as tyrannical and illegitimate.

Boxer uprising Uprising in China led by the Boxers, an antiforeign society, in which 30,000 Chinese converts and 250 foreign Christians were killed. An international force rescued foreigners in Beijing, and European powers imposed the humiliating Boxer Protocol on China in 1901.

Brown v. Board of Education 1954 Supreme Court ruling that overturned the "separate but equal" precedent established in *Plessy v. Ferguson* in 1896. The Court declared that separate educational facilities were inherently unequal and thus violated the Fourteenth Amendment.

burial mounds Earthen mounds constructed by ancient American peoples, especially throughout the gigantic drainage of the Ohio and Mississippi rivers, after about 2500 BP and often used to bury important leaders and to enact major ceremonies.

Cahokia The largest ceremonial site in ancient North America located on the eastern bank of the Mississippi River across from present-day St. Louis where thousands of inhabitants built hundreds of earthen mounds between about AD 700 and AD 1400.

California gold rush Mining rush initiated by James Marshall's discovery of gold in the foothills of the Sierra Nevada in 1848. The hope of striking it rich drew over 250,000 aspiring miners to California between 1849 and 1852 and accelerated the push for statehood.

Calvinism Christian doctrine of Swiss Protestant theologian John Calvin. Its chief tenet was predestination, the idea that God had determined which human souls would receive eternal salvation. Despite this, Calvinism promoted strict discipline in daily and religious life.

Camp David accords Agreements between Egypt and Israel reached at the 1979 talks hosted by President Carter at Camp David. In the accords, Egypt became the first Arab state to recognize Israel, and Israel agreed to gradual withdrawal from the Sinai Peninsula.

Carlisle Indian School Institution established in Pennsylvania in 1879 to educate and assimilate American Indians. It pioneered the "outing system," in which Indian students were sent to live with white families in order to accelerate acculturation.

carpetbaggers Southerners' pejorative term for northern migrants who sought opportunity in the South after the Civil War. Northern migrants formed an important part of the southern Republican Party.

Central Intelligence Agency (CIA) Agency created by the National Security Act of 1947 to expand the government's espionage capacities and ability to thwart communism through covert activities, including propaganda, sabotage, economic warfare, and support for anti-Communist forces around the world.

Chicano movement Mobilization of Mexican Americans in the 1960s and 1970s to fight for civil rights, economic justice, and political power and to combat police brutality. Most notably, the movement worked to improve the lives of migrant farmworkers and to end discrimination in employment and education.

chiefdom Hierarchical social organization headed by a chief. Archaeologists posit that the Woodland cultures were organized into chiefdoms because the construction of their characteristic burial mounds likely required one person having command over the labor of others.

Chinese Exclusion Act 1882 law that effectively barred Chinese immigration and set a precedent for further immigration restrictions. The Chinese population in America dropped sharply as a result of the passage of the act, which was fueled by racial and cultural animosities.

chivalry The South's romantic ideal of male-female relationships. Chivalry's underlying assumptions about the weakness of white women and the protective authority of men resembled the paternalistic defense of slavery.

Civil Rights Act of 1866 Legislation passed by Congress in 1866 that nullified the black codes and affirmed that black Americans should have equal benefit of the law. This expansion of black rights and federal authority drew a veto from President Johnson, which Congress later overrode.

Civil Rights Act of 1964 Law that responded to demands of the civil rights movement by making discrimination in employment, education, and public accommodations illegal. It was the strongest such measure since Reconstruction and included a ban on sex discrimination in employment.

civil service reform Effort in the 1880s to end the spoils system and reduce government corruption. The Pendleton Civil Service Act of 1883 created the Civil Service Commission to award government jobs under a merit system that required examinations for office and made it impossible to remove jobholders for political reasons.

Civilian Conservation Corps (CCC) Federal relief program established in March 1933 that provided assistance in the form of jobs to millions of unemployed young men and a handful of women. CCC workers worked on conservation projects throughout the nation.

Clean Air Act of 1990 Environmental legislation signed by President George H. W. Bush. The legislation was the strongest and most comprehensive environmental law in the nation's history.

Clovis point Distinctively shaped spearhead used by Paleo-Indians and named for the place in New Mexico where the points were first excavated.

Coercive (Intolerable) Acts Four British acts of 1774 meant to punish Massachusetts for the destruction of three shiploads of tea. Known in America as the Intolerable Acts, they led to open rebellion in the northern colonies.

Cold War Term given to the tense and hostile relationship between the United States and the Soviet Union from 1947 to 1989. The term *cold* was apt because the hostility stopped short of direct armed conflict.

Columbian exchange The transatlantic exchange of goods, people, and ideas that began when Columbus arrived in the Caribbean, ending the age-old separation of the hemispheres.

Comanchería Indian empire based on trade in horses, hides, guns, and captives that stretched from the Canadian plains to Mexico in the eighteenth century. By 1865, fewer than five thousand Comanches lived in the empire, which ranged from west Texas north to Oklahoma.

Committee for Industrial Organization (CIO) Coalition (later called Congress of Industrial Organizations) of mostly unskilled workers formed in 1935 that mobilized massive union organizing drives in major industries. By 1941, through the CIO-affiliated United Auto Workers, organizers had overcome violent resistance to unionize the entire automobile industry.

committees of correspondence A communications network established among towns in Massachusetts and also among colonial capital towns in 1772–1773 to provide for rapid dissemination of news about important political developments. These committees politicized ordinary townspeople, sparking a revolutionary language of rights and duties.

Common Sense Pamphlet written by Thomas Paine in 1776 that laid out the case for independence. In it, Paine rejected monarchy, advocating its replacement with republican government based on the consent of the people. The pamphlet influenced public opinion throughout the colonies.

Compromise of 1850 Laws passed in 1850 meant to resolve the dispute over the spread of slavery in the territories. Key elements included the admission of California as a free state and the Fugitive Slave Act. The Compromise soon unraveled.

Compromise of 1877 Informal agreement in which Democrats agreed not to block Hayes's inauguration and to deal fairly with freedmen, and Hayes vowed not to use the army to uphold the remaining Republican regimes in the South and to provide the South with substantial federal subsidies for railroads. The Compromise brought the Reconstruction era to an end.

Comstock Lode Silver ore deposit discovered in 1859 in Nevada. Discovery of the Comstock Lode touched off a mining rush that brought a diverse population into the region and led to the establishment of a number of boomtowns, including Virginia City, Nevada.

Confederate States of America Government formed by Lower South states on February 7, 1861, following their secession from the Union. Secessionists argued that the election of a Republican to the presidency imperiled slavery and the South no longer had political protection within the Union.

conquistadors Term, literally meaning "conqueror," that refers to the Spanish explorers and soldiers who conquered lands in the New World.

containment The post–World War II foreign policy strategy that committed the United States to resisting the influence and expansion of the Soviet Union and communism. The strategy of containment shaped American foreign policy throughout the Cold War.

Continental army The army created in June 1775 by the Second Continental Congress to oppose the British. Virginian George Washington, commander in chief, had the task of turning local militias and untrained volunteers into a disciplined army.

contraband of war General Benjamin F. Butler's term for runaway slaves, who were considered confiscated property of war, not fugitives, and put to work in the Union army. This policy proved to be a step on the road to emancipation.

cotton kingdom Term for the South that reflected the dominance of cotton in the southern economy. Cotton was particularly important in the tier of states from South Carolina west to Texas. Cotton cultivation was the key factor in the growth of slavery.

court-packing plan Law proposed by Franklin Roosevelt to add one new Supreme Court justice for each existing judge who was over the age of seventy. Roosevelt wanted to pack the Court with up to six New Dealers who could protect New Deal legislation, but the Senate defeated the bill in 1937.

Coxey's army Unemployed men who marched to Washington, D.C., in 1894 to urge Congress to enact a public works program to end unemployment. Jacob S. Coxey of Ohio led the most publicized contingent. The movement failed to force federal relief legislation.

Creek War Part of the War of 1812 involving the Creek nation in Mississippi Territory and Tennessee militiamen. General Andrew Jackson's forces gained victory at the Battle of Horseshoe Bend in 1814, forcing the Creeks to sign away much of their land.

creoles Children born to Spanish parents in the New World who, with the *peninsulares*, made up the tiny portion of the population at the top of the colonial social hierarchy.

Cripple Creek miners' strike of 1894 Strike led by the Western Federation of Miners in response to an attempt to lengthen their workday to ten hours. With the support of local businessmen and the Populist governor of Colorado, the miners successfully maintained an eight-hour day.

Cuban missile crisis 1962 nuclear standoff between the Soviet Union and the United States when the Soviets attempted to deploy nuclear missiles in Cuba. In a negotiated settlement, the Soviet Union agreed to remove its missiles from Cuba, and the United States agreed to remove its missiles from Turkey.

Cuban revolution Uprising led by Fidel Castro that drove out U.S.-supported dictator Fulgencio Batista and eventually allied Cuba with the Soviet Union.

cult of domesticity Nineteenth-century belief that women's place was in the home, where they should create havens for their families. This sentimentalized ideal led to an increase in the hiring of domestic servants and freed white middle-class women to spend time in pursuits outside the home.

Dawes Allotment Act 1887 law that divided up reservations and allotted parcels of land to individual Indians as private property. In the end, the American government sold almost two-thirds of "surplus" Indian land to white settlers. The Dawes Act dealt a crippling blow to traditional tribal culture.

D Day June 6, 1944, the date of the Allied invasion of northern France. D Day was the largest amphibious assault in world history. The invasion opened a second front against the Germans and moved the Allies closer to victory in Europe.

Declaration of Independence A document containing philosophical principles and a list of grievances that declared separation from Britain. Adopted by the Second Continental Congress on July 4, 1776, it ended a period of intense debate with moderates still hoping to reconcile with Britain.

Declaratory Act 1766 law issued by Parliament to assert Parliament's unassailable right to legislate for its British colonies "in all cases whatsoever," putting Americans on notice that the simultaneous repeal of the Stamp Act changed nothing in the imperial powers of Britain.

Democrats Political party that evolved out of the Democratic Republicans after 1834. Strongest in the South and West, the Democrats embraced Andrew

Jackson's vision of limited government, expanded political participation for white men, and the promotion of an ethic of individualism.

détente Term given to the easing of conflict between the United States and the Soviet Union during the Nixon administration by focusing on issues of common concern, such as arms control and trade.

domino theory Theory of containment articulated by President Eisenhower in the context of Vietnam. He warned that the fall of a non-Communist government to communism would trigger the spread of communism to neighboring countries.

Double V campaign World War II campaign in America to attack racism at home and abroad. The campaign pushed the federal government to require defense contractors to integrate their workforces. In response, Franklin Roosevelt authorized a committee to investigate and prevent racial discrimination in employment.

***Dred Scott* decision** 1857 Supreme Court decision that ruled the Missouri Compromise unconstitutional. The Court ruled against slave Dred Scott, who claimed travels with his master into free states made him and his family free. The decision also denied the federal government the right to exclude slavery in the territories and declared that African Americans were not citizens.

Earned Income Tax Credit (EITC) Federal antipoverty program initiated in 1975 that assisted the working poor by giving tax breaks to low-income, fulltime workers or a subsidy to those who owed no taxes. President Clinton pushed through a significant increase in the program in 1993.

Economic Recovery Tax Act Legislation passed by Congress in 1981 that authorized the largest reduction in taxes in the nation's history. The tax cuts benefited affluent Americans disproportionately and widened the distribution of American wealth in favor of the rich.

Eighteenth Amendment (prohibition) Amendment banning the manufacture, transportation, and sale of alcohol. Congress passed the amendment in December 1917, and it was ratified in January 1920. World War I provided a huge boost to the crusade to ban alcohol.

Eisenhower Doctrine President Eisenhower's 1957 declaration that the United States would actively combat communism in the Middle East. Following this doctrine, Congress approved the policy, and Eisenhower sent aid to Jordan in 1957 and troops to Lebanon in 1958.

Ellis Island Immigration facility opened in 1892 in New York harbor that processed new immigrants coming into New York City. In the late nineteenth century, some 75 percent of European immigrants to America came through New York.

Emancipation Proclamation President Lincoln's proclamation issued on January 1, 1863, declaring all slaves in Confederate-controlled territory free. The proclamation made the Civil War a war to free slaves though its limitations—exemptions for loyal border states and Union-occupied areas of the Confederacy—made some ridicule the act.

Embargo Act of 1807 Act of Congress that prohibited U.S. ships from traveling to foreign ports and effectively banned overseas trade in an attempt to deter Britain from halting U.S. ships at sea. The embargo caused grave hardships for Americans engaged in overseas commerce.

encomienda A system for governing used during the Reconquest and in New Spain. It allowed the Spanish *encomendero*, or "owner" of a town, to collect tribute from the town in return for providing law and order and encouraging "his" Indians to convert to Christianity.

English Reformation Reform effort initiated by King Henry VIII that included banning the Catholic Church and declaring the English monarch head of the new Church of England but little change in doctrine. Henry's primary concern was consolidating his political power.

Enlightenment An eighteenth-century philosophical movement that emphasized the use of reason to reevaluate previously accepted doctrines and traditions. Enlightenment ideas encouraged examination of the world and independence of mind.

Environmental Protection Agency (EPA) Federal agency created by President Nixon in 1970 to enforce environmental laws, conduct environmental research, and reduce human health and environmental risks from pollutants.

Equal Rights Amendment (ERA) Constitutional amendment passed by Congress in 1972 requiring equal treatment of men and women under federal and state law. Facing fierce opposition from the New Right and the Republican Party, the ERA was defeated as time ran out for state ratification in 1982.

Erie Canal Canal finished in 1825, covering 350 miles between Albany and Buffalo and linking the port of New York City with the entire Great Lakes region. The canal turned New York City into the country's premier commercial city.

family economy Economic contributions of multiple members of a household that were necessary to the survival of the family. From the late nineteenth century into the twentieth, many working-class families depended on the wages of all family members, regardless of sex or age.

Farmers' Alliance Movement to form local organizations to advance farmers' collective interests that gained wide popularity in the 1880s. Over time, farmers' groups consolidated into the Northwestern Farmers' Alliance and the Southern Farmers' Alliance. In 1892, the Farmers' Alliance gave birth to the People's Party.

Federal Deposit Insurance Corporation (FDIC) Regulatory body established by the Glass-Steagall Banking Act that guaranteed the federal government would reimburse bank depositors if their banks failed. This key feature of the New Deal restored depositors' confidence in the banking system during the Great Depression.

Federalists One of the two dominant political groups that emerged in the 1790s. Federalist leaders supported Britain in foreign policy and commercial interests at home. Prominent Federalists included George Washington, Alexander Hamilton, and John Adams.

feme covert Legal doctrine grounded in British common law that held that a wife's civic life was subsumed by her husband's. Married women lacked independence to own property, make contracts, or keep wages earned. The doctrine shaped women's status in the early Republic.

Fifteenth Amendment Constitutional amendment passed in February 1869 prohibiting states from depriving any citizen of the right to vote because of "race, color, or previous condition of servitude." It extended black suffrage nationwide. Woman suffrage advocates were disappointed the amendment failed to extend voting rights to women.

finance capitalism Investment sponsored by banks and bankers that typified the American business scene at the end of the nineteenth century. After the panic of 1893, bankers stepped in and reorganized major industries to stabilize them, leaving power concentrated in the hands of a few influential capitalists.

fireside chats Series of informal radio addresses Franklin Roosevelt made to the nation in which he explained New Deal initiatives. The chats helped bolster Roosevelt's popularity and secured popular support for his reforms.

First Continental Congress September 1774 gathering of colonial delegates in Philadelphia to discuss the crisis precipitated by the Coercive Acts. The congress produced a declaration of rights and an agreement to impose a limited boycott of trade with Britain.

first transcontinental railroad Railroad completed in 1869 that was the first to span the North American continent. Built in large part by Chinese laborers, this railroad and others opened access to new areas, fueled land speculation, and actively recruited settlers.

Five-Power Naval Treaty of 1922 Treaty that committed Britain, France, Japan, Italy, and the United States to a proportional reduction of naval forces, producing the world's greatest success in disarmament up to that time. Republicans orchestrated its development at the 1921 Washington Disarmament Conference.

Fort Sumter Union fort on an island at the entrance to Charleston harbor in South Carolina. After Confederate leaders learned President Lincoln intended to resupply Fort Sumter, Confederate forces attacked the fort on April 12, 1861, thus marking the start of the Civil War.

Fourteen Points Woodrow Wilson's plan, proposed in 1918, to create a new democratic world order with lasting peace. Wilson's plan affirmed basic liberal ideals, supported the right to self-determination, and called for the creation of a League of Nations. Wilson compromised on his plan at the 1919 Paris peace conference, and the U.S. Senate refused to ratify the resulting treaty.

Fourteenth Amendment Constitutional amendment passed in 1866 that made all native-born or naturalized persons U.S. citizens and prohibited states from abridging the rights of national citizens. The amendment hoped to provide guarantee of equality before the law for black citizens.

free black An African American who was not enslaved. Southern whites worried about the increasing numbers of free blacks. In the 1820s and 1830s, state legislatures stemmed the growth of the free black population and shrank the liberty of free blacks.

free labor Term referring to work conducted free from constraint and according to the laborer's own inclinations and will. The ideal of free labor lay at the heart of the North's argument that slavery should not be extended into the western territories.

free silver Term used in the late nineteenth century by those who advocated minting silver dollars in addition to supporting the gold standard and the paper currency backed by gold. Western silver barons and poor farmers from the West and South hoped this would result in inflation, effectively providing them with debt relief.

Freedmen's Bureau Government organization created in March 1865 to distribute food and clothing to destitute Southerners and to ease the transition of slaves to free persons. Early efforts by the Freedmen's Bureau to distribute land to the newly freed blacks were later overturned by President Johnson.

Fugitive Slave Act A law included in the Compromise of 1850 to help attract southern support for the legislative package. Its strict provisions for capturing runaway slaves provoked outrage in the North and intensified antislavery sentiment in the region.

Ghost Dance Religion founded in 1889 by Paiute shaman Wovoka that combined elements of Christianity and traditional Indian religion and served as a nonviolent form of resistance for Indians in the late nineteenth century. The Ghost Dance frightened whites and was violently suppressed.

GI Bill of Rights Legislation passed in 1944 authorizing the government to provide World War II veterans with funds for education, housing, and health care, as well as loans to start businesses and buy homes.

Gilded Age A period of enormous economic growth and ostentatious displays of wealth during the last quarter of the nineteenth century. Industrialization dramatically changed U.S. society and created a newly dominant group of rich entrepreneurs and an impoverished working class.

global migration Movement of populations across large distances such as oceans and continents. In the late nineteenth century, large-scale immigration from southern and eastern Europe into the United States contributed to the growth of cities and changes in American demographics.

good neighbor policy Foreign policy announced by Franklin Roosevelt in 1933 that promised the United States would not interfere in the internal or external affairs of another country, thereby ending U.S. military interventions in Latin America.

gospel of wealth The idea that the financially successful should use their wisdom, experience, and wealth as stewards for the poor. Andrew Carnegie promoted this view in an 1889 essay in which he maintained that the wealthy should serve as stewards for society as a whole.

gradual emancipation A law passed in five northern states that balanced civil rights against property rights by providing a multistage process for freeing slaves, distinguishing persons already alive from those not yet born and providing benchmark dates when freedom would arrive for each group.

Great Awakening Wave of revivals that began in Massachusetts and spread through the colonies in the 1730s and 1740s. The movement emphasized vital religious faith and personal choice. It was characterized by large, open-air meetings at which emotional sermons were given by itinerant preachers.

Great Railroad Strike A violent multicity strike that began in 1877 with West Virginia railroad brakemen who protested against sharp wage reductions and quickly spread to include roughly 600,000 workers. President Rutherford B. Hayes used federal troops to break the strike. Despite the strike's failure, union membership surged.

Gulf of Tonkin Resolution Resolution passed by Congress in 1964 in the wake of a naval confrontation in the Gulf of Tonkin. It gave the president virtually unlimited authority in conducting the Vietnam War. The Senate terminated the resolution following outrage over the U.S. invasion of Cambodia in 1970.

Haitian Revolution The 1791–1804 conflict involving diverse Haitian participants and armies from three

European countries. At its end, Haiti became a free, independent, black-run country. The Haitian Revolution fueled fears of slave insurrections in the United States.

Halfway Covenant A Puritan compromise established in Massachusetts in 1662 that allowed the unconverted children of the "visible saints" to become "halfway" members of the church and baptize their own children even though they were not full members of the church themselves.

Hartford Convention A secret meeting of New England Federalist politicians held in late 1814 to discuss constitutional changes to reduce the South's political power and thus help block policies that injured northern commercial interests.

Haymarket bombing May 4, 1886, conflict in which both workers and policemen were killed or wounded during a labor demonstration in Chicago. The violence began when someone threw a bomb into the ranks of police at the gathering. The incident created a backlash against labor activism.

headright Fifty acres of free land granted by the Virginia Company to planters for each indentured servant they purchased.

Helsinki accords 1975 agreement signed by U.S., Canadian, Soviet, and European leaders, recognizing the post–World War II borders in Europe and pledging the signatories to respect human rights and fundamental freedoms.

Hernandez v. Texas 1954 Supreme Court decision that found that the systematic exclusion of Mexican Americans from juries violated the constitutional guarantee of equal protection.

Holocaust German effort during World War II to murder Europe's Jews, along with other groups the Nazis deemed "undesirable." Despite reports of the ongoing genocide, the Allies did almost nothing to interfere. In all, some 11 million people were killed in the Holocaust, most of them Jews.

Homestead Act of 1862 Act that promised 160 acres in the trans-Mississippi West free to any citizen or prospective citizen who settled on the land for five years. The act spurred American settlement of the West. Altogether, nearly one-tenth of the United States was granted to settlers.

Homestead lockout 1892 lockout of workers at the Homestead, Pennsylvania, steel mill after Andrew Carnegie refused to renew the union contract and workers prepared to strike. Union supporters attacked the Pinkerton National Detective Agency guards hired to protect the mill, but the National Guard soon broke the strike.

House of Burgesses Organ of government in colonial Virginia made up of an assembly of representatives elected by the colony's male inhabitants. It was established by the Virginia Company and continued by the crown after Virginia was made a royal colony.

House Un-American Activities Committee (HUAC) Congressional committee especially prominent during the early years of the Cold War that investigated Americans who might be disloyal to the government or might have associated with Communists or other radicals. It was one of the key institutions that promoted the second Red scare.

Housing Act of 1949 Law authorizing the construction of 810,000 units of government housing. This landmark effort marked the first significant commitment of the federal government to meet the housing needs of the poor.

hunter-gatherer A way of life that involved hunting game and gathering food from naturally occurring sources, as opposed to engaging in agriculture and animal husbandry. Archaic Indians and their descendants survived in North America for centuries as hunter-gatherers.

Immigration and Nationality Act of 1965 Legislation passed during Lyndon Johnson's administration abolishing discriminatory immigration quotas based on national origins. Although it did limit the number of immigrants, including those from Latin America for the first time, it facilitated a surge in immigration later in the century.

impressment A British naval practice of seizing sailors on American ships under the claim they were deserters from the British navy. Some 2,500 British and American men were taken by force into service, a grievance that helped propel the United States to declare war on Britain in 1812.

Incan empire A region under the control of the Incas and their emperor, Atahualpa, that stretched along the western coast of South America and contained more than nine million people and a wealth in gold and silver.

indentured servants Poor immigrants who signed contracts known as indentures, in which they committed to four to seven years of labor in North America in exchange for transportation from England, as well as food and shelter after they arrived in the colony.

Indian Removal Act of 1830 Act that directed the mandatory relocation of eastern tribes to territory west of the Mississippi. Jackson insisted his goal was to save the Indians. Indians resisted the controversial act, but in the end most were forced to comply.

Industrial Workers of the World (IWW) Umbrella union and radical political group founded in 1905 that was dedicated to organizing unskilled workers to oppose capitalism. Nicknamed the Wobblies, it advocated direct action by workers, including sabotage and general strikes, in hopes of triggering a widespread workers' uprising.

intermediate-range nuclear forces (INF) agreement Nuclear disarmament agreement reached between the United States and the Soviet Union in 1987, signifying a major thaw in the Cold War. The treaty eliminated all short- and medium-range missiles from Europe and provided for on-site inspection for the first time.

internment camps Makeshift prison camps, to which Americans of Japanese descent were sent as a result of Roosevelt's Executive Order 9066, issued in February 1942. In 1944, the Supreme Court upheld this blatant violation of constitutional rights as a "military necessity."

Interstate Commerce Commission (ICC) Federal regulatory agency designed to oversee the railroad industry. Congress created it through the 1887 Interstate Commerce Act after the Supreme Court decision in *Wabash v. Illinois* (1886) effectively denied states the right to regulate railroads. The ICC proved weak and did not immediately pose a threat to the industry.

Interstate Highway and Defense System Act of 1956 Law authorizing the construction of a national highway system. Promoted as essential to national defense and an impetus to economic growth, the national highway system accelerated the movement of people and goods and changed the nature of American communities.

Iran-Contra scandal Reagan administration scandal that involved the sale of arms to Iran in exchange for Iran's help securing the release of hostages held in Lebanon and the redirection of the sale's proceeds to finance the Nicaraguan Contras who wanted to unseat an elected government.

Iran hostage crisis Crisis that began in 1979 after the deposed shah of Iran was allowed into the United States following the Iranian revolution. Iranians broke into the U.S. Embassy in Teheran and took sixty-six Americans hostage, imprisoning most of them for more than a year.

Iraq War War launched by the United States, Britain, and several smaller countries in March 2003 against the government of Iraqi dictator Saddam Hussein. It was based on claims (subsequently refuted) that Hussein's government had links to Al Qaeda, harbored terrorists, and possessed weapons of mass destruction.

iron curtain Metaphor coined by Winston Churchill in 1946 to demark the line dividing Soviet-controlled countries in Eastern Europe from democratic nations in Western Europe following World War II.

Jamestown The first permanent English settlement in North America, established in 1607 by colonists sponsored by the Virginia Company.

Jay Treaty 1795 treaty between the United States and Britain, negotiated by John Jay. It secured limited trading rights in the West Indies but failed to ensure timely removal of British forces from western forts and reimbursement for slaves removed by the British after the Revolution.

Jim Crow System of racial segregation in the South lasting from after the Civil War into the twentieth century. Jim Crow laws segregated African Americans in public facilities such as trains and streetcars, curtailed their voting rights, and denied other basic civil rights.

Johnson-Reed Act 1924 law that severely restricted immigration to the United States to no more than 161,000 a year with quotas for each European nation. The racist restrictions were designed to staunch the flow of immigrants from southern and eastern Europe and Asia.

Kansas-Nebraska Act 1854 law that divided Indian territory into Kansas and Nebraska, repealed the Missouri Compromise, and left the new territories to decide the issue of slavery on the basis of popular sovereignty. The law led to bloody fighting in Kansas.

King Cotton diplomacy Confederate diplomatic strategy built on the hope that European nations starving for cotton would break the Union blockade and recognize the Confederacy. This strategy failed as Europeans held stores of surplus cotton and developed new sources outside the South.

King Philip's War War begun by Metacomet (King Philip), in which the Wampanoag Indians attacked colonial settlements in western Massachusetts in 1675. Colonists responded by attacking the Wampanoag and other tribes they believed conspired with them. The colonists prevailed in the brutal war.

Knights of Labor The first mass organization of America's working class. Founded in 1869, the Knights of Labor attempted to bridge the boundaries of ethnicity, gender, ideology, race, and occupation to build a "universal brotherhood" of all workers.

Korean War Conflict between North Korean forces supported by China and the Soviet Union and South Korean and U.S.-led United Nations forces over control of South Korea. Lasting from 1950 to 1953, the war represented the first time that the United States went to war to implement containment.

Ku Klux Klan Secret society that first thwarted black freedom after the Civil War as a paramilitary organization supporting Democrats. It was reborn in 1915 to fight against perceived threats posed by blacks, immigrants, radicals, feminists, Catholics, and Jews. The new Klan spread well beyond the South in the 1920s.

Ladies Association A women's organization in Philadelphia that collected substantial money donations in 1780 to reward Continental soldiers for their service. A woman leader authored a declaration, "The Sentiments of an American Woman," to justify women's unexpected entry into political life.

League of Nations International organization proposed in Woodrow Wilson's Fourteen Points designed to secure political independence and territorial integrity for all states and thus ensure enduring peace. The U.S. Senate refused to ratify the Treaty of Versailles, and the United States never became a member.

Lend-Lease Act Legislation in 1941 that enabled Britain to obtain arms from the United States without cash but with the promise to reimburse the United States when the war ended. The act reflected Roosevelt's desire to assist the British in any way possible, short of war.

Lewis and Clark expedition 1804–1806 expedition led by Meriwether Lewis and William Clark that explored the trans-Mississippi West for the U.S. government. The expedition's mission was scientific, political, and geographic.

Lincoln-Douglas debates Series of debates on the issue of slavery and freedom between Democrat Stephen Douglas and Republican Abraham Lincoln, held as part of the 1858 Illinois senatorial race. Douglas won the election, but the debates helped catapult Lincoln to national attention.

Lone Star Republic Independent republic, also known as the Republic of Texas, that was established by a rebellion of Texans against Mexican rule. The victory at San Jacinto in April 1836 helped ensure the region's independence and recognition by the United States.

Louisiana Purchase 1803 purchase of French territory west of the Mississippi River that stretched from the Gulf of Mexico to Canada. The Louisiana Purchase nearly doubled the size of the United States and opened the way for future American expansion west.

Lowell mills Water-powered textile mills constructed along the Merrimack River in Lowell, Massachusetts, that pioneered the extensive use of female laborers. By 1836, the eight mills there employed more than five thousand young women, living in boardinghouses under close supervision.

loyalists Colonists who remained loyal to Britain during the Revolutionary War, probably numbering around one-fifth of the population in 1776. Colonists remained loyal to Britain for many reasons, and loyalists could be found in every region of the country.

Lusitania British passenger liner torpedoed by a German U-boat on May 7, 1915. The attack killed 1,198 passengers, including 128 Americans. The incident challenged American neutrality during World War I and moved the United States on a path toward entering the war.

Manhattan Project Top-secret project authorized by Franklin Roosevelt in 1942 to develop an atomic bomb ahead of the Germans. The thousands of Americans who worked on the project at Los Alamos, New Mexico, succeeded in producing a successful atomic bomb by July 1945.

manifest destiny Term coined in 1845 by journalist John L. O'Sullivan to justify American expansion. O'Sullivan claimed that it was the nation's "manifest destiny" to transport its values and civilization westward. Manifest destiny framed the American conquest of the West as part of a divine plan.

Marbury v. Madison 1803 Supreme Court case that established the concept of judicial review in finding that parts of the Judiciary Act of 1789 were in conflict with the Constitution. The Supreme Court assumed legal authority to overrule acts of other branches of the government.

Marshall Plan Aid program begun in 1948 to help European economies recover from World War II. Between 1948 and 1953, the United States provided $13 billion to seventeen Western European nations in a project that helped its own economy as well.

Mason-Dixon line A surveyor's mark that had established the boundary between Maryland and Pennsylvania in colonial times. By the 1830s, the boundary divided the free North and the slave South.

mechanical reapers Tools usually powered by horses or oxen that enabled farmers to harvest twelve acres of wheat a day, compared to the two or three acres a day possible with manual harvesting methods.

Medicare and Medicaid Social programs enacted as part of Lyndon Johnson's Great Society. Medicare provided the elderly with universal compulsory medical insurance financed primarily by Social Security taxes. Medicaid authorized federal grants to supplement state-paid medical care for poor people of all ages.

Mexica An empire that stretched from coast to coast across central Mexico and encompassed as many as 25 million people. Their culture was characterized by steep hierarchy and devotion to the war god Huitzilopochtli.

Middle Passage The crossing of the Atlantic by slave ships traveling from West Africa to the Americas. Slaves were crowded together in extremely unhealthful circumstances, and mortality rates were high.

military-industrial complex A term President Eisenhower used to refer to the military establishment and defense contractors who, he warned, exercised undue influence in city, state, and federal government.

Military Reconstruction Act Congressional act of March 1867 that initiated military rule of the South. Congressional reconstruction divided the ten unreconstructed Confederate states into five military districts, each under the direction of a Union general. It also established the procedure by which unreconstructed states could reenter the Union.

miscegenation Interracial sex. Proslavery spokesmen played on the fears of whites when they suggested that giving blacks equal rights would lead to miscegenation. In reality, slavery led to considerable sexual abuse of black women by their white masters.

Missouri Compromise 1820 congressional compromise engineered by Henry Clay that paired Missouri's entrance into the Union as a slave state with Maine's as a free state. The compromise also established Missouri's southern border as the permanent line dividing slave from free states.

Monroe Doctrine President James Monroe's 1823 declaration that the Western Hemisphere was closed to further colonization or interference by European powers. In exchange, Monroe pledged that the United States would not become involved in European struggles. The United States strengthened the doctrine during the late nineteenth century.

Montgomery bus boycott Yearlong boycott of Montgomery's segregated bus system in 1955–1956 by the city's African American population. The boycott brought Martin Luther King Jr. to national prominence and ended in victory when the Supreme Court declared segregated transportation unconstitutional.

Mormons Members of the Church of Jesus Christ of Latter-Day Saints founded by Joseph Smith in 1830. Most Americans deemed the Mormons heretics. After Smith's death at the hands of an angry mob in 1844, Brigham Young moved the people to Utah in 1846.

muckraking Early-twentieth-century style of journalism that exposed the corruption of big business and government. Theodore Roosevelt coined the term after a character in Pilgrim's Progress who was too busy raking muck to notice higher things.

mutually assured destruction (MAD) Term for the standoff between the United States and Soviet Union based on the assumption that a nuclear first strike by either nation would result in massive retaliation and mutual destruction for each. Despite this, both countries pursued an ever-escalating arms race.

National American Woman Suffrage Association (NAWSA) Organization formed in 1890 that united the National Woman Suffrage Association and the American Woman Suffrage Association. The NAWSA pursued state-level campaigns to gain the vote for women. With successes in Idaho, Colorado, and Utah, woman suffrage had become more accepted by the 1890s.

National Energy Act of 1978 Legislation that penalized manufacturers of gas-guzzling automobiles and provided additional incentives for energy conservation and development of alternative fuels, such as wind and solar power. The act fell short of the long-term, comprehensive program that President Carter advocated.

National Organization for Women (NOW) Women's civil rights organization formed in 1966. Initially, NOW focused on eliminating gender discrimination in public institutions and the workplace, but by the 1970s it also embraced many of the issues raised by more radical feminists.

National Recovery Administration (NRA) Federal agency established in June 1933 to promote industrial recovery. It encouraged industrialists to voluntarily adopt codes that defined fair working conditions, set prices, and minimized competition. In practice, large corporations developed codes that served primarily their own interests rather than those of workers or the economy.

natural increase Growth of population through reproduction, as opposed to immigration. In the eighteenth century, natural increase accounted for about three-fourths of the American colonies' population growth.

Navigation Acts English laws passed in the 1650s and 1660s requiring that English colonial goods be shipped through English ports on English ships in order to benefit English merchants, shippers, and seamen.

neutrality acts Legislation passed in 1935 and 1937 that sought to avoid entanglement in foreign wars while protecting trade. It prohibited selling arms to nations at war and required nations to pay cash for nonmilitary goods and to transport them in their own ships.

New (Christian) Right Politically active religious conservatives who became particularly prominent in the 1980s. The New Right criticized feminism, opposed abortion and homosexuality, and promoted a larger role for religion in public life, "family values," and military preparedness.

New Deal coalition Political coalition that supported Franklin D. Roosevelt's New Deal and the Democratic Party, including farmers, factory workers, immigrants, city folk, women, African Americans, and progressive intellectuals. The coalition dominated American politics during and long after Roosevelt's presidency.

"The New Freedom" Woodrow Wilson's 1912 campaign slogan, which reflected his belief in limited government and states' rights. Wilson promised to use antitrust legislation to eliminate big corporations and to improve opportunities for small businesses and farmers.

"The New Nationalism" Theodore Roosevelt's 1912 campaign slogan, which reflected his commitment to federal planning and regulation. Roosevelt wanted to use the federal government to act as a "steward for the people" to regulate giant corporations.

New Jersey Plan Alternative plan drafted by delegates from small states, retaining the confederation's single-house congress with one vote per state. It shared with the Virginia Plan enhanced congressional powers, including the right to tax, regulate trade, and use force to stop popular uprisings.

New Negro Term referring to African Americans who challenged American racial hierarchy through the arts. The New Negro emerged in New York City in the 1920s in what became known as the Harlem Renaissance, which produced dazzling literary, musical, and artistic talent.

new Negroes Term given to newly arrived African slaves in the colonies. Planters usually maintained only a small number of recent arrivals among their slaves at any given time in order to accelerate their acculturation to their new circumstances.

New Netherland Dutch colony on Manhattan Island. New Amsterdam was its capital and colony headquarters.

New Spain Land in the New World held by the Spanish crown. Spain pioneered techniques of using New World colonies to strengthen the kingdom in Europe and would become a model for other European nations.

new woman Alternative image of womanhood that came into the American mainstream in the 1920s. The mass media frequently portrayed young, college-educated women who drank, smoked, and wore skimpy dresses. New women also challenged American convictions about separate spheres for women and men and the sexual double standard.

New York City draft riots Four days of rioting in New York City in July 1863 triggered by efforts to enforce the military draft. Democratic Irish workingmen, suffering economic hardship, infuriated by the draft, and opposed to emancipation, killed at least 105 people, most of them black.

New York Female Moral Reform Society An organization of religious women inspired by the Second Great Awakening to eradicate sexual sin and male licentiousness. Formed in 1833, it spread to hundreds of auxiliaries and worked to curb male licentiousness, prostitution, and seduction.

Newburgh Conspiracy A bogus threatened coup staged by Continental army officers and leaders in the congress in 1782–1783, who hoped that a forceful demand for military back pay and pensions would create pressure for stronger taxation powers. General Washington defused the threat.

Nineteenth Amendment (woman suffrage) Amendment granting women the vote. Congress passed the amendment in 1919, and it was ratified in August 1920. Like proponents of prohibition, the advocates of woman suffrage triumphed by linking their cause to the war.

No Child Left Behind Act 2002 legislation championed by President George W. Bush that expanded the role of the federal government in public education. The law required every school to meet annual testing standards, penalized failing schools, and allowed parents to transfer their children out of such schools.

North American Free Trade Agreement (NAFTA) 1993 treaty that eliminated all tariffs and trade barriers among the United States, Canada, and Mexico. NAFTA was supported by President Clinton, a minority of Democrats, and a majority of Republicans.

North Atlantic Treaty Organization (NATO) Military alliance formed in 1949 among the United States, Canada, and Western European nations to counter any possible Soviet threat. It represented an unprecedented commitment by the United States to go to war if any of its allies were attacked.

Northwest Ordinance Land act of 1787 that established a three-stage process by which settled territories would become states. It also banned slavery in the Northwest Territory. The ordinance guaranteed that western lands with white population would not become colonial dependencies.

NSC 68 Top-secret government report of April 1950 warning that national survival required a massive military buildup. The Korean War brought nearly all of the expansion called for in the report, and by 1952 defense spending claimed nearly 70 percent of the federal budget.

nullification Theory asserting that states could nullify acts of Congress that exceeded congressional powers. South Carolina advanced the theory of nullification in 1828 in response to an unfavorable federal tariff. A show of force by Andrew Jackson, combined with tariff revisions, ended the crisis.

Oneida community Utopian community organized by John Humphrey Noyes in New York in 1848. Noyes's opposition to private property led him to denounce marriage as the root of the problem. The community embraced sexual and economic communalism, to the dismay of its mainstream neighbors.

Open Door policy Policy successfully insisted upon by Secretary of State John Hay in 1899–1900 recommending that the major powers of the United States, Britain, Japan, Germany, France, and Russia should all have access to trade with China and that Chinese sovereignty be maintained.

Oregon Trail Route from Independence, Missouri, to Oregon traveled by American settlers starting in the late 1830s. Disease and accidents caused many more deaths along the trail than did Indian attacks, which migrants feared.

Paleo-Indians Archaeologists' term for the first migrants into North America and their descendants who spread across the Americas between 15,000 BP and 13,500 BP, approximately.

Panama Canal treaty 1977 agreement that returned control of the Panama Canal from the United States to Panama in 2000. To pass the treaty, President Carter overcame stiff opposition in the Senate from conservatives who regarded control of the canal as vital to America's interests.

panic of 1837 First major economic crisis of the United States that led to several years of hard times from 1837 to 1841. Sudden bankruptcies, contraction of credit, and runs on banks worked hardships nationwide. Causes were multiple and global and not well understood.

partible inheritance System of inheritance in which land was divided equally among sons. By the eighteenth century, this practice in Massachusetts had subdivided plots of land into units too small for subsistence, forcing children to move away to find sufficient farmland.

paternalism The theory of slavery that emphasized reciprocal duties and obligations between masters and their slaves, with slaves providing labor and obedience and masters providing basic care and direction. Whites employed the concept of paternalism to deny that the slave system was brutal and exploitative.

Patient Protection and Affordable Care Act Sweeping 2010 health care reform bill that established nearly universal health insurance by providing subsidies and compelling larger businesses to offer coverage to employees. Championed by President Obama, it also imposed new regulations on insurance companies and contained provisions to limit health care costs.

Peace Corps Program launched by President Kennedy in 1961 through which young American volunteers helped with education, health, and other projects in developing countries around the world. More than 60,000 volunteers had served by the mid-1970s.

Pennsylvania Dutch Name given by other colonists to German immigrants to the middle colonies; an English corruption of the German term Deutsch. Germans were the largest contingent of migrants from continental Europe to the middle colonies in the eighteenth century.

Pentagon Papers Secret government documents published in 1971 containing an internal study of the Vietnam War. The documents further disillusioned the public by revealing that officials harbored pessimism about the war even as they made rosy public pronouncements about its progress.

People's Party (Populist Party) Political party formed in 1892 by the Farmers' Alliance to advance the goals of the Populist movement. Populists sought economic democracy, promoting land, electoral, banking, and monetary reform. Republican victory in the presidential election of 1896 effectively destroyed the People's Party.

Persian Gulf War 1991 war between Iraq and a U.S.-led international coalition. The war was sparked by the 1990 Iraqi invasion of Kuwait. A forty-day bombing campaign against Iraq followed by coalition troops storming into Kuwait brought a quick coalition victory.

Personal Responsibility and Work Opportunity Reconciliation Act Legislation signed by President Clinton in 1996 that replaced Aid to Families with Dependent Children with Temporary Assistance for Needy Families. It provided grants to the states to assist the poor and limited welfare payments to two years, with a lifetime maximum of five years.

plantation Large farm worked by twenty or more slaves. Although small farms were more numerous, plantations produced more than 75 percent of the South's export crops.

plantation belt Flatlands that spread from South Carolina to east Texas and were dominated by large plantations.

planter A substantial landowner who tilled his estate with twenty or more slaves. Planters dominated the social and political world of the South. Their values and ideology influenced the values of all southern whites.

Plessy v. Ferguson 1896 Supreme Court ruling that upheld the legality of racial segregation. According to the ruling, blacks could be segregated in separate schools, restrooms, and other facilities as long as the facilities were "equal" to those provided for whites.

Pontiac's Rebellion A coordinated uprising of Native American tribes in 1763 in the Northwest after the end of the Seven Years' War. The rebellion heightened Britain's determination to create a boundary between Americans and Indians, embodied in the Proclamation of 1763.

popular sovereignty The idea that government is subject to the will of the people. Applied to the territories, popular sovereignty meant that the residents of a territory should determine, through their legislatures, whether to allow slavery.

predestination Doctrine stating that God determined whether individuals were destined for salvation or damnation before their birth. According to the doctrine, nothing an individual did during his or her lifetime could affect that person's fate.

presidios Spanish forts built to block Russian advance into California.

progressivism A reform movement that often advocated government activism to mitigate the problems created by urban industrialism. Progressivism reached its peak in 1912 with the creation of the Progressive Party. The term *progressivism* has come to mean any general effort advocating for social welfare programs.

prohibition The ban on the manufacture and sale of alcohol that went into effect in January 1920 with the Eighteenth Amendment. Prohibition proved almost impossible to enforce. By the end of the 1920s, most Americans wished it to end, and it was finally repealed in 1933.

Protestant Reformation The reform movement that began in 1517 with Martin Luther's critiques of the Roman Catholic Church, which precipitated an enduring schism that divided Protestants from Catholics.

Pueblo Bonito The largest residential and ceremonial site, containing more than 600 rooms and thirty-five kivas, in the major Anasazi cultural center of Chaco Canyon in present-day New Mexico.

Pueblo Revolt An effective revolt of Pueblo Indians in New Mexico, under the leadership of Popé, against the Spaniards in 1680. Particularly targeting symbols of Christianity, they succeeded in killing two-thirds of

Spanish missionaries and driving the Spaniards out of New Mexico.

pueblos Multiunit dwellings, storage spaces, and ceremonial centers—often termed kivas—built by ancient Americans in the Southwest for centuries around AD 1000.

Pullman boycott Nationwide railroad workers' boycott of trains carrying Pullman cars in 1894 after Pullman workers, suffering radically reduced wages, joined the American Railway Union (ARU) and union leaders were fired in response. The boycott ended after the U.S. Army fired on strikers and ARU leader Eugene Debs was jailed.

Puritan Revolution English civil war that arose out of disputes between King Charles I and Parliament, which was dominated by Puritans. The conflict began in 1642 and ended with the execution of Charles I in 1649, resulting in Puritan rule in England until 1660.

Puritans Dissenters from the Church of England who wanted a genuine Reformation rather than the partial Reformation sought by Henry VIII. The Puritans' religious principles emphasized the importance of an individual's relationship with God developed through Bible study, prayer, and introspection.

Quakers Epithet for members of the Society of Friends. Their belief that God spoke directly to each individual through an "inner light" and that neither ministers nor the Bible was essential to discovering God's Word put them in conflict with orthodox Puritans.

Reconquest The centuries-long drive to expel Muslims from the Iberian Peninsula undertaken by the Christian kingdoms of Spain and Portugal. The military victories of the Reconquest helped the Portuguese gain greater access to sea routes.

Reconstruction Finance Corporation (RFC) Federal agency established by Herbert Hoover in 1932 to help American industry by lending government funds to endangered banks and corporations, which Hoover hoped would benefit people at the bottom through trickle-down economics. In practice, this provided little help to the poor.

Red scare The widespread fear of internal subversion and Communist revolution that swept the United States in 1919 and resulted in suppression of dissent. Labor unrest, postwar recession, the difficult peacetime readjustment, and the Soviet establishment of the Comintern all contributed to the scare.

Redeemers Name taken by southern Democrats who harnessed white rage in order to overthrow Republican rule and black political power and thus, they believed, save southern civilization.

redemptioners A variant of indentured servants. In this system, a captain agreed to provide passage to Philadelphia, where redemptioners would obtain money to pay for their transportation, usually by selling themselves as servants.

reform Darwinism Sociological theory developed in the 1880s that argued humans could speed up evolution by altering their environment. A challenge to the laissez-faire approach of social Darwinism, reform Darwinism insisted the liberal state should play an active role in solving social problems.

Report on Manufactures A proposal by Treasury Secretary Alexander Hamilton in 1791 calling for the federal government to encourage domestic manufactur-ers with subsidies while imposing tariffs on foreign imports. Congress initially rejected the measure.

Report on Public Credit Hamilton's January 1790 report recommending that the national debt be funded—but not repaid immediately—at full value. Hamilton's goal was to make the new country creditworthy, not debt-free. Critics of his plan complained that it would benefit speculators.

republicanism A social philosophy that embraced representative institutions (as opposed to monarchy), a citizenry attuned to civic values above private interests, and a virtuous community in which individuals work to promote the public good.

Republican Party Antislavery party formed in 1854 following passage of the Kansas-Nebraska Act. The Republicans attempted to unite all those who opposed the extension of slavery into any territory of the United States.

Republicans One of the two dominant political groups that emerged in the 1790s. Republicans supported the revolutionaries in France and worried about monarchical Federalists at home. Prominent Republicans included Thomas Jefferson and James Madison.

reservations Land given by the federal government to American Indians beginning in the 1860s in an attempt to reduce tensions between Indians and western settlers. On reservations, Indians subsisted on meager government rations and faced a life of poverty and starvation.

rock and roll A music genre created from country music and black rhythm and blues that emerged in the 1950s and captivated American youth.

Roe v. Wade 1973 Supreme Court ruling that the Constitution protects the right to abortion, which states cannot prohibit in the early stages of pregnancy. The decision galvanized social conservatives and made abortion a controversial policy issue for decades to come.

Roosevelt Corollary Theodore Roosevelt's 1904 follow-up to the Monroe Doctrine in which he declared the United States had the right to intervene in Latin America to stop "brutal wrongdoing" and protect American interests. The corollary warned European powers to keep out of the Western Hemisphere.

royal colony A colony ruled by a king or queen and governed by officials appointed to serve the monarchy and represent its interests.

scalawag A derogatory term that Southerners applied to southern white Republicans, who were seen as traitors to the South. Most were yeoman farmers.

Schenck v. United States 1919 Supreme Court decision that established a "clear and present danger" test for restricting free speech. The Court upheld the conviction of socialist Charles Schenck for urging resistance to the draft during wartime.

Scopes trial 1925 trial of John Scopes, a biology teacher in Dayton, Tennessee, for violating his state's ban on teaching evolution. The trial created a nationwide media frenzy and came to be seen as a showdown between urban and rural values.

Scottsboro Boys Nine African American youths who were arrested for the alleged rape of two white women in Scottsboro, Alabama, in 1931. After an all-white jury sentenced the young men to death, the Communist Party took action that saved them from the electric chair.

Scots-Irish Protestant immigrants from northern Ireland, Scotland, and northern England. Deteriorating economic conditions in their European homelands contributed to increasing migration to the colonies in the eighteenth century.

second Bank of the United States National bank with multiple branches chartered in 1816 for twenty years. Intended to help regulate the economy, the bank became a major issue in Andrew Jackson's reelection campaign in 1832, framed in political rhetoric about aristocracy versus democracy.

Second Continental Congress Legislative body that governed the United States from May 1775 through the war's duration. It established an army, created its own money, and declared independence once all hope for a peaceful reconciliation with Britain was gone.

Second Great Awakening Unprecedented religious revival in the 1820s and 1830s that promised access to salvation. The Second Great Awakening proved to be a major impetus for reform movements of the era, inspiring efforts to combat drinking, sexual sin, and slavery.

Selective Service Act Law enacted in 1940 requiring all men who would be eligible for a military draft to register in preparation for the possibility of a future conflict. The act also prohibited discrimination based on "race or color."

Seneca Falls Declaration of Sentiments Declaration issued in 1848 at the first national woman's rights convention in the United States, which was held in Seneca Falls, New York. The document adopted the style of the Declaration of Independence and demanded equal rights for women, including the franchise.

Separatists People who sought withdrawal from the Church of England. The Pilgrims were Separatists.

settlement houses Settlements established in poor neighborhoods beginning in the 1880s. Reformers like Jane Addams and Lillian Wald believed that only by living among the poor could they help bridge the growing class divide. College-educated women formed the backbone of the settlement house movement.

Seven Years' War War (1754–1762) between Britain and France that ended with British domination of North America; known in America as the French and Indian War. Its high expense laid the foundation for conflict that would lead to the American Revolution.

sharecropping Labor system that emerged in the South during reconstruction. Under this system, planters divided their plantations into small farms that freedmen rented, paying with a share of each year's crop. Sharecropping gave blacks some freedom, but they remained dependent on white landlords and country merchants.

Shays's Rebellion Uprising (1786–1787) led by farmers centered in western Massachusetts. Dissidents protested taxation policies of the eastern elites who controlled the state's government. Shays's Rebellion caused leaders throughout the country to worry about the confederation's ability to handle civil disorder.

Sherman Antitrust Act 1890 act that outlawed pools and trusts, ruling that businesses could no longer enter into agreements to restrict competition. Government inaction, combined with the Supreme Court's narrow reading of the act in the *United States v. E. C. Knight Company* decision, undermined the law's effectiveness.

Sherman's March to the Sea Military campaign from September through December 1864 in which Union forces under General Sherman marched from Atlanta, Georgia, to the coast at Savannah. Carving a path of destruction as it progressed, Sherman's army aimed at destroying white Southerner's will to continue the war.

siege of Vicksburg Six-week siege by General Grant intended to starve out Vicksburg. On July 4, 1863, the 30,000 Confederate troops holding the city surrendered. The victory gave the Union control of the Mississippi River and, together with Gettysburg, marked a major turning point of the war.

Six-Day War 1967 conflict between Israel and the Arab nations of Egypt, Syria, and Jordan. Israel attacked Egypt after Egypt had massed troops on its border and cut off the sea passage to Israel's southern port. Israel won a stunning victory, seizing territory that amounted to twice its original size.

slave codes Laws enacted in southern states in the 1820s and 1830s that required the total submission of slaves. Attacks by antislavery activists and by slaves convinced southern legislators that they had to do everything in their power to strengthen the institution.

slavery Coerced labor. African slavery became the most important form of coerced labor in the New World in the seventeenth century.

social Darwinism A social theory popularized in the late nineteenth century by Herbert Spencer and William Graham Sumner. Proponents believed only relentless competition could produce social progress and wealth was a sign of "fitness" and poverty a sign of "unfitness" for survival.

social gospel A vision of Christianity that saw its mission not simply to reform individuals but to reform society. Emerging in the early twentieth century, it offered a powerful corrective to social Darwinism and the gospel of wealth, which fostered the belief that riches signaled divine favor.

Social Security A New Deal program created in August 1935 that was designed to provide a modest income for elderly people. The act also created unemployment insurance with modest benefits. Social Security provoked sharp opposition from conservatives and the wealthy.

Socialist Party Political party formed in 1900 that advocated cooperation over competition and promoted the breakdown of capitalism. Its members, who were largely middle-class and native-born, saw both the Republican and the Democratic parties as hopelessly beholden to capitalism.

Spanish-American War 1898 war between Spain and the United States that began as an effort to free Cuba from Spain's colonial rule. This popular war left the United States an imperial power in control of Cuba and colonies in Puerto Rico, Guam, and the Philippines.

spoils system System in which politicians doled out government positions to their loyal supporters. This patronage system led to widespread corruption during the Gilded Age.

Stamp Act 1765 British law imposing a tax on all paper used for official documents, for the purpose of raising revenue. Widespread resistance to the Stamp Act led to its repeal in 1766.

Strategic Arms Limitation Talks (SALT) Negotiations begun in 1969 that produced an agreement between the United States and the Soviet Union in 1972, limiting antiballistic missiles (ABMs) to two each. The treaty prevented either nation from building an ABM system defense so secure against a nuclear attack that it would risk a first strike.

Strategic Defense Initiative (SDI) Project launched by President Reagan to deploy lasers in space that would prevent enemy missiles from reaching their targets. Critics protested that it violated the 1972 Antiballistic Missile Treaty. The project cost billions of dollars without producing a working system.

Stono Rebellion Slave uprising in Stono, South Carolina, in 1739 in which a group of slaves armed themselves, plundered six plantations, and killed more than twenty whites. Whites quickly suppressed the rebellion.

Sugar (Revenue) Act 1764 British law that decreased the duty on French molasses, making it more attractive for shippers to obey the law, and at the same time raised penalties for smuggling. The Sugar Act regulated trade but was also intended to raise revenue.

Sun Belt Name applied to the West, Southwest, and parts of the South, which grew rapidly after World War II as a center of defense industries and non-unionized labor.

supply-side economics Economic theory that justified the Reagan administration's large tax cuts on the grounds that they would encourage investment and production (supply) and stimulate consumption (demand) because individuals could keep more of their earnings. Reagan's supply-side economics created a massive federal budget deficit.

sweatshop A small room used for clothing piecework beginning in the late nineteenth century. As mechanization transformed the garment industry with the introduction of foot-pedaled sewing machines and mechanical cloth-cutting knives, independent tailors were replaced with sweatshop workers hired by contractors to sew pieces into clothing.

Taft-Hartley Act Law passed by the Republicancontrolled Congress in 1947 that amended the Wagner Act and placed restrictions on organized labor that made it more difficult for unions to organize workers.

Tainos The Indians who inhabited San Salvador and many Caribbean islands and who were the first people Columbus encountered after making landfall in the New World.

task system A system of labor in which a slave was assigned a daily task to complete and allowed to do as he wished upon its completion. This system offered more freedom than the carefully supervised gang-labor system.

Tea Act of 1773 British act that lowered the existing tax on tea to entice boycotting Americans to buy it. Resistance to the Tea Act led to the passage of the Coercive Acts and imposition of military rule in Massachusetts.

Teapot Dome Nickname for scandal in which Interior Secretary Albert Fall accepted $400,000 in bribes for leasing oil reserves on public land in Teapot Dome, Wyoming. It was part of a larger pattern of corruption that marred Warren G. Harding's presidency.

Tet Offensive Major campaign of attacks launched throughout South Vietnam in early 1968 by the North Vietnamese and Vietcong. A major turning point in the war, it exposed the credibility gap between official statements and the war's reality, and it shook Americans' confidence in the government.

three-fifths clause Clause in the Constitution that stipulated that all free persons plus "three-fifths of all other Persons" would constitute the numerical base for apportioning both representation and taxation. The clause tacitly acknowledged the existence of slavery in the United States.

Townshend duties British law that established new duties on tea, glass, lead, paper, and painters' colors imported into the colonies. The Townshend duties led to boycotts and heightened tensions between Britain and the American colonies.

Trail of Tears Forced westward journey of Cherokees from their lands in Georgia to present-day Oklahoma in 1838. Despite favorable legal action, the Cherokees endured a grueling 1,200-mile march overseen by federal troops. Nearly a quarter of the Cherokees died en route.

Treaty of Fort Stanwix 1784 treaty with the Iroquois Confederacy that established the primacy of the American confederation (and not states) to negotiate with Indians and resulted in large land cessions in the Ohio Country (northwestern Pennsylvania). Tribes not present at Fort Stanwix disavowed the treaty.

Treaty of Greenville 1795 treaty between the United States and various Indian tribes in Ohio. The United States gave the tribes treaty goods valued at $25,000. In exchange, the Indians ceded most of Ohio to the Americans. The treaty brought only temporary peace to the region.

Treaty of Guadalupe Hidalgo February 1848 treaty that ended the Mexican-American War. Mexico gave up all claims to Texas north of the Rio Grande and ceded New Mexico and California to the United States. The United States agreed to pay Mexico $15 million and to assume American claims against Mexico.

Treaty (Peace) of Paris, 1783 September 3, 1783, treaty that ended the Revolutionary War. The treaty acknowledged America's independence, set its boundaries, and promised the quick withdrawal of British troops from American soil. It failed to recognize Indians as players in the conflict.

Treaty of Tordesillas The treaty negotiated in 1494 to delineate land claims in the New World. The treaty drew an imaginary line west of the Canary Islands; land discovered west of the line belonged to Spain, and land to the east belonged to Portugal.

tribute The goods the Mexica collected from conquered peoples, from basic food products to candidates for human sacrifice. Tribute engendered resentment among the Mexica's subjects, creating a vulnerability the Spaniards would later exploit.

Triple Alliance Early-twentieth-century alliance between Germany, Austria-Hungary, and Italy, formed as part of a complex network of military and diplomatic agreements intended to prevent war in Europe by balancing power. In actuality, such alliances made largescale conflict more likely.

Triple Entente Early-twentieth-century alliance between Great Britain, France, and Russia, which was formed as part of a complex network of military and diplomatic agreements intended to prevent war in Europe by balancing power. In actuality, such alliances made large-scale conflict more likely.

Truman Doctrine President Harry S. Truman's commitment to "support free peoples who are resisting attempted subjugation by armed minorities or outside pressures." First applied to Greece and Turkey in 1947, it became the justification for U.S. intervention into many countries during the Cold War.

trust A system in which corporations give shares of their stock to trustees who hold the stocks "in trust" for their stockholders, thereby coordinating the industry to ensure profits to the participating corporations and curb competition.

"typewriters" Women who were hired by businesses in the decades after the Civil War to keep records and conduct correspondence, often using equipment such as typewriters. Secretarial work constituted one of the very few areas where middle-class women could use their literacy for wages.

Uncle Tom's Cabin Enormously popular antislavery novel written by Harriet Beecher Stowe and published in 1852. It helped to solidify northern sentiment against slavery and to confirm white Southerners' sense that no sympathy remained for them in the free states.

underconsumption New Dealers' belief that the root cause of the country's economic paralysis was that factories and farms produced more than they could sell, causing factories to lay off workers and farmers to lose money. The only way to increase consumption, they believed, was to provide jobs that put wages in consumers' pockets.

underground railroad Network consisting mainly of black homes, black churches, and black neighborhoods that helped slaves escape to the North by supplying shelter, food, and general assistance.

Union blockade The United States' use of its navy to patrol the southern coastline to restrict Confederate access to supplies. Over time, the blockade became increasingly effective and succeeded in depriving the Confederacy of vital supplies.

United States Constitution The document written in 1787 and subsequently ratified by the original thirteen states that laid out the governing structure of the United States in separate legislative, executive, and judicial branches.

upcountry The hills and mountains of the South whose higher elevation, colder climate, rugged terrain, and poor transportation made the region less hospitable than the flatlands to slavery and large plantations.

USA Patriot Act 2001 law that gave the government new powers to monitor suspected terrorists and their associates, including the ability to access personal information. Critics charged that it represented an unwarranted abridgment of civil rights.

Versailles treaty Treaty signed on June 28, 1919, that ended World War I. The agreement redrew the map of the world and assigned Germany sole responsibility for the war and saddled it with a debt of $33 billion in war damages. Many Germans felt betrayed by the treaty.

Virginia and Kentucky Resolutions 1798 resolutions condemning the Alien and Sedition Acts submitted to the federal government by the Virginia and Kentucky state legislatures. The resolutions tested the idea that state legislatures could judge the constitutionality of federal laws and nullify them.

Virginia Company A joint-stock company organized by London investors in 1606 that received a land grant from King James I in order to establish English colonies in North America. Investors hoped to enrich themselves and strengthen England economically and politically.

Virginia Plan Plan drafted by James Madison, presented at the opening of the Philadelphia constitutional convention. Designed as a powerful three-branch government, with representation in both houses of the congress to be tied to population, this plan eclipsed the voice of small states in national government.

virtual representation The theory that all British subjects were represented in Parliament, whether they had elected representatives in that body or not. American colonists rejected the theory of virtual representation, arguing that only direct representatives had the right to tax the colonists.

visible saints Puritans who had passed the tests of conversion and church membership and were therefore thought to be among God's elect.

Voting Rights Act of 1965 Law passed during Lyndon Johnson's administration that empowered the federal government to intervene to ensure minorities access to the voting booth. As a result of the act, black voting and officeholding in the South shot up, initiating a major transformation in southern politics.

Wagner Act 1935 law that guaranteed industrial workers the right to organize into unions; also known as the National Labor Relations Act. Following passage of the act, union membership skyrocketed to 30 percent of the workforce, the highest in American history.

War Hawks Young men newly elected to the Congress of 1811 who were eager for war against Britain in order to end impressments, fight Indians, and expand into neighboring British territory. Leaders included Henry Clay of Kentucky and John C. Calhoun of South Carolina.

War on Poverty President Lyndon Johnson's efforts, organized through the Office of Economic Opportunity, to ameliorate poverty primarily through education and training as well as by including the poor in decision making.

Warren Court The Supreme Court under Chief Justice Earl Warren (1953–1969), which expanded the Constitution's promise of equality and civil rights. It issued landmark decisions in the areas of civil rights, criminal rights, reproductive freedom, and separation of church and state.

Watergate Term referring to the 1972 break-in at Democratic Party headquarters in the Watergate complex in Washington, D.C., by men working for President Nixon's reelection, along with Nixon's efforts to cover it up. The Watergate scandal led to President Nixon's resignation.

welfare capitalism Industrial programs for workers that became popular in the 1920s. Some businesses improved safety and sanitation inside factories. They also instituted paid vacations and pension plans. This encouraged loyalty to companies rather than to independent labor unions.

Whigs Political party that evolved out of the National Republicans after 1834. With a Northeast power base, the Whigs supported federal action to promote commercial development and generally looked favorably on the reform movements associated with the Second Great Awakening.

Whiskey Rebellion July 1794 uprising by farmers in western Pennsylvania in response to enforcement of an unpopular excise tax on whiskey. The federal government responded with a military presence that caused dissidents to disperse before blood was shed.

Wilmot Proviso Proposal put forward by Representative David Wilmot of Pennsylvania in August 1846 to ban slavery in territory acquired from the Mexican-American War. The proviso enjoyed widespread support in the North, but Southerners saw it as an attack on their interests.

Woman's Christian Temperance Union (WCTU) All-women organization founded in 1874 to advocate for total abstinence from alcohol. The WCTU provided important political training for women, which many used in the suffrage movement.

Works Progress Administration (WPA) Federal New Deal program established in 1935 that provided government-funded public works jobs to millions of unemployed Americans during the Great Depression, in areas ranging from construction to the arts.

World Trade Organization (WTO) International economic body established in 1994 through the General Agreement on Tariffs and Trade to enforce substantial tariff and import quota reductions. Many corporations welcomed these trade barrier reductions, but critics linked them to job loss and the weakening of unions.

World's Columbian Exposition World's fair held in Chicago in 1893 that attracted millions of visitors. The elaborately designed pavilions of the "White City" included exhibits of technological innovation and of cultural exoticism. They embodied an urban ideal that contrasted with the realities of Chicago life.

Wounded Knee 1890 massacre of Sioux Indians by American cavalry at Wounded Knee Creek, South Dakota. Sent to suppress the Ghost Dance, the soldiers opened fire on the Sioux as they attempted to surrender. More than two hundred Sioux men, women, and children were killed.

XYZ affair 1797 incident in which American negotiators in France were rebuffed for refusing to pay a substantial bribe. The incident led the United States into an undeclared war with France, known as the Quasi-War, which intensified antagonism between Federalists and Republicans.

yellow journalism Term first given to sensationalistic newspaper reporting and cartoon images rendered in yellow. A circulation war between two New York City papers provoked the yellow journalism tactics that fueled popular support for the Spanish-American War in 1898.

yeomen Farmers who owned and worked on their own small plots of land. Yeomen living within the plantation belt were more dependent on planters than were yeomen in the upcountry, where small farmers dominated.

Acknowledgments

Index

Abington School District v. Schempp (1963), 803

ABMs. *See* Antiballistic Missile Treaty

Abolition and abolitionism, Lincoln and, 435–436

Abortion and abortion rights, 820–821, 864, 876, 876*(i),* 896, 907

Abraham Lincoln Brigade, 711

Abstract expressionism, 787

Abu Ghraib prison, 910

Abundance. *See also* Consumers; Prosperity; Wealth
  era of, 651
  politics and culture of, 767–793

Accommodation
  in big-city government, 547
  by Indians, 470
  Washington, Booker T., and, 610, 611

Acheson, Dean, 748, 755–756, 763, 841

Activism. *See also* Protest(s); Revolts and rebellions
  civil rights, 787–793
  consumer, 801
  feminist, 817–821
  gay and lesbian, 816
  Latino, 810–811
  Native American, 809–810
  presidential, 602
  by women, 512–513, 564–566
  youth, 811–816

ADA. *See* Americans with Disabilities Act

Addams, Jane, 604
  Hull House and, 583, 584, 584*(i),* 588
  woman suffrage and, 590
  World War I and, 628

Adding machine, 536

Adenauer, Konrad, 750*(b)*

Advanced Research Project Agency (ARPA), 902*(i)*

Advertising
  in 1920s, 651, 652–653*(b),* 660
  on television, 785

Aerospace industry, 781, 783

AFDC. *See* Aid to Families with Dependent Children

Affirmative action. *See also* African Americans
  Bakke case and, 863

Johnson, L. B., executive order for (1965), 806

  Nixon and, 796, 824
  for women, 818

Affluent society. *See* Prosperity; Wealth

Afghanistan, 909*(m)*
  Bush, G. W., and, 905, 908
  Soviets and, 871, 872, 885
  stabilization of, 913
  Taliban in, 908
  United States and, 883

AFL. *See* American Federation of Labor

Africa
  fascism in, 711
  mandate system in, 633
  Nixon and, 846
  Peace Corps workers in, 831*(i)*
  U.S. embassy bombings in, 901

African Americans. *See also* Africa; Civil rights; Civil rights movement; Freedmen; Race and racism; Race riots; Slaves and slavery
  in 1950s, 768–769, 779
  1968 Columbia University demonstrations and, 842–843
  in armed forces, 620, 621–622
  black codes and, 441–442
  as buffalo soldiers, 480
  in cities, 658
  civil rights and, 444, 755–756, 756*(i),* 787–793, 804–809
  communities of, 480, 640
  in Congress, 449
  as cowboys, 487–488
  discrimination against, 480, 610
  farmers' groups and, 556
  in Great Depression, 671, 672*(i),* 698
  Harlem Renaissance and, 658
  in higher education, 783
  Jim Crow laws and, 449–450, 509, 530, 610
  labor unions and, 539, 695*(b),* 696
  median income of, 899
  middle class of, 803
  migrations by, 530, 640, 641*(i),* 662*(m),* 779
  in military, 756
  New Deal and, 698–699, 699*(i)*

"New Negro" and, 646, 658

Nixon and, 861

Obama and, 888, 911

as officeholders, 897

People's Party and, 568

poverty of, 772

in Progressive Era, 584

protests by, 804–805, 806, 807–809

rock and roll and, 787

school integration and, 861–862

segregation and, 449, 457, 531, 660–661*(b),* 661*(i),* 781

sharecropping and, 450*(b),* 453

Social Security and, 698

in Vietnam War, 838–839

voting rights for, 509, 795–796, 805, 806, 807*(m)*

in West, 480

women and, 512, 534, 640, 699, 699*(i),* 780, 793

in World War I, 620, 621–622

in World War II, 718, 719*(i),* 726–727

after World War II, 755

African Methodist Episcopal Church, 440

Afrikaners. *See* Boers

Age. *See* Elderly

Agencies. *See* Government (U.S.); specific agencies

Agent Orange, 834, 835*(i),* 839, 854

Agnew, Spiro T., 844, 865

Agrarianism, transformation of, 490

Agribusiness, 489, 490
  bracero program and, 782

Agricultural Adjustment Act (AAA)
  first (1933), 685–686, 687*(t),* 688
  second (1938), 704

Agricultural Adjustment Administration (AAA), 690, 690*(i)*

Agricultural Marketing Act (1929), 668

Agriculture. *See also* Crops; Farms and farming
  commercial, 464, 482–483, 488, 489, 490
  free trade and, 903
  in Great Depression, 668
  immigrant labor in, 903
  income (1920–1940), 668*(f)*
  Japanese immigrants in, 482
  labor for, 663

Agriculture (*continued*)
  migrant workers in, 488, 670, 691
  in New Deal, 685–686, 690, 704
  plantation, 450(*b*)
  price supports for, 647
  sharecropping system of, 450(*b*), 453, 488, 670, 686, 690, 690(*i*)
  technology and, 489, 779, 779(*i*)
Agriculture Department, Farm Security Administration of, 704
Aguinaldo, Emilio, 579
AIDS (acquired immune deficiency syndrome), 878, 906
Aid to Families with Dependent Children (AFDC), 800, 898
AIM. *See* American Indian Movement
Air-conditioning, 781, 781(*i*)
Air force
  German, 714, 729, 734(*b*)
  in World War II, 729, 732
Airplanes, in World War II, 734(*b*)
Air pollution, 505(*i*), 823
  Clinton and, 896
  Reagan and, 875
Alabama, 459, 476. *See also* Montgomery; Selma
Alaska, 580(*m*)
  environmental preservation in, 869
  Indians of, 824
Albanians, ethnic, 900–901
Alcatraz, Indian seizure of, 809–810, 810(*i*)
Alcohol and alcoholism. *See also* Temperance
  consumption of, 565
  progressivism and, 586–587
  prohibition and, 614, 625, 653–654
  World War I and, 614, 625
Alexander II (Russia), 528(*b*)
Alfred E. Murrah Federal Building (Oklahoma City), explosion of, 897(*i*)
Algeciras, Spain, conference in, 599
Ali, Muhammad, 839
Alien Land Law (California, 1913), 609
Aliens. *See* Illegal immigrants
Alito, Samuel A., 907
Allen, Doris, 854
Allende, Salvador, 846
Alliance(s). *See also* specific alliances
  peacetime military, 749–750
  in World War I, 617, 618(*m*)
  in World War II, 716
Alliance Independent (newspaper), 557(*i*)
Allies (World War I), 617, 618(*m*), 619, 620, 622. *See also* World War I
  loans and, 619, 667
  at Paris Peace Conference, 632–634
  in Russia, 638(*b*)
Allies (World War II), 708, 721, 728. *See also* World War II
  Holocaust and, 728
  reasons for winning war, 734–735(*b*)
  second front and, 724
  war effort by, 732(*i*)
  weapons produced by, 722(*f*)
Allotment policy, 471, 474–475
Al Qaeda, 901, 909, 913
Altgeld, John Peter, 564
Amalgamated Association of Iron and Steel Workers, 539, 558, 560
Amalgamated Butchers and Meat Cutters, 695(*b*)
Amalgamated Clothing Workers, 696
Amendments to Constitution. *See also* specific amendments
  equal rights, 818

American Association of University Women, 755
American Bell (telephone company), 503
American Civil Liberties Union (ACLU), 639–640
American Communist Party. *See* Communist Party
American Enterprise Institute, 857
American Equal Rights Association, 445
American Expeditionary Force (AEF), 613, 621, 622, 623, 623(*m*)
American Federation of Labor (AFL), 537, 539, 553, 558, 560, 695(*b*). *See also* Labor unions; Strikes
  in Great Depression, 671, 696
  women workers and, 588, 589
  in World War I, 625
American GI Forum, 757, 757(*i*)
American Historical Association, 463
American Independent Party, 844
American Indian Movement (AIM), 810
American Indians. *See* Native Americans
Americanization
  immigrants and, 529
  of Vietnam War, 841
American Liberty League, 688, 697
American Medical Association, 656, 697, 755
American Psychiatric Association, gays classified by, 816
American Railway Union (ARU), Pullman strike and, 561, 562(*b*), 563(*b*), 564
American Recovery and Reinvestment Act (2009), 911
American Sugar Refining Company, 517
Americans with Disabilities Act (ADA, 1990), 889–890, 890(*b*)
American Telephone and Telegraph (AT&T), 503–504
American Tobacco Company, 593
American Woman Suffrage Association (AWSA), 565–566
Ames, Adelbert, 459
Amusement parks, 543, 544, 544(*i*), 550–551
Anarchism, 559–560, 592
  Sacco and Vanzetti trial and, 663, 664(*i*)
  unionism and, 539, 560
Anderson, John B., 873
Angel Island immigration station, 530
Anglo-Americans, in West, 480
Anglo-Zulu War (1879), 466(*b*)
Angola, 883, 885
Annexation, Hawai'i and, 570, 572(*b*), 573(*b*), 579, 580(*m*)
Anthony, Susan B.
  on "negro first" strategy, 447
  woman's suffrage movement and, 444(*i*), 445, 512, 566
Anthracite coal strike (1902), 593
Antiballistic Missile Treaty (1972), 883, 909
Anticommunism, 765
  crusade of, 760–761(*b*)
  Eisenhower and, 769–770
  of Nixon, 845
Antidiscrimination ordinance, for gays and lesbians, 816
Antifeminists, 820–821
Anti-German sentiment, during World War I, 628–629
Antigovernment sentiment, 897
Anti-immigrant sentiment, 447, 479, 481–482, 663
Antilynching legislation, 658, 704
Antin, Mary, 527

Antipoverty programs
  of Clinton, 896
  of Johnson, L. B., 799, 800
Antiradicalism, after World War I, 637–640, 638(*b*), 639(*b*), 663
Anti-Saloon League, 587
Anti-Semitism. *See also* Jews and Judaism; Nazi Germany
  atomic bomb and, 730–731(*b*)
  of Hitler, 680(*b*)
  in Nazi Germany, 710
  in 1930s, 691
  in Russia, 528(*b*)
Antisodomy laws, 882
Antitrust activities
  legislation, 502, 517, 605
  New Deal and, 687
  Roosevelt, T., and, 584, 593, 604
  Taft and, 592, 604, 606
  of Wilson, 605
Antiwar movement, in Vietnam War, 839–840, 840(*i*), 847, 850
Antonucci, Joseph, 531(*i*)
Apache Indians, 476
Apartheid, end in South Africa, 893
Apollo program, 830–831
Appeasement, before World War II, 712, 713
Appliances, in 1950s, 768
Apprenticeship, laws in black codes, 442
Arab-Israeli wars
  Six-Day War (1967), 846–847, 846(*m*)
  Yom Kippur War (1973), 847
Arab League, 894(*m*)
  2011 rebellions and, 913
Arab Spring (2011), 902(*i*), 913
Arab world. *See also* Arab-Israeli wars; Middle East; Palestine
  Eisenhower and, 775–776
  Iraq War (2003–) and, 894(*m*)
  Jews and, 633
  Nixon and, 846–847
Arafat, Yasir, 902
Arapaho Indians, 469, 472(*b*), 476
Arbenz, Jacobo, 774
Architecture, Chicago school of, 545
Arctic National Wildlife Refuge, 869
Aristide, Jean-Bertrand, 900
Arizona, 465, 476, 490
Arkansas, 436
  Clinton and, 899
  political killings in, 451(*b*)
  Redeemers in, 459
  school integration in, 790–791
Armed forces. *See* Military; Militia; specific battles and wars
Armed neutrality, 619
Armenian immigrants, 525, 526(*f*)
Armistice
  after Korean War, 764–765
  after World War I, 623
Arms and armaments. *See* Weapons
Arms race, 748–749, 832. *See also* Nuclear weapons
  Eisenhower and, 776–778
  freeze on, 882(*i*)
  Kennedy and, 831, 832
Armstrong, Louis, 752(*i*)
Army of the Republic of Vietnam. *See* ARVN
Arsenal of democracy, U.S. as, 714–715, 720
Art(s). *See also* Literature; Poets and poetry; specific writers and works
  in 1950s, 787
  federal funding of, 801
  in Harlem Renaissance, 658

Lost Generation and, 660–662
WPA and, 696
Arthur, Chester A., 514
Artisans, 533
ARVN (Army of the Republic of Vietnam), 774, 837, 839, 847
Aryans, Nazis on, 710, 730(b)
Asia
   immigrants from, 480–482, 525, 525(m), 530, 663, 903
   Japan and, 599, 715, 715(m)
   mandate system in, 633
   Open Door policy in, 573–574, 574(i), 598–599
   Spanish-American War and, 578, 578(m), 579
   trade with, 571, 573–574, 574(i), 598–599
Asians and Asian Americans
   in cabinet, 897
   citizenship and, 481, 482, 699, 759
   New Deal and, 699
   prejudice against, 717
   in Progressive Era, 530, 584, 609
   segregation of, 599
Aspirin Age, 647
Assassinations
   of Garfield, 514
   of Kennedy, J. F., 799
   of Kennedy, R. F., 843
   of King, Martin Luther, Jr., 809, 842(b)
   of Lincoln, 440
   of Long, Huey, 692
   of McKinley, 592
Assembly lines, 645, 646, 649
Assimilation
   immigrants and, 482, 529, 530
   of Indians, 467(b), 471–475, 699, 770–772
Aswan Dam, 775
Atlanta, race riot in, 610, 611
Atlanta Compromise, 610
Atlanta Constitution, 509
Atlantic Charter (1941), 715
Atlantic Ocean region, in World War II, 717, 721, 723
Atomic bomb. *See also* Arms race; Nuclear weapons
   Chinese, 855
   Nazi anti-Semitism and, 730–731(b)
   Soviet, 748–749
   in World War II, 708, 708(i), 729, 737–738, 737(i)
Audiotapes, in Watergate scandal, 864–865
Auschwitz, Poland, concentration camp in, 728
Australia, in World War II, 722, 734
Austria, 632
   Nazi Germany and, 712(m)
Austria-Hungary, World War I and, 617, 632
Automobiles and automobile industry
   in 1920s, 647, 649
   in 1950s, 779
   dating and, 657(b)
   energy crisis (1979) and, 868
   filling stations and, 649, 650(i)
   Ford and, 645–646
   interstate highway system and, 770, 771(m)
   Obama and, 911
   UAW strike in (1937), 696
Axis powers, 712(m), 716, 722(f), 725, 728.
   See also World War II

B-17 Flying Fortress (airplane), 729
B-29, 708

Babbitt (Lewis), 662
Baby boom, 785
"Back to Africa" movement, 658
Bad Heart Bull, Amos, 472(b), 472(i)
Baer, George, 593
Baker, Ella, 796(i), 804
Baker v. Carr (1963), 803
Bakke case, 863
Balance of power
   naval, 649
   Roosevelt, T., and, 599
   World War I and, 617, 633
Balch, Emily Greene, 628
Baldwin, Roger, 640, 901
Balkan region, 633
"Ballad of Pretty Boy Floyd, The," 671
Ballparks, 543
Baltimore and Ohio Railroad, 537
"Banana republics," 572
Bank(s) and banking. *See also* Federal Reserve Board; Great Depression; Panics
   credit to foreign customers, 667
   deregulation and, 705, 875
   failures of, 667, 683(f)
   farms and, 670
   gold standard and, 555
   in Great Depression, 668, 669
   housing segregation and, 660(b)
   interlocking directorships and, 505, 606
   Morgan and, 505, 595
   New Deal and, 682–683
   railroads and, 505
   securities, insurance, and, 898
   Wilson and, 606
Bankruptcies, of farmers (1920s), 647
Banks, Dennis, 810
Banky, Vilma, 656(i)
Bannock Shoshoni Indians, 479
Baptists, 440
Barbed wire, 487, 622
Barboncito (Navajo leader), 467
Barrios, in California, 480
Barrow plantation, in 1860 and 1881, 455(m)
Barry, Leonora, 539, 541(b)
Baruch, Bernard, 625
Baseball, 544, 659, 755
Bastogne, in World War II, 729
Bataan Death March, 722
Battle of Britain (1940), 714
Battle of the Atlantic, 721
Battle of the Bulge, 729
Battles. *See* specific battles and wars
Bay of Pigs invasion (1961), 829–830
"Bayonet Constitution" (Hawai'i), 572(b)
Bayonet rule, in South, 458, 459
Beals, Melba Patillo, 790
Beat generation, 787
Beautification, environmental, 801
Beaux Arts school, 548(b)
Begin, Menachem, 870
Beijing, Tiananmen Square demonstration in, 893
Belgium, in World War II, 713
Bell, Alexander Graham, 503–504
Belleau Wood, battle at, 622, 623(m)
Bends (medical condition), building of Brooklyn Bridge and, 521, 522, 522(i)
Bentley, Elizabeth, 759
Benton, Thomas Hart (artist), 693(i)
Berger, Victor, 639
Berkeley, California, free speech movement in, 813–814
Berkman, Alexander, 559

Berlin
   blockade and airlift in, 748, 749(i)
   Treaty of (1899), 573, 575(m)
   after World War II, 730, 748(m)
Berliner, Emile, 548(b)
Berlin Wall, 831, 893(i)
Bessemer, Henry, 500
Bethune, Mary McLeod, 699, 699(i)
"Big Bonanza," 479, 479(i)
Big business. *See also* Business; Economy
   New Dealers and, 682
   railroads as, 494–497, 505
   regulation of, 502, 517, 594–595
   Roosevelt, T., and, 593, 594, 595
"Big stick" foreign policy, of Roosevelt, Theodore, 597, 599(i), 600(b), 615
"Big Three" (World War II), 729–730
"Billion Dollar Congress," 516
Bill of Rights (U.S.). *See also* Amendments; Constitution (U.S.)
   states subject to, 803
Bimetallism system, 518
Bin Laden, Osama, 896, 901, 913
"Birds of passage" (immigrants), 527
Birmingham, Alabama, 509
   King campaign in, 805
Birth control
   movement for, 608–609, 608(i), 655–656
   pill for, 816, 816(i)
   sexual intercourse and (1920s), 657(b)
Birthrate. *See also* Baby boom
   in 1800s, 608
   after World War II, 754
Bisno, Abraham, 528–529(b), 529(i)
Bison (buffalo)
   Plains Indians and, 465
   slaughter of, 465, 469–470, 469(i)
Black Bottom, Detroit, 660(b)
Black codes, 441–442, 442(i), 443
Black Elk (Oglala holy man), 471
Black Hills, Indians and, 465, 470–471
Black Kettle (Cheyenne leader), 469
Blacklist
   of "Hollywood Ten," 761
   of union members, 560, 689(b)
Black Panther Party for Self-Defense, 809(i)
Black people. *See* Africa; African Americans; Slaves and slavery
Black power movement, 807, 808–809, 809(i)
Black Star Line, 658
Black suffrage. *See also* African Americans; Voting and voting rights
   Fifteenth Amendment and, 447
Black Thursday (October 24, 1929), 667
Black Tuesday (October 29, 1929), 667
Blaine, James G., 493(i), 513, 514–515, 516, 571, 572(b)
Blair, Francis P., Jr., 458(i)
Blitzkrieg ("lightning war"), 713
Block, Herbert Lawrence, 759(i)
Blockades
   of Berlin, 748
   of Cuba, 832
   in World War I, 617–618, 619
"Bloody Sunday" (Alabama), 805
Blue-collar workers, in 1950s, 780
Blue Eagle campaign (NRA), 687
Bly, Nellie, on Pullman strike, 562(b), 563(b)
Boarding schools, for Indians, 471–474
Board of Indian Commissioners, 473
Boat people, from Vietnam, 852(b)
Boers, in South Africa, 466(b)
Bolshevik Revolution, 638(b), 639(b)

Bolsheviks and Bolshevism
    withdrawal from World War I by, 620
    after World War I, 637, 638–639(b)
Bombs and bombings. See also Atomic bomb;
        Embassies; Nuclear weapons
    of Cambodia and Laos, 851
    domestic, after World War I, 637, 639(b)
    of England, 713–714
    at Haymarket Square, 542, 542(i)
    of Iraq, 895, 910
    of Vietnam, 833–834, 837, 841, 845, 847,
        851
    in World War II, 707–708, 729, 734(b)
Bonanza farms, 489
Bond, Julian, 865
Bonds, to finance railroads, 497
Bonfield, John ("Blackjack"), 542
Bonus Marchers, in Great Depression, 671,
        694
Bookbinders' union, 588
Books, Texas textbooks and, 860
Boom and bust cycles, 497
Bootblacks, 534
Booth, John Wilkes, 440
Bootlegging, in prohibition, 654
Borah, William, 635(i), 638(b)
Borrowing, in 1950s, 784
Bosch, Juan, 836, 836(i), 837
Bosnia, 900–901
Bosque Redondo Reservation (New Mexico),
        467
Bossism, 546, 547
Boston, 527
    police strike in, 636
Boston (ship), 572(b)
Boston Public Library, 545, 546, 546(i)
Bougainville campaign, 719(i)
Bow, Clara ("It Girl"), 658
Boxer Protocol (1901), 571
Boxer uprising (China), 548(b), 570
Boxing, 659
    Ali and, 839
Boycotts
    of college classes (1970), 848
    economic, of Soviet Union, 638(b)
    of grapes by farmworkers, 811
    Montgomery bus boycott, 792–793, 804
    of Pullman cars, 561, 562(b), 564
    of stores, 589
Boyer, LaNada, 810
Bozeman Trail, 470
Bracero program, 782, 783(i)
Brains Trust, in New Deal, 681, 682
Brandeis, Louis, 607
Bray, Rosemary, 801
"Breaker boys," 593, 594(i)
Brezhnev, Leonid, 871
Briand, Aristide, 649
Bridges. See Brooklyn Bridge
Bridges, Ruby, 790(b)
Briggs, Laura, 744
Brinksmanship strategy, 773
Britain. See also England (Britain)
    Battle of, 714
British Guiana, Venezuela and, 571
Brooke, Edward, 822(i)
Brooklyn Bridge, 521, 521(i), 522, 522(i),
        533, 545
Brooks, Gwendolyn, 755
Brotherhood of Sleeping Car Porters, 726
Brown, Oliver, 789–790
Browne, George ("Brownie"), 613–614,
        614(i), 620, 623, 643
Brown power, 811

Brownsville (Brooklyn, New York), birth
        control clinic in, 608–609, 608(i)
Brown v. Board of Education (1954),
        788–789(b), 789–790, 790(b), 803
Brunauer, Esther, 760
Bryan, William Jennings
    election of 1896 and, 568, 569, 569(i),
        569(m), 581
    election of 1900 and, 569(i)
    election of 1904 and, 594
    election of 1908, 569(i), 601
    Scopes trial and, 664–665
    as secretary of state, 615, 618
    on U.S expansionism, 579
Bryce, James, 547
Buchanan, Pat, 821, 906(m)
"Buckwheats," 524
Buddhists, in Vietnam, 774, 833
Budget. See Federal budget
Buffalo. See Bison (buffalo)
Buffalo, New York, 592
Buffalo soldiers, 480
Buffalo Telegraph, 515
Bulgaria
    in World War II, 734
    after World War II, 744
Bulge, Battle of the (1944–1945), 729
Bull Moose Party. See Progressive Party, of
        1912
"Bully pulpit," 592, 592(i)
Bunche, Ralph J., 755
Bundy, McGeorge, 834
Bureau of Corporations, 593
Bureau of Indian Affairs, 476
    Indian relocation and, 470
Bureau of Refugees, Freedmen, and
        Abandoned Lands. See Freedmen's
        Bureau
Burger, Warren E., 863
Burleson, Albert, 629
Burlington Mills, 689(b)
Burma, 722, 731
Burnham, Daniel, 547, 550
Bus boycott, in Montgomery, 792–793,
        804
Bush, George H. W., 905–910
    CIA and, 889
    economy and, 889
    election of 1988 and, 889
    election of 1992 and, 896
    foreign policy of, 891–896
    Iran-Contra and, 884
    new world order and, 900
    Persian Gulf War and, 895–896, 895(i)
    taxation and, 890–891
    as vice president, 873, 889
Bush, George W.
    economy and, 905, 911
    election of 2000 and, 905, 906, 906(m)
    election of 2004 and, 910
    foreign policy of, 905
    Hurricane Katrina and, 907–908
    Iraq War and, 888, 909–910
    on presidential powers, 909
    Supreme Court and, 907
    trade and, 902
    war on terror and, 912–913
Business. See also Big business; Corporations;
        Finance capitalism
    in 1920s, 646, 647–648, 667
    in 1990s, 899
    city bosses and, 546–547
    foreign policy and, 570, 572–573
    in Gilded Age, 504, 506–507, 519

    government and, 495, 500, 506(b), 508,
        513, 593
    Great Depression and, 667–668
    mechanization in, 533–534
    monopolies in, 502, 517
    in New Deal, 686–687, 687–688
    NRA codes and, 686–687
    regulation of trusts and, 502, 516, 554,
        592, 606
    Republicans and, 507, 513, 516
    telephones and, 494, 503–504, 548(b)
    trade barriers and, 902
    after World War I, 636, 647
Business organization
    horizontal integration, 502
    vertical integration, 501, 501(f)
Busing, school integration and, 861, 861(i),
        862
Butler, Nicholas Murray, 628
Buxton, Myron, 694–695(b)
Byrd, Harry F., election of 1960 and, 798(m)

CAFTA-DR. See Central American–
        Dominican Republic Free Trade
        Agreement
Caissons, 521, 522, 522(i)
California, 664, 676. See also Los Angeles
    ban on housing discrimination in, 806
    Chinese in, 481–482
    gold rush in, 477
    growth of, 781
    Hispanics in, 480
    manifest destiny and, 465
    Mexican Americans in, 488, 691
    Reagan as governor of, 873
    taxes in, 860, 860(i)
Californios, 480
Calley, William, 850
Cambodia
    immigrants from, 903
    Vietnam War and, 833, 847, 847(i), 849,
        851
Campaigns (political). See also Elections
    donations for, 866
    Hoover poster (1928), 666(i)
    pins in (1884), 493(i)
    Roosevelt, F. D., poster (1936), 675(i)
Camp David accords, 870
Canada
    immigrants from, 524, 525(m)
    NAFTA and, 902
Canals, Panama Canal, 597–598, 602(m)
Canal Zone. See Panama Canal Zone
Cannon, Joseph, 595
Cannon Textile Mills, 689(i)
Cantigny, battle at, 622, 623(m)
Cao, Anh Quang ("Joseph"), 852–853(b),
        853(i)
CAP. See Community Action Program
Cape Colony (Africa), 466(m)
Cape of Good Hope, 466(b)
Capitalism
    effort to "Christianize," 586
    finance, 504, 505–506
    in Gilded Age, 495
    industrial, 461
    New Dealers and, 682
    Roosevelt, F. D., and, 705
    welfare capitalism, 650
    after World War II, 752
Capone, Alphonse ("Big Al"), 654
Caribbean region
    immigrants from, 903
    people from, 810

Roosevelt, T., and, 597–598
U.S. involvement in, 616(m), 830(m)
Carkin, Theona, 485(b)
Carlisle Indian School, 473, 474(i)
Carmichael, Stokely, 796(i), 808
Carnegie, Andrew, 494, 495, 500(i)
and gospel of wealth, 508
Homestead strike and, 558, 559, 560
Morgan, J. P., and, 505
social Darwinism and, 506–507(b), 508
steel industry and, 500, 501, 501(f), 505, 509, 524, 535–536
Carpetbaggers, 433(i), 434, 448
Carson, Rachel, 822
Carter, James Earl ("Jimmy"), **Jr.,** 866–872
domestic policy of, 867–869
election of 1976 and, 866, 866(m)
energy and, 868–869
environment and, 869
foreign policy of, 869–872
human rights and, 869–870, 871
Carter, Rosalyn, 867(i)
Carter Doctrine, 871
Casablanca meeting (1943), 725
Cash-and-carry policy, 711
Cash register, 536
Caste system, New Negro and, 658
Castle & Cooke (sugar producers), 572(b)
Castro, Fidel, 774–775
Cuban refugees from, 776–777(b), 777(i)
Casualties
in Iraq War, 910
in Korean War, 765
Soviet, in World War II, 735(b)
in Vietnam War, 834, 839, 847
Catholicism. See also Missions and missionaries
on gay rights, 880(b)
of Smith, Alfred, 665
Catt, Carrie Chapman, 628, 630(b), 631(b)
Cattell, James McKeen, 628
Cattle. See Ranching
Cattle trails, 486
Census Bureau, racial categories on forms of, 904
Central America
Reagan and, 883
United Fruit in, 572
U.S. intervention in, 597–598, 602(m), 893–894
Central American–Dominican Republic Free Trade Agreement, 902
Centralia, Washington, IWW in, 638–639
Central Intelligence Agency (CIA)
creation of, 749(i), 751
Cuba and, 774–775, 829–830, 832
Middle East and, 775
Watergate and, 864
Central Pacific Railroad, 481, 483(i)
Central Park (New York City), 545
Central Powers (World War I), 618(m)
Century of Dishonor, A (Jackson), 474
Cession, of Indian land. See Land; Native Americans
Chamberlain, Neville, 712
Chamberlain, Wilt, 822(i)
Chamber of Commerce, 648, 688, 697
Chambers, Whittaker, 759
Chaplin, Charlie, 658–659
Chase, Salmon P., 440, 447
Château-Thierry, battle at, 622, 623(m)
Chavez, Cesar, 811, 811(i)
Checks and balances, on executive, 864
Chelmsford, (Lord), 466(b)

Cheney, Richard B.
Iraq War and, 909
Persian Gulf War and, 895
as vice president, 906
Cherokee Indians, 465
Cherokee strip, land rush in, 486
Cheyenne Indians, 467, 468–469, 470, 476
Chiang Kai-shek. See **Jiang Jieshi**
(Chiang Kai-shek)
Chicago
1968 Democratic National Convention in, 842(b), 843–844, 844(i)
African Americans in, 640, 641(i)
architecture in, 545
gangsters in (1920s), 654
Great Fire of 1871 in, 545
Haymarket bombing in, 529, 542–543, 542(i)
Hull House in, 583, 584, 584(i)
immigrants in, 527, 528(b), 529(b)
King, Martin Luther, Jr., in, 806
Pullman Strike in, 560–564, 561(i), 588
World's Columbian Exposition in, 463, 547–551, 549(i), 550(i)
Chicago Bears (football team), 659
Chicago Cloak Makers' Union, 529
Chicago's White City (Nichols), 550
Chicago Times, on Pullman strike, 562(b), 563(b)
Chicago Tribune
on 1948 election, 757
on Pullman strike, 562(b), 563(b), 564
Chicanos and Chicano movement, 811
Chickasaw Indians, 465
Chief Joseph. See Joseph (Nez Percé chief)
Child care, 820, 864
Child labor
in coal mines, 593, 594(i)
efforts to reform, 585, 607
Fair Labor Standards Act and, 704
Keating-Owen Act and, 607
in late 19th century, 533, 534, 535(i)
in textile mills, 509
Children
black codes, apprenticeship laws, and, 442
as Cuban refugees, 776–777(b), 777(i)
of freedmen, 453
Indian, 468, 469, 471–474, 474(i)
in poverty, 534
in textile mills, 509
working class, 534
Children's Bureau (Labor Department), 603–604
Child Support Enforcement Amendments Act, 877
Chile, 846(m)
Carter and, 869
China
atomic bomb of, 855
Boxer uprising in, 570, 571
Carter and, 871
civil war in, 752
communism in, 739, 759
dependence on, 906
Japan and, 633, 709, 711
Korean War and, 763, 763(i)
missionaries in, 571
Nationalists in, 752
Nixon and, 828, 845–846, 845(i)
Open Door policy in, 573–574, 574(i), 598–599
Tiananmen Square protests in, 893
World War II and, 729, 731, 739
Chinese Americans, in World War II, 718

Chinese Exclusion Act (1882, 1902), 482, 488, 530, 609, 640
Chinese immigrants
in California, 481–482
in cities, 530
on Comstock, 479
in mining, 481
railroads and, 481, 482(i)
restrictions on, 663
work of, 530
Chiricahua Apache Indians, 476
Chisholm, Shirley, 864
Chisholm Trail, 486
Chivington, John M., 468–469
Choctaw Indians, 465
Choice Not an Echo, A (Schlafly), 858
Christianity. See also Missions and missionaries
in China, 571
fundamentalist, 873
Christian Right, 858, 873
gays and, 882
sex education and, 862–863(b)
Chrysler, bailout of, 911
Churches. See also Religion
black, 440
Churchill, Winston, 638(b), 713–714. See also World War II
at Casablanca, 725
iron curtain speech of, 744, 745(m), 746–747(b)
at Teheran, 729
at Yalta, 729
Church of Jesus Christ of Latter-Day Saints. See Mormons
CIA. See Central Intelligence Agency
Cigarettes, 509, 652–653(b), 653(i). See also Tobacco and tobacco industry
CIO. See Congress of Industrial Organizations
Cisler, Lucinda, 820
Cities and towns. See also Rural areas; Urban areas
in 1920s, 662(m), 663
African American movement to, 779
automobiles and, 649
bosses (political) in, 546–547
decline of, 780–781
electric lights in, 545, 548(b)
in Gilded Age, 508, 519
in Great Depression, 704
immigrants in, 527, 528–533
Indian relocation to, 475
mass transit in, 531, 532
mining boomtowns, 478–480
movement to, 523, 527, 662(m)
neighborhoods in, 531
poor in, 584, 704
population in, 646
progressivism and, 590–592
public works in, 545, 546, 546(i)
race riots in 1960s, 807, 808(m)
rise of, 522, 523–533
world's fairs in, 548(b)
Citizens and citizenship
Asians and, 481, 482, 699
for Californios, 480
Fourteenth Amendment and, 444
for Japanese Americans, 759
for Mexicans, 782–783
Native Americans and, 474, 663
Supreme Court and, 457
Civil Defense Administration, 778
Civil disobedience, in Vietnam War, 850

Civilian Conservation Corps (CCC), 684, 684(i)
Civilian Conservation Corps Act (1933), 687(t)
Civil liberties
  Red scare and, 637, 638, 639–640
  World War I and, 614, 624, 628–629
Civil rights. See also Civil rights movement
  for African Americans, 444, 755–756, 756(i), 787–793, 804–809
  Eisenhower and, 770, 772, 790
  for gays and lesbians, 882
  Johnson, L. B, and, 800–801, 805–806
  Kennedy and, 799, 805
  for Latinos, 810–811
  for Native Americans, 809–810
  Reagan and, 876
  during Reconstruction, 449–450
  Rockwell's painting about, 790(b), 791(i)
  Supreme Court and, 803
  Truman and, 755
Civil Rights Act
  of 1866, 444
  of 1875, 457
  of 1957, 772, 791
  of 1960, 791
  of 1964, 799, 801, 806, 817, 824, 860
  of 1968, 801, 806
Civil Rights Commission, Reagan and, 876
Civil rights movement. See also King, Martin Luther, Jr.
  in 1950s, 787–793
  freedom rides and, 805(m)
  Kennedy, Robert F., and, 805
  protests during, 795–796, 795(i), 807–809
  Rockwell painting during, 790(b), 791(i)
Civil Rights Restoration Act (1988), 876
Civil service, 456
  reforms of, 513, 514, 514(i)
Civil Service Commission, 514
Civil war(s)
  in China, 752
  in Guatemala, 774
  in Mexico, 640
  in Rwanda, 900
  in Spain, 711
  in Syria, 913
  Vietnam War as, 827, 853–854
Civil Works Administration (CWA), 684
Claiborne, Liz, 875
Clamshell Alliance, 868
Classes, in Vietnam War military, 838–839
Classical liberalism, Gilded Age and, 584
Clayton Antitrust Act (1914), 606
Clean Air Act
  of 1970, 823
  of 1990, 889
Clean Water Act (1972), 823, 907
"Clear and present danger" test, 639
Clemenceau, Georges, 632
Clemens, Samuel Langhorne. See Twain, Mark
Clerical jobs, 780
  women in, 533, 534, 535(f), 536, 536(i)
Cleveland, Grover
  election of 1884 and, 493(i), 515, 516, 516(i), 516(m)
  election of 1888 and, 516
  election of 1892 and, 516–517, 568(m)
  election of 1896 and, 568
  gold standard and, 518, 519
  Hawai'i and, 570, 573
  on immigration restriction, 530
  Monroe Doctrine and, 571

Pullman strike and, 564
  tariff reform and, 516–517
Cleveland, Ohio, 530–531
  progressive government in, 590–591, 591(i)
Clinton, Hillary Rodham, 914(b), 914(i)
  election of 2008 and, 911
  as secretary of state, 915(b)
Clinton, William Jefferson ("Bill"), 573(i)
  cabinet of, 897
  caricatures of, 914–915(b), 914(i), 915(i)
  economy and, 896–897, 899
  election of 1992 and, 896
  election of 1996 and, 898
  foreign policy of, 900–905
  globalization and, 902–903
  impeachment of, 896, 898–899
  presidency of, 896–904
  right wing and, 897–898
Clodfelter, Mike, 838
Closed shops, 648
Clothing. See also Garment industry; Textiles and textile industry
  anti-Establishment, 814–815(b), 814(i), 815(i)
  of flappers, 655
  Lakota vest as, 463(i)
  WPA and, 696
Coal and coal industry
  child labor in, 593, 594(i)
  shortages of, 593
  strikes against, 593, 671, 671(m)
Coalitions
  in New Deal, 679, 679(m), 682
  of reformers, 565, 583, 589, 611
Cobb, Beth, 484(b)
Cochran, Elizabeth Jane. See Bly, Nellie
Cochrane, Charles, Jr., 881(b)
Cockran, Bourke, 579
Codes, NRA, 686–687, 688(b), 690
Cody, William F. ("Buffalo Bill"), 464, 464(i)
Cold War, 742, 743–745, 746–747(b). See also Korean War; Nuclear weapons; Soviet Union; Vietnam War
  beginning of, 639(b)
  end of, 885, 887, 891–892
  racial issues during, 755–756
  Reagan and, 882, 884–885
  U.S. intervention during, 830(m)
  Vietnam War and, 828
Cole, Jim, 695(b)
Colfax massacre, 458
Collapse of the Armed Forces, The, 850
Collective bargaining, 625
Collective security, 649, 749–750
College(s). See Universities and colleges
Collier, John, 699–700
Colombia, Panama Canal and, 597
Colonialism
  third world and, 524, 524(m)
  treatment of Sioux and Zulu and, 466–467(b)
  in West, 465
Colonies and colonization, after World War I, 633
Colorado, 465, 486, 490
  voting rights for women in, 566(i)
Color-blind hiring, 876
Color-blind laws, 449
Colored Farmers' Alliance, 556
Colt company, 548(b)
Columbia (female symbol of U.S.), 579(i)
Columbia University, protests at, 812–813(b), 842–843, 842(b)
Columbus, New Mexico, Villa raid on, 616

Comanche Indians, 465, 469, 470, 475
Comanchería, 470
Combines (farm machine), 489
Coming of Age in Mississippi (Moody), 804(i)
Comintern, 637
Commerce and Labor Department, 593
Commercial agriculture, 464, 482–483, 488, 489, 490
Commercial banks, 683
Commercialization, of leisure, 544
Commission on the Status of Women (UN), 817, 818(b)
Committee for Industrial Organization (CIO), 696
Committee on Civil Rights (1946). See President's Committee on Civil Rights (1946)
Committee on Fair Employment Practices (1941), 726
Committee on Public Information (CPI), 628
Commodity Credit Corporation, 686
Common economic market, in Western Europe, 892
Common laborers, 533
Commonwealth of Independent States, 893
Communication(s)
  telegraph and, 498, 499, 503
  telephone and, 503–504
Communism
  in Cambodia, 852
  in China, 739
  in Eastern Europe, 744, 748, 892–893
  in East Germany, 744
  Guatemala and, 774
  Johnson, L. B., and, 834–837
  in Laos, 852
  Nicaragua and, 869
  Nixon and, 764
  Popular Front of, 700–701
  Red scare after World War I and, 637–640
  Red scare of 1950s and, 759–762
  in Russia, 638(b)
  in Vietnam, 774, 852
  after World War I, 638–639(b)
  after World War II, 742
Communist Party, 638(b)
  Great Depression and, 671
  New Deal and, 691, 700–701, 705
  Truman and, 761–762
Community Action Program (CAP), 800
Compassionate conservatism, of Bush, G. W., 906–909
Competition
  Morgan and, 505
  in petroleum industry, 506
  in railroad industry, 499–500
Compromise of 1877, 460
Compulsory free labor, 437
Computers, 899
  foreign-born software developers and, 904
  Internet and, 902(i)
Comstock, Anthony, 608
Comstock, Henry, 478
Comstock Lode, 464, 477, 478–480, 479(i)
Concentration camps
  in Cuba, 575
  in Holocaust, 728
Condren, Don, 754–755
Coney Island, New York, 544, 544(i), 550–551
Confederate Congress, 443
Confederate States of America (Civil War South), war debts of, 441

Confiscation Act
of 1861, 437
of 1862, 437
Conger, Sarah, 571
Congress (U.S.). *See also* Elections
bipartisan cooperation in, 888
election of 1876 and, 460
ex-Confederates in, 443
presidential vetoes and, 443, 444
Reconstruction and, 443–444, 457
southern congressional delegations
(1865–1877), 449(f)
Supreme Court and, 876
wartime Reconstruction plan of, 436
Congressional Reconstruction, 444–447
Congress of Industrial Organizations (CIO),
695(b)
Congress of Racial Equality (CORE), 727,
792, 805
Conkling, Roscoe, 513
Conoco filling station, 650(i)
Conscientious objectors, in Vietnam War,
839
Consciousness-raising groups, women in,
817
Conservation. *See also* Environment
Hetch Hetchy Valley and, 600–601(b)
Roosevelt, T., and, 584, 595–596
Taft and, 603
Conservatives and conservatism, 859–865
Bush, G. W., and, 905–910
Clinton and, 897
in education, 862–863(b)
on Great Depression, 678
laissez-faire and, 508, 581
New Deal and, 700, 701–702, 703–704,
705
Nixon and, 821, 825, 858, 859–865
progressivism and, 607
Reagan and, 872–873
Republican "Old Guard" and, 594
Schlafly and, 857–858
Social Security and, 697
Consolidation, 483, 496, 501(f), 504, 505,
506
Constitution. *See also* Constitution (U.S.)
Cuban, 579
Reconstruction, in South, 441, 446,
448–449
Constitution (U.S.). *See also* Amendments;
Supreme Court (U.S.)
election of senators and, 558
strict construction of, 863
term *male* in, 445
Consumer goods
in 1950s, 784–785
production of (1921–1929), 651(f)
revolution in, 650
in World War II, 725–726
Consumers
in 1920s, 650–652, 667
in 1950s, 767, 768, 768(i), 784
activism by, 801
advertising and, 651, 652–653(b)
critique of, 787
passive, 651
prices and farm income (1865–1910), 555,
556(f)
women and, 655
after World War I, 636
after World War II, 754, 784–785
Consumption
by farm families, 685
inequality of wealth and, 667, 682

mass production and, 651
underconsumption and, 682
Container shipping, 887(i)
Containment policy, 742, 745–746
Eisenhower and, 772–778
Kennan and, 744–745
Korean War and, 764
Nixon and, 845–846
toward Vietnam, 773–774
Contraception. *See* Birth Control
Contract labor
Asian immigrants and, 530
freedmen and, 437
Contract with America, 897
Contras, in Nicaragua, 883
Cooke, Amos Starr, 572(b)
Coolidge, Calvin, 636, 647, 648, 666,
667
"Coolie labor," 530
Cooperatives, farmers', 556
Coral Sea, battle of (1942), 722
CORE. *See* Congress of Racial Equality
Corliss, Alonzo B., 450(b)
Cornish pumps, in mining, 479
Corporate consolidation, 504
Corporate liberalism, 595
Corporations. *See also* Business
bailouts of, 911
interlocking directorships and, 505, 606
legislation and, 502, 517, 605
pensions and, 697
Rockefeller and, 501–502
trade barriers and, 902
Corruption
in city government, 547
in Gilded Age, 500, 501–502
under Grant, 456(i), 513
under Harding, 648, 648(i)
prohibition and, 654
in southern Republican governments, 434,
451
in territorial governments, 490
Cost of living, in 1920s, 650
Cotton and cotton industry
sharecropping and, 453, 488
in Texas, 488
Cotton Club, 658, 659(i)
Coughlin, Charles, 691, 697
Council of Economic Advisers, 753–754
Counterculture, 816
Counterinsurgency strategy, in Vietnam,
832
Coups
against Diem, 834
in Dominican Republic, 836
in Haiti, 900
in Iran, 775, 775(i)
in Latin America, 835–836
Court(s). *See also* Supreme Court (U.S.)
disabled and, 890–891(b)
Court-packing plan, of Roosevelt, Franklin
D., 701
Covert operations, of CIA, 750–751
Cowboys, 486, 487–488
industrial, 490
Cox, Archibald, 864–865
Cox, James M., 642, 677
Coxey, Jacob S., 566
Coxey's army, 566–567, 567(i)
Craft unions, 539, 558
Crane, Stephen, 593
Crashes (financial). *See* Depressions
(financial); Panics; Recessions
Crater Lake National Park, 598(m)

Crazy Horse (Sioux chief), 471, 472(b),
472(i)
Credit, 667
farmers and, 555, 557, 607
installment buying, 651–652, 667
Obama and, 911
sex discrimination in, 821
sharecropping and, 453
Credit Mobilier scandal of 1872, 500,
513
Creditor, U.S. as, 649
Creek Indians, removal of, 465
Creel, George, 628
Crime and criminals
conservatives on, 860
in Great Depression, 670–671
during prohibition, 653, 654
Crimes against humanity
Milosevic and, 901
by Nazis, 728
Cripple Creek, Colorado, 479, 560
Croatia, 900–901
Crocker, Charles, 481, 482(i)
Crogman, William, 611
Croix de Guerre, 627(b)
Croly, Jane Cunningham (Jennie June),
512
Cronkite, Walter, 839, 841
Crook, George, 471, 476
Crop lien system, 453, 509, 555
subtreasury and, 557–558
Crops
markets for, 555
price decline for, 555
in West, 489
Cross-class alliance, 583, 589
"Cross of gold" speech, of Bryan, 568
Crow Dog, Mary, 810
Crow Indians, 475
Crusade for Justice (Wells), 511
Cuba. *See also* Cuban missile crisis
in 1930s, 710
Angola and, 885
Bay of Pigs invasion in, 829–830
Carter and, 869
Castro in, 774–775
immigrants from, 903
intervention in, 574, 575, 576, 577–578,
578(m)
Kennedy and, 829–830
Platt Amendment and, 579, 580(m)
revolution in (1895), 575, 576
revolution in (1959), 775
Spain and, 574, 575, 576, 578
Spanish-American War and, 548(b), 554,
574–579
United States and, 579
U.S. naval base in, 579
Cuban missile crisis, 832, 832(m), 833(i)
Cullen, Countee, 658
Cult(s)
of domesticity, 543, 565
in Waco, 897
Cultural revolution, by students, 815–816
Culture(s)
in 1920s, 658–660
of abundance, 784–787
African American, 658
consumer, 548–549(b), 650–652
mass, 544
national, 658
politics and, 508–513
television and, 785
U.S. representatives of, 752(i)

Currency. *See also* Money
    gold standard for, 518
    "In God We Trust" on, 785
    paper, 518
Curriculum
    sex education in public schools and,
        862–863(b)
    student-won reforms in, 815
Cushman, Belle, 536
Custer, George Armstrong, 466(b), 469,
        471, 472(b), 473(b)
"Custer's Last Stand," 471, 472–473(b),
        472(i), 473(i)
Czechoslovakia, 632
    Prague Spring in (1968), 842(b), 843(b),
        843(i)
    Sudetenland and, 712
    after World War II, 744, 748
Czolgosz, Leon, 592

Dakotas, female homesteaders in, 484–485(b)
Dakota Sioux, 470
Dakota territory, 490
Dams
    Hetch Hetchy valley and, 600–601(b),
        601(i)
    for hydroelectricity, 684–685, 685(m)
Dana, Charles, 500
Dance halls, 543
Darlington Agency (Indian Territory), 477(i)
Darrow, Clarence, 660(b), 664
Darwin, Charles, 506–507, 506(b), 664.
        See also Reform Darwinism; Social
        Darwinism
Davis, Henry Winter, 436
Davis, James J., 533
Davis, John W., 648
Dawes, Charles, 649
Dawes, Henry, 474
Dawes Allotment Act (1887), 474–475, 699,
        771
Dawes Plan, 649
Day care. *See* Child care
D Day, invasions on, 729, 734
Dean, John, 864
Death camps, Nazi, 708
Death penalty, 876
Death rate. *See* Mortality rate
Debs, Eugene V.
    election of 1912 and, 605, 606(m), 607
    Espionage Act and, 629
    as progressive, 605
    Pullman strike and, 561, 562(b), 564
    Socialist Party and, 607
Debt
    Bush, G. W., and, 906
    Confederate, 441
    farm, 453, 458, 509
    Reagan and, 875
    after World War I, 667
Defender (Chicago newspaper), 530
Defense. *See also* National security
    interstate highway system and, 770,
        771(m)
    in World War II, 717
Defense industry
    discrimination in, 725
    Eisenhower on, 778
Defense of Marriage Act (DOMA, 1996),
        897, 898
Defense spending
    in 1950s, 749, 781–782
    in 2005, 900(f)
    by Reagan, 883

by Soviets, 777
    after World War II, 754
Deficit. *See* Federal budget
Deficit spending, recession of 1937 and,
        702–703
Deforestation, logging and, 489(i)
Demilitarized zone, in Korea, 764
Demobilization
    after Civil War, 448
    after World War I, 636
Democracy, in South Africa, 893
Democratic National Convention
    of 1896, 568–569
    of 1948, 742(i)
    of 1960, 797
    of 1964, 796, 796n(i)
    of 1968, 842(b), 843–844, 844(i)
Democratic Party (Democrats), 635. *See also*
        Elections
    bossism and, 547
    Catholics and, 508
    challenge to New Deal, 692, 692(i)
    in Gilded Age, 518
    immigrants in, 508
    Jews and, 508
    Roosevelt coalition and, 679, 679(m), 682
    sectionalism and, 514
    South and, 449, 458–459, 508, 759
    splits in, 568
    vote buying by, 609–610
    Watergate break-in and, 864–865
    white supremacy and, 458–459, 609
Demonstration(s). *See* Protest(s); Revolts
        and rebellions
Dempsey, Jack, 659
Denby, Charles, 571
Denmark, 713
Dennis, John Q. A., 438(b)
Deportation
    of Mexican Americans, in Great
        Depression, 670, 699
    during Red scare, 638
Depressions (financial). *See also* Great
        Depression; Panics; Recessions
    in 1870s, 457, 497, 525–526, 533
    in 1890s, 464, 489, 518, 519, 525–526,
        533, 560, 566–569, 570
Deregulation
    of banking industry, 875
    Carter and, 868
    of financial institutions and 2008
        recession, 705
    Reagan and, 874–875
Desegregation. *See also* Segregation
    of armed services, 756
    Eisenhower and, 769
    Nixon and, 824
    of schools, 757, 788–789(b), 788–791,
        790(b), 824
Détente policy, 845–846, 866, 872
Detroit
    auto industry in, 649, 649(m)
    housing and segregation in (1920s),
        660–661(b)
    race riot in (1943), 727
    race riot in (1967), 807
Devaluation, of U.S. dollar, 821
Developing nations
    foreign aid to, 752
    United States and, 902–903
Dewey, George, 578(m)
Dewey, Thomas E., 727, 757
DeWitt, John, 710(b)
Díaz, Porfirio, 640

Dictatorships
    in Guatemala, 774
    of Hitler, 680–681(b)
    in Latin America, 710, 744
    in Nicaragua, 869
Diem, Ngo Dinh, 774, 833, 834
Dien Bien Phu, 774
Diet (food). *See* Food(s)
Dioxin, in Agent Orange, 835(i)
Diplomacy. *See also* Foreign policy
    dollar diplomacy and, 615
    private sector (1920s), 649
    of Wilson, 618–619
Direct election, of senators, 513, 558, 604
Directorships, interlocking, 505, 606
Direct primary, 604
Dirksen, Everett, 799
Disabled people
    ADA and, 889–890
    courts and, 890–891(b)
Disarmament. *See also* Arms race
    calls for, 883
    Reagan and, 884–885
    Washington Disarmament Conference
        and, 649
Discrimination. *See also* Civil rights; Civil
        rights movement; Integration; Race
        and racism; Segregation
    against African Americans, 441–442, 457,
        480, 620, 658, 660–661(b)
    in armed forces, 620, 756
    against Asians, 530, 599, 609
    black codes and, 441–442
    against Chinese immigrants, 480–482
    Civil Rights Act (1964) and, 799, 801
    against disabled, 889–890
    Grove City case and, 876
    against Hispanics, 480
    homosexuals and, 816, 879–880, 911
    in housing, 801, 806
    immigrants and, 525, 529
    in jury selection, 806
    Mexican Americans and, 480, 699, 756–757,
        782–783
    in public employment, 898
    during Reconstruction, 449–450
    reverse, 876
    women and, 670, 814, 817
    in women's clubs, 512
    during World War II, 718, 726–727
    after World War II, 755, 756
Disease
    AIDS and, 878
    Indians and, 466–467
    venereal, 586
    in World War I, 623
Disfranchisement. *See also* Voting and
        voting rights
    of African Americans, 698
    in Reconstruction South, 448
Disney World, 781
Dissent. *See also* Protest(s)
    in 1950s, 786–787
    in World War I, 624, 629, 639(b)
Dissenters, Holocaust and, 727–728
Dissidents, in Eastern Europe, 846
District of Columbia, minimum wage in,
        648
Diversity, in West, 464, 478, 480–482
Dixiecrats, 757
Dobson, James, 873
Doctors, foreign-born, 904
Dodge, Richard, 469(i)
"Dole" (money for needy), in Britain, 668

Dole, Robert, 898
Dollar (U.S.), gold standard and, 821
Dollar diplomacy (Taft), 604, 604(m), 615
"Domestic allotment plan" in New Deal, 686
Domesticity
    in 1950s, 785
    cult of, 543, 565
    women and, 543
Domestics (domestic servants). See also
        Servants
    black women as, 534, 543, 640
    New Deal and, 698
    women as, 534, 535(f), 543
Domestic violence, 821
Dominican Republic
    coup in, 836
    U.S. intervention in, 598, 604, 604(m),
        615, 834, 836, 836(i)
Dominis, Lydia Kamakaeha. See
        Liliuokalani
Domino theory, 774
Donnelly, Ignatius, 553, 567–568
Double standard, of sexual behavior, 657(b)
Double V campaign, 726–727, 805
"Doughboys," 613, 614(i), 620
Douglas, Aaron, 658, 742(i)
Douglas, Helen Gahagan, 741–742, 757
    containment and, 765
    election loss to Nixon, 742
    Fair Deal reforms and, 754
    "Hollywood Ten" and, 761
Douglas, Melvyn, 741
Douglass, Frederick, 445
Doves, in Vietnam War, 840
Downs, Frederick, 827–828, 838, 839, 853
Draft (military)
    Carter and, 871
    in Cold War, 749
    Kennedy and, 831
    in Vietnam War, 838, 851
    in World War I, 620, 621(i)
    in World War II, 718–719
Drift and Mastery (Lippmann), 590
Drought
    in Dust Bowl, 691
    on Great Plains (1880s-1890s), 486
Drugs (legal). See Prescription medication
Dubček, Alexander, 842
Du Bois, W. E. B., 511, 611, 620, 658
Dukakis, Michael, 889
Duke family, 509
Dulles, John Foster, 772, 774, 775(i)
Dunkirk, withdrawal from, 713
Du Pont, 593
Dupree, Jack, 450–451(b)
Durant, Thomas, 500
Dust Bowl, in Great Depression, 676, 691,
        691(m)
Dutch East Indies, 716, 722. See also East
        Indies
Duties. See also Taxation
Dynamic Sociology (Ward), 590

Earned Income Tax Credit (EITC), 896
Earth Day (1970), 822, 823(i)
East (U.S. region), immigrants in, 527
East Berlin, 748, 748(m)
Eastern Europe. See also Europe
    after communism, 900
    end of communism in, 892–893
    events in (1989–2002), 892(m)
    immigration from, 524, 525, 525(m), 663
    Soviet control of, 739
    after World War II, 729, 744, 745(m)

Eastern front
    in World War I, 620
    in World War II, 723, 724, 735(i)
Eastern Hemisphere, competition for trade
        in, 572–573
East Germany, 748(m). See also Germany
    end of communism in, 892
East Indies
    Dutch, 716, 722
    Japan and, 716
Ecology, of Great Plains, 469
Economic Opportunity Act (1964), 799, 800
Economic Recovery Tax Act (1981), 874
Economics
    Keynesian, 703
    supply-side, 874
    trickle-down, 668
Economy. See also Depressions; Globalization;
        Panics; Recessions; Tariffs; Trade
    in 1920s, 648, 667
    in 1930s, 710
    in 1950s, 779–781
    of 1980s, 875–876
    of 1990s, 899
    auto industry and, 649
    Bush, G. H. W., and, 889
    Carter and, 867–868
    Clinton and, 896–897, 899
    in Eisenhower years, 772
    in Gilded Age, 516–519
    global comparison of, 703(f)
    global regions of, 523, 524, 524(m)
    Kennedy and, 798
    Nixon and, 821–822
    Obama and, 911–912
    postwar boom in (1945–1970), 784(f)
    Reagan and, 873, 874–875
    in Reconstruction South, 450–451
    regulation of, 796
    underconsumption and, 682
    of West, 489–490
    World War I and, 617
    after World War I, 636
    World War II and, 717, 719–720, 725–726
    after World War II, 738–739, 743–744,
        748, 753–755
Edison, Thomas Alva, 503, 504
Education. See also Higher education; Schools
    Bush, G. W., and, 907
    ESEA and, 800
    free secondary, 545
    for Indians, 471–474, 474(i)
    Klan and black, 450(b)
    for Mexican American children, 757
    about sex, 860, 862–863, 863(i)
    in South, 449
Education Amendments Act (1972), Title
        IX of, 821, 876
EEOC. See Equal Employment Opportunity
        Commission
Efficiency, 590
Egypt
    Israel recognized by, 870
    rebellion in (2011), 913
    Six-Day War and, 846–847
    Suez crisis and, 775–776, 775(m)
    in World War II, 724
    Yom Kippur War and, 847
Eiffel, Alexandre-Gustav, 548(b)
Eighteenth Amendment, 625, 653
    repeal of, 654
Eight-hour workday, 539, 542, 543, 558, 560,
        604, 625, 636
Eighty-ninth Congress (1965–1966), 800

Einstein, Albert, 730–731(b), 731(i), 749
Eisenhower, Dwight D.
    civil rights and, 770, 772, 790
    containment policy and, 772–778
    desegregation and, 769, 790–791
    domestic policy of, 768, 779–783
    election of 1952 and, 764, 764(i)
    election of 1956 and, 772
    foreign policy of, 768, 772–778
    "middle way" of, 769–772
    on military-industrial complex, 778
    "Moderate Republicanism" of, 769–772
    television and, 786
    Vietnam and, 774, 828
    in World War II, 724, 729
Eisenhower Doctrine, 776
EITC. See Earned Income Tax Credit
Elderly
    Great Society and, 801–802
    prescription medication for, 907
    Social Security for, 697–698
Elections. See also Voting and voting rights
    of 1865, 443
    of 1866, 446
    of 1868, 433–434, 455–456, 456(m), 458(i)
    of 1872, 434, 456–457
    of 1874, 434, 457
    of 1876, 455, 459–460, 460(m)
    of 1880, 514
    of 1884, 483(i), 514–516, 515(i), 515(m)
    of 1888, 516
    of 1890, 516
    of 1892, 516–517, 568(m)
    of 1896, 554, 567–569, 569(i), 569(m)
    of 1900, 564, 592
    of 1904, 594
    of 1908, 601
    of 1910, 591, 603
    of 1912, 584, 604–606, 605(i), 606(m), 615
    of 1914, 607
    of 1916, 607, 619, 629
    of 1918, 629
    of 1920, 635, 642, 642(m), 647–648
    of 1924, 648
    of 1928, 665, 665(m)
    of 1932, 678–679, 679(m)
    of 1934, 692, 698
    of 1936, 682, 692, 701
    of 1938, 704
    of 1940, 682, 714
    of 1944, 682, 727
    of 1948, 757–758, 758(m)
    of 1950, 742
    of 1952, 764, 764(i), 785
    of 1956, 772
    of 1960, 785–786, 797, 798(m)
    of 1964, 800, 857, 859
    of 1968, 822(i), 839, 843–844, 843(b), 844
    of 1972, 864
    of 1976, 866, 866(m)
    of 1980, 872–873
    of 1984, 875
    of 1988, 889
    of 1992, 896
    of 1994, 897
    of 1996, 898
    of 2000, 905, 906, 906(m)
    of 2004, 910
    of 2006, 910
    of 2008, 911
    of 2012, 888, 912, 913(m)
    direct election of senators, 513, 558, 604
    electoral shift (1928–1932), 679(m)
    primary, 604

Electoral college, election of 1932 and, 679
Electoral commission, for 1876 election, 460
Electoral reforms, 558
Electric industry, 503
Electricity
    at Columbian Exposition, 548(b)
    dangers of, 504(i)
    hydroelectricity and, 595, 596, 603, 684–685, 685(m)
    in rural areas, 685, 686(i)
    in urban life, 504, 532
Electric streetcar, 531, 532(i)
Elementary and Secondary Education Act (ESEA, 1965), 800
Eleventh Amendment, 890(b)
Elkins Act (1903), 593, 594
Ellington, Duke, 659(i)
Ellis, Havelock, 657(b)
El Paso, 642(i)
El Salvador, 883(m)
    Carter and, 869
    uprising in, 883
Emancipation, whites and, 439
Embargo
    before World War II, 711
    in World War II, 716
Embassies, attacks on U.S., 872, 883, 901
Emergency Banking Act (1933), 683, 687(t)
Emergency Brigade, sit-down strike and, 697(i)
Emigration, from Europe (1870–1910), 525, 526(f)
Emissions controls, 823
Emmons, Glenn, 770
Empires
    Comanchería, 470
    Spanish, 579
    of United States, 464, 465–471, 477, 579, 580(m)
    after World War I, 632, 633
Employees, Reagan and, 874
Employment. See also Unemployment; Women
    in 1950s, 780
    in auto industry, 649
    black codes limitations on, 441–442
    discrimination in, 726, 806, 876
    of gays and lesbians, 816
    public, 898
    of women, 627, 655
    after World War I, 636, 636(i)
    in World War II, 719, 738
    after World War II, 753
Employment Act (1946), 753
Endangered Species Act (1973), 823
Energy
    Bush, G. W., and, 906
    Carter and, 867
    consumption of, 869(f)
    nuclear, 770
    resources of, 822
Energy crisis, 822
England (Britain). See also World War I (1914–1918); World War II (1939–1945)
    alliances of, 617
    immigrants from, 524, 525, 525(m), 526(f), 663
    Iraq War and, 910
    Nazi bombings of, 713–714
    Suez crisis and, 775–776
    Venezuelan-British Guiana borders and, 571, 598
    in World War I, 617, 619, 620, 624

in World War II, 713–714, 734
    Zulu subjugation and, 466–467(b)
Enola Gay (airplane), 708(i), 737(i)
Entertainment. See also Leisure
    in 1920s, 658–660
    commercialization of, 544, 544(i)
Environment. See also Air pollution
    Agent Orange and, 839
    Bush, G. W., and, 906–907
    globalization and, 902–903
    Johnson, L. B., and, 801
    Nixon and, 822–823
    Obama and, 912
    Reagan and, 874–875
    suburban growth and, 781
    in Sun Belt, 782
    water pollution and, 875
Environmental Protection Agency (EPA), 823, 875
Epidemics, Spanish influenza, 637, 637(i)
Equal Employment Opportunity Commission (EEOC), 811, 824, 891
Equality. See also Civil rights movement; Gender and gender issues; Slaves and slavery
    gender, 655
    World War II, 725
Equal Pay Act (1963), 817
Equal protection guarantee, 803, 898
Equal rights, for African Americans, 434
Equal Rights Amendment (ERA)
    of 1923, 655
    of 1972, 818, 818(b), 820, 876(m)
    reasons for failure, 878–879(b)
    Republican Party and, 873, 876–877
Ervin, Samuel J., 864–865, 878(b)
Escalation, of Vietnam War, 833, 837
Espionage. See Spies and spying
Espionage Act (1917), 629
Establishment, anti-Establishment clothing and, 814–815(b), 814(i), 815(i)
Estey Organ Company, 652(b), 652(i)
Ethiopia, Italian conquest of, 711
Ethnic Albanians, 900–901
Ethnic cleansing, of Comanche, 470
Ethnic groups. See also specific groups
    in cities, 531
    fighting by, 900–901, 901(i)
    in mining boomtowns, 478, 479
    politics and, 508
Eugenics, birth control and, 609, 656
Europe. See also World War I; World War II
    expatriates in, 661–662
    immigrants from, 524, 525(m), 526(f), 530
    Roosevelt, T., and, 598–599
    after World War I, 632–633, 634(m), 667
    after World War II, 745(m)
European Recovery Program. See Marshall Plan
European Union, 751(b)
Evangelicalism
    in 1950s, 785
    in 1970s, 873, 874(i)
Evans, Hiram Wesley, 664
Everett, Wesley, 638
Evers, Medgar, 755, 805
Evictions, AAA and, 690(i)
"Evil empire," Reagan on, 874(i), 882
Evolution, 590, 664
Exceptionalism, 463, 465
Executive Orders
    8802, 726
    9066, 717–718, 718(i)
    9835, 760

abortion rights and, 896
    desegregating armed services, 756
Exodusters, 488
Expansion and expansionism. See also Imperialism; Monroe Doctrine; Open door policy
    as foreign policy, 570
    Hawai'i and, 570, 573
    of Japan, 599
    missionaries and, 570–571
    Spanish-American War and, 577, 579, 579(i), 580(m)
    trade and, 570–571, 570(f)
    U.S. overseas through 1900, 579, 580(m)
Expatriates, in 1920s, 660–662
Expertise, 590
Exploration. See Space exploration
Exports
    expansion of (1870–1910) of, 570, 570(f)
    to Latin America, 710
    after World War I, 667
Expressionism, abstract, 787

Factionalism, 451, 513, 514
Factions. See Political parties
Factories
    assembly-line production in, 649
    workers and, 490, 696
    in World War II, 725
Fair Deal, 753–762
Fair Labor Standards Act (1938), 704
Fall, Albert, 648
Falwell, Jerry, 873, 878(b)
Families
    in 1950s, 784–785
    birth control movement and, 608
    farm, 685
    female-headed, 876
    of freedmen, 438(b), 440, 440(i), 453
    in Great Depression, 670, 675–676, 676(i)
    Native American, 471–472
    in World War II, 725–726
Family and Medical Leave Act (1993), 896
Family economy, 534
Family Research Council, 873
Farewell address
    of Eisenhower, 778
    of Reagan, 885
Farm Board, 668
Farm Credit Act (FCA, 1933), 686
Farmers' Alliance, 554, 555–556, 557(i)
Farms and farming. See also Agriculture; Rural areas; Tenant farmers
    in 1920s, 662–663, 667
    in 1950s, 779
    agrarian revolt in, 555
    commercial, 464, 482–483, 488, 489, 490
    cooperatives and, 556
    credit and, 555, 557, 607
    crop lien system and, 509
    debt of, 509
    electricity for, 685
    Grange and, 517
    in Great Depression, 668, 671, 683(f), 690
    income (1920–1940), 668(f)
    income decline and, 555, 556(f)
    labor for, 641, 663
    land for, 486
    mechanization of, 488
    Mexican American farm workers and, 811, 811(i)
    migratory labor and, 488, 675–676
    in New Deal, 685–686, 690, 690(i), 704
    railroads and, 486, 555

sharecropping and, 450(b), 453, 488, 670, 686, 690, 690(i)
in South, 458, 509
tenant, 488, 670
in West, 486, 488–490
Farm Security Administration (FSA, 1937), 704
Fascism, 678, 708. See also Mussolini, Benito; Nazi Germany
in Africa, 711
Hitler and, 680–681(b)
U.S. isolationism and, 711–712
Faubus, Orval, 790
Faulkner, William, 662
FBI. See Federal Bureau of Investigation
FCA. See Farm Credit Act
Federal assistance, Great Depression and, 670
Federal budget
deficit in, 875, 890–891, 896, 906, 912
Reagan and, 875
surplus in, 897
Federal Bureau of Investigation (FBI)
King, Martin Luther, Jr., and, 805, 866
Watergate and, 864
Federal Communications Commission, 786
Federal Deposit Insurance Corporation (FDIC), 683
Federal Emergency Relief Act (1933), 687(t)
Federal Emergency Relief Administration (FERA), 684
Federal government. See Government (U.S.)
Federal Republic of Germany. See West Germany
Federal Reserve Act (1913), 606
Federal Reserve Board, 606, 867, 899
Federal Trade Commission (FTC), 606, 648
Federal Writers Project, interviews about New Deal, 694–695(b)
Females. See Feminism and feminists; Women
Feminine Mystique, The (Friedan), 785
Feminism and feminists, 447, 656(b), 811, 817–819, 817–821. See also Women
in 1920s, 655
countermovement to, 819–821
Fifteenth Amendment and, 447
Nineteenth Amendment and, 655
transnational, 818–819(b), 819(i)
Fences, ranching and, 487, 488
Ferraro, Geraldine A., 875
Ferris wheel, 544(i), 548(b), 550
Fetterman, William, 470
Fifteenth Amendment, 434, 447
Filipinos. See also Philippines
as migrant workers, 488, 676
Films. See Movies
"Final Report on Removing the Wreck of Battleship *Maine* from the Harbor of Habana, Cuba," 576(b)
Finance capitalism, 504, 505–506
Finances. See also Economy
banking and, 875
Clinton and, 898
Eisenhower and, 779
Obama and, 912
Reagan and, 875
Financial Services Modernization Act (1999), 898
Fireside chats, of Roosevelt, Franklin D., 682(i), 683
First Amendment, Red Scare (1950s) and, 761, 762
First transcontinental railroad, 482

First World War. See World War I
Fitzgerald, F. Scott, 655, 662
"Five Cents a Spot" (Riis), 596(i), 597(b), 597(i)
Five Civilized Tribes, 465
Five-Power Naval Treaty (1922), 649
Flaming Youth, 647
Flappers, 655, 655(i), 657(b)
Flexible response program, 831
Flint, Michigan, sit-down strike at GM, 696, 697(i)
Florida
election of 1876 and, 460
election of 2000 and, 906
Indians in, 476
population in, 662(m)
Flowers, Andrew, 450(b)
Flu. See Spanish influenza epidemic
Folk music, 816
Food(s). See also Crops
at Columbian Exposition, 548(b)
inspection of, 595
in New Deal, 702(i), 704
in World War II, 734(b), 735(b)
Food Administration, in World War I, 625
Food stamp program, 803, 821
Football, 659
Ford, Betty, 865(i)
Ford, Gerald, 859, 865, 865(i), 866, 866(m)
Ford, Henry, 645–646, 649, 651, 660
Ford Motor Company, 645, 646
Foreclosures
on farms, 670, 671, 683(f), 686
in Great Depression, 670, 671, 683(f)
Foreign aid
to developing nations, 752
Marshall Plan and, 742, 743, 750–751(b)
to Middle East, 776
Truman Doctrine and, 748
after World War II, 746–748
Foreign policy. See also Cold War; Containment; Diplomacy
business and, 570, 572–573
isolationism and expansionism in, 570
Monroe Doctrine and, 571–572
after World War I, 649, 709–711
after World War II, 744, 752–753
Forest reserves, 596
Forrestal, James V., 744
Fortas, Abe, 799(i)
Fort Laramie
Treaty of (1851), 466
Treaty of (1868), 470, 471
Founding Fathers. See Constitution (U.S.)
"Four-Minute Men," 628
Fourteen Points, 631–632
Fourteenth Amendment, 434, 444, 457
Mexican American rights and, 783
ratification by southern states, 445, 446, 449
school segregation and, 790
voting rights and, 444–445, 803
France
1968 protests in, 842(b)
Morocco crisis and, 599
Ruhr occupation by, 649
Suez crisis and, 775–776
Universal Exposition in, 548(b)
Vietnam and, 774
World War I and, 617, 621–623, 623(m), 624
World War II and, 713, 729
Franchise. See Voting and voting rights
Franco, Francisco, 711

Franz Ferdinand (Archduke, Austria-Hungary), 617
Freedmen, 435, 436, 437(i), 454(i), 460–461
black codes and, 441–442, 442(i)
education and, 437(i), 440, 449, 452(i)
as Exodusters, 488
freedom and, 438–439(b), 438–440, 452–453
Klan and, 450(b)
labor code and, 437
land for, 437–438
marriage and, 438(b)
in Republican Party, 448
search for families by, 438(b), 440
sharecropping by, 450(b), 453
voting rights for, 436–437, 444, 446
Freedmen's Bureau, 437–438, 443, 444
Freedom(s). See also Rights
freedmen and, 438–439(b), 438–440
McCarthyism and, 762
Freedom Rides, 805, 805(m)
Freedom schools, for Mexican American children, 811
Free enterprise, Reagan and, 874–875
Free labor
immigrants and, 530
in postwar South, 437, 448
Free market, Supreme Court and, 648
Free silver, 516, 517–518, 558, 568
Free speech, 608, 639
"Free speech" movement, 813–814
Free trade, 902
Frémont, John C., 490
Freud, Sigmund, 657(b)
Frick, Henry Clay, 558, 559–560
Friedan, Betty, 785, 817
Frontier thesis (Turner), 463, 464, 491
FTC. See Federal Trade Commission
Fuel Administration, 625
Fuels. See also Energy; Oil and oil industry
alternative, 869
"chips" as, 486
resources of, 822
shortage of, 868–869, 868(i)
Führer, Hitler as, 681(b)
Fundamentalism
Christian, 873
Islamic, 872
Scopes trial and, 664–665
Fusco, Charles, 694(b)

Gabler, Mel and **Norma,** 860
Gabon, Peace Corps in, 831(i)
Al-Gaddafi, Muammar, 913
Gadsden Purchase (1853), 465
Gangster profiteering, after World War I, 647
Garcia, Héctor, 757(i)
Garfield, James A., 446, 456, 514
Garland, Hamlin, 550
Garment industry, 533–534, 534(i), 588, 588(i), 589
Garrison, William Lloyd, 460
Garvey, Marcus, 658
Gary, Martin, 458
Gas. See Poison gas
Gas mask, 613(i)
Gasoline. See Energy; Oil and oil industry
Gates, Bill, 875
Gates, Merrill, 473–474
GATT. See General Agreement on Tariffs and Trade
Gay Liberation Front, 816
Gay marriage, 898

Gays and lesbians. *See also* Homosexuals and homosexuality
  Clinton and, 897
  gay rights protests and (1960s), 816
  in military, 897, 911
  protecting rights of, 880–881(b)
  rights movement for, 877(i), 878–882
Gaza Strip, 847, 870, 902
Gender and gender issues. *See also* Men; Sex discrimination; Women
  new woman and, 654–657
  politics and, 509–512, 512(i)
  separate spheres and, 509, 543
  sexual integration in speakeasies and, 654
  voting rights and, 796
  women in colleges and, 783
Gender equality, 434
General Agreement on Tariffs and Trade (GATT), 902
General Electric, 504, 548(b), 904(b)
General Federation of Women's Clubs (GFWC), 512
General Managers Association, 561, 564
General Motors (GM), 767(i), 911
  sit-down strike against, 696, 697(i)
General strike, in Seattle, 636
Geneva accords (1954), 774, 774(m)
Geneva meeting (1955), 777
Genocide, Holocaust in World War II as, 728
Georgia, 441
  Klan in, 451(b)
  Redeemers in, 459
German Americans
  Pennsylvania Dutch as, 587
  World War I and, 628–629
Germany. *See also* East Germany; Nazi Germany; West Germany
  colonies of, 633
  immigrants from, 525, 525(m), 526(f)
  League condemnation of, 710
  Morocco crisis and, 599
  rearmament by, 680–681(b)
  reparations of, 632, 649
  revolt in, 623
  U-boats of, 618, 619, 623
  unification of, 617, 892
  Venezuela confrontation and, 571, 598
  war guilt assigned to, 632
  World War I and, 613–614, 617–619, 622, 623, 623(m), 624
  after World War I, 632, 633, 649, 709
  after World War II, 744
Geronimo (Apache shaman), 476
Gestapo (Nazi secret police), 680(b)
Ghettos
  in Detroit, 660(b)
  Harlem as, 658
Ghost Dance, 476–477, 477(i)
Gibbon, John, 471
GI Bill (1944), 727, 739, 754–755
Gideon v. Wainwright (1963), 803
GI Forum. *See* American GI Forum
Gilbert Islands, 732
Gilded Age
  cities in, 508, 519, 530–531
  classical liberalism and, 584
  consolidation in, 496, 501(f), 504, 505, 506
  corruption in, 500, 501–502
  depression of 1890s in, 518, 519
  economy during, 516–519
  free silver issue in, 516, 517–518
  gender, race, and politics in, 509–512, 512(i)

  industry during, 500–501, 509
  materialism of, 493, 548(b)
  New South during, 508–509
  politics in, 509–513, 512(i)
  presidency during, 516, 518–519
  presidential politics in, 513–516
  Republicans in, 498, 507, 508, 513–514
  social Darwinism and, 494, 506–507(b), 506–508
  Supreme Court during, 504, 506, 508, 517
  wealthy in, 497–498, 498–499(b), 532–533
  West in, 490–491, 495, 496, 496(m), 497
  women in, 498–499(b), 499(i), 503, 503(i), 510–511, 512–513, 512(i)
Gilded Age, The (Twain and Warner), 490–491, 493
Gilman, Charlotte Perkins, 656(b)
Gingrich, Newt, 897
Ginsberg, Allen, 787
Gish, Lillian, 629(i)
Glasnost, 884
Glass-Steagall Banking Act (1933), 683, 687(t), 898
Global comparison
  casualties of World War I, 624(f)
  European emigration (1870–1890), 525, 526(f)
  national populations and economies ca. 1938, 703(f)
Globalization, 887–888
  debates over, 902–903
  of terrorism, 908–909
  U.S. world role and, 900–905
Global markets, for western agriculture, 489
Global warming, 909
Glover, Cathleen, 897
God's Trombones (James Weldon Johnson), 658
Golan Heights, 847
Gold
  discoveries of, 478(m)
  Indians and discoveries of, 470–471
  U.S. reserves of, 518, 821
Goldman, Emma, 638
Goldmark, Josephine, 590
Gold rush (California), 477
Gold standard, 555
  election of 1896 and, 568
  vs. free silver, 517–518, 519, 568
Goldthorpe, Lucy, 484–485(b)
Goldwater, Barry M., 800, 822(i), 857, 859
Gompers, Samuel, 539, 542, 543, 636
Gonzales, Rodolfo ("Corky"), 811
Goode, G. Brown, 549(b)
Good neighbor policy, 710, 710(i)
"Goodwill mission," 599–600
Goodwin, Francis, 541(b)
"Goo goos" (good government proponents), 547
Gorbachev, Mikhail, 884–885, 884(i)
  end of Cold War and, 888, 891–892
Gordon, John B., 450(b)
Gore, Albert, Jr., 896, 906, 906(m)
Gospel of wealth, 508, 585
Gould, Jay, 494, 495, 496–497, 496(m), 497(i), 499, 556
Gould and Curry mine, 479
Government. *See also* Government (U.S.)
  business and, 495, 500, 506(b), 508, 513, 593
  centralized, 584
  city, 546, 547
  limited, 519, 605

  Reconstruction, in South, 448–452, 458
  shadow, 547
  territorial, 490
Government (U.S.). *See also* Constitution (U.S.); Federal budget
  activist, 705
  business and, 647–648
  Eisenhower and, 770
  Great Depression and, 668, 678
  Indians and, 771
  New Deal and, 681, 682, 684, 704–705
  Reagan and, 875, 885
  separation of powers in, 602
  support for labor organization, 696
Governors, territorial, 490
Gradualism policy, of Washington, Booker T., 611
Grady, Henry, 509
Graham, Billy, 785, 785(i)
Grand Alliance. *See* Allies (World War II)
Grand Canyon National Park, 598(m)
Grand Old Party (GOP), 605(i)
Grange, 517, 555
Grange, Harold ("Red"), 659
Grant, Ulysses S.
  corruption and, 456, 456(i), 513
  election of 1868 and, 455–456, 456(m), 458(i)
  election of 1872 and, 456–457
  peace policy for Indians, 470
  presidency of, 455–457
  Reconstruction and, 457
  tariffs and, 570(f)
Grape boycott, 811
Grapes of Wrath, The (Steinbeck), 691
Grassroots, movements for reform, 585–590, 591
Grassroots conservatism, 859–860
Great American Desert, farmers in, 486
Great Britain. *See* England (Britain)
Great Depression (1930s). *See also* New Deal; Roosevelt, Franklin Delano
  crash of 1929 and, 646, 667
  economy during, 668, 668(f), 669
  global productivity in, 703(f)
  Hoover and, 667–669, 673
  labor unions during, 671
  lifestyle in, 669–670, 675–676
  migrant labor during, 670, 675, 691
  recession during (1937–1938), 701, 702–703
  tariffs and, 667, 668
  welfare state and, 693–698
  working-class militancy in, 671–672
  World War II and, 738
"Great Die Up," 488
Great East River Bridge. *See* Brooklyn Bridge
Greater East Asia Co-Prosperity Sphere, 715–716
Great Plains. *See also* Plains Indians
  bison hunters in, 469–470, 469(i)
  drought in, 486
  dust storms in, 676, 691, 691(m)
  farming in, 486
  Indians of, 465–471
Great Railroad Strike (1877), 537–539, 537(m), 538(i), 560
Great Sioux Uprising (1862), 470
Great Society
  assessment of, 800–803
  legislation of (1964–1968), 802(t)
  Nixon and, 859
  policymaking for, 796, 800–801
  reforms of (1964–1968), 799–801
Great Trek, 466(b)

"Great War." *See* World War I
Great White Fleet, 599–600
Greece, 633
  after World War II, 742, 747–748
Greeley, Horace, 456–457, 523
Green, William, 671
Greenback Labor Party, 518, 518(i), 555
Greenbacks (paper money), 518
Green Berets, 832
Greenfield Village, 646
Greensboro, North Carolina, Woolworth
  sit-ins and, 804
Grenada, invasion of, 883
Grey, Edward, 617
Griffith, D. W., 629(i)
Grinnell, Julius S., 543
Gross domestic product, global comparison
  c. 1938, 703(f)
Gross national product (GNP)
  in 1937, 702
  in 1950s, 784, 784(f), 915
Grove City v. Bell (1984), 876
Guadalupe Hidalgo, Treaty of (1848), 480
Guam, 579, 579(i), 580(m), 722
Guantánamo, Cuba, U.S. base at, 579, 909
Guatemala, 572, 710, 774
Guerrilla warfare
  by Apaches, 496
  with Filipino nationalists, 574
  by Ku Klux Klan, 450(b)
  in Vietnam, 774, 832, 833–834, 853–854
Guevara, Ernesto ("Che"), 842
Guiteau, Charles, 514
Gulf of Tonkin Resolution (1964), 835
Gulf War. *See* Persian Gulf War
Gun control, 896, 907
Guthrie, Woody, 670–671, 700
Gypsies, Holocaust and, 727–728

Haiti
  coup in, 900
  intervention in, 615, 710
Halvorsen, Gail S., 749(i)
Hamer, Fannie Lou, 795–796, 796(i), 805
Hamilton, Alice, lead poisoning crusade
  and, 586–587(b), 587(i)
Hamilton, Grant, 575(i)
Hampton Institute (Indian boarding school),
  471
Hancock, Winfield Scott, 514
Haney-López, Ian, 783
Hanna, Mark, 569, 576–577, 592
Hanoi. *See* North Vietnam; Vietnam; Vietnam
  War
Haole/hapa haole, in Hawai'i, 572(b)
Harding, Warren Gamaliel, 642, 642(m),
  647, 666
Harlan County coal strike, 671, 671(m)
Harlem, migration to, 640, 658
Harlem Renaissance, 658
Harper's Weekly, 445(i), 454(i), 469(i)
Harrington, Michael, 798
Harris, Frank, 522
Harrison, Benjamin, 476, 516, 568(m),
  600
Harrison, Carter, 542
Harrison, William Henry, 516
Harrows, 489
Hawai'i. *See also* Pearl Harbor
  annexation and, 570, 572(b), 573(b), 579,
    580(m)
  Japanese Americans in, 717
  regime change in, 570, 572–573(b), 573(i)
  sugar industry in, 570, 572(b)

Hawks, in Vietnam War, 840
Hawley-Smoot tariff (1930), 668
Hay, John, 573–574, 598
Hay, Mary Garrett, 630(b)
Hayes, Rutherford B.
  election of 1876 and, 459–460, 460(m)
  Great Railroad Strike and, 538, 539
  presidency of, 513–514
Haymarket bombing, 537, 542–543, 542(i)
Haymarket martyrs, 529
Haywood, William Dudley ("Big Bill"),
  607–608
Head Start, 799
Health, Education, and Welfare, Department
  of, 770
Health and health care
  Clinton and, 897
  for gays and lesbians, 898
  Johnson, L. B., and, 800
  Obama and, 911–912, 912(i)
Health insurance, national, 770, 867, 888,
  897
Hearst, William Randolph, 575, 576–577(b)
Hearts of the World (film), 629(i)
Helicopters, in Vietnam War, 837(i)
Helsinki accords (1975), 846
Hemingway, Ernest, 661–662
Hendricks, Thomas A., 457
Henry Street settlement, 585
Hepburn Act (1906), 594
Herbicide, Agent Orange as, 834, 835(i)
Hernandez, Aileen, 817
Hernandez v. Texas (1954), 783
Hetch Hetchy Valley, 600–601(b), 601(i)
Hezbollah, 883
Higher education. *See also* Universities and
    colleges
  democratization of, 783
  GI Bill and, 754
  women in, 817, 820
Higher Education Act (1965), 800
Highways. *See* Roads and highways
Hill, Anita, 891
Hillman, Sidney, 696
Hippies, 814–815(b), 814(i), 815–816, 815(i)
Hirohito (Japan), 716
Hiroshima, bombing of, 708, 708(i), 729,
    731(b), 737(i), 738
Hispanics and Hispanic Americans. *See also*
    Latinos
  New Deal and, 699
  use of term, 810
  in West, 480
"History of the Standard Oil Company"
    (Tarbell), 502–503, 503(i)
Hitler, Adolf, 709, 712(m). *See also* Nazi
    Germany
  anti-Semitism of, 680(b), 710, 730(b)
  fascist dictatorship of, 680–681(b), 705
Hoarding, 593
Hobos, in Great Depression, 669–670, 669(i)
Ho Chi Minh, 773–774, 832, 833
Ho Chi Minh Trail, 833
Hodel, Donald, 601(b)
Holding companies, 502, 517
"Hollywood Ten," 761
Holmes, Oliver Wendell (poet), 596(b)
Holmes, Oliver Wendell (Supreme Court
    Justice), 639
Holocaust, 727–728, 727(m), 753. *See also*
    Nazi Germany
Home front
  in World War I, 624–630
  in World War II, 725–728

Homeland Security, Department of, 909
Homelessness, in Great Depression, 669–670,
    669(i)
Homer, Winslow, 454(b), 454(i)
Home rule, for South, 456, 458
Homestead Act (1862), 482, 484(b)
Homesteaders, 483–486
  women as, 483(i), 484–485(b), 485–486
Homestead steelworks, strike at, 558–560
Homosexuals and homosexuality. *See also*
    Gays and lesbians
  AIDS and, 878
  attitudes toward, 897–898
  Holocaust and, 727–728
  in military, 897, 911
  Red Scare and, 761
  in World War II armed forces, 719
Honduras, 572
Hoover, Herbert
  Bonus Marchers and, 671
  crash of 1929 and, 667
  election of 1928 and, 665, 665(m)
  election of 1932 and, 678–679, 679(m)
  as Food Administration head, 625, 666
  in Great Depression, 667–669, 673
  on New Deal, 701–702
  on prohibition, 654
  as Secretary of Commerce, 647, 648, 666
Hoovervilles, 670
Horizontal integration, 502
Horowitz, Carl F., 881(b)
Horse car, 531
Hostages
  in Iran, 872, 872(i)
  in Lebanon, 884
Hotchkiss rapid-fire guns, 477
House of Representatives, 434, 457. *See also*
    Impeachment
House Un-American Activities Committee
    (HUAC), 761, 764
Housing
  in 1950s, 780–781, 780(i)
  in California, 783
  discrimination in, 801, 806
  federal government and urban, 704
  of freedmen, 453
  on plains, 484–485, 486
  in Pullman, 560–561
  in rural areas, 663
  segregation in, 660–661(b), 661(i)
  slums and, 758
  sod houses, 483(i), 484, 486
  working class, 560–561
Howard University, African Americans
    students at, 814–815
Howe, Eleanor, 860
How the Other Half Lives (Riis), 531, 532,
    596(b), 597(b)
Hue, Vietnam, battle for, 841(i)
Huerta, Dolores, 811, 811(i)
Huerta, Victoriano, 615–616
Hughes, Charles Evans, 619, 649
Hughes, Langston, 658
Hull House, 583, 584, 584(i), 586(b), 587(i),
    588
Human rights, Carter and, 869–870, 871
Humphrey, Hubert H., 831, 844
Hundred Days, 693
Hungary, 632
  immigrants from, 524, 526(f)
  in NATO, 892
  revolt in (1956), 773
  in World War II, 734
  after World War II, 744

Hunger
  in Great Depression, 669
  on reservations, 467
  during World War II, 726
Hurricane Katrina, 907–908, 907(i)
Hurston, Zora Neale, 658
Hussein (Jordan), 902
Hussein, Saddam, 894–895
  arms inspections and, 895, 901
  Iraq War and, 909–910
  in Persian Gulf War, 895
Hydroelectricity, 595, 596, 603
  New Deal programs for, 684–685,
    685(m)
Hydrogen bomb, 749

ICBMs. See Intercontinental ballistic
    missiles
Idaho, 490, 691
  voting rights for women in, 566(i)
"I Have a Dream" speech (King), 805
Illegal immigrants, 782, 903–904
Illinois, 586(b), 664
  ERA in, 878, 879(i)
Illiteracy, 449
Illness. See Disease
Immigrants and immigration, 646. See also
    Migration; Slaves and slavery
  anti-immigrant sentiment and, 908–909
  Asian, 481–482, 599, 903
  in cities, 527, 528–533, 547, 583, 584
  as domestic servants, 543
  employment of, 522, 525–526
  European, 525, 525(m), 526(f), 530
  German, 525
  illegal, 903–904
  impact to 1910, 525, 525(m)
  Japanese, 599
  of Jews from Europe, 525
  labor unions and, 696
  Mexican, 640–642, 642(i), 782
  as migratory workers, 488
  to North America, 525, 525(m)
  poverty of, 531
  quotas on, 663
  racism and, 481–482, 525, 530, 903–904
  restrictions on, 530, 663
  rural views of, 663
  Truman and, 759
  U.S. policy toward, 903–904
  in western mining boom towns, 478–479
Immigration and Nationality Act (1965),
    801, 903
Impeachment
  of Clinton, 896, 898–899
  of Johnson, Andrew, 444, 446–447, 899
  of Nixon, 865
Imperialism
  Japanese, 715(m)
  mandate system and, 633
  Sioux, Zulu, and, 466–467(b)
  by United States, 836
  in West, 465
Imperial presidency, 864
Imports
  expansion in 1870–1910 of, 570(f)
  tariffs and, 570(f)
Inauguration
  of Hoover (1929), 665
  of Kennedy, 798
  of Roosevelt, F. D. (1933), 680, 683
  of Roosevelt, F. D. (1937), 701
  of Roosevelt, T., 476
Incandescent light bulb, 504

Income
  in 1920s, 667
  inequality of, 899(f), 900(f), 912
  national, 669
  women in workforce and, 725
Income tax, 604, 606, 860(i)
Independence, after World War II, 752
Independent magazine, 533, 538
India
  British withdrawal from, 752
  nuclear test ban treaty and, 893
  outsourcing to, 904(b)
Indian(s). See Native Americans
Indian Citizenship Act (1924), 663
Indian Claims Commission (1946), 771
Indian policy. See also Native Americans
  allotment as, 471, 474–475
  assimilation as, 467(b), 471–475
  peace policy as, 470
  removal as, 465, 467
  reservations and, 464, 465–469, 467–468,
    468(m), 470, 475
Indian Relocation Program (1948), 771
Indian Reorganization Act (1934), 699, 700
Indian Rights Association, 474
Indian Territory, 475(i), 486
Indian wars, in West, 464, 465, 470, 471, 476
Indigenous people. See Native Americans
Individualism
  Indians and, 474
  after World War I, 647
Indochina, 715
Indonesia. See Dutch East Indies
Industrial capitalism, 461
Industrial core (global economic region),
    523, 524, 524(m)
Industrial cowboys, 490
Industrial hygiene, 587
Industrialism
  urban, 564, 583
  in West, 489–490
Industrial Workers of the World (IWW),
    607–608, 636, 637
Industry
  in 1920s, 648, 649–650
  in 1980s, 875
  buffalo slaughter and, 469
  in Gilded Age, 500–501, 509
  New Deal and, 686–687
  in South, 509
  technology and, 779
  worker safety in, 586–587(b)
  in World War I, 625, 640
  in World War II, 725, 734(b), 735(b)
  after World War II, 784
Inequality. See also Equality
  economic, 899(f)
  social Darwinism and, 506–508
  wealth and, 667, 682
Inflation. See also Stagflation
  in 1980s, 875
  Carter and, 867
  Clinton and, 899
  Nixon and, 821
  after World War I, 636
Influenza. See Spanish influenza epidemic
Infrastructure, WPA jobs and, 696
"In God We Trust," on currency, 785
In His Steps (Sheldon), 587
Injunctions, against labor unions, 564, 607
Installment buying, 651–652, 667
Insurance
  national health, 770, 867, 888, 897
  for prescription drugs, 907

Integration. See also Military; Segregation
  busing and, 861(i)
  Eisenhower and, 790, 791
  of public schools, 789–791, 861
  after World War II, 755
Intellectual thought. See also Education;
    Literature
  criticism of American culture, 662
Intercontinental ballistic missiles (ICBMs),
    777, 778
Intermediate-range nuclear forces (INF)
    agreement (1987), 885
International Criminal Court, 909
Internationalism
  of Roosevelt, F.D., 709
  of Wilson, 614, 648
International Monetary Fund, 903
International Women's Year (1975), 818(b),
    819(i)
Internet, 902(i)
Internment camps, 716, 717–718, 718(i),
    720–721(b)
Interstate Commerce Act (1887), 517
Interstate Commerce Commission (ICC),
    517, 594–595
Interstate Highway and Defense System
    Act (1956), 770, 771(m)
"In the Depths of a Coal Mine" (Crane),
    593
Inventions and inventors. See also Electricity
  from 1865–1899, 503
  telegraph and, 498, 499, 503
  telephone and, 503–504
Investment(s), from China, 906
Investment banks, 683
Iran. See also Iran hostage crisis
  Bush, G. W., and, 910
  Carter and, 869, 871–872
  CIA and, 775
  Obama and, 913
  oil in, 744
  revolution in (1979), 868(i)
  Shah in, 775, 775(i), 846
  after World War II, 744
Iran-Contra scandal, Reagan and, 883–884
Iran hostage crisis, 872, 872(i), 873
Iran-Iraq war, 894
Iraq, 633, 909(m). See also Iraq War
    (2003–2011)
  Bush, G. W., and, 905, 909–910
  Clinton and, 901
  Iran-Iraq war and, 895
  Persian Gulf War and, 895
  U.S. air strikes against, 901–902
Iraq War (2003–2011), 888, 894(m), 905,
    909–910
Ireland, immigrants from, 478, 479, 525,
    525(m), 527, 533
Irish Americans, 515, 587
Iron and iron industry, 501(f), 509, 533
Iron curtain, 744, 745(m), 746–747(b). See
    also Soviet Union
Irreconcilables, in Congress, 635
Isaacs, Norma, 877(i)
Isandhlwana, Battle of, 466–467(b)
Islam. See also Muslims
  fundamentalists in, 872
Islamic terrorists, 901
Island-hopping campaign, in World War II,
    731, 736(m)
Isolationism
  in 1920s, 649
  in 1930s, 709–711
  foreign policy and, 560

Israel
in 1948, 753, 753(m)
Clinton and, 902
Egypt and, 870
Eisenhower and, 775
Six-Day War and (1967), 846–847, 846(m)
terrorism against, 883
Yom Kippur War and (1973), 847
Italian Americans, 587
Italy. See also Mussolini, Benito
CIA and, 751
immigrants from, 525, 525(m), 526(f), 527, 527(i), 533
unification of, 617
in World War I, 617
after World War I, 617, 632, 709
in World War II, 725, 734
Iwo Jima, battle of, 732
IWW. See Industrial Workers of the World

Jackson, Helen Hunt, 474
Jackson, Jesse, 889
Jackson State College, killings at, 848
Japan
aggression through 1941, 715(m)
atomic bombing of, 708, 708(i), 737–738, 737(i)
China and, 573
immigrants from, 482, 488, 530, 609, 663
League condemnation of, 710
Manchuria and, 599, 709, 711, 715(m)
Pearl Harbor attack by, 707, 715–716, 716(m)
Roosevelt, T., and, 599
Smyrna, Tennessee, plant of, 905(b)
Vietnam and, 774
in World War I, 617
after World War I, 633, 709
in World War II, 722–723, 722(f)
World War II defeat of, 729, 731–738
after World War II, 739, 753
Japanese Americans
citizenship for, 759
discrimination against, 699
internment of, 716, 717–718, 718(i), 718(m), 720–721(b)
World War II and, 716, 717–718, 718(i), 720–721(b)
Jarvis, Howard, 860(i)
Jazz, 658, 659(i)
Jazz Age, 647
Jefferson, Thomas, 490
Jericho, 902
Jerusalem, 902
Jesuits, in California, 481(i)
Jews and Judaism, 633. See also Anti-Semitism
Einstein, atomic bomb, and, 730–731(b)
Holocaust and, 727–728, 728(i)
as immigrants, 525, 527, 528–529(b), 529(i)
Nazi Germany and, 680(b), 710
pogroms against, 527, 528–529(b), 529(i)
in United States, 691
after World War II, 753
Jiang Jieshi (Chiang Kai-Shek), 711, 729, 731, 752
Jim Crow laws, 449–450, 509, 530, 610
Job Corps, 799
Jobs. See also Employment; Unemployment
Carter and, 867–868
Jobs, Steven, 875
Johns, Barbara, 790
Johnson, Andrew, 436(i), 455
assumption of presidency, 440–441

black codes and, 442
Fourteenth Amendment and, 445
Freedmen's Bureau bill and, 443, 444
impeachment of, 444, 446–447, 899
reconstruction plan of, 441
Johnson, Dorothy, 726(i)
Johnson, Eastman, 437(i)
Johnson, Hiram, 591, 592, 600(b), 604, 609, 635(i)
Johnson, James Weldon, 658
Johnson, Lyndon B.
assumption of presidency, 799
civil rights and, 800–801, 805–806
education and, 800
election of 1960 and, 797
election of 1964 and, 800, 859
environment and, 801
equal rights and, 801
Great Society and, 800–803
Latin America and, 835–837
Mexican Americans and, 811
political skill of, 799, 799(i)
Vietnam War and, 801, 828, 834–835, 837, 855
War on Poverty of, 799, 800
Warren commission and, 799
Johnson, Martha, 613, 614
Johnson, Thomas Loftin (Tom), 590–591, 591(i)
Johnson-Reed Act (1924), 663
Joint Chiefs of Staff, MacArthur removal and, 764
Jones, Beverly, 890(b), 891(i)
Jones, William ("Billy"), 535
Jordan
Eisenhower aid to, 776
Six-Day War and, 847
Joseph, Chief (Nez Percé), 475–476, 475(i)
Journalism. See also Newspapers
muckraking in, 567, 595
photojournalism, 595, 596–597(b), 596(i), 597(i)
yellow, 575, 575(i)
Judaism. See Jews and Judaism
Judge (magazine), 575(i)
Judiciary. See also Supreme Court
Reagan and, 876
Jungle, The (Sinclair), 595
Juries, discrimination in, 806
Justice Department, 640
conservatives appointed to, 876

Kamikaze pilots, 732
Kanawha County, West Virginia, sex education in, 862–863(b)
Kansas, 480, 486, 488, 555, 557(i), 664
Katrina, Hurricane, 907–908, 907(i)
Kearney, Denis, 481
Keating-Owen Act (1916), 607
Kelley, Florence, 590
Kellogg, Frank, 649
Kellogg-Briand Pact (1928), 649
Kennan, George F., 744–745, 749
Kennedy, John F., 683, 798(i)
assassination of, 799
Bay of Pigs invasion and, 829–830
civil rights and, 797, 805
Cuban missile crisis and, 832
domestic policy of, 798–799
election of 1960 and, 797, 798(i), 798(m)
foreign policy of, 829–834
Freedom Rides and, 805
New Frontier of, 797–799

Soviet Union and, 830
space program and, 830–831
television and, 786
Vietnam War and, 828, 832–834
Kennedy, Joseph P., 683
Kennedy, Robert F., 805, 811(i), 843
Kent State University, killings at, 848
Kenya, U.S. embassy bombing in, 901
Kerouac, Jack, 787
Kerry, John, 848–849(b), 910
Kettle Hill, Rough Riders at, 578
Keynes, John Maynard, 670, 703
Keynesian economics, 703
Khomeini, Ayatollah Ruholla, 868(i), 872
Khrushchev, Nikita
arms race and, 776–777
Cuban missile crisis and, 832
Kennedy, J. F., and, 831
Nixon and, 767–768, 768(i)
Kikuchi, Charles, 720–721(b)
Kim Il-sung, 762–763
King, Coretta Scott, 867(i)
King, Martin Luther, Jr., 804, 867(i)
assassination of, 809, 842(b)
in Birmingham, 805
black power and, 808–809
in Chicago, 806
in Detroit, 661(b)
FBI surveillance of, 805, 866
Montgomery bus boycott and, 792–793
King, Martin Luther, Sr., 867(i)
Kings Canyon National Park, 598(m)
Kinsey, Alfred, 787
Kiowa Indians, 469, 475
Kissinger, Henry A., 845, 847, 855
Klan. See Ku Klux Klan
Knights of Labor, 529, 530, 537, 539, 542, 543, 553
songs of, 540–541(b), 542
WCTU and, 565
Kodak camera, 596(b)
Korea. See also Korean War; North Korea; South Korea
after World War II, 729
Korean War (1950–1953), 762–765, 762(m), 763(i)
military desegregation during, 756
soldiers in, 763, 764
Korematsu decision, 718
Kosovo, 900–901, 901(i)
Ku Klux Klan, 433–434, 448, 450–451(b), 451(i), 646
rebirth of, 663–664
Ku Klux Klan Acts (1870 and 1871), 451(b), 457
Kurds, in Iraq, 895, 901, 910
Kuwait
Bush, G. H. W., and, 889
Persian Gulf War and, 894, 894(m)
Kyoto Protocol, Bush, George W., and, 909

Labor. See also Child labor; Free labor; Labor unions; Servants; Strikes
in 1920s, 650
African American, 640
agricultural, 663
black codes and, 441–442
Chinese, 479, 481, 482(i), 530
common laborers and, 533
of freed slaves, 437
globalization and, 902–903
global population of, 524

Labor (*continued*)
in Great Depression, 667–668, 675–676, 696–697, 698
immigrant, 524, 525–526, 903(*i*)
mechanization and, 533–534
Mexican, 640–641, 641(*i*), 782
migrant, 483, 488, 675–676, 691
in mining, 593
Native American, 481(*i*)
organization of, 564
standards for, 704
Taft-Hartley Act and, 757
Truman and, 754
in World War I, 625
after World War I, 663
in World War II, 697, 727
Labor code, for freed slaves, 437
Labor Department
affirmative action and, 824
Children's Bureau of, 603–604
Labor unions. *See also* Labor; Strikes; specific unions
in 1950s, 779, 780
African Americans in, 549
antitrust laws used against, 517
closed shops and, 648
during Great Depression, 671
immigrants and, 663
injunctions and, 564, 607
in mining, 479
New Deal and, 688(*b*), 689–690, 696–697
Reagan and, 875
in textile industry, 688(*b*)
union label and, 588(*i*)
welfare capitalism and, 650
women and, 549
during World War I, 625
after World War I, 636–637
during World War II, 697, 719
after World War II, 754
Labor wars, 558–564
Lady Liberty (Statue of Liberty), 530
La Follette, Robert M. ("Fighting Bob"), 591, 595, 605, 648
Laissez-faire
depression of 1890s and, 566–569, 581
Great Depression and, 678
Hoover on, 666
People's Party and, 554, 566
progressive challenges to, 584(*i*), 590, 594
social Darwinism and, 506–508, 517, 566
Lakewood development, in California, 783
Lakota Sioux Indians, 463(*i*), 470–471, 472(*b*), 810
imperialism, colonialism and, 466(*b*), 467(*b*)
Land. *See also* Agriculture; Conservation; Farms and farming
Asian Americans and, 530, 609
of Californios, 480
Dawes Act and, 474–475
for freedmen, 437–438, 441
Homestead Act and, 482
Indian, 464, 466, 468(*m*), 824
Indian cessions of, 771
speculation in, 482, 486
in West, 463, 482–483, 486, 557
Land grants
to railroads, 486, 487(*m*), 495, 498
Spanish and Mexican, 480
Landlords, in sharecropping, 452, 453, 686
Landon, Alfred ("Alf"), 701

Land rush
in Oklahoma, 486
in trans-Mississippi West, 482
Lane, Franklin, 600(*b*)
Lane, George, 890
Lange, Dorothea, 676, 676(*i*)
Language(s), of immigrants, 528(*b*), 531
Lansing, Robert, 619, 632
Laos
immigrants from, 903
Vietnam War and, 833, 851
Laramie, Fort
Treaty of (1851), 466
Treaty of (1868), 470, 471
Las Manos Negras (the Black Hands), 480
Lassen Volcanic National Park, 598(*m*)
Latin America. *See also* Central America; South America
good neighbor policy and, 710, 710(*i*)
immigrants from, 525(*m*), 903
interventions in, 571, 572
Johnson, L. B., and, 835–837
Monroe Doctrine and, 571–572, 597–598, 602(*m*)
revolutions in 1930s, 710
Roosevelt Corollary and, 598
U.S. involvement in, 615–617, 616(*m*), 744, 774–775, 830(*m*)
Latinos/Latinas. *See also* Hispanics and Hispanic Americans
equal rights struggle by, 810–811
median income of, 899
as officeholders, 897
Law(s). *See also* Legislation; specific acts
women and, 655
Law and order, conservatives on, 860
Lawless Decade, 647
Lawson, James, 804
Lazarus, Emma, 530
Lead poisoning, 586–587(*b*)
League of Nations, 632, 633–634, 635, 635(*i*), 649, 709–710
League of United Latin-American Citizens (LULAC), 642, 756–757, 810
League of Women Voters, 655
League on Urban Conditions, 641(*i*)
Lease, Mary Elizabeth, 557(*i*)
Lebanon
American hostages in, 884
Eisenhower aid to, 776
Hezbollah in, 883
intervention in, 883
Lee, Robert E., 458
Leftist movements, Reagan and, 883
Left wing (political). *See* Communism; Socialism and socialists
Legislation. *See also* Law(s); specific acts
of New Deal's first Hundred Days, 687(*t*)
to protect working women, 589–590
Legislatures, in Reconstruction South, 449–450
Leisure. *See also* Entertainment
of working class, 543
Lemlich, Clara, 588
Lend-Lease Act (1941), 714, 717
Lenin, Vladimir Ilyich, 638(*b*), 639(*b*)
Leningrad, battle at, 733(*m*)
Lesbians. *See* Gays and lesbians; Homosexuals and homosexuality
Leslie's Illustrated Weekly (magazine), 559(*i*)
Levi Strauss, 905(*b*)
Levitt, William J., 780–781, 780(*i*)
Levittown, 780–781, 780(*i*)
Lewelling, Lorenzo, 568

Lewis, John (SNCC), 805
Lewis, John L. (United Mine Workers), 696
Lewis, Sinclair, 662
Leyte Gulf, Battle of, 732
Liberal Party, 456–457
Liberals and liberalism. *See also* Classical liberalism; Progressivism
in 1960s, 797–803
Nixon's reforms and, 796, 821–824
after World War II, 741–742
Liberty(ies). *See* Civil liberties; Freedom(s)
Libraries, public, 500, 501, 545, 546(*i*)
Libya, rebellion in (2011), 913
Lien, crop, 453, 509, 555, 557–558
Lifestyle. *See also* Society
in Great Depression, 669–672, 669(*i*)
after World War II, 753
Lifestyles of the Rich and Famous (TV program), 875
"Lift Every Voice" (Johnson), 658
Lili'uokalani (Hawai'i), 570, 572–573(*b*), 573(*i*)
Limited government, 519, 605
Lin, Maya, 854
Lincoln, Abraham (president)
assassination of, 440
Reconstruction plan of, 435–440, 436(*i*)
"Lincoln states," 436
Lindbergh, Charles, 659
Lindsay, John, 847(*i*)
Lippmann, Walter, 590
Liquor. *See* Alcohol and alcoholism
Literacy
for freedmen, 437(*i*), 440, 452(*i*)
of immigrants, 530
in South, 449
tests of, 530, 610
for voting, 610
of women, 536
Literature. *See also* specific works and writers
in Harlem Renaissance, 658
Lost Generation and, 661–662
Western, 487–488
Little Big Horn, Battle of (1876), 467(*b*), 471, 472–473(*b*), 472(*i*), 473(*i*)
"Little Boy" (bomb), 708
Little Crow (Dakota Sioux), 470
Little Rock, Arkansas, school integration in, 790–791
"Little Rock Nine," 790
Lloyd, Henry Demarest, 513
Loans. *See also* Bank(s) and banking; Economy
to Allies (World War I), 619, 667
Lobbying, 589, 606
Locke, Alain, 658
Lodge, Henry Cabot, 530, 635, 635(*i*), 649
Loggers, 489(*i*)
Lonely Crowd, The (Riesman), 786
Long, Huey, 692, 692(*i*), 697
"Long Walk" of Navajo, 467
Loom, 533
López, Julio, 904(*b*)
Lord Is My Shepherd, The (Johnson), 437(*i*)
Los Alamos, New Mexico, 737
Los Angeles, 781. *See also* Watts riots
Lost Cause, 457
Lost Generation, 647, 660–662
Louisiana, 436, 460, 664. *See also* New Orleans
political violence in, 451(*b*), 458
Love, Nat (Deadwood Dick), 487

Love Canal, 869
Loving v. Virginia (1967), 803
Low-income housing, 801
Loyalists (Spain), 711
Lozen (Apache female warrior), 476
Lucky Strikes, advertising for, 652–653(b), 653(i)
Luftwaffe (Germany), 714, 729, 734(b)
LULAC. *See* League of United Latin-American Citizens
Lumber industry, 595
   loggers in, 489(i)
Lunch counter sit-ins, 804, 804(i)
Lusitania (ship), 618, 619(m), 620(i)
Lutz, Alfred, 750(b)
Lux, Charles, 490
Lynchings
   of African Americans, 640
   antilynching laws and, 655, 658, 704
   of Prager, Robert, 629
   in South, 509–510, 510–511(b), 511, 512(i), 530
   after World War I, 638, 640
   after World War II, 755

MacArthur, Douglas, 763–764
Machinery, farm, 489
MacKenzie, Kathleen, 909
MAD. *See* Mutually assured destruction
Mahan, Alfred Thayer, 570–571
Mail service. *See also* Postal system
   birth control publications and, 608
   political information and, 629
   Pullman boycott and, 564
   for soldiers, 707(i)
Maine (ship), explosion of, 575(i), 576–577(b), 577(i)
Main Street (Lewis), 662
Malcolm X, 808
Male, use of word in Constitution, 445
Male suffrage. *See* Suffrage; Voting and voting rights
Manchuria, 599, 709, 711, 715, 729
Mandate system, after World War I, 632, 633
Mandela, Nelson, 893
Manhattan Project, 731(b), 737
Manifest destiny, Indian removal and, 465
Manila, U.S. navy in, 577, 578, 578(m)
Mansfield, Mike, 835
Manufacturing
   automobile, 646(m), 649, 649(m), 779
   at Columbian Exposition, 548(b)
   income (1920–1940), 668(f)
   women in, 533–534, 534(i), 535(f)
   workers in, 904(b)
Mao Zedong, 752
Marble House, 498–499(b), 498(i)
March on Washington (1941), 726
March on Washington for Jobs and Freedom (1963), 805
Marines (U.S.). *See also* Military
   in Beirut, 883
   in Dominican Republic, 834
   in Hawai'i, 572(b)
   in Lebanon, 883
   in Mexico, 616
   in Nicaragua, 894
   in World War I, 622, 636(i)
Market(s)
   domestic, 572(b)
   expansion of, 570–571, 570(f), 651
   international, 555, 570, 651
   for tobacco, 509

for western agriculture, 489
   after World War II, 744
Marne River, battle at, 622, 623(m)
Marriage
   freedmen and, 438(b)
   gay, 898
   in Great Depression, 670
   plural (polygamy), 480
   women and, 534, 657(b)
Married women, in workforce, 534, 670
Marshall, George C., 759
Marshall, Thurgood, 757, 790, 891
Marshall Islands, 732
Marshall Plan, 742, 743, 750–751(b), 750(b)
Martin, Joseph W., Jr., 753
Massive retaliation policy, 773
Mass production
   in auto industry, 646, 649
   consumer goods revolution and, 650
Mass transit, 531
Materialism, in Gilded Age, 493, 548(b)
Mathews, Mary McNair, 479
May Day rally (Chicago, 1886), 542
Mazo, Ike, 875–876
McCain, John, 853(b), 911
McCarran-Walter Act (1952), 759
McCarthy, Eugene, 843
McCarthy, Joseph R., and McCarthyism, 759–762, 769–770
McClure's Magazine, 502–503, 503(i)
McCormick, Cyrus, Jr., 542
McCormick, Katharine Dexter, 816(i)
McCormick reaper works, strike at, 542
McDonough, Clarence, 861
McGovern, George S., 864
McKay, Claude, 658
McKim, Charles F., 546(i)
McKinley, William
   assassination of, 592
   election of 1896 and, 568, 569, 569(m)
   Hawai'ian annexation and, 573
   Spanish-American War and, 577–578, 579
   tariffs and, 570, 570(f), 572(b)
McMaster, Bobby, 838(i)
McNamara, Robert, 834, 841
McVeigh, Timothy, 897
Meat Inspection Act (1906), 595
Meatpacking industry, 595
Mechanization
   of farming, 488
   in garment industry, 533–534
   in textile industry, 533
Mediation, Roosevelt, T., and, 593, 599
Medicaid (1965), abortion coverage under, 800, 821
Medicare (1965), 800, 800(i), 801
   poverty of elderly and, 876
   prescription medication for elderly and, 907, 915
Medicine. *See also* Disease
   drug prescriptions for elderly and, 907, 915
Medicine Lodge Creek, Treaty of (1867), 469
Mediterranean region, in World War II, 724
Mein Kampf (Hitler), 730(b)
Mellon, Andrew, 647, 648
Memphis, race riot in (1866), 445(i)
Men. *See also* Gender
   in Great Depression, 670
   as immigrants, 479, 527
   separate spheres for, 509
Mencken, H. L., 665
Mendez v. Westminster (1947), 757

Merchant marine, World War I, 625
Merchants, in sharecropping, 453
Mergers, 505
   Reagan and, 874, 875
Mesa Verde National Park, 598(m)
Mescalero Apache Agency, 471–472
Methodists, 440, 508
Meuse-Argonne offensive, 614, 623, 623(m)
Mexican Americans
   as agricultural labor, 663, 782
   civil rights for, 810–811
   as cowboys, 488
   discrimination against, 699
   in Great Depression, 670, 699
   land grants of, 480
   as migrant workers, 488, 676, 691, 700(i)
   New Deal and, 699
   as ranchers, 487
   in Southwest, 480, 641–642
   in World War II, 718
   after World War II, 756–757
Mexican-American War (1846–1848)
   land cessions after, 465, 480, 490
   manifest destiny and, 465
Mexican immigrants, 488, 670, 699
   to Southwest, 640–642, 642(i)
Mexico
   NAFTA and, 902
   nationalization of oil in, 710
   revolution in, 640, 700(i)
   Texas and, 465
   U.S. intervention in, 604, 604(m), 615–617, 617(m)
   Wilson and, 615–617
   Zimmermann telegram and, 619
Mexico City, protests in (1968), 842(b)
Michigan, 691
Middle class
   by 1960, 784
   black, 640, 803
   consumer culture and, 549(b)
   in Gilded Age, 494
Middle East. *See also* Arab world; Israel
   1948–1989, 871(m)
   1989–2011, 894(m)
   Bush, G. H. W., and, 895
   Carter and, 870, 871
   CIA and, 775
   Iran revolution in, 868, 868(i)
   Nixon and, 846
   oil in, 752
   Reagan and, 885
   terrorism in, 883
   U.S. interventions in, 775–776
Middletown (1929), 651
"Middle way," of Eisenhower, 769–772
Midway Island, Battle of, 721, 722
Midway Plaisance, 550, 551
Midwest, 686
   auto industry in, 646(m)
   settlement before 1862, 486(m)
Migrant Mother (Lange photo), 676, 676(i)
Migrant workers, 483, 488, 489, 670, 691
   in Great Depression, 670, 675–676, 691, 701(i)
   Social Security and, 698
Migration
   African American, 640, 641(i), 662(m), 727
   during Great Depression, 691
   by Jews, 527, 528(b)
   Mexican to Southwest, 640–642, 642(i)
Miles, Dora, 726(i)
Miles, Nelson, 475(i), 476

Milholland, Inez, 609(i)
Militancy. *See also* Activism; Protest(s)
　working-class, 671–672
Military. *See also* Draft (military); Soldiers;
　specific battles and wars
　African Americans in, 480, 756
　in Boxer uprising (China), 571
　in Cold War, 749
　countries with highest expenditures (2005),
　　900(f)
　equipment for (World War II), 719–720
　gays and lesbians in, 897, 911
　in Great Railroad Strike, 538
　in Japan, 711
　morale in Vietnam War, 850
　NSC 68 and, 765
　in Pullman strike, 563, 564
　Reagan and, 882–883
　in South, 448
　special forces in, 832
　spending on, 765
　volunteer army and, 851–852
　women in, 749, 838, 895(i)
　in World War I, 613–614, 620–621
　in World War II, 718–719, 734
Military districts, in South, 446, 446(m)
Military-industrial complex, 778
Military Reconstruction Act (1867), 446
Militia. *See also* National Guard
　in Great Railroad Strike, 537, 538, 538(i)
Militia movement, 897
Miller, Henry, 490
Miller & Lux (corporate ranching), 490
Mills, textile, 688–689(b), 689(i)
Milosevic, Slobodan, 900–901
Mines and mining
　accidents in, 479
　Chinese immigrants and, 481
　Comstock Lode and, 478–480, 479(i)
　Indians and, 464, 471
　strikes and, 560, 671
　technology for, 479
　in West, 477–480, 478(m), 489
Miniconjou Sioux Indians, 477
Minimum wage, 625, 648, 704, 896, 899
Mining towns, 479
Minneapolis, gay and lesbian rights in, 880(b)
Minnesota, 470
Minnick, Will, 541(b)
Minorities. *See also* Ethnic groups; specific
　　groups
　feminists in, 817–819
　in higher education, 783
　Hispanics as, 480
　poverty and, 803, 876
　Social Security and, 698
Minow, Newton, 786
Miranda v. Arizona (1966), 803
Miscegenation, Garvey on, 658
Miss America pageant, 817
Missiles. *See also* Cuban missile crisis;
　　Intercontinental ballistic missiles
　in 1950s, 773(i)
　Clinton and, 901
　in Iraq, 895
　SDI and, 883
　in Turkey, 832
Missions and missionaries
　in California, 481(i)
　in China, 571
　in Hawai'i, 572(b)
Mission Santa Clara, 481(i)
Mississippi, 449
　political violence in, 459

Mississippi Freedom Democratic Party
　(MFDP), 796
Mississippi Freedom Summer Project (1964),
　805
Mississippi River region, Civil War in, 437
Mitchell, George (Chippewa Indians), 810
Mixed economy, 780
Mixed marriages, 904
Mizocz, Ukraine, World War II execution of
　Jews in, 728(i)
Mobility, social, 754–755
Mobilization
　for World War I, 617, 624–625
　for World War II, 697, 716–720, 725
Model T Ford, 645(i)
"Modern Republicanism" (Eisenhower),
　769–770
Mohammed, Shanaz, 908
Mondale, Walter F., 866, 875
Money
　gold standard and, 517–518
　hard money, 518
　paper, 518
　tight money policy and, 518, 558
　after World War I, 647
Money supply
　Carter and, 867
　contraction of, 518
"Money trust" of Morgan, 505
Mongella, Gertrude, 818(b)
"Monkey trial." *See* Scopes trial
Monnet, Jean, 750(b)
Monopolies
　business, 502, 517
　Reagan and, 874
Monroe Doctrine (1823)
　foreign policy and, 571–572
　Roosevelt Corollary to, 598, 598(m), 599(i),
　　604
　Spanish-American War and, 574
　Wilson and, 615
Montana, 490
Montgomery, Alabama
　bus boycott in, 792–793, 804
　march to (1965), 805
Montgomery Improvement Association
　(MIA), 792
Moody, Anne, 804(i)
Moore, Alice, 862–863, 863(i)
Moore, Paul, 880(b)
Morality
　in 1920s, 656–657(b), 663
　Clinton impeachment over, 899
　conservatives and, 860
Moral Majority, 873
Moral reform movement, 508
Morgan, Anne, 588
Morgan, J. P., and Company, 606
Morgan, J. P., 505–506
　gold standard and, 519
　panic of 1907 and, 595, 604, 606
　U.S. Steel and, 505, 505(i), 506
Mormons, 480
Morocco, 599
　in World War II, 724
Morrow, E. Frederick, 791
Morse, Samuel F. B., 498, 499
Mortality rate, infant, 655
Mortgages
　in 1950s, 781
　foreclosures of, 911
Mosher, Clelia Duel, 657(b)
Mossadegh, Mohammed (Iran), 775, 775(i),
　871

Mothers. *See also* Women
　against Vietnam War, 840(i)
Motion picture camera, 504. *See also* Movies
Moudy, Ross, 479
Movies
　in 1920s, 658–659
　during Great Depression, 670
　World War I propaganda in, 628, 629(i)
Ms. magazine, 818, 820(i)
Mubarak, Hosni, 913
Muckraking, 567, 595
Mugwumps, 513, 515
Muir, John, 595, 600(b), 601(i)
Muir Woods, 600(b)
Muller v. Oregon (1908), 589–590
Mumford, Lewis, 781
Muncie, Indiana, study of, 651
Munich Olympics, Israelis murdered at, 883
Municipal government, 545, 546
Munn v. Illinois (1877), 517
Murals, of city activities (Benton, 1930s),
　693(i)
Murray, Pauli, 817
Music
　in 1950s, 787
　in 1960s, 816
　jazz as, 658, 659(i)
　of Knights of Labor, 540–541(b)
　rock and roll, 787, 816
Music halls, 543
Muslims. *See also* Islam
　in Afghanistan, 871
　Obama and, 913
Mussolini, Benito, 709, 712(m), 725
Mutually assured destruction (MAD), 773
Myer, Dillon S., 771
My Lai massacre, 850, 854

NAACP. *See* National Association for the
　Advancement of Colored People
Nader, Ralph, 906(m)
NAFTA. *See* North American Free Trade
　Agreement
Nagasaki, bombing of, 729, 738
Names, of Indian children, 472–473
Nanjing (Nanking), Japan capture of, 711
Napalm, 834
NASA. *See* National Aeronautics and Space
　Administration
Nasser, Gamal Abdel, 775
Nast, Thomas, on Grant and scandal, 456(i)
National Aeronautics and Space
　Administration (NASA), 777
National American Woman Suffrage
　Association (NAWSA), 566, 609, 628,
　630(b)
National Arts and Humanities Act (1965),
　801
National Association for the Advancement
　of Colored People (NAACP), 512(i),
　611, 658, 660(b), 727, 755
　Brown v. Board of Education and, 788(b),
　789–790
National Association of Evangelicals, 874(i)
National Association of Manufacturers, 688,
　697
National Conference of Catholic Bishops,
　883
National Consumers' League (NCL), 589
National Council of Negro Women, 699
National debt. *See* Debt
National defense. *See* Defense
National Defense Education Act (NDEA),
　777

National Energy Act (1978), 868
National Farmers' Holiday Association (1932), 671
National forests and parks, 896
National Gay and Lesbian Task Force, 816
National Geographic, 577(b)
National government. *See* Government (U.S.)
National Guard
  Berlin crisis and, 831
  at Boston police strike, 636
  at Homestead strike, 559, 560
  at Kent State, 848
  in Little Rock, 790–791
  Selma civil rights marchers and, 805
  textile workers' strike and, 688(b)
  Vietnam War soldiers and, 838
  violence against strikers by, 696
National health insurance
  Carter and, 867
  Clinton and, 897
  Eisenhower and, 770
  Obama and, 888
National Housing Act, of 1937, 704
National Industrial Recovery Act (NIRA, 1933), 686, 687(t)
Nationalist China, 752
Nationalities. *See also* Ethnic groups; specific groups
  immigration quotas on, 663
National Labor Relations (Wagner) Act (NLRA, 1935), 693, 696, 698
National Liberation Front (NFL, Vietnam), 833, 837, 842
National liberation movements
  in third world, 829
  after World War II, 739
National Miners Union, 671
National Organization for Women (NOW), 817, 878(b)
National origins, immigration quotas based on, 801
National parks, 596, 598(m)
National Park Service Act (1916), 601(b)
National Plan of Action, 818
National Recovery Administration (NRA, 1933), 686–687, 688, 688(b), 689–690
National security
  Eisenhower and, 772
  in World War II, 717
National Security Act (1947), 749, 751
National Security Council (NSC)
  creation of, 749
  Iran-Contra and, 884
  NSC 68 and, 765
National security state, 748–752
National self-determination. *See also* Self-determination
  Persian Gulf War and, 895
National Socialism. *See also* Nazi Germany
  Hitler and, 680–681(b)
National Union for Social Justice (Union Party), 691
National War Labor Policies Board, 625
National Welfare Rights Organization, 800
National Woman's Party (NWP), 609, 655, 878
National Woman Suffrage Association (NWSA), 512, 554, 565
National Women's Political Caucus, 796
National Youth Administration, Division of Negro Affairs, 699
Nation building, in Somalia, 900
Native Americans
  Alcatraz seizure by, 809–810, 810(i)

assimilation of, 467(b), 471–475, 699
buffalo and, 469–470
buffalo soldiers and, 480
citizenship and suffrage for, 663
Comstock Lode discovery and, 479
cultures of, 471, 474
Dawes Act and, 474–475
diseases among, 466–467
Ghost Dance of, 476–477, 477(i)
Grant's peace policy for, 470
lands of, 464, 466, 468(m), 700
manifest destiny and, 465
mass execution of, 470
New Deal and, 699–700
Nixon and, 796, 824
Plains Indians, 465–471
protests by, 809–810
removal of, 465, 467
reservations for, 464, 467–468, 468(m), 470, 475
resistance by, 464, 470–471, 475–477
Sand Creek massacre against, 468–469
schools for, 471–474, 474(i)
termination and relocation of, 770–772, 771(m), 772(i)
U.S. westward expansion and, 465
warfare by, 464, 465, 470, 471, 476
Washita River massacre against, 469
in World War II, 718
Wounded Knee Massacre against, 477
Nativism, 481–482, 587, 663
NATO. *See* North Atlantic Treaty Organization
Naturalization. *See* Citizens and citizenship
Natural resources. *See* Resources
Navajo Indians, 467, 476
Navies. *See also* Navy (U.S.)
  British, 617
  German, 619
  Japanese, 710, 711
  reduction of, 649
Navy (U.S.). *See also* Ships and shipping; Submarines
  Great White Fleet of, 599–600
  at Guantánamo, 579
  in Manila, 577, 578, 578(m)
  Panama Canal and, 597, 602(m)
  at Pearl Harbor, 716
  in Samoan Islands, 573
  SEALs of, 832
  in Spanish-American War, 575(i), 576–577(b), 577(i), 578, 578(m)
  in World War II, 721, 732
Nazi Germany. *See also* Germany; Hitler, Adolf; World War II
  in 1930s, 680–681(b), 712–713
  Allied World War II victory and, 729
  anti-Semitism in, 680(b), 710
  Czechoslovakia and, 712–713
  fascism in, 680–681(b)
  Hitler in, 705
  Holocaust in, 727–728
  militarization of, 680–681(b)
  Poland and, 712(m), 713, 713(i)
  in World War II, 722(f)
  World War II surrender, 730
Nebraska, 486
"Negro domination," southern politics and, 447, 449
"Negro first" strategy, 447
"Negro rule," 449
Neighborhoods, 480, 531
Nelson, Gaylord, 823(i)
Nelson, Knute, 579

Netherlands, in World War II, 713
Neutrality, in World War I, 614, 617–619, 618(m)
Neutrality Acts, of 1935–1937, 711
Nevada
  Comstock Lode in, 477, 478–480
  statehood for, 490
Newark, race riot in (1967), 807
New Deal, 676, 681–682. *See also* Economy; Great Depression; Roosevelt, Franklin Delano
  achievements and limitations of, 704–705
  agriculture in, 685–686, 690, 690(i)
  allies of, 700–701
  banking and finance reform in, 682–683
  challenges to, 687–692
  conservation programs in, 684–685
  industry in, 686–687
  labor unions and, 688(b), 689–690, 696–697
  later period in, 703–704
  legislation of first hundred days, 687(t)
  neglected people during, 698–700
  objectives of, 680–681, 682
  photographs of, 676, 676(i)
  reaction and recession in, 701–703
  relief programs in, 684, 693–696
  Supreme Court and, 690, 698, 701
  welfare state and, 693–698
New Deal coalition, 679, 679(m), 682, 700–701
New England, manufacturing in, 509
"New Era," 1920s as, 647–652, 666
New Freedom (Wilson), 605
New Frontier (Kennedy), 797–799
New Guinea, in World War II, 722, 732
New Left, 813, 817
"New Look" (Eisenhower), 773
New Mexico
  Hispanics in, 480
  Indians of, 824
  manifest destiny and, 465
  territorial government in, 490
New Nationalism (Roosevelt, T.), 605, 606
"New Negro," 646, 658
New Orleans
  Hurricane Katrina in, 907–908
  school integration in, 790(b)
New (Christian) Right, 860. *See also* Christian Right
  Reagan and, 873
Newsboys, 534
New South, 508–509
Newspapers. *See also* Journalism
  muckraking by, 567, 595
  photojournalism in, 596–597(b), 596(i), 597(i)
  populist, 557(i)
  Pullman strike coverage in, 562–563(b), 564
  yellow journalism in, 575–576, 575(i), 576(b)
New woman, 646, 654–657, 656–657(b)
New York (city)
  African Americans in, 640, 648
  Central Park in, 545
  Ellis Island in, 530
  Harlem Renaissance in, 658
  immigrants in, 527, 530
  September 11, 2001, terrorist attacks in, 888, 908, 908(i)
  settlement houses in, 585
  Tammany Hall in, 547, 665
  vice in, 608
  world finance and, 649

New York (state), Roosevelt, F. D., as governor of, 678
New York Journal, 575(b), 576(b)
New York Stock Exchange, 497, 667
New York Sun, 500
New York Times, 474, 538, 594, 839, 850
New York World, 532, 575, 577(i)
  on Pullman strike, 562(b), 563(b)
New Zealand, in World War II, 722
Nez Percé Indians, 475–476, 475(i)
Ngoza (Zulu chief), 467(i)
Niagara movement (1905), 611
Nicaragua, 883(m)
  in 1930s, 710
  Reagan, Contras, and, 883
  Sandinistas in, 869
  Taft and, 604, 604(m)
  U.S. intervention in, 615
Nicholas II (Russia), 620
Nichols, H. D., 550
Nicodemus, Kansas, 480
Niedermeyer, George, 800(i)
Nightclubs, in Harlen, 658
Night riders, 458
Nike, overseas production by, 903, 904(b), 905(i)
Nimitz, Chester W., 722
Nineteenth Amendment, 628, 628(m), 630–631(b), 655
92nd Division, in World War I, 621–622
Nixon, E. D., 792
Nixon, Isaac, lynching of, 755
Nixon, Pat, 845(i), 865(i)
Nixon, Richard M.
  as anti-Communist, 742
  China and, 828, 845–846, 845(i)
  conservatism and, 821, 825, 858, 859–865
  détente policy and, 845–846
  economy and, 821–822
  election of 1950 and, 742
  election of 1952 and, 764, 764(i)
  election of 1960 and, 797, 798(m)
  election of 1968 and, 822(i), 839, 843–844, 843(b), 844
  election of 1972 and, 864
  environment and, 822–823
  foreign policy of, 828, 845–854
  Great Society and, 859
  Khrushchev and, 767–768, 768(i)
  liberal reform and, 796, 821–824
  Native Americans and, 796, 824
  pardon of, 865
  resignation of, 865, 865(i)
  right wing and, 861–864
  social justice under, 823–824
  Supreme Court and, 862–863
  Vietnam War and, 821, 847–852, 848(b)
  Watergate and, 864–865
  welfare state and, 821–822
Nobel Peace Prize
  for Bunche, R., 755
  for Roosevelt, T., 599
  for Wilson, Woodrow, 635
Noble, Elaine, 816
Noble and Holy Order of the Knights of Labor. *See* Knights of Labor
"Noble Knights of Labor, The" (Stephens), 540(b)
No Child Left Behind (NCLB) Act (2002), 907, 915
Nonviolent resistance
  by Chavez and Huerta, 811(i)
  in civil rights movement, 804–805
  by Indians, 476–477

Nonwhites, immigrant, 481, 482
Noriega, Manuel, 894
"Normalcy," Harding on, 642
Norman, Icy, 688(b), 689(b)
Normandy, D Day invasion at, 729, 733(m)
North (U.S. region)
  African Americans in, 530, 727
  black migration to, 530, 640, 641(i)
  civil rights activism in, 792(i)
  domestics in, 543
  Reconstruction and, 448, 455, 457
North Africa, in World War II, 721, 724, 724(i), 725, 733(m)
North American Free Trade Agreement (NAFTA), 902
North Atlantic Treaty Organization (NATO)
  Eastern European countries in, 742, 749–750, 892
  in former Yugoslavia, 901, 901(i)
North Carolina, 509
  Democrats in, 458
Northern Alliance (Afghanistan), 908
Northern Pacific Railroad, 471
Northern Paiute Indians, 479
Northern Securities Company, 593
North Korea. *See also* Korean War
  Bush, G. W., and, 910
  communism in, 893
North Vietnam. *See also* Vietnam; Vietnam War
  formation of, 774
  Vietnam War and, 833, 837, 842
Northwestern Farmers' Alliance, 556
Norton, Eleanor Holmes, 796(i)
Norway
  immigrants from, 483(i)
  in World War II, 713
NOW. *See* National Organization for Women
NRA codes, 686–687, 688(b), 690
NSC 68, 765
Nuclear arms race. *See* Arms race
Nuclear disarmament. *See* Disarmament
Nuclear power plants, 770, 868–869
Nuclear test ban treaty, 832, 893
Nuclear weapons. *See also* Arms race; Atomic bomb
  anxiety over, 778
  Cuban missile crisis and, 832, 832(i), 832(m)
  Eisenhower and, 777–778
  freeze on, 882(i), 883
  hydrogen bomb as, 749
  Johnson, L. B., and, 834
  Kennedy and, 831
  missiles and, 773(i)
  Reagan and, 882–883
  religion and, 785
Nursing, in World War I, 625
Nye, Gerald, and Nye Committee, 711

Oath of allegiance, in Lincoln's Reconstruction plan, 435
Obama, Barack, 911–913
  caricatures of, 914–915(b), 914(i), 915(i)
  domestic policy of, 911–912
  economy and, 911–912
  election of 2008 and, 911
  election of 2012 and, 888, 912, 913(m)
  foreign policy of, 912–913
  Guantánamo and, 909
Occupation (military)
  of Germany, 649, 744
  of Korea, 762

Occupational Disease Commission (Illinois), 586(b)
Occupational Safety and Health Act (OSHA, 1970), 587, 823
Occupations (jobs). *See* Employment
O'Connor, Sandra Day, 891(b), 907
O'Donnell, Hugh, 558, 560
Officeholders
  African American, 434, 449, 806, 897
  ex-Confederate, 443, 457
  Latino, 897
  in Reconstruction, 449, 449(f)
Oglala Sioux Indians, 472(b)
Ohio gang, of Harding, 647, 648
Oil and oil industry. *See also* Energy crisis
  energy shortage and, 868–869, 868(i)
  Iran and, 744, 775
  in Mexico, 710
  in Middle East, 752, 871(m), 895
  Rockefeller in, 501–503
  in World War II, 734(b)
  after World War II, 744, 752
  worldwide reserves of (1980), 870(m)
Okies, 676, 691
Okinawa, battle of, 732
Oklahoma, 486, 664, 691. *See also* Indian Territory
  Indian removal to, 465
Oklahoma City, terrorism in, 897, 897(i)
Oklahoma Tenant Farmers' Union, 686
Old Age Revolving Pension, 691–692
Older Americans. *See* Elderly
"Old Guard" in Republican Party, 594, 605
Olesdater, Beret, 483(i)
Olmsted, Frederick Law, 545, 547, 550
Olney, Richard B., 564
Olympic Games
  Israelis murdered at (1972), 883
  protests at (Mexico, 1968), 842(b)
  U.S. non-participation in 1980, 871
Oñate, Juan de, 480
"100% American" campaigns, 628–629
"Only the Working Class" (Barry), 541(b)
On the Origin of Species (Darwin), 506–507
Open Door policy, 573–574, 574(i), 598–600
Open-housing law, 806
Open range, 480, 487
Operation Pedro Pan, 776–777(b)
Operation Rolling Thunder, 835, 839
Operation Wetback, 782
Oppenheimer, J. Robert, 737
Opper, Fredrick Burr, 497(i)
Orange Free State, 466(b)
Oregon, 465, 664
Organization Man, The (Whyte), 787
Organization of American States (OAS), 837, 894
Organized labor. *See* Labor unions
"Organize the Hosts of Labor" (Minnick), 541(b)
Ortega, Daniel, 883
OSHA. *See* Occupational Safety and Health Act
O'Shaughnessy Dam, 600(b)
O'Sullivan, Mary Kenney, 588
Oswald, Lee Harvey, 799
Other America, The (Harrington), 798
Ottoman Empire, after World War I, 632
"Outing system," at Carlisle Indian School, 473
Overcapitalization, 904(b)
Overlord campaign, 729

Owens, Florence, and family, in Great Depression, 675–676, 676(i), 686, 691, 705

P-51 Mustang fighter, 729
Pacific Gas and Electric Company (PG&E), Hetch Hetchy and, 600(b)
Pacific Ocean region
  Hispanics in, 480
  tenancy and migratory labor in, 488, 676
  U.S. acquisitions in, 579, 580(m)
  World War II in, 716, 719(i), 721, 722–723, 728, 732, 734
Pago Pago, Samoa, naval base in, 573
Pahlavi, Mohammad Reza (Shah of Iran), 775, 775(i), 846, 871–872
Painting. *See also* Art(s)
  in 1950s, 786(i), 787
  in Harlem Renaissance, 658
Paiute Indians, 476, 479
Pakistan
  bin Laden in, 908
  nuclear test ban treaty and, 893
Palestine. *See also* Israel; Middle East
  Clinton and, 902
  Israel and, 753, 753(m), 870, 902
  refugees from, 847
  after World War I, 632
  after World War II, 753
Palestine Liberation Organization (PLO), 883, 902
Palin, Sarah, 911
Palmer, A. Mitchell, 637, 638(b), 640
Palo Duro Canyon, Battle of, 470
Panama
  Carter and, 869–870
  intervention in, 597, 602(m), 894
  Isthmus of, 597
  Noriega and, 894
Panama Canal, 597–598, 602(m), 869
Panama Canal treaty, 869–870
Panama Canal Zone, U.S. control of, 616(m), 836
Pan-American Exposition, 592
Panics. *See also* Depressions (financial)
  of 1873, 494, 518
  of 1893, 489, 494, 516, 566–569
  of 1907, 595, 606
Pan Indian movement, 474, 772
Pan-Slavic union, Russia and, 617
Paper money. *See* Money
Pardons
  for Confederates, 435
  for Iran-Contra officials, 884
  by Johnson, Andrew, 441, 443, 446
  for Nixon, 865
Paris
  Eisenhower-Khrushchev meeting in, 778
  liberation in World War II, 729
Paris, Treaty of, of 1898, 579
Paris Exposition (1889), 548(b)
Paris Peace Conference (1919), 614, 632–634
Parker, Alton B., 594
Parks, Rosa, 792
Parsons, Albert, 542, 543
Partitions
  of Palestine, 753(m)
  of Vietnam, 774
Patient Protection and Affordable Care Act (2010), 912(i)
Patriarchy, 510–511
Patriot Act (2001). *See* USA Patriot Act
Patriotism, 646
  in Spanish-American War, 578, 581

symbols of, 549, 574, 579(i)
  in World War I, 624, 628–629
  in World War II, 717
Patronage, 513
Patrons of Husbandry. *See* Grange
Patton, George, 718, 724
Paul, Alice, 609, 628
Pawnee Indians, 476
Payne-Aldrich bill, 602
Peace
  accords in Vietnam War, 850–852
  after World War I, 649
Peace Corps, 831–832, 831(i)
Peacekeeping, UN and, 729–730
Peace movement. *See also* Antiwar movement
  in World War I, 628
Peace talks, in Vietnam War, 841–842, 850–852
Pearl Harbor, Japanese attack on, 707, 715–716, 716(i)
Pell grants, 821
Pendleton Civil Service Act (1883), 514
Pennsylvania
  anthracite coal strike in, 593
  September 11, 2001, terrorist attacks and, 908
Pennsylvania Railroad, 497, 500
"Penny sales," in Great Depression, 671
Pensions
  military, 671
  Social Security and, 697
  Townsend on, 691–692
Pentagon, September 11, 2001, terrorist attack on, 908
Pentagon Papers, 850
People of color. *See also* Minorities
  women as, 817–818
  in World War II, 718
People's (Populist) Party. *See also* Populist movement
  election of 1892 and, 557–558, 568(m)
  election of 1896 and, 568, 569, 569(i), 569(m)
  in reform coalition, 565
  St. Louis convention of, 553–554, 553(i), 554(i), 557, 567–568
  subtreasury plan of, 557–558
People's Popular Monthly magazine, 656(i)
People's Republic of China (PRC), 752–753, 775. *See also* China
People's Republic of North Korea, 762. *See also* North Korea
Pepper, Claude, 800(i)
Per capita income, increase in, 650
Peréz García, Héctor, 757
Perot, H. Ross, 896, 898
Pershing, John J. ("Black Jack")
  in Mexico, 616–617
  in World War I, 621, 622, 623
Persian Gulf region, Carter Doctrine and, 871
Persian Gulf War (1991), 895–896, 895(i)
Personal Responsibility and Work Opportunity Reconciliation Act (1996), 898
Peterson, Esther, 817
"Petition 'to the Union Convention of Tennessee Assembled in the Capital at Nashville,'" 439(b)
Petrified Forest National Park, 598(m)
Petroleum. *See* Oil and oil industry
Petting (sexual), 657(b)
Phelan, James, 600(b)

Philadelphia, 527, 637(i)
Philadelphia Centennial Exposition (1876), 503
Philippines
  Carter and, 869
  independence of, 752
  Spanish-American War and, 574, 578, 578(m), 579
  Taft as governor of, 601
  U.S. acquisition of, 579, 579(i), 580(m)
  in World War II, 722, 732
Phillips, Wendell, 435–436
Phonograph, 548(b)
Photography
  of immigrants, 527
  by Lange (Great Depression), 676, 676(i)
  of tenements, 596(b), 596(i), 597(b), 597(i)
Photojournalism, 596(b), 596(i), 597(b), 597(i)
Phyllis Schlafly Report, The, 858, 858(i)
Physicians. *See* Doctors
Piecework, 533, 561, 561(i)
Pill, the. *See* Birth control
Pinchot, Gifford, 595, 596, 600(b), 603
Pine Ridge Reservation, 470, 471, 476
Pinkerton Detective Agency, 542
  Homestead lockout and, 558, 559(i)
Pinochet, Augusto, 846
Pittsburgh, 538(i)
Pittsburgh Courier, The, 726
Plains Indians, 465–471, 476–477. *See also* Great Plains
  buffalo decimation and, 465, 469–470, 469(i)
Planters and plantations
  Johnson, Andrew, and, 441
  Klan and, 450(b)
  labor code and, 437
  during Reconstruction, 450(b), 452, 453, 455(m)
Platt Amendment (1898), 579, 580(m)
Playboy magazine, 787
Plenty Coups (Crow chief), 475
Plessy v. Ferguson (1896), 610, 788(b), 790
PLO. *See* Palestine Liberation Organization
Plow, steel, 489
Plural marriage (polygamy). *See* Polygamy
Plutocracy, 500(i), 533
Poets and poetry, in Harlem Renaissance, 658
Pogroms, against Jews, 527, 528–529(b), 529(i)
Poison gas
  in Syria, 913
  in World War I, 613(i), 614, 621
Poland
  immigrants from, 525, 526(f)
  in NATO, 892
  Nazi Germany and, 712(m), 713, 713(i)
  after World War I, 632
  in World War II, 713
  after World War II, 744
Polaris nuclear submarines, 778
Police
  Miranda v. Arizona and, 803
  strike in Boston (1919), 636
Polio
  Roosevelt, Franklin, and, 677
  vaccine for, 770, 770(i)
Political action committees (PACs), 866
Political campaigns. *See* Campaigns (political)
Political parties. *See also* specific parties
  in Gilded Age, 516–517
  Mexican American, 811

Political parties (*continued*)
  realignment of, 516
  women and, 655
Political refugees. *See* Refugees
Politics. *See also* Political parties
  of abundance, 767–793
  culture and, 508–513
  in depression of 1890s, 566–569
  gender and, 509–513, 512(*i*)
  in Gilded Age, 516–517
  in Great Depression, 691–692
  Ku Klux Klan and, 664
  polarization of, 912
  race and, 509–512, 512(*i*)
  in Reconstruction, 448
  sectionalism in, 516
  television and, 785–786
  women and, 448, 628, 630(*b*), 655
  during World War I, 629–630
  after World War I, 642
  during World War II, 727
Pollock, Jackson, 786(*i*), 787
Poll tax, for voting, 610, 704
Pollution. *See* Air pollution; Environment;
  Water
Polygamy, 480
Pony Express, 499
Poor people. *See* Poverty
Popular culture, Vietnam War in, 854
Popular Front, in 1930s, 700–701
Popular vote. *See* Elections
Population
  in 1950s, 784, 785
  baby boom and, 785
  of Californios, 480
  of Chinese immigrants, 482
  immigrants in, 663
  Mexican American, 640
  rural and urban (1870–1900), 488(*f*)
  rural and urban (1920–1930), 662(*m*),
    663
  of Virginia City, 478, 480
Populist movement, 556–558, 557(*i*), 564.
  See also People's (Populist) Party
Pork barrel, 516
Portraits. *See* Painting
Postal system. *See also* Mail service
  segregation of, 610
Poverty
  in 1950s, 772
  1960–1974, 801(*f*)
  in 1980s, 875–876
  of African Americans, 727
  of Chicanos, 811
  in cities, 547, 704
  Clinton and, 898
  in Great Depression, 670, 697, 704
  housing and, 758
  of immigrants, 527, 531, 532
  income inequality and, 899(*f*)
  of Indians, 467, 699
  Johnson, L. B., and, 799, 800
  Kennedy and, 799
  on reservations, 467, 474
  Roosevelt, F. D., and, 678
  rural, 779
  settlement house movement and, 583,
    584
  social Darwinism and, 507–508, 566
  of working-class families, 534
Powderly, Terence V., 530, 539, 542, 553
Powell, Colin L., 893
  on America's global role, 913–914
  Panama and, 894

Persian Gulf War and, 895
  after Soviet Union, 887–888
  unilateralism and, 888, 909
Power (energy). *See* Energy; Energy crisis
Power (political)
  balance of, 599
  separation of powers and, 602
Prager, Robert, lynching of, 629
Prague Spring (1968), 842(*b*), 843(*b*), 843(*i*)
Prayer, in public schools, 803
PRC. *See* People's Republic of China
Preemption doctrine, of Bush, G. W., 909,
  910
Prejudice. *See* Discrimination
Premarital sex, in 1920s, 657(*b*)
Presbyterians, 508
Prescription medication, for elderly, 907, 915
Preservationists, Hetch Hetchy,
  conservationists, and, 600–601(*b*)
Presidency
  Roosevelt, F. D., and, 703
  Roosevelt, T., and, 592, 592(*i*), 602
President. *See also* Executive; specific
  individuals
  African American as, 911
Presidential debates, of 1960, 797
Presidential Reconstruction, 440–444
President's Commission on the Status of
  Women (PCSW, 1963), 817
President's Committee on Civil Rights (1946),
  756
Presley, Elvis, 787
Price controls, 754
Price supports, for agriculture, 647
Primary elections, 604
Prisoners of war (POWs), 909
Private property
  Indians and, 474
  vs. workers' rights, 559
Private welfare state, 780
Problem We All Live With, The (Rockwell),
  790(*b*), 791(*i*)
Proclamation of Amnesty and Reconstruction
  (1863), 435
Production
  of consumer goods (1921–1929), 651(*f*)
  global, 703(*f*)
  industrial (1929–1933), 686
  industrial (1945–1960), 779
  overproduction and, 685
  underconsumption and, 682, 685
Productivity
  agricultural, 685
  in Great Depression, 667, 668
  in manufacturing, 649
  after World War II, 784(*f*)
Professional Air Traffic Controllers
  Organization (PATCO), strike by, 874
Profiteering, 593
Progressive Era, World War I and, 614, 646
Progressive Party
  of 1912, 583(*i*), 584, 604, 607
  of 1924, 648
  of 1948, 757
  woman suffrage and, 628
Progressivism, 605, 643, 646
  Addams, Jane, and, 583, 584
  African Americans and, 584, 609–610
  Asians and, 584, 609
  conservation and, 584
  election of 1912 and, 584, 604–606, 605(*i*),
    606(*m*)
  grassroots, 585–590, 591
  limitations of, 607–611

nativism and, 587
racism and, 584, 609
reform Darwinism and, 590
on robber barons, 646
Roosevelt, T., and, 584, 593, 594, 595
Taft and, 602, 604
theoretical basis for, 590–592
Wilson and, 635–636
woman suffrage and, 609, 628
working class and, 588–590
World War I and, 614, 621, 624–625
Prohibition, 614, 625, 646, 653–654, 663,
  665. *See also* Temperance
Prohibition Party, 513, 565
Propaganda
  in Nazi Germany, 681(*b*)
  in World War I, 620(*i*), 628–629, 629(*i*)
  after World War II, 752
Property, as voting qualification, 449
Property rights
  state intervention in, 560
  workers' rights and, 559
Property taxes, 860, 860(*i*)
Proposition 13, 860(*i*)
Prosperity. *See also* Abundance; Wealth
  in 1920s, 647–648, 650, 667
  in 1950s, 785
  Johnson, L. B., and, 803
  in World War II, 726, 738–739
Prostitution, 586
Protective tariffs, 668. *See also* Tariffs
Protest(s). *See also* Civil rights movement;
  Resistance
  in 1960s, 795–796, 795(*i*)
  in 1968, 842–843(*b*), 843(*i*)
  by African Americans, 804–805, 806,
    807–809
  at Columbia University, 812–813(*b*),
    842–843, 842(*b*)
  by farmers, 555
  by gays and lesbians, 816
  in Great Depression, 671–672, 690
  by Native Americans, 809–810
  against segregation, 791–793
  over sex education, 862–863(*b*)
  student, 811–816, 812–813(*b*)
  against taxation, 860, 860(*i*)
  by Vietnam veterans, 849–850
  for Vietnam War, 847(*i*)
  against Vietnam War, 839–840, 840(*i*)
Protestants and Protestantism, 646
Provisional Revolutionary Government
  (Vietnam), 851
Pro-war demonstrations (1970), 847(*i*)
Public credit. *See* Credit
Public debt. *See* Debt
Public education. *See* Public schools
Public employment, discrimination ban in,
  898
Public facilities, segregation of, 457
Public libraries, 500, 501, 545, 546(*i*)
Public parks, 545
Public schools. *See also* Education; Schools
  in cities and towns, 545
  prayer in, 803
  segregation of Asians in, 599
  in South, 449
Public works
  in cities, 545, 546
  in Great Society, 803
  Hoover administration and, 668
  New Deal programs for, 694–696
Puck (magazine), 579(*i*), 603(*i*)
Puddlers, in iron industry, 533

Puerto Rican people, 810
as immigrants, 904(b)
Puerto Rico, 579, 579(i), 580(m)
Pulaski, Tennessee, Klan in, 450(b)
Pulitzer, Joseph, 575
Pullman (town), 560–561
Pullman, George M., 560, 561, 562(b), 564
Pullman boycott, 561, 562(b), 564
Pullman Palace cars, 561(i)
Pullman strike (1894), 560–564, 561(i), 588
Punishment, of blacks, 437, 450(b)
Pure Food and Drug Act (1906), 595
Pushcarts, immigrant livelihood and, 527, 527(i), 531(i)

Qian Xuesen (Hsien Hsue-shen, immigrant scientist), 760–761(b)
Quarantine policy, 530
Quotas, on immigration, 663, 801

Rabin, Yitzak, 902
Race and racism. See also African Americans; Civil rights; Civil rights movement; Discrimination; Segregation
against African Americans, 433–434, 480, 509, 530, 609
against Asians, 480–482, 530, 717
Fifteenth Amendment and, 447
in Great Depression, 671–672
immigrants and, 525, 528–533, 903–904
of Johnson, Andrew, 441
labor unions and, 695(b)
in Levittowns, 781
lynchings and, 509–510, 510–511(b), 511, 512(i), 640, 655, 658
New Deal and, 695(b), 704
of Northerners, 530
politics and, 509–512, 512(i)
Populists and, 568
progressivism and, 530, 609
racial mixing and, 509
Reconstruction and, 433–434, 457
social Darwinism and, 529
southern Democratic Party and, 458
during Vietnam War, 850
in West, 480–482
during World War II, 726–727
after World War II, 755
Race music, 786
Race riots
in 1943, 727
in Detroit (1967), 807
in East St. Louis, Illinois, 640
after King's death, 843
in Memphis, 445(i)
in Newark (1967), 807
in Watts (1965), 807
after World War I, 658
Racial code, Klan and, 450(b)
Racial equality clause, in Versailles treaty, 633
Racial segregation. See Race and racism; Segregation
Radar, in World War II, 723
Radical feminists, 817
Radical Reconstruction, 446
Radical Republicans, 446, 447, 595
Radicals and radicalism. See also Communism
black, 808–809
in Great Depression, 671, 691–692, 701
students and, 816
women and, 444(i)
after World War I, 637–638, 638–639(b)

Radical suffragists, 628, 630(b)
Radio
advertising on, 650
fireside chats on, 682(i), 683
mass culture and, 659–660
Scopes trial on, 664
Radioactivity, nuclear test ban and, 832
Railroad Administration, 625
Railroads
as big business, 497, 505
buffalo hunting and, 469
Chinese workers on, 481, 482(i)
competition and, 499–500
expansion of, 495, 496(m), 519, 524
farming and, 486, 489, 555
financing of, 498
General Managers Association and, 561, 564
land grants to, 486, 487(m), 495, 498
Morgan, J. P., and, 505
Populist efforts to reform, 558
Pullman boycott of, 561, 562(b), 564
ranching and, 486
rebates from, 501, 502, 503(i), 517, 593
regulation of, 517, 594–595
safety legislation for, 603
segregation in, 610
in South, 509
strikes against, 537–539, 537(m), 538(i), 556, 560
telegraph communication and, 498
transcontinental, 469, 496–497
in West, 464(i), 483(i), 486, 487(m)
Rainbow Coalition, 889
Raker Act (1913), 600(b)
Ranching, 486–488, 595
corporate, 490
Tejanos and, 488
vaqueros in, 488
Ranchos, 480
Randall, A. B., 438(b)
Randolph, A. Philip, 726, 805
Rape, victims of, 821
"Rape of Nanking," 711
Rapier, James T., 433–434, 434(i), 449, 457, 460
Rapier, John, 433
Ratification
of ERA (1972–1982), 820
of Versailles Treaty, 635
Raza Unida, La, 811
Readjusters, 509
Reagan, Ronald, 857(i), 858
cabinet of, 877
as California governor, 873
conservatism and, 857(i), 872–882
economy and, 873, 874–875
election of 1976 and, 866, 866(m)
election of 1980 and, 872–873
election of 1984 and, 875
end of Cold War and, 887
foreign policy of, 882–885
Iran-Contra scandal and, 883–884
Lebanon and, 883
Middle East and, 885
New Right and, 873
on Panama Canal, 870
rights and freedoms under, 876–882
Soviet Union and, 882, 884–885, 884(i)
Supreme Court and, 876
U.S. Government and, 875, 885
women's rights and, 877
Reapers, 489
Rearmament, of Nazi Germany, 680–681(b)

Rebates, railroad, 501, 502, 503(i), 517, 593, 594–595
Rebellions. See Protest(s); Revolts and rebellions
Recessions. See also Depressions; Economy; Panics
in 1913, 617
in 1937–1938, 701, 702–703
in 1957, 772
in 1980s, 875
of 2008–, 705, 911
after World War I, 637
Reconstruction (1863–1877), 443(i), 461
African Americans during, 433–434
carpetbaggers and, 433(i), 434, 448
collapse of, 455–460
congressional, 444–447
Johnson impeachment and, 446–447
Ku Klux Klan and, 448, 450–451(b), 451(i)
labor code and, 437
military rule during, 446, 446(m)
North and, 448, 455, 457
politics in, 448
presidential, 440–444
Radical, 446
Redeemers and, 460–461
scalawags and, 448
second, 804–809
South and, 441–443, 448–453, 454(i), 459(m)
southern Republican Party and, 446, 448–452, 455, 457
wartime, 435–440, 436(i)
white supremacy and, 442, 457–459
Reconstruction Acts (1867), 446, 447, 448
Reconstruction Finance Corporation (RFC, 1932), 668
Recovery
economic, in New Deal, 680–681, 705
industrial, in New Deal, 686–687
Recreation. See Leisure
Red Army (Soviet Union), 728, 729, 734, 744
Redbook magazine, "flappers" in, 655(i)
Red Cloud (Sioux chief), 470–471
Red Cross, 626, 626(b), 669
Redeemers, in South, 458–459, 460–461
Red power, 809
Red scare
after World War I, 637–640, 638–639(b)
after World War II, 742, 759–762, 759(i)
Red Stockings, 544
Reform and reform movements. See also Civil rights movement; Great Society
in cities, 547
civil service, 513, 514, 514(i)
coalitions of, 565, 583, 589
for direct election of senators, 513
Great Society and, 799–803, 802(t)
in Guatemala, 774
Hoover and, 666
moral reformers and, 508
Mugwumps as, 513
in New Deal, 681
Nixon and, 821–824
Obama and, 911–912
progressive, 558, 568, 584–587
Roosevelt, T., and, 593, 594–595
settlement house movement and, 584
social Darwinism and, 590
suffrage, 590
Taft and, 570(f), 602–603
tariff, 570(f), 602–603
temperance and, 512

Reform and reform movements (*continued*)
  Wilson and, 584, 606, 607
  women and, 590, 655
  after World War II, 753
Reform Darwinism, 590
Refugee Act (1980), 852(*b*)
Refugees
  from Cuba, 775–776(*b*)
  Jewish, 728, 753
  Palestinian, 847
  Vietnam War and, 852(*b*)
Regents of the University of California v. Bakke (1978), 863
Regulation
  in 1920s, 648
  of economy, 796
  of employee health and safety, 874
  of insurance companies, 911
  in New Deal, 683, 687
  progressives and government, 593, 594
  of railroads, 517, 594
  Supreme Court on, 648
  of trusts, 516, 517, 593
Relief programs, in New Deal, 676, 680, 684, 693–696, 694–695(*b*), 705
Religion(s). *See also* Churches
  in 1950s, 785, 785(*i*)
  Bush, G. W., and, 906
  of freedmen, 440
  of Indians, 476–477
  politics and, 508
  in rural and urban areas, 663
  Supreme Court on, 803
Relocation. *See also* Removal policy
  of Indians, 770–772, 771(*m*), 772(*i*), 809
  of Japanese Americans, 717–718, 718(*i*), 718(*m*)
Remington, Frederic, 575–576
Removal policy, for Indians, 465, 467
Rent controls, 754
Reparations, after World War I, 632, 649, 667
Republic(s)
  in former Yugoslavia, 900
  independence of Soviet, 893
Republican National Convention (1912), 604–605
Republican Party, 448. *See also* Elections
  black rights and, 457
  conservatism in, 873
  under Eisenhower, 769–770
  ERA and, 872, 876–877
  ex-Confederates in Congress and, 443
  factionalism in, 513, 514
  during Gilded Age, 498, 507, 508, 513–514
  Hoover in, 666
  Klan and political violence against, 450–451(*b*)
  Liberal Party and, 456–457
  New Deal and, 687, 691
  Northern Protestants and, 508
  "Old Guard" in, 594
  presidential Reconstruction and, 443–444
  progressives in, 584, 595
  Radical Reconstruction and, 446, 447
  in South, 446, 448–452, 455, 457, 458
  splits in, 513, 514, 584, 604, 605, 607
  tariffs and, 516, 570(*f*)
  woman suffrage and, 628
  World War I and, 629
  after World War I, 647–648
Republicans (Spain), 711
Republic Steel, strike at, 696

Reservationists, in Congress, 635
Reservations (Indian), 464, 465–469, 468(*m*), 470, 475
  division of, 474
Reserve Officers Training Corps (ROTC), 839, 887
Resistance. *See also* Revolts and rebellions
  by Indians, 464, 470–471, 475–477
Resources
  conservation of, 595–596
  World War I and, 625
Reston, James, 799
Restrictive covenants, 660(*b*), 781
Retirement Equity Act (1984), 877
Reuther, Walter, 780
Revenue. *See* Finances
Revenue agents, during prohibition, 654, 654(*i*)
Reverse discrimination, 876
Revolts and rebellions. *See also* Resistance
  in Hungary (1956), 773
  by students, 811–816
Revolution(s)
  Bolshevism and, 637, 638(*b*), 639(*b*)
  in Cuba, 775
  in Iran (1979), 868, 868(*i*)
  in Latin America, 710
  in Russia (1917), 620, 638(*b*)
Rhee, Syngman, 762, 763
Rhineland, 632
  Nazis in, 711
Rhodesia, 869
Rickover, Hyman, 576(*b*)
Ridgway, Matthew B., 765
Riefenstahl, Leni, 681(*b*)
Riesman, David, 786
Righter, Robert, 600(*b*)
Rights. *See also* Women
  Double V campaign and, 726–727
  of gays and lesbians, 880–881(*b*)
  Indian, 770
  of Japanese Americans, 718
  Reagan and, 876–882
  Supreme Court on, 457
  of workers to organize, 564
Right-to-life view, 821, 864
Right-to-work laws, 757
Right wing (political). *See also* Conservatives and conservatism
  Clinton and, 897–898
  Nixon and, 861–864
Riis, Jacob, 531, 532, 596(*b*), 596(*i*), 597(*b*), 597(*i*)
Riots. *See also* Protest(s); Race riots
  in 1968, 842–843(*b*)
  at Democratic National Convention (1968), 842(*b*), 843–844, 844(*i*)
River Rouge factory (Ford), 646, 671
Road maps, 650(*i*)
Roads and highways
  auto use and, 649
  interstate system and, 770, 771(*m*)
Roaring Twenties, 647, 652–653, 672
"Robber barons," 504, 646
Robertson, Pat, 873
Robinson, Jackie, 755
Robinson, Jo Ann, 792
Rock and roll music, 787, 816
Rockefeller, John D., 494, 495, 501–503, 502(*i*), 531, 593
  on government aiding trade, 570
Rockefeller, John D., Jr., 506
Rockefeller, Nelson, 822(*i*)
Rockne, Knute, 659

Rockwell, Norman, school desegregation and, 790(*b*), 791(*i*)
Roebling family
  Emily Warren, 522
  John, 522
  Washington, 522
Roe v. Wade (1973), 820–821, 876, 876(*i*)
Rolling Thunder (Vietnam War), 835
Roman Catholicism. *See* Catholicism
Romania, 632
  in World War II, 734
Rommel, Erwin, 724
Romney, Mitt, 911, 912, 912(*i*)
Roosevelt, Eleanor, 677
  New Deal and, 681–682, 684, 699
Roosevelt, Franklin Delano, 680(*b*). *See also* Great Depression; New Deal
  about, 677–678
  Atlantic Charter and, 715
  atomic bomb development and, 730–731(*b*)
  campaigning by, 678(*i*)
  at Casablanca, 725
  court-packing plan of, 701
  death of, 730–731
  Democratic coalition of, 679, 679(*m*), 682
  discrimination in defense industries and, 726
  economy and, 678
  election of 1920 and, 642
  election of 1932 and, 678–679, 678(*m*)
  election of 1936 and, 682, 701
  election of 1940 and, 682, 714
  election of 1944 and, 682, 727
  fireside chats of, 682(*i*), 683
  good neighbor policy in Latin America and, 710, 710(*i*)
  isolationism and, 709–711
  presidential power and, 703
  recession of 1937–1938 and, 701, 702–703
  Social Security and, 697–698
  Teheran meeting and, 729
  at Yalta, 729
Roosevelt, Theodore, 476, 677
  as assistant navy secretary, 576–577
  assumption of presidency, 592, 592(*i*)
  conservation and, 584, 595–596, 600(*b*), 601(*i*)
  election of 1900 and, 592
  election of 1904 and, 594, 600
  election of 1912 and, 584, 584(*i*), 604, 605, 605(*i*), 606, 606(*m*)
  foreign policy of, 596–600, 598(*m*), 615
  government intervention by, 593
  mediation by, 593, 599
  Monroe Doctrine and, 597–598, 598(*m*), 599(*i*)
  New Nationalism of, 605, 606
  Nobel Peace Prize for, 599
  Open Door Policy and, 599–600
  Panama Canal and, 597–598, 602(*m*)
  progressivism and, 584, 593, 594, 595
  as reformer, 593, 594–595
  Spanish-American War and, 576–577, 578–579
  Square Deal of, 594
  Taft and, 601, 603, 604
  as trustbuster, 584, 593
  Washington, Booker T., and, 610(*i*)
Roosevelt Corollary, 598, 598(*m*), 599(*i*), 604
Root-Takahira agreement (1908), 600
Rosebud, Battle of (1876), 471
Rosenberg, Ethel and **Julius,** 759
"Rosie the Riveter", 725, 726(*i*)
ROTC. *See* Reserve Officers Training Corps

Roughing It (Twain), 490
Rough Riders, 578
Royal Navy. *See* Navies, British
Ruhr Valley region, France and, 649
Rumsfeld, Donald, 909
Rural areas. *See also* Farms and farming
   in 1920s, 646, 662–663, 672–673
   automobiles and, 649
   clean water in, 686*(i)*
   electricity and, 684–685, 685*(m)*, 686*(i)*
   in Great Depression, 668, 670, 690, 690*(i)*
   population in, 488*(f)*, 662*(m)*
   poverty in, 670
Rural Electrification Administration (REA),
   685
Rusk, Dean, 834
Russell, Harold, 743
Russia, 617. *See also* Bolshevik Revolution;
   Soviet Union
   Bolshevism in, 620, 637, 638*(b)*
   immigrants from, 525, 526*(f)*, 528–529*(b)*,
     529*(i)*, 663
   pogroms in, 527, 528–529*(b)*, 529*(i)*
   World War I and, 617, 620, 624, 638*(b)*
Russian Revolution. *See* Bolshevik
   Revolution
Russo-Japanese War, 599
Ruth, Herman ("Babe"), 659
Rwanda, civil war in, 900

Sacco, Nicola, 663, 664*(i)*
Sadat, Anwar, 870
Saddam Hussein. *See* Hussein, Saddam
Safety, in mining, 479
Safety legislation. *See also* Occupational
   Safety and Health Act
   for mines and railroads, 603
Saigon. *See* Vietnam War
Saint-Gaudens, August, 546*(i)*
St. Louis, Missouri, People's Party 1892
   convention in, 553, 553*(i)*, 554, 554*(i)*,
   557, 567–568
St. Louis Exposition (1904), 476
St.-Mihiel, battle at, 614, 623*(m)*
St. Valentine's Day massacre, 654
SALT. *See* Strategic Arms Limitation Talks
Salter, John, Jr., 804*(i)*
Saltonstall, Nora, in World War I France,
   626–627*(b)*, 627*(i)*
Salvation Army, 626
Samoan Islands, 573, 575*(m)*
San Carlos Reservation, 476
Sand Creek massacre (1864), 468–469
San Diego, 480
Sandinistas, in Nicaragua, 869, 883
S&L crisis. *See* Savings and loan crisis
Sandoz, Jules, 477
Sandwich Islands (Hawai'i). *See* Hawai'i
Sanfilippo, Peter, 724*(i)*
San Francisco, 530
   Hetch Hetchy Valley and, 600*(b)*, 601*(b)*,
     601*(i)*
   stock market in, 478
Sanger, Margaret, 608–609, 608*(i)*,
   655–656, 816*(i)*
San Juan Hill, Roosevelt, Theodore, at, 578
Santa Clara, University of, 481*(i)*
Santee (Dakota) Indians, 470
Santee Uprising (1862), 470
Sarajevo, World War I and, 617
Satellite countries, Soviet, in Eastern Europe,
   744, 748
Satellites. *See* Space exploration
Saturday Evening Post, 654, 790*(b)*

Saudi Arabia, 895*(i)*
   U.S. soldiers in, 908
Savings and loan (S&L) crisis, 875
"Scabs" (strikebreakers), 538, 542, 558
Scalawags, 448
Scandinavia, 525, 525*(m)*, 526*(f)*
   immigrants from, 691
Schenck, Charles, 639
Schenck v. United States (1919), 639
Schlafly, Phyllis, 820, 857–858, 859, 861,
   873, 878–879*(b)*, 879*(i)*
Schools. *See also* Desegregation; Education;
   Integration; Public schools
   desegregation of, 757, 788–789*(b)*, 788–791,
     824
   ESEA and, 800
   Freedmen's, 452*(i)*
   Indian, 471–474, 474*(i)*
   Klan and black, 450*(b)*
   segregation of, 449, 699
   "separate but equal" doctrine and, 788*(b)*,
     790
Schreiber, Marie, 754
Schuman, Robert, 750*(b)*
Schurz, Carl, 434, 460
Schwartz, Edward, on student power
   (1967), 812*(b)*
Science and scientists
   anti-Communist crusade and, 760–761*(b)*
   Jewish scientists and, 730–731*(b)*
SCLC. *See* Southern Christian Leadership
   Conference
Scopes, John, 664, 665
Scopes trial, 660*(b)*, 664–665
Scorched-earth policy, against Indians, 470
Scott, Hugh, 865
Scott, Tom, 500
Scottsboro Boys, 671, 672*(i)*
SDI. *See* Strategic Defense Initiative
SDS. *See* Students for a Democratic Society
Seabrook nuclear power plant, 868
SEALs, 832
Seasonal laborers. *See* Migrant workers
Seattle, general strike in, 636
SEC. *See* Securities and Exchange
   Commission
Secession, 441
Secondary schools, 545
Second front, in World War II, 724, 729, 743
Second Reconstruction, 804–809
Second World War. *See* World War II
Secretarial work, women in, 536, 536*(i)*
Sectionalism
   efforts to reduce, 514
   New South and, 508–509
   in politics, 516
Securities and Exchange Commission (SEC,
   1934), 683
Security. *See* Defense; National security
   state
Security Council (UN), 730
Sedition Act, of 1918, 629
Segregation
   of African Americans, 509, 530, 531,
     788–793
   of armed forces, 620
   of Asians, 599
   in California, 480
   in Chicago, 806
   in cities, 530, 531
   of federal workforce, 610
   in housing, 660–661*(b)*, 661*(i)*, 781
   Jim Crow and, 449–450, 509, 610
   protests against, 791–793

of public transportation, 457
   in railroads, 610
   social, 531
   in South, 449, 457, 509
   after World War II, 755–756, 756*(i)*
Seitz, Charles, 904*(b)*
Selective Service Act
   of 1917, 620
   of 1940, 718–719
Self-determination, 615, 632, 633, 710, 752
*Selling a Freeman to Pay His Fine at
   Monticello, Florida,* 442*(i)*
Selma, Alabama, voting rights march in,
   805, 806*(i)*
Seminole Indians, 465
Senate (U.S.), 649
   direct election to, 513, 558, 604
   election to, 558
   federal officials tried in, 447
   Foreign Relations Committee, 635
   Versailles treaty and, 635
Seneca Falls, New York, women's rights
   convention at, 566
"Separate but equal" doctrine, 610, 788*(b)*,
   790
Separate spheres idea, 509, 543
Separation of church and state, Bush, G.
   W., and, 906
Separation of powers, 602
September 11, 2001, terrorist attacks, 888,
   908, 908*(i)*
Sequoia National Park, 598*(m)*
Serbs and Serbia, 617
   in former Yugoslavia, 900–901
Servants. *See also* Domestics
   women as, 534, 536*(f)*, 543
Servicemen's Readjustment Act (1944). *See*
   GI Bill (1944)
Service occupations, in 1950s, 780
Settlement house movement, 583, 584, 584*(i)*,
   585
Settler(s), transportation for, 482
Seventeenth Amendment, 604
Sewall, Arthur M., 568
Sewing machine, 533–534
Sewing rooms, WPA and, 696
Sex and sexuality. *See also* Homosexuals
   and homosexuality
   in 1920s, 656–657*(b)*
   double standard of, 657*(b)*
   gender integration in speakeasies, 654
   Kinsey on, 787
   middle class, 657*(b)*
   Sanger and, 655–656
   sex education and, 860, 862–863, 863*(i)*
   working class women and, 544
Sex discrimination, 796, 821, 877, 907
Sexual Behavior in the Human Female
   (Kinsey), 787
Sexual Behavior in the Human Male (Kinsey),
   787
Sexual harassment, in workplace, 877, 891
Sexual orientation, 898
Sexual revolution
   1920s, 656–657*(b)*
   1960s, 816
Seymour, Horatio, 455–456, 458*(i)*
Shafter, William, 579
Shahn, Ben, 664*(i)*
Shah of Iran. *See* Pahlavi, Mohammad
   Reza
Shaka (Zulu king), 466*(b)*
"Shame of the Cities, The" (Steffens), 547
Shanks, Daren, 905*(b)*

Shantung Peninsula, as Japanese mandate, 633
Sharecroppers and sharecropping, 450(b), 453, 461, 488, 670, 686, 690, 690(i), 704
"Share Our Wealth" plan (Long), 692
Sheldon, Charles M., 586
Shelters, for women, 821
Sheppard-Towner Act (1921), 655
Shepstone, Theophilus, 466(b), 467(b)
Sherman, William Tecumseh, 437, 470
Sherman Antitrust Act (1890), 517, 593, 874
Sherman Silver Purchase Act (1890), 518
Shiite Muslims
    Hezbollah and, 883
    in Iran, 872
    in Iraq, 895, 910
Shipping Board, 625
Ships and shipping. See also Navies; Navy (U.S.)
    Panama Canal and, 597, 602(m)
    steamboat travel, 528(b)
    in World War I, 617–619
    in World War II, 714, 723–724
Shoe industry, 904(b)
Shoshoni Indians, 475, 476, 479
Sicily, in World War II, 725
Sierra Club, 595, 600(b), 601(b)
Sierra Nevada Mountains, 481
Sigsbee, Charles Dwight, 576(b)
Silent Spring (Carson), 822
Silver
    Comstock Lode and, 477, 478–480
    free silver issue, 516, 517–518
    mining of, 478(m)
Sinai Peninsula, 870
Sinclair, Upton, 595, 691
Singapore, 722
Sioux Indians, 469, 474(i), 475, 476
    Black Hills and, 470–471
    imperialism, colonialism and, 466(b), 467(b)
Sit-down strike, at GM, 696, 697(i)
Sit-ins, 804, 804(i)
Sitting Bull (Sioux leader), 469, 471, 477, 477(i)
Six-Day War (1967), 846–847, 846(m), 870
Sixteenth Amendment, 604, 606
Skilled workers, 533, 535, 537, 539, 543, 551, 558, 561, 561(i), 696
    Johnson, L. B., training for, 800
Slaughterhouse cases (1873), 457
Slaveholders, Reconstruction and former, 434
Slaves and slavery. See also Abolition and abolitionism; African Americans; Revolts and rebellions
    Civil War and, 437–438
    families and, 440
    Johnson, Andrew, and, 441
    Thirteenth Amendment and, 441
Slavic immigrants, 524, 525, 525(m), 526(f), 533, 558
Slums, 523
    slum clearance and, 758, 803
Smith, Alfred E. (Al), 665, 665(m)
Smith, E. G, 877(i)
Smith, Effie Vivian, 485(b)
Smith, Joseph, Jr., 480
Smithsonian Institution, 577(b)
Smoking. See Tobacco and tobacco industry
SNCC. See Student Nonviolent Coordinating Committee

Snelling, Fort, mass execution at, 470
Social Darwinism, 494, 506–507(b), 506–508
    depression of 1890s and, 566–569
    People's Party and, 566
    racism and, 529
    reform Darwinism and, 590
    social gospel and, 585–586
Social Democratic Party. See Socialist Party
Social engineering, 590
Social geography, of cities, 530–533
Social gospel, 585–586
Socialism and socialists, 539, 639
    in Great Depression, 671
    New Deal and, 691, 700, 705
Socialist Labor Party, 607
Socialist Party
    in 1936, 701
    Debs and, 564, 605, 606(m), 629
    as middle-class and native-born, 607
    in 1912, 605, 606(m)
    racism and, 671
Social justice
    Nixon and, 823–824
    progressives and, 584(i)
Social mobility, after World War II, 754–755
Social purity movement, 585
Social Security, 693, 697–698, 701, 758
    poverty of elderly and, 876
Social Security Act (1935), 697–698
Social segregation, 531
Social welfare. See Welfare and welfare system
Social work, as profession, 585
Society. See also Culture(s); Great Society; Progressivism
    speakeasies and, 654
    suburbs and, 781
    of Zulu, 466(b)
"Sodbusters," 484
Sod houses, 483(i), 484, 486
Sodomy, laws against, 882
Solar power, 868, 869
Soldiers. See also Military; specific battles and wars
    black, 480
    in Korean War, 763, 764
    mail for, 707(i)
    in Vietnam War, 828, 837(i), 838–839, 838(i), 841, 841(i)
    in World War I, 613–614, 620–621, 621–622, 622(i), 636, 636(i)
    in World War II, 718, 719(i), 722, 723(i), 724(i), 729, 730, 735(i), 739
Solid South, 864
Solomon Islands, 719(i), 723(i), 732
Somalia, 900
Somme, Battle of (1916), 621
Sonnek, Christine, 484(b)
Sonoran Desert, 476
Soros, George, 903
Sorosis Club, 512
Souls of Black Folk, The (Du Bois), 611
Sousa, John Philip, 575
South (U.S. region). See also Civil rights; Civil rights movement; Reconstruction; Segregation; Solid South; Sun Belt
    African Americans and, 433–434, 448, 530, 543, 609–610, 640, 662(m), 698, 727, 791–793, 804–806
    allotment program in, 685, 686, 690
    black codes in, 441–442, 442(i)
    black migration from, 640, 641(i)
    civil rights in, 803
    crop lien system in, 509, 555

Democrats in, 759
    disfranchisement of blacks in, 609–610
    economy in, 517–518
    Fourteenth Amendment and, 445, 446
    freedmen, land, and labor in, 437–438
    Great Depression in, 670
    home rule for, 456, 458
    immigration to, 525, 525(m)
    Indian removal from, 465
    industry in, 509
    Jim Crow laws in, 509, 530, 610
    lynchings in, 509–511, 510–511(b), 512(i)
    military rule in, 446, 446(m)
    New Deal agricultural benefits in, 686, 698
    Populists in, 557(i), 568
    poverty in 1950s, 779
    progressivism in, 609–610
    racial violence in, 509–510, 510–511(b), 511, 512(i), 610, 611
    railroads in, 509
    Reconstruction and, 441–443, 448–454, 454(i), 457–459, 459(m)
    Redeemers in, 458–459
    Republican governments in, 448–452, 455, 458, 460
    Republican Party in, 446, 448, 455, 456, 457
    sectionalism and, 508–509
    segregation in, 449, 457, 509, 530
    sharecropping in, 450(b), 453, 488, 670, 686
    Sun Belt and, 781, 782(m)
    tariffs and, 516
    tobacco and, 509
    violence against blacks in, 509–510, 510–511(b), 511, 512(i), 610
    voting in, 509, 609–610
South Africa, 466(b)
    Carter and, 869
    democracy in, 893
    Reagan and, 883
South America, 615. See also Latin America; North America
South Boston, busing and, 861(i)
South Carolina, 441, 460
Southeast Asia. See also Vietnam War
    containment policy in, 773–774
Southern Arapaho Indians, 469
Southern Christian Leadership Conference (SCLC), 793, 796(i), 804
Southern Europe, immigrants from, 663
Southern Farmers' Alliance, 556
Southern Farm Tenants Union, 690
Southern Manifesto on Integration (1956), 788(b)
Southern Pacific Railroad, 591
Southern strategy, of Nixon, 861, 864
South Korea. See also Korean War
    Carter and, 869
    Nike in, 904(b)
South Vietnam. See also Vietnam War
    army of (ARVN), 774
    formation of, 774
    U.S. evacuation of, 851(i)
Southwest
    Hispanics in, 480
    Indians in, 467, 476
    Mexican Americans in, 757, 810
    Mexican migration to, 640–642, 642(i)
    population in, 662(m)
    vaqueros in, 488
Sovereign immunity, of states, 890(b)

Soviet Union. *See also* Bolsheviks and
        Bolshevism; Cold War; Russia
    Afghanistan and, 871, 872, 885
    arms race with, 748–749
    Bolshevism in, 638*(b)*, 639*(b)*
    Carter and, 871
    Cold War and, 742
    Cuba and, 828, 829–830
    détente with, 845–846
    dissolution of, 892–893
    Eastern Europe and, 744, 748
    end of, 888
    Germany after World War II, 744
    Nazi invasion of, 714, 723
    nuclear missiles of, 773*(i)*
    Popular Front and, 700–701
    Prague Spring and, 843
    Reagan and, 874*(i)*, 882, 884–885
    Roosevelt, F. D., and, 709
    Stalingrad battle and, 728
    Wilson and, 638*(b)*
    World War II and, 713, 730, 734, 734–735*(b)*
    after World War II, 739
Space exploration
    Apollo program and, 830–831
    Soviet orbit of earth and, 830
    Sputnik and, 777
Spain. *See also* Spanish-American War
    civil war in, 711
    Cuba and, 574, 575, 576, 578, 578*(m)*, 579
    Monroe Doctrine and, 574
    Treaty of Paris (1898) and, 579
    Spanish-American War (1898), 548*(b)*, 554,
        574–577, 575*(i)*, 578*(m)*
    treaty ending, 579
Spanish civil war, 711
Spanish empire, 579
Spanish influenza epidemic, 637, 637*(i)*
"Speakeasy," 654
"Speak softly but carry a big stick" (Roosevelt,
        T.), 597, 599*(i)*, 600
Special Forces
    bin Laden and, 913
    Kennedy and, 832
Speculation
    in land, 482, 486
    in mining, 478
    in railroads, 496, 496*(m)*
    stock, 667
Spencer, Herbert, 506–507*(b)*, 506*(i)*
Spending. *See* Defense spending; Deficit
        spending; Finances; Military
Spheres of influence
    in China, 573
    of Russia, 599
    Western Hemisphere and, 570, 571
Spies, August, 542, 543
Spies and spying, 750–751
    in Cold War, 749*(i)*
    U-2 incident and, 778
Spoils system, 456, 508, 513
Sports, in 1920s, 659
Sputnik, 777
Square Deal, 594
Squatters, 480
Stagflation, 821, 867
Stalin, Joseph, 713
    at Teheran, 729, 734
    after World War II, 743
    at Yalta, 729
Stalingrad, battle at, 728, 733*(m)*
Stalwarts, 513, 514
Stamping mills, in mining, 479
Standard of living. *See* Lifestyle; Wealth

Standard Oil Company, 501–503, 502*(i)*,
        503*(i)*, 506, 513, 570, 593
Standing Bear, Henry, 474*(i)*
Standing Bear, Luther, 470, 472–473, 474
Standing Rock Reservation, 477
Stanton, Edwin M., 438*(b)*, 447
Stanton, Elizabeth Cady
    on "negro first" strategy, 447
    on term *male* in Constitution, 445
    woman's suffrage movement and, 444*(i)*,
        445, 512, 566
Starr, Kenneth, 899
START treaty. *See* Strategic Arms Reduction
        Talks treaty
Starvation
    during Great Depression, 670
    on reservations, 467
"Star Wars," SDI as, 883, 885
State(s)
    Bill of Rights and, 803
    business regulation and, 648
    Eisenhower and, 770
    during Reconstruction, 446, 446*(m)*,
        448–452
    regulation by, 517
    restoration to Union, 435, 436, 441, 445,
        449, 459*(m)*
    rights derived from, 457
    Social Security financing for, 698
State Department, pro-Communists in,
        753
Statehood, for territories, 490
States' rights
    Johnson, Andrew, on, 441, 444
    Wilson and, 605, 606
States' Rights (Dixiecrats) Party, 757
Statue of Liberty, 530, 663
Steam power
    engines in mining, 479
    in farming, 489
    steamships, global migration, and, 526
Steel and steel industry
    Bessemer process in, 500, 501*(f)*
    Carnegie in, 500, 501, 524, 558–560
    in New South, 509
    production in, 501*(f)*
    strikes against, 558–560, 636–637,
        696–697
    structural steel and, 501, 545
Steffens, Lincoln, 547
Stein, Gertrude, 661
Steinbacher, Joseph, 731–732, 737
Steinbeck, John, 691
Steinem, Gloria, 818, 820*(i)*
Stephens, Alexander, 443
Stephens, Harry, and family, 440*(i)*
Stephens, Uriah, 540*(b)*
Stephenson, David, 664
Stern, Edith, 785
Stevens, John L. (American minister to
        Hawai'i), 572*(b)*
Stevens, Thaddeus, 446
Stevenson, Adlai E., 772
Stock(s)
    of railroads, 500
    speculation in, 667
Stock market
    in 1990s, 899
    crash of (1929), 665, 667, 673
    in San Francisco, 478
Stone Mountain, Georgia, Klan in, 664
Stonewall riots (1969), 816
STOP ERA, 878*(b)*, 879*(i)*
"Storm the Fort" (Taylor), 540*(b)*

Strategic Arms Limitation Talks (SALT),
        846
Strategic Arms Reduction Talks (START)
        treaty (1990), 893
Strategic Defense Initiative (SDI, "Star
        Wars"), 883, 885, 909
Streetcars, 531, 532*(i)*, 590, 591, 591*(i)*, 649
"Stretch-out system," in mills, 688*(b)*, 689*(b)*
Strikebreakers, 538, 542, 558, 559*(i)*, 561,
        637, 689*(i)*
Strikes. *See also* Labor; Labor unions
    in 1946, 754
    in auto industry, 696
    by coal miners, 593, 671, 671*(m)*
    by Cripple Creek miners, 560
    Gompers and, 542
    in Great Depression, 671, 671*(m)*,
        688–689*(b)*, 696–697
    Great Railroad Strike (1877), 537–539,
        537*(m)*, 538*(i)*, 560
    Knights of Labor and, 542, 543
    at McCormick reaper works, 542
    by PATCO, 874
    against railroads, 537–539, 537*(m)*, 538*(i)*,
        556
    in textile mills, 688–689*(b)*, 689*(i)*
    after World War I, 636–637
    during World War II, 719
Student Nonviolent Coordinating Committee
        (SNCC), 804, 805
Students. *See also* Young people
    at Freedmen's school, 452*(i)*
    protests by, 789*(b)*, 811–816, 812–813*(b)*,
        842*(b)*
Students for a Democratic Society (SDS),
        811–812, 813, 839
Submarines
    nuclear, 778
    in World War I, 618–619, 619*(m)*, 623,
        714, 717, 723
    in World War II, 707, 714, 717, 723
Subsidies
    for home ownership, 781
    for poor mothers, 898
Subtreasury plan, of Populists, 557–558
Suburbs
    African Americans in, 660–661*(b)*
    automobiles and, 649
    growth of, 780–781
Subversives, Red Scare and, 760
Sudetenland, 712
Suez Canal, 724, 775
Suez crisis (1956), 775–776, 775*(i)*
Suffrage. *See also* Voting and voting rights;
        Woman suffrage
    black, 436–437, 446
    Fourteenth Amendment and, 444–445
    for men, 449
    for Native Americans, 663
    in states, 564
Suffragists, 444*(i)*, 628
Sufronko, Paul, 894*(b)*
Sugar and sugar industry
    Cuba and, 576
    in Hawai'i, 570, 572*(b)*
    monopoly in, 517
Sullivan, Louis, 548*(b)*
Sultzer, William, 576*(b)*
Summit meetings
    Eisenhower-Khrushchev (Geneva, 1955),
        777
    Reagan-Gorbachev (1985), 777
Sumner, Charles, 436, 445, 446
Sumner, William Graham, 507, 507*(b)*

Sun Also Rises, The (Hemingway), 662
Sun Belt, 768, 781–783, 782(*m*)
   air conditioning and, 781
   conservatism in, 860
Sunday laws, 587–588
Sunni Muslims, in Iraq, 910
Superfund, 869
Superpowers
   global rivalry of, 752–753, 832, 872
   U.S. as, 738
   after World War II, 739, 749
Supply and demand, law of, 678
Supply-side economics, 874
Supreme Court (U.S.)
   2000 election and, 906
   ADA and, 890, 891(*b*)
   on antisodomy laws, 882
   antitrust law and, 504, 593
   Bush, G. H. W., and, 891
   Bush, G. W., and, 907
   business and, 504, 508, 648
   on busing, 861
   on bus segregation, 793
   civil rights and, 788–790, 803
   "clear and present danger" test and, 639
   on Colfax massacre attackers, 458
   in Gilded Age, 504, 506, 508, 517
   on labor unions, 593
   laissez-faire and, 506–508, 517
   National Recovery Administration and, 689
   Nixon and, 862–863
   Obama and, 911
   on railroad regulation, 504, 517
   Reagan and, 876
   Reconstruction and, 457
   on religion, 803
   Roosevelt, F. D., and, 701
   segregated housing and, 660(*b*)
   on segregation, 610
   on seizure of Black Hills, 471
   separate but equal doctrine and, 610, 788(*b*)
   Social Security and, 698
   on Spanish and Mexican land grants, 480
   women on, 877, 897
   on workday, 589–590
Surplus (agricultural), in Great Depression, 668, 669
Surplus (financial), 897
"Survival of the fittest," 506(*i*), 507
Sweatshops, 533, 534(*i*), 588(*i*), 903
Sweet, Gladys, 660(*b*)
Sweet, Ossian, 660(*b*), 661(*b*), 661(*i*)
Syria
   rebellion in (2011), 913
   Six-Day War and, 847
   Yom Kippur War and, 847
Szilard, Leo, 731(*b*)

Taft, Robert A., 764
Taft, William Howard
   dollar diplomacy of, 604, 604(*m*), 615
   election of 1908 and, 601
   election of 1912 and, 584, 603(*i*), 604, 605, 606, 606(*m*)
   foreign policy of, 604, 604(*m*)
   presidency of, 584, 592, 602–603, 603(*i*), 604
   Roosevelt and, 601, 603, 604
   tariffs and, 570(*f*), 602–603
Taft-Hartley Act (1947), 757
Taiwan, Nationalist Chinese on, 752–753
Taliban (Afghanistan), 908

Tammany Hall, 547, 665
Tanks, in World War II, 724
Tanzania, U.S. embassy bombing in, 901
Tarbell, Ida M., 502–503, 503(*i*), 602
Tariffs
   globalization and, 902
   Harding and, 647
   Hawley-Smoot (1930), 668
   Latin American reductions on (1930s), 710
   McKinley, 516, 517, 570, 570(*f*), 572(*b*)
   Payne-Aldrich, 602
   reduction of, 516, 602
   social Darwinism and, 508
   Taft and, 570(*f*), 602–603
   Underwood (1913), 606
   Wilson and, 606
   after World War I, 667
Taxation
   in 1920s, 648, 667
   Bush, G. H. W., and, 890–891
   Bush, G. W., and, 906
   Carter and, 867
   Coolidge and, 667
   income tax and, 604, 606
   Johnson, L. B., and, 799
   Kennedy and, 798
   Mellon and, 648
   Proposition 13 and, 860(*i*)
   protests against, 860, 860(*i*)
   Reagan and, 874
   in South, 451, 458
   on wealth, 698
   of windfall profits, 868
Tax Reform Act (1986), 874
Taylor, Frederick Winslow, 590
Taylor, Horace, 502(*i*)
Taylor, Thomas W. ("Old Beeswax"), 540(*b*)
Teachers
   in black schools, Klan and, 450(*b*)
   women and, 536
Tea Party movement, 912
Teapot Dome scandal, 648, 648(*i*)
Technology. *See also* Weapons
   agricultural, 489, 779, 779(*i*)
   at Columbian Exposition, 548(*b*)
   for mining, 479
   in Vietnam War, 854
Teheran
   hostage crisis in, 872
   World War II meeting in, 729, 734(*b*)
Tejanos, 480, 488
Telegraph, 498, 499, 503, 558
Telephone, 503–504, 548(*b*)
Television
   culture, politics, and (1950s), 785–786
   presidential debates on, 797
Temperance. *See also* Prohibition
   movement, 512
   "pledge" about, 512
   women and, 512–513, 513(*i*), 564–565
Temporary Assistance for Needy Families, 898
Tenant farmers
   New Deal and, 686, 704
   in South, 670, 686
   in West, 488
Tenements, 584
   photography of, 596(*b*), 596(*i*), 597(*b*), 597(*i*)
Tennessee, 436, 445
   ADA and, 890–891(*b*)
   Democrats in, 458
Tennessee Coal and Iron Company, 595, 604

Tennessee v. Lane, 890–891(*b*)
Tennessee Valley Authority (TVA), 684–685, 685(*m*)
Tennessee Valley Authority Act (1933), 687(*t*)
Tenure of Office Act (1867), 447
Termination program, for Indians, 770–772, 809, 824
Territories. *See also* Indian Territory
   government in, 490
Terrorism
   Bush, G. W., and, 905, 912
   globalization of, 908–909
   Islamic, 901
   by Klan, 450–451(*b*)
   in Middle East, 883
   Obama and, 912–913
   in Oklahoma City, 897, 897(*i*)
   of September 11, 2001, 888, 908, 908(*i*)
   southern Democratic party and, 458, 459(*i*)
   after World War I, 637
Tet Offensive (1968), 841
Texas, 664
   Hispanics in, 480
   manifest destiny and, 465
   Mexican Americans in, 691
   Redeemers in, 459
   Tejanos in, 488
   textbooks in, 860
Texas Rangers, 480
Textbooks
   sex education in, 862–863(*b*)
   in Texas, 860
Textiles and textile industry
   immigrants in, 533
   mechanization in, 533
   in South, 509
   strikes in, 688–689(*b*), 689(*i*)
   unions and, 697
   women workers in, 533, 565, 688(*b*), 698
Textile Workers' Union, 688(*b*)
Thatcher, Margaret, 873
Their Eyes Were Watching God (Hurston), 658
Thieu, Nguyen Van, 851(*i*)
Third parties, 701
Third world, 523, 524, 524(*m*), 752
   Kennedy and, 831–832
Thirteenth Amendment, 441
This Side of Paradise (Fitzgerald), 655, 662
Thomas, Clarence, 891
Thomas, Lorenzo, 438(*b*)
Thomas, Norman, 671
Thor Ballistic Missile, 773(*i*)
369th Regiment, in World War I, 622
Threshers, 489
Thurber, James, 662
Thurmond, J. Strom, 757
Thurston, Lorrin, 572(*b*)
Thygeson, Sylvie, 536
Tiananmen Square demonstrations, Beijing, 893
Tianjin (Tientsin) treaty (1858), 571
Tibbets, Paul, 707–708, 717, 731(*b*), 738
Tiffany, Louis Comfort, 548(*b*)
Tight money, 518
Tilden, Samuel J., 459–460, 460(*m*)
Till, Emmett, 790
Tillman, Benjamin, 568
Tilyou, George, 544
Timber Yellow Robe, 474(*i*)
Title VII, of Civil Rights Act (1964), 806, 817
Title IX, of Education Amendments Act (1972), 821, 824, 876

Tobacco and tobacco industry, 509
   advertising for, 652–653(b)
   in South, 509
Tojo, Hideki (Japan), 716
Tourism, 650(i)
Townsend, Francis, 691–692, 697
Toxic wastes, Love Canal disaster and, 869
Trade. *See also* Commerce; Free trade;
      Ships and shipping; Transportation
   Bush, G. W., and, 902
   China, 571, 573–574, 574(i), 598–599
   Clinton and, 902
   expansion of (1870–1910), 570–571, 570(f)
   missionaries and, 571, 572(b)
   during World War I, 617
   before World War II, 711
Trade associations, 648
Trade barriers, globalization and, 902
Trade unions, 696
Trading with the Enemy Act (1917), 629
Trail(s)
   Bozeman, 470
   cattle, 486
   Chisholm, 486
Transcontinental railroad, 469, 481, 496–497, 498
   first, 482
Trans-Mississippi West, 465
Transportation
   improvements in, 524
   public, 868
   segregation of, 457
Treasury Department, prohibition
      enforcement by, 653–654, 654(i)
Treaties. *See also* specific treaties
   Indian, 466, 475
Trench warfare, in World War I, 621, 622(i)
Triangle Shirtwaist Company, fire at, 589, 589(i)
Tribes. *See* Native Americans
Trickle-down economics, 668
Tripartite Pact (1940), 716
Triple Alliance, 617
Triple Entente, 617
Troubled Asset Relief Program (2008), 911
Truman, Harry S.
   assumption of presidency, 727, 731, 742
   atomic bomb and, 737–738
   civil rights and, 756
   containment and, 746
   election of 1944 and, 727
   election of 1948 and, 757–758, 758(i), 758(m)
   Fair Deal and, 753–762
   foreign policy of, 744
   Indian termination program under, 771
   Korean War and, 762–764
   labor and, 754
   national security state and, 748–753
   Vietnam and, 774, 828
Truman Doctrine, 748
Trumbull, Lyman, 443
Trumpauer, Joan, 804(i)
Trust(s), 502, 516, 592, 606
Tunisia
   rebellion in (2011), 913
   in World War II, 724(i)
Tunney, Gene, 659
Tuolumne River, 600(b)
Turkey
   Greece and, 633
   immigrants from, 526(f)
   U.S. missiles in, 832
   after World War II, 742, 747–748

Turner, Frederick Jackson, 463, 464, 465, 491
Tuskegee Institute, 610
Twain, Mark (Samuel Langhorne Clemens), 496
   on baseball, 544
   on Comstock Lode, 478
   on Gilded Age, 490–491, 493
   on West, 490
Tweed, William Marcy ("Boss"), 547
Twenty-sixth Amendment, 838
Twenty Years at Hull-House (Addams), 584(i)
Two Moons (Cheyenne chief), 471
Typewriter (machine), 536

U-2 spy plane incident, 778
U-boats. *See* Submarines
UFW. *See* United Farm Workers
UN. *See* United Nations
Uncle Sam (male symbol of US), 549, 574
Underconsumption
   Great Depression and, 682
   unemployment and, 533, 696
Undocumented migrants, 783(i)
Unemployment. *See also* Employment; Great
      Depression
   in 1890s depression, 519, 533, 560, 566–567, 567(i)
   in 1920s, 647, 650
   Carter and, 867
   Clinton and, 798, 899
   in Great Depression, 668, 669, 670, 686, 693–694, 698, 702
   Nixon and, 821
   Obama and, 912
   after World War I, 636
   in World War II, 727
Unemployment compensation, 754
Unemployment insurance, 698
Unification, of Germany, 892
Unilateralism, in foreign policy of Bush,
      George W., 909–910
Unionism, 593
   anarchism and, 560
Unionists, in South, 439(b), 448
Union Pacific Railroad, 500
Union Party, 691, 692
Unions. *See* Labor unions
Union Signal, 565
United Auto Workers (UAW), 696
United Farm Workers (UFW), 811, 811(i)
United Fruit Company, 774
United Garment Workers of America, 588(i)
United Mine Workers (UMW), 593, 696
United Nations (UN), 729–730, 738
   2011 rebellions and, 913
   Charter of, 730
   Decade for Women, 818(b)
   Iraq weapons inspections by, 895, 901
   Korean War and, 762
   Persian Gulf War and, 895
   total nuclear test ban treaty and, 893
UN International Criminal Court, 909
United States. *See also* Constitution (U.S.);
      Government (U.S.)
   developing nations and, 902–903
   global role of, 913–915
   internationalization of, 903–904
   NAFTA and, 902
   as superpower, 739
   as world creditor, 649
   as world power, 584, 599
U.S. Chamber of Commerce, 646
U.S. Communist Party. *See* Communist Party

U.S. Congress. *See* Congress (U.S.)
U.S. Constitution. *See* Constitution (U.S.)
U.S. Government. *See* Government (U.S.)
U.S. Steel, 505, 505(i), 506, 595, 604
U.S. Supreme Court. *See* Supreme Court
      (U.S.)
United States v. Cruikshank (1876), 457
United States v. E. C. Knight Company (1895), 517
United Students against Sweatshops, 903
Universal Exposition (Paris), 548(b)
Universal male suffrage, 449
Universal Negro Improvement Association
      (UNIA), 658
Universities and colleges. *See also* Higher
      education
   democratization of, 783
   football in, 659
   government aid for, 896
   sexuality in 1920s and, 657(b)
   student protests in, 813–815
   women in, 817, 820
University of California, Berkeley, free
      speech movement in, 813–814
University of Illinois, Grange at, 659
Unskilled workers, 525, 528, 558, 607–608, 696
Uprisings. *See* Protest(s); Revolts and
      rebellions
Urban areas. *See also* Cities and towns
   in 1920s, 646, 663
   population in (1870–1900), 488, 488(f)
   population in (1920–1930), 662(m)
   riots in, 807, 808(m)
Urban industrialism, 477–478, 543
   social problems of, 583
   women activists and, 564, 583
Urban League, 641(i)
USA Patriot Act (2001), 909
Utah, 465, 480, 490
   voting rights for women in, 480, 566(i)

Vaccines, polio, 770, 770(i)
Vagrancy, black codes and, 442
Valentino, Rudolph, 656(i), 658
Vandenberg, Arthur, 748
Vanderbilt family
   Alice, 532
   Alva, 498–499(b), 499(i), 532
   Cornelius ("Commodore"), 497(b), 498(b), 532
   William K., 498(b), 532–533
Vanzetti, Bartolomeo, 663, 664(i)
Vaqueros, 488
Vaux, Calvert, 545
Venezuela, 571, 598
Veracruz, Marines in, 616
Versailles, Paris Peace Conference at, 632–634
Versailles treaty (1919), 634–635
Vertical integration, 501, 501(f)
Veterans
   African American, 640, 755
   bonus for, 671, 695
   in Great Depression, 671, 694
   higher education for, 783
   Maine sinking and, 576(b)
   of Vietnam War, 848–849(b), 849–850, 853, 854
   after World War I, 636
   after World War II, 636(i), 727
Vetoes, by Johnson, Andrew, 443, 444, 446
Vice, urban, 663

Vichy France, 713
Victory Gardens, in World War II, 725
Vietcong, 832, 837, 851
Vietminh, 773–774
Vietnam
    containment policy toward, 773–774
    immigrants from, 903
    outsourcing to, 905(b)
    partition of, 774
    U.S. involvement in, 774
Vietnamization policy, in Vietnam War,
        841–842, 848(b)
Vietnam Veterans Memorial (1982), 854
Vietnam War (1964–1975), 796, 827–828,
        827(i), 834(m). See also Vietnam
    antiwar protests against, 839–840
    costs and effects of, 852–855
    fall of Saigon and, 851(i), 852–853(b)
    Johnson, L. B., and, 801, 855
    Kennedy and, 828, 832–834
    legacy of defeat after, 852–854
    Nixon and, 821, 844, 847–852
    opposition to, 839
    peace accords and, 850–852
    peace negotiations in (1968), 842
    pro-war demonstrations in, 847(i)
    soldiers in, 837(i), 838–839, 838(i), 841,
        841(i)
    U.S. troops in (1962–1972), 836(f)
    veterans of, 849–850, 853, 854
    women in, 838
Villa, Francisco ("Pancho"), 616–617
Violence. See Protest(s); Race riots; Riots;
        Strikes
Violence against Women Act (1994), 896
Virginia. See also Tobacco and tobacco
        industry
    Democrats in, 458
    as "Lincoln state," 436
    Readjusters in, 509
Virginia City, 478–480
Visit from the Old Mistress, A (Homer),
        454(i)
VISTA. See Volunteers in Service to America
Volunteers, in Spanish-American War,
        578
Volunteers in Service to America (VISTA),
        799
Voter Education Project (1962), 805
Voting and voting rights. See also Elections;
        Woman suffrage
    African Americans and, 444, 446, 448,
        509, 609–610, 698, 795–796, 805,
        807(m)
    disfranchisement of blacks and, 509,
        609–610
    Fourteenth Amendment and, 444–445,
        803
    Fifteenth Amendment and, 447
    for freedmen, 436–437, 441, 446
    gender and, 796
    literacy tests for, 610
    for Native Americans, 663
    Nineteenth Amendment and, 628, 630–
        631(b), 655
    poll tax and, 610, 704
    Selma march and, 805, 806(i)
    in South, 433–434, 459(i), 698, 805
    Twenty-sixth Amendment and, 838
    voter turnout in, 508, 569
    for women, 444(i), 445, 447, 480, 509, 564,
        565, 590, 628, 628(m), 630–631(b)
Voting Rights Act (1965), 801, 805, 806
    extension of, 824, 876

Wabash v. Illinois (1886), 517
Waco, Texas, religious cult in, 897
Wade, Benjamin, 436
Wade-Davis bill (1864), 436
Wage(s)
    in 1920s, 648, 649
    for auto workers, 651
    for farm workers, 811
    in Great Depression, 686, 698, 699, 704
    industrial (1912–1920), 625(f)
    of industrial workers, 667
    for men vs. women, 817, 876
    for miners, 479
    minimum, 625, 648
    in Pullman, 561, 562(b)
    in steel industry, 501, 524
    for women, 586, 648, 655, 698, 754
Wage labor, 487, 488, 525. See also Free
        labor; Labor
    freedmen and, 437
Wagner, Robert, 696, 704
Wagner Act (NLRA, 1935), 693, 696, 698, 757
Wagon trains, 464(i)
Waite, Davis H., 560
Wake Island, 580(m), 722
Wald, Lillian, 585
Wallace, George C., 844
Wallace, Henry A., 745, 747(b), 757
Wall Street
    bombing of, 637
    New Deal and, 683
    Roosevelt, T., and, 593
    SEC and, 683
Wall Street Reform and Consumer Protection
        Act (2010), 911
Walt Disney World, 781
War crimes
    by Milosevic, 901
    by Nazis, 728
Ward, Lester Frank, 590
War debts. See also Debt
    Confederate, 441
War Industries Board (WIB), 625, 629
Warm Springs, Georgia, 677
Warner, Charles Dudley, 493, 497
War on Poverty, 799, 800
War on terror, 912–913
War Powers Act (1973), 851
War Production Board, 719
Warren, Earl, and Warren Court, 790, 799,
        803, 862–863
Wars and warfare. See Guerrilla war;
        specific battles and wars
Wartime Reconstruction, 435–440, 436(i)
Washington (state), 490
Washington, Booker T., 452(i), 610, 610(i),
        611
Washington, D.C
    Bonus Marchers in, 671
    September 11, 2001, terrorist attack in,
        888
Washington Disarmament Conference
        (1921–1922), 649
Washington Post, on U.S. empire, 579
Washita River, massacre at, 469
Waste, toxic, 869
Water
    Hetch Hetchy Valley damming and, 600–
        601(b), 601(i)
    hydroelectricity and, 595, 596, 603
    on plains, 485–486
    pollution of, 875
    in rural areas, 686(i)
Watergate scandal, 851, 859, 864–865

Watson, Tom, 556, 568, 569
Watt, James, 874–875
Watts riots (1965), 807, 808(m)
"Waving the bloody shirt," 456, 508, 516
WCTU. See Woman's Christian Temperance
        Union
We (Lindbergh), 659
Wealth. See also Gold; Silver
    in 1920s, 662, 667
    1952–1960, 767
    in 1980s, 875
    Bush, G. W., and, 906
    distribution of, 650
    in Gilded Age, 495, 497, 498–499(b)
    Long on, 692
    New Dealers and, 682
    Reagan and, 874
    Roosevelt, F. D., and, 698
    social Darwinism on, 507–508
    social needs and, 903
    tax cuts and, 648, 667
Wealth gap, 522, 523, 667. See also Income,
        inequality of
Weapons. See also Arms race; Atomic bomb;
        Nuclear weapons
    Hotchkiss rapid-fire guns, 477
    in Iran-Contra, 884
    Iraq inspections and, 895, 901
    in Vietnam War, 833–834
    in World War I, 614, 621
    in World War II, 722(f), 734(b)
Weapons of mass destruction, 909–910
    after Persian Gulf War, 895
Weaver, James, 568(m)
Wehrmacht (German army), 714, 728, 734(b)
Welch, Jack, 902
Welfare and welfare system
    Carter and, 867
    Clinton and, 898, 898(i)
    Johnson, L. B., and, 799–801, 803
    Kennedy and, 798
    limits on, 898
    Nixon and, 821–822
    Truman and, 754
Welfare capitalism, 650
Welfare state, New Deal and, 693–698, 700,
        705
Wells, Ida B., antilynching campaign of,
        509–510, 510–511, 510–511(b), 519
West (U.S. region). See also Pacific Ocean
        region; Sun Belt
    African Americans in, 727
    anti-Asian bigotry in, 479, 609
    conservatism in, 591, 860
    diversity in, 464, 478, 480–482
    farming in, 486, 488
    in Gilded Age, 490–491
    homesteaders in, 483–486, 483(i),
        484–485(b)
    Indians and, 464, 465–469, 468(m)
    land in, 464, 482–483, 486
    manifest destiny and, 465
    mining in, 477–480, 478(m)
    population in, 662(m)
    Populists and, 557–558, 557(i)
    railroads in, 464(i), 483(i), 486, 487(m)
    ranching in, 486–488
    Sun Belt and, 782, 782(m)
    territorial government in, 490
    Turner on, 463, 464
West Bank, 847, 870, 883, 902
West Berlin, 748, 748(m)
    protests in 1968, 842(b)
    Soviets and, 831

West Coast. *See* Pacific Ocean region
Western Europe. *See also* Europe
   common economic market in, 892
Western Federation of Miners (WFM), 560,
   607–608
Western Hemisphere. *See also* Latin America
   immigration and, 663, 801
   Monroe Doctrine and, 571–572, 597–598,
      598(*m*), 599(*i*), 615
Western Union, 499
Western world, U.S. dominance in, 739
West Germany, 744, 748(*m*). *See also*
   Germany
   protests of 1968 and, 842(*b*)
   unification with East Germany, 892
Westinghouse, George W., 504
Westmoreland, William, 837
Weyler, Valeriano ("Butcher"), 575(*b*),
   576(*b*), 577
What Social Classes Owe to Each Other
   (Sumner), 507
Wheat, 489
White, William Allen, 578
White City (World's Columbian Exposition),
   463, 547–551, 549(*i*), 550(*i*)
White-collar workers, 650
   in 1950s, 780
   female, 536, 536(*i*), 627, 655
White House, Office of Faith-Based and
   Community Initiatives, 906
Whites
   California ban on housing discrimination
      and, 806
   as feminists, 817–818
   in Harlem, 658
   in Indian lands, 465
   poverty and, 803, 899
   school integration and, 861–862
   social Darwinism and, 529
   in South, 460, 640
   in southern Democratic Party, 458–459
   in southern Republican Party, 448
White supremacy
   Johnson, Andrew, and, 442
   Ku Klux Klan and, 450(*b*), 664
   in South, 451(*b*), 457–459, 510
"White terror," 448
Whyte, William H., Jr., 787
Wilderness, preservation of, 600(*b*)
Wild West show, 464, 464(*i*)
Wilhelm II (Germany), 617, 623
Willard, Frances, 553, 554, 554(*i*)
   Woman's Christian Temperance Union
      and, 512–513, 564, 565
Williamsburg Bridge (New York City), 545
Willkie, Wendell, 714
Wilson, Edith, 628, 629(*i*)
Wilson, Woodrow, 630–631, 642, 643, 666
   banking and, 606
   Bolsheviks and, 638(*b*)
   election of 1912 and, 584, 604–606, 606(*m*),
      615
   election of 1916 and, 607, 619, 629
   foreign policy of, 615–617
   Fourteen Points of, 631–632
   as governor of New Jersey, 603
   Hetch Hetchy and, 600(*b*)
   internationalism of, 614, 649
   labor and, 607
   neutrality of, 617–619
   New Freedom of, 605
   at Paris Peace Conference, 632–634
   progressivism and, 584, 606, 607
   reforms and, 584, 606, 607

segregation and, 610
self-determination and, 615, 632, 633
states' rights and, 605, 606
tariffs and, 606
trusts and, 606–607
Versailles treaty and, 634–635
on women's rights, 607, 609, 628,
   630–631(*b*)
World War I and, 614, 619–620, 628, 629
Wind Cave National Park, 598(*m*)
Windfall profits, tax on, 868
Wind power, 868
Winnemucca, Sarah, 470
Wisconsin, 591
   sexual orientation as protected category,
      882
Wives. *See also* Women
Wobblies. *See* Industrial Workers of the
   World
Wolfensohn, James D., 903
Woman Rebel (newspaper), 608
Woman's Christian Temperance Union
   (WCTU), 512, 513, 553, 554(*i*), 564–
   565, 565(*i*), 587
Woman's rights. *See also* Feminism; Women
Woman suffrage, 614
   documentation of, 630–631(*b*)
   Fourteenth Amendment and, 445
   Fifteenth Amendment and, 447
   march for, 609, 609(*i*)
   movement for, 441(*i*), 445, 512
   Nineteenth Amendment and, 628, 628(*m*),
      630(*b*), 655
   progressivism and, 628
   in West, 566(*i*)
   Willard and, 512–513, 564, 565
   Wilson and, 607, 609, 628, 630–631(*b*)
   World War I and, 614
Women. *See also* Feminism and feminists;
   Gender and gender issues; Slaves
   and slavery; Voting and voting rights
   in 1950s, 768, 785
   activism of, 512–513, 513(*i*), 564–566
   birth control and, 608, 608(*i*), 655–656,
      657(*b*)
   black, 450(*b*), 534, 699, 699(*i*), 780, 793
   in cabinet, 877, 897
   in combat support, 895(*i*)
   Comstock Lode and, 479
   cult of domesticity and, 543
   discrimination against, 806, 814
   earnings in 1950s, 780
   ex-slave, 452–453, 453(*i*), 454(*i*)
   families headed by, 803
   feminism and, 817–821
   as flappers, 655, 655(*i*)
   Fourteenth Amendment and, 445
   in garment industry, 533–534, 534(*i*),
      588(*i*), 589, 589(*i*)
   in Great Depression, 670, 675–676, 676(*i*)
   in higher education, 783, 817, 820
   as homesteaders, 483(*i*), 484–485(*b*),
      485–486
   as immigrants, 527
   Indian, 476
   labor unions and, 539, 696, 697(*i*)
   leisure and, 543
   married, 534, 670
   Mexican American, 642(*i*)
   in military, 749, 838, 895(*i*)
   in mining towns, 479
   in New Deal, 684, 695, 696, 698
   "new woman" and, 646, 654–657
   politics and, 553

polygamy and, 480
poverty of, 876
separate spheres doctrine and, 509, 543
as servants, 534, 536(*f*), 543, 640
in settlement house movement, 583, 584,
   584(*i*), 585
Social Security and, 698
southern, 509, 510
on Supreme Court, 877, 897
in sweatshops, 533, 535(*i*), 588(*i*)
in teaching, 536
in temperance movement, 512–513, 513(*i*)
in textile industry, 509, 565
in Vietnam War, 838
voting rights for, 444(*i*), 445, 447, 480,
   509, 628, 628(*m*), 630–631(*b*)
workday for, 589–590
as workers, 533–534, 534(*i*), 535(*f*), 536,
   536(*i*), 754(*f*), 768, 784, 875–876
working class, 534
in World War I, 625–628, 626–627(*b*)
in World War II, 725–726
after World War II, 754, 755(*i*)
Women of color, as feminists, 817–818
Women's clubs, 512
Women's movement, 817–819. *See also*
   Feminism
Women's Political Council (WPC), 792
Women's rights, movement for, 793
Women's shelters, 821
Women's Trade Union League (WTUL), 588,
   589
Women Strike for Peace (WSP), 840
Wood, Leonard, 476
Wooden Leg (Cheyenne warrior), 472(*b*)
Woodley, Arthur E., Jr., 838–839
Woodstock Music Festival (1969), 816
Woolworth's, lunch counter sit-ins at, 804,
   804(*i*)
Work. *See also* Labor
   seasonal, 533
   women and (1870–1890), 534, 535(*f*)
Workday
   eight-hour, 539, 542, 543, 558, 560, 604,
      625, 636
   in garment industry, 533–534
   of miners, 560, 604
   in steel industry, 501, 535–536
   ten-hour, for women, 589–590
   twelve- vs. eight-hour, 560
Workers. *See also* Child labor; Factories;
   Labor; Labor unions; Strikes; Women;
   Working class
   in 1980s, 875
   African American, 640
   in caissons, 521, 522, 522(*i*)
   Carnegie and, 524, 558
   as common laborers, 533
   computer and, 899
   in factories, 533
   Ford, Henry, and, 651
   in Gilded Age, 497
   in Great Depression, 667–668, 669, 670
   immigrants in, 524
   in labor unions, 780
   in manufacturing jobs, 904(*b*)
   in New Deal, 675–676, 696–697, 698
   private property vs. rights of, 559
   at Pullman, 560–561
   in railroads, 497, 537, 539, 556
   seasonal, 533
   segregation of federal, 610
   skilled, 533, 535, 537, 539, 543, 551, 558
   in Sun Belt, 782

Workers (continued)
  unionization in, 696
  unskilled, 525, 528, 558, 607–608
  wealth gap and, 522, 523
  welfare capitalism for, 650
  white-collar, 534–536, 536(i)
  women as, 479, 533–534, 534(i), 535(f),
    536, 536(i), 565, 627, 655, 670, 754(f),
    768, 784
  in World War I, 626–627
  after World War I, 636–637
  in World War II, 725
  after World War II, 784(f)
Workers' compensation, 607
Working class
  baseball and, 659
  families in, 534, 608
  leisure of, 543, 544
  militancy of, 671–672
  women in, 534, 535(f), 583, 584, 608
Workingmen's Party, 481
Workplace. See also Workers
  lead poisoning in, 586–587(b)
  separate spheres and, 543
Works Progress Administration (WPA),
    694–696, 698
  Federal Writers Project interviews on,
    694–695(b)
World Bank, 903
World Jewish Congress, 728
World's Columbian Exposition (Chicago,
    1893), 463, 547–551, 549(i), 550(i)
World Trade Center, September 11, 2001,
    destruction of, 908, 908(i)
World Trade Organization (WTO), 902
World War I (1914–1918), 621(i). See also
    Allies (World War I)
  African Americans and, 620, 621–622,
    640
  alliances in, 617, 618(m)
  American Expeditionary Force in, 621,
    622, 623(m)
  armistice in, 623
  casualties in, 614, 617, 621, 623

eastern front in, 620
events leading to, 617
in France, 620, 621–623, 623(m)
home front during, 624–630
patriotism during, 624, 628–629
Red Scare after, 637–640, 638–639(b)
Russian withdrawal from, 620, 638(b)
society after, 709–711
submarine warfare in, 618–619, 619(m)
trench warfare in, 621, 622(i)
United States entry in, 619–620
U.S. neutrality and, 617–619
western front in, 620
World War II (1939–1945), 707–739. See
    also Allies (World War II)
  air bombings in, 713–714
  alliances in, 716
  Allied win in, 734–735(b), 735(i)
  in Atlantic Ocean region, 717, 721, 723
  atomic bomb and, 730–731(b), 737–738,
    737(i)
  Axis powers in, 712(m)
  Cold War after, 743–745
  economy and, 717, 719–720, 725–726,
    738–739, 753–755, 784(f)
  in Europe, 723–725, 733(m)
  Europe after, 745(m)
  families in, 725–726
  German surrender in, 730
  home front in, 725–728
  Japan defeated in, 731–738
  mobilization for, 716–720
  opening of, 711–716
  in Pacific Ocean region, 722–723, 736(m)
  politics during, 727
  second front in, 729
  soldiers in, 718, 719(i), 722, 723(i), 724(i),
    729, 730, 735(i), 739
  Soviet Union in, 714, 734–735(b)
  submarines in, 707, 714, 717, 723
  veterans' rights and, 727
  women in, 725
Wounded Knee, South Dakota, massacre at
    (1890), 477

Wounded Yellow Robe, 474(i)
Wovoka (Paiute shaman), 476
Wright, Frank Lloyd, 548(b)
WTO. See World Trade Organization
Wyoming, 490
  voting by women in, 564, 566(i)

Ximenes, Vicente T., 811

Yalta meeting, 729
Yamamoto, Isoroku (Japan), 722, 723
Yellow journalism, 575–576, 575(i), 576(b)
Yellowstone National Park, 598(m)
Yellow Wolf (Nez Percé), 475
Yeltsin, Boris, 892–893
Yeomen, 449
  in southern Republican Party, 448
  taxation and, 458
Yom Kippur War (1973), 822, 847
Yosemite National Park, 598(m), 600(b),
    601(i)
Young, Andrew, 867
Young, Brigham, 480
Young Men's Christian Association (YMCA),
    626
Young people. See also Students
  in 1920s, 657(b)
  in Great Depression, 684, 684(i)
Youth culture
  in 1950s, 768, 793
  in 1960s, 814–815(b), 814(i), 815(i)
Yugoslavia, 632
  breakup of, 900, 901(m)

Zimmermann, Arthur, and Zimmermann
    telegram, 619
Zion National Park, 598(m)
Zitkala-Sa, 474
Zones
  in Germany, 744, 748(m)
  in Korea, 762
Zululand (Africa), 466(b), 466(m), 467(b)
Zulu people, imperialism, colonialism and,
    466–467(b), 467(i)

ATLAS OF THE TERRITORIAL GROWTH OF THE UNITED STATES

THE ORIGINAL THIRTEEN COLONIES IN 1776 ....M-2

THE UNITED STATES IN 1783 ....M-3

THE UNITED STATES IN 1819 ....M-4

THE UNITED STATES IN 1853 ....M-6

THE CONTEMPORARY UNITED STATES M-8

Lake Superior

Lake Michigan

Lake Huron

Lake Ontario

Lake Erie

St. Lawrence R.

N.H.

MASS.

NEW YORK

Connecticut R.

Hudson R.

RHODE
ISLAND

CONNECTICUT

PENN.

Delaware R.

Susquehanna R.

NEW JERSEY

DELAWARE

MARYLAND

Potomac R.

Chesapeake
Bay

THE ORIGINAL THIRTEEN COLONIES

Proclamation Line of 1763

James R.

VIRGINIA

NORTH
CAROLINA

Cape Fear R.

Ohio R.

Cumberland R.

Tennessee R.

SOUTH
CAROLINA

ATLANTIC
OCEAN

Missouri R.

Arkansas R.

Mississippi R.

Savannah R.

GEORGIA

**THE ORIGINAL
THIRTEEN COLONIES
IN 1776**

0	150	300 miles
0	150	300 kilometers

Gulf of Mexico

M-2

Lake Superior

Lake Michigan

Lake Huron

Lake Ontario

Lake Erie

St. Lawrence R.

Connecticut R.

N.H.

MASS.

NEW YORK

Hudson R.

RHODE ISLAND

CONNECTICUT

PENN.

Delaware R.

Susquehanna R.

NEW JERSEY

DELAWARE

MARYLAND

Potomac R.

Chesapeake Bay

Missouri R.

James R.

VIRGINIA

Ohio R.

Gained by treaty with Britain, 1783

NORTH CAROLINA

Cape Fear R.

Cumberland R.

Tennessee R.

Proclamation Line of 1763

THE ORIGINAL THIRTEEN COLONIES

Arkansas R.

Mississippi R.

SOUTH CAROLINA

ATLANTIC OCEAN

Savannah R.

GEORGIA

THE UNITED STATES IN 1783

| 0 | 150 | 300 miles |

| 0 | 150 | 300 kilometers |

Gulf of Mexico

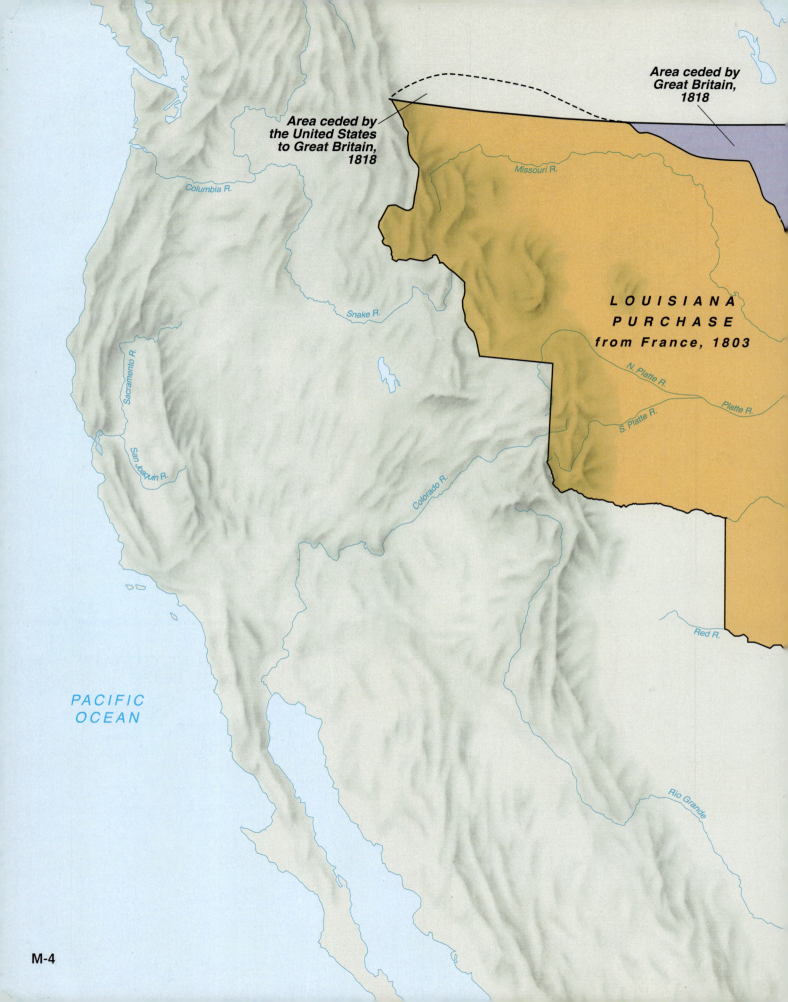

Area ceded by
Great Britain,
1818

Area ceded by
the United States
to Great Britain,
1818

Columbia R.

Missouri R.

Snake R.

**L O U I S I A N A
P U R C H A S E**
from France, 1803

N. Platte R.

S. Platte R.

Platte R.

Sacramento R.

San Joaquin R.

Colorado R.

Red R.

PACIFIC
OCEAN

Rio Grande

Lake Superior

(MICHIGAN TERRITORY)

Lake Michigan

Lake Huron

St. Lawrence R.

Lake Ontario

Lake Erie

Maine
(part of Mass.)

VERMONT
(1791)

NEW YORK
(1788)

Connecticut R.

N.H.
(1788)

MASS.
(1788)

RHODE
ISLAND
(1790)

CONNECTICUT
(1788)

NEW JERSEY
(1787)

DELAWARE
(1787)

MARYLAND
(1788)

Chesapeake
Bay

PENN.
(1787)

Susquehanna R.

Delaware R.

Hudson R.

THE ORIGINAL THIRTEEN COLONIES

Proclamation Line of 1763

Potomac R.

James R.

VIRGINIA
(1788)

NORTH
CAROLINA
(1789)

Cape Fear R.

Savannah R.

SOUTH
CAROLINA
(1788)

GEORGIA
(1788)

ATLANTIC
OCEAN

ILLINOIS
(1818)

INDIANA
(1816)

OHIO
(1803)

Ohio R.

KENTUCKY
(1792)

**Gained by treaty
with Britain, 1783**

Cumberland R.

Tennessee R.

TENNESSEE
(1796)

Missouri R.

Mississippi R.

MISSISSIPPI
(1817)

ALABAMA
(1819)

LOUISIANA
(1812)

**Areas taken from Spain
in 1810, 1813**

**FLORIDA
Treaty with Spain,
1819**

Gulf of Mexico

THE UNITED STATES
IN 1819

0   150   300 miles

0   150   300 kilometers

(1789)   Date of statehood

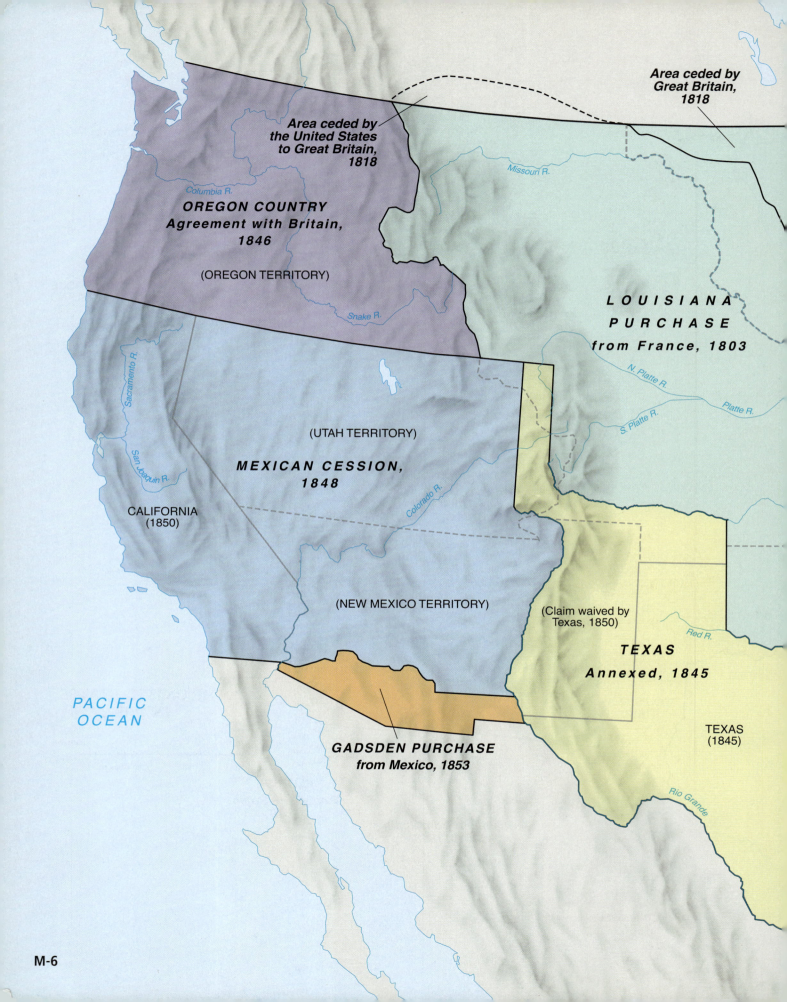

Area ceded by
Great Britain,
1818

Area ceded by
the United States
to Great Britain,
1818

Missouri R.

OREGON COUNTRY
Agreement with Britain,
1846

(OREGON TERRITORY)

Columbia R.

Snake R.

LOUISIANA
PURCHASE
from France, 1803

N. Platte R.

S. Platte R.

Platte R.

Sacramento R.

(UTAH TERRITORY)

MEXICAN CESSION,
1848

San Joaquin R.

CALIFORNIA
(1850)

Colorado R.

(NEW MEXICO TERRITORY)

(Claim waived by
Texas, 1850)

Red R.

TEXAS
Annexed, 1845

PACIFIC
OCEAN

GADSDEN PURCHASE
from Mexico, 1853

TEXAS
(1845)

Rio Grande

Areas ceded by Britain, 1842
(Webster-Ashburton Treaty)

Lake Superior

MAINE
(1820)

St. Lawrence R.

VERMONT
(1791)

Lake Huron

Lake Ontario

NEW YORK
(1788)

Connecticut R.

N.H.
(1788)

MASS.
(1788)

Lake Michigan

MICHIGAN
(1837)

Lake Erie

Hudson R.

RHODE
ISLAND
(1790)

(MINNESOTA
TERRITORY)

WISCONSIN
(1848)

PENN.
(1787)

Delaware R.

CONNECTICUT
(1788)

NEW JERSEY
(1787)

IOWA
(1846)

Missouri R.

OHIO
(1803)

INDIANA
(1816)

Susquehanna R.

DELAWARE
(1787)

ILLINOIS
(1818)

Potomac R.

MARYLAND
(1788)

Chesapeake
Bay

Ohio R.

KENTUCKY
(1792)

James R.

VIRGINIA
(1788)

Proclamation Line of 1763

THE ORIGINAL THIRTEEN COLONIES

MISSOURI
(1821)

Gained by treaty
with Britain, 1783

Cumberland R.

Tennessee R.

NORTH
CAROLINA
(1789)

Cape Fear R.

ARKANSAS
(1836)

TENNESSEE
(1796)

Mississippi R.

ATLANTIC
OCEAN

(INDIAN
TERRITORY)

SOUTH
CAROLINA
(1788)

Savannah R.

MISSISSIPPI
(1817)

ALABAMA
(1819)

GEORGIA
(1788)

**THE UNITED STATES
IN 1853**

LOUISIANA
(1812)

0		150		300 miles

0	150	300 kilometers

FLORIDA
(1845)

FLORIDA
Treaty with Spain,
1819

**Areas taken from Spain
in 1810, 1813**

Gulf of Mexico

(1789)   Date of statehood

M-7

Area ceded by the United States to Great Britain, 1818

Area ceded by Great Britain, 1818

WASHINGTON (1889)
★ Olympia

★ Salem

OREGON COUNTRY
Agreement with Britain, 1846

OREGON (1859)

Columbia R.

★ Helena

MONTANA (1889)

Missouri R.

IDAHO (1890)
★ Boise

Snake R.

WYOMING (1890)

NORTH DAKOTA (1889)
Bismarck ★

SOUTH DAKOTA (1889)
Pierre ★

LOUISIANA PURCHASE
from France, 1803

N. Platte R.

NEBRASKA (1867)

Cheyenne ★

Platte R.

Sacramento R.

★ Carson City
★ Sacramento

NEVADA (1864)

★ Salt Lake City

UTAH (1896)

S. Platte R.

★ Denver

COLORADO (1876)

KANSAS (1861)

San Joaquin R.

MEXICAN CESSION 1848

Colorado R.

CALIFORNIA (1850)

PACIFIC OCEAN

ARIZONA (1912)
★ Phoenix

★ Santa Fe

NEW MEXICO (1912)

TEXAS
Annexed, 1845

Red R.

GADSDEN PURCHASE
from Mexico, 1853

TEXAS (1845)

ARCTIC OCEAN

RUSSIA

ALASKA (1959)
Purchased from Russia, 1867

CANADA

Yukon R.

Bering Sea

Gulf of Alaska

★ Juneau

0   250   500 miles
0 250 500 kilometers

HAWAII (1959)
Annexed, 1898

★ Honolulu

PACIFIC OCEAN

0   50   100 miles
0 50 100 kilometers

Rio Grande

M E X I C O

M-8

Areas ceded by Britain, 1842
(Webster-Ashburton Treaty)

CANADA

Lake Superior

MAINE
(1820)

★ **Augusta**

VERMONT
(1791)

Montpelier ★

Lake Huron

St. Lawrence R.

Concord
★ **N.H.**
(1788)

NEW YORK
(1788)

Lake Ontario

Albany ●

MASS. ★ **Boston**
(1788)

★
Hartford

★ **Providence**

**RHODE
ISLAND**
(1790)

St. Paul

WISCONSIN
(1848)

Lake Michigan

MICHIGAN
(1837)

Lake Erie

PENN.
(1787)

CONNECTICUT
(1788)

MINNESOTA
(1858)

★ **Madison**

★ **Lansing**

Harrisburg
★

● **Trenton**

NEW JERSEY
(1787)

IOWA
(1846)

ILLINOIS
(1818)

INDIANA
(1816)

OHIO
(1803)

★ **Columbus**

● **Dover**

Annapolis ●

DELAWARE (1787)

MARYLAND (1788)

★ **Des
Moines**

★ **Indianapolis**

**WEST
VIRGINIA**
(1863)

WASHINGTON, D.C.

*Chesapeake
Bay*

Lincoln

★ **Springfield**

Frankfort
★

Charleston
●

Richmond
●

VIRGINIA
(1788)

Topeka

**Jefferson
City**
★

KENTUCKY (1792)

***Gained by treaty
with Britain, 1783***

**NORTH
CAROLINA**
(1789)

★ **Raleigh**

MISSOURI
(1821)

● **Nashville**

TENNESSEE
(1796)

**ATLANTIC
OCEAN**

**Oklahoma
City**

ARKANSAS
(1836)

Atlanta
★

**SOUTH
CAROLINA**
(1788)

● **Columbia**

OKLAHOMA
(1907)

★ **Little
Rock**

ALABAMA
(1819)

MISSISSIPPI
(1817)

Montgomery ★

GEORGIA
(1788)

Jackson
★

LOUISIANA
(1812)

Austin

**Baton
Rouge** ●

★ **Tallahassee**

FLORIDA
(1845)

***Areas taken
from Spain
in 1810, 1813***

FLORIDA
**Treaty with Spain,
1819**

Gulf of Mexico

THE CONTEMPORARY
UNITED STATES

| 0 | 150 | 300 miles |
| 0 | 150 | 300 kilometers |

THE ORIGINAL THIRTEEN COLONIES

Proclamation Line of 1763

U.S. Territories

*ATLANTIC
OCEAN*

**San
Juan**
★

***VIRGIN
ISLANDS***
**Acquired
from
Denmark,
1916–1917**

***PUERTO RICO
Acquired from
Spain, 1898***

Caribbean Sea

| 0 | 50 | 100 miles |
| 0 | 50 | 100 kilometers |

(1789)   Date of statehood

BAHAMAS

CUBA

M-9

About the authors

JAMES L. ROARK (Ph.D., Stanford University) is Samuel Candler Dobbs Professor of American History at Emory University. In 1993, he received the Emory Williams Distinguished Teaching Award, and in 2001–2002 he was Pitt Professor of American Institutions at Cambridge University. He has written *Masters without Slaves: Southern Planters in the Civil War and Reconstruction* and with Michael P. Johnson coauthored *Black Masters: A Free Family of Color in the Old South* and coedited *No Chariot Let Down: Charleston's Free People of Color on the Eve of the Civil War*.

MICHAEL P. JOHNSON (Ph.D., Stanford University) is professor of history at Johns Hopkins University. His publications include *Toward a Patriarchal Republic: The Secession of Georgia; Abraham Lincoln, Slavery, and the Civil War: Selected Speeches and Writings;* and *Reading the American Past: Selected Historical Documents,* the documents reader for *The American Promise.* With James L. Roark he has coauthored *Black Masters: A Free Family of Color in the Old South* and coedited *No Chariot Let Down: Charleston's Free People of Color on the Eve of the Civil War.*

PATRICIA CLINE COHEN (Ph.D., University of California, Berkeley) is professor of history at the University of California, Santa Barbara, where she received the Distinguished Teaching Award in 2005–2006. She has written *A Calculating People: The Spread of Numeracy in Early America* and *The Murder of Helen Jewett: The Life and Death of a Prostitute in Nineteenth-Century New York,* and she has coauthored *The Flash Press: Sporting Male Weeklies in 1840s New York.*

SARAH STAGE (Ph.D., Yale University) has taught U.S. history at Williams College and the University of California, Riverside, and she was visiting professor at Beijing University and Szechuan University. Currently she is professor of Women's Studies at Arizona State University. Her books include *Female Complaints: Lydia Pinkham and the Business of Women's Medicine* and *Rethinking Home Economics: Women and the History of a Profession.*

SUSAN M. HARTMANN (Ph.D., University of Missouri) is Arts and Humanities Distinguished Professor of History at Ohio State University. In 1995 she won the university's Exemplary Faculty Award in the College of Humanities. Her publications include *Truman and the 80th Congress; The Home Front and Beyond: American Women in the 1940s; From Margin to Mainstream: American Women and Politics since 1960;* and *The Other Feminists: Activists in the Liberal Establishment.*